THE UNITED STATES

The American Nation

The American Nation

A History of the United States

SIXTH EDITION

JOHN A. GARRATY
Columbia University

ROBERT A. McCAUGHEY
Barnard College, Columbia University

1817

HARPER & ROW, PUBLISHERS, New York
Cambridge, Philadelphia, San Francisco, Washington,
London, Mexico City, São Paulo, Singapore, Sydney

Sponsoring Editor: Marianne J. Russell / Robert Miller
Development Editor: Mary Lou Mosher
Project Editor: Susan Goldfarb
Text Design: Leon Bolognese
Cover Design: Ron Gross
Text Art: Vantage Art, Inc.
Photo Research: Elsa Peterson
Production: Willie Lane
Compositor: Arcata Graphics/Kingsport
Printer and Binder: Arcata Graphics/Kingsport

The American Nation: A History of the United States
Sixth Edition

Picture credits begin on page C-1.

The authors make grateful acknowledgment to:

New Directions Publishing Corporation for permission to quote from "Hugh Selwyn Mauberley" by Ezra Pound. From Ezra Pound, *Personae.* Copyright 1926 by Ezra Pound. Reprinted by permission of New Directions Publishing Corporation.

Liveright Publishing Corporation for permission to quote from "the first president to be loved by his . . ." by e. e. cummings. Reprinted from *ViVa* by E. E. Cummings by permission of Liveright Publishing Corporation. Copyright 1931, 1959 by E. E. Cummings. Copyright © 1979, 1973 by the Trustees for the E. E. Cummings Trust. Copyright © 1979, 1973 by George James Firmage.

Cover illustration: George Inness, *Delaware Water Gap* (1861): The Metropolitan Museum of Art, Morris Jessup Collection.

Library of Congress Cataloging-in-Publication Data

Garraty, John Arthur, 1920–
The American nation.

Includes bibliographies and index.
1. United States—History—1865–
I. McCaughey, Robert A. II. Title.
E178.1.G24 1987b 973 86–25613
ISBN 0–06–042298–X

86 87 88 89 9 8 7 6 5 4 3 2 1

For Kathy, Jack, and Sarah

Contents in Brief

Contents

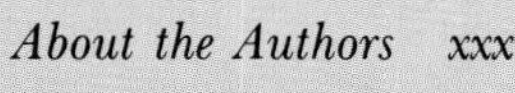

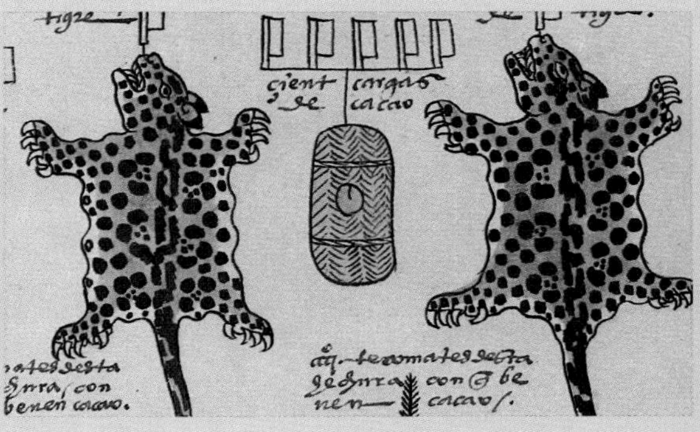

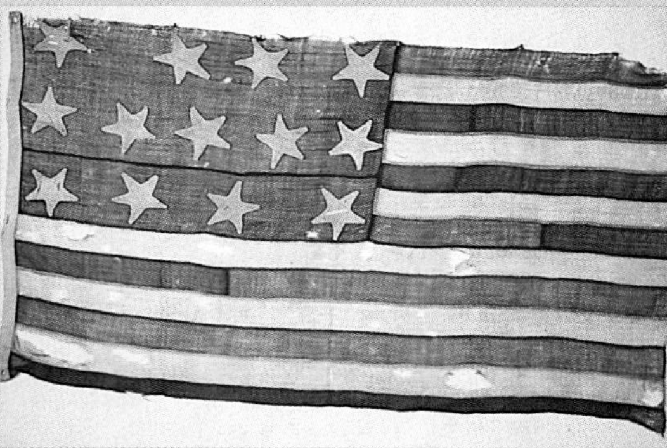

7 America Escapes from Europe *202*

8 The Cords of Union *226*

9 Jacksonian Democracy *262*

WANTED
1.000.000
MEN
GOOD WAGES
CASTLE GARDEN
UNITED STATES

12 Expansion and Slavery *346*

13 The Sections Go Their Ways *370*

14 The Coming of the Civil War *396*

HOLY BIBLE
PROCLAMATION

PROVIENCE NORFOLK AND

Girls get together and ORGANIZE
Do you want Fair Treatment? ORGANIZE
Do you want Fire Protection? ORGANIZE

Buy a
Liberty
BOND

GET BEHIND THE GOVERNMENT
LIBERTY LOAN OF 1917

Louis

Aleppo
Nicosia
SYRIA
PRUS
LEBANON
Beirut
Damascus
IRAQ
ISRAEL
Tel-Aviv
Jerusalem
Port Said
Amman
JORDAN
Suez
Elath

Maps

Graphs

Preface

In preparing this sixth edition of *The American Nation,* I have asked Robert A. McCaughey of Barnard College and Columbia University to join me as co-author. Professor McCaughey specializes in social and intellectual history, and his main work on this edition has been in those fields. In particular, the restructuring of Chapters 2, 10, and 11 has been his responsibility. But he has made useful contributions to every chapter in the book.

Throughout, however, the additions and changes in this edition have been the result of our combined efforts. This has been a true collaboration. I have worked with McCaughey almost line by line on the sections he has concentrated on, and he has read and commented upon all of my own revisions. In particular, I have assumed the task of making sure that the uniform style and tone of earlier editions have been preserved; as a result, like its predecessors, this is one book, written now by two historians rather than by me alone.

In short, this edition has been constructed on the same principles as all the others. It assumes, to begin with, that American history is important for its own sake—as an epic and unique tale of the experience of hundreds of millions of people in a vast land. Beyond this, our history provides an object lesson in how the past affects the present, or rather, how a series of pasts has changed a series of presents in an unending pattern of development. Thus, while historians have never been any better at foretelling the future than politicians, economists, or soothsayers, good ones have always been able to illuminate their own times, adding depth and perspective to their readers' understanding of how they got to be where they were at any particular point.

Telling the story of the American past clearly and intelligibly, but with adequate attention to its complexities and subtleties, is another of our objectives. Of course, this is not the final word—that will never be written. This edition, however, is up-to-date and as accurate and thoughtful and wide-ranging as we could make it. The theory that a few great individuals, cut from larger cloth than the general run of human beings, have shaped the course of past events oversimplifies history. But the story of the past becomes more comprehensible when attention is paid to how the major figures on the historical stage have reacted to events and to one another. Since generalizations require concrete illustration if they are to be grasped fully, readers will find many anecdotes and quotations on the following pages along with the facts and dates and statistics that every good history must contain. This illustrative material is interesting, and most of it is entertaining, but it is instructive too.

Finally, one need not be an uncritical admirer of the American nation and its people to recognize that the history of the United States deserves to be treated with dignity and respect. However, a subject of such magnitude is not well served by patriotic hoopla or by ignoring or slighting or excusing its dark and discreditable aspects. The English radical Oliver Cromwell is said to have told an artist who was painting his picture to portray him "warts and all." Cromwell wanted to be remembered as he was, confident that, on balance, history would judge him fairly. That is another principle on which *The American Nation* continues to be based.

JOHN A. GARRATY

About the Authors

John A. Garraty is Professor of History and Chair of the Department of History at Columbia University. He received his B.A. from Brooklyn College, an M.A. and Ph.D. from Columbia, and an L.H.D. from Michigan State University. He taught at Michigan State before joining the Columbia faculty. Professor Garraty is the author, co-author, and editor of scores of books and articles, among them biographies of Silas Wright, Henry Cabot Lodge, Woodrow Wilson, George W. Perkins, and Theodore Roosevelt. He contributed a volume, *The New Commonwealth,* to the New American Nation series. He edited *Quarrels That Shaped the Constitution.* He has been editor of Supplements IV through VII of the *Dictionary of American Biography,* and is on the Board of Advisers of *American Heritage* magazine. Professor Garraty has recently been vice-president and head of the teaching division of the American Historical Association. His areas of special research interest include the Gilded Age, unemployment (in an historical sense), and the Great Depression of the 1930s.

Robert A. McCaughey is Professor of History and Chair of the Department of History at Barnard College, Columbia University. After receiving a B.A. in history from the University of Rochester, he served as an officer in the U.S. Navy. He taught in the NROTC Program at the University of North Carolina, where he completed his M.A. degree. Upon completion of military service, he earned his Ph.D. at Harvard University, and then joined the Barnard faculty. He has since received fellowships from the Charles Warren Center at Harvard and from the Guggenheim Foundation. Professor McCaughey's major books include *Josiah Quincy: The Last Federalist* and, more recently, *International Studies and Academic Enterprise: A Chapter in the Enclosure of American Learning.* His areas of special interest include American intellectual history, with a particular focus on colleges and universities; he is also actively exploring the uses of computers in historical studies.

The American Nation

1
Europe Discovers America

In the beginning, all the world was America. JOHN LOCKE

Who discovered America? This is not as easy a question to answer as one might think. The first human beings to set foot on the continents of North and South America were the ancestors of the modern Indians. These people came from Asia; they entered the North American continent tens of thousands of years ago during the Ice Age, when a land bridge connected northeastern Asia with Alaska. They did not, however, think of themselves as discoverers or even explorers. Being hunters and herders, they were simply moving from camp to camp in search of game and green grass. No doubt the first humans in other parts of the world found their way in the same manner and at about the same time to what are now Egypt, Iran, India, China, Australia, and for that matter England, France, and the rest of Europe. Almost certainly the settlers of the Americas were unaware that they were entering "new" territory. So we must look elsewhere (and much later in time) for the "discoverer" of America as we use that word. Several claimants have been advanced.

Probably the first European to reach America was a Norseman, Leif Ericson. He ventured before the day of the compass into the void of the North Atlantic and, around the year 1000, found the shores of Labrador. Yet Ericson's discovery passed practically unnoticed for centuries, and to most modern inhabitants of the New World he lives only in legend.

Amerigo Vespucci, a clever Italian with an eye for publicity, visited the northern coast of South America in 1499. He wrote an account of his experiences that was widely circulated. In 1507, after reading a distorted copy of Vespucci's tale, a German geographer, Martin Waldseemüller, concluded that the author was the discoverer of the New World and suggested that it be named America in his honor. Today millions call themselves Americans, but few know much about Amerigo Vespucci.

Another Italian mariner, Cristoforo Colombo, brave, persistent, an inspired sailor but a fumbling administrator, spent a decade cruising in the Caribbean Sea under the mistaken impression that he was next door to China. He killed some natives, established a few rickety settlements, ventured no nearer to North America than Cuba, and died poor, embittered, and frustrated, hotly denying that he had found anything more than a new route to the Orient. Today, whether he be known as Colombo, Colón, or Columbus, he is honored in the Old World and the New as the discoverer of the Western Hemisphere.

Why Columbus rather than Ericson, the real European pioneer, or Vespucci, whose name has become immortal? The answer is that Ericson came upon the scene too soon and Vespucci too late. Europe in the year 1000 was not yet ready to find a new world, and by 1499 it had already found one. Amerigo Vespucci gave his name to the region, but the adventures of Christopher Columbus inspired the European invasion and development of the whole area between Hudson Bay and the Strait of Magellan.

Columbus and the Discovery of America

About two o'clock on the morning of October 12, 1492, a sailor named Roderigo de Triana, clinging in a gale to the mast of the ship *Pinta,* saw a gleam of white on the moonlit horizon and shouted: "*Tierra! Tierra!*" The land he had spied was an island in the West Indies called Guanahaní by its inhabitants, a place distinguished neither for beauty nor size. Nevertheless, when Triana's master, Christopher Columbus, went ashore bearing the flag of Castile, he named it San Salvador, or Holy Saviour. Columbus selected this imposing name for the island out of gratitude and wonder at having found it—he had sailed with three frail vessels more than 3,000 miles for 33 days without sight of land. The name was appropriate, too, from history's far larger viewpoint. Neither Columbus nor any of his men suspected it, but the discovery of San Salvador was probably the most important event in the history of western civilization since the birth of Christ.

San Salvador was the gateway to two continents. Columbus did not know it, and he refused to learn the truth, but his voyage threw open to exploitation by the peoples of western Europe more than a quarter of all the land in the world, a region of more than 16 million square miles, an area lushly endowed with every imaginable resource. He made possible a mass movement from Europe (and later from Africa and to a lesser extent from other regions) into the New World. Gathering force rapidly, this movement did not slacken until the present

In this 1590 engraving by Theodor de Bry, Columbus is about to depart from Palos; Ferdinand and Isabella, at right, bid him farewell.

century, and it still has not ceased entirely; something on the order of 70 million persons have been involved in the migration.

Columbus was an intelligent as well as a dedicated and skillful mariner. He failed to grasp the significance of his accomplishment because he had no idea that he was on the edge of two huge continents previously unknown to Europeans. He was seeking a way to China and Japan and the Indies, the amazing countries described by the Venetian Marco Polo in the late 13th century.

Having read carefully Marco Polo's account of his adventures in the service of Kublai Khan, Columbus had decided that these rich lands could be reached by sailing directly west from Europe. The idea was not original, but while others merely talked about it (in the jawbreaking phrase of one scholar, experts had been slow to consider "the cosmographical implications of the earth's sphericity"), Columbus pursued it with brilliant persistence.

If one could sail to Asia directly, the trading possibilities and the resulting profits would be limitless. Oriental products were highly valued all over Europe. Spices such as pepper, cinnamon, ginger, nutmeg, and cloves were of first importance, their role being not so much to titillate the palate as to disguise the taste of spoiled meats in regions that had little ice. Europeans also prized such tropical foods as rice, figs, and oranges, as well as perfumes (often used as a substitute for soap), silk and cotton, rugs, textiles such as muslin and damask, dyestuffs, fine steel products, precious stones, and various drugs.

These products flowed into western Europe by way of the Italian city-states. By the 11th century Venice had established a thriving trade with Constantinople, shipping large quantities of European foodstuffs to the great metropolis on the Bosporus. The Venetians also supplied young Slavs, captured or purchased along the nearby Dalmatian coast, to the markets of Egypt and Syria (the word *slave* originally meant a Slav).

The Venetians brought back oriental products from these voyages, and the effect was like that of tossing a stone into a pond. Europeans bestirred themselves, searching for more goods to offer in exchange. They possessed surpluses of grain and food, but these bulky products were expensive to transport over long distances. However, in Flanders, in the Low Countries, woolen cloth of high quality was being manufactured. Other areas were producing furs and lumber. Demand led to increased output; thus the flow of commerce stimulated manufacturing, which in turn spurred the growth of towns. As towns became larger and more numerous, the market for food expanded and surrounding rural areas increased their agricultural output.

Urban growth also created a demand for more clothmakers. The resulting labor shortage in both town and country produced important changes in the structure of medieval society. The manorial system, based on serfdom, soon began to change. As their labor became more valuable, serfs won the right to pay off their traditional obligations in money rather than in service and to leave the manors and move to the towns or to newly opened farmland. The lords themselves often instituted this change, for they wished to increase agricultural output by draining swamps and clearing forests, and they willingly granted freedom to serfs who would move to the new lands. And they needed money rather than the services of serfs to buy the expensive oriental luxuries being dangled before their eyes by traders.

The Crusades further accelerated the tempo of this new activity. Genuine religious motives seem to have inspired these mighty efforts, protracted over two centuries from 1095 to about 1290, to drive the Moslems from the Holy Land. Once the crusading armies had won a foothold in Asia Minor, the commerce of Venice and of other Italian cities increased still more, and their merchant fleets expanded. The business of transporting and supplying the European armies was itself extremely profitable. Furthermore, when the waves of Crusaders returned home, they brought with them more oriental products and a taste for these things that persisted after the goods themselves had been consumed.

The volume of this trade cannot be exactly determined. It was large enough to keep the fleets of the thriving Italian cities busy, and it tended to grow with the years. Yet it was not impressive by modern standards. In the 1920s the Belgian historian Henri Pirenne estimated that the entire tonnage of the 13th-century Venetian fleet would scarcely fill a single freighter, the cargo of which, in turn, would scarcely serve as ballast for a modern supertanker. Nor did the increase in trade cause universal prosperity or even a steady economic expansion in western Europe. In fact, the period of the 14th and early 15th centuries seems to have been marked by depression and economic decline in the West.

This decline resulted principally from the terrible losses occasioned by the plague known as the Black Death, which ravaged Europe in the mid-14th century. Part of the difficulty, however, stemmed from the steady drain of precious metals to the Orient (because of the unfavorable balance of east-west trade) and from the high cost of oriental goods. It was easy to blame this on the greed of the Italians, who monopolized east-west trade. Certainly the Venetians have never possessed a reputation for altruism nor the Pisans for being poor businessmen. However, even if the Italians had labored only for the joy of serving their fellow human beings, or if other merchants had been able to break the Italian monopoly, the cost of eastern products would have remained high. To transport spices from the Indies, silk from China, or rugs, cloth, and steel from the Middle East was extremely costly. The combined sea-land routes were long and complicated—across strange seas, through deserts, over high mountain passes—with pirates or highwaymen a constant threat. Every petty tyrant through whose domain the caravans passed levied taxes, a quasi-legal form of robbery. Few merchants operated on a continental scale; typically, goods passed from hand to hand and were loaded and unloaded many times between eastern producer and western consumer, with each middleman exacting as large a profit as he could. In the end the western European consumer had to pay for all this.

As time went on, merchants in the West began to cast about for a cheaper way of obtaining oriental products. If they could be carried by sea by one merchant in one ship, the cost would be far less, for the goods would be loaded and unloaded only once. A small number of sailors could provide all the necessary labor, and the free wind would supply the power to move the cargo to its destination. By the 15th century, this idea was beginning to be transformed into action.

The great figure in the transformation was Prince Henry the Navigator, third son of John I, king of Portugal. After distinguishing himself in 1415 in the capture of Ceuta, on the African side of the Strait of Gibraltar, he became interested in navigation and exploration. Sailing a vessel out of sight of land was still, in Henry's day, more an art than a science and was extremely hazardous. Ships were small and clumsy. Primitive compasses and instruments for reckoning latitude existed, but

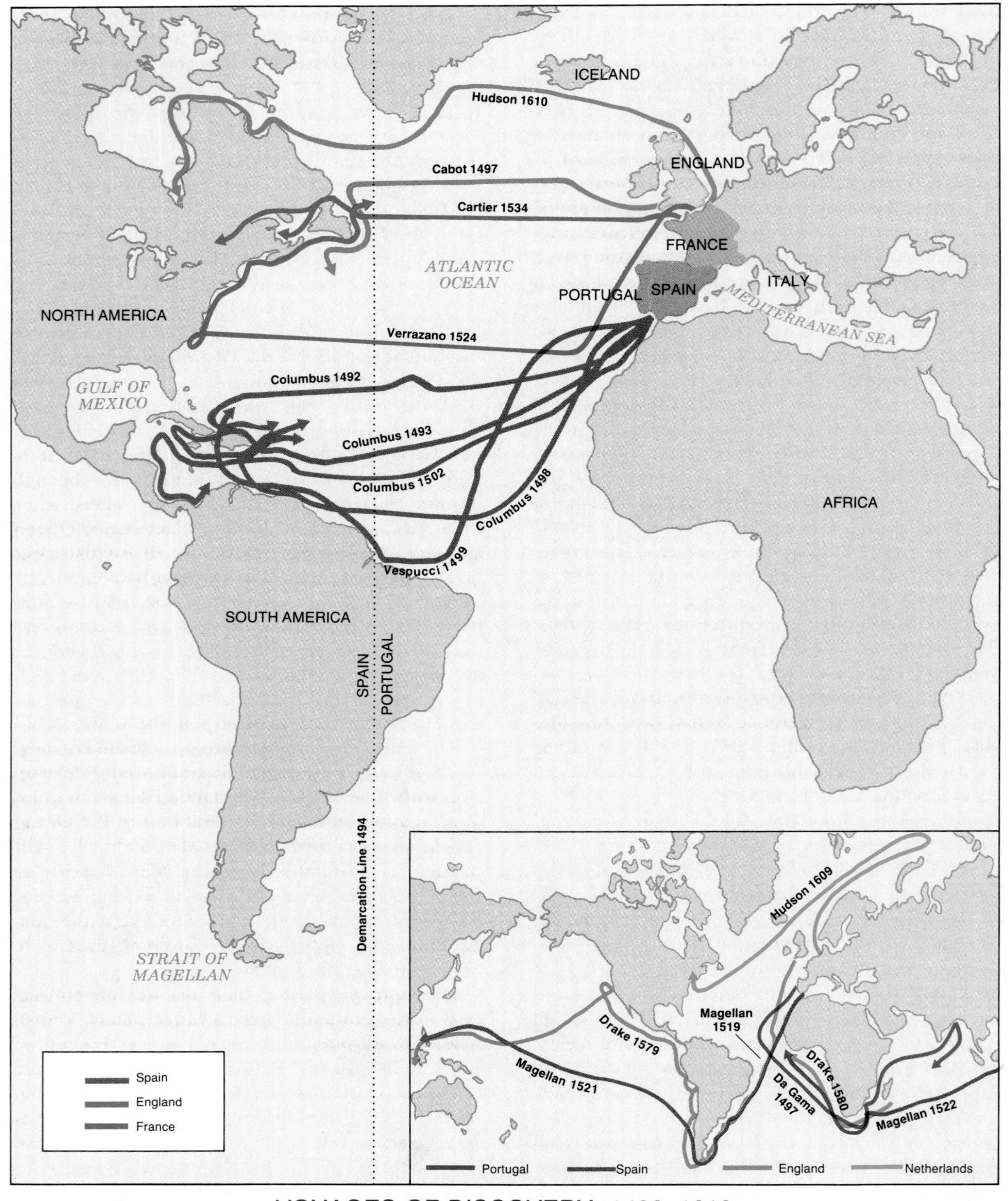
ICELAND
Hudson 1610
ENGLAND
Cabot 1497
Cartier 1534
FRANCE
ATLANTIC
OCEAN
PORTUGAL
SPAIN
ITALY
MEDITERRANEAN SEA
NORTH AMERICA
Verrazano 1524
Columbus 1492
GULF OF
MEXICO
Columbus 1493
Columbus 1502
Columbus 1498
Vespucci 1499
AFRICA
SOUTH AMERICA
SPAIN
PORTUGAL
Demarcation Line 1494
STRAIT OF
MAGELLAN
Spain
England
France
Hudson 1609
Magellan
1519
Drake 1579
Magellan 1521
Drake 1580
Da Gama
1497
Magellan 1522
Portugal
Spain
England
Netherlands

VOYAGES OF DISCOVERY, 1492–1610

under shipboard conditions they were very inaccurate. Navigators could determine longitude only by keeping track of direction and estimating speed; even the most skilled could place little faith in their estimates.

Henry attempted to improve and codify navigational knowledge. To his court at Sagres, hard by Cape St. Vincent, the extreme southwestern point of Europe, he brought geographers, astronomers, and mapmakers, along with Arab and Jewish mathematicians. He built an observatory and supervised the preparation of tables measuring the declination of the sun and other navigational data. Searching for a new route to the Orient, Henry's captains sailed westward to the Madeiras and the Canaries and south along the coast of Africa, seeking a way around that continent. In 1445 Dinis Dias reached Cape Verde, site of present-day Dakar.

Henry was interested in trade, but he cared more for the advancement of knowledge, for the glory of Portugal, and for spreading Christianity. When his explorers developed a profitable business in slaves, he tried to stop it. Nevertheless, the movement he began had, like the Crusades, important commercial overtones. Probably half of the Portuguese voyages were undertaken by private merchants. Without the gold, ivory, and other African goods, which brought great prosperity to Portugal, the explorers would probably not have been so bold and persistent. Yet, like Henry, they were idealists, by and large. The Age of Discovery was in a sense the last Crusade; its leaders displayed mixed religious and material motives along with a love of adventure. In any case the Portuguese realized that if they could find a way around Africa, they might well sail directly to India and the Spice Islands.* The profits from such a voyage would surely be spectacular.

For 20 years after Henry's death in 1460, the Portuguese concentrated on exploiting his discoveries. In the 1480s King John II undertook systematic new explorations focused on reaching India. Gradually his caravels probed southward along the sweltering coast—to the equator, to the region of Angola, and beyond.

Into this bustling, prosperous, expectant little country in the corner of Europe came Christopher Columbus in 1476. Columbus was a weaver's son from Genoa, born in 1451. He had taken to the sea early, ranging widely in the Mediterranean. His arrival in Portugal was unplanned, since it resulted from the loss of his ship in a battle off the coast. For a time he became a chartmaker in Lisbon. He married a local woman. Then he was again at sea. He cruised northward, perhaps as far as Iceland, south to the equator, westward in the Atlantic to the Azores. Had his interest lain in that direction, he might well have been the first person to reach Asia by way of Africa, for in 1488, in Lisbon, he met and talked with Bartholomeu Dias, just returned from his voyage around the southern tip of Africa, which had demonstrated that the way lay clear for a voyage to the Indies. But by this time Columbus had committed himself to the westward route. When King John II refused to finance him, he turned to the Spanish court, where, after many disappointments, he finally persuaded Queen Isabella to equip his expedition. In August 1492 he set out from the port of Palos with his tiny fleet, the *Santa María,* the *Pinta,* and the *Niña.* A little more than two months later, after a stopover in the Canary Islands to repair the *Pinta*'s rudder, his lookout sighted land.

Columbus's success was due in large part to his single-minded conviction that the Indies could be reached by sailing westward for a relatively short distance and that a profitable trade would develop over this route. He had persuaded Isabella to grant him, in addition to the title Admiral of the Ocean Sea, political control over all the lands he might discover and 10 percent of the profits of the trade that would follow in the wake of his expedition. Now the combination of zeal and tenacity that had got him across the Atlantic cost him dearly. He refused to accept the plain evidence, which everywhere confronted him, that this was an entirely new world. All about were strange plants, known neither to Europe nor to Asia. The copper-colored people who paddled out to inspect his fleet could no more follow the Arabic widely understood in the East than they could Spanish. Yet Columbus, consulting his charts, convinced himself that he had reached the Indies. That is why he called the natives Indians.

Searching for treasure, he pushed on to Cuba.

* The Moluccas, west of New Guinea. In the geography of the 15th century the Spice Islands were part of the Indies, a vague term that encompassed the southeast rim of Asia from India to what is now Indonesia.

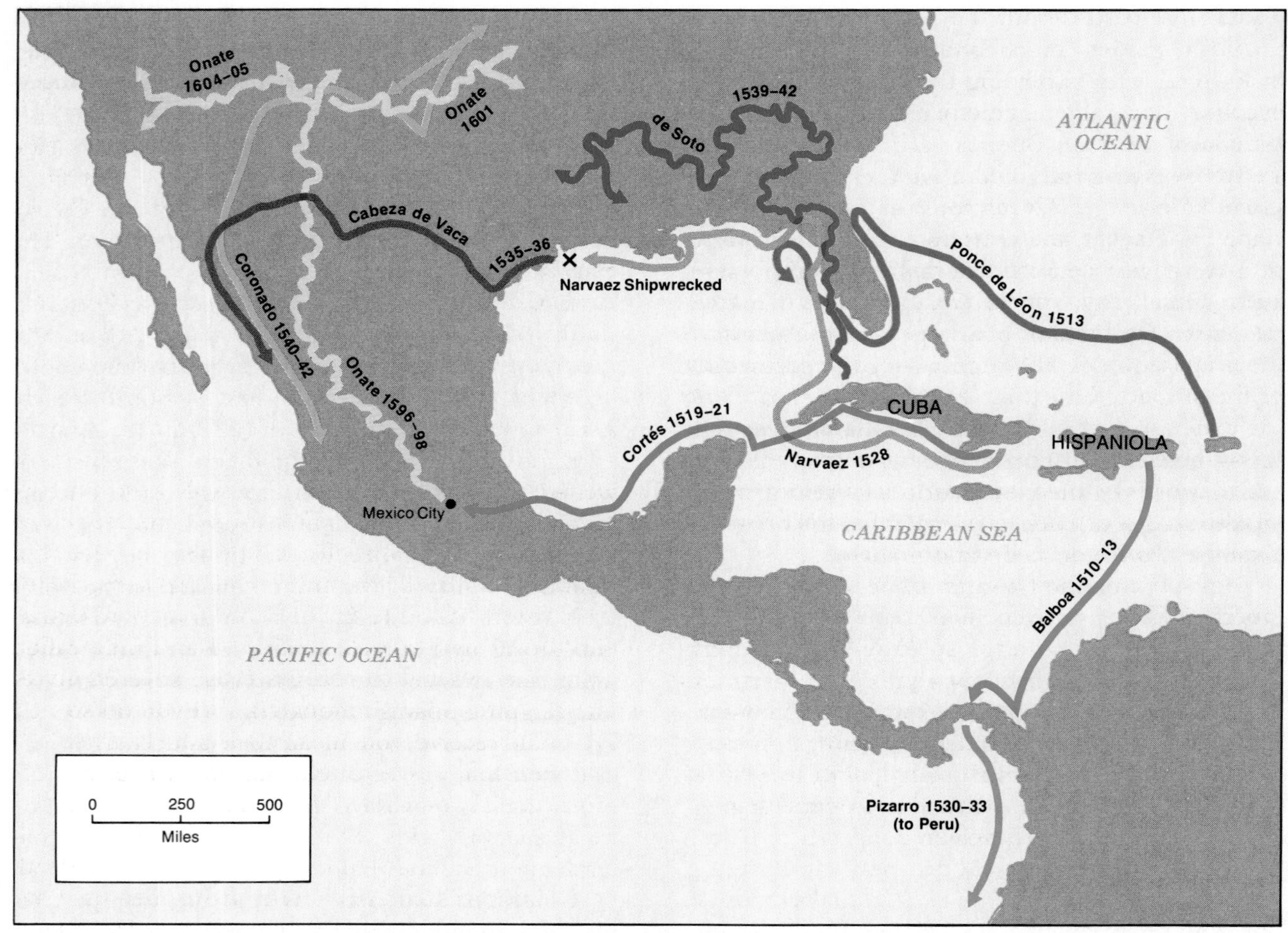

SPANISH EXPLORATIONS, 1510–1605

When he heard the native word *Cubanocan,* meaning "middle of Cuba," he mistook it for *El Gran Can* (Marco Polo's "Grand Khan") and sent emissaries on a fruitless search through the tropical jungle for the khan's palace. He finally returned to Spain relatively empty-handed but certain that he had explored the edge of Asia. Three later voyages failed to shake his conviction.

Columbus died in 1506. By that time other captains had taken up the work, most of them more willing than he to accept the New World on its own terms. As early as 1493, Pope Alexander VI had divided the non-Christian world between Spain and Portugal. The next year, in the Treaty of Tordesillas, these powers negotiated an agreement about exploiting the new discoveries. In effect, Portugal continued to concentrate on Africa, leaving the New World, except for what eventually became Brazil, to the Spanish. Thereafter, from their base on Hispaniola (Santo Domingo), founded by Columbus, the Spaniards quickly fanned out through the Caribbean and then over large parts of the two continents that bordered it.

In 1513 Juan Ponce de León made the first Spanish landing on the mainland of North America, exploring the east coast of Florida. In the same year Vasco Nuñez de Balboa crossed the Isthmus of Panama and discovered the Pacific Ocean. In 1519 Hernán Cortés landed an army in Mexico and overran the empire of the Aztecs, rich in gold and silver. That same year Ferdinand Magellan set out on his epic three-year voyage around the world. By discovering the strait that bears his name, at the southern tip of South America, he gave the

Spanish a clear idea of the size of the continent. In the 1530s Francisco Pizarro subdued the Inca empire in Peru, providing the Spaniards with still more treasure, drawn chiefly from the silver mines of Potosí. In 1536 Buenos Aires was founded by Pedro de Mendoza. Within another decade Francisco Vásquez de Coronado had marched as far north as Kansas and west to the Grand Canyon, and Hernando de Soto had discovered the Mississippi River. Fifty years after Columbus's first landfall, Spain was master of a huge American empire.

What explains this mighty surge of exploration and conquest? Greed for gold and power, a sense of adventure, the desire to Christianize the Indians—mixed motives propelled the *conquistadores* onward. Most saw the New World as a reincarnation of the Garden of Eden, a kind of fairyland of infinite promise. Ponce de León and many others actually expected to find the Fountain of Youth in America. Their vision, at once so selfish and so exalted, reveals the central paradox of New World history. This immense land brought out both the best and the worst in human beings. Virgin America—like all virgins—inspired conflicting feelings in men's hearts. They worshiped it for its purity and promise, yet they could not resist the opportunity to take advantage of its innocence.

The Indian and the European

The *conquistadores* were brave and imaginative men, well worthy of their fame. It must not, however, be forgotten that they wrenched their empire from innocent hands; in an important sense, the settlement of the New World, which the historian Francis Jennings has called "the invasion of America," ranks among the most flagrant examples of unprovoked aggression in human history. When Columbus landed on San Salvador he planted a cross, "as a sign," he explained to Ferdinand and Isabella, "that your Highnesses held this land as your own." Of the Lucayans, the native inhabitants of San Salvador, Columbus wrote: "The people of this island . . . are artless and generous with what they have, to such a degree as no one would believe. . . . If it be asked for, they never say no, but rather invite the person to accept it, and show as much lovingness as though they would give their hearts."

The Indians of San Salvador behaved this way because the Spaniards seemed the very gods. "All believe that power and goodness dwell in the sky," Columbus reported, "and they are firmly convinced that I have come from the sky." The products of Europe fascinated them. For a bit of sheet copper an inch square, they would part with a bushel of corn, while knives, hatchets, and even fishhooks made of metal were beyond price to a people whose own technology was still in the Stone Age.

But the Spaniards would not settle for the better of the bargain. Columbus also remarked of the Lucayans: "These people are very unskilled in arms . . . with fifty men they could all be subjected and made to do all that one wished." He and his compatriots tricked and cheated the Indians at every turn. Before entering a new area, Spanish generals customarily read a *Requerimiento* (requirement) to the inhabitants. This long-winded document recited a Spanish version of the history of the human race from the Creation to the division of the non-Christian world by Pope Alexander VI and then called upon the Indians to recognize the sovereignty of the reigning Spanish monarch. ("If you do so . . . we shall receive you in all love and charity.") If this demand was rejected, the Spanish promised: "We shall powerfully enter into your country, and . . . shall take you, your wives, and your children, and shall make slaves of them. . . . The death and losses which shall accrue from this are your fault." This arrogant harangue was read in Spanish and often out of earshot of the Indians. When they responded by fighting, the Spaniards decimated them, drove them from their lands, and held the broken survivors in contempt. As Bartolomé de las Casas, a priest among them, said, the *conquistadores* behaved "like the most cruel Tygres, Wolves, and Lions, enrag'd with a sharp and tedious hunger."

Wherever they went, the Europeans mistreated the people they encountered. When the Portuguese reached Africa, they carried off thousands into slavery. The Dutch behaved shamefully in the East Indies, as did the French in their colonial possessions—although, in North America at least, the French record was better than most.

English settlers described the Indians as being "of a tractable, free, and loving nature, without guile or treachery," yet in most instances they exploited and all but exterminated them. "Why should you take by force from us that which you can obtain by love?" one puzzled chief asked an early Virginia colonist, according to the latter's own account. The first settlers of New England dealt fairly with the local inhabitants. They made honest, if somewhat misguided, efforts to Christianize and educate them and to respect their rights. But within a few years their relations with the Indians deteriorated, and in King Philip's War (1675–1676), proportionately the bloodiest in American history, they destroyed the tribes as independent powers.

Native American Civilizations

Of course the victims of the Europeans' cruelty were not innocent "noble savages." Being human, Indians suffered from all the human failings in one form or another. During thousands of years they had multiplied, occupying the hemisphere from Alaska to Tierra del Fuego. By 1500 there were somewhere between 50 and 60 million Indians, 1 or 2 million living in what is now the United States. (Exactly how many is impossible to discover. As the anthropologist Bruce Trigger has written, "It is notoriously difficult to determine the size of aboriginal American populations.")

In the course of many centuries the Indians' cultures had evolved in different ways. Climate, soil conditions, wars, and other factors, including pure chance, shaped their ways of life profoundly, just as these forces shaped the civilizations that had developed over the ages in Asia, Africa, and Europe. More than a thousand languages were spoken in North and South America at the time of Columbus, some as different from one another as English is from Russian or Chinese.

Even in the relatively limited area that the first Spanish explorers visited, the native cultures displayed an extraordinary variety. If the Lucayans who greeted Columbus were a naive people, their institutions relatively primitive, the civilizations of the Incas of Peru and the Aztecs of Mexico were in many respects as highly developed as any in Europe or Asia. The Incas built roads as enduring as those of the Romans. Montezuma, the Aztec emperor, lived in a great palace surrounded by courti-

The architectural genius of the Aztecs is evident in this view of the Great Temple and Plaza of Tenochtitlán, based on a modern reconstruction from archeological evidence.

ers and servants in a city as large as and far more impressive architecturally than Madrid, the home of Cortés's master, Charles V.

In the immense land north of Mexico no such imposing civilizations existed, but there, too, the number of different patterns of life was enormous. About 200 languages were spoken. Some groups were nomads who traveled in small bands and lived by hunting and fishing. Others lived settled lives based on a combination of hunting and agriculture. "Political organization among Indians varied from the simple family groups of the remote Arctic and desert West to the complex confederacies of tribes in the East," Wilcomb Washburn writes in *The Indian in America.* It is therefore difficult to generalize, and the problem of describing the lives and attitudes of these original Americans is made more difficult still by the absence of written records before the arrival of the Europeans and the fact that most of the accounts written by European explorers and settlers are biased and incomplete.

Certain traits the Indians had in common, and many of these the Europeans shared. Cruelty and war, slavery and plunder existed in the New World long before Columbus. When the good father las Casas wrote that Indians were "without evil and without guile," he was as far off the mark as the Spaniard who claimed that they indulged in "every kind of intemperance and wicked lust." Indian men were by our standards chauvinists, as indeed were most Europeans of that day. Hunting and fishing—which, again like many Europeans, the Indians regarded as sports as well as sources of food—were usually male occupations, as was warfare. In agricultural communities, men and women shared other tasks; in general the men did the heavy work of clearing land and building shelters; the women did the planting, cultivating, and harvesting. When Indians observed European men planting seeds and weeding their fields they scoffed at them for being effeminate.

Most of the terrible decimation that was everywhere the Indians' fate was caused by European diseases such as smallpox and measles. The population of Mexico was at least 20 million when Cortés invaded the country and only 2 million a century later. European germs killed far more of the inhabitants than European gunpowder and steel. The Arawak population of Hispaniola fell from perhaps 8 million when Columbus first touched there to a couple of hundred 50 years later.

The Europeans could not be blamed for these deaths. They did not understand the diseases any better than the Indians did. The fact remains that in conflicts between Indians and whites, far more often than not, the whites were the main cause of the trouble.

Most Europeans had what the historian David B. Quinn described as "almost complete confidence in the rectitude of whatever they did." They simply assumed that non-Europeans were inferior beings. This was their fundamental misconception, their fatal sin. Apparently their prejudices were not always of racial origin; some early colonists seemed to have considered Indians members of the white race whose skin had been darkened by exposure to the elements. The term *red man* did not become current until the 18th century.

The relativity of cultural values escaped all but a handful of the Europeans. If some of the natives were naive in thinking that the invaders, with their huge ships and their potent fire sticks, were gods, these "gods" were equally naive in their thinking. Since the Indians did not worship the Christian God and indeed worshiped a large number of other gods, the Europeans dismissed them as contemptible heathens. Some insisted that the Indians were servants of Satan. "Probably the devil decoyed these miserable savages hither in hopes that the Gospel of the Lord Jesus Christ would have come here to destroy or disturb his absolute empire over them," one English colonist explained. This man, obviously, was determined to frustrate the devil's nefarious scheme.

In fact, most Indians were deeply religious people. But their religious values were so different from those of the Europeans that many of the latter believed that even if the Indians were not minions of Satan, they were unworthy of becoming Christians. Others, such as the Spanish friars, did try to convert the Indians, and with considerable success; but as late as 1569, when Spain introduced the Inquisition into its colonies, the natives were exempted from its control on the ground that they were incapable of rational judgment and thus not responsible for their "heretical" religious beliefs.

Most Indians lived in close harmony with their surroundings. They adjusted to and took advantage of existing ecologies (for example, by trapping furbearing animals in winter and netting fish during spring spawning runs), whereas the Europeans sought to change ecologies to their advantage (as

The watercolor paintings of John White, one of the earliest English settlers, provide a glimpse of the Indians through European eyes. Here White depicts "their sitting at meat"—"deer's flesh, or of some other beast, and fish."

by plowing fields and building fences). Indians who depended on hunting and fishing lived nomadic lives and therefore had small use for personal property that was not easily portable. They had little interest in amassing wealth, as individuals or as tribes. Even the Aztecs, with their treasures of gold and silver, valued the metals for their durability and the beautiful things that could be made with them rather than as objects of commerce.

This lack of concern for material things led Europeans to conclude that the native people of America were childlike creatures, not to be treated as equals. "[Indians] do but run over the grass, as do also foxes and wild beasts," an Englishman wrote in 1622, "so it is lawful now to take a land, which none useth, and make use of it." The first part of this statement contained a grain of truth, though of course the second did not follow from it logically.

Other troubles grew out of similar misunderstandings. English colonists assumed that Indian chiefs ruled with the same authority as their own kings. When Indians, whose loyalties were shaped by complex kinship relations more than by identification with any one leader, sometimes failed to honor commitments made by their chiefs, the English accused them of treachery.

The Europeans' inability to grasp the communal nature of land tenure among Indians also led to innumerable quarrels. Traditional tribal boundaries were neither spelled out in deeds or treaties nor marked by fences or any other sign of occupation. Often corn grown by a number of families was stored in a common bin and drawn upon by all as needed. Such practices were utterly alien to the European mind. On the other hand, Indians put more emphasis on who was using land than on who first obtained or "owned" it. Among some agricultural tribes, if a farmer failed to cultivate a plot of land, another could take over no matter how long the first had previously used it.

The Indians, writes William Cronon in his fascinating book *Changes in the Land: Indians, Colonists, and the Ecology of New England,* "moved from habitat to habitat to find maximum abundance through minimal work, and so reduce their impact on the land." The English colonists, Cronon goes on to say, "believed in and required permanent settlements." And he concludes: "English fixity sought to replace Indian mobility; here was the central conflict in the ways Indians and colonists interacted with their environments."

The Spanish Decline

While Spain waxed fat on the wealth of the Americas, the other nations of western Europe did little. In 1497 and 1498 King Henry VII of England sent

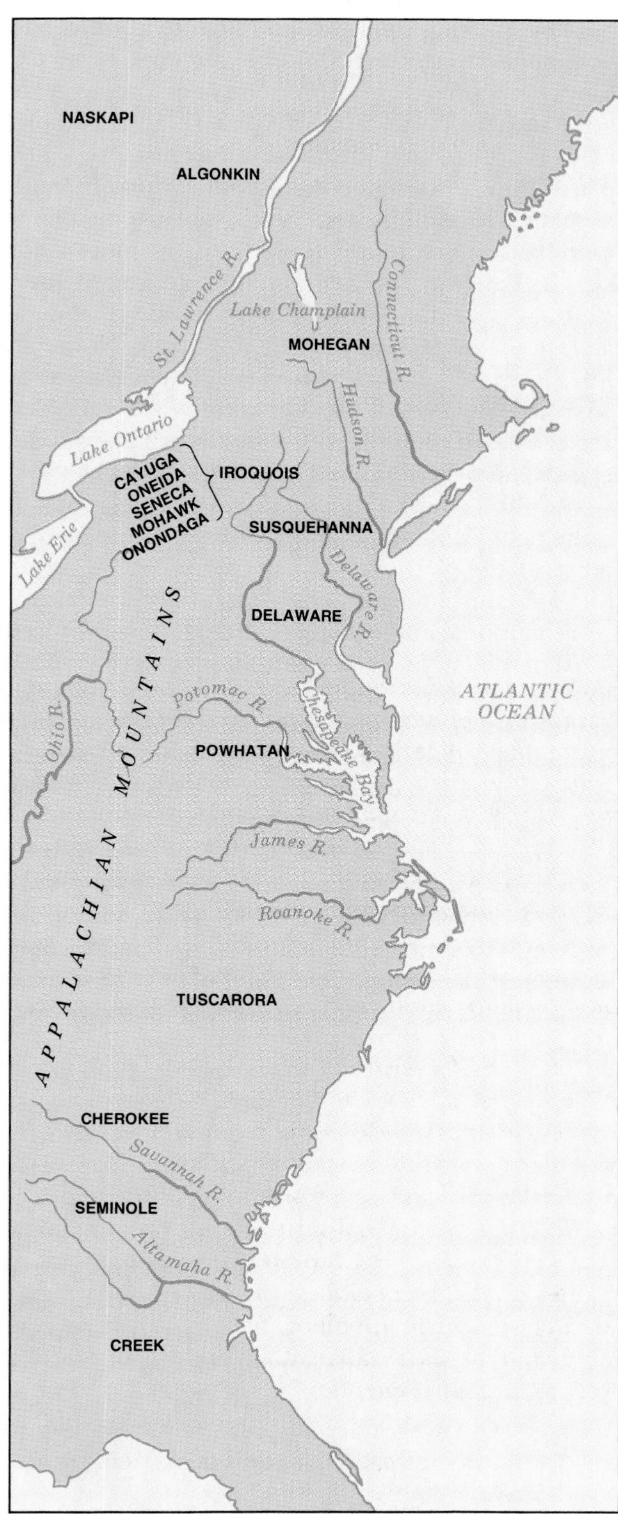

PRIMARY EAST COAST INDIAN TRIBES IN THE 1600s

John Cabot to the New World. Cabot visited Newfoundland and the northeastern coast of the continent. His explorations formed the basis for later British claims in North America, but they were not followed up for many decades. In 1524 Giovanni da Verrazano made a similar voyage for France, coasting the continent from Carolina to Nova Scotia. Some ten years later the Frenchman Jacques Cartier explored the St. Lawrence River as far inland as present-day Montreal. During the 16th century, fishermen from France, Spain, Portugal, and England began exploiting the limitless supplies of cod and other fish they found in the cold waters off Newfoundland. They landed at many points along the mainland coast from Nova Scotia to Labrador to collect water and wood and to dry their catches, but they made no permanent settlements until the next century.

There were many reasons for this delay, the most important probably the fact that Spain had achieved a large measure of internal tranquillity by the 16th century, while France and England were still torn by serious religious and political conflicts. The Spanish also profited from having seized upon those areas in America best suited to producing quick returns. Furthermore, in the first half of the 16th century, Spain, under Charles V, dominated Europe as well as America. Charles controlled the Low Countries, most of central Europe, and part of Italy. Reinforced by the treasure of the Aztecs and the Incas, Spain seemed too mighty to be challenged in either the New World or the Old.

Under Philip II, who succeeded Charles in 1556, Spanish strength seemed at its peak, especially after Philip added Portugal to his domain in 1580. But beneath the pomp and splendor (so well captured by such painters as Velázquez and El Greco) the great empire was in trouble. The corruption and vacuity of the Spanish court had much to do with this. So did the ever-increasing dependence of Spain upon the gold and silver of its colonies, which tended to undermine the local Spanish economy. Even more important was the disruption of the Catholic church throughout Europe by the Protestant Reformation.

The Protestant Reformation

The spiritual lethargy and bureaucratic corruption besetting the Roman Catholic church in the early

16th century made it a fit target for reform. A thriving business in the sale of indulgences, payments that were supposed to win for departed loved ones forgiveness for their earthly sins and thus release from purgatory, was a public scandal. The luxurious life-style of the popes and the papal court in Rome was another. Yet there had been countless earlier religious reform movements that had led to little or no change. The fact that the movement launched by Martin Luther in 1517 and carried forward by men like John Calvin addressed genuine shortcomings in the Roman Catholic church does not entirely explain why it led so directly to the rupture of Christendom.

The charismatic leadership of Luther and the compelling brilliance of Calvin made their protests more effective than earlier efforts at reform. Probably more important, so did the political possibilities let loose by their challenge to Rome's spiritual authority. German princes seized upon Luther's campaign against the sale of indulgences to stop *all* payments to Rome and to confiscate church property within their domains. Swiss cities like Geneva, where Calvin took up residence in 1536, and Zurich joined the Protestant revolt for spiritual reasons, but also to establish their political independence from Catholic kings. Francis I of France remained a Catholic, but he took advantage of Rome's troubles to secure control over the clergy of his kingdom. The efforts of Spain to suppress Protestantism in the Low Countries only further stimulated nationalist movements there, especially among the Dutch.

The decision of Henry VIII of England to break with Rome was at bottom a political one. The refusal of Pope Clement VII to agree to an annulment of Henry's marriage of 20 years to Catherine of Aragon, the daughter of Ferdinand and Isabella, provided the occasion. Catherine had given birth to six children, but all were girls and only Mary survived childhood; Henry was without a male heir. By repudiating the pope's spiritual authority and declaring himself head of the English (Anglican) church in 1534, Henry freed himself to divorce Catherine and to marry whomever—and however often—he saw fit. By the time of his death five wives and 13 years later, England had become a Protestant nation. More important for our story, the dominant character of the future English colonies in America had also been determined.

The growing political and religious conflict had economic overtones. Modern students have exploded the theory that the merchant classes were attracted to Protestantism because the Catholic church, preaching outdated concepts like "just price" and frowning on the accumulation of wealth as an end in itself, stifled their acquisitiveness. Few merchants were more devoted to the quests for riches than the Italians, yet they remained loyal Catholics. So did the wool merchants of Flanders, among the most important in all Europe. Nonetheless, in some lands the business classes tended to support Protestant leaders, in part because the new sects, stressing simplicity, made fewer financial demands upon the faithful than the Catholics did.

As the commercial classes rose to positions of influence, England, France, and the United Provinces of the Netherlands experienced a flowering of trade and industry. The Dutch built the largest merchant fleet in the world. Dutch traders captured most of the Far Eastern business once monopolized by the Portuguese, and they infiltrated Spain's Caribbean stronghold. A number of English merchant companies, soon to play a vital role as colonizers, sprang up in the last half of the 16th century. These joint-stock companies, ancestors of the modern corporation, enabled groups of investors to pool their capital and limit their individual responsibilities to the sums actually invested—a very important protection in such risky enterprises. The Muscovy Company, the Levant Company, and the East India Company were the most important of these ventures.

English Beginnings in America

English merchants took part in many kinds of international activity. The Muscovy Company spent large sums searching for a passage to China around Scandinavia and dispatched six overland expeditions in an effort to reach the Orient by way of Russia and Persia. In the 1570s Martin Frobisher made three voyages across the Atlantic, hoping to discover a northwest passage to the Orient or new gold-bearing lands.

Such projects, particularly in the area of America, received strong but concealed support from the Crown. Queen Elizabeth I invested heavily in

Sir Francis Drake, one of the boldest sea captains to serve Queen Elizabeth I, sailed around the world from 1577 to 1580 and gratified his sovereign by plundering the Spanish-held west coast of South America.

Frobisher's expeditions. England was still too weak to challenge Spain openly, but Elizabeth hoped to break the Spanish overseas monopoly just the same. She encouraged her boldest sea dogs to plunder Spanish merchant ships on the high seas. When Captain Francis Drake was about to set sail on his fabulous round-the-world voyage in 1577, the queen said to him: "Drake! . . . I would gladly be revenged on the King of Spain for divers injuries that I have received." Drake, who hated the Spaniards because of a treacherous attack they had once made on the fleet of his kinsman and former chief, Sir John Hawkins, took her at her word. He sailed through the Strait of Magellan and terrorized the west coast of South America, capturing the Spanish treasure ship *Cacafuego,* heavily laden with Peruvian silver. After exploring the coast of California, which he claimed for England, Drake crossed the Pacific and went on to circumnavigate the globe, returning home in triumph in 1580. Although Elizabeth took pains to deny it to the Spanish ambassador, Drake's voyage was officially sponsored. Elizabeth being the principal shareholder in the venture, most of the ill-gotten Spanish bullion went into the Royal Treasury rather than Drake's pocket.

When schemes to place settlers in the New World began to mature at about this time, the queen again became involved. The first English effort was led by Sir Humphrey Gilbert, an Oxford-educated soldier and courtier with a lifelong interest in far-off places. Gilbert owned a share of the Muscovy Company; as early as 1566 he was trying to get a royal grant for an expedition in search of a northeast passage to the Orient. But soon his interests concentrated on the northwest route. He read widely in navigational and geographical lore and in 1576 wrote a persuasive *Discourse . . . to prove a passage by the north west to Cathaia.* Two years later the queen authorized him to explore and colonize "heathen lands not actually possessed by any Christian prince."

We know almost nothing about Gilbert's first attempt except that it occurred in 1578–1579; in 1583 he set sail again with five ships and over 200 settlers. He landed them on Newfoundland, then evidently decided to seek a more congenial site farther south. However, no colony was established, and on his way back to England his ship went down in a storm off the Azores.

Gilbert's half brother, Sir Walter Raleigh, took up the work. Handsome, ambitious, and impulsive, Raleigh was a great favorite of Elizabeth. He sent a number of expeditions to explore the east coast of North America, a land he named Virginia in honor of his unmarried sovereign. In 1585 he settled about a hundred men on Roanoke Island, off the North Carolina coast, but these settlers returned home the next year. In 1587 Raleigh sent another group to Roanoke, including a number of women and children. Unfortunately, the supply ships sent to the colony in 1588 failed to arrive; when help did get there in 1590, not a soul could be found. The fate of these pioneers has never been determined.

One reason for the delay in getting aid to the Roanoke colonists was the attack of the Spanish Armada on England in 1588. Angered by English raids on his shipping and by the assistance Elizabeth was giving to the rebels in the Netherlands, King Philip II had decided to invade England. His motives were religious as well as political and economic, for England was now seemingly committed to Protestantism. His great fleet of some 130 ships bore huge crosses on the sails as if on another crusade. The Armada carried 30,000 men and 2,400 guns, the largest naval force ever assembled up to that time. However, the English fleet badly mauled this armada, and a series of storms completed its destruction. Thereafter, although the war continued and Spanish sea power remained formidable, Spain could no longer block English penetration of the New World.

Experience had shown that the cost of planting settlements in a wilderness 3,000 miles from England was more than any individual purse could bear. (Raleigh lost about £40,000 in his overseas ventures; early in the game he began to advocate government support of colonization.) As early as 1584 Richard Hakluyt, England's foremost authority on the Americas, made a convincing case for royal aid. In his *Discourse on Western Planting,* Hakluyt stressed the military advantages of building "two or three strong fortes" along the Atlantic coast of North America. Ships operating from such bases would make life uncomfortable for "king Phillipe" by intercepting his treasure fleets—a matter, Hakluyt added coolly, "that toucheth him indeede to the quicke." Colonies in America would also provide a market for English woolens, bring in valuable tax revenues, and perhaps offer employment for the swarms of "lustie youthes that be turned to no provitable use" at home. From the great American forests would come the timber and naval stores needed to build a bigger navy and merchant marine.

Queen Elizabeth read Hakluyt's essay, but she was too cautious and too devious to act boldly on his suggestions. Only after her death in 1603 did full-scale efforts to found English colonies in America begin, and even then the organizing force came from merchant capitalists, not from the Crown. This was unfortunate, because the search for material rewards, and especially for quick profits, dominated the thinking of these enterprisers. Larger national ends (while not neglected, because the Crown was always involved) were subordinated. On the other hand, if private investors had not taken the lead, no colony would have been established at this time.

The Settlement of Virginia

In September 1605 two groups of English merchants petitioned the new king, James I, for a license to colonize Virginia, as the whole area claimed by England was then named. This was granted the following April, and two joint-stock companies were organized, one controlled by London merchants, the other by a group from the area around Plymouth and Bristol.* Both were under the control of a Royal Council for Virginia, but James appointed prominent stockholders to the council, which meant that the companies had considerable independence.

This first chapter revealed the commercial motivation of both king and company in the plainest terms. Although it spoke of spreading Christianity and bringing "the Infidels and Savages, living in those Parts, to human Civility," it stressed the right "to dig, mine, and search for all Manner of Mines of Gold, Silver, and Copper." On December 20, 1606, the London Company dispatched about 100 settlers aboard the *Susan Constant, Discovery,* and *Godspeed.* This little band reached the Chesapeake Bay area in May 1607 and founded Jamestown, the first permanent English colony in the New World.

From the start everything seemed to go wrong. The immigrants established themselves in what was practically a malarial swamp simply because it appeared easily defensible against Indian attack. They failed to get a crop in the ground because of the lateness of the season and were soon almost without food. Their leaders, mere deputies of the London merchants, did not respond to the challenges of the wilderness. The settlers lacked the skills that pioneers need. More than a third of them were "gentlemen" unused to manual labor, and many of the rest were the gentlemen's body servants, almost equally unequipped for the task of colony building. During the first winter more than half of the settlers died.

All the land belonged to the company, and aside from the gentlemen and their retainers, most of the settlers were only hired laborers who had contracted to work for it for seven years. This was

---

* The London Company was to colonize south Virginia, while the Plymouth Company, the Plymouth-Bristol group of merchants, was granted northern Virginia.

most unfortunate. The situation demanded people skilled in agriculture, and the tragedy was that such a labor force was available. In England times were bad. The growth of the textile industry had led to an increased demand for wool, and great landowners were dismissing laborers and tenant farmers and shifting from labor-intensive agriculture to sheep raising. Inflation, caused by a shortage of goods to supply the needs of a growing population and by the influx of large amounts of American silver into Europe, worsened the plight of the dispossessed. Many landless farmers were eager to migrate if offered a decent opportunity to obtain land and make new lives for themselves.

The merchant directors of the London Company, knowing little or nothing about Virginia, failed to provide the colony with effective guidance. They set up a council of settlers, but they kept all real power in their own hands. Instead of stressing farming and public improvements, they directed the energies of the colonists into such futile labors as searching for gold (the first supply ship devoted precious space to two goldsmiths and two "refiners"), glassblowing, silk raising, wine making, and exploring the local rivers in hopes of finding a water route to the Pacific and the riches of China.

One colonist, Captain John Smith, tried to stop some of this foolishness. Smith had come to Virginia after a fantastic career as a soldier of fortune in eastern Europe, where he had fought many battles, been enslaved by a Turkish pasha, and triumphed in a variety of adventures, military and amorous. He quickly realized that building houses and raising food were essential to survival, and he soon became an expert forager and Indian trader. In dealing with Indians he was stern but by his standards fair-minded. It was necessary to dominate what he called the "proud Savages" yet to avoid bloodshed.

Smith pleaded with company officials in London to send over more people accustomed to working with their hands, such as farmers, fishermen, carpenters, masons, and "diggers up of trees," and fewer gentlemen and "Tuftaffety humorists."* "A plaine soldier who can use a pickaxe and a spade is better than five knights," he said.

Captain John Smith recounted his rescue by Pocahontas in his illustrated Generall Historie of Virginia, *published in London in 1624.*

Whether Smith was actually rescued from death at the hands of the Indians by the princess Pocahontas is not certain, but there is little doubt that without him the colony would have perished in the early days. However, he stayed in Virginia only two years.

Lacking intelligent direction and faced with appalling hardships, the Jamestown colonists failed to develop a sufficient sense of common purpose. Each year they died in wholesale lots. The causes of death were disease, starvation (there was even a case of cannibalism among the desperate survivors), Indian attack, and above all, ignorance and folly. Between 1606 and 1622 the London Company invested more than £160,000 in Virginia and sent over about 6,000 settlers. Yet no dividends were ever earned, and of the 6,000, fewer than 2,000 were still alive in 1622. In 1625 the population was down to about 1,300. The only profits were those taken by certain shrewd investors who had organized a joint-stock company to transport

* Smith was referring to the gold tassels worn by titled students at Oxford and Cambridge at that time.

women to Virginia "to be made wives" by the colonists.

One major problem, the mishandling of the local Indians, was largely the colonists' doing. It is quite likely that the settlement would not have survived if the Powhatan Indians had not given the colonists food in the first hard winters, taught them the ways of the forest, introduced them to valuable new crops such as corn and yams, and showed them how to clear dense timber by girdling the trees and burning them down after they were dead. The settlers accepted Indian aid, then took whatever else they wanted by force. "[They] conciliated the Powhatan people while they were of use," one historian has written, "and pressed them remorselessly, facelessly, mechanically, as innocent of conscious ill will as a turning wheel, when they became of less value than their land." The Indians did not submit meekly to such treatment. They proved brave, skillful, and ferocious fighters, once they understood that their very existence was at stake. The burden of Indian fighting might easily have been more than the frail settlement could bear.

What saved the Virginians was not the brushing aside of the Indians but the gradual realization that they must produce their own food—cattle raising was especially important—and the cultivation of tobacco, which flourished there and could be sold profitably in England. Once the settlers discovered tobacco, no amount of company pressure could keep them at wasteful tasks like looking for gold. The "restraint of plantinge Tobacco," one company official commented, "is a thinge so distastefull to them that they will with no patience indure to heare of it."

John Rolfe, who is also famous for marrying Pocahontas, introduced West Indian tobacco—much milder than the local "weed" and thus more valuable—in 1612. With money earned from the sale of tobacco, the colonists could buy the manufactured articles they could not produce in a raw new country; this freed them from dependence on outside subsidies. It did not mean profit for the London Company, however, for by the time tobacco caught on, the surviving original colonists had served their seven years and were no longer hired hands. To attract more settlers, the company had permitted first tenancy and then outright ownership of farms. Thus the profits of tobacco went largely to the planters, not to the "adventurers" who had organized the colony.

Important administrative reforms helped Virginia to forge ahead. A revised charter in 1612 extended the London Company's control over its own affairs in Virginia. Despite serious intracompany rivalry between groups headed by Sir Thomas Smythe and Sir Edwin Sandys, a somewhat more intelligent direction of Virginia's affairs resulted. First the merchants appointed a single resident governor and gave him sufficient authority to control the settlers. Then they made it much easier for settlers to obtain land of their own. In 1619 a rudimentary form of self-government was instituted: a House of Burgesses, consisting of delegates chosen in each district, met at Jamestown to advise the governor on local problems. The company was not bound by the actions of the burgesses, but from this seed sprang the system of representative government that became the American pattern.

These reforms, however, came too late to save the fortunes of the London Company. In 1619 the Sandys faction won control and started an extensive development program, but in 1622 a bloody Indian attack took the lives of 347 colonists. Morale sank and James I, who disliked Sandys, decided that the colony was being badly managed. In 1624 the charter was revoked and Virginia became a royal colony. As a financial proposition the company was a fiasco; the shareholders lost every penny they had invested. Nonetheless, by 1624 Virginia was firmly established and beginning to prosper.

The sociologist Sigmund Diamond has offered an interesting theoretical explanation of how and why the Virginia colony changed from a mere commercial organization to a real society. In the beginning, he asserts, there was no cement binding the colonists into a community; either employees or bosses, they were all oriented toward company headquarters in London. In order to attract more settlers and motivate them to work, the company had to grant them special privileges and status, such as political power and the right to own land, which had the effect of making them more dependent upon one another. By thus destroying the reliance of the colonists on the company, these actions undermined company control over the colonists. "The new relationships in which [the Virginians] were now involved," Diamond explains, "were of greater importance than the company relationship. . . . It was the company's fate to have created a country and to have destroyed itself in the process."

Remnants of Popery

Through all the social and political reshuffling that occurred in Virginia in its opening decades, the people, by and large, kept their eyes fixed on the main chance. But although the prospect of a better material life brought most English settlers to America, for some, economic opportunity was not the only reason they abandoned what their contemporary, William Shakespeare, called "dear mother England." A profound unease with England's spiritual state—and therefore with their own while they remained there—explains why many colonists embarked on their "errand in the wilderness."

Despite the attempt of Henry VIII's older daughter, Queen Mary, to reinstall Catholicism during her brief reign (1553–1558), the Anglican church became once and for all the official Church of England during the long reign of Elizabeth I (1558–1603). Like her father, Elizabeth took more interest in politics than in religion. So long as England had its own church, with her at its head, and with English rather than Latin as its official language, she was content. Aside from these changes, the Anglican church under Elizabeth closely resembled the Catholic church it had replaced.

This middle way satisfied most, but not all, of Elizabeth's subjects. Steadfast Catholics could not accept it. Some left England; the rest practiced their faith in private. At the other extreme, more radical Protestants, including a large percentage of England's university-trained clergy, insisted that Elizabeth had not gone far enough. The Anglican church was still too much like the Church of Rome, they claimed. They objected to the richly decorated vestments worn by the clergy and to the use of candles, incense, and music in church services. They insisted that emphasis should be put on reading the Bible and analyzing the meaning of the Scriptures in order to encourage ordinary worshipers to truly understand their faith. Since they wanted to "purify" Anglicanism, these critics were called Puritans. At first the name was a pejorative assigned to them by their opponents. Later it became a badge of honor.

Puritans objected to the way Elizabeth's bishops interpreted the Protestant doctrine of predestination. Their reading of the Book of Genesis convinced them that all human beings were properly damned by Adam's original sin and that what one did on earth had no effect on a person's fate after death. To believe otherwise was to limit God's power, which was precisely what the Catholic church did in stressing its ability to forgive sins by granting indulgences. The Anglicans implied that while God had already decided whether or not a person was saved, an individual's efforts to lead a good life could somehow cause God to change His mind. The Anglican clergy did not come right out and say that good works could win a person admission to Heaven—that heresy was called Arminianism. But they encouraged people to hope that good works were somehow something more than ends in themselves.

Puritans differed as to whether or not the ideal church should have any structure beyond the local congregation. Some—later called Congregationalists—favored a completely decentralized arrangement, with the members of each church and their chosen minister beholden only to one another. Others, called Presbyterians, favored some organization above the local level, but one controlled by elected laymen, not by the clergy.

Puritans were also of two minds as to whether reform could be accomplished within the Anglican church. During Elizabeth's reign most hoped that it could. Whatever they did in their local churches, the Puritans remained professed Anglicans. After King James I succeeded Elizabeth I in 1603, however, their fears that the royal court might be backsliding into its old "popish" ways mounted. James was a Scot of the Stuart clan, and the Stuarts had supported Queen Mary's attempts to restore Catholicism 50 years earlier. He was married to a Catholic, and the fact that he favored toleration for Catholics gave further substance to the rumor that he was himself a secret member of that church. This rumor proved to be false, but in his 22-year reign (1603–1625) James did little to advance the Protestant cause. His one contribution—which had a significance far beyond what he or anyone else anticipated—was to authorize a new translation of the Bible. The King James Version (1611) was both a monumental scholarly achievement and a literary masterpiece of the first order.

"Of Plymouth Plantation"

In 1606, worried about the future of their faith, members of the church in Scrooby, Nottinghamshire, "separated" from the Anglican church, declaring it corrupt beyond salvage. In 17th-century England, Separatists had to go either underground or into exile. Since only the second would permit them to practice their religious faith openly, exile it was. In 1608 some 125 of the group departed England for the Low Countries. They were led by their pastor, John Robinson; church elder William Brewster; and a young man of 16, William Bradford. After a brief stay in Amsterdam, the group settled in the town of Leyden. In 1619, however, disheartened by the difficulties they had encountered in making a living, disappointed by the failure of others in England to join them, and distressed because their children were being "subjected to the great licentiousness of the youth" in Holland, these "Pilgrims" decided to move again—to seek "a place where they might have liberty and live comfortably."

Negotiations between the Pilgrims in Leyden and the head of the Virginia Company in London, Sir Edwin Sandys, raised the possibility of America. Although unsympathetic to their religious views, Sandys appreciated the Pilgrims' inherent worth and supported their request to establish a settlement near the mouth of the Hudson River, on the northern boundary of the Virginia Company's grant. Since the Pilgrims were short of money, they formed a joint-stock company with other prospective emigrants and some optimistic investors who agreed to pay the expenses of the group in return for half the profits of the venture. In September 1620, about 100 strong—only 35 of them Pilgrims from Leyden—they set out from Plymouth, England, on the ship *Mayflower.*

Had the *Mayflower* reached its intended destination, the Pilgrims might have been soon forgotten. Instead their ship touched America slightly to the north, on Cape Cod Bay. Unwilling to remain longer at the mercy of storm-tossed December seas, they decided to settle where they were. Since they were outside the jurisdiction of the London Company, some members of the group claimed to be free of all governmental control. Therefore, before going ashore, the Pilgrims drew up the Mayflower Compact. "We whose names are underwritten," the Compact ran,

> do by these Presents, solemnly and mutually in the presence of God and one another covenant and combine ourselves under into a civil Body Politick . . . and by Virtue hereof do enact . . . such just and equal laws . . . as shall be thought most meet and convenient for the general Good of the Colony.

The Pilgrims chose William Bradford as their first governor. In this simple manner, ordinary people created a government that they hoped would enable them to cope with the unknown wilderness confronting them.

The story of the first 30 years of the colony has been preserved in *Of Plymouth Plantation,* written by Bradford. Having landed on the bleak Massachusetts shore in December, at a place called Plymouth, the Pilgrims had to endure a winter of desperate hunger. About half of them died. But by great good luck there was an Indian in the area, named Squanto, who spoke English! Squanto had been kidnapped in 1615 by an English sea captain, Thomas Hunt, who took him to Spain and sold him as a slave. Squanto soon escaped, however, and somehow made his way to England, where he was well treated. He fell in with people involved in colonization and exploring. He spent some time in Newfoundland in 1617–1618, returned to England, and in 1619 made another voyage to America as a pilot. This time he remained.

It is easy to understand why the Pilgrims believed that Squanto was "a special instrument sent of God for their good." In addition to serving as an interpreter, he showed them the best places to fish, and what to plant and how to cultivate it. In general, he provided them with all kinds of advice and support in an unfamiliar world. They, in turn, worked hard, got their crops in the ground in good time, and after a bountiful harvest the following November, they treated themselves and their Indian neighbors to the first Thanksgiving feast.

But if the Pilgrims had quickly secured themselves a safe place in the wilderness, what followed was hardly all cranberries and drumsticks. Bradford's flock grew neither rich nor numerous on the thin New England soil. By 1650 there were still fewer than 1,000 settlers, most of them living beyond the reach of the original church. Among them were a few who tried to take advantage of the freedom from social control afforded by the wilderness. In 1628 one Thomas Morton declared himself "Lord of Misrule" of the outlying community of Mount Wollaston, which he renamed Merrymount. He and kindred spirits declared their liberation from all restraints by setting up a maypole. They then invited neighboring Indian women to join them, provided drinks all round, and began (as the disapproving Bradford described the doings) "dancing and frisking together like so many fairies." Troops were dispatched to break up the carousing and take Morton into custody, after which he was expelled from the colony. In 1640 a teenager, Thomas Granger, was "detected of buggery" with various farmyard animals, including, according to Bradford, "a mare, a cow, two goats, five sheep, two calves, and a turkey"! Young Granger was convicted of bestiality and executed, but not before the animals in question—to the consternation of their owners—were destroyed in his presence.

Such lapses humanize the Pilgrims without jeopardizing their place in American history. That place is one of honor for, among other reasons, the integrity that characterized their dealings with the Indians. Theirs were victories won not with sword and gunpowder like those of Cortés or with bulldozer and dynamite like those of modern pioneers, but with simple courage and practical piety.

A 1641 English cartoon comments on the religious turmoil of the period. The Roman Catholic, "The Papist," at lower right joins in a game of "abusing" the Bible along with three Protestant sects opposed to the Church of England.

A Puritan Commonwealth

The Pilgrims were not the first English colonists to inhabit the northern regions. The Plymouth Company had settled a group on the Kennebec River in 1607. These colonists gave up after a few months, but fishermen and traders continued to visit the area, which was christened New England by Captain John Smith after an expedition there in 1614.

In 1620 the Plymouth Company was reorganized as the Council for New England, which had among its principal stockholders Sir Ferdinando Gorges and his friend John Mason, former governor of an English settlement on Newfoundland. Their particular domain included a considerable part of what is now Maine and New Hampshire. More interested in real estate deals than in colonizing, the council disposed of a number of tracts in the area north of Cape Cod. The most significant of these grants was a very small one made to a group of Puritans from Dorchester, who established a settlement at Salem in 1629.

Later that year these same Dorchester Puritans organized the Massachusetts Bay Company and obtained a royal grant to the area between the Charles and Merrimack rivers. The Massachusetts Bay Company was organized like any other commercial venture, but its Puritan investors regarded it less as a device for making money than as the shelter behind which they might take religious refuge in America should the need arise.

Unlike the Separatists in Plymouth, most Puritans had managed to satisfy both Crown and conscience while James I was king. The England of his son Charles I, who succeeded to the throne in 1625, posed a more serious challenge. Whereas James had been content to keep Puritans at bay, Charles and his favorite Anglican cleric, William Laud, intended to bring them to heel. With the king's support, Laud proceeded to further embellish the already elaborate Anglican ritual and to tighten the central control that the Puritans found so distasteful. He removed ministers with Puritan leanings from their pulpits and threatened church elders who harbored such ministers with imprisonment. No longer able to remain within the Anglican fold in good conscience and now facing prison if they tried to worship in the way they thought right, the Puritans decided to migrate to America in force. In the summer of 1630 nearly 1,000 of them set out from England, carrying the charter of the Massachusetts Bay Company with them. By the fall, they had founded Boston and several other towns. The Puritan commonwealth was under way.

Massachusetts settlers suffered fewer hardships in the early years than had the early Jamestown and Plymouth colonists. Luck played a part in this, but so did the careful planning that went into the transplantation. They also benefitted from a constant influx of new recruits, who came with families and worldly possessions in tow. Continuing bad times and the persecution of Puritans at home led to the Great Migration of the 1630s. Only a minority came to Massachusetts (many thousands more poured into new English colonies in the West Indies), but by 1640 well over 10,000 had arrived. This concentrated group of industrious, well-educated, and fairly prosperous colonists swiftly created a complex and distinct civilization on the very edge of what one of the pessimists among them called "a hideous and desolate wilderness, full of wild beasts and wild men."

The directors of the Massachusetts Bay Company believed their enterprise to be divinely inspired. Before leaving England, they elected John Winthrop, a 29-year-old Oxford-trained attorney, as governor of the colony. Throughout his 20 years of almost continuous service as governor, Winthrop spoke for the solid and sensible core of the Puritans and their high-minded experiment. His lay sermon, "A Modelle of Christian Charity," delivered in mid-Atlantic on the deck of the *Arbella* in 1630, made clear his sense of the momentousness of that experiment:

> Wee must Consider that wee shall be as a Citty upon a Hill, the eies of all people are upon us; soe that if wee shall deale falsely with our god in this worke wee have undertaken and soe cause him to withdrawe his present help from us, wee shall be made a story and a by-word through the world, wee shall open the mouthes of enemies to speake evill of the wayes of god and all professours for Gods sake.

Besides the governorship, the founders created an elected legislature, the General Court. Their system was not democratic in the modern sense because the right to vote and hold office was limited to church members. But this did not mean that the government was run by clergymen or that it did not reflect the popular will. Clergymen were influential, but since they were not allowed to hold public office, their authority was indirect and based on the respect of their parishoners, not on law or force. At least until the mid-1640s, most families contained at least one adult male church member. Since these "freemen" soon secured the right to choose the governor and elect the representatives ("deputies") to the General Court, a kind of practical democracy existed.

The Puritans had a clear sense of what their churches should be like. After getting permission from the General Court, a group of colonists who wished to form a new church could select a minister and conduct their spiritual affairs as they saw fit. Membership, however, was not open to everyone or even to all who led outwardly blameless lives. It was restricted to those who could present satisfactory evidence of their having experienced "saving grace," such as the compelling recounting of some extraordinary emotional experience, some mystical sign of intimate contact with God. This meant that full membership in the churches of early Massachusetts was reserved for "visible saints." During the 1630s, however, few applicants were denied membership. Having removed oneself from England was considered in most cases sufficient proof of spiritual purity. Indeed, as Winthrop had more than one occasion to lament, most of the colony's early troublemakers came not from those of doubtful spiritual condition but from its certified saints.

Troublemakers

The "godly and zealous" Roger Williams was a prime example. The Pilgrim leader William Bradford described Williams as possessed of "many precious parts, but very unsettled in judgment." Even by Plymouth's standards Williams was an extreme separatist. He was ready to bring down upon New England the wrath of Charles I rather than accept the charters signed by him or his father, even if these documents provided the only legal basis for the governments of Plymouth and Massachusetts Bay. Williams had arrived in Massachusetts in 1631. Following a short stay in Plymouth, he joined the church in Salem, which elected him minister in 1635. Well before then, however, his outspoken opposition to the alliance of church and civil government turned both ministers and magistrates against him. Part of his contrariness stemmed from his religious libertarianism. Magistrates should have no voice in spiritual matters, he insisted—"forced religion stinks in God's nostrils." He also offended the property owners of the commonwealth (which meant nearly everyone) by advancing the radical idea that it was "a Nationale sinne" for anyone, including the king, to take possession of any American land without buying it from the Indians.

A page from this New England primer reflects the pervasive influence of religion on every aspect of Puritan life, from politics to the education of the young.

N *Noah* did view
The old World & new

O Young *Obadias*,
David, *Josias*,
All were pious.

P *Peter* deny'd
His Lord, and cry'd.

Q Queen *Esther* sues,
And saves the *Jews*.

R Young pious *Ruth*,
Left all for Truth.

S Young *Samuel* dear
The Lord did fear.

As long as Williams enjoyed the support of his Salem church, there was little the magistrates could do to silence him. But his refusal to heed those who counselled moderation—"all truths are not seasonable at all times" Governor Winthrop reminded him—swiftly eroded that support. In the fall of 1635, economic pressure put on the town of Salem by the General Court turned his congregation against him. The General Court then ordered him to leave the colony within six weeks.

Williams departed Massachusetts in January 1636, traveling south to the head of Narragansett Bay. There he worked out mutually acceptable arrangements with the local Indians and founded the town of Providence. In 1644, after obtaining a charter in England from Parliament, he established the colony of Rhode Island and Providence Plantations. The government was relatively democratic, all religions were tolerated, and church and state were rigidly separated. Whatever Williams's temperamental excesses, he was more than ready to practice what he preached when given the opportunity.

Anne Hutchinson, who arrived in Boston in 1631, was another "visible saint" who, in the judgment of the Puritan establishment, went too far. Hutchinson was not to be taken lightly. According to Governor Winthrop, her husband William was "a man of mild temper and weak parts, wholly guided by his wife." (He was not so weak as to prevent him from fathering her 15 children.) Duties as a midwife brought her into the homes of other Boston women, with whom she discussed and more than occasionally criticized the sermons of their minister, John Wilson. Where Wilson and virtually all the ministers in the Bay Colony except her favorite, John Cotton, went wrong, she contended, was in emphasizing the obligation of the saved to lead morally pure lives as a model for the unregenerate. By taking the Puritan view that there was no necessary relationship between moral conduct and salvation to its extreme limits, she concluded to her own satisfaction that those possessed of saving grace were exempt from the rules of good behavior and the laws of the commonwealth.

As her detractors pointed out, this was the same conclusion some of the earliest German Protestants had reached, for which they were judged guilty of the heresy of antinomianism ("against the law") and burned at the stake. In 1636 the General Court charged Hutchinson with defaming the clergy and brought her to trial. When her accusers quoted the Bible ("Honor thy father and thy mother") to make their case, she coolly announced that even the Ten Commandments must yield to one's own insights if these were directly inspired by God. When pressed for details, she acknowledged that she was a regular recipient of such divine insights, communicated, as they were to Abraham, "by the voice of His own spirit in my soul." The General Court, upon hearing this shocking claim, promptly banished her from the commonwealth.

Hutchinson, together with her large family and a group of supporters, left Massachusetts in the spring of 1637 for Rhode Island, thereby adding to the growing reputation of that colony as the "sink" of New England. After her husband died in 1642 she and six of her children moved to the Dutch colony of New Netherland, where, the following year, she and all but her youngest daughter were killed by Indians.

The banishments of Roger Williams, whom some historians have championed as the first American democrat, and Anne Hutchinson, who, if not a feminist in the modern sense, refused to defer to her male "betters," did not endear the Massachusetts Puritans to posterity. In both cases outspoken individualists seem to have been done in by frightened politicians and self-serving ministers. Yet Williams and Hutchinson posed genuine threats to the new community. Massachusetts was truly a social experiment. Could it accommodate such uncooperative spirits and remain intact? When forced to choose between the peace of the commonwealth and sending dissenters packing, Winthrop, the magistrates, and the ministers did not hesitate. Such was the price of holding together a self-governing people whose only protections against anarchy were those they imposed upon themselves.

Other New England Colonies

From the successful Massachusetts Bay Colony, settlement radiated outward to other areas of New England because of population growth and Puritan intolerance. In 1629 Sir Ferdinando Gorges and John Mason divided their holdings, Gorges taking the Maine section (enlarged in 1639) and Mason New Hampshire, but neither succeeded in making much of his claim. Massachusetts gradually took over these areas. The heirs of Gorges and Mason managed to regain legal possession briefly in the 1670s, but Massachusetts bought title to Maine for a pittance (£1,250) in 1677. New Hampshire became a royal colony in 1680.

Meanwhile, beginning in 1635, a number of Massachusetts congregations had pushed southwestward into the fertile valley of the Connecticut River. A group headed by the Reverend Thomas Hooker founded Hartford in 1636. Hooker was influential in the drafting of the Fundamental Orders, a sort of constitution creating a government for the valley towns, in 1639. The Fundamental Orders resembled the Massachusetts system, except that they did not limit voting to church members. Other groups of Puritans came directly from England to settle towns in and around New Haven in the 1630s. These were incorporated into Connecticut shortly after the Hooker colony obtained a royal charter in 1662.

Competition between Connecticut and Massachusetts Bay over land led to quarrels that exacerbated Indian troubles, and Hooker and some of the other Connecticut pioneers quarreled with the Massachusetts leaders about religious questions.

French and Dutch Settlements

While the English were settling Virginia and New England, other European powers were challenging Spain's monopoly in the New World. French explorers had pushed up the St. Lawrence as far as the site of Montreal in the 1530s, and beginning in 1603, Samuel de Champlain made several voyages to the region. In 1608 he founded Quebec, and he had penetrated as far inland as Lake Huron before the Pilgrims left Leyden. The French also planted colonies in St. Christopher, Guadeloupe, Martinique, and other islands in the West Indies after 1625.

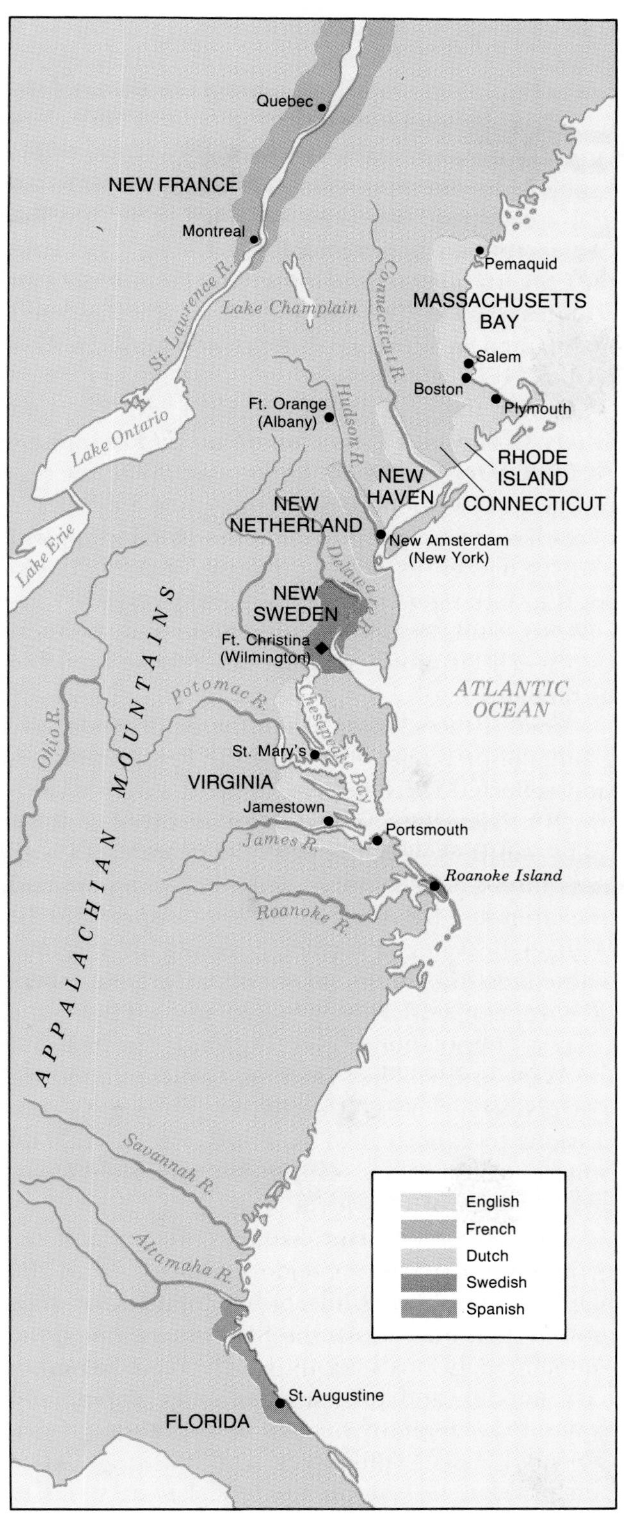

NORTH AMERICAN COLONIES TO 1650

Through their West India Company, the Dutch also established themselves in the West Indies. On the mainland they founded New Netherland in the Hudson Valley, basing their claim to the region on the explorations of Henry Hudson in 1609. As early as 1624 there was a Dutch outpost, Fort Orange, on the site of present-day Albany. Two years later New Amsterdam was located at the mouth of the Hudson River, and Manhattan Island was purchased from the Indians by Peter Minuit, the director-general of the West India Company, for trading goods worth about 60 guilders.

The Dutch traded with the Indians for furs and plundered Spanish colonial commerce enthusiastically. Through the Charter of Privileges of Patroons, which authorized large grants of land to individuals who would bring over 50 settlers, they tried to encourage large-scale agriculture. Only one such estate—Rensselaerswyck, on the Hudson south of Fort Orange, owned by the rich Amsterdam merchant Kiliaen Van Rensselaer—was successful. Peter Minuit was removed from his post in New Amsterdam in 1631; he organized a group of Swedish settlers several years later and founded the colony of New Sweden on the lower reaches of the Delaware River. New Sweden was in constant conflict with the Dutch, who finally overran it in 1655. But the Dutch were never deeply committed to colonizing America; their chief activity was in the Far East, where they took over the role formerly played by the Portuguese.

Maryland and the Carolinas

The Virginia and New England colonies were essentially corporate ventures. Most of the other English colonies in America were founded by individuals or by a handful of partners who obtained charters from the ruling sovereign. It was becoming easier to establish settlements in America, for experience had taught the English a great deal about the colonization process. Settlers knew better what to bring with them and what to do after they arrived. Moreover, the psychological barrier was much less formidable. Like a modern athlete seeking to run a mile in less than four minutes, colonizers knew after about 1630 that what they were attempting *could* be accomplished. And conditions in Europe in the mid-17th century encouraged thousands to migrate. Both in England and on the Continent the economic future seemed unpromising, while political and religious persecution erupted in one country after another, each time supplying America with new waves of refugees.

Numbers of influential Englishmen were eager to try their luck as colonizers. The grants they received made them "proprietors" of great estates which were, at least in theory, their personal property. By granting land to settlers in return for a small annual rent, they hoped to obtain a steadily increasing income while holding a valuable speculative interest in all undeveloped land. At the same time their political power, guaranteed by charter, would become increasingly important as their colonies expanded. In practice, however, the realities of life in America limited their freedom of action and their profits.

One of the first of the proprietary colonies was Maryland, granted by Charles I to George Calvert, Lord Baltimore. Calvert had a deep interest in America, being a member both of the London Company and of the Council for New England and owner of a colony called Avalon in Newfoundland. He hoped to profit financially from Maryland but, since he was a Catholic, he also intended the colony to be a haven for his coreligionists.

Calvert died shortly before Charles approved his charter, so the grant went to his son Cecilius. The first settlers arrived in 1634, founding St. Mary's just north of the Potomac. The presence of the now well-established Virginia colony nearby greatly aided the Marylanders; they had little difficulty in getting started and in developing an economy based, like Virginia's, on tobacco. However, an acrimonious dispute raged for some years between the two colonies over their common boundary. Despite the emptiness of the American wilderness, settlers could squabble over a few acres as bitterly as any European peasants.

The Maryland charter was similar to that of the isolated county palatine of Durham in the north of England, whose bishop-overlords had almost regal authority. Lord Baltimore had the right to establish feudal manors, hold people in serfdom, make laws, and set up his own courts. He soon discovered, however, that to attract settlers he had to allow them to own their farms and that to maintain any political influence at all he had to give the settlers considerable say in local affairs. Other wise concessions marked his handling of the religious question. He would have preferred an exclusively Catholic colony, but while Catholics did go to Maryland, there existed from the beginning a large Protestant majority. Baltimore solved this problem by "accepting" a Toleration Act (1649) that guaranteed freedom of religion to anyone "professing to believe in Jesus Christ." Because the Calverts adjusted their pretensions to American realities, they made a fortune out of Maryland and maintained an influence in the colony until the Revolution.

During the period of the English Civil War and Oliver Cromwell's Protectorate, no important new colonial enterprises were undertaken. With the restoration of the monarchy in 1660 came a new wave of settlement, for the government wished to expand and strengthen its hold on North America. To do so, it granted generous terms to settlers—easy access to land, religious toleration, and political rights—all far more extensive than those available in England.

Most of the earlier colonies were organized by groups of merchants; those of the Restoration period reflected the concerns of great English landowners. The first new venture involved a huge grant south of Virginia to eight proprietors with large interests in colonial affairs, including the Earl of Clarendon, Sir Anthony Ashley Cooper, and Sir William Berkeley, a former governor of Virginia. These men did not intend to recruit large numbers of European settlers, depending instead upon the "excess" population of New England, Virginia, and the West Indies. They (and the Crown) hoped for a diversified economy, the charter granting tax concessions to exporters of wine, silk, oil, olives, and other exotic products. The region was called Carolina in honor of Charles I.

The Carolina charter, like that of Maryland, accorded the proprietors wide authority. With the help of the political philosopher John Locke, they drafted a grandiose plan of government called the Fundamental Constitutions, which created a hereditary nobility and provided for huge paper land grants to a hierarchy headed by the lords proprietors and lesser "landgraves" and "caciques." The human effort to support the feudal society was to be supplied by peasants called leet-men.

This pretentious system proved unworkable. The landgraves and caciques got grants, but they

Engraved "prospects" of New World settlements served to attract immigrants. This rather lavish example shows Philadelphia in the 1730s, when the city was a half-century old.

could not find leet-men willing to toil on their domains. Probably the purpose of all this elaborate feudal nonsense was promotional; the proprietors hoped to convince investors that they could make fortunes in Carolina rivaling those of English lords. In reality, life followed the pattern established in Virginia and Maryland, with nearly all white men owning their own property and possessing a good deal of political power.

The first settlers arrived in 1670, most of them from the sugar plantations of Barbados, where slave labor was driving out small independent farmers. Charles Town (now Charleston) was founded in 1680. Another center of population sprang up in the Albemarle district, just south of Virginia, settled largely by individuals from that colony. Two quite different societies grew up in these areas. The Charleston colony, with an economy based on a thriving trade in furs and on the export of foodstuffs to the West Indies, was prosperous and cosmopolitan. The Albemarle settlement was poorer and more "backwoodsy." Eventually, in 1712, the two were formally separated, becoming North and South Carolina.

The Middle Colonies

Gradually it became clear that the English would dominate the entire stretch of coast between the St. Lawrence Valley and Florida. After 1660 only the Dutch challenged their monopoly. The two nations, once allies against Spain, had fallen out because of the fierce competition of their textile manufacturers and merchants. England's efforts to bar Dutch merchant vessels from its colonial trade also brought the two countries into conflict in America. Charles II precipitated a showdown by granting his brother James, Duke of York, the entire area between Connecticut and Maryland. This was tantamount to declaring war. In 1664 English forces captured New Amsterdam without a fight—there were only 1,500 people in the town—and soon the rest of the Dutch settlements capitulated. New Amsterdam became New York. The duke did not interfere much with the way of life of the Dutch settlers, and they were quickly reconciled to English rule. New York had no local assembly until the 1680s, but there had been no such body under the Dutch either.

In 1664, even before the capture of New Amsterdam, the Duke of York gave New Jersey, the region between the Hudson and the Delaware, to John, Lord Berkeley and Sir George Carteret. To attract settlers, these proprietors offered land on easy terms and established freedom of religion and a democratic system of local government. A considerable number of Puritans from New England and Long Island moved to the new province.

In 1674 Berkeley sold his interest in New Jersey to two Quakers. The Quakers were left-wing Separatists who believed that they could communicate directly with their Maker; their religion required neither ritual nor ministers. Originally a sect emotional to the point of fanaticism, by the 1670s the Quakers had come to stress the doctrine of the Inner Light—the direct, mystical experience of religious truth—which they believed possible for all persons. They were at once humble and fiercely proud, pacifistic yet unwilling to bow before any person or to surrender their right to worship as they pleased. They distrusted the intellect in religious matters and, while ardent proselytizers of their own beliefs, they tolerated those of others cheerfully. When faced with opposition, they resorted to passive resistance, a tactic that embroiled them in grave difficulties in England and in most of the American colonies. In Massachusetts Bay, for example, four Quakers were executed when they refused either to conform to Puritan ideas or to leave the colony.

The acquisition of New Jersey (when Sir George Carteret died in 1680, they purchased the rest of the colony) gave the Quakers a place where they could practice their religion in peace. The proprietors, in keeping with their principles, drafted an extremely liberal constitution for the colony, the Concessions and Agreements of 1677, which created an autonomous legislature and guaranteed settlers freedom of conscience, the right of trial by jury, and other civil rights.

The main Quaker effort at colonization came in the region immediately west of New Jersey, a fertile area belonging to William Penn, the son of a wealthy English admiral. Penn had early rejected a life of ease and had become a Quaker missionary. As a result, he was twice jailed. Yet he possessed qualities that enabled him to hold the respect and friendship of people who found his religious ideas abhorrent. From his father, Penn had inherited a claim to £16,000 that the admiral had lent Charles II. The king, reluctant to part with that much cash, paid off the debt in 1681 by giving Penn the region north of Maryland and west of the Delaware River, insisting only that it be named Pennsylvania, in honor of the admiral. The Duke of York then added Delaware, the region between Maryland and Delaware Bay, to Penn's holdings.

William Penn considered his colony a "Holy Experiment." He treated the Indians fairly, buying title to their lands and trying to protect them in their dealings with settlers and traders. Anyone who believed in "one Almighty and Eternal God" was entitled to freedom of worship. His political ideas were paternalistic rather than democratic—the assembly he established could only approve or reject laws proposed by the governor and council—but individual rights were as well protected in Pennsylvania as in New Jersey.

Penn's altruism, however, did not prevent him from taking excellent care of his own interests. He sold land to settlers large and small on easy terms but reserved huge tracts for himself and attached quitrents (see page 44) to the land he disposed of. He promoted Pennsylvania tirelessly, writing a series of glowing, although perfectly honest, descriptions of the colony which were circulated widely in England and, in translation, on the Continent. These attracted many settlers, including large numbers of Germans—the Pennsylvania "Dutch" (a corruption of *Deutsch,* meaning "German").

Penn was neither a doctrinaire nor an ivory-tower philosopher. He came himself to Pennsylvania and agreed to adjustments in his first Frame of Government when local conditions demonstrated the need for change. His combination of wisdom, liberality, and good salesmanship helped the colony to prosper and grow rapidly. Of course the presence of well-settled colonies on all sides and the richness of the soil had much to do with this happy state of affairs. By 1685 there were almost 9,000 settlers in Pennsylvania, and by 1700 twice that number, a heartening contrast to the early history of Virginia and Plymouth. Pennsylva-

In a letter dated 1682, William Penn assured the native inhabitants of his newly acquired land that "I have already taken care that none of my people wrong you, by good laws I have provided for that purpose. . . ." He signed himself "Your loveing Freind [sic], Wm Penn."

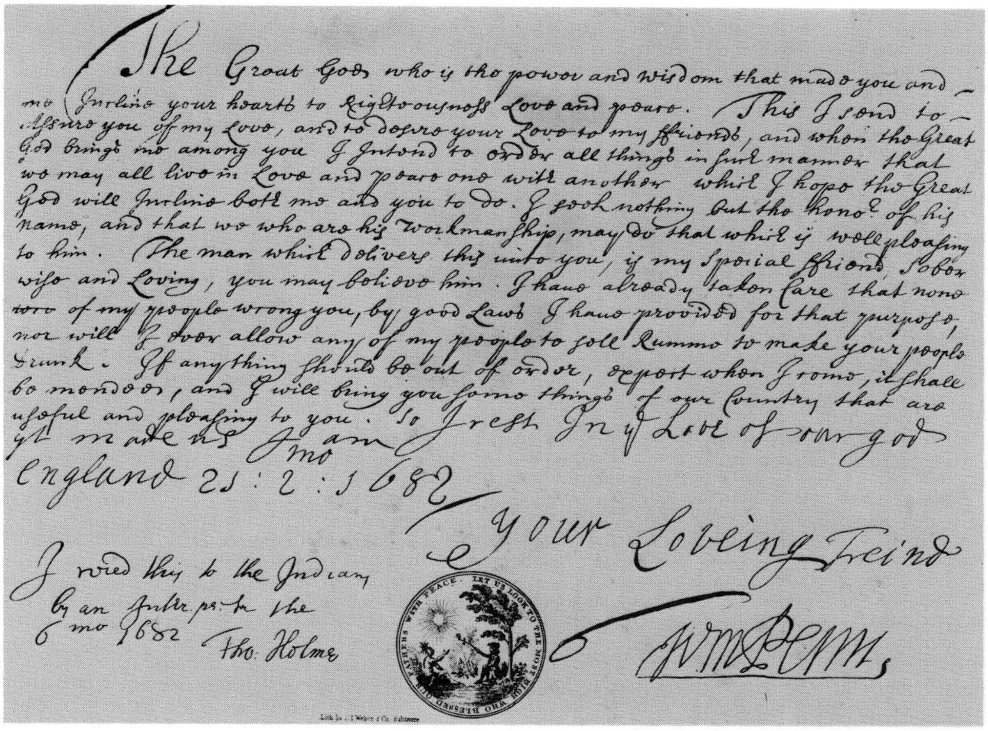
The Great God who is the power and wisdom that made you and me, Incline your hearts to Righteousness Love and peace. This I send to Assure you of my Love, and to desire your Love to my friends, and when the Great God brings me among you I intend to order all things in such manner that we may all live in Love and peace one with another which I hope the Great God will Incline both me and you to do. I seek nothing but the hono^r of his name, and that we who are his workmanship, may do that which is well pleasing to him. The man which delivers this unto you, is my Special friend, Sober wise and Loving, you may believe him. I have already taken Care that none of my people wrong you, by good Laws I have provided for that purpose, nor will I ever allow any of my people to sell Rumme to make your people Drunk. If any thing should be out of order, expect when I come, it shall be mended, and I will bring you some things of our Country that are useful and pleasing to you. So I rest In ye Love of our god yt made us I am

England 21 : 2 : 1682

Your Loveing Freind
Wm Penn

I read this to the Indians by an Interpreter the 6 mo 1682 Tho: Holme

nia produced wheat, corn, rye, and other crops in abundance and found a ready market for its surpluses on the sugar plantations of the West Indies.

Indians as "Americanizers"

Interaction with the native peoples was characteristic of life in all the English colonies. *Interaction* is the key word in this sentence. The so-called Columbian exchange between Indian and European was a two-way street. The colonists learned a great deal about how to live in the American forest from the Indians: the names of plants and animals (hickory, pecan, raccoon, skunk, moose); what to eat in their new home and how to catch or grow it; what to wear (leather leggings and especially moccasins); how best to get from one place to another; how to fight; in some respects how to think.

The colonists learned from the Indians how best to use many wild plants and animals for food and clothing, but they would probably have discovered most of these if the continent had been devoid of human life when they arrived. Corn, however, the staple of the diet of agricultural tribes, was something the Indians had domesticated. Its contribution to the success of English colonization was enormous.

The colonists also took advantage of that marvel of Indian technology, the birchbark canoe. An early explorer, Martin Pring, brought one back to England in 1603; it was 17 feet long and 4 feet wide and capable, according to Pring, of carrying nine full-grown men. Yet it weighed "not at the most above sixtie pounds," a thing, Pring added, "almost incredible in regard to the largenesse and capacitie thereof."

For their part the Indians adopted European technology eagerly. All metal objects were indeed of great usefulness to them, though the products and tools that metals replaced were neither crude nor inefficient in most cases. (To say that a gun is a more deadly weapon than a bow and arrow is a far more accurate statement about *modern* guns than about a 17th-century firelock. A bowman could get off six times as many shots in a given time as a soldier armed with a firelock and would probably hit the target more frequently.)

Indians took on many of the whites' attitudes along with their tools, clothing, weapons, alcohol,

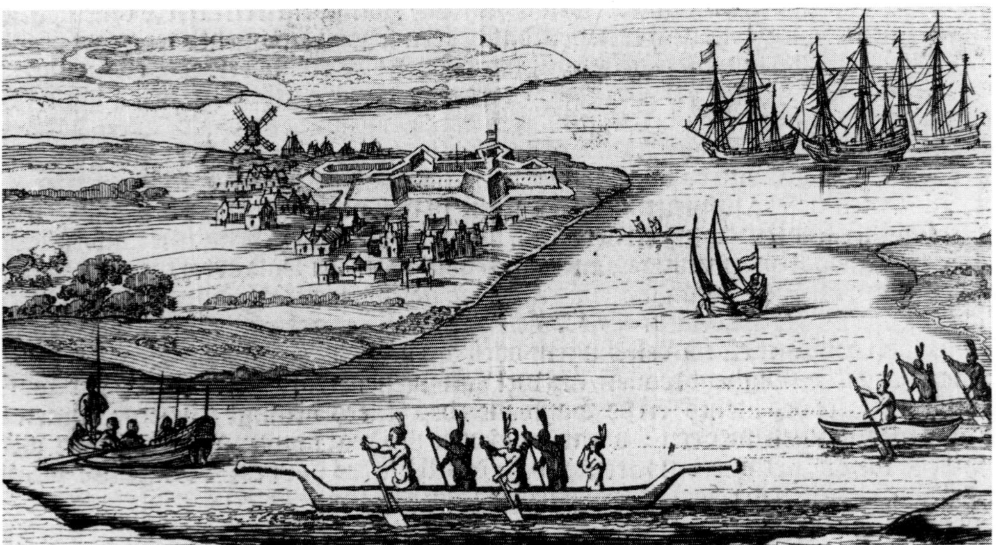

This 1651 engraving, the first known view of Manhattan Island, shows the new fort of New Amsterdam in the 1620s. Indians bring beaver pelts in their canoes to sell to the Dutch.

and ornaments. Some tribes used the products of European technology to tyrannize over tribes in more remote areas. During wars, as we shall soon be pointing out, Indians fought almost as often with whites against other Indians as with other Indians against whites.

The fur trade illustrates the pervasiveness of Indian-white interaction. It was in some ways a perfect business arrangement. Both groups profited greatly—the colonists got "valuable" furs for "cheap" European products, while the Indians got "priceless" tools, knives, and other trade goods in exchange for "cheap" beaver pelts and deerskins. The demand for furs caused the Indians to become more efficient hunters and trappers and even to absorb some of the whites' ideas about private property and capitalist accumulation. Hunting parties became larger. Farming tribes shifted their villages in order to be nearer trade routes and waterways. In some cases tribal organization was altered: small groups combined into confederations in order to control more territory when their hunting reduced the supplies of furs nearer home. Early in the 17th century, Huron Indians in the Great Lakes region, who had probably never seen a Frenchman, owned French products obtained from eastern tribes in exchange for Huron corn. All in all, as one historian puts it, "the fur trade set off a chain reaction . . . within the Indian world."

In *The European and the Indian,* James Axtell makes an important point about the relative impact of the two cultures on each other. Although the colonists learned much from the Indians and adopted certain elements of Indian culture and technology eagerly, their objective was *not* to be like the Indians, whom they considered the epitome of savagery and barbarism. That they feared they might become "Indianized," Axtell notes, is clear from the adage "It is very easy to make an Indian out of a white man, but you cannot make a white man out of an Indian." Yet this very fear, the colonial rejection of Indian ways, caused what Axtell calls "reactive changes" that are at the heart of what made them Americans rather than transplanted Europeans. The constant conflicts with Indians forced the colonists to band together and in time gave them a sense of having shared a common history. And later, when they broke away from Great Britain, they used the image of the Indian to symbolize the freedom and independence they sought for themselves.

In sum, during the 200-odd years that followed Columbus's first landfall in the Caribbean a complex development had taken place in the Americas, one that profoundly affected the civilizations of the people who preceded Columbus and those who followed him. We shall now turn to a more detailed look at how this happened in one part of that vast region, the part on which our own civilization has evolved.

SUPPLEMENTARY READING

Titles marked with an asterisk have been published in paperback.

On the explorers and the world they opened up, see D. B. Quinn, **North America from Earliest Discovery to First Settlements*** (1977), S. E. Morison, **The European Discovery of America** (1971–1974), J. H. Parry, **The Spanish Seaborne Empire** (1966), and C. O. Sauer, **Sixteenth-Century North America*** (1971). Morison's biography of Columbus, **Admiral of the Ocean Sea** (1942), is a model of sound scholarship and good writing.

Accounts of the English background of colonization can be found in Wallace Notestein, **The English People on the Eve of Colonization*** (1954), A. L. Rowse, **The Elizabethans and America*** (1959), and Carl Bridenbaugh, **Vexed and Troubled Englishmen*** (1968). J. H. Elliott, **The Old World and the New*** (1970), analyzes the impact of the discovery of America on Europe.

On French and Spanish colonization, see W. J. Eccles, **France in America*** (1972), and Charles Gibson, **Spain in America*** (1966). On the interactions of European and Indian civilizations, consult James Axtell, **The European and the Indian** (1981), Karen Kupperman, **Settling with the Indian** (1980), and William Cronon, **Changes in the Land** (1981). W. E. Washburn, **The Indian in America** (1975), contains a good discussion of the culture and history of North American Indian groups. Francis Jennings, **The Invasion of America*** (1975), is extremely critical of white dealings with the Indians. A. T. Vaughan, **New England Frontier*** (1965), argues that New Englanders treated the Indians fairly. On the African background of black slaves, see B. Davison and K. Buah, **History of West Africa to the 19th Century*** (1967); on the slave trade, P. D. Curtin, **The Atlantic Slave Trade*** (1970), and H. S. Klein, **The Middle Passage** (1978).

The classic account of the history of English colonization is C. M. Andrews's **The Colonial Period of American History*** (1934–1938). W. F. Craven's **The Colonies in Transition*** (1968) is a first-rate study of late 17th- and early 18th-century developments. On the southern colonies, W. F. Craven's **The Southern Colonies in the Seventeenth Century*** (1949) is excellent. On Virginia, E. S. Morgan, **American Slavery, American Freedom** (1975), is outstanding, while G. F. Willison's **Behold Virginia** (1951) is popular history at its best. For Maryland, consult G. T. Main, **Tobacco Colony** (1982).

Historians have always been of two minds about the Puritan colonies. S. E. Morison, in **Builders of the Bay Colony*** (1930), presents a favorable account. D. R. Rutman, **Winthrop's Boston** (1965), is more up-to-date and balanced. For the middle colonies, see Michael Kammen, **Colonial New York** (1975), and G. B. Nash, **Quakers and Politics** (1968). The Georgia experiment is covered well in Phinizy Spalding, **Oglethorpe in America** (1977). No student should miss at least dipping into the works of Francis Parkman on the French in America. His **Pioneers of France in the New World** (1855) covers the early period.

Biographies worth noting include A. T. Vaughan, **American Genesis: Captain John Smith*** (1975), E. S. Morgan, **The Puritan Dilemma: The Story of John Winthrop*** (1958), Morgan's **Roger Williams: The Church and the States*** (1967), and M. M. Dunn, **William Penn** (1967).

Three "Different" Cultures

The idea that the New World was a "melting pot" in which people from vastly different cultures became "Americans" was never entirely correct. Most retained many of their "foreign" attitudes and beliefs, however much they were influenced by their surroundings. Nevertheless, the idea that America was and is a place where people of different geographic and cultural backgrounds live and interact is fundamentally correct.

The civilizations depicted here do not figure largely in the modern mainstream. After Columbus, people from western Europe came to dominate both North and South America. Their culture and the story of how it evolved in the New World dominate the pages of this book. But these civilizations represent three types of influence. The Ashanti of West Africa never came to America themselves. But since they were slave traders, they were partly responsible for forcing thousands of other blacks to become Americans. The complex Aztec civilization was destroyed by the conquistadors. It exists today mainly in museums. But the descendants of the Aztecs still live in the "melting pot" of modern Mexico. The Hopi were far less rich and powerful than either the Aztecs or the Ashantis. Yet they still exist relatively unchanged in their original homeland.

European—and eventually American—traders were attracted to the Gold Coast by the Ashanti people's gold resources and also by the slave trade. The brass figures on the facing page were used to weigh gold dust; they show scenes of everyday Ashanti life—pounding yams, climbing a palm tree, doing carpentry. The gold mask is from the Ashanti treasury.

The yam festival witnessed by T. E. Bowdich in 1817 celebrated the harvest of that staple food. The Union Jack and the red-coated British strike a brilliant note in an already exotic scene.

En route to the New World, blacks suffered unspeakable conditions. An officer of an English slave ship painted this watercolor during a voyage. It is one of the few known depictions of a slave ship's hold.

Slave traders were active in West Africa from the fifteenth century on. This illustration from a 1698 French book shows a white trader bargaining for the pair of shackled blacks. The woman at left pounds "coscou"; compare her actions with those of the family-group gold weight on the facing page.

When the Spanish arrived in Mexico, they found the Aztec civilization in full flower. The Aztecs produced beautiful objects for ceremonial purposes, like the shield at left, intricately formed with the brilliantly colored feathers of native birds. The human skull, inlaid with obsidian and turquoise, was found in an Aztec treasure horde. It may be Mixtec.

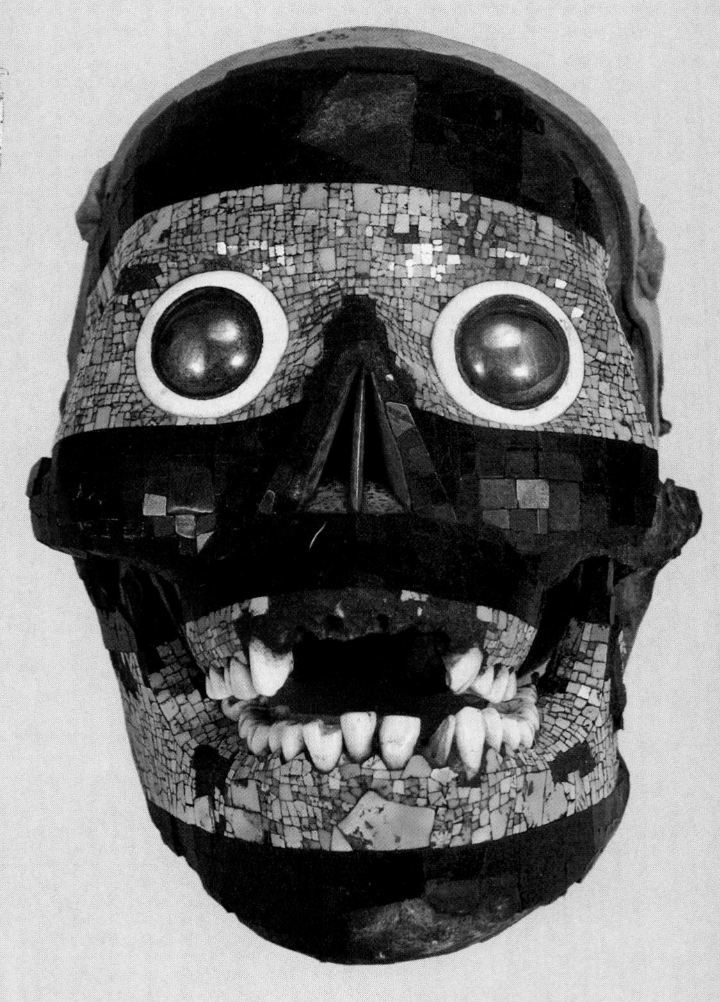

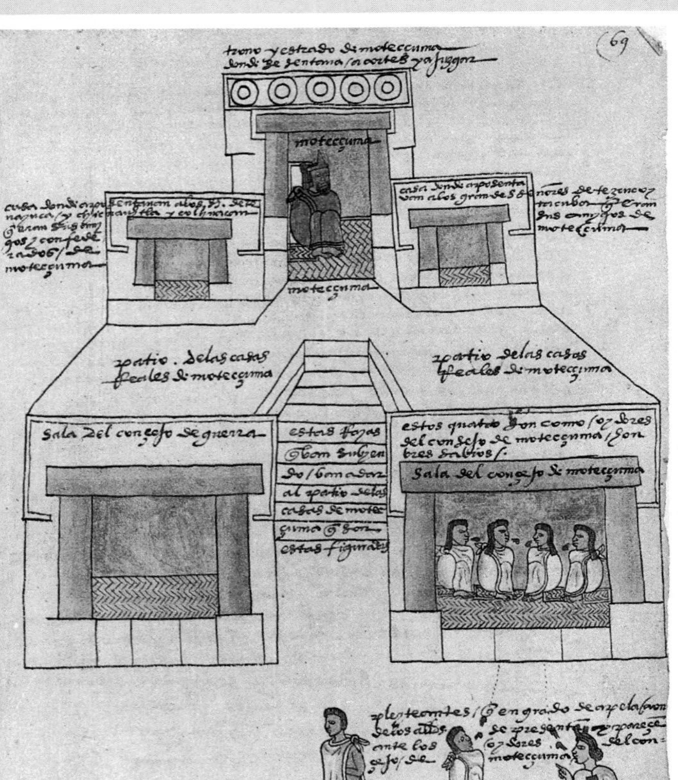

The Aztecs had an elaborate legal system. Here Montezuma, in blue robes at the top of the drawing, presides over the law court that meets in his palace.

A page from a codex (illustrated manuscript) shows Cortés's troops with their native allies advancing on Tenochtitlán, now Mexico City. The four major attacking divisions surround Montezuma's capital as dismembered Aztecs are trampled underfoot.

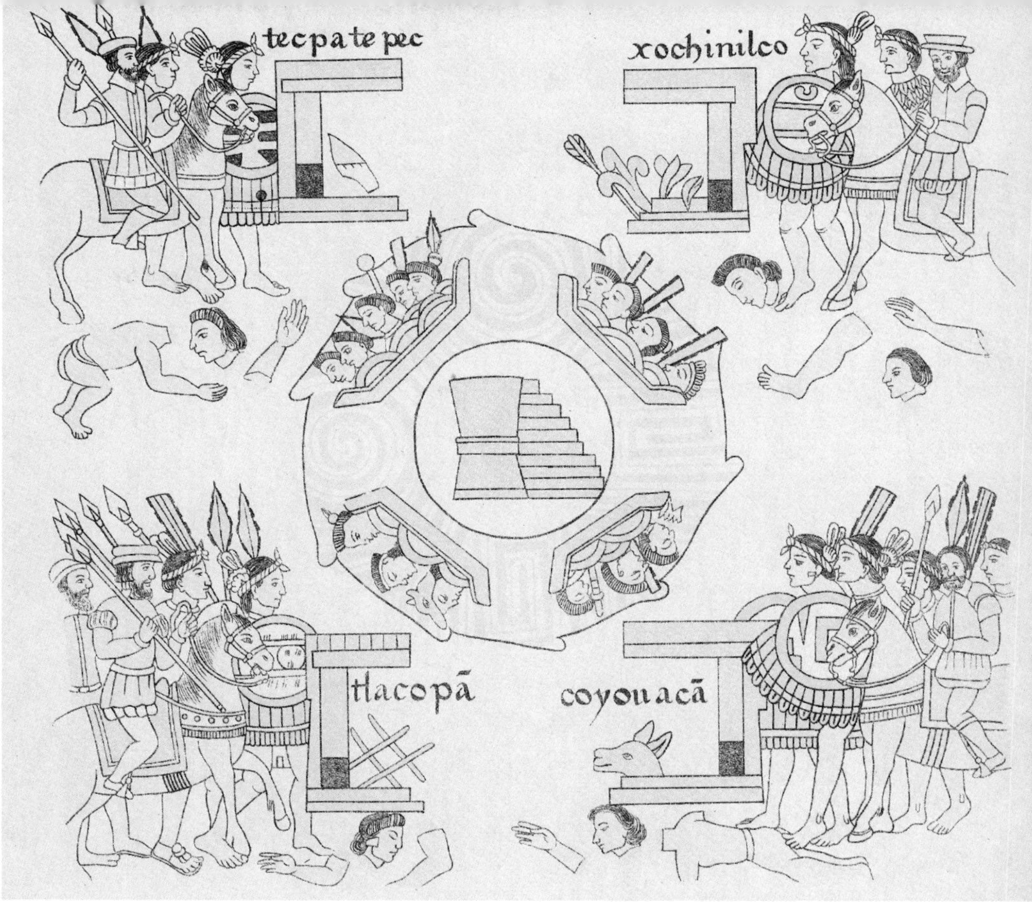

tecpatepec

xochinilco

tlacopā

coyouacā

Among the Aztecs and neighboring peoples, a form of picture writing existed. The types of images and the number of times they are repeated convey a message without the use of a true alphabet. This is a Mixtec pictograph.

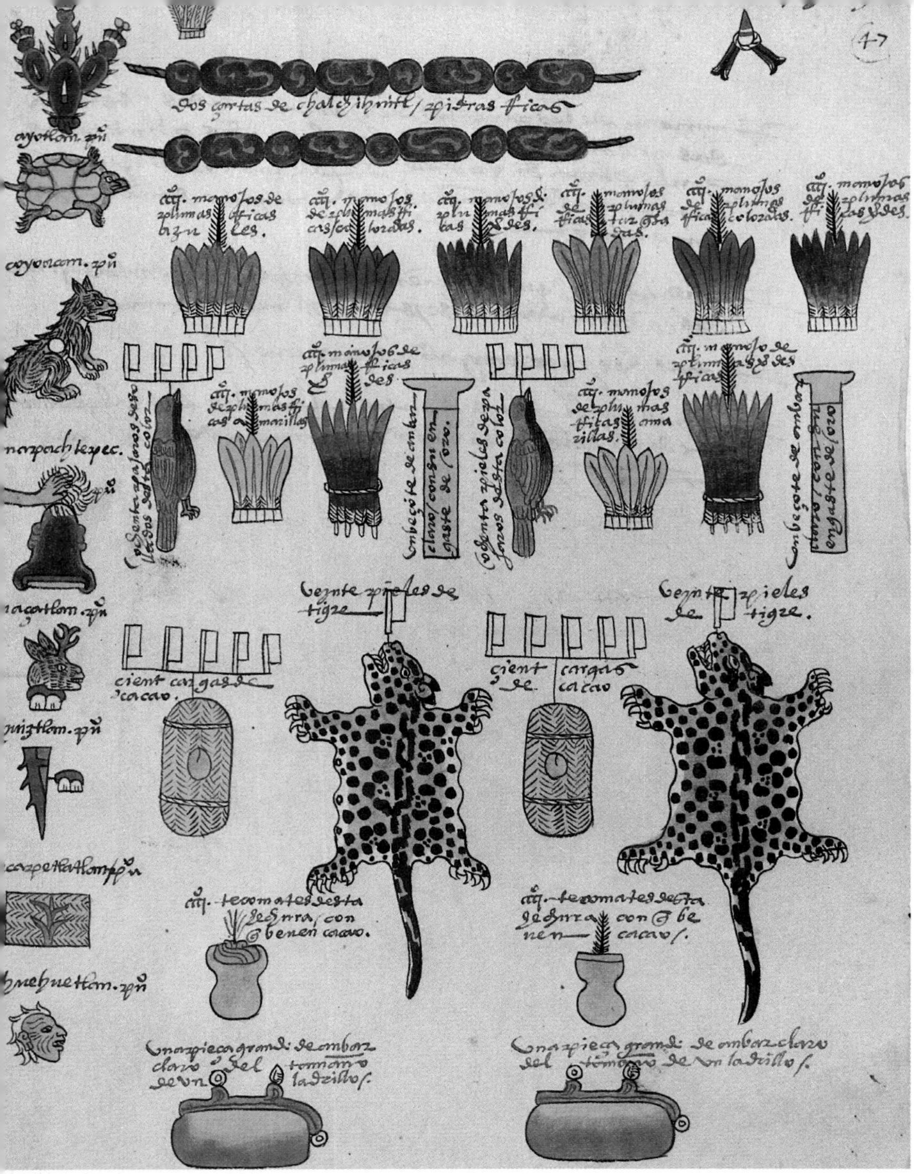

After the Spanish conquered Mexico, they collected the tribute that had formerly been paid the Aztecs by subject peoples. The Spanish notations on the above tribute roll record the quantities of semiprecious stones, feathers, jaguar skins, baskets of cacao, and other goods received in one such tribute. The drawing at right, from a Spanish codex, shows European influence on spinning—note the wheel—and weaving, both activities supervised by a Spanish overseer.

Despite the persistent Spanish and Mexican influences in the Southwest, the Hopi people of what is now Arizona preserved many traditional elements in their culture virtually unchanged until the 20th century. This pueblo on a mesa at Walpi, photographed in the late 1800s, looked very much as it might have looked before the time of Columbus.

Cotton yarn was spun on a spindle rather than a wheel (see the Spanish-influenced spinning wheel on the opposite page). The work was done by men. Weaving was also primarily a man's job. Both photos date from the early 20th century.

The Kachina ritual dances are still a centerpiece of Hopi life. The men participating wear masks, body paint, feathers, and special garments representing a particular animal, spirit, or element. Kachina "dolls" are dressed in replicas of these costumes. This modern doll represents Kwa, the Eagle Kachina. Most such figures are 12 to 24 inches high.

Many Kachina ceremonies took place in underground rooms called *kivas.* Kiva walls were decorated with ceremonial images, such as this mural of a Corn Maiden. Corn is the symbolic Mother of the Hopi.

Another essential part of Hopi life was catching small game. In this modern painting by Hopi artist Leroy Kewanyama, the hunter has just killed a rabbit with the traditional throwing stick. A woman, perhaps his wife, runs up to put it in a sack.

The coming of the Anglos from the East brought profound changes in Hopi life. These three Hopi men, photographed in the mid-19th century, were delegates sent to meet with Brigham Young and arrange for increased trade with the Mormon settlers of Utah and the intermountain West.

2

American Society in the Making

The great Increase of Offspring in particular Families is not always owing to greater Fecundity of Nature, but sometimes to Examples of Industry in the Heads, and industrious Education; by which the Children are enabled to provide better for themselves, and their marrying earlier is encouraged from the Prospect of good Subsistence. BENJAMIN FRANKLIN, *1751*

The colonies were settled chiefly by English people at first, with a leavening of Germans, Scots, Scotch-Irish, Dutch, French, Swedes, Finns, a scattering of other nationalities, a handful of Sephardic Jews, and a gradually increasing number of black African slaves. The cultures these people brought with them varied according to the nationality, social status, intelligence, and taste of the individual. The newcomers never lost this heritage entirely, but they—and certainly their descendants—became something quite different from their relatives who remained in the Old World. They became what we call Americans.

But not right away.

What Is an American?

The subtle but profound changes that occurred when Europeans moved to the New World were hardly self-willed. Most of the settlers came, it is true, hoping for circumstances different from those they left behind—for a more bountiful existence, and sometimes also for nonmaterialistic reasons, such as the opportunity to practice their religions in ways barred to them at home. For some whose alternative was prison or execution, there was really no choice. Still, even the most rebellious or alienated seldom intended to develop an entirely new civilization; rather, they wished to reconstruct the old on terms more favorable to themselves. Nor did a single "American" type result from the careful selection of particular kinds of Europeans as colonizers. Settlers came from every walk of life and in rough proportion to their numbers in Europe (if we exclude the very highest social strata). Certainly there was no systematic selection of the finest grain to provide seed for cultivating the wilderness.

Why then did America become something more than another Europe? Why was New England not merely a new England, Virginia not simply an English province west of Ireland? If not just another "poor European immigrant" away from home, the French visitor Hector St. John de Crèvecoeur wondered in 1762, "What then is the American, this new man?" And how did he—and she—come to be?

The fact of physical separation provides an important part of the answer. America was isolated from Europe by 3,000 miles of ocean. The Atlantic served as an umbilical cord but also as a barrier; it was practically closed to commerce during the stormy winter months and dangerous enough in any season. The crossing took anywhere from a few weeks to several months, depending on wind and weather. No one undertook an ocean voyage lightly in colonial times, and few who made the westward crossing ever thought seriously of returning. The modern mind can scarcely grasp the awful isolation that enveloped the settler, the sense of being alone, of having cut all ties with home and past. One had to face forward (westward) and construct a new life or perish—if not of hunger, then of loneliness.

More than physical separation went into the process by which the people Crèvecoeur called this "promiscuous breed" fashioned for themselves a new national identity and the outlines of a distinctive civilization. Unlike separation from Europe, some factors affected some settlers differently than others. Factors as material as the landscape encountered, as quantifiable as population patterns, as elusive as chance and calculation all shaped colonial social arrangements. Their cumulative impact did not at first produce anything like a uniform society throughout the 2,000-mile-long and 50-mile-wide corridor that contained England's American colonies. Two quite different societies developed, one at each end of the corridor. A third society in the middle shared elements of both. The "Americans" who evolved in these regional societies were in many ways as different from each other as all were from their European cousins. The national identity Crèvecoeur happened upon in 1762 had been a century and a half in the making. It was an amalgam of regional identities that were no longer European but not yet wholly something else. The process by which these identities merged into an American nation remained incomplete. It was—and is—ongoing.

The Southern Colonies: A Hustling People

The southern parts of English North America comprised three regions: the Chesapeake Bay, consisting of "tidewater" Virginia and Maryland; the "low country" Carolinas; and the "back country," a vast territory that extended from the fall line of the tidal rivers to the farthest point of western settlement, eventually including Georgia. Not until well into the 18th century would the emergence of common features—export-oriented agricultural economies, a labor force in which black slaves figured prominently, the absence of towns of any size—prompt people to think of the "South" as a single region.

The Chesapeake: "Seasoning Time"

When the English philosopher Thomas Hobbes wrote in 1651 that human life tended to be "nasty, brutish, and short," he might well have had in mind the royal colony of Virginia. Although the colony grew from about 1,300 to nearly 5,000 in the decade after the crown took it over in 1624, the death rate remained appalling. Since more than 9,000 immigrants had entered the colony, nearly half the population died during that decade.

The climate helped make Virginia a death trap. "Hot and moist" is how Robert Beverly described the weather in *The History and Present State of Virginia* (1705), the dampness "occasioned by the abundance of low grounds, marshes, creeks, and rivers." Among the "annoyances" attending these circumstances, Beverly listed thunder and "troublesome vermin." Europeans found that these conditions took getting used to. Almost without exception

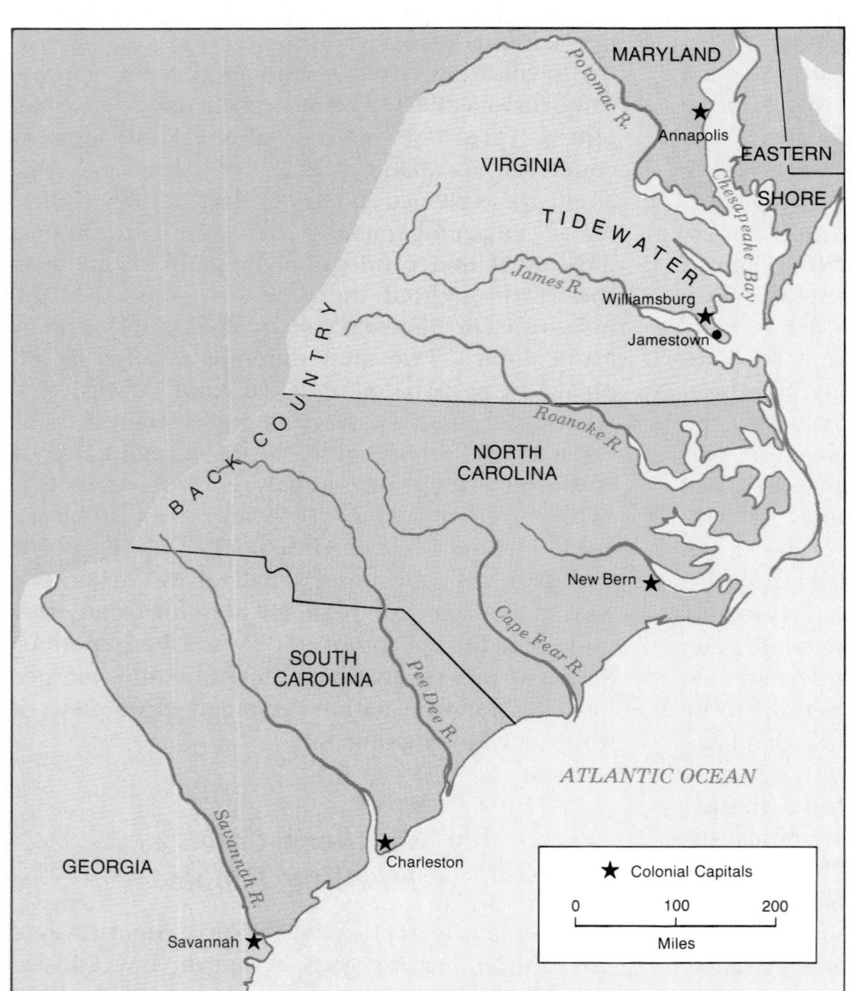

THE SOUTHERN COLONIES

The "Indian menace" was always uppermost in the minds of those living on the frontier. A drawing made in 1711 by Christopher von Graffenried, the founder of a Swiss-German colony in North Carolina, shows Graffenried, his surveyor, and their black servant held captive by the Tuscarora. A tribal dance (right) was followed by the torture of the bound prisoners. Graffenried and his companions were later ransomed.

newcomers underwent "seasoning," a period of illness which in its mildest form consisted of "two or three fits of a feaver and ague." Once safely over this threshold, settlers ran the seasonal risk of contracting malaria, a disease spread by mosquitos. Though seldom fatal in itself, malaria could so debilitate its victims that they often died of dysentery and other ailments.

Long after food shortages and Indian warfare had ceased to be serious problems, life in the Chesapeake remained precarious. Well into the 1700s a white male of 20 in Middlesex County could look forward to about 25 more years of life. Across Chesapeake Bay, in Charles County, Maryland, the average life expectancy was even lower. Survival often turned on little more than luck, the presence of someone healthy to nurse a person laid low by sickness.

Because of the persistent shortage of women in the Chesapeake region (men outnumbered women by three to two even in the early 1700s), widows easily found new husbands. Many men stayed single, spending their lives alone or in the company of other men. Others married Indian women and became part of Indian society. Still others improvised life-styles unimaginable in Europe. William Byrd encountered one of the more original in 1728 along the border between Virginia and North Carolina. "Not far from the inlet," Byrd recorded, "dwelt a marooner [mulatto] that modestly call'd himself a hermit, tho' he forfeited that Name by Suffering a wanton Female to cohabit with Him."

> His Habitation was a bower, cover'd with Bark after the Indian Fashion, which in that mild Situation protected him pretty well from the Weather. . . . As for raiment, he depended mostly upon the length of beard, and she upon her Length of Hair, part of which she brought decently forward, and the rest dangled behind quite down to her Rump.

If few Cheasapeake settlers took up what might be called common-law beachcombing, all felt the psychological effects of their precarious and frustrating existence. Random mayhem and calculated violence posed a continuous threat to life and limb. Social arrangements were rude at best and often as "brutish" as Hobbes had claimed, even allowing for the difficulties involved in carving out a community in the wilderness. Those who survived and prospered in such a "dirty State of Nature" were those who learned quickest how to avoid its pitfalls and exploit its possibilities.

The Lure of Land

Agriculture was the bulwark of life for the Chesapeake settlers and the rest of the colonial south; the tragic experiences of the Jamestown settlement revealed this quickly enough. Jamestown also suggested that a colony could not succeed unless its inhabitants were allowed to own their own land. The first colonists, it will be recalled, were employees of the London Company who had agreed to work for seven years in return for a share of the profits. When their contracts expired there were few profits. To satisfy these settlers and to attract new capital, the company declared a "dividend" of land, its only asset. The surviving colonists each received 100 acres. Thereafter, as prospects continued poor, the company relied more and more on grants of land to attract both capital and labor. A number of wealthy Englishmen were given immense tracts, some running to several hundred thousand acres. Lesser persons willing to settle in Virginia received more modest grants. Whether dangled before a great tycoon, a country squire, or a poor farmer, the offer of land had the effect of encouraging migration to the colony. This was a much-desired end, for without the labor to develop it the land was worthless.

Soon what was known as the headright system became entrenched in Virginia, and when the Crown took over in 1624 the system was not disturbed. Behind it lay the eminently sound principle that land should be parceled out according to the availability of labor to cultivate it. For each "head" entering the colony the government issued a "right" to take any 50 acres of unoccupied land. To "seat" a claim and receive title to the property, the holder of the headright had to mark out its boundaries, plant a crop, and construct some sort of habitation. This system was adopted in all the southern colonies and in Pennsylvania and New Jersey.

The first headrights were issued with no strings attached, but generally the grantor demanded a small annual payment called a quitrent. A quitrent was not rent at all, for the person who paid it was not a tenant. It was a tax, perhaps a shilling for 50 acres, which provided a way for the proprietors to derive incomes from their colonies. By the middle of the 18th century the Calvert family was collecting over £4,000 a year in Maryland from this source.

A quitrent differed from a modern tax in that it bore little relation to the value of the property and was not assessed to pay for public services. It was a tribute paid in recognition of the "sovereignty" of the grantor, a commutation of feudal obligations that had never really existed in America. Quitrents were therefore resented and always hard to collect.

The headright system encouraged landless Europeans to migrate to America. More often than not, however, those most eager to come could not afford passage across the Atlantic. In order to bring together those with money who sought land and labor and those without funds who wanted to go to America, the indentured servant system was developed. Indenture resembled apprenticeship. In return for transportation the indentured servants agreed to work for a stated period, usually about five years. During that time they were subject to strict control by the master and received no compensation beyond their keep. Servants therefore lacked any incentive to work hard, whereas masters tended to "abuse their servantes . . . with intollerable oppression." In this clash of wills the advantage lay with the master; servants lacked full political and civil rights, and masters could administer physical punishment and otherwise abuse them with almost total impunity.

Servants who completed their years of labor became free. Usually the ex-servant was entitled to an "outfit" (a suit of clothes, some farm tools, seed, and perhaps a gun). Custom varied from colony to colony and according to the bargain struck by the two parties when the indenture was signed. In the Carolinas and in Pennsylvania, for example, servants received small grants of land from the colony when their service was completed.

The headrights issued when indentured servants entered the colonies went to whoever paid their passage, not to the servants. Thus the system gave a double reward to capital—land and labor for the price of the labor alone. Since well over half of the white settlers of the southern colonies came as indentured servants, the effect on the structure of southern society was enormous. Most servants eventually became landowners, but with the passage of time their lot became harder. The best land belonged to the large planters, and low tobacco prices and high local taxes combined to keep many ex-servants in dire poverty. Some were forced to become "squatters" on land along the fringes of settlement that no one had yet claimed. Squatting often led to trouble; eventually someone was sure to turn up with a legal title to the squatter's property. Squatters then demanded what they called squatters' rights, the privilege of buying the land from the legal owner without paying for the improvements they had made upon it. This led to arguments and lawsuits and sometimes to violence.

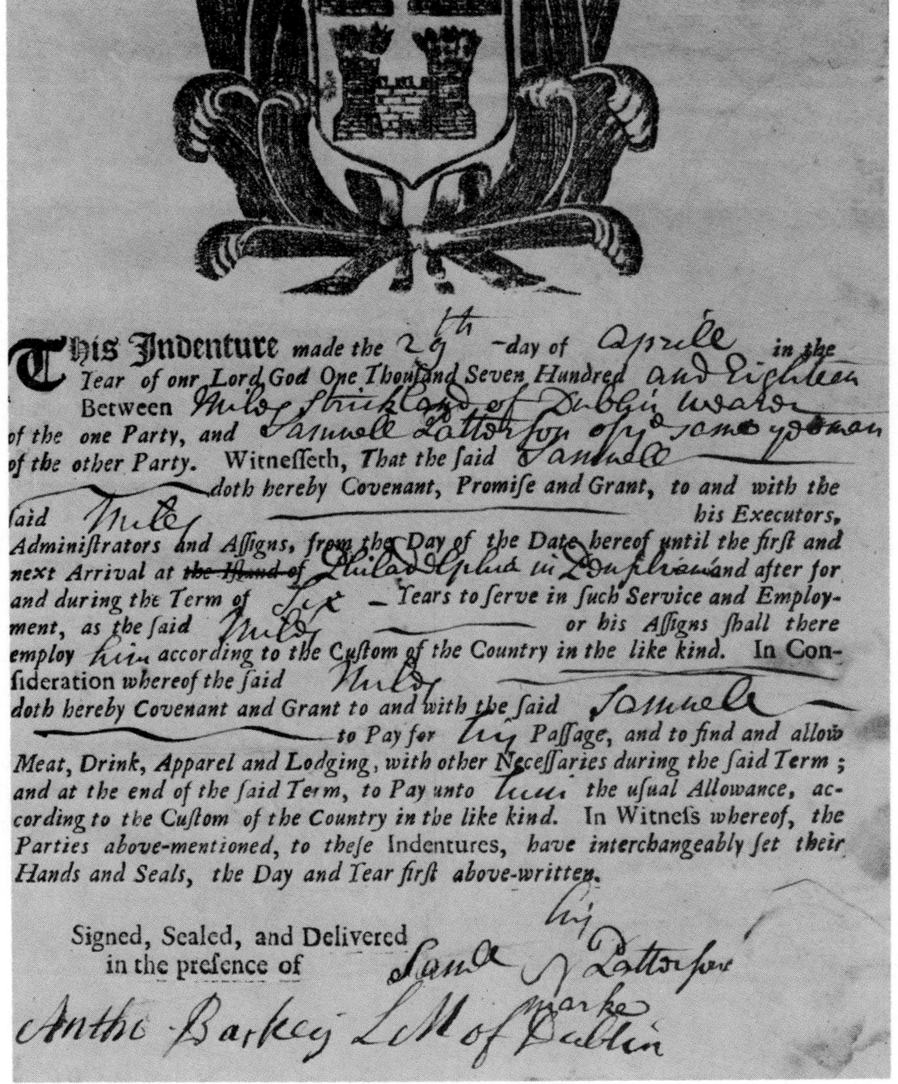

This Indenture made the 29th day of Aprile in the Year of our Lord God One Thouſand Seven Hundred and Eighteen Between Miles Strickland of Dublin weaver of the one Party, and Samuell Patterson of ye same yeoman of the other Party. Witneſſeth, That the ſaid Samuell doth hereby Covenant, Promiſe and Grant, to and with the ſaid Miles his Executors, Adminiſtrators and Aſſigns, from the Day of the Date hereof until the firſt and next Arrival at ~~the Iſland of~~ Philadelphia in Pensilvania and after for and during the Term of Six Years to ſerve in ſuch Service and Employment, as the ſaid Miles or his Aſſigns ſhall there employ him according to the Cuſtom of the Country in the like kind. In Conſideration whereof the ſaid Miles doth hereby Covenant and Grant to and with the ſaid Samuell to Pay for his Paſſage, and to find and allow Meat, Drink, Apparel and Lodging, with other Neceſſaries during the ſaid Term; and at the end of the ſaid Term, to Pay unto him the uſual Allowance, according to the Cuſtom of the Country in the like kind. In Witneſs whereof, the Parties above-mentioned, to theſe Indentures, have interchangeably ſet their Hands and Seals, the Day and Year firſt above-written.

Signed, Sealed, and Delivered in the preſence of

Saml his marke Patterson

Anth. Barkey ... of Dublin

The indentured servant system allowed those with little money to emigrate to America, sometimes on the same ship as their new master. In this 1718 indenture, Samuel Patterson agrees to serve Miles Strickland for six years in return for his passage to Pennsylvania as well as food, clothing, and other necessary effects.

By the 1670s conflicts between Virginians who owned choice land and ex-servants on the outer edge of settlement brought the colony to the brink of class warfare. The costs of meeting the region's ever-growing need for labor with indentured servants were becoming prohibitive. Some other solution was needed. - But, was brought in long before the indenture problem.

The Resort to Slavery

The first African blacks brought to English North America arrived on a Dutch ship and were sold at Jamestown in 1619. Early records are vague and incomplete, so it is not possible to say whether these Africans were treated as slaves or freed after a period of years like indentured servants. What is certain is that by about 1640 *some* Virginia blacks were slaves (a few, with equal certainty, were free) and that by the 1660s local statutes had firmly established the institution in Virginia.

Whether slavery produced race prejudice in America or prejudice slavery is a hotly debated, important, and difficult-to-answer question. Most 17th-century Europeans were prejudiced against Africans; the usual reasons that led them to look

Kingdoms—Large Capital Letters ("GHANA")
Peoples—Smaller Capital Letters ("**FULANI**")
Cities—Initial Capitals ("Bonny")

0 500 1000
Miles

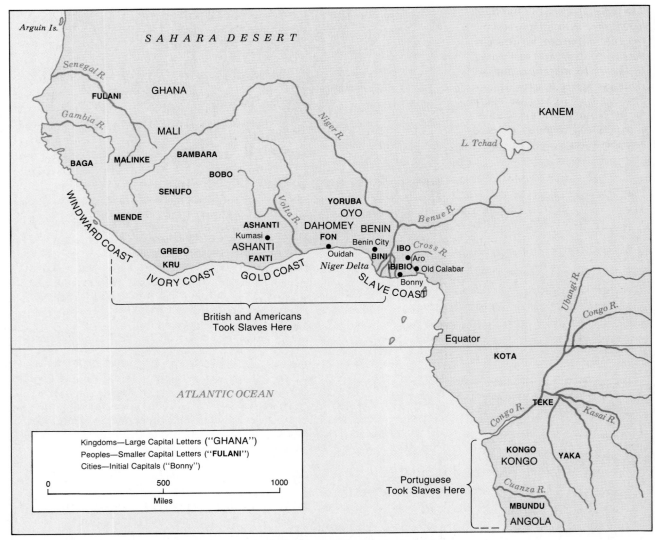

THE WEST COAST OF AFRICA

down on "heathens" with customs other than their own were in the case of Africans greatly reinforced by their blackness, which the English equated with dirt, the Devil, danger, and death. "Black is the Colour of Night, Frightful, Dark and Horrid," a popular disquisition of 1704 proclaimed. That Africa was also the habitat of the great apes suggested, furthermore, that blacks were somehow related to these human-appearing creatures and were thus inherently bestial and inferior.

Yet the English knew that the Portuguese and

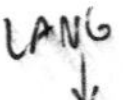

Spaniards had enslaved blacks—*negro* is Spanish for black. Since the English adopted the word as a name for Africans, their treatment of Africans in the New World may also have derived from the Spanish.

Probably the Africans' blackness lay at the root of the tragedy. Winthrop D. Jordan, whose researches have added enormously to our understanding of the question, has stressed the process by which prejudice and existing enslavement interacted with each other as both cause and effect, bringing about the total debasement of the African. "The concept of Negro slavery," Jordan writes with specific reference to the Chesapeake region,

> was neither borrowed from foreigners, nor extracted from books, nor invented out of whole cloth, nor extrapolated from servitude, nor generated by English reaction to Negroes as such, nor necessitated by the exigencies of the New World. Not any one of these made the Negro a slave, *but all.*

Slavery soon made its appearance throughout English America. As early as 1626 there were 11 slaves in New Netherland, and when the English conquered the colony in 1664 there were 700 slaves in a population of about 8,000. The Massachusetts Body of Liberties of 1641—strange title—provided that "there shall never be any bond-slavery . . . amongst us; unlesse it be lawful captives taken in just warrs [*i.e.,* Indians] and such strangers as willingly sell themselves, or *are solde* to us." However, relatively few blacks were imported until late in the 17th century, even in the southern colonies. In 1650 there were only 300 blacks in Virginia and as late as 1670 no more than 2,000.

White servants were much more highly prized. The African, after all, was utterly alien to both the European and the American ways of life. In a country starved for capital, the cost of slaves—roughly five times that of servants—was another disadvantage. In 1664 the governor of Maryland informed Lord Baltimore that local planters would use more "neigros" "if our purses would endure it."

For these reasons, so long as white servants could be had in sufficient numbers, there were few slaves in the Chesapeake. In the 1670s, however, the flow of new servants slackened, the result of improving economic conditions in England and the competition of other colonies for servants. At the same time, the formation of the Royal African Company (1672) made slaves more readily available. The indenture system began to give way to slavery as the "permanent" solution to the region's chronic need for labor. An additional inducement causing planters and politicians to switch was the recognition that, unlike white servants, black slaves (and their offspring) would be forever barred from competing with whites for land or political power.

Announcements for the sale of newly imported slaves were plentiful in Colonial newspapers—notice the claim that these captives are free from smallpox, an important selling point.

TO BE SOLD, on board the Ship *Bance-Yland*, on tueſday the 6th of *May* next, at *Aſhley-Ferry*; a choice cargo of about 250 fine healthy

NEGROES,

juſt arrived from the Windward & Rice Coaſt. —The utmoſt care has already been taken, and ſhall be continued, to keep them free from the leaſt danger of being infected with the SMALL-POX, no boat having been on board, and all other communication with people from *Charles-Town* prevented.

Auſtin, Laurens, & Appleby.

N. B. Full one Half of the above Negroes have had the SMALL-POX in their own Country.

"Their Darling Tobacco"

Labor and land made agriculture possible, but it was necessary to find a market for American crops in the Old World if the colonists were to enjoy anything but the crudest sort of existence. They could not begin to manufacture all the articles they required; to obtain from England such items as plows and muskets and books and chinaware, they had to have cash crops, what their English creditors called "merchantable commodities." Here, at least, fortune favored the Chesapeake.

The founders of Virginia tried to produce all sorts of things that were needed in the old country: grapes and silk in particular, indigo, cotton, oranges, olives, sugar, and many other plants. But it was tobacco, unwanted, even strongly opposed at first, that became for farmers on both sides of Chesapeake Bay "their darling."

Tobacco was unknown in Europe until Spanish

explorers brought it back from the West Indies. It was not common in England until the time of Sir Walter Raleigh. Then it quickly proved irrestible to thousands of devotees. However, since it clearly contained some habit-forming drug, many people opposed its use.

At first the London Company discouraged its colonists from growing tobacco. King James I wrote a pamphlet attacking the weed, in which, among other things, he anticipated the findings of modern cancer researchers by saying that smoking was a "vile and stinking" habit "dangerous to the Lungs." But English smokers and partakers of snuff ignored their king, and the Virginians ignored their company. By 1617 a pound of tobacco was worth more than 5 shillings in London. Company and Crown then changed their tune, granting the colonists a monopoly and encouraging them in every way. Unlike wheat, which required expensive plows and oxen to clear the land and prepare the soil, tobacco plants could be set on semicleared land and cultivated with a simple hoe. But tobacco required lots of human labor. Constant weeding was essential. During the growing season, shoots ("suckers") had to be removed and the top bud clipped off at the proper time or the plant would become a spindly "Frenchman" instead of a valuable broad-leaved specimen. Nevertheless, a single laborer working two or three acres could produce as much as 1,200 pounds of cured tobacco, which, in a good year, yielded a profit of more than 200 percent. This being the case, production in America leaped from 2,500 pounds in 1616 to 500,000 in 1627 and to nearly 30 million pounds in the late 17th century, or roughly 400 pounds of tobacco for every man, woman, and child in the Chesapeake colonies. Such a tremendous expansion of the supply caused the price to plummet. By the middle of the 17th century the English market was glutted and the colonists already established in the market were seeking deperately to curb production.

The low price of tobacco in the last decades of the 17th century did not stop the expansion of the tobacco colonies, but it did alter the structure of their society. Small farmers found it more difficult to make a decent living. At the same time a number of favored individuals were engrossing large tracts of land. If well managed, a big plantation gave its owner important competitive advantages over the small farmer. Tobacco was notorious for the speed with which it exhausted the fertility of the soil. Growers with a lot of land could shift frequently to new fields within their holdings and thus maintain high yields, but the only option that small farmers had when their land gave out was to pack up and move to unsettled land on the frontier. To do that in the 1670s was to risk trouble with properly indignant Indians. It might also violate colonial laws designed to slow westward migration and limit tobacco production. Not that either was about to stop settlement.

Bacon's Rebellion

From the start, Chesapeake settlers showed little respect for constituted authority. The first Virginians often ignored directives of the London Company, while early Marylanders regularly disputed the right of the Calverts' agents to direct the affairs of the proprietorship. In 1635, a group of Virginia planters, angered by the policies of the recently arrived Governor John Harvey, accomplished his "thrusting out" by putting him on a ship bound for England. The most serious challenge to standing authority took place in Virginia in 1676. Planters in the outlying counties had many reasons for disliking the officials in Jamestown who ran the colony. The royal governor, Sir William Berkeley, and his "Green Spring" faction (the organization took its name from the governor's plantation, where the leaders customarily met) had ruled Virginia for more than 30 years. Outsiders resented the way Berkeley and his henchmen used their offices to line their pockets. They also resented their social pretensions. The Green Springers made no effort to conceal their opinion, which had considerable basis in fact, that western planters were a crude and vulgar lot.

Early in 1676 planters on the western edge of settlement, always looking for excuses to grab land by doing away with the Indians who owned it, asked Berkeley to authorize an expedition against Indians who had been attacking nearby plantations. Berkeley refused. The planters then took matters into their own hands. Their leader, Nathaniel Bacon, was (and remains today) a controversial figure. His foes described him as extremely ambitious and possessed "of a most imperious and dangerous hidden Pride of heart." But even his sharpest critics conceded that he was "of an inviting aspect and powerful elocution" and well qualified "to lead a giddy and unthinking multitude."

When Berkeley refused to authorize him to attack the Indians, Bacon promptly showed himself only too willing to lead that multitude not only against Indians, but against the governor. Without permission he raised an army of 500 men, described by the Berkeley faction as "rabble of the basest sort." Berkeley then declared him a traitor.

Several months of monumental confusion followed. Bacon murdered some peaceful Indians, marched on Jamestown and forced Berkeley to legitimize his authority, then headed west again to kill more Indians. In September he returned to Jamestown and burned it to the ground. Berkeley fled across Chesapeake Bay to the Eastern Shore. The Baconites plundered the estates of some of the Green Spring faction. But a few weeks after the destruction of Jamestown, Bacon came down with a "violent flux"—probably it was a bad case of dysentery—and he died. Soon thereafter an English naval squadron arrived with enough soldiers to restore order. Bacon's Rebellion ended.

On the surface, the uprising changed nothing. No sudden shift in political power occurred. Berkeley returned to his post as royal governor. For that matter, Bacon had not sought to change either the political system or the social and economic structure of the colony. Although a "frontiersman" in the geographical sense, and a relative newcomer to Virginia, he was a member of the upper class both in economic status and in social background. Some who sided with him had comparable credentials.

But if the *rebellion* did not change anything, nothing was ever again quite the same after it ended. With seeming impartiality, the Baconites had warred against Indians and against other planters. In retrospect, we might wonder which was the real enemy of anyone interested in growing tobacco. Surely Baconite and Green Springer had no differences that could not be compromised. And their common interest extended beyond the question of how to deal with Indians. "For men bent on the maximum exploitation of labor," the historian Edmund S. Morgan has written, "the implication should have been clear."

There is every reason to think that it was clear. In the quarter-century following Bacon's Rebellion the entire Chesapeake region became committed to black slavery. Large differences in the wealth and life-styles of growers of tobacco resulted. The few who succeeded in accumulating 20 or more slaves and enough land to keep them occupied could live like lords. Most of them put the management of their plantations in the hands of overseers; they did not dirty their hands in the fields, though unless they kept a close watch on what was going on, their fine situation might end in bankruptcy. The majority of planters owned no more than five or six slaves, and many had fewer still. They lived much less grandly and indeed tended to work side by side in the tobacco fields with their slaves.

The large slaveowners also controlled politics; they, not the far more numerous small holders, held the commissions in the militia, the county judgships, and the seats in the House of Burgesses. The control that these "leading families" exercised over their neighbors was not entirely unearned and it was never total. They were, in general, responsible leaders. And they recognized the necessity of throwing open their houses and serving copious amounts of rum to ordinary voters when election time rolled around. Such gatherings served to acknowledge the representative character of the system. More important, they sealed an implicit contract between the inhabitants of the "great houses" and those who lived in more modest lodgings: The southern whites might differ greatly in wealth and influence, but they stood as one and forever behind the principle that blacks must have neither. This was the basis—the price—of the harmony and prosperity achieved by those who survived the century-long "seasoning" in the Chesapeake colonies.

The Carolinas: "More Like a Negro Country"

The English and, in increasing proportions after 1700, the Scotch-Irish settlers of the tidewater parts of the Carolinas turned to agriculture as enthusiastically as had their Chesapeake neighbors. In South Carolina, after two decades in which furs and cereals were chief products, Madagascar rice was introduced into the low-lying coastal areas in 1696. It quickly proved its worth as a cash crop. By 1700 almost 100,000 pounds were being exported annually; by the eve of the Revolution rice exports from

South Carolina and Georgia exceeded 65 million pounds a year.

Rice culture required water for flooding the fields. At first freshwater swamps were adapted to the crop, but by the middle of the 18th century the chief rice fields lay along the tidal rivers and inlets. A series of dikes and floodgates allowed fresh water to pour across the fields with the rising tide; when the tide fell, the gates closed automatically to keep the water in. The process was reversed when it was necessary to drain the land. Then the water ran out as the tide ebbed, and the pressure of the next flood pushed the gates shut.

In the 1740s a second cash crop, indigo, was introduced in South Carolina by Eliza Lucas. Indigo did not compete with rice either for land or labor. It prospered on high ground and needed care in seasons when the slaves were not busy in the rice paddies. The British were delighted to have a new source of indigo because the blue dye was important in their woolens industry. Parliament quickly placed a bounty on it to stimulate production.

The production of tobacco, rice, and indigo, along with furs and forest products such as tar and resin, meant that the southern colonies had no difficulty in obtaining manufactured articles from abroad. Planters dealt with agents in England and Scotland, called factors, who managed the sale of their crops, filled their orders for manufactures, and supplied them with credit. This was a great convenience but not necessarily an advantage, for it made southerners dependent upon European intermediaries, who naturally exacted a price for their services. It tended to prevent the development of a diversified economy. Throughout the colonial era, while small-scale manufacturing developed rapidly in the north, it was stillborn in the south. Even in the decade before the Revolution it was not unheard-of for a Virginia planter to send a fine piece of silk—itself an import—all the way to London to be dyed because it had become soiled.

Reliance on European middlemen also retarded the development of urban life. Until the rise of Baltimore in the 1750s, Charleston was the only city of importance in the entire South. But according to Carl Bridenbaugh's *The Colonial Craftsman,* even Charleston, a town of nearly 12,000 in 1760, "did not nourish an outstanding craft or produce a single eminent workman before the Revolution." Despite its rich export trade, its fine harbor, and the easy availability of excellent lumber, Charleston's shipbuilding industry never remotely rivaled that of Boston, New York, or Philadelphia.

On the South Carolina rice plantations, slave labor predominated from the beginning, for free workers would not submit to its backbreaking and unhealthy regimen. The first quarter of the 18th century saw an enormous influx of Africans into all the southern colonies. By 1730 roughly three out of every ten people south of Pennsylvania were black, and in South Carolina the blacks were the majority. "Carolina," remarked a newcomer in 1737, "looks more like a negro country than like a country settled by white people."

Given the existing race prejudice and the degrading impact of slavery, this demographic change had an enormous impact on life wherever blacks were concentrated. In each colony regulations gov-

Introduced in the 1740s, indigo quickly became an important cash crop. The labor and land it required were different from those needed to grow rice.

erning the behavior of blacks, both free and slave, were gradually worked out. These increased in severity as the density of the black population increased. The blacks had no civil rights under these codes, and punishments were sickeningly severe. How to punish a particular offense—or suspected offense—was for the slave's owner to decide. Whipping was common for minor offenses, death by hanging or by being burned alive for serious crimes. Blacks were sometimes castrated for sexual offenses—even for lewd talk about white women—or for repeated attempts to escape. The following "melancholy encounter" occurred in the 1760s near Charleston. A French visitor, Hector St. John de Crèvecoeur, hearing the clamor of vultures in a nearby tree, drove them off with a gunshot, then investigated to see what they had been up to. He found a slave suspended in a cage, whom he later discovered had been condemned on mere suspicion of having killed an overseer. "Horrid to think and painful to repeat," Crèvecoeur reported,

An idealized view of slave life shows the black family when work for the master is finished, catching their own fish, harvesting fruits from their own garden plot. In reality most slaves had time to pursue such tasks only at the end of an exhausting day in the master's fields.

> the birds had already picked out his eyes, his cheekbones were bare; his arms had been attacked in several places and his body seemed covered with a multitude of wounds. . . . The living spectre, though deprived of his eyes, could still distinctly hear, and in his uncouth dialect begged me to give him some water. . . . "Tanke, you white man, tanke you, pute some poison and give me. . . . Two days and me no die; the birds, the birds; aaah me!"

That blacks resented slavery goes without saying, but since slavery did not mean the same thing to all of them, their reactions to it varied. Throughout the 18th century a constant stream of new slaves was arriving from Africa. These "outlandish" blacks tended to respond differently than American-born slaves. Among the latter, field hands experienced a different kind of slavery than did household servants, and skilled artisans faced still another set of circumstances. In short, the slaves' places in society influenced their behavior.

The master race sought to acculturate the slaves in order to make them more efficient workers. A slave who could understand English was easier to order about; one who could handle farm tools or wait on table was more useful than one who could not; a carpenter or a mason was more valuable still. But acculturation increased the slave's independence and mobility, and this posed problems. Field hands seldom tried to escape; they expressed their dissatisfactions by pilferage and petty sabotage, by laziness, or by feigning stupidity. Most runaways were artisans who hoped to "pass" as free in a nearby town. It was one of the many paradoxes of slavery that the more valuable a slave became, the harder that slave was to control.

On the other hand, few runaway slaves became rebels. Indeed, organized slave rebellions were rare, and while individual assaults by blacks on whites were common enough, it must be remembered that personal violence was also common among whites throughout American history. But the masters had sound reasons for fearing their slaves; the particular viciousness of the system lay in the fact that oppression bred resentment, which in turn produced still greater oppression.

What is superficially astonishing is that the whites—absolute masters of their human property—grossly exaggerated the danger of slave revolts. They pictured the black as a kind of malevolent ogre, powerful, bestial, and lascivious, a caldron of animal emotions that had to be restrained at any cost. Probably the characteristics they attributed to the blacks were really projections of their own passions. The most striking illustration of this process was the universal white fear of the "mongrelization" of the race: if blacks were free, they would breed with whites. Yet in practice the interbreeding, which indeed took place, was almost exclusively the result of white men using their power as masters to have sexual relations with female slaves.

Thus the "peculiar institution" was fastened upon America with economic, social, and psychic barbs. Ignorance and self-interest, lust for gold and for the flesh, primitive prejudices and complex social and legal ties, all combined to convince the whites that black slavery was not so much good as a fact of life. With the passage of time a barely perceptible trend toward ameliorating the harshness of bondage emerged, but talk of abolishing slavery was almost nonexistent until the eve of the Revolution. A few isolated reformers, mostly Quakers, attacked the institution on the religious ground that all human beings are equal before God: "*Christ* dyed for all, both *Turks, Barbarians, Tartarians,* and *Ethyopians.*" Yet a few Quakers owned slaves, and even the majority who did not usually succumbed to color prejudice. Blackness was a defect, but it was no justification for enslavement, they argued. And they attracted little attention anywhere—none in areas where slavery was important.

The Back Country

West of the fall line of the rivers that irrigated tidewater Chesapeake and Carolina lay the back country or "back parts." This region comprised a territory larger than that of the Chesapeake and Carolina regions combined. It included the Great Valley of Virginia, the Piedmont, and what became the final English colony to be founded in North America, Georgia.

The circumstances of the founding of Georgia were most unusual. A group of London philanthropists concerned over the plight of honest persons imprisoned for debt conceived of settling these unfortunates in the New World, where they might make a fresh start. (Here is striking proof that Europeans were still beguiled by the prospect of regenerating their society in the New World.) They petitioned for a grant south of the Carolinas, and the government, eager to create a buffer between South Carolina and the hostile Spanish in Florida, readily granted a charter (1732) to a group of "trustees" who were to manage the colony without profit to themselves for a period of 21 years.

In 1733 the leader of the trustees, James Oglethorpe, founded Savannah. Oglethorpe was a complicated person, vain, high-handed, and straitlaced, yet hardworking and idealistic. He hoped to people the colony with sober and industrious yeoman farmers. Land grants were limited to 50 acres and made nontransferable. To insure sobriety, rum and other "Spirits and Strong Waters" were banned. To guarantee that the colonists would have to work hard, the entry of "any Black . . . Negroe" was prohibited. The Indian trade was to be strictly regulated in the interest of fair dealing. Oglethorpe intended that silk, wine, and olive oil be the main products—none of which, unfortunately, could be profitably produced in Georgia. His noble intentions came to naught. The settlers refused to endure the Spartan existence he envisaged; they swiftly found ways to circumvent all restrictions. Rum flowed, lawyers argued, slaves were imported, large landholdings were amassed, and Georgia developed an economy much like South Carolina's. Oglethorpe returned to England in 1743; in 1752 the trustees, disillusioned, abandoned their responsibilities. Georgia then became a royal colony.

It was only about this time that settlers in any numbers penetrated the rest of the southern back country. So long as cheap land remained available closer to the coast and Indians along the frontier remained a threat, only the most footloose hunters or fur traders lived far inland. But when the movement began, in the 1750s and 1760s, it became a rush. Chief among those making the trek were Scotch-Irish and German immigrants, many of the latter wagoning down from Pennsylvania, which, by their lights, already seemed too crowded. By 1770 the back country contained about 250,000 settlers, 10 percent of the population of the colonies.

This internal migration did not proceed altogether peacefully. In 1771 a pitched battle was fought in the back-country precincts of North Carolina between frontiersmen calling themselves Regulators and 1,200 troops dispatched by the Carolina assembly, which was dominated by low-country interests. The Regulators were protesting their lack of representation in the assembly. They were crushed and their leaders executed. This was not to be either the last or the bloodiest sectional conflict in American history.

Intellectual and Religious Life in the Colonial South

The rural gentry that laid claim to political power throughout the south in the opening decades of the 18th century also set the region's intellectual tone. Theirs was a provincial culture; virtually everything meant to divert them from their workday lives, the artifacts of both culture and ideas, came from Great Britain. Their literary output consisted primarily of personal correspondence and descriptions of the country, most of which, like Robert Beverley's *History of Virginia,* was directed at English readers.

"Southerners," one historian has written, "were not a reading people." This is not to say they had no interest in affairs of the mind. The efforts of the Virginia planter and public official William Byrd II (1674–1744) indicate otherwise. During his lifetime Byrd collected at his Westover estate one of the largest libraries in the colonies, some 3,600 titles. His diaries (incidentally a major source of our knowledge of southern life) attest to its regular use.

> Feb. 7, 1709—I rose at 5 o'clock this morning, and read a chapter in Hebrew and 200 verses in Homer's Odyssey. I ate milk for breakfast.

Thirty-three years later, during which Byrd spent several years in England pursuing the literary lions of London, only the hour of rising and the drink had changed.

> Feb. 7, 1742—I rose about 6, read Hebrew and Greek. I prayed and had tea.

Although born in Virginia, Byrd received his formal schooling in England. He, in turn, sent his children, including his daughters, to English schools. This was the pattern for young southerners whose families had the inclination and wherewithal to provide them with a higher education. Prominent Catholic families in Maryland like the Carrolls of Carrollton sent their sons to Jesuit schools on the Continent, while the Pinckneys in South Carolina sent theirs to London to study law at one of the Inns of Court. The founding of the College of William and Mary in Williamsburg, Virginia, in 1693, represented an effort to provide the region with its own institution of higher learning. But staffing problems and insufficient funding kept it from offering much more than a grammar school education for decades.

Education at the primary and secondary level was also hard to come by. Virtually all instruction in reading and writing remained the responsibility of parents, private tutors, or local ministers. Many white children, and just about all black children, went without. The rural character of southern society, with the population scattered along countless rivers and bays, helps explain this limited intellectual development. So does the preoccupation of its most ambitious members with attaining a secure position in a rapidly changing and unpredictable economy. Still another contributing factor, however, was the limited role of formal religion.

By the middle of the 18th century the Anglican church had been legally established in all the southern colonies, which meant that it was the official religion, its ministers supported by public funds. The Virginia assembly had made attendance at Anglican services compulsory in 1619, and in later years it deprived dissenters of the right to vote. Many non-Anglicans were driven from the colony. In Maryland, Lord Baltimore, although intolerant of non-Christians, had sought to persuade the Protestant majority to adopt a live-and-let-live attitude toward Catholics by imposing stiff fines on individuals who used terms like "heretick" and "papist" in what his Toleration Act defined as "a reproachful manner." This law did not survive the invasion of the colony by militant Puritans. It was repealed in 1654 during the Cromwellian period, reenacted in 1657, then repealed again in 1692 when the Anglican church was established. Catholics, who made up less than 10 percent of Maryland's population, were repeatedly discriminated against; in 1704 priests were forbidden to say mass, and in 1718 Catholics lost the right to vote. In the Carolinas the proprietor's original desire to encourage the immigration of people of all faiths—including Jews and Quakers—could not be carried out in practice. The Anglican church was established in 1706. In Georgia, where no state religion existed at the start, Anglicanism was established in 1758.

For all its legal standing, the Anglican church was not a very powerful force in the south. The English hierarchy neglected their American parishes. Since there was no Anglican bishop in the colonies, would-be ministers had to sail to England to be ordained, something few colonists chose to do. These English pastors who emigrated to America were mostly second-rate men unable to obtain a decent living at home. If they had intellectual ambitions when they arrived, their rural circumstances provided little opportunity to develop them. All too regularly, they found themselves in conflict with the vestrymen of their parishes. When such conflict threatened to become violent, or merely tiresome, some ministers abandoned their pulpits and became planters.

In Virginia, Anglican ministers were usually paid in tobacco vouchers worth the market value of 17,280 pounds of the crop. In 1758, after a drought drove up the price of tobacco, the House of Burgesses passed a law providing that "tobacco debts" for the year 1759 be honored at a rate of 2 pence per pound. Since tobacco was selling at more than twice that price in 1759, this Two-Penny Act deprived the ministers of a much-desired windfall.

Indignant clergmen appealed to the Privy Council in London, which voided the law. Thereupon several ministers went to court to sue for back pay. One test case, involving the claim of Reverend James Maury, revealed how thoroughly the Anglican clergy had failed to win the respect of the populace. The judge ruled in Maury's favor, but a young lawyer, Patrick Henry, beclouded the issue with oratorical pyrotechnics, attacking the clergy as unpatriotic, money-grubbing "enemies of the community." The jury awarded Maury only one penny in damages. The "Parson's Cause," settled in 1763, has long been regarded as one of the earliest portents of the Revolution, for it demonstrated that in a clash of royal and local authority, most Americans would stand by their local leaders.

Colonial New England: A Covenanted People

What if the Pilgrims and Puritans had settled on the shores of Chesapeake Bay rather than Massachusetts Bay? Would the "Puritan society" established in New England have worked 600 miles to the south? The second question has no answer because the first violates the facts. But like many "what-if" or contrafactual questions, these lead to other questions for which at least tentative answers exist. For example, what was the relative importance of the experiences and values settlers brought

Patrick Henry first gained public recognition when he argued against the Anglican clergy's claim for higher wages in 1763.

with them to America as against what they encountered there? If survival in the Chesapeake required junking European notions about social arrangements and submitting to the dictates of the wilderness, was this also true in Massachusetts and Connecticut? Ultimately it probably was, but in the early going, Puritan ideas certainly fought the New England reality to a draw.

The town of Boston is located slightly more than 5° latitude north of Jamestown and almost 10° north of Charleston. Like other early New England towns and unlike these southern settlements, Boston had a dependable and safe water supply. The surrounding landscape, a patchwork of forest and parkland, pond and bog, dunes and tidemarsh, was much more open than the often swampy and malaria-infected terrain of the tidewater and low country South. These differences alone made New England a much healthier habitat for 17th-century English settlers than either the Chesapeake or the Carolinas. "Seasoning" proceeded so imperceptibly as almost to escape notice. One consequence of this relatively painless entry into what the minister Cotton Mather called "the Lord's 'almost perfect garden' " was that New Englanders escaped "the agues and fevers" that beset settlers to the south, leaving them free to attend to their spiritual and social well-being.

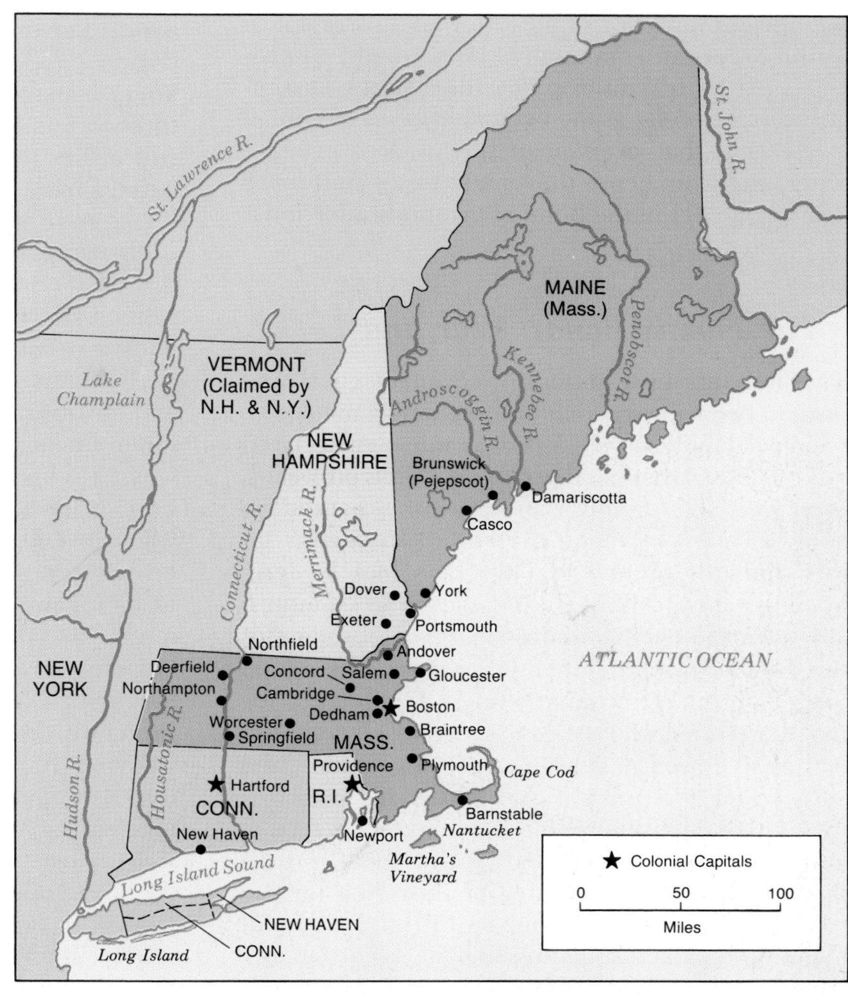

COLONIAL NEW ENGLAND

The Stamp of Puritanism

New England's Puritans were set apart from other English settlers by how much—and how long—they lived out of their baggage. The supplies the first arrivals brought with them eased their adjustment, as did the wherewithal of later, equally heavily laden arrivals. The Puritans' baggage, however, included more than pots and pans, saws and shovels. It also included a comprehensive plan for the proper ordering of society.

At the center of the plan was the Biblical concept of the covenant. Unlike the Covenant of Grace that God made with Abraham so that he and his "seed" might be spared damnation in the next world, all other covenants concentrated on this world. Their purpose was all-embracing—to insure the upright behavior of all who took up residence within a Puritan community. They sought to provide what John Winthrop described to the passengers on the *Arbella* as the two imperatives of human existence: "that every man might have need of other, and from hence they might be all knitt more nearly together in the Bond of brotherly affection."

The Family Bonds: Fear and Love

The first and most important covenant governing Puritan behavior was that binding family members. "Such as families are," a Boston minister declared in 1653, "at last the Church and Common-wealth must be." The family's authority was backed by its own Commandment, the Fifth: "Honor thy father and thy mother, that thy days may be long upon the land." Ministers and magistrates continually warned New Englanders that any loosening of this family covenant put all other covenants at risk.

In a properly ordered Puritan family and, for that matter, anywhere else in the English colonies, authority flowed downward. Sociologists describe such a family as nuclear and patriarchal, which is to say that each household contained one family, and in it, the father was boss. The husband's principal responsibilities consisted of providing for the physical welfare of all members of the household, including any servants, and making sure they behaved properly, in private and in public. The political views of the family were his to voice through his vote. Economic dealings between the family and other parties were also transacted by the husband, even when the property had been owned by his wife prior to their marriage.

John Cotton's outline of a woman's responsibilities clearly establishes her subordinate position: she should keep house, educate the children, and improve "what is got by the industry of the man." And Cotton, please recall, had been Anne Hutchinson's favorite minister! The poet Anne Bradstreet reduced the functions of a Puritan woman to two: "loving Mother and obedient Wife." Colonial New England, and the southern colonies as well, did have their female blacksmiths, silversmiths, shipwrights, gunsmiths, and butchers as well as shopkeepers and teachers. Such early cases of domestic "liberation," however, were for the most part confined to widows and the wives of incapacitated husbands. For exceptional women, the labor shortage created opportunities to develop their talents. Some managed large plantations; Eliza Lucas ran three in South Carolina for her absent father while still in her teens, and after the death of her husband, Charles Pinckney, she successfully managed his large properties. Even so, most widows, especially young ones, quickly remarried. According to the historian Laurel Thatcher Ulrich, colonial women generally, and New England women particularly, "were by definition basically domestic."

Dealings with neighbors and nearby relatives and involvement in church activities marked the outer limits of the social range of most Puritan women. This does not mean they went unoccupied. Care of the children was a full-time occupation when several were involved, and broods of twelve or fourteen were more common than those of one or two. Fewer children died in New England than in the Chesapeake or in Europe, though few families escaped a miscarriage or a child's death along the way. Childbearing and active motherhood, therefore, likely extended over two decades of a woman's life. Meanwhile, she also functioned as the chief operating officer of the household. Cooking, baking, sewing, and supervising servants, as well as mastering such arcane knowledge as the chemistry needed to make cheese from milk, bacon from pork, and beer from malt, all fell to her. These jobs were physically demanding, though not so debilitating as to prevent large numbers of New England wives from seeing one or more husbands off to the hereafter.

New England children like David, Joanna, and Abigail Mason (painted by an unknown artist about 1670) were expected to emulate adults in their chores and their appearance. Nevertheless, indications are that they were cherished by their parents in a way closer to modern family love than what their European contemporaries experienced.

As Puritan social standards required husbands to rule over wives, so parents ruled over children. The virtue most insistently impressed upon New England children was obedience. Refusal to submit to parental direction was disturbing in itself and for what it implied about the child's eternal condition. Cotton Mather's advice, "better whipt, than damned," graced many a New England rod taken up by a parent in anger, from there to be rapidly transferred to the afterparts of misbehaving offspring. Besides the generous use of corporal punishment, early assignments of household chores kept children out of mischief. By age 6 or 7 girls were set to sewing and helping with housework and boys were put to work outdoors. When a few years older a child might be sent to live with another family to take up the duties of a servant or apprentice. Only when well into adulthood and ready to begin families of their own would children emerge from under parental control.

Such practices, particularly when set beside surviving portraits of early New England families which depict toddlers as somber-faced miniature adults wearing clothes indistinguishable from those of their parents, convey the impression that Puritans moved their young through childhood with as much speed and as little love as possible. That colonial New Englanders harbored no illusions about childhood is clear enough. "Innocent vipers" is how one Puritan minister described children, having 14 of his own to submit as evidence. Anne Bradstreet, mother of eight, characterized one as harboring "a perverse will, a love of what's forbid / a serpent's sting in pleasing face lay hid."

Yet for all their acceptance of the Calvinist doctrine of infant damnation, Puritan parents were not indifferent to the fate of their children. "I do hope," Cotton Mather confessed at the burial of one of the eight children he lost before the age of 2, "that when my children are gone they are not lost; but carried unto the Heavenly Feast with Abraham." Even the dour Michael Wigglesworth assigned children who died in infancy "the easiest room in hell." Compared with their European contemporaries, or with the Virginian William Byrd, who marked the death of his firstborn son in 1710 with the laconic diary entry "God gives and God takes away," New England Puritans possessed parental affections close to those we honor today by calling them "modern."

The character of New England population growth reinforced Puritan ideas about the family. With the end of the Great Migration in the early 1640s, immigration virtually ceased. Thereafter population growth was entirely due to the region's extraordinarily high birthrate (50 births for every 1,000 population, which is more than three times the rate today) and strikingly low mortality rate (about 20 per 1,000). This resulted in a population much more evenly distributed by age and sex than that in the south. The fact that New England women married relatively late, in their early twenties rather than their late teens, suggests that the demand for unmarried women matched the supply. Demographic realities joined with Puritan expectations to create in New England a society of nuclear families. This pattern was neither European nor generally "American" but distinct to the region.

Visible Saints and Others

"In the best of families," John Cotton acknowledged, "you shall find a mixture of good and bad together." But when it came to their churches, Puritans hoped to be more choosy. They agreed that membership ought not to be a presumptive right, as in Catholic countries or in Anglican England, but the joint decision of a would-be member and those already in the church.

Obvious sinners and those ignorant of Christian doctrine were rejected out of hand. But what of "outwardly just" and scripturally knowledgeable applicants who lacked compelling evidence that they had experienced God's saving grace? In the late 1630s, with the Great Migration in full swing and new arrivals clamoring for admission to the churches, New England Puritans decided that such "merit-mongers" might safely be excluded, thereby limiting church membership to the community's "visible saints." A decade later, the Great Migration over and applications down, some of the saints began to have second thoughts.

By the early 1650s fewer than half of Boston's adults were church members, and other towns in Massachusetts and Connecticut experienced the same proportionate decline. So exacting had the examination for membership become, particularly in churches where the minister and elders tried to outdo each other in the ferocity of their questioning, that most young people simply declined to submit themselves to such scrutiny. How these growing numbers of nonmembers could be compelled to attend church services was a problem ministers could not long defer. Meanwhile, the magistrates found it harder to defend the policy of withholding the vote from otherwise qualified taxpayers because they were not church members. But what really forced reconsideration of the membership policy was the concerns of nonmember parents about the souls of their children, who could not be baptized.

At first the New England churches permitted baptism of the children of church members. Later, some Biblical purists (including a Harvard president fired for insisting as much) came out against infant baptism altogether. But most early Puritans approved the practice, which allowed them the hope that a child who died after receiving baptism might at least be spared Hell's hottest precincts. Since most of the first generation were church members, nearly all the second-generation New Englanders were baptized, whether they became church members or not. The problem began with the third generation, the offspring of parents who had been baptized but who did not become church members. By the mid-1650s it was clear that if nothing were done, soon a majority of the people would be living in a state of original sin. If that happened, how could Puritan values, and for that matter the churches themselves, remain the dominant force in New England life?

Fortunately, a way out was at hand. In 1657 an assembly of Massachusetts and Connecticut ministers recommended a form of intermediate church membership that would permit the baptism of people who were not visible saints. Five years later, some 80 ministers and laymen from 34 churches met at Boston's First Church to hammer out what came to be called the Half-Way Covenant. It provided for limited—or halfway—membership for any applicant not known to be a sinner who was willing to "own" (accept the provisions of) the church covenant. Such members and their children could be baptized, but the sacrament of communion and a voice in church decision making were reserved for full members. Halfway types could later apply for full membership, if the Spirit moved them. The General Court of Massachusetts promptly endorsed the recommendations of the Half-Way Synod and urged all the churches of the Commonwealth to adopt them. Two years later it quietly extended the right to vote to halfway church members.

Opponents of the Half-Way Covenant argued that it reflected a slackening of religious fervor. Michael Wigglesworth gave poetic voice to these views in his 32-verse "God's Controversy with New England" and his even more evocatively entitled "The Day of Doom," both written in 1662. The historian Perry Miller, a leading authority on Puritan New England, argued that the early 1660s marked the beginning of the decline, or "declension," of the Puritan experiment. Some loss of religious intensity there may have been, but the rise in church memberships, the continuing prestige accorded ministers, and the lessening of the intrachurch squabbling in the decades after the Half-Way Covenant was adopted suggest that the secularization of New England society had a long way to go. Like its families, New England's churches made it through their first half-century in the American wilderness impressively intact.

Democracies Without Democrats

Along with their families and churches, Puritans looked to government to order their communal lives. They left England out of opposition not to government as such but to that of Charles I, which failed to satisfy their civil as well as their spiritual needs. Several hundred returned to England in the 1640s when the Puritan-led Parliamentary opposition deprived Charles first of his royal authority and then, in 1649, of his head. But most of the Puritans who came to New England stayed on, convinced that the government that would best serve their needs lay closest at hand.

Like their Chesapeake neighbors, the governments of Massachusetts, Connecticut, Rhode Island, and New Hampshire derived their authority from charters granted by the Crown or Parliament. Each resembled closely the structure of government in England. Where in England stood the monarch atop the governmental pyramid, in a New England colony stood a governor; where there the House of Lords represented the aristocracy, in New England a governor's council represented people of wealth and social position; where there a House of Commons represented everyone else, in New England a popularly elected assembly did the same. Resemblances to England aside, the provincial governments went about their business as if they were independent. Except for rare fits of Parliamentary meddling, they largely were.

Freedom from English supervision allowed the colonial assemblies to focus on the needs of New Englanders. Well into the 18th century these needs typically involved calls to maintain order by regulating how people behaved. "Were it not for government," a minister reminded Connecticut lawmakers in 1718, "the world would soon run into all manner of disruptions and confusions." According to Puritan theory, government was both a civil covenant, entered into by all who came within its jurisdiction, and the principal mechanism for policing all the institutions upon which the maintenance of the social order depended. When the Massachusetts and Connecticut general courts passed laws requiring church attendance, levying taxes for the support of the clergy, and banning Quakers from practicing their faith, they were acting as "shield of the churches." When they provided the death penalty both for adultery and for blaspheming a parent, they were defending the integrity of the family and its role as "nurseries of the commonwealth." When they set the price a laborer might charge for his services or even the amount of gold braid that servants might wear on their jackets, they believed they were enforcing the Puritan ideal that people must accept their assigned stations in life. "When Sin and Iniquity prevails over the laws already made," another Connecticut minister insisted in 1717, "nature . . . call[s] for the Addition of Further."

Most of these colonial laws went unnoticed in England. Those upholding the privileged position of the Congregational church, however, came under sharp attack from English Anglicans, Presbyterians, and Quakers. When the Massachusetts General Court imposed the death penalty on four stubborn Quakers who returned after being expelled from the colony, a royal order of 1662 forbade further executions.

Laws like these have prompted historians and Americans generally to characterize New England colonial legislation as socially repressive and personally invasive. Yet many of the laws remained in force through the colonial period without rousing much local opposition. Others, particularly those upholding religious discrimination or restricting economic activity, were repealed at the insistence of Parliament.

A healthy respect for the backsliding ways of humanity obliged New Englanders not to depend too much on provincial governments, whose jurisdiction extended over several thousand square miles. Almost of necessity, the primary responsibility for maintaining "Good Order and Peace" fell to the more than 500 towns of the region. These differed greatly in size and development. By the early 18th century the largest and most economically advanced, Boston, Newport, and Portsmouth, were well along toward becoming urban centers. This was before "frontier" towns like Amherst, Kent, and Hanover had even been founded. Nonetheless, as recent studies of specific towns have documented, the towns gave the New England region the distinctiveness it has still not wholly lost.

Dedham, Massachusetts, whose early history has

been meticulously reconstructed by Kenneth Lockridge, illustrates how this worked. In 1634 the heads of 30 households, already feeling crowded in the then–two-year-old village of Watertown, petitioned the General Court for a grant of land to establish a new town. A year later they became the proprietors of a 200-square-mile tract west of Watertown on the condition that they all move there, "gather" a church, and organize a town government. The proprietors then drew up a town covenant, the first clause of which committed all who signed it to conduct themselves "according to that most perfect rule, the foundation wherof is everlasting love." Other clauses bound them to keep out the "contrary minded," to submit personal differences to the judgment of the town, and to conduct their business so as to create a "loving and comfortable society in our said town."

The covenant provided that town business be decided at semiannual town meetings, at which all male adults who had subscribed to the covenant could vote. At these meetings a representative to the General Court was elected and seven selectmen were chosen to administer community affairs between town meetings. In addition, matters relating to town lands were decided, taxes to pay the minister's salary set, and provisions for poor and incompetent people made. The next century brought many changes to Dedham. Yet when the town's 1,200 residents celebrated its centenary in 1736, they were governing themselves much as had their great-grandparents. Looking back, they could only be struck by the continuities that shaped their lives.

But was colonial New England democratic? To be considered democratic, a government must at least offer those subject to its authority a voice in its operations. This condition New England governments met. With the possible exception of the 1670s and 1680s, when a stiff property holding requirement (£80 of taxable estate) was introduced in Massachusetts and Connecticut, most adult male New Englanders were qualified to vote. Compared with England, where property qualifications prevented most people from voting, or with the southern colonies, where blacks—"free" or slave—had no political rights, the New England governments were democratic. Relatively few voters, however, actually bothered to participate in provincial or town elections because most offices went uncontested. Furthermore, those elected to office consistently came from the wealthiest and most established levels of the community. In Dedham, 5 percent of the adult males filled 60 percent of the town's positions. Even in Rhode Island, widely regarded as almost too democratic, Providence and Newport voters usually elected their wealthiest and longest-settled townsmen. Important families, such as the Otises of Barnstable, the Quincys of Braintree, and the Wolcotts of Windsor, had members serving as moderator of the town meeting or deputy to the General Court so often as to make these offices almost hereditary. Ordinary voters tended to choose their "betters," while those they selected took seriously the responsibilities of public office. Together they created what one voter approvingly called "a speaking aristocracy in the face of a silent democracy."

The most serious threat to these arrangements occurred in the 1680s. Following the execution of Charles I in 1649, the Parliament-led Puritan Revolution devolved into rule by one man, the Lord Protector, Oliver Cromwell. Cromwell's death in 1658 and dissatisfaction with Puritan rule led to the restoration of the Stuart monarchy in the person of Charles II (1660–1685). During his reign and the abbreviated one of his brother, James II (1685–1688), royal officials sought to bring the colonies under effective royal supervision. Massachusetts seemed in particular need of such supervision. Accordingly, in 1684 the Massachusetts Bay Charter of 1630 was annulled and the colony, along with all those north and east of Pennsylvania, became part of the Dominion of New England, which was to have as its governor Edmund Andros.

Andros sailed into Boston Harbor in late 1686 with orders to make the northern colonies, Massachusetts most of all, behave in ways consistent with their status as colonies. Specifically, he set out to abolish popular assemblies, to change the land-grant system so as to provide the king with quitrents, and to enforce religious toleration, particularly of his fellow Anglicans. He promptly forced the congregation of the Old South Meeting House in Boston to permit its use for Anglican services. The historian Stephen Saunders Webb has characterized the Dominion as designed to bring about nothing less than the political and cultural "anglicization" of New England. A professional military man and a skilled colonial administrator, as he had shown earlier as governor of New York, Andros dismissed resistance to his authority. "Knoweing no other government then their owne, [they] think it best, and are wedded to . . . it."

Fortunately for New Englanders so wedded, the Dominion fell victim two years later to yet another political turnabout in England, the Glorious Revolution. In 1688 Parliament decided it had had enough of the Catholic-leaning Stuarts and sent James II packing. In his place it installed a more resolutely Protestant Dutchman, William of Orange, and his wife, James's daughter Mary. When news of these events reached Boston in the spring of 1689, the Andros regime was routed by a force of more than 1,000 armed colonists led by a contingent of ministers. Two years later, in 1691, Massachusetts got a new charter, which, except for its insistence upon the religious rights of all Protestants, once again extended to the Bay Colony the luxury of existing under "no other government then their owne."

Crisis in Salem Village

Many New England towns resembled "peaceable kingdoms." But not all of them. In some, like Andover, tensions developed between generations when they ran out of land sufficient to support the grandchildren of the founders. Others, like Braintree and Worcester, allowed petty disputes over a minister's salary or the location of the meetinghouse to divide townspeople into rival camps. Still others seemed doomed to serious discord. Among these, Salem village provides a singular example.

In 1666, families living in the rural outback of the thriving town of Salem petitioned the General Court for the right to establish their own church rather than attend and contribute to the support of the Salem church. For political and economic reasons this was a questionable move. Most of the families were among the poorest in Essex County, while the two most prosperous, the Porters and the Putnams, disagreed about everything except having a separate church. In addition, the Salem selectmen, fearing the loss of taxes, vigorously objected. But in 1672 the General Court authorized the establishment of a separate parish in "Salem Village." In so doing the Court put the 600-odd inhabitants of the village politically on their own as well.

All did not go well for either parish or village. Over the next 15 years three preachers came and went before, in 1689, one Samuel Parris, after some mutually unbecoming haggling over salary, became minister. It was said at the time that Parris and Salem Village deserved each other. A Harvard College dropout, Parris had spent 20 years in the Caribbean as a merchant and had taken up preaching only three years before coming to Salem Village. Accompanying him were his wife; a daughter, Betty; a niece, Abigail; and the family's West Indian slave, Tituba, who told fortunes and practiced magic on the side.

Parris proved as incapable of bringing peace to the feuding factions of Salem Village as had his predecessors. In January 1692, less than two years after his appointment, a faction opposed to Parris and the Putnams won control of the church and called for his dismissal. The selectmen blocked his salary and, despite the season, even stopped delivery of his firewood.

At this point Betty and Abigail, now 9 and 11, along with Ann Putnam, the 12-year-old daughter of their father's principal supporter, started acting strangely. Earlier that winter they had begun, under the tutelage of Tituba, to experiment with fortune-telling and other "little sorceries." From these they soon advanced to taking on "odd postures and antic gestures," and from there to "uttering foolish, ridiculous speeches which neither they themselves nor any others could make sense of." When Parris sought medical advice, the doctor diagnosed the girls' ravings as the work of the "Evil Hand." Then, after calling in parish allies and nearby ministers to observe the girls in action, he declared them bewitched.

But who had done the bewitching? The hunt began cautiously enough, likely because the "afflicted" and their elders only slowly realized its full possibilities. The first persons accused were three women whose unsavory reputations and frightening appearances made them likely candidates. Sarah Good was a pauper with a nasty tongue; Sarah Osborne was a bedridden widow. The third was the slave Tituba, who had brought suspicion on herself at the first sign of the girls' distress by volunteering to bake a "witch cake," made of rye meal and the urine of the girls. The cake should be fed to a dog, Tituba said. If the girls were truly afflicted, the dog would show signs of bewitchment!

The Salem witch trials have fascinated artists and writers, as well as historians, over the years. In this 19th-century painting, a judge examines the "mark of the devil" on the skin of an accused witch while others in the courtroom go into contortions.

On the last day of February 1692, the three women were brought before the local deputies to the General Court to determine whether they should be formally charged. As each was questioned, the girls went into contortions; "their arms, necks and backs turned this way and that way . . . their mouths stopped, their throats choaked, their limbs wracked and tormented." With only the slightest urging, Tituba, likely impressed by the powers ascribed to her, promptly confessed to being a witch. Sarah Good and Sarah Osborne each claimed to be innocent, although Sarah Good expressed doubts about Sarah Osborne. All three were sent to jail on suspicion of witchcraft.

These proceedings triggered new accusations. By the end of April, 24 more people had been charged with practicing witchcraft, among them several prominent residents of the town of Salem. The feuding Putnams and Porters accused each other of harboring witches in their families. Elsewhere others seized upon the witchcraft scare to settle old scores. Officials in neighboring Andover, lacking their own "bewitched," invited the Parris and Putnam girls to their village to help with their investigations. The girls obliged by providing grounds for the indictment of 40 persons. By May the hunt had extended beyond Essex County to Maine and Boston and up the social ladder to some of the colony's most prominent citizens, including Lady Mary Phips, whose husband, William, had just been appointed governor under the colony's new royal charter.

By June, when Governor Phips convened a special court consisting of members of his council, more than 150 persons (Lady Phips no longer among them) stood formally charged with practicing witchcraft. In the next four months the court found grounds for convicting 28 persons, most of them women, of witchcraft. Of these, five "confessed" and were spared; the rest were condemned to death. One woman won a reprieve because she was pregnant. Two others escaped. Because anyone who spoke in defense of the accused was in danger of being charged with witchcraft, hostile testimony dominated the proceedings. Even so, some brave souls did challenge both the procedures and the findings of the court. As the summer wore on, the contortions of the girls became less convincing as they became less novel. Their trustworthiness slumped further after a defense witness testified that one girl had boasted that they "did it for sport, they must have some sport."

Growing skepticism, however, did not halt the carrying out of sentences. Nineteen persons were hanged, most in batches of four or five. The husband of a convicted witch refused to enter a plea when charged with being a "wizard." He was executed by having stones piled upon him until he suffocated. Finally, in October, at the urging of the leading ministers of the Commonwealth, Governor Phips adjourned the court and forbade any further executions.

No one involved in these gruesome proceedings escaped with reputation intact. From Phips on down, political leaders failed to exercise the judgment those they represented had a right to expect from them. The court, presided over by the lieutenant governor, seemed more intent on reaching speedy verdicts that would empty the jails than on seeing justice done. Those whose reputations suffered most were the ministers. Parris behaved so badly that even his parish allies turned against him. Within a year of the last execution, the church sent him packing. Among the clergy called in to oversee the proceedings, only Increase Mather deserves any credit. He persuaded Phips to halt the executions, arguing that "it were better that ten witches should escape, than that one innocent person should be condemned." That needed to be said, but it took the elder Mather an awfully long time to say it.

The behavior of his son Cotton defies apology. It was not that Cotton Mather accepted the existence of witches—at the time everyone did—or even that he took such pride in being the resident expert on demonology. It was rather his vindictiveness. Despite his sound advice to the court to discount "spectral evidence," that offered by witnesses supposedly acquired while bewitched, he insisted repeatedly that only the most "vigorous prosecution" could rid the Commonwealth of its demonic afflictions. He even stood at the foot of the gallows bullying hesitant hangmen into doing "their duty."

Life went on in New England after the trials much as it had before. Nearly three decades passed before anyone publicly claimed that what had happened in Salem Village was a tragic case of mass hysteria and official panic, not, as the Mathers insisted, an appropriate response to the "molestations of evil spirits." It was, Perry Miller wrote of Salem after the witchcraft episode, "as though no such thing ever happened."

But such a thing had happened. "What will be the issue of these troubles, God only knows," the treasurer of Harvard College, Thomas Brattle, wrote within a week of the last hanging. "I am afraid that ages will not wear off that reproach which these things will leave behind upon our land."

Would the troubles have occurred if New Englanders had been less quick to pass critical judgment on their neighbors and more willing to tolerate nonconformity? Would society be better off if people minded their own business, instead of worrying about everyone else's business? At the time, New Englanders would have judged such questions heretical. Even later they represented quite radical views. The second thoughts prompted by the witchcraft crisis did not mark the point at which the Puritan ideal of a community "knitt together" by covenant was abandoned. They do mark the point in New England's history where those who persisted in upholding that ideal were put permanently on the defensive.

"To Advance Learning"

Along with the farmers and artisans who settled in New England with their families during the Great Migration came nearly 150 university-trained colonists. The majority had attended one of the Puritan-leaning colleges at Cambridge. Nearly all had studied divinity. Most of the older ones had started out as Anglican ministers, but by the 1620s all had become Puritans. The younger ones despaired of securing pulpits in the England of King Charles and Bishop Laud. For both generations, New England gave promise of religious freedom and also professional fulfillment.

These men became the first ministers in Massachusetts and Connecticut. In the late 1630s, churches were being founded in New England at a rate of more than 15 a year. A brisk "seller's market" existed for would-be ministers. Larger churches began stockpiling candidates by hiring newly arrived Cambridge and Oxford graduates as assistants or teachers in anticipation of the retirement of their senior ministers. But what to do when the initial supply of English-educated immigrants ran out? As a 1643 promotional pamphlet, *New Englands First Fruits,* put it, what would happen "when our present ministers shall lie in the dust"? More than any other factor, fear of leaving "an illiterate Ministry to the Churches" turned the first generation of New Englanders early and resolutely to finding a way to "advance learning and perpetuate it to Posterity."

In 1636 the Massachusetts General Court appropriated £400 to found "a schoole or colledge." Two years later, just as the first freshmen gathered in Cambridge, John Harvard, a recent arrival who had died of tuberculosis, left the college £800 and his library. After a shaky start, during which students conducted a hunger strike against a sadistic and larcenous headmaster, Harvard settled into an annual pattern of admitting a dozen or so 14-year-old boys, stuffing their heads with four years of theology, logic, and mathematics, and then sending them out into the wider world of New England. In 1650 Harvard received from the General Court the charter under which it is still governed.

Although the charter made no mention of training ministers, Harvard's governing board and the entire faculty were clergymen. Of its first 465 graduates, about two of every three became ministers. On this count alone, one 17th-century Harvard alumnus declared his "colledge the best Thing that ever New England thought upon."

Immediately below Harvard on the educational ladder came the grammar schools, where boys spent seven years learning Latin and Greek "so far as they may be fitted for the Universitie." Boston founded the first—Boston Latin School—in 1636. Massachusetts and Connecticut soon passed education acts which required all towns of any size to establish such schools. New Englanders hoped, as the preamble to the Massachusetts law of 1647 stated, to thwart "that old deluder, Satan," whose "chief object was to keep men from the knowledge of the Scriptures," by insuring "that Learning may not be buried in the graves of our forefathers."

Not every New England town required to maintain a school actually did so. Those that did often paid their teachers poorly. Only the most dedicated or least otherwise employable Harvard graduates took up teaching as a career. Some parents kept their children at their chores rather than at school. Yet the cumulative effect of the Puritan community's educational institutions—the family and the church as well as the school—was impressive. Historians estimate that a majority of men in 17th-century New England could read and write. Moreover, literacy increased thereafter faster than the population. By the middle of the 18th century, New England was approaching universal male literacy. In Europe only Scotland and Sweden had achieved this happy state so early. Literacy among women also improved steadily, despite the almost total neglect of formal education for girls. A New England woman was considerably more likely to know how to read and write than her counterparts in England.

Spreading literacy created a thriving market for the printed word. Many of the first settlers brought impressive libraries with them, and large numbers of English books were imported throughout the colonial period. The first printing press in the English colonies was founded in Cambridge in 1638, and by 1700 Boston's many presses were producing a very avalanche of printed matter. Most of these early publications were reprints of sermons, whose authors required only the smallest encouragement from their congregations to send off last Sunday's remarks to the local printer. But if ministers exercised a near-monopoly of the printed word, they did not limit their output entirely to religious topics. They also produced modest amounts of history, poetry, reports of scientific investigations, and treatises on political theory.

By the early 18th century the intellectual life of New England had taken on a character different from and potentially at odds with the ideas of the first Puritans. In the 1690s Harvard acquired a reputation for encouraging liberal ideas about religious toleration. According to orthodox Puritans, its graduates were unfit for the ministry and its professors were no longer interested in training young men for the clergy. In 1701 several Connecticut ministers, most of them Harvard graduates, founded a new "Collegiate School" designed to uphold the Puritan values that Harvard seemed ready to abandon. The new college, which eventually settled in New Haven, was named after its first English benefactor, Elihu Yale. It fulfilled its founders' hopes by sending more than half of its early graduates into the ministry. Nonetheless, as became all too clear at commencement ceremonies in 1722 when its president and six tutors announced themselves Anglicans, Yale quickly acquired purposes well beyond those assigned it by its creators.

The assumption that the clergy had the last word on learned matters, still operative at the time of the witchcraft episode, came under direct challenge in 1721. When a smallpox epidemic swept through Boston that summer, Cotton Mather, at the time the most prestigious clergyman in New England, recommended that the citizenry be inoculated. He favored a method described in the *Transactions* of the Royal Society in England, of which, he informed the community, he was a member.

But instead of accepting Mather's authority, his heretofore silent critics seized on his support of the then-radical idea of inoculation to challenge both his motives and his professional credentials. They filled the unsigned contributor columns of New England's first newspaper, the *Boston Gazette,* and the *New England Courant,* which opened in the midst of the inoculation controversy, with their views.

The *Courant* was published by James Franklin, a printer just back from London, where he had been impressed by the commercial possibilities of journalistic satire. He was soon joined in the enterprise by his 16-year-old brother, Benjamin. They attacked both the advisability of inoculation (in which they were wrong) and the logic of paying much attention to the pronouncements of ministers on scientific subjects (which made eminent good sense). The younger Franklin's "Silence Dogood" essays were particularly infuriating to Mather (who some years earlier had published a collection of *Essays to do Good*) and to other members of the Boston intellectual establishment. Franklin described Harvard as an institution where rich and lazy "blockheads . . . learn little more than how to carry themselves handsomely . . . and from whence they return, after Abundance of Trouble, as Blockheads as ever, only more proud and conceited."

James Franklin was jailed in 1722 for criticizing the General Court, and shortly thereafter the *New England Courant* went out of business. Ben then departed Boston for Philadelphia, where, as everyone knows, fame and fortune awaited him. Before shaking the dust of Boston from his sandals, however, the young Franklin had introduced an element of anticlericalism into the intellectual life of New England, which thereafter would never be wholly rooted out. It remained unclear at the time whether this marked, as an ancient upholder of the Puritan way lamented, "a very great degeneracy from our forefathers" or the first stirrings in America of an intellectual life free of ministerial domination. We now know it was both.

Benjamin Franklin is most often depicted as he looked in later life, with his own thinning hair rather than the wig which was de rigueur for an 18th-century man of good family. In this 1767 portrait, a younger Franklin follows the fashion.

The Serpent Prosperity

Prior experience (and the need to eat) turned the first New Englanders to farming. Laws providing for the establishment of towns required that households be allocated land sufficient for their subsistence. Everyone assumed that families would devote the bulk of their collective energies to agriculture. They grew barley (used to make beer), rye, oats, green vegetables, and also native crops such as potatoes, pumpkins, and, most important, Indian corn, or maize. Corn was easily cultivated and its yield per acre under rough frontier conditions exceeded that of other grains. It proved versatile and tasty when prepared in a variety of ways and also made excellent fodder for livestock. In the form of corn liquor, it was easy to store, to transport, and, in a pinch, to imbibe.

The colonists also had plenty of meat. They grazed cattle, sheep, and hogs on the common pastures or in the surrounding woodlands. Deer, turkey, and other game birds abounded. The Atlantic provided fish, especially cod, which was easily preserved by salting. In short, New Englanders ate an extremely nutritious diet. Abundant surpluses of firewood kept the winter cold from their doors.

The combination contributed significantly to their good health and longevity.

The trouble was that virtually everything that New England farmers grew could be grown in Europe—and was. The shortness of the growing season, the rocky and often hilly terrain, and careless methods of cultivation, which exhausted the soil, meant that farmers did not produce large surpluses. Thus, while New Englanders could feed themselves without difficulty, they had relatively little to spare and no place to sell it.

The earliest Puritans accepted this economic marginality. The more pious positively welcomed it as insurance against "the serpent prosperity" which might otherwise deflect their spiritual mission into commercial opportunism. No prominent English merchants joined the Great Migration, though many were devoted Puritans and some had invested in the Massachusetts Bay Company. Settlers who turned to business upon arrival attracted suspicion, if not open hostility, as in the case of the aspiring merchants who allied themselves with Anne Hutchinson in 1637 and departed with her to Rhode Island. Laws against usury (lending money at excessive rates) and profiteering in scarce commodities were in effect from the first days of settlement. In 1639, and again in 1643, Robert Keayne, a prosperous Boston merchant, was fined £200 by the General Court and admonished by his church for "taking above six-pence in the shilling profit; in some above eight-pence; and in some small things, above two for one." Keayne paid the fines and made "penitential acknowledgment" to his church, all the while convinced that "my goods and prices were cheap pennyworths."

Winthrop and the other early leaders resisted the argument of people like Keayne that business was a calling no less socially useful than the ministry or public office. They wished instead to maintain a community in which economic activity was less prestigious than religion and government. Differences in wealth should be modest and should favor those to whom the community looked for leadership. In the Puritan scheme of things, since Governor Winthrop was a far more valuable member of the community than Robert Keayne, he should stand higher than Keayne in all rankings, wealth included. But Winthrop died in 1649 broke and in debt, whereas Keayne died three years later in sufficient prosperity (despite those stiff fines) to leave the town of Boston and Harvard College impressive benefactions. The gap between the Puritan ideal and the emerging reality was becoming embarrassingly clear.

Winthrop's generation had tried to minimize dependence on European-manufactured goods such as iron tools, glass, and cloth by producing their own. When their efforts failed, they next pinned their hopes on establishing direct trade links with European suppliers by offering the skins of beaver and such other fur-bearing animals as otter, muskrat, and mink. Several towns in the Connecticut Valley and New Hampshire became collection centers for these furs. Unfortunately, the beavers soon caught wind of what was going on and took off for points west and north. By the end of the 1650s the New Englanders were back where they started. As one English merchant wrote, as trading partners "they have noe returns."

The colonists then turned to indirect trading schemes, in which merchants like Robert Keayne played a central role and from which they derived stature as well as wealth. The anticommercial bias of the early Puritans did not, however, vanish as quickly as the elusive beaver had. At the beginning of the 18th century a Boston minister could still tell his congregation this story with every confidence that they shared his belief that his colleague got the better of the Maine fisherman: Once, some years after Keayne's death, a minister in Maine was reminding his flock that "the main end of planting this wilderness" was religion. A prominent member of the congregation could not contain his disagreement. "Sir," he cried out, "you are mistaken. You think you are preaching to the people of the Bay; our main end was to catch fish."

Actually, fish, caught offshore on grounds that extended from Cape Cod to Newfoundland, provided merchants with their opening into the world of transatlantic commerce. In 1643 five New England vessels set out with their holds packed with fish which they sold in Spain and the Canary Islands; they took payment in sherry and madeira, for which a market existed in England. One of these ships also had the dubious distinction of initiating New England into the business of trafficking in human beings when her captain took payment in African slaves, whom he subsequently sold in the West Indies.

This was the start of the famous "triangular

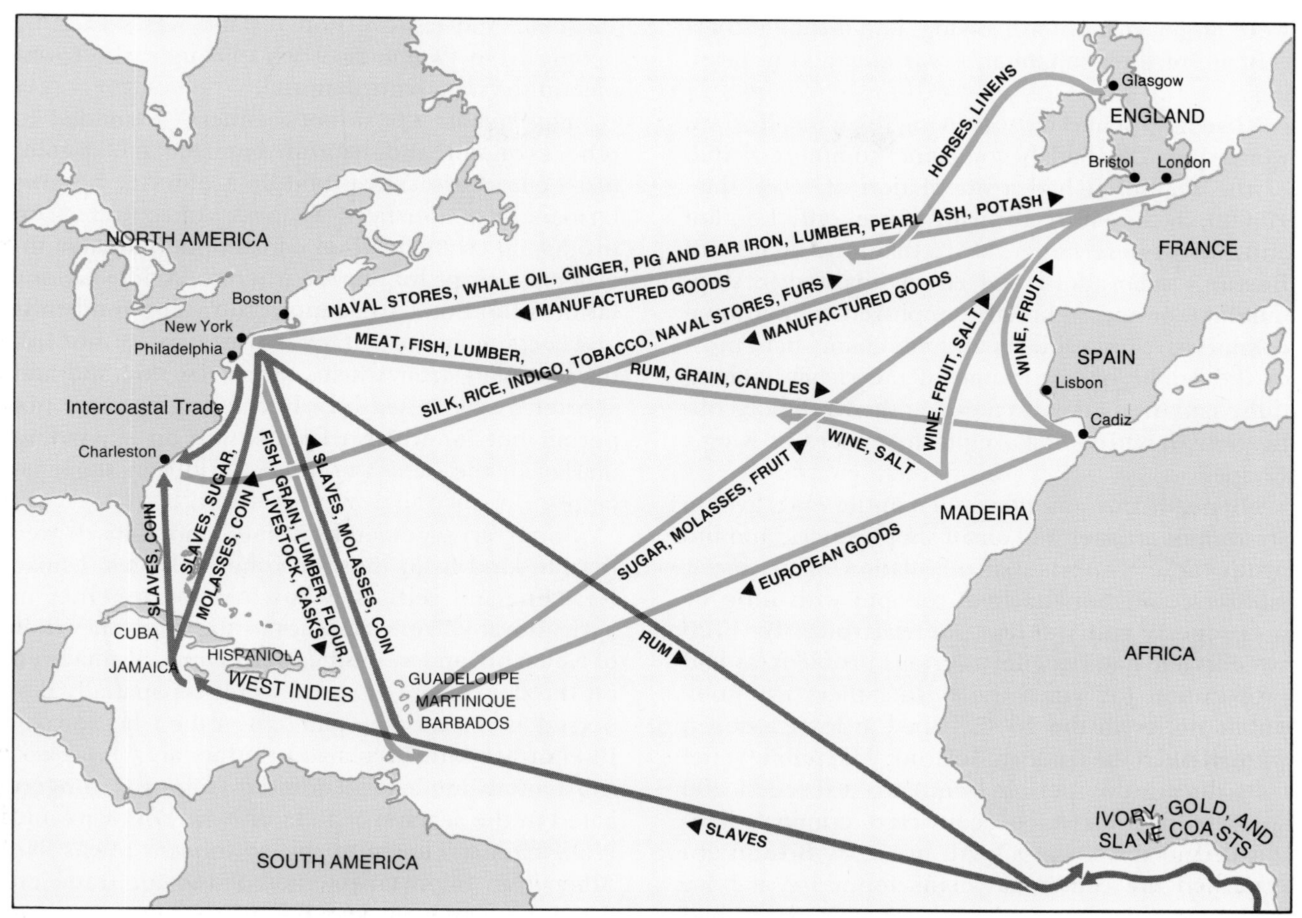

COLONIAL OVERSEAS TRADE

This map summarizes the chief routes of colonial trade in the 1700s. An instance of the so-called triangular slave trade is shown in black for clarity. Most southern exports went to England, but a lack of suitable English markets led the northern and middle colonies to seek outlets for their products in the West Indies and southern Europe.

trade," for once New England merchants discovered that access to English markets was no less feasible—or less profitable—for being indirect, they were in business for keeps. Only occasionally was the pattern truly triangular; more often, intermediate legs gave it a polygonal character. So long as their ships ended up with something that could be exchanged for English goods needed at home, it did not matter what they started out with or how many things they bought and sold along the way. Success required more than, as critics had it, complying with the rule "to buy as cheap as they could, and sell as dear." The profits of years of effort could be lost on the turning of a tide. Daring, good business connections, capital, knowledge of market conditions, and not a little luck all went into these voyages.

So maritime trade and those who engaged in it became the driving force of the New England economy, important all out of proportion to the number of persons directly involved. Because those engaged congregated in Portsmouth, Salem, Boston, Newport, and New Haven, these towns soon differed greatly from towns in the interior. They were larger and faster growing, and a smaller percentage of their inhabitants was engaged in farming.

The largest and most thriving town was Boston, which by 1720 had become the commercial hub of the region. It had a population of more than 10,000; in the entire British Empire, only London and Bristol were larger. More than one-quarter of Boston's male adults had either invested in shipbuilding or were directly employed in maritime commerce. Ship captains and merchants held most of the public offices. Some of the richest among these had even taken to meeting their religious obligations by attending Anglican services at King's Chapel!

Beneath this emergent mercantile elite lived a stratum of artisans and small shopkeepers, and beneath these a substantial population of mariners, laborers, and "unattached" people with little or no property and still less political voice. By 1720 street crime had become a serious problem, as had prostitution (of which the town fathers first took public notice in the 1670s, when at least a dozen women plied the trade in Boston). The public relief rolls during this period frequently exceeded 200 souls, while dozens of convicted criminals languished in the town jail. All in all, as Boston approached the centennial of its founding, it bore little resemblance to what the first Puritans had in mind when they planted their "Citty upon a Hill." But neither was it like any European city of the time. It stood there on Massachusetts Bay, midway between its Puritan origins and its American future.

The Middle Colonies: A Rising People

New York, New Jersey, Pennsylvania, and Delaware owe their collective name, the Middle Colonies, to geography. Sandwiched between New England and the Chesapeake region, they often receive only passing notice in accounts of colonial America. The lack of a distinctive institution, such as slavery or the town meeting, explains part of this neglect.

Actually, both institutions existed there. Black slaves made up about 10 percent of the population; indeed, one New York county in the 1740s had proportionally more blacks than large sections of Virginia. And eastern Long Island was settled by people from Connecticut who brought the town-meeting system with them.

This quality of "in-betweenness" extended to other economic and social arrangements. Like colonists elsewhere, most Middle Colonists became farmers. But northern farmers concentrated on producing crops for local consumption and southerners on crops for export, whereas Middle Colony farmers did both. In addition to raising foodstuffs and keeping livestock, farmers throughout the Middle Colonies grew wheat, which the thin soil and shorter growing season of New England did not permit but for which there existed an expanding market in the densely settled Caribbean sugar islands.

Social arrangements differed more in degree than in kind from those in other colonies. Unlike New England settlers, who clustered together in agricultural villages, families in the Hudson Valley of New York and in southeastern Pennsylvania lived on the land they cultivated, often as spatially dispersed as the tobacco planters of the Chesapeake. In contrast with Virginia and Maryland, however, substantial numbers of Middle Colonists congregated in the seaport centers of New York City and Philadelphia. They also settled interior towns like Albany, an important center of the fur trade on the upper Hudson, and Germantown, an "urban village" northwest of Philadelphia where many citizens were engaged in trades like weaving and tailoring and in agriculturally related businesses like flour milling rather than in farming itself.

"This Promiscuous Breed"

The Middle Colonists also possessed traits that later would be seen as distinctly "American." Their ethnic and religious heterogeneity is a case in point. Traveling through Pennsylvania in 1744, the Swedish botanist Peter Kalm encountered "a very mixed company of different nations and religions." In addition to "Scots, English, Dutch, Germans, and Irish," he reported, "there were Roman Catholics, Presbyterians, Quakers, Methodists, Seventh day men, Moravians, Anabaptists, and one Jew." In New York City an embattled English resident complained: "Our chiefest unhappiness here is too

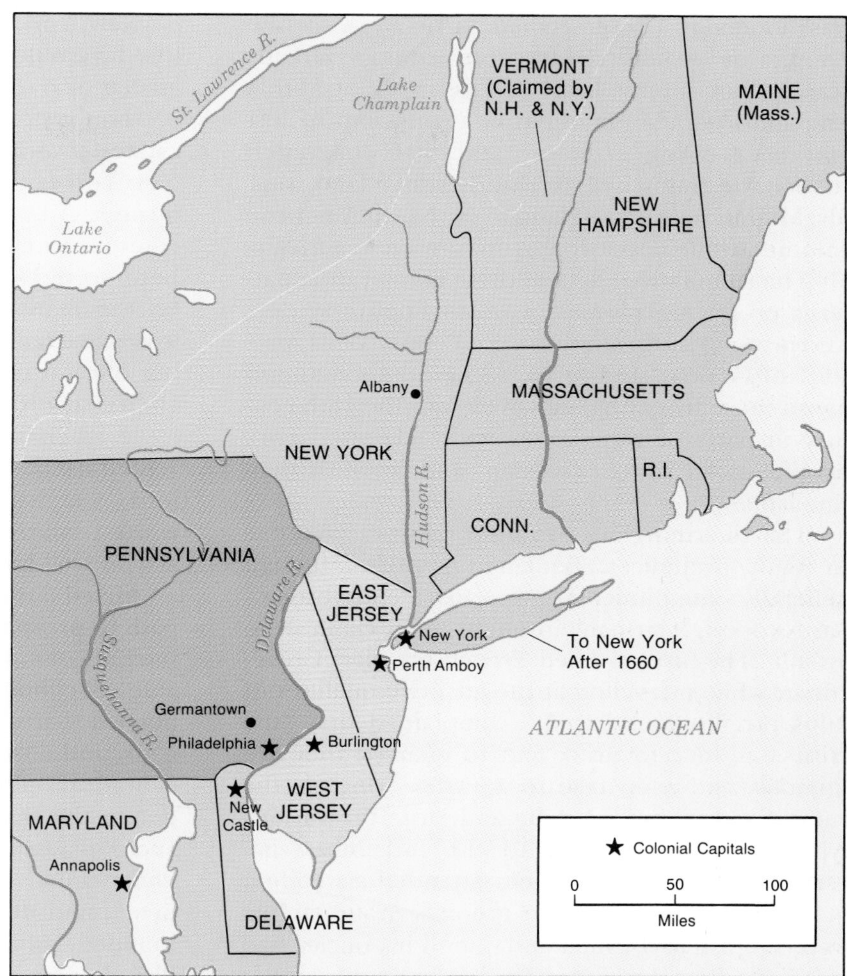

THE MIDDLE COLONIES

great a mixture of nations, & English the least part."

Three of the Middle Colonies had substantial numbers of non-English settlers. The English population of New York City was smaller than the Dutch until 1698, and Scandinavian and Dutch settlers outnumbered the English in New Jersey and Delaware for decades. Even after the English took over these colonies, most settlers came from countries other than England. Penn's first success in attracting colonists was with German Quakers and other persecuted religious sects, among them Mennonites and Moravians from the Rhine Valley. The first substantial influx of immigrants into New York after it became a royal colony consisted of French Huguenots.

Early in the 18th century, hordes of Scotch-Irish settlers from Northern Ireland and Scotland descended on Pennsylvania. These colonists spoke English but felt little loyalty to the English government, which had treated them badly back home, and less to the Anglican church, since most of them were Presbyterians.

Why so few English? Here, again, timing provides the best answer. In the 1640s, England had been experiencing a depression. Many people were unemployed. The government therefore encouraged emigration. But in the 1680s, the economy was booming. There seemed to be work for all. Emigration would reduce the nation's already scarce labor supply. Later still, fears surfaced that England's population might be insufficient to sustain its growing economy and that emigration robbed the country of its already scarce labor supply. Migration from England to the North American colonies, while never drying up, slowed to a trickle.

The cumulative effect of these immigration patterns produced colonies in which English settlers were a minority. In southeastern Pennsylvania, persons of German and Swiss backgrounds outnumbered those from England. Well into the 18th century in parts of New Jersey and Delaware, more people spoke Dutch, German, and Swedish than English.

The intermingling of ethnic groups gave rise to many prejudices. Benjamin Franklin, though generally complimentary toward Pennsylvania's hard-working Germans, thought them clannish to a fault. The already cited French traveler, Crèvecoeur, while marveling at the adaptive qualities of "this promiscuous breed," complained that "the Irish . . . love to drink and to quarrel; they are litigious, and soon take to the gun, which is the ruin of everything." Yet by and large the various types managed to get along with each other successfully enough. Crèvecoeur attended a wedding in Pennsylvania where the groom's grandparents were English and Dutch and one of his uncles had married a Frenchwoman. The groom and his three brothers, Crèvecoeur added with some amazement, "now have four wives of different nations."

"The Best Poor Man's Country"

Ethnic differences seldom caused conflict in the Middle Colonies because they seldom limited opportunity. The promise of prosperity—promotional pamphlets proclaimed Pennsylvania "the best poor man's country in the world"—had attracted all in the first place, and achieving prosperity was relatively easy, even for those who came with only a willingness to work. From its founding, Pennsylvania granted upwards of 500 acres of land to families upon arrival, provided they would pay the proprietor an annual quitrent. Similar arrangements existed in New Jersey and Delaware. Soon travelers in the Middle Colonies were being struck by "a pleasing uniformity of decent competence."

New York was something of an exception to this favorable economic situation. When the English took over New York, they extended the Dutch patroon system (page 25) by creating 30 manorial estates covering 2-million-odd acres. But ordinary New Yorkers never lacked ways of becoming landowners. A hundred acres along the Hudson River could be bought in 1730 for what an unskilled laborer could earn in three months. Even tenants on the manorial estates could obtain long-term leases that had most of the advantages of ownership but did not require the investment of any capital. Unlike serfs or slaves, a tenant could pack up and leave when a better economic opportunity presented itself. "One may think oneself to be a great lord," one frustrated "lord" of a New York manor wrote a colleague, "but it does not amount to much, as you well know."

Mixed farming offered the most commonly trod path to prosperity in the Middle Colonies, but not the only one. Inland communities offered comfortable livelihoods for artisans. Farmers always needed barrels, candles, rope, horseshoes and nails, and dozens of other articles in everyday use. Countless opportunities awaited the ambitious settler in the shops, yards, and offices of New York and Philadelphia. Unlike Boston, New York and Philadelphia profited from navigable rivers that penetrated deep into the back country. Although founded half a century after New York and Boston, Philadelphia grew more rapidly than either. In the 1750s, when its population reached 15,000, it passed Boston to become the largest city in English America.

Most Philadelphians who stuck to their business, particularly if it happened to be maritime commerce, did well for themselves. John Bringhurst, a merchant, began his career as a clerk. At his death in 1751 he left an estate of several thousand pounds. According to the historian Gary Nash, the city's "leather-apron" artisans often accumulated estates of more than £400, a substantial sum at the time. By way of contrast, in Boston after 1710, economic stagnation made it much more difficult for a skilled artisan to rise in the world.

The Politics of Diversity

"Cannot more friendly and private courses be taken to set matters right in an infant province?" an exasperated William Penn asked the people of

Pennsylvania in 1704. "For the love of God, me, and the poor country, be not so *governmentish.*" However well-intentioned Penn's advice, however justified his annoyance, the Pennsylvanians ignored him. Instead, they and their fellows throughout the region constructed a political culture that diverged sharply from the patterns of New England and the south both in contentiousness and in the sophistication required of local politicians.

Superficially the governments of the Middle Colonies closely resembled those of earlier settlements. All had popularly elected representative assemblies and appointed governors and councils. Most male adults could vote. In Pennsylvania, where Penn had insisted that there be no religious test and where 50 acres constituted a freehold, something close to universal manhood suffrage existed. In New York even non-property-holding white male residents voted in local elections, and rural tenants with lifetime leases enjoyed full voting rights.

Except in places where people from New England had settled, local government was relatively unimportant and the emphasis on maintaining a communal consensus that characterized the politics of New England towns was absent. In Germantown, Pennsylvania, according to historian Stephanie Wolf, "there was no true formal town government at all."

In Pennsylvania and most of New York, representatives were elected by counties. In this they resembled Virginia and Maryland. But unlike the southerners, voters did not tend to defer in politics to the landed gentry. Instead, they seemed addicted to precisely the kind of political contentiousness and instability that colonists elsewhere sought to avoid.

In New York, in 1689, during the political vacuum following the abdication of King James II and the absence of a royal governor, Jacob Leisler, a disgruntled merchant and militia captain, seized control of the government. "Leisler's Rebellion" did not amount to much. He held power for less than two years before he was overthrown and sent to the gallows. Yet for two decades New York politics continued to be a struggle between the Leislerians, and other self-conscious "outs" who shared Leisler's dislike of English rule, and anti-Leislerians, who had in common only that they had opposed his takeover. Each group sought the support of a succession of ineffective governors, and the one that failed to get it invariably proceeded to make that poor man's tenure as miserable as possible. (Governor Edward Cornbury [1702–1708] had an especially difficult time asserting the royal authority after being spotted on the streets of New York wearing a dress.)

New York lapsed into political tranquility during the governorship of Robert Hunter (1710–1719), who joined forces with Lewis Morris, a prominent landholder and sometime leader of the colonial assembly. But the early 1730s New York politics again became polarized, this time less on ethnic or class lines than on regional and economic ones. The merchants, led by James DeLancey, dominated the Governor's Council. The large landowners, led by Morris, controlled the assembly. Conflict broke out in 1732 over a claim for back salary by Governor William Cosby. When Morris, who was also chief justice of the supreme court, opposed Cosby's claim, the governor replaced him with DeLancey. Morris and his assembly allies responded by establishing the *New York Weekly Journal.* To edit the paper they hired an itinerant German printer, John Peter Zenger. The editorial policy of the paper rested in the hands of the lawyer James Alexander, an ally of the Morrisites.

Cosby might have tolerated the *Weekly Journal*'s front-page lectures on the right of the people to criticize their rulers had the back pages not contained advertisements referring to his supporters as spaniels and to him as a monkey. After submitting to two months of "open and implacable malice against me," he shut down the paper, arrested Zenger, and charged him with seditious libel.

What began as a squalid salary dispute became one of the most celebrated tests of freedom of the press in the history of journalism. At the trial Zenger's attorney, James Hamilton, using a brief prepared by Alexander, argued that the truth of his client's criticisms of Cosby constituted a proper defense against seditious libel. This reasoning (though contrary to English law at the time) persuaded the jury to acquit Zenger.

Meanwhile, Morris, who had gone to England seeking Cosby's removal, got himself appointed governor of New Jersey! In colonial New York flexibility, not consistency, was the way to get ahead in politics. Having acquired political prominence first as the defender of one royal governor and then as the critic of another, that Morris should end up a governor himself seems only fitting.

ADVERTISEMENT.

A Large Spaneil, of about Five Foot Five Inches High, has lately ſtray'd from his Kennell with his Mouth full of fulſom Panegericks, and in his Ramble dropt them in the NEW-YORK-GAZETTE; when a Puppy, he was mark'd thus J T, and a Croſs in his Forehead, but the Mark being worn out, he has taken upon him in an heatheniſh Manner to abuſe Mankind, by impoſing a great many groſs Falſhoods upon them. Whoever will ſtrip the ſaid Panagericks of all their Fulſomneſs, and ſend the Beaſt back to his Kennell, ſhall have the Thanks of all honeſt Men, and all reaſonable Charges.

Appearing on the back page of the New York Weekly Journal *of November 26, 1733, this advertisement was a thinly veiled taunt aimed at one of Governor Cosby's supporters. When a less flamboyant piece appeared several weeks later, characterizing Cosby himself as a monkey, the governor shut down the paper and had the printer arrested.*

Politics in Pennsylvania also turned on conflict between two interest groups. One clustered around the proprietor, the other around the assembly, which was controlled by a coalition of Quaker representatives from Philadelphia and the German-speaking Pennsylvania Dutch.

Neither the proprietary party nor the Quaker party (nor for that matter either the Morrisites or the DeLanceyites in New York) qualifies as a political party in the modern sense of being organized and maintained for the purpose of winning elections. Nor can they be categorized as standing for "democratic" or "aristocratic" interests. But their existence guaranteed that the political leaders had to take popular opinion into account. Moreover, having once appealed to public opinion, they had to be prepared to defer to it. Success turned as much on knowing how to follow as on knowing how to lead.

The 1763 uprising of the "Paxton Boys" of western Pennsylvania put this policy to a full test. The uprising was triggered by eastern indifference to Indian attacks on the frontier—an indifference made possible by the fact that the east outnumbered the west in the assembly, 26 to 10. Fuming because they could obtain no help from Philadelphia against the Indians, a group of Scotch-Irish from Lancaster county fell upon a village of peaceful Conestoga Indians and murdered them in cold blood. Then these Paxton Boys marched on the capital, several hundred strong. Fortunately a delegation of burghers, headed by Benjamin Franklin, talked them out of attacking the town, by acknowledging the legitimacy of their grievances about representation and by promising to vote a bounty on Indian scalps! It was just such fancy footwork that established Franklin, the leader of the assembly party, as Pennsylvania's consummate politician. "Tell me, Mr. Franklin," a testy member of the proprietary party asked, "how is it that you are always with the majority?"

The Great Awakening

By the early 18th century, religious fervor had slackened in all the colonies. Prosperity turned many colonists away from their forebears' preoccupation with the rewards of the next world to the more tangible ones of this. John Winthrop invested his faith in God and his own efforts in the task of creating a spiritual community; his grandsons, Fitzhugh and Wait Still, invested in Connecticut real estate. The proliferation of religious denominations, all competing for members and political influence, made it impracticable to enforce laws requiring regular religious observances. Even in South Carolina, the colony that came closest to having an "Anglican Establishment," only a minority of persons were churchgoers. Settlers in frontier districts, particularly in the south but in New York and New England too, lived beyond the reach of church or clergy. The result was a large and growing number of "persons careless of all religion."

This state of affairs came to an abrupt end with

the Great Awakening of the 1740s. The Awakening began in the Middle Colonies as the result of religious developments that originated in Europe. In the late 1720s two newly arrived ministers—Theodore Frelinghuysen, a Calvinist from Westphalia, and William Tennent, an Irish-born Presbyterian—sought to instill in their sleepy Pennsylvania and New Jersey congregations the evangelical zeal and spiritual enthusiasm they had witnessed among the pietists in Germany and the Methodist followers of John Wesley in England. Their example inspired other clergymen, including Tennent's two sons. A more significant surge of religious enthusiasm followed the arrival in 1738 in Georgia of the Reverend George Whitefield, a young Oxford-trained Anglican minister. Whitefield was a marvelous pulpit orator and no mean actor. He played on the feelings of his audience the way a conductor directs a symphony. David Garrick, king of the London stage, is supposed to have said that he would give a hundred guineas to be able to say "Oh" the way Whitefield did.

In Georgia, Whitefield built an orphanage. He then undertook a series of fund-raising tours throughout the colonies. His most successful trip began in Philadelphia in 1739. Benjamin Franklin, not a very religious person and not easily moved by emotional appeals, was struck by the way Whitefield's visit changed the "manners of our inhabitants." Most people had been "thoughtless or indifferent about religion," Franklin wrote. Now "one could not walk through the town in an evening without hearing psalms sung in different families of every street."

Wherever Whitefield went he filled the churches. If no local clergyman offered his pulpit, he attracted thousands to meetings out of doors. During a three-day visit to Boston, 19,000 people (more than the population of the town) thronged to hear him. According to the Reverend Ezra Stiles, "multitudes were seriously, soberly, and solemnly out of their wits."

His oratorical brilliance aside, Whitefield succeeded in releasing an epidemic of religious emotionalism because his message was so well suited to American ears. By preaching a theology that one critic said was "scaled down to the comprehension of twelve-year olds," he spared his audiences the rigors of hard thought. Though he usually began by chastising his listeners as sinners, "half animals and half devils," he invariably took care to leave them with the hope that eternal salvation could be theirs. While not denying the doctrine of predestination, he preached a God responsive to good intentions. He disregarded sectarian differences and encouraged his listeners to do the same. "God

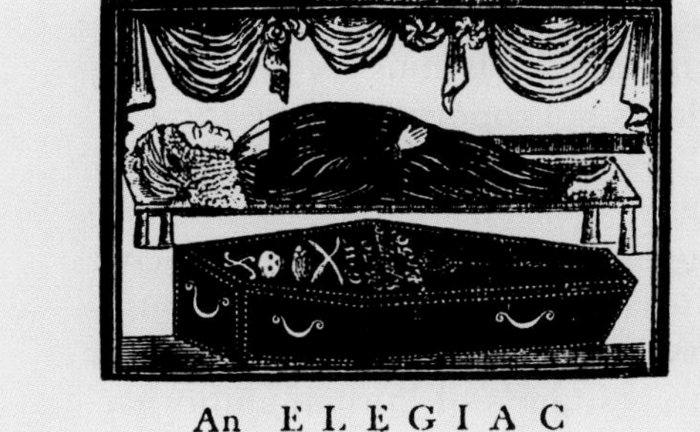

An ELEGIAC

POEM,

On the DEATH of that celebrated Divine, and eminent Servant of JESUS CHRIST, the late Reverend, and pious

GEORGE WHITEFIELD,

Chaplain to the Right Honourable the Counteſs of HUNTINGDON, &c. &c.

Who made his Exit from this tranſitory State, to dwell in the celeſtial Realms of Bliſs, on LORD's-Day, 30th of September, 1770, when he was ſeiz'd with a Fit of the Aſthma, at NEWBURY-PORT, near BOSTON, in NEW-ENGLAND. In which is a Condolatory Addreſs to His truly noble Benefactreſs the worthy and pious Lady HUNTINGDON,---and the Orphan-Children in GEORGIA; who, with many Thouſands, are left, by the Death of this great Man, to lament the Loſs of a Father, Friend, and Benefactor.

By PHILLIS, a Servant Girl of 17 Years of Age, belonging to Mr. J. WHEATLEY, of BOSTON:--And has been but 9 Years in this Country from Africa.

Phyllis Wheatley, one of America's first black poets, was a 17-year-old slave when she wrote this testimony to George Whitefield: "Thou didst, in strains of eloquence refin'd,/Inflame the soul, and captivate the mind."

help us to forget party names and become Christians in deed and truth," he prayed.

Whitefield attracted some supporters among ministers with established congregations, but many more from among younger "itinerants," as preachers who lacked permanent pulpits were called. A visit from him or one of his followers inevitably prompted comparisons between this new, emotionally charged style and the more restrained "plaine style" favored by the typical settled minister. Parishoners who had heard a revivalist preacher listened the next Sunday to the droning of their regular minister with what one of Whitefield's imitators claimed was the fear that their souls were at risk because they had been "living under the ministry of dead men."

Of course not everyone found the Whitefield style edifying. When those who did not spoke up, churches sometimes split into factions. Those who supported the incumbent minister were called, among Congregationalists, "Old Lights," and among Presbyterians, "Old Sides," while those who favored revivalism were known as "New Lights" and "New Sides." When the factions could not agree they separated, usually with the minority going off to build a new church.

These splits often ran along class lines. The richer, better-educated, and more influential members of the church tended to stay with the traditional arrangements. In the hands of some of Whitefield's disciples, revivalism became openly radical. "The rich," one such minister proclaimed, "grow in Wickedness in Proportion to the Increase in their Wealth."

The strains these divisions put upon communities already struggling to maintain a sense of civic unity produced what the historian Richard Bushman called a "psychological earthquake." Persons chafing under the restraints of Puritan authoritarianism and made guilt-ridden by their rebellious feelings now found release. For some the release was more than spiritual; Timothy Cutler, a conservative Anglican clergyman, complained that as a result of the Awakening "our presses are forever teeming with books and our women with bastards." Whether or not Cutler was correct, the Great Awakening helped some people to rid themselves of the idea that disobedience to authority entailed damnation. Anything that God justified, human law could not condemn.

Other institutions besides the churches were affected by the Great Awakening. In 1741 the president of Yale College criticized the theology of itinerant ministers. One of these promptly retorted that a Yale faculty member had no more divine grace than a chair! Other revivalists called upon the New Light churches of Connecticut to withdraw their support from Yale and endow a college of their own. The result was the College of New Jersey (now Princeton), founded in 1746 by New Side Presbyterians. Three other educational by-products of the Great Awakening followed: the College of Rhode Island (Brown), founded by Baptists in 1765; Queen's College (Rutgers), founded by Dutch Reformers in 1766; and Dartmouth, founded by New Light Congregationalists in 1769.

All of these institutions promptly set about to refute the charge, made then and since, that the evangelical temperament was hostile to learning. Jonathan Edwards, the most famous native-born revivalist of the Great Awakening, was living proof that it need not be. Edwards, though a deeply pious person, was passionately devoted to intellectual pursuits. He once admitted that he might have been temperamentally better suited to the scholar's study than to the pulpit. But in 1725, four years after graduating from Yale, he was offered the position of assistant at his grandfather Solomon Stoddard's church in Northampton, Massachusetts. He accepted, and when Stoddard died two years later, Edwards became pastor.

Solomon Stoddard had been no ordinary clergyman. During his six decades in Northampton, he so dominated the ministers of the Connecticut Valley that some referred to him as "pope." His prominence came in part from the "open enrollment" admission policy he adopted for his own church. Evidence of saving grace was neither required nor expected of members: mere good behavior sufficed. As a result, the grandson inherited a congregation whose members were possessed of an "inordinate engagedness after this world." How ready they were to meet their Maker in the next was another question.

Edwards set out to change this, but he began cautiously. His first revival efforts were directed at the young people of Northampton. By 1734 he could report that he had succeeded "by degrees" in getting them "to leave off their frolicking." When several town rowdies took up the study of the Bible and sought admission in the church, he was encouraged. When a 5-year-old girl begged her mother to take her to church so she could "hear Mr. Edwards preach," he knew he was on the right track.

For all his learning and intellectual brilliance, Edwards did not stick at dramatizing what unconverted listeners had to look forward to. The heat of Hell's consuming fires and the stench of brimstone became palpable at his rendering. That he offered it in a high, piercing voice, his lean frame perfectly still, and his eyes fixed on the bell rope at the back of the church, made it all the more frightening. In his most famous sermon, "Sinners in the Hands of an Angry God," delivered at Enfield, Connecticut, in 1741, he pulled out all the stops, depicting a "dreadfully provoked" God holding the unconverted over the pit of Hell, "much as one holds a spider, or some loathsome insect." Later, on the off chance that his listeners did not recognize themselves among those God held, he declared that "this is the dismal case of every soul in this congregation that has not been born again, however moral and strict, sober and religious, they may otherwise be." A great moaning reverberated through the church. People cried out, "What must I do to be saved?"

Edwards next began to work on older people, calling upon them to repent before it was too late. Unfortunately, some church members disturbed by Edwards's warnings about the state of their souls were unable to recognize any signs of their conversion. For them his sermons caused much anxiety. In the midst of the "extraordinary breaking forth of the work of God," one disconsolate member, Joseph Hawley, slit his throat. Edwards took the suicide calmly. "Satan seems to be in a great rage," he declared. "I hope it is because he knows that he has a short time." But for some of Edwards's most prominent parishioners, Hawley's death roused doubts. They began to miss the easy, Arminian ways of Solomon Stoddard. Attendance at Edwards's church fell off. The influx of new members came to an end.

Rather than soften his message, Edwards persisted in depicting the citizens of Northampton in "the blackest colours." Finally, in 1749 his parishioners voted unanimously to dismiss him. He became a missionary to some Indians in Stockbridge, Massachusetts. In 1759 he was appointed president of Princeton, but he died of smallpox before he could take office.

By the early 1750s, a reaction had set in against religious "enthusiasm" in all its forms. Except in the south, where New Side Presbyterians and Baptists continued their evangelizing efforts, the Great Awakening had run its course. Whitefield's last tour of the colonies in 1754 attracted little notice.

Although it caused divisions, the Great Awakening also fostered religious toleration. If one group claimed the right to worship in its own way, how could it deny to other Protestant churches equal freedom to practice the common faith as they wished? From New Hampshire to Georgia, the Awakening also loosened traditional ties between the churches and civil governments. By its nature, politics tended to divide people; it seemed, therefore, a corrupting influence in religion.

The Great Awakening was the first truly national event in American history. It marks the time when the previously distinct histories of New England, the Middle Colonies, and the South began to intersect. Powerful links were being forged. As early as 1691 there was a rudimentary intercolonial postal system. In 1754, not long after the Awakening, the farsighted Benjamin Franklin advanced his Albany Plan for a colonial union to deal with common problems, such as defense against Indian attacks on the frontier. Thirteen once-isolated colonies, expanding to the north and south as well as westward, were merging.

The Enlightenment in America

The Great Awakening pointed ahead to an America marked by religious pluralism and to the strict separation of church and state. Jonathan Edwards rejected the easy Arminianism of his Stoddard grandfather and embraced the sternest aspects of Calvinism, but by the 1740s many colonists were experimenting with a different, far less forbidding theology, one more in keeping with the ideas of the European Enlightenment.

The Enlightenment had an enormous impact in America. The founders of the colonies were contemporaries of the astronomer Galileo Galilei (1564–1642), the philosopher-mathematician René Descartes (1596–1650), and Sir Isaac Newton (1642–1727), the genius who revealed to the world

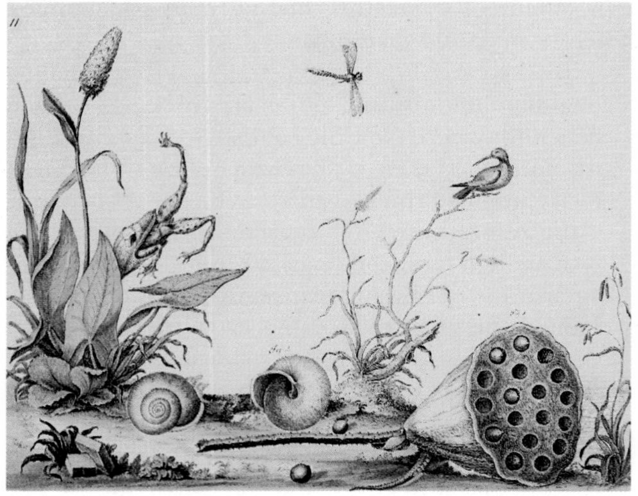

The pioneering work of naturalist John Bartram was carried on after his death by his son William. These drawings by William show a study of snails and Florida alligators.

the workings of gravity and other laws of motion. American society developed amid the excitement generated by these great discoverers, who provided both a new understanding of the natural world and a new mode of thought. Their discoveries implied that instead of responding to the caprice of an omnipotent and unpredictable Deity, the universe was based on impersonal, scientific laws that governed the behavior of all matter, animate and inanimate. Earth and the heavens, human beings and the lower animals—all seemed parts of an immense, intricate machine. God had set it all in motion and remained the master technician (the divine watchmaker) overseeing it, but had fewer and fewer occasions to interfere with its immutable operation. When Edwards published his *Thoughts Concerning the Present Revival of Religion in New England* in 1742, the Boston minister Charles Chauncy criticized him for stressing the supernatural aspects of religion and neglecting the role of reason.

To Americans like Chauncy, human reasoning powers and direct observation of natural phenomena, rather than God's revelations, provided the key to knowledge; it followed that knowledge of the laws of nature, by enabling people to understand the workings of the universe, would enable them not only to control their temporal destinies, but also to have at least a voice in their eternal destinies.

Most creative thinkers of the European Enlightenment realized that human beings were not entirely rational and that a complete understanding of the physical world was beyond their grasp. They did, however, believe that human beings were becoming more rational and would be able, by using their rational powers, to discover the laws governing the physical world. Their faith in these ideas produced the so-called Age of Reason. And while their confidence in human rationality seems to us naive and the "laws" they formulated no longer appear so mechanically perfect (the universe is far less orderly than they imagined), they added immensely to knowledge.

Many churchgoing colonists, especially better-educated ones, accepted the assumptions of the Age of Reason wholeheartedly. Some, like Chauncy, repudiated the doctrine of original sin and asserted the benevolence of God. Others came to doubt the divinity of Christ and eventually declared themselves Unitarians. Still others, among them Benjamin Franklin, embraced Deism, a faith that revered God for the marvels of His universe rather than for His power over humankind.

"Here is my creed," Franklin wrote:

> I believe in one God, Creator of the Universe. That he governs it by his providence. That he ought to be worshipped. That the most acceptable service we render to him is doing good to his other Children. That the soul of Man is immortal, and will be treated with Justice in another Life respecting its Conduct in this.

The impact of Enlightenment ideas went far beyond religion. The writings of John Locke and other political theorists found a receptive audience. So did the work of the Scottish philosophers Francis Hutcheson and David Hume and the French *philosophes* Montesquieu and Voltaire. Ideas generated in Europe often reached America with startling speed. *Cato's Letters,* a series of essays attacking political and religious corruption, written in the 1720s by the Englishmen John Trenchard and Thomas Gordon, appeared only months later in America, where they were quoted in newspapers from Massachusetts to Georgia. No colonial political controversy really heated up in America until all involved had published pamphlets citing half a dozen European authorities. Radical ideas that in Europe were discussed only by an intellectual elite became almost commonplace in the colonies.

As the topics of learned discourse expanded, ministers lost their monopoly on intellectual life. By the 1750s, only a minority of Harvard and Yale graduates were becoming ministers. The College of Philadelphia (later the University of Pennsylvania), founded in 1751, and King's College (later Columbia), founded in New York in 1754, added two institutions to the growing ranks of American colleges which were never primarily training grounds for clergymen.

Lawyers, who first appeared in any number in colonial towns in the 1740s, swiftly asserted their intellectual authority in public affairs. Physicians and the handful of professors of natural history declared themselves better able to make sense of the new scientific discoveries than clergymen. Yet because fields of knowledge were far less specialized than in modern times, self-educated amateurs could also make useful contributions.

The most famous instances of popular participation occurred in Philadelphia. It was there, in 1727, that Benjamin Franklin founded the Junto, a club to which young artisans gathered on Friday evenings to discuss "any point of morals, politics, or natural philosophy." In 1743, Franklin established an expanded version of the Junto, the American Philosophical Society, which he hoped would "cultivate the finer arts and improve the common stock of knowledge."

Colonial America produced no Galileo or Newton, but Americans contributed significantly to the collection of scientific knowledge. The unexplored continent provided a laboratory for the study of natural phenomena. The Philadelphia Quaker, John Bartram, a "down right plain Country Man," ranged from Florida to the Great Lakes during the middle years of the 18th century, gathering and classifying hundreds of plants. Bartram also studied Indians closely, speculating about their origins and collecting information about their culture. Cadwallader Colden, lieutenant governor of New York from 1761 to 1776, made important contributions to the systematic study of American flora and fauna and carried on an extensive correspondence with the Swedish botanist Linnaeus and other European scientists. The South Carolina physician Alexander Garden added to the modest reputation Americans had acquired in Europe as careful collectors of natural history specimens.

Astronomy was another science to which 18th-century Americans were able to contribute, by virtue of their distance from Europe. In 1761 Professor John Winthrop of Harvard, a descendant of the first governor of the Massachusetts Bay Colony, led a scientific expedition to Newfoundland, the only place in British North America from which the transit of the planet Venus could be observed. Winthrop's observations enabled him to calculate the distance of the sun from the earth with an error of only 2 percent. Another transit of Venus passed directly over several colonies in 1769. It attracted the attention of amateur astronomers from Massa-

The first orrery (model of the solar system) constructed in America was built by David Rittenhouse in 1767 as a teaching tool. This is a modern restoration.

chusetts to Maryland. The most accurate observations were made by David Rittenhouse of Philadelphia. Thomas Jefferson later described Rittenhouse somewhat hyperbolically as "second to no astronomer living." Rittenhouse's other claim to scientific eminence was his construction of the first orrery (a mechanical model of the solar system) in America.

Jefferson was on firmer ground when he said of Benjamin Franklin that "no one of the present age has made more important discoveries." Franklin had retired from business in his early 40s to concentrate on his many other interests. One of his biographers has called him a "harmonious human multitude." His studies of electricity, which he capped in 1752 with his famous kite experiment, established him as a scientist of international stature. He also invented the lightning rod, the iron Franklin stove (a far more efficient way to heat a room than an open fireplace), bifocal spectacles, and several other ingenious devices. In addition he served 14 years (1751–1764) in the Pennsylvania assembly and for part of that time was agent for the colony in London. He founded a circulating library and helped to get the first hospital in Philadelphia built, and he was an organizer of a volunteer fire company. In his spare time he taught himself Latin, French, Spanish, and Italian.

Franklin wrote so much about the virtues of hard work and thrift that some historians have described him as stuffy and straitlaced. Nothing could be further from the truth. He recognized the social value of conventional behavior, but he was no slave to convention. He fathered two illegitimate children, wrote satirical essays on such subjects as the advantage of having affairs with older and plain-looking women (who were, he claimed, more likely to appreciate the attention). And he had the perfect temperament, being open-minded and imaginative as well as shrewd and judicious—an unbeatable combination.

Franklin's international fame notwithstanding, the theoretical contributions of American scientists were modest. Most were practical rather than speculative types, tinkerers rather than constructors of grand designs. As one observer noted, they were easily diverted "by Business or Inclination from profound Study, and prying into the Depth of Things." Thomas Jefferson, for example, made no theoretical discovery of importance, but his range was almost without limit: linguist, bibliophile, political scientist, architect, inventor, scientific farmer and—above all—apostle of reason. "Fix reason firmly in her seat," he wrote, "and call to her tribunal every fact, every opinion."

Involvement at even the most marginal level in the intellectual affairs of Europe gave influential New Englanders, Middle Colonists, and southerners a chance to get to know one another. Although their role in what Jefferson called "the Republic of Letters" was still minor, by mid-century their influence on the intellectual climate of the colonies was growing. That climate was one of eager curiosity, flexibility of outlook, and confidence.

SUPPLEMENTARY READING

Titles marked with an asterisk have been published in paperback.

Among general interpretations of colonial society, Daniel J. Boorstin's **The Americans: The Colonial Experience*** (1958), and Howard Munford Jones's **O Strange New World*** (1964), remain stimulating. David Hawke, **The Colonial Experience** (1966), provides a good survey of colonial history generally, while Richard Hofstadter, **America at 1750*** (1971), offers a compelling social portarit of the colonies at mid-century. Stephen Saunders Webb, **1676—The End of American Independence** (1984), is similarly pointed in time and comprehensive in regional coverage.

John A. Henretta, **The Evolution of American Society*** (1973), Robert V. Wells, **The Population of the British Colonies in America before 1776** (1975), and Gary B. Nash, **The Urban Crucible*** (1979), present the results of the recent demographic research on the period. Among older interpretations, those of Frederick Jackson Turner on the influence of the frontier on American history, collected in R. A. Billington, ed., **Frontier and Section*** (1961), and David Potter's **People of Plenty*** (1954), which stresses economic abundance as a shaping influence on American development, remain illuminating.

On economic conditions, E. J. Perkins, **The Economy of Colonial America** (1980), is an up-to-date survey, while Stuart Bruchey, **The Roots of American Economic**

Growth (1965), explores the dynamics of American economic development. On the institution of slavery generally, see Herbert Klein, **The Middle Passage** (1978), David B. Davis, **The Problem of Slavery in Western Culture** (1966), and Winthrop D. Jordan, **White Over Black: American Attitudes Toward the Negro*** (1968). A. E. Smith, **Colonists in Bondage** (1947), is a good study of indentured servitude, while Robert B. Morris, **Government and Labor in Early America** (1946), remains the standard account.

On life in the colonial South, one might begin with W. F. Craven, **The Southern Colonies in the Seventeenth Century** (1949), Carl Bridenbaugh, **Myths and Realities: Societies of the Colonial South** (1952), and Verner M. Crane, **The Southern Frontier, 1670–1732** (1928). More recent interpretations include Thad W. Tate and David Ammerman (eds.), **The Chesapeake in the Seventeenth Century** (1979), Darrett B. Rutman and Anita H. Rutman, **A Place in Time: Middlesex County, Virginia, 1650–1750** (1984), Peter H. Wood, **Black Majority: Negroes in Colonial South Carolina** (1974), and T. H. Breen and Stephen Innes, **"Myne Owne Ground": Race and Freedom on Virginia's Eastern Shore*** (1980).

The family and community life of colonial New England are considered in Edmund S. Morgan, **The Puritan Family*** (1966 ed.), John Demos, **A Little Commonwealth: Family Life in Plymouth County*** (1970), Richard L. Bushman, **From Puritan to Yankee: Character and Social Order in Connecticut*** (1967), Kenneth A. Lockridge, **A New England Town: The First Hundred Years*** (1970), and Philip Greven, **Four Generations: Population, Land and Family in Colonial Andover*** (1970). The places of women and children are effectively presented in Laurel Thatcher Ulrich, **Good Wives: Image and Reality in the Lives of Women in Northern New England** (1982), and Philip Greven, **The Protestant Temperament: Patterns of Child-Rearing, Religious Experience, and the Self in Early America** (1980).

For the evolution of the New England landscape and ideas about it, see William Cronon, **Changes in the Land: Indians, Colonists, and the Ecology of New England*** (1983). On the region's economic development, Darrett B. Rutman, **Winthrop's Boston*** (1965), and Bernard Bailyn, **The New England Merchants in the 17th Century*** (1955), are useful.

The works of Perry Miller remain the starting point for any serious study of the cultural life of colonial New England. Among them, **Errand into the Wilderness*** (1956), provides a good introduction. More recent studies, most of which seek to modify Miller's judgments, include Edmund S. Morgan, **Visible Saints: The History of a Puritan Idea*** (1963), and Robert G. Pope, **The Half-Way Covenant: Church Membership in Puritan New England** (1969). On Anne Hutchinson, see David D. Hall (ed.), **The Antinomian Controversy** (1968).

On the interplay of religion and social thought, see Stephen Foster, **Their Solitary Way: The Puritan Social Ethic in the First Century of Settlement in New England** (1971), and T. H. Breen, **The Character of the Good Ruler: Puritan Political Ideas in New England** (1970). Neither displaces, however, Edmund S. Morgan's biography of John Winthrop, **The Puritan Dilemma*** (1958), which remains the best introduction to Puritan society. See also Michael Zuckerman, **Peaceable Kingdoms: New England Towns in the 18th Century*** (1970). The disturbances in Salem Village are discussed in great detail in Paul Boyer and Stephen Nissenbaum, **Salem Possessed: The Social Origins of Witchcraft*** (1974), while the subject is considered generally in John Demos, **Entertaining Satan: Witchcraft and the Culture of Early New England*** (1982).

Educational and intellectual developments are treated in Samuel Eliot Morison, **The Intellectual Life of Colonial New England*** (1956), Bernard Bailyn, **Education in the Forming of American Society*** (1960), and in rich detail in Lawrence A. Cremin, **American Education: The Colonial Experience*** (1970). Robert Middlekauff's **The Mathers: Three Generations of Puritan Intellectuals*** (1971) provides an effective biography.

On the Middle Colonies see Robert C. Ritchie, **The Duke's Province** (1977), Patricia Bonomi, **A Factious People: Politics and Society in Colonial New York** (1971), Frederick B. Tolles, **Meeting House and Counting House: The Quaker Merchants of Colonial Philadelphia** (1948), and Gary B. Nash, **Quakers and Politics** (1968). Stephanie G. Wolf, **Urban Village: Population, Community, and Family Structure in Germantown, Pennsylvania** (1977), and James Lemon, **The Best Poor Man's Country** (1972), provide detailed social analyses, while E. Digby Baltzell, **Puritan Boston and Quaker Philadelphia** (1979), focuses on the differences between the respective urban elites. The best brief biographical account of the region's leading citizen is Verner W. Crane, **Benjamin Franklin and a Rising People*** (1954).

The sources of the Great Awakening are discussed in Patricia Tracey, **Jonathan Edwards, Pastor*** (1980), and in Rhys Isaac, **The Transformation of Virginia*** (1982); its consequences are discussed in Alan Heimert, **Religion and the American Mind** (1966), J. William T. Youngs, Jr., **God's Messengers: Religious Leadership in Colonial New England** (1976), and Edmund S. Morgan, **The Gentle Puritan: A Life of Ezra Stiles** (1962).

Henry F. May, **The Enlightenment in America*** (1976), is the best recent account of later colonial intellectual developments. Brook Hindle, **The Pursuit of Science in Revolutionary America*** (1956), remains authoritative. On Jefferson and his circle, see Daniel Boorstin, **The Lost World of Thomas Jefferson*** (1948).

Patterns of Development

Climate, wealth, family size, and many other influences shaped the patterns of life that developed in the colonies. The three sections—north, middle, south—were distinct entities throughout the period, and this was true despite the fact that in each region the people came from diverse social and economic backgrounds and encountered widely different experiences after they arrived.

At the same time, the colonists became increasingly American (as distinct from European or African) as the generations passed. By the middle of the 18th century they were beginning to notice the uniqueness of some aspects of their civilization, and this was certainly a stage in their transition from dependence on Great Britain (psychological as well as material) to independence.

But if the sectional differences were ultimately less significant than the trends common to all the colonies, they were nonetheless important. In all three sections farming was the principal occupation, but in New England and the Middle Colonies the growing towns were exerting political and cultural influence out of proportion to their population. In most families, fathers ruled the roost; children, while cherished, were expected to obey orders and work hard. However, growing up on a New England farm was a far different experience from growing up on a southern plantation. Foreigners were always struck by the general prosperity of the people compared to conditions in Europe, but the gap between the circumstances of a well-to-do eastern merchant and a frontier farmer was large, and widening. Religion played an important role in people's lives everywhere, but the difference, architectural and doctrinal, between a Massachusetts Puritan congregation and a Virginia Anglican one was great indeed.

This panorama of the Van Bergen farm in New York's Catskill Mountains was painted by an unknown artist about 1735. The picture graced the farm's living room mantel. It gives a clear sense of the family's self-sufficiency, with their house, outbuildings, servants, and domestic animals, and of their general prosperity.

Before Europeans like the Van Bergens settled on the land, the Indians had their own types of dwellings, all attuned to the climate of the area in which they lived. John White's watercolor shows the houses of Pomeiock, in the Virginia tidewater region; they are made of poles covered with bark and woven mats. Shade and fresh air could be controlled by adjusting these coverings.

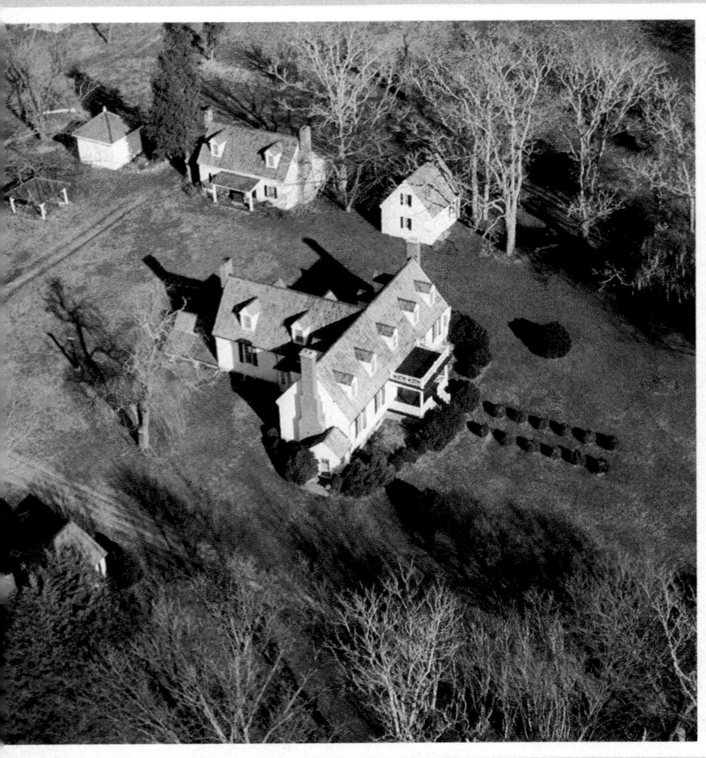

The Virginia plantation "Greenway," later owned by President John Tyler, is typical of southern plantations, with its large but unostentatious main house and its numerous outbuildings. Far different were the slave cabins of a South Carolina plantation, which provided only the minimum shelter needed in a warm climate.

New England houses—this parsonage in Newington, New Hampshire, is typical—tended to be built as a single "saltbox" in order to conserve heat during the long, hard winters. As families grew and prospered, rooms were added, hugging the original structure.

Then, as now, couples had to obtain a marriage certificate from the civil authorities before having a religious ceremony. This preprinted version issued in the name of Richard Penn (William Penn's son) is addressed to any Protestant minister, and is good for the province of Pennsylvania and the counties of Delaware.

BY THE HONORABLE

RICHARD PENN, Esq;

Lieutenant Governor and Commander in Chief of the Province of PENNSYLVANIA, *and Counties of* NEW-CASTLE, KENT, *and* SUSSEX, *on* DELAWARE.

To any PROTESTANT MINISTER.

Rich.d Penn

WHEREAS Application hath been made unto me by

to be joined together in HOLY MATRIMONY, and there appearing no lawful Let or Impediment, by Reaſon of *Pre-Contract, Conſanguinity, Affinity*, or any juſt Cauſe whatſoever, to hinder the ſaid Marriage; Theſe are therefore to licence and authoriſe you to join the ſaid

in the HOLY BANDS OF MATRIMONY, and them to pronounce MAN and WIFE.

GIVEN *under my Hand and Seal at Arms, at* Philadelphia, *the* *Day of* *in the Year of our LORD One Thouſand Seven Hundred and Seventy*

A charming primitive painting of a toddler napping in a red high chair gives an idyllic picture of colonial childhood.

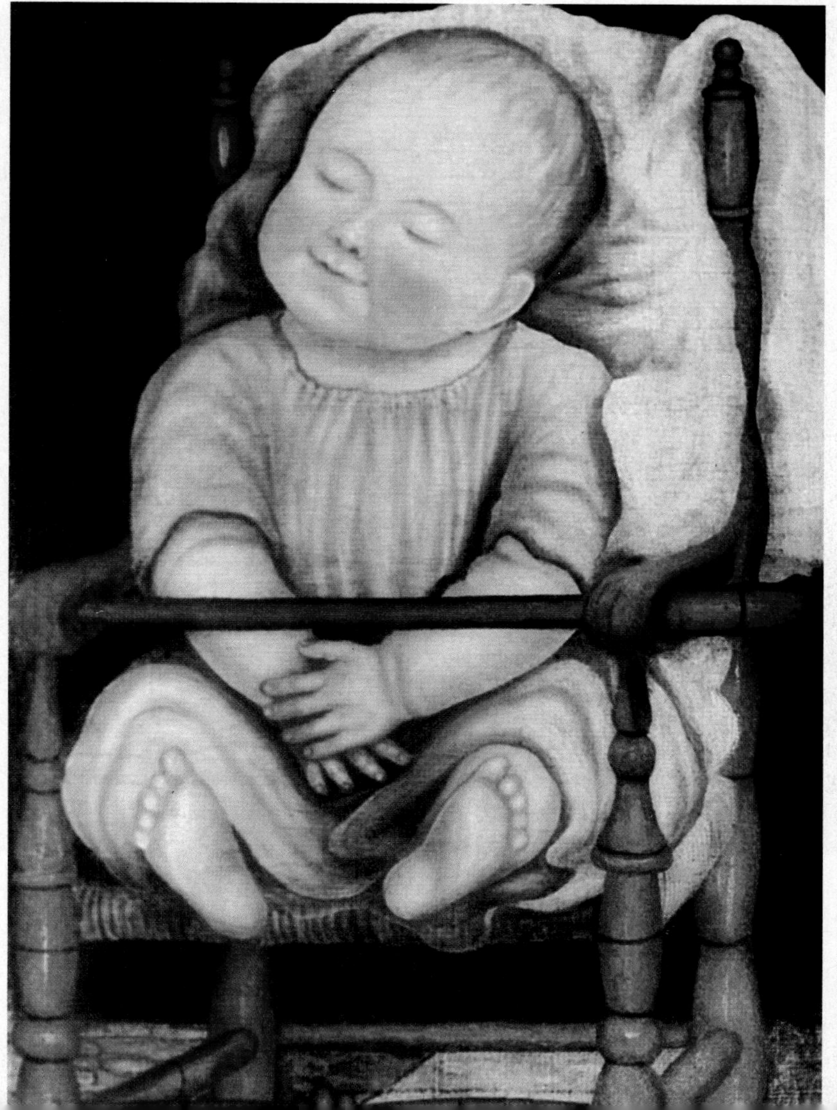

Two contrasting views of prosperous families of the late 1700s, one from New England and one from the South.

The handsome painting of Alexander Spotswood Payne and his younger brother John Robert Dandridge Payne, with their black nurse and their dog, provides a glimpse of youth in an upper-class Virginia family.

The group portrait of the New England Cheneys shows what is apparently three generations of the family. Genealogies indicate that Dr. Samuel Cheney's first wife had seven children. Since his second wife (in the white cap) had none, the youngest children are presumably her stepgrandchildren.

Variety and intensity were the hallmarks of colonial religion. The three buildings shown here illustrate the variety. In the 18th century, Conrad Beissel, a German mystic, founded the Ephrata Society, a communal venture in which the members practiced celibacy, in Pennsylvania. The large wooden building contains the Sisters' House (Saron) and the meeting house (Saal). The community existed into the 20th century.

A sharp contrast to the mysticism of Ephrata is represented by the cool, classical Georgian features of the carefully restored Bruton Parish Church in colonial Williamsburg. In Virginia, the Anglican church was the official established religion.

Another aspect of colonial religion is reflected by the unornamented interior of the Rocky Hill Meeting House in Amesburg, Massachusetts, dating from the late 1700s. The church was used for town meetings as well as worship until the 1870s.

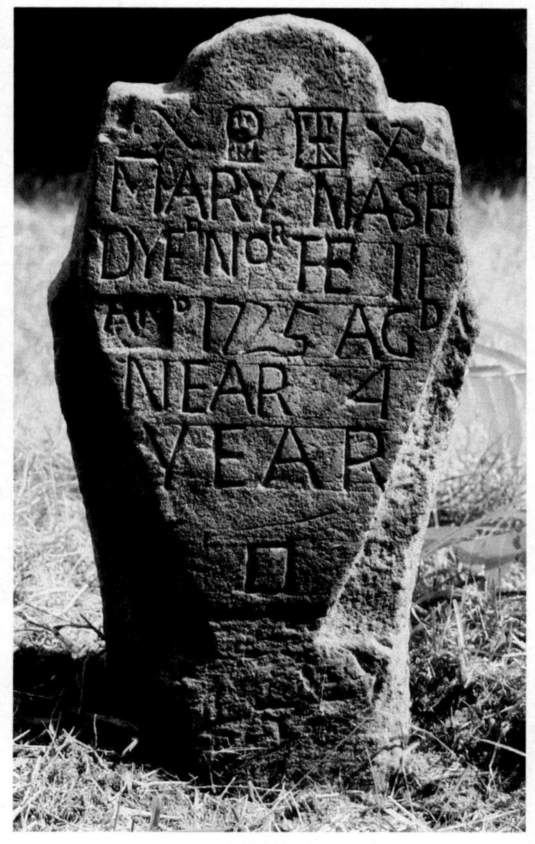

Death was never far away in colonial America. The headstone for 3-year-old Mary Nash (right), who died in western Massachusetts in 1725, was roughly carved in local stone, all that was available in a frontier region. In contrast, William Dickson's elegant monument (above), dating from 1692, shows the work of a skilled Boston-area stonecutter.

3

America in the British Empire

North America was once indeed a great strength to this nation. . . . We found her a sound, an active, a vigorous member of the empire. I hope, by wise management, she will again be so. But one of our capital present misfortunes is her discontent and disobedience. EDMUND BURKE, *1769*

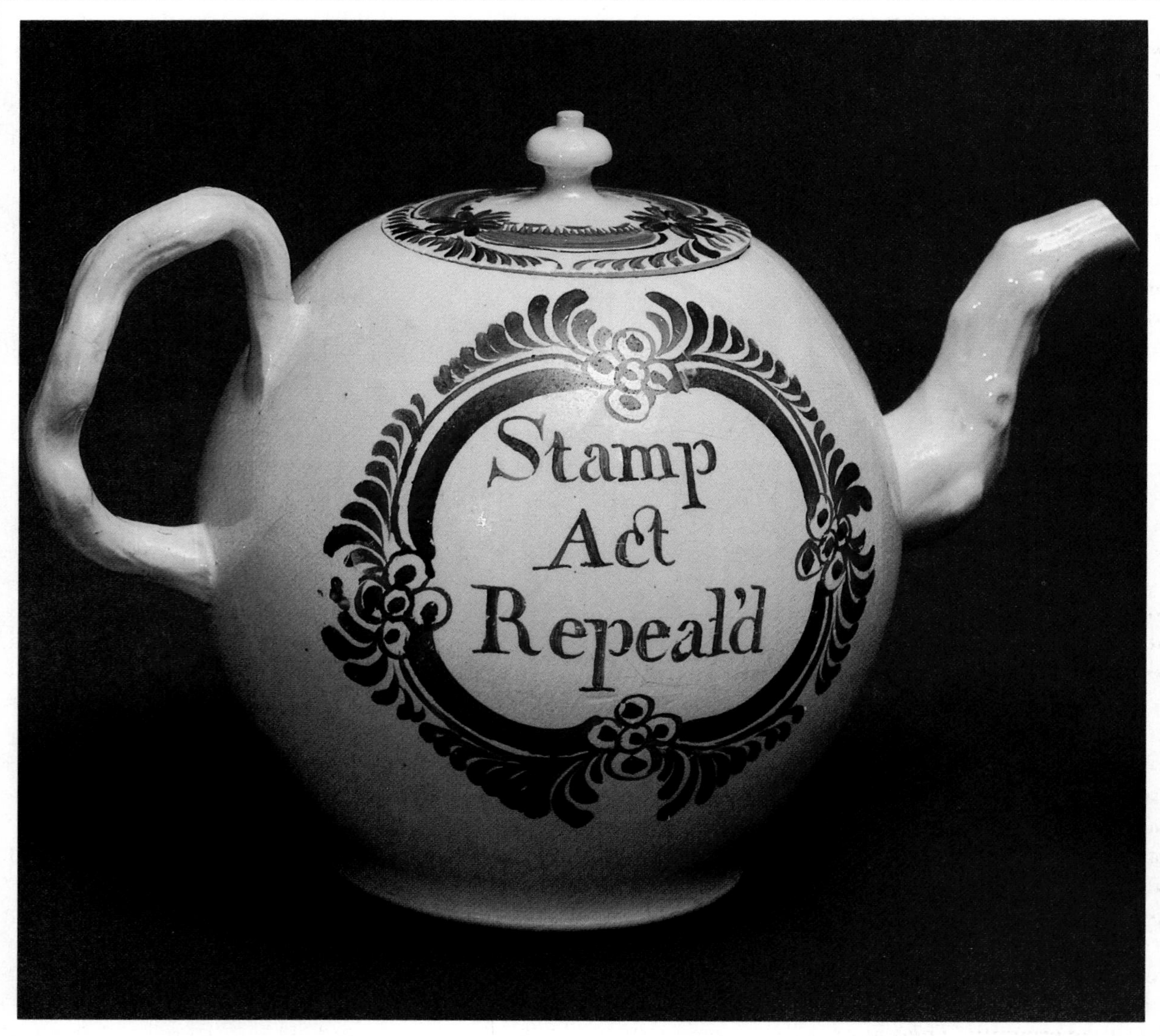

Since the colonies were founded piecemeal by persons with varying motives and backgrounds, common traditions and loyalties developed slowly. For the same reason, the British government was slow to think of its American possessions as a unit or to deal with them in any centralized way. From the time in 1497 when Henry VII authorized John Cabot and his sons to search out new lands, the "rule, title, and jurisdiction" over these lands had resided in the Crown. They were the *king's* possessions. As a good sovereign he was obligated to use them in a manner consonant with the national interest, but it was left to him and his advisers to decide what that interest was. No authority challenged his right to dispose of one section of his American domain to this group of merchants under such-and-such terms and another to that personal friend or creditor under a different arrangement. The specific form of each colony's government and the degree of local independence permitted it depended on how this was done.

The British Colonial System

There was a pattern basic to all colonial governments and a general framework of imperial control for all the king's overseas plantations. English political and legal institutions (common law, private property, more or less representative legislative assemblies, systems of local administration) took hold everywhere in British America. While the colonists and the home authorities often had different motives in establishing new settlements, they were seldom conflicting motives. Colonists might leave home with grievances, bent on securing certain rights denied them in England, but prosperity, political and economic expansion, and the reproduction of Old World civilization were aims common to ruler and ruled, to Englishman and American.

In the earliest days of any settlement, the need to rely upon home authorities was so obvious that few besides Roger Williams questioned England's political sovereignty. Thereafter, as the fledglings grew strong enough to think of using their own wings, distance and British political inefficiency combined to allow them a great deal of freedom. Although royal representatives in America tried to direct policy, the Crown generally yielded the initiative in local matters to the colonies while reserving the right to veto actions it deemed to be against the national interest. External affairs were controlled entirely in London.

Each colony had a governor. By the 18th century he was an appointed official, except in Rhode Island and Connecticut. Governors were chosen by the king in the case of the royal colonies and by the proprietors of Maryland, Delaware, and Pennsylvania. The governors' powers were much like those of the king in Great Britain. They executed the local laws, appointed many minor officials, summoned and dismissed the colonial assemblies, and proposed legislation to them. They possessed the right to veto colonial laws, but in most colonies, again like the king, they were financially dependent on their "subjects."

Each colony also had a legislature. Except in Pennsylvania, these assemblies consisted of two houses. The lower house, chosen by qualified voters, had general legislative powers, including control of the purse. In all the royal colonies except Massachusetts, members of the upper house, or council, were appointed by the king. (In Massachusetts the council members were elected by the General Court.) The councils served primarily as advisors to the governors, but they also had some judicial and legislative powers. Judges were appointed by the king and served at his pleasure. Yet both councillors and judges were normally selected from among the leaders of the local communities; London had neither the time nor the will to investigate their political beliefs. The system, therefore, tended to strengthen the influence of the entrenched colonials.

Although the power of the lower houses of the legislatures was severely restricted in theory, the assemblies tended to dominate the government in nearly every colony. Financial power—including the right to set the governor's salary—gave them some importance, and the fact that the assemblies usually had the backing of public opinion was significant. Most colonial legislators were practical men. Knowing their own interests, they pursued them steadily, without much regard for political theories or the desires of the royal authorities. In the words of one Virginia governor, they were "Expedient Mongers in the highest Degree." They extended their influence by slow accretion. Governors came and went, but the lawmakers remained, accumulating experience, building upon precedent, widening decade by decade their control over colonial affairs.

The official representatives of the Crown, whatever their powers, whatever their intentions, were prisoners of their surroundings. A royal governor lived thousands of miles from London, alone in a *colonial* world. To defend the British position at every turn when one had to make one's life amid a vigorous and strong-willed people, who usually had solid practical arguments to buttress their side if it clashed with the Crown's, was no easy task. Governors had no security of tenure; they served at the whim of the government in London. In their dealings with the assemblies they were often bound by rigid and impractical royal instructions that restricted their ability to maneuver. They had few jobs and favors to offer in their efforts to influence the legislators. Judges might interpret the law according to English precedents, but in local matters colonial juries had the final say. And juries were seldom awed by precedents that clashed with their own conceptions of justice.

Colonial governors exercised powers much like the King's in Great Britain's constitutional monarchy. John Winthrop, first governor of Massachusetts, was elected before sailing from England and reelected eleven times.

Within the British government the king's Privy Council had the responsibility for formulating colonial policy. It did so on an ad hoc basis, treating each situation as it arose and seldom generalizing. Everything was decentralized: the Treasury had charge of financial matters, the army of military affairs, and so on. The Privy Council could and did disallow (annul) specific colonial laws, but it did not proclaim constitutional principles to which all colonial legislatures must conform. It acted as a court of last appeal in colonial disputes and handled each case individually. One day the council might issue a set of instructions to the governor of Virginia, the next a different set to the governor of South Carolina. No one office directed colonial affairs, no one person or committee thought broadly about the administration of the overseas empire. Parliamentary legislation applied to the colonies, yet there was little distinctively *American* legislation. For example, Parliament passed laws regulating the trade of the entire British empire and until late in the colonial period directed its attention specifically to North American conditions only on rare occasions.

At times the British authorities, uneasy about their lack of control over the colonies, attempted to create a more effective system. Whenever possible the original, broadly worded charters were revoked. To transform proprietary and corporate colonies into royal colonies (whose chief officials were appointed by the king) seems to have been London's official policy by the late 17th century. The Privy Council appointed a number of subcommittees to advise it on colonial affairs at this time. The most important was the Lords of Trade. In the 1680s when James II brought New York, New Jersey, and all of New England under one administration, the Dominion of New England, he apparently planned to unify the southern colonies in a similar manner. James's actions were deeply resented by the colonists, and after the Glorious Revolution and the collapse of the Dominion of New England, no further important efforts at unification were attempted. Instead, the tendency was in the other direction. Delaware partially separated from Pennsylvania in 1704, and the two Carolinas formally split in 1712.

In 1696 a new Board of Trade took over the

functions of the Lords of Trade and expanded them considerably. It nominated colonial governors and other high officials. It reviewed all the laws passed by the colonial legislatures, recommending the disallowance of those that seemed to conflict with imperial policy. The efficiency, assiduousness, and wisdom of the Board of Trade fluctuated over the years, but the Privy Council and the Crown nearly always accepted its recommendations.

Colonists naturally disliked having their laws disallowed, and London exercised this power with considerable restraint; only about 5 percent of the laws reviewed were rejected. Furthermore, the board served as an important intermediary for colonists seeking to influence king and Parliament. All the colonies in the 18th century maintained agents in London to present the colonial point of view before board members. The most famous colonial agent was Benjamin Franklin, who represented Pennsylvania, Georgia, New Jersey, and Massachusetts at various times during his long career.

The British never developed an effective, centralized government for the American colonies. By and large, their American "subjects" ran their own affairs. This fact more than any other explains our present federal system and the wide areas in which the state governments are sovereign and independent. Local and colonywide government in America evolved from English models. Had a rational central authority been superimposed in the early days, the colonies would almost certainly have accepted it. Then, even in revolt, they would probably have followed a different path.

Mercantilism

The Board of Trade, as its name implies, was concerned with commerce as well as colonial administration. According to prevailing European opinion, colonies were important chiefly for economic reasons. The 17th century being a period of hard times and considerable unemployment, some authorities saw the colonies as excellent dumping grounds for surplus people. If only two idlers in each parish were shipped overseas, one clergyman calculated in 1624, England would be rid of 16,000 undesirables. But most 17th-century economic thinkers envisaged colonies more as potential sources of raw materials. To obtain these, they developed a number of loosely related policies that later economists called mercantilism. The most important raw materials in the eyes of mercantilists were gold and silver, since these metals, being universally valued and relatively rare, could be exchanged at any time for anything the owner desired, or, being durable and compact, stored indefinitely for future use. For these reasons how much gold and silver ("treasure" according to mercantilists) a nation possessed was considered the best barometer of its prosperity and power.

Since gold and silver could not be mined in significant amounts in western Europe, every early colonist dreamed of finding "El Dorado." The Spanish were the winners in this search; from the mines of Mexico and South America a treasure in gold and silver poured into the Iberian Peninsula. Failing to control the precious metals at the source, the other powers tried to obtain them by guile and warfare (witness the exploits of Francis Drake).

In the mid-17th century another method, less hazardous and in the long run far more profitable, called itself to the attention of the statesmen of western Europe. If a country could make itself as nearly self-sufficient as possible and at the same time keep all its citizens busy producing items marketable in other lands, it could sell more abroad than it imported. This state of affairs was known as "having a favorable balance of trade." The term is misleading; in reality, trade, which means exchange, always balances unless one party simply gives its goods away (a practice not recommended by mercantilists). A country with a favorable balance in effect made up the difference by "importing" money in the form of gold and silver. Nevertheless, mercantilism came to mean concentrating on producing for export and limiting imports of ordinary goods and services in every way possible. Colonies that did not have deposits of precious metals were well worth having if they supplied raw materials that would otherwise have to be purchased from foreign sources or if their people bought substantial amounts of the manufactured goods produced in the mother country.

Of the English colonies in the New World, those in tropical and subtropical climes were valued for their raw materials. The more northerly ones were important as markets, but because they were small in the 17th century, in English eyes they took second place. In 1680 the sugar imported from the single West Indian island of Barbados was worth more than the goods sent to England by all the mainland colonies.

If the possession of gold and silver signified wealth, trade was the route that led to riches, and merchants were the captains who would pilot the ship of state to prosperity. "Trade is the Wealth of the World," Daniel Defoe wrote in 1728. "Trade makes the difference as to Rich and Poor, between one Nation and another; Trade nourishes Industry . . . and Trade raises new Species of Wealth, which Nature knew nothing of. . . ." One must, of course, have something to sell, so internal production must be stimulated. Parliament encouraged the British people to concentrate on manufacturing by placing tariffs on foreign-manufactured goods and subsidizing British-made textiles, iron, and other products.

The Navigation Acts

The nurture of commerce was fundamental. Toward this end Parliament enacted the Navigation Acts. These laws, put into effect over a period of half a century and more, were designed to bring money into the Royal Treasury, to develop the imperial merchant fleet, to channel the flow of colonial raw materials into England, and to keep foreign goods and vessels out of colonial ports (since the employment of foreign ships in the carrying trade was as much an import as the consumption of foreign wheat or wool).

The system originated in the 1650s during the Cromwell period in response to the stiff commercial competition offered by the Dutch. Having won their independence from Spain, the Dutch had constructed a magnificent merchant fleet of more than 10,000 ships. Their sailors roamed the world's oceans in search of business. The Dutch dominated the coastal trade of France, threatened to do the same with that of England, and practically monopolized the whale fisheries of the North Atlantic. They established themselves in South America, in India, and in the East and West Indies. Before 1650 a large share of the produce of the English colonies in America reached Europe in Dutch vessels; the first slaves in Virginia, it will be recalled, arrived on a Dutch ship and were doubtless paid for in tobacco that was later burned in the clay pipes of the burghers of Amsterdam and Rotterdam.

Dismayed by this trend, Parliament in 1650 and 1651 barred foreign ships from the English colonies (except when specially licensed) and prohibited the importation into England of goods that were not carried in English ships or those of the country where the goods had been originally produced. All foreign vessels were excluded from the English coastal trade. Although phrased in general terms, this legislation struck primarily at the Dutch, and in 1652 the English provoked the first of three wars with the Dutch Republic that were only extensions of the policy laid down in the first Navigation Acts.

The laws of 1650–1651 were not rigidly enforced because England did not have enough ships to supply its overseas possessions. The colonies protested vigorously and then ignored the regulations. Nevertheless, the English persisted. New laws were passed after the accession of Charles II in 1660, and as the merchant marine expanded (tonnage doubled between 1660 and 1688) and the Royal Navy gradually reduced Dutch power in the New World, enforcement became fairly effective.

The Navigation Act of 1660 reserved the entire trade of the colonies to English ships and required that the captain and three-quarters of his crew be English. (Colonists, of course, were English, and their ships were treated on the same terms as those sailing out of London or Liverpool.) The act also provided that certain colonial "enumerated articles"—sugar, tobacco, cotton, ginger, and dyes like indigo and fustic—could not be "shipped, carried, conveyed or transported" outside the empire. Three years later Parliament required that with trifling exceptions all European products destined for the colonies be brought to England before being shipped across the Atlantic. Since trade between England and the colonies was reserved to English vessels, this meant that the goods would have to be unloaded and reloaded in England. Legislation in 1673 and 1696 was concerned with enforcing these laws: it dealt with the posting of bonds, the registration of vessels, and the appointment of customs officials. Early in the 18th century the list of enumerated articles was expanded to include rice, molasses, naval stores, furs, and copper.

The English looked upon the empire broadly; they envisioned the colonies as part of an economic unit, not as servile dependencies to be exploited for England's selfish benefit. The growing of tobacco in England was prohibited, and valuable bounties were paid to colonial producers of indigo and naval stores. A planned economy, England specializing in manufacturing and the colonies in the production of raw materials, was the grand design. By and large the system suited the realities of life in an underdeveloped country rich in raw materials and suffering from a chronic labor shortage.

Much has been made by some historians of the restrictions that the British placed on colonial manufacturing. The Wool Act of 1699 prohibited the export (but not the manufacture for local sale) of colonial woolen cloth. A similar law regarding hats was passed in 1732, and in 1750 an Iron Act outlawed the construction of new rolling and slitting mills in America. No other restrictions on manufacturing were imposed. At most the Wool Act stifled a potential American industry; the law was directed chiefly at Irish woolens rather than American. The hat industry cannot be considered a major one. Iron, however, was important; by 1775 the industry was thriving in Virginia, Maryland, New Jersey, and Pennsylvania, and America was turning out one-seventh of the world supply. Yet the Iron Act was designed to steer the American iron industry in a certain direction, not to destroy it. Eager for iron to feed English mills, Parliament eliminated all duties on colonial pig and bar iron entering England, a great stimulus to the basic industry. A similar system had been set up with regard to West Indian sugar as early as 1651, when the English fixed the duty on semirefined sugar at a level more than three times higher than that on raw sugar.

The Effects of Mercantilism

All this legislation reflected, more than it molded, the imperial economy. It made England the colonies' main customer and chief supplier of manufactures, but that would have happened in any case, and it remained the case after the Revolution, when the Navigation Acts no longer applied to America. The chronic colonial shortage of hard money was superficially caused by the flow of specie to England to meet the "unfavorable" balance that resulted from this trade, and this, too, reflected natural conditions. The rapidly growing colonial economy consumed far more manufactured products than it could pay for out of current production. To be "in debt" to England really meant that the English were investing capital in America, a state of affairs that continued until World War I.

Important colonial products for which no market existed in England (such as fish, wheat, and corn) were never enumerated and moved freely and directly to foreign ports. Most colonial manufacturing was untouched by English law. Shipbuilding benefited from the Navigation Acts, since many English merchants bought vessels built in the colonies. Between 1769 and 1771, Massachusetts, New Hampshire, and Rhode Island yards constructed perhaps 250 ships of 100 to 400 tons for transatlantic commerce and twice that many sloops and schooners for fishermen and coastal traders. The manufacture of rum for local consumption and for the slave trade was significant; so were barrelmaking, flour milling, shoemaking, and dozens of other crafts that operated without restriction.

Two forces that worked in opposite directions must be considered before arriving at any judgment about English mercantilism. While the theory presupposed a general imperial interest above that of both colony and mother country, when conflicts of interest arose the latter nearly always predominated. Whenever Parliament or the Board of Trade resolved an Anglo-American disagreement, the colonists tended to lose out. "It cannot be expected," the Board of Trade announced in 1706, "that encouragement should be given by law to the making of any manufactures made by England in the plantations, it being against the advantage of England."

The Hat Act may have been good mercantilism, but Parliament passed it because English feltmakers were concerned over the news that Massachusetts and New York were turning out 10,000 hats a year. The requirement that foreign goods destined for the colonies must first be unloaded in England increased the cost of certain goods to Americans for the benefit of English merchants and dockworkers. The enumeration of tobacco and other colonial products meant that English merchants could profit by reexporting surpluses to the Continent; by 1700 this reexport trade amounted to 30 percent of the value of all England's exports.

Complementary interests conspired to keep conflicts at a minimum, but in the long run, as the American economy became more complex, the colonies would have been seriously hampered and much more trouble would have occurred had the system continued to operate.

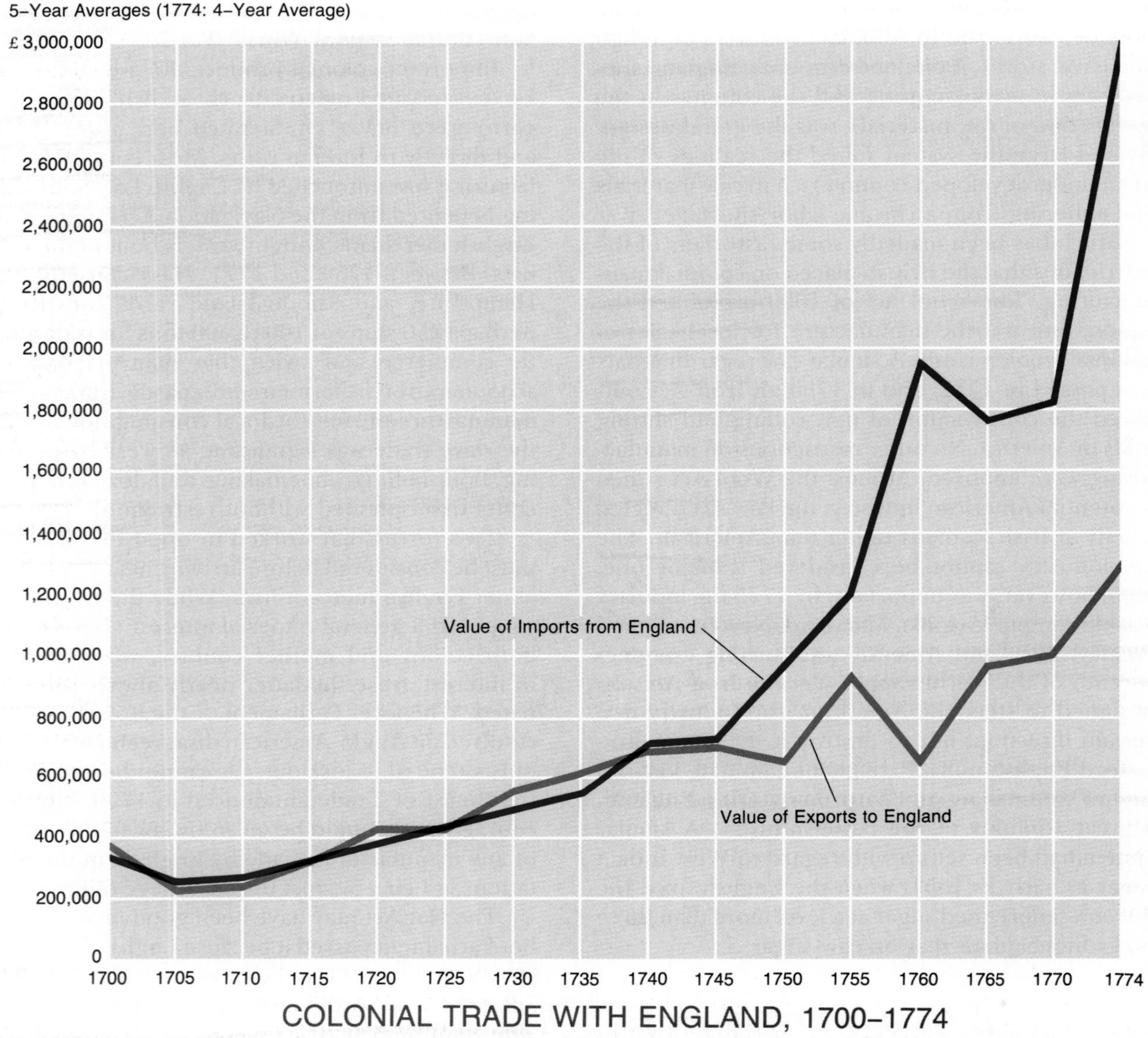

COLONIAL TRADE WITH ENGLAND, 1700–1774

On the other hand, the restrictions of English mercantilism were greatly lessened by inefficiency. The English government was by modern standards incredibly cumbersome and corrupt. The king and his ministers handed out government posts to win political favor or to repay political debts, regardless of the recipient's ability to perform the duties of the office. Transported to remote America, this bumbling and cynical system scarcely functioned at all when local opinion resisted it. Smuggling became a respected profession, bribery of English officials standard practice. Despite a supposedly prohibitive duty of sixpence a gallon imposed by the Molasses Act of 1733, molasses from the French West Indies continued to be imported. The duty was seldom collected. A customs officer in Salem offered to pass French molasses for 10 percent of the legal tax, and in New Jersey the collectors "entered into a composition with the Merchants and took a Dollar a Hogshead or some such small matter."

Mercantilistic policies hurt some colonists such as the tobacco planters, who grew far more than British consumers could smoke. But the policies helped others, and most people proved adept at getting around those aspects of the system that

The value of sugar from the West Indies far outweighed the value of imports to Britain from the mainland American colonies. Refining the sugar before shipping, as shown in this engraving, resulted in far higher import duties.

threatened them. In any case, the colonies enjoyed almost continuous prosperity in the years between 1650 and the Revolution, as even so dedicated a foe of mercantilistic restrictions as Adam Smith admitted.

By the same token England profited greatly from its overseas possessions. With all its inefficiencies, mercantilism worked. Prime Minister Sir Robert Walpole's famous policy of "salutary neglect," which involved looking the other way when Americans violated the Navigation Acts, was partly a bowing to the inevitable, partly the result of complacency. English manufactures were better and cheaper than those of other nations. This fact, together with ties of language and a common heritage, predisposed Americans toward doing business in England. All else followed naturally; the mercantilistic laws merely steered the American economy in a direction it had already taken. On balance they benefited both the colonies and the mother country. They were not a cause of serious discontent in any part of America. At least this was the case until the end of the French and Indian War.

As the colonies matured, their relations with Crown and Parliament remained reasonably harmonious. The great majority of the settlers were of British descent, and their interests generally coincided with those of their cousins in the mother country. This was fortunate because the British authorities were poorly equipped to deal with trouble in America. As one leading authority on 18th-century English politics has said, there was "immense ignorance and even vaster indifference" in the government with regard to all American questions. When trouble did come, intelligence and diligence would be called for—and found lacking.

Early Colonial Wars

The British colonies were part of a great empire that was part of a still larger world. Seemingly isolated in their remote communities, scattered like a broken string of beads between the wide Atlantic and the trackless Appalachian forests, Americans were constantly affected by outside events both in the Old World and in the New. Under the spell of mercantilistic logic, the western European nations competed fiercely for markets and colonial raw materials. War—hot and cold, declared and undeclared—was almost a permanent condition of 17th- and 18th-century life, and when the powers clashed they fought wherever they could get at one another, in America, in Europe, and elsewhere.

Although the American colonies were minor pieces in the game and were sometimes casually exchanged or sacrificed by the masterminds in London, Paris, and Madrid in pursuit of some supposedly more important objective, the colonists quickly generated their own international animosities. North America, a huge and, compared to densely populated Europe, an almost empty stage, evidently did not provide enough room for French, Dutch, Spanish, and English companies to perform. Frenchmen and Spaniards clashed savagely in Florida in the 16th century. Before the landing of the Pilgrims, Samuel Argall of Virginia was sacking French settlements in Maine and carrying off Jesuit priests into captivity at Jamestown. Instead of fostering tranquility and generosity, the abundance of America seemed to make the settlers belligerent and greedy.

The North Atlantic fisheries quickly became a source of trouble between Canadian and New England colonists, despite the fact that the waters of the Grand Banks teemed with cod and other fish. To dry and salt their catch the fishermen needed land bases, and French and English Americans struggled constantly over the harbors of Maine, Nova Scotia, and Newfoundland.

British ties with the Iroquois nation were long-lasting; this Seneca chief, Cornplanter, aided the British in the American Revolution. In this romanticized portrait by F. Bartoli, he is shown wearing metal jewelry inspired by European fashion.

Even more troublesome was the fur trade. The yield of the forest was easily exhausted by indiscriminate slaughter, and traders contended bitterly to control valuable hunting grounds. The French in Canada conducted their fur trading through tribes such as the Algonquins and the Hurons. This brought them into conflict with the Five Nations, the powerful Iroquois confederation centered in what is now New York State. As early as 1609 the Five Nations were at war with the French and their Indian allies. For decades this struggle flared sporadically, the Iroquois more than holding their own both as fighters and as traders. They combined, according to one terrified Frenchman, the stealth and craftiness of the fox, the ferocity and courage of the lion, and the speed of a bird in flight. The Iroquois brought quantities of beaver pelts to the Dutch at Albany, some obtained by their own trappers, others taken by ambushing the fur-laden canoes of their enemies. They preyed on and ultimately destroyed the Hurons in the land north of Lake Ontario and dickered with Indian trappers in far-off Michigan. When the English took over the New Amsterdam colony they eagerly adopted the Iroquois as allies, buying their furs and supplying them with trading goods and guns.

The French managed to bypass the Iroquois by sending their trappers into the Illinois country and even beyond the Mississippi in search of skins, but in the final showdown for control of North America, the friendship of the Iroquois was vitally important to the English.

By the last decade of the 17th century it had become clear that the Netherlands lacked the strength to maintain a big empire and that Spain was fast declining. The future, especially in North America, belonged to England and France. In the wars of the next 125 years European alliances shifted dramatically, yet the English and what the Boston lawyer John Adams called "the turbulent Gallicks" were always on opposite sides.

In the first three of these conflicts colonists played only minor parts. The fighting in America consisted chiefly of sneak attacks on isolated outposts. In King William's War (1689–1697), the American phase of the War of the League of Augsburg, French forces raided Schenectady in New

York and frontier settlements in New England. English colonists retaliated by capturing Port Royal, Nova Scotia, only to lose that outpost in a counterattack in 1691. The Peace of Ryswick in 1697 restored all captured territory in America to the original owners.

The next struggle was the War of the Spanish Succession (1702–1713), fought to prevent the union of Spain and France under the Bourbons. The Americans named this conflict Queen Anne's War. French-inspired Abenaki Indians razed Deerfield, Massachusetts. A party of Carolinians burned St. Augustine in Spanish Florida. The New Englanders retook Port Royal. However, in Europe the forces of England, Holland, and Austria, led by the Duke of Marlborough, won a series of decisive victories. In the Treaty of Utrecht in 1713, France yielded Nova Scotia, Newfoundland, and the Hudson Bay region to Great Britain.

If the colonies were mere pawns in these wars, the people of New England (and of Canada) paid heavily in them. Many frontier settlers were killed in the raids. Hundreds of townspeople died during the campaigns in Nova Scotia. Massachusetts taxes went up sharply and the colony issued large amounts of paper currency to pay its bills, causing an inflation that ate into the living standards of wage earners.

The American phase of the third Anglo-French conflict, the War of the Austrian Succession (1740–1748), was called King George's War. The usual Indian raids were launched in both directions across the lonely forests that separated the St. Lawrence settlements from the New York and New England frontier. A New England force captured the strategic fortress of Louisbourg on Cape Breton Island, guarding the entrance to the Gulf of St. Lawrence. The Treaty of Aix-la-Chapelle in 1748, however, required the return of Louisbourg, much to the chagrin of the New Englanders.

As this incident suggests, the colonial wars generated a certain amount of trouble between England and the colonies; matters that seemed unimportant in London might loom large in American eyes, and vice versa. But the conflicts were seldom serious. The wars did, however, increase the bad feelings between settlers north and south of the St. Lawrence. Every Indian raid was attributed to French provocateurs, although more often than not the English colonists themselves were responsible for the Indian troubles. Conflicting land claims further aggravated the situation. Massachusetts, Connecticut, and Virginia possessed overlapping claims to the Ohio Valley, and Pennsylvania and New York also had pretensions in the region. Yet the French, ranging broadly across the midcontinent, insisted that the Ohio country was exclusively theirs.

The Great War for the Empire

In this beautiful, almost untouched land, a handful of individuals determined the future of the continent. Over the years the French had established a chain of forts and trading posts running from Mackinac Island in northern Michigan to Kaskaskia on the Mississippi and Vincennes on the Wabash, and from Niagara in the east to the Bourbon River, near Lake Winnipeg, in the west. By the 1740s, however, Pennsylvania fur traders, led by George Croghan, a rugged Irishman, were setting up posts north of the Ohio River and dickering with Miami and Huron Indians who ordinarily sold their furs to the French. In 1748 Croghan built a fort at Pickawillany, deep in the Miami country, in what is now western Ohio. That same year agents of a group of Virginia land speculators who had recently organized what they called the Ohio Company reached this area.

With trifling exceptions, an insulating band of wilderness had always separated the French and English in America. Now the two powers came into contact. The immediate result was a showdown battle for control of North America, the "great war for the empire." Thoroughly alarmed by the presence of the English on land they had long considered their own, the French struck hard. Attacking suddenly in 1752, they wiped out Croghan's post at Pickawillany and drove his traders back into Pennsylvania. Then they built a string of barrier forts south from Lake Erie along the Pennsylvania line: Fort Presque Isle, Fort Le Boeuf, Fort Venango. The Pennsylvania authorities chose to ignore this action, but Lieutenant Governor Robert Dinwiddie of Virginia (who was an investor in the Ohio Company) dispatched a 21-year-old surveyor named George Washington to warn the French that they were trespassing on Virginia territory.

Washington, a gangling, inarticulate, yet courageous and intensely ambitious young planter, made his way northwest in the fall of 1753 and delivered Dinwiddie's message to the commandant at Fort Le Boeuf. It made no impression. "[The French] told me," Washington reported, "that it was their absolute Design to take Possession of the *Ohio,* and by G–– they would do it." Governor Dinwiddie thereupon promoted Washington to lieutenant colonel and sent him back in the spring of 1754 with 150 men to seize a strategic junction south of the new French forts, where the Allegheny and Monongahela rivers join to form the Ohio.

Eager but inexperienced in battle, young Washington botched his assignment. As his force labored painfully through the tangled mountain country southeast of the fork of the Ohio, he received word that the French had already occupied the position and were constructing a powerful post, Fort Duquesne. Outnumbered by perhaps four to one, Washington foolishly pushed on. He surprised and routed a French reconnaissance party, but this brought upon him the main body of enemy troops.

Hastily he threw up a defensive position, aptly named Fort Necessity, but the ground was ill chosen; the French easily surrounded the fort and Washington had to surrender. After tricking the young officer, who could not read French, into signing an admission that he had "assassinated" the leader of the reconnaissance party, his captors, with the gateway to the Ohio country firmly in their hands, permitted him and his men to march off. Nevertheless, Washington returned to Virginia a hero, for although still undeclared, this was war, and he had struck the first blow against the hated French.

In the resulting conflict—which they named the French and Indian War—the English colonists outnumbered the French by about 1.5 million to 90,000. But the English were divided and disorganized, the French disciplined and united. The French controlled the disputed territory, and most of the Indians took their side. As a colonial official wrote, together they made formidable forest fighters, "sometimes in our Front, sometimes in our Rear, and often on all sides of us, Hussar Fashion, taking the Advantage of every Tree and Bush." With an ignorance and arrogance typical of 18th-century colonial administration, the British mismanaged the war and failed to make effective use of local resources. For several years they stumbled from one defeat to another.

General Edward Braddock, a competent but uninspired soldier, was dispatched to Virginia to take command. In June 1755 he marched against Fort Duquesne with 1,400 Redcoats and a smaller number of colonials, only to be ambushed and decisively defeated by a much smaller force of French and Indians. Braddock died bravely in battle, and only 500 of his men, led by Colonel Washington, who was serving as his aide-de-camp, made their way back to Virginia.

Elsewhere Anglo-American arms fared little better in the early years of the war. Expeditions against Fort Niagara, key to all French defenses in the west, and Crown Point, gateway to Montreal, bogged down. Meanwhile the Indians, armed by the French, bathed the frontier in blood. Venting the frustration caused by 150 years of white advance, they attacked defenseless outposts with unrestrained brutality. Crazed with hatred, they poured molten lead into their victims' wounds, ripped off the fingernails of captives, raped, kidnaped—even drank the blood of captives who endured their tortures stoically.* The most feared of the "French" Indians were the Delawares, a once-peaceful Pennsylvania tribe that had been harried from their homelands by English and Iroquois. General Braddock paid his Indian allies only £5 each for French scalps but offered £200 for the hair of Shinngass, the Delaware chieftain.

In 1756 the conflict spread to Europe to become the Seven Years' War. Prussia sided with Great Britain, Austria with the French. On the world stage, too, things went badly for the British. Finally, in 1757, as defeat succeeded defeat, King George II was forced to allow William Pitt, whom he detested, to take over leadership of the war effort. Pitt, grandson of "Diamond" Pitt, a *nouveau riche* East India merchant, was an unstable man who spent much of his life on the verge of madness, but he was an imaginative planner and a passionate orator, capable of inspiring the entire nation in its hour of trial.

Pitt recognized, as few contemporaries did, the potential value of North America. Instead of relying on the tightfisted and shortsighted colonial assem-

---

* The anthropologist Bruce Trigger writes: "If the prisoner had been a brave man, his heart was cooked and eaten by the young [Huron] warriors, who believed that they would acquire his courage in this manner. . . . It was an act of religious significance."

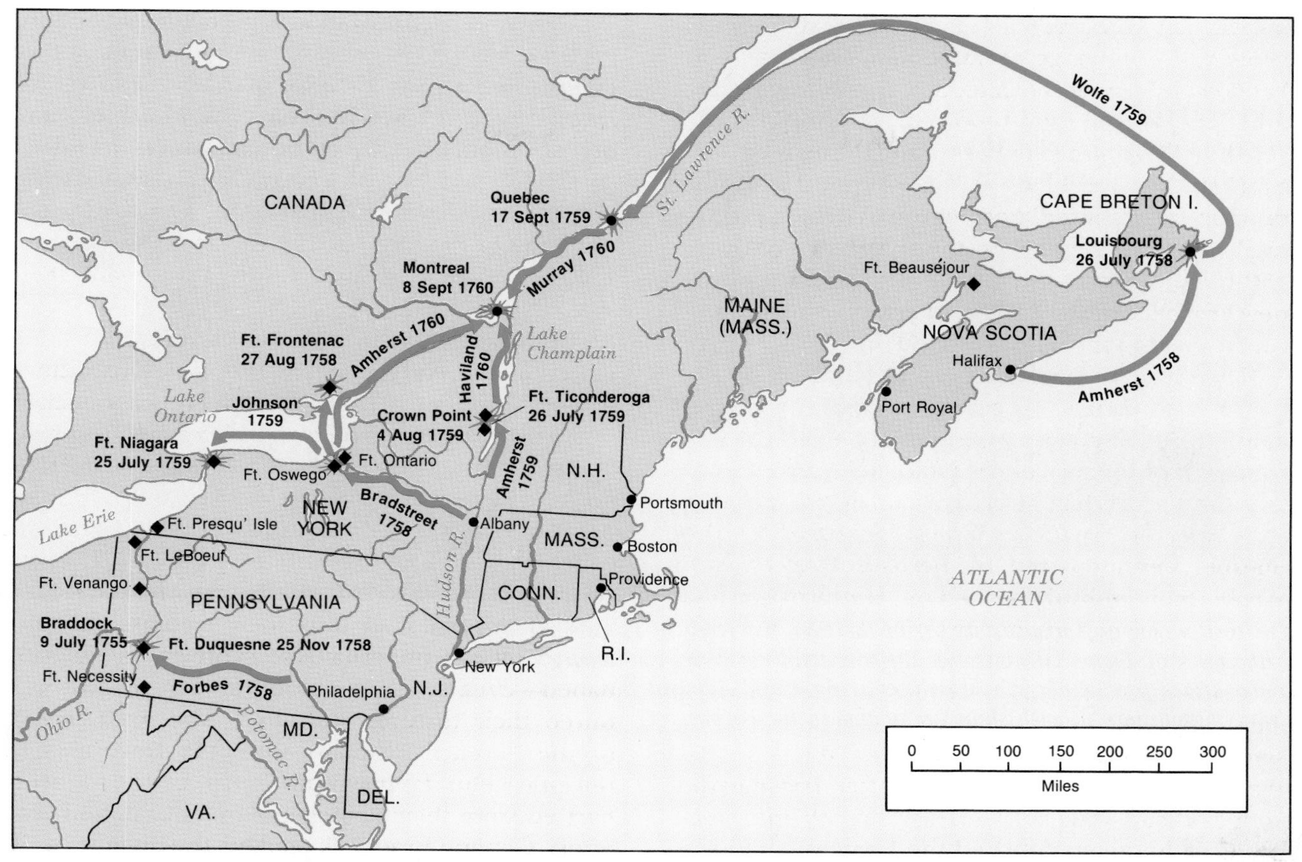

PITT'S STRATEGY, FRENCH AND INDIAN WAR, 1758–1760

A key phase of Pitt's American strategy involved capturing the French strongpoints guarding the approaches to Canada: Louisbourg, protecting the St. Lawrence; Fort Ticonderoga and Crown Point, on Lake Champlain; and Fort Duquesne, in the Ohio country. Colonial forces played a significant role in this strategy, with John Forbes seizing Fort Duquesne, John Bradstreet winning control of Lake Ontario, and William Johnson taking Fort Niagara.

blies for men and money, he poured regiment after regiment of British regulars and the full resources of the British treasury into the contest, mortgaging the future recklessly to secure the prize. Grasping the importance of sea power in fighting a war on the other side of the Atlantic, he used the British navy to bottle up the enemy fleet and hamper French communications with Canada. He possessed a keen eye for military genius, and when he discovered it, he ignored seniority and the outraged feelings of mediocre generals and promoted talented young officers to top commands. His greatest find was James Wolfe, whom he made a brigadier at 31. Wolfe and Major General Jeffrey Amherst, only ten years his senior and another of Pitt's discoveries, recaptured the Louisbourg fortress in July 1758.

That winter, as Pitt's grand strategy matured, Fort Duquesne fell. It was appropriately renamed Fort Pitt, the present Pittsburgh. The following summer Fort Niagara was overrun. Amherst took Crown Point, and Wolfe sailed up the St. Lawrence to Quebec. There the French General Montcalm had prepared a formidable defense, but after months of probing and planning, Wolfe found and exploited a chink in the city's armor and on the

This watercolor of Amherst's seizure of the French fortress of Louisbourg in 1758 is the work of Thomas Davies, an English artillery officer. Louisbourg is at center, under attack from Amherst's siege lines at right and Admiral Boscawen's British fleet lying offshore. French ships are aflame in the harbor.

Plains of Abraham defeated the French—although both he and Montcalm died in the battle. In 1760 Montreal fell and the French abandoned all Canada to the British.

Spain attempted to stem the British advance but failed utterly. A Far Eastern fleet captured Manila in 1762, and another British force took Cuba. The French sugar islands in the West Indies were also captured, while in India, British troops reduced the French posts one by one.

Peace was restored in 1763 by the Treaty of Paris. Its terms were moderate considering the extent of the British triumph. France abandoned all claim to North America except for two small islands near Newfoundland; Great Britain took over Canada and the eastern half of the Mississippi Valley. Although the British considered the French sugar islands, Guadeloupe and Martinique, more economically valuable than the cold Canadian wilderness, they kept Canada for military and strategic reasons and returned the islands to France, along with some of the captured French possessions in India and Africa. Spain got back both the Philippine Islands and Cuba but in exchange ceded East and West Florida to Great Britain. In a separate treaty, Spain also got New Orleans and the huge area of North America west of the Mississippi River. France and Spain thus remained important colonial powers.

"Half the continent," the historian Francis Parkman wrote, "had changed hands at the scratch of a pen." From the point of view of the English colonists in America, the victory was overwhelming. All threat to their frontiers seemed to have been swept away. Surely, they believed in the first happy moments of victory, their peaceful and prosperous expansion was assured for countless generations.

No honest American could deny that the victory had been won chiefly by British troops and with British gold. Colonial militiamen fought well in defense of their homes or when some highly prized objective seemed ripe for the plucking; they lacked discipline and determination when required to fight far from home and under commanders they did not know. As one American official admitted to the British commander in chief, it was difficult to get New Englanders to enlist "unless assurances can be given that they shall not march to the southward of certain limits."

Colonials were certainly happy to see scarlet-clad British regulars bear the brunt of the fighting and happier still when the Crown shouldered most of the financial burden of the long struggle. The local assemblies contributed to the cost, but except for Massachusetts and Virginia their outlays were trivial compared with the £82 million poured into the worldwide conflict by the British.

Little wonder that the great victory produced a burst of praise for king and mother country throughout America. Parades, cannonading, fireworks, banquets, the pealing of church bells—these were the order of the day in every colonial town. Ezra Stiles, later president of Yale, extolled "the illustrious House of Hanover," whose new head, the young George III, had inherited the throne in 1760. "Nothing," said Thomas Pownall, wartime governor of Massachusetts and a student of colonial administration, "can eradicate from [the colonists'] hearts their natural, almost mechanical affection to Great Britain."

Putting the Empire Right

In London peace proved a time for reassessment; that the empire of 1763 was not the same as the empire of 1754 was obvious. The new, far larger dominion would be much more expensive to maintain. Pitt had spent a huge sum winning and securing it, much of it borrowed money. Great Britain's national debt had doubled between 1754 and 1763. Now this debt must be serviced and repaid, and the strain that this would place upon the economy was clear to all. Furthermore, the day-to-day cost of administering an empire that extended from Hudson Bay to India was far larger than that which the already burdened British taxpayer could be expected to bear. Before the great war for the empire, Britain's North American possessions were administered for about £70,000 a year; after 1763 the cost was five times as much.

The American empire had also grown far more complex. A system of administration that treated it as a string of separate plantations struggling to exist on the edge of the forest would no longer suffice. The war had been fought for control of the Ohio Valley. Now that the prize had been secured, ten thousand hands were eager to make off with it. The urge to expand was, despite the continent's enormous empty spaces, an old American drive. As early as the 1670s, eastern stay-at-homes were lamenting the "insatiable desire after Land" that made people willing to "live like Heathen, only that so they might have Elbow-room enough in the world." Frontier warfare had frustrated this urge for seven long years. How best could it be satisfied now that peace had come?

Conflicting colonial claims, based on charters drafted by men who thought the Pacific lay over the next hill, threatened to make the great valley a battleground once more. The Indians remained unpacified, urged to fight on by Spaniards in the area around New Orleans who sought to check and throw back the American advance. Rival land companies contested for charters, while fur traders, eager to absorb the riches formerly controlled by France, strove to hold back the wave of settlement that must inevitably destroy the world of the beaver and the deer. One Englishman who traveled through America at this time predicted that if the colonists were left to their own devices, "there would soon be civil war from one end of the continent to the other."

Apparently only Great Britain could deal with these problems and rivalries, for when a farsighted man like Franklin had proposed a rudimentary form of colonial union—the Albany Plan of 1754—it was almost universally rejected by the Americans. Unfortunately, the British government did not rise to the challenge. Perhaps this was to be expected, given the singularly ineffective character of 18th-century British politics. The government, according to the historian J. H. Plumb, was "an extremely complex system of political bargaining and blackmail." A handful of aristocrats (fewer than 150 peers were active in government affairs) dominated politics, and they were more concerned with local offices and personal advantage than with large questions of policy. An American who spent some time in London in 1764 trying to obtain approval for a plan for the development of the west reported: "The people hear Spend thire time in Nothing but abuseing one Another and Striveing who shall be in power with a view to Serve themselves and Thire friends." George I and George II were not indifferent to national affairs and George III, while determined to be a strong leader, was not a tyrant, as once was commonly believed, but the first two were stupid and the third an inept politician and the victim of frequent bouts of illness.

Even the best-educated English leaders were nearly all monumentally ignorant of American conditions. The British imperial system lacked effective channels of communication. Information about American attitudes came from royal officials in the colonies and others with special interests to protect or advance, or from the colonial agents and merchants in London, whose information was often out of date. Serene in their ignorance, most English leaders insisted that colonials were uncouth and generally inferior beings. During the French and Indian War, General Wolfe characterized colonial troops as "the dirtiest, most contemptible cowardly dogs you can conceive," and another English officer compared the ordinary run to "broken innkeepers, horse jockeys and Indian traders."

Any officer with a royal commission outranked all officers of the colonial militia, regardless of title. Young Colonel Washington, for example, had to travel all the way from Virginia to the headquarters of the commander in chief in Boston to establish his precedence over one Captain John Dagworthy, a Maryland officer who had *formerly* held a royal commission and who did not propose to let a mere colonial colonel outrank him.

Many English people resented the colonists because they were rapidly becoming rich and powerful. Shortly after the war, John Adams predicted that within a century America would be wealthier and more populous than Great Britain.* If the English did not say much about this possibility, they too considered it from time to time—without Adams's relish.

Tightening Imperial Controls

The attempt of the inefficient, ignorant, envious, and indignant British government to deal with the intricate colonial problems that resulted from the great war for the empire led to the American Revolution—a rebellion that was costly but which produced excellent results for the colonists, for Great Britain, for the rest of the empire, and eventually for the entire world. Trouble began when the British decided after the war to intervene more actively in American affairs. Theoretically the colonies were entirely subordinate to Crown and Parliament, yet except for the disastrous failure of the Dominion of New England to centralize control of the colonies in the 1680s they had been allowed a remarkable degree of freedom to manage their own affairs. Of course they had come to expect this as their right.

Parliament had never attempted to raise a revenue in America. "Compelling the colonies to pay money without their consent would be rather like raising contributions in an enemy's country than taxing Englishmen for their own benefit," Benjamin Franklin wrote. That shrewd judge of human nature, Sir Robert Walpole, initiator of the policy of salutary neglect, recognized the colonial viewpoint. He responded to a suggestion that Parliament tax the colonies by saying: "I will leave that for some of my successors, who may have more courage than I have." Nevertheless, the *legality* of parliamentary taxation, or of other parliamentary intervention in colonial affairs, had not been seriously contested. During King George's War and again during the French and Indian War many British officials in America suggested that Parliament tax the colonies.

Nothing was done until 1759, when British victories had made ultimate triumph sure. Then a general tightening of imperial regulations began. Important Virginia and South Carolina laws were disallowed and royal control over colonial courts was strengthened. In Massachusetts the use of general search warrants (writs of assistance) was authorized in 1761. These writs enabled customs officers searching for smuggled goods to invade homes and warehouses without evidence or specific court orders. The British believed this necessary because many colonial merchants were trading openly with the French in the West Indies. With French shipping driven from the seas by the Royal Navy and American privateers, the price of food and other necessities in the Indies soared, and some Americans took advantage of the opportunities that resulted. But nearly all Americans resented the invasions of privacy that the writs caused. In 1761 a Boston lawyer, James Otis, argued in a case involving 63 merchants that the writs were "against the Constitution" and therefore void. Otis lost the case but by boldly suggesting that Parliament's authority over the colonies was not absolute, he became a colonial hero.

After the signing of the peace treaty in 1763, events pushed the British authorities to still more

---

* As early as 1751, Franklin predicted that in a century "the greatest number of Englishmen will be on this Side of the Water."

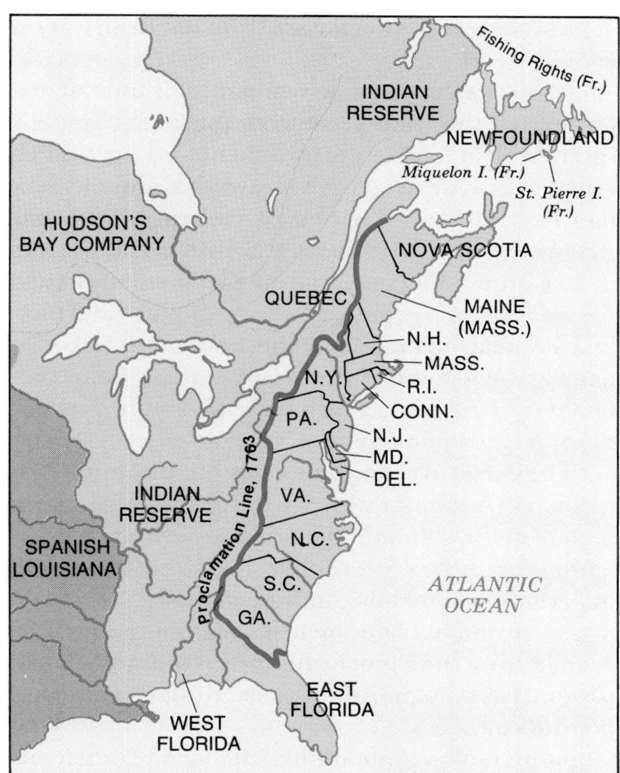

EASTERN NORTH AMERICA, 1763

George III's Proclamation of 1763 in effect reserved for the Indians the vast area across the Appalachians (except for the new royal colonies of Quebec, East Florida, and West Florida) as far west as Spanish Louisiana and as far north as the Hudson's Bay Company preserve.

vigorous activity in America. Freed of the restraint imposed by French competition, Englishman and colonist increased their pressure on the Indians. Cynical fur traders now cheated them outrageously, while callous military men hoped to exterminate them like vermin. The Brtish commander in the west, Lord Jeffrey Amherst, suggested infecting the Indians with smallpox; another officer expressed the wish that they could be hunted down with dogs.

Led by an Ottawa chief named Pontiac, the desperate tribes made one last effort to drive the whites back across the mountains. Pontiac's Rebellion caused much havoc, but it failed. By 1764 most of the western tribes had accepted the peace terms offered by a royal commissioner, Sir William Johnson, one of the few whites who understood and sympathized with the Indians. The British government then decided to maintain 15 regiments, some 6,000 soldiers, in posts along the entire arc of the frontier, as much to protect the Indians from the settlers as the settlers from the Indians. It proclaimed a new western policy: no settlers were to cross the Appalachian divide. Only licensed traders might do business with the Indians beyond that line. The purchase of Indian land was forbidden. In compensation, three new colonies—Quebec, East Florida, and West Florida—were created, but they were not permitted to set up local assemblies.

This Proclamation of 1763 excited much indignation in America. The frustration of dozens of schemes for land development in the Ohio Valley angered many influential colonists. Colonel Wash-

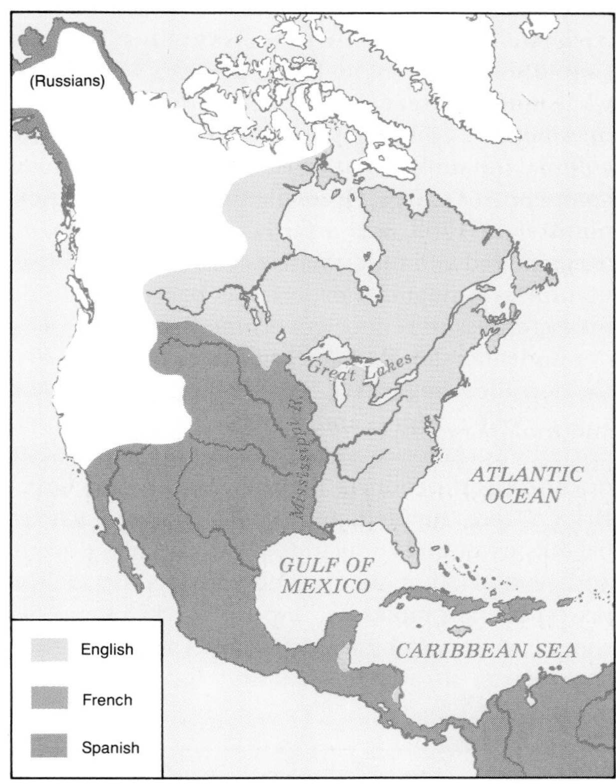

EUROPEAN CLAIMS IN ALL OF NORTH AMERICA, 1763

ington referred to the proclamation contemptuously as "a temporary expedient to quiet the minds of Indians," and he continued to stake out claims to western lands. The licensing of fur traders aroused opposition, especially when the British mishandled the task of regulating the trade.

Originally the British had intended the proclamation to be temporary. With the passage of time, however, checking westward expansion seemed a good way to save money, prevent trouble with the Indians, and keep the colonies tied closely to the mother country. The proclamation line, the Board of Trade declared, was "necessary for the preservation of the colonies in due subordination."* Naturally this attitude caused resentment in America. To close off the west temporarily in order to pacify the Indians made some sense; to keep it closed was like trying to contain a tidal wave.

The Sugar Act

Americans disliked the new western policy but realized that the problems were knotty and that no simple solution existed. Their protests were somewhat muted. Great Britain's effort to raise money in America to help support the increased cost of colonial administration caused far more vehement complaints. George Grenville, who became prime minister in 1763, was a fairly able man, although long-winded and rather narrow in outlook. His reputation as a financial expert was based chiefly on his eagerness to reduce government spending. Under his leadership Parliament passed, in April 1764, the so-called Sugar Act. This law placed tariffs on sugar, coffee, wines, and many other products imported into America in substantial amounts. Taxes on European products imported by way of Great Britain were doubled, and the enumerated articles list was extended to include iron, raw silk, potash, and several other items. The sixpence-per-gallon tax on foreign molasses, imposed in 1733 and designed to be prohibitively high, was reduced to threepence, at which level the foreign product could compete with molasses from the British West Indies.

At the same time, new measures aimed at enforcing all the trade laws were put into effect. (A threepenny molasses duty would not produce much revenue if it were as easy to avoid as the old levy had been.) Those accused of violating the Sugar Act were to be tried before British naval officers in vice-admiralty courts. Grenville was determined to end both smuggling and the corruption and inefficiency that had plagued the customs service for decades. Soon the customs service was collecting each year 15 times as much in duties as it had before the war.

The Sugar Act and the decision of the government in London to restrict the printing of paper money in the colonies disturbed Americans deeply. Throughout the 18th century local assemblies had issued paper currency in anticipation of tax payments to finance emergencies such as wars. The act of 1764 merely imposed restrictions on colonial paper; it did not prevent its use. But it came at a bad time. During the war the seaports prospered mightily, and shipbuilding boomed. Merchants earned fat profits supplying the British forces with food and other goods. British soldiers and sailors, 40,000 of them, spent most of their wages in the colonies.

When the fighting shifted to the Caribbean after the fall of Canada, most of this spending stopped. The soldiers "are gone to drink [rum] in a warmer Region, the place of its production," a New York merchant mourned. A depression increased the impact of the new laws. Hard-hit merchants and artisans found British policy alarming.

Far more alarming was the nature of the Sugar Act and the manner of its passage. The Navigation Acts had imposed duties of many kinds, but they had been intended to regulate commerce and the sums collected had not cut deeply into profits. Indeed, the Navigation Acts might well be considered an instrument of imperial foreign policy, an area of government that everyone willingly conceded to London. Yet few Americans were willing to concede that Parliament had the right to tax them. As *Englishmen* (and as readers of John Locke) they believed that no one should be deprived arbitrarily of property and that, as James Otis put it in his stirring pamphlet *The Rights of the British Colonies Asserted and Proved,* written during the controversy

* The British were particularly concerned about preserving the colonies as markets for their manufactures. They feared that the spread of population beyond the mountains would stimulate local manufacturing because the high cost of land transportation would make British goods prohibitively expensive.

over writs of assistance, everyone should be "free from all taxes but what he consents to in person, or by his representative." John Locke had made clear in his *Second Treatise of Government* (1690) that property ought never be taken from people without their consent, not because material values transcend all others but because human liberty can never be secure when arbitrary power of any kind exists. "If our Trade may be taxed why not our Lands?" the Boston town meeting asked when news of the Sugar Act reached America. "Why not the produce of our Lands and every Thing we possess or make use of?"

"Essential Rights and Liberties"

To most people in Great Britain the colonial protest against taxation without representation seemed a hypocritical quibble, and it is probably true that in 1764 many of the protesters had not thought the argument through. The distinction between tax laws and other types of legislation was artificial, the British reasoned. Either Parliament was sovereign in America or it was not, and only a fool or a traitor would argue that it was not. If the colonists were loyal subjects of George III, as they claimed, they should bear cheerfully their fair share of the cost of governing his widespread dominions. As to representation, the colonies *were* represented in Parliament; every member of that body stood for the interests of the entire empire. If Americans had no say in the election of members of Commons, neither did most English subjects.

This concept of "virtual" representation accurately described the British system. But it made no sense in America, where from the time of the first settlements members of the colonial assemblies had represented the people of the districts in which they stood for office. The confusion between virtual and actual (geographically based) representation revealed the extent to which colonial and British political practices had diverged over the years.

The British were partly correct in concluding that selfish motives influenced colonial objections to the Sugar Act. The colonists denounced taxation without representation, but they would have rejected the offer of a reasonable number of seats in Parliament if it had been made, and they would probably have complained about paying taxes to support imperial administration even if imposed by their own assemblies. American abundance and the simplicity of colonial life had enabled them to prosper without assuming any considerable tax burden. Now their maturing society was beginning to require communal rather than individual solutions to the problems of existence. Not many of them were prepared to face up to this hard truth.

Over the course of colonial history Americans had taken a significantly narrow view of imperial concerns. They had avoided complying with the Navigation Acts whenever they could profit by doing so. Colonial militiamen had compiled a sorry record when asked to fight for Britain or even for the inhabitants of colonies other than their own. True, most Americans professed loyalty to the Crown, but not many would voluntarily open their purses except to benefit themselves. In short they were provincials, in attitude and in fact. Many of the difficulties they faced after they won their independence resulted from this narrowness of outlook.

Nevertheless, the colonists were opposed in principle to taxation without representation. They failed, however, to agree upon a common plan of resistance. Many of the assemblies drafted protests, but these varied in force as well as in form. Merchant groups that tried to organize boycotts of products subject to the new taxes met with indifferent success. Then in 1765 Parliament provided the flux necessary for welding colonial opinion by passing the Stamp Act.

The Pot Set to Boiling

The Stamp Act placed stiff excise taxes on virtually all kinds of printed matter—colonial newspapers, legal documents, licenses, even playing cards. Stamp duties were intended to be relatively painless and cheap to collect; in England similar taxes brought in about £100,000 annually. Grenville hoped the Stamp Act would produce £60,000 a year in America, and the law provided that all revenue should be applied to "defraying the necessary expenses of defending, protecting, and securing, the . . . colonies."

Hardly a farthing was collected. As the Boston clergyman Jonathan Mayhew explained, "almost every British American . . . considered it as an infraction of their rights, or their dearly purchased privileges." The Sugar Act had been related to Parliament's uncontested power to control colonial trade, but the Stamp Act was a direct tax. When Parliament ignored the politely phrased petitions of the colonial assemblies, more vigorous protests quickly followed.

Virginia took the lead. In late May 1765 Patrick Henry, fresh from his triumph in the Parson's Cause controversy, introduced resolutions asserting redundantly that the House of Burgesses possessed "the only and sole and exclusive right and power to lay taxes" on Virginians and suggesting that Parliament had no legal authority to tax the colonies at all. Henry spoke for what the royal governor called the "Young, hot and Giddy Members" of the legislature. The more extreme of his resolutions failed of enactment, but the debate they occasioned attracted wide and favorable attention. On June 6 the Massachusetts assembly proposed an intercolonial Stamp Act Congress, which, when it met in New York City in October, passed another series of resolutions of protest. The Stamp Act and other recent acts of parliament were "burthensome and grievous," the delegates declared. "It is unquestionably essential to the freedom of a people . . . that no taxes be imposed on them but with their own consent."

During the summer an irregular organization known as the Sons of Liberty began to agitate against the act. Although led by men of character and position, the "Liberty Boys" frequently resorted to violence to achieve their aims. In Boston they staged vicious riots, looting and then wantonly vandalizing the houses of the stamp master and Lieutenant Governor Thomas Hutchinson and destroying important government records. In Connecticut the stamp master Jared Ingersoll, a man of great courage and dignity, faced an angry mob demanding his resignation. When threatened with death if he refused, he coolly replied that he was prepared to die "perhaps as well now as another Time." Probably his life was not really in danger, but the size and determination of the crowd convinced him that resistance was useless, and he capitulated.

The stamps were printed in England and shipped to stamp masters (all Americans) in the colonies well in advance of November 1, 1765, the date the law was to go into effect. The New York

Outrage at the Stamp Act was demonstrated all over the colonies in incidents like this, where the effigy of a New Hampshire stamp master is ridiculed by the townspeople.

stamp master had resigned, but the stamps were stored in the city under military guard. Radicals distributed placards reading "The first Man that either distributes or makes use of Stampt Paper let him take care of his House, Person, and Effects. We dare." When Major Thomas James, the officer who had charge of the stamps, promised that "the stamps would be crammed down New Yorkers' throats," a mob responded by breaking into his house, drinking all his wine, and smashing his furniture and china, reducing the place to a shambles.

In some colonies the stamps were snatched by mobs and put to the torch amid rejoicing. Elsewhere they were locked up in secret by British officials or held on shipboard. For a time no business requiring stamped paper was transacted; then, gradually, people began to defy the law by issuing and accepting unstamped documents. Threatened by mob action should they resist, British officials stood by helplessly. The law was a dead letter.

The looting associated with this crisis alarmed many colonists, including some prominent opponents of the Stamp Act. "When the pot is set to boil," John Adams remarked sadly, "the scum rises to the top." Another Bostonian called the vandalizing of Thomas Hutchinson's house a "flagrant instance of to what a pitch of infatuation an incensed populace can rise." Such people began to fear that the protests might be aimed at the wealthy and powerful in America as well as at British tyranny. Historians still debate this question.

That many of the poor resented the colonial elite goes without saying, as does the fact that in many instances the rioting got out of hand and took on a social as well as a political character. Times were hard, and the colonial elite, including most of the leading critics of British policy, had little compassion for the poor, whom they feared could be corrupted by anyone who offered them a square meal or a glass of rum. Once roused, laborers and artisans may well have directed their energies toward righting what they considered local wrongs.

Yet the mass of the people, being owners of property and capable of influencing political decisions, were not social revolutionaries. They might envy and resent the wealth and power of the great landowners and merchants, but there is no evidence that they wished to overthrow the established order.

The British were not surprised that Americans disliked the Stamp Act. They had not anticipated, however, that Americans would react so violently and so unanimously. Americans did so for many reasons. Business continued poor in 1765, and at a time when 3 shillings was a day's wage for an urban laborer, the stamp tax was 2 shillings for an advertisement in a newspaper, 5 shillings for a will, and 20 shillings for a license to sell liquor. The taxes would hurt the business of lawyers, merchants, newspaper editors, and tavernkeepers. Even clergymen dealt with papers requiring stamps. The protests of such influential and articulate people had a powerful impact on public opinion.

The greatest cause of alarm to the colonists was Great Britain's flat rejection of the principle of no taxation without representation. To buy a stamp was to surrender all claim to self-government. Almost no colonist in 1765 wished to be independent of Great Britain, and nearly all accepted George III as "the best of sovereigns." Yet all valued highly their local autonomy and what they called "the rights of Englishmen." They saw the Stamp Act as only the worst in a series of invasions of these rights. Already Parliament had passed still another measure, the Quartering Act, requiring local legislatures to house and feed new British troops sent to the colonies. Reluctantly, many Americans were beginning to fear that the British authorities had organized a conspiracy to deprive them of their liberties—indeed, to subvert the liberties of all English subjects.

In the 18th century the English were universally recognized to be the freest people in the world. In Mozart's opera *The Abduction from the Seraglio* (1782), when the Turk Osmin tells the kidnapped Blonda that she is his slave, a "gift" from his master, she replies contemptuously: "A slave! I am an Englishwoman, born to freedom." Americans, like their English cousins, attributed their freedom to what they called their balanced government. In England power appeared to be shared by the Crown, the House of Lords (representing the aristocracy), and the House of Commons (representing the rest of the realm). The governors, councils, and assemblies seemed to play analogous roles in the colonies. In reality this balance of separate forces never existed, either in Britain or in America. The apparent harmony of society was in both instances the product of a lack of seriously divisive issues, not of dynamic tension between rival forces. But the new laws seemed to Americans to threaten the balance, and this idea was reinforced by their observations of the corruption of English elections. Benjamin Franklin, being a colonial agent in London, knew British politics well. He complained that the entire country was "at market" and "might be bought . . . by the Devil himself" for about £2 million. A clique seeking unlimited power was trying to destroy balanced government in Britain and in America, or so many colonists thought.

There was no such conspiracy; yet to the question, Were American rights actually in danger? no certain answer can be made. Grenville and his successors were English politicians, not tyrants. They looked down on bumptious colonials but surely had no wish to destroy either them or their prosperity. The British attitude was like that of a parent making a recalcitrant youngster swallow a bitter medicine: protests were understandable, but in the patient's own interest they must be ignored.

At the same time, British leaders believed that the time had come to assert royal authority and centralize imperial power at the expense of colonial autonomy. The need to maintain a substantial British army in America to control the western Indians tempted the government to use some of the troops to "control" white Americans as well. And psychologically the leaders were not ready to deal with Americans as equals or to consider American inter-

The distress of British merchants at the repeal of the Stamp Act is mocked in this cartoon "funeral" for the act.

ests on a par with their own. In the long run, American liberty would be destroyed if this attitude were not changed.

Besides refusing to use stamps, Americans responded to the Stamp Act by boycotting British goods. Nearly a thousand merchants signed nonimportation agreements. These struck British merchants hard in their pocketbooks, and they in turn began to bring pressure on Parliament for repeal. After a hot debate—Grenville, whose ministry had fallen over another issue, advocated using the army to enforce the act—the hated law was repealed in March 1766. In America there was jubilation at the news. The ban on British goods was lifted at once. Colonists congratulated themselves on having stood fast in defense of a principle and having won their point.

The Declaratory Act

The great controversy over the constitutional relationship of colony to mother country was only beginning. The same day that it repealed the Stamp Act, Parliament passed a Declaratory Act stating that the colonies were "subordinate" and that Parliament could enact any law it wished "to bind the colonies and people of *America.*"

To most Americans this bald statement of parliamentary authority seemed unconstitutional—a flagrant violation of their understanding of how the British imperial system was supposed to work. Actually the Declaratory Act highlighted the degree to which British and American views of the system had drifted apart. The English and the colonials were using the same words but giving them different meanings. Their conflicting definitions of the word *representation* was a case in point. Another involved the word *constitution,* the term that James Otis had used in his attack on writs of assistance. To the British the Constitution meant the totality of laws, customs, and institutions that had developed over time and under which the nation functioned. In America, partly because governments were based upon specific charters, the word meant a written document or contract spelling out, and thus limiting, the powers of government. If in England Parliament passed an "unconstitutional" law, the result might be rebellion, but that the law existed none would deny. "If the parliament will positively enact a thing to be done which is unreasonable," the great 18th-century English legal authority Sir William Blackstone wrote, "I know of no power that can control it." In America people were beginning to think that an unconstitutional law simply had no force.

Even more basic were the differing meanings that English and Americans were giving to the word *sovereignty.* As Bernard Bailyn has explained in *The Ideological Origins of the American Revolution,* 18th-century English political thinkers believed that sovereignty (ultimate political power) could not be divided. Government and law being based ultimately on force, some "final, unqualified, indivisible" authority had to exist if social order was to be preserved. The Glorious Revolution in England had settled the question of where sovereignty resided—in Parliament. The Declaratory Act, so obnoxious to Americans, seemed to the English the mere explication of the obvious. That colonial governments had passed local laws the English did not deny, but they had done so at the sufferance of the sovereign legislative power, Parliament.

Given these ideas and the long tradition out of which they had sprung, one can sympathize with the British failure to follow the colonists' reasoning (which had not yet evolved into a specific proposal for constitutional reform). But most responsible British officials refused even to listen to the American argument.

The Townshend Acts

Despite the repeal of the Stamp Act, the British did not abandon the idea of taxing the colonies. If direct taxes were inexpedient, indirect ones like the Sugar Act certainly were not. To persuade Parliament to repeal the Stamp Act, some Americans (most notably Benjamin Franklin) had claimed that the colonists objected only to direct taxes. To draw such a distinction as a matter of principle was absurd, and in fact few colonists had done so. British leaders saw the absurdity but easily convinced themselves that Americans were making the distinction.

The government was hard pressed for funds to cover an annual budget of over £8.5 million. Therefore, in June 1767, the chancellor of the exchequer, Charles Townshend, introduced a series of new levies on glass, lead, paints, paper, and tea imported into the colonies. Townshend was a charming and witty man experienced in colonial administration, but he was something of a playboy (his nickname was Champagne Charlie), and he lacked both integrity and common sense. He liked to think of Americans as ungrateful children; he once said he would rather see the colonies turned into "Primitive Desarts" than treat them as equals. Townshend thought it "perfect nonsense" to draw a distinction between direct and indirect taxation, yet in his arrogance he believed the colonists were stupid enough to do so.

By this time the colonists were thoroughly on guard, and they responded quickly to the Townshend levies with a new boycott of British goods. In addition they made elaborate efforts to stimulate colonial manufacturing. By the end of 1769 imports from the mother country had been almost halved. Meanwhile, administrative measures enacted along with the Townshend duties were creating more ill will. A Board of Customs Commissioners, with headquarters in Boston, took charge of enforcing the trade laws, and new vice-admiralty courts were set up at Halifax, Boston, Philadelphia, and Charleston to handle violations. These courts operated without juries, and the new commissioners proved to be a gang of rapacious racketeers who systematically attempted to obtain judgments against honest merchants in order to collect the huge forfeitures—one-third of the value of ship and cargo—that were their share of all seizures.

The struggle forced Americans to do some deep thinking about both American and imperial political affairs. The colonies' common interests and growing economic and social interrelationships probably made some kind of union inevitable. Trouble with England speeded the process. In 1765 the Stamp Act Congress had brought the delegates of nine colonies to New York. Now, in 1768, the Massachusetts General Court took the next step. It sent the legislatures of the other colonies a "Circular Letter" expressing the "humble opinion" that the Townshend Acts "imposing Duties on the People . . . with the sole & express purpose of raising a Revenue are Infringements of their natural & constitutional Rights." The question of the limits of British power in America was much debated, and this too was no doubt inevitable, again because of change and growth. As the colonies matured, the balance of Anglo-American power *had* to shift or the system would become tyrannical. Even in the late 17th century the assumptions that led Parliament to pass the Declaratory Act would have been unrealistic. By 1766 they were absurd.

After the passage of the Townshend Acts, John Dickinson, a Philadelphia lawyer, wrote a series of *Letters from a Farmer in Pennsylvania to the Inhabitants of the British Colonies.* Dickinson considered himself a loyal British subject trying to find a solution to

In Copley's flattering portrait painted in 1771, Samuel Adams points to the Massachusetts charter as if reminding Great Britain of the colonists' rights.

colonial troubles. "Let us behave like dutiful children, who have received unmerited blows from a beloved parent," he wrote. Nevertheless, he stated plainly that while Parliament was sovereign, it had no right to tax the colonies, though it might collect incidental revenues in the process of regulating commerce.

Some Americans were much more radical than Dickinson. Samuel Adams of Boston, a genuine revolutionary agitator, believed by 1768 that Parliament had no right at all to legislate for the colonies. If few were ready to go that far, fewer still accepted the reasoning behind the Declaratory Act.

The British ignored American thinking. The Massachusetts Circular Letter had been framed in moderate language and clearly reflected the convictions of most of the people in the Bay Colony, yet when news of it reached England, the secretary of state for the colonies, Lord Hillsborough, ordered the governor to dissolve the legislature. Two regiments of British troops were transferred from the frontier to Boston, part of the aforementioned policy of bringing the army closer to the centers of colonial unrest.

The Boston Massacre

These acts convinced more Americans that the British were conspiring to destroy their liberties. Bostonians found it galling that with the country at peace and no enemy in sight, Redcoats should patrol their streets and (still worse) compete with them for scarce jobs when off duty.

Crowding 4,000 tough British soldiers into a town of 16,000 people, many of them as capable of taking care of themselves when challenged as any Redcoat, was a formula for disorder. How many scuffles and minor riots took place in waterfront taverns and darkened alleys during the winter of 1770 is lost to history. But on March 5, 1770, real trouble erupted. Late that afternoon a crowd of idlers began tossing snowballs at a company of Redcoats guarding the Custom House. Some of these missiles had been carefully wrapped around suitably sized rocks. Gradually the crowd increased in size and its mood grew meaner. The soldiers panicked and began firing their muskets. When the smoke cleared, five Bostonians lay dead and dying on the bloody ground.

This so-called Boston massacre infuriated the populace. The violence played into the hands of radicals like Samuel Adams. But just as at the time of the Stamp Act riots, cooler heads prevailed. Announcing that he was "defending the rights of man and unconquerable truth," John Adams volunteered his services to make sure the soldiers got a fair trial. Most were acquitted; the rest were treated leniently by the standards of the day. In Great Britain, confrontation also gave way to adjustment. In April 1770 all the Townshend duties except the threepenny tax on tea were repealed. The tea tax was maintained as a matter of principle.

"A peppercorn in acknowledgment of the right was of more value than millions without it," one British peer declared smugly—a glib fallacy.

At this point the nonimportation movement collapsed; although the boycott on tea was continued, many merchants imported British tea and paid the tax too. "Drank green tea," one patriot wrote in describing an afternoon at the merchant John Hancock's. "From Holland, I hope, but don't know."

A kind of postmassacre truce settled over Boston and the rest of British America. During the next two years no serious crisis erupted. Imports of British goods were nearly 50 percent higher than before the nonimportation agreement. So long as the British continued to be conciliatory, the colonists seemed satisfied with their place in the empire.

Paul Revere's engraving of the Boston Massacre was potent propaganda fully exploited by the Boston radicals. Many copies were made. His view of a deliberately ordered, concerted volley fired into a group of innocent citizens bore slight resemblance to fact. At the trial of the British soldiers, the jury was warned against "the prints exhibited in our houses" that added "wings to fancy." Two soldiers were punished mildly, the rest acquitted.

The Pot Spills Over

In 1772 this informal truce ended and new troubles broke out. The first was plainly the fault of the colonists involved. Early in June the British patrol boat *Gaspee* ran aground in Narragansett Bay, south of Providence, while pursuing a suspected smuggler. The *Gaspee's* commander, Lieutenant Dudingston, had antagonized everyone in the area by his officiousness and zeal; that night a gang of local people boarded the helpless *Gaspee* and put it to the torch. This action was clearly criminal, but when the British attempted to bring the culprits to justice no one would testify against them. The British, frustrated and angry, were strengthened in their conviction that the colonists were uterly lawless.

Then Thomas Hutchinson, now governor of Massachusetts, announced that henceforth the Crown rather than the local legislature would pay his salary. Since control over the salaries of royal officials gave the legislature a powerful hold on them, this development was disturbing. Colonial suspicions of British motives mounted again, especially after it was revealed that judges would also be paid by the London government. Groups of radicals formed "committees of correspondence" and stepped up communications with one another, planning joint action in case of trouble.

The Tea Act Crisis

In the spring of 1773 an entirely unrelated event precipitated the final crisis. The British East India Company held a monopoly of all trade between India and the rest of the empire. This monopoly had yielded fabulous returns, but decades of corruption and inefficiency together with heavy military expenses in recent years had weakened the company until it was almost bankrupt.

Among the assets of this venerable institution were some 17 million pounds of tea stored in English warehouses. The decline of the American market, a result first of the boycott and then of the smuggling of cheaper Dutch tea, partly accounted for the glut. Normally, East India Company tea was sold to English wholesalers. They in turn sold it to American wholesalers, who distributed it to local merchants for sale to the consumer. A substantial British tax was levied on the tea as well as the threepenny Townshend duty. Now Lord North, the new prime minister, decided to remit the British tax and to allow the company to sell directly in America through its own agents. The savings would permit a sharp reduction of the retail price and at the same time yield a nice profit to the company. The Townshend tax was retained, however, to preserve (as Lord North said when the East India Company directors suggested its repeal) the principle of Parliament's right to tax the colonies.

The company then shipped 1,700 chests of tea to colonial ports. Though the idea of high-quality tea offered at bargain prices was tempting, after a little thought nearly everyone in America appreciated the dangers involved in buying it. If Parliament could grant the East India Company a monopoly of the tea trade, it could parcel out all or any part of American commerce to whomever it pleased. More important, the act appeared utterly diabolical, a dastardly trick to trap them into paying the tea tax. The plot seemed obvious: the real price of Lord North's tea was American submission to parliamentary taxation.

Public indignation was so great in New York and Philadelphia that when the tea ships arrived, the authorities ordered them back to England without attempting to unload. The tea could only be landed "under the Protection of the Point of the Bayonet and Muzzle of the Cannon," the governor of New York reported. "Even then," he added, "I do not see how the Sales or Consumption could be effected."

The situation in Boston was different. The tea ship *Dartmouth* arrived on November 27. The radicals, marshaled by Sam Adams, were determined to prevent it from landing its cargo; Governor Hutchinson was equally determined to collect the tax and enforce the law. For days the town seethed. Crowds milled in the streets, harangued by Adams and his friends, while the *Dartmouth* and two later arrivals swung with the tides on their moorings. Then, on the night of December 16, as Hutchinson was preparing to seize the tea for nonpayment of the duty, a band of colonists disguised as Indians rowed out to the ships and dumped the hated tea chests in the harbor.

The destruction of the tea was a serious crime and it was obvious that a solid majority of the people of Boston approved of it. The painted "Patriots" who jettisoned the chests were a veritable cross section of society, and a huge crowd gathered at wharfside and cheered them on. The British burned with indignation when news of the "Tea Party" reached London. People talked (fortunately it was only talk) of flattening Boston with heavy artillery. Nearly everyone, even such a self-described British friend of the colonists as Edmund Burke, agreed that the colonists must be taught a lesson. George III himself said, "We must master them or totally leave them to themselves." What particularly infuriated the British was the certain knowledge that no American jury would render a judgment against the criminals; the memory of the *Gaspee* affair was fresh in everyone's mind in England, as undoubtedly it was in the minds of those Bostonians who, wearing the thinnest of disguises, brazenly destroyed the tea.

BOSTON, *December* 2, 1773.

WHEREAS it has been reported that a Permit will be given by the Cuſtom-Houſe for Landing the Tea now on Board a Veſſel laying in this Harbour, commanded by Capt. HALL: THIS is to Remind the Publick, That it was ſolemnly voted by the Body of the People of this and the neighbouring Towns aſſembled at the Old-South Meeting-Houſe on Tueſday the 30th Day of *November*, that the ſaid Tea never ſhould be landed in this Province, or pay one Farthing of Duty: And as the aiding or aſſiſting in procuring or granting any ſuch Permit for landing the ſaid Tea or any other Tea ſo circumſtanced, or in offering any Permit when obtained to the Maſter or Commander of the ſaid Ship, or any other Ship in the ſame Situation, muſt betray an inhuman Thirſt for Blood, and will alſo in a great Meaſure accelerate Confuſion and Civil War: This is to aſſure ſuch public Enemies of this Country, that they will be conſidered and treated as Wretches unworthy to live, and will be made the firſt Victims of our juſt Reſentment.

The PEOPLE.

N. B. Captain *Bruce* is arrived laden with the ſame deteſtable Commodity; and 'tis peremptorily demanded of him, and all concerned, that they comply with the ſame Requiſitions.

The inflammatory handbill shown here, attributing to the "Enemies of this Country" an "inhuman Thirst for Blood," typified the propaganda that flooded Boston from the presses of the Sons of Liberty during the tea crisis.

From Resistance to Revolution

Parliament responded in the spring of 1774 by passing the Coercive Acts. The Boston Port Act closed the harbor of Boston to all commerce until its citizens paid for the tea. The Administration of Justice Act provided for the transfer of cases to courts outside Massachusetts when the governor felt that an impartial trial could not be had within the colony. The Massachusetts Government Act revised the colony's charter drastically, strengthening the power of the governor, weakening that of the local town meetings, making the council appointive rather than elective, and changing the method by which juries were selected. These were unwise laws—they cost Great Britain an empire. All of them, and especially the Port Act, were unjust laws as well. Parliament was punishing the entire community for the crimes of individuals. These were acts of tyranny, a denial of English principles of justice.

The Americans named the laws (together with a new, more extensive Quartering Act and the Quebec Act, an unrelated measure that attached the area north of the Ohio River to Canada and gave the region an authoritarian, centralized government) the Intolerable Acts. That the British answer to the crisis was coercion the Americans found unendurable. The result was revolution.

Who must bear the blame for the rupture? Both sides in part, but the major share belongs on British shoulders. Although no one had thought it through in detail, the Americans were trying to work out a federal system with certain powers centered in London and others in the colonial capitals. Nearly every colonist was willing to see Great Britain continue to control, or at least regulate, such things as foreign relations, commercial policy, and other matters of general American interest. Parliament, however—and in the last analysis George III and most Britons—insisted that their authority over the colonies was unlimited. Behind their stubbornness lay the arrogant psychology of the European: "*Colonists are inferior. . . . We own you.*"

Lord North directed the Coercive Acts at Massachusetts alone because he thought that the other colonies, profiting from the discomfiture of Massachusetts, would not intervene, and because of the British tendency to think of the colonies as separate units connected only through London. His strategy failed because his assumption was incorrect: the colonies began at once to act in concert.

In June 1774 Massachusetts called for a meeting of delegates from all the colonies to consider common action. This First Continental Congress met at Philadelphia in September; only Georgia failed to send delegates. Many points of view were represented, but even the so-called conservative proposal, introduced by Joseph Galloway of Pennsylvania, called for a thorough overhaul of the empire. Galloway suggested an *American* government, consisting of a president general appointed by the king and a grand council chosen by the colonial assemblies, that would manage intercolonial affairs and possess a veto over parliamentary acts affecting the colonies.

This was not what the majority wanted. Pro-

A British cartoon shows Bostonians, caged by the Port Act of 1774, receiving sustenance from residents of the neighboring colonies.

Among the positions espoused by the First Continental Congress was a resolution to boycott British goods and to cease exports to the empire.

longed thought and discussion, and sporadic outbursts of violence, had produced a marked shift in opinion. If taxation without representation was tyranny, so was all legislation. Therefore Parliament had no right to legislate in any way for the colonies. James Wilson, born in Scotland and a resident of America for less than a decade, made the argument in a pamphlet, *Considerations on the . . . Legislative Authority of the British Parliament,* published in the summer of 1774. "All the different members of the British empire are distinct states, independent of each other, but connected together under the same sovereign," Wilson insisted. John Adams, while prepared to *allow* Parliament to regulate colonial trade, now believed that Parliament had no inherent right to control it. "The foundation . . . of all free government," he declared, "is a right in the people to participate in their legislative council." Americans "are entitled to a free and exclusive power of legislation in their several provincial legislatures."

Propelled by the reasoning of Wilson, Adams, and others, the Congress passed a declaration of grievances and resolves that amounted to a complete condemnation of Britain's actions since 1763. A Massachusetts proposal that the people take up arms to defend their rights was endorsed. The delegates also organized a "Continental Association" to boycott British goods and to stop all exports to the empire. To enforce this boycott, committees were appointed locally "to observe the conduct of all persons touching this association" and to expose violators to public scorn.

To the extent that the Continental Congress reflected the views of the majority—there is no reason to suspect that it did not—it may be said that by the fall of 1774 the American Revolution had already begun. The committees set up to enforce the boycott were, in a sense, extralegal governments. Americans had decided that drastic changes must be made. Fumblingly yet inexorably, they were becoming aware of their common interests, their *Americanism.* It was not merely a question of mutual defense against the threat of British power, not only (in Franklin's aphorism) a matter of hanging together lest they hang separately. A nation was being born.

Looking back many years later, one of the delegates to the First Continental Congress made just these points. He was John Adams of Massachusetts, and he said: "The revolution was complete, in the minds of the people, and the Union of the colonies, before the war commenced."

SUPPLEMENTARY READING

Titles marked with an asterisk have been published in paperback.

The fullest analysis of the British imperial system can be found in the early volumes of L. H. Gipson's **British Empire Before the American Revolution** (1936–1968), while the British political system is described in L. B. Namier, **The Structure of Politics at the Accession of George III*** (1929) and **England in the Age of the American Revolution*** (1930). For a briefer account, see J. H. Plumb, **England in the 18th Century*** (1950). See also J. A. Henretta, **Salutary Neglect** (1972), and Michael Kammen, **Empire and Interest** (1974). J. P. Greene, **The Quest for Power: The Lower Houses of Assembly in the Southern Royal Colonies*** (1963), describes how the colonists extended their control of political affairs.

The best study of mercantilism is Eli Heckscher, **Mercantilism** (1935); the fullest analysis of the Navigation Acts is G. L. Beer, **The Origins of the British Colonial System** (1908) and **The Old Colonial System** (1912). O. M. Dickerson, **The Navigation Acts and the American Revolution*** (1951), claims that mercantilism did not injure the colonial economy, but L. A. Harper, **The English Navigation Laws** (1939), concludes that it did. C. P. Nettels, **The Money Supply of the American Colonies Before 1720** (1934), is an important study.

The colonial wars are described in H. H. Peckham, **The Colonial Wars*** (1963), but see also Fred Anderson, **A People's Army: Massachusetts Soldiers and Society in the Seven Years' War** (1984). On the French and Indian War, L. H. Gipson's multivolume work is particularly useful. Washington's role receives full treatment in Volume II of D. S. Freeman, **George Washington** (1948). On the problems posed for the British by the acquisition of French Canada, see T. P. Abernethy, **Western Lands and the American Revolution** (1937), and J. M. Sosin, **Whitehall and the Wilderness** (1961).

On the causes of the Revolution, two brief treatments are L. H. Gipson, **The Coming of the Revolution*** (1954), and E. S. Morgan, **The Birth of the Republic*** (1956), a better-balanced analysis. Fuller discussions can be found in Merrill Jensen, **The Founding of a Nation** (1968), in J. C. Miller, **Origins of the American Revolution*** (1943), a most entertaining volume, and in Bernhard Knollenberg, **Origin of the American Revolution*** (1960), which is more argumentative but at some points more penetrating. Bernard Bailyn's **The Ideological Origins of the American Revolution*** (1967) and **The Origins of American Politics*** (1968) are brilliant analyses of the political thinking and political structure of 18th-century America, while his edition of the **Pamphlets of the American Revolution** (1965) should be sampled by every student. G. B. Nash, **The Urban Crucible*** (1979), contains valuable data on political, social, and economic conditions in the largest towns, which Nash calls "crucibles of revolutionary agitation." See also Pauline Maier's **From Resistance to Revolution** (1972) and **The Old Revolutionaries** (1980) and A. F. Young (ed.), **The American Revolution: Explorations in the History of American Radicalism*** (1976).

Important special studies of the period include E. S. and H. M. Morgan, **The Stamp Act Crisis*** (1953), B. W. Labaree, **The Boston Tea Party*** (1964), John Shy, **Toward Lexington: The Role of the British Army in the Coming of the American Revolution*** (1965), J. M. Sosin, **Agents and Merchants: British Colonial Politics and the Origins of the American Revolution** (1965), and M. G. Kammen, **A Rope of Sand: The Colonial Agents, British Politics, and the American Revolution** (1968).

The first of several time lines in this volume appears on pages 116–117. (There are seven time lines in the combined volume; Volumes One and Two each have four.) These time lines are designed to convey in graphic form the relationships over time among key events and notable people, as shown in distinct, chronologically parallel areas of historical development. Each time line is laid out so that it can be read across or down. To read down the time line on a specific date, use a ruler or the edge of a piece of paper.

The dark red center band lists the reigns of English monarchs or the terms of U.S. presidents. It serves as an anchor. Apart from the center band, no two time lines give exactly the same information, but the top and bottom event lines carry identical date scales. The first time line spans 200 years; the others span a century or less. Between the center band and the upper and lower event lines are "lifelines," which often cite prominent world or national figures at the upper level and local or more private figures at the lower level. Within some lifelines there are partitions marking off the span of time during which those particular people fulfilled their most well-known function (for example, as Supreme Court justice).

TIME LINE 1 ▪ Imperial Struggles and Colonial Tumults in English North America, 1575–1775

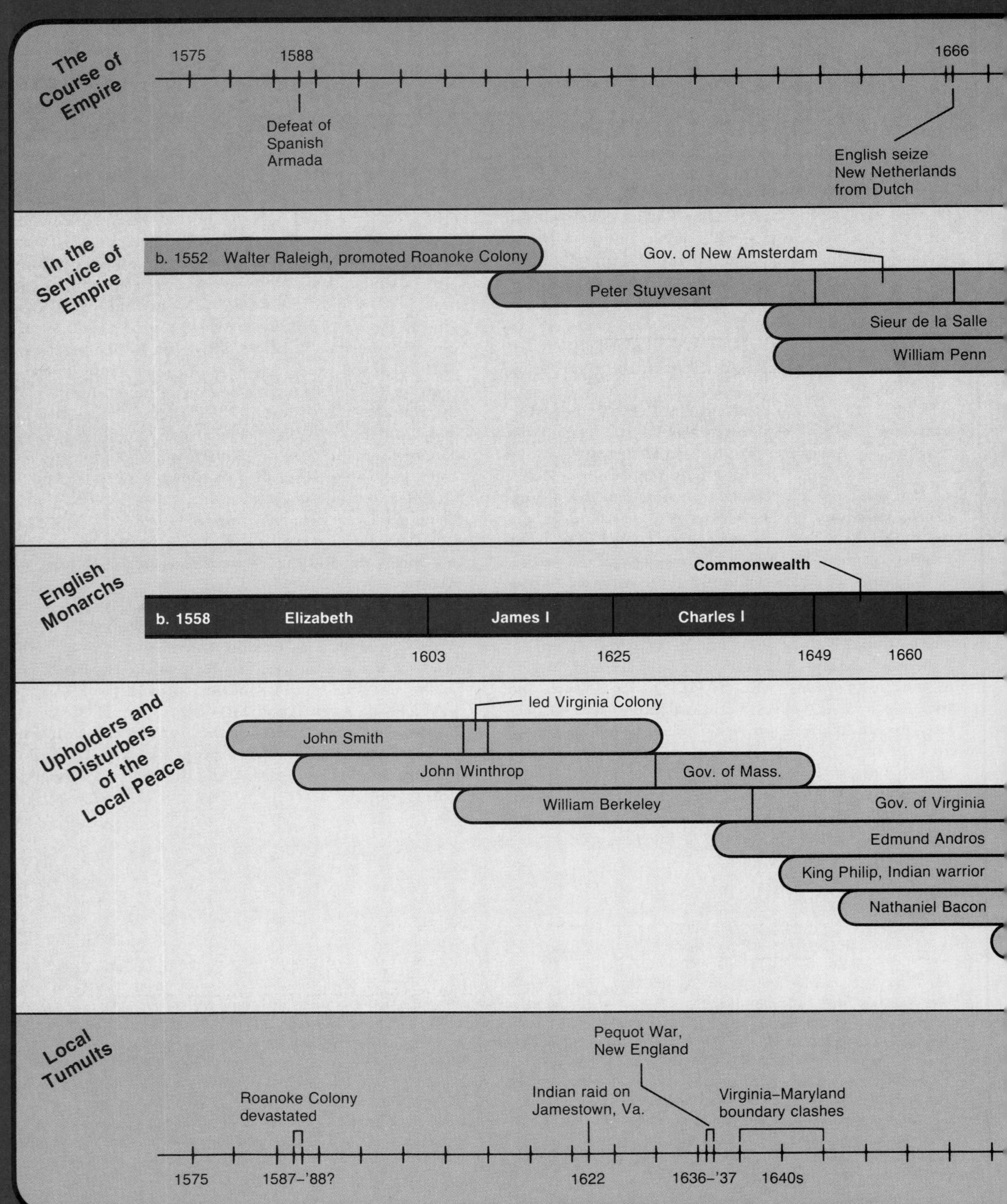

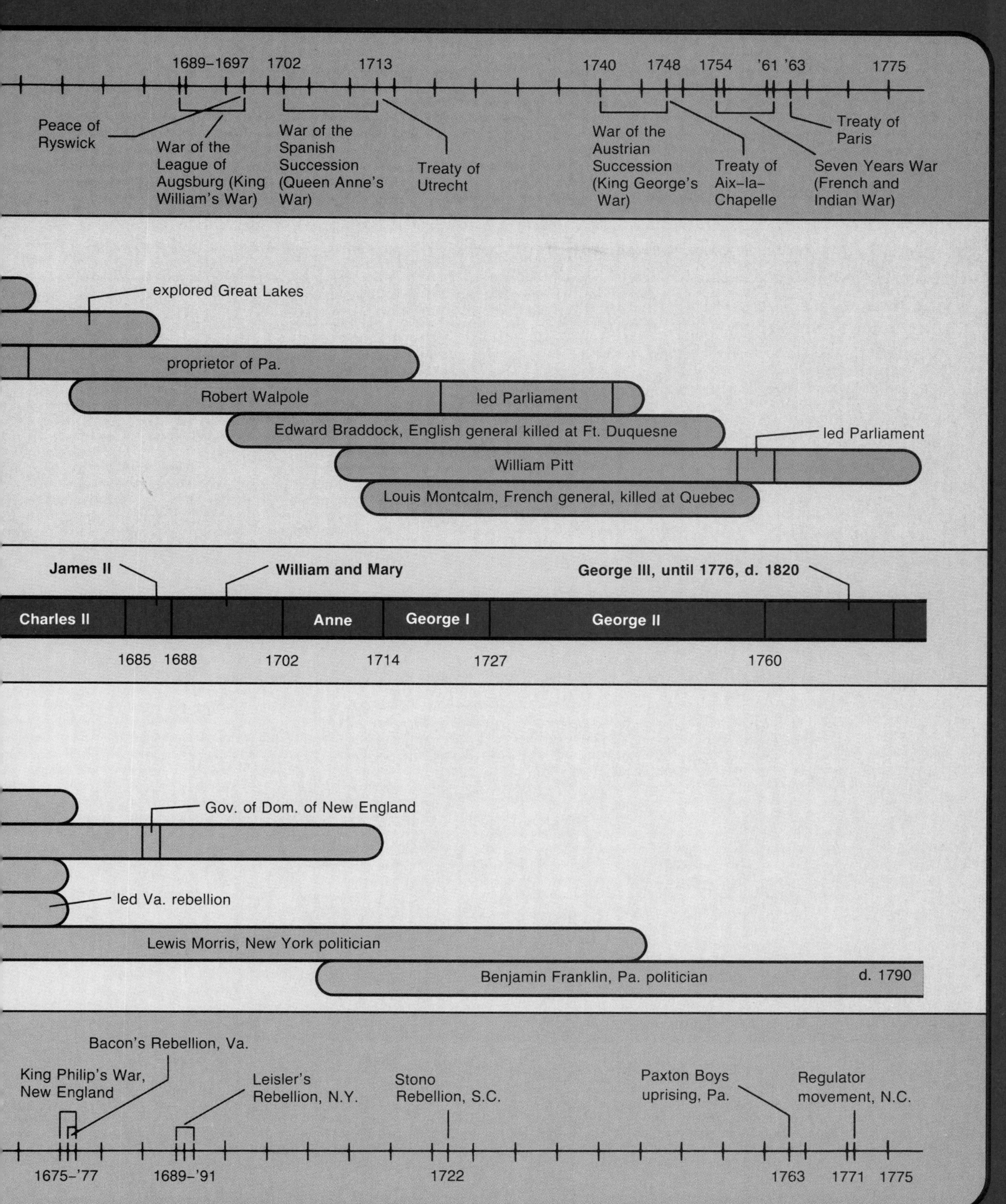
1689–1697
1702
1713
1740
1748
1754
'61
'63
1775
Peace of Ryswick
War of the League of Augsburg (King William's War)
War of the Spanish Succession (Queen Anne's War)
Treaty of Utrecht
War of the Austrian Succession (King George's War)
Treaty of Aix-la-Chapelle
Treaty of Paris
Seven Years War (French and Indian War)
explored Great Lakes
proprietor of Pa.
Robert Walpole
led Parliament
Edward Braddock, English general killed at Ft. Duquesne
led Parliament
William Pitt
Louis Montcalm, French general, killed at Quebec
James II
William and Mary
George III, until 1776, d. 1820
Charles II
Anne
George I
George II
1685
1688
1702
1714
1727
1760
Gov. of Dom. of New England
led Va. rebellion
Lewis Morris, New York politician
Benjamin Franklin, Pa. politician
d. 1790
Bacon's Rebellion, Va.
King Philip's War, New England
Leisler's Rebellion, N.Y.
Stono Rebellion, S.C.
Paxton Boys uprising, Pa.
Regulator movement, N.C.
1675–'77
1689–'91
1722
1763
1771
1775

4
The American Revolution

By referring the matter from argument to arms, a new era for politics is struck; a new method of thinking hath arisen.
THOMAS PAINE, Common Sense, *1776*

The actions of the First Continental Congress led the British authorities to force a showdown with their bumptious colonial offspring. "The New England governments are in a state of rebellion," George III announced. "Blows must decide whether they are to be subject to this country or independent." Already General Thomas Gage, veteran of Braddock's ill-fated expedition against Fort Duquesne and now commander in chief of all British forces in North America, had been appointed governor of Massachusetts. New redcoated regiments poured into Boston, camping on the town common once peacefully reserved for the citizens' cows. Parliament echoed with demands for a show of strength in America. General James Grant announced that with a thousand men he "would undertake to go from one end of America to the other, and geld all the males, partly by force and partly by a little coaxing." Some opposed the idea of crushing the Americans, and others believed that it could not be easily managed, but they were a small minority. The House of Commons listened to Edmund Burke's magnificent and sensible speech on conciliating the colonies and then voted 270 to 78 against him.

"The Shot Heard Round the World"

The decision to use troops against Massachusetts was made in January 1775, but the order did not reach General Gage until April. In the interim both sides were active. Parliament voted new troop levies, declared Massachusetts to be in a state of rebellion, and closed the Newfoundland fisheries and all seaports except those in Great Britain and the British West Indies, first to the New England colonies and then to most of the others. The Massachusetts Patriots, as they were now calling themselves, formed an extralegal provincial assembly, reorganized the militia, and began training "Minute Men" and other fighters. Soon companies armed with anything that would shoot were drilling on town commons throughout Massachusetts and in other colonies too.

When Gage received his orders on April 14, he acted swiftly. The Patriots had been accumulating arms at Concord, some 20 miles west of Boston. On the night of April 18 Gage dispatched 700 crack troops to seize these supplies. The Patriots were forewarned. Paul Revere set out on his famous ride to alert the countryside and warn John Hancock and Sam Adams, leaders of the provincial assembly, whose arrests had been ordered. When the Redcoats reached Lexington early the next morning, they found the common occupied by about 70 Minute Men. After an argument the Americans began to withdraw. Then someone fired a shot. There was a flurry of gunfire and the Minute Men fled, leaving eight of their number dead.

The British marched on to Concord, where they destroyed whatever supplies the Patriots had been unable to carry off. Now militiamen were pouring into the area from all sides. A hot skirmish at Concord's North Bridge forced the Redcoats to yield that position. Becoming alarmed, they began to march back to Boston. Soon they were being subjected to a withering fire from American irregulars along their line of march. A strange battle developed on a "field" 16 miles long and only a few hundred yards wide. Gage was obliged to send out an additional 1,500 men, and total disaster was avoided only by deploying skirmishers to root out snipers hiding in barns and farmhouses along the road to Boston. When the first day of the Revolutionary War ended, the British had sustained 273 casualties, the Americans fewer than 100.

For a brief moment of history tiny Massachusetts stood alone at arms against an empire that had humbled France and Spain. Yet Massachusetts assumed the offensive! The provincial government organized an expedition that captured Fort Ticonderoga and Crown Point, on Lake Champlain. The other colonies rallied quickly to the cause, sending reinforcements to Cambridge.

The Second Continental Congress

On May 10 (the day Ticonderoga fell) the Second Continental Congress met in Philadelphia. It was a distinguished group, more radical than the First Congress. Besides John and Sam Adams, Patrick Henry and Richard Henry Lee of Virginia, and Christopher Gadsden of South Carolina, all holdovers from the First Congress, there was Thomas Jefferson, a lanky, sandy-haired young planter from Virginia. Jefferson, an indifferent debater but a brilliant writer, had recently published *A Summary View of the Rights of British America,* an essay criticizing

In this engraving by Amos Doolittle, made from a sketch by Ralph Earle, British forces at the North Bridge in Concord fight a rear-guard action. A line of riflemen hold off the Massachusetts militia on the left, while the mass of the Redcoats retreat toward Boston.

the institution of monarchy and warning George III that "kings are the servants, not the proprietors of the people." Virginia had also sent George Washington, who could neither write well nor make good speeches, but who knew more than any other colonist about commanding men. He wore his buff and blue colonel's uniform, a not-too-subtle indication of his willingness to place his skill at the disposal of the Congress. The renowned Benjamin Franklin was a delegate and moving rapidly to the radical position. The Boston merchant John Hancock was chosen president of the Congress.

This Congress had no legal authority, yet it had to make agonizing decisions under the pressure of rapidly unfolding military events—with the future of every American depending on its actions. Delicate negotiations and honeyed words might yet persuade king and Parliament to change their ways, but precipitate, bold effort was essential to save Massachusetts.

In this predicament Congress naturally dealt first with the military crisis. It organized the forces gathering around Boston into a Continental Army and appointed George Washington commander in chief. After Washington and his assistants left for the front on June 23, the Congress turned to the task of requisitioning men and supplies.

Meanwhile, in Massachusetts the first major battle of the war had been fought. The British position on the peninsula of Boston was impregnable to direct assault, but high ground north and south, at Charlestown and Dorchester Heights, could be used to pound the city with artillery. When the Patriots seized Bunker Hill and Breed's Hill at Charlestown and set up defenses on the latter, Gage determined at once to drive them off. This was accomplished on June 17. Twice the Redcoats marched in close ranks up Breed's Hill, each time being driven back after suffering heavy losses. Stubbornly they came again, and this time they carried the redoubt, for the defenders had run out of ammunition. However, more than 1,000 Redcoats fell in a couple of hours, out of a force of some 2,500, while the Patriots lost only 400 men, most of them cut down by British bayonets after the hill was taken.

The British had cleared the Charlestown peninsula, but the victory was really the Americans', for they had proved themselves against professional soldiers and had exacted a terrible toll. "The day ended in glory," a British officer wrote, "but the loss was uncommon in officers for the number engaged."

The Battle of Bunker Hill, as it was called for no good reason, greatly reduced whatever hope remained for a negotiated settlement. The spilling of so much blood left each side determined to force the other's submission. The British recalled General Gage, replacing him with General Sir William Howe, a respected veteran of the French and Indian War, and George III formally proclaimed the colonies to be "in open rebellion." The Continental Congress dispatched one last plea to the king (the Olive Branch Petition), but this was a sop to the moderates. Immediately thereafter it adopted the Declaration of the Causes and Necessity of Taking Up Arms, which condemned everything the British had done since 1763. Americans were "a people attacked by unprovoked enemies"; the time had come to choose between "submission" to "tyranny" and "resistance by force." Congress then ordered an attack on Canada and created a special committee to seek foreign aid and another to buy munitions abroad. It authorized the outfitting of a navy under Commodore Esek Hopkins of Rhode Island.

Congress (and the bulk of the people) still hung back from a break with the Crown. To declare for independence would be to burn the last bridge, to become traitors in the eyes of the mother country. Aside from the word's ugly associations, everyone knew what happened to traitors when their efforts failed. It was sobering to think of casting off everything that being English meant: love of king, the traditions of a great nation, pride in the power of a mighty empire. "Where shall we find another Britain?" John Dickinson asked at the time of the Townshend Acts crisis. "Torn from the body to which we are united by religion, liberty, laws, affections, relation, language and commerce, we must bleed at every vein."

Then, too, rebellion might end in horrors worse than submission to *British* tyranny. The disturbances following the Stamp Act and the Tea Act had revealed an alarming fact about American society. The organizers of the protests, mostly persons of wealth and status, had thought in terms of "ordered resistance." They countenanced violence only as a means of forcing the British authorities to pay attention to their complaints. But protest meetings and mob actions had brought out every thief, every ne'er-do-well, every demagogue in the colonies. Property had been destroyed, not all of it owned by Loyalists and British officials. Too much exalted talk about "rights" and "liberties" might well give the poor (to say nothing of the slaves) an exaggerated impression of their importance. Finally, in a world where every country had some kind of monarch, could common people *really* govern themselves? The most ardent defender of American rights might well hesitate after considering all the implications of independence.

The Great Declaration

Independence was probably inevitable by the end of 1775. The belief that George III had been misled by evil or stupid advisers on both sides of the Atlantic became progressively more difficult to sustain. Mistrust of Parliament—indeed, of the whole of British society—grew apace.

Two events in January 1776 pushed the colonies a long step toward a final break. First came the news that the British were sending hired Hessian soldiers to fight against them. Colonists associated mercenaries with looting and rape and feared that the German-speaking Hessians would run amok among them. Such callousness on the part of Britain made reconciliation seem out of the question.

The second decisive event was the publication of *Common Sense.* This tract was written by Thomas Paine, a onetime English corsetmaker and civil servant turned pamphleteer, a man who had been in America scarcely a year. *Common Sense* called boldly for complete independence. It attacked not only

George III but the idea of monarchy itself. Paine applied the uncomplicated logic of the zealot to the recent history of America. Where the colonists had been humbly petitioning George III and swallowing their resentment when he ignored them, Paine called George a "Royal Brute" and "the hardened sullen-tempered Pharaoh of England." Where many Americans had wanted to control their own affairs but feared the instability of untried republican government, Paine stated plainly that monarchy was a corrupt institution. "A government of our own is our natural right," he insisted. "O! ye that love mankind! Ye that dare oppose not only tyranny but the tyrant, stand forth!"

Virtually everyone in the colonies must have read *Common Sense* or heard it explained and discussed. About 150,000 copies were sold in the critical period between January and July. Not every Patriot was impressed by Paine's arguments. John Adams dismissed *Common Sense* as "a tolerable summary of arguments which I had been repeating again and again in Congress for nine months." But no one disputed the impact of Paine's pamphlet on public opinion.

The tone of the debate changed sharply as Paine's slashing attack had its effect. The Continental Congress began to act more boldly. In March it unleashed privateers against British commerce; in April it opened American ports to foreign shipping; in May it urged the provincial assemblies to frame constitutions and establish state governments.

On June 7 Richard Henry Lee of Virginia introduced a resolution:

> RESOLVED: That these United Colonies are, and of right ought to be, free and independent States, that they are absolved from all allegiance to the British

A detail from John Trumbull's Declaration of Independence *portrays the five-man drafting committee presenting its handiwork to the Congress: from left, Massachusetts's John Adams, Connecticut's Roger Sherman, New York's Robert Livingston, Virginia's Thomas Jefferson, and Pennsylvania's Benjamin Franklin. Trumbull's skillful composition "ranks" the contributors, with Jefferson dominating.*

> Crown, and that all political connection between them and the State of Great Britain is, and ought to be, totally dissolved.

This momentous resolution was not passed at once; Congress first appointed a committee consisting of Thomas Jefferson, Benjamin Franklin, John Adams, Roger Sherman, and Robert Livingston to frame a suitable justification of independence. Livingston, a member of one of the great New York landowning families, was put on the committee in an effort to push New York toward independence. Sherman, a self-educated Connecticut lawyer and merchant, was a conservative who opposed parliamentary control over colonial affairs. Franklin, the best known of all Americans and an experienced writer, was a natural choice; so was John Adams, whose devotion to the cause of independence combined with his solid conservative qualities made him perhaps the typical man of the Revolution.

Thomas Jefferson was probably placed on the committee because politics required that a Virginian be included and because of his literary skill and quality of mind. Aside from writing *A Summary View of the Rights of British America,* he had done little to attract notice. At 33 he was the youngest member of the Continental Congress and was only marginally interested in its deliberations. He had been slow to take his seat in the fall of 1775, and he had gone home to Virginia before Christmas. He put off returning several times and arrived in Philadelphia only on May 14. Had he delayed another month, someone else would have written the Declaration of Independence. Nevertheless the committee asked Jefferson to prepare a draft. (Jefferson wanted John Adams to do it, but Adams refused, saying, "You can write ten times better than I can.") His draft, with a few amendments made by Franklin and Adams and somewhat toned down by the whole Congress, was officially adopted by the delegates on July 4, 1776.

Jefferson's Declaration consisted of two parts. The first was by way of introduction: it justified the abstract right of any people to revolt and described the theory on which the Americans based their creation of a new, republican government. The second, much longer, section was a list of the "injuries and usurpations" of George III, a bill of indictment explaining why the colonists felt driven to exercise the rights outlined in the first part of the document. Here Jefferson stressed George's interference with the functioning of representative government in America, his harsh administration of colonial affairs, his restrictions on civil rights, and his maintenance of troops in the colonies without their consent. The king was blamed for Parliament's efforts to tax the colonies and to restrict their trade. Jefferson sought to marshal every possible evidence of British perfidy and to make the king, rather than Parliament, the villain. He held George III responsible for many actions by subordinates that George had never deliberately authorized and for some things that never happened. He even blamed the king for the existence of slavery in the colonies, a charge Congress cut from the document not entirely because of its concern for accuracy. The long bill of particulars reads more like a lawyer's brief than a careful analysis; it holds relatively little interest for the modern reader except as an indication of how deeply Jefferson and his compatriots believed that the British were conspiring against their liberties.

Jefferson's general statement of the right of revolution, however, has inspired oppressed peoples all over the world for more than 200 years:

> We hold these truths to be self-evident, that all men are created equal, that they are endowed by their Creator with certain unalienable Rights, that among these are Life, Liberty and the pursuit of Happiness. That to secure these rights, Governments are instituted among Men, deriving their just powers from the consent of the governed, That whenever any Form of Government becomes destructive of these ends, it is the Right of the People to alter or to abolish it, and to institute new Government. . . .

Why has this statement had so much influence on modern history? Not because the thought was original with Jefferson. As John Adams later pointed out—Adams viewed his great contemporary with a mixture of affection, respect, and jealousy—the basic idea was commonplace among 18th-century liberals. "I did not consider it any part of my charge to invent new ideas," Jefferson explained, "but to place before mankind the common sense of the subject, in terms so plain and firm as to command their assent. . . . It was intended to be an expression of the American mind."

Revolution was not new, but the spectacle of a people solemnly explaining and justifying their right, in an orderly manner, to throw off their oppressors and establish a new system on their own authority was almost without precedent. Soon the French would be drawing upon this example in their revolution, and rebels everywhere have since done likewise. And if Jefferson did not create the concept, he gave it a nearly perfect form.

1776: The Balance of Forces

A formal declaration of independence merely cleared the way for tackling the problems of founding a new nation and maintaining it in defiance of Great Britain. Lacking both traditions and authority based in law, the Congress had to create political institutions and a new national spirit—all in the midst of war.

Always the military situation took precedence over other tasks, for a single disastrous setback might make everything else meaningless. At the start the Americans had what we might call the home-court advantage. They already possessed their lands (except for the few square miles occupied by British troops). Although thousands of colonists fought for George III, the British soon learned that to put down the American rebellion they would have to bring in men and supplies from bases on the other side of the Atlantic. This was a most formidable task. On the other hand, many colonists who favored independence lacked much *national* feeling. As in the wars against the French, some who would fight stoutly when their own district was threatened refused to help out at all when other regions came under British attack.

For a time, the initiative remained with the Americans. An expedition under General Richard Montgomery had captured Montreal in November 1775, and another small force under Benedict Arnold advanced to the gates of Quebec after a grueling march across the wilderness from Maine. Montgomery and Arnold attempted to storm the Quebec defenses on December 31, 1775, but were repulsed with heavy losses. Even so, the British troops in Canada could not drive the remnants of the American army—perhaps 500 men in all—out of the province until reinforcements arrived in the spring.

Certain long-run factors operated in America's favor. Although His Majesty's soldiers were brave and well disciplined, the army was as inefficient and ill directed as the rest of the British government. Whereas nearly everyone in Great Britain wanted to crack down on Boston after the Tea Party, many boggled at engaging in a full-scale war against all the colonies. Aside from a reluctance to spill so much blood, there was the question of expense. Finally, the idea of dispatching the cream of the British army to America while powerful enemies on the Continent still smarted from past defeats seemed risky. For all these reasons the British approached gingerly the task of subduing the rebellion. When Washington fortified Dorchester Heights overlooking Boston, General Howe withdrew his troops to Halifax rather than risk another Bunker Hill. On March 17, 1776, Washington marched his troops into the city. For the moment the 13 colony-states were clear of Redcoats.

Awareness of Britain's problems undoubtedly spurred the Continental Congress to the bold actions of the spring of 1776. However, on the very day that Congress voted for independence (July 2), General Howe was back on American soil, landing in force on Staten Island in New York harbor in preparation for an assault on the city. Soon Howe had at hand 32,000 well-equipped troops and a powerful fleet commanded by his brother, Richard, Lord Howe. Washington realized that if the British controlled New York City and the Hudson River they could "stop intercourse between the northern and southern Colonies, upon which depends the Safety of America."

Suddenly the full strength of the empire seemed to have descended on the Americans. Superior British resources (a population of 9 million to the colonies' 2.5 million, large stocks of war materials and the industrial capacity to boost them further, mastery of the seas, a well-trained and experienced army, a highly centralized and, when necessary, ruthless government) were now all too evident.

The demonstration of British might accentuated American military and economic weaknesses: both money and the tools of war were continually in short supply in a predominantly agricultural country. Many of Washington's soldiers were armed with weapons no more lethal than spears and tomahawks. Few had proper uniforms. Even

The troop count shown here includes militias as well as regular Continental army forces. Washington's troop strength varied greatly from month to month and year to year, and at times militias accounted for more than one-third of the total.

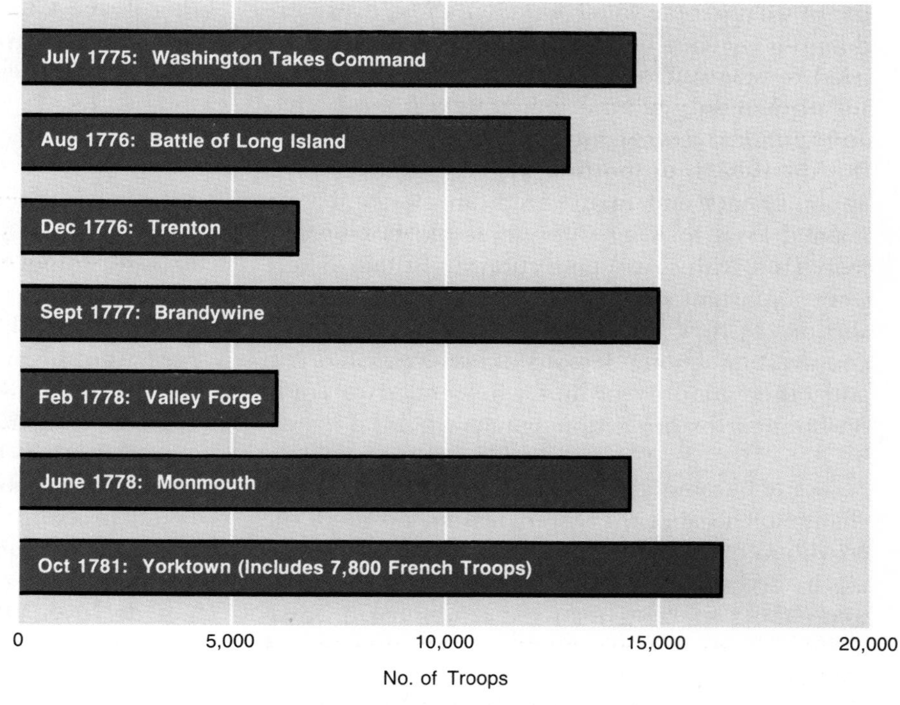

WASHINGTON'S TROOP STRENGTH

the most patriotic resisted conforming to the conventions of military discipline; the men hated drilling and all parade-ground formality.

Supply problems were handled inefficiently and often corruptly. Few officers knew much about such mundane but vital matters as how to construct and maintain proper sanitary facilities when large numbers of soldiers were camped at one place for extended periods of time. What was inelegantly known as "the Itch" afflicted soldiers throughout the war.

Loyalists

Behind the lines, the country was far from united. Whereas nearly all colonists had objected to British policies after the French and Indian War, many still hesitated to take up arms against the mother country. Even Massachusetts harbored many Loyalists, or Tories, as they were called; about 1,000 Americans fled Boston with General Howe, abandoning their homes rather than submit to the rebel army.

No one knows exactly how the colonists divided on the question of independence. John Adams's off-the-cuff estimate was that a third of the people were ardent Patriots, another third loyal to Great Britain, and the rest neutral or tending to favor whichever side seemed to be winning. This guess is probably as useful as any, though in keeping with Adams's character he may have understated the number who agreed with him and overstated those opposed to his position. Most historians think that about a fifth of the people were Loyalists and about two-fifths Patriots, but there are few hard figures to go by. What is certain is that large elements, perhaps a majority of the people, were more or less indifferent to the conflict or, in Tom Paine's famous phrase, were summer soldiers and sunshine patriots—they supported the Revolution when all was going well and lost their enthusiasm in difficult hours.

The divisions cut across geographic, social, and economic lines. Edward Countryman makes this clear in *A People in Revolution:* "The positions that people took grew out of the lives they had led and out of what people who counted in those lives were doing. . . . They became rebels or Tories or they tried to stay out of it by reference to the whole set of material, cultural, geographical, economic, and political complexities that had been their world." A high proportion of those holding royal appointments and many Anglican clergymen remained loyal to King George, as did numbers of merchants with close connections in Britain. There were important pockets of Tory strength in rural sections of New York, in the North Carolina back country, and among persons of non-English origin and other minority groups who tended to count on London for protection against the local majority.

Many became Tories simply out of distaste for change or because they were pessimistic about the condition of society and the possibility of improving it. "What is the whole history of human life," wrote the Tory clergyman and schoolmaster Jonathan Boucher of Virginia, "but a series of disappointments?" Still others believed that the actions of the British, however unfair and misguided, did not justify rebellion. Knowing that they possessed a remarkably free and equitable system of government, they could not stomach shedding blood merely to avoid paying a few new taxes or to escape from what they considered minor restrictions on their activities. "The Annals of no Country can produce an Instance of so virulent a Rebellion . . . originating from such trivial Causes," one Loyalist complained.

The Tories lacked organization. While Patriot leaders worked closely together, many of the Tory "leaders" did not even know one another. They had no central committee to lay plans or coordinate their efforts. When the revolutionaries took over a colony, some Tories fled; others sought the protection of the British army; others took up arms; others accommodated themselves silently to the new regime.

If the differences separating Patriot from Loyalist are unclear, feelings were nonetheless bitter. Individual Loyalists were often set upon by mobs, tarred and feathered, and otherwise abused. Some were thrown in jail for no legitimate reason; others were exiled, their property confiscated. Battles between Tory units and the Continental Army were often exceptionally bloody. "Neighbor was against neighbor, father against son and son against father," one Connecticut Tory reported. "He that would not thrust his own blade through his brother's heart was called an infamous villain."

Early Defeats

General Howe's campaign against New York brought to light another American weakness—the lack of military experience. Washington, expecting Howe to attack New York, had moved south to meet the threat, but both he and his men failed badly in this first major test. Late in August Howe crossed from Staten Island to Brooklyn. In the Battle of Long Island he easily outflanked and defeated Washington's army. Had he acted decisively, he could probably have ended the war on the spot, but Howe, who could not make up his mind whether to be a peacemaker or a conqueror, was not decisive. When he hesitated in consolidating his gains, Washington managed to withdraw his troops to Manhattan Island.

Howe could have trapped Washington simply by using his fleet to land troops on the northern end of Manhattan; instead he attacked New York City directly, leaving the Americans an escape route to the north. Again Patriot troops proved no match for British regulars. Though Washington threw his hat to the ground in a rage and threatened to shoot cowardly Connecticut soldiers as they fled the battlefield, he could not stop the rout and had to fall back on Harlem Heights in upper Manhattan. And once more Howe failed to pursue his advantage promptly.

Still Washington refused to see the peril in remaining on an island while the enemy commanded the surrounding waters. Only when Howe shifted a powerful force to Westchester, directly threatening his rear, did Washington move north to the mainland. Finally, after several narrow escapes, he crossed the Hudson River to New Jersey, where the British could not use their naval superiority against him.

The battles in and around New York City seemed to presage an easy British triumph. Yet somehow Washington salvaged a moral victory from these ignominious defeats. He learned rapidly; seldom thereafter did he place his troops in such vulnerable positions. And his men, in spite of repeated failure, had become an army. In No-

The events in and around New York, so nearly disastrous to Washington and his army, are detailed in this map.

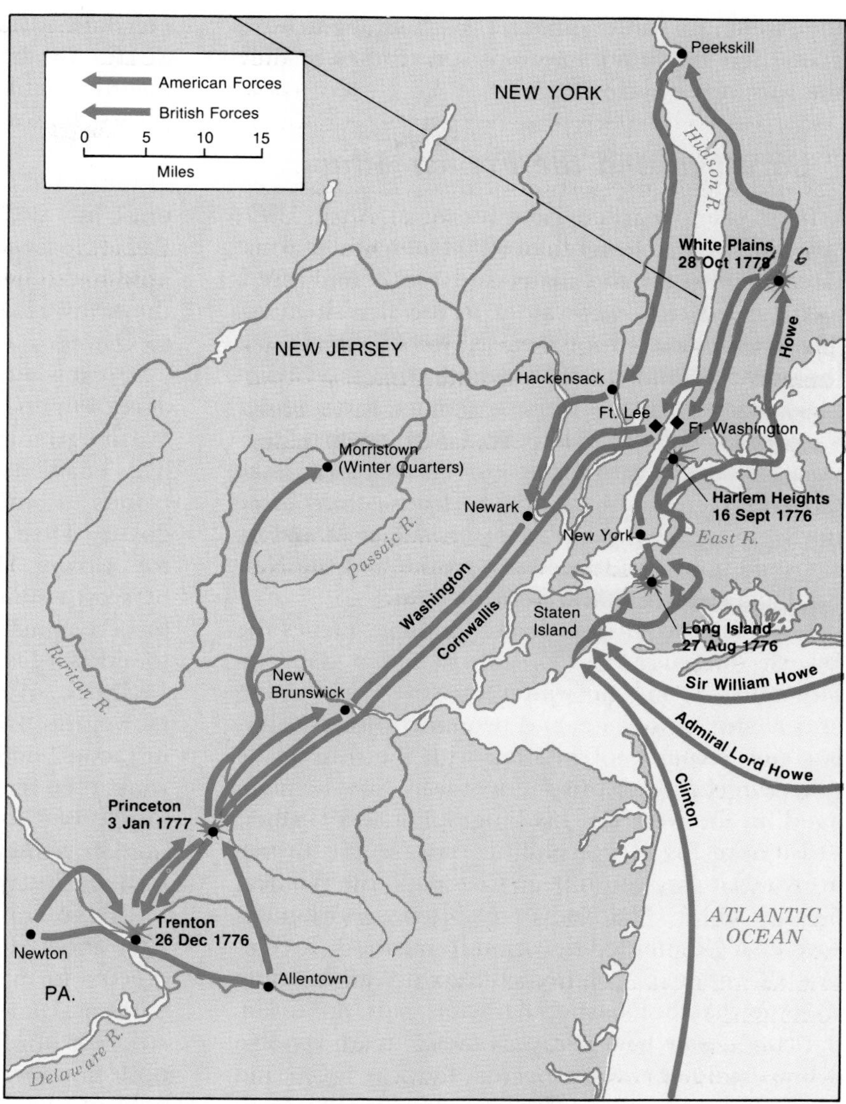

NEW YORK–NEW JERSEY CAMPAIGNS, 1776–1777

vember and December 1776 they retreated across New Jersey and into Pennsylvania. General Howe then abandoned the campaign, going into winter quarters in New York but posting garrisons at Trenton, Princeton, and other strategic points. The troops at Trenton were hated Hessian mercenaries, and Washington decided to attack them. He crossed the ice-clogged Delaware River with 2,400 men on Christmas night during a wild storm. The little army then marched 9 miles to Trenton, arriving at daybreak in the midst of a sleet storm. The Hessians were taken completely by surprise. Those who could fled in disorder; the rest—900 of them—surrendered.

The Hessians were first-class professional soldiers, probably the most competent troops in Europe at that time. The victory gave a boost to American morale. A few days later Washington outmaneuvered General Cornwallis, who had rushed to Trenton with reinforcements, and won another battle at Princeton. These engagements had little strategic importance, since both armies then went into winter quarters. Without them, however, there might not have been an army to resume the war in the spring.

Saratoga and the French Alliance

When spring reached New Jersey in April 1777, Washington had fewer than 5,000 men under arms. Great plans—far too many and too complicated, as it turned out—were afoot in the British camp. The strategy called for General John Burgoyne to lead a large army from Canada down Lake Champlain toward Albany while a smaller force under Lieutenant Colonel Barry St. Leger pushed eastward toward Albany from Fort Oswego on Lake Ontario. General Howe was to lead a third force north up the Hudson. Patriot resistance would be smashed between these three armies and the New England states isolated from the rest.

As a venture in coordinated military tactics the British campaign of 1777 was a fiasco. General Howe had spent the winter in New York wining and dining his officers and prominent local Loyalists and having a torrid affair with the wife of the officer in charge of prisoners of war. Now he managed, in the words of his biographer, Ira Gruber, "to ignore his responsibilities toward the British army advancing south from Canada." (Sir William, Gruber notes, "had never inspired subordinates with a single-minded devotion to business.") General "Gentleman Johnny" Burgoyne, a charming if somewhat bombastic character, part politician, part poet, part gambler, part ladies' man, yet also a brave soldier who respected and was loved and admired by his men, had begun his march from Canada in mid-June. By early July his army, which consisted of 500 Indians, 650 Loyalists, and 6,000 regulars, had captured Fort Ticonderoga, at the southern end of Lake Champlain. He quickly pushed beyond Lake George, but then bogged down. Burdened by a huge baggage train that included 138 pieces of generally useless artillery, more than 30 carts laden with his personal wardrobe and supply of champagne, and his mistress,* he could advance at but a snail's pace through the dense woods north of Saratoga. Patriot forces, mainly militia, impeded his way by felling trees across the forest trails.

St. Leger was also slow in carrying out his part of the grand design. He did not leave Fort Oswego until July 26, and when he stopped to besiege a Patriot force at Fort Stanwix, General Benedict Arnold had time to march west with 1,000 men from the army resisting Burgoyne and drive him back to Oswego.

Meanwhile, with magnificent disregard for the agreed-upon plan, Howe wasted time trying to trap Washington into exposing his army in New Jersey. This enabled Washington to send some of his best troops to buttress the militia units opposing Burgoyne. Then, just when St. Leger was setting out for Albany, Howe took the bulk of his army off by sea to attack Philadelphia, leaving only a small force commanded by General Sir Henry Clinton to aid Burgoyne.

When Washington moved south to oppose Howe, the Britisher taught him a series of lessons in tactics, defeating him at the Battle of Brandywine, then feinting him out of position and moving unopposed into Philadelphia. But by that time it was late September, and disaster was about to befall General Burgoyne.

The American forces under Philip Schuyler and later under Horatio Gates and Benedict Arnold had erected formidable defenses immediately south of Saratoga near the town of Stillwater. Burgoyne struck at this position twice and was thrown back both times with heavy losses. Each day more local militia swelled the American forces. Soon Burgoyne was under siege, his troops pinned down by withering fire from every direction, unable even to bury their dead. The only hope was General Clinton, who had finally started up the Hudson from New York. Clinton got as far as Kingston, about 80 miles below Saratoga, but on October 16 he decided to return to New York for reinforcements. The next day, at Saratoga, Burgoyne surrendered. Some 5,700 British prisoners were marched off to Virginia.

This overwhelming triumph changed the course and character of the war, for when news of the victory reached France, Louis XVI immediately recognized the United States. The French had been eager to stir up trouble between the Americans and the hated British since the 1760s. When the

* Many soldiers, enlisted men as well as officers, were accompanied by their wives or other women on campaigns. More than 2,000 accompanied the Burgoyne expedition. At one point Washington complained of "the multitude of women . . . especially those who are pregnant, or have children [that] clog upon every movement." Actually, women in 18th-century armies worked hard, doing most of the cooking, washing, and other "housekeeping" tasks.

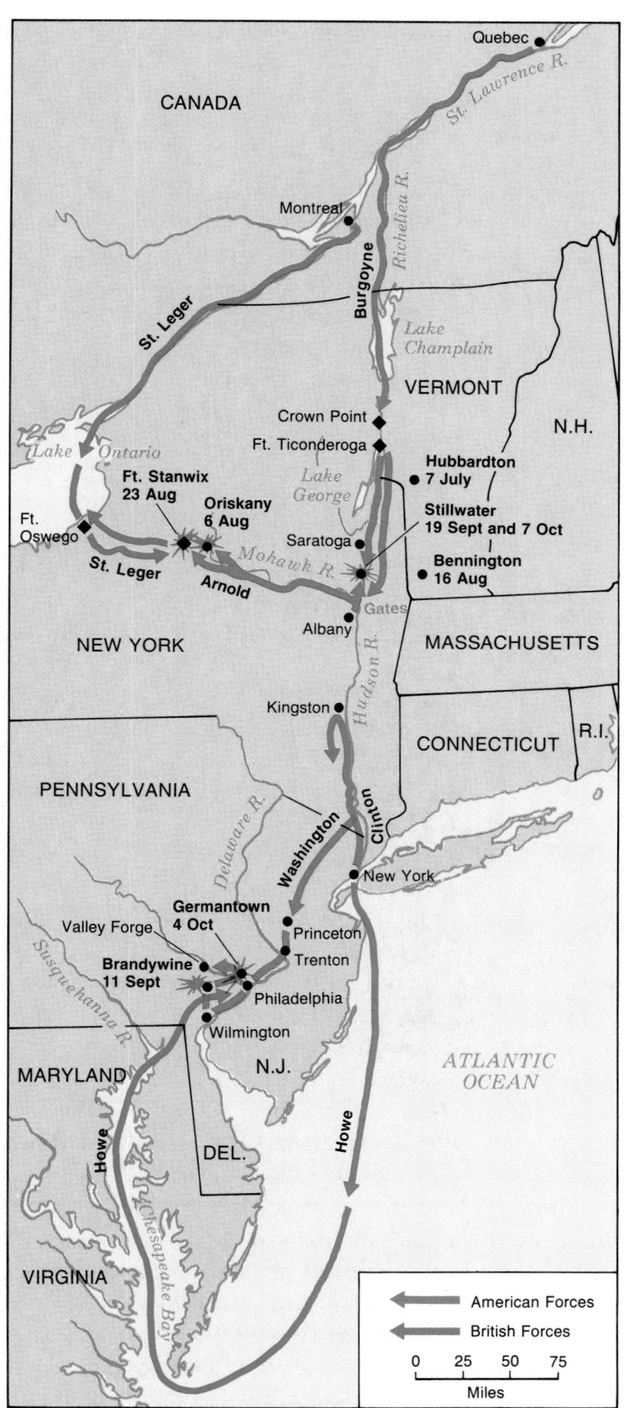

SARATOGA AND PHILADELPHIA CAMPAIGNS, 1777

Howe's attack on Philadelphia and Burgoyne's simultaneous fatal attempt at grand strategy are shown here. Lacking definite orders from London to participate in Burgoyne's campaign, and already resentful that his own strategic plans had been ignored, Howe set sail for the Chesapeake, leaving behind in New York a token force to cooperate with Burgoyne in the north.

fighting started they hastened to take advantage of it. In May 1776 the Comte de Vergennes, France's foreign minister, persuaded Louis XVI to authorize the expenditure of a million livres for munitions for America, and more was added the next year. Spain also contributed to the cause. Soon vital supplies were being funneled secretly to the rebels through a dummy company, Roderigue Hortalez et Cie.

After France was officially allied to the United States, Vergennes and three American commissioners in Paris, Benjamin Franklin, Arthur Lee, and Silas Deane, had drafted a commercial treaty and a formal treaty of alliance. The two nations agreed to make "common cause and aid each other mutually" should war "break out" between France and Great Britain. Meanwhile, France guaranteed "the sovereignty and independence absolute and unlimited" of the United States.

When the news of Saratoga reached England, Lord North realized that a Franco-American alliance was almost inevitable. To forestall it he was ready to give in on all the issues that had agitated the colonies before 1775. Both the Coercive Acts and the Tea Act would be repealed; Parliament would pledge never to tax the colonies.

Instead of implementing this proposal promptly, Parliament delayed until March 1778. Royal Peace Commissioners did not reach Philadelphia until June, a month after Congress had ratified the French treaty. The British proposals were icily rejected, and while the peace commissioners were still in Philadelphia war broke out between France and Great Britain.

The war, however, if no longer being lost, had yet to be won. After the Battle of Germantown, Washington had settled his army for the winter at Valley Forge, 20 miles northwest of Philadelphia. The army's supply system collapsed. Often the men had nothing to eat but "Fire Cake," a mixture of ground grain and water molded on a stick or in a pan and baked in the campfire. According to the Marquis de Lafayette, one of many European liberals who volunteered to fight on the American side, "the unfortunate soldiers . . . had neither coats, nor hats, nor shirts, nor shoes; their feet and legs froze till they grew black, and it was often necessary to amputate them."

To make matters worse, there was grumbling in Congress over Washington's failure to win victories and talk of replacing him as commander in chief with Horatio Gates, the "hero" of Saratoga. (In fact, Gates was an indifferent soldier, lacking in decisiveness and unable to instill confidence in his subordinates. "Historical accounts of the Saratoga campaign have given abundant reasons for the American victory other than the military skill of Horatio Gates," one of his biographers has confessed.)

As the winter dragged on, the Continental Army melted away. So many officers resigned that Washington was heard to say that he was afraid of "being left Alone with the Soldiers only." Since enlisted men could not legally resign, they deserted by the hundreds. Yet the army survived. Gradually the soldiers who remained became a tough, professional fighting force. Their spirit has been described by the historian Charles Royster as a "mixture of patriotism, resentment, and fatalism."

The War Moves South

Spring brought a revival of American hopes in the form of more supplies, new recruits, and, above all, word of the French alliance. In May the British replaced General Howe as commander with General Clinton, who decided to transfer his base back to New York. While Clinton was moving across New Jersey, Washington attacked him at Monmouth Court House. The fight was inconclusive, but the Americans held the field when the day ended and were able to claim a victory. Clinton marched on to New York.

Thereafter British strategy changed. Fighting in the northern states practically ceased. Instead, relying on sea power and the supposed presence of many Tories in the south, the British concentrated their efforts in South Carolina and Georgia. Savannah fell late in 1778 and most of the settled parts of Georgia were overrun during 1779. In

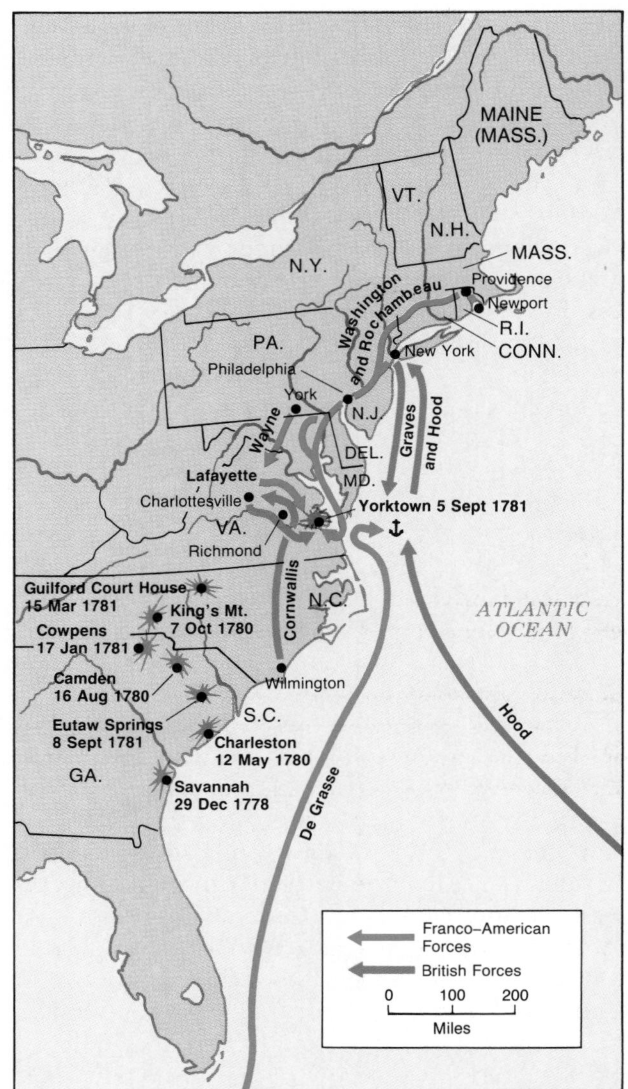

YORKTOWN AND THE WAR IN THE SOUTH, 1778–1781

In an era when communications were slow and erratic at best, the coordination between the American and French land and naval forces that sealed up Cornwallis in Yorktown was nothing short of remarkable.

1780 Clinton led a massive expedition against Charleston. When the city surrendered in May, more than 3,000 soldiers were captured, the most overwhelming American defeat of the war. Leaving General Cornwallis and some 8,000 men to carry on the campaign, Clinton sailed back to New York.

The Tories of South Carolina and Georgia came closer to meeting British expectations than did those of any other region. Nevertheless, the callous behavior of the British troops rapidly persuaded large numbers of hesitating citizens to join the Patriot cause. Guerrilla bands led by men like Francis Marion, the "Swamp Fox," and Thomas Sumter, after whom Fort Sumter, famous in the Civil War, was named, provided a nucleus of resistance in areas that had supposedly been subdued.

In June 1780 Congress placed the highly regarded Horatio Gates in charge of a southern army consisting of the irregular militia units and a hard core of Continentals transferred from Washington's command. Gates encountered Cornwallis at Camden, South Carolina. Foolishly, he entrusted a key sector of his line to untrained militiamen, who promptly panicked when the British charged with fixed bayonets. Gates suffered heavy losses and had to fall back. Congress then recalled him, sensibly permitting Washington to replace him with General Nathanael Greene, a first-rate officer.

A band of militiamen had trapped a contingent of Tories at King's Mountain and forced its surrender. Greene, avoiding a major engagement with Cornwallis's superior numbers, divided his troops and staged a series of raids on scattered points. In January 1781, at the Battle of Cowpens in northwestern South Carolina, General Daniel Morgan inflicted a costly defeat on Colonel Banastre Tarleton, one of Cornwallis's best officers. Cornwallis pursued Morgan hotly, but the American rejoined Greene and at Guilford Court House they inflicted heavy losses on the British. Then Cornwallis withdrew to Wilmington, North Carolina, where he could rely on the fleet for support and reinforcements. Greene's Patriots quickly regained control of the Carolina back country.

Victory at Yorktown

Seeing no future in the Carolinas and unwilling to vegetate at Wilmington, Cornwallis marched north into Virginia, where he joined forces with troops under Benedict Arnold. (Disaffected by what he considered unjust criticism of his generalship, Arnold had sold out to the British in 1780. He intended to betray the bastion of West Point on the Hudson River. The scheme was foiled when incriminating papers were found on the person of a British spy, Major John André. Arnold fled to the British and André was hanged.) As in the Carolina campaign, the British had numerical superiority at first but lost it rapidly when local militia and Continental forces concentrated against them. Cornwallis soon discovered that Virginia Tories were of little help in such a situation. "When a Storm threatens, our friends disappear," he grumbled.

General Clinton ordered Cornwallis to take up a defensive position at Yorktown, where he could be supplied by sea. Cornwallis objected; Yorktown, he said, was "an unhealthy swamp" where his army would be "liable to become a prey to a Foreign enemy with a temporary superiority at sea." But Clinton insisted.

It was a terrible mistake. The British navy in American waters far outnumbered American and French vessels, but the Atlantic is wide, and in those days communication was slow. The French had a fleet in the West Indies under Admiral De Grasse and another squadron at Newport, Rhode Island, where a French army was stationed. In the summer of 1781 Washington, De Grasse, and the Comte de Rochambeau, commander of French land forces, designed and carried out with an efficiency unparalleled in 18th-century warfare a complex plan to bottle up Cornwallis.

The British navy in the West Indies and at New York might have forestalled this scheme had it moved promptly and in force. But Admiral Sir George Rodney sent only part of his Indies fleet. As a result De Grasse, after a battle with a British fleet commanded by Admiral Thomas Graves, won control of the Chesapeake and cut Cornwallis off from the sea.

The next move was up to Washington, and this was his finest hour as a commander. He desperately wanted to attack the British base at New York, but at the urging of Rochambeau he agreed instead to strike at Yorktown. After tricking Clinton into thinking he was going to strike at New York, he pushed boldly south. In early September he reached Yorktown and joined up with an army commanded by Lafayette and troops from De Grasse's fleet. He soon had nearly 17,000 French and American veterans in position.

Cornwallis was helpless. He held out until October 17 and then asked for terms. On the 19th more

A French view of De Grasse's fleet blockading the bay at Yorktown. The French ships, in the right foreground, have long pennants streaming from their masts.

than 7,000 British soldiers marched out of their lines and laid down their arms while their band played "The World Turned Upside Down." Then the jubilant Lafayette ordered his military band to play "Yankee Doodle."

The Peace of Paris

The British gave up trying to suppress the rebellion after Yorktown, but the event that confirmed the existence of the United States as an independent nation was the signing of a peace treaty with Great Britain. Yorktown had been only one of a string of defeats suffered by British arms in the Mediterranean, the West Indies, Africa, and Asia. The national debt had doubled again since 1775. In March 1782 Lord North resigned after Parliament renounced all further efforts to coerce the colonies. At once the new ministry of Lord Rockingham attempted to negotiate a peace settlement with America.

The problem of peacemaking was complicated. The United States and France had pledged not to make a separate peace. Spain, at war with Great Britain since 1779, was allied with France but not with America. Although eager to profit at British expense, the Spanish hoped to limit American expansion beyond the Appalachians, for they had ambitions of their own in the eastern half of the Mississippi Valley. France, while ready enough to see America independent, did not want the new country to become *too* powerful; in a conflict of interest between America and Spain, France tended to support Spain.

The Continental Congress appointed John Adams, Benjamin Franklin, John Jay, Thomas Jefferson, and Henry Laurens as a commission to conduct peace talks. Franklin and Jay did most of the actual negotiating. Congress, grateful for French aid during the Revolution, had instructed the commissioners to rely on the advice of the Comte de Vergennes, subject only to the limitation that they must hold out at all costs for independence.

In Paris, however, the commissioners soon discovered that Vergennes was not the perfect friend of America that Congress believed him to be. When they did, they did not hesitate to violate their instructions. Vergennes "means to keep his hand under our chin to prevent us from drowning," Adams complained, "but not to lift our head out of the water." Franklin, perhaps because as a famous scientist and sage he was wined and dined by the cream of Paris and petted and fussed over by some of the city's most beautiful women, was neither aggressive nor suspicious enough to press fully the American point of view. John Jay, who had spent two years dealing with Spanish duplicity as unacknowledged American minister in Madrid, was more tough-minded. When he realized that Spain and France were less than entirely committed to American interests, he took Franklin aside and convinced him they must stop consulting Vergennes at every step. They hinted to the British representative, Richard Oswald, that they would consider a separate peace if it were a generous one and suggested that Great Britain would be far better off with America, a nation that favored free trade, in control of the trans-Appalachian region than with a mercantilist power like Spain.

The British government reacted favorably, authorizing Oswald "to treat with the Commissioners appointed by the Colonys, under the title of Thirteen United States." Soon the Americans were deep in negotiations with Oswald. They told Vergennes what they were doing but did not discuss details.

Oswald was cooperative, and the Americans drove a hard bargain. One scrap of conversation reveals the tenor of the talks.

> OSWALD: We can never be such damned sots as to disturb you.
>
> ADAMS: Thank you. . . . But nations don't feel as you and I do, and your nation, when it gets a little refreshed from the fatigues of the war, and when men and money become plentiful, and allies at hand, will not feel as it does now.
>
> OSWALD: We can never be such damned sots as to think of differing again with you.
>
> ADAMS: Why, in truth I have never been able to comprehend the reason why you ever thought of differing with us.

" 'Tis lost! irrecoverably lost!" cries John Bull as America flies away in the hands of the devil. Spain, France, and Holland chide the Briton for his negligence.

By the end of November 1782 a preliminary treaty had been signed. "His Britannic Majesty," Article I began, "acknowledges the said United States . . . to be free, sovereign and independent States." Other terms were equally in line with American hopes and objectives. The boundaries of the nation were set at the Great Lakes, the Mississippi River, and 31° north latitude (roughly the northern boundary of Florida). Britain recognized the right of Americans to take fish on the Grand Banks off Newfoundland and—far more important—to dry and cure their catch on unsettled beaches in Labrador and Nova Scotia. The British agreed to withdraw their troops from American soil "with all convenient speed." Where the touchy problem of Tory property seized during the Revolution was concerned, the Americans agreed only that Congress would "earnestly recommend" that the states "provide for the restitution of all estates, rights and properties which have been confiscated." They promised to prevent further property confiscation and prosecutions of Tories—certainly a wise as well as a humane policy—and they agreed not to impede the collection of debts owed British subjects. Vergennes was flabbergasted by the success of the Americans. "The English buy the peace more than they make it," he wrote. "Their concessions . . . exceed all that I should have thought possible."

The American commissioners obtained favorable terms because they were shrewd diplomats, and because of the rivalries that existed among the great European powers. In the last analysis Britain preferred to have a weak nation of English-speaking people in command of the Mississippi Valley rather than France or Spain. From their experience at the peace talks, the American leaders learned the importance of playing one power against another without committing themselves completely to any. This policy demanded constant contact with European affairs and skill at adjusting policies to changes in the European balance of power. It enabled the United States, a young and relatively feeble country, to grow and prosper.

Forming a National Government

Independence was won on the battlefield and at the Paris Peace Conference, but it could not have been achieved without the work of the Continental Congress and the new state governments. The delegates recognized that the Congress was a legislative body rather than a complete government and from the start they struggled to create a true central authority. But their effort was handicapped by much confusion and bickering, and early military defeats sapped their energy and morale. In July 1776 John Dickinson prepared a draft national constitution, but it could not command much support. The larger states objected to equal representation of all the states, and the states with large western land claims refused to cede them to the central government. It was not until November 1777 that the Articles of Confederation were submitted to the states for ratification.

It was necessary to obtain the approval of all the states before the Articles could go into effect. All but Maryland acted fairly promptly, but that state did not ratify the document until 1781. Maryland held out in order to force a change that would authorize Congress to determine the western limits of states with land claims beyond the Appalachians. There were many good reasons why this should be done. The state claims to the west were overlapping, vaguely defined, and in some instances preposterous. To have permitted a few states to monopolize the west would have unbalanced the union from the start.

Many people in the "landed" states recognized the justice of Maryland's suggestion, yet Maryland had a more selfish motive. Land speculators in the state had obtained from the Indians rights to large tracts in the Ohio Valley claimed by Virginia. Under Virginia, the Maryland titles would be worthless, but under a national administration they might be made to stand up.

Virginia resented its neighbor's efforts to grasp these valuable lands by indirection, but with the British about to advance into the state, Virginia agreed to surrender its claim to all land west and north of the Ohio River. It thwarted the Maryland speculators by insisting that all titles based on Indian purchases be declared void. Maryland then had no recourse but to ratify the Articles.

The Articles merely provided a legal basis for authority that the Continental Congress had already been exercising. Each state, regardless of size, was to have but one vote; the union it created was only a "league of friendship." Article II defined the limit of national power: "Each state retains its sovereignty, freedom, and independence, and every Power, Jurisdiction, and right, which is not by this confederation expressly delegated to the United States, in Congress assembled." Time would prove this an inadequate arrangement, chiefly because the central government had no way of enforcing its authority. As the historian David Ramsay explained in 1789, "No coercive power was given to the general government, nor was it invested with any legislative power over individuals."

Financing the War

In practice, Congress and the states carried on the war cooperatively. General officers were appointed by the Congress, lesser ones locally. The Continental Army, the backbone of Washington's force, was supported by Congress. The states raised militia chiefly for short-term service. Militiamen fought well at times but often proved unreliable. Washington continually fretted about their "dirty mercenary spirit" and their "intractable" nature, yet he could not have won the war without them.

The fact that Congress's requisitions of money often went unhonored by the states does not mean that the states failed to contribute heavily to the war effort. Altogether they spent about $5.8 million in hard money, and they met Congress's demands for beef, corn, rum, fodder, and other military supplies. In addition Congress raised large sums by borrowing. Americans bought bonds worth between $7 and $8 million during the war. Foreign governments lent another $8 million, most of this furnished by France. Congress issued more than $240 million in paper money, the states over $200 million more. This currency fell rapidly in value, resulting in an inflation that caused hardship and grumbling. The people, in effect, paid much of the cost of the war through the depreciation of their savings, but it is hard to see how else the war could have been financed, given the prejudice of the populace against paying taxes to fight a war against British taxation.

At about the time the Articles of Confederation were ratified, Congress established departments of Foreign Affairs, War, and Finance, with individual heads responsible to it. The most important of the new department heads was the superintendent of

BY HIS EXCELLENCY

GEORGE WASHINGTON, ESQUIRE,

GENERAL and COMMANDER in CHIEF of the FORCES of the UNITED STATES OF AMERICA.

BY Virtue of the Power and Direction to Me eſpecially given, I hereby enjoin and require all Perſons reſiding within ſeventy Miles of my Head Quarters to threſh one Half of their Grain by the 1ſt Day of February, and the other Half by the 1ſt Day of March next enſuing, on Pain, in Caſe of Failure, of having all that ſhall remain in Sheaves after the Period above mentioned, ſeized by the Commiſſaries and Quarter-Maſters of the Army, and paid for as Straw.

GIVEN *under my Hand, at Head Quarters, near the Valley Forge, in Philadelphia County, this 20th Day of December,* 1777.

G. *WASHINGTON.*

By His Excellency's Command,

ROBERT H. HARRISON, Sec'y.

LANCASTER; PRINTED BY JOHN DUNLAP.

The Continental Army's lack of financial support is demonstrated in requisitions like this one, issued by General Washington the day after his troops limped into Valley Forge.

finance, a Philadelphia merchant named Robert Morris. When Morris took office, the Continental dollar was worthless, the system of supplying the army chaotic, the credit of the government exhausted. He set up an efficient method of obtaining food and uniforms for the army, persuaded Congress to charter a national Bank of North America, and somehow—aided by the slackening of military activity after Yorktown—got the country back on a specie basis. New foreign loans were obtained, partly because Morris's efficiency and industry inspired confidence.

State Governments

However crucial the role of Congress, in an important sense the *real* revolution occurred when the individual colonies broke the official ties with Great Britain. Using their colonial charters as a basis, the states began framing new constitutions even before the Declaration of Independence. By early 1777 all but Connecticut and Rhode Island, which continued under their colonial charters well into the 19th century, had taken this decisive step.

On the surface the new governments were not drastically different from those they replaced. The most significant change was the removal of *outside* control, which had the effect of making the governments more responsive to public opinion. Gone were the times when a governor could be appointed and maintained in office by orders from London. The new constitutions provided for an elected legislature, an executive, and a system of courts. In general the powers of the governor and of judges were limited, the theory being that elected rulers no less than those appointed by kings were subject to the temptations of authority, that, as one Patriot put it, all men are "tyrants enough at heart." The typical governor had no voice in legislation and little in appointments. Pennsylvania went so far as to eliminate the office of governor, replacing it with an elected council of 12.

Power was concentrated in the legislature, which the people had come to count on to defend their interests. In addition to the lawmaking authority exercised by the colonial assemblies, the state constitutions gave the legislatures the power to declare war, conduct foreign relations, control the courts, and perform many other essentially executive functions. While continuing to require that voters be property owners or taxpayers, the constitution makers remained suspicious even of the legislature. The British concept of virtual representation they rejected out of hand. They saw legislators as *representatives,* that is, agents carrying out the wishes of the voters of a particular district rather than superior persons chosen to decide public issues according to their own best judgment. Gordon S. Wood, whose *The Creation of the American Republic* throws much light on the political thinking of the period, describes the concept as "acutely actual representation." Where political power was involved, the common American principle was every man for himself. The constitutions contained bills of rights protecting the people's civil liberties against all branches of the government. In Britain such guarantees checked only the Crown; the

Americans invoked them against their elected representatives as well.

The state governments combined the best of the British system, including its respect for status, fairness, and due process, with the uniquely American stress on individualism and a healthy dislike of too much authority. The idea of drafting written frames of government—contracts between the people and their representatives that carefully spelled out the powers and duties of the latter—grew out of the experience of the colonists after 1763, when the vagueness of the unwritten British Constitution had caused so much controversy, and from the compact principle described in the Declaration of Independence. It represented one of the most important innovations of the Revolutionary era: a peaceful method for altering the political system. In the midst of violence the states changed their frames of government in an orderly, legal manner—a truly remarkable achievement that became a beacon of hope to reformers all over the world.

Social Reform

Back in 1909 the historian Carl Becker wrote that the American Revolution was not merely a fight for "home rule," that is, for independence from Great Britain. It was also, Becker insisted, a fight to determine "who should rule at home." It is certainly true that there were many riots and numerous other indications of social conflict in America during the Revolutionary era, especially in the cities. The destruction of property by mobs during the Stamp Act crisis is only the best-known case where well-to-do people had cause to fear that popular resentment was not entirely directed at the British.

Many states seized the occasion of constitution making to introduce important political and social reforms. In Pennsylvania, Virginia, North Carolina, and other states the seats in the legislature were reapportioned in order to give the western districts their fair share. Primogeniture, entail (the right of an owner of property to prevent heirs from ever disposing of it), and quitrents were abolished wherever they had existed. Steps toward greater freedom of religion were taken, especially in states where the Anglican church had enjoyed a privileged position. In Virginia the movement to separate church and state was supported by a galaxy of Revolutionary leaders, including Washington, Patrick Henry, and Jefferson. It was given the force of law by Jefferson's Statute of Religious Liberty, enacted in 1786. "Our civil rights have no dependence on our religious opinions, any more than our opinions in physics or geometry," the statute declared. "Truth is great and will prevail if left to herself." Therefore "no man shall be compelled to frequent or support any religious worship, place, or ministry . . . nor shall otherwise suffer on account of his religious opinions or belief."

With this measure, wrote Jefferson's friend James Madison, "the ambitious hope of making laws for the human mind" was "extinguished forever." Of course Madison's optimistic expectation did not come to pass even in America. Most states continued to support religion; Massachusetts did not end public support of Congregational churches until the 1830s. But after the Revolution the states usually distributed the money roughly in accordance with the numerical strength of the various Protestant denominations.

Many states moved tentatively against slavery. In attacking British policy after 1763, colonists had frequently claimed that Parliament was trying to make slaves of them. No less a personage than George Washington wrote in 1774: "We must assert our rights, or submit to every imposition, that can be heaped upon us, till custom and use shall make us tame and abject slaves." However exaggerated the language, such reasoning led to denunciations of slavery, often vague but significant in their effects on public opinion. The fact that practically every important thinker of the European Enlightenment had criticized slavery on moral and economic grounds (Montesquieu, Voltaire, Diderot, and Rousseau in France, David Hume, Samuel Johnson, and Adam Smith in England, to name a few) had an impact on educated opinion. Then, too, the forthright statements in the Declaration of Independence about liberty and equality seemed impossible to reconcile with slaveholding. "How is it," asked Dr. Johnson, who opposed independence vehemently, "that we hear the loudest *yelps* for liberty among the drivers of negroes?"

The war opened direct paths to freedom for some slaves. In November 1775 Lord Dunmore, the royal governor of Virginia, proclaimed that all slaves "able and willing to bear arms" for the British would be liberated. In fact, the British treated slaves as captured property, seizing them by the thousands in their campaigns in the south. The

WILLIAMSBURG, *Nov.* 25.

By his Excellency the Right Honourable JOHN *Earl of* DUNMORE, *his Majeſty's Lieutenant and Governor General of the Colony and Dominion of* Virginia, *and Vice Admiral of the ſame:*

A PROCLAMATION.

AS I have ever entertained hopes that an accommodation might have taken place between *Great Britain* and this colony, without being compelled, by my duty, to this moſt diſagreeable, but now abſolutely neceſſary ſtep, rendered ſo by a body of armed men, unlawfully aſſembled, firing on his Majeſty's tenders, and the formation of an army, and that army now on their march to attack his Majeſty's troops, and deſtroy the well diſpoſed ſubjects of this colony: To defeat ſuch treaſonable purpoſes, and that all ſuch traitors, and their abettors may be brought to juſtice, and that the peace and good order of this colony may be again reſtored, which the ordinary courſe of the civil law is unable to effect, I have thought fit to iſſue this my proclamation, hereby declaring, that untill the aforeſaid good purpoſes can be obtained, I do, in virtue of the power and authority to me given, by his Majeſty, determine to execute martial law, and cauſe the ſame to be executed throughout this colony; and to the end that peace and good order may the ſooner be reſtored, I do require every perſon capable of bearing arms to reſort to his Majeſty's STANDARD, or be looked upon as traitors to his Majeſty's crown and government, and thereby become liable to the penalty the law inflicts upon ſuch offences, ſuch as forfeiture of life, confiſcation of

In this proclamation urging the colonists to remain loyal to the Crown, Royal Governor Lord Dunmore called for "all indented servants, Negroes, or others . . . free, that are able and willing to bear arms" to join "his Majesty's troops, as soon as may be."

fate of these blacks is obscure. Some ended up in the West Indies, still slaves. Others were evacuated to Canada and liberated, and some of them settled the British colony of Sierra Leone in West Africa, founded in 1787. Probably many more escaped from bondage by running away during the confusion accompanying the British campaigns in the south.

About 5,000 blacks served in the Patriot army and navy. Most black soldiers were assigned noncombat duties, but some fought in every major battle from Lexington to Yorktown.

Beginning with Pennsylvania in 1780, the northern states all did away with slavery. In most cases slaves born after a certain date were to become free upon reaching maturity. Since New Jersey did not pass its emancipation act until 1804, there were numbers of slaves in the so-called free states well into the 19th century—more than 3,500 as late as 1830. But the institution was on its way toward extinction. All the states prohibited the importation of slaves from abroad, and except for Georgia and South Carolina, the southern states passed laws removing restrictions on the right of individual owners to free their slaves. The greatest success of voluntary emancipation came in Virginia, where, between 1782 and 1790, 10,000 blacks were freed.

These advances encouraged foes of slavery to hope that the institution would soon disappear. But slavery died only where it was not economically important. Except for owners whose slaves were "carried off" by the British, only in Massachusetts, where the state supreme court ruled slavery unconstitutional in 1783, were owners deprived of existing slaves against their will.

After the publication of *Common Sense* and the Declaration of Independence, with their excoriations of that "Royal Brute," King George III, it became fashionable to denounce the granting of titles of nobility, all "aristocrats," and any privilege based on birth. In 1783 a group of army officers founded a fraternal organization, the Society of Cincinnati. Although the revered George Washington was its president, many citizens found the mere existence of a club restricted to officers alarming; the fact that membership was to be hereditary, passing on the death of a member to his oldest son, caused a furor.

Despite the continuing subordination of blacks, there is no question that the Revolution permanently changed the tone of American society. In the way they dressed, their manner of speech, and in the way they dealt with one another in public places, Americans paid at least lip service to the idea of equality to a degree unknown elsewhere in the world.

Nevertheless, little of the social and economic upheaval usually associated with revolutions occurred, before, during, or after 1776. At least part of the urban violence of the period (just how large a part is difficult to determine at this distance) had no social objective. America had its share of criminals, mischievous youths eager to flex their muscles, and other people unable to resist the temptation to break the law when it could be done without much risk of punishment. Certainly there was no wholesale proscription of any class, faith, or profession.

The property of Tories was frequently seized by the state governments, but almost never with the idea of redistributing wealth or providing the poor with land. While some large Tory estates were broken up and sold to small farmers, others passed intact to wealthy individuals or to groups of speculators. The war disrupted many traditional business relationships. Some merchants were unable to cope with the changes; others adapted well and grew rich. But the changes occurred without regard for the political beliefs or social values of either those who profited or those who lost.

That the new governments were liberal but moderate reflected the spirit of the times, a spirit typified by Thomas Jefferson, who had great faith in the democratic process yet owned a large estate and many slaves and had never suggested a drastic social revolution. More individuals of middling wealth were elected to the legislatures than in colonial times because the Revolution stimulated popular interest in politics and republican forms subtly undermined the tendency of farmers and artisans to defer automatically to great planters and merchants. Nevertheless, relatively high property qualifications for office holding remained the general rule. Few "ordinary" people wanted radical changes. If they were becoming more skeptical about "their betters," they continued to look down their noses at unskilled laborers, servants, and others lower on the social ladder. There were three classes in Philadelphia society, a writer in the Pennsylvania *Packet* noted in 1781: "The first class consists of commercial projectors . . . speculators, riotous livers, and a kind of loungers. . . . The second class are a set of honest sober men, who mind their business. . . . The third class are thieves, pick-pockets, low-cheats and dirty sots."

In the late 18th century there was a worldwide trend, barely perceptible at the time, toward increasing the legal rights of women. For example, it became somewhat easier for women to obtain divorces. In 1791 a South Carolina judge went so far as to say that the law protecting "the absolute dominion" of husbands was "the offspring of a rude and barbarous age." The "progress of civilization," he continued, "has tended to ameliorate the condition of women, and to allow even to wives, something like personal identity."

As the tone of this "liberal" opinion indicates, the change in male attitudes that took place in America because of the Revolution was small. When John Adams's wife Abigail warned him in 1776 that if he and his fellow rebels did not "Remember the Ladies" when reforming society, the women would "foment a Rebellion" of their own, he treated her remarks as a joke. However, the war effort increased the influence of women in several ways. With so many men in uniform, women took over the management of countless farms, shops, and businesses, and they became involved in the handling of other day-to-day matters that men had normally conducted. Their experiences made them more aware of their ability to take on all sorts of chores previously considered exclusively masculine in character. At the same time, women wanted to contribute to the winning of independence, and their efforts to do so made them conscious of their importance. Furthermore, the rhetoric of the Revolution, with its stress on liberty and equality, affected women in the same way that it caused many whites of both sexes to question the morality of slavery.

Attitudes toward the education of women changed because of the Revolution. According to the best estimates, at least half the white women in America could not read or write as late as the 1780s. But as the historian Linda K. Kerber writes, "the republican experiment demanded a well-educated citizenry." In a land of opportunity like the United States, women seemed particularly important because of their role in training the young. "You distribute 'mental nourishment' along with physical," one orator told the women of America in 1795. "The reformation of the world is in your power. . . . The solidity and stability of your country rest with you." Therefore the idea of female education began to catch on. Schools for girls were founded and the level of female literacy gradually rose.

During the war, conflicts erupted over economic issues involving land and taxation, yet no single class or interest triumphed in all the states or in the national government. In Pennsylvania, where the western radical element was strong, the constitution was extremely democratic; in Maryland and South Carolina the conservatives maintained control handily. Throughout the country, many great landowners were ardent Patriots but others became Tories—and so did many small farmers.

In some cases the state legislatures wrote the new constitutions. In others the legislatures ordered special elections to choose delegates to conventions empowered to draft the charters. The convention method was a further important product of the Revolutionary era, an additional illustration of the idea that constitutions are contracts between the people and their leaders. Massachusetts even required that its new constitution be ratified by the people after it was drafted.

Finally, the new governments became more responsive to public opinion, no matter what the particular shape of their political institutions. This was true principally because *Common Sense,* the Declaration of Independence, and the experience of participating in a revolution had made people conscious of their rights in a republic and of their power to enforce those rights. Conservatives swiftly discovered that state constitutions designed to insulate legislators and officials from popular pressures were ineffective when the populace felt strongly about any issue. In other words, the Revolution produced a more nearly democratic society, not one that satisfies modern standards of fairness and justice entirely, but a distinct advance toward popular rule.

Growth of a National Spirit

American independence and control of a wide and rich domain were the most obvious results of the Revolution. Changes in the structure of society, as we have seen, were relatively minor. Economic developments, such as the growth of new trade connections and the expansion of manufacturing in an effort to replace British goods, were of only modest significance. By far the most important social and economic changes involved the Tories and were thus by-products of the political revolution rather than a determined reorganization of a people's way of life.

There was another important result of the Revolution: the growth of American nationalism. Most modern revolutions have been *caused* by nationalism and have *resulted* in independence. In the case of the American Revolution the desire to be free antedated any very intense national feeling. The colonies entered into a political union not because they felt an overwhelming desire to bring all Americans under one rule but because unity offered the only hope of winning a war against Great Britain. That they remained united after throwing off British rule reflects the degree to which nationalism had developed during the conflict.

By the middle of the 18th century the colonists had begun to think of themselves as a separate society distinct from Europe and even from Britain. Benjamin Franklin described himself not as a British subject but as "an American subject of the King," and in 1750 a Boston newspaper could urge its readers to drink "American" beer in order to free themselves from being "beholden to Foreigners" for their alcoholic beverages. Little political nationalism existed before the Revolution, however. Local ties remained predominant. A few might say, with Patrick Henry in 1774, "The distinctions between Virginians, Pennsylvanians, New Yorkers, and New Englanders are no more. I am not a Virginian, but an American." But such people were rare before the final break with Great Britain.

The new nationalism rose from a number of sources and expressed itself in different ways. Common sacrifices in war certainly played a part; the soldiers of the Continental Army fought in the summer heat of the Carolinas for the same cause that had led them to brave the ice floes of the Delaware in order to surprise the Hessians. Such men lost interest in state boundary lines; they became Americans. John Marshall of Fauquier County, Virginia, for example, was a 20-year-old militiaman in 1775. The next year he joined the Continental Army. He served in Pennsylvania, New Jersey, and New York and endured the winter of 1777–1778 at Valley Forge. "I found myself associated with brave men from different states who were risking life and everything valuable in a common cause," he later wrote. "I was confirmed in the habit of considering America as my country and Congress as my government." Andrew Jackson, child of the Carolina frontier, was only 9 when the Revolution broke out. One brother was killed in battle; another died as a result of untreated wounds. Young Andrew took up arms and was captured by the Redcoats. A British officer ordered Jackson to black his boots and, when the boy refused, struck him across the face with the flat of his sword. Jackson bore the scar to his grave—and became an ardent nationalist on the spot. He and Marshall had very different ideas and came to be bitter enemies in later life. Nevertheless they were both American nationalists—and for the same reason.

Civilians as well as soldiers reacted in this way. A Carolina farmer whose home and barn were protected against British looters by men who spoke

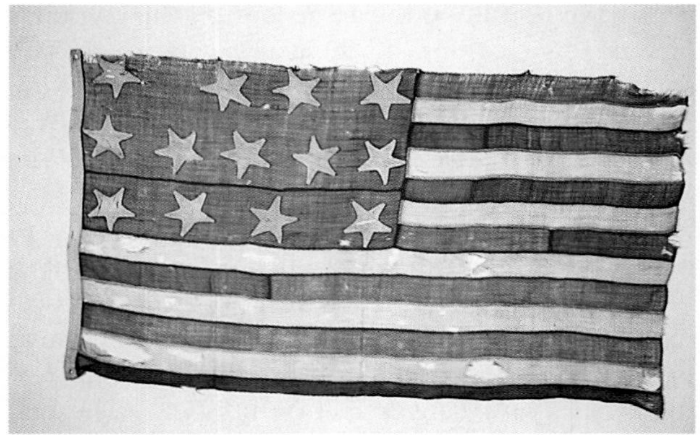

The Continental Congress adopted the basic pattern for the 13-star flag in June 1777. This example, associated with the merchant ship Bedford, *is typical of the replicas that were made generations later.*

with the harsh nasal twang of New England adopted a broader outlook toward politics. When the news came that thousands of Redcoats had stacked their arms in defeat after Yorktown, few people cared what state or section had made the victory possible—it was an American triumph.

The war caused many people to move from place to place. Soldiers traveled as the tide of war fluctuated; so too—far more than in earlier times—did prominent leaders. Members of Congress from every state had to travel to Philadelphia; in the process they saw much of the country and the people who inhabited it. Listening to their fellows and serving with them on committees almost inevitably broadened these men, most of them highly influential in their local communities.

With its 13 stars and 13 stripes representing the states, the American flag symbolized national unity and reflected the common feeling that such a symbol was necessary. After much experimentation (one version pictured the Union as a snake made up of 13 segments), the Continental Congress adopted the basic pattern in June 1777.

Certain practical problems that demanded common solutions also drew the states together. No one seriously considered having 13 postal systems or 13 sets of diplomatic representatives abroad. Every new diplomatic appointment, every treaty of friendship or commerce signed, committed all to a common policy and thus bound them more closely together. And economic developments had a unifying effect. Cutting off English goods encouraged manufacturing, making America more self-sufficient and stimulating both interstate trade and national pride.

The Great Land Ordinances

The western lands, which had divided the states in the beginning, became a force for unity once they had been ceded to the national government. Everyone realized what a priceless national asset they were, and while many greedily sought to possess them by fair means or foul, all now understood that no one state could determine the future of the west.

The politicians argued hotly about how these lands should be developed. Some advocated selling the land in township units in the traditional New England manner to groups or companies; others favored letting individual pioneers stake out farms in the helter-skelter manner common in the colonial south. The decision was a compromise. The Land Ordinance of 1785 provided for surveying western territories into six-mile-square townships before sale. Every other township was to be further subdivided into 36 sections of 640 acres (one square mile) each. The land was sold at auction at a minimum price of one dollar an acre. The law favored speculative land-development companies, for even the 640-acre units were far too large and expensive for the typical frontier family. But the fact that the land was to be surveyed and sold by the central government was a nationalizing force. Congress set aside the sixteenth section of every township for the maintenance of schools, another important and farsighted decision.

Still more significant was the Northwest Ordinance of 1787, which established governments for the west. As early as 1780 Congress had resolved that all lands ceded to the nation by the states should be "formed into distinct republican States" with "the same rights of sovereignty, freedom and independence" as the original 13. In 1784 a committee headed by Thomas Jefferson worked out a plan for doing this, and in 1787 it was enacted into law. The area bounded by the Ohio, the Mississippi, and the Great Lakes was to be carved into not less than three or more than five territories. Until the adult male population of the entire area

New York and Virginia gave up their claims to the vast area that became the Northwest Territory, and thus set a precedent for trans-Appalachian land policy. By 1802 the various state claims had been ceded to the national government. The original Northwest Territory (the Old Northwest) was bounded by the Ohio River, the Mississippi, and the Great Lakes.

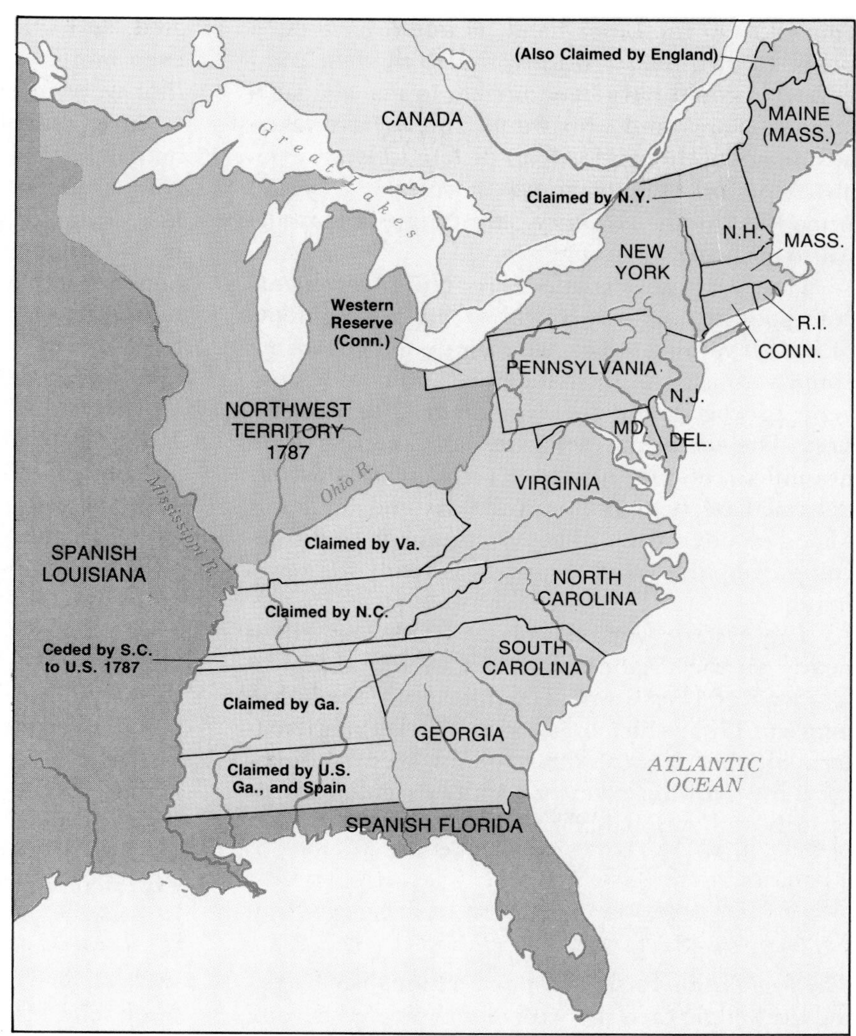

THE UNITED STATES
UNDER THE ARTICLES OF CONFEDERATION, 1787

reached 5,000, it was to be ruled by a governor and three judges, all appointed by Congress. Acting together, these officials would make and enforce the necessary laws. When 5,000 men of voting age had settled in the territory, the ordinance authorized them to elect a legislature and send a nonvoting delegate to Congress. Finally, when 60,000 persons had settled in any one of the political subdivisions, it was to become a state. It could draft a constitution and operate in any way it wished, save that the government had to be "republican" and that slavery was prohibited.

Seldom has a legislative body acted more wisely. That the western districts must become states everyone conceded from the start. The people had had their fill of colonialism under British rule, and the rebellious temper of frontier settlers made it impossible even to consider maintaining the west in a dependent status. (When North Carolina ceded its trans-Appalachian lands to the United States in 1784, the settlers there, uncertain how they would fare under federal rule, hastily organized an extralegal "State of Franklin," and it was not until 1789 that the national government obtained control.) On the other hand, it would have been unfair to turn the territories over to the first comers, who would have been unable to manage such large domains and who would surely have taken advantage of their priority to dictate to later arrivals. A period of tutelage was necessary, a period when the "mother country" must guide and nourish its growing offspring.

Thus the intermediate territorial governments corresponded almost exactly to the governments of British royal colonies. The appointed governors could veto acts of the assemblies and could "convene, prorogue, and dissolve" them at their discretion. The territorial delegates to Congress were not unlike colonial agents. Yet it was vital that this intermediate stage end and that its end be determined in advance so that no argument could develop over when the territory was ready for statehood.

The system worked well and was applied to nearly all the regions absorbed by the nation as it advanced westward. Together with the Ordinance of 1785, which branded its checkerboard pattern on the physical shape of the west, this law gave the growing country a unity essential to the growth of a national spirit.

National Heroes

The Revolution further fostered nationalism by giving the people their first commonly revered heroes. Benjamin Franklin was widely known before the break with Great Britain through his experiments with electricity, his immensely successful *Poor Richard's Almanack,* and his invention of the Franklin stove. His staunch support of the Patriot cause, his work in the Continental Congress, and his diplomatic successes in France, where he was extravagantly admired, added to his fame. Franklin demonstrated, to Europeans and to Americans themselves, that not all Americans need be ignorant rustics.

Thomas Jefferson was also a national figure by the 1780s. His writing of the Declaration of Independence (to which, it will be recalled, Franklin contributed) made him a hero to all Americans. When in retrospect the boldness of the document and its felicity of expression could be fully appreciated, and when the success of the revolt made it even more significant, the Declaration and its author were revered in every state.

Most notable of all was Washington, "the chief human symbol of a common Americanism." Stern, cold, a man of few words, the great Virginian did not seem a likely candidate for hero worship. Yet he had qualities that made people name babies after him and call him "the Father of his Country" long before the war was won: his personal sacrifices in the cause of independence, his integrity, his devotion to duty, his commanding presence, and above all, perhaps, his obvious desire to retire to his Mount Vernon estate (for many Americans feared *any* powerful leader and worried lest Washington seek to become a dictator). He was, one contemporary explained, "discreet and Virtuous, no harum Starum ranting Swearing fellow but Sober, steady, and Calm."

As a general, Washington was not a brilliant strategist like Napoleon, although his design for the complicated Yorktown campaign was superb. Neither was he a tactician of the quality of Caesar or Robert E. Lee. His lack of genius made his achievements all the more impressive. He held his forces together in adversity, avoiding both useless slaughter and catastrophic defeat. He learned from experience and won the respect—if not the love—of his men and the cooperation of Congress and his French allies. People of all sections, from every walk of life, looked upon Washington as the embodiment of American virtues: a man of deeds rather than words; a man of substance accustomed to luxury yet capable of enduring great hardships stoically and as much at home in the wilderness as an Indian; a bold Patriot, quick to take arms against British tyranny, yet eminently respectable. The Revolution might have been won without Washington, but it is unlikely that the free United States would have become so easily a true nation had he not been at its call.

A National Culture

Breaking away from Great Britain accentuated certain trends toward social and intellectual independence and strengthened the national desire to create an *American* culture. The Anglican church in

"The chief human symbol of a common Americanism," George Washington attained heroic status perhaps as much for his modesty as for his devotion to the new nation.

America had to form a new organization once the connection with the Crown was severed; in 1786 it became the Protestant Episcopal church. The Dutch and German Reformed churches also became independent of their European connections. Roman Catholics in America had been under the administration of the vicar apostolic of England; after the Revolution, Father John Carroll of Baltimore assumed these duties, and in 1789 he became the first American Roman Catholic bishop.

The impact of post-Revolutionary nationalism on American education was best reflected in the immense success of the textbooks of Noah Webster, later famous for his American dictionary. The first of these, the famous *Spelling Book,* appeared in 1783 when Webster was a young schoolteacher in Goshen, New York. It emphasized American forms and usage and contained a patriotic preface urging Americans to pay proper respect to their own literature. Webster's *Reader,* published shortly thereafter, included selections from the speeches of Revolutionary leaders who, according to the compiler, were the equals of Cicero and Demosthenes as orators. Some 15 million copies of the *Speller* were sold in the next five decades, several times that number by 1900. The *Reader* was also a continuing best-seller.

Webster's work was not the only sign of nationalism in education. In 1787 John M'Culloch published the first American history textbook. The colleges saw a great outburst of patriotic spirit. King's College (founded in 1754) received a new name, Columbia, in 1784. Everywhere it was recognized that the republic required educated and cultivated leaders. Many new colleges were founded in the two decades or so following the Revolution.

Nationalism affected the arts and sciences in the years after the Revolution. Jedidiah Morse's popular *American Geography* (1789) was a paean in praise of the "astonishing" progress of the country, all the result of the "natural genius of Americans." The American Academy of Arts and Sciences, founded at Boston during the Revolution, was created "to advance the interest, honor, dignity and happiness of a free, independent and virtuous people."

American painters and writers of the period usually chose extremely patriotic themes. John Trumbull helped capture Dorchester Heights and force the evacuation of Boston, took part in the defense of northern New York against Burgoyne, and fought in Pennsylvania and Rhode Island. When he took up painting he produced such pictures as *The Battle of Bunker's Hill, The Surrender of Lord Cornwallis at Yorktown,* and *The Declaration of Independence.* Trumbull referred to these and similar efforts as his "national work." Joel Barlow intended his *Vision of Columbus,* written between 1779 and 1787, to prove that America was "the noblest and most elevated part of the earth." Royall Tyler's play *The Contrast,* which was produced in New York in 1787, compared American virtue (the hero was called Colonel Manly) with British vice and contained such chauvinistic lines as:

> *Why should our thoughts to distant countries roam*
> *When each refinement may be found at home?*

The United States in the 1780s was far from being the powerful centralized nation it has since become. Probably most citizens still gave their first loyalty to their own states. In certain important respects the Confederation was pitifully ineffectual. However, people were increasingly aware of their common interests and increasingly proud of their common heritage. The motto of the new nation, *E pluribus unum*—"from many, one"—perfectly describes a process that was rapidly taking place in the years after Yorktown.

SUPPLEMENTARY READING

Titles marked with an asterisk have been published in paperback.

The best brief survey of the Revolutionary years is E. S. Morgan, **The Birth of the Republic*** (1956); Robert Middlekauf, **The Glorious Cause** (1982), is more detailed. Don Higgenbotham, **The War of American Independence*** (1971), provides an up-to-date account of the military aspects of the Revolution and Charles Royster, **A Revolutionary People at War** (1979), describes the attitudes of soldiers and civilians toward the army. See also Robert A. Gross, **The Minutemen and Their World** (1976). H. S. Commager and R. B. Morris (eds.), **The Spirit of Seventy-Six** (1958), is a rich collection of source materials. For Washington's role, see J. R. Alden, **George Washington** (1984), and Marcus Cunliffe, **George Washington: Man and Monument*** (1958).

On the Continental Congress and the Articles of Confederation, see E. C. Burnett, **The Continental Congress*** (1941), and two books by Merrill Jensen, **The Articles of Confederation*** (1940) and **The New Nation*** (1950). Eric Foner, **Tom Paine and Revolutionary America*** (1976), is an excellent brief biography. The classic analysis of the Declaration of Independence is C. L. Becker, **The Declaration of Independence*** (1922). Jefferson's ideas are thoughtfully analyzed in Gilbert Chinard, **Thomas Jefferson: The Apostle of Americanism*** (1929), and Adrienne Koch, **Jefferson and Madison*** (1950).

The early history of the state governments is covered in Elisha P. Douglas, **Rebels and Democrats*** (1955). Edward Countryman, **A People in Revolution** (1982), deals with conditions in New York. The development of political ideas is admirably described and analyzed in G. S. Wood, **The Creation of the American Republic*** (1969), and in D. J. Boorstin, **The Genius of American Politics*** (1953). The financial problems of this period are covered in E. J. Ferguson, **The Power of the Purse*** (1968), and Clarence Ver Steeg, **Robert Morris, Revolutionary Financier** (1954). For federal policy toward western lands, see R. M. Robbins, **Our Landed Heritage*** (1942), and W. D. Pattison, **The Beginnings of the American Rectangular Land Survey** (1957).

The classic account of the social and economic effects of the Revolution is J. F. Jameson, **The American Revolution Considered as a Social Movement*** (1926). R. E. Brown takes issue with Jameson's view in **Middle-Class Democracy and the Revolution in Massachusetts** (1955), as does R. P. McCormick, **Experiment in Independence: New Jersey in the Critical Period** (1950). J. T. Main, **The Social Structure of Revolutionary**

America* (1965), provides a general picture against which to evaluate the views of Jameson and his critics. On the Tories, see W. H. Nelson, **The American Tory*** (1962), M. B. Norton, **The British-Americans** (1972), R. M. Calhoun, **The Loyalists in Revolutionary America** (1973), and Wallace Brown, **The King's Friends** (1965). P. H. Smith, **Loyalists and Redcoats*** (1965), treats the fumbling efforts of the British to make use of their American supporters. The effects of the Revolution on slavery are treated in W. D. Jordan, **White Over Black*** (1968), Arthur Zilversmit, **The First Emancipation: The Abolition of Slavery in the North*** (1967), and Benjamin Quarles, **The Negro in the American Revolution*** (1961). See also Ira Berlin and Ronald Hoffman (eds.), **Slavery and Freedom in the Age of the American Revolution** (1983). L. K. Kerber, **Women of the Republic** (1980), and M. B. Norton, **Liberty's Daughters** (1980), discuss the effects of the Revolution on women.

On the diplomacy of the Revolution, see S. F. Bemis, **The Diplomacy of the American Revolution*** (1935). The definitive account of the peace treaty is R. B. Morris, **The Peacemakers*** (1965).

On the emergence of American nationalism and cultural history generally, see E. B. Greene's **Revolutionary Generation** and R. B. Nye, **The Cultural Life of the New Nation*** (1960). R. L. Merritt, **Symbols of American Community** (1966), concludes from a study of colonial newspapers that a sense of national identity was well developed before 1763. P. C. Nagel, **One Nation Indivisible: The Union in American Thought** (1964), discusses the various views of the nature of the Union advanced in this period, and Paul Varg, **Foreign Policies of the Founding Fathers** (1963), is instructive.

5
Nationalism Triumphant

You and I have been sent into life at a time when the greatest lawgivers of antiquity would have wished to live. How few of the human race have ever enjoyed an opportunity of making an election of government . . . for themselves or their children! When, before the present epoch, had three millions of people full of power and a fair opportunity to form and establish the wisest and happiest government that human wisdom can contrive? JOHN ADAMS *to George Wythe*

WASHINGTON'S TRIUMPHAL ENTRY INTO NEW YORK IN 1783

At first, only a relative handful of Americans resented the constraints imposed by the Articles of Confederation on the power of the central government. Once the war was over, the need for unity seemed less pressing and sectional conflicts reasserted themselves. Modern research has modified the thesis, advanced by John Fiske in *The Critical Period of American History* (1888), that the national government was demoralized and inadequate. If as Washington said it moved "on crutches . . . tottering at every step," it *did* move. The negotiation of a successful peace treaty ending the Revolutionary War, the humane and farsighted federal land policies, and even the establishment of a federal bureaucracy to manage routine affairs were remarkable achievements, all carried out under the Articles. Yet the country's evolution placed demands upon the national government that its creators had not anticipated.

Border Problems

The government had to struggle to win actual control over the territory granted the United States in the treaty ending the Revolution. Both Great Britain and Spain stood in the way of this objective. The British had promised to withdraw all their troops from American soil promptly, and so they did—within the settled portions of the 13 states. Beyond the frontier, however, they had established a string of seven military posts, running from the northern end of Lake Champlain through Niagara and Detroit to the tip of the Michigan peninsula (see map, page 167). These, despite the Treaty of Paris, they refused to surrender. Pressing against America's exposed frontier like hot coals, the posts seared national pride. They threatened to set off another Indian war, for the British intrigued constantly to stir up the tribes against the Americans. The great prize was the rich fur trade of the region, which the British now controlled but which might be drained off through Albany and other American centers if British military influence was removed.

The British justified holding on to these positions by citing the failure of the Americans to live up to some terms of the peace treaty. The United States had agreed not to impede British creditors seeking to collect prewar debts in America and to "earnestly recommend" that the states restore Tory property confiscated during the revolt. The national government complied with both requirements (which called for nothing more than words on Congress's part), but the individual states did not cooperate. Many passed laws making it impossible for British creditors to collect debts, and in general the property of Tory émigrés was not returned.

Yet those violations of the peace terms, which resulted more from the state of public opinion than from the weakness of the central authority, had little to do with the continued presence of the British on American soil. They would not have evacuated the posts at this time even if every farthing of the debt had been paid and every acre of confiscated land restored. Not internal dissension or the absence of congressional determination but the lack of military might accounts for the failure of the United States to compel the British to withdraw. Although Britain had been unable to conquer the colonies, it was a much simpler task to hold posts far removed from centers of American power, and in a region swarming with Indians hostile to settlers but willing to deal with white men interested in buying furs.

Americans found the presence of British troops galling, even in the western wilderness. When the French had pushed a line of forts into the Ohio country in the 1750s, it had seemed to most colonists only a matter of local concern, to be dealt with by Virginia or Pennsylvania. Three decades later the inability to eject the British seemed a national disgrace.

Then there was the question of the Spanish in the southwest. Spain had been a cobelligerent, not an ally, in the war with Great Britain. In the peace negotiations it had won back Florida and the Gulf Coast region east of New Orleans. Spanish troops had captured Natchez during the war, and although the post lay north of the boundary, Spain refused to turn it over to the United States. Far more serious, the Spaniards had closed the lower Mississippi River to American commerce. Because of the prohibitive cost of moving bulky farm produce over the mountains, settlers beyond the Appalachians depended on the Mississippi and its network of tributaries to get their corn, tobacco, and other products to eastern and European markets. If Spain closed the river, or even if it denied them the right to "deposit" goods at New Orleans while awaiting

The Mississippi teems with commerce in this watercolor, based on a sketch made about 1790 by Christophe Colomb. Two flatboats (on the right) and a keelboat are in the improbably narrow river; in the center left foreground Colomb sits on a log, sketching his father-in-law's plantation house on the other side of the river.

oceangoing transportation, westerners could not sell their surpluses.

Frontier settlers fumed when Congress failed to win concessions from Spain. A few of the unscrupulous and shortsighted among their leaders, such as General James Wilkinson, a handsome, glib, hard-drinking veteran who had moved to Kentucky after the Revolution, accepted Spanish bribes and tried to swing the southwest into the Spanish orbit.

A stronger central government might have dealt with these foreign problems more effectively, but it could not have eliminated them. United or decentralized, America was too weak in the 1780s to challenge a major European nation. Until the country grew more powerful, or until the Europeans began to fight among themselves, the United States was bound to suffer at their hands.

Foreign Trade

The fact that the Revolution freed American trade from the restrictions of British mercantilism proved a mixed blessing in the short run. The commercial benefits that Tom Paine had described in *Common Sense* did not materialize. Americans could now trade directly with the Continental powers, and commercial treaties were negotiated with a number of them. Beginning in 1784, when the 360-ton *Empress of China* reached Canton with a cargo of furs and cotton to be exchanged for silks, tea, and spices, a valuable Far Eastern trade sprang up where none had existed before. At the same time, exclusion from Britain's imperial trade union brought losses of a much larger magnitude.

Immediately after the Revolution a controversy broke out in Great Britain over fitting the former colonies into the mercantilistic system. Some people, influenced by Adam Smith's brilliant exposition of the subject in *The Wealth of Nations,* published in 1776, argued that any restriction on the buying and selling of goods was wasteful; if people could trade freely, all parties would benefit. Others, while remaining mercantilists, realized how important the American trade was for British prosperity and argued that special treatment should be afforded the former colonists. Unfortunately, a proud empire recently humbled in war could hardly be expected to exercise such forbearance. Persuaded in part by the reasoning of Lord Sheffield, who claimed in his influential pamphlet *Observations on the Commerce of the American States* that Britain could get all the American commerce it wished without making concessions, Parliament voted to try building up exports to America while holding imports to a minimum, all according to the best tenets of mercantilism.

The British atttitude hurt American interests severely. In the southern states the termination of royal bounties hit North Carolina producers of naval stores and South Carolina indigo planters hard, and a new British duty on rice reduced the export of that product by almost 50 percent. Rice and tobacco growers were also afflicted by a labor shortage in the 1780s because of the wartime British seizure of so many slaves.

British Orders in Council in 1783 struck at the northern states, barring American cured meat, fish, and dairy products from the British West Indies and permitting other American products to enter the islands only in British ships. The British hoped that Canada and Newfoundland would replace New England as the supplier of food for their sugar islands, and they counted on their own merchant fleet to carry the commerce of the region. Fishermen lost the lucrative West Indian market, merchants a host of profitable opportunities. Shipbuilding slumped because of these facts and because British merchants stopped ordering American-made vessels.

At the same time British merchants, eager to regain markets closed to them during the Revolution, poured low-priced manufactured goods of all kinds into the United States. Americans, long deprived of British products, rushed to take advantage of the bargains. Soon imports of British goods were approaching the levels of the early 1770s, while exports to the empire reached no more than half their earlier volume.

American had always had an unfavorable balance of trade. The economy was essentially colonial; the people produced bulky, relatively cheap raw materials and voraciously consumed expensive manufactured goods. Throughout the first three-quarters of the 18th century, imports consistently exceeded exports by a large margin. This is another way of saying that foreigners were investing heavily in America. These investments speeded the growth and development of the country. But the unfavorable trade balance also resulted in a constant shortage of hard money in the colonies. Gold and silver tended to flow to Europe to pay interest on loans and to purchase manufactured goods.

The influx of British goods after the Revolution aggravated the situation just when the economy was suffering a certain dislocation as a result of the ending of the war. From 1784 to 1786 the country went through a period of bad times. The inability of the central government to pay its debts undermined confidence and caused grave hardships for veterans and others dependent on the Confederation. In some regions crop failures compounded the difficulties. The depression made the states stingier than ever about supplying the requisitions of Congress; at the same time many of them levied heavy property taxes in order to pay off their own war debts. Everywhere people were hard pressed for cash. "As Money has ever been considered the root of all evils," one Massachusetts man commented sourly, "may we not presage happy times, as this source is almost done away?"

The depression of the mid-1780s was not by any stretch of the imagination a major economic collapse. By 1786 all signs were pointing toward a revival of good times. Nevertheless, dislike of British trade policy remained widespread. The obvious tactic would have been to place tariffs on British goods in order to limit imports or force the British to open the West Indies to all American goods, but the Confederation lacked the authority to do this. When individual states erected tariff barriers, British merchants easily got around them by bringing their goods in through states that did not. That the central government lacked the power to control commerce disturbed merchants, other businessmen, and the ever-increasing number of national-minded citizens in every walk of life.

Thus a movement developed to give the Confederation the power to tax imports. In 1781 Congress sought authority to levy a 5 percent tariff duty. Eleven states agreed—a remarkable indication of the growth of national feeling, considering that local control of taxation and trade had been primary objectives of the Revolution. However, the measure required the unanimous consent of the states and therefore failed. Another request for the same power made in a more moderate form won the approval of all the states by 1786, but conditions imposed by New York were unacceptable to Congress, and again the measure failed.

Defeat of the "impost" pointed up the need for revising the Articles of Confederation, for here was a case where a large percentage of the states were ready to increase the power of the national government yet were unable to do so. Although many individuals in every region were worried about creating a centralized monster that might

The postwar depression made it difficult to finance projects to rebuild property destroyed in battle. This "view of part of the ruins of Norfolk" was painted by Benjamin Latrobe more than a decade after the war's end.

gobble up the sovereignty of the states, the practical needs of the times convinced most that this risk must be taken. Not a *general* devotion to local sovereignty but the existence of pockets of resistance—as in Rhode Island—to a broader, more national outlook hamstrung the Confederation.

The Specter of Inflation

The depression and the unfavorable balance of trade led to increased pressures in the states for the printing of paper money and the passage of laws designed to make life easier for debtors. Before the Revolution the colonists had grappled with the chronic shortage of hard money in many ways, declaring various staple products such as furs, tobacco, and even Indian wampum to be legal tender, deliberately overvaluing foreign coins to discourage their export, making it illegal to ship coins abroad, and printing paper currency. In response to wartime needs, both the Continental Congress and the states issued large amounts of paper money during the Revolution, with inflationary results (the Continental dollar became utterly worthless by 1781, and Virginia eventually called in its paper at 1,000 to 1).

After the war some states set out to restore their credit by imposing heavy taxes and severely restricting new issues of money. Combined with the postwar depression and the increase in imports, this policy had a powerful deflationary effect on prices and wages. Soon debtors, especially farmers, were crying for relief, both in the form of stay laws designed to make it difficult to collect debts (these laws were popular because of the anti-British feeling of the times) and through the printing of more paper money.

More than half the states yielded to this pressure in 1785 and 1786. Issues in South Carolina, New York, and Pennsylvania were conservatively handled and succeeded, but in some states the money depreciated rapidly: Georgia's currency lost 75 percent of its value in one year, and issues in North Carolina and New Jersey also failed.

The most disastrous experience was that of Rhode Island, where the government attempted to legislate public confidence in £100,000 of paper. Any landowner could borrow a share of this money from the state for 14 years, using real estate as security. Creditors feared that the loans would never be repaid, and had no confidence in the money, but the legislature established a system of fines in cases where people refused to accept it. When creditors fled the state to avoid being confronted, the legislature authorized debtors to discharge their obligations by turning the necessary currency over to a judge. Of course these measures further weakened public confidence; when the state tried to use paper money to meet its obligations to the federal government, Congress refused to accept it. Indeed, no one accepted the currency freely. The Rhode Island Supreme Court, in *Trevett v. Weeden,* declared that it was unconstitutional to fine a creditor for refusing it, and soon there was a reaction. The element of compulsion was withdrawn, and the paper depreciated rapidly.

"A Little Rebellion"

Although the Rhode Island case was atypical, it alarmed conservatives. Then, close on its heels, came a disturbing outbreak of violence in Massachusetts. The Massachusetts legislature was determined to pay off the state debt and maintain a sound currency. Taxes amounting to almost £1.9 million were levied between 1780 and 1786, the burden falling most heavily on those of moderate income. The historian Merrill Jensen estimates that the average Massachusetts farmer paid about a third of every year's income in taxes. Bad times and deflation led to many foreclosures, and the prisons were crowded with honest men unable to pay their debts. "Our Property is torn from us," one town complained, "our Gaols filled & still our Debts are not discharged."

In the summer of 1786 mobs in the western communities began to stop foreclosures by forcibly preventing the courts from holding their sessions. Under the leadership of Daniel Shays, veteran of Bunker Hill, Ticonderoga, and Saratoga, the "rebels" marched on Springfield and prevented the state supreme court from meeting. When the state government sent troops against them, they attacked the Springfield arsenal. They were routed, and the uprising then collapsed. Shays fled to Vermont.

In itself, "Shays' Rebellion" did not amount to much. As Thomas Jefferson observed at safe remove from the trouble in Paris, where he was serving as minister to France, it was only "a *little* rebellion" and as such "a medicine necessary for the sound health of government." Shays and his fellows were genuinely exasperated by the refusal of the government even to try to provide relief for their troubles. By taking up arms they forced the authorities to heed them: at its next session the legislature made some concessions to their demands. Good times soon returned and the uprising was forgotten. Yet the episode had an impact far beyond the borders of Massachusetts and all out of proportion to its intrinsic importance. Unlike Jefferson, most well-to-do Americans considered the uprising "Liberty run mad." "What, gracious God, is man! that there should be such inconsistency and perfidiousness in his conduct?" the usually unexcitable George Washington asked when news of the riots reached Virginia. "We are fast verging to anarchy and confusion!" During the crisis, private persons had had to subscribe funds to put the rebels down, and when Massachusetts had appealed to Congress for help there was little Congress could legally do. The lessons seemed plain: liberty must not become an excuse for license; greater authority must be vested in the central government.

The reactions to the Rhode Island excesses and the uprising in Massachusetts illustrated the continuing development of American nationalism. Citizens everywhere were concerned with what was going on in other parts of the country. Newspapers in all the states followed the bizarre spectacle of debtors in Rhode Island pursuing their creditors with fistfuls of paper money. The tragicomic revolt of Daniel Shays worried planters in far-off Virginia and the Carolinas almost as much as it did the merchants of Boston. All were becoming more conscious of their common interests, their national identity. Bacon's Rebellion, a far more serious affair, had evoked no such reaction in the 17th century, nor had the Regulator War in North Carolina as late as 1771.

The Road to Philadelphia

If most people wanted to increase the power of Congress, many were afraid to shift the balance too far lest they destroy the sovereignty of the states. The machinery for change etablished in the Articles of Confederation, which required the unanimous consent of the states for all amendments, posed a particularly delicate problem. Experience had shown it unworkable, yet to bypass it would be revolutionary and therefore dangerous.

The first fumbling step toward reform was taken in March 1785, when representatives of Virginia and Maryland, meeting at the home of George Washington to settle a dispute over the improvement of navigation on the Potomac River, suggested a conference of all the states to discuss common problems of commerce. In January 1786 the Virginia legislature sent out a formal call for such a gathering, to be held in September at Annapolis. However, the meeting disappointed advocates of reform; delegates from only five states appeared, and being so few they did not feel it worthwhile to propose changes.

Among the delegates was a young New York lawyer named Alexander Hamilton, a brilliant, imaginative, and daring man who was convinced that only drastic centralization would save the nation from disintegration. Instead of giving up, he proposed calling another convention to meet at Philadelphia to deal generally with constitutional reform. Delegates to the new convention should be empowered to work out a broad plan for correcting "such defects as may be discovered to exist" in the Articles of Confederation.

The Annapolis group approved Hamilton's suggestion, and Congress reluctantly endorsed it. This time all the states but Rhode Island sent delegates. On May 25, 1787, the convention opened its proceedings at the State House in Philadelphia and unanimously elected George Washington its president. When it adjourned four months later, it had drafted the Constitution.

The Great Convention

As the decades have passed and the Constitution has grown more and more tradition-encrusted without losing any of its flexibility, each generation has tried to explain how a people so young and inexperienced, so free-swinging and unruly, could have produced it. At the time of the hundredth anniversary of its signing, the British statesman William E. Gladstone called it "the most wonderful work ever struck off at a given time by the brain of man." One reason for its durability was the ability of those who drafted it. The Founding Fathers were remarkable men. Jefferson, who was on a foreign assignment and did not attend the convention, called them "demigods," though he later had reason to quarrel with certain aspects of their handiwork. Collectively they possessed a rare combination of talents. Although remarkably youthful—the typical delegate was in his early 40s—they had none of the weaknesses so often associated with youth: instability, overoptimism, half-cocked radicalism, and the refusal to heed the suggestions of others. But most of them had had considerable experience in politics and the many lawyers among them were skilled in negotiation. Furthermore, the times made them mature beyond their years and acutely aware of their opportunities. It was, John Adams wrote, "a time when the greatest lawgivers of antiquity would have wished to live," an opportunity to "establish the wisest and happiest government that human wisdom can contrive." "We . . . decide for ever the fate of republican government," James Madison said during the deliberations.

If these remarks overstated the importance of their deliberations, they nonetheless represented the opinion of most of those present. At the same time the delegates recognized the difficulties they faced. The ancient Roman republic was their model, and all knew that it had been overthrown by tyrants and eventually overrun by barbarians.

Fortunately, they were nearly all of one mind on basic questions. That there should be a federal system, with both independent state governments and a national government with limited powers to handle matters of common interest, was accepted by all but one or two of them. Republican government, drawing its authority from the people and remaining responsible to them, was a universal assumption. A measure of democracy followed inevitably from this principle, for even the most aristocratic delegates agreed that ordinary citizens should share in the process of selecting those who were to make and execute the laws.

All agreed that no group within society, no matter how numerous, should have *unrestricted* authority. They looked upon political power much as we today view nuclear energy: a force with tremendous potential value for mankind, but one easily misused and therefore dangerous to unleash. People meant well and had limitless possibilities, the constitution makers believed, but they were selfish by nature and could not be counted on to respect the interests of others. The poor, therefore, should have a say in government in order to be able to protect themselves against those who would exploit their weakness, and somehow the majority must be prevented from plundering the rich, for property must be secure or no government could be stable. No single state or section must be allowed to predominate, nor should the legislature be supreme over the executive or the courts. Power, in short, must be divided, and the segments must be balanced one against the other.

Although the level of education among them was high and a number might fairly be described as learned, the delegates' approach was pragmatic rather than theoretical. This was perhaps their most useful asset, for their task called for reconciling clashing interests. It could never have been accomplished without compromise and an acute sense of what was possible (as distinct from what was ideally best).

At the outset the delegates decided to keep the proceedings secret. That way no one was tempted to play to the gallery or seek some personal political advantage at the expense of the common good. Next they agreed to go beyond their instructions to revise the Articles of Confederation and draft an entirely new frame of government. This was a bold, perhaps illegal act, but it was in no way irresponsible because nothing the convention might recommend was binding on anyone. Alexander Hamilton, eager to scrap the Confederation in favor of a truly national government, captured the mood of the gathering when he said: "We can only propose and recommend—the power of ratifying or rejecting is still in the States. . . . We ought not to sacrifice the public Good to narrow Scruples."

James Madison was a key figure at the 1787 convention. This miniature was painted by Charles Willson Peale ca. 1783, when Madison was in his early thirties.

The Settlement

The delegates voted on May 30 that "a *national* Government ought to be established" and then set to work hammering out a specific plan. Two big questions had to be answered. The first—*What powers should this national government be granted?*—occasioned relatively little discussion. The right to levy taxes and to regulate interstate and foreign commerce was assigned to the central government almost without debate. So was the power to raise and maintain an army and navy and to summon the militia of the states to enforce national laws and suppress insurrections. With equal absence of argument, the states were deprived of their rights to issue money, to make treaties, and to tax either imports or exports without the permission of Congress. Thus, in summary fashion, was brought about a massive shift of power, a shift made necessary by the problems that had brought the delegates to Philadelphia and made practicable by the new nationalism of the 1780s.

The second major question—*Who shall control the national government?*—proved more difficult to answer in a manner satisfactory to all. Led by Virginia, the larger states pushed for representation in the national legislature based on population. The smaller states wished to maintain the existing system of equal representation for each state regardless of population. The large states rallied behind the Virginia Plan, drafted by James Madison and presented to the convention by Edmund Randolph, governor of the state. The small states supported the New Jersey Plan, prepared by William Paterson, a former attorney general of that state.

The question was important; equal state representation would have been undemocratic, while a proportional system would have effectively destroyed the influence of all the states *as states.* But the delegates saw it in terms of combinations of large or small states, and this was unrealistic: when the states combined, they did so on geographic, economic, or social grounds that seldom had any

On Friday, May 25, 1787, 29 delegates from 9 of the 13 states assembled in Philadelphia to deal with constitutional reform. New Hampshire, Connecticut, and Maryland were not yet there; Rhode Island never did appear. On Monday, September 17, of that same year, 39 of the 42 delegates still in attendance signed the final document. They had met in 88 sessions and taken 569 votes in all.

What backgrounds did these men have? What do we know about them? Here are . . .

FACTS ON THE

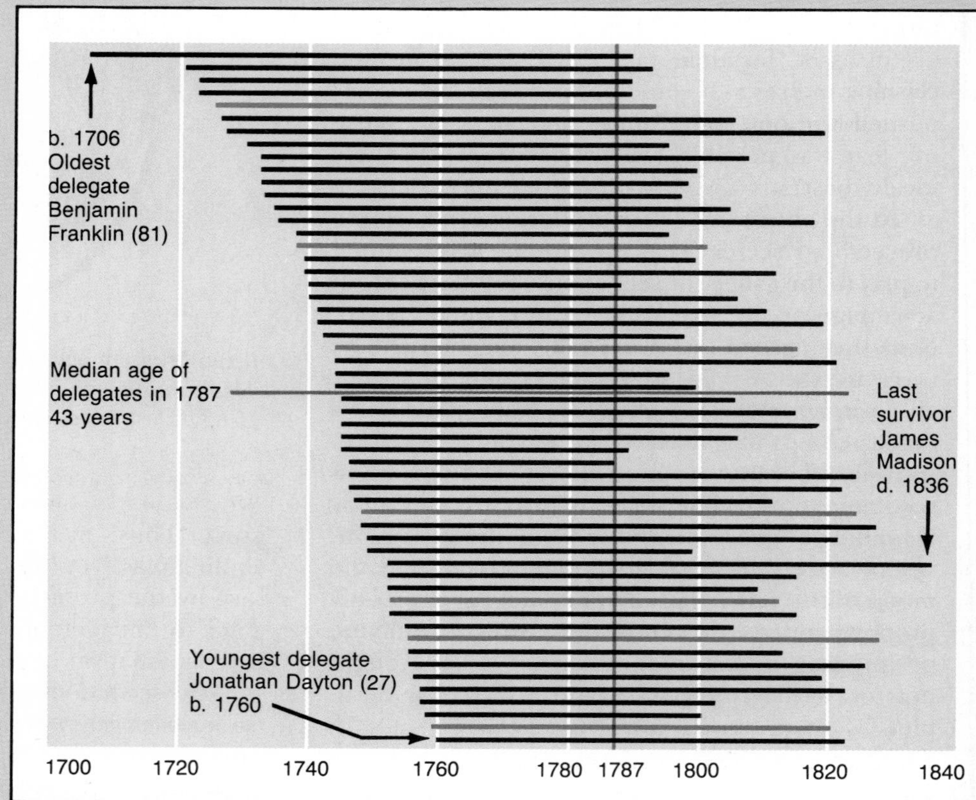

The median age of the U.S. population in 1790 was 16.

The mean age of death in 1800 was about 56.

How Old Were They?

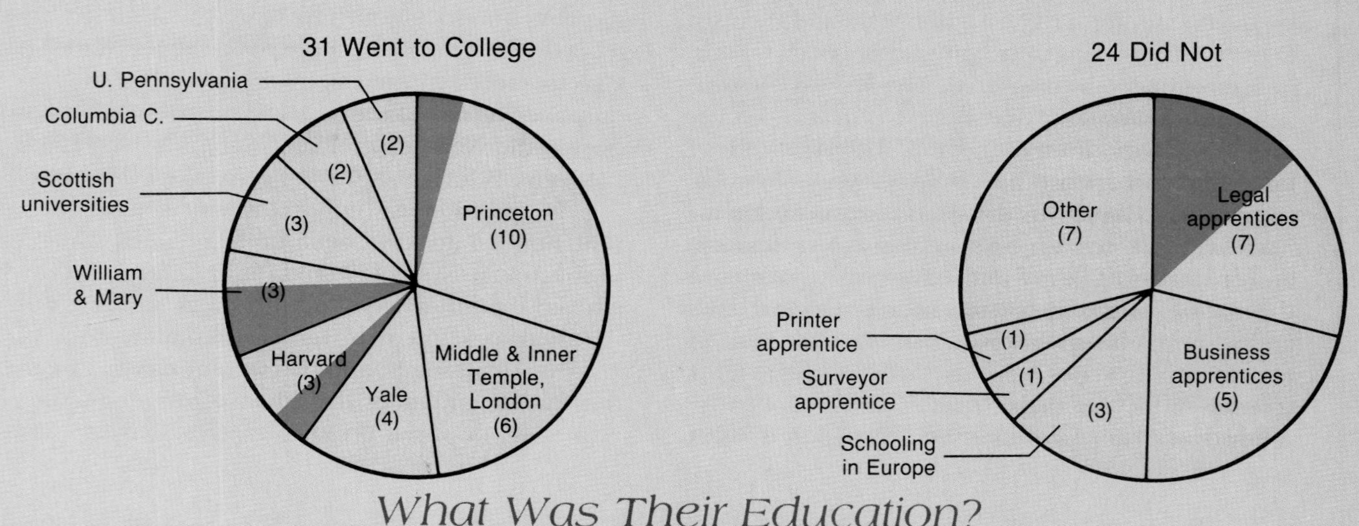

What Was Their Education?

The color red applies to those who opposed the Constitution.

FRAMERS

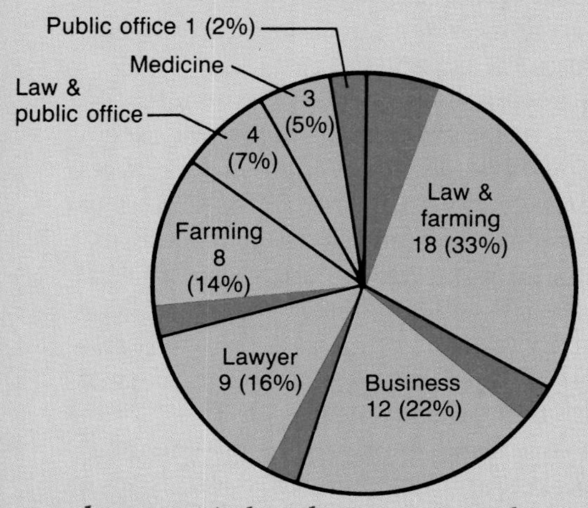

What Did They Do for a Living?

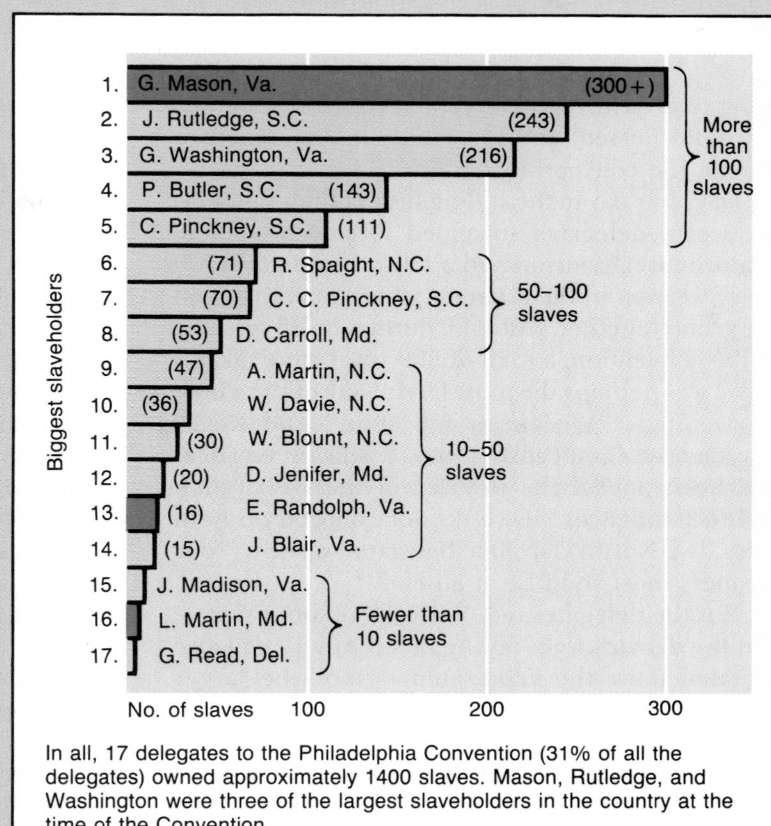

In all, 17 delegates to the Philadelphia Convention (31% of all the delegates) owned approximately 1400 slaves. Mason, Rutledge, and Washington were three of the largest slaveholders in the country at the time of the Convention.

How Many Were Slaveholders?

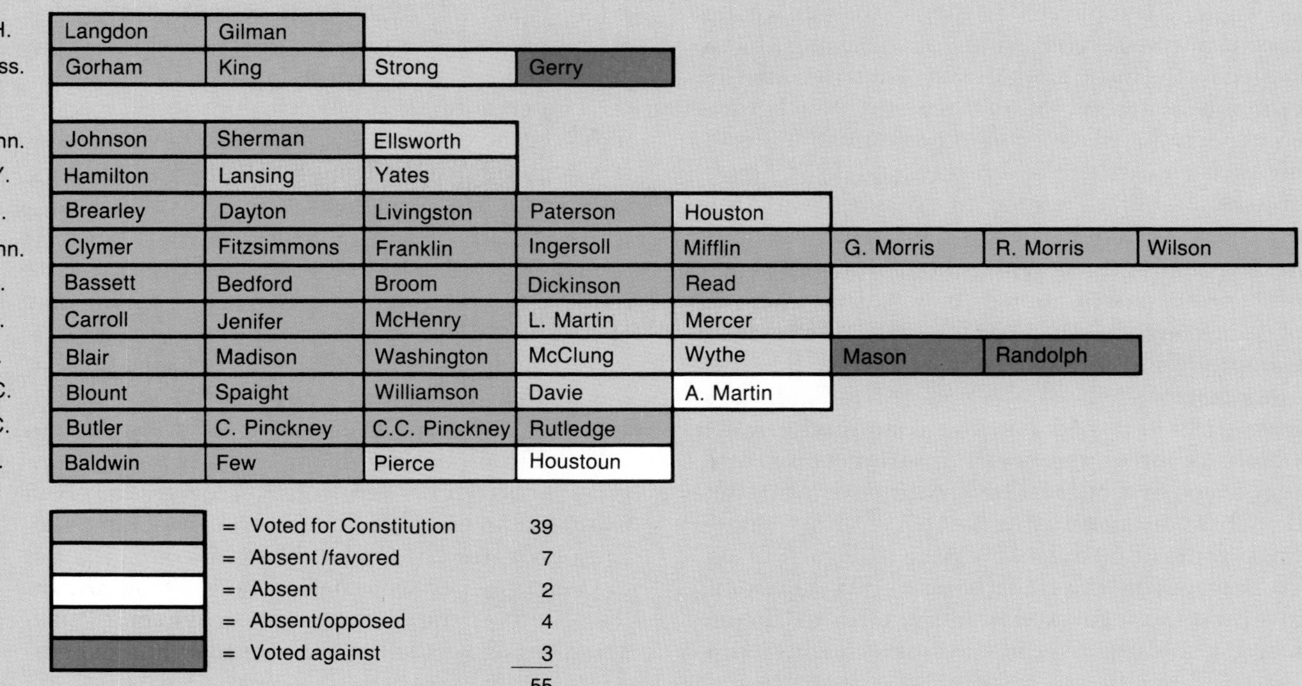

N.H.	Langdon	Gilman						
Mass.	Gorham	King	Strong	Gerry				
R.I.								
Conn.	Johnson	Sherman	Ellsworth					
N.Y.	Hamilton	Lansing	Yates					
N.J.	Brearley	Dayton	Livingston	Paterson	Houston			
Penn.	Clymer	Fitzsimmons	Franklin	Ingersoll	Mifflin	G. Morris	R. Morris	Wilson
Del.	Bassett	Bedford	Broom	Dickinson	Read			
Md.	Carroll	Jenifer	McHenry	L. Martin	Mercer			
Va.	Blair	Madison	Washington	McClung	Wythe	Mason	Randolph	
N.C.	Blount	Spaight	Williamson	Davie	A. Martin			
S.C.	Butler	C. Pinckney	C.C. Pinckney	Rutledge				
Ga.	Baldwin	Few	Pierce	Houstoun				

	= Voted for Constitution	39
	= Absent /favored	7
	= Absent	2
	= Absent/opposed	4
	= Voted against	3
		55

How Did They Vote?

thing to do with size. Nevertheless, the debate was long and heated, and for a time it threatened to disrupt the convention.

Day after day in the stifling heat of high summer, the weary delegates struggled to find a suitable compromise. Madison and a few others had to use every weapon in their arsenal of argument to hold the group together. (All told, during the 88 sessions of the convention, a total of 569 votes were taken.) July 2 was perhaps the most fateful day of the whole proceedings. "We are at full stop," said Roger Sherman of Connecticut, who, it will be recalled, had been one of the drafters of the Declaration of Independence. "If we do not concede on both sides," a North Carolina delegate warned, "our business must soon be at an end."

But the delegates did "concede on both sides," and the debates went on. Again on July 17 collapse threatened as the representatives of the larger states caucused to consider walking out of the convention. Fortunately they did not walk out, and finally the delegates adopted what is known as the Great Compromise. In the lower house of the new legislature—the House of Representatives—places were to be assigned according to population and filled by popular vote. In the upper house—the Senate—each state was to have two members, elected by its legislature.

Then a complicated struggle took place between northern and southern delegates, occasioned by the institution of slavery and the differing economic interests of the regions. Northerners contended that slaves should be counted in deciding each state's share of direct federal taxes. Southerners, of course, wanted to exclude slaves from the count. Yet southerners wished to include slaves in determining their representation in the House of Representatives, though they had no intention of permitting the slaves to vote. In the Three-fifths Compromise it was agreed that "three-fifths of all other Persons" should be counted for both purposes. (As it turned out, the compromise was a victory for the southerners, for no direct taxes were ever levied by Congress before the Civil War.) Settlement of the knotty issue of the African slave trade was postponed by a clause making it illegal for Congress to outlaw the trade before 1808. Questions involving the regulation of less controversial commerce also caused sectional disagreement. Southerners disliked export taxes because their staple products were largely sold abroad. In return for a clause prohibiting such taxes, they dropped their demand that all laws regulating foreign commerce be approved by two-thirds of both houses of Congress. Many other differences of opinion were resolved by the give-and-take of practical compromise. As the historian David M. Potter once said, the Constitution was "an exchange of promises" whereby different interests gained large advantages by making large concessions.

The final document, signed on September 17, established a legislature of two houses; an executive, consisting of a president with wide powers and a vice-president whose only function was to preside over the Senate; and a national judiciary, consisting of a Supreme Court and such "inferior courts" as Congress might decide to create. The lower, popularly elected branch of the Congress was supposed to represent especially the mass of ordinary citizens. It was given the sole right to introduce bills for raising revenue. The 26-member Senate was looked upon by many as a sort of advisory council similar to the upper houses of the colonial legislatures. Its consent was required before any treaty could go into effect and for major presidential appointments. The Founding Fathers also intended the Senate to represent in Congress the interests not only of the separate states but of what Hamilton called "the rich and the well-born" as contrasted with "the great mass of the people."

The creation of a powerful president was the most drastic departure from past experience, and it is doubtful that the Founding Fathers would have gone so far had everyone not counted on Washington, a man universally esteemed for character, wisdom, and impartiality, to be the first to occupy the office. Besides giving him general responsibility for executing the laws, the Constitution made the president commander in chief of the armed forces of the nation and general supervisor of its foreign relations. He was to appoint federal judges and other officials, and he might veto any law of Congress, although his veto could be overridden by a two-thirds majority of both houses. While not specifically ordered to submit a program of legislation to Congress, he was to deliver periodic reports on the "State of the Union" and recommend "such Measures as he shall judge necessary and expedi-

The room in Independence Hall where the constitutional convention was held has been scrupulously restored.

ent." Most modern presidents have interpreted this requirement as authorizing them to submit detailed legislative proposals and to use the full power and prestige of the office to get Congress to enact them.

Looking beyond Washington, whose choice was sure to come about under any system, the Constitution established a cumbersome method of electing presidents. Each state was to choose a number of "electors" equal to its representation in Congress. The electors, meeting separately in their own states, were to vote for two persons for president. Supposedly the procedure would prevent anyone less universally admired than Washington from getting a majority in the "electoral college," in which case the House of Representatives would choose the president from among the leading candidates, each state having but one vote. However, the swift rise of national political parties prevented the expected fragmentation of the electors' votes, and only two elections have ever gone to the House for settlement.

The national court system was set up to adjudicate disputes under the laws and treaties of the United States. No such system had existed under the Articles, a major weakness. Although the Constitution did not specifically authorize the courts to declare laws void when they conflicted with the Constitution, the courts soon exercised this right of "judicial review" in cases involving both state and federal laws.

That the Constitution reflected the commonly held beliefs of its framers is everywhere evident in the document. It greatly expanded the powers of the central government yet did not seriously threaten the independence of the states. Foes of centralization, at the time and ever since, have predicted the imminent disappearance of the states as sovereign bodies. But despite a steady trend toward centralization, probably inevitable as American society has grown ever more complex, the states remain powerful political organizations that are sovereign in many areas of government.

The Founders believed that since the new powers of government might easily be misused, each should be held within safe limits by some countervailing force. The Constitution is full of ingenious devices ("checks and balances") whereby one power controls and limits another without reducing it to impotence. The separation of legislative, executive, and judicial functions is the fundamental example of this principle. Others are the president's veto; Congress's power of impeachment, cleverly divided between House and Senate; the Senate's power over treaties and appointments; judicial review; and the balance between Congress's right to declare war and the president's control of the armed forces.

Ratification of the Constitution

Influenced by the widespread approval of the decision of Massachusetts to submit its state constitution of 1780 to the voters for ratification, the framers of the Constitution provided (Article VII) that their handiwork be ratified by special state conventions. This procedure gave the Constitution what Madison called "the highest source of authority"—the endorsement of the people, expressed through representatives chosen specifically to pass upon it. The framers may also have been motivated by a desire to bypass the state legislatures, where many members might resent the reductions being made in state authority. This was not of central importance because the legislatures could have blocked ratification by refusing to call conventions. Only Rhode Island did so, and since the Constitution was to go into operation when nine states had approved it, Rhode Island's stubbornness did no vital harm.

Such a complex and controversial document as the Constitution naturally excited argument throughout the country. Those who favored it called themselves Federalists, thereby avoiding the more accurate but politically unattractive label of Centralizers. Their opponents thus became the Antifederalists. It is difficult to generalize about the members of these groups. The Federalists tended to be substantial individuals, members of the professions, well-to-do, active in commercial affairs, and somewhat alarmed by the changes wrought by the Revolution. They were more interested, perhaps, in orderly and efficient government than in safeguarding the maximum freedom of individual choice, but they were, as a group, about as friendly to popular government as the Antifederalists.

The Antifederalists were more often small farmers, debtors, and persons to whom free choice was more important than power. But many rich and worldly citizens opposed the Constitution, and many poor and obscure persons were for it. It seems likely that most did not support or oppose the new system for narrowly selfish reasons. The historian David Ramsay, who lived at the time when these groups were forming, was probably correct when he wrote that "the great body of independent men who saw the necessity of an energetic government" swung the balance in favor of the Constitution.

Whether the Antifederalists were more democratic than the Federalists is an interesting question. Those who are loud for local autonomy do not necessarily believe in equal rights for all the locals. Many Antifederalist leaders had reservations about democracy. On the other hand, even Hamilton, no admirer of democracy, believed that the humblest citizens should have *some* say about their government. In general, practice still stood well ahead of theory when it came to popular participation in politics.

Various Antifederalists criticized many of the specific grants of authority in the new Constitution, some concocting farfetched arguments to show what disasters might ensue should it be put into effect. The routine clause (Article I, Section 4) giving Congress the power to regulate "the times, places, and manner of holding elections" threatened to "destroy representation entirely," a North Carolina Antifederalist claimed. The chief force behind the opposition was a vague fear that the new system would destroy the independence of the states.

It is important to keep in mind that the country was large and sparsely settled, that communication was primitive, and that the central government did not influence the lives of most people to any great degree. Many persons, including some who had been in the forefront of the struggle for independence, believed that a centralized republican system would not work in a country so large and with so many varied interests as the United States. Patrick Henry considered the Constitution "horribly frightful." It "squints toward monarchy," he added. That Congress could pass all laws "necessary and proper" to carry out the functions assigned it and legislate for the "general welfare" of the country seemed alarmingly all-inclusive. The first sentence of the Constitution, beginning "We the *people* of the United States" rather than "We the states," convinced many that the document represented centralization run wild. Another old revolutionary who expressed doubts was Samuel Adams, who remarked: "As I enter the Building I stumble at the Threshold."

Many members of the Convention were well-to-do and stood to profit from the establishment of a sound and conservative government that would honor its obligations, foster economic development, and preserve a stable society. Since the Constitution was designed to do all these things, it has been suggested that the Founders were not true patriots but selfish men out to protect their own interests. Charles A. Beard advanced this thesis in 1913 in *An Economic Interpretation of the Constitution*, arguing that most members of the Convention owned large amounts of depreciated government securities that were bound to rise in price if the Constitution was approved. The thesis does not stand up under close examination. The Founders wanted to advance their own interests as every normal human being does. Most of them, however, had no special involvement in securities, being far more concerned with land. The closest thing to a general spirit at Philadelphia was a public spirit. To call men like Washington, Franklin, and Madison self-seeking would be absurd.

Beard's book is important. It provided a necessary corrective to the 19th-century tendency to deify the Founding Fathers. The book properly called attention to the role of economic motivation in the framing of the Constitution. But it ought not to obscure the greatness of the Constitution or the men who made it.

Very little of the opposition to the Constitution grew out of economic issues. Most people wanted the national debt paid off; nearly everyone opposed an unstable currency; most favored uniform trade policies. Aside from a few doctrinaires, most were ready to give the new government a chance if they could be convinced that it would not destroy the states. When backers agreed to add amendments guaranteeing the civil liberties of the people against challenge by the national government and reserving all unmentioned power to the states, much of the opposition disappeared. Sam Adams ended up voting for the Constitution in the Massachusetts convention after the additions had been promised.

No one knows exactly how public opinion divided on the question of ratification. The Federalists were usually able to create an impression of strength far beyond their numbers and to overwhelm doubters with the mass of their arguments. They excelled in political organization and in persuasiveness. James Madison, for example, demolished the thesis that a centralized republican government could not function efficiently in a large country. In rule by the majority lay protection against the "cabals" of special interest groups. "Extend the sphere," Madison argued, "and you take in a greater variety of parties and interests; you make it less probable that a majority of the whole will have a common motive to invade the rights

New York's approval of the Constitution on July 26, 1788, inspired this cartoon in the Massachusetts Centinel. *Hopes were high that North Carolina would "rise" to ratify, but prospects in Rhode Island were not as bright—and, as expected, Rhode Island did not ratify the Constitution.*

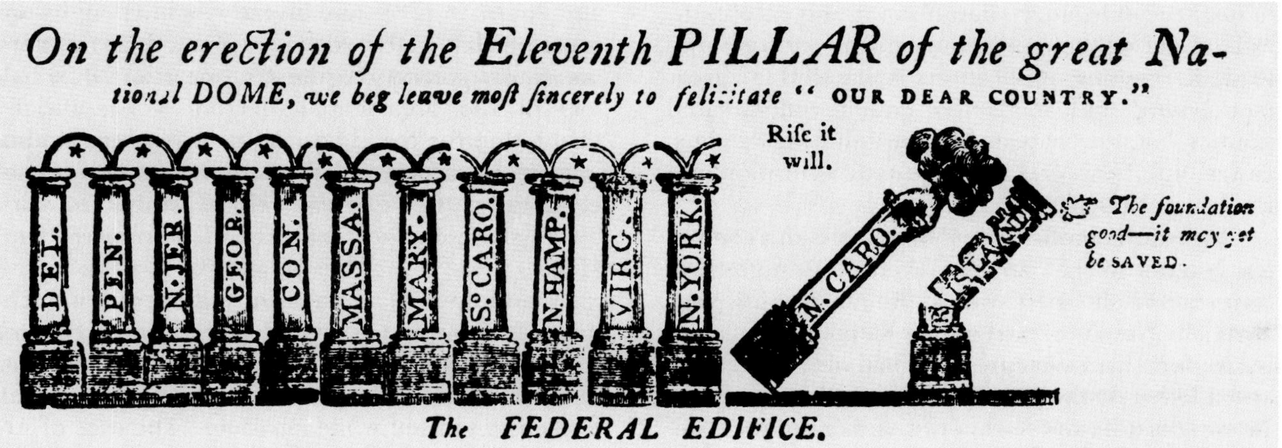

of other citizens." Moreover, the management of national affairs would surely attract leaders of greater ability and sounder character to public service than the handling of petty local concerns ever could in a decentralized system.

The Constitution met with remarkably little opposition in most of the state ratifying conventions, considering the importance of the changes it instituted. Delaware acted first, ratifying unanimously on December 7, 1787. Pennsylvania followed a few days later, voting for the document by a two-to-one majority. New Jersey approved unanimously on December 18; so did Georgia on January 2, 1788. A week later Connecticut fell in line, 128 to 40.

The Massachusetts convention provided the first close contest. Early in February, by a vote of 187 to 168, the delegates decided to ratify. In April Maryland accepted the Constitution by nearly six to one, and in May South Carolina approved, 149 to 73. New Hampshire came along on June 21, voting 57 to 47 for the Constitution. This was the ninth state, making the Constitution legally operative. On June 25, before the news from New Hampshire had spread throughout the country, the Virginia convention ratified, 89 to 79. Aside from Rhode Island, this left only New York and North Carolina outside the Union.

New York politics presented a complex and baffling picture during the entire Revolutionary era. Resistance to independence had been strong there in 1776 and remained a problem all through the war. Although New York was the third largest state, with a population rapidly approaching 340,000, it sided with the small states at Philadelphia, and two of its three delegates (Hamilton was the exception) walked out of the convention in July and took the lead in resisting ratification. A handful of great landowning and mercantile families dominated politics, but they were divided into shifting factions. In general, New York City favored ratification and the rural areas were against it.

The Antifederalists, well organized and competently led in New York by Governor George Clinton, won 46 of the 65 seats at the ratifying convention. The New York Federalists had one great asset in the fact that so many states had already ratified and another in the person of Alexander Hamilton. Although contemptuous of the *weakness* of the Constitution, Hamilton supported it with all his energies as being incomparably stronger than the old government. Working with Madison and John Jay, he produced the *Federalist Papers,* a brilliant series of essays explaining and defending the new system. These were published in the local press and later in book form. Although generations of judges and lawyers have treated them almost as parts of the Constitution, their impact on contemporary public opinion was probably slight. Open-minded members of the convention were undoubtedly influenced, but few delegates were open-minded.

Hamilton became virtually a one-man army in defense of the Constitution, plying hesitating delegates with dinners and drinks, facing obstinate ones with the threat that New York City would secede from the state if the Constitution were rejected. He spoke, one of the leading Antifederalists at the convention remarked, "frequently, very long, and very vehemently" on every aspect of the Constitution, posing as a devoted supporter of republican government and scoffing at the idea that the Constitution represented a threat to liberty. Once New Hampshire and Virginia had ratified, opposition in New York became a good deal less intransigent. In the end, by promising to support a call for a second national convention to consider amendments, the Federalists carried the day, 30 to 27. With New York in the fold, the new government was free to get under way. North Carolina finally ratified in November 1789, Rhode Island the following May.

Washington as President

Elections took place in the states during January and February 1789, and by early April enough congressmen had gathered in New York, the temporary national capital, to commence operation. The ballots of the presidential electors were officially counted in the Senate on April 6, Washington being the unanimous choice. John Adams, with 34 electoral votes, won the vice-presidency. On April 30 Washington took the oath of office at Federal Hall.

Washington made a firm, dignified, conscientious, but cautious president. His acute sense of responsibility and his sensitivity to the slightest criticism made it almost impossible for him to relax and enjoy himself while in office. "The eyes of Argus are upon me," he complained, "and no slip

Amos Doolittle's engraving of "Federal Hall, the Seat of Congress" is the only known contemporary depiction of Washington's inauguration. Note the newly designed United States seal above the assembled dignitaries.

will pass unnoticed." Each presidential action must of necessity establish a precedent. Hoping to make the presidency appear respectable in the eyes of the world, he saw to it that his carriage was drawn by six cream-colored horses, and when he rode (he was a magnificent horseman), it was upon a great white charger, with the saddle of leopardskin and the cloth edged in gold. Twenty-one servants (seven of them slaves) attended his needs at the presidential mansion on Broadway. When guests arrived for state functions, they were met at the entry by powdered lackeys.

Washington meticulously avoided treading upon the toes of Congress, for he took seriously the principle of the separation of powers. Never would he speak for or against a candidate for Congress, nor did he think that the president should push or even propose legislation. When he knew a controversial question was to be discussed in Congress, he avoided the subject in his annual message. The veto, he believed, should be employed only when the president considered a bill unconstitutional.

Although the Constitution said nothing about a presidential cabinet, Washington established the system of calling his department heads together for general advice, a practice that was followed by his successors. In selecting these department heads and other important administrators, he favored no particular faction. He insisted only that appointees be competent and "of known attachment to the Government we have chosen." He picked Hamilton for secretary of the treasury, Jefferson for secretary of state, General Henry Knox of Massachusetts for secretary of war, and Edmund Randolph for attorney general. He called upon them for advice according to the logic of his particular needs and frequently without regard for their own specialties. Thus he sometimes consulted Jefferson about financial matters and Hamilton about foreign affairs.

This system caused resentment and confusion, especially when rival factions began to coalesce around Hamilton and Jefferson. Nevertheless, Washington persisted in acting as though no political organizations existed, for he wished to minimize conflict.

Despite his respect for the opinions of others, Washington was a strong chief executive. As Hamilton put it, he "consulted much, pondered much, resolved slowly, resolved surely." His stress on the dignity of his office suited the needs of a new country whose people tended to be perhaps too informal. It was indeed important that the *first* president be particularly concerned about establishing precedents. His scrupulous care lest he overstep the bounds of presidential power helped erase the prejudices of those who feared that republican government must inevitably succumb to dictatorship and tyranny. When each step is an experiment, when foreign dangers loom at the end of every errant path, it is surely wise to go slowly. And no one should forget that Washington's devotion to duty did not always come easily. Occasionally he exploded. Thomas Jefferson has left us a graphic picture of the president at a Cabinet meeting, in a rage because of some unfair criticism, swearing that "by god he had rather be on his farm than to be made *emperor of the world.*"

Congress Under Way

The first Congress had the task of constructing the machinery of government. By September 1789 it had created the State, Treasury, and War departments and passed a Judiciary Act establishing 13 federal district courts and three circuit courts of appeal. The number of Supreme Court justices was set at six, and Washington named John Jay chief justice.

True to Federalist promises—for a large majority of both houses were friendly to the Constitution—Congress prepared a list of a dozen amendments (10 were ratified) guaranteeing what Congressman James Madison, who drafted the amendments, called the "great rights of mankind." These amendments, known as the Bill of Rights, provided that Congress should make no law infringing freedom of speech, the press, or religion. The right of trial by jury was reaffirmed, the right to bear arms guaranteed. No one was to be subject to "unreasonable" searches or seizures nor compelled to testify against himself in a criminal case. No one was to "be deprived of life, liberty, or property, without due process of law." The Bill of Rights was unique; the English Bill of Rights of 1689 was much less broad-gauged and, being an act of Parliament, was subject to repeal by Parliament at any time. The Tenth Amendment—not, strictly speaking, a part of the Bill of Rights—was designed to mollify those who feared that the states would be destroyed by the new government. It provided that powers not delegated to the United States or denied specifically to the states by the Constitution were to reside either in the states or in the people.

As experts pointed out, the amendments were not logically necessary because the federal government had no authority to act in such matters to begin with. But many had wanted to be reassured. Experience has proved repeatedly that whatever the logic of the situation, the protection afforded individuals by the Bill of Rights has been anything but unnecessary.

The Bill of Rights did much to convince doubters that the new government would not become too powerful. More complex was the task of proving that it was powerful enough to deal with those national problems that the Confederation had not been able to solve: the threat to the west posed by the British, Spaniards, and Indians; the disruption of the pattern of American foreign commerce resulting from independence; the collapse of the financial structure of the country.

Hamilton and Financial Reform

One of the first acts of Congress in 1789 was to employ its new power to tax. The simplest means of raising money seemed to be that first attempted by the British after 1763, a tariff on foreign imports. Congress levied a 5 percent duty on all foreign products entering the United States, applying higher rates to certain products, such as hemp, glass, and nails, as a measure of protection for American producers. The Tariff Act of 1789 also placed heavy tonnage duties on all foreign shipping, a mercantilistic measure designed to stimulate the American merchant marine.

Raising money for current expenses was a small and relatively simple aspect of the financial problem faced by Washington's administration. The nation's debt was large, its credit shaky, its economic future uncertain. In October 1789 Congress deposited upon the slender shoulders of Secretary of the Treasury Hamilton the task of straightening out the fiscal mess and stimulating the country's economic development.

Hamilton at 34 had already proved himself a remarkable man. Born in the British West Indies, the illegitimate son of a shiftless Scot who was little better than a beachcomber, and raised by his mother's family, he went to New York in 1773 to attend King's College. When the Revolution broke out, he joined the army. At 22 he was a staff colonel, aide-de-camp to Washington. Later, at Yorktown, he led a line regiment, displaying a bravery approaching foolhardiness. He married the daughter of Philip Schuyler, a wealthy and influential New Yorker, and after the Revolution he practiced law in that state.

Hamilton was a bundle of contradictions. Witty, charming, possessed of a mind like a sharp knife, he was sometimes the soul of practicality, sometimes an incurable romantic. No more hard-headed realist ever lived, yet he was quick to resent any slight to his honor, even—tragically—ready to fight a duel though he abhorred the custom of dueling. A self-made man, he admired aristocracy and disparaged the abilities of the common run of mankind who, he said, "seldom judge or determine right." Although granting that Americans must be allowed to govern themselves, he was as apprehensive of the "turbulence" of the masses as a small boy passing a graveyard in the dark. "No popular government was ever without its Catilines and its Caesars," he warned—a typical example of that generation's concern about the fate of the Roman republic.

The country, Hamilton insisted, needed strong national government. "I acknowledge," he wrote in one of the *Federalist Papers,* "my aversion to every project that is calculated to disarm the government of a single weapon, which in any possible contingency might be usefully employed for the general defense and security." That government should be "a great Federal Republic," not "a number of petty states, with the appearance only of union, jarring, jealous, perverse, without any determined direction." He wished to reduce the states to mere administrative units, like English counties.

As secretary of the treasury, Hamilton proved to be a farsighted economic planner. The United States, a "Hercules in the cradle," needed capital to develop its untapped material and human resources. To persuade investors to commit their funds in America, the country would have to convince them that it would meet every obligation in full. His *Report on the Public Credit* outlined the means for accomplishing this objective. The United States owed more than $11 million to foreigners and over $40 million to its own citizens. Hamilton suggested that this debt be funded at par, which meant calling in all outstanding securities and issuing new bonds to the same face value in their stead, and establishing an untouchable sinking fund to assure payment of interest and principal. Further, the remaining state debts should be assumed (taken over) by the United States on the same terms.

"To confess my weakness," Hamilton wrote when he was only 14, "my ambition is prevalent." This pastel drawing by James Sharples was made about 1796.

While most members of Congress agreed, albeit somewhat grudgingly, that the debt should be funded at par, many believed that at least part of the new issue should go to the original holders of the old securities: the soldiers, farmers, and merchants who had been forced to accept them in lieu of cash for goods and services rendered the Confederation during the Revolution. Many of these people had sold their securities for a fraction of their face value to speculators; under Hamilton's proposal, the speculators would make a killing. To the argument for divided payment, Hamilton answered coldly: "[The speculator] paid what the commodity was worth in the market, and took the risks. . . . He . . . ought to reap the benefit of his hazard."

Hamilton was essentially correct, and in the end Congress had to go along. After all, the speculators had not caused the securities to fall in value; indeed, as a group they had favored sound money and a strong government. The best way to restore the nation's credit was to convince investors that the government would honor all obligations in full. What infuriated his contemporaries and still attracts the scorn of many historians was Hamilton's motive. He deliberately intended his plan to give a special advantage to the rich. The government would be strong, he thought, only if well-to-do Americans enthusiastically supported it. What better way to win them over than to make it worth their while financially to do so?

In part, opposition to the funding plan was sectional, for citizens of the northern states held more than four-fifths of the national debt. The scheme for assuming the state debts aggravated the controversy, since most of the southern states had already paid off much of their Revolutionary War obligations. For months Congress was deadlocked. Finally, in July 1790, Hamilton worked out a compromise with Representative James Madison of Virginia and Secretary of State Jefferson. The two Virginians swung a few southern votes, and Hamilton induced some of his followers to support the southern plan for locating the permanent capital of the Union on the Potomac River.

Jefferson later claimed that Hamilton had hoodwinked him. Having only recently returned from Europe, he said, "I was really a stranger to the whole subject." Hamilton had persuaded him to "rally around" by the false tale that "our Union" was threatened with dissolution. This was nonsense; Jefferson agreed to the compromise because he expected that Virginia and the rest of the south would profit from having the capital so near at hand.

The assumption bill passed, and the entire funding plan was a great success. Soon the United States had the highest possible credit rating in the world's financial centers. Foreign capital poured into the country.

Hamilton next proposed that Congress charter a national bank. Such an institution would provide safe storage for government funds and serve as an agent for the government in the collection, movement, and expenditure of tax money. Most important, it would issue bank notes, thereby providing a vitally needed medium of exchange for the specie-starved economy. This Bank of the United States was to be partly owned by the government, but 80 percent of the $10 million stock issue was to be sold to private individuals.

The country had much to gain from such a bank, but again—Hamilton's devilish cleverness was never more in evidence—the well-to-do commercial classes would gain still more. Government balances in the bank belonging to all the people would earn dividends for a handful of rich investors. Manufacturers and other capitalists would profit from the bank's credit facilities. Public funds would be invested in the bank, but control would remain in private hands, since the government would appoint only 5 of the 25 directors. Nevertheless, the bill creating the bank passed both houses of Congress with relative ease in February 1791.

President Washington, however, hesitated to sign it, for the bill's constitutionality had been questioned during the debate in Congress. Nowhere did the Constitution specifically authorize Congress to charter corporations or engage in the banking business. As was his wont when in doubt, Washington called upon Jefferson and Hamilton for advice.

Hamilton defended the legality of the bank. Since a logical connection existed between the purpose of the bill and powers clearly stated in the Constitution, he wrote, the bill was constitutional. "A bank has a natural relation to the power of collecting taxes—to that of regulating trade to that of providing for the common defence." Jefferson disagreed. Congress could only do what the Constitution specifically authorized, he said. The "elastic clause" granting it the right to pass "all Laws which shall be necessary and proper" to carry out the specified powers must be interpreted literally or Congress would "take possession of a boundless field of power, no longer susceptible to any definition." Because a bank was obviously not *necessary,* it was not authorized.

Although not entirely convinced, Washington accepted Hamilton's reasoning and signed the bill. He could just as easily have followed Jefferson, for the Constitution is not clear. If one stresses *proper* in the "necessary and proper" clause, one ends up a Hamiltonian; if one stresses *necessary,* then Jefferson's view is correct. Historically (and this is the important point) politicians have nearly always adopted the "loose" Hamiltonian interpretation when they favor a measure and the "strict" Jeffersonian one when they do not. Jefferson disliked the bank; therefore he claimed it was unconstitutional. Had he approved, he doubtless would have taken a different tack. In 1819 the Supreme Court officially sanctioned Hamilton's construction of the "necessary and proper" clause (see pages 258–260), and in general that interpretation has prevailed. Because the majority tends naturally toward an argument that increases its freedom of action, the pressure for this view has been continual and formidable.

The Bank of the United States succeeded from the start. When its stock went on sale, investors snapped up every share in a matter of hours. People eagerly accepted its bank notes at face value. Business ventures of all kinds found it easier to raise new capital. Soon state-chartered banks entered the field. There were only 3 state banks in 1791; by 1801 the number was 32.

Hamilton had not finished. In December 1791 he submitted his *Report on Manufactures,* a bold call for economic planning. The pre-Revolutionary nonimportation agreements and wartime shortages had stimulated interest in manufacturing. Already a number of joint-stock companies had been founded to manufacture textiles, and an elaborate argument for economic diversification had been worked out by American economists such as Tench Coxe and Mathew Carey. Hamilton was familiar with these developments. In his *Report* he called for government tariffs, subsidies, and awards to encourage American manufacturing. He hoped to change an essentially agricultural nation into one with a complex, self-sufficient economy.

Once again business and commercial interests in particular would benefit. They would be protected against foreign competition and otherwise subsidized, whereas the general taxpayer, particularly the farmer, would pay the bill in the form of higher taxes and higher prices on manufactured goods. Hamilton argued that in the long run every interest would profit, and he was undoubtedly sincere, being too much the nationalist to favor one section at the expense of another. A majority of the Congress, however, balked at so broad-gauged a scheme. Hamilton's *Report* was pigeonholed, though many of the specific tariffs he recommended were enacted into law in 1792.

Nevertheless, the secretary of the treasury had managed to transform the financial structure of the country and to prepare the ground for an economic revolution. The constitutional reforms of 1787 had made this possible, and Hamilton turned possibility into reality.

Foreign Affairs

The western issues and those related to international trade proved more difficult because other nations were involved. The British showed no disposition to evacuate their posts on American soil simply because the American people had decided to strengthen their central government, nor did the western Indians suddenly agree to abandon their hunting grounds to the white invaders. Military campaigns against the Indians were at first unsuccessful. When a bill was introduced in Congress to bring economic pressure on the British by placing discriminatory tonnage duties on British ships, it was defeated because of the opposition of northern business interests.

However, events that had nothing to do with the new Constitution enabled the United States to achieve most of its objectives. In 1789 revolution broke out in France. By 1793 a republic had been proclaimed, King Louis XVI had been beheaded, and France had become embroiled in a war with the chief European nations. The war caused a great deal of trouble for the United States, but it presented the United States with a marvelous opportunity to play one side off against the other.

With France fighting Great Britain and Spain, there arose the question of America's obligations under the Alliance of 1778. That treaty required the United States to defend the French West Indies "forever against all other powers." Suppose the British attacked Martinique; must America then go to war? Morally the United States was so obligated, but no responsible American statesman urged such a policy. With the British in Canada and Spanish forces to the west and south, the nation would be in serious danger if it entered the war. Instead, in April 1793, Washington issued a proclamation of neutrality committing the United States to "conduct friendly and impartial" toward both sides in the war.

Meanwhile the French had sent a special representative, Edmond Charles Genet, to the United States to seek support. The French Revolution had excited much enthusiasm in the United States, for it seemed to indicate that American democratic ideas were already engulfing the world. The increasing radicalism in France tended to dampen some of the enthusiasm, yet when "Citizen" Genet landed at Charleston, South Carolina, the majority of Americans probably wished the revolutionaries well. As Genet, a charming ebullient young man, made his way northward to present his credentials, cheering crowds welcomed him in every town. Quickly concluding that the proclamation of neutrality was "a harmless little pleasantry designed to throw dust in the eyes of the British," he began, in plain violation of American law, to license American vessels to operate as privateers against British shipping and to grant French military commissions to a number of American adventurers in order to mount expeditions against Spanish and British possessions in North America.

Washington received Genet coolly, and soon thereafter he flatly ordered him to stop his illegal activities. Genet, whose capacity for self-deception was monumental, appealed to public opinion over the president's head and continued to commission privateers. Washington then demanded his recall. The incident ended on a ludicrous note. When Genet left France, he had been in the forefront of the Revolution. Now events had marched swiftly leftward, and the new leaders in Paris considered him a dangerous reactionary. His replacement arrived in America with an order for his arrest. To return might well mean the guillotine, so Genet asked the government that was expelling him for political asylum! Washington agreed, for he was not a vindictive man. A few months later the bold revolutionary married the daughter of the governor of New York and settled down to become a farmer on Long Island.

The Genet affair was incidental to a far graver problem. Although the European war increased the foreign demand for American products, it also led to attacks on American shipping by both France and Great Britain. Each power captured American vessels headed for the other's ports whenever it could. In 1793 and 1794 perhaps 600 United States ships were seized. The British attacks caused far more damage, both physically and psychologically, because the British fleet was much larger than France's, and France at least professed to be America's friend and to favor freedom of trade for neutrals. In addition the British issued secret orders late in 1793 turning their navy loose on neutral ships headed for the French West Indies. Pouncing without warning, British warships captured about 250 American vessels and sent them off as prizes to British ports. The merchant marine, one American diplomat declared angrily, was being "kicked, cuffed, and plundered all over the Ocean."

The attacks roused a storm in America, reviving hatreds that had been smoldering since the Revolution. The continuing presence of British troops in the northwest (in 1794 the British began to build a *new* fort in the Ohio country) and the restrictions imposed on American trade with the British West Indies raised tempers still further. To try to avoid a war, for he wisely believed that the United States should not become embroiled in the Anglo-French conflict, Washington sent Chief Justice John Jay to London to seek a settlement with the British.

Jay's Treaty

Jay spent months in England in 1794 discussing various issues. The British genuinely wanted to keep the peace—as one minister quipped, the Americans "are so much in debt to this country that we scarcely dare to quarrel with them." At the same time they were concerned about American intentions. Despite Washington's neutrality proclamation, the British feared that the two new republics, France and the United States, would draw together in a battle against Europe's monarchies. Furthermore, the British were riding the crest of a wave of important victories in the war, whereas the United States was pitifully unprepared.

The treaty that Jay brought home contained one major concession: the British agreed to evacuate the posts in the west. They also promised to compensate American shipowners for seizures in the West Indies and to open up their colonies in Asia to American ships. The British conceded nothing, however, to American demands that the rights of

The United States on the eve of the Louisiana Purchase. In 1804 Georgia's cession became part of the Mississippi Territory. The seven British western forts were evacuated as a result of Jay's Treaty (1795).

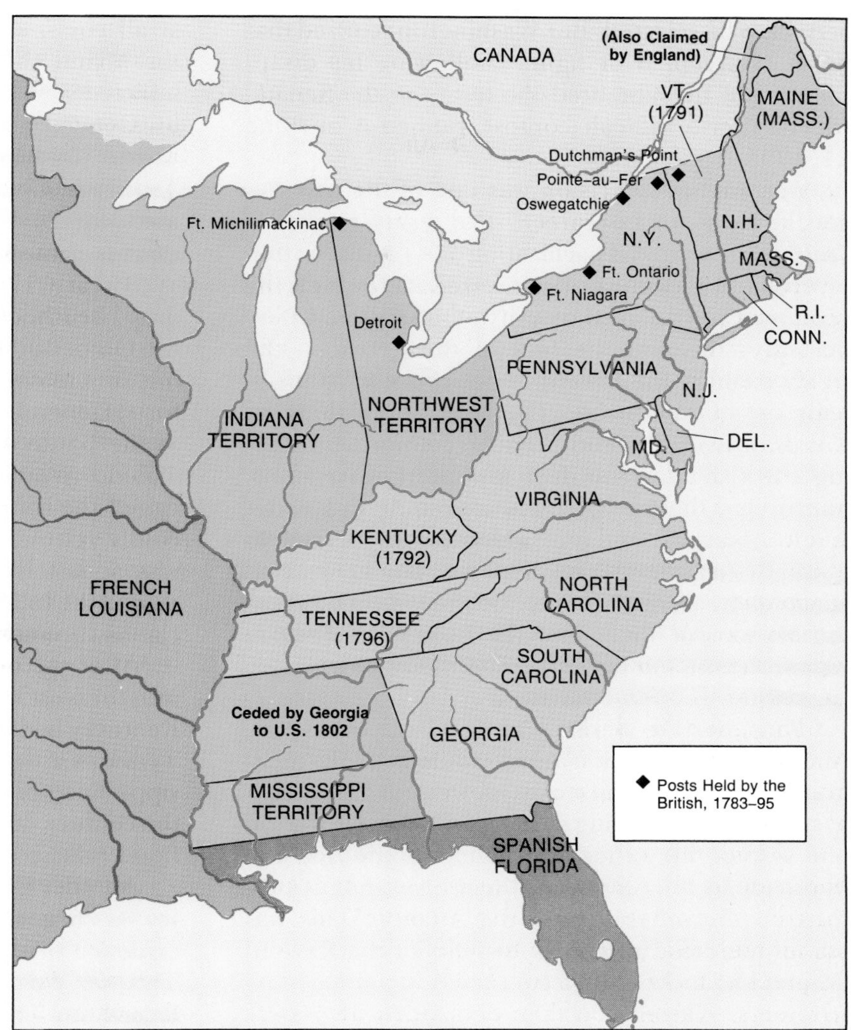

THE UNITED STATES, 1787–1802

neutrals on the high seas be respected; in effect, Jay submitted to the "Rule of 1756," a British regulation stating that neutrals could not trade in wartime with ports normally closed to them by mercantilistic restrictions in time of peace. A provision opening the British West Indies to American commerce was so hedged with qualifications limiting the size of American vessels and the type of goods allowed that the United States refused to accept it. Jay assented to an arrangement that prevented the United States from imposing discriminatory duties on British goods, an idea that a number of congressmen had proposed as a means of forcing Great Britain to treat American commerce more gently. He committed the United States government to paying pre-Revolutionary debts still owed British merchants, a slap in the face to many states whose courts had been impeding their collection. Yet nothing was said about the British paying for the slaves they had "abducted" during the fighting in the south.

Although Jay was perhaps too pro-British to have driven the hardest possible bargain, this was a valuable treaty for the United States. It was also a humiliating one. Most of what the United States gained already legally belonged to it, and the treaty sacrificed principles of tremendous importance to a nation dependent on foreign trade. It seemed certain to be rejected. But Washington realized that he must accept it or fight. Swallowing his disappointment, he submitted the treaty to the Senate, which, after a difficult contest, ratified it on June 24, 1795.

Washington's decision was one of the wisest—and luckiest—of his career. The treaty marked a long step toward the pacification and regularization of Anglo-American relations, essential for both the economic and political security of the nation. Unexpectedly—this was the luck of the decision—the treaty enabled the United States to solve its problems in the southwest. The Spanish, wishing to withdraw from the anti-French coalition and fearing a British attack on their American possessions, interpreted the Jay Treaty as a prelude to a wider Anglo-American entente. They quickly agreed to a treaty (negotiated by Thomas Pinckney) that granted the United States the free navigation of the Mississippi River and the right of deposit at New Orleans, and they accepted the American version of the Florida boundary.

Thus, despite alarms and divisive controversy, Americans for the first time avoided involvement in a war between the major powers of Europe. It had been a close thing, for many believed war on one side or the other desirable; but the decision was made by the Americans themselves, not by persons on the other side of the Atlantic. This was one of the most important benefits of the Revolution and of independence.

Federalism Militant

Jay's and Pinckney's treaties cleared the title of the United States to the vast region between the Appalachians and the Great River. At the same time the long struggle with the Indians, which had consumed a major portion of the government's revenues and had held back settlement of the Northwest Territory, was finally ended. The government's policy was "expansion with honor," with the emphasis on expansion. In 1789 Congress put Indian relations under the War Department rather than the State Department, a clear indication that force, not diplomacy, would be the main instrument of federal policy.

Trouble came swiftly when white settlers moved onto the land north of the Ohio River in large numbers. The Indians, determined to hold this country at all costs, struck hard at the invaders. In 1790 the Miami chief Little Turtle, a gifted strategist, inflicted a double defeat on troops commanded by General Josiah Harmar. The next year Little Turtle and his men defeated the forces of General Arthur St. Clair still more convincingly. Both Harmar and St. Clair resigned from the army, their careers ruined.

By early 1792 the Indians had driven the whites into "beachheads" at Marietta and Cincinnati on the Ohio. But in August 1794, while Jay was dickering in London for the evacuation of the British forts, General Anthony Wayne defeated the Indians at the Battle of Fallen Timbers, near present-day Toledo. When the British at Fort Miami, who had egged the tribesmen on with promises of aid, now coldly refused to help, the Indians' will to resist was at last broken. In the Treaty of Greenville, signed the following summer, they abandoned their claims to much of the Northwest Territory.

After the events of 1794–1795, settlers poured into the west as water bursts through a broken dike. Kentucky had become a state in 1792; now, in 1796, Tennessee was admitted. Two years later, Mississippi Territory was organized, and at the end of the century, Indiana Territory. The great westward flood reached full tide.

Another event that took place in the west while Jay was negotiating with the British offered further evidence of the growth of American nationalism. This was Washington's suppression of the Whiskey Rebellion. To help pay for the cost of assuming the state debts, Hamilton had persuaded Congress to put a stiff excise tax on whiskey. This hurt western farmers, who turned much of their grain into whiskey in order to cope with the high cost of transportation. When Hamilton frivolously replied to western complaints by suggesting that farmers drank too much to begin with and should cut down on their consumption if they found the tax oppressive, resentment increased. In the summer of 1794 rioting broke out in western Pennsylvania. Much like the Shaysites a few years earlier, the "rebels" interfered with judicial proceedings and terrorized local law enforcement officers. But the new Constitution made possible prompt and effective action against them. Washington, in an uncharacteristically harsh and precipitous decision, called up nearly 13,000 militiamen (more men than he had ever commanded during the Revolution) and marched westward. At this tremendous show of force the rebels vanished. There was no fighting. A few minor figures were thrown in jail, and thereafter the tax was peaceably collected until it was repealed during Jefferson's administration. The contrast with Shays' Rebellion warmed the hearts of all who feared "anarchy." Thus the events of the mid-1790s seemed to demonstrate that independence had been fully established and that the United States was well on its way to becoming a nation in fact as well as in name.

SUPPLEMENTARY READING

Titles marked with an asterisk have been published in paperback.

On the "critical period," see J. T. Main, **Political Parties before the Constitution** (1973). J. L. Davis, **Sectionalism in American Politics** (1977), is also useful. For the western problems of this period, see B. W. Bond, **The Foundations of Ohio** (1941), A. P. Whitaker, **The Spanish American Frontier*** (1927), and J. A. James, **Life of George Rogers Clark** (1928). On economic problems, E. J. Ferguson, **The Power of the Purse*** (1968), R. A. East, **Business Enterprise in the American Revolutionary Era** (1938), and T. C. Cochran, **New York in the Confederation** (1932), are useful, while C. P. Nettels, **The Emergence of a National Economy*** (1962), puts this subject in the broader perspective of the period 1775–1815. A lively treatment of Shays' Rebellion is M. L. Starkey, **A Little Rebellion** (1955); D. P. Szatmary, **Shays' Rebellion** (1980), is a more recent study.

The political thinking of the period is discussed lucidly in G. S. Wood, **The Creation of the American Republic*** (1969), and Richard Buel, Jr., **Securing the Revolution: Ideology in American Politics*** (1972). As for the making of the Constitution, the records kept by Madison and other delegates to the Constitutional Convention are reprinted in C. C. Tansill (ed.), **Documents Illustrative of the Formation of the Union . . .** (1927). A good general account of the convention is Clinton Rossiter, **1787: The Grand Convention*** (1966). The best treatment of Alexander Hamilton's connection with the Constitution and of his political views generally is Clinton Rossiter, **Alexander Hamilton and the Constitution** (1964). For Madison, Irving Brant, **James Madison: Father of the Constitution** (1950), provides the fullest account.

C. A. Beard, **An Economic Interpretation of the Constitution*** (1913), caused a veritable revolution in the thinking of historians about the motives of the Founding Fathers, but recent studies have caused a major reaction away from the Beardian interpretation; see especially R. E. Brown, **Charles Beard and the Constitution*** (1956), and a more detailed critique, Forrest McDonald, **We the People: The Economic Origins of the Constitution*** (1958). Two books by R. A. Rutland, **The Birth of the Bill of Rights*** (1955) and **The Ordeal of the Constitution: The Anti-Federalists and the Ratification Struggle** (1966), and also J. T. Main, **The Antifederalists*** (1961), are helpful in understanding the opposition to the Constitution, while the **Federalist Papers*** of Hamilton, Madison, and Jay, available in many editions, are essential for the arguments of the supporters of the new government. For the Bill of Rights, consult Bernard Schwartz, **The Great Rights of Mankind** (1977).

On the organization of the federal government and the history of the Washington administration, see L. D. White, **The Federalists** (1948), an administrative history, and J. C. Miller, **The Federalist Era*** (1960), a more general history of the period. Nathan Schachner, **The Founding Fathers*** (1954), is a somewhat fuller study of these years. Washington's presidency is treated in detail in the latter volumes of D. S. Freeman, **George Washington** (1948–1957). Joseph Charles, **Origins of the American Party System*** (1961), is thought-provoking, and the early chapters of W. N. Chambers, **Political Parties in a New Nation*** (1963), are also useful.

Hamilton's **Reports** as secretary of the treasury are conveniently collected in Samuel McKee, Jr. (ed.), **Papers on Public Credit, Commerce, and Finance by Alexander Hamilton*** (1934). The best of the many biographies of Hamilton are Broadus Mitchell, **Alexander Hamilton*** (1976), J. E. Cooke, **Alexander Hamilton** (1982), an up-to-date brief biography, and J. C. Miller, **Alexander Hamilton: A Portrait in Paradox*** (1959). For foreign affairs during the Washington administration, see Alexander De Conde, **Entangling Alliance: Politics and Diplomacy under George Washington** (1958), Felix Gilbert, **To the Farewell Address*** (1961), Harry Ammon, **The Genet Mission** (1973), and two volumes by S. F. Bemis, **Jay's Treaty*** (1923) and **Pinckney's Treaty*** (1926). Hannah Arendt, **On Revolution*** (1963), provides an interesting discussion of the relative influence of the French and American revolutions on later history.

TIME LINE 2 ▪ The Age of Democratic Revolution, 1735–1835

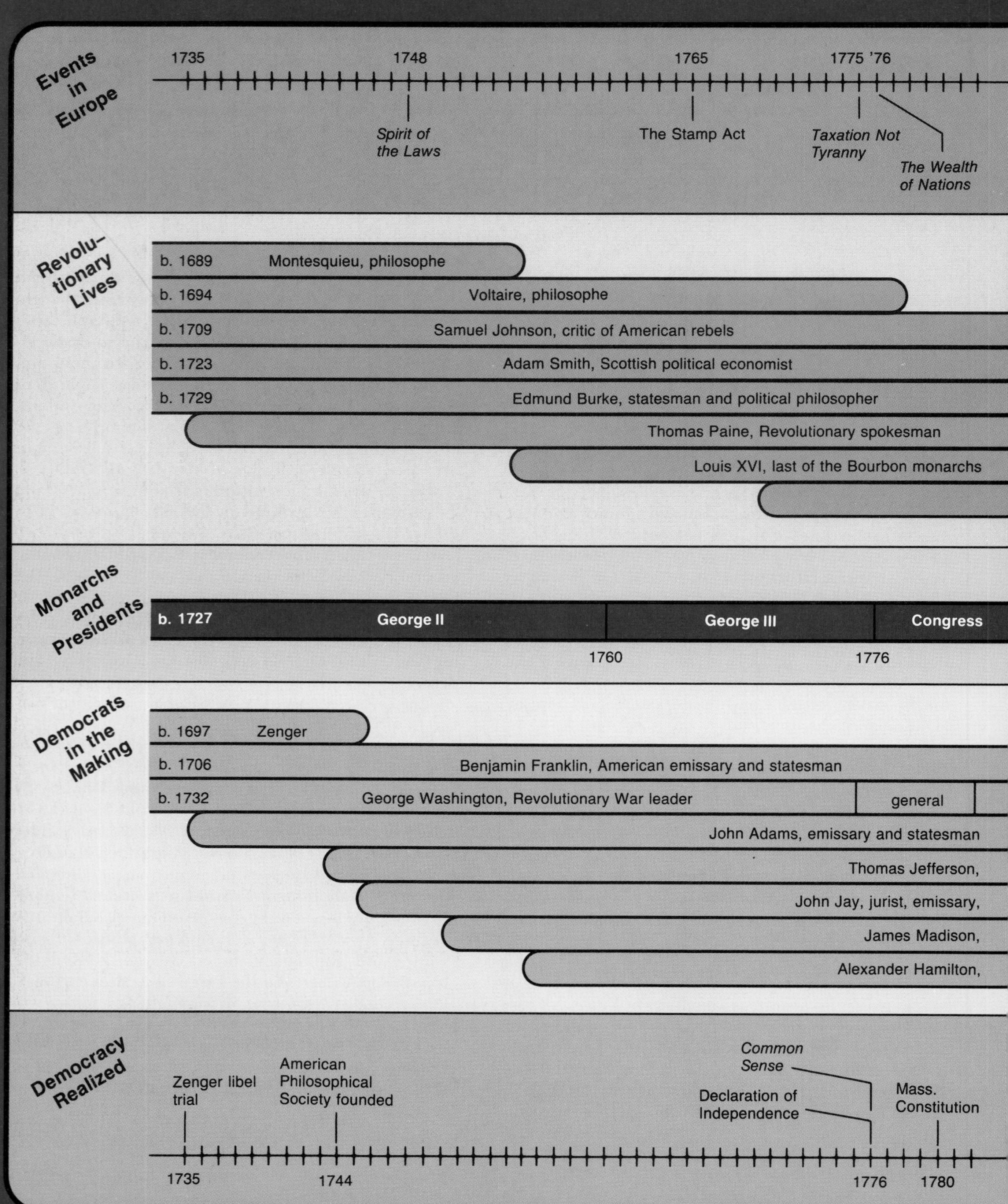

Events in Europe
1735
1748
1765
1775 '76
Spirit of the Laws
The Stamp Act
Taxation Not Tyranny
The Wealth of Nations
Revolutionary Lives
b. 1689 Montesquieu, philosophe
b. 1694 Voltaire, philosophe
b. 1709 Samuel Johnson, critic of American rebels
b. 1723 Adam Smith, Scottish political economist
b. 1729 Edmund Burke, statesman and political philosopher
Thomas Paine, Revolutionary spokesman
Louis XVI, last of the Bourbon monarchs
Monarchs and Presidents
b. 1727 George II
George III
Congress
1760
1776
Democrats in the Making
b. 1697 Zenger
b. 1706 Benjamin Franklin, American emissary and statesman
b. 1732 George Washington, Revolutionary War leader
general
John Adams, emissary and statesman
Thomas Jefferson,
John Jay, jurist, emissary,
James Madison,
Alexander Hamilton,
Democracy Realized
Zenger libel trial
American Philosophical Society founded
Common Sense
Declaration of Independence
Mass. Constitution
1735
1744
1776
1780

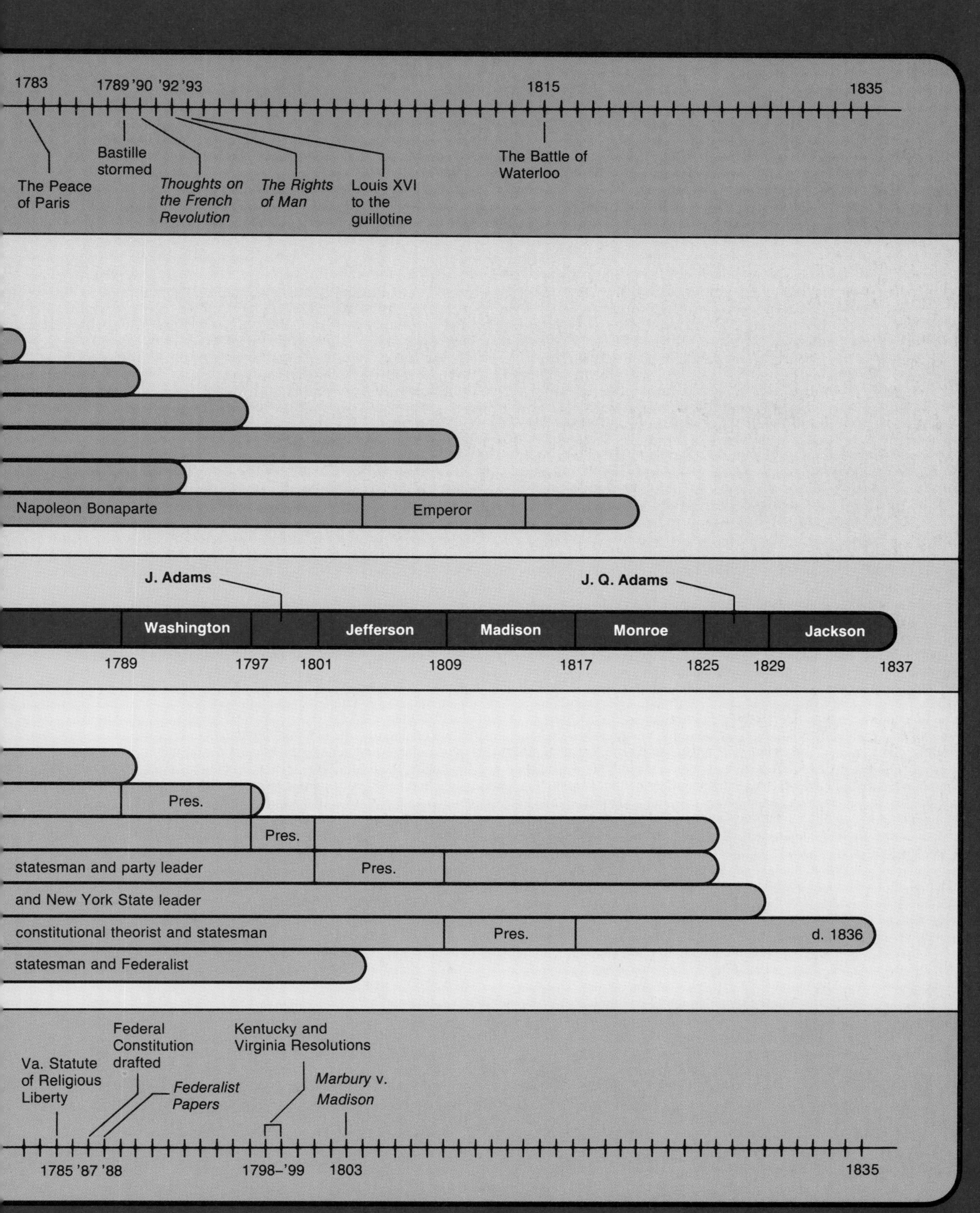

1783
1789
'90
'92
'93
1815
1835
The Peace of Paris
Bastille stormed
Thoughts on the French Revolution
The Rights of Man
Louis XVI to the guillotine
The Battle of Waterloo
Napoleon Bonaparte
Emperor
J. Adams
J. Q. Adams
Washington
Jefferson
Madison
Monroe
Jackson
1789
1797
1801
1809
1817
1825
1829
1837
Pres.
Pres.
statesman and party leader
Pres.
and New York State leader
constitutional theorist and statesman
Pres.
d. 1836
statesman and Federalist
Va. Statute of Religious Liberty
Federal Constitution drafted
Federalist Papers
Kentucky and Virginia Resolutions
Marbury v. Madison
1785
'87
'88
1798–'99
1803
1835

Jeffersonian Democracy

Nor is it true that Jefferson is zealot enough to do anything in pursuance of his principles, which will contravene his popularity or his interest. He is as likely as any man I know to temporize; to calculate what will be likely to promote his own reputation and advantage. . . . He is too much in earnest with his democracy. ALEXANDER HAMILTON, *1801*

No one had a better right to rejoice in the course of events in the mid-1790s than Alexander Hamilton. His financial reforms had achieved a dramatic success. Jay's Treaty had extinguished the danger of war with Great Britain, a conflict that in his opinion would have been catastrophic. And the Mississippi had been opened, another advance toward the national greatness he desired. Yet Hamilton was far from content, for a formidable opposition to himself and to everything he believed in had developed. The opposition was coalescing into a political party headed by Thomas Jefferson. A savage struggle for power was under way, the prize being the mantle of Washington, who was determined to retire at the end of his second term in 1797.

Thomas Jefferson: Political Theorist

Jefferson hardly seemed cut out for politics. Although in some ways a typical, pleasure-loving southern planter, he had in him something of the Spartan. He grew tobacco but did not smoke, and he partook only sparingly of meat and alcohol. Unlike most planters he never hunted or gambled, though he was a fine horseman and enjoyed dancing, music, and other social diversions. His practical interests ranged enormously—from architecture and geology to natural history and scientific farming—yet he displayed little interest in managing men. Controversy dismayed him, and he tended to avoid it by assigning to some thicker-skinned associate the task of attacking his enemies. Nevertheless, he wanted to have a say in shaping the future of the country, and once engaged he fought stubbornly and at times deviously to get and hold power.

Like Hamilton, Jefferson thought human beings basically selfish. "Lions and tigers are mere lambs compared with men," he once said. Although he claimed to have some doubts about the subject, he suspected that blacks were "inferior to whites in the endowments both of body and mind." (Hamilton, who also owned slaves, stated flatly of blacks: "Their natural faculties are as good as ours.") The historian Winthrop Jordan, who has made a careful study of white attitudes during this period, claims that Jefferson's opinion, however tenuous, was "the strongest suggestion of inferiority expressed by any native American of the time." Yet, like a good child of the Enlightenment, Jefferson believed that "no definite limits can be assigned to the improvability of the human race" and that unless people were free to follow the dictates of reason, the march of civilization would grind quickly to a halt. "To preserve the freedom of the human mind," he wrote, "every spirit should be ready to devote itself to martyrdom." Democracy seemed to him not so much an ideal as a practical necessity. If people could not govern themselves, how could they be expected to govern their fellows? He had no patience with Hamilton's fondness for magnifying the virtues of the rich and the well-born. He believed that "genius" was a rare quality but one "which nature has shown as liberally among poor as rich." When a very old man he wrote: "The mass of mankind has not been born with saddles on their backs, nor a favored few booted and spurred, ready to ride them legitimately, by the grace of God."

Jefferson believed *all* government a necessary evil at best, for by its nature it restricted the freedom of the individual. For this reason, he wanted the United States to remain a society of small independent farmers.* Such a nation did not need much political organization.

Jefferson's main objection to Hamilton was that Hamilton wanted to commercialize and centralize the country. This Jefferson feared, for it would mean the growth of cities, which would complicate society and hence require more regulation. "When we get piled upon one another in large cities, as in Europe," he wrote Madison in 1787, "we shall become corrupt as in Europe, and go to eating one another as they do there." Twenty years later he warned a nephew to avoid "populous cities" because, he said, in such places young men acquire "habits and partialities which do not contribute to the happiness of their afterlife." Like Hamilton, he believed that city workers were easy prey for demagogues. "I consider the class of artificers as the panders of vice, and the instruments by which the liberties of a country are usually overturned," he said. "Those who labor in the earth," he also said, "are the chosen people of God, if ever He had a chosen people."

---

* To Jefferson, agriculture was both the fundamental and the noblest of callings. "The greatest service which can be rendered to any country is to add a useful plant to its culture," he once said.

The Federalists often attacked Jefferson for his pro-French attitudes. A dog-eared cartoon, ca. 1790, shows Washington in the national chariot leading troops against an invasion of bloodthirsty French "Cannibals" at the left. The figures trying to halt the chariot are, from left, Albert Gallatin, Citizen Genet (holding the spoke of the wheel), and Jefferson.

Jefferson objected to what he considered Hamilton's pro-British orientation. Despite his support of the Revolution, Hamilton admired English society and the orderliness of the British government, and he modeled much of his financial program on the British example. To the author of the Declaration of Independence, these attitudes passed all understanding. Jefferson thought English society immoral and decadent, the British system of government fundamentally corrupt. Toward France, the two took opposite positions. Jefferson was in Paris when the French Revolution broke out; he was delighted to see another blow struck at tyranny. Leading French liberals consulted him at every turn. Later, as secretary of state, he excused the excesses of the French upheaval far more than did most Americans. To Hamilton, the violence and social disruption caused by the French Revolution were anathema.

The conflict between Hamilton and Jefferson came to a head slowly. At the start, Hamilton had the ear of the president, and his allies controlled a majority in Congress. Jefferson, who disliked controversy, avoided a direct confrontation as long as he could. He went along with Hamilton's funding plan and, as we have seen, traded the assumption of state debts for a capital on the Potomac. However, when Hamilton proposed the Bank of the United States and the Whiskey Tax, he dug in his heels. These measures seemed designed to benefit the northeastern commercial classes at the expense of southern and western farmers. He sensed a dastardly plot to milk the producing masses for the benefit of a few capitalists and suspected that Hamilton wanted to turn America into a monarchy.

Late in the spring of 1791 Jefferson and James Madison, the real organizer of the anti-Hamilton faction in Congress, began to sound out other politicians. He appointed a friend of Madison, the poet Philip Freneau, to a minor State Department post. Settling in Philadelphia, the new temporary capital, Freneau established a newspaper, the *National Gazette,* and was soon describing that "illustrious patriot" Thomas Jefferson as the "Colossus of Liberty" and flailing away editorially at Hamilton and his policies. Furious, Hamilton hit back hard at Jefferson through the columns of another Philadelphia paper, John Fenno's *Gazette of the United States.*

As their quarrel became more and more personal, first Jefferson and then Hamilton appealed to Washington for support. The poor president, who hated controversy even more than Jefferson, tried to get them to bury their differences—to no avail. The two now agreed on only one thing: Washington, who was in ill health and wished desperately to retire, must serve a second term.

Federalists and Republicans

Around the striking personalities of these quarreling leaders, two political camps began to gather. Jefferson's friends were the first to organize and of the two groups by far the more efficient. They called themselves Democratic Republicans. Congressional supporters of Hamilton took the name Federalists. Why national political parties emerged after the ratification of a Constitution that made no provision for such organizations is a question that has long intrigued historians. Probably the main reason was the obvious one: by creating a strong central government the Constitution produced national issues and a focus for national discussion and settlement of these issues. Furthermore, by failing to create machinery for nominating candidates for federal offices, the Constitution left a vacuum, which informal party organizations promptly filled.

In the early stages neither the Federalist nor the Democratic Republican was a party in the modern sense; there were no national committees, no conventions, no state "machines." In large measure the two parties were alliances of local and state groups, greatly influenced by parochial issues and the personalities of local leaders. Over time, however, closer-knit organizations developed.

What determined a voter's party allegiance in the 1790s is hard to pin down. No simple dichotomy between "forward looking" Hamiltonian business interests and "backward" Jeffersonian agrarian interests makes sense. The divisions were close, and since 90 percent of the citizens were farmers, a sharp commercial-agrarian split would have produced an overwhelming victory for the Democratic Republicans. Probably the most significant differences between Federalists and Republicans were psychological, or perhaps social. Both groups expected change and looked forward to it. But the typical Federalist preferred to think of change as an orderly progression presided over by established authority, while the Republican view was more free-form—one that emphasized individual ability and individual effort. Farmers who produced for commercial markets were somewhat more likely to respond to Federalist arguments, settlers in remote areas to those of the Democratic Republicans, but the division was far from clear. A majority of the privileged group that Hamilton appealed to voted Federalist, but numbers of merchants and other businessmen supported the Jeffersonians. As in the divisions over ratifying the Constitution, individuals of status with established interests tended to be Federalists, while those on the periphery of society (and those on the make) were more often on the other side. The problem was enormously complicated by conditions and traditions in the separate states.

In short, no clear-cut social or economic alignments appeared, although social and economic issues were certainly discussed by the politicians. The parties stood for their leaders more than for principles, and these men, dealing with a series of practical problems, were not always consistent in their attitudes.

The personal nature of early American political controversies goes far toward explaining why the party battles of the era were so bitter. So does the continuing anxiety that plagued partisans of both persuasions about the supposed frailty of a republican government. The United States was still very much an experiment; leaders who sincerely proclaimed their own devotion to its welfare suspected that their opponents wanted to undermine its institutions. Federalists feared that the Jeffersonians sought a dictatorship based on mob rule, Democratic Republicans that the Hamiltonians hid "under the mask of Federalism hearts devoted to monarchy."

The growing controversy over the French Revolution and the resulting war between France and Great Britain widened the split between the parties. After the radicals in France executed Louis XVI and instituted the Reign of Terror, American conservatives were horrified. The Jeffersonians, however, continued to defend the Revolution. Slaveowners could be heard singing the praises of *liberté, égalité, fraternité,* and great southern landlords, whose French counterparts were losing their estates—some their heads—were extolling "the glorious successes of our Gallic brethren." In the same way the Federalists began to idealize the British, whom they considered the embodiment of the forces that were resisting French radicalism.

This created an explosive situation. Enthusiasm for a foreign country might tempt Americans, all unwittingly, to betray their own. Hamilton came to believe that Jefferson was so prejudiced in favor of France as to be unable to conduct foreign affairs rationally, and Jefferson could say contemptuously: "Hamilton is panick struck, if we refuse our breech to every kick which Great Britain may choose to give it."

In fact, Jefferson never lost his sense of perspective. When the Anglo-French war erupted, he recommended neutrality. In the Genet affair, although originally sympathetic to the young envoy, Jefferson ended by characterizing him as "hot-headed, all imagination, no judgment, passionate, disrespectful and even indecent." He cordially approved Washington's decision to send Genet packing. Although he objected to the Jay Treaty, he did so not out of fondness for France but because he believed peace with Great Britain could not be purchased by surrendering American rights. "Acquiescence under insult is not the way to escape war," he wrote in 1795.

Hamilton perhaps went a little too far in his friendliness to Great Britain, but the real danger was that some of Hamilton's and Jefferson's excitable followers might become so committed as to forget the true interests of the United States.

Washington's Farewell

As long as Washington remained president, his popularity inhibited the solidification of party lines. On questions of finance and foreign policy he usually sided with Hamilton and thus increasingly incurred the anger of Jefferson. But he was, after all, a Virginian. Only the most rabid partisan could think him a tool of northern commercial interests. He remained as he intended himself to be, a symbol of national unity. But he was determined to put away the cares of office at the end of his second term. In September 1796 he announced his retirement in a "Farewell Address" to the nation.

Washington had found the acrimonious rivalry between Federalists and Republicans very disturbing. "I had no conceptions that Parties would . . . go the length I have been witness to," he complained to Jefferson. Hamilton advocated national unity, yet he seemed prepared to smash any individual or faction that disagreed with his vision of the country's future. Jefferson had risked his neck for independence, but he opposed the economic development needed to make America strong enough to defend that independence. Washington was less brilliant than either Hamilton or Jefferson but wiser. He appreciated how important it was that the new nation remain at peace—with the rest of the world and and with itself. In his farewell he deplored the "baneful effects of the spirit of party" that led honest people to use unscrupulous means to win a mean advantage over fellow Americans. He tried to show how the north benefited from the prosperity of the south, the south from that of the north, and the east and west also, in reciprocal fashion. It is significant that he drew on the suggestions of both Hamilton and Madison in preparing his farewell.

Washington urged the people to avoid both "inveterate antipathies" and "passionate attachments" to any foreign nation. Nothing had alarmed him more than the sight of Americans dividing into "French" and "English" factions. Furthermore, France had repeatedly interfered in American domestic affairs. First there had been Genet, childish and exasperating. Later another French minister, Citizen Adet, had tried to prejudice both Congress and public opinion against the Jay Treaty. Adet had attempted to organize on American soil an expedition to conquer Louisiana for France. "Against the insidious wiles of foreign influence," Washington now warned, "the jealousy of a free people ought to be *constantly* awake." America should develop its foreign trade but steer clear of foreign political connections as far as possible. "Permanent alliances" should be avoided, although "temporary alliances for extraordinary purposes" might sometimes be useful.

The Election of 1796

Washington's Farewell Address was destined to have a long and important influence on American thinking, but its immediate impact was small. He had intended it to cool political passions. Instead, in the words of one Federalist congressman, people took it as "a signal, like dropping a hat, for the party racers to start." By the time the presidential campaign had ended, many Federalists and Republicans were refusing to speak to one another.

Jefferson was the only Republican candidate seriously considered in 1796. The logical Federalist was Hamilton, but, as was to happen so often in American history with powerful leaders, he was not considered "available" because his controversial policies had made him many enemies. Gathering in caucus, the Federalists in Congress nominated Vice-President John Adams for the top office and Thomas Pinckney of South Carolina, negotiator of the popular Spanish treaty, for vice-president. In the election the Federalists won a majority.

Hamilton, hoping to run the new administration

from the wings, preferred Pinckney, a relatively weak character, to the tough-minded Adams. He arranged for some of the Federalist electors from South Carolina to vote only for Pinckney. Catching wind of this, a number of New England electors retaliated by cutting Pinckney. As a result, Adams won in the electoral college, 71 to 68, over Jefferson, who had the solid support of the Republican electors. Pinckney got only 59 electoral votes. Jefferson thus became vice-president.

The unexpected result seemed to presage a decline in partisanship. Adams actually preferred the Virginian to Pinckney for the vice-presidency, while Jefferson said that if Adams would "reliquish his bias to an English constitution," he might make a fine chief executive. The two had in common a distaste for Hamilton—a powerful bond.

However, the closeness of the election indicated a trend toward the Republicans, who were making constant and effective use of the canard that the Federalists were "monocrats" (monarchists) determined to destroy American liberty. Without Washington to lead them, the Federalist politicians were already quarreling among themselves; honest, able, hardworking John Adams was too caustic and too scathingly frank to unite them. The unpopularity of the Jay Treaty hurt the Federalists further. In March 1797 everything seemed to indicate a Republican victory at the next election.

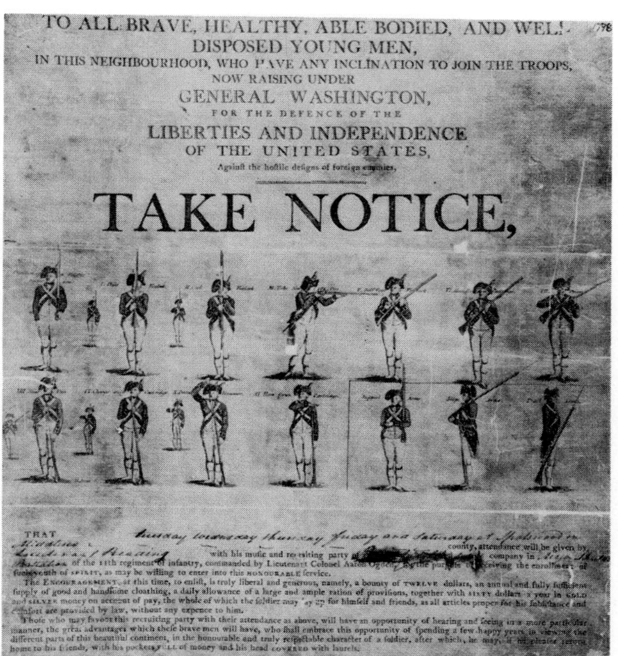

A recruiting poster of 1798 appealed for volunteers to defend the nation "against the hostile designs of foreign enemies," the "enemies" being the French.

The XYZ Affair

At this point occurred one of the most remarkable reversals of public feeling in American history. French attacks on American shipping, begun out of irritation at the Jay Treaty and in order to influence the election, continued after Adams took office. Hoping to stop them, Adams appointed three commissioners (Charles Pinckney, United States minister to France and elder brother of Thomas; John Marshall, a prominent Virginia Federalist; and Elbridge Gerry of Massachusetts, a former congressman who was a friend of Jefferson but was not closely identified with either party) to try to negotiate a settlement. Their mission was a fiasco. Talleyrand, the French foreign minister, sent three agents (later spoken of as X, Y, and Z) to demand a huge bribe as the price of making a deal. The Americans refused, more because they suspected Talleyrand's good faith than because of any distaste for bribery. "No, no, not a sixpence," Pinckney told the agents. The talks broke up, and in April 1798 President Adams released the commissioners' reports.

They caused a sensation. Americans' sense of national honor, perhaps overly tender because the country was so young and insecure, was outraged. Pinckney's laconic refusal to pay a bribe was translated into the grandiose phrase "Millions for defense, but not one cent for tribute!" and broadcast throughout the land. John Adams, never a man with mass appeal, suddenly found himself a national hero. Federalist hotheads burned for a fight. Congress unilaterally abrogated the French Alliance, created a Navy Department, and appropriated enough money to build 40-odd warships and triple the size of the army. Washington came out of retirement to lead the forces, with Hamilton, now a general, as second in command. On the seas American privateers began to attack French shipping.

Adams did not much like the French and he could be extremely stubborn. A declaration of war would have been immensely popular. But perhaps—it is not an entirely illogical surmise about John Adams—the president did not want to be popular. And whatever other qualities he possessed, he was a realist. He knew that the United States had only 3,500 men under arms and a navy of exactly three vessels. Instead of calling for war, he contented himself with approving the buildup of the armed forces.

The Republicans, however, committed to friendship with France, did not appreciate Adams's moderation. Although angered by the XYZ Affair, they tried, one angry Federalist said, "to clog the wheels of government" by opposing the military appropriations. Their newspapers spewed abuse on Adams and his administration. They referred to Adams derisively as "His Rotundity," a term that particularly annoyed the somewhat plump president. Benjamin Bache, editor of the Philadelphia *Aurora,* referred to him as "blind, bald, toothless, querulous," which was three-quarters true but irrelevant. John Daly Burk of the New York *Time Piece* called him a "mock Monarch" surrounded by a "*court* composed of tories and speculators," which was a flat lie.

In light of this virulent reaction, many Federalists expected the Republicans to side with France if war broke out. Hysterical and near panic, these Federalists easily persuaded themselves that the danger of subversion was acute. The French Revolution and the resulting war were churning European society to the depths, stirring the hopes of liberals and striking fear in the hearts of conservatives. Refugees of both persuasions were often forced to flee their homes, and many of them came to the United States. Suddenly the presence of the foreigners seemed threatening to "native" Americans. Benjamin Bache was a grandson of Benjamin Franklin, but Burk, for example, was Irish-born. The most important leader of the Republican opposition in Congress was Albert Gallatin, an immigrant from Switzerland.

Alien and Sedition Acts

Conservative Federalists saw in this situation a chance to smash the opposition. In June and July 1798 they pushed through Congress a series of repressive measures known as the Alien and Sedition Acts. The least offensive of these laws, the Naturalization Act, increased the period a foreigner had to reside in the United States before being eligible for citizenship from 5 to 14 years. The Alien Enemies Act gave the president the power to arrest or expel aliens in time of "declared war," but since the quasi-war with France was never declared, this measure had no practical importance. The Alien Act authorized the president to expel *all* aliens whom he thought "dangerous to the peace and safety of the United States." (Adams never invoked this law, but a number of aliens left the country out of fear that he might.) Finally, there was the Sedition Act. Its first section, making it a crime "to impede the operation of any law" or to attempt to instigate a riot or insurrection, was reasonable enough; but the act made it illegal to publish, or even to utter, any "false, scandalous and malicious" criticism of high government officials.

Although milder than British sedition laws, this proviso rested, as James Madison said, on "the exploded doctrine" that government officials "are the masters and not the servants of the people." To criticize a king is to try to undermine the respect of his subjects for the establishment over which he rules, and that is seditious. To criticize an elected official in a republic is to express dissatisfaction with the way one's agent is performing an assigned task—certainly no threat to the state itself. The difference between the two modes of thought escaped the Federalists of 1798.

This is mere theory; far worse was the Federalists' practice under the Sedition Act. As the election of 1800 approached, they made a systematic attempt to silence the leading Republican newspapers. Twenty-five persons were prosecuted and ten convicted, all in patently unfair trials. In typical cases, the editor Thomas Cooper was sentenced to six months in jail and fined $400, the editor Charles Holt got three months and a $200 fine, the editor James Callender got nine months and a $200 fine. In some instances the criticisms of the Adams administration had been very raw, yet equally harsh things were being said with impunity by Federalist editors about Vice-President Jefferson. When Cooper, a distinguished English-born radical and later president of the University of South Carolina, attempted after serving his sentence to have Hamilton prosecuted for *his* intemperate attacks on President Adams, he got nowhere.

While Thomas Jefferson did not object to *state* sedition laws, he believed that the Alien and Sedition Acts violated the First Amendment's guarantees of freedom of speech and the press and were an invasion of the rights of the states. He conferred with Madison, and they decided to draw up resolutions arguing that the laws were unconstitutional. Madison's draft was presented to the Virginia legislature and Jefferson's to the legislature of Kentucky. Since the Constitution was a compact made by sovereign states, each state had "an equal right to judge for itself" when the compact had been violated, the Kentucky Resolves declared. Thus a state could declare a law of Congress unconstitutional. The Virginia Resolves took an only slightly less forthright position.

Neither Kentucky nor Virginia tried to implement these resolves or to interfere with the enforcement of the Alien and Sedition Acts. Jefferson and Madison were protesting Federalist high-handedness and firing the opening salvo of Jefferson's campaign for the presidency, not advancing a new constitutional theory of extreme states' rights. "Keep away all show of force," Jefferson advised his supporters.

This was sound advice, for events were again playing into the hands of the Republicans. Talleyrand had never wanted war with the United States. When he finally realized how vehemently the Americans had reacted to his little attempt to replenish his personal fortune, depleted during the Revolution, he let Adams know that new negotiators would be properly received.

President Adams quickly grasped the importance of the French change of heart, for like Washington before him he never forgot that the country needed peace and tranquillity in order to grow stronger and more closely knit. Other leading Federalists, however, had lost their heads. By shouting about the French danger, they had roused the country against radicalism, and they did not intend to surrender this advantage tamely. Hamilton in particular wanted war at almost any price—if not against France, then against Spain. He saw himself at the head of the new American army sweeping first across Louisiana and the Floridas, then on to the south. "We ought to squint at South America," he suggested. "Our game will be to attack where we can," he added. "Tempting objects will be without our grasp."

One of the most flattering likenesses of John Adams is this portrait by John Trumbull done in 1793. Public criticism of Adams ran high throughout his term of office.

The British cleverly played upon Federalist ambitions, hinting at further commercial concessions, talking of convoying American merchant vessels in case of a Franco-American war, even suggesting to the United States minister in London, Rufus King, the idea of a British-American attack on South America.

But the Puritan Adams was a specialist at resisting temptation. At this critical point his intelligence, his fundamentally moderate political philosophy, and above all his stubborn integrity stood him in good stead. He would neither go to war merely to destroy the political opposition in America nor follow "the fools who were intriguing to plunge us into an alliance with England . . . and wild expeditions to South America." Instead he submitted to the Senate the name of a new minister plenipotentiary to France, and when the Federalists tried to block the appointment, he threatened to resign. That would have made Jefferson president! So the furious Federalists had to give in, though they forced Adams to send three men instead of one.

Napoleon had taken over France by the time the Americans arrived, and he drove a harder bargain than Talleyrand would have. In the end he signed an agreement (the Convention of 1800) abrogating the Franco-American treaties of 1778. Nothing was said about the damage done to American shipping by the French, but the war scare was over.

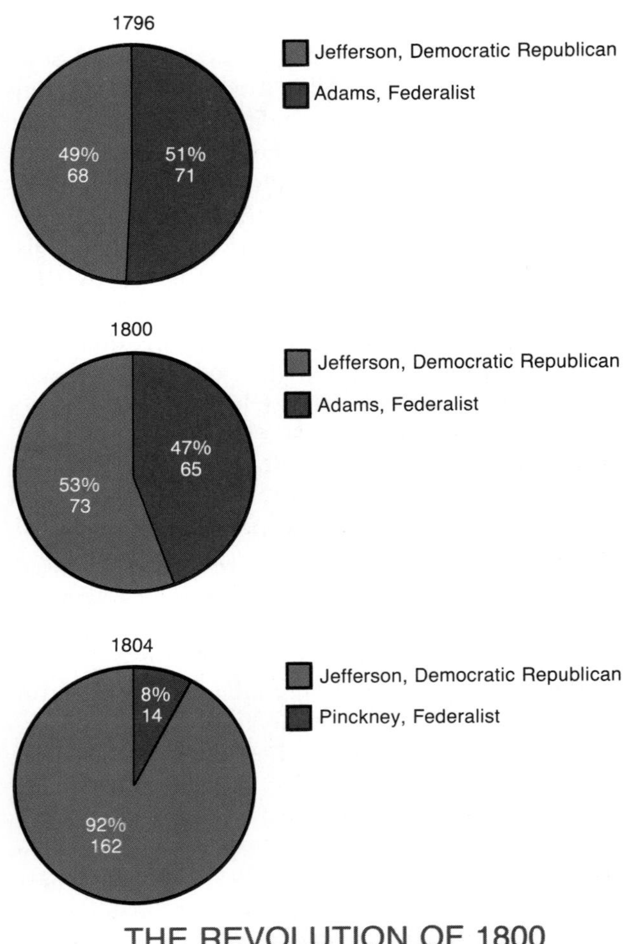

THE REVOLUTION OF 1800

The upper percentage figures show the percent of the electoral vote received by the candidate, and the lower figures the actual electoral votes for that candidate. Before the Twelfth Amendment of 1804, the Electoral College voted for two presidential candidates; the runner-up became vice-president.

The Revolution of 1800

Suddenly the public realized that the furor over war and subversion had been concocted almost out of thin air. Nevertheless, the presidential contest between Adams and Jefferson was close. Because of his stand for peace, Adams personally escaped the brunt of popular indignation against the Federalist party. His solid qualities had a strong appeal to conservatives, and fear that the Republicans would introduce radical "French" social reforms did not disappear. Many nationalist-minded voters worried lest the strong government established by the Federalists be weakened by the Jeffersonians in the name of states' rights. The economic progress stimulated by Hamilton's financial reforms also seemed threatened. When the electors' votes were counted in February 1801, the Republicans were discovered to have won narrowly, 73 to 65.

But *which* Republican? The Constitution did not distinguish between presidential and vice-presidential candidates; it provided only that each elector should vote for two candidates, the one with the most votes becoming president and the runner-up vice-president. The vice-presidential candidate of the Republicans was Aaron Burr of New York, a former senator and a rival of Hamilton in law and politics. And Republican party solidarity had been perfect: Jefferson and Burr received 73 votes each. Because of the tie, the House of Representatives (voting by states) had to choose between them.

In the House the Republicans could control only 8 of the 16 state delegations. On the first ballot Jefferson got these 8 votes, one short of election, while 6 states voted for Burr. Two state delegations, being evenly split, lost their votes. Through 35 ballots the deadlock persisted; the Federalists, fearful of Jefferson's radicalism, voted solidly for Burr. Pressures were exerted on both candidates to make deals to win additional support. Officially at least, both refused. Burr put on a great show of remaining above the battle. (Had he been an honorable man, he would have withdrawn, since the voters had clearly intended him for the second spot.) Whether Jefferson made any promises is uncertain; there is some evidence that to break the deadlock he assured the Federalists that he would preserve Hamilton's financial system and continue the Washington-Adams foreign policy. Hamilton played an important part behind the scenes; he detested Burr and threw his weight to Jefferson.

Finally, on February 17, 1801, Jefferson was elected. Burr became vice-president.

To make sure that this deadlock would never be repeated, the Twelfth Amendment was drafted, providing for separate balloting in the electoral college for president and vice-president. This change was ratified in 1804, shortly before the next election.

The Federalist Contribution

On March 4, 1801, in the raw new national capital on the Potomac River named in honor of the Father of his Country, Thomas Jefferson took the presidential oath and delivered his inaugural address. The new president believed that a revolution as important as that heralded by his immortal Declaration of Independence had occurred, and for once most of his enemies agreed with him.

Certainly an era had ended. In the years between the Peace of Paris and Jay's Treaty the Federalists had practically monopolized the political good sense of the nation. In the perspective of history they were "right" in strengthening the federal government, in establishing a sound fiscal system, in trying to diversify the economy, in seeking an accommodation with Great Britain, and in refusing to be carried away with enthusiasm for France despite the bright dreams inspired by the French Revolution. The Federalists had displayed remarkable self-control and moderation at least until 1798. They were nationalists who did not try to destroy local patriotism, artistocrats willing to live with the spirit of democracy. The Constitution is their monument, with its wise compromises. its balance of forces, its restraints, its practical concessions to local prejudices.

But the Federalists were unable to face up to defeat. When they saw the Jeffersonians gathering strength by developing clever new techniques of party organization and propaganda, mouthing slogans about "monocrats," glorifying both the past with its satisfying simplicity and the future with its promise of a glorious day when all men would be free, equal, and brothers, they panicked. Abandoning the sober wisdom of their great period, they fought to save themselves at any cost. The effort turned defeat into rout. Jefferson's victory, fairly close in the electoral college, approached landslide proportions in the congressional elections, where popular feeling could express itself directly.

Jefferson erred, however, in calling this triumph a revolution. The real upheaval had been attempted in 1798; it was Federalist inspired, and it failed. In 1800 the voters expressed a preference for the old over the new; that is, for individual freedom and limited national power. And Jefferson, despite Federalist fears that he would destroy the Constitution and establish a radical social order, presided instead over a regime that confirmed the great achievements of the Federalist era.

What was most significant about the election of 1800 was that it was *not* a revolution. After a bitter contest the Jeffersonians took power and proceeded to change the policy of the government. They did so peacefully. Thus American republican government passed a crucial test: control of its machinery had changed hands in a democratic and

This anti-Jefferson cartoon shows the newly elected president kneeling before the altar of Gallic Despotism, whereon he is burning the writings of prominent Enlightenment philosophers. The American eagle appears to be wresting the Constitution from Jefferson's grasp.

THE PROVIDENTIAL DETECTION

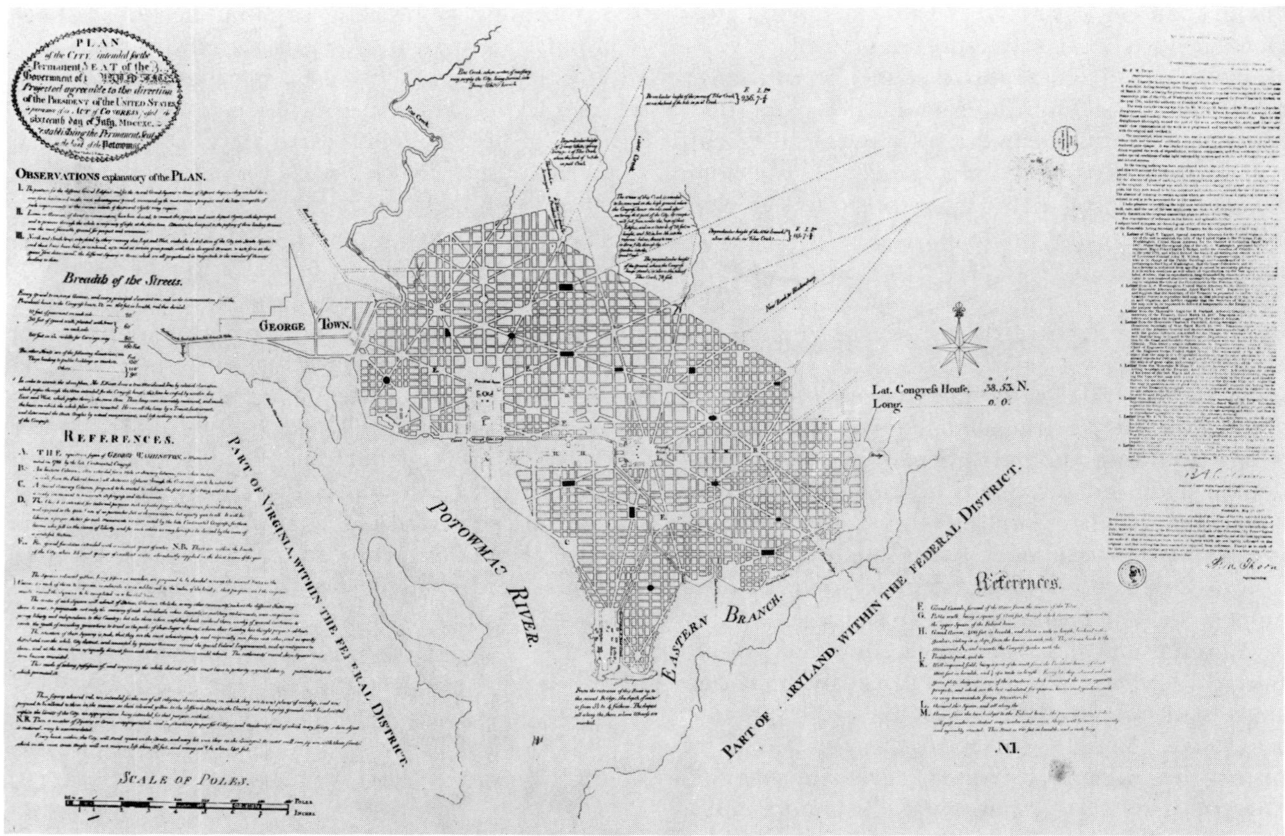

This map of Washington, based on L'Enfant's original plan, was adopted by Congress as the city's official layout. One notation about the plan says that the main streets and avenues "are from 130 to 160 feet wide, and may be conveniently divided into foot ways, walks of trees, and a carriage way."

orderly way. And only less significant, the informal party system had demonstrated its usefulness. The Jeffersonians had organized popular dissatisfaction with Federalist policies, formulated a platform of reform, chosen leaders to put their plans into effect, and elected those leaders to office.

Jefferson as President

The novelty of the new administration lay in its style and its moderation. Both were apparent in Jefferson's inaugural address. The new president's opening remarks showed that he was neither a demagogue nor a firebrand. "The task is above my talents," he said modestly, "and . . . I approach it with . . . anxious and awful presentiments." The people had spoken, and their voice must be heeded, but the rights of dissenters must be respected. "All . . . will bear in mind this sacred principle," he said, "that though the will of the majority is in all cases to prevail, that will to be rightful must be reasonable; that the minority possess their equal rights, which equal law must protect, and to violate would be oppression."

Jefferson spoke at some length about specific policies. He declared himself against "entangling alliances" and for economy in government, and he promised to pay off the national debt, preserve the government's credit, and stimulate both agriculture and its "handmaid," commerce. His main stress was on the cooling of partisan passions. "Every difference of opinion is not a difference of principle. We have called by different names brethren of the same principle. We are all Republicans—we are all Federalists." And he promised the country "a wise and frugal Government, which shall restrain men from injuring one another . . . [and] leave them otherwise free to regulate their own pursuits."

Jefferson quickly demonstrated the sincerity of his remarks. He saw to it that the Whiskey Tax and other Federalist excises were repealed, and he made sharp cuts in military and naval expenditures to keep the budget in balance. The national debt was reduced from $83 million to $57 million during his eight years in office. The Naturalization Act of 1798 was repealed and the old five years' residence requirement for citizenship restored. The Sedition Act and the Alien Act expired of their own accord in 1801 and 1802.

The changes were not drastic. Jefferson made no effort to tear down the fiscal structure that Hamilton had erected. "We can pay off his debt," the new president confessed, "but we cannot get rid of his financial system." Nor did the author of the Kentucky Resolves try to alter the balance of federal-state power.

Yet there was a different tone to the new regime. Jefferson had no desire to surround himself with pomp and ceremony; the excessive formality and punctilio of the Washington and Adams administrations had been distasteful to him. He made sure that his own household was less cluttered by ritual and display. From the moment of his election he played down the ceremonial aspects of the presidency. He asked that he be notified of his election by mail rather than by a committee, and he would have preferred to have taken the oath at Charlottesville, near Monticello, his home, rather than at Washington. After the inauguration he returned to his boardinghouse on foot and took dinner in his usual seat at the common table.

In the White House he often wore a frayed coat and carpet slippers, even to receive the representatives of foreign powers when they arrived, resplendent with silk ribbons and a sense of their own importance, to present their credentials. At social affairs he paid little heed to the status and seniority of his guests. When dinner was announced, he offered his arm to whichever lady he was talking to at the moment and placed her at his right; other guests were free to sit wherever they found an empty chair. During business hours congressmen,

Jefferson appears more relaxed and approachable in this drawing by the French expatriate Charles Saint-Mémin than he does in more formal portraits.

friends, foreign officials, and plain citizens coming to call took their turn in the order of their arrival. "The principle of society with us," Jefferson explained, "is the equal rights of all. . . . Nobody shall be above you, nor you above anybody, *pell-mell* is our law."

"Pell-mell" was also good politics, and Jefferson was a superb politician. He gave dozens of small stag dinner parties for congressmen, serving the food personally from a dumbwaiter connected with the kitchen. The guests, carefully chosen to make congenial groups, were seated at a round table to encourage general conversation; the food and wine were first-class. These were ostensibly social occasions—shoptalk was avoided—yet they paid large political dividends. Jefferson learned to know every congressman personally, Democratic Republican and Federalist alike, and not only their political views but their strengths, their quirks, their flaws. And he worked his personal magic upon them, displaying the breadth of his knowledge, his charm and wit, his lack of pomposity. "You see, we are alone and *our walls have no ears,*" he would say, and while the wine flowed and the guests sampled delicacies prepared by Jefferson's French chef, the president manufactured political capital. "You drink as you please and converse at your ease," one guest reported.

Jefferson made effective use of his close supporters in Congress, and of Cabinet members as well, in persuading Congress to go along with his proposals. His state papers were models of sweet reason, minimizing conflicts, stressing areas where all honest people must agree. After all, as he indicated in his inaugural address, nearly all Americans *were* both federalists and republicans; no great principle divided them into irreconcilable camps. Jefferson set out to bring them all into *his* camp, and he succeeded so well in four years that when he ran for reelection against Charles Pinckney, he got 162 of the 176 electoral votes cast. Eventually even John Quincy Adams, son of the second president, became a Jeffersonian.

At the same time Jefferson was anything but nonpartisan in the sense that Washington had been. His Cabinet consisted exclusively of men of his own party. He exerted almost continuous pressure on Congress to make sure that his legislative program was enacted into law. He did not remove many Federalist officeholders, and at one point he remarked ruefully that government officials seldom died and never resigned; but when he could, he used his power of appointment to reward his friends and punish his enemies.

Attack on the Judiciary

Although notably open-minded and tolerant, Jefferson had a few stubborn prejudices. One was against kings, another against the British system of government. A third was against judges, or rather, against entrenched judicial power. While recognizing that judges must have a degree of independence, he feared what he called their "habit of going out of the question before them, to throw an anchor ahead, and grapple further hold for future advances of power." The biased behavior of Federalist judges during the trials under the Sedition Act enormously increased this basic distrust. It burst all bounds when the Federalist majority of the dying Congress rammed through the Judiciary Act of 1801 in a last-ditch effort to "protect" the country against Jeffersonian radicalism.

The Judiciary Act created 6 new circuit courts, presided over by 16 new federal judges and a small army of attorneys, marshals, and clerks. The expanding country needed the judges, but with the enthusiastic cooperation of President Adams the Federalists made shameless use of the opportunity to fill all the new positions with conservative Federalists, and this angered Jefferson. The new appointees were dubbed midnight justices because, according to rumor, Adams stayed up till midnight on March 3, his last day as president, feverishly signing their commissions.

The Republicans retaliated as soon as the new Congress met by repealing the Judiciary Act of 1801, but President Jefferson still fumed. Upon taking office he had discovered that in the confusion of Adams's last hours the commissions of a number of justices of the peace for the new District of Columbia had not been distributed. While these were small fry indeed, Jefferson was so angry that he ordered the commissions held up even though they had been signed by Adams. One of the appointees, William Marbury, then petitioned the Supreme Court for a writ of mandamus (Latin for "we order") directing the new secretary of state, James Madison, to give him his commission.

The case of *Marbury* v. *Madison* placed Chief Justice John Marshall in an embarrassing position. Marbury had a strong claim. If Marshall refused to issue a mandamus, everyone would say he dared not stand up to Jefferson, and the prestige of the Court would suffer. If he issued the writ, he would place the Court in direct conflict with the executive. Jefferson particularly disliked Marshall. He would probably tell Madison to ignore the order, and in the prevailing state of public opinion nothing could be done about it. This would be a still more staggering blow to the judiciary. What should the chief justice do?

Marshall, like Jefferson and Madison a Virginian, had studied law only briefly and had no judicial experience, but in this crisis he first displayed the genius that was to mark him as a great judge. By right Marbury should have his commission, he announced. However, the Court could not require Madison to give it to him. Marbury's request for a mandamus had been based on an ambiguous clause in the Judiciary Act of 1789. That clause was unconstitutional, Marshall declared, and therefore void. Congress could not legally give the Supreme Court the right to issue writs of mandamus in such circumstances.

With the skill and foresight of a chess grand master, Marshall turned what had looked like a trap into a triumph. By sacrificing the pawn, Marbury, he established the power of the Supreme Court to invalidate federal laws that conflicted with the Constitution. Jefferson could not check him because Marshall had *refused* power instead of throwing an anchor ahead, as Jefferson had feared. Yet he had certainly grappled a "further hold for future advances of power," and the president could do nothing to stop him.

The Marbury case made Jefferson more determined to strike at the Federalist-dominated courts. He decided to press for the impeachment of some of the more partisan judges. First he had the House of Representatives bring charges against District Judge John Pickering. Pickering was clearly insane—he had frequently delivered profane and drunken harangues from the bench—and the Senate quickly voted to remove him. Then Jefferson went after a much larger fish, Samuel Chase, associate justice of the Supreme Court. Chase had been prominent for decades, an early leader of the Sons of Liberty, a signer of the Declaration of Independence, active in the affairs of the Continental Congress. Washington had named him to the Supreme Court in 1796, and he had delivered a number of important opinions. But his handling of cases under the Sedition Act had been outrageously high-handed. Defense lawyers had become so exasperated as to throw down their briefs in disgust at some of his prejudiced rulings. But the trial demonstrated that Chase's actions had not constituted the "high crimes and misdemeanors" required by the Constitution to remove a judge. Even Jefferson became disenchanted with the efforts of some of his more extreme followers and accepted Chase's acquittal with equanimity.

The Barbary Pirates

Aside from these perhaps salutary setbacks, Jefferson's first term was a parade of triumphs. Although he cut back the army and navy sharply in order to save money, he temporarily escaped the consequences of leaving the country undefended because of the lull in the European war signalized by the treaty of Amiens between Great Britain and France

The frigate Philadelphia *had been captured in October of 1803 by Tripolitanian pirates. In February of 1804, Stephen Decatur managed to steal into the harbor of Tripoli with a small boarding party (the ship at lower left) and set fire to the vessel.*

in March 1802. Despite the fact that he had only seven frigates in commission, he even managed to fight a small naval war with the Barbary pirates without damage to American interests or prestige.

The North African Arab states of Morocco, Algiers, Tunis, and Tripoli had for decades made a business of piracy, seizing vessels all over the Mediterranean and holding crews and passengers for ransom. The European powers found it simpler to pay them annual protection money than to crush them. Under Washington and Adams, the United States joined in the payment of this tribute; while large, the sums were less than the increased costs of insurance for shippers when the protection was not purchased. Such pusillanimity ran against Jefferson's grain—"When this idea comes across my mind, my faculties are absolutely suspended between indignation and impatience," he said—and when the pasha of Tripoli tried to raise the charges, he balked. Tripoli then declared war in May 1801, and Jefferson dispatched a squadron to the Mediterranean.

In the words of one historian, the action was "halfhearted and ill-starred." The pirates were not overwhelmed, and a major American warship, the frigate *Philadelphia,* had to be destroyed after running aground off the Tripolitanian coast. The payment of tribute continued until 1815. Just the same, America, though far removed from the pirate bases, was the only maritime nation that tried to resist the blackmail. Although the war failed to achieve Jefferson's purpose of ending the payments, its final effect was positive. The pasha agreed to a new treaty more favorable to the United States, and American sailors led by Commodore Edward Preble won valuable experience and a large portion of fame. The greatest hero was Lieutenant Stephen Decatur, who captured two pirate ships, led ten men in a daring raid on another in which he took on a gigantic sailor in a wild battle of cutlass against boarding pike,* and snatched the stricken *Philadelphia* from the pirates by sneaking aboard and setting her afire.

The Louisiana Purchase

The major achievements of Jefferson's first term had to do with the American west, and of these the greatest by far was the acquisition of the huge area between the Mississippi River and the Rocky Mountains. In a sense the purchase of this region, called Louisiana, was fortuitous, an accidental by-product of European political adjustments and the whim of Napoleon Bonaparte. Certainly Jefferson had not planned it, for in his inaugural address he had expressed the opinion that the country already had all the land it would need for a thousand generations. It was nonetheless the perfectly logical—one might almost say inevitable—result of a long series of events in the history of the Mississippi Valley.

Along with every other American who had even a superficial interest in the west, Jefferson understood that the United States must have access to the mouth of the Mississippi and the city of New Orleans or eventually lose everything beyond the Appalachians. "There is on the globe one single spot, the possessor of which is our natural and habitual enemy," he was soon to write. "It is New Orleans." Thus, when he learned shortly after his inauguration that Spain had given Louisiana back to France, he was immediately on his guard. Control of Louisiana by Spain, a "feeble" country with "pacific dispositions," could be tolerated; control by a resurgent France dominated by Napoleon, the greatest military genius of the age, was entirely different. Did Napoleon have designs on Canada? Did he perhaps mean to resume the old Spanish and British game of encouraging the Indians to harry the American frontier? And what now would be the status of Pinckney's precious treaty? Deeply worried, the president instructed his minister to France, Robert R. Livingston, to seek assurances that American rights in New Orleans would be respected and to negotiate the purchase of West Florida in case that region had also been turned over to France.

Jefferson's concern was well founded; France was indeed planning new imperial ventures in North America. Immediately after settling its difficulties with the United States through the Convention of 1800, France signed the secret Treaty of San Ildefonso with Spain, which returned Louisiana to France. Napoleon hoped to use this region as a breadbasket for the French West Indian sugar plantations, just as colonies like Pennsylvania and Massachusetts had fed the British sugar islands before the Revolution.

However, the most important French island,

* Decatur killed the pirate by firing a small pistol from his pocket as his opponent was about to skewer him.

Saint Domingue, or Haiti, had slipped from French control. At the time of the French Revolution the slaves of the island had revolted. In 1793 they were granted personal freedom, but they fought on under the leadership of the "Black Napoleon," a self-taught genius named Toussaint L'Ouverture, and by 1801 the island was entirely in their hands. The original Napoleon, taking advantage of the slackening of war in Europe, dispatched an army of 20,000 men under General Charles Leclerc to reconquer it.

When Jefferson learned of the Leclerc expedition, he had no trouble divining its relationship to Louisiana. His uneasiness became outright alarm. In April 1802 he again urged Minister Livingston to attempt the purchase of New Orleans and Florida or, as an alternative, to buy a tract of land near the mouth of the Mississippi where a new port could be constructed. Of necessity, the mild-mannered, idealistic president now became an aggressive realist. If the right of deposit could not be preserved through negotiation, it must be purchased with gunpowder, even if that meant acting in conjuction with the despised British. "The day that France takes possession of New Orleans," he warned, "we must marry ourselves to the British fleet and nation."

In October 1802 the Spanish, who had not yet actually turned Louisiana over to France, heightened the tension by suddenly revoking the right of deposit at New Orleans. We now know that the French had no hand in this action, but it was beyond reason to expect Jefferson or the American people to believe it at the time. With the west clamoring for relief, Jefferson appointed his friend and disciple James Monroe minister plenipotentiary and sent him to Paris with instructions to offer up to $10 million for New Orleans and Florida. If France refused, he and Livingston should open negotiations for a "closer connection" with the British.

Before Monroe reached France the tension was broken. General Leclerc's Saint Domingue expedition ended in disaster. Although Toussaint surrendered, Haitian resistance continued. Yellow fever raged through the French army; Leclerc himself fell before the fever, which wiped out practically his entire force.

When news of this calamity reached Napoleon early in 1803, he began to have second thoughts about reviving French imperialism in the New World. Without Saint Domingue the wilderness of Louisiana seemed of little value. Napoleon was preparing to reopen his campaigns in Europe. He could no longer spare troops to recapture a rebellious West Indian island or to hold Louisiana against a possible British attack, and he needed money. For some weeks the commander of the most powerful army in the world mulled the question without consulting anyone. Then, with characteristic suddenness, he made up his mind. On April 10 he ordered Foreign Minister Talleyrand to offer not merely New Orleans but all of Louisiana to the Americans. The next day Talleyrand summoned Livingston to his office on the rue du Bac and dropped this bombshell. Livingston was almost struck speechless but quickly recovered his composure. When Talleyrand asked what the United States would give for the province, he suggested the French equivalent of about $5 million. Talleyrand pronounced the sum "too low" and urged Livingston to think about the subject for a day or two.

Livington faced a situation that could never confront a modern diplomat. His instructions said nothing about buying an area almost as large as the entire United States, and there was no time to write home for new instructions. The offer staggered the imagination. Luckily, Monroe arrived the next day to share the responsibility. The two Americans consulted, dickered with the French, and finally agreed—they could scarcely have done otherwise—to accept the proposal. Early in May they signed a treaty. For 60 million francs—about $15 million—the United States was to have all Louisiana.

No one knew exactly how large the region was or what it contained. When Livingston asked Talleyrand about the boundaries of the purchase, he replied: "I can give you no direction. You have made a noble bargain for yourselves, and I suppose you will make the most of it." Never, as the historian Henry Adams wrote, "did the United States government get so much for so little."

Napoleon's unexpected concession caused consternation in America, though there was never real doubt that the treaty would be ratified. Jefferson did not believe that the government had the power under the Constitution to add new territory or to grant American citizenship to the 50,000 residents of Louisiana by executive act, as the treaty required. He even drafted a constitutional amendment: "The province of Louisiana is incorporated with the

United States and made part thereof," but his advisers convinced him that it would be dangerous to delay approval of the treaty until an amendment could be acted upon by three-fourths of the states. Jefferson then suggested that the Senate ratify the treaty and submit an amendment afterward "confirming an act which the nation had not previously authorized." This idea was so obviously illogical that he quickly dropped it. Finally, he came to believe "that the less we say about constitutional difficulties the better." Since what he called "the good sense of our country" clearly wanted Louisiana, he decided to "acquiesce with satisfaction" while Congress overlooked the "metaphysical subtleties" of the problem and ratified the treaty.

Some of the more partisan Federalists, who had been eager to fight Spain for New Orleans, attacked Jefferson for undermining the Constitution. One such critic described Louisiana contemptuously as a "Gallo-Hispano-Indian" collection of "savages and adventurers." Even Hamilton expressed hesitation about absorbing "this new, immense, unbounded world," though he had dreamed of seizing still larger domains himself. In the end Hamilton's nationalism reasserted itself, and he urged ratification of the treaty, as did such other important Federalists as John Adams and John Marshall. And in a way the Louisiana Purchase was as much Hamilton's doing as Jefferson's. Napoleon accepted payment in United States bonds, which he promptly sold to European investors. If Hamilton had not established the nation's credit so soundly, such a large issue could never have been so easily disposed of.

It was ironic—and a man as perceptive as Hamilton must surely have recognized the irony—that the acquisition of Louisiana assured Jefferson's reelection and further contributed to the downfall of Federalism. The purchase was popular even in the New England bastions of that party. While the negotiations were progressing in Paris, Jefferson had written of partisan political affairs: "If we can settle happily the difficulties of the Mississippi, I think we may promise ourselves smooth seas during our time." These words turned out to be no more accurate than most political predictions, but the Louisiana Purchase drove another spike into Federalism's coffin.

Federalism Discredited

The west and south were solid for Jefferson, and the north was rapidly succumbing to his charm. The addition of new western states would soon further reduce New England's power in national affairs. So complete did the Republican triumph seem that a handful of die-hard Federalists in New England began to think of secession. Led by former secretary of state Timothy Pickering, a sour, implacable conservative, a group known as the Essex Junto organized in 1804 a scheme to break away from the Union and establish a "Northern Confederacy."

Even within the dwindling Federalist ranks the Junto had little support. Nevertheless, Pickering and his friends pushed ahead, drafting a plan whereby, having captured political control of New York, they would take the entire northeast out of the Union. Since they could not begin to win New York for anyone in their own ranks, they hit on the idea of supporting Vice-President Aaron Burr, who was running against the "regular" Republican candidate for governor of New York. Although Burr did not promise to bring New York into their

In the most significant duel in American history, Aaron Burr fatally wounded Alexander Hamilton on the cliffs of Weehawken, New Jersey, on July 11, 1804. This depiction is from a 19th-century magic lantern slide.

confederacy if elected, he encouraged them enough to win their backing. The foolishness of the plot was revealed in the April elections: Burr was overwhelmed by the regular Republican. The Junto's scheme collapsed.

The incident, however, had a tragic aftermath. Hamilton had campaigned against Burr, whom he considered "an embryo Caesar." When he continued after the election to cast aspersions on Burr's character (not a very difficult assignment, since Burr, despite being a grandson of the preacher Jonathan Edwards, frequently violated both the political and sexual mores of the day), Burr challenged him to a duel. It was well known that Hamilton opposed dueling in principle, his own son having been slain in such an affair, and he certainly had no need to prove his courage. But he believed his honor at stake. The two met with pistols on July 11, 1804, at Weehawken, New Jersey, across the Hudson from New York City. Hamilton made no effort to hit the challenger, but Burr took careful aim. Hamilton fell, mortally wounded. Thus a great, if enigmatic, man was cut off in his prime. His work, in a sense, had been completed, and his philosophy of government was being everywhere rejected, yet the nation's loss was large.

Lewis and Clark

While the disgruntled Federalists dreamed of secession, Jefferson was planning the exploration of Louisiana and the region beyond. Early in 1803 he got $2,500 from Congress and obtained the permission of the French to send his exploring party across Louisiana. To command the expedition he appointed his private secretary, Meriwether Lewis, a young Virginian who had seen considerable service with the army in the west and who possessed, according to Jefferson, "a great mass of accurate information on all the subjects of nature." Lewis chose as his companion officer William Clark, another soldier (he had served with General Anthony Wayne at the Battle of Fallen Timbers) who had much experience in negotiating with Indians.

Jefferson, whose interest in the west was scientific as well as political, issued minute instructions to Lewis:

> Other objects worthy of notice will be, the soil and face of the country . . . the remains and accounts of any animals which may be deemed rare or extinct; the mineral productions of every kind, but particularly metals . . . volcanic appearances; climate, as characterized by the thermometer, by the proportion of rainy, cloudy, and clear days, by lightning, hail, snow, ice, by the access and recess of frost, by the winds prevailing at different seasons, the dates at which particular plants put forth or lose their flower or leaf, times of appearance of particular birds, reptiles or insects. . . .

Scientific matters were inextricably intertwined with practical ones, such as the fur trade, for in his nature studies Jefferson concentrated on "useful" plants and animals. He was haunted by imperialistic visions of an expanding America that were not unlike those of Hamilton. After the consummation of the Louisiana Purchase, he instructed Lewis to try to establish official relations with the Indians in the Spanish territories beyond. Lewis should assure the tribes that "they will find in us faithful friends and protectors," Jefferson said. That the expedition would be moving across Spanish territory need not concern the travelers because of "the expiring state of Spain's interests there."

Lewis and Clark gathered a group of 48 experienced men near St. Louis during the winter of 1803–1804. In the spring they set forth, pushing slowly up the Missouri River in a 55-foot keelboat and two dugout canoes called pirogues. By late fall they had reached what is now North Dakota, where they built a small station, Fort Mandan, and spent the winter. In April 1805, having shipped back to the president more than 30 boxes of plants, minerals, animal skins and bones, and Indian artifacts, they struck out again toward the mountains, accompanied by a Shoshone squaw, Sacagawea, and her French-Canadian husband, Toussaint Charbonneau, who acted as interpreters and guides. They passed the Great Falls of the Missouri and then clambered over the Continental Divide at Lemhi Pass, in southwestern Montana. Soon thereafter the going became easier, and they descended to the Pacific by way of the Clearwater and Columbia rivers, reaching their destination in November. They had hoped to return by ship, but during the long, damp winter not a single vessel appeared. In the spring of 1806 they headed back by land, reaching St. Louis on September 23.

The country greeted the news of their return with delight. Besides locating several passes across

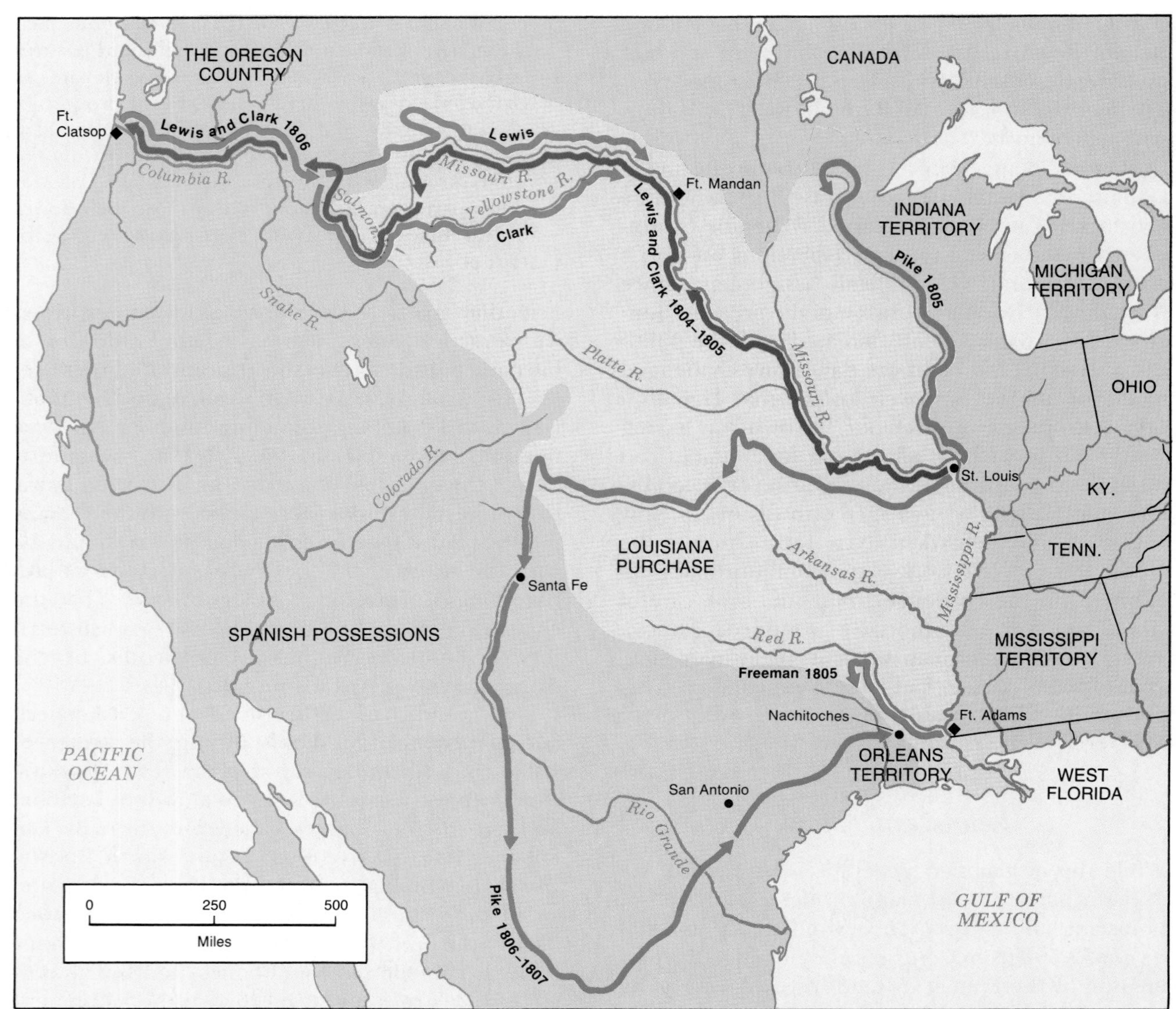

EXPLORING THE LOUISIANA PURCHASE

The explorations of Lewis and Clark, as well as those of Freeman and Pike, are traced in the map. The yellow shading shows the Louisiana Purchase as delineated by its "natural" boundaries. On their return journey, Lewis and Clark divided their party to explore more thoroughly the area around the upper Missouri and Yellowstone rivers.

the Rockies, Lewis and Clark had established friendly relations with a great many Indian tribes to whom they presented gifts, medals, American flags, and a sales talk designed to promote peace and the fur trade. They brought back a wealth of data about the country and its resources. The journals kept by members of the group were published and, along with their accurate maps, became major sources for scientists, students, and future explorers. To Jefferson's great personal satisfaction, Lewis provided him with many specimens of the local wildlife, including two grizzly bear cubs, which he kept for a time in a stone pit in the White House lawn.

The success of Lewis and Clark did not open the gates of Louisiana very wide. Other explorers sent out by Jefferson accomplished far less. Thomas Freeman, an Irish-born surveyor, led a small party up the Red River but ran into a powerful Spanish force near the present junction of Arkansas, Oklahoma, and Texas and was forced to retreat. Between 1805 and 1807 Lieutenant Zebulon Pike explored the upper Mississippi Valley and the Colorado region. (He discovered but failed to scale the peak south of Denver that bears his name.) Pike eventually made his way to Santa Fe and the upper reaches of the Rio Grande, but he was not nearly so careful and acute an observer as Lewis and Clark were and consequently brought back much less information. By 1808 fur traders based at St. Louis were beginning to invade the Rockies, and by 1812 there were 75,000 people in the southern section of the new territory. That year it was admitted to the Union as the state of Louisiana. The northern region lay almost untouched until much later.

Lewis and Clark kept meticulous records of the many plants and animals they discovered. The notes accompanying the drawing of the fish describe the plentiful supply of this species, and declare that the likeness is "as perfect as I can make it with my pen."

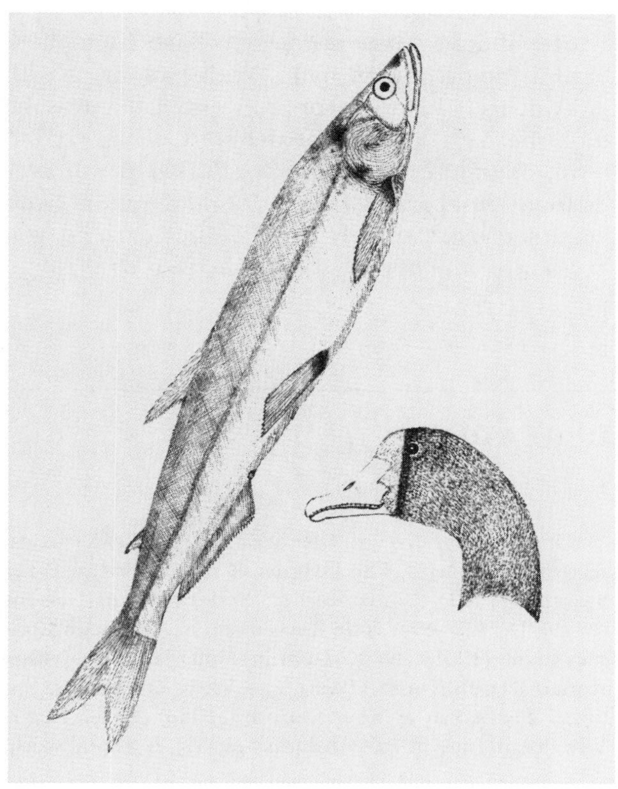

Jeffersonian Democracy

With the purchase of Louisiana, Jefferson completed the construction of the political institution known as the Republican party and the philosophy of government known as Jeffersonian Democracy. From what sort of materials had he built his juggernaut? In part his success was a matter of personality; in the march of American democracy he stood halfway, temperamentally, between Washington and Andrew Jackson, perfectly in tune with the thinking of his times. The colonial American had practiced democracy without really believing in it; hence, for example, the maintenance of property qualifications for voting in regions where nearly everyone owned property. Stimulated by the libertarian ideas of the Revolution, Americans were rapidly adjusting their beliefs to conform with their practices. However, it took a Jefferson, a man of large estates, possessed of the general prejudice in favor of the old-fashioned citizen rooted in the soil, yet deeply committed to majority rule, to oversee the transition.

Jefferson's marvelous talents as a writer help to explain his success. He expounded his ideas in language that few could resist. He had a remarkable facility for discovering practical arguments to justify his beliefs—as when he suggested that by letting everyone vote, elections would be made more honest because with large numbers going to the polls bribery would become prohibitively expensive.

Jefferson prepared the country for democracy by proving that a democrat could establish and maintain a stable regime. The Federalist tyranny of 1798 was compounded of selfishness and stupidity, but it was also based in part on honest fears that an egalitarian regime would not protect the fabric of society from hotheads and crackpots. The impact of the French Revolution on conservative thinking in the mid-1790s can scarcely be overestimated. America had fought a seven-year revolution without executing a single Tory, yet during the few months that the Terror ravaged France, nearly 17,000 persons were officially put to death for political "crimes," and many thousands more were killed in civil disturbances. Worse, in the opinion of many, the French extremists had attempted to destroy Christianity, substituting for it a "Cult of Reason." They confiscated property, imposed price controls, abolished slavery in the French colonies. Little wonder that many Americans feared that the Jeffersonians, lovers of France and of *liberté, égalité, fraternité,* would try to remodel American society in a similar way.

Jefferson calmed these fears. "Pell-mell" might scandalize the British and Spanish ministers and a few other mossbacks, but it was scarcely revolutionary. The most partisan Federalist was hard put to see a Robespierre in the amiable president scratching out state papers at his desk or chatting with a Kentucky congressman at a "republican" dinner party. Furthermore, Jefferson accepted Federalist ideas on public finance, even learning to live with Hamilton's bank. As a good democrat, he drew a nice distinction between his own opinions and the wishes of the majority, which he felt must always take priority. Even in his first inaugural he admitted that manufacturing and commerce were, along with agriculture, the "pillars of our prosperity," and while believing that these activities would best thrive when "left most free to individual enterprise," he accepted the principle that the government should protect them when necessary from "casual embarrassments." Eventually he gave his backing to modest proposals for spending federal money on roads, canals, and other projects that, according to his political philosophy, ought to have been left to the states and private individuals.

During his term the country grew and prospered, the commercial classes sharing in the bounty along with the farmers so close to Jefferson's heart. Blithely he set out to win the support of all who could vote. "It is material to the safety of Republicanism," he wrote in 1803, "to detach the mercantile interests from its enemies and incorporate them into the body of its friends."

Thus Jefferson undermined the Federalists all along the line. They had said that the country must pay a stiff price for prosperity and orderly government, and they demanded prompt payment in full, both in cash (taxes) and in the form of limitations on human liberty. Under Jefferson these much-desired goals had been achieved cheaply and without sacrificing freedom. A land whose riches could only be guessed at had been obtained without firing a shot and without burdening the people with new taxes. "What farmer, what mechanic, what laborer, ever sees a taxgatherer in the United States?" the president could ask in 1805, without a single Federalist rising to challenge him. Order without discipline, security without a large military establishment, prosperity without regulatory legislation, freedom without license—truly the Sage of Monticello appeared to have led his fellow Americans into a golden age.

Republican virtue seemed to have triumphed, both at home and abroad. "With nations as with individuals," Jefferson proudly proclaimed as he took the oath of office at the start of his second term, "our interests soundly calculated, will ever be found inseparable from our moral duties." And he added more smugly still: "Fellow citizens, you best know whether we have done well or ill."

SUPPLEMENTARY READING

Titles marked with an asterisk have been published in paperback.

No student interested in Jefferson's political and social philosophy should miss sampling his writings. A useful compilation is Adrienne Koch and William Peden, **The Life and Selected Writings of Thomas Jefferson** (1944). Lance Banning, **The Jeffersonian Persuasion** (1978), is valuable, as are Joyce Appleby, **Capitalism and a New Social Order** (1984), and M. D. Peterson, **Thomas Jefferson and the New Nation*** (1970).

On the Federalist and Democratic Republican parties, see Joseph Charles, **The Origins of the American Party System*** (1961), Linda Kerber, **Federalists in Dissent** (1970), D. H. Fischer, **The Revolution of American Conservatism** (1965), N. E. Cunningham, Jr., **The Jeffersonian Republicans*** (1958), and W. N. Chambers, **Political Parties in a New Nation*** (1963). S. G. Kurtz, **The Presidency of John Adams*** (1957), is a solid work, and Peter Shaw, **The Character of John Adams** (1976), is an interesting psychological study. See also R. A. McCaughey, **Josiah Quincy: The Last Federalist** (1974).

For the diplomatic conflicts of the late 1790s, see Bradford Perkins, **The First Rapprochement: England and the United States** (1967), Alexander De Conde, **The Quasi-War*** (1966), and William Stinchcombe, **The XYZ Affair** (1980). On the Alien and Sedition Acts, both J. M. Smith, **Freedom's Fetters: The Alien and Sedition Laws and American Civil Liberties*** (1956), and J. C. Miller, **Crisis in Freedom: The Alien and Sedition Acts*** (1951), are excellent. L. W. Levy, **Freedom of Speech and Press in Early American History*** (1963), provides valuable background for understanding the acts, for it demonstrates that modern conceptions of civil liberties are very different from those commonly held in the 18th century. Levy's **Jefferson and Civil Liberties: The Darker Side*** (1963) is a lawyer's brief for the prosecution.

The most recent general treatment of the Jeffersonian era is Marshall Smelser, **The Democratic Republic*** (1968). On the parties of the era, see N. E. Cunningham, Jr., **The Jeffersonian Republicans in Power*** (1963), and D. H. Fischer, **The Revolution of American Conservatism: The Federalist Party in the Era of Jeffersonian Democracy*** (1965); on the structure of Jefferson's administration, L. D. White, **The Jeffersonians*** (1951); on Jefferson's management of the administration and of Congress, J. S. Young, **The Washington Community*** (1966), a fascinating book.

Jefferson's battle with the judges can be followed in A. J. Beveridge, **Life of John Marshall** (1916–1919). For *Marbury* v. *Madison,* see J. A. Garraty (ed.), **Quarrels That Have Shaped the Constitution*** (1964), and D. O. Dewey's more detailed **Marshall Versus Jefferson*** (1970).

The war with the Barbary pirates is covered in R. W. Irwin, **The Diplomatic Relations of the United States with the Barbary Powers** (1931). On the Louisiana Purchase, see Henry Adams's **History,** E. W. Lyon, **Louisiana in French Diplomacy*** (1934), A. P. Whitaker, **The Mississippi Question** (1934), Irving Brant, **James Madison: Secretary of State** (1953), and George Dangerfield, **Chancellor Robert R. Livingston of New York** (1960).

Jefferson's interest in the west is discussed in E. T. Martin, **Thomas Jefferson: Scientist*** (1952). An excellent general treatment of western exploration is contained in R. A. Billington, **Westward Expansion** (1967). On Lewis and Clark, see P. R. Cutright, **Lewis and Clark: Pioneering Naturalists** (1976), Richard Dillon, **Meriwether Lewis** (1965), and J. O. Steffen, **William Clark** (1977). The career of Pike is traced in W. E. Hollon, **The Lost Pathfinder: Zebulon Montgomery Pike** (1949).

PORTFOLIO THREE
Jefferson at Monticello

The magnificent portrait of Jefferson at left, painted by Gilbert Stuart in 1805, is the official image of Jefferson that is currently reproduced on stamps. It is known as the Edgehill portrait, and it hung at Monticello for many years. The bust at right was made by the French sculptor Houdon when Jefferson was in France in 1789. It deliberately copies the look of the portrait busts so popular during the republican era of ancient Rome.

Monticello, designed in nearly every detail by Jefferson himself, was his home from 1772, the year he married the young widow Martha Skelton Wales, until his death in 1826.

could the dead feel any interest in Monu-
-ments or other remembrances of them, when, as
Anacreon says Ολιγη δε κεισομεσθα
Κονις, οστεων λυθεντων
the following would be to my Manes the most
gratifying.
On the grave
a plain die or cube of 3.f without any
mouldings, surmounted by an Obelisk
of 6.f. height, each of a single stone:
on the faces of the Obelisk the following
inscription, & not a word more
"Here was buried
Thomas Jefferson
Author of the Declaration of American Independance
of the Statute of Virginia for religious freedom
& Father of the University of Virginia."

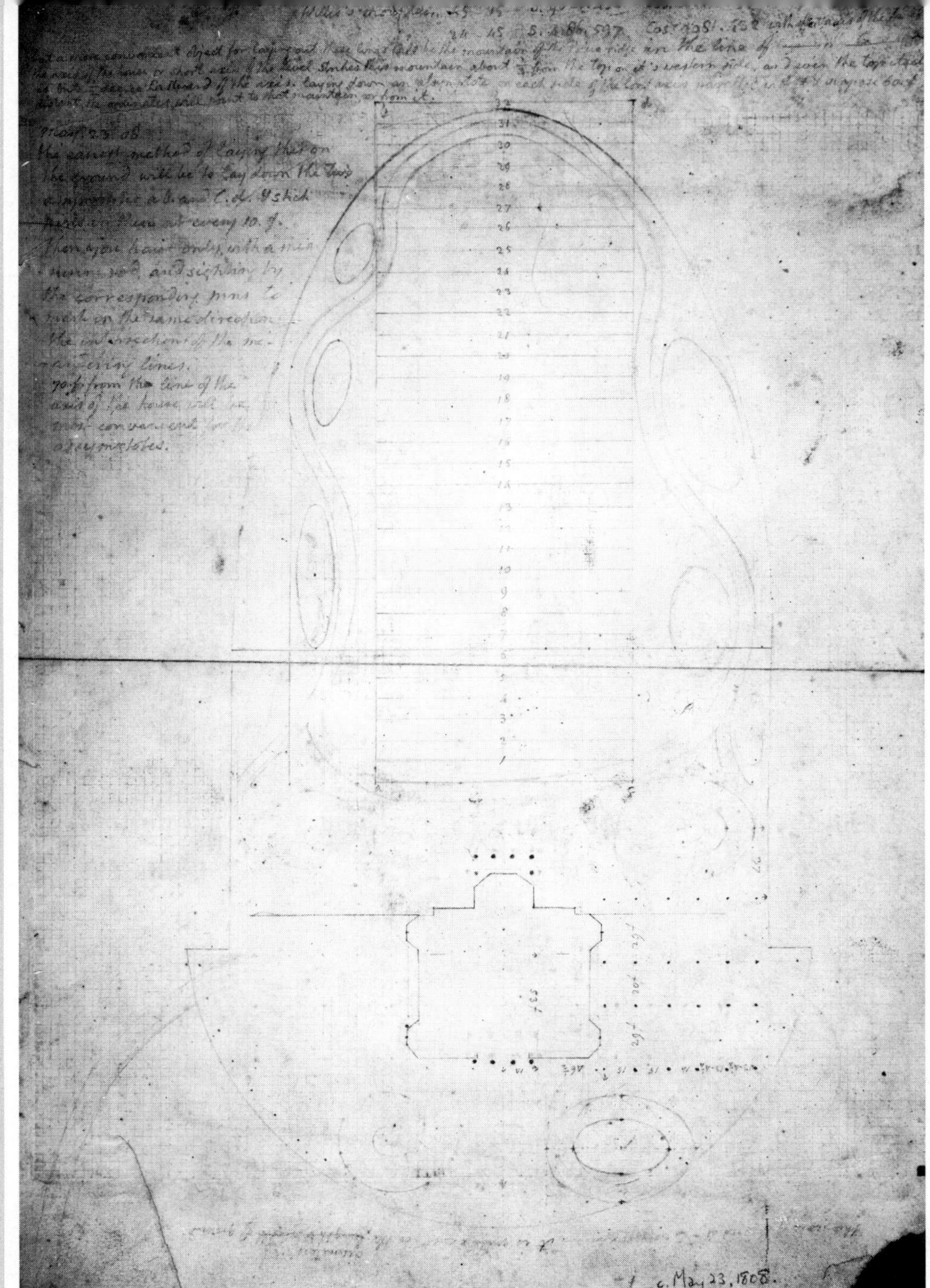

Jefferson started planning the grounds for Monticello in 1767, two years before construction on the house itself began. His detailed sketches of the front elevation of the house (compare the sketch here to the photo on page 195) and of the layout of the grounds show his wide-ranging interests. The notations on the plan, drawn in 1803, indicate how the house is oriented in relation to the surrounding hills and mountains. He even sketched his own gravestone and epitaph, writing: ". . . on the face of the Obelisk the following inscription, & not a word more

'Here was buried
Thomas Jefferson

author of the Declaration of American Independence
of the Statute of Virginia for religious freedom
& Father of the University of Virginia.' "

Jefferson, a musician as well as a statesman and scientist, owned a number of instruments, including a harpsichord. The music stand to the right of the harpsichord was designed by Jefferson. It allows four players to sit in a circle around it, while two more can stand and read their music from the upper tier.

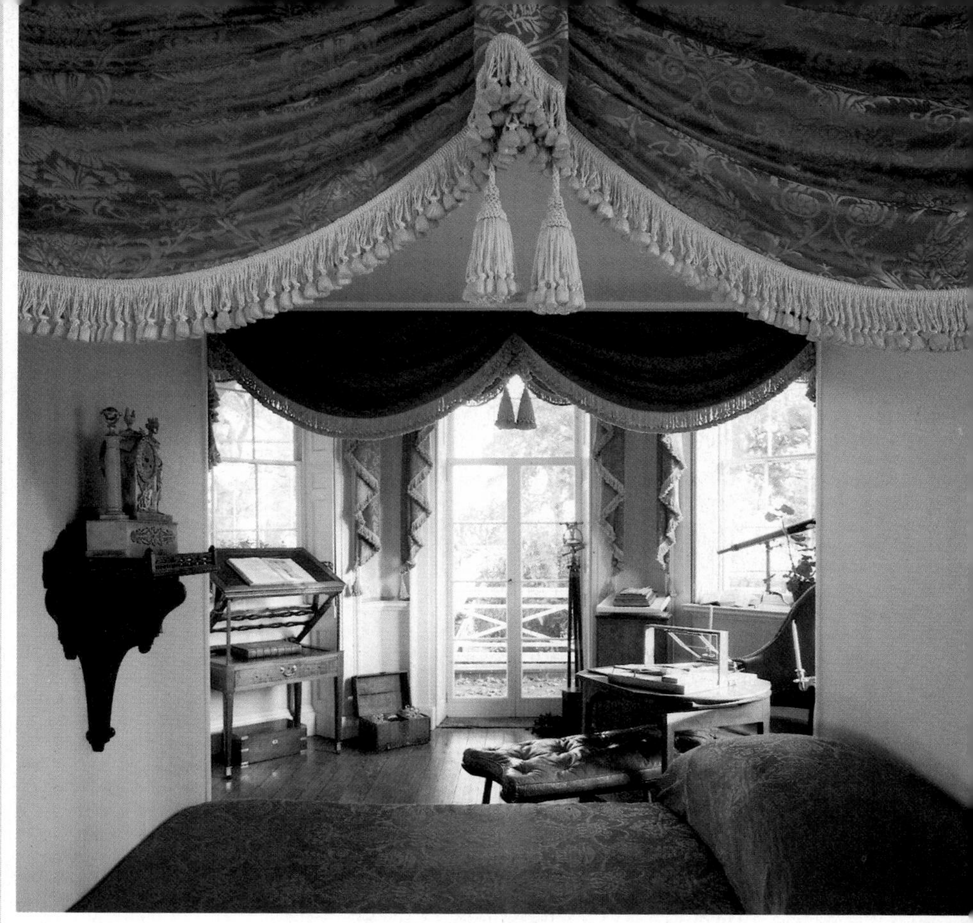

Jefferson's bed was conveniently set in an alcove, so that he could get in and out of it on either side. A clock is handy on the wall at the foot of the bed. In the background, his surveying equipment stands beside the glass door, and his telescope is aimed out the window. The table has a revolving surface, like a lazy Susan.

The cluttered entry hall of Monticello greeted visitors in the years after the Lewis and Clark expedition with western mementos: the antlers of a deer and a stuffed bison's head, as well as a tableful of bones, rocks, and other natural history objects. One visitor commented, "There is no private gentleman in the world in possession of so complete a scientific, useful and ornamental collection."

Supremely practical, Jefferson devised a way to make more than one copy of a letter or document at a time. This apparatus, called a polygraph, holds a second pen, which moves over a second piece of paper as the writer composes on the first piece. Jefferson had three polygraphs.

Isaac Jefferson was born in 1775; this daguerreotype was taken about 1845. He was a Monticello slave who worked as a blacksmith and made nails for the plantation. His stories are the source of many details of Jefferson's domestic life.

A Roll of the proper slaves of Thomas Jefferson. Jan. 14. 1774.

Monticello.

* Goliah.
* Hercules.
\+ Jupiter. 1743.

* Gill.
* Fanny
\+ Ned. 1760.
Suckey 1765.
Frankey. 1767.
Gill. 1769.

* Quash
* Nell.
* Bella. 1757.
* Charles. 1760.
Jenny. 1768.

* Betty

– Juno
* Toby junr. 1753.
– Luna. 1758.

* Cate. about 1747.
Hannah 1770.
Rachael. 1773.

Monticello.

\+ George
\+ Ursula.
George.
Bagwell.
Archy. 1773.

\+ Frank 1757.

\+ Bett. 1759
\+ Scilla. 1762.

* denotes a labourer in the ground.

\+ denotes a titheable person following some other occupation

– denotes a person discharged from labor on acct of age or infirmity.

A household as large as Monticello could not have been maintained without the help of many servants, and like other wealthy southerners Jefferson was a slave owner. Twenty-nine slaves are listed on the roll at left dated January 14, 1774. The persons not otherwise designated by a footnote were children under 10.

7
America Escapes from Europe

Our policy in regard to Europe . . . remains the same, which is, not to interfere in the internal concerns of any of its powers, . . . to leave the parties to themselves, in the hope that other powers will insure the same course. Monroe Doctrine, *1823*

Smugness and complacency are luxuries that politicians can seldom afford. Jefferson, beginning his second term with pride in the past and confidence in the future and with the mass support of the nation, soon found himself in trouble at home and abroad. In part his difficulties rose from the extent of the Republican victory. In 1805 the Federalists had neither useful ideas nor intelligent leadership nor effective numbers. They held only a quarter of the seats in Congress. As often happens in such situations, lack of opposition weakened party discipline and encouraged factionalism among the Republicans. At the same time, Napoleon's renewed aggressiveness in Europe, to which the sale of Louisiana had been a prelude, produced a tangle of new problems for the neutral United States. Jefferson could not solve these problems merely by being "just" and "moral," as he had suggested in his second inaugural address. At the end of his second term he was suffering from rheumatism and recurrent headaches that were no doubt of psychosomatic origin, and he wrote feelingly to a friend: "Never did a prisoner, released from his chains, feel such relief as I shall on shaking off the shackles of power."

John Randolph of Roanoke

Jefferson's domestic troubles were not of critical importance, but they were vexing. To a considerable extent they resulted from the elements in his makeup that explain his success: his facility in adjusting his principles to practical conditions, his readiness to take over the best of Federalism. This flexibility got him in trouble with some of his disciples, who were less ready than he to surrender principle to expediency.

The most prominent of the Republican critics was John Randolph of Roanoke, congressman from Virginia and majority leader during Jefferson's first term. Randolph was unique. Although he had wit, charm, and imagination, he was also intellectually rigid, and when he thought some principle at stake he was a vitriolic and unyielding obstructionist. Randolph made a fetish of preserving states' rights against invasion by the central government. "Asking one of the States to surrender part of her sovereignty is like asking a lady to surrender part of her chastity," he remarked in one of his typical epigrams.

Randolph first clashed with Jefferson in 1804, over an attempted settlement of the so-called Yazoo land frauds. In 1795 the Georgia legislature had sold a huge area in what is now Alabama and Mississippi to four land companies for a tiny fraction of its value, something less than 2 cents an acre. When it was revealed that many of the legislators had been corrupted, the next legislature canceled the grants, but not before the original grantees had unloaded large tracts on various third parties. These innocents turned to the federal government for relief when the grants were canceled. Jefferson favored a bill giving 5 million acres to these interests, but Randolph would have none of this. Rising in righteous wrath, he denounced in his shrill soprano all those who would countenance such fraud. The compromise bill was defeated.*

By the beginning of Jefferson's second term, Randolph was fretting about how the president's adversaries were taking advantage of his "easy credulity." Then, in December 1805, he broke with the administration over a request that Jefferson had made for $2 million to be used in unspecified dealings designed to obtain West Florida from Spain. Randolph—correctly, it turned out—suspected chicanery and from that date could be counted on to oppose every administration measure. He seldom mustered more than a handful of supporters in Congress, but his stabbing, nerve-shattering assaults grievously disturbed the president's peace of mind.

The Burr Conspiracy

Another Republican who caused trouble for Jefferson was Aaron Burr, and again the president was partially to blame for the difficulty. After their contest for the presidency in 1801, Jefferson pursued Burr vindictively, depriving him of federal patronage in New York and replacing him as the 1804 Republican vice-presidential candidate with Governor George Clinton, Burr's chief rival in the state.

While still vice-president, Burr began to flirt

* The controversy then entered the courts, and in 1810 Chief Justice Marshall held in *Fletcher* v. *Peck* that in rescinding the grant Georgia had committed an unconstitutional breach of contract. Before Marshall's ruling, however, the federal grant was finally approved by Congress. Had it not been, *Fletcher* v. *Peck* would have provided the "victims" of the Yazoo frauds with an area considerably larger than the state of Mississippi!

John Randolph of Roanoke (as he signed his name to avoid being mistaken for his cousin "Possum" John) was painted in 1805, when he was 32, by Gilbert Stuart.

with treason. He approached Anthony Merry, the British minister in Washington, and offered to "effect a separation of the Western part of the United States." His price was £110,000 and the support of a British fleet off the mouth of the Mississippi. The British did not fall in with his scheme, but he went ahead nonetheless. Exactly what he had in mind has long been in dispute. Certainly he dreamed of acquiring a western empire for himself; whether he intended to wrest it from the United States or from Spanish territories beyond Louisiana is unclear. He joined forces with General James Wilkinson, whom Jefferson unfortunately had appointed governor of Louisiana Territory, and who, it will be recalled, was secretly in the pay of Spain (see page 148).

In 1806 Burr and Wilkinson organized a small force at a place called Blennerhassett Island, in the Ohio River. Some six dozen men began to move downriver toward New Orleans under Burr's command. Whether the objective was New Orleans or some part of Mexico, the scheme was clearly illegal. For some reason, however—possibly because he was incapable of loyalty to anyone* —Wilkinson betrayed Burr to Jefferson at the last moment. The president issued a proclamation warning the nation and ordering Burr's arrest. Burr tried to escape to Spanish Florida but was captured in February 1807, brought to Richmond, Virginia, under guard, and charged with high treason.

Any president will deal summarily with traitors, but Jefferson's attitude during Burr's trial reveals the depth of his hatred. He "made himself a party to the prosecution," personally sending evidence to the United States attorney who was handling the case and offering blanket pardons to associates of Burr who would agree to turn state's evidence. On the other hand, Chief Justice Marshall, presiding at the trial in his capacity as judge of the circuit court, repeatedly showed favoritism to the prisoner. The proceedings quickly lost all appearance of impartiality.

In this contest between two great men at their worst, Jefferson as a vindictive executive and Marshall as a prejudiced judge, the victory went to the judge. Organizing "a military assemblage," Marshall declared on his charge to the jury, "was not a levying of war." To "advise or procure treason" was not in itself treason. Unless two independent witnesses testified to an overt act of treason as thus defined, the accused should be declared innocent. In the light of this charge, the jury, deliberating only 25 minutes, found Burr not guilty.

Burr was also tried and acquitted on the charge of conspiring to invade Spanish territory. Throughout his ordeal he never lost his self-possession and seemed to view the proceedings with amiable cynicism. Then, since he was wanted either for murder or for treason in six states, he went into exile in Europe. Some years later he returned to New York, where he spent an unregenerate old age, fathering two illegitimate children in his seventies and being divorced by his second wife on grounds of adultery at 80.

The Burr affair was a blow to Jefferson's prestige; it left him more embittered against Marshall and the federal judiciary, and it added nothing to his reputation as a statesman.

* John Randolph said of him: "Wilkinson is the only man that I ever saw who was from the bark to the very core a villain."

Aaron Burr was sketched in 1805 by Charles Saint-Mémin, who was well-known for his profile portraits. (See the Jefferson portrait on page 183.)

Napoleon and the British

Jefferson's difficulties with Randolph and Burr may be traced at least in part to the purchase of Louisiana. His easy success in obtaining the region encouraged him to think that West Florida could be snapped up with equal ease, and this error brought upon him the shrill wrath of Randolph of Roanoke. Louisiana itself, fat, empty, and unknown, excited the cupidity of men like Burr and Wilkinson. But problems infinitely more serious were also related to Louisiana.

Napoleon had jettisoned Louisiana to clear the decks before resuming the battle for control of Europe. This war had the effect of stimulating the American economy, for the warring powers needed American goods and American vessels. Shipbuilding boomed; foreign trade, which had quintupled since 1793, nearly doubled again between 1803 and 1805. By the summer of 1807, however, the situation had changed: a most unusual stalemate had developed in the war. In October 1805 Britain's Horatio Nelson demolished the combined Spanish and French fleets in the Battle of Trafalgar, off the coast of Spain. Napoleon, now at the summit of his powers, quickly redressed the balance, smashing army after army thrown against him by Great Britain's continental allies. First he attacked the Austrians, capturing 50,000 at Ulm in Bavaria. Then he shattered a great Austrian and Russian army in the Battle of Austerlitz (December 1805), perhaps the most brilliant victory of his career. In 1806 he overwhelmed the Prussians at Jena and the following June, the Russians at Friedland in East Prussia. Thereafter Napoleon was master of Europe, while the British controlled the seas around the Continent. Neither nation could strike directly at the other.

They therefore resorted to commercial warfare, striving to disrupt each other's economy. Napoleon struck first with his Berlin Decree (November 1806), which made "all commerce and correspondence" with Great Britain illegal. The British retaliated with a series of edicts called Orders in Council, blockading most continental ports and barring from them all foreign vessels unless they first stopped at a British port and paid customs duties. Napoleon then issued his Milan Decree (December 1807), declaring any vessel that submitted to the British rules "to have become English property" and thus subject to seizure.

The blockades and counterblockades seemed designed to stop commerce completely, yet this was not the case. Napoleon's "Continental System" was supposed to make Europe self-sufficient and isolate Great Britain, yet he was willing to sell European products to the British (if the price was right); his chief objective was to deprive them of their continental markets. The British were ready to sell anything on the Continent, and to allow others to do so too, provided they first paid a toll. In effect this commercial warfare amounted to the organized exploitation of foreign merchants, who were enjoying unprecedented opportunities for profit because of the prolonged conflict. The Continental System was, in John Quincy Adams's pithy phrase, "Little more than extortion wearing the mask of prohibition," and British policy was equally immoral—a kind of piracy practiced with impunity because the Royal Navy controlled the seas.

When war first broke out between Britain and

France in 1792, the colonial trade of both sides had fallen largely into American hands because the danger of capture drove many belligerent merchant vessels from the seas. This commerce had engaged Americans in some rather devious practices. Under the Rule of War of 1756, it will be recalled, the British denied to neutrals the right to engage in trade during time of war from which they were barred by mercantilistic regulations in time of peace. If an American ship carried sugar from the French colony of Martinique to France, for example, the British claimed the right to capture it because such traffic was normally confined to French bottoms by French law.

To avoid this risk, American merchants brought the sugar first to the United States, a legal peacetime voyage under French mercantilism. Then they reshipped it to France as *American* sugar. Since the United States was a neutral and sugar was not contraband of war, the Americans expected the British to let their ships pass with impunity. Continental products likewise reached the French West Indies by way of United States ports, and the American government encouraged the traffic in both directions by refunding customs duties on foreign products reshipped within a year. Between 1803 and 1806 the annual value of foreign products reexported from the United States jumped from $13 million to $60 million! In 1806 the United States exported 47 million pounds of coffee—none, of course, of local origin. An example of this type of trade is offered by Samuel Eliot Morison in his *Maritime History of Massachusetts*:

> The brig *Eliza Hardy* of Plymouth enters her home port from Bordeaux, on May 20, 1806, with a cargo of claret wine. Part of it is immediately re-exported to Martinique in the schooner *Pilgrim,* which also carries a consignment of brandy that came from Alicante in the brig *Commerce,* and another of gin that came from Rotterdam in the barque *Hannah* of Plymouth. The rest of the *Eliza Hardy's* claret is taken to Philadelphia by coasters, and thence re-exported in seven different vessels to Havana, Santiago de Cuba, St. Thomas, and Batavia.

This underhanded commerce irritated the British. In the cases of the *Essex* and the *William* (1805–1806), a British judge, Sir William Grant, decreed that American ships could no longer rely on "mere voluntary *ceremonies*" to circumvent the Rule of 1756. Thus, just when Britain and France were cracking down on direct trade by neutrals, Britain determined to halt the American reexport trade, thereby gravely threating American prosperity.

The Impressment Controversy

More dismaying were the cruel indignities being visited upon American seamen by the British practice of impressment. Under British law, any able-bodied subject could be drafted for service in the Royal Navy in an emergency. Normally, when the commander of a warship found himself short-handed he put into a British port and sent a "press gang" ashore to round up the necessary men in harborside pubs. When far from home waters he might hail any passing British merchant ship and commandeer the necessary men, though this practice was understandably unpopular in British maritime circles. He might also stop a *neutral* merchant vessel on the high seas and remove any British subject. Since the United States owned by far the largest merchant fleet among the neutrals, its vessels bore the brunt of this practice.

Impressment had been a cause of Anglo-American conflict for many years; American pride suffered every time a vessel carrying the flag was forced to back topsails and heave to at the command of a British man-of-war. Still more galling was the contemptuous behavior of British officers when they boarded American ships. In 1796 an American captain named Figsby was stopped twice by British warships while carrying a cargo of poultry and other livestock to Guadeloupe. First a privateer, the *Sea Nymph,* impressed two of his crew, confiscated most of his chickens, "abused" him, and stole his ship's flag. Two days later H.M.S. *Unicorn* took another of Figsby's men, the rest of his poultry, four sheep, and three hogs.

Many British captains made little effort to be sure they were impressing British subjects; any likely looking lad might be taken when the need was great. Furthermore, there were legal questions in dispute. When did an English immigrant become an American? When he was naturalized, the United States claimed. Never, the British retorted; "once an Englishman, always an Englishman."

America's lax immigration laws compounded the problem. A foreigner could become a citizen with ridiculous ease; those too impatient to wait the required five years could purchase false naturalization papers for as little as a dollar. Because working conditions in the American merchant marine were superior to those of the British, at least 10,000 British-born tars were serving on American ships. Some became American citizens legally; others obtained false papers; some admitted to being British subjects; some were deserters from the Royal Navy. From the British point of view, all were liable to impressment.

The Jefferson administration conceded the right of the British to impress their own subjects from American merchant ships. When naturalized Americans were impressed, however, the administration was irritated, and when native-born Americans were taken, it became incensed. Impressment, Secretary of State Madison said in 1807, was "anomalous in principle . . . grievous in practice, and . . . abominable in abuse." Between 1803 and 1812 at least 5,000 sailors were snatched from the decks of United States vessels and forced to serve in the Royal Navy. Most of them—estimates run as high as three out of every four—were Americans. The British did not claim the right to impress native-born Americans, and when it could be proved that boarding officers had done so, the men in question were released by higher authority. During the course of the controversy, the British authorities freed 3,800 impressed Americans, which suggests that a much larger number were seized. However, the British refused to abandon impressment. "The Pretension advanced by Mr. Madison that the American Flag should protect every Individual sailing under it," one British foreign secretary explained, "is too extravagant to require any serious Refutation."

The combination of impressment, British interference with the reexport trade, and the general harassment of neutral commerce instituted by both Great Britain and France would have perplexed the most informed and hardheaded of leaders, and in dealing with these problems Jefferson was neither informed nor hardheaded. Fundamentally he was an isolationist, ready "to let every treaty we have drop off without renewal"; he even considered closing down all overseas diplomatic missions. He believed it much wiser to stand up for one's rights than to compromise, yet he hated the very thought of war. Perhaps, being a southerner, he was less sensitive than he might have been to the needs of New England commercial interests. While the American merchant fleet passed 600,000 tons and continued to grow at an annual rate of over 10 percent, Jefferson kept only a skeleton navy on active service, despite the fact that the great powers were fighting a worldwide, no-holds-barred war. Instead of building a navy that other nations would have to respect, he relied on a tiny fleet of frigates and a swarm of gunboats that were useless against the Royal Navy—"a macabre monument," in the words of one historian, "to his hasty, ill-digested ideas" about defense.*

The Embargo Act

The frailty of Jefferson's policy became obvious once the warring powers began to attack neutral shipping in earnest. Between 1803 and 1807 the British seized over 500 American ships, Napoleon over 200 more. The United States could do nothing. "We have principles from which we shall never depart," Jefferson boasted. "Our neutrality should be respected." He added immediately: "On the other hand, we do not want war, and all this is very embarrassing."

The ultimate in frustration came on June 22, 1807, off Norfolk, Virginia. The American 46-gun frigate *Chesapeake* had just left port for patrol duty in the Mediterranean. Among its crew were a British sailor who had deserted from H.M.S. *Halifax* and three Americans who had been illegally impressed by the captain of H.M.S. *Melampus* and had later escaped. The *Chesapeake* was barely out of sight of land when H.M.S. *Leopard* (56 guns) approached and signaled it to heave to. Thinking that *Leopard* wanted to make some routine communication, Captain James Barron did so. A British officer came aboard and demanded that the four "deserters" be handed over to him. Barron refused, whereupon as soon as the officer was back on board, *Leopard* opened fire on the unsuspecting American ship, killing three sailors. Barron had to surrender. The "deserters" were seized and then the crippled *Chesapeake* was allow to limp back to port.

---

* The gunboats had performed effectively against the Barbary pirates, but Jefferson was enamored of them mainly because they were cheap. A gunboat cost about $10,000 to build, a frigate well over $300,000.

The Ograbme ("embargo" spelled backwards), a unique snapping turtle created by cartoonist Alexander Anderson, effectively frustrates an American tobacco smuggler.

The attack was in violation of international law, for no nation claimed the right to impress sailors from warships. The British government admitted this, though it delayed making restitution for years. The American press clamored for war, but the country had nothing to fight with. Jefferson contented himself with ordering British warships out of American territorial waters. However, he was determined to put a stop to the indignities being heaped upon the flag by Great Britain and France. The result was the Embargo Act.

The Embargo Act prohibited all exports. American vessels could not clear for any foreign port, and foreign vessels could do so only if empty. Importing was not forbidden, but few foreign ships would come to the United States if they had to return without a cargo. Although the law was sure to injure the American economy, Jefferson hoped that it would work in two ways to benefit the nation. By keeping U.S. merchant ships off the seas, it would end all chance of injury to them and to the national honor. By cutting off American goods and markets, it would put great economic pressure on Britain and France to moderate policies toward American shipping. The fact that boycotts had repeatedly wrested concessions from the British during the crises preceding the Revolution was certainly in Jefferson's mind when he devised the embargo.

Seldom has a law been so bitterly resented and resisted by a large segment of the public. It demanded of the maritime interests far greater sacrifices than they could reasonably be expected to make. Massachusetts-owned ships alone were earning over $15 million a year in freight charges by 1807, and Bay State merchants were making far larger gains from the buying and selling of goods. Foreign commerce was the most expansive force in the economy, the chief reason for the nation's prosperity. Losses through seizure were exasperating, but they could be insured against. Impressment excited universal indignation, but it hit chiefly at the defenseless, the disreputable, and the obscure and never caused a labor shortage in the merchant marine. The profits of commerce were still tremendous. A Massachusetts senator estimated that if only one vessel in three escaped the blockade, the owner came out ahead. As John Randolph remarked in a typical sally, the administration was trying "to cure the corns by cutting off the toes."

The Embargo Act had catastrophic effects. Exports fell from $108 million in 1807 to $22 million in 1808, imports from $138 million to less than $57 million. Prices of farm products and manufactured goods reacted violently; seamen were thrown out of work; merchants found their businesses disrupted.

How many Americans violated the law is difficult

to determine, but they were ingenious at discovering ways to do so. The most obvious way was to smuggle goods back and forth between Canada and the northeastern states. As Madison recalled in later years, the political boundary lost all significance. People on both sides made the region "a world of itself," treating the Embargo Act as though the laws of Congress did not apply to them.

As for ocean commerce, American ships made hastily for blue water before the machinery of enforcement could be put into operation, not to return until the law was repealed. Shipping between American ports had not been outlawed, and coasting vessels were allowed to put into foreign ports when in distress. Suddenly, mysterious storms began to drive experienced skippers leagues off their courses, some as far as Europe. The brig *Commerce*, en route from Massachusetts to New Orleans, was

The embargo's effects are shown graphically here. The brief foreign trade spurt in 1810 was due to congressional passage of Macon's Bill No. 2. The space between the upper (import) line and the lower (export) line indicates a persistent foreign-trade deficit.

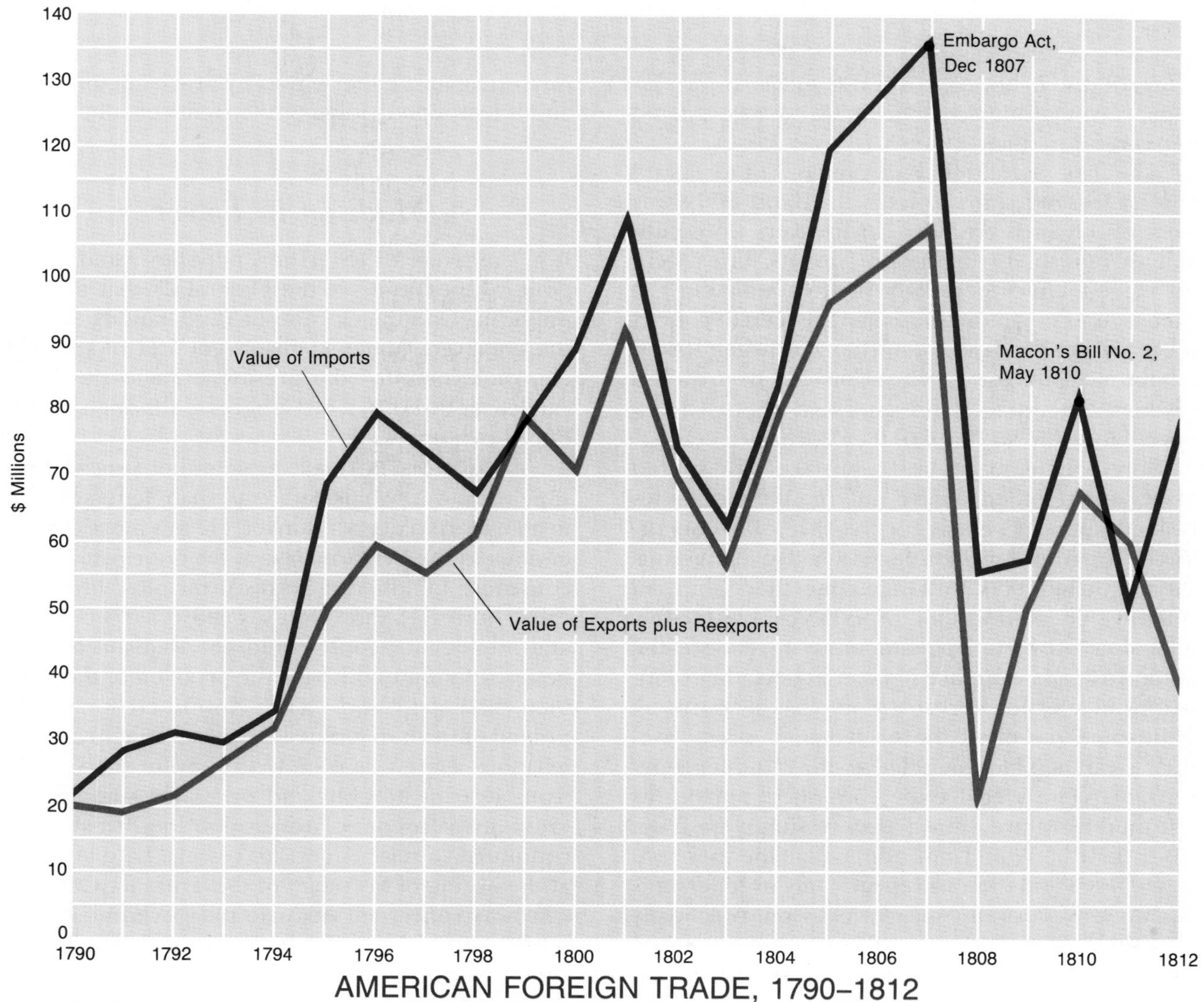

AMERICAN FOREIGN TRADE, 1790–1812

The state of the art in ship-to-ship communications during the Embargo Act is shown in Benjamin Latrobe's sketch of "A Conversation at Sea." Ships wishing to put into foreign ports could easily fabricate stories of sudden storms or other emergencies.

"forced" by a shortage of water to make for Havana. Having replenished her casks, she exchanged her cargo for sugar.

The law permitted merchants with property abroad to send ships to fetch it. About 800 ships went off on such errands. Lawbreakers were difficult to punish. In the seaport towns juries were no more willing to convict men of violating the Embargo Act than their fathers had been to convict those charged with violating the Townshend Acts. A mob at Gloucester, Massachusetts, destroyed a revenue cutter in the same spirit that Rhode Islanders exhibited in 1772 when they burned the *Gaspee.*

Surely the embargo was a mistake. The United States ought either to have suffered the indignities heaped upon its vessels for the sake of profits or, by constructing a powerful navy, made it dangerous for the belligerents to treat its merchant ships so roughly. Jefferson was too proud to choose the former alternative, too parsimonious to choose the latter. Instead he applied harsher and harsher regulations in a futile effort to accomplish his purpose. Militiamen patrolled the Canadian border; revenuers searched out smuggled goods without proper warrants. The illegal trade continued, and in his last months as president Jefferson simply gave up. Even then he would not admit that the embargo was a fiasco and urge its repeal. Only in Jefferson's last week in office did a leaderless Congress finally abolish it, substituting the Non-Intercourse Act, which forbade trade only with Great Britain and France and authorized the president to end the boycott against either power by proclamation when and if it stopped violating the rights of Americans.

Madison in Power

It is a measure of Jefferson's popularity and of the political ineptitude of the Federalists that the Republicans won the election of 1808 handily despite the embargo. James Madison got 122 of the 173 electoral votes for the presidency, and the party carried both houses of Congress, although by reduced majorities.

Madison was a small, neat, rather precise person, narrower in his interests than Jefferson but in many ways a deeper thinker. He was more conscientious in the performance of his duties and more consistent in adhering to his principles. Ideologically, however, they were as close as two active and intelligent people could be. Madison had no better solution to offer for the problem of the hour than had Jefferson. The Non-Intercourse Act proved difficult to enforce—once an American ship left port, there was no way to prevent the skipper from steering for England or France—and it exerted little economic pressure on the British, who continued to seize American vessels. Late in 1809, at the urging of Secretary of the Treasury Gallatin, who was concerned because the government was operating at a deficit, Representative Nathaniel Macon of North Carolina introduced a bill permitting American ships to go anywhere but closing United

States ports to the ships of Britain and France. After protracted bickering in Congress, this measure was replaced by another, known as Macon's Bill No. 2, which removed all restrictions on commerce with France and Britain, though French and British warships were still barred from American waters. It authorized the president to reapply the principle of nonintercourse to either of the major powers if the other should "cease to violate the neutral commerce of the United States." This bill became law in May 1810.

The volume of United States commerce with the British Isles swiftly zoomed to preembargo levels. Trade with France remained much more limited because of the British fleet. Napoleon therefore announced that the Berlin and Milan decrees would be revoked in November on the understanding that Great Britain would abandon its own restrictive policies. Treating this ambiguous proposal as a statement of French policy (which it decidedly was not), Madison reapplied the nonintercourse policy to Great Britain. Napoleon, having thus tricked Madison into closing American ports to British ships and goods, continued to seize American ships and cargoes whenever it suited him to do so.

The British grimly refused to modify the Orders in Council unless it could be shown that the French had actually repealed the Berlin and Milan decrees—and this despite mounting complaints from their own businessmen that the new American nonimportation policy was cutting off a major market for their manufactures. Madison, on the other hand, could not afford either to admit that Napoleon had deceived him or to reverse American policy still another time. Reluctantly he came to the conclusion that unless Britain repealed the Orders, the United States must declare war.

Tecumseh and the Prophet

There were other reasons for fighting besides British violations of neutral rights. The Indians were again making trouble, and western farmers believed that the British in Canada were egging them on. This had been true in the past but was no longer the case in 1811–1812. American domination of the southern Great Lakes region was no longer in question. Canadian officials had no desire to force a showdown between the Indians and the Americans, for that could have but one result. Aware of their own vulnerability, the Canadians wanted to preserve Indian strength in case war should break out between Great Britain and the United States.

American political leaders tended to believe that Indians should be encouraged to become farmers and to copy the "civilized" ways of whites. However, no government had been able to control the frontiersmen, who by bribery, trickery, and force were driving the tribes back year after year from the rich lands of the Ohio Valley. General William Henry Harrison, governor of Indiana Territory, a tough, relentless soldier, kept a constant pressure on them. He wrested land from one tribe by promising it aid against a traditional enemy, from another as a penalty for having murdered a white man, from others by corrupting a few chiefs. Harrison justified his sordid behavior by citing the end in view—that "one of the fairest portions of the globe" be secured as "the seat of civilization, of science, and of true religion." The "wretched savages" should not be allowed to stand in the path of this worthy objective. As early as 1805 it was clear that unless something drastic was done, Harrison's aggressiveness, together with the corroding effects of white civilization, would soon obliterate the tribes.

At this point the Shawnee chief Tecumseh made a bold and imaginative effort to reverse the trend by binding all the tribes east of the Mississippi into a great confederation. Traveling from the Wisconsin country to the Floridas, he persuaded tribe after tribe to join him. "Let the white race perish," Tecumseh declared. "They seize your land; they corrupt your women. . . . Back whence they came, upon a trail of blood, they must be driven!"

To Tecumseh's political movement his brother Tenskwatawa, known as the Prophet, added the force of a moral crusade. Instead of aping white customs, the Prophet said, Indians must give up white ways, white clothes, and white liquor and reinvigorate their own culture. Ceding lands to the whites must stop because the Great Spirit intended that the land be used in common by all.

The Prophet was a fanatic who saw visions and claimed to be able to control the movement of heavenly bodies. Tecumseh, however, possessed true genius. A powerful orator and a great orga-

The Prophet, also called "The Open Door," lent religious fervor to his brother Tecumseh's antiwhite doctrine.

nizer, he had deep insight into the needs of his people. Harrison himself said of Tecumseh: "He is one of those uncommon geniuses which spring up occasionally to produce revolutions and overturn the established order of things." The two brothers made a formidable team. By 1811 thousands of Indians were organizing to drive the whites off their lands. Alarms swept through the west.

With about a thousand soldiers, General Harrison marched boldly against the brothers' camp at Prophetstown, where Tippecanoe Creek joins the Wabash, in Indiana. Tecumseh was away recruiting men, and the Prophet recklessly ordered an assault on Harrison's camp outside the village on November 7, 1811. When the white soldiers held their ground despite the Prophet's magic, the Indians lost confidence and fell back. Harrison then destroyed Prophetstown. While the Battle of Tippecanoe was pretty much a draw, it disillusioned the Indians and shattered their confederation. Frontier warfare continued, but in the disorganized manner of former times. Like all such fighting it was brutal and bloody.

Unwilling as usual to admit that their own excesses were the chief cause of the trouble, the settlers directed their resentment at the British in Canada. "This combination headed by the Shawanese prophet is a British scheme," a resolution adopted by the citizens of Vincennes, Indiana, proclaimed. As a result, the cry for war with Great Britain rang along the frontier.

Depression and Land Hunger

Some westerners pressed for war because they were suffering an agricultural depression. The prices they received for their wheat, tobacco, and other products in the markets of New Orleans were falling, and they attributed the decline to the loss of foreign markets and the depredations of the British. American commercial restrictions had more to do with the western depression than the British, and in any case the slow and cumbersome transportation and distribution system that western farmers were saddled with was the major cause of their difficulties. But the farmers were no more inclined to accept these explanations than they were to absolve the British from responsibility for the Indian difficulties. If only the seas were free, they reasoned, costs would go down, prices would rise, and prosperity would return.

To some extent western expansionism also heightened the war fever. The west contained immense tracts of virgin land, but westerners wanted more. Canada would surely fall to American arms in the event of war, the frontiersmen believed. So, apparently, would Florida, for Spain was now Britain's ally. Florida in itself provided no cause for a war, for it was sure to fall into American hands before long. In 1810 Madison had snapped up the extreme western section without eliciting any effective response from Spain. So it was primarily because of Canada, nearby and presumably vulnerable, that westerners wanted war. It is also likely that President Madison saw an attack on Canada as a way to force the British to respect neutral rights. If Napoleon's Continental System cut Great Britain off from trade with northern Europe, Canada would be its only source of lumber and naval stores. Between 1808 and 1812 Canadian exports of lumber to Britain soared. Still more important in Madison's mind, if the United States conquered

Canada, Britain's hope of obtaining food in Canada for its West Indian sugar islands would be shattered. Then it would have to end its hateful assaults and restrictions on American merchant ships or the islands' economy would collapse.

But westerners, and many easterners too, were more patriots than imperialists or merchants in 1811 and 1812. When the "War Hawks" (their young leaders in Congress) called for war against Great Britain, they did so because they saw no other way to defend the national honor and force repeal of the Orders in Council. The choice seemed to lie between war and surrender of true independence. As Madison put it, to bow to British policy would be to "recolonize" American foreign commerce.

Resistance to War

There were, however, large numbers of people who thought that a war against Great Britain would be a national calamity. Some Federalists would have resisted anything the administration proposed; Congressman Josiah Quincy of Massachusetts declared that he "could not be kicked" into the war, which he considered a cowardly, futile, and unconstitutional business designed primarily to insure the reelection of Madison. (Quincy saw no inconsistency between this opinion and his conviction that Madison was a pacifist.) According to Quincy the War Hawks were "backwoodsmen" willing to wage a "cruel, wanton, senseless and wicked" war in order to swallow up Canada.

But other people based their objections on economics and a healthy realism. Powerful interests in the eastern maritime states were dead set against fighting, for the same reasons that had led them to resist the Embargo Act. No shipowner could view with equanimity the idea of taking on the largest navy in the world. Such persons complained sincerely enough about impressment and the Orders in Council, but war seemed worse to them by far. Self-interest led them to urge patience.

Such a policy would have been wise, for Great Britain did not represent a real threat to the United States. British naval officers were high-handed, officials in London complacent, British diplomats in Washington second-rate and obtuse. Yet language, culture, and strong economic ties bound the two countries. Napoleon, on the other hand, represented a tremendous potential danger. He had offhandedly turned over Louisiana, but even Jefferson, the chief beneficiary of his largess, hated everything he stood for. Jefferson called Napoleon "the Attila of the age" and "an unprincipled tyrant who is deluging the continent of Europe with blood."

No one understood the Napoleonic danger to America more clearly than the British; part of the stubbornness and arrogance of their maritime policy grew out of their conviction that Napoleon was a threat to all free nations. The *Times* of London declared: "The Alps and the Apennines of America are the British Navy. If ever that should be removed, a short time will suffice to establish the headquarters of a [French] Duke-Marshal at Washington." Yet by going to war with Britain, the United States was aiding Napoleon.

What made the situation even more unfortunate was the fact that by 1812 conditions had changed in England in a way that made a softening of British maritime policy likely. A depression caused chiefly by the increasing effectiveness of Napoleon's Continental System was plaguing the country. Manufacturers, blaming the slump on the loss of American markets, were urging repeal of the Orders in Council. Gradually, though with exasperating slowness, the government prepared to yield. On June 23, after a change of ministries, the new foreign secretary, Lord Castlereagh, suspended the Orders. Five days earlier, alas, the United States had declared war.

The War of 1812

The illogic of the War Hawks in pressing for a fight was exceeded only by their ineffectiveness in planning and managing the struggle. By what possible strategy could the ostensible objective of the war be achieved? To construct a navy capable of challenging the British fleet would have been the work of many years and a more expensive proposition than the War Hawks were willing to consider. So hopeless was that prospect that Congress failed to undertake *any* new construction in the first year of the conflict. Several hundred merchant ships lashed a few cannon to their decks and sailed off as privateers to attack British commerce. The

In Ambroise Louis Garneray's painting, Oliver Hazard Perry's squadron (right) drives through the British line in the Battle of Lake Erie. When Perry's flagship Lawrence *was knocked out of action, he transferred under fire to the* Niagara *and, attacking aggressively, pounded the two largest British vessels into submission.*

navy's seven modern frigates, built during the war scare after the XYZ Affair, put to sea. But these forces could make no pretense of disputing Britain's mastery of the Atlantic.

For a brief moment the American frigates held center stage, for they were faster, tougher, larger, and more powerfully armed than their British counterparts. Barely two months after the declaration of war, Captain Isaac Hull in U.S.S. *Constitution* chanced upon H.M.S. *Guerrière* in mid-Atlantic, outmaneuvered her brilliantly, brought down her mizzenmast with his first volley, and then gunned her into submission, a hopeless wreck. In October U.S.S. *United States,* captained by Stephen Decatur, hero of the war against the Barbary pirates, caught H.M.S. *Macedonian* off the Madeiras, pounded her unmercifully at long range, and forced her surrender. *Macedonian* was taken into New London as a prize; over a third of her 300-man crew were casualties, while American losses were but a dozen. Then, in December, *Constitution,* now under Captain William Bainbridge, took on the British frigate *Java* off Brazil. "Old Ironsides" shot away the *Java's* mainmast and reduced her to a hulk too battered for salvage.

These victories had little influence on the outcome of the war. The Royal Navy had 34 frigates, 7 more powerful ships of the line, and dozens of smaller vessels. As soon as these forces could concentrate against them, the American frigates were immobilized, forced to spend the war gathering barnacles at their moorings while powerful British squadrons ranged offshore. The privateering merchantmen were more effective because they were so numerous; they captured more than 1,300 British vessels during the war. The best of them—vessels like *America* and *True-Blooded Yankee*—were redesigned, given more sail to increase their speed, and formidably armed. *America* captured 26 prizes valued at more than a million dollars. *True-Blooded Yankee* took 27 and destroyed 7 more in a Scottish harbor.

Great Britain's one weak spot seemed to be Canada. The colony had but half a million inhabitants to oppose 7.5 million Americans. Only 2,257 British regulars guarded the long border from Montreal to Detroit. The Canadian militia was feeble, and many of its members, being American-born, sympathized with the "invaders." According to the War Hawk congressman Henry Clay of Kentucky, the west was one solid horde of ferocious frontiersmen, armed to the teeth and thirsting for Canadian blood. Yet such talk was mostly brag and bluster; when Congress authorized increasing the army by 25,000 men, Kentucky produced 400 enlistments.

American military leadership proved extremely disappointing. Madison relied on officers who had served with distinction in the Revolution, but in most cases, as one biographer suggested, their abil-

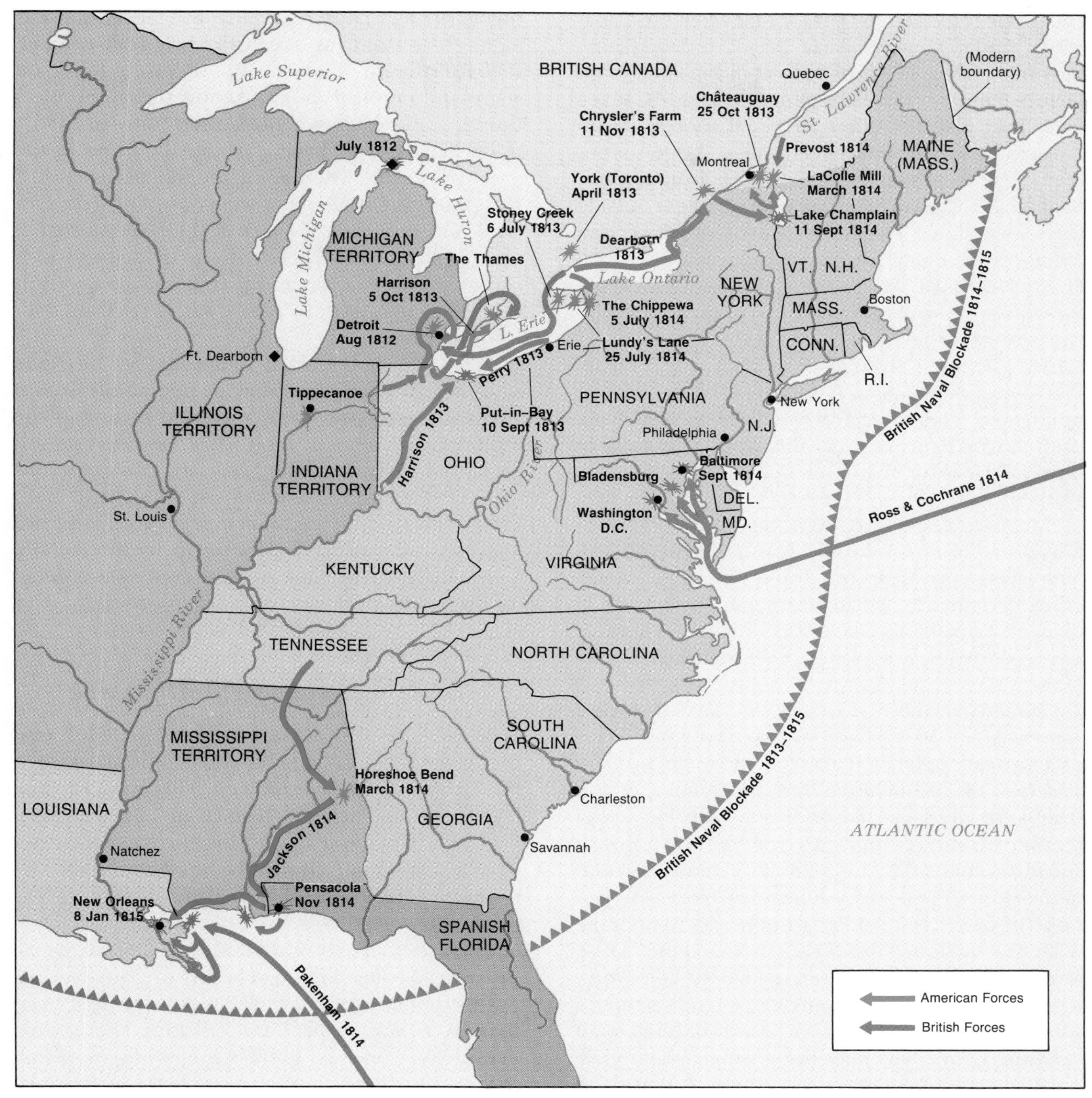

THE WAR OF 1812

ities "appeared to have evaporated with age and long disuse." Instead of a concentrated strike against Canada's St. Lawrence River lifeline, the generals planned a complicated three-pronged attack. It was a total failure. In July 1812 General William Hull, veteran of the battles of Trenton, Saratoga, and Monmouth and now governor of Michigan Territory, marched forth with 2,200 men against the Canadian positions facing Detroit. Hoping that the Canadian militia would desert, he delayed his assault, only to find his communications threatened by hostile Indians led by Tecumseh.

Hastily he retreated to Detroit, and when the Canadians, under General Isaac Brock, pursued him, he surrendered the fort without firing a shot! In October another force attempted to invade Canada from Fort Niagara. After an initial success it was crushed by superior numbers, while a large contingent of New York militiamen watched from the east bank of the Niagara River, unwilling to fight outside their own state. The third arm of the American "attack" was equally unsuccessful. Major General Henry Dearborn, who had fought honorably in the Revolution from Bunker Hill to Yorktown but who had grown so fat that he needed a specially designed cart to get from place to place, set out from Plattsburg, New York, at the head of an army of militiamen. Their objective was Montreal, but when they reached the border, the troops refused to cross. Dearborn meekly marched them back to Plattsburg.

Meanwhile, the British had captured Fort Michilimackinac in northern Michigan, and the Indians had taken Fort Dearborn (now Chicago), massacring 85 captives. Instead of sweeping triumphantly through Canada, the Americans found themselves trying desperately to keep the Canadians out of Ohio.

Stirred by these disasters, westerners rallied somewhat in 1813. General Harrison, the victor of Tippecanoe, headed an army of Kentuckians in a series of inconclusive battles against British troops and Indians led by Tecumseh. He found it impossible to recapture Detroit because a British squadron controlling Lake Erie threatened his communications. President Madison therefore assigned Captain Oliver Hazard Perry to the task of building a fleet to challenge this force. In September 1813, at Put-in-Bay near the western end of the lake, Perry destroyed the British vessels in a bloody battle in which 85 of the 103 men on Perry's flagship were casualties. "We have met the enemy and they are ours," he reported modestly. About a quarter of Perry's 400 men were blacks, which led him to remark that "the color of a man's skin" was no more an indication of his worth than "the cut and trimmings" of his coat.

With the Americans in control of Lake Erie, Detroit became untenable for the British, and when they fell back, Harrison gave chase and defeated them at the Thames River, some 60 miles northeast of Detroit. Although little more than a skirmish, this battle had large repercussions. Tecumseh was among the dead (an eccentric American colonel, Richard Mentor Johnson, was to base a long and successful political career, culminating in his election as vice-president of the United States in 1836,* upon his claim of having personally done in the great chief), and without him the Indians lost heart. But American attempts to win control of Lake Ontario and to invade Canada in the Niagara region were again thrown back. Late in 1813 the British captured Fort Niagara and burned the town of Buffalo. The conquest of Canada was as far from realization as ever.

The British fleet had intensified its blockade of American ports, extending its operations to New England waters previously spared to encourage the antiwar sentiments of local maritime interests. All along the coast, patrolling cruisers, contemptuous of Jefferson's puny gunboats, captured small craft, raided shore points to commandeer provisions, and collected ransom from port towns by threatening to bombard them. One captain even sent a detail ashore to dig potatoes for his ship's mess.

Britain Assumes the Offensive

Until 1814 the British put relatively little effort into the American war, being concerned primarily with the struggle against Napoleon. However, in 1812 Napoleon had invaded Russia and been thrown back; thereafter, one by one, his European satellites rose against him. Gradually he relinquished his conquests; the Allies marched into France, Paris fell, and in April 1814 the emperor abdicated. Then the British, free to strike hard at the United States, dispatched some 14,000 veterans to Canada.

By the spring of 1814 British strategists had devised a master plan for crushing the United States. One army, 11,000 strong, was to march from Montreal, tracing the route that General Burgoyne had followed to disaster in the Revolution. A smaller amphibious force was to make a feint at the Chesapeake Bay area, destroying coastal towns and threatening Washington and Baltimore.

* Of Johnson, a biographer writes: "His career as vice-president was inconspicuous. . . . As a politician, though not lacking in sagacity, he was lacking in purpose."

A third army was to assemble at Jamaica and sail to attack New Orleans and bottle up the west.

It is necessary, in considering the War of 1812, to remind oneself repeatedly that in the course of the conflict many brave young men lost their lives. Without this sobering reflection it would be easy to dismiss the conflict as a great farce compounded of stupidity, incompetence, and brag. For the British, despite their years of experience against Napoleon, were scarcely more effective than the Americans when they assumed the offensive. They achieved significant success only in the diversionary attack in Chesapeake Bay.

While the main British army was assembling in Canada, 4,000 veterans under General Robert Ross sailed from Bermuda for the Chesapeake. After making a rendezvous with a fleet commanded by Vice Admiral Sir Alexander Cochrane and Rear Admiral Sir George Cockburn, which had been terrorizing the coast, they landed in Maryland at the mouth of the Patuxent River, southeast of Washington. A squadron of gunboats "protecting" the capital promptly withdrew upstream; when the British pursued, their commander ordered them blown up to keep them from being captured.

The British troops marched rapidly toward Washington. At Bladensburg, on the outskirts of the city, they came upon an army twice their number, commanded by General William H. Winder, a Baltimore lawyer who had already been captured and released by the British in the Canadian fighting. While President Madison and other officials watched, the British charged—and Winder's army turned tail almost without firing a shot. The British swarmed into the capital and put most public buildings to the torch. Before personally setting fire to the White House, Admiral Cockburn took one of the president's hats and a cushion from Dolley Madison's chair as souvenirs, and, finding the table set for dinner, derisively drank a toast to "Jemmy's health," adding, an observer coyly recalled, "pleasantries too vulgar for me to repeat."

This was the sum of the British success. When they attempted to take Baltimore, they were stopped by a formidable line of defenses devised by General Samuel Smith, a militia officer. General Ross fell in the attack. The fleet then moved up the Patapsco River and pounded Fort McHenry with its cannon, raining 1,800 shells upon it in a 25-hour bombardment on September 13 and 14. While this attack was in progress, an American civilian, Francis Scott Key, who had been temporarily detained on one of the British ships, watched anxiously through the night. Key had boarded the vessel before the attack in an effort to obtain the release of an American doctor who had been taken into custody in Washington. As twilight faded, Key had seen the Stars and Stripes flying proudly over the battered fort. During the night the glare of rockets and bursting of bombs gave proof that the defenders were holding out. Then, by the first light of the new day, Key saw again the flag, still waving over Fort McHenry. Drawing an old letter from his pocket, he dashed off the words to "The Star-Spangled Banner," which, when set to music, was to become the national anthem of the United States.

To Key that dawn seemed a turning point in the war. He was roughly correct, for in those last weeks of the summer of 1814 the struggle began to move toward resolution. Unable to crack the defenses of Baltimore, the British withdrew to their ships; shortly after, they sailed to Jamaica to join the forces preparing to attack New Orleans. The destruction of Washington had been a profound shock. Thousands came forward to enlist in the army. The new determination and spirit were strengthened by news from the northern front, where General Sir George Prevost had been leading the main British invasion force south from Montreal. At Plattsburg, on the western shore of Lake Champlain, his 11,000 Redcoats came up against a well-designed defense line manned by 3,300 Americans under General Alexander Macomb. Prevost called up his supporting fleet of four ships and a dozen gunboats. An American fleet of roughly similar strength under Captain Thomas Macdonough, a youthful officer who had served with Decatur against the Barbary pirates, came forward to oppose the British. On September 11, in a brutal battle at point-blank range, Macdonough destroyed the British ships and drove off the gunboats. With the Americans now threatening his flank, Prevost lost heart. Despite his overwhelming numerical superiority, he retreated to Canada.

The Treaty of Ghent

The war might as well have ended with the battles of Plattsburg, Washington, and Baltimore, for later

This American cartoon sarcastically portrays "the humane British and their worthy allies" the Indians. The latter are delivering Yankee scalps for a promise of reward from the King.

military developments had no effect on the outcome. Earlier in 1814 both sides had agreed to discuss peace terms. Commissioners were appointed and negotiations begun during the summer at Ghent, in Belgium. The American delegation consisted of former secretary of the treasury Albert Gallatin; Speaker Henry Clay of the House of Representatives; James A. Bayard, a former senator; and two veteran diplomats, Jonathan Russell, minister to Sweden, and John Quincy Adams, minister to Russia. Adams was chairman. The British commissioners were lesser men by far, partly because they could refer important questions to the Foreign Office in nearby London for decision and partly because Britain's topflight diplomats were engaged in settling the future of Europe at the Congress of Vienna.

The talks at Ghent were drawn out and frustrating. The British were in no hurry to sign a treaty, believing that their three-pronged offensive in 1814 would swing the balance in their favor. They demanded at first that the United States abandon practically all the Northwest Territory to the Indians and cede other points along the northern border to Canada. As to impressment and neutral rights, they would make no concessions at all. The Americans would yield no territory, for public opinion at home would have been outraged if they had. Old John Adams, for example, told President Madison at this time, "I would continue this war forever rather than surrender an acre. . . ."

Fortunately, the British came to realize that by pressing this point they would only spur the Americans to fight on. News of the defeat at Plattsburg modified their ambitions, and when the Duke of Wellington advised that from a military point of view they had no case for territorial concessions so long as the United States controlled the Great Lakes, they agreed to settle for *status quo ante bellum*, which is what the Americans sought. The other issues, everyone suddenly realized, had simply evaporated. The mighty war triggered by the French Revolution seemed finally over. The seas were free to all ships, and the Royal Navy no longer had need to snatch sailors from the vessels of the United States or of any other power. On Christmas Eve 1814 the treaty, which merely ended the state of hostilities, was signed. Although, like other members of his family, he was not noted for tact, John Quincy Adams rose to the spirit of the occasion. "I hope," he said, "it will be the last treaty of peace between Great Britain and the United States." And so it was.

The Hartford Convention

Before news of the treaty could cross the Atlantic, two events took place that had important effects but that would not have occurred had the news reached America more rapidly. The first was the Hartford Convention, a meeting of New England Federalists held in December 1814 and January 1815 to protest the war and to plan for a convention of the states to revise the Constitution.

Sentiment in New England had opposed the war from the beginning. The governor of Massachusetts titled his annual address in 1813 "On the Present Unhappy War," and the General Court went on record calling the conflict "impolitic, improper, and unjust." The Federalist party had been quick to employ the discontent to revive its fortunes. Federalist-controlled state administrations refused to provide militia to aid in the fight and discouraged individuals and banks from lending money to the hard-pressed national government. Trade with the enemy flourished as long as the British fleet did not crack down on New England ports, and goods flowed across the Canadian line in as great or greater volume as during Jefferson's embargo.

Their attitude toward the war made the Federalists even more unpopular with the rest of the country, and this in turn encouraged extremists to talk of seceding from the Union. After Massachusetts summoned the meeting of the Hartford Convention, the fear was widespread that the delegates would propose a New England Confederacy, thereby striking at the Union in a moment of great trial.

Luckily for the country, moderate Federalists controlled the convention. They approved a statement that in case of "deliberate, dangerous and palpable infractions of the Constitution" a state has the right "to interpose its authority" to protect itself. This concept, similar to that expressed in the Kentucky and Virginia resolves by the Republicans when they were in the minority, was accompanied by a list of proposed constitutional amendments designed to make the national government conform more closely to the New England ideal. These would have: (1) repealed the Three-fifths Compromise on representation and direct taxes, which favored the slaveholding states, (2) required a two-thirds vote of Congress for the admission of new states and for declaring war, (3) reduced Congress's power to restrict trade by measures such as an embargo, (4) limited presidents to a single term, and (5) made it illegal for naturalized citizens to hold national office. Nothing formally proposed at Hartford was treasonable, but the proceedings were kept secret, and rumors of impending secession were rife. In this atmosphere came the news from Ghent of an honorable peace. The Federalists had been denouncing the war and predicting a British triumph; now they were discredited.

The Battle of New Orleans

Still more discrediting to Federalists was the second event that would not have happened had communications been more rapid: the Battle of New Orleans. During the fall of 1814 the British had gathered an army at Negril Bay in Jamaica, commanded by Major General Sir Edward Pakenham, brother-in-law of the Duke of Wellington. Late in November an armada of 60 ships set out for New Orleans with 11,000 soldiers. Instead of sailing directly up from the mouth of the Mississippi as the Americans expected, Pakenham approached the city by way of Lake Borgne, to the east. Proceeding through a maze of swamps and bayous, he advanced close to the city's gates before being detected. Early on the afternoon of December 23, three mud-spattered local planters burst into the headquarters of General Andrew Jackson, commanding the defenses of New Orleans, with the news.

For once in this war of error and incompetence the United States had the right man in the right place at the right time. After his Revolutionary War experiences, Jackson had studied law, then moved west, settling in Nashville, Tennessee. He served briefly in both houses of Congress and was active in Tennessee affairs. Jackson was a hard man and fierce-tempered, frequently involved in brawls and duels, but honest and, by western standards, a good public servant. When the war broke out, he was named major general of volunteers. Almost alone among nonprofessional troops during the conflict, his men won impressive victories, crushing the Creek Indians in a series of battles in Alabama.

Jackson's success was due to his toughness and determination, a determination that his biographer Robert Remini describes as "virtually demonic . . . sheer, total, concentrated." Discipline based on fear, respect, and their awareness of his genuine concern for their well-being made his individualistic frontier militiamen into an army. His men called

Jackson Old Hickory; the Indians called him Sharp Knife.

Following these victories, Jackson was assigned the job of defending the Gulf Coast against the expected British strike. Although he had misjudged Pakenham's destination, he was ready when the news of the British arrival reached him. "By the Eternal," he vowed, "they shall not sleep on our soil." "Gentlemen," he told his staff officers, "the British are below, we must fight them tonight."

While the British rested and waited reinforcements, planning to take the city the next morning, Jackson rushed up men and guns. At 7:30 P.M. on December 23 he struck hard, taking the British by surprise. But Pakenham's veterans rallied quickly, and the battle was inconclusive. With Redcoats pouring in from the fleet, Jackson fell back to a point five miles below New Orleans and dug in.

He chose his position wisely. On his right was the Mississippi, on his left an impenetrable swamp, to the front an open field. On the day before Christmas (while the commissioners in Ghent were signing the peace treaty), Jackson's army, which included a segregated unit of free black militiamen, erected an earthen parapet about ten yards behind a dry canal bed. Here the Americans would make their stand.

For two weeks Pakenham probed the American line. Jackson strengthened his defenses daily. At night, patrols of silent Tennesseans slipped out with knife and tomahawk to stalk British sentries. They called this grim business "going hunting." On January 8, 1815, Pakenham ordered an all-out frontal assault. The American position was formidable, but his men had defeated Napoleon. At dawn, through the lowland mists, the Redcoats moved forward with fixed bayonets. Pakenham assumed that the undisciplined Americans—about 4,500 strong—would run at the sight of bare steel.

The Americans did not run. Perhaps they feared the wrath of their commander more than enemy bayonets. Artillery raked the advancing British, and when the range closed to about 150 yards, the riflemen opened up. Jackson had formed his men in three ranks behind the parapet. One rank fired, then stepped down as another took its place. By the time the third had loosed its volley, the first had reloaded and was ready to fire again. Nothing could stand against this rain of lead. General Pakenham was wounded twice, then killed by a shell fragment while calling up his last reserves. During the battle a single brave British officer reached the top of the parapet. When retreat was finally sounded, the British had suffered almost 2,100 casualties, including nearly 300 killed. Thirteen Americans lost their lives, and 58 more were wounded or missing.

Fruits of "Victory"

Word of Jackson's magnificent triumph reached Washington almost simultaneously with the good

An engineer in the Louisiana militia named Hyacinthe Laclotte painted the Battle of New Orleans from sketches made during the action. The main British thrust is shown in progress against the left side of the American line. In the foreground a column of troops carrying scaling ladders is caught in a withering fire. In addition to turning back the British infantry, Jackson's big guns silenced their artillery.

news from Ghent. People found it easy to confuse the chronology and consider the war a victory won on the battlefield below New Orleans instead of the standoff it had been. Jackson became the "Hero of New Orleans"; his proud fellow citizens rated his military abilities superior to those of the Duke of Wellington, the conqueror of Napoleon. The entire nation rejoiced. One sour Republican complained that the Federalists of Massachusetts had fired off more powder and wounded more men celebrating the victory than they had during the whole course of the conflict. The Senate ratified the peace treaty unanimously, and the frustrations and failures of the past few years were forgotten. Moreover, American success in holding off Great Britain despite internal frictions went a long way toward convincing European nations that both the United States and its republican form of government were here to stay. The powers might accept these truths with less pleasure than the Americans, but accept them they did.

The nation had suffered relatively few casualties and little economic loss, except to the shipping interests. The Indians were the main losers in the contest. When Jackson defeated the Creeks, for example, he forced them to cede 23 million acres to the United States.

The war completed the destruction of the Federalist party. The success of the Jeffersonians' political techniques had inspired younger Federalists in many parts of the country to adopt the rhetoric of democracy and (more important) to perfect local organizations. In 1812 the party made significant gains in the northeast, electing numbers of congressmen and winning many state and local offices. They did not run a candidate for president, but their support enabled the dissident New York Republican DeWitt Clinton to obtain 89 electoral votes to Madison's 128.

Their private correspondence reveals that these Federalists were no more enchanted by the virtues of mass democracy than their elders, but by mouthing democratic slogans they revived the party in many districts. Now the results of the war undermined their efforts. They had not supported the war effort; they had argued that the British could not be defeated; they had dealt clandestinely with the enemy; they had even threatened to break up the Union. So long as the issue remained in doubt, these policies won considerable support, but New Orleans made the party an object of ridicule and scorn. It soon disappeared even in New England, swamped beneath a wave of patriotism that flooded the land.

The chief reason for the happy results of the war had little to do with American events. After 1815 Europe settled down to what was to be a century of relative peace. With peace came an end to serious foreign threats to America and a revival of commerce. European emigration to the United States, long held back by the troubled times, spurted ahead, providing the expanding country with its most valuable asset—strong, willing hands to do the work of developing the land. The mood of Jefferson's first term, when democracy had reigned amid peace and plenty, returned with a rush. And the nation, having had its fill of international complications, turned in on itself as Jefferson had wished. The politicians, ever sensitive to public attitudes, had learned what seemed at the time a valuable lesson. Foreign affairs were a potent cause of domestic conflict. The volatile character of sectional politics was thus another reason why America should escape from involvement in European affairs.

Anglo-American Rapprochement

There remained a few matters to straighten out with Great Britain, Spain, and Europe generally. Since no territory had changed hands at Ghent, neither signatory had reason to harbor a grudge. There was no sudden flowering of Anglo-American friendship. British conservatives continued, in the words of the historian George Dangerfield, to view the United States as "little more than a grimy republican thumbprint" on the pages of history, and the device of "twisting the British lion's tail" remained an important tool in the workchest of many an American politician for the rest of the century. Yet for years no serious trouble marred Anglo-American relations. The war had taught the British to respect Americans, if not to love them.

In this atmosphere the two countries worked out peaceful solutions to a number of old problems. American trade was becoming ever more important to the British, that of the sugar islands less so. In July 1815 they therefore signed a commercial convention ending discriminatory duties and making other adjustments favorable to trade. Boundary difficulties also moved toward resolution. At Ghent the diplomats had created several joint commissions to settle the disputed boundary between the United States and Canada. Many years were to pass before the line was finally drawn, but establishing the principle of defining the border by negotiation was important. In time, a line extending over 3,000 miles was agreed to without the firing of a single shot.

Immediately after the war the British reinforced their garrisons in Canada and began to rebuild their shattered Great Lakes fleet. The United States took similar steps. But both nations found the cost of rearming more than they cared to bear. When the United States suggested demilitarizing the lakes, the British agreed. The Rush-Bagot Agreement of 1817 limited each country to one 100-ton vessel armed with a single 18-pounder on Lake Champlain and another on Lake Ontario. They were to have two each for all the other Great Lakes. Gradually, as an outgrowth of this decision, the entire border was demilitarized, a remarkable achievement. In 1818 the two countries agreed to the 49th parallel as the northern boundary of Louisiana Territory between Lake of the Woods and the Rockies, and to the joint control of the Oregon country for ten years. The question of the rights of Americans in the Labrador and Newfoundland fisheries, which had been much disputed during the Ghent negotiations, was settled amicably.

Transcontinental Treaty

The acquisition of Spanish Florida and the settlement of the western boundary of Louisiana were also accomplished as an aftermath of the War of 1812, but in a far different spirit. Spain's control of the Floridas was feeble. West Florida had passed into American hands by 1813, and frontiersmen in Georgia were eyeing East Florida greedily. Indians struck frequently into American territory from Florida, then fled to sanctuary across the line. American slaves who escaped across the border could not be recovered. In 1818 President James Monroe ordered General Andrew Jackson to clear raiding Seminole Indians from American soil and to pursue them into Florida if necessary. Seizing on these instructions, Jackson marched into Florida and easily captured two Spanish forts.

Although Jackson eventually withdrew from Florida, the impotence of the Spanish government made it obvious even in Madrid that if nothing were done, the United States would soon fill the power vacuum by seizing the territory. The Spanish also feared for the future of their tottering Latin American empire, especially the northern provinces of Mexico, which stood in the path of American westward expansion. Spain and the United States had never determined where Louisiana Territory ended and Spanish Mexico began. In return for American acceptance of a boundary as far east of the Rio Grande as possible, Spain was ready to surrender Florida.

For these reasons the Spanish minister in Washington, Luis de Onís, undertook in December 1817 to negotiate a treaty with John Quincy Adams, Monroe's secretary of state. Adams pressed the minister mercilessly on the question of the western boundary, driving a bargain that would have done credit to the most tightfisted of his Yankee ancestors. Onís opened their talks by proposing a line in the middle of what is now Louisiana, and when Adams countered by demanding a boundary running through present-day Texas, Onís professed to be shocked. Abstract right, not power, should determine the settlement, he said. "Truth is of all times, and reason and justice are founded upon immutable principles." To this Adams replied: "That truth is of all times and that reason and justice are founded upon immutable principles has never been contested by the United States, but neither truth, reason, nor justice consists in stubbornness of assertion, nor in the multiplied repetition of error."

In the end Onís could only yield. He saved Texas for his monarch but accepted a boundary to Louisiana Territory that followed the Sabine, Red, and Arkansas rivers to the Continental Divide and the 42nd parallel to the Pacific, thus abandoning Spain's claim to a huge area beyond the Rockies that had no connection at all with the Louisiana Purchase. Adams even compelled him to agree that when the boundary followed rivers, United States territory was to extend to the farthest bank, not merely to midstream. The United States obtained Florida in return for a mere $5 million, and that paid not to Spain but to Americans who held claims against the Spanish government.

This "Transcontinental Treaty" was signed in 1819, though ratification was delayed until 1821.

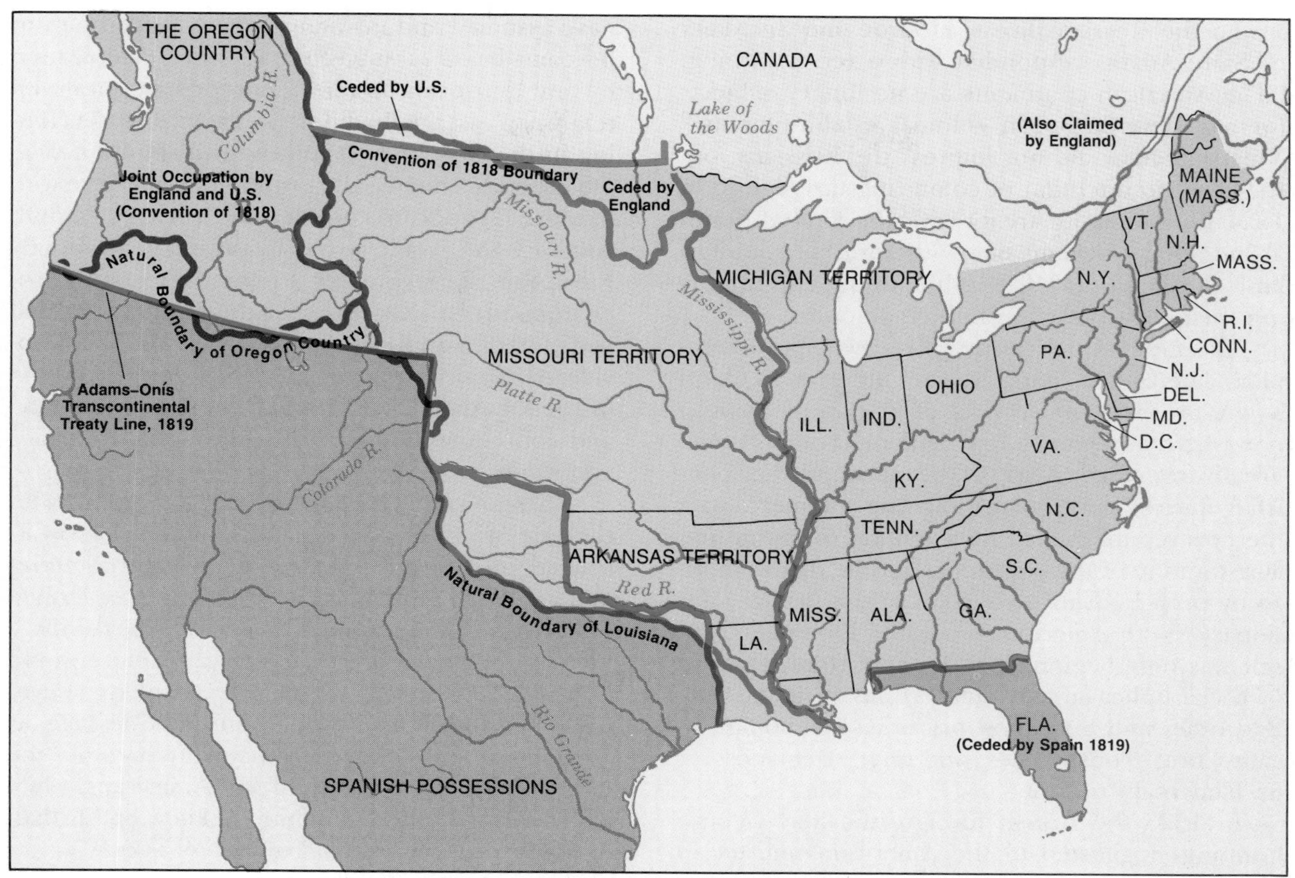

THE UNITED STATES, 1819

Most Americans at the time thought the acquisition of Florida the most important part of the treaty, but Adams, whose vision of America's future was truly continental, knew better. "The acquisition of a definite line of boundary to the [Pacific] forms a great epoch in our history," he recorded in his diary.

The Monroe Doctrine

Concern with defining the boundaries of the United States did not reflect a desire to limit expansion; rather, the feeling was that there should be no more quibbling and quarreling with foreign powers that might distract the people from the great task of national development. The classic enunciation of this point of view, the completion of America's withdrawal from Europe, was the Monroe Doctrine.

Two separate strands met in this pronouncement. The first led from Moscow to Alaska and down the Pacific Coast to the Oregon country. Beginning with the explorations of Vitus Bering in 1741, the Russians had maintained an interest in fishing and fur trading along the northwest coast of North America. In 1821 the czar extended his claim south to the 51st parallel and forbade the ships of other powers to enter coastal waters north of that point. This announcement was disturbing.

The second strand ran from the courts of the European monarchs to Latin America. Between 1817 and 1822 practically all of the region from the Rio Grande to the Strait of Magellan had won its independence. Spain, former master of all the area except Brazil, was too weak to win it back by force, but Austria, Prussia, France, and Russia decided at the Congress of Verona in 1822 to try to regain the area for Spain in the interests of "legitimacy." There was talk of sending a large French army to South America. This possibility also caused grave concern in Washington.

To the Russian threat, Monroe and Secretary of State Adams responded with a terse warning: "The American continents are no longer subjects for any new European colonial establishments." This statement did not impress the Russians, but they had no intention of colonizing the region. In 1824 they signed a treaty with the United States abandoning all claims below the present southern limit of Alaska (54°40′ north latitude) and removing their restrictions on foreign shipping.

The Latin American problem was more complex. The United States was not alone in its alarm at the prospect of a revival of French or Spanish power in that region. Great Britain, having profited greatly from the breakup of the mercantilistic Spanish empire by developing a thriving commerce with the new republics, had no intention of permitting a restoration of the old order. But the British monarchy preferred not to recognize the new revolutionary South American republics, for England itself was only beginning to recover from a period of social upheaval as violent as any in its history. Bad times and high food prices had combined to cause riots, conspiracies, and angry demands for parliamentary reform.

In 1823 the British foreign minister, George Canning, suggested to the American minister in London that the United States and Britain issue a joint statement opposing any French interference in South America, pledging that they themselves would never annex any part of Spain's old empire, and saying nothing about recognition of the new republics. This proposal of joint action with the British was flattering to the United States but scarcely in its best interests. The United States had already recognized the new republics, and it had no desire to help Great Britain retain its South American trade. As Secretary Adams pointed out, to agree to the proposal would be to abandon the possibility of someday adding Cuba or any other part of Latin America to the United States. America should act independently, Adams urged. "It would be more candid, as well as more dignified, to avow our principles explicitly . . . than to come in as a cockboat in the wake of the British man-of-war."

Monroe heartily endorsed Adams's argument and decided to include a statement of American policy in his annual message to Congress in December 1823. "The American continents," he wrote, "by the free and independent condition which they have assumed and maintain, are henceforth not to be considered as subjects for future colonization by any European powers." Europe's political system was "essentially different" from that developing in the New World, and the two should not be mixed. The United States would not interfere with existing European colonies in North or South America and would avoid involvement in strictly European affairs, but any attempt to extend European control to countries in the hemisphere that had already won their independence would be considered, Monroe warned, "the manifestation of an unfriendly disposition toward the United States" and consequently a threat to the nation's "peace and safety."

This policy statement—it was not dignified with the title Monroe Doctrine until decades later—attracted little notice in Europe or Latin America and not much more at home. Obviously the United States, whose own capital had been overrun by a mere raiding party less than ten years before, could not police the entire Western Hemisphere. European statesmen dismissed Monroe's message as "arrogant" and "blustering," worthy only of "the most profound contempt." Latin Americans, while appreciating the intent behind it, knew better than to count on American aid in case of attack.

Nevertheless, the principles laid down by President Monroe so perfectly expressed the wishes of the people of the United States that when the country grew powerful enough to enforce them, there was little need to alter or embellish his pronouncement. However understood at the time, the doctrine may be seen as the final stage in the evolution of American independence.

The famous Declaration of 1776, in this perspective, merely began a process of separation and self-determination. The peace treaty ending the Revolutionary War was a further step, and Washington's neutrality proclamation of 1793 was another, demonstrating as it did the capacity of the United States to determine its own best interests despite the treaty of alliance with France. The removal of British troops from the northwest forts, achieved by the otherwise ignominious Jay Treaty, marked the next stage. Then the Louisiana Purchase made a further advance toward true independence by assuring that the Mississippi River could not be closed to the commerce so vital to the development of the western territories. The standoff

War of 1812 ended any lingering British hope of regaining control of America, and the Transcontinental Treaty pushed the last European power from the path of westward expansion. Monroe's "doctrine" was a kind of public announcement that the sovereign United States had completed its independence and wanted nothing better than to be left alone to concentrate on its own development. Better yet if Europe could be made to allow the entire hemisphere to follow its own path.

SUPPLEMENTARY READING

Titles marked with an asterisk have been published in paperback.

Most of the volumes dealing with Jefferson's first administration continue to be useful for this period. On John Randolph, see W. C. Bruce, **John Randolph of Roanoke** (1939). C. P. Magrath, **Yazoo: Law and Politics in the New Republic*** (1966), is the best treatment of the case of ***Fletcher* v. *Peck*.** The most satisfactory life of Burr is T. P. Abernethy, **The Burr Conspiracy** (1954), and F. F. Beirne, **Shout Treason: The Trial of Aaron Burr** (1959). Raymond Walters, Jr., **Albert Gallatin: Jeffersonian Financier and Diplomat*** (1957), is an excellent biography of one of the key figures of the age.

By far the best account of the controversy over neutral rights is Bradford Perkins, **Prologue to War*** (1961), which combines careful research with lucid interpretation. Madison's actions can be followed in Irving Brant, **James Madison: The President** (1956). S. E. Morison, **The Maritime History of Massachusetts*** (1921), contains excellent chapters on the embargo and war periods. J. W. Pratt first played up the role of the west in triggering the War of 1812 in his **Expansionists of 1812** (1925). The best modern account of the causes and course of the war is J. C. A. Stagg, **Mr. Madison's War** (1983). A good brief treatment is H. L. Coles, **The War of 1812*** (1965). Irving Brant, **James Madison: Commander-in Chief** (1961), vigorously defends Madison's handling of the war. Jackson's part in the conflict is described in Marquis James, **Andrew Jackson: The Border Captain** (1933), and R. V. Remini, **Andrew Jackson and the Course of American Empire, 1767–1821** (1977).

On the Treaty of Ghent, see F. L. Engelman, **The Peace of Christmas Eve** (1962). Bradford Perkins, **Castlereagh and Adams** (1964), S. F. Bemis, **John Quincy Adams and the Foundations of American Foreign Policy*** (1949), and George Dangerfield, **The Era of Good Feelings*** (1952), also discuss the settlement intelligently. For the Hartford Convention, consult J. M. Banner, **To the Hartford Convention** (1981).

For the postwar diplomatic settlements, see Bradford Perkins, **Castlereagh and Adams,** S. F. Bemis, **John Quincy Adams,** and Harry Ammon, **James Monroe: The Quest for National Identity** (1971); for the Monroe Doctrine specifically, see Dexter Perkins, **The Monroe Doctrine: 1823–1826** (1927), and E. R. May, **The Making of the Monroe Doctrine** (1975).

8
The Cords of Union

Our confederacy comprehends within its vast limits, great diversity of interests; agricultural, planting, farming, commercial, navigating, fishing, manufacturing. . . . Some of these are peculiar to particular sections of the country. But all these great interests are confided to the protection of one government—to the fate of one ship; and a most gallant ship it is, with a noble crew. HENRY CLAY, *1824*

James Monroe, of Westmoreland County, Virginia, was a lucky man. He lived a long life in good health; he was happily married to a beautiful and cultivated woman; he saw close up most of the great events in the history of the young republic. Washington looked upon him with favor when Monroe was a youthful soldier and sent him on his first diplomatic mission in 1794. He studied law at the feet of Jefferson, who became his lifelong friend. Monroe's chief ambition, like that of so many Virginians of his generation, was to serve his country, and this end he achieved in full measure. At the age of 18 he shed his blood for liberty at the glorious Battle of Trenton. He was twice governor of his state, a United States senator, and a Cabinet member. He was at various times the nation's representative in Paris, where he helped engineer the Louisiana Purchase, and in Madrid and London. In 1816 he was elected president, defeating Rufus King of New York, 183 electoral votes to 34.

The Era of Good Feelings

As president, Monroe's good fortune continued. The world was finally at peace, the country united and prosperous. A man of good feeling who would keep a steady hand on the helm and hold to the present course seemed called for, and Monroe possessed exactly the qualities that the times required. "He is a man whose soul might be turned wrongside outwards, without discovering a blemish," Jefferson said, and John Quincy Adams, a harsh critic of public figures, praised Monroe's courtesy, sincerity, and sound judgment.

Courtesy and purity of soul do not always suffice to make a good president. In more troubled times Monroe might well have brought disaster, for he was neither a person of outstanding intellect nor a forceful leader. He blazed few paths, presented few important state papers, organized no personal machine. Speaking of his various policies and beliefs, the historian Ernest R. May concludes: "None was unique to Monroe." May adds that Monroe had "less than total confidence in his opinions." The Monroe Doctrine, by far the most significant achievement of his administration, was as much the work of Secretary of State Adams as his own. No one ever claimed that Monroe was better than second-rate, yet when his first term ended, he was reelected without organized opposition.

Monroe seemed to epitomize the resolution of the conflicts that had divided the country between the end of the Revolution and the Peace of Ghent. In his long career he had frequently taken strong positions on controversial issues; always, however, he was a nationalist—his biographer Harry Ammon has subtitled the story of Monroe's life "The Quest for National Identity."

By 1817 the divisive issues of earlier days had vanished. Monroe dramatized their disappearance by beginning his first term with a goodwill tour of New England, heartland of the opposition. The tour was a triumph. Everywhere the president was greeted with tremendous enthusiasm. After he visited Boston, once the headquarters and now the graveyard of Federalism, a Federalist newspaper, the *Columbian Centinel,* gave the age its name. Pointing out that the celebrations attending Monroe's visit had brought together in friendly intercourse many persons "whom party politics had long severed," it dubbed the times the "Era of Good Feelings."

It has often been said that the harmony of Monroe's administrations was superficial, that beneath the calm lay potentially disruptive issues that had not yet begun to influence national politics. The dramatic change from the unanimity of Monroe's second election to the fragmentation of four years later, when four candidates divided the vote and the House of Representatives had to choose the president, supports the point.

Nevertheless, the people of the period had good reasons for thinking it extraordinarily harmonious. Peace, prosperity, liberty, and progress: all flourished in 1817 in the United States. The heirs of Jefferson had accepted, with a mixture of resignation and enthusiasm, most of the economic policies advocated by the Hamiltonians. In 1816 Madison put his signature to a bill creating a new national bank almost exactly in the image of Hamilton's, which had expired before the War of 1812, and to a protective tariff which, if less comprehensive than the kind Hamilton had wanted, marked an important concession to the rising manufacturing interests. Monroe accepted the principle of federal aid for transportation projects, approving a bill authorizing Congress to invest $300,000 in the Chesapeake and Delaware Canal Company.

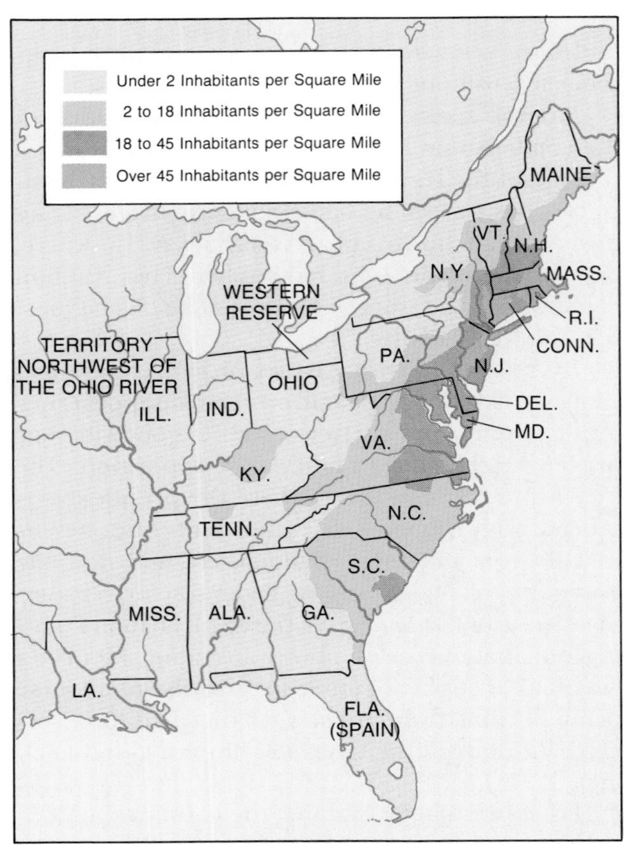

POPULATION DENSITY, 1790

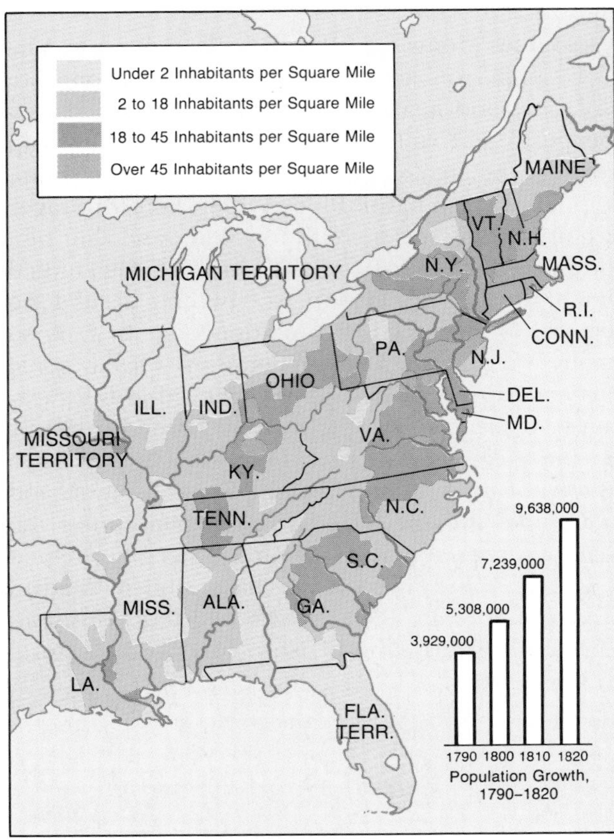

POPULATION DENSITY, 1820

The thirty years from 1790 to 1820 saw a sizable increase in population. The growth was especially great in the decade from 1810 to 1820, with a 33.1 percent increase in national population. Some of the largest increases were in what was earlier called the Old Northwest; the population of the area making up Illinois, Indiana, and Michigan territories, for example, grew from 31,000 to more than 200,000 during that decade.

The Jeffersonian balance between individual liberty and responsible government, having survived both bad management and war, had justified itself to the opposition. The new unity was symbolized by the restored friendship of Jefferson and John Adams. In 1801 Adams had slipped sulkily out of Washington without waiting to attend his successor's inauguration, but after ten years of icy silence, the two old collaborators, abetted by Dr. Benjamin Rush, effected a reconciliation. Although they continued to disagree vigorously about matters of philosophy and government, the bitterness between them disappeared entirely. By Monroe's day, Jefferson was writing long letters to "my dear friend," ranging over such subjects as theology, the proper reading of the classics, and agricultural improvements, and receiving equally warm and voluminous replies. "Whether you or I were right," Adams wrote amiably to Jefferson, "Posterity must judge."

When political divisions appeared again, as they soon did, it was not because the old balance had been shaky. Few of the new controversies challenged Republican principles or revived old issues. Instead, these controversies were children of the present and the future, products of the continuing growth of the country.

National unity speeded national expansion, yet

expansion, paradoxically, endangered national unity. For as the country grew, new differences appeared within its sections even as the ties binding the parts became stronger and more numerous.

Growth in the 30 years after the ratification of the Constitution had been phenomenal even for a country that took growth for granted. The area of the United States doubled, increasing from nearly 9 million to almost 18 million square miles, but this figure is deceptive because very little of the Louisiana Purchase had been settled by 1820. More significant, the population of the nation had more than doubled, from 4 million to 9.6 million. Perhaps the most remarkable feature of this growth was that nearly all of it resulted from natural increase. Only about 250,000 immigrants entered the United States between 1790 and 1820, for the turbulent conditions in Europe during the wars had slowed the flow of humanity across the Atlantic to a trickle. The pace of the westward movement had also quickened; by 1820 more than 2.2 million people had settled in the Mississippi Valley, and the moving edge of the frontier ran in a long, irregular curve from Michigan to Arkansas.

The Subsidence of Sectionalism

The War of 1812 and the depression that struck the country in 1819 shaped many of the controversies that agitated political life during the Era of Good Feelings. The tariff question was affected by both. Before the War of 1812 the level of duties averaged about 12.5 percent of the value of dutiable products, but to meet the added expenses occasioned by the conflict, Congress doubled all tariffs. In 1816, when the revenue was no longer needed, a new act kept duties close to wartime levels. Infant industries that had grown up during the years of embargo, nonintercourse, and war were able to exert considerable pressure, for they could show that imports had rocketed from $12 million in 1814 to $113 million in 1815 and were still rising. The act especially favored textiles because the British were dumping cloth in America at bargain prices in their attempt to regain lost markets. The depression added to the strength of the protectionists. Unemployed workers and many farmers became convinced that prosperity would return only if American industry were shielded against foreign competition.

There was backing for high duties in every section. Except for New England, where the shipping interests favored free trade and where the booming mills of the Boston Associates were not seriously injured by foreign competition, the North favored protection. A few southerners hoped that textile mills would spring up in their region; more supported protection on the ground that national self-sufficiency was necessary in case of war. In the West small manufacturers in the towns added their support, and so did farmers, who were counting on workers in the new eastern factories to consume much of their wheat and corn and hogs. But with the passage of time the South rejected protection almost completely. Industry failed to develop, and since they exported most of their cotton and tobacco, southerners soon concluded that besides increasing the cost of nearly everything they bought, high duties on imports would limit the foreign market for southern staples by inhibiting international exchange. As this fact became clear, the West tended to divide on the tariff question: the Northwest and much of Kentucky, which had a special interest in protecting its considerable hemp production, favored high duties; the Southwest, where cotton was the major crop, favored low duties.

National banking policy was another important political issue affected by the war and the depression. Presidents Jefferson and Madison had managed to live with the Bank of the United States despite its dubious constitutionality, but its charter was not renewed when it expired in 1811. Aside from the constitutional question, the major opposition to recharter came from state banks eager to take over the business of the Bank for themselves. The fact that English investors owned most of the Bank's stock (the government had sold 2,200 shares to the British banking house of Baring Brothers in 1802) was also used as an argument against recharter.

The war played havoc with American banking. Many more state banks were created after 1811, and most extended credit recklessly. When the British raid on Washington and Baltimore in 1814 sent panicky depositors scurrying to convert their deposits into gold or silver, the overextended financiers could not oblige them. All banks outside New England suspended specie payments; that is, they stopped exchanging their bank notes for hard money on demand. Paper money immediately fell in value; a paper dollar was soon worth only 85

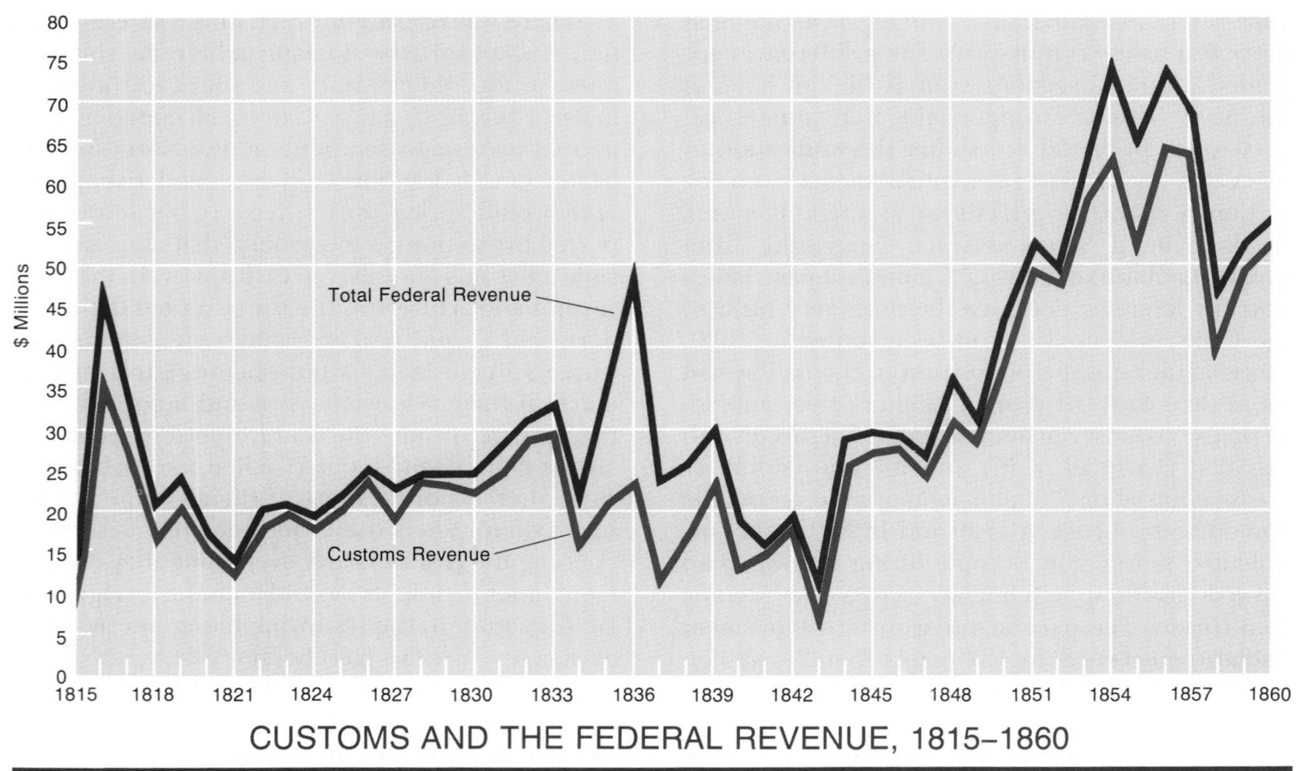

CUSTOMS AND THE FEDERAL REVENUE, 1815–1860

In some years—1841, for example—the amounts received from customs duties supplied nearly all the federal revenues, so it is no surprise that the tariff was a major political and sectional issue in the years between the War of 1812 and the Civil War. The jump in federal revenues in the mid-1830s, over and above the usual customs duties, was caused largely by increased public land sales (*see chart on page 280*).

cents in coin in Philadelphia, less in Baltimore. Government business also suffered from the absence of a national bank. In October 1814 Secretary of the Treasury Alexander J. Dallas submitted a plan for a second Bank of the United States, and after considerable wrangling over its precise form, the institution was authorized in April 1816.

The new Bank was much larger than its predecessor, being capitalized at $35 million. However, unlike Hamilton's creation, it was badly managed at the start. Its first president, William Jones, a former secretary of the treasury, was as inept as he was easygoing. He displayed, according to the historian George Dangerfield, "a kindheartedness which, in his new position, was tantamount to corruption." All kinds of chicanery went on under Jones's nose. According to the charter, no shareholder could have more than 30 votes, regardless of the number of shares owned, yet one director who owned 1,172 shares registered each in a different name, with himself as "attorney" for all, and successfully cast 1,172 votes at meetings. More important, Jones allowed his institution to join in the irresponsible creation of credit. By the summer of 1818 the Bank's 18 branches had issued notes in excess of ten times their specie reserves, far more than was prudent, considering the Bank's responsibilities. When depression struck the country in 1819, the Bank of the United States was as hard pressed as many of the state banks. Jones resigned.

The new president, Langdon Cheves of South Carolina, was as rigid as Jones had been permissive. During the bad times, when easy credit was needed, he pursued a policy of stern curtailment. The Bank thus regained a sound position at the expense of hardship to borrowers. "The Bank was saved," the contemporary economist William Gouge wrote somewhat hyperbolically, "and the people were ruined." Just at the time when John Marshall was establishing its constitutionality, it reached a low point in public favor. Irresponsible state banks resented it, as did the advocates of hard money.

Regional lines were less sharply drawn on the Bank issue than on the tariff. Northern congressmen voted against the Bank 53 to 44 in 1816—many of them because they objected to the particular proposal, not because they were against *any* national bank. Those from other sections favored it, 58 to 30. The collapse occasioned by the Panic of 1819 produced further opposition to the institution in the West.

Land policy also caused sectional controversy. No one wished to eliminate the system of survey and sale, but there was continuous pressure to reduce the price of public land and the minimum unit offered for sale. The Land Act of 1800 set $2 an acre as the minimum price and 320 acres (a half section) as the smallest unit. Buyers could pay for the land in four annual installments, which meant that one needed only $160 to take possession of a good-sized farm. In 1804 the minimum was cut to 160 acres, which could be had for about $80 down, roughly a quarter of what the average artisan could earn in a year.

Since banks were pursuing an easy-credit policy, land sales boomed. The outbreak of the War of 1812 caused a temporary slump, but by 1814 sales had reached an all-time high and were increasing rapidly. Postwar prices of agricultural products were excellent, for the seas were now free and European agriculture had not yet recovered from the ravages of the Napoleonic wars. In 1818 the government sold nearly 3.5 million acres. Thereafter, continuing expansion and the rapid shrinkage of the foreign market as European farmers resumed production led to disaster. Prices fell, the panic struck, and western debtors were forced to the wall by the hundreds.

Sectional attitudes toward the public lands were fairly straightforward. The West wanted cheap land; the North and South tended to look upon the national domain as an asset that should be converted into as much cash as possible. Northern manufacturers feared that cheap land in the West would drain off surplus labor and force wages up, while southern planters were concerned about the competition that would develop when the virgin lands of the Southwest were put to the plow to make cotton. The West, however, was ready to fight to the last line of defense over land policy, while the other regions would usually compromise on the issue to gain support for their own vital interests. Sectional alignments on the question of internal improvements were almost identical, but this issue, soon to become very important, had not greatly agitated national affairs before 1820. As we have seen, the only significant federal internal improvement project undertaken before that date was the National Road.

The most divisive issue was slavery. After the compromises affecting the "peculiar institution" made at the Constitutional Convention, it caused remarkably little conflict in national politics before 1819. Although the importation of blacks rose in the 1790s, Congress abolished the African slave trade in 1808 without major incident. As the nation expanded, free and slave states were added to the Union in equal numbers, Ohio, Indiana, and Illinois being balanced by Louisiana, Mississippi, and Alabama. In 1819 there were 22 states, 11 slave and 11 free. The expansion of slavery occasioned by the cotton boom led southerners to support it more aggressively, which tended to irritate many northerners, but most persons considered slavery mainly a local issue. To the extent that it was a national question, the North opposed it and the South defended it ardently. The West leaned toward the southern point of view, for in addition to the southwestern slave states, the Northwest was sympathetic, partly because much of its produce was sold on southern plantations and partly because at least half of its early settlers came from Virginia, Kentucky, and other slave states.

By 1824 the giants of the Revolutionary generation had completed their work. Washington, Hamilton, Franklin, Samuel Adams, Patrick Henry, and most of their peers were dead. John Adams (88), Thomas Jefferson (81), and James Madison (73) were passing their declining years quietly on their ancestral acres, full of memories and sage advice, but no longer active in national affairs. In every section new leaders had come forward, men shaped by the past but chiefly concerned with the present. Quite suddenly, between the war and the panic, they had inherited power. They would shape the future of the United States.

Those Who Would Be President

John Quincy Adams was the best-known political leader of the North in the early 1820s. Just completing his brilliant work as secretary of state under Monroe, he had behind him a record of public service dating to the Confederation period. At 11 he was giving English lessons to the French minister to the Continental Congress and his secretary. ("He shows us no mercy and makes us no compliments," the minister remarked.) While in his teens he served as secretary of legation in Russia and Great Britain. After graduating from Harvard in 1787, he practiced law for some years, then became American minister to the Netherlands and to Prussia. Chosen United States senator from Massachusetts in 1803 as a Federalist, he gradually switched to the Republican point of view, supporting the Louisiana Purchase and even the Embargo Act. Madison sent him back to Europe as minister to Russia in 1809. His work at Ghent on the Peace Commission and as Madison's secretary of state has already been mentioned.

Asher B. Durand's portrait of an uncompromising John Quincy Adams dates from 1835, when the former president was a congressman from Massachusetts.

Adams was farsighted, imaginative, hardworking, and extremely intelligent, but he was inept in personal relations. He had all the virtues and most of the defects of the Puritan, being suspicious both of others and of himself. He suffered in two ways from being his father's child: as the son of a president he was under severe pressure to live up to the Adams name, and his father expected a great deal of him. When the boy was only 7, John Adams wrote his wife: "Train [the children] to virtue. Habituate them to industry, activity, and spirit. Make them consider vice as shameful and unmanly. Fire them with ambition to be useful. . . . Fix their ambition upon great and solid objects, and their contempt upon little, frivolous and useless ones."

Such training made John Quincy an indefatigable worker. Even in winter he normally rose at 5 A.M., and he could never convince himself that most of his associates were not lazy dolts. He was tense, compulsive, conscience-ridden. He set a standard no one could meet and consequently was continually dissatisfied with himself. As one of his grandsons remarked, "he was disappointed because he was not supernatural." Adams had what one Englishman called "a vinegar aspect," passing through life "like a bull-dog among spaniels." Toward enemies he was merciless and overwhelming, toward friends inspiring but demanding.

Like his father and the other great men of the preceding generation, John Quincy Adams was a strong nationalist. While New England was still antiprotectionist, he was at least open-minded on the subject of high tariffs. He supported the second Bank of the United States and, unlike most easterners, he believed that the federal government should spend freely on roads and canals in the West. To slavery he was, like most New Englanders, personally opposed. As Monroe's second term drew toward its close, Adams seemed one of the most likely candidates to succeed him, and at this period his ambition to be president was his great failing. He said he would like to be elected because it would please his father, but he did not deny that being president would please him too. His ambition led him to make certain compromises with his principles, which in turn plagued his oversensitive conscience and had a corrosive effect upon his peace of mind.

Eyes like "anthracite furnaces," the English historian Thomas Carlyle remarked of Daniel Webster; this is the "Black Dan" portrait by Francis Alexander.

Daniel Webster was less prominent in the 1820s than Adams, but he was recognized as one of the coming leaders of New England. Born in New Hampshire in 1782, he graduated from Dartmouth College in 1801, and by the time of the War of 1812 he had made a local reputation as a lawyer and orator. After serving two terms in Congress during the conflict, he moved to Boston to concentrate on his legal practice. He soon became one of the leading constitutional lawyers of the country, prominent in the Dartmouth College controversy, *McCulloch* v. *Maryland,* and other important cases. In 1823 he was again elected to Congress.

Webster owed much of his reputation to his formidable presence and his oratorical skill. Dark, large-headed, craggy of brow, with deep-set, brooding eyes and a firm mouth, he projected a remarkable appearance of heroic power and moral strength. His thunderous voice, his resourceful vocabulary, his manner—all backed by the mastery of every oratorical trick—made him unique. "He . . . is never averse, whilst traversing the thorny paths of political disputation," one contemporary admirer recorded, "to scatter the flowers of rhetorical elegance around him."

Webster had a first-rate mind, powerful and logical. His faults were largely those of temperament. He was too fond of good food and fine broadcloth, of alcohol and adulation. Hard work over an extended period of time was beyond him; generally he bestirred himself only with great effort and then usually to advance his own cause. Webster could have been a lighthouse in the night, guiding his fellow citizens to safe harbor. More often he was a weather vane, shifting to accommodate the strongest breeze. The good opinion of "the best people" meant so much to him that he rarely used his gifts to shape and guide that opinion in the national interest.

Unlike the independent-minded Adams, Webster nearly always reflected the beliefs of the dominant business interests of New England. His opposition to the embargo and the War of 1812 got him into Congress, where he faithfully supported the views of New England merchants. He opposed the high tariff of 1816 because the merchants favored free trade, and he voted against establishing the Bank chiefly on partisan grounds. (His view changed when the Bank hired him as its lawyer.) He was against cheap land and federal construction of internal improvements. His opposition to slavery accorded with the opinion of most of his constituents, but on this question he stood more solidly for principle. Basically he was a nationalist (as was seen in his arguments before the Supreme Court), yet he sometimes allowed political expediency and the prejudices of New England to obscure his feelings. Ahead of him lay fame, considerable constructive service, but also bitter frustration. And one hour of greatness.

Elsewhere in the North there were few outstanding figures among the younger politicians. DeWitt Clinton of New York had served briefly in the United States Senate and had run unsuccessfully for the presidency against Madison in 1812, but he was primarily concerned with state and local affairs, especially during the 1820s when the Erie Canal was being constructed. New York's man of the future was a little sandy-haired politico named Martin

Van Buren. The Red Fox, as people sometimes called him, was one of the most talented politicians ever to play a part in American affairs. He was born in 1782 and in his teens campaigned for Thomas Jefferson. He studied law and prospered for he was clever and hardworking, but his ambitions were always political. From 1812 to 1820 he served in the state legislature; in 1820 he was elected United States senator.

Van Buren had great charm and immense tact. By nature affable, he never allowed partisanship to mar his personal relationships with other leaders. The historian Richard Hofstadter once described him as the type of politician whose influence "comes in large part out of his taste for political association, his liking for people, and his sportsmanlike ability to experience political conflict without taking it as ground for personal rancor." The members of his political machine, known as the Albany Regency, were almost fanatically loyal to him, and even his enemies could seldom dislike him as a man.

Somehow Van Buren could reconcile deviousness with honesty. He "rowed to his objective with muffled oars," as Randolph of Roanoke said, yet he was neither crooked nor venal. Politics for him was like a game or a complex puzzle: the object was victory, but one must play by the rules or lose all sense of achievement. Only a fool will cheat at solitaire, and despite his gregariousness Van Buren was at heart a solitary operator.

His positions on the issues of the 1820s are hard to determine because he never took a position if he could avoid doing so. In part this was his politician's desire to straddle every fence; it also reflected his quixotic belief that issues were means rather than ends in the world of politics. He opposed rechartering the first Bank, yet was not conspicuous among those who fought the second. He did not oppose internal improvements, but DeWitt Clinton was his political enemy. No one could say with assurance what he thought about the tariff, and since slavery did not arouse much interest in New York, it is safe to suppose that at this time he had no opinion at all about the institution. Any intelligent observer in the 1820s would have predicted that "the Little Magician" would go far, for he was obviously a master of his craft. How far, and in what direction, no one could have guessed.

Southern Leaders

The most prominent southern leader was William H. Crawford, Monroe's secretary of the treasury. Born in 1772 in the shadow of Virginia's Blue Ridge, he was taken to the Deep South while still a lad, settling finally in Georgia. For a brief time he taught school, then studied law. A giant of a man, ruddy-faced and strong-jawed, he prospered in the law and became a leader in the conservative faction in the state, speaking for the large planters against the interests of the yeomen farmers. Following service in the legislature, he was elected to the Senate in 1807. Later he put in a tour of duty as minister to France, and in 1816 he was appointed secretary of the treasury.

Crawford was direct and friendly, a marvelous storyteller, and a superb manipulator of people. He was one of the few persons in Washington who could teach the fledgling senator Martin Van Buren anything about politics, and Van Buren supported him enthusiastically in the contest for the 1824 presidential nomination. (So, although not publicly, did Jefferson and Madison.) Crawford was one of the first politicians to try to build a national machine. "Crawford's Act" of 1820, limiting the term of minor federal appointees to four years, was passed, as the name suggests, largely through his efforts, for he realized before nearly anyone else that a handful of petty officers, properly distributed, could win the allegiance of thousands of voters.

Crawford had something interesting to say on most of the important issues of the times. Although predisposed toward the states' rights position, he favored recharter of the Bank and was willing to go along with a moderately protective tariff. During the depression that began in 1819 he devised an excellent relief plan for farmers who were unable to meet installment payments due on land purchased from the government. He suggested a highly original scheme for a flexible paper currency not convertible into hard money. Crawford was controversial. Many of his contemporaries considered him no more than a cynical spoilsman, though his administration of the Treasury was first-rate. Yet he had many friends. His ambition was vast, his power great. Fate, however, was about to strike Crawford a crippling blow.

This striking portrait of John C. Calhoun was painted sometime between 1818 and 1825, probably by Charles Bird King. The handsome Calhoun was in his thirties.

John C. Calhoun, the other outstanding southern leader, was born in South Carolina in 1782 and graduated from Yale in 1804. He studied law at Tapping Reeve's remarkable law school in Litchfield, Connecticut, which in half a century turned out 15 future United States senators, 10 governors, 2 Supreme Court justices, and a number of other men prominent in public affairs. Returning to South Carolina, Calhoun served in the state legislature; in 1811 he went to Washington as a congressman. A prominent War Hawk, he took a strong nationalist position on all the issues of the day. In 1817 Monroe made him secretary of war.

Although devoted to the South and its institutions, Calhoun took the broadest possible view of political affairs. John Quincy Adams, seldom charitable in his private opinions of colleagues (he called Crawford "a worm" and Henry Clay a "gamester" with an "undigested system of ethics"), praised Calhoun's "quick understanding" and "enlarged philosophic views." "He is above all sectional and factional prejudices," Adams wrote. "Our true system is to look to the country," Calhoun said in 1820, "and to support such measures and such men, without regard to sections, as are best calculated to advance the general interest."

Calhoun was intelligent, bookish, and given to the study of abstractions. Basically a gentle person, he was cold and restrained in most of his relationships. He had no hobbies and was utterly humorless. Legend has it that he once tried to write a poem but after putting down the word "Whereas" gave it up as beyond his powers. Some obscure failing made it impossible for him to grasp the essence of the human condition. An English observer once said that Calhoun had "an imperfect acquaintance with human nature." Yet he burned to lead his fellows. Few contemporaries could maintain themselves in debate against his powerful intelligence, yet that mind—so sharp, so penetrating—was the blind bondsman of his ambition.

Western Leaders

The outstanding western leader of the 1820s was Henry Clay of Kentucky, one of the most charming and colorful of American statesmen. Tall, lean, gray-eyed, Clay was the kind of person who made men cheer and women swoon. On the platform he ranked with Webster; behind the political scenes he was the peer of Van Buren. In every environment he was warm and open—what a modern political scientist might call a charismatic personality. Clay loved to drink, swear, tell tales, and play poker. It was characteristic that at one sitting he won $40,000 from a friend and then cheerfully told him that a note for $500 would wipe out the obligation. He was a reasonable man, skilled at arranging political compromises, but he possessed a reckless streak: like so many westerners, his sense of honor was exaggerated. Twice in his career he called men out for having insulted him. Fortuntely, all concerned were poor shots.

Virginia-born Clay moved to Lexington, Kentucky, in 1797 at the age of 20 and developed a thriving law practice. After some years in the state legislature, he won a seat in Congress in 1810.

This portrait of Henry Clay was completed in 1824, when he was Speaker of the House. An unidentified artist painted it after a portrait by John Neagle.

He led the War Hawks in 1811–1812 and was Speaker of the House from 1811 to 1820 and from 1823 to 1825.

Intellectually the inferior of Adams and Calhoun, or even of Webster, Clay had few original ideas. But he had a perfect temperament for politics. He loved power and understood that in the United States it had to be shared to be exercised. His great gift was in seeing national needs from a broad perspective and fashioning a program that could inspire ordinary citizens with something of his vision. In the early 1820s he was just developing his "American System." In return for eastern support of a policy of federal aid in the construction of roads and canals, the West would back the protective tariff. He justified this deal on the widest national grounds. By stimulating manufacturing, it would increase the demand for western raw materials, while western prosperity would lead to greater consumption of eastern manufactured goods. Washington did not describe the interdependence of the sections better in his Farewell Address than did Clay, repeatedly, in Congress and upon the stump. And, like Washington, Clay was conservative. He opposed the national bank in 1811 on constitutional grounds but supported the new one in 1816 and thereafter, saying, with typical candor and shrewdness, that "the force of circumstance and the lights of experience" had convinced him that he had previously misread the Constitution. His view of slavery, as his biographer Glyndon Van Deusen has said, was "a combination of theoretical dislike and practical tolerance." He would have preferred to ignore the subject. Nevertheless, slavery repeatedly played a crucial role in Clay's career.

The West had other spokesmen in the 1820s. Thomas Hart Benton, elected to the Senate by the new state of Missouri, was an expansionist and a hard-money man of the uncompromising sort, suspicious of paper currency and therefore of all banks. He championed the small western farmer, favoring free homesteads for pioneers and an extensive federal internal improvements program. Opposed in principle to high tariffs, he tended to vote for them "with repugnance and misgiving" to obtain protection for Missouri's lead and furs. Poor workers should cast aside their tools and head west, he believed.

For 30 years Benton advocated his ideas in the Senate in bluff, colorful language. "Nobody opposes Benton but a few black-jack prairie lawyers," he would roar. "Benton and democracy are one and the same, sir; synonymous terms, sir; synonymous terms, sir." A largehearted man, though vain and pompous, he remained essentially a sectional rather than a national figure.

Another western leader was General William Henry Harrison. Although he sat in the Ohio legislature and in both houses of Congress between 1816 and 1828, Harrison was primarily a soldier. During the Panic of 1819 he took an anti-Bank and pro-high-tariff stand, but he did not identify himself closely with any policy other than the extermination of the Indians. He had little to do with the newly developing political alignments of the 1820s.

Much like Harrison was Andrew Jackson, the "Hero of New Orleans," whose popularity greatly exceeded Harrison's. He had many friends, shrewd in the ways of politics, who were working devotedly, if not entirely unselfishly, to make him president. No one knew his views on most questions, but few cared. His chief assets as a presidential candidate were his military reputation and his forceful personality, but both, and especially the latter, were equally likely to get him into political hot water.

The Missouri Compromise

The sectional concerns of the 1820s repeatedly influenced politics. The depression of 1819–1822 increased tensions by making people feel more strongly about the issues of the day. For example, manufacturers who wanted high tariffs in 1816 were more vehemently in favor of protection in 1820 when their business fell off. Even when economic conditions improved, geographical alignments on key issues tended to solidify.

One of the first and most critical of the sectional questions concerned the admission of Missouri as a slave state. When Louisiana entered the Union in 1812, the rest of the Louisiana Purchase was organized as Missouri Territory. Building upon a nucleus of Spanish and French inhabitants, the region west and north of St. Louis grew rapidly, and in 1817 the Missourians petitioned for statehood. A large percentage of the settlers—the population exceeded 60,000 by 1818—were southerners who had moved into the valleys of the Arkansas and Missouri rivers. Since many of them owned slaves, Missouri would become a slave state.

The admission of new states had always been a routine matter, in keeping with the admirable pattern established by the Northwest Ordinance. But during the debate on the Missouri Enabling Act in February 1819, Congressman James Tallmadge of New York introduced an amendment prohibiting "the further introduction of slavery" and providing that all slaves born in Missouri after the territory became a state should be freed at age 25.

While Tallmadge was merely seeking to apply in the territory the pattern of race relations that had developed in the states immediately east of Missouri, his amendment represented, at least in spirit, something of a revolution. The Northwest Ordinance had prohibited slavery in the land between the Mississippi and the Ohio, but that area had only a handful of slaveowners in 1787 and little prospect of attracting more. Elsewhere no effort to restrict the movement of slaves into new territory had been attempted. If one assumed (as whites always had) that the slaves themselves should have no say in the matter, it appeared democratic to let the settlers of Missouri decide the slavery question for themselves. Nevertheless, the Tallmadge amendment passed the House, the vote following sectional lines closely. The Senate, however, resoundingly rejected it. The less populous southern part of Missouri was then organized separately as Arkansas Territory, and an attempt to bar slavery there was stifled. The Missouri Enabling Act failed to pass before Congress adjourned.

When the next Congress met in December 1819, the Missouri issue came up at once. The vote on Tallmadge's amendment had shown that the rapidly growing North controlled the House of Representatives. It was vital, southerners felt, to preserve a balance in the Senate. Yet northerners objected to the fact that Missouri extended hundreds of miles north of the Ohio River, which they considered slavery's natural boundary. Angry debate raged in Congress for months.

The debate did not turn on the morality of slavery or the rights of blacks. Northerners objected to adding new slave states because under the Three-fifths Compromise these states would be overrepresented in Congress (60 percent of their slaves would be counted in determining the size of the states' delegations in the House of Representatives) and because they did not relish competing with slave labor. Since the question was political influence rather than the rights and wrongs of slavery, a compromise was worked out in 1820. Missouri entered the Union as a slave state and Maine, having been separated from Massachusetts, was admitted as a free state to preserve the balance in the Senate.

To prevent further conflict, Congress adopted a proposal of Senator Jesse B. Thomas of Illinois, which "forever prohibited" slavery in all other parts of the Louisiana Purchase north of 36°30′ north latitude, the westward extension of Missouri's southern boundary. Although this division would keep slavery out of most of the territory, southerners accepted it cheerfully. The land south of the line, the present states of Arkansas and Oklahoma, seemed ideally suited for the expanded plantation economy, and most persons considered the

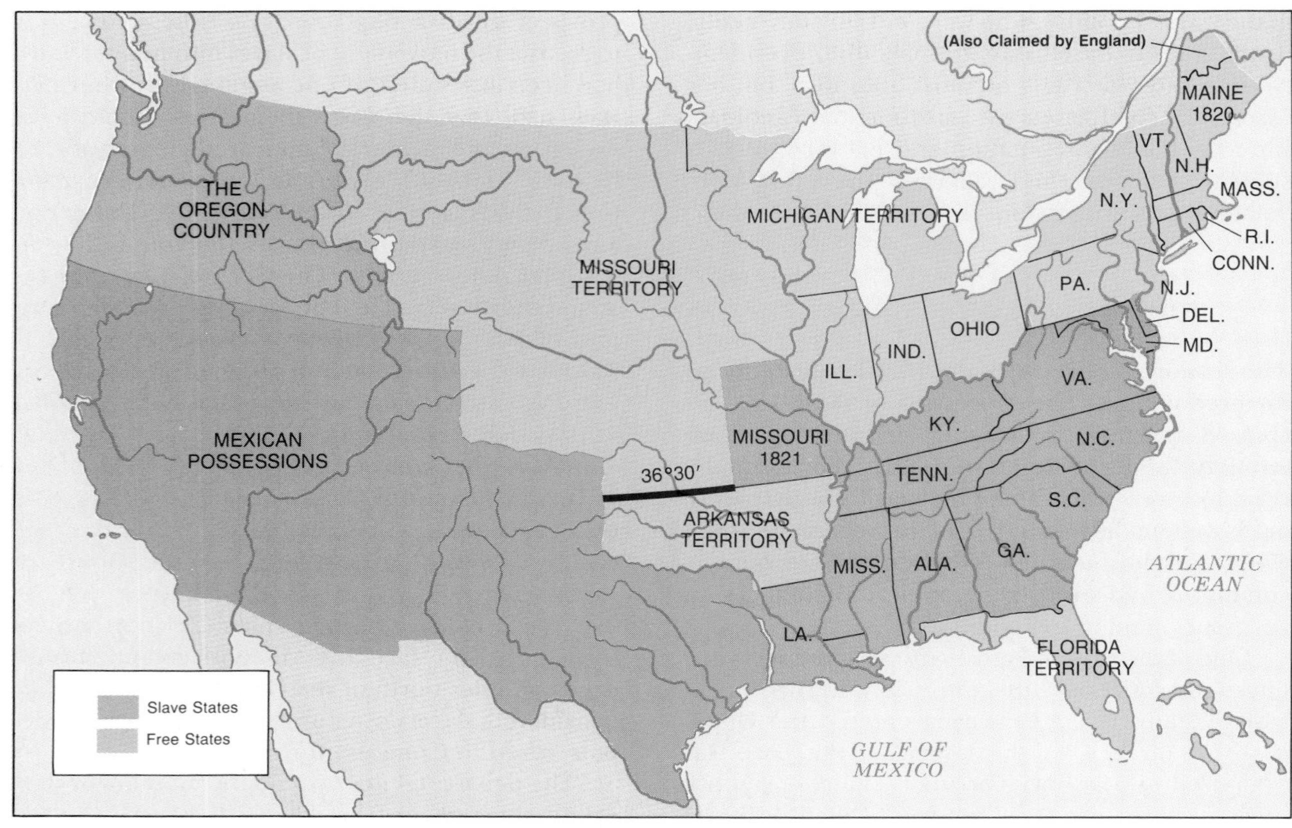

THE MISSOURI COMPROMISE, 1820–1821

This was the lineup of the slave and free states resulting from the Missouri Compromise. The Compromise was repealed by the Kansas-Nebraska Act (1854) and declared unconstitutional in the Dred Scott Case (1857).

treeless northern regions little better than a desert. One northern senator, decrying the division, contemptuously described the land north and west of Missouri, today one of the world's richest agricultural regions, as "a prairie without food or water."

The Missouri Compromise did not end the crisis. When Missouri submitted its constitution for approval by Congress (the final step in the admission process), the document, besides authorizing slavery and prohibiting the emancipation of any slave without the consent of the owner, *required* the state legislature to pass a law barring free blacks and mulattos from entering the state "under any pretext whatever." This provision plainly violated Article IV, Section 2 of the United States Constitution: "The Citizens of each State shall be entitled to all Privileges and Immunities of Citizens in the several States." It did not, however, represent any more of a break with established racial patterns, north or south, than the Tallmadge amendment; many states east of Missouri barred free blacks without regard for the Constitution.

Nevertheless, northern congressmen hypocritically refused to accept the Missouri constitution. Once more the debate raged. Again, since few northerners cared to defend the rights of blacks seriously, the issue was compromised. In March 1821 Henry Clay found a face-saving formula: out of respect for the "supreme law of the land," Congress accepted the Missouri constitution with the demurrer that no law passed in conformity to it should be construed as contravening Article IV, Section 2. Of course this was pure cant.

Every thinking person recognized the political

dynamite inherent in the Missouri controversy. The sectional lineup had been terrifyingly compact. What meant the Union if so trivial a matter as one new state could so divide the people? Moreover, despite the timidity and hypocrisy of the North, everyone realized that the rights and wrongs of slavery lay at the heart of the conflict. "We have the wolf by the ears, and we can neither safely hold him, nor safely let him go," Jefferson wrote a month after Missouri became a state. The dispute, he said, "like a fire bell in the night, awakened and filled me with terror." Jefferson knew that the compromise had not quenched the flames ignited by the Missouri debates. "This is a reprieve only," he said. John Quincy Adams called it the "title page to a great tragic volume." Yet one could still hope that the fire bell was only a false alarm, that Adams's tragic volume would remain unread.

The "Corrupt Bargain" of 1824

Other controversies that aroused strong feelings did not seem to divide the country so deeply. The question of federal internal improvements caused endless debate that split the country on geographical lines. In 1816 the nationalist-minded Calhoun had pressed a plan to set up a $1.5 million fund for roads and canals. Congress approved this despite strong opposition in New England and a divided South. In 1822 a bill providing money for the upkeep of the National Road caused another sectional split. Both measures were vetoed, but in 1824 Monroe approved a differently worded internal improvement act. Such proposals excited intense reactions. John Randolph, opposing the 1824 bill with his usual ferocity, threatened to employ "every . . . means short of actual insurrection" to defeat it. Yet other prominent southerners favored internal improvements, and no one—not even Randolph, it will be noted—threatened the Union on this issue.

The tariff continued to divide the country. When a new, still higher tariff was enacted in 1824, the slave states voted almost unanimously against it, the North and Northwest in favor, and New England remained of two minds. Clay, who expounded the case for his American System brilliantly in the debates, provided arguments for the tariff that his foes found hard to counter. Webster, continuing to speak for the merchants of New England (he conducted a poll of business leaders before deciding how to vote), made a powerful speech against the act, but the measure passed without creating a major storm.

The divisions on the questions were not severely disruptive, in part because the major politicians, competing for the presidency, did not dare risk alienating any section by taking too extreme a position. Calhoun, for example, had changed his mind about protective tariffs by 1824, but he avoided declaring himself because of his presidential ambitions. Another reason was that the old party system had broken down; the Federalists had disappeared as a national party and the Jeffersonians, lacking an organized opposition, had become less aggressive and more troubled by factional disputes.

The presidential fight was therefore waged on personal grounds, though the heat generated by the contest began the process of reenergizing party politics. Besides Calhoun the candidates were Jackson, Crawford, Adams, and Clay. The maneuvering among them was complex, the infighting savage. In March 1824 Calhoun, who was young enough to wait for the White House, withdrew and declared for the vice-presidency, which he won easily. Crawford, who had the support of many congressional leaders, seemed the likely winner, but he suffered a series of paralytic strokes that gravely injured his chances.

Despite the bitterness of the contest, it attracted relatively little public interest; barely a quarter of those eligible took the trouble to vote. In the electoral college Jackson led with 99, Adams had 84, Crawford 41, and Clay 37. Since no one had a majority, the contest was thrown into the House of Representatives, which, under the Constitution, had to choose from among the three leaders, each state delegation having one vote. By employing his great influence in the House, Clay swung the balance. Not wishing to advance the fortunes of a rival westerner like Jackson and feeling, with reason, that Crawford's health made him unavailable, Clay gave his support to Adams, who was thereupon elected.

Although deeply marked by his New England heritage, Adams was a man of the broadest experience and interests. He took a Hamiltonian view of the future of the country and hoped to use the national authority to foster all sorts of useful projects. He asked Congress for a federal program

A comment by David Claypoole Johnston on the 1824 presidential "foot-race" has Adams leading by a head, trailed by Crawford and Jackson. Clay (far right, hand on head), well behind, pulls up in dismay. The many figures and the dreadful puns ("How is Clay now?" "Oh dirt cheap" and "Hurra for our son Jack*" "Hurra for our Jack-*son*") are typical of cartoons of the era.*

of internal improvements so vast that even Clay boggled when he realized its scope. He came out for aid to manufacturing and agriculture, a variety of scientific and educational projects (including expeditions to explore the West, a national university, and an astronomical observatory), and many administrative reforms. For a nationalist of unchallengeable Jeffersonian origins like Clay or Calhoun to have pressed for so extensive a program would have been politically risky. For the son of John Adams to do so was disastrous; every doubter remembered his Federalist background and decided that he was trying to overturn the glorious "Revolution of 1800."

Adams proved to be his own worst enemy, for he was as inept a politician as ever lived. Although capable on occasion of turning a phrase—in his first annual message to Congress he described astronomical observatories as "light-houses of the skies"—his general style of public utterance was bumbling and cumbersome. Knowing that many citizens considered things like observatories impractical extravagances, he urged Congress not to be "palsied by the will of our constituents." To persuade Americans, who were almost pathological on the subject of monarchy, to support his road-building program, he cited with approval the work being done abroad by "the nations of Europe and . . . their rulers," which revived fears that all Adamses were royalists at heart. He was insensitive to the ebb and flow of public feeling; even when he wanted to move with the tide, he seldom managed to dramatize and publicize his stand effectively. There was wide support in the country for a federal bankruptcy law, but instead of describing himself in plain language as a friend of poor debtors, Adams called for the "amelioration" of the "often oppressive codes relating to insolvency" and buried the recommendation at the tail end of a dull state paper. He refused to use his power of appointment to win support. "I will not dismiss. . . able and faithful political opponents to provide for my own partisans," he said. The attitude was traditional at the time, but Adams carried it to extremes—in four years he removed only 12 men from office. Nevertheless, by appointing Henry Clay secretary of state, he laid himself open to the charge that he had won the presidency by a "corrupt bargain." Thus, despite his politically suicidal attitude toward federal jobs, he was subject to the annoyance of a congressional investigation of his appointments, out of which came no less than six bills designed "to reduce the patronage of the executive."

Toward a National Economy

Politicians might attribute the growth of the country and the preservation of the Union to their own patriotism and ingenuity, but without the economic and technological developments of the period, neither of these much-to-be-desired objectives could have been attained. The country was still overwhelmingly rural in 1820. Fewer than 700,000 people lived in centers of more than 2,500 in that year and the percentage of urban dwellers had declined in the previous decade. But the nation was on the brink of a major economic readjustment, for certain obscure seeds planted in the early years of the republic had taken root. Almost unnoticed in a country that lived by agriculture and maritime commerce, new ways of producing goods and making a living were beginning to take hold. The industrial revolution was coming to America with a rush.

The growth of industry required certain technological advances and the development of a new type of business organization. Both elements existed in Europe by the time of the Revolution, but it was only after the ratification of the Constitution that they crossed the Atlantic. In 1790 a young English-born genius named Samuel Slater, employed by the Rhode Island merchant firm of Almy & Brown, began to spin cotton thread by machine in the first effective factory in the United States. In 1800 a youthful graduate of Yale College, Eli Whitney, having contracted to make 10,000 rifles for the government, succeeded in manufacturing them by such precise methods that the parts were interchangeable, a major step toward the perfection of the assembly-line system of production. Three years later Oliver Evans, a Philadelphia inventor, had come close to achieving automation in flour milling. A worker poured wheat down a chute at one end of the plant and a second worker headed the barrels of superfine flour which emerged at the other end. The intervening steps of weighing, cleaning, grinding, and packing were all performed by machines.

Other important technological advances included John Fitch's construction and operation of the world's first regularly scheduled steamboat in 1790 and Eli Whitney's invention of the cotton gin in 1793. The steamboat and the gin affected American history almost as much as the factory system and mass production. The former, when employed on western waters, cut the cost of transportation dramatically and brought the West into the national economy. The latter made possible the widespread cultivation of cotton, which transformed the South and fed the world's cotton factories for decades.

Innovations in the way businesses were organized and financed accompanied technological developments. The most spectacular step was the sudden flowering of American banking. Here the establishment of the Bank of the United States was of key importance. Aside from aiding government financial operations, the Bank provided an important source of credit for private business. Its success led to the founding of many state-chartered banks. When the great Bank was created in 1791, there were only 3 banks in the entire country. By 1800 there were 29, located in all the major towns and in such minor centers of commerce and industry as Nantucket, Massachusetts, and Hudson, New York. Bank credit, in the historian Bray Hammond's words, "was to Americans a new source of energy, like steam." Yet many citizens failed to grasp this truth. "Every dollar of a bank bill that is issued beyond the quantity of gold and silver in the vaults represents nothing and is therefore a cheat upon somebody," John Adams remarked as late as 1809.

America was not industrialized overnight. Slater's factory did not signal the disappearance of the family spinning wheel or the spread of the factory system to other forms of manufacturing. Most commercial and manufacturing businesses were still managed by a single owner or a few partners. Methods of distributing goods, keeping records, and accounting remained primitive. Interchangeable firing pins for rifles did not lead at once to the spark plug or even to matching pairs of shoes. More than 15 years were to pass after the invention of Fitch's steamboat before it was widely accepted, and it was the better part of another decade before it found its true home beyond the Appalachians.

Samuel Slater "smuggled a textile mill out of England in his head." Two decades after its founding, the mill and its surroundings looked like this.

Birth of the Factory

The stirrings of America's industrial revolution were slow in coming. By the 1770s British manufacturers, especially those in textiles, had made astonishing progress in mechanizing their operations, bringing workers together in buildings called factories where waterpower, and later steam, supplied the force to run new spinning and weaving devices that increased productivity and reduced labor costs. John Kay's flying shuttle, James Hargreaves's spinning jenny, and Richard Arkwright's perfection of the water frame were the major technological improvements. Arkwright in particular was responsible for the efficient installation of these machines in factories.

Since machine-spun cotton was cheaper and of better quality than that spun by hand, producers in other countries were eager to adopt British methods. Americans had depended on Great Britain for such products until the Revolution cut off supplies; then the new spirit of nationalism gave impetus to the development of local industry. A number of state legislatures offered bounties to anyone who would introduce the new machinery. The British, however, guarded their secrets vigilantly. It was illegal to export any of the new machines or to send their plans abroad. Workers skilled in their construction and use were forbidden to leave the country. These restrictions were effective for a time; the principles on which the new machines were based were simple enough, but to construct workable models without plans was another matter. Although a number of persons tried to do so, it was not until Samuel Slater installed his machines in Pawtucket that a successful factory was constructed.

Slater, trained by one of Arkwright's partners, was more than a skilled mechanic. Attracted by stories of the rewards offered in the United States, he slipped out of England in 1789. Not daring to carry any plans, he depended on his memory and his mechanical sense for the complicated specifications of the necessary machines. When Moses Brown brought him to Rhode Island, he insisted on scrapping the crude machinery Almy & Brown had assembled. Then, working in secrecy with a carpenter who was "under bond not to steal the patterns nor disclose the nature of the work," he built and installed Arkwright-type water frames and other machinery. In December 1790 all was ready, and the first American factory began production.

It was a humble beginning indeed. Slater's machines made only cotton thread, which Almy & Brown sold in its Providence store and "put out" to individual artisans, who, working for wages, wove it into cloth in their homes. The machines were tended by a labor force of nine children, for the work was simple and the pace slow. The young operatives' pay ranged from 33 to 67 cents a week, about what a youngster could earn in other occupations.

The factory was profitable from the start. Slater soon branched out on his own, and others trained by him opened their own establishments. By 1800 seven mills possessing 2,000 spindles were in operation; by 1815, after production had been stimulated by the War of 1812, there were 130,000 spindles turning in 213 factories. Many of the new factories were inefficient, but the well-managed ones earned large profits. Slater began with almost nothing. When he died in 1835 he owned mill properties in Rhode Island, Massachusetts, Connecticut, and New Hampshire in addition to other interests, and by the standards of the day he was a rich man.

Before long the Boston Associates, a group of merchants headed by Francis Cabot Lowell, added a new dimension to factory production. Beginning at Waltham, Massachusetts, where the Charles River provided the necessary waterpower, they built between 1813 and 1850 a number of large factories that revolutionized textile production. Some early factory owners had set up hand looms in their plants, but the weavers could not keep pace with the whirring jennies. Lowell, after an extensive study of British mills, smuggled the plans for an efficient power loom into America. His Boston Manufacturing Company at Waltham, capitalized at $300,000, combined machine production, large-scale operation, efficient management, and centralized marketing procedures. It concentrated on the mass production of a standardized product.

Lowell's cloth, though plain and rather coarse, was durable and cheap. His profits averaged almost 20 percent a year during the Era of Good Feelings. In 1823 the Boston Associates began to harness the power of the Merrimack River, setting up a new $600,000 corporation at the sleepy village of East Chelmsford, Massachusetts (population 300), where there was a fall of 32 feet in the river. Within three years the town, appropriately renamed Lowell, had 2,000 inhabitants.

The Persistence of the Household System

The efficiency of the "Lowell System" was obvious, yet it led to no immediate transformation of American manufacturing. While the embargo and the war with Great Britain aided the new factories by limiting foreign competition, they also stimulated nonfactory production. In Monroe's time the "household-handicraft-mill complex" was still dominant nearly everywhere. Except in the manufacture of textiles, factories employing as many as 50 workers did not exist. Traveling and town-based artisans produced goods ranging from hats, shoes, and other articles of clothing to barrels, clocks, pianos, ships' supplies, cigars, lead pencils, and pottery. Ironworks, brickyards, flour mills, distilleries, and lumberyards could be found even in the most rural parts of the country. The historian George Rogers Taylor reports that in and about a single tiny Ohio town in 1815, more than 30 craftsmen of the shoemaker-baker-druggist type plied their trades.

Nearly all these "manufacturers" produced only to supply local needs, but in some instances large industries grew up without advancing to the factory stage. In the neighborhood of the Connecticut town of Danbury, hundreds of small shops turned out hats by handicraft methods. The hats were sold in all sections of the country, the trade being organized by wholesalers. The shoe industry followed a related pattern, with centers of production in Pennsylvania, New Jersey, and especially eastern Massachusetts. Merchants in these regions bought leather in wholesale lots, had it cut to patterns in central workshops, and then distributed it to craftsmen who made the shoes in their homes or shops on a piecework basis. The finished product was returned to the central shops for inspection and packaging and then shipped throughout the United States. Some strange combinations of production techniques appeared, none more peculiar than in the manufacture of stockings. Frequently the feet and legs were knit by machine in separate factories and then "put out" to handworkers who sewed the parts together in their homes.

Since technology affected American industry unevenly, contemporaries found the changes difficult to evaluate. Few people in the 1820s appreciated how profound the impact of the factory system would be. The city of Lowell seemed remarkable and important but not necessarily a herald of future trends. Yet in nearly every field apparently minor changes were being made. Beginning around 1815, small improvements in the design of waterwheels, such as the use of leather transmission belts and metal gears, made possible larger and more efficient machinery in mills and factories. The woolens industry gradually became as mechanized as the cotton. Iron production advanced beyond the stage of the blacksmith's forge and the small foundry only slowly; nevertheless, by 1810 machines were stamping out nails at a third the cost of the hand-forged type, and a few years later sheet iron, formerly hammered out laboriously by hand, was being produced in efficient rolling mills. At about this time the puddling process for refining pig iron made it possible to use coal for fuel instead of expensive charcoal.

Improvements were made soon after the War of 1812 in the manufacture of paper, glass, and pottery. The commercial canning of sterilized foods in airtight containers began about 1820. The invention in that year of a machine for cutting ice, which reduced the cost by over 50 percent, had equally important effects on urban eating habits.

Corporations

Besides the competition of other types of production and the inability of technology to supply instant solutions to every industrial problem, there were other reasons why the factory took hold so slowly in the United States. Mechanization required substantial capital investment, and capital was chronically in short supply. The modern method of organizing large enterprises, the corporation, was rarely used in this period. Between 1781 and 1801 only 326 corporations were chartered by the states, and only a few of them were engaged in manufacturing. The general opinion was that only quasi-public projects, such as roads and waterworks, were entitled to the privilege of incorporation. Anyone interested in organizing a corporation had to obtain a special act of a state legislature. And even among businessmen there was a tendency to associate corporations with monopoly, with corruption, and with the undermining of individual enterprise. In 1820 the economist Daniel Raymond wrote: "The very object . . . of the act of incorporation is to produce inequality, either in rights, or in the division of property. *Prima facie,* therefore all money corporations are detrimental to national wealth. They are always created for the benefit of the rich. . . ." Such feelings help to explain why as late as the 1860s most manufacturing was being done by unincorporated companies.

While the growth of industry did not suddenly revolutionize American life, it reshaped society in various ways. For many years it lessened the importance of foreign commerce. Some relative decline from the lush years immediately preceding Jefferson's embargo was no doubt inevitable, especially in the fabulously profitable reexport trade, but industrial growth reduced the need for foreign products and thus the business of merchants. Only in the 1850s, when the wealth and population of the United States were more than three times what they had been in the first years of the century, did the value of American exports climb back to the levels of 1807. As the country moved closer to self-sufficiency (a point it never reached), nationalistic and isolationist sentiments were subtly augmented. During the embargo and the War of 1812 a great deal of capital had been transferred from commerce to industry; afterward new capital continued to prefer industry, attracted by the high profits and growing prestige of manufacturing. The rise of manufacturing affected farmers too, for as cities grew in size and number, commercial agriculture flourished. Dairy farming, truck gardening, and fruit growing began to thrive around every manufacturing center.

Cotton Revolutionizes the South

By far the most important indirect effect of industrialization occurred in the South, which soon began to produce cotton to supply the new textile factories of Great Britain and New England. The possibility of growing large amounts of this crop in America had not been seriously considered in colonial times, but by the 1780s the demand for raw cotton to feed the voracious British mills was causing many American farmers to experiment with the crop. Most of the world's cotton at this time came from Egypt, India, and the East Indies. The plant was considered tropical, most varieties being unable to survive the slightest frost. Hamilton, who missed nothing that related to the economic growth of the country, reported: "It has been observed . . . that the nearer the place of growth to the equator, the better the quality of the cotton."

Beginning in 1786, "sea-island" cotton was

grown successfully in the mild, humid lowlands and offshore islands along the coasts of Georgia and South Carolina. This was a high-quality cotton, silky and long-fibered like the Egyptian. But its susceptibility to frost severely limited the area of its cultivation. Elsewhere in the South, "green-seed," or upland, cotton flourished, but this plant had little commercial value because the seeds could not be easily separated from the lint. When sea-island cotton was passed between two rollers, its shiny black seeds simply popped out; with upland cotton the seeds were pulled through with the lint and crushed, the oils and broken bits destroying the value of the fiber. To remove the seeds by hand was laborious; a slave working all day could clean scarcely a pound of the white fluff. This made it an uneconomical crop. In 1791 the usually sanguine Hamilton admitted in his *Report on Manufactures* that "the extensive cultivation of cotton can, perhaps, hardly be expected."

Early American cotton manufacturers used the sea-island variety or imported the foreign fiber, in the latter case paying a duty of 3 cents a pound. However, the planters of South Carolina and Georgia, suffering from hard times after the Revolution, needed a new cash crop. Rice production was not expanding, and indigo, the other staple of the area, had ceased to be profitable when it was no longer possible to claim the British bounty. Cotton seemed an obvious answer. Farmers were experimenting hopefully with varieties of the plant and mulling the problem of how upland cotton could be more easily deseeded.

This was the situation in the spring of 1793, when Eli Whitney was a guest at Mulberry Grove, the plantation of Catherine Greene, widow of General Nathanael Greene, some dozen miles from Savannah.* Whitney had accepted a position as private tutor at 100 guineas a year with a nearby family and had stopped to visit a friend, Phineas Miller, who was overseer of the Greene plantation. While at Mulberry Grove, Whitney, who had never seen a cotton plant before, met a number of the local landowners.

> I heard [he wrote his father] much of the extreme difficulty of ginning Cotton, that is, separating it from its seed. There were a number of very respectable Gentlemen at Mrs. Greene's who all agreed that if a machine could be invented that would clean the Cotton with expedition, it would be a great thing both to the Country and to the inventor.

Whitney thought about the problem for a few days and then "struck out a plan of a machine." He described it to Miller, who enthusiastically offered to finance the invention. Since Whitney had just learned that his job as tutor would pay only 50 guineas, he accepted Miller's proposal.

Within ten days he had solved the problem that had baffled the planters. His gin (engine) consisted of a cylinder covered with rows of wire teeth rotating in a box filled with cotton. As the cylinder turned, the teeth passed through narrow slits in a metal grating. Cotton fibers were caught by the teeth and pulled through the slits. The seeds, too thick to pass through the openings, were left behind. A second cylinder, with brushes rotating in the opposite direction to sweep the cotton from the wires, prevented matting and clogging.

This "absurdly simple contrivance" almost instantly transformed southern agriculture. With a gin a slave could clean 50 times as much cotton as by hand; soon larger models driven by mules and horses were available. The machines were so easy to construct (once the basic idea was understood) that Whitney and Miller were never able to enforce their patent rights effectively. Rival manufacturers shamelessly pirated their work, and countless farmers built gins of their own. Cotton production figures tell the story: in 1790 about 3,000 bales (the average bale weighed 500 pounds) were produced in the United States. In 1793, 10,000 bales were produced; two years later, 17,000; by 1801, 100,000. The embargo and the War of 1812 temporarily checked expansion, but in 1816 output spurted ahead by more than 25 percent, and in the early 1820s annual production averaged well over 400,000 bales.

Despite this avalanche, the price of cotton remained high. During the 1790s it ranged between 26 and 44 cents a pound, a veritable bonanza. In the next decade the price was lower (15 to 19 cents), but it still provided high profits even for inefficient planters. It was higher again after 1815 and fell below 14 cents only once before 1826. With prices at these levels, profits of $50 an acre were not unusual, and the South boomed.

* The property, formerly owned by a prominent Georgia Tory, had been given to Greene by the state in gratitude for his having driven out the British during the Revolution.

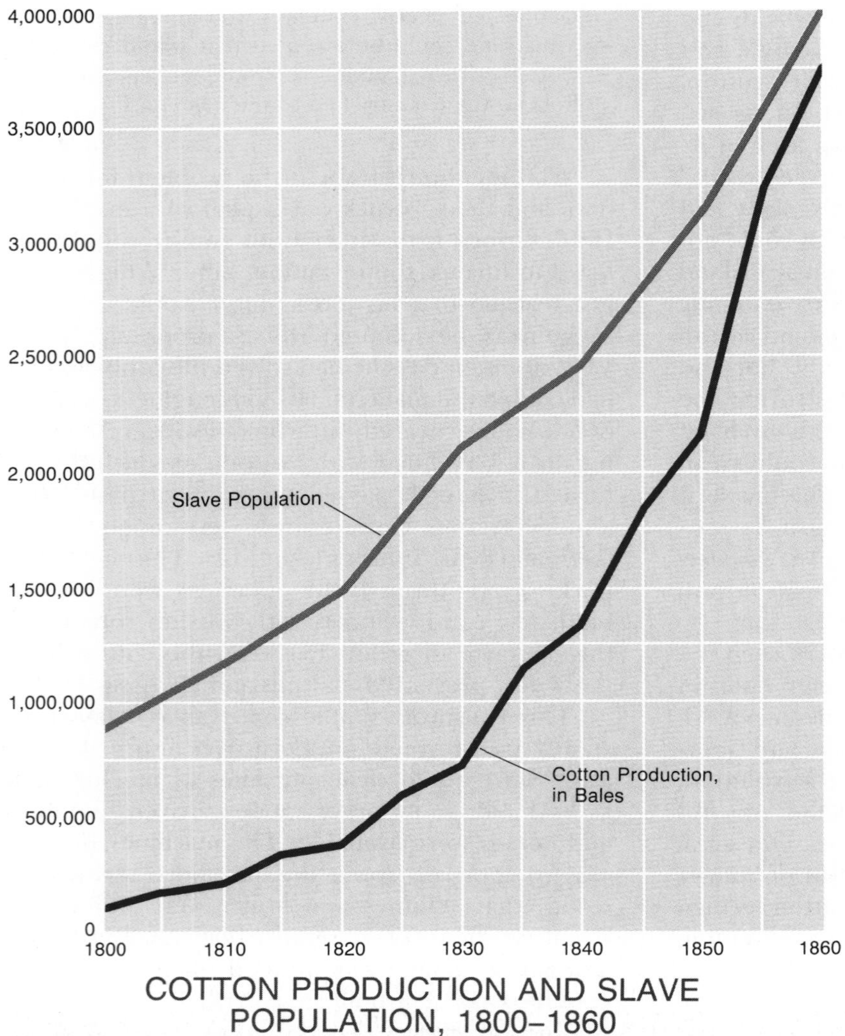

COTTON PRODUCTION AND SLAVE POPULATION, 1800–1860

Upland cotton would grow wherever there were 200 consecutive days without frost and 24 inches of rain. The crop engulfed Georgia and South Carolina and spread north into parts of Virginia. After Andrew Jackson smashed the southwestern Indians during the War of 1812, the rich "Black Belt" area of central Alabama and northern Mississippi and the delta region along the lower Mississippi River were rapidly taken over by the fluffy white staple. In 1821 Alabama alone raised 40,000 bales. Central Tennessee also became important cotton country.

Cotton stimulated the economy of the rest of the nation as well. Most of it was exported, the sale paying for much-needed European products. The transportation, insurance, and final disposition of the crop fell largely into the hands of northern merchants, who profited accordingly. And the surplus corn and hogs of western farmers helped feed the slaves of the new cotton plantations. As Douglass North explained in *The Economic Growth of the United States: 1815–1860,* cotton was "the major expansive force" in the economy for a generation, beginning about 1815. "The demands for western foodstuffs and northeastern services and manufactures were basically dependent upon the income received from the cotton trade."

Revival of Slavery

Amid the national rejoicing over this prosperity, one aspect both sad and ominous was easily overlooked. Slavery, a declining or at worst stagnant institution in the decade of the Revolution, was revitalized in the following years.

Libertarian beliefs inspired by the Revolution ran into the roadblock of race prejudice as soon as some of the practical aspects of freedom for blacks became apparent. As disciples of John Locke, the Revolutionary generation had a deep respect for property rights; in the last analysis most white Americans placed these rights ahead of the personal liberty of black Americans in their constellation of values. Forced abolition of slavery therefore attracted few recruits. Moreover, the rhetoric of the Revolution had raised the aspirations of blacks. Increasing signs of rebelliousness appeared among them, especially after the slave uprising in Saint Domingue, which culminated, after a great bloodbath, in the establishment of the black Republic of Haiti in 1804. This example of a successful slave revolt filled white Americans with apprehension. Their fears were irrational (Haitian blacks outnumbered whites and mulattos combined by seven to one) but nonetheless real. And fear led to repression; the exposure of a plot to revolt in Virginia, led by the slave Gabriel, resulted in some three dozen executions even though no actual uprising had occurred.

The mood of the Revolutionary decade had led to the manumission of many slaves; unfortunately this led many whites to have second thoughts about ending slavery. "If the blacks see all of their color slaves, it will seem to them a disposition of Providence, and they will be content," a Virginia legislator, apparently something of an amateur psychologist, claimed. "But if they see others like themselves free . . . they will repine." As the number of free blacks rose, restrictions on them were everywhere tightened.

In the 1780s many opponents of slavery began to think of solving the "Negro problem" by colonizing freed slaves in some distant region—in the western districts or perhaps in Africa. The colonization movement had two aspects. One, a manifestation of an embryonic black nationalism, reflected the disgust of black Americans with local racial attitudes and their interest in African civilization. Paul Cuffe, a Massachusetts Quaker, managed to finance the emigration of 38 of his fellow blacks to Sierra Leone in 1815, but few others followed. The other colonization movement, led by whites, was paternalistic. Some white colonizationists genuinely abhorred slavery. Others could not stomach living with free blacks; to them colonization was merely a polite word for deportation. Most white colonizationists were conservatives who considered themselves realists. Whether they thought blacks degenerate by nature or the victims of their surroundings, they were sure that American conditions gave them no chance to better their lot and that both races would profit from separation.

The colonization idea became popular in Virginia in the 1790s, but nothing was achieved until

The notion that blacks would be content if they "saw all of their color slaves" led to abuse of free blacks. In this frontispiece from American Slave Trade *(1822), the author interviews "freeborn people of colour who had been kidnapped" into slavery.*

after the founding of the American Colonization Society in 1817. The society purchased African land and established the Republic of Liberia. However, despite the cooperation of a handful of black nationalists and the patronage of many important white southerners, including presidents Madison and Monroe and Chief Justice Marshall, it accomplished little. Although some white colonizationists expected ex-slaves to go to Africa as enthusiastic Christian missionaries who would convert and "civilize" the natives, few blacks in fact wished to migrate to a land as alien to their own experience as to their masters'. Only about 12,000 went to Liberia, and the toll taken among them by tropical diseases was large. As late as 1850 the black American population of Liberia was only 6,000.

The cotton boom of the early 19th century acted as a brake on the colonization movement. As cotton production expanded, the need for labor in the South grew apace. The price of slaves doubled between 1795 and 1804. As it rose, the inclination of even the most kindhearted masters to free their slaves began to falter. Although the importation of slaves from abroad had been outlawed by all the states, perhaps 25,000 were smuggled into the country in the 1790s. In 1804 South Carolina reopened the trade, and between that date and 1808, when the constitutional prohibition of importation became effective, some 40,000 were brought in. Thereafter the miserable traffic in human beings continued clandestinely, though on a very small scale (see page 376).

Equally obnoxious was the interstate slave trade that resulted from the cotton boom. While it had always been legal for owners to transport their own slaves to a new state if they were settling there, many states forbade, or at least severely restricted, interstate commercial transactions in human flesh. A Virginia law of 1778, for example, prohibited the importation of slaves for purposes of sale, and persons entering the state with slaves had to swear that they did not intend to sell them. Once cotton became important, these laws were systematically evaded. There was a surplus of slaves in one part of the United States and an acute shortage in another. A migration from the Upper South to the cotton lands quickly sprang up. Slaves from "free" New York and New Jersey and even from New England began to appear on the auction blocks of Savannah and Charleston. Early in the Era of Good Feelings, newspapers in New Orleans were carrying reports such as: "Jersey negroes appear to be particularly adapted to this market. . . . We have the right to calculate on large importations in the future, from the success which hitherto attended the sale."

By about 1820 the letter of the law began to be changed. Soon the slave trade became an organized business, cruel and shameful, frowned on by the "best" people of the South, managed by the depraved and the greedy, yet patronized by nearly anyone who needed labor. "The native land of Washington, Jefferson, and Madison," one disgusted Virginian told a French visitor, "[has] become the Guinea of the United States."

The lot of blacks in the northern states was almost as bad as that of southern free blacks. Except in New England, where there were few blacks to begin with, most were denied the vote, either directly or by extralegal pressures. They could not testify in court, intermarry with whites, obtain decent jobs or housing, or get even a rudimentary education. Some states prohibited the migration of free blacks into their territories. Most segregated blacks in theaters, hospitals, and churches and on public transportation facilities. They were barred from hotels and restaurants patronized by whites.

Northern blacks could at least protest and try to convince the white majority of the injustice of their treatment. These rights were denied their southern brethren. They could and did publish newspapers and pamphlets, organize for political action, petition legislatures and the Congress for redress of grievance—in short, they applied methods of peaceful persuasion in an effort to improve their position in society.

Roads to Market

Inventions and technological improvements were extremely important in the settlement of the West. On superficial examination, this may not seem to have been the case, for the hordes of settlers who struggled across the mountains immediately after the War of 1812 were no better equipped than their ancestors who had pushed up the eastern slopes in previous generations. Many plodded on foot over hundreds of miles, dragging crude carts laden with their meager possessions. More fortu-

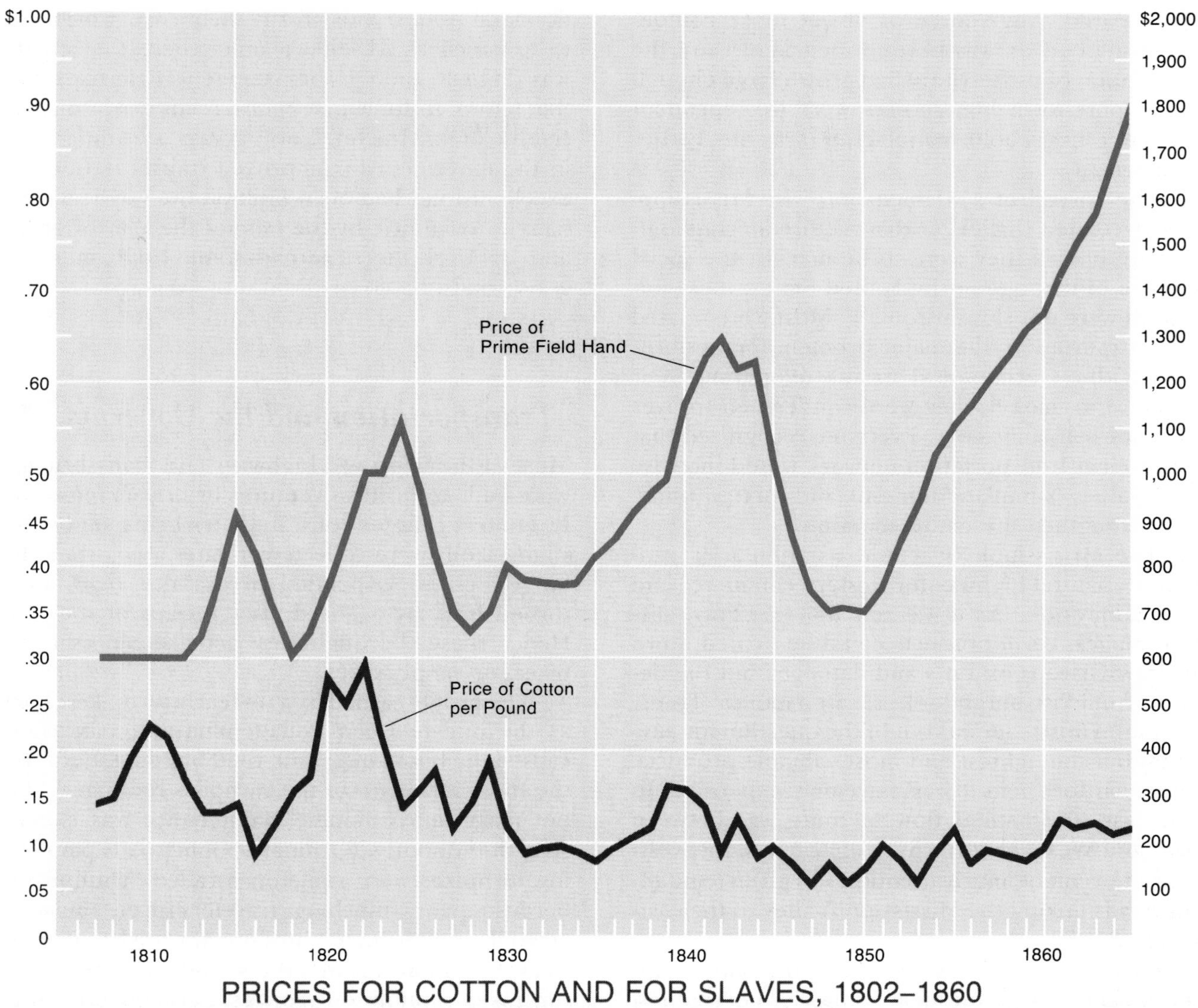

The vertical axis on the left shows cents, and the curve for the price of cotton should be read against it; the right vertical axis shows dollars, and the price of slaves should be read against it. These prices are from New Orleans records. According to Conrad and Meyer, the rising trend of slave prices (and a growing slave population) shows the continuing profitability and viability of slavery up to 1860.

nate pioneers traveled on horseback or in heavy, cumbersome wagons, the best known being the hearselike, canvas-topped Conestoga "covered wagons," pulled by horses or oxen.

In many cases the pioneers followed trails and roads no better than those of colonial days—quagmires in wet weather, rutted and pitted with potholes a good part of the year. When they settled down, their way of life was no more advanced than that of the Pilgrims. At first they were creatures of the forest, feeding upon its abundance, building their homes and simple furniture with its wood, clothing themselves in the furs of forest animals. They usually planted the first crop in a natural glade; thereafter, year by year, they pushed back the trees with ax and saw and fire until the land was cleared. Any source of power more complicated than an ox was beyond their ken. Until the population of the territory had grown large enough to support town life, settlers were as dependent on crude household manufacturers as any earlier pioneer.

The spread of settlement into the Mississippi Valley created challenges that required technological advances if they were to be met. In the social climate of that age in the United States, these advances were not slow in coming. Most were related to transportation, the major problem for westerners. Without economical means of getting their produce to market, they were condemned to lives of crude self-sufficiency. Everyone recognized that an efficient transportation network would increase land values, stimulate domestic and foreign trade, and strengthen the entire economy.

The Mississippi River and its tributaries provided a natural highway for western commerce and communication, but it was one that had grave disadvantages. Farm products could be floated down to New Orleans on rafts and flatboats, but the descent from Pittsburgh took at least a month. Transportation upstream was out of the question for anything but the lightest and most valuable products, and even for them it was extremely expensive. In any case, the natural flow of trade was between East and West. That is why, from early in the westward movement, much attention was given to building roads linking the Mississippi Valley to the eastern seaboard.

Constructing decent roads over the rugged Appalachians was a formidable task. The steepest grades had to be reduced by cutting through hills and filling in low places, all without modern blasting and earth-moving equipment. Streams had to be bridged. Drainage ditches were essential if the roads were not to be washed out by the first rains, and a firm foundation of stones, topped with a well-crowned gravel dressing, had to be provided if they were to stand up under the pounding of heavy wagons. The skills required for building roads of this quality had been developed in Great Britain and France, and the earliest American examples, constructed in the 1790s, were similar to good European highways. The first such road, connecting Philadelphia and Lancaster, Pennsylvania, opened to traffic in 1794.

In heavily populated sections the volume of traffic made good roads worth their cost, which ran to as much as $13,000 a mile where the terrain was difficult, though the average was perhaps half that figure. In some cases good roads ran into fairly remote areas. In New York, always a leading state in the movement for improved transportation, an excellent road had been built all the way from Albany to Lake Erie by the time of the War of 1812, and by 1821 the state had some 4,000 miles of good roads.

Transportation and the Government

Most of the improved highways and many bridges were built as business ventures by private interests. Promoters charged tolls, the rates being set by the states. Tolls were collected at gates along the way; hinged poles suspended across the road were turned back by a guard after receipt of the toll. Hence these thoroughfares were known as turnpikes, or simply pikes.

The profits earned by a few early turnpikes, such as the one between Philadelphia and Lancaster, caused the boom in private road building, but even the most fortunate of the turnpike companies did not make much money. Maintenance was expensive, traffic spotty. (Ordinary public roads paralleling turnpikes were sometimes called "shunpikes" because penny-pinching travelers used them to avoid the tolls.) Some states bought stock to bolster weak companies, and others built and operated turnpikes as public enterprises. Local governments everywhere provided considerable support, for every town was eager to develop efficient communication with its neighbors.

Despite much talk about individual self-reliance and free enterprise, local, state, and national governments contributed heavily to the development of what in the jargon of the day were called "internal improvements." They served as "primary entrepreneurs," supplying capital for risky but socially desirable enterprises, with the result that a fascinating mixture of private and public energy went into the building of these institutions. At the federal level even the parsimonious Jeffersonians became deeply involved. In 1808 Secretary of the Treasury Albert Gallatin drafted a comprehensive plan for constructing much-needed roads at a cost of $16 million. This proposal was not adopted, but the government poured money in an erratic and unending stream into turnpike companies and other organizations created to improve transportation.

Logically, the major highways, especially those over the mountains, should have been built by the national government. Strategic military requirements alone would have justified such a program. One major artery, the Old National Road, running from Cumberland, Maryland, to Wheeling, in western Virginia, was constructed by the United States between 1811 and 1818. In time it was extended as far west as Vandalia, Illinois. However, further federal road building was hampered by political squabbles in Congress, usually phrased in constitutional terms but in fact based on sectional rivalries and other economic conflicts. Thus no comprehensive highway program was undertaken in the 19th century.

While the National Road, the New York Pike, and other, rougher trails such as the Wilderness Road into the Kentucky country were adequate for the movement of settlers, they did not begin to answer the West's need for cheap and efficient transportation. Wagon freight rates averaged at least 30 cents a ton-mile around 1815. At such rates, to transport a ton of oats from Buffalo to New York would have cost 12 times the value of the oats! To put the problem another way, four horses could haul a ton and a half of oats about 18 or 20 miles a day over a good road. If they could obtain half their feed by grazing, the horses would still consume about 50 pounds of oats a day. It requires little mathemtaics to figure out how much oats would be left in the wagon when it reached New York City, almost 400 miles away.

Turnpikes made it possible to transport such goods as clothing, hardware, coffee, and books across the Appalachians, but the expense was considerable. It cost more to ship a ton of freight 300 miles over the mountains from Philadelphia to Pittsburgh than from Pittsburgh to Philadelphia by way of New Orleans, more than ten times as far. Until the coming of the railroad, which was just being introduced in England in 1825, shipping bulky goods by land over the great distances common in America was uneconomical. Businessmen and inventors concentrated instead on improving water transport, first by designing better boats and then by developing artificial waterways.

"Organs of Communication"

Rafts and flatboats were adequate for downstream travel, but the only practical solution to upstream travel was the steamboat. After John Fitch's work around 1790, a number of others made important contributions to the development of steam navigation. One early enthusiast was John Stevens, a wealthy New Jerseyite, who designed an improved steam boiler for which he received one of the first patents issued by the United States. Stevens got his brother-in-law, Robert R. Livingston, interested in the problem, and the latter used his political influence to obtain an exclusive charter to operate steamboats on New York waters. In 1802, while in France trying to buy New Orleans from Napoleon, Livingston got to know Robert Fulton, a young American artist and engineer who was experimenting with steam navigation, and agreed to finance his work. In 1807, after returning to New York, Fulton constructed the *North River Steam Boat,* famous to history as the *Clermont.*

The *Clermont* was 142 feet long, 18 feet abeam, and drew 7 feet of water. With its towering stack belching black smoke, its side wheels could push it along at a steady 5 miles an hour. Nothing about it was radically new, but Fulton brought the essentials—engine, boiler, paddle wheels, and hull—into proper balance and thereby produced an efficient vessel.

No one could patent a steamboat; soon the new vessels were plying the waters of every navigable river from the Mississippi east. After 1815 steamers were making the run from New Orleans as far as Ohio. By 1820 at least 60 vessels were operating between New Orleans and Louisville, and by the end of the decade there were more than 200 steamers on the Mississippi.

The day of the steamboat had dawned, and although the following generation would experience its high noon, even in the 1820s its major effects were clear. The great Mississippi Valley, in the full tide of its development, was immensely enriched. Produce poured down to New Orleans, which soon ranked with New York and Liverpool among the world's great ports. Only 80,000 tons of freight reached New Orleans from the interior in 1816–1817, more than 542,000 tons in 1840–1841. Upriver traffic was affected even more spectacularly. Freight charges plummeted, in some cases to a

Artist as well as inventor, Robert Fulton painted these miniature portraits of himself and his wife, Harriet Livingston, on ivory, after canvas portraits by Elizabeth Emmett.

tenth of what they had been after the War of 1812. Around 1818 coffee cost 16 cents a pound more in Cincinnati than in New Orleans, a decade later less than 3 cents more. The Northwest emerged from self-sufficiency with a rush and became part of the national market.

Steamboats were far more comfortable than any contemporary form of land transportation, and competition soon led builders to make them positively luxurious. The *General Pike,* launched in 1819, set the fashion. Marble columns, thick carpets, mirrors, and crimson curtains adorned its cabins and public rooms. Soon the finest steamers were floating palaces where passengers could dine, drink, dance, and gamble in luxury as they sped smoothly to their destinations. Yet raft and flatboat traffic *increased.* Farmers, lumbermen, and others with goods from upriver floated down in the slack winter season and returned in comfort by steamer after selling their produce—and their rafts as well, for lumber was in great demand in New Orleans. Every January and February New Orleans teemed with westerners and Yankee sailors, their pockets jingling, bent on a fling before going back to work. The shops displayed everything from the latest Paris fashions to teething rings made of alligator teeth mounted in silver. During the carnival season the city became one great festival, where every human pleasure could be tasted, every vice indulged. "Have you ever been in New Orleans?" one visiting bard sang in the late 1820s.

> *. . . If not you'd better go,*
> *It's a nation of a queer place; day and night a show!*
> *Frenchmen, Spaniards, West Indians, Creoles, Mustees,*
> *Yankees, Kentuckians, Tennesseeans, lawyers and trustees.*
> *Clergymen, priests, friars, nuns, women of all stains;*
> *Negroes in purple and fine linen, and slaves in rags and chains.*

This "front view of St. Louis" may be the earliest print of that city; it appeared as frontispiece in the first atlas published west of the Mississippi (Eugene Charles Dupré's Atlas . . . , *St. Louis, 1838).*

Ships, arks, steamboats, robbers, pirates, alligators,
Assassins, gamblers, drunkards, and cotton speculators;
Sailors, soldiers, pretty girls, and ugly fortunetellers;
Pimps, imps, shrimps, and all sorts of dirty fellows;
White men with black wives, et vice-versa *too,*
A progeny of all colors—an infernal motley crew! . . .

The Canal Boom

While the steamboat was conquering western rivers, canals were being constructed that further improved the transportation network. Since the midwestern rivers all emptied into the Gulf of Mexico, they did not provide a direct link with the eastern seaboard. If an artificial waterway could be cut between the great central valley and some navigable stream flowing into the Atlantic, all sections would profit immensely.

Canals were more expensive than roads, but so long as the motive power used in overland transportation was the humble horse, they offered enormous economic advantages to shippers. Because there is less friction to overcome, a team plodding along a towpath could pull a canal barge with a 100-ton load and make better time over long distances than it could pulling a single ton in a wagon on the finest road.

Although canals were as old as Egypt, only about 100 miles of them existed in the United States as late as 1816. Construction costs aside, in a rough and mountainous country canals presented formidable engineering problems. To link the Mississippi Valley and the Atlantic meant somehow circumventing the Appalachian Mountains. Most people thought this impossible.

Mayor DeWitt Clinton of New York believed that such a project was feasible in New York State. In 1810, while serving as canal commissioner, he traveled across central New York and convinced himself that it would be practicable to dig a canal from Buffalo, on Lake Erie, to the Hudson River. The Mohawk Valley cuts through the Appalachian chain just north of Albany, and at no point along the route to Buffalo does the land rise more than 570 feet above the level of the Hudson. Marshaling a mass of technical, financial, and commercial information (and using his political influence cannily), Clinton placed his proposal before the New York legislature. In its defense he was eloquent and far-sighted:

> As an organ of communication between the Hudson, the Mississippi, the St. Lawrence, the great lakes of the north and west, and their tributary rivers, [the canal] will create the greatest inland trade ever witnessed. The most fertile and extensive regions of America will avail themselves of its facilities for a market. All their surplus . . . will concentrate in the city of New York. . . . That city will, in the course of time, become the granary of the world, the emporium of commerce, the seat of manufactures, the focus of great moneyed operations. . . . And before the revolution of a century, the whole island of Manhattan, covered with habitations and replenished with a dense population, will constitute one vast city.

The legislators were convinced, and in 1817 the state began construction along a route 363 miles long, most of it across densely forested wilderness. At the time the longest canal in the United States ran less than 28 miles!

The construction of the Erie Canal, as it was called, was a remarkable accomplishment. The chief engineer, Benjamin Wright, a surveyor-politician from Rome, New York, had had almost no experience with canal building. One of his chief associates, James Geddes, possessed only an elementary school education and knew virtually nothing about surveying. Both learned rapidly by trial and error. Fortunately, Wright proved to be a good organizer and a fine judge of engineering talent. He quickly spotted young men of ability among the workers and pushed them forward. One of his finds, Canvass White, was sent to study British canals. White became an expert on the design of

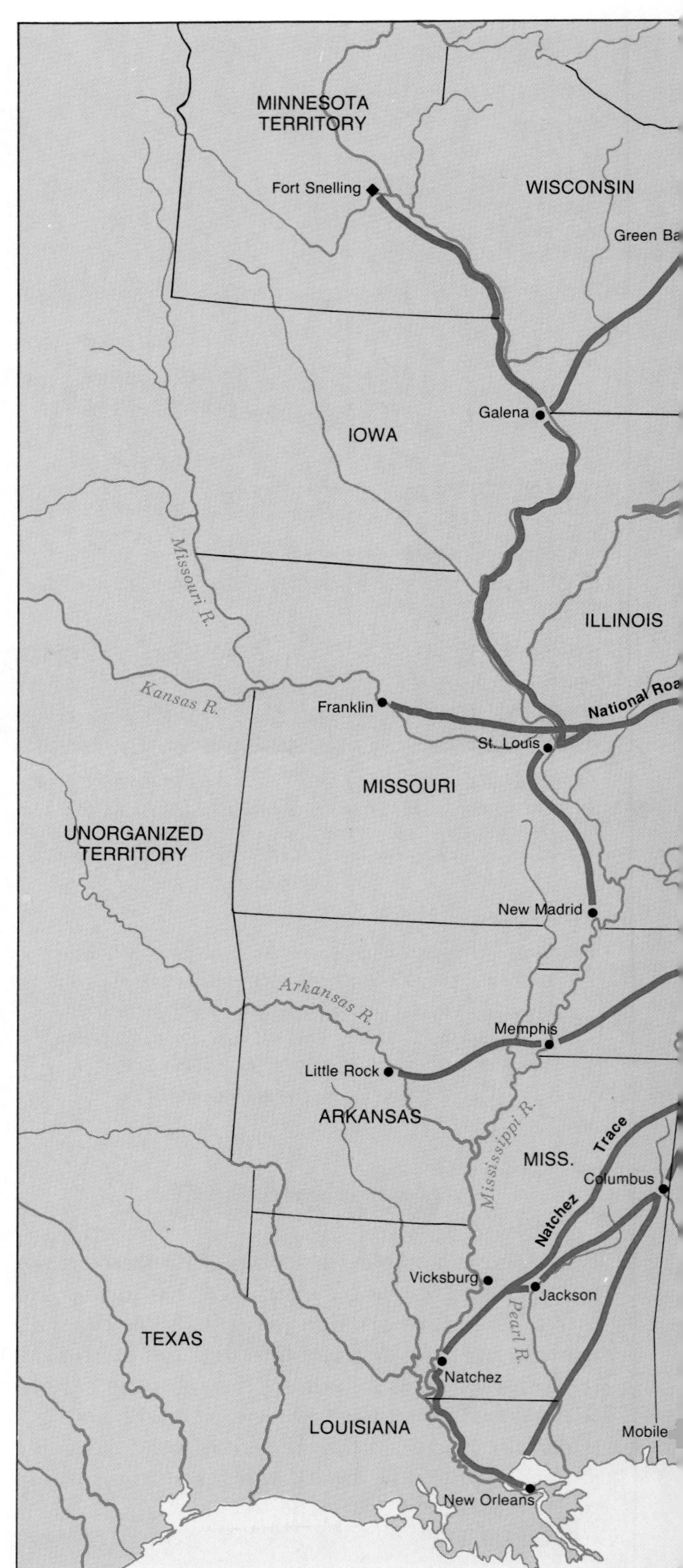

CANALS AND ROADS, 1820–1850

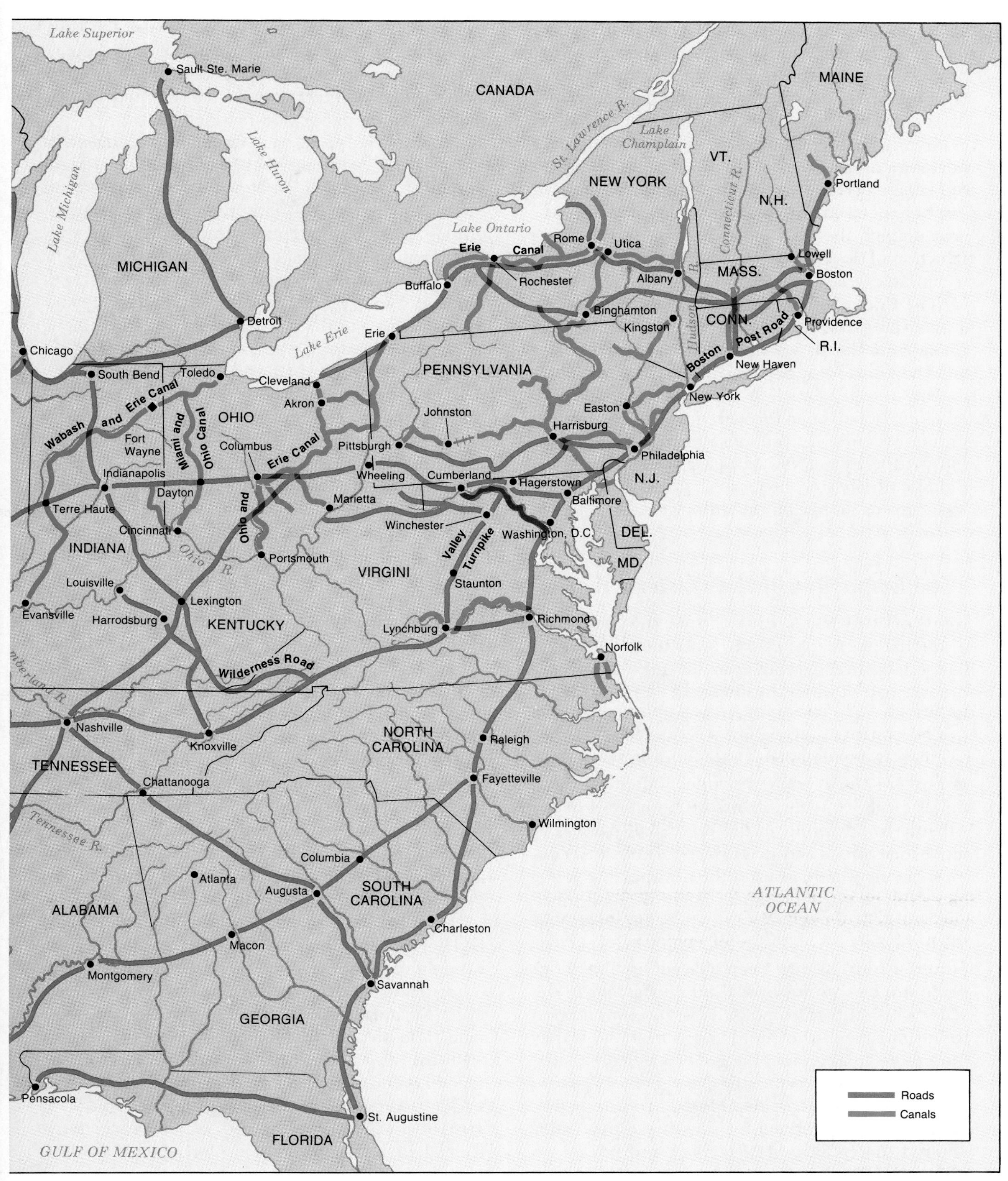
Lake Superior
Sault Ste. Marie
CANADA
MAINE
St. Lawrence R.
Lake Champlain
VT.
Lake Huron
Lake Michigan
NEW YORK
N.H.
Portland
Lake Ontario
Connecticut R.
Rome
Utica
Erie Canal
Lowell
MICHIGAN
Rochester
Albany
MASS.
Buffalo
Boston
Binghamton
Detroit
Kingston
CONN.
Providence
Erie
Hudson R.
Post Road
Chicago
Lake Erie
R.I.
Boston
New Haven
South Bend
Toledo
PENNSYLVANIA
Cleveland
New York
Wabash and Erie Canal
Akron
Easton
Miami and Ohio Canal
OHIO
Johnston
Fort Wayne
Harrisburg
Columbus
Erie Canal
Pittsburgh
Philadelphia
Indianapolis
Wheeling
Cumberland
N.J.
Hagerstown
Dayton
Baltimore
Terre Haute
Marietta
Ohio and
Winchester
Cincinnati
Washington, D.C.
DEL.
INDIANA
Ohio R.
Valley Turnpike
Portsmouth
MD.
VIRGINI
Louisville
Staunton
Lexington
Evansville
Harrodsburg
KENTUCKY
Richmond
Lynchburg
Norfolk
Wilderness Road
Cumberland R.
Nashville
NORTH CAROLINA
Raleigh
Knoxville
TENNESSEE
Fayetteville
Chattanooga
Tennessee R.
Wilmington
Columbia
Atlanta
SOUTH CAROLINA
ATLANTIC OCEAN
Augusta
ALABAMA
Charleston
Macon
Montgomery
Savannah
GEORGIA
Pensacola
St. Augustine
FLORIDA
GULF OF MEXICO
Roads
Canals

locks; he also discovered an American limestone that could be made into waterproof cement, a vital product in canal construction that had previously been imported at a substantial price from England. Another of Wright's protégés, John B. Jervis, began as an axman, rose in two years to resident engineer in charge of a section of the project, and went on to become perhaps the outstanding American civil engineer of his time. Workers who learned the business digging the "Big Ditch" supervised the construction of dozens of canals throughout the country in later years.

The Erie, completed in 1825, was immediately a financial success. Together with the companion Champlain Canal, which linked Lake Champlain and the Hudson, it brought in over half a million dollars in tolls in its first year. Soon its entire $7 million cost had been recovered, and it was earning profits of about $3 million a year. The effect of this prosperity on New York State was enormous. Buffalo, Rochester, Syracuse, and half a dozen lesser towns along the canal flourished.

The Emporium of the Western World

New York City had already become the largest city in the nation, thanks chiefly to its merchants, who had established a reputation for their rapid and orderly way of doing business. In 1818 the Black Ball Line opened the first regularly scheduled freight and passenger service between New York and England. Previously, shipments might languish in port for weeks while a skipper waited for additional cargo. Now merchants on both sides of the Atlantic could count on the Black Ball packets to move their goods between Liverpool and New York on schedule whether or not the transporting vessel had a full cargo. This improvement brought much new business to the port. In the same year New York enacted an auction law requiring that imported goods having been placed on the block could not be withdrawn if a bid satisfactory to the seller was not forthcoming. This, too, was a boon to businessmen, who could be assured that if they outbid the competition, the goods would be theirs.

Now the canal cemented New York's position as the national metropolis. Most European-manufactured goods destined for the Mississippi Valley entered the country at New York and passed on to the west over the canal. The success of the Erie also sparked a nationwide canal-building boom. Most canals were constructed either by the states, as in the case of the Erie, or as "mixed enterprises" that combined public and private energies.

No state profited as much from this construction as New York, for none possessed New York's geographical advantages. In New England the terrain was so rugged as to discourage all but fanatics. Canals were built connecting Worcester and Northampton, Massachusetts, with the coast, but they were failures financially. The Delaware and Hudson Canal, running from northeastern Pennsylvania across northern New Jersey and lower New York to the Hudson, was completed by private interests in 1828. It managed to earn respectable dividends by barging coal to the eastern seaboard, but it made no attempt to compete with the Erie for the western trade. Pennsylvania, desperate to keep up with New York, engaged in an orgy of construction. In 1834 it completed a complicated system, part canal and part railroad, over the mountains to Pittsburgh. This Mainline Canal cost a staggering sum for that day. With its 177 locks and its cumbersome "inclined-plane railroad" it was slow and expensive to operate and never competed effectively with the Erie. Efforts of Maryland to link Baltimore with the West by water failed utterly.

Beyond the mountains there was even greater zeal for canal construction in the 1820s and still more in the 1830s. Once the Erie opened the way across New York, farmers in the Ohio country demanded that links be built between the Ohio River and the Great Lakes so that they could ship their produce by water directly to the East. Local feeder canals seemed equally necessary; with corn worth 20 cents a bushel at Columbus selling for 50 cents at Marietta, on the Ohio, the value of cheap transportation became obvious to Ohio farmers.

Even before the completion of the Erie, Ohio had begun construction of the Ohio and Erie Canal running from the Ohio River to Cleveland. Another, from Toledo to Cincinnati, was begun in 1832. Meanwhile, Indiana had undertaken the 450-mile Wabash and Erie Canal. These canals were well conceived, but the western states overextended themselves building dozens of feeder lines, trying, it sometimes seemed, to supply all farmers west of the Appalachians with water connections from their barns to the New York docks. Politics made such programs almost inevitable, for in order to win support for their pet projects, legislators had to back the schemes of their fellows. The result was frequently financial disaster. There was not enough traffic to pay for all the waterways that were dug. By 1844, $60 million in state "improvement" bonds were in default. Nevertheless, the canals benefited both western farmers and the national economy.

Government Aid to Business

Throughout this period both the United States and the states were active in areas that directly affected the economy. Federal banking, tariff, and land legislation had considerable influence on economic expansion. These political activities, which also contributed to the growth of sectional conflicts in the nation, will be considered in Chapter 10; here a number of legal and judicial developments require consideration.

While prejudice against corporations in the manufacturing field continued, the device was such a useful means of bringing together the substantial amounts of capital needed for building roads and canals and for organizing banks and insurance companies that a steadily increasing number of promoters applied for charters. Bills authorizing incorporations became so numerous in some eastern states that legislators found themselves devoting a disconcertingly large portion of their time to them. Therefore they were tempted to issue blanket, though restricted, authorizations. In 1809 Massachusetts passed a law establishing strict rules for all manufacturing corporations in the state. One rule made shareholders individually liable for their companies' debts beyond their actual investment. While still requiring separate authorizations for each charter, the Massachusetts legislature could now dispose of applications in a more routine fashion.

Two years later New York enacted the first general incorporation law, permitting the issuance of charters without specific legislative action in each case. Although they held stockholders liable only "to the extent of their respective shares in the . . . company," which was the basic privilege sought by all incorporators, these general charters were not available to companies capitalized at more than $50,000, and they ran for only five years. This was unsatisfactory; after an initial period of enthusiasm (122 charters were issued between 1811 and 1816), the law became nearly a dead letter. Other states did not begin to permit general incorporation until 1837, and businessmen continued to seek, and obtain, special charters for decades thereafter.

Manufacturers in some states recieved valuable tax benefits. In Vermont no industrial concern paid local taxes. A New York law of 1817 exempted textile mills, and in 1823 Ohio extended similar privileges to textile, iron, and glass companies. Manufacturers benefited from the protection granted inventors by the United States Patent Office, created in 1790, and the attitude of most courts and juries toward labor unions and strikes in this period favored employers. Before the end of the 1820s craft unions had become numerous and active, yet judges tended to consider strikes unlawful conspiracies and to find against unions that tried to establish the closed shop. Though the public's attitude toward organized labor was beginning to change, the legal right of unions to exist was not fully established until the 1840s.

The Marshall Court

The most important legal advantages bestowed upon businessmen in the period were the gift of Chief Justice John Marshall. Historians have tended to forget he had six colleagues on the Supreme Court, and that is easy to understand. Marshall's particular combination of charm, logic, and forcefulness made the Court during his long reign, if not a rubber stamp, remarkably submissive to his view of the Constitution. Marshall's belief in a powerful central government explains his tendency to hand down decisions favorable to manufacturing and business interests. He also thought that "the business community was the agent of order and progress" and tended to interpret the Constitution in a way that would advance its interests.

A series of extremely important cases came before the Court between 1819 and 1824, and in each one Marshall's decision was applauded by most of the business community. The cases involved two major principles: the "sanctity" of contracts and the supremacy of federal legislation over the laws of the states.

Marshall shared the conviction of the Revolutionary generation that property had to be protected against arbitrary seizure if liberty was to be preserved. Contracts between private individuals and between individuals and the government must be strictly enforced, he believed, or chaos will result. He therefore gave the widest possible application to the constitutional provision that no state could pass any law "impairing the Obligation of Contracts."

Two controversies settled in February 1819 illustrate Marshall's views on the subject of contracts. In *Sturges* v. *Crowninshield* he found a New York bankruptcy law unconstitutional. States could pass such laws, he conceded, but they could not make them applicable to debts incurred before the laws were passed, for debts were contracts. In *Dartmouth College* v. *Woodward* he held that a charter granted by a state was a contract and might not be canceled or altered without the consent of both

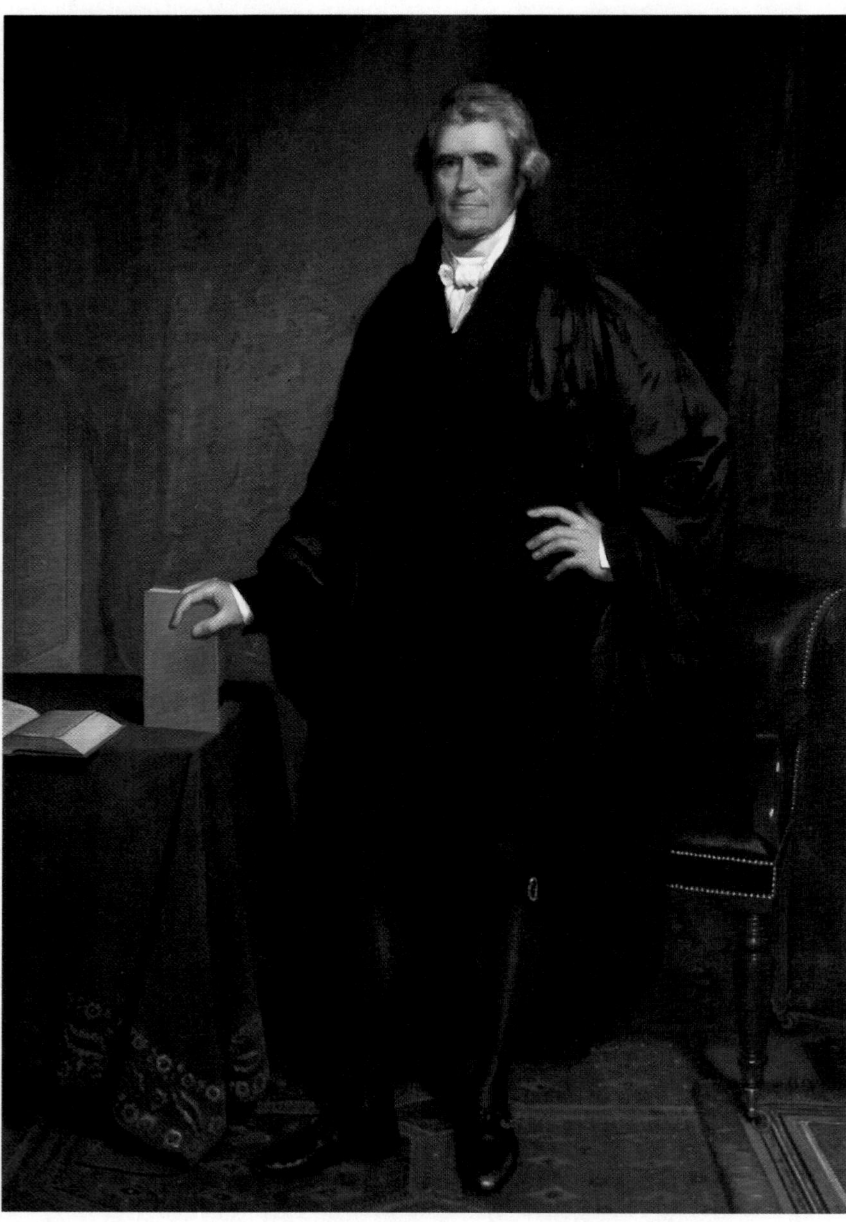

The artist Chester Harding painted John Marshall in 1828, during the chief justice's twenty-seventh year on the Supreme Court. "The unpretentious dignity [and] the sober factualism" of Harding's style (as art historian Oliver Larkin describes it) was well suited to capturing Marshall's character.

parties. Contracts could scarcely be more sacred than Marshall made them in the Dartmouth College case, which involved an attempt by New Hampshire to alter the charter granted to Dartmouth by King George III in 1769. The state had sought not to destroy the college but to change it from a private to a public institution, yet Marshall held that to do so would violate the contract clause. In the light of this decision, corporations licensed by the states seemed immune against later attempts to regulate their activities, although, of course, restrictions imposed at the time of the chartering were not affected. As a result, states began to spell out the limitations of corporate charters in greater detail.

Marshall's decisions concerning the division of power between the federal government and the states were even more important. The question of the constitutionality of a national bank, first debated by Hamilton and Jefferson, had not been submitted to the courts during the life of the first Bank of the United States. By the time of the second Bank there were many state banks, and some of them felt that their interests were threatened by the national institution. Responding to pressure from local banks, the Maryland legislature placed an annual tax of $15,000 on "foreign" banks. The Maryland branch of the Bank of the United States refused to pay, whereupon the state brought suit against its cashier, John W. McCulloch. *McCulloch* v. *Maryland* was crucial to the Bank, for five other states had levied taxes on its branches, and others would surely follow suit if the Maryland law were upheld.

Marshall extinguished the threat. The Bank was constitutional, he announced in phrases taken almost verbatim from Hamilton's 1791 memorandum to Washington on the subject; its legality was implied in many of the powers specifically granted to Congress. Full "discretion" must be allowed Congress in deciding exactly how its powers "are to be carried into execution." Since the Bank was legal, the Maryland tax was unconstitutional. Marshall found a "plain repugnance" in the thought of "conferring on one government a power to control the constitutional measures of another." He put this idea in the simplest possible language: "The power to tax involves the power to destroy . . . the power to destroy may defeat and render useless the power to create." The long-range significance of the decision lay in its strengthening of the implied powers of Congress and its confirmation of the Hamiltonian or "loose" interpretation of the Constitution. By establishing the legality of the Bank, it also aided the growth of the economy.

In 1824 Marshall handed down an important decision involving the regulation of interstate commerce. This was the "steamboat case," *Gibbons* v. *Ogden.* In 1815 Aaron Ogden, former United States senator and governor of New Jersey, had purchased the right to operate a ferry between Elizabeth Point, New Jersey, and New York City from Robert Fulton's backer, Robert R. Livingston, who held a New York monopoly of steamboat navigation on the Hudson. When Thomas Gibbons, who held a federal coasting license, set up a competing line, Ogden sued him. Ogden argued in effect that Gibbons could operate his boat (whose captain was Cornelius Vanderbilt, later a famous railroad magnate) on the New Jersey side of the Hudson but had no right to cross into New York waters. After complicated litigation in the lower courts, the case reached the Supreme Court on appeal. Marshall decided in favor of Gibbons, effectively destroying the New York monopoly. A state can regulate commerce which begins and ends in its own territory but not when the transaction involves crossing a state line; then the national authority takes precedence. "The act of Congress," he said, "is supreme; and the law of the state . . . must yield to it."

This decision threw open the interstate steamboat business to all comers, and since an adequate 100-ton vessel could be built for as little as $7,000, dozens of small operators were soon engaged in it. Their competition tended to keep rates low and service efficient, to the great advantage of the country. More important in the long run was the fact that in order to include the ferry business within the federal government's power to regulate interstate commerce, Marshall had given the word the widest possible meaning. "Commerce, undoubtedly, is traffic, but it is something more,—it is intercourse." By construing the "commerce" clause so broadly, he made it easy for future generations of judges to extend its coverage to include the control of interstate electric power lines and even radio and television transmission.

Many of Marshall's decisions aided the economic development of the country in specific ways, but his chief contribution lay in his broadly national view of economic affairs. When he tried consciously to favor business by making contracts inviolable, his influence was important but limited—and, as it worked out, impermanent. In the steamboat case and in *McCulloch* v. *Maryland,* where he was really deciding between rival property interests, his work was more truly judicial in spirit and far more lasting. In such matters his nationalism enabled him to add form and substance to Hamilton's vision of the economic future of the United States.

Marshall and his colleagues firmly established the principle of judicial limitation on the power of legislatures and made the Supreme Court a vital part of the American system of government. In an age plagued by narrow sectional jealousies, Marshall's contribution was of immense influence and significance, and upon it rests his claim to greatness.

John Marshall died in 1835. Two years later, in the Charles River Bridge case, the court handed down another decision that aided economic development. The state of Massachusetts had built a bridge across the Charles River between Boston and Cambridge that drew traffic from an older, privately owned toll bridge nearby. Since no tolls were collected from users of the state bridge after construction costs were recovered, owners of the older bridge sued for damages on the ground that the free bridge made the stock in their company worthless. They argued that in building the bridge, Massachusetts had violated the contract clause of the Constitution.

The Court, however, now speaking through the new Chief Justice, Roger B. Taney, decided otherwise. The state had a right to place "the comfort and convenience" of the whole community over that of a particular company, Taney declared. "Improvements" that add to public "wealth and property" take precedence. How John Marshall would have voted in this case, in which he would have had to choose between his Dartmouth College and steamboat case arguments, will never be known. But like most of the decisions of the Court that were made while Marshall was Chief Justice, the Charles River Bridge case advanced the interests of those who favored economic development. Whether they were pursuing political advantage or economic, the Americans of the early 19th century seemed committed to a policy of compromise and accommodation.

SUPPLEMENTARY READING

Titles marked with an asterisk have been published in paperback.

Two splendid works by George Dangerfield provide the best introduction to the Era of Good Feelings: **The Era of Good Feelings*** (1952) and **The Awakening of American Nationalism*** (1965). The best biography of Monroe is Harry Ammon, **James Monroe: The Quest for National Identity** (1971). Shaw Livermore, Jr., **The Twilight of Federalism** (1962), is also useful.

On the tariff, see F. W. Taussig, **The Tariff History of the United States*** (1923); on banking, Bray Hammond, **Banks and Politics in America from the Revolution to the Civil War*** (1957); on land policy, R. M. Robbins, **Our Landed Heritage*** (1942).

The outstanding study of the career of Adams is S. F. Bemis, **John Quincy Adams** (1949–1956). R. N. Current, **Daniel Webster and the Rise of National Conservatism*** (1955), is an excellent brief biography. M. G. Baxter, **One and Indispensable: Daniel Webster and the Union** (1984), is more detailed. Van Buren's early career is treated in John Nivens, **Martin Van Buren** (1983), Jackson's in R. V. Remini's **Andrew Jackson and the Course of American Empire, 1767–1821** (1977). Van Buren's **Autobiography** (1920), edited by J. C. Fitzpatrick, is candid and amusing.

For Crawford, see C. C. Mooney, **William H. Crawford** (1974). On Calhoun, the standard study of his early career is C. M. Wiltse, **John C. Calhoun: Nationalist** (1949), an excellent work. Richard Hofstadter, **The American Political Tradition*** (1948), contains a thought-provoking essay on Calhoun; see also R. N. Current, **John C. Calhoun*** (1963), and G. M. Capers, **John C. Calhoun, Opportunist*** (1960). The best biography of Clay is G. G. Van Deusen, **The Life of Henry Clay*** (1937), while Clement Eaton, **Henry Clay and the Art of American Politics*** (1957), is a stimulating and judicious brief account. W. N. Chambers, **Old Bullion Benton: Senator from the New West** (1956), is first-rate. Freeman Cleaves, **Old Tippecanoe** (1939), covers the life of William Henry Harrison adequately.

On the Missouri Compromise, see Glover Moore, **The Missouri Controversy*** (1953). The election of

1824 can be studied in the biographies of Adams, Clay, and Calhoun mentioned above and in Dangerfield's volumes. See also Shaw Livermore, **The Twilight of Federalism** (1962). On the presidency of John Quincy Adams, in addition to the Bemis biography, see Henry Adams, **The Degradation of the Democratic Dogma** (1919). R. V. Remini, **The Election of Andrew Jackson*** (1964), provides an excellent survey of the election of 1828; Remini's **Andrew Jackson and the Course of American Empire** presents new evidence on Jackson's marriage.

On the forces changing the American economy and stimulating the development of industry, see Stuart Bruchey, **The Roots of American Economic Growth*** (1965), and D. C. North, **The Economic Growth of the United States*** (1961). G. R. Taylor, **The Transportation Revolution*** (1951), a book far broader in scope than its title indicates, also discusses this subject intelligently. On government aid to business, see Oscar and M. F. Handlin, **Commonwealth: A Study of the Role of Government in the American Economy** (1947), Louis Hartz, **Economic Policy and Democratic Thought: Pennsylvania*** (1948), and E. M. Dodd, **American Business Corporations Until 1860** (1954). F. J. Turner, **Rise of the New West*** (1906), is still the best volume on the expansion of the west during the Era of Good Feelings, but see also the appropriate chapters of R. A. Billington, **Westward Expansion** (1967).

On the industrial revolution in America, see A. D. Chandler, Jr., **The Visible Hand: The Managerial Revolution in American Business** (1977), B. M. Tucker, **Samuel Slater and the Origins of the American Textile Industry** (1984), V. S. Clark, **History of Manufactures in the United States** (1929), T. C. Cochran and William Miller, **The Age of Enterprise*** (1942), Roger Burlingame, **March of the Iron Men*** (1938), and C. F. Ware, **The Early New England Cotton Manufacture** (1931).

On the "Lowell girls," see Thomas Dublin, **Women at Work** (1977). B. M. Wertheimer, **We Were There: The Story of Working Women in America** (1977), is a more general history. See also R. A. Mohl, **Poverty in New York** (1971), and A. F. C. Wallace, **Rockdale: The Growth of an American Village** (1978).

On the spread of cotton cultivation in the south, see L. C. Gray, **History of Agriculture in the Southern United States** (1933). There are two excellent biographies of Eli Whitney: Allan Nevins and Jeannette Mirsky, **The World of Eli Whitney*** (1952), and C. McL. Green, **Eli Whitney and the Birth of American Technology*** (1956). W. D. Jordan, **White over Black*** (1968), and L. F. Litwack, **North of Slavery: The Negro in the Free States*** (1961), discuss the fate of blacks. On the colonization movement, see P. J. Staudenraus, **The African Colonization Movement** (1961).

Taylor's **Transportation Revolution** is the best introduction to the changes in transportation that took place. P. D. Jordan, **The National Road** (1948), is useful, as are L. D. Baldwin, **The Keelboat Age on Western Waters** (1941), and Walter Havighurst, **Voice on the River: The Story of the Mississippi Waterways** (1964). George Dangerfield, **Chancellor Robert R. Livingston of New York** (1960), contains an excellent account of the planning and operation of the ***Clermont***, while L. C. Hunter, **Steamboats on the Western Rivers** (1949), is good on later developments. No student should miss Mark Twain, **Life on the Mississippi*** (1883).

On the Erie Canal, see R. E. Shaw, **Erie Water West: A History of the Erie Canal** (1966), Nathan Miller, **The Enterprise of a Free People** (1962), and R. G. Albion, **The Rise of New York Port** (1939). Albion's **Square-Riggers on Schedule** (1938) is also good on the growth of New York City, while Blake McKelvey, **Rochester: The Water-Power City** (1945), discusses the impact of the Erie on that community. Carter Goodrich (ed.), **Canals and American Economic Development** (1961), describes the role of government aid in canal construction authoritatively.

On Marshall, see F. N. Stites, **John Marshall: Defender of the Constitution** (1981). The most important decisions of the Marshall court in this period are discussed in J. A. Garraty (ed.), **Quarrels That Have Shaped the Constitution*** (1964), and R. K. Newmyer, **The Supreme Court under Marshall and Taney*** (1968).

9
Jacksonian Democracy

The best government rests on the [whole] people and not on the few, on persons and not on property, on the free development of public opinion and not on authority, . . . the munificent Author of our being has conferred the gifts of mind upon every member of the human race without distinction of outward circumstance. George Bancroft, The Office of the People, *1842*

At 11 A.M. on March 4, 1829, a bright sunny day, Andrew Jackson, hatless and dressed severely in black, left his quarters at Gadsby's Hotel. Accompanied by a few close associates, he walked up Pennsylvania Avenue to the Capitol. At a few minutes after noon he emerged on the East Portico with the justices of the Supreme Court and other dignitaries. Before a throng of more than 15,000 people he delivered an almost inaudible and thoroughly commonplace inaugural address and then took the presidential oath. The first man to congratulate him was Chief Justice Marshall, who had administered the oath. The second was "Honest George" Kremer, a Pennsylvania congressman best known for the leopardskin coat that he affected, who led the cheering crowd that brushed past the barricade and scrambled up the Capitol steps to wring the new president's hand.

Jackson shouldered his way through the crush, mounted a splendid white horse, and rode off to the White House. A reception had been announced, to which "the officially and socially eligible as defined by precedent" had been invited. The day was unseasonably warm after a hard winter, and the streets of Washington were muddy. As Jackson rode down Pennsylvania Avenue, the crowds that had turned out to see the Hero of New Orleans followed—on horseback, in rickety wagons, and on foot. Nothing could keep them out of the executive mansion, and the result was chaos. Long tables laden with cakes, ice cream, and orange punch had been set up in the East Room, but these scarcely deflected the well-wishers. Jackson was pressed back helplessly as men tracked mud across valuable rugs and clambered up on delicate chairs to catch a glimpse of him. The White House shook with their shouts. Glassware splintered, furniture was overturned, women fainted.

Jackson was a thin old man despite his toughness, and soon he was in danger. Fortunately, friends formed a cordon and managed to extricate him through a rear door. The new president spent his first night in office at Gadsby's.

Only a generation earlier Jefferson had felt obliged to introduce pell-mell to encourage informality in the White House. Now a man whom John Quincy Adams called "a barbarian" held Jefferson's office, and, as one Supreme Court justice complained, "The reign of King 'Mob' seemed triumphant."

The changes that produced this state of affairs had come quickly. They could scarcely have been imagined in 1825 when John Quincy Adams took over the White House. But Adams was not well equipped either to lead King Mob or to hold it in check. In any case, the battle to succeed Adams began almost on the day of his selection by the House of Representatives. Jackson quickly established himself as the candidate of what can best be characterized as the "opposition." He felt that he, the man with the largest vote, had been cheated of the presidency in 1824 by "the corrupt bargain" that he believed Adams had made with Henry Clay, promising to name him secretary of state in exchange for the votes Clay controlled in the House, votes that made Adams president. Jackson sought vindication. Relying heavily on his military reputation and on Adams's talent for making enemies, Jackson avoided taking a stand on issues as much as possible. Senator Benton of Missouri urged him to shrink from any "particular confession" on internal improvements and on other questions where his views might displease one or another political faction. The political situation thus became monumentally confused, one side unable to marshal support for its policies, the other unwilling to adopt policies for fear of losing support. The tariff question added to the confusion. High duties, so repulsive to the export-conscious South, attracted more and more favor in the North and West. Besides manufacturers, lead miners in Missouri, hemp raisers in Kentucky, woolgrowers in New York, and many other interests demanded protection against foreign competition. The lack of party discipline provided an ideal climate for "logrolling" in Congress. Legislators who like Senator Benton opposed high tariffs in principle found themselves under constant pressure from their constituents to raise the duties on products of local importance; to satisfy these demands, they traded votes with other congressmen similarly situated. In this way massive "support" for protection was generated.

In 1828 a new tariff was hammered into shape by the House Committee on Manufactures. Northern and western agricultural interests were in command; they wrote into the bill extremely high duties on raw wool, hemp, flax, fur, and liquor. New England manufacturers protested vociferously, for although their products were protected, the proposed law would increase the cost of their raw materials. This gave southerners, now hopelessly in the minority on the tariff question, a chance to block the bill. When the New Englanders proposed amendments lowering the duties on raw materials, the southerners voted nay, hoping to force them to reject the measure on the final vote. This desperate strategy failed. New England had by this time committed its future to manufacturing, a change signalized by the somersault of Webster, who, ever responsive to local pressures, now voted for protection. After winning some minor concessions in the Senate, largely through the intervention of Van Buren, enough New Englanders accepted the so-called Tariff of Abominations to assure its passage.

Vice-President Calhoun, who had watched the debate from the vantage point of his post as president of the Senate, now came to a great turning point in his career. He had thrown in his lot with Jackson, whose running mate he was to be in the coming election, and had been assured that the Jacksonians would oppose the bill. Yet northern Jacksonians had been responsible for drafting and passing it. The new tariff would impoverish the South, he believed. He warned Jackson that relief must soon be provided or the Union would be shaken to its foundations. Then he returned to his South Carolina plantation and wrote an essay, the *South Carolina Exposition and Protest,* repudiating the nationalist philosophy he had previously championed.

The South Carolina legislature released this document to the country in December 1828, along with eight resolutions denouncing the protective tariff as unfair and unconstitutional. The theorist Calhoun, however, was not content with outlining the case against the tariff. His *Exposition* provided an ingenious defense of the right of the people of a state to reject a law of Congress. Starting with John Locke's revered concept of government as a contractual relationship, he argued that since the states had created the Union, logic dictated that they be the final arbiters of the meaning of the Constitution which was its framework. If a special state convention, representing the sovereignty of the people, decided that an act of Congress violated the Constitutiton, it could interpose its authority and "nullify" the law within its boundaries. Calhoun did not seek to implement this theory in 1828, for he hoped that the next administration would lower the tariff and make nullification unnecessary.

The Election of 1828

The new president was to be Jackson, who defeated Adams handily, though by no means overwhelmingly, in a contest disgraced by character assassination and lies of the worst sort on both sides. Administration supporters denounced Jackson as a bloodthirsty military tyrant, a drunkard, and a gambler. His wife Rachel, ailing and shy, was dragged into the campaign, her good name heartlessly besmirched. Previously married to a cruel, unbalanced man named Lewis Robards, she had begun living with Jackson (whether a marraige ceremony had been performed is to this day uncertain) before her divorce from Robards had been legally completed. When this fact came to light, she and Jackson had to remarry. Seizing upon this incident, an Adams pamphleteer wrote: "Ought a convicted adulteress and her paramour husband be placed in the highest offices of this free and christian land?"

Furious, the Jacksonians (now calling themselves Democrats) replied in kind. They charged that Adams had lived with his wife before marriage and that, while American minister to Russia, he had supplied a beautiful American virgin for the delectation of the czar. Discovering that the president had purchased a chess set and a billiard table for the White House, they accused him of squandering public money on gambling devices. They translated his long and distinguished public service into the statistic that he had received over the years a sum equal to $16 for every day of his life in government pay. The great questions of the day were largely ignored.

All this was inexcusable, and both sides must share the blame. When inauguration day arrived, Adams refused to attend the ceremonies because Jackson had failed to pay the traditional preinaugural courtesy call on him at the White House, but the Old Puritan may have been equally if unconsciously motivated by shame at tactics he had countenanced during the campaign. In any case, deep personal feelings were uppermost in everyone's mind at the formal changing of the guard. The real issues, however, remained. Andrew Jackson would now have to deal with them.

The Jacksonian Appeal

Some historians claim that Andrew Jackson was not a democrat at all and anything but a consistent friend of the weak and underprivileged. They point out that he was a wealthy land speculator and the owner of a fine Tennessee plantation, the Hermitage, and of many slaves. Before becoming president he had opposed cheap-money schemes, favored the big speculators, and pressed lawsuits against more than a hundred individuals who owed him money. Although his supporters liked to cast him as the political heir of Jefferson, he was in many ways like the conservative Washington: a soldier first, an inveterate speculator in western lands, a man with few intellectual interests and only sketchily educated.

Nor was Jackson quite the roughhewn frontier character he sometimes seemed. He could not spell (again, like Washington); he possessed the unsavory habits of the tobacco chewer; and he had a violent temper. But his manners and life-style were those of a southern planter. As president he spent money lavishly, entertaining guests at great feasts in halls bedecked with flowers and glowing in the light of hundreds of candles. His judgment was intuitive yet usually sound; his reputation for unbridled irascibility was not really deserved. His frequent rages were often feigned—designed to accomplish some carefully thought out purpose. "He would sometimes extemporize a fit of passion in order to overwhelm an adversary," one contemporary noted, "but his self-command was always perfect." Once, after scattering a delegation of protesters with an exhibition of Jovian wrath, he turned to an observer and said impishly, "They thought I was mad."

A figurehead of Andrew Jackson carved by Laban S. Beecher for the frigate Constitution. *Soon after it was mounted on the ship, an anti-Jackson agitator sawed off the head just below the nose! (It was later neatly mended.) The figurehead is almost 12 feet tall.*

It is of small importance to anyone interested in Jacksonian Democracy to know exactly how "democratic" Jackson was, or how sincere his interest in the welfare of the "common man." Whatever his personal convictions, he stood as the symbol for a movement supported by a new, democratically oriented generation that had grown up under the spell of the American and French revolutions. That he was both a great hero and in many ways a very ordinary man helps explain his mass appeal. He had defeated a mighty British army and killed hosts of Indians, but he acted on hunches and not always consistently, shouted and pounded his fist when angry, put loyalty to old comrades above efficiency in making appointments, distrusted "aristocrats" and all special privilege. Perhaps he was rich, perhaps conservative, but he was a man of the people, born in a frontier cabin, familiar with the problems of the average citizen.

Jackson epitomized many American ideals. He was intensely patriotic, generous to a fault, natural and democratic in manner (at home alike in the forest and in the ballroom of a fine mansion). He admired good horseflesh and beautiful women, yet no sterner moralist ever lived; he was a fighter, a relentless foe, but a gentleman in the best American sense. That some special providence watched over him (as over the United States) appeared beyond argument to those who had followed his career. He seemed, in short, both an average and an ideal American, one the people could identify with and still revere.

For these reasons Jackson drew support from every section and every social class: western farmers and souther planters, urban workers and bankers and merchants. In this sense he was profoundly democratic—and in the sense, too, that whatever his position on public issues, he believed in equality of opportunity, distrusted entrenched status of every sort, and rejected no free American because of humble origins or inadequate education.

"Democratizing" Politics

Having been taught by Jefferson that all men are created equal, the Americans of Jackson's day found it easy to believe that every man was as good as his neighbor. The difference between Jeffersonian Democracy and the Jackson variety was one of attitude rather than practice. Jefferson had believed that ordinary citizens could be educated to determine right. Jackson insisted that they knew what was right by instinct. Jefferson's pell-mell encouraged the average citizen to hold up his head; by the time of Jackson, the "common man" gloried in ordinariness and made mediocrity a virtue. The slightest hint of distinctiveness or servility became suspect. That President Washington required his footmen to wear uniforms was taken as a matter of course in the 1790s, but the British minister in Jackson's day found it next to impossible to find American servants willing to don his splendid livery. The word "servant" itself fell out of fashion, replaced by the egalitarian "help."

The Founding Fathers had not foreseen all the implications of political democracy for a society like that which existed in the United States. They believed that the ordinary man should have political power in order to protect himself against the superior man, but they assumed that the latter would always lead. The people would naturally choose the best men to manage public affairs. In Washington's day and even in Jefferson's this was generally the case, but the inexorable logic of democracy gradually produced a change. The new western states, unfettered by systems created in a less democratic age, drew up constitutions that eliminated property qualifications for voting and holding office; the eastern states revised their own frames of government to accomplish the same purpose. More public offices were made elective rather than appointive.

Even the presidency, designed to be removed from direct public control by the electoral college, felt the impact of the new thinking. By Jackson's day only two states, Delaware and South Carolina, still provided for the choice of presidential electors by the legislature; in all others they were selected by popular vote. The system of permitting the congressional caucus to name the candidates for the presidency came to an end before 1828. Jackson and Adams were put forward by state legislatures, and soon the still more democratic system of nomination by national party conventions was adopted.

Certain social changes reflected a new way of looking at political affairs. The final disestablishment of churches reveals a dislike of special privilege. The beginnings of the free-school movement, the earliest glimmerings of interest in adult education, and the slow spread of secondary education all bespeak a concern for improving the knowledge and judgment of the ordinary citizen. The rapid increase in the number of newspapers, their declining prices (the first successful penny papers appeared in the 1830s), and their ever-greater concentration on political affairs indicate that an effort was being made to bring political news to the common man's attention.

All these changes emphasized the idea that every citizen was equally important and the conviction that all should participate actively in government. Officeholders began to stress the fact that they were *representatives* as well as leaders and to appeal more frankly and much more intensively for votes. The public responded with a surge of interest. At each succeeding presidential election, a larger percentage of the population went to the polls. Roughly 300,000 ballots were cast in 1824, 1.1 million four years later.

As voting became more important, so did party politics, for it took organized effort to run the campaigns and get out the vote. Parties became powerful institutions; as a result, they attracted voters' loyalties powerfully. This development took place first at the state level and at different times in differ-

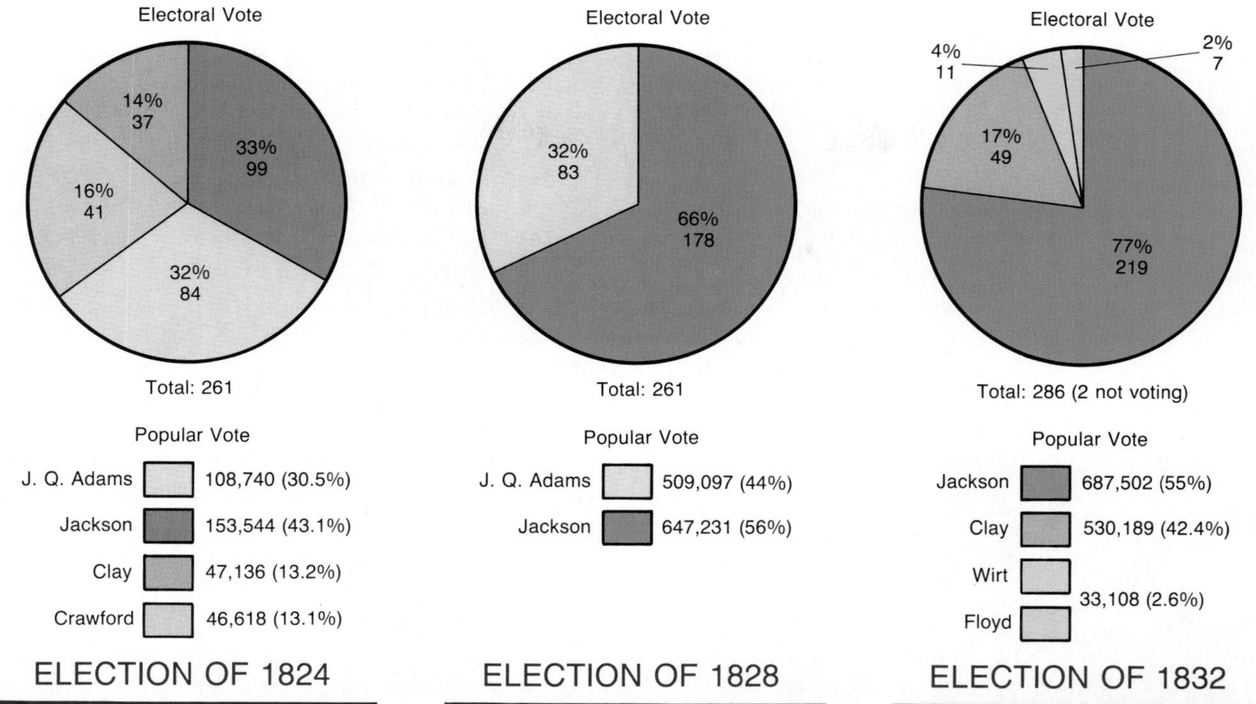

ent states. According to Richard P. McCormick, whose book *The Second American Party System* describes the process, the 1828 election stimulated party formation because it pitted two well-known men against each other, forcing local leaders to make a choice and then convince local voters to accept their judgment. This was especially true in states where neither Adams nor Jackson had a preponderance. Thus the new system established itself much faster in New York and Pennsylvania than in New England, where Adams was strong, or Tennessee, where the "native son" Jackson had overwhelming support.

The Spoils System

Like most institutions, the parties created bureaucracies to keep them running smoothly. Devoted party workers were rewarded with political office when their efforts were successful. "To the victors belong the spoils," said the New York politician William L. Marcy, and the image, drawn from war and piracy, was appropriate. Although the vigorous wooing of voters constituted a recognition of their importance and commitment to keeping them informed, campaigning—another military term—frequently degenerated into demagoguery. The most effective way to attract the average voter, politicians soon decided, was by flattery.

Jackson took office with the firm intention of punishing the "vile wretches" who had attacked him so viciously during the campaign. (Rachel Jackson died shortly after the election, and her devoted husband was convinced that the indignities heaped upon her by Adams partisans had speeded her decline.) The concept of political office as a reward for victory seemed to justify a housecleaning in Washington. Henry Clay captured the fears of anti-Jackson government workers. "Among the official corps here there is the greatest solicitude and apprehension," he said. "The members of it feel something like the inhabitants of Cairo when the plague breaks out; no one knows who is next to encounter the stroke of death."

Eager for "the spoils," an army of politicians invaded Washington. "I am ashamed of myself," one such character confessed when he met a friend on the street. "I feel as if every man I meet knew what I came for." "Don't distress yourself," his friend replied, "for every man you meet is on the same business." There was nothing especially inno-

Jackson's spoils-system policies were repeatedly attacked by opposition cartoonists. "Office Hunters for the Year 1834," for example, portrays the president as a demon dangling the spoils of his office, including banquets, money, weapons, appointments, and—for some obscure reason—millinery, above his greedy supporters.

vative about this invasion, for the principle of filling offices with one's partisans was almost as old as the republic. However, the long lapse of time since the last real political shift, and the recent untypical example of John Quincy Adams, who rarely removed or appointed anyone for political reasons, made Jackson's policy appear revolutionary. His removals were not entirely unjustified, for many government workers had grown senile and others corrupt. A number of officials were found to be short in their accounts; a few were hopeless drunks. Jackson was determined to root out the thieves. Even Adams admitted that some of those Jackson dismissed deserved their fate.

Aside from going along with the spoils system and eliminating crooks and incompetents, Jackson advanced another reason for turning experienced government employees out of their jobs—the principle of rotation. "No man has any more intrinsic right to official station than another," he said. Those who hold government jobs for a long time "are apt to acquire a habit of looking with indifference upon the public interests and of tolerating conduct from which an unpracticed man would revolt." By "rotating" jobholders periodically, more citizens could participate in the tasks of government, an obvious advantage in a democracy. The danger of creating an entrenched bureaucracy would also be eliminated. The problem was that the constant replacing of trained workers by novices was not likely to increase the efficiency of the government. Jackson's response to this argument was typical: "The duties of all public officers are . . . so plain and simple that men of intelligence may readily qualify themselves for their performance."

Contempt for expert knowledge and the belief that ordinary Americans can do anything they set their minds to became fundamental tenets of Jacksonian Democracy. To apply them to present-day government would be to court disaster, but in the early 19th century it was not so preposterous, for the role that government played in American life was simple and nontechnical.

Furthermore, Jackson did not practice what he preached. By and large his appointees were anything but "common men." A majority came from the same social and intellectual elite as those they replaced. As the historian Sidney H. Aronson pointed out, "circumstances made it difficult for him to locate such common men in the crowd." He did not try to rotate civil servants in the War and Navy departments, where to do so might have been harmful. In general he left pretty much alone what a modern administrator would call "middle management," the backbone of every organization. During his two terms he dismissed less than 20 percent of the 10,000-odd government workers.

Nevertheless, the spoilsmen roamed the capital in force during the spring of 1829, seeking, as the forthright Jackson said, "a tit to suck the treasury pap." Their philosophy was well summarized by a New Yorker: "No d----d rascal who made use of his office . . . for the purpose of keeping Mr. Adams in, and Genl. Jackson out of power is entitled to the least lenity or mercy. . . . Whether or not I shall get anything in the general scramble for plunder, remains to be proven, but I rather *guess* I shall."

President of All the People

President Jackson was not cynical about the spoils system. As a strong man who intuitively sought to increase his authority, the idea of making government workers dependent on him made excellent sense. His opponents had pictured him as a simple soldier fronting for a rapacious band of politicians, but he soon proved he would exercise his authority directly. Except for Martin Van Buren, the secretary of state, his Cabinet was not distinguished, and he did not rely on it for advice. He turned instead to an informal "Kitchen Cabinet," which consisted of the influential Van Buren and a few close friends. But these men were advisers, not directors; Jackson was clearly master of his own administration.

More than any earlier president, he conceived of himself as the direct representative of all the people and therefore the embodiment of national power. From Washington to John Quincy Adams, his predecessors together had vetoed only 9 bills, always on the ground that the measures were unconstitutional. Jackson vetoed 12, some simply because he thought the legislation inexpedient. He was the first president to employ the "pocket veto," the device of killing a bill at the tag end of a session of Congress by refusing either to sign or veto it. Yet he had no ambition to expand the scope of federal authority at the expense of the states. Furthermore, he was a poor administrator, given to penny-pinching and lacking in imagination. His strong prejudices and his contempt for expert advice, even in fields such as banking where his ignorance was almost total, did him no credit and the country considerable harm.

Jackson's great success (not merely his popularity) was primarily the result of his personality. A shrewd French observer, Michel Chevalier, after commenting on "his chivalric character, his lofty integrity, and his ardent patriotism," pointed out what was probably the central element in Jackson's appeal. "His tactics in politics, as well as in war," Chevalier wrote in 1824, "is to throw himself forward with the cry of *Comrades, follow me!*" Sometimes he might be wrong, but always he was a leader.

Sectional Tensions Revived

In office Jackson had to say something about western lands, the tariff, and other issues. He tried to steer a moderate course, urging a slight reduction of the tariff and "constitutional" internal improvements. He suggested that once the rapidly disappearing federal debt had been paid off, the surplus revenues of the government might be "distributed" among the states.

Even these cautious proposals caused conflict, so complex were the interrelations of sectional disputes. If the federal government turned its ex-

"Liberty and *Union, now and forever, one and inseparable." With these rousing words, Daniel Webster ended his impassioned speech refuting the states' rights arguments of Robert Hayne. Vice-President Calhoun listens intently, seated at his desk as president of the Senate.*

pected surplus over to the states, it could not afford to reduce the price of public land without going into the red. This disturbed some westerners, notably Senator Thomas Hart Benton of Missouri. Western anxiety in turn suggested to southern opponents of the protective tariff an alliance of South and West. The southerners argued that a tariff levied only to raise revenue would increase foreign imports, bring more money into the Treasury, and thus make it possible to reduce the price of public land.

The question came up in the Senate in December 1829, when an obscure Connecticut senator, Samuel A. Foot, suggested restricting the sale of government land. Benton promptly denounced the proposal as a plot concocted by eastern manufacturers to check the westward migration of their workers. On January 19, 1830, Senator Robert Y. Hayne of South Carolina, a spokesman for Vice-President Calhoun, supported Benton vigorously, suggesting an alliance of South and West based on cheap land and low tariffs. Daniel Webster then rose to the defense of northeastern interests, cleverly goading Hayne by accusing South Carolina of advocating disunionist policies. Responding to this attack, the South Carolinian, a glib speaker but a rather imprecise thinker, launched into an impassioned exposition of the states' rights doctrine.

Webster then took the floor again and for two days, before galleries packed with the elite of Washington society, cut Hayne's argument to shreds. The Constitution was a compact of the American people, not merely of the states, he insisted, the Union perpetual and indissoluble. Webster made the states' rights position appear close to treason; his "second reply to Hayne" effectively prevented the formation of a West-South alliance.

Jackson Versus Calhoun

The Webster-Hayne debate revived discussion of the idea of nullification. Although southern-born, Jackson had devoted too much of his life to fighting for the entire United States to countenance disunion. Therefore, when the states' rights faction invited him to a dinner to celebrate the anniversary of Jefferson's birth, he came prepared. The evening reverberated with speeches and toasts of a states' rights tenor, but when the president was called upon to volunteer a toast, he raised his glass, fixed his eyes grimly on John C. Calhoun, and said: "Our *Federal* Union: It must be preserved!" Calhoun took up the challenge at once. "The Union," he retorted, "next to our liberty, most dear!"

It is difficult to measure the importance of the animosity between Jackson and Calhoun in the crisis to which this clash was a prelude. Calhoun wanted very much to be president. He had failed to inherit the office from John Quincy Adams and had accepted the vice-presidency again under Jackson in hopes of succeeding him at the end of one term, if not sooner, for Jackson's health was known to be frail. Yet Old Hickory showed no sign of passing on or retiring. Jackson also seemed to place special confidence in the shrewd Van Buren, who, as secretary of state, also had claim to the succession.

A silly social fracas in which Calhoun's wife appeared to take the lead in the systematic snubbing of Peggy Eaton, wife of the secretary of war, had estranged Jackson and Calhoun. (Peggy was supposed to have had an affair with Eaton while she was still married to another man, and Jackson, undoubtedly sympathetic because of the attacks he and Rachel had endured, stoutly defended her good name.) Then, shortly after the Jefferson Day dinner, Jackson discovered that in 1818, when he invaded Florida (see page 222), Calhoun, then secretary of war, had recommended to President Monroe that Jackson be summoned before a court of inquiry and charged with disobeying orders. Since Calhoun had repeatedly led Jackson to believe that he had supported him at the time, the revelation convinced the president that Calhoun was not a man of honor.

The personal difficulties are worth stressing because Jackson and Calhoun were not far apart ideologically except on the ultimate issue of the right of a state to overrule federal authority. Jackson was a strong president, but he did not believe that the area of national power was large or that it should be expanded. His interests in government economy, in the distribution of federal surpluses to the states, and in interpreting the powers of Congress narrowly were all similar to Calhoun's. Like most westerners, he favored internal improvements, but he preferred that local projects be left to the states. In 1830 he vetoed a bill providing aid for the construction of the Maysville Road because the route was wholly within Kentucky. There were political reasons for this veto, which was a slap at Kentucky's hero, Henry Clay, but it could not fail to please Calhoun.

Indian Removals

The president also took a states' rights position in the controversy that arose between the Cherokee Indians and Georgia. While he shared many of the typical westerner's feelings about Indians, Jackson insisted that he did not hate them. He subscribed to the theory, advanced by Jefferson, that Indians were "savage" because they roamed wild in a trackless wilderness. The "original inhabitants of our forests" were "incapable of self-government," Jackson claimed, ignoring the fact that they had governed themselves without trouble before the whites arrived. If they settled on small farms they would become "civilized," and all would be well between them and the whites.

Most Indians preferred to maintain their tribal ways, so Jackson pursued a policy of "removing" them from the path of western settlement. This policy seems heartless to modern critics, but since few Indians were willing to adopt the white way of life, most contemporary whites considered removal the only humane solution if the nation was to continue to expand. Jackson was well aware that removal would impose hardships on what he called "this unhappy race—the original dwellers in our land." He insisted that the Indians receive fair prices for their lands and that the government bear the expense of resettling them. He believed that moving them beyond the Mississippi would protect them from the "degradation and destruction to

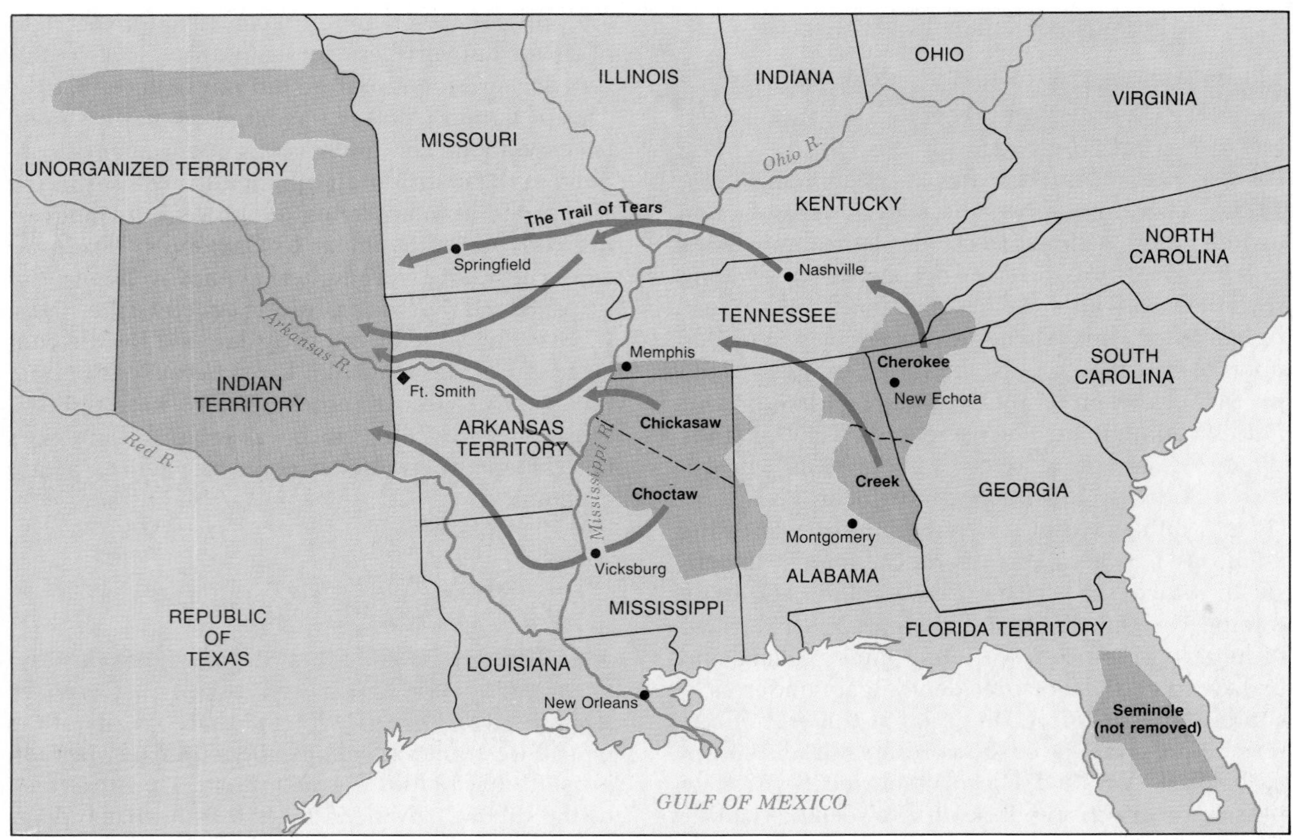

INDIAN REMOVALS

which they were rapidly hastening . . . in the States."

Many tribes resigned themselves to removal without argument. Between 1831 and 1833, 15,000 Choctaws migrated from their lands in Mississippi to the region west of Arkansas Territory.

In *Democracy in America,* written at this time, the Frenchman Alexis de Tocqueville commented on "the frightful sufferings that attend these forced migrations," and he added sadly that the migrants "have no longer a country, and soon will not be a people." In the book Tocqueville penned a vivid description of a group of Choctaws crossing the Mississippi River at Memphis in the dead of winter.

> The cold was unusually severe; the snow had frozen hard upon the ground, and the river was drifting huge masses of ice. The Indians had their families with them, and they brought in their train the wounded and the sick, with children newly born and old men upon the verge of death. They possessed neither tents nor wagons, but only their arms and some provisions. I saw them embark to pass the mighty river, and never will that solemn spectacle fade from my remembrance. No cry, no sob, was heard among the assembled crowd; all were silent.

Tocqueville was particularly moved by the sight of an old woman whom he described in a letter to his mother. She was "naked save for a covering which left visible, at a thousand places, the most emaciated figure imaginable. . . . To leave one's country at that age to seek one's fortune in a foreign land, what misery!" "In the whole scene," he went on, "there was an air of ruin and destruction, something which betrayed a final and irrevocable adieu; one couldn't watch without feeling one's heart wrung."

A few tribes, such as Black Hawk's Sac and Fox in Illinois and Osceola's Seminoles in Florida, re-

In 1832, fighting to retain tribal lands in Illinois, Black Hawk and his followers were attacked by militia. This lithograph by Henry Lewis depicts the Indians' slaughter as they fled across the Mississippi.

sisted being "removed" and were subdued by troops. One Indian nation, the Cherokees, sought to hold on to their lands by adjusting to white ways. They took up farming and cattle raising, developed a written language, drafted a constitution, and tried to establish a state within a state in northwestern Georgia. Several treaties with the United States seemed to establish the legality of their government. But Georgia would not recognize the Cherokee Nation. It passed a law in 1828 declaring all Cherokee laws void and the region part of Georgia.

The Indians challenged this law in the Supreme Court. In *Cherokee Nation* v. *Georgia* (1831) Chief Justice John Marshall refused to hear the case. However, in *Worcester* v. *Georgia* (1832), a case involving two missionaries to the Cherokees who had not procured licenses required by Georgia law, he ruled that the state could not control the Cherokees or their territory. Later, when a Cherokee named Corn Tassel, convicted in a Georgia court of the murder of another Indian, appealed on the ground that the crime had taken place in Cherokee territory, Marshall declared the Georgia action unconstitutional on the same ground.

Jackson backed Georgia's position. No independent nation could exist within the United States, he insisted. As for *Worcester* v. *Georgia,* he said: "John Marshall has made his decision. Now let him enforce it." Georgia thereupon hanged poor Corn Tassel. In 1838, after Jackson had left the White House, the United States forced 15,000 Cherokees to leave Georgia for Oklahoma. About 4,000 of them died on the way; the route has been named the Trail of Tears.

Jackson's willingness to allow Georgia to ignore decisions of the Supreme Court persuaded extreme southern states' righters that he would not oppose the doctrine of nullification should it be formally applied to a law of Congress. They deceived themselves egregiously. Jackson did not challenge Georgia because he approved of the state's position. He spoke of "the poor deluded . . . Cherokees" and called William Wirt, the distinguished lawyer who defended their cause, a "truly wicked" man. Jackson was not one to worry about being inconsistent. When South Carolina revived the talk of nullification in 1832, he acted in quite a different manner.

The Nullification Crisis

The proposed alliance of South and West to reduce the tariff and the price of land had not materialized, partly because Webster had discredited the South in the eyes of western patriots and partly because the planters of South Carolina and Georgia, fearing the competition of fertile new cotton lands in Alabama and Mississippi, opposed the rapid exploitation of the West almost as vociferously as northern manufacturers did. When a new tariff law was passed in 1832, it lowered duties much less than

This is Charles Lesueur's 1830 study of a Choctaw, one of the southeastern peoples removed to Indian territory in what is now Oklahoma.

the southerners desired. At once talk of nullifying it began to be heard in South Carolina.

In addition to the economic woes of the up-country cotton planters, the great planter-aristocrats of the rice-growing Tidewater, though relatively prosperous, were troubled by northern criticisms of slavery. In the rice region, blacks outnumbered whites by two to one; it was the densest concentration of blacks in the United States. Thousands of these slaves were African-born, brought in during the burst of importations before Congress outlawed the trade in 1808. Controlled usually by overseers of the worst sort, the slaves seemed to the master race like savage beasts straining to rise up against their oppressors. In 1822 the exposure in Charleston of a planned revolt organized by Denmark Vesey, who had bought his freedom with money won in a lottery, had alarmed many whites. News of a far more serious uprising in Virginia led by the slave Nat Turner in 1831, just as the tariff controversy was coming to a head, added to popular concern. Radical South Carolinians saw protective tariffs and agitation against slavery as the two sides of one coin; against both aspects of what appeared to them the tyranny of the majority, nullification seemed the logical defense. Yield on the tariff, editor Henry L. Pinckney of the influential Charleston *Mercury* warned, and "abolition will become the order of the day."

Endless discussions of Calhoun's doctrine after the publication of his *Exposition and Protest* in 1828 had produced much interesting theorizing without clarifying the issue. William H. Freehling, a modern student of the controversy, sums it up aptly: "The theory of nullification was a veritable snarl of contradictions." Admirers of Calhoun praised his "power of analysis & profound philosophical reasonings," but his idea was ingenious rather than profound. Plausible at first glance, it was based on false assumptions: that the Constitution was subject to definitive interpretation; that one party could interpret a compact unilaterally without destroying it; that a minority of the nation could reassume its sovereign independence but that a minority of a state could not.

President Jackson was in this respect Calhoun's exact opposite. The South Carolinian's mental gymnastics he brushed aside; intuitively he realized the central reality: if a state could nullify a law of Congress, the Union could not exist. "Tell . . . the Nullifiers from me that they can talk and write resolutions and print threats to their hearts' content," he warned a South Carolina representative when Congress adjourned in July 1832. "But if one drop of blood be shed there in defiance of the laws of the United States, I will hang the first man of them I can get my hands on to the first tree I can find."

The warning was not taken seriously in South Carolina. In October the state legislature provided for the election of a special convention, which, when it met, contained a solid majority of nullifiers. On November 24, 1832, the convention passed an Ordinance of Nullification, prohibiting the collection of tariff duties in the state after February 1, 1833. The legislature then authorized the raising of an army and appropriated money to supply it with weapons.

Jackson quickly began military preparations of his own, telling friends that he would have 50,000 men ready to move in a little over a month. He also made a statesmanlike effort to end the crisis peaceably. First he suggested to Congress that it lower the tariff further. On December 10 he addressed a "Proclamation to the People of South Carolina." Nullification could only lead to the destruction of the Union, he said. "The laws of the United States must be executed. I have no discretionary power on the subject. . . . Those who told you that you might peaceably prevent their execution deceived you." Old Hickory added sternly: "Disunion by armed force is *treason.* Are you really ready to incur its guilt?"

Attention now shifted to Congress, where administration leaders introduced both a new tariff bill and a Force Bill granting the president additional authority to execute the revenue laws. Calhoun, having resigned as vice-president to accept appointment as senator from South Carolina, led the fight against the Force Bill. Jackson was eager to see the tariff reduced but determined to enforce the law. As the February 1 deadline approached, he claimed that he could raise 200,000 men if needed to suppress resistance. "Union men, fear not," he said. *"The Union will be preserved."*

Jackson's determination sobered the South Carolina radicals. Their appeal for the support of other southern states fell on deaf ears: all rejected the idea of nullification. The unionist minority in South Carolina added to the radicals' difficulties by threatening civil war if federal authority were defied. Calhoun, though a brave man, was alarmed for his own safety, for Jackson had threatened to "hang him as high as Haman" if nullification were attempted. He was suddenly eager to avoid a showdown. Ten days before the deadline, South Carolina postponed nullification pending the outcome of the tariff debate. Then Calhoun joined forces with Henry Clay to push a compromise tariff through Congress. Its passage early in March 1833 reflected the willingness of the North and West to make concessions in the interest of national harmony. Senator Silas Wright of New York, closely affiliated with Van Buren, explained the situation: "People will neither cut throats nor dismember the Union for protection. There is more patriotism and love of country than that left yet. The People will never balance this happy government against ten cents a pound upon a pound of wool."

And so the Union weathered the storm. Having approached the brink of civil war, the nation had drawn hastily back. The South Carolina legislature professed to be satisfied with the new tariff (in fact it made few immediate reductions, providing for a gradual lowering of rates over a ten-year period) and repealed the Nullification Ordinance, saving face by nullifying the Force Bill, which was now a dead letter. But the radical South Carolina planters—not Calhoun, who continued to count himself a nationalist—were becoming convinced that only secession would protect slavery. The nullification fiasco had proved that they could not succeed without the support of other slave states. Thereafter they devoted themselves ceaselessly to obtaining it.

"The Bank . . . I Will Kill It!"

Jackson's strong stand against South Carolina was the more effective because in the fall of 1832 he had been reelected president. The main issue in this election, aside from Jackson's personal popularity, was the president's determination to destroy the second Bank of the United States. In the "Bank War" Jackson won as complete a victory as in his battle with the nullifiers, yet the effects of his triumph were anything but beneficial to the country.

After *McCulloch* v. *Maryland* had presumably established its legality and the conservative Langdon Cheves had gotten it on a sound footing, the Bank of the United States had flourished. In 1823 Cheves was replaced as president by Nicholas Biddle, who managed it brilliantly. A charming and talented Philadelphian, only 37 when he took over the Bank, Biddle was experienced in literature, the law, and diplomacy as well as in finance. At the suggestion of his friend William Clark, he prepared the first scholarly account of the Lewis and Clark expedition, based on the explorers' voluminous journals.

Almost alone in the United States, Biddle realized that his institution could act as a rudimentary central bank, regulating the availability of credit throughout the nation by controlling the lending policies of the state banks. Small banks, possessing limited amounts of gold and silver, sometimes overextended themselves in making large amounts of bank notes available to borrowers in order to earn interest. All this paper money was legally convertible into hard cash on demand, but in the ordinary run of business people seldom bothered to convert their notes so long as they thought the issuing bank was sound. Bank notes passed freely from hand to hand and from bank to bank in every section of the country.

Eventually much of the paper money of the local banks came across the counter of one or another of the 22 branches of the Bank of the United States. By collecting these notes and presenting them for conversion into specie, Biddle could compel the local banks to maintain adequate reserves of gold and silver—in other words, make them hold their lending policies within bounds. "The Bank of the United States," he explained, "has succeeded in keeping in check many institutions which might otherwise have been tempted into extravagant and ruinous excesses." By exerting what he described as "a mild and gentle but efficient control," he compelled local banks to operate upon "a scale . . . commensurate with their real means."

Biddle's policies in the 1820s were good for his own institution, which earned substantial profits, for the state banks, and probably for the country. Pressures on local bankers to make loans were enormous. The nation had an insatiable need for capital, and the general mood of the people was optimistic. Everyone wanted to borrow, and everyone expected values to rise, as *in general* they did. But by making liberal loans to produce merchants, for example, rural bankers indirectly stimulated farmers to expand their output beyond current demand, which eventually led to a decline in prices and an agricultural depression. In every field of economic activity, reckless lending caused inflation and greatly exaggerated the ups and downs of the business cycle. It can be argued, however, that by restricting the lending of state banks, Biddle was slowing the rate of economic growth and that in a predominantly agricultural society an occasional slump was not a large price to pay for rapid economic development.

This miniature of Nicholas Biddle, president of the Bank of the United States, is by Henry Inman, who was considered the nation's finest portraitist in his day.

Thus Biddle's policies acted to stabilize the economy, and many interests, including a substantial percentage of state bankers, supported them. They also roused a great deal of opposition. In part the opposition originated in pure ignorance: distrust of paper money did not disappear, and those who disliked *all* paper saw the Bank as merely the largest (and thus the worst) of many bad institutions. At the other extreme, some bankers chafed under Biddle's restraints because by discouraging them from lending freely, he was limiting their profits. Few financiers realized what Biddle was trying to accomplish. Bray Hammond, whose researches have thrown much light on the history of American banking, estimated that in this period no more than one banker in four understood what was happening when he made a loan. What *was* "sound" banking practice? Honest people disagreed, and many turned against the ideas of Nicholas Biddle.

Many bankers who understood what Biddle was doing also resisted him. New York bankers resented the fact that a Philadelphia institution could wield so much power over their affairs. New York was the nation's largest importing center; huge amounts of tariff revenue were collected there. Yet, since this money was all deposited to the credit of the Bank of the United States, Biddle controlled it from Philadelphia. Finally, some objected to the Bank because it was a monopoly. Distrust of chartered corporations as agents of special privilege tended to focus on the Bank, which had a monopoly of public funds but was managed by a private citizen and controlled by a handful of rich men. Biddle's wealth and social position aggravated this feeling. Like many brilliant people, he sometimes appeared arrogant. He was unused to criticism and disdainful of ignorant and stupid attacks, failing to see that they were sometimes the most dangerous.

Jackson's Bank Veto

This formidable opposition to the Bank was diffuse and unorganized until Andrew Jackson brought it together. When he did, the Bank was quickly destroyed. Jackson belonged among the ignorant enemies of the institution, a hard-money man suspicious of all commercial banking. "I think it right to be perfectly frank with you," he told Biddle in 1829. "I do not dislike your Bank any more than all banks. But ever since I read the history of the South Sea Bubble I have been afraid of banks."

Jackson's attitude dismayed Biddle. It also mystified him, since the Bank was the country's best defense against a speculative mania like the 18th-century South Sea Bubble, in which hundreds of naive British investors had been fleeced. Almost against his will, Biddle found himself gravitating toward Clay and the National Republicans, offering advantageous loans and retainers to politicians and newspaper editors in order to build up a following. Thereafter events moved inevitably toward a showdown, for the president's combative instincts were easily aroused. "The Bank," he told Van Buren, "is trying to kill me, *but I will kill it!*"

Henry Clay, Daniel Webster, and other prominent National Republicans hoped to use the Bank controversy against Jackson. They reasoned that the institution was so important to the country that Jackson's opposition to it would undermine his popularity. They therefore urged Biddle to ask Congress to renew the Bank's charter. The charter would not expire until 1836, but by pressing the issue before the 1832 presidential election they could force Jackson either to approve the recharter bill or to veto it (which would give candidate Clay a lively issue in the campaign). The banker yielded to this strategy reluctantly, for he would have preferred to postpone the showdown, and a recharter bill passed Congress early in July 1832. Jackson promptly vetoed it.

Jackson's message explaining why he had rejected the bill was immensely popular. It adds nothing to his reputation as a statesman. Being a good Jeffersonian—and no friend of John Marshall—he insisted that the Bank was unconstitutional. (*McCulloch* v. *Maryland* he brushed aside, saying that as president he had sworn to uphold the Constitution as *he* understood it.) The Bank was inexpedient, he argued. Being a dangerous private monopoly that allowed a handful of rich men to accumulate "many millions" of dollars, the Bank was making "the rich richer and the potent more powerful." Furthermore, many of its stockholders were foreigners: "If we must have a bank . . . it should be *purely American.*" Little that he said made any more sense than this absurdity.*

The most unfortunate aspect of Jackson's veto was that he could have reformed the Bank instead of destroying it. The central banking function was too important to be left in private hands. Biddle once boasted that he could put nearly any bank in the United States out of business simply by forcing it to exchange specie for its bank notes; he thought he was demonstrating his forbearance, but in fact he was revealing a dangerous flaw in the system. When the Jacksonians called him Czar Nicholas, they were not far from the mark. Moreover, private bankers *were* making profits that in justice belonged to the people, for the government received no interest from the large sums it kept on deposit in the Bank. Jackson would not consider reforms. He set out to smash the Bank of the United States without any real idea of what might be put in its place—a most foolhardy act.

Biddle considered Jackson's veto "a manifesto of anarchy," its tone like "the fury of a chained panther biting the bars of his cage." A large majority of the voters, however, approved of Jackson's hard-hitting attack. He was easily reelected president, defeating Clay 219 to 49 in the electoral college.

Buttressed by his election triumph, Jackson acted swiftly. "Until I can strangle this hydra of corruption, the Bank, I will not shrink from my duty," he said. Shortly after the start of his second term, he decided to withdraw the government

* The country needed all the foreign capital it could attract. Foreigners owned only $8 million of the $35 million stock, and in any case they could not vote their shares.

The "Set To Between Old Hickory and Bully Nick" is pictured in this cartoon of 1834–1835. Jackson's seconds are "Little Van" Martin Van Buren and Major Jack Downing; Biddle is seconded by "Long Harry" (Henry Clay) and "Black Dan" Webster.

funds deposited in its vaults. Under the law only the secretary of the treasury could remove the deposits. When Secretary Louis McLane refused to do so, believing that the alternative depositories, the state banks, were less safe, Jackson promptly "promoted" him to secretary of state and appointed William J. Duane, a Pennsylvania lawyer, to the Treasury post. Foolishly, he failed to ask Duane his views on the issue before appointing him. Too late he discovered that the new secretary agreed with McLane! It would not be "prudent" to entrust the government's money to "local and irresponsible" banks, Duane said.

Believing that Cabinet officers should obey the president as automatically as a colonel obeys a general, Jackson dismissed Duane, replacing him with Attorney General Roger B. Taney, who had been advising him closely on Bank affairs. Taney carried out the order by depositing new federal receipts in seven state banks in eastern cities while continuing to meet government expenses with drafts on the Bank of the United States.

The situation was confused and slightly unethical. Set on winning the "Bank War," Jackson lost sight of his fear of unsound paper money. Taney, however, knew exactly what he was doing. One of the state banks receiving federal funds was the Union Bank of Baltimore. Taney owned stock in this institution, and its president was his close friend. Little wonder that Jackson's enemies were soon calling the favored state banks "pet" banks. This charge was not entirely fair because Taney took pains to see that the deposits were placed in financially sound institutions. Furthermore, by 1836 the government's funds had been spread out reasonably equitably in about 90 banks. But neither was the charge entirely unfair; the administration certainly favored institutions that were politically sympathetic to it.

When Taney began to remove the deposits, the government had $9,868,000 to its credit in the Bank of the United States; within three months the figure fell to about $4 million. Faced with the withdrawal of so much cash, Biddle had to contract his operations. He decided to exaggerate the contraction, pressing the state banks hard by presenting all their notes and checks that came across his counter for conversion into specie and drastically limiting his own bank's business loans. He hoped that the resulting shortage of credit would be blamed on Jackson and that it would force the president to return the deposits. "Nothing but the evidence of suffering . . . will produce any effect," he reasoned.

For a time the strategy appeared to be working. Paper money became scarce, specie almost unobtainable. A serious panic threatened. New York banks were soon refusing to make any loans at all. "Nobody buys; nobody can sell," a French visitor to the city observed. Memorials and petitions poured in on Congress. Worried and indignant delegations of businessmen began trooping to Washington seeking "relief." Clay, Webster, and Calhoun thundered against Jackson in the Senate.

The president would not budge. "I am fixed in my course as firm as the Rockey Mountain," he wrote Vice-President Van Buren. No "frail mortals" who worshipped "the golden calf" could change his mind. To others he swore he would sooner cut off his right arm and "undergo the torture of ten Spanish inquisitions" than restore the deposits. When delegations came to him, he roared at them harshly: "Go to Nicholas Biddle. . . . Biddle has all the money!" And in the end—because he was right—business leaders began to take the old general's advice. Pressure on Biddle mounted swiftly, and in July 1834 he suddenly reversed his policy and began to lend money freely. The artificial crisis ended.

Boom and Bust

While the government insisted that its pet banks maintain large reserves, other state banks began to offer credit on easy terms, aided by a large increase in their reserves of gold and silver resulting from causes unconnected with the policies of either the government or Biddle's Bank.* Bank notes in circulation jumped from $82 million in January 1835 to $120 million in December 1836. Bank deposits rose even more rapidly.

Much of the new money flowed into speculation in land; a mania to invest in property swept the country. The increased volume of currency caused prices to soar 15 percent in six months, buoying investors' spirits and making them ever more optimistic about the future. By the summer of 1835 one observer estimated that in New York City, which had about 250,000 residents, enough house lots had been laid out and sold to support a population of 2 million. Chicago at this time had only 2,000 to 3,000 inhabitants, yet most of the land for 25 miles around the village had been sold and resold in small lots by speculators anticipating the growth of the area. Throughout the West farmers borrowed money from local banks by mortgaging their land, used the new bank notes to buy more land from the government, and then borrowed still more money from the banks on the strength of their new deeds.

So long as prices rose, the process could be repeated endlessly. In 1832, while the Bank of the United States still regulated the money supply, federal income from the sale of land was $2.6 million. In 1834 it was $4.9 million; in 1835, $14.8 million. In 1836 it rose to $24.9 million, and the government found itself totally free of debt and with a surplus of $20 million!

Finally Jackson became alarmed by the speculative mania. In the summer of 1836 he issued the Specie Circular, which provided that purchasers must henceforth pay for public land in gold or silver. At once the rush to buy land ground to a halt. When demand slackened, prices sagged. Speculators, unable to dispose of lands mortgaged to the banks, had to abandon them to the banks, but the banks could not realize enough on the foreclosed property to recover their loans. Suddenly the public mood changed. Commodity prices tumbled 30 percent between February and May. Hordes of depositors sought to withdraw their money in the form of specie, and soon the banks exhausted their supplies. Panic swept the country in the spring of 1837 as every bank in the nation was forced to suspend specie payments. The boom was over.

Major swings in the business cycle can never be attributed to the actions of a single person, however powerful, but there is no doubt that Jackson's war against the Bank exaggerated the swings of the economic pendulum, not so much by its direct effects as by the impact of its ill-considered policies on popular thinking. His Specie Circular did not *prevent* speculators from buying land—at most it caused purchasers to pay a premium for gold or silver. But it convinced potential buyers that the

* A decline in the Chinese demand for Mexican silver led to increased exports of the metal to the United States, and the rise of American interest rates attracted English capital into the country. Heavy English purchases of American cotton at high prices also increased the flow of specie into American banks.

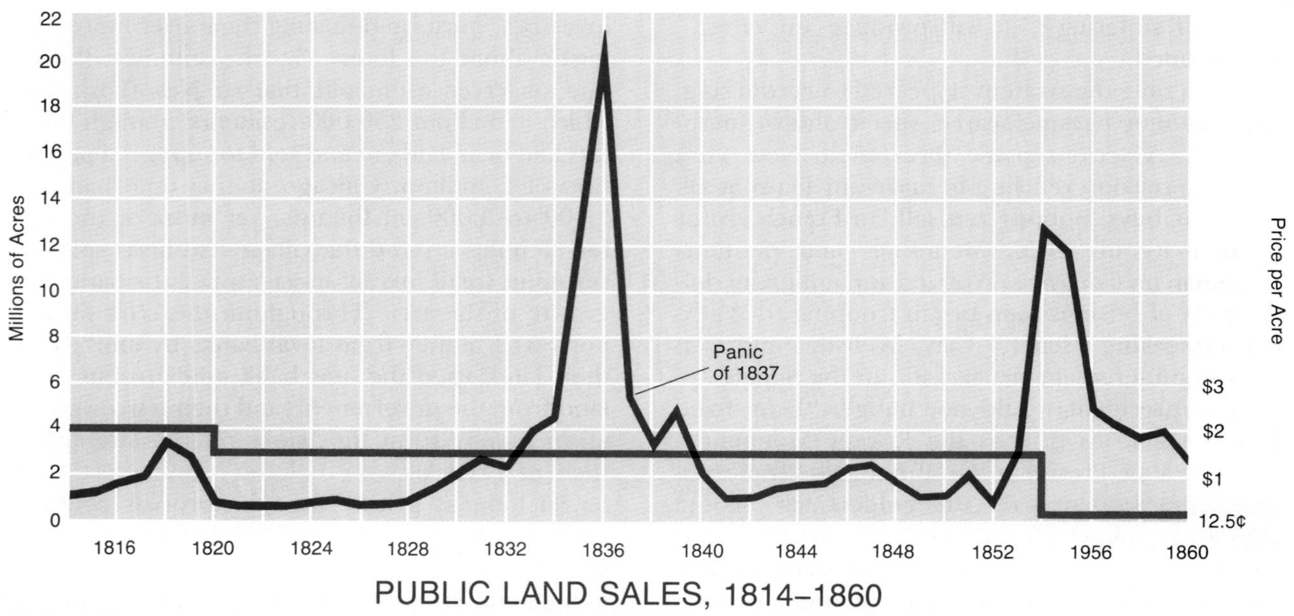

The left axis shows millions of acres of public land; the right axis price per acre. The speculative peak of 1836 burst with the Panic of 1837. The size of land parcels offered varied from 160 acres in 1830 to 40 or more acres in 1832 and at later times. Starting in 1830, squatters on public land were allowed to buy it at the minimum price. The 12.5¢ price per acre in 1854 applied to land on the market for 30 years or more.

boom was going to end and led them to make decisions that in fact ended it. Old Hickory's combination of impetuousness, combativeness, arrogance, and ignorance rendered the nation he loved so dearly a serious disservice. He lacked, as Glyndon Van Deusen wrote in *The Jacksonian Era,* "the capacity for that slow and often painful balancing of opposite viewpoints, the fruit of philosophic reflection, which is the characteristic of the man of culture." This was his greatest failing, as a president and as a man.

Jacksonianism Abroad

Jackson's emotional and dogmatic side also influenced his handling of foreign affairs. His patriotism was often so extravagant as to be ludicrous; in less peaceful times he might well have embroiled the country in far bloodier battles than his war with Nicholas Biddle produced. By pushing relentlessly for the solution of minor problems, he won a number of diplomatic successes. Several advantageous reciprocal trade agreements were negotiated, including one with Great Britain that finally opened British West Indian ports to American ships. American claims dating from the Napoleonic wars were pressed vigorously. The most important result of this policy came in 1831, when France agreed to pay about $5 million to compensate for damages to American property during that long conflict.

This settlement, however, led to trouble because the French Chamber of Deputies refused to appropriate the necessary funds. When the United States submitted a bill for the first installment in 1833, it was unable to collect. Jackson at once adopted a belligerent stance, his ire further aroused by a bill for $170,041.18 submitted by Nicholas Biddle for the services of the Bank of the United States in attempting to collect the money. When France ignored the second installment, Jackson sent a blistering message to Congress, full of such phrases as "not to be tolerated" and "take redress into our own hands." He asked for a law "authorizing reprisals upon French property" if the money was not paid.

Jackson's case was ironclad, yet the matter did not merit such vigorous prosecution. Congress wisely took no action. Jackson suspended diplomatic relations with France and ordered the navy readied. The French—in part, no doubt, because they were clearly in the wrong—were insulted by Jackson's manner. Irresponsible talk of war was heard in both countries. Fortunately the French Chamber finally appropriated the money, Jackson moderated his public pronouncements, and the issue subsided.

Similarly, when a snag delayed the negotiation of the West Indian treaty, Jackson had suggested forcing Great Britain to make concessions by imposing a boycott on trade with Canada. In both cases he showed poor judgment, being ready to take monumental risks to win petty victories. His behavior reinforced the impression held by foreigners that the United States was a rash young country with a chip on its shoulder, pathologically mistrustful of the good faith of European powers.

The Jacksonians

Jackson's personality had a large impact on the shape and tone of American politics. When he came to office, nearly everyone professed to be a follower of Jefferson. By 1836 being a Jeffersonian no longer meant much; what mattered was how one felt about Andrew Jackson. He had ridden to power at the head of a diverse political army, but he left behind him an organization with a fairly cohesive, if not necessarily consistent, body of ideas. This democratic party contained rich citizens and poor, easterners and westerners, abolitionists as well as slaveholders. It was not yet a close-knit national organization, but—always allowing for individual exceptions—the Jacksonians agreed on certain underlying principles. These included suspicion of special privilege and large business corporations, both typified by the Bank of the United States; freedom of economic opportunity, unfettered by private or governmental restrictions; absolute political freedom, at least for white males; and the conviction that any ordinary man is capable of performing the duties of most public offices.

Jackson's ability to reconcile his belief in the *supremacy* of the Union with his conviction that the *area* of national authority should be held within narrow limits tended to make the Democrats the party of those who believed that the powers of the states should not be diminished. Tocqueville caught this aspect of Jackson's philosophy perfectly: "Far from wishing to extend Federal power," he wrote, "the president belongs to the party that wishes to limit that power."

Although the Locofoco,* or radical, wing of the party championed the idea, nearly all Jacksonians, like their leader, favored giving the small man his chance—by supporting public education, for example, and by refusing to place much weight on a person's origin, dress, or manners. "One individual is as good as another" (again we must insert the adjective "white") was axiomatic with them. This attitude helps explain why immigrants, Catholics, and other minority groups usually voted Democratic. However, the Jacksonians showed no tendency either to penalize the wealthy or to intervene in economic affairs to aid the underprivileged. The motto "That government is best which governs least" graced the masthead of the chief Jacksonian newspaper, the Washington *Globe,* throughout the era.

Rise of the Whigs

The opposition to Jackson was far less cohesive. Henry Clay's National Republican party provided a nucleus, but Clay never dominated that party as Jackson dominated the Democrats. Its orientation was basically anti-Jackson. It was as though the American people were a great block of granite from which some sculptor had just fashioned a statue of Jackson, the chips scattered about the floor of the studio representing the opposition.

While Jackson was president the impact of his personality delayed the formation of a true two-party system, but as soon as he surrendered power, the opposition, taking heart, began to coalesce. Many Democrats could not accept the odd logic of Jacksonian finance. As early as 1834 these men, together with the Clay element, the extreme states' righters who followed Calhoun, and other dissident groups, were calling themselves Whigs, the name (harking back to the Revolution) implying patriotic

* A locofoco was a type of friction match. The name was first applied in politics when a group of New York Jacksonians used these matches to light candles when a conservative faction tried to break up their meeting by turning off the gaslights.

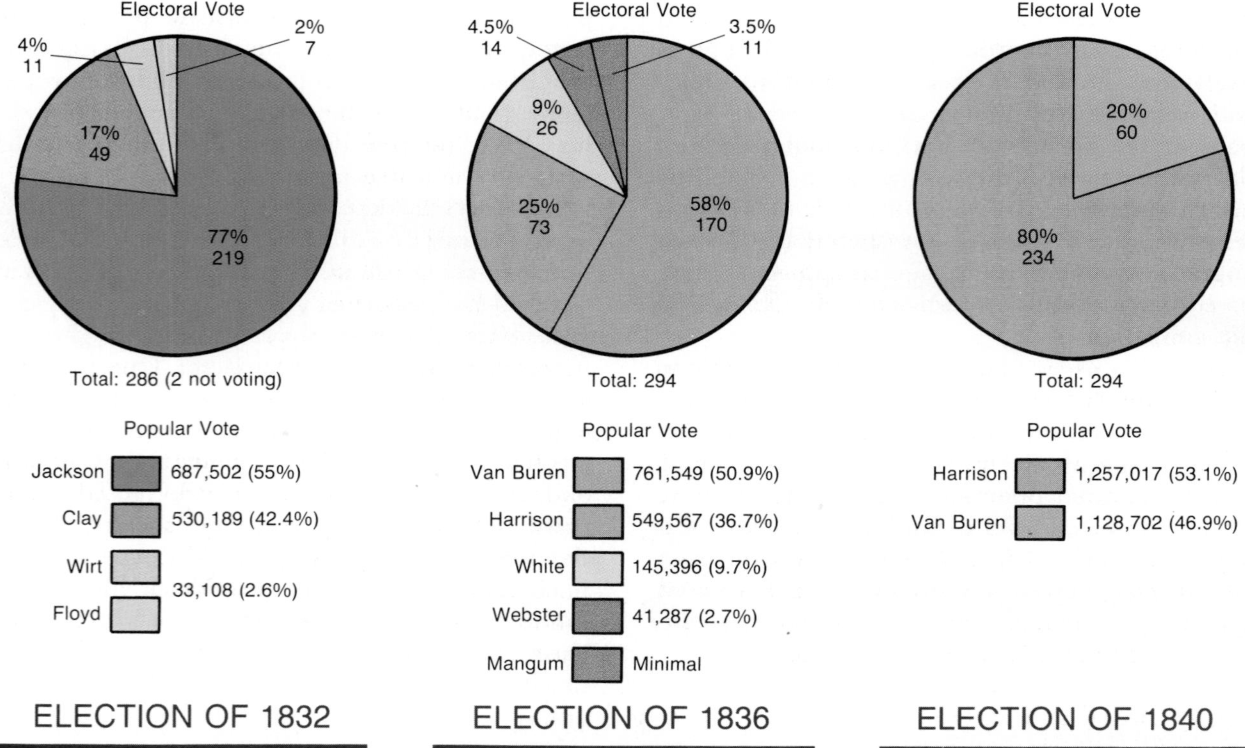

resistance to the tyranny of "King Andrew." This coalition possessed great resources of wealth and talent. Anyone who understood banking was almost obliged to become a Whig unless he was connected with one of Jackson's "pets." Those spiritual descendants of Hamilton who rejected the administration's refusal to approach economic problems from a broadly national perspective also joined in large numbers. Those who found the coarseness and "pushiness" of the Jacksonians offensive were another element in the new party. The anti-intellectual and antiscientific bias of the administration (Jackson rejected proposals for a national university, an observatory, and a scientific and literary institute) drove many well-educated people into the Whig fold. Whig arguments also appealed to ordinary voters who were predisposed to favor strong governments that would check the "excesses" of unrestricted individualism.

The Whigs were slow to develop an effective party organization. They had too many generals and not enough troops. It was hard for them to agree on any issue more complicated than opposition to Jackson. Furthermore, they stood in conflict with the major trend of their age: the glorification of the common man.

Lacking a dominant leader in 1836, the Whigs relied on "favorite sons," hoping to throw the presidential election into the House of Representatives. Daniel Webster ran in New England. For the West and South, Hugh Lawson White of Tennessee, a former friend who had broken with Jackson, was counted on to carry the fight. General William Henry Harrison was supposed to win in the Northwest and to draw support everywhere from those who liked to vote for military heroes. This sorry strategy failed; Jackson's handpicked candidate, Martin Van Buren, won a majority of both the popular and the electoral votes.

Jacksonianism Without Jackson

The Red Fox, the Little Magician—Van Buren's brilliance as a political manipulator has tended to obscure his statesmanlike qualities and his engaging personality. High office sobered Van Buren and improved his judgment. He fought the Bank of the

United States as a monopoly, but he also opposed irresponsbile state banks. New York's "Safety Fund System," requiring all banks to contribute to a fund, supervised by the state, to be used to redeem the notes of any member bank that failed, was established largely through his efforts. Van Buren believed in public construction of internal improvements, but he favored state rather than national programs, and he urged a rational approach: each project must stand on its own as a useful and profitable public utility.

He continued to equivocate spectacularly on the tariff—in his *Autobiography* he described two of his supporters walking home after listening to him talk on the tariff, each convinced that it had been a brilliant speech, but neither having obtained the slightest idea as to where Van Buren stood on the subject—but he was never in the pocket of any special interest group or tariff lobbyist. He accounted himself a good Jeffersonian, tending to prefer state action to federal, but he was by no means doctrinaire. Basically he approached most questions rationally and pragmatically.

Van Buren had outmaneuvered Calhoun easily in the struggle to succeed Jackson, winning the old hero's confidence and serving him well. In 1832 he was elected vice-president and thereafter was conceded to be the "heir apparent." In 1835 the Democratic National Convention nominated him for president unanimously.

Van Buren took office just as the Panic of 1837 struck the country. Its effects were frightening but short-lived. When the banks stopped converting paper money into gold and silver, they outraged conservatives but in effect eased the pressure on the money market: interest rates declined and business loans again became relatively easy to obtain. In 1836, at the height of the boom in land sales, Congress had voted to "distribute" the new Treasury surplus to the states, and this flow of money, which the states promptly spent, also stimulated the revival. Late in 1838 the banks resumed specie payments.

In 1839 a bumper crop caused a sharp decline in the price of cotton. Then a number of state governments that had overextended themselves in road- and canal-building projects were forced to default on their debts. This discouraged investors, particularly foreigners. A general economic depression ensued that lasted until 1843.

Van Buren was not responsible for the panic or the depression, but his manner of dealing with economic issues was scarcely helpful. He saw his role as being concerned only with problems plaguing the *government,* ignoring the economy as a whole. "The less government interferes with private pursuits the better for the general prosperity," he pontificated. As Daniel Webster scornfully pointed out, Van Buren was following a policy of "leaving the people to shift for themselves," one which many Whigs rejected.

Such a hands-off approach to the depression seems foolish by modern standards. Van Buren's refusal to assume any responsibility for the general welfare appears to explode the theory that the Jacksonians were deeply concerned with the fate of ordinary citizens. In *The Concept of Jacksonian Democracy,* Lee Benson argues that the Whigs, rather than the Democrats, were the "positive liberals" of the era. Benson cites many statements by Whigs about giving "free scope to the employment of capital

By the 1840s the daguerreotype—"the mirror with a memory," as Oliver Wendell Holmes described it—was all the rage. This is Martin Van Buren as he looked in 1848.

and credit" and applying "the means of the state boldly and liberally to aid . . . public works."

This approach helps correct past oversimplifications, but it judges the period by the standards of a later age. The country in the 1830s was still mainly agricultural, and for most farmers the depression, while serious, did not spell disaster. The means, even the statistical information, necessary for regulating the economy effectively did not exist. Moreover, many Jacksonians were perfectly willing to see the *states* act to stimulate economic growth in bad times—as indeed most of them did.

Van Buren's chief goal as president was to find an acceptable substitute for the state banks as a place to keep federal funds. The depression and the suspension of specie payments embarrassed the government along with private depositors. He soon settled on the idea of "divorcing" the government from all banking activities. His Independent Treasury Bill called for the construction of government-owned vaults where federal revenues could be stored until needed. To insure absolute safety, all payments to the government were to be made in hard cash. After a battle that lasted until the summer of 1840, the Independent Treasury Act passed both the House and the Senate.

Opposition to the Independent Treasury had been bitter, and not all of it was partisan. Bankers and businessmen objected to the government's withholding so much specie from the banks, which needed all the hard money they could get to support loans that were the lifeblood of economic growth. It seemed irresponsible for the federal government to turn its back on the banks, which so obviously performed a semipublic function. These criticisms made good sense, but through a lucky combination of circumstances, the system worked reasonably well for many years. By creating suspicion in the public mind, officially stated distrust of banks acted as a useful damper on their tendency to overexpand. No acute shortage of specie developed because heavy agricultural exports and the investment of much European capital in American railroads beginning in the mid-1840s brought in large amounts of new gold and silver. After 1849 the discovery of gold in California added another important source of specie. The supply of money and bank credit kept pace roughly with the growth of the economy, but through no fault of the government. "Wildcat" banks proliferated. Fraud and counterfeiting were common, and the operation of everyday business affairs was inconvenienced in countless ways. The disordered state of the currency remained a grave problem until corrected by Civil War banking legislation.

The Log Cabin Campaign

It was not his financial policy that led to Van Buren's defeat in 1840. The depression naturally hurt the Democrats, and the Whigs were far better organized than in 1836. The Whigs also adopted a different strategy, cynical but effective. The Jacksonians had come to power on the coattails of a popular general whose views on public questions they concealed or ignored. They had maintained themselves by shouting the praises of the common man. Now the Whigs seized upon these techniques and carried them to their logical—or illogical—conclusion. Not even bothering to draft a program, and passing over Clay and Webster, whose views were known and therefore controversial, they nominated General Harrison for president. The Hero of Tippecanoe was counted on to conquer the party created in the image of the Hero of New Orleans. To "balance" the ticket, the Whigs chose a former Democrat, John Tyler of Virginia, an ardent supporter of states' rights, as their vice-presidential candidate.

The Whig argument was specious but effective: General Harrison is a plain man of the people who lives in a log cabin (where the latchstring is always out). Contrast him with the suave Van Buren, luxuriating amid "the Regal Splendor of the President's Palace." Harrison drinks ordinary hard cider and eats hog meat and grits, while Van Buren drinks expensive foreign wines and fattens on fancy concoctions prepared by a French chef. The general's furniture is plain and sturdy; the president dines off gold plates and treads on Royal Wilton carpets that cost the people $5 a yard. In a country where all are equal, the people will reject an aristocrat like "Martin Van Ruin" and put their trust in General Harrison, a simple, brave, honest, public-spirited common man.

Such nonsense created an irrelevant and misleading impression. Harrison came from a distin-

A cornerstone of Whig strategy in the 1840 campaign was the mass political rally; this one was held in Cincinnati a month before election day. A "triumphal arch" was erected across Main Street for the occasion, with Harrison banners, flags, and slogans, both patriotic and political, much in evidence.

guished family, being the son of Benjamin Harrison, a signer of the Declaration of Independence and a former governor of Virginia. He was well educated and in at least comfortable financial circumstances, and he certainly did not live in a log cabin. The Whigs ignored these facts. The log cabin and the cider barrel became their symbols, which every political meeting saw reproduced in a dozen forms. The leading Whig campaign newspaper, edited by a vigorous New Englander named Horace Greeley, was called the *Log Cabin.* Cartoons, doggerel, slogans, and souvenirs were everywhere substituted for argument.

The Democrats used the same methods as the Whigs and were equally well organized, but they had little heart for the fight. The president tried to run on his record and to focus public attention on issues. His voice could not be heard above the huzzas of the Whigs. When the Whigs chanted "Tippecanoe and Tyler too!" and "Van, Van, is a used-up man" and rolled out another barrel of hard cider, the best the Democrats could come up with was:

Rumpsey, Dumpsey,
Colonel Johnson
Killed Techumseh.

A huge turnout (four-fifths of the eligible voters, more than 2.4 million as against 1.5 million four years earlier) carried Harrison to victory by a margin of almost 150,000. The electoral vote was 234 to 60.

The Democrats had been blown up by their own bomb. In 1828 they had portrayed John Quincy Adams as a bloated aristocrat and Jackson as a simple western farmer. The lurid talk of Van Buren dining off golden plates was no different from the stories that made Adams out to be a passionate gambler. If Van Buren was a lesser man than Adams, Harrison was a pale imitation indeed of Andrew Jackson.

The Whigs continued to repeat history by rushing to gather the spoils of victory. Washington was again flooded by office seekers, the political confusion monumental. Harrison had no ambition to be an aggressive leader. He believed that Jackson had misused the veto and professed to put as much emphasis as had Washington on the principle of the separation of legislative and executive powers. This delighted the Whig leaders in Congress, who had had their fill of the "executive usurpation" of Jackson. Either Clay or Webster seemed destined to be the real ruler of the new administration, and soon the two were squabbling over their old general like sparrows over a crust.

At the height of their squabble, less than a month after his inauguration, Harrison fell gravely ill. Pneumonia developed, and on April 4 he died. John Tyler of Virginia, honest, conscientious, but doctrinaire, became president of the United States. The political climate of the country was changed dramatically. Events began to march in a new direction, and one that led ultimately to Bull Run, to Gettysburg, and to Appomattox.

SUPPLEMENTARY READING

Titles marked with an asterisk have been puhlished in paperback.

On Jackson's presidency, see G. G. Van Deusen, **The Jacksonian Era*** (1959), and R. V. Remini, **Andrew Jackson and the Course of American Freedom** (1981) and **Andrew Jackson and the Course of American Democracy** (1984). The nature of Jacksonian Democracy was analyzed brilliantly by Alexis de Tocqueville, **Democracy in America*** (1835–1840). A. M. Schlesinger, Jr., **The Age of Jackson*** (1945), stresses the democratic character of Jacksonianism. J. W. Ward, **Andrew Jackson: Symbol for an Age*** (1955), pictures Jackson as typifying certain basic aspects of the American character. D. T. Miller, **Jacksonian Aristocracy** (1967), and two works by Edward Pessen, **Riches, Class and Power Before the Civil War** (1973) and **Jacksonian America*** (1969), describe the growth and extent of economic and class distinctions. T. P. Abernethy, **From Frontier to Plantation in Tennessee** (1932), portrays Jackson as a conservative, chiefly by stressing his early career.

A number of contemporary commentaries by foreigners throw much light on Jacksonian Democracy. See especially, in addition to Tocqueville, Frances Trollope, **Domestic Manners of the Americans*** (1832), Michel Chevalier (J. W. Ward, ed.), **Society, Manners and Politics in the United States*** (1961), Harriet Martineau, **Retrospect of Western Travel** (1838) and **Society in America*** (1837), and F. J. Grund, **Aristocracy in America*** (1959).

On Jackson's administration of the government and the development of the spoils system, see L. D. White, **The Jacksonians*** (1954), and S. H. Aronson, **Status and Kinship in the Higher Civil Service** (1964); on the development of parties, R. P. McCormick, **The Second American Party System*** (1966). For his Indian policy, consult F. P. Prucha, **American Indian Policies in the Formative Years*** (1962), B. W. Sheehan, **Seeds of Extinction*** (1973), R. N. Satz, **American Indian Policy in the Jacksonian Era** (1975), and Grant Foreman, **Indian Removal: The Emigration of the Five Civilized Tribes*** (1953).

By far the best treatment of the nullification controversy is W. W. Freehling, **Prelude to Civil War: The Nullification Controversy in South Carolina*** (1966), which shows the close relationship between the nullifiers and the slavery issue. Also helpful is C. M. Wiltse, **John C. Calhoun: Nullifier** (1949). C. S. Sydnor, **The Development of Southern Sectionalism*** (1948), locates the crisis in a broader context. Calhoun's character and personality are well described in M. L. Coit, **John C. Calhoun: American Portrait*** (1950).

The struggle with the Bank is discussed in Bray Hammond, **Banks and Politics in America from the Revolution to the Civil War*** (1957), J. M. McFaul, **The Politics of Jacksonian Finance** (1972), and Walter Smith, **Economic Aspects of the Second Bank of the United States**

(1953). Peter Temin, **The Jacksonian Economy*** (1969), minimizes the effects of Jackson's policies on economic conditions. Temin also provides an interesting analysis of economic trends throughout the period. T. P. Govan's **Nicholas Biddle: Nationalist and Public Banker*** (1959) is excellent on Biddle's view of banking but too apologetic. C. B. Swisher's **Roger B. Taney** (1935) is a good biography.

The political and economic ideas of Whigs and Democrats are discussed in Lee Benson, **The Concept of Jacksonian Democracy*** (1961), R. P. Formisano, **The Transformation of Political Culture** (1983), and D. W. Howe, **The Political Culture of the American Whigs** (1980). For Jackson's foreign policy, see R. A. McLemore, **Franco-American Diplomatic Relations** (1941). Walter Hugins's **Jacksonian Democracy and the Working Class*** (1960) is a fine scholarly study. On the development of the Whig party, in addition to the biographies of leading Whigs, see E. M. Carroll, **Origins of the Whig Party** (1925), G. R. Poage, **Henry Clay and the Whig Party** (1936), and McCormick's **Second American Party System.**

For the Van Buren administration see John Niven, **Martin Van Buren** (1983), and M. L. Wilson, **The Presidency of Martin Van Buren** (1984). The election of 1840 is treated in R. G. Gunderson. **The Log-Cabin Campaign** (1957), Freeman Cleaves, **Old Tippecanoe** (1939), O. P. Chitwood, **John Tyler: Champion of the Old South** (1939), J. A. Garraty, **Silas Wright** (1949), and the biographies of Clay and Webster.

TIME LINE 3 ▪ The Political Economy of the New Republic, 1760–1860

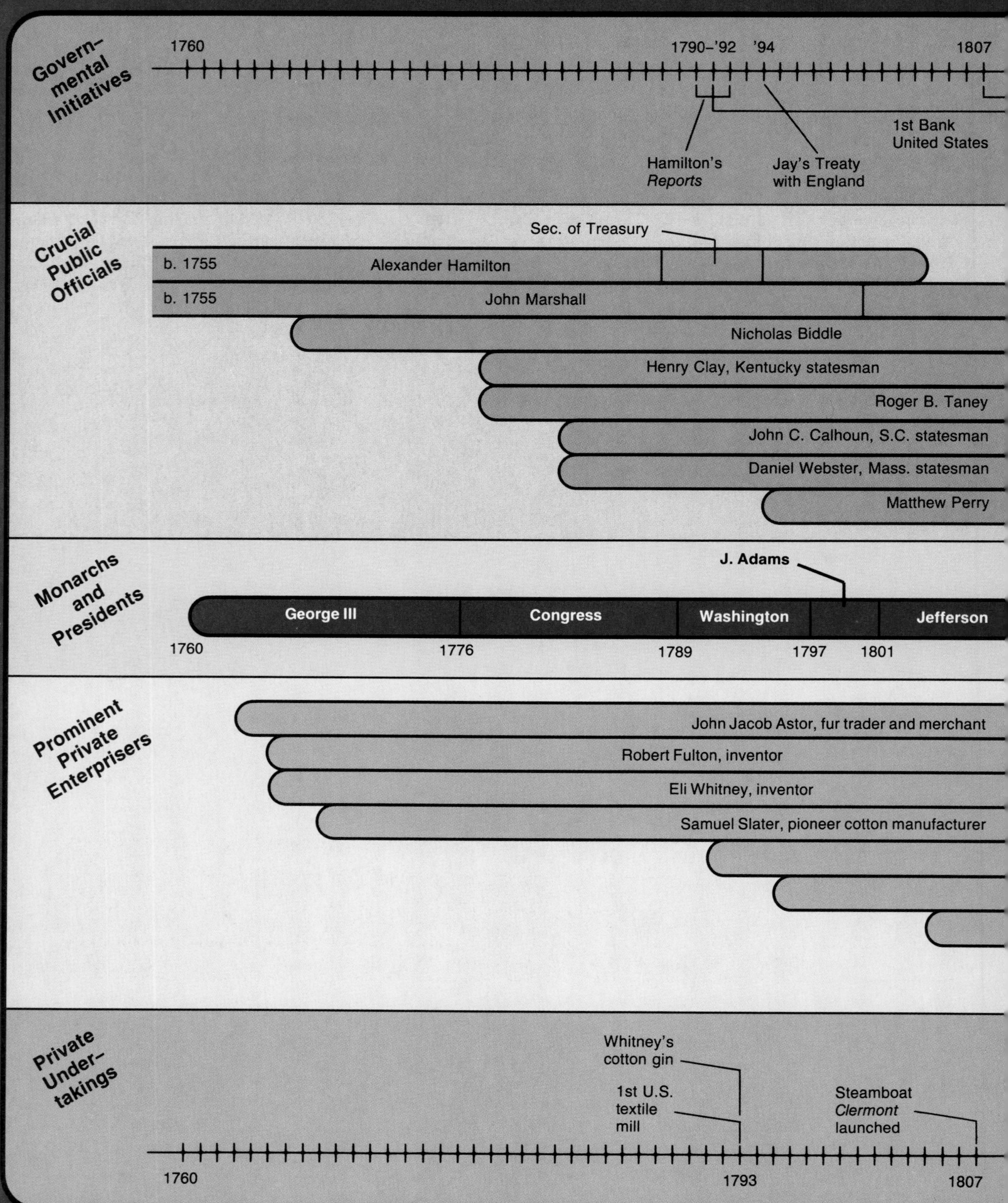

Governmental Initiatives
1760
1790–'92
'94
1807
1st Bank United States
Hamilton's *Reports*
Jay's Treaty with England
Crucial Public Officials
Sec. of Treasury
b. 1755 Alexander Hamilton
b. 1755 John Marshall
Nicholas Biddle
Henry Clay, Kentucky statesman
Roger B. Taney
John C. Calhoun, S.C. statesman
Daniel Webster, Mass. statesman
Matthew Perry
Monarchs and Presidents
J. Adams
George III
Congress
Washington
Jefferson
1760
1776
1789
1797
1801
Prominent Private Enterprisers
John Jacob Astor, fur trader and merchant
Robert Fulton, inventor
Eli Whitney, inventor
Samuel Slater, pioneer cotton manufacturer
Private Undertakings
Whitney's cotton gin
1st U.S. textile mill
Steamboat *Clermont* launched
1760
1793
1807

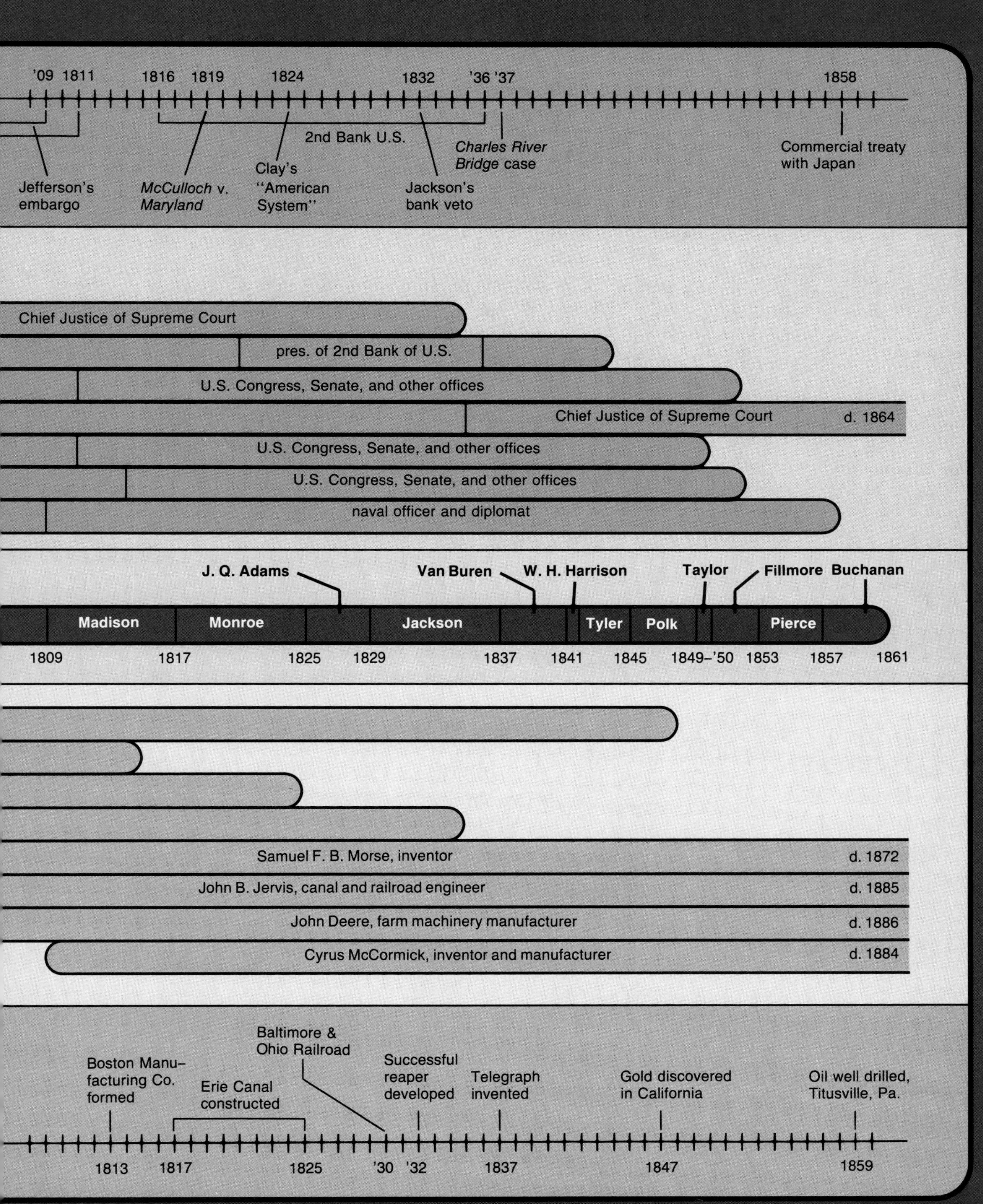

'09
1811
1816
1819
1824
1832
'36 '37
1858
2nd Bank U.S.
Charles River Bridge case
Commercial treaty with Japan
Jefferson's embargo
McCulloch v. Maryland
Clay's "American System"
Jackson's bank veto
Chief Justice of Supreme Court
pres. of 2nd Bank of U.S.
U.S. Congress, Senate, and other offices
Chief Justice of Supreme Court
d. 1864
U.S. Congress, Senate, and other offices
U.S. Congress, Senate, and other offices
naval officer and diplomat
J. Q. Adams
Van Buren
W. H. Harrison
Taylor
Fillmore
Buchanan
Madison
Monroe
Jackson
Tyler
Polk
Pierce
1809
1817
1825
1829
1837
1841
1845
1849–'50
1853
1857
1861
Samuel F. B. Morse, inventor
d. 1872
John B. Jervis, canal and railroad engineer
d. 1885
John Deere, farm machinery manufacturer
d. 1886
Cyrus McCormick, inventor and manufacturer
d. 1884
Baltimore & Ohio Railroad
Boston Manu- facturing Co. formed
Erie Canal constructed
Successful reaper developed
Telegraph invented
Gold discovered in California
Oil well drilled, Titusville, Pa.
1813
1817
1825
'30
'32
1837
1847
1859

10
The Making of Middle-Class America

A great democratic revolution is taking place in our midst; everybody sees it, but by no means everybody judges it in the same way. . . . No man on earth can affirm, absolutely and generally, that the new state of societies is better than the old, but it is already easy to see that it is different. ALEXIS DE TOCQUEVILLE, *1836*

On May 12, 1831, two French aristocrats, Alexis de Tocqueville and Gustave de Beaumont, arrived in New York City from Le Havre on the packet *President.* Their official purpose was to make a study of American prisons for the French government. But they really came, as Tocqueville explained, "to see what a great republic is like."

Tocqueville and Beaumont were only the most insightful of dozens of Europeans who came to the United States during the first half of the 19th century in order to study the "natives." Their visit, for example, overlapped with that of Mrs. Frances Trollope, whose *Domestic Manners of Americans* (1834) advised English readers that Americans were just as uncouth as they had imagined. A decade later, the English novelist Charles Dickens made what by then had become an almost obligatory pass through this crude outpost of civilization, before publishing his report on his "sharp dealing" cousins in *American Notes* (1842). A little later, in a novel, Dickens described the United States as a "Republic . . . full of sores and ulcers."

Unlike Trollope, Dickens, and other uncharitable foreign visitors, Tocqueville and Beaumont did not come to America chock-full of preconceived notions. Both believed that Europe was passing from its aristocratic past into a democratic future. How better to prepare for the change, they believed, than by studying the United States, where democracy was already the "enduring and normal state" of the land.

Tocqueville and Beaumont made a far more systematic effort to understand their American hosts than most foreign commentators. In the nine months they spent in America, they traveled from New York to Boston, then back through New York in order to inspect the state prison at Auburn, then on to Ohio. ("No one has been born there; no one wants to stay there," Tocqueville later said of Ohio.) They examined conditions on the frontier in Michigan Territory, then sailed down the Mississippi River to New Orleans, where they heard an opera good enough to make them imagine they were back in France. They also attended a "Quadroon ball," where, according to Tocqueville, "all the men [were] white, all the women coloured." From New Orleans they went on to "semi-barbarous" Alabama before turning north to Washington, a city that Beaumont declared to be "very ugly." Finally back to New York, whence they sailed for France on February 20, 1832. All told, they had met and interviewed some 250 individuals, ranking from President Jackson—Beaumont insisted on referring to Old Hickory as "Monsieur"—to a number of Chippewa Indians. "I leave America after having employed my time here usefully and agreeably," Tocqueville wrote.

It had indeed been a "useful" trip for the two Frenchmen. It resulted in their prison report and in *Marie, ou l'Esclavage aux Etats Unis* (1835), Beaumont's account of American race problems, cast in the form of a novel. But above all else, the visit provided the material for Tocqueville's classic two-volume *De la Démocratie en Amérique,* which appeared in France in 1835 and a year later in an English translation. *Democracy in America* has been the starting point for virtually all subsequent writers who have tried to describe the workings of American society and what Tocqueville called "the creative elements" of American institutions.

Tocqueville in Judgment

The gist of *Democracy in America* is contained in the book's first sentence: "No novelty in the United States struck me more vividly during my stay there than the equality of conditions." Tocqueville meant not that Americans lived in a state of total equality, but that the inequalities that did exist among white Americans were not enforced by institutions or supported by public opinion. Moreover, the inequalities paled when compared with those of Europe. "In America," he concluded, "men are nearer equality than in any other country in the world." The circumstances of one's birth meant little, one's education less, and one's intelligence scarcely anything. Economic differences, while real and certainly "paraded" by those who enjoyed "a pre-eminence of wealth," were transitory. "Such wealth," Tocqueville assured his readers, "is not at all permanent; it is within reach of all."

These sweeping generalizations, however comforting to Americans then and since, are simplifications. Few modern students of Jacksonian America would accept them without qualification. The historian Edward Pessen has pointed out that in the 1830s and 1840s a wide and growing gap existed between the rich and poor in the larger eastern

Among the scores of noted Europeans who visited the United States in its first fifty years, Alexis de Tocqueville is perhaps the best remembered, thanks to his exhaustive and insightful published account of his travels. This lithograph portrait is by Léon Noël.

cities. According to Pessen, the wealthiest 4 percent of the population of New York controlled about half the city's wealth in 1828, about two-thirds in 1845. The number of New Yorkers worth $100,000 or more tripled in that period. A similar concentration of wealth was occurring in Philadelphia and Boston.

Moreover, there was substantial poverty in Jacksonian America that Tocqueville did not recognize. Particularly in the cities, bad times forced many unskilled laborers and their families into dire poverty. Tocqueville took little notice of such inequalities, in part because he was so captivated by the theme of American equality. He also had little interest in how industrialization and urbanization were affecting society. When he did take notice of working conditions, he remarked that wages were higher in America than in Europe and the cost of living was lower, facts obvious to the most obtuse European visitor. Furthermore, as with most foreign visitors, nearly all his contacts were with members of the upper crust. "We hardly see anyone," he acknowledged, "except people of distinction."

Despite his blind spots, Tocqueville realized that America was undergoing some fundamental social changes. These changes, he wrote in *Democracy,* were being made by "an innumerable crowd who are . . . not exactly rich nor yet quite poor, [and who] have enough property to want order and not enough to excite envy." In his notes he put it even more succinctly: "The whole society seems to have turned into one middle class."

A Restless People

"In America, men never stay still," Tocqueville noted; "Something is almost always provisional about their lives." Other European observers came away equally struck by the restlessness of Americans, without necessarily agreeing that their democratic institutions made them so. Mrs. Trollope thought their "incessant bustling" of a piece with their eating too fast and spitting too often. It stemmed from their "universal pursuit of money," she claimed.

One reason Americans seemed continually on the move was that every year there were more of them. The first federal census in 1790 recorded that there were 3.9 million people in the country. In 1850 there were more than 23 million. The population was doubling every 22 years—just about what Franklin had predicted in 1751!

Yet by contemporary European standards (or ours today), even the settled parts of the United States were sparsely populated in the 1830s and 1840s. But for those who had accustomed themselves to the wide open spaces, the presence of more than a handful of neighbors provided reason enough for moving on. The knowledge that cheap land existed on the edge of settlement provided sufficient economic inducement to pull up stakes. Abraham Lincoln's father Thomas (1778–1851) was typical. He grew up in Kentucky, pioneered in Indiana, and died in Illinois.

The Move to Town

The urge to move had an urban dimension as well. For every "young man" who took the advice of the New York newspaperman Horace Greeley to "go west," several young men and women went

The Dinner Party *was painted about 1825 by Boston artist Henry Sargent. Tocqueville tolerated but rarely praised American haute cuisine. After one banquet, he recorded that the dinner represented the infancy of the art: "the vegetables and fish before the meat, the oysters for dessert. In a word, complete barbarism."*

instead to town. By the tens of thousands they exchanged the rigors of farming for the uncertain risks and rewards of city life. Boston, New York, and Philadelphia had a combined population of 50,000 at the time of the Revolution. Each expanded rapidly during the first half of the next century. Boston had 40,000 residents in 1820, nearly 140,000 in 1850. Philadelphia grew even more rapidly, from just under 100,000 in 1820 to almost 400,000 in 1850. New York, which forged ahead of Philadelphia around 1810, grew from 125,000 in 1820 to more than 500,000 in 1850.

However spectacular the growth of the largest cities, the emergence of new towns was more significant. In 1820 the Northeast contained 5 cities with populations above 25,000 and 13 with populations above 10,000. Thirty years later, 26 cities had more than 25,000 residents and 62 had more than 10,000.

While the Old Northwest remained primarily agricultural, its towns grew as fast as its farms. Pittsburgh, St. Louis, Cincinnati, Louisville, and Lexington, each founded before 1800, attracted settlers in such numbers that by 1850 all but Lexington had populations of over 35,000. Cincinnati, "the Emporium of the West," with a population of 100,000, ranked seventh in the country.

Those who filled the western cities struck foreigners as no less restless than the farmers of the frontier. Mrs. Trollope lived in Cincinnati from 1829 to 1832. She was amazed by the local practice of moving houses from place to place. With his customary eye for significant trends, Tocqueville pointed out that the westward migration was only the most obvious sign of the wanderlust to which Americans were prone. "In the United States, a man builds his house to spend his old age, and sells it before the roof is on," he wrote. "He brings

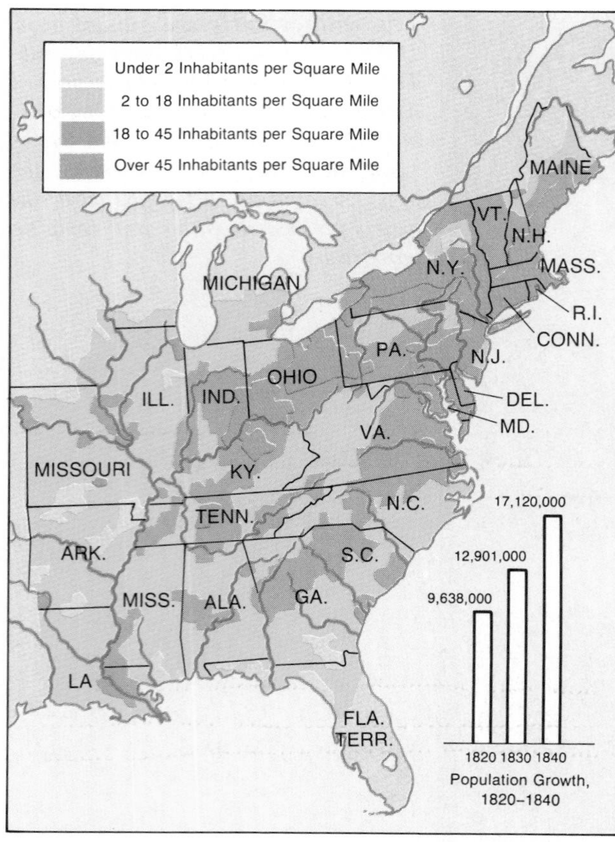

POPULATION DENSITY, 1840

The accelerating westward movement is evident in this map. Arkansas entered the Union in 1836, Michigan in 1837. During the 1830s the population of the nation as a whole increased by nearly one-third. Of the 4.2 million increase, a little over 10 percent were immigrants.

a field into tillage and leaves other men to gather the crops; . . . he settles in a place, which he soon afterwards leaves. . . ."

The trek to town that was transforming the Northeast did not occur in the South. There were four cities of respectable size in the region—Mobile, Savannah, Charleston, and Baltimore—and one large city, New Orleans, which had a population of 120,000 in 1850. Yet all these cities were located on the region's perimeter. Neither Virginia nor North Carolina had an urban center of even modest dimensions. Charleston, the oldest and most typically southern city, scarcely grew at all after 1830.

Strangers at the Door

Between 1790 and 1820 the population of the United States more than doubled to 9.6 million. The most remarkable feature of this growth was that it resulted almost entirely from natural increase. The birthrate in the early 19th century, though already declining, exceeded 50 per 1,000 population, a rate substantially higher than that of any country in the world today. Fewer than 250,000 immigrants entered the United States between 1790 and 1820. European wars, the ending

As the balance of rural and urban population began to shift during the years from 1820 to 1860, the number of cities with populations over 100,000 grew from one in 1820—New York—to nine in 1860, including southern and western cities like New Orleans and San Francisco.

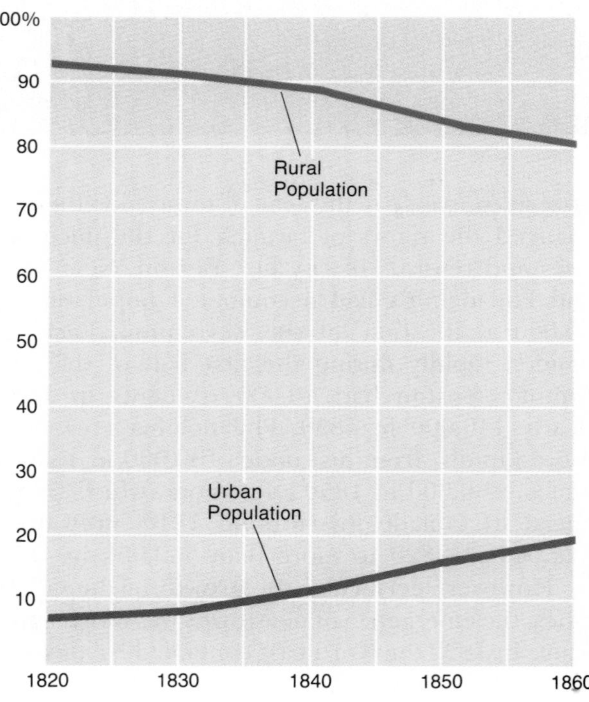

RURAL VERSUS URBAN POPULATION, 1820–1860

of the slave trade, and doubts about the viability of the new republic slowed the flow of humanity across the Atlantic to a trickle.

But soon after the final defeat of Napoleon in 1815, immigration began to pick up. In the 1820s, 150,000 European immigrants arrived; in the 1830s, 600,000; in the 1840s, 1,700,000. The 1850 census, the first to make the distinction, estimated that of the nation's population of 23 million, more than 10 percent were foreign-born. In the Northeast the proportion exceeded 15 percent.

Most of this human tide came from Germany and Ireland, but substantial numbers also came from Great Britain and the Scandinavian countries. As with earlier immigrants, many of these were drawn to America by the prospect of abundant land, high wages, and economic opportunity generally. Some, too, were attracted by the promise of political and religious freedom. But many came simply because to stay where they were meant to face starvation. This was particularly true of those from Ireland, where a potato blight triggered the desperate flight of tens of thousands. This exodus continued throughout the century, by which time there were more people of Irish origin in America than in Ireland.

Once ashore in New York, Boston, or Philadelphia, most relatively prosperous immigrants pushed directly westward. Others found work in the new factory towns along the route of the Erie Canal, in the lower Delaware Valley southeast of Philadelphia, or along the Merrimack River north of Boston. But most of the Irish immigrants, "the poorest and most wretched population that can be found in the world," one of their priests called them, lacked the means to go west. Aside from the cost of transportation, starting a farm required far more capital than they could raise. Like it or not, they had to settle in the eastern cities and accept any work they could get.

Viewed in historical perspective, this massive wave of immigration stimulated the American economy. In the short run, however, the influx of the 1830s and 1840s depressed living standards and strained the social fabric. For the first time the nation had acquired a culturally distinctive, city-bound, and propertyless class. The poor Irish immigrants had to accept whatever wages employers

Immigration before the Civil War was primarily from the northern European countries of Britain, Ireland, and Germany. Between 1820 and 1860, about 800,000 immigrants came from Britain, 3.5 million from Ireland, and 1.5 million from Germany. Famine in Ireland and political upheavals and economic hard times in Germany during the 1840s and 1850s accounted for much of the flow.

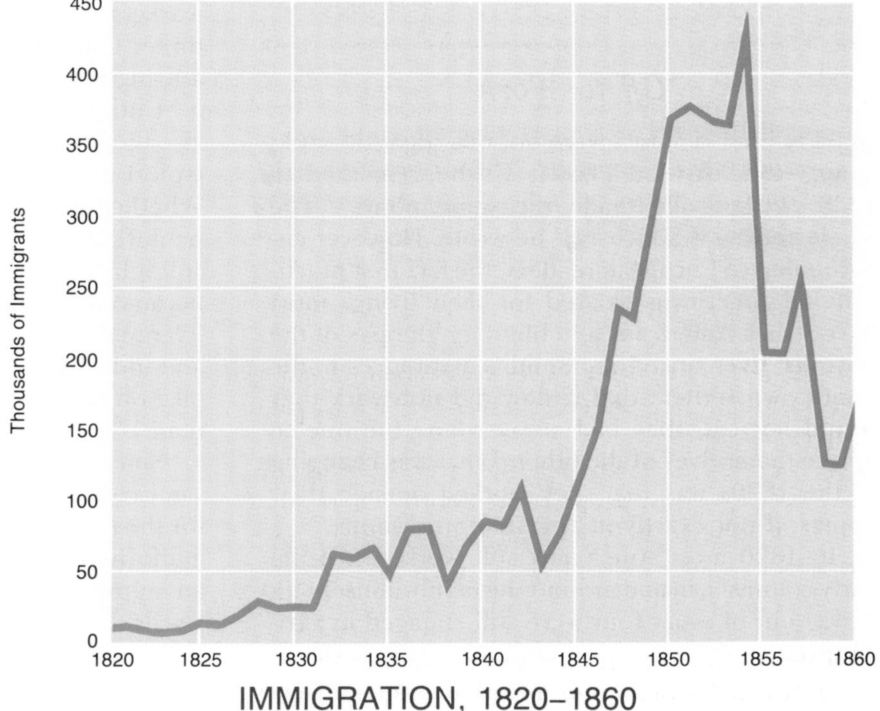

IMMIGRATION, 1820–1860

As the United States became an industrial nation, waves of immigrants—many from Ireland in the 1830s and 1840s—were attracted by the promise of better wages.

offered them. By doing so they roused resentment among native workers, resentment exacerbated by the unfamiliarity of the Irish with city ways and by their Roman Catholic faith, which the Protestant majority associated with European authoritarianism and corruption.

Off to Work

"It is as if all America were but one gigantic workshop," the Austrian Francis Grund remarked in 1838. Tocqueville made the same point. "The whole society is a factory," he wrote. However enlightening to European readers, the fact that practically all Americans worked for their livings must have struck Americans as a blinding glimpse of the obvious. Ever since John Smith's assurances to the Jamestown settlers that if they did not work they would not eat, they had always done the one to assure themselves of the other. What was changing in the 1830s was that they worked outside their homes, if not exactly in "gigantic workshops."

In 1820 most Americans still worked like the early colonists, in and around the family household. Three out of every four were still engaged in agriculture. An efficient farming family used the labor of all its members, with chores assigned according to age, strength, and experience. Parents, children, and sometimes grandparents lived in the same house, or in adjoining houses, together with unrelated hired hands, when such existed. Except on large southern plantations run by overseers, farming remained a family enterprise.

By 1850, however, fewer than two out of three workers were farmers, in Massachusetts one of three. Outside the South, the way people earned a living had been transformed.

Until the 1820s and 1830s, the household was also the focus of most nonagricultural pursuits. The typical urban worker was a self-employed artisan. Whether a tailor, shoemaker, printer, baker, or carpenter, he had been apprenticed to a master while still a lad. After five to seven years of training, he became a journeyman and began to earn wages. Eventually, if he was reasonably talented, frugal, and industrious, he could open a shop of his own, take on apprenctices, and thus perpetuate the system.

Since an apprentice lived and worked under the same roof as his master and his family, it was natural for the master to have familial as well as occupation authority over him. So intertwined did the life of an apprentice and his master become that the words "employee" and "employer" do not describe the relationship accurately. The historian Sean Wilentz has characterized the preindustrial workshop as "a benevolent hierarchy of skill."

What each member owed to and received from the others could not be measured in hours of labor and dollars and cents. Apprentices were sometimes exploited and even physically abused. But just as often, as in any family, strong, personal bonds developed. Some apprentices married one of the master's daughters, thus helping to keep the trade in the family.

Forced reliance on domestically manufactured goods during the Embargo and the War of 1812, and the improvements in transportation that were taking place steadily in the 1820s and 1830s, prompted many master craftsmen and artisans to expand production. They took on more workers, in some cases as apprentices, more often as relatively unskilled wage earners. Work was broken down into a series of simple tasks that the unskilled help could learn easily and repeat endlessly. As a business grew bigger and the division of labor became more complex, the master-turned-businessman spent less time working side by side with his employees and more marketing his products. Elaborate rules evolved regulating the hours of labor and the on-the-job behavior of workers. Drinking on the job, which in an earlier day had been considered normal and even desirable, was by 1850 almost universally forbidden.

Larger operations required more work space, and the need to locate near suppliers, customers, or a source of waterpower meant that the owner's home could no longer serve as a workplace. During the second quarter of the 19th century, Boston, New York, Philadelphia, and other cities sorted themselves into commercial and residential districts; the residential districts further separated into working-class and employer-class neighborhoods.

The first mill operations performed only the task of spinning wool, cotton, and other fibers into thread; soon weaving was also mechanized, so that fabric ready to be cut and sewn was manufactured. Note the child at left, working under the spindles where an adult could not stand.

Even before the widespread use of machinery, large economies of scale were possible. Until the introduction of sewing machines in the 1850s shoes were made entirely by hand, yet by the 1830s the shoe manufacturers of Lynn, Massachusetts, had shifted from making finely finished shoes for individual customers to mass-producing the rough brogans worn by slaves and other farmers. Custom-fitted shoes required the undivided attention of a skilled craftsman, but brogans were made by several unskilled laborers, each performing a different function. Only the last ever saw the finished product.

An Industrial Proletariat?

As the importance of skilled labor declined, so did the ability of workers to influence working conditions. Skilled workers either became employers and developed entrepreneurial and managerial skills or they descended into the mass of wage earners. Simultaneously, the changing structure of work widened the gap between owners and workers and erased the distinction between skilled and unskilled workers.

These trends might have been expected to generate hostility between workers and those who hired them and to foster feelings of class solidarity among workers. To some extent they did. There were strikes for higher wages and to protest work speedups throughout the 1830s and again in the 1850s. Efforts to found unions and to create political organizations dedicated to advancing the interests of workers were also undertaken.

But well into the 1850s few Americans displayed much resentment of the employer class. They lacked the class solidarity that so many European workers had developed by this time. Why American workers did not become a self-conscious working class is a question that has long intrigued historians. As with most such large questions, no single answer has been forthcoming. Some historians argue that the existence of the frontier siphoned off displaced and dissatisfied workers. Other historians believe that ethnic and racial differences kept workers from seeing themselves as a distinct class with common needs and common enemies. Still others have suggested that the influx of needy immigrants willing to accept any job available at almost any wage undercut the organizational efforts of the native-born workers. The fact that the expanding economy created many opportunities for laborers to rise out of the working class was another reason why so few of them developed strong class feelings.

No doubt all these answers help explain the

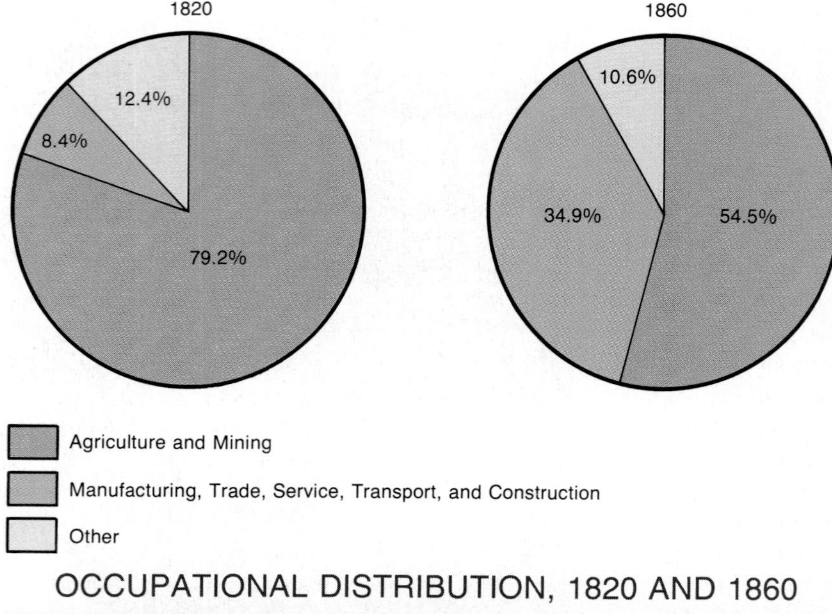

OCCUPATIONAL DISTRIBUTION, 1820 AND 1860

relative absence of class conflict during the early stages of the Industrial Revolution in America. But so does the fact that conditions in the early shops and factories, for all their drawbacks, represented an improvement for the people who worked in them.

Most factory workers, especially in the textile industry, were drawn from outside the regular labor market. Relatively few hand spinners and weavers became factory workers; indeed, some of them continued to work as they had, for it was many years before the factories could even begin to satisfy the ever-increasing demand for cloth. Nor did immigrants attend the new machines. Instead, the mill owners relied chiefly on women and children. They did so because machines lessened the need for skill and strength and because the labor shortage made it necessary to tap unexploited sources. By the early 1820s about half the cotton textile workers in the factories were under 16 years of age.

Most people of that generation considered this a good thing. They reasoned that the work was easy and that it kept youngsters busy at useful tasks while providing their families with extra income. Roxanna Foote, whose daughter Harriet Beecher Stowe wrote *Uncle Tom's Cabin,* came from a solid middle-class family in Guilford, Connecticut. Nevertheless, she worked full-time before her marriage in her grandfather's small spinning mill. "This spinning-mill was a favorite spot," a relative recalled many years later. "Here the girls often received visitors, or read or chatted while they spun." Roxanna explained her daily regimen as a "mill girl" matter-of-factly: "I generally rise with the sun, and, after breakfast, take my wheel, which is my daily companion, and the evening is generally devoted to reading, writing, and knitting." A society accustomed to seeing the children of fairly well-to-do farmers working full-time in the fields was not shocked by the sight of children working all day in mills. In some factories laborers were hired in family units. No member earned very much, but with a couple of adolescent daughters and perhaps a son of 9 or 10 helping out, a family could take home enough to live decently. For most working Americans, then as now, that was success enough.

Instead of hiring children, the Boston Associates developed the "Waltham System" of employing young, unmarried women in their new textile mills. The young women were lodged in company boardinghouses, which, like college dormitories, became centers of social life and not merely places to eat and sleep. Unlike college dormitories, the boardinghouses were strictly supervised; strait-laced New Englanders did not hesitate to permit their daughters to live in them. The regulations laid down by one company, for example, required that all employees "show that they are penetrated by a laudable love of temperance and virtue." "Ardent spirits" were "banished" from company prop-

The cover page of a periodical collection of articles by New England "factory girls"; the Lowell (Massachusetts) publishers listed were Misses Curtis and Farley. A prominent feature in the design is the beehive, a popular symbol representing industriousness.

LOWELL
OFFERING
December, 1845.
" Is Saul also among the prophets ?"
A REPOSITORY
OF ORIGINAL ARTICLES, WRITTEN BY
"FACTORY GIRLS."
LOWELL: MISSES CURTIS & FARLEY.
BOSTON: JORDAN & WILEY, 121
Washington street.
1845.

erty, "games of hazard and cards" prohibited. A 10 P.M. curfew was strictly enforced.

For a generation after the opening of the Merrimack Manufacturing Company in 1823, the thriving factory towns of Lowell, Chicopee, and Manchester provided the background for a remarkable industrial idyll. Young women came from farms all over New England to work for a year or two in the mills. They earned between $2.50 and $3.25 a week, about half of which went for room and board. Some of the remainder they sent home, the rest (what there was of it) they could spend as they wished.

Most of these young women did not have to support themselves. They worked to save for a trousseau, to help educate a younger brother, or simply for the experience and excitement of meeting new people and escaping the confining environment of the farm. "The feeling that at this new work the few hours they had of every-day leisure was entirely their own was a satisfaction to them," one Lowell worker recalled. Anything but an industrial proletariat, they filled the windows of the factories with flowering plants, organized sewing circles, edited their own literary periodicals, and attended lectures on edifying subjects. That such activity was possible on top of a 70-hour workweek is a commentary on both the resiliency of youth and the leisurely pace of these early factories. Dickens, though scarcely enchanted by other American ways, was impressed by his visit to Lowell, which he compared most favorably to "those great haunts of misery," the English manufacturing towns. "They were all well dressed," he wrote of the workers. "They were healthy in appearance, many of them remarkably so, and had the manners and deportment of young women. . . . The rooms in which they worked were as well ordered as themselves."

Life in the mills was not all it might have been—or we might wish it to have been. Though they made up 85 percent of the work force, women were kept out of all supervisory positions. In 1834 workers in several mills "turned out" to protest cuts in their wages and a hike in board. This work stoppage did not force a reversal of management policy. Another strike two years later in response to a work speedup was somewhat more successful. But when a drop in prices in the 1840s led the owners to introduce new rules designed to increase production, workers lacked the organizational strength to prevent their implementation. By then young women of the kind that had flocked to the mills in the 1820s and 1830s were able to find work as schoolteachers or clerks. Mill owners turned increasingly to Irish immigrants to operate their machines.

The Family Recast

The factory system and the growth of cities undermined the importance of home and family as the unit of economic production. This happened first in the cities of the Northeast, then in the West, and eventually wherever nonagricultural jobs occupied a substantial percentage of the work force. More and more people did their work in shops, in offices, or on factory floors. Whether a job was skilled or unskilled, white-collar or blue-collar, or strictly professional it took the family breadwinner out of the house during working hours six days a week. The social consequences of this change were enormous for the traditional "head of the family" and for his wife and children.

Because he was away so much the husband had to surrender much of the power and authority he had formerly possessed to his wife, if for no other reason than that she was always there. This explains why Tocqueville concluded that "a sort of equality reigns around the domestic hearth" in America.

The new power that the wife and mother enjoyed was not obtained without cost. Since she was exercising day-to-day control over household affairs, she was expected to tend only to those affairs. Anything that might take her away from the family hearth was frowned upon. Where she had formerly been a partner in a family enterprise, she now left earning a living entirely to her husband. Time spent away from home or devoted to matters unrelated to the care of husband and family was, according to the new doctrine of "separate spheres," time misappropriated. For a middle-class wife and mother to take a job or, still worse, to devote herself to any "frivolous" activity outside the home was considered a dereliction of duty.

Some women objected to the discrimination implicit in what the historian Barbara Welter has called "the cult of true womanhood." Others escaped its more suffocating aspects by forming close and enduring friendships with other women. But most women, including such forceful proponents of women's rights as Catharine Beecher and Sarah

Family structure changed as a result of the industrial revolution. Not only did couples have fewer children, but husbands were expected to earn the family's living and concern themselves with worldly business while wives assumed all domestic duties.

Hale, subscribed in their writing to the view that a woman's place was in the home.

Another reason for the switch in power and influence from husbands to wives was that women began to have fewer children. Here again, the change happened earliest and was most pronounced among families in the rapidly urbanizing Northeast. But the birthrate gradually declined all over the country. People married later than in earlier periods. Long courtships and broken engagements were common, probably because prospective marriage partners were becoming more choosy. On average, women began having their children two or three years later than their mothers had, and they stopped having children two or three years earlier. Apparently many middle-class couples made a conscious effort to limit family size, even when doing so required sexual abstinence.

Having fewer children led parents to value children more highly, or so it would seem from the additional time and affection they lavished on them. Here again, the mother provided most of both. Child rearing fell within her "sphere" and occupied the time that earlier generations of mothers had devoted to such tasks as weaving, sewing, and various farm chores. Not least of these new responsibilities was overseeing the children's education, both secular and religious.

As families became smaller, relations within them became more caring. Parents ceased to think of their children mostly as future workers. The earlier tendency even among loving parents to keep their children at arm's length, yet within reach of the strap, gave way to more intimate relationships. Gone was the Puritan notion that children possessed "a perverse will, a love of what's forbid," and with it the belief that parents were responsible for crushing all juvenile resistance to their authority (see page 57). In its place arose the view (described by Lydia Maria Child in *The Mother's Book* [1831]) that children "come to us from heaven, with their little souls full of innocence and peace." Mothers "should not interfere with the influence of angels," Child advised her readers.

Bronson Alcott, another proponent of gentle child-rearing practices, went still further. Children, he insisted, were the moral superiors of their parents. Alcott banished "the rod and all its appendages" from his own household, wherein four daughters were raised, and urged other parents to follow his example. "Childhood hath saved me!," he wrote. The English poet William Wordsworth's "Ode on Intimations of Immortality," in which babies entered the world "trailing clouds of glory," served some American parents as an indispensable child-rearing manual.

The Church Almost Revolutionized

Belief in the innate goodness of children was of course in direct conflict with the Calvinist doctrine of infant damnation, to which most American churches formally subscribed. "Of all the impious

Louisa May Alcott's father, Bronson Alcott, advocated benevolent child-rearing practices, teaching that children were the moral superiors of their parents.

doctrines which the dark imagination of man ever conceived," Bronson Alcott wrote in his journal, "the worst [is] the belief in original and certain depravity of infant nature." Alcott was far from alone in thinking infant damnation a "debased doctrine," despite its standing as one of the central tenets of orthodox Calvinism. In point of fact, almost no Calvinist ministers, going back to the Mathers, made any more of the doctrine than they had to. Even Jonathan Edwards was known to have softened its edges when consoling bereaved parents.

The inclination to set aside other Calvinist tenets, such as predestination, became more pronounced as a new wave of revivalism took shape in the 1790s. The Second Great Awakening began as a counteroffensive to the deistic thinking and other forms of "infidelity" which New England Congregationalists and southern Methodists alike identified with the French Revolution. Prominent New England ministers, who considered themselves traditionalists but also revivalists, men such as Yale's Timothy Dwight and Lyman Beecher, placed less stress in their sermons on God's arbitrary power over mortals, more on His mercy, love, and "disinterested benevolence." When one of Dwight's students, Horace Bushnell, declared in a sermon on "Christian Nurture" in 1844 that Christian parents should prepare their children "for the skies," he meant that parents could contribute to their children's salvation. If Bushnell did not intend to discredit Calvinism (and clearly he did not), his argument implied that God was not nearly as stern and wrathful as his Puritan forebears had believed.

Calvinism came under more direct assault from Charles Grandison Finney, probably the most effective of a number of charismatic evangelists who brought the Second Great Awakening to its crest in the early 1830s. In 1821 Finney abandoned a promising career as a lawyer and became an itinerant preacher. His most spectacular successes occurred during a series of revivals conducted in towns along the Erie Canal, a region Finney called "the burned-over district" because it had been the site of so many revivalist efforts before his own. From Utica, where his revival began in 1826, to Rochester, where it climaxed in 1831, he exhorted his listeners to take their salvation into their own hands. He insisted that people could control their own fate. He dismissed Calvinism as a "theological fiction." Salvation was available to anyone. But the day of judgment was just around the corner; there was little time to waste.

During and after Finney's efforts in Utica, declared conversions increased sharply, particularly among women. In Rochester, church membership doubled in six months. Elsewhere in the country, churches capitalized upon the efforts of other evangelists to fill their pews. In 1831 alone, church membership increased by 100,000, making it, according to a New England minister, "unparalleled in the history of the church." Little wonder that Tocqueville declared the United States "the most religious country in the world."

The success of the evangelists of the Second Great Awakening stemmed from the timeliness of their assault on Calvinist doctrines, which were ripe for discrediting, and even more from their methods. Finney, for example, consciously set out to be entertaining as well as edifying. Unlike Jonathan Edwards, who believed that revivals came from God as "surprises" and were not subject to human direction, Finney insisted that they could be "worked up" by evangelists like himself and thereafter carefully orchestrated. The singing of hymns and the solicitation of personal testimonies provided his meetings with emotional release and human interest. Prominent among his innovations was the "anxious bench," where leading members of the community awaited the final prompting from within before coming forward to declare themselves saved. He encouraged young men and young women to pray together in "small circles," well out of sight of their elders. "Who is not aware," wrote a prominent Calvinist editor in 1838, "that the Church has been almost revolutionized within four or five years by means of such excitements?"

Finney took swipes at the pretensions of Protestant ministers who unlike himself had "the advantages of the higher schools of learning" and at all members of the Catholic faith. These tactics went over well with listeners, who were in the main neither professionals nor college graduates and who feared being inundated by German and Irish Catholic immigrants. In short, Finney was one with his age.

Charles Grandison Finney was a major force in the Second Great Awakening of the 1830s. He severely criticized Calvinist strictness and preached the availability of salvation to all.

The Era of Associations

Alongside the recast family and the "almost revolutionized" church, as a third pillar of the emerging American middle class, was the voluntary association. Unlike the other two, it had neither colonial precedents nor contemporary European equivalents. The voluntary association of early 19th-century America was unique to both the country and the era. "In France," Tocqueville wrote of this phenomenon, "if you want to proclaim a truth or propagate some feeling . . . you would find the government or in England some territorial magnate." In America, however, "you are sure to find an association."

Tocqueville may have exaggerated when he wrote that "Americans of all ages, all stations in life, and all types of disposition are forever forming associations," but not by much. In 1828 Utica, New York (population 12,000), supported 21 religious or charitable societies, 3 reform societies, 5 benefit associations, 6 fraternal orders, and 6 self-improvement associations! The leaders of these associations tended to be ministers, lawyers, or merchants, but the rank and file consisted of tradesmen, foremen, clerks, and their wives. Some of these associations were formed around a local cause which some townspeople wished to advance, such as the provision of religious instruction for orphaned children; others were affiliated with associations elsewhere for the purposes of combating some national evil, such as drunkenness. Some, such as the American Board of Commissioners of Foreign Missions, founded in Boston in 1810, quickly became large and complex enterprises. (By 1860 the Board had sent 1,250 missionaries into the "heathen world" and raised $8 million to support them.) Others lasted only as long as it took to accomplish a specific good work, such as the construction of a school or a library. Taken all in all, these associations constituted a "benevolent empire," eager to make society over into their members' idea of how God wanted it to be. "In the history of the world," a popular lecturer informed the Mechanics' Apprentices' Library Association of Boston in 1841, "the doctrine of reform has never had such scope as at the present hour."

Backwoods Utopias

Americans frequently belonged to several associations at the same time and more than a few made "reform" their life's work. The most adventuresome were those who tested their reform theories by withdrawing from workaday American society and establishing experimental communities. The "communitarian" point of view aimed at "commencing a wholesale social reorganization by first establishing and demonstrating its principles completely on a small scale." The first communitarians were religious reformers. In a sense the Pilgrims fall into this category, along with a number of other groups in colonial times, but only in the 19th century did the idea flourish.

One of the earliest significant groups was founded by George Rapp, who brought some 600 Germans to western Pennsylvania in 1804. Rappites renounced marriage and sex and took every word in the Bible literally. They believed that the millennium was at hand; people must have their affairs constantly in order so as to be ready to meet their Maker on short notice. Industrious, pious, and isolated from other Americans by their language and beliefs, the Rappites prospered but had little influence on their neighbors.

More influential were the Shaker communities founded by an English woman, Ann Lee, who came to America in 1774. Mother Ann, as she was called, saw visions which convinced her that Christ would come to earth again as a woman and that she was that woman. With a handful of followers she founded a community near Albany, New York. The group grew rapidly, and after her death in 1784 her movement continued to expand. By the 1830s her followers had established about 20 successful communities.

Like the Rappites, the Shakers practiced celibacy; believing that the millennium was imminent, they saw no reason for perpetuating the human race. Each group lived in a large Family House, the sexes strictly segregated. Property was held in common but controlled by a ruling hierarchy. So much stress was placed on equality of labor and reward and on voluntary acceptance of the rules, however, that the system does not seem to have been oppressive.

The Shaker religon, joyful and fervent, was marked by much group singing and dancing, which provided the members with emotional release from their tightly controlled regimen. An industrious, skillful people, they made a special virtue of simplicity; some of their designs for buildings and, especially, furniture achieved a classic beauty seldom equaled among untutored artisans. Despite their odd customs, the Shakers were universally tolerated and even admired.

The simplicity of Shaker life is apparent in this spartan bedroom, with its plain, narrow bed, its washstand, and the hanging pegs which are a practical way of storing articles such as hats, towels, and even a looking glass.

There were many other religious colonies, such as the Amana Community, which flourished in New York and Iowa in the 1840s and 1850s, and John Humphrey Noyes's Oneida Community, where the members practiced "complex" marriage—a form of promiscuity based on the principle that every man in the group was married to every woman—and prospered by developing a number of manufacturing skills. Brook Farm, the famous transcendental retreat founded "to combine the thinker and the worker" and "do away with the necessity of menial services," was essentially a religious experiment at the start. Brook Farm experimenters tried to accomplish through cooperation what Thoreau sought to do at Walden by himself, "to impart," as their constitution stated, "a greater freedom, simplicity, truthfulness, refinement, and moral dignity, to our mode of life."

The most important of the religious communitarians were the Mormons. A remarkable Vermont farm boy, Joseph Smith, founded the religion in western New York in the 1820s. Smith saw visions; he claimed to have discovered and translated an ancient text, the *Book of Mormon,* written in hieroglyphics on plates of gold, which described the adventures of a tribe of Israelites that had populated America from biblical times until their destruction in a great war in 400 A.D. With a small band of followers, Smith established a community in Ohio in 1831. The Mormons' dedication and economic efficiency attracted large numbers of converts, but their unorthodox religious views and their exclusivism, product of their sense of being a chosen people, roused resentment among unbelievers. They were forced to move first to Missouri and then back to Illinois, where in 1839 they founded the town of Nauvoo.

Nauvoo flourished—by 1844 it was the largest city in the state, with a population of 15,000—but once again the Mormons ran into local trouble. They quarreled among themselves, especially after Smith secretly authorized polygamy (he called it "celestial marriage") and a number of other unusual rites for members of the "Holy Order," the top leaders of the church.* They created a paramilitary organization, the Nauvoo Legion, headed by Smith, envisaging themselves as a kind of semi-independent state within the federal Union. Smith announced that he was a candidate for president of the United States. Rumors circulated that the Mormons intended to take over the entire Northwest for their "empire." Once again local "gentiles" rose against them; Smith was arrested, then murdered by a mob.

Under a new leader, Brigham Young, the Mormons sought a haven beyond the frontier. In 1847 they marched westward, pressing through the mountains until they reached the desolate wilderness on the shores of Great Salt Lake. There, at last, they established their Zion and began to make their truly significant impact on American history. Irrigation made the desert flourish, precious water wisely being treated as a community asset. Hard, cooperative, intelligently directed effort spelled growth and prosperity; more than 11,000 people were living in the area when it became part of Utah Territory as a result of the Compromise of 1850. In time the communal Mormon settlement broke down, but the religion has remained, along with a distinctive Mormon culture that has been a major force in the shaping of the West. The Mormon church is still by far the most powerful single influence in Utah and is a thriving organization in many other parts of the United States and in Europe.

Despite their many common characteristics, the religious communities varied enormously; subordination of the individual to the group did not destroy group individualism. Their sexual practices, for example, ranged from the "complex marriage" of the Oneidans through Mormon polygamy and the ordinary monogamy of the Brook Farmers to the reluctant acceptance of sexual intercourse by the Amana Community and the absolute celibacy of the Rappites and Shakers. The communities are more significant as reflections of the urgent reform spirit of the age than they are for their accomplishments.

The communities had some influence on reformers who wished to experiment with social organization. When Robert Owen, a British utopian socialist who believed in economic as well as political equality and who considered competition debasing, decided to create an ideal community in America, he purchased the Rappite settlement at New Harmony, Indiana. Owen's advocacy of free love and "enlightened atheism" did not add to the stability

* The justification of polygamy, paradoxically, was that marriage was a sacred, eternal state. If a man remarried after his wife's death, eventually he would have two wives in Heaven. Therefore why not on earth?

The Mormon town of Nauvoo, founded in 1839 and within six years the largest city in Illinois, boasted this imposing temple, which was burned by the mob that murdered Joseph Smith in 1844.

of his group or to its popularity among outsiders. The colony was a costly failure.

The American followers of Charles Fourier, a French utopian socialist who proposed that society should be organized in cooperative units called phalanxes, fared better. Fourierism did not seek to tamper with sexual and religious mores. Its advocates included important journalists, such as Horace Greeley of the New York *Tribune* and Parke Godwin of the New York *Evening Post,* and many of the leading Massachusetts transcendentalists. In the 1840s several dozen Fourierist colonies were established in the northern and western states; Brook Farm, in its last years, became one of them. Members worked at whatever tasks they wished and only as much as they wished. Wages were paid according to the "repulsiveness" of the tasks performed; the person who "chose" to clean out a cesspool would receive more than someone hoeing corn or mending a fence or engaging in some task requiring complex skills. As might be expected, none of the communities lasted very long. Ralph Waldo Emerson's epitaph for Brook Farm serves them all:

> It was a perpetual picnic, a French Revolution in small, an Age of Reason in a patty-pan.

The Age of Reform

The communitarians were the most colorful of the reformers, their proposals the most spectacular. More effective, however, were the many individuals who took upon themselves responsibility for caring for the physically and mentally disabled and for the rehabilitation of criminals. The work of Thomas Gallaudet in developing methods for educating deaf people reflects the spirit of the times. Gallaudet's school in Hartford, Connecticut, opened its doors in 1817; by 1851 similar schools for the deaf had been established in 14 states.

Dr. Samuel Gridley Howe did similar work with the blind, devising means for making books with raised letters (Louis Braille's system of raised dots was not introduced until later in the century) that the blind could "read" with their fingers. Howe headed a school for the blind in Boston, the pioneering Perkins Institution, which opened in 1832. Of all that Charles Dickens observed in America, nothing so favorably impressed him as Howe's success in educating 12-year-old Laura Bridgman, who was deaf, dumb, and blind. Howe was also interested in trying to educate the mentally defective and in other causes, including antislavery. "Every creature in human shape should command our respect," he insisted. "The strong should help the weak, so that the whole should advance as a band of brethren."

One of the most striking aspects of the reform movement was the emphasis reformers placed on establishing special institutions for dealing with social problems. In the colonial period, orphans, indigent persons, the insane, and the feebleminded were usually cared for by members of their own families or boarded in a neighboring household. They remained part of the community. Even criminals were seldom "locked away" for extended jail terms; punishment commonly consisted of whipping, being placed in stocks in the town square, or (for serious crimes) execution. But once persuaded that people were primarily shaped by their surroundings, reformers demanded that deviant and dependent members of the community be taken from their present corrupting circumstances and placed in specialized institutions where they could be trained or rehabilitated. The result, according to the historian David J. Rothman, was "the discovery of the asylum." Almshouses, orphanages, reformatories, prisons, and lunatic asylums sprang up throughout the United States like mushrooms in a forest after a summer rain.

The rationale for this movement was scientific; elaborate statistical reports attested to the benefits that such institutions would bring to both inmates and society as a whole. The motivating spirit of the founders of these asylums was humane, though many of the institutions seem anything but humane to the modern eye. The highly regarded Philadelphia prison system was based on strict solitary confinement, which was supposed to lead culprits to reflect upon their sins and then reform their ways. The prison was literally a penitentiary, a place to repent. In fact, the system drove some inmates mad, and soon a rival Auburn system was introduced in New York State, which allowed for some social contact among prisoners and for work in shops and stone quarries. Absolute silence was required at all times. The prisoners were herded about in lock step and punished by flogging for the slightest infraction of the rules. Regular "moral and religious instruction" was provided, which the authorities believed would lead inmates to reform their lives. Tocqueville and Beaumont, in their report on American prisons, concluded that the Philadelphia system produced "the deepest impression on the soul of the convict," while the Auburn system made the convict "more conformable to the habits of man in society."

The hospitals for mental patients were intended to cure inmates, not merely to confine them. The emphasis was on isolating them from the pressures of society; on order, quiet, routine; on control but not on punishment. The unfortunates were seen

A daguerreotype of Dorothea Lynde Dix, the pioneer reformer who worked to improve the lot of the insane in the United States. She also traveled to Europe, where she urged Queen Victoria and Pope Pius IX to support her efforts.

as *de*ranged; the task was to *ar*range their lives in a rational manner. In practice, shortages of trained personnel, niggardly legislative appropriations, and the inherent difficulty of managing violent and irrational patients often produced deplorable conditions in the asylums. This situation led Dorothea Dix, a woman of almost saintlike selflessness, to devote 30 years of her life to a campaign to improve the care of the insane. She traveled to every state in the Union and as far afield as Turkey and Japan, inspecting asylums and poorhouses. Insane persons in Massachusetts, she wrote in a memorial intended to shock state legislators into action, were being kept in cages and closets, "*chained, naked, beaten with rods, and lashed into obedience!*" Her reports led to some improvement in conditions in Massachusetts and other states, but in the long run the bright hopes of the reformers were never realized. Institutions founded to uplift the deviant and dependent all too soon lost their reformist intentions and became instead places where society's "misfits" might safely be kept out of sight.

"Demon Rum"

Reformers must of necessity interfere with the affairs of others; thus there is often something of the busybody and arrogant meddler about them. How they are regarded usually turns on the observer's own attitude toward their objectives. What is to some an unjustified infringement upon a person's private affairs is to others a necessary intervention for that person's own good and for the good of society. Consider the temperance movement, the most widely supported and successful reform of the age of reforms.

Americans in the 1820s consumed prodigious amounts of alcohol, more than ever before or since. Not that the colonists had been teetotalers. Liquor, mostly in the form of rum or hard apple cider, was cheap and everywhere available; taverns were an integral part of colonial society. There were alcoholics in colonial America, but because neither political nor religious leaders considered drinking dangerous there was no alcohol "problem." Most doctors recommended the regular consumption of alcohol as healthy. John Adams, certainly the soul of propriety, drank a tankard of hard cider every day for breakfast. Dr. Benjamin Rush's *Inquiry into the Effects of Ardent Spirits* (1784), which questioned the medicinal benefits of alcohol, fell on deaf ears.

However, alcohol consumption increased markedly in the early years of the new republic, thanks primarily to the availability of cheap corn and rye whiskey distilled in the new states of Kentucky and Tennessee. In the 1820s the per capita consumption of hard liquor reached 5 gallons, well over twice what it is today. Since many people did not drink that much, others must have drunk a great deal more. Many women drank, if mostly at home; and reports of carousing among 14-year-old college freshmen show that youngsters did too. But the bulk of the heavy drinking occurred when men got together, at taverns or grog shops and at work.

Artisans and common laborers regarded their twice-daily "dram" of whiskey as part of their wages. In workshops masters were expected to halt production periodically to drink with their apprentices and journeymen. Trips to the neighborhood grog shop also figured into the workaday routine. In 1829 Secretary of War John Eaton estimated that three-quarters of the nation's laborers drank at least 4 ounces of distilled spirits a day. Lawyers and doctors had a running argument as to which profession contained the larger proportions of sots.

The foundation of the American Temperance Union in 1826 signaled the start of a national crusade against drunkenness. Employing lectures, pamphlets, rallies, essay contests, and other techniques, the union set out to persuade people to "sign the pledge" not to drink liquor. Primitive sociological studies of the effects of drunkenness (as early as 1833, reformers were able to show a high statistical correlation between alcohol consumption and crime) added to the effectiveness of the campaign. Revivalist ministers like Lyman Beecher and Charles Grandison Finney argued that alcohol was one of the great barriers to conversion. Employers also signed on, declaring their businesses henceforward to be "cold-water" enterprises. Soon the temperance movement claimed a million members. In 1840 an organization of reformed drunkards, the Washingtonians, began a campaign of their own to reclaim alcoholics. One of the most effective of its workers was John B. Gough, rescued by the organization after seven years in the gutter. "Crawl from the slimy ooze, ye drowned drunkards," Gough would shout, "and with suffocation's blue and livid lips speak out against the drink!"

The methods and the objectives of the temperance people roused bitter opposition, particularly after they moved beyond calls for restraint to demands for prohibition of all alcohol. German and Irish immigrants, for the most part Catholic, objected to being told by reformers, for the most part Protestant, that their drinking would have to stop. Their objections only confirmed what many temperance reformers already believed, that the rapidly growing Catholic church was out to defeat them.

By the early 1840s the reformers had secured legislation in many states which imposed strict licensing systems and heavy liquor taxes. Local option laws permitted towns and counties to ban the sale of alcohol altogether. In 1851 Maine passed the first effective law prohibiting the manufacture and sale of alcoholic beverages. The leader of the campaign was Mayor Neal Dow of Portland, a businessman who became a prohibitionist after seeing the damage done by drunkenness among workers in his tannery. By 1855 a dozen other states had passed laws based on the Maine statute, and the nation's per capita consumption of alcohol had dropped to 2 gallons a year.

The Abolitionist Crusade

No reform movement of this era was more significant, more ambiguous in character, or more provocative of later historical investigation than the drive to abolish slavery. That slavery should have been a cause of indignation to reform-minded Americans was inevitable. Humanitarians were outraged by the master's whip and by the practice of disrupting families. Democrats protested the denial of political and civil rights to slaves. Perfectionists of all stripes deplored the fact that slaves had no chance to improve themselves. However, well into the 1820s, the abolitionist cause attracted few followers because there seemed to be no way of getting rid of slavery short of revolution. While a few theorists argued that the Fifth Amendment, which provides that no one may be "deprived of life, liberty, or property, without due process of law" could be interpreted to mean that the Constitution outlawed slavery, the great majority believed that the institution was not subject to federal control.

Particularly in the wake of the Missouri Compromise, antislavery northerners neatly compartmentalized their thinking. Slavery was wrong; they would not tolerate it in their own communities. But since the Constitution obliged them to tolerate it in states where it existed, they felt no responsibility to fight it. The issue was explosive enough even when limited to the question of the expansion of slavery into the territories. Those who advocated any kind of *forced* abolition in states where it was legal and backed by nearly all voters were judged irresponsible in the extreme. In 1820 presidential hopeful John Quincy Adams called slavery "the great and foul stain upon the North American Union." "If the Union must be dissolved," he added, "slavery is precisely the question upon which it ought to break." But Adams expressed these opinions in the privacy of his diary, not in a public speech.

Most critics of slavery therefore confined themselves to urging "colonization" or persuading slaveowners to treat their property humanely. Meanwhile, they advised, slaves should "cultivate feelings of piety and gratitude" for the "blessings" they enjoyed. What these blessings were their northern sympathizers seldom specified. As the historian Benjamin Quarles remarked acidly, such advice came down to "bear and forbear."

One of the few Americans in the 1820s to go further was the Quaker Benjamin Lundy, editor of the Baltimore-based newspaper *The Genius of Universal Emancipation.* Lundy was no fanatic; he urged the use of persuasion in the South rather than interference by the federal government. He also explored the possibility of colonizing free blacks and slaves in Haiti and Canada. But he refused to mince words and consequently he was subject to frequent harassment.

Even more provocative and less accommodating to local sensibilities was Lundy's youthful assistant, William Lloyd Garrison of Massachusetts. Garrison pronounced himself for "immediate" abolition. When his absolutely unyielding position made continued residence in Baltimore impossible, he returned to Boston where in 1831 he established his own newspaper, *The Liberator.* "I am in earnest,"

William Lloyd Garrison founded The Liberator *and edited it for 35 years; the newspaper was one of the nation's leading antislavery publications.*

he announced in the first issue. "I will not equivocate—I will not excuse—I will not retreat a single inch—and *I will be heard.*"

Garrison's position, and that espoused by the New England Anti-Slavery Society, which he organized in 1831, was absolutely unyielding: slaves must be freed immediately and treated as equals; compensated emancipation was unacceptable, colonization unthinkable. Because the United States government countenanced slavery, Garrison refused to engage in political activity to achieve his ends. Burning a copy of the Constitution—that "agreement with hell"—became a regular feature at Society-sponsored public lectures.

Few white Americans found Garrison's line of argument convincing, and many were outraged by his confrontational tactics. Whenever he spoke in public he risked being mobbed by what newspaper accounts approvingly described as "gentlemen of property and standing." In 1833 a Garrison meeting in New York City was broken up by colonizationists. Two years later a mob dragged Garrison through the streets of his own Boston. That same day a mob broke up the convention of the New York Anti-Slavery Society in Utica. In 1837 Elijah Lovejoy, a Garrisonian newspaper editor in Alton, Illinois, first saw his press destroyed by fire and then was himself murdered by a mob. When the proprietors of Philadelphia's Pennsylvania Hall booked an abolitionist meeting in 1838, a mob burned the hall to the ground to prevent the meeting from taking place. The historian Leonard L. Richard has located more than 100 attacks on abolitionists in the North between 1833 and 1838.

In the wake of this violence some of Garrison's backers had second thoughts about his strategy of immediatism. The wealthy New York businessmen Arthur and Lewis Tappan, who had subsidized *The Liberator,* turned instead to Theodore Dwight Weld, a young minister who was part of Charles Grandison Finney's "holy band" of revivalists. Weld and his followers spoke of "immediate" emancipation "gradually" achieved and they were willing to engage in political activity to achieve that goal.

In 1840 the Tappans and Weld openly broke with Garrison over the issue of involvement in politics and the use of female abolitionists as public lecturers. Garrison, ever the radical, supported the women; Weld thought they would needlessly antagonize would-be supporters. The Tappans then organized the Liberty Party, which nominated as its presidential candidate James G. Birney, a Kentucky slaveholder who had been converted to evangelical Christianity and abolitionism by Weld. Running on a platform of universal emancipation to be gradually brought about through legislation, Birney received only 7,000 votes.

Many blacks were abolitionists long before the white movement began to attract attention. In 1830 some 50 black antislavery societies existed, and thereafter these groups grew in size and importance, being generally associated with the Garrisonian wing. White abolitionists eagerly sought out black speakers, especially runaway slaves, whose heartrending accounts of their experiences roused sympathies and who, merely by speaking clearly and with conviction, stood as living proof that blacks were neither animals nor fools.

Frederick Douglass, a former slave who had escaped from Maryland, was one of the most remarkable Americans of his generation. While a bondsman he had received a full portion of beatings and other indignities; but he had been allowed to learn to read and write and to master a trade, opportunities denied the vast majority of slaves. Settling in Boston, he became an agent of the Massachusetts Anti-Slavery Society and a featured speaker at its public meetings.

Douglass was a tall, majestically handsome man who radiated determination and indignation. Slavery, he told white audiences, "brands your republicanism as a sham, your humanity as a base pretense, your Christianity as a lie." In 1845 he published his *Narrative of the Life of Frederick Douglass,* one of the most gripping autobiographical accounts of a slave's life ever written. The book attracted wide attention in America and Europe. Douglass insisted that freedom for blacks required not merely emancipation but full equality, social and economic as well as political. Not many white northerners accepted his reasoning, but few who heard him or read his works could afterward maintain the illusion that all blacks were dull-witted or resigned to inferior status.

Former slave Frederick Douglass was one of the most effective spokesmen of the Massachusetts Anti-Slavery Society in the 1840s.

At first Douglass was, in his own words, "a faithful disciple" of Garrison, prepared to tear up the Constitution and destroy the Union to gain his ends. In the late 1840s, however, he changed his mind, deciding that the Constitution, created to "establish Justice, insure domestic Tranquility . . . and secure the Blessings of Liberty," as its preamble states, "could not well have been designed at the same time to maintain and perpetuate a system of rapine and murder like slavery." Thereafter he fought slavery and race prejudice from within the system. This Garrison was never willing to do.

Garrison's importance cannot be measured by the number of his followers, which was never large. Unlike more moderately inclined enemies of slavery, he recognized that abolitionism was a revolutionary movement, not merely one more middle-class reform. He also understood that achieving racial equality, not merely "freeing" the slaves, was the only way to reach the abolitionists' professed objective: full justice for blacks. And he saw clearly that few whites, even among abolitionists, believed that blacks were their equals.

At the same time, Garrison seemed utterly indifferent to what effect the "immediate" freeing of the slaves would have on the South. He and his followers came close to claiming that all southern whites were villains, all blacks saints. Garrison said he would rather be governed by "the inmates of our penitentiaries" than by southern congressmen, whom he characterized as "desperadoes." The life of the slaveowner, he wrote, is "one of unbridled lust, of filthy amalgamation, of swaggering braggadocio, of haughty domination, of cowardly ruffianism, of boundless dissipation, of matchless insolence, of infinite self-conceit, of unequalled oppression, of more than savage cruelty." His followers were no less fanatical in their judgments. "Slavery and cruelty cannot be disjoined," one wrote. "Consequently every slaveholder must be inhuman."

Both Garrison's insights into the limits of northern racial egalitarianism and his blind contempt for southern whites led him to the conclusion that American society was rotten to the core. Hence his refusal to make any concession to the existing establishment, religious or secular. He was hated in the North as much for his explicit denial of the idea that a Constitution which supported slavery merited respect as for his implicit denial of the idea that a professed Christian who tolerated slavery for even an instant could hope for salvation. He was, in short, a perfectionist, a trafficker in moral absolutes who wanted his Kingdom of Heaven in the here and now. By contrast, most other American reformers were willing to settle for perfection on the installment plan.

Women's Rights

The question of slavery was related to another major reform movement of the era, the crusade for women's rights. The relationship was personal and ideological, direct and indirect, simple and profound. Superficially, the connection can be explained in this way: Women were as likely as men to find slavery offensive and to protest against it. When they did so, they ran into even more adamant resistance, the prejudices of those who objected to abolitionists being reinforced by their feelings that women should not speak in public or participate in political affairs. Thus female abolitionists, driven by the urgencies of conscience, were almost forced to become advocates of women's rights. "We have good cause to be grateful to the slave," the feminist Abby Kelley wrote. "In striving to strike his irons off, we found most surely, that we were manacled *ourselves.*"

At a more profound level, the reference that abolitionists made to the Declaration of Independence to justify their attack on slavery radicalized women with regard to their own place in society. Were only all *men* created equal and endowed by God with unalienable rights? For many women the question was a consciousness-raising experience; they began to believe that, like blacks, they were imprisoned from birth in a caste system, legally subordinated and assigned menial social and economic roles that prevented them from developing their full potentialities. Such women considered themselves in a sense worse off than blacks, who had at least the psychological advantage of confronting an openly hostile and repressive society rather than one concealed behind the cloying rhetoric of romantic love.

With the major exception of Margaret Fuller, whose book *Women in the Nineteenth Century* (1844) made a frontal assault on all forms of sexual discrimination, the leading advocates of equal rights for women began their public careers in the abolitionist movement. Among the first were Sarah and Angelina Grimké, South Carolinians who abandoned their native state and the domestic sphere to devote themselves to speaking out against slavery. (In 1841 Angelina married Theodore Dwight Weld.) Male objections to the Grimkés' activities soon made them advocates of women's rights. Similarly, the refusal of delegates to the World Anti-Slavery Convention held in London in 1840 to let women participate in their debates precipitated the decision of two American abolitionists, Lucretia Mott and Elizabeth Cady Stanton, to turn their attention to the women's rights movement.

Slavery aside, there were other aspects of feminist consciousness-raising. Some women rejected the idea that they should confine themselves to a "sphere" of activity consisting mostly of child rearing and housekeeping. As the historian Nancy Cott has shown, the very effort to enforce this kind of specialization made women aware of their second-class citizenship and thus more likely to be dissatisfied. They lacked not merely the right to vote, of which they did not make a major issue, but if married, the right to own property or to make a will. Lydia Maria Child, a popular novelist, found this last restriction particularly offensive. It excited her "towering indignation" that her husband had to sign her will. David Child was not what today would be called a chauvinist, but, as she explained, "I was indignant for womankind made chattels personal from the beginning of time."

As Lydia Child noted, the subordination of women was as old as civilization. The attack on it came not because of any new discrimination but for the same reasons that roused reformers against other forms of injustice: belief in progress, a sense of personal responsibility, the conviction that institutions *could* be changed and that the time for changing them was limited.

When women sought to involve themselves in reform, they became aware of perhaps the most serious handicap that society imposed upon them—the conflict between their roles as wives and mothers and their urge to participate in the affairs of the larger world. Elizabeth Cady Stanton has left a striking description of this dilemma. She lived

Elizabeth Cady Stanton at the age of 41 with her youngest daughter. In 1848 she helped draft the Declaration of Principles, spelling out the injustices of man to woman. The conclusion: "He has endeavored, in every way he could, to destroy her confidence in her own powers, to lessen her self-respect, and to make her willing to lead a dependent and abject life."

in the 1840s in Seneca Falls, a small town in central New York. Her husband was frequently away on business; she had a brood of growing children and little domestic help. When, stimulated by her interest in abolition and women's rights, she sought to become active in the movements, her family responsibilities made it almost impossible even to read about them.

"I now fully understood the practical difficulties most women had to contend with," she recalled in her autobiography, *Eighty Years and More* (1898). "The general discontent I felt with woman's portion as wife, mother, housekeeper, physician, and spiritual guide, the chaotic condition into which everything fell without her constant supervision, and the wearied, anxious look of the majority of women, impressed me with the strong feeling that some active measures should be taken." Active measures she took. Together with Lucretia Mott and a few others of like mind, she organized a meeting, the Seneca Falls Convention (July 1848), and drafted a Declaration of Principles patterned on the Declaration of Independence. "We hold these truths to be self-evident: that all men and women are created equal," it stated, and it went on to list the "injuries and usurpations" of men, just as Jefferson had outlined those of George III.

From this seed the movement grew. During the 1850s a series of national conventions was held; more and more reformers, including William Lloyd Garrison, joined the cause. Of the recruits Susan B. Anthony was the most influential, for she was the first to see the need for thorough organization if effective pressure was to be brought to bear on male-dominated society. Her first campaign, mounted in 1854–1855 in behalf of a petition to the New York legislature calling for reform of the property and divorce laws, accumulated 6,000 signatures. But the petition did not persuade the legislature to act. Indeed, the feminists achieved very few practical results during the age of reform. Their leaders, however, were persevering types, most of them extraordinarily long-lived. Their major efforts lay in the future.

Despite the aggressiveness of many reformers and the extremity of some of their proposals, little social conflict blighted these years. Most citizens readily accepted the need for improving society and showed a healthy tolerance for even the most harebrained schemes for doing so. When Sylvester Graham, inventor of the graham cracker, traveled up and down the land praising the virtues of hard mattresses, cold showers, and homemade bread, he was mobbed by professional bakers, but otherwise, as his biographer says, "he was the subject of jokes, lampoons, and caustic editorials" rather than violence. Americans argued about everything from prison reform to vegetarianism, from women's rights to phrenology (a pseudoscience much occupied with developing the diagnostic possibilities of measuring the bumps on people's heads). But they seldom came to blows. Even the abolitionist movement might not have caused serious social strife if the territorial expansion of the late 1840s had not dragged the slavery issue back into politics. When that happened, politics again assumed center stage, public discourse grew embittered, and the first great age of reform came to an end.

SUPPLEMENTARY READING

Titles marked with an asterisk have been published in paperback.

On Tocqueville and his views of America, Alexis de Tocqueville, **Democracy in America,*** J. P. Mayer, ed. (1966 edition), Tocqueville's Travel Notes in J. P. Mayer (ed.), **Journey to America** (1960), and George W. Pierson, **Tocqueville and Beaumont in America** (1938). For other visitor accounts, see Frances Trollope, **Domestic Manners of the Americans** (1832), Francis J. Grund, **Aristocracy in America** (1839), Charles Dickens, **American Notes** (1847), and Harriet Martineau, **Retrospect of Western Travel** (1838). Edward Pessen, **Riches, Class, and Power Before the Civil War*** (1973), and Rowland Berthoff, **An Unsettled People: Social Order and Disorder in American History*** (1971), offer views different from Tocqueville's.

The growth of cities in the Jacksonian era can be traced in Richard C. Wade, **The Urban Frontier*** (1957) and **Slavery in the Cities*** (1964), and Howard Chudacoff, **The Evolution of American Urban Society*** (1981). Allen F. Davis and Mark Haller (eds.), **The Peoples of Philadelphia*** (1973), Sam Bass Warner, Jr., **The Private City: Philadelphia in Three Periods of Its Growth*** (1968), Oscar Handlin, **Boston's Immigrants*** (1968 ed.), and Peter R. Knights, **The Plain People of Boston*** (1971), deal with individual cities.

On immigration and ethnicity, see Maldwyn Jones, **American Immigration*** (1960), Ray A. Billington, **Protestant Crusade*** (1938), Jay P. Dolan, **Immigrant Church: New York's Irish and German Catholics*** (1982), and, generally, Stephan Thernstrom (ed.), **Harvard Encyclopedia of American Ethnic Groups** (1980).

On changes in the nature of work in America, consult A. F. C. Wallace, **Rockdale: The Growth of an American Village*** (1978), Alan Dawley, **Class and Community: The Industrial Revolution in Lynn, Massachusetts*** (1976), Thomas Dublin, **Women at Work: The Transformation of Work and Community in Lowell, Massachusetts** (1979), and Sean Wilencz, **Chants Democratic: New York City and the Rise of the American Working Class** (1984). On the changing place of the family and the changes within it, see Mary P. Ryan, **Cradle of the Middle Class: The Family in Oneida, New York*** (1981), Nancy Cott, **The Bonds of Womanhood*** (1977), and Philip Greven, **The Protestant Temperament: Patterns of Child-Rearing, Religious Experience, and the Self in Early America** (1980). On demographic developments, see Walter Nugent, **Structures in American Social History** (1981), and Maris A. Vinovskis, **Fertility in Massachusetts from the Revolution to the Civil War** (1981).

The Second Great Awakening has been examined both as a religious and as a social phenomenon. Still useful are Whitney Cross, **The Burned-Over District: Enthusiastic Religion in Western New York*** (1950), and Bernard Weisberger, **They Gathered at the River** (1958), but see also William McLoughlin, **Modern Revivalism: Finney to Graham** (1959), Timothy Smith, **Revivalism and Reform** (1965), and Paul E. Johnson, **A Shopkeeper's Millennium: Societies and Revivals in Rochester, New York, 1815–1837*** (1978).

On the overseas missions, see Clifton Phillips, **Protestant America and the Pagan World** (1964), and on utopianism generally, Arthur Bestor, **Backwoods Utopias** (1950). Newell G. Bringhurst, **Brigham Young and the Expanding American Frontier*** (1985), is useful on the Mormons, while Fawn W. Brodie, **No Man Knows My History: The Life of Joseph Smith the Mormon Prophet*** (1945), is a critical account of the Mormon leader.

On reform movements generally, see Ronald G. Walters, **American Reformers, 1815–1860*** (1978). On the social-control implications of reform, see Clifford S. Griffin, **Their Brothers' Keepers*** (1960), and David J. Rothman, **Age of the Asylum: Social Order and Disorder in the New Republic*** (1971). Three lively accounts of the temperance movement are F. L. Bryne, **Prophet of Prohibition: Neal Dow and his Crusade** (1961), Ian Tyrrell, **Sobering Up: From Temperance to Prohibition in Ante-Bellum America** (1979), and W. J. Rorabaugh, **The Alcoholic Republic: An American Tradition*** (1979).

For sharply contrasting views of the abolitionist movement, see Stanley Elkins, **Slavery: A Problem in American Institutional and Intellectual Life*** (1975), and Aileen Kraditor, **Means and Ends in American Abolitionism*** (1967). Lewis Perry and Michael Fellman (eds.), **Anti-Slavery Reconsidered: New Perspectives**

on the Abolitionists* (1979), provides just that. Biographical accounts include John L. Thomas, **The Liberator: William Lloyd Garrison*** (1963), Gerda Lerner, **The Grimke Sisters from South Carolina*** (1967), and Nathan Huggins, **Slave and Citizen: The Life of Frederick Douglass*** (1980). On anti-abolitionists, see Leonard L. Richards, **"Gentlemen of Property and Standing": Anti-Abolitionist Mobs in Jacksonian America*** (1970).

Two recent interpretive accounts of the history of women and women's rights are Carl Degler, **At Odds: Women and Family in America from the Revolution to the Present*** (1980), and Nancy Woloch, **Women and the American Experience*** (1984); and Eleanor Flexner, **Century of Struggle: The Women's Rights Movement in the United States*** (1959), is still useful. Elizabeth Griffith, **In Her Own Rights: The Life of Elizabeth Cady Stanton** (1984), and Kathryn K. Sklar, **Catharine Beecher: A Study in American Domesticity** (1973), are solid biographies of important women in the Jacksonian era.

PORTFOLIO FOUR

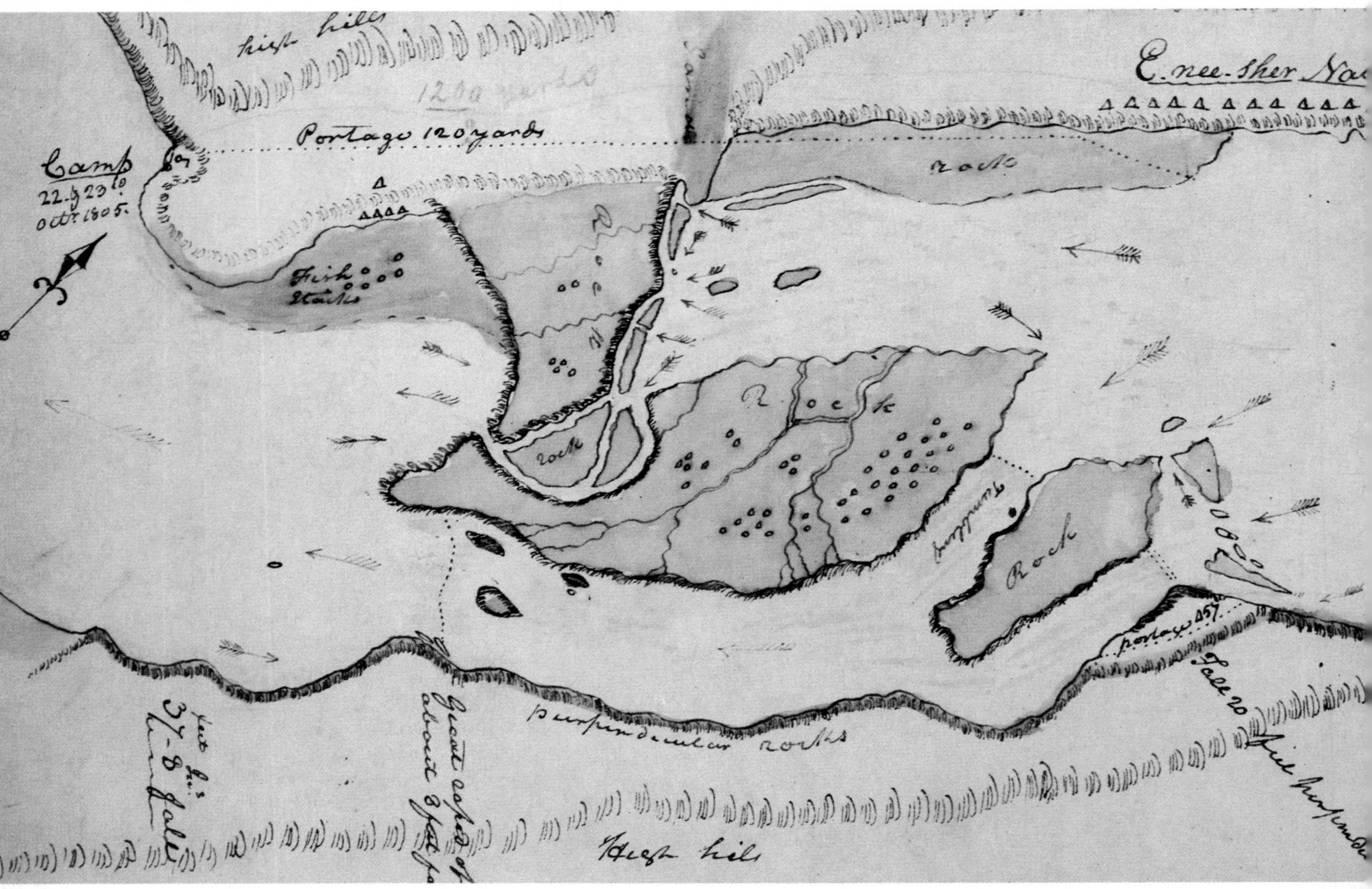

Westward Ho!

The "conquest" of the West, completed in a great rush during the middle decades of the 19th century, was only the final chapter of a story that began when the first Europeans set foot on North American soil in the 16th century. But beginning with the explorations of Lewis and Clark, the scale of western development changed dramatically. Thereafter, the stage on which the western drama was played out was of giant size; one might almost say larger than life.

By the 1830s the western epic was approaching its climax. The West was a land of infinite distances, its climate harsh, its Indian inhabitants brave and skillful fighters, its resources difficult to extract, yet it was explored, mapped, conquered, and settled with unprecedented rapidity. The mighty Rockies dwarfed the ridges of the Appalachians that had long checked the westward advance, but they were surmounted far more swiftly.

This portfolio illustrates some of the many elements that made up the conquest of the West—the grandeur and dignity of the region and its native peoples, the interactions of white and native inhabitants in a constantly changing situation, the driving energy of the pioneers and their stop-at-nothing commitment to the task of winning control of the region.

During Lewis and Clark's 1804 expedition to the Louisiana Purchase country (see Chapter 6), the explorers kept extensive records of their trip. This watercolor map of the Great Falls of the Columbia River is one of hundreds such drawings they made.

For many years after the Louisiana Purchase, Indian tribal life west of the Mississippi River continued almost unchanged. Buffalo and elk, beautifully portrayed in this painting by Karl Bodmer, were major sources of food and clothing. Great Plains tribes used horses for transportation, hunting, and warfare. They were famous horsemen. Alfred Jacob Miller's painting *Throwing the Lasso* portrays one of their tricky maneuvers.

Violence was an accepted part of life in the West. In this facsimile of an Indian painting, the Mandan chief Mató-Tópe battles and kills a fur-hatted Cheyenne chief in a bloody hatchet fight.

By 1820, expeditions into the far reaches of the Louisiana Purchase country were becoming common. Above, a group of white men visit a Kiowa encampment on the Yellowstone River. The flag, with its interracial handclasp and peace pipes, was almost surely a gift from the visitors. By 1834, stout wooden stockades like that surrounding Ft. Laramie on the North Fork of the Platte River (below) showed that white settlers were establishing themselves in country that had previously been dominated by Indians.

Back country Indiana still had the look of the frontier in the 1830s, as can be seen from Karl Bodmer's watercolor of an isolated farmstead (above). But by the 1840s and 1850s the search for more land and better opportunities had led Americans across the prairies and the mountains to Oregon and California. The covered Conestoga wagon had gained the nickname "prairie schooner." The romanticized 1853 view of a pause in the trip to talk over plans and problems at immediate right is titled *Advice on the Prairie.* When the pioneers arrived at the end of the trail, they found raw settlements, like Oregon City huddled on the banks of the Willamette River. The watercolor at upper right was made in 1845 by an English visitor.

W. R. H.

The discovery of gold in California in 1848 brought still more people to the West Coast. In 1847, San Francisco (see sketch at upper left) was a sleepy village with a few houses scattered along the shore and straggling up the hills. After gold was discovered, thousands flocked in, some by clipper ship from the East Coast (see poster at right). By 1850, San Francisco, as portrayed in the drawing at lower left, had become a booming community of hastily constructed boardinghouses, taverns, and general stores, all designed to satisfy the needs of the gold seekers headed for the Mother Lode country. In 1853 alone, 33,000 people arrived.

Merchants' Express Line of Clipper Ships

FOR

SAN FRANCISCO!

NONE BUT A 1 FAST SAILING CLIPPERS LOADED IN THIS LINE.

THE EXTREME CLIPPER SHIP

OCEAN EXPRESS

WATSON, COMMANDER,

AT PIER 9, EAST RIVER.

This splendid vessel is one of the fastest Clippers afloat, and a great favorite with all shippers. Her commander, Capt. WATSON, was formerly master of the celebrated Clipper "FLYING DRAGON," which made the passage in **97 days**, and of the ship POLYNESIA, which made the passage in **103 days.**

She comes to the berth one third loaded, and has very large engagements.

RANDOLPH M. COOLEY,

118 WATER ST., cor. Wall, Tontine Building.

Agents in San Francisco, De Witt, Kittle & Co.

11
A Democratic Culture

We have listened too long to the courtly muses of Europe. Ralph Waldo Emerson, *1837*

It's good to be shifty in a new country. J. J. Hooper, The Adventures of Simon Suggs, *1846*

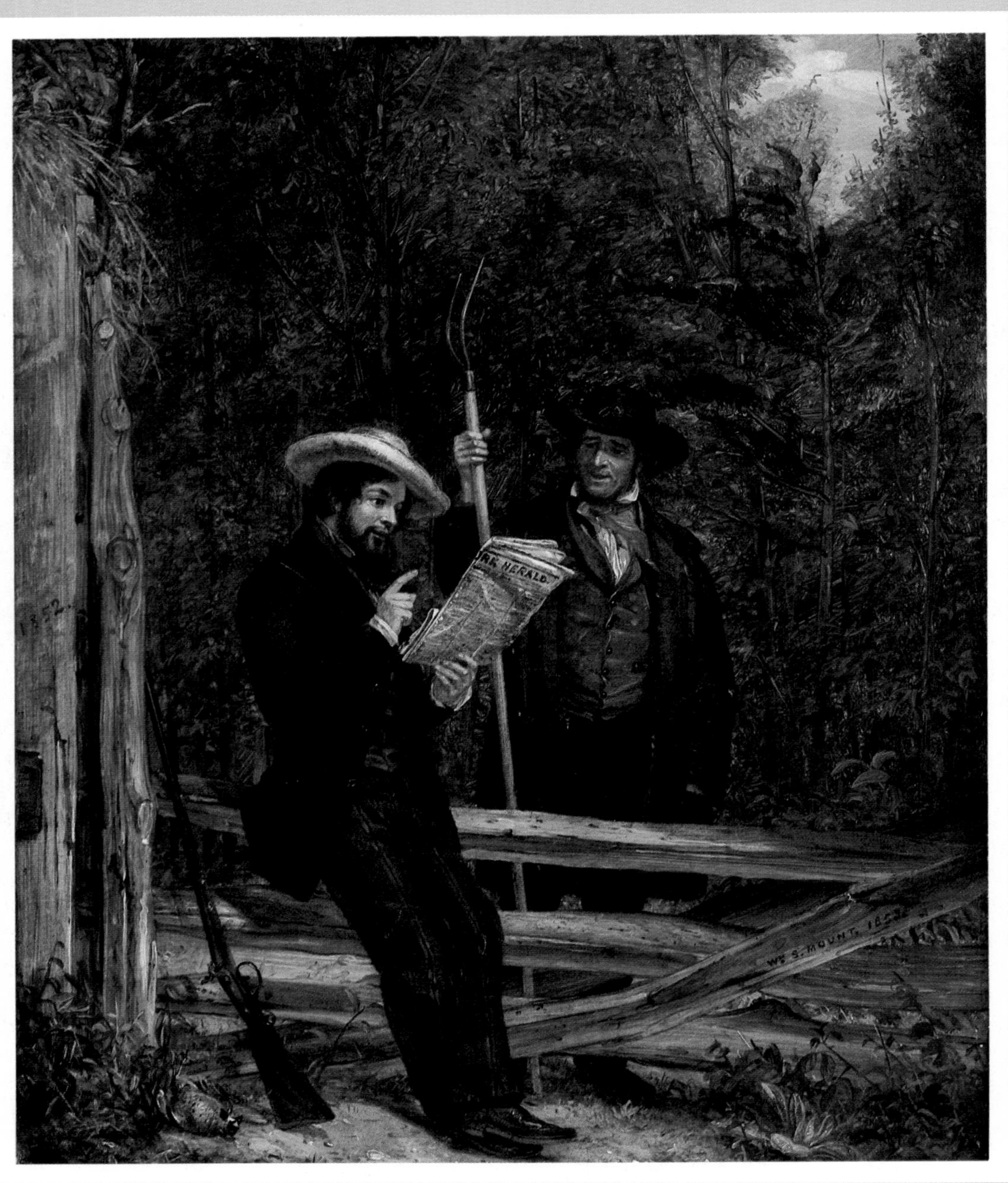

As the United States grew larger, richer, and more centralized, it began to evolve a more distinctive culture. Still the child of Europe, by mid-century it was clearly the offspring rather than an imitation of the parent society. Jefferson had drawn most of his ideas from classical authors and 17th-century English thinkers. He gave to these doctrines an American cast, as when he stressed the separation of church and state or the pursuit of happiness instead of property in describing the "unalienable rights" of men. But Ralph Waldo Emerson, whose views were roughly similar to Jefferson's and who was also influenced by European thinkers, was an *American* philosopher. He and his generation drew quite self-consciously on native sources and inspirations. In doing so they described convincingly the emergence of a distinctly democratic culture.

In Search of Native Grounds

Early 19th-century literary groups such as Boston's Anthology Club and the Friendly Club in New York consciously set out to "foster American genius" and to encourage the production of a distinctively American literature. According to the historian Russel B. Nye, in the period between the Revolution and 1830 "every author of note made at least one effort to use American history in a major literary work."

Yet as Nye admits, in nearly every case "nothing of consequence appeared." Of the novelists before 1830, only James Fenimore Cooper made successful use of the national heritage. Beginning with *The Spy* (1821), *The Pioneers* (1823), and *The Last of the Mohicans* (1826), he wrote a long series of tales of Indians and settlers that presented a vivid, if romanticized, picture of frontier life. (Cooper's Indians, Mark Twain quipped, belonged to "an extinct tribe that never existed.") Cooper's work marked a shift from the classicism of the 18th century, which emphasized reason and orderliness in writing, to the romanticism of the early 19th century, with its stress on highly subjective emotional values and its concern for the beauties of nature and the freedom of the individual.

Most novelists of the period slavishly imitated British writers. Some looked to the sentimental novels of Samuel Richardson for a model; others aped satirical writers like Daniel Defoe and Tobias Smollett. Most popular were historical romances done in the manner of the Waverley novels of Sir Walter Scott. None approached the level of the best British writers, and as a result American novelists were badly outdistanced in their own country by the British, both in prestige and popularity. Since foreign copyrights were not recognized in the United States, British books were shamelessly pirated and sold cheaply. Half a million volumes of Scott were sold in America before 1823. American readers benefited but not American writers. Cooper even encouraged a rumor that his first novel, *Precaution* (1820), had been written by an Englishman because he thought this a good way to get it a fair hearing.

New York City was the literary capital of the country during the first three decades of the century. Its leading light was Washington Irving, whose comical *Diedrich Knickerbocker's History of New York* (1809) made its young author famous on both sides of the Atlantic. Yet Irving soon abandoned the United States for Europe. *The Sketch Book* (1819), which included "Rip Van Winkle" and other well-known tales and legends of the Dutch in the Hudson Valley, was written while the author was residing in Birmingham and London. Outside New York there was much less literary activity. New England was only on the verge of its great literary flowering. The Massachusetts-born poet William Cullen Bryant made a stir with "Thanatopsis," published in the *North American Review* in 1817, but he soon moved to New York, where he became editor of the *Evening Post.* In Philadelphia Philip Freneau continued to write excellent verse, and, before his premature death in 1810, Charles Brockden Brown produced some mildly interesting novels, but that was all that was worthy of even passing mention.

American painting in this period reached a level comparable to that of contemporary European work. Like the writers, nearly all American artists came from the North. All received most of their training in Europe. Benjamin West of Philadelphia, the first and in his day the most highly regarded, went to Europe before the Revolution and never returned; he can scarcely be considered an American. John Singleton Copley, whose stern, straightforward portraits display a more distinctly American character than the work of any of his

The Peale family about 1790, in a group portrait by patriarch Charles Willson Peale. Many of his numerous children were named after famous painters: Raphaelle, Titian, Rembrandt, Rubens, Angelica (for Angelica Kauffman, a well-known 18th-century artist).

contemporaries, was a Bostonian. No one so well captured the vigor and integrity of the Revolutionary generation. Charles Willson Peale was born in Maryland, but after studying under West in London, he settled in Philadelphia, where he established a museum containing fossils, stuffed animals, and various natural curiosities as well as paintings. Peale helped found the Pennsylvania Academy of the Fine Arts, and he did much to encourage American painting. Not the least of his achievements was the production of a large brood of artistic children to whom he gave such names as Rembrandt, Titian, and Rubens. The most talented of Peale's children was (appropriately) Rembrandt, whose portrait of Jefferson, executed in 1800, is one of the finest likenesses of the Sage of Monticello.

Another outstanding artist of this generation was Gilbert Stuart of Rhode Island, best known for his many studies of George Washington. Stuart studied in England with Benjamin West, and his brush was much in demand in London. In America he worked in New York, Philadelphia, and Boston. Stuart was probably the most technically accomplished of the early American portrait painters. He was fond of painting his subjects with ruddy complexions (produced by means of a judicious mixture of vermilion, purple, and white pigment), which made many of his elderly sitters appear positively cherubic. Stuart once remarked that the pallid flesh tones used by a rival looked "like putrid veal a little blown with green flies."

John Vanderlyn of New York was one of the

first Americans to study in Paris, where the icy neoclassicism of Jacques Louis David influenced him greatly. Originally a portraitist, in later life he painted a number of curious panoramas covering thousands of square feet of canvas. Henry Inman, who learned his trade as an apprentice to the prolific miniaturist-engraver John Wesley Jarvis, lived most of his life in New York and Philadelphia. Among the many prominent men who sat for Inman were Chief Justice Marshall, President Van Buren, the artist-naturalist John Audubon (whose *Birds of America* [1827–1838] is a landmark in the history of American art), the writer Nathaniel Hawthorne, and Nicholas Biddle, president of the second Bank of the United States (see page 276).

In general the painting of the period was less obviously imitative of European models than the national literature—and of far higher quality. Wealthy merchants, manufacturers, and planters wished their likenesses preserved, and the demand for portraits of the nation's Revolutionary heroes seemed insatiable. Since paintings could not be reproduced as books could be, American artists did a flourishing business. And they remained unmistakably in the European tradition.

Exceptions to this generalization can be found in the work of a number of self-trained artists like Jonathan Fisher, Charles Octavius Cole, and J. William Jennys. These primitive painters supplied rural and middle-class patrons in the same way that Copley and Stuart catered to the tastes of the rich and prominent. Jennys, for example, received $24 in 1801 for portraits of Dr. William Stoddard Williams of Deerfield, Massachusetts, and his wife. Cole specialized in New England sea captains, whom he often painted holding brassbound spyglasses. One historian has discovered traces of more than 20 artisan-painters within the single state of Maine in the 1830s and 1840s. Some of these primitive canvases have great charm and distinction. All show little sign of European influence, yet they are not especially American either. They reflect rather the characteristics of all primitive art: simplicity and distinctiveness.

The Romantic View of Life

In the western world the romantic movement was a revolt against the bloodless logic of the Age of Reason. It was a noticeable if unnamed point of view in Germany, France, and England as early as the 1780s and in America a generation later; by the second quarter of the 19th century few intellectuals were unmarked by it. "Romantics" believed that change and growth were the essence of life, for individuals and for institutions. They valued feeling and intuition over pure thought, and they stressed the differences between individuals and societies rather than the similarities. Ardent love of country characterized the movement; individualism, optimism, ingenuousness, emotion were its bywords. Whereas the Puritans, believing that nearly everyone was destined to endure the tortures of Hell for all eternity, contemplated death with dread, romantics, assuming that good people would go to Heaven, professed to look forward to death.

Romanticism perfectly fitted the mood of 19th-century America. Interest in raw nature and in primitive peoples, worship of the individual, praise of folk culture, the subordination of intellect to feeling—were these primarily romantic ideas or American ideas? Jacksonian Democracy with its self-confidence, careless prodigality, contempt for learning, glorification of the ordinary—was it a product of the American experience or a reflection of a wider world view?

The romantic way of thinking found its fullest American expression in the transcendentalist movement. Transcendentalism, a New England creation, is difficult to describe because it emphasized the indefinable and the unknowable. It was a mystical, intuitive way of looking at life that subordinated facts to feelings. Its literal meaning was "to go beyond the world of the senses," by which the transcendentalists meant the material and observable world. To the transcendentalists, human beings were truly divine because they were part of nature, itself the essence of divinity. Their intellectual capacities did not define their capabilities, for they could "transcend" reason by having faith in themselves and in the fundamental benevolence of the universe. Transcendentalists were complete individualists, seeing the social whole as no more than the sum of its parts. Organized religion, indeed all institutions were unimportant if not counterproductive; what mattered was the single person and that people aspire, stretch *beyond* their known capabilities. Failure resulted only from lack of effort. The expression "hitch your wagon to a star" is of transcendentalist origin.

Emerson and Thoreau

The leading transcendentalist thinker was Ralph Waldo Emerson. Born in 1803 and educated at Harvard, Emerson became a minister, but in 1832 he gave up his pulpit, deciding that "the profession is antiquated." After traveling in Europe, where he met many romantic writers, including Samuel Taylor Coleridge, William Wordsworth, and (especially important) Thomas Carlyle, he settled in Concord, Massachusetts, to a long career as essayist, lecturer, and sage.

Emerson managed to restore to what he called "corpse-cold" Unitarianism the fervor and purposefulness characteristic of 17th-century Puritanism. His philosophy was at once buoyantly optimistic and rigorously intellectual, self-confident and conscientious. In a notable address at Harvard in 1837 on "The American Scholar," he urged Americans to put aside their devotion to things European and seek inspiration in their immediate surroundings. He saw himself as pitting "spiritual powers" against "the mechanical powers and the mechanical philosophy of this time." The new industrial society of New England disturbed him profoundly.

Ralph Waldo Emerson was largely responsible for generating the transcendentalist movement, and in a broader sense for fostering romantic thought in the United States.

Emerson favored change and believed in progress. It was America's destiny to fulfill "the postponed expectations of the world." Temperamentally, however, he was too serene and too much his own man to fight for the causes other reformers espoused, and he was too idealistic to accept the compromises that most reformers make to achieve their ends. To abolitionist friends who sought his aid he said: "God must govern his own world. . . . I have quite other slaves to face than those Negroes, to wit, imprisoned thoughts . . . which have no watchman or lover or defender but me."

Because he put so much emphasis on self-reliance, Emerson disliked powerful governments. "The less government we have the better," he said. In a sense he was the prototype of some modern alienated intellectuals, so repelled by the world as it was that he would not actively try to change it. Nevertheless he thought strong leadership essential, perhaps being influenced in this direction by his friend Carlyle's glorification of the role of great men in history. "The wise man is the State," Emerson argued. He also had a strong practical streak. He made his living by lecturing, tracking tirelessly across the country, talking before every type of audience for fees ranging from fifty to several hundred dollars.

Closely identified with Emerson was his Concord neighbor Henry David Thoreau. After graduating from Harvard in 1837, Thoreau taught school for a time and helped out in a small pencil-making business run by his family. He was a strange man, gentle, a dreamer, content to absorb the beauties of nature almost intuitively, yet stubborn and individualistic to the point of selfishness. "He is the most unmalleable fellow alive," one acquaintance wrote. The hectic scramble for wealth that Thoreau saw all about him he found disgusting—and alarming, for he believed it was destroying both the natural and the human resources of the country.

Like Emerson, Thoreau objected to many of society's restrictions on the individual. "That government is best which governs not at all," he said, going both Emerson and the Jeffersonians one better. He was perfectly prepared to see himself as a majority of one. Emerson reduced him to a phrase when he called him "a born protestant." "When

Walden Pond was Thoreau's refuge for two years of solitary living. Of the view from his cabin he wrote, "From this point, I could not see over or beyond the woods which surrounded me. It is well to have some water in your neighborhood, to give buoyancy to and float the earth."

were the good and the brave ever in a majority?" Thoreau asked. "If a man does not keep pace with his companions," he wrote on another occasion, "perhaps it is because he hears a different drummer."

In 1845 Thoreau decided to put to the test his theory that a person need not depend on society for a satisfying existence. He built a cabin at Walden Pond on some property owned by Emerson and lived there alone for two years. He did not try to be entirely self-sufficient: he was not above returning to his family or to Emerson's for a square meal on occasion, and he generally purchased the building materials and other manufactured articles that he needed. Instead he set out, by experimenting, to prove that *if necessary* an individual could get along without the products of civilization. He used manufactured plaster in building his Walden cabin, but he also gathered a bushel of clamshells and made a small quantity of lime himself, to prove that it could be done.

At Walden Thoreau wrote *A Week on the Concord and Merrimack Rivers* (1849), which utilized an account of a trip he had taken with his brother as a vehicle for a discussion of his ideas about life and literature. He spent much time observing the quiet world around the pond, thinking, and writing in his journal. The best fruit of this period was that extraordinary book *Walden* (1854). Superficially, *Walden* is the story of Thoreau's experiment, moving and beautifully written. It is also an acid indictment of the social behavior of the average American, an attack on unthinking conformity, on subordinating one's own judgment to that of the herd.

The most graphic illustration of Thoreau's confidence in his own values occurred while he was living at Walden. At that time the Mexican War was raging (see pages 356–361). Thoreau considered the war immoral because it advanced the cause of slavery. To protest he refused to pay his Massachusetts poll tax. For this he was arrested and lodged in jail, although only for one night because an aunt promptly paid the tax for him. His essay "Civil Disobedience," explaining his view of the proper relation between the individual and the state, resulted from this experience. Like Emerson, however, Thoreau refused to participate in practical reform movements. "I love Henry," one of his friends said, "but I cannot like him; and as for taking his arm, I should as soon think of taking the arm of an elm tree."

Edgar Allan Poe

The work of all the imaginative writers of the period reveals romantic influences, and it is possibly an indication of the affinity of the romantic approach to American conditions that a number of excellent writers of poetry and fiction first appeared

Edgar Allan Poe, widely appreciated in his lifetime, inspired generations of later writers with his detective stories and horror tales.

in the 1830s and 1840s. Edgar Allan Poe, one of the most remarkable, seems almost a caricature of the romantic image of the tortured genius. Poe was born in Boston in 1809, the son of poor actors who died before he was 3. He was raised by a wealthy Virginian, John Allan.

Few persons as neurotic as Poe have been able to produce first-rate work. In college he ran up debts of $2,500 in less than a year and had to withdraw. He won an appointment to West Point but was discharged after a few months for disobedience and "gross neglect of duty." He was a lifelong alcoholic and an occasional taker of drugs. He married a child of 13. Once he attempted to poison himself; repeatedly he was down and out even to the verge of starvation. He was haunted by melancholia and hallucinations. Yet he was an excellent magazine editor, a penetrating critic, a poet of unique if somewhat narrow talents, and a fine short story writer. Although he died at 40, he turned out a large volume of serious, highly original work.

Poe responded strongly to the lure of romanticism. In his youth he aped Lord Byron, and Coleridge profoundly influenced his approach to writing. His works abound with examples of wild imagination and fascination with mystery, fright, and the occult. He was not, however, an imitator. If he did not invent the detective story, he perfected it; his tales "The Murders in the Rue Morgue" and "The Purloined Letter" stressed the thought processes of a clever detective in solving a mystery by reasoning from evidence. Poe was one of the earliest writers to deal with what are today called science fiction themes, and "The Pit and the Pendulum" and "The Cask of Amontillado" show that he was a master of the horror tale.

Although dissolute in his personal life, when Poe touched pen to paper, he became a disciplined craftsman. The most fantastic passages in his works are the result of careful, reasoned selection; not a word, he believed, could he removed without damage to the whole. And despite his rejection of most of the values prized by middle-class America, Poe was widely read in his own day. His poem "The Raven" won instantaneous popularity when it was published in 1845. Had he been a little more stable, he might have made a good living with his pen—but in that case he might not have written as he did.

Nathaniel Hawthorne

Another product of the prevailing romanticism was Nathaniel Hawthorne of Salem, Massachusetts. Hawthorne was born in 1804. When he was a small child, his father died and his grief-stricken mother became a recluse. Left largely to his own devices, he grew to be a lonely, introspective person, bookish and imaginative. Wandering about New England by himself in summertime, he soaked up local lore, which he drew upon in writing short stories. For a time he lived in Concord, where he came to know most of the leading transcendentalists. However, he disliked the egoism of the transcendental point of view and rejected its bland optimism outright. "Emerson," he said, was an "everlasting rejector of all that is, and seeker for he knows not what." Emerson, for his part, could not enjoy Hawthorne's writings because of their pervasive air of gloom.

Hawthorne was fascinated by the past, particularly by the Puritan heritage of New England and its continuing influence on his own generation. He scorned "minute fidelity" to the real world in his fiction, seeking "a severer truth . . . the truth of the human heart." But he was active in politics and an admirer of Andrew Jackson. Three Democratic presidents—Van Buren, Polk, and Franklin Pierce, the last a classmate of his at Bowdoin College—appointed him to minor political offices.

Hawthorne's early stories, originally published in magazines, were brought together in *Twice-Told Tales* (1837). They made excellent use of New England culture and history for background but were concerned chiefly with the struggles of individuals with sin, guilt, and especially the pride and isolation that often afflict those who place too much reliance on their own judgment. His greatest works were two novels written after the Whigs turned him out of his government job in 1849. *The Scarlet Letter* (1850), a grim yet sympathetic analysis of adultery, condemned not the woman, Hester Prynne, but the people who presumed to judge her. *The House of the Seven Gables* (1851) was a gripping account of the decay of an old New England family brought on by the guilt feelings of the current owners of the house, caused by the way their ancestors had cheated the original owners of the property.

Like Poe, Hawthorne was appreciated in his own day and widely read; unlike Poe, he made a modest amount of money from his work. Yet he was never very comfortable in the society he inhabited. Thoreau considered him "simple and childlike," and another writer spoke of his "tenderness" and "boundless sympathy with all forms of being." Nevertheless, there was a certain gruffness in him too. He had no patience with the second-rate. And despite his success in creating word pictures of a somber, mysterious world, he considered America too prosaic a country to inspire good literature. "There is no shadow, no antiquity, no mystery, no picturesque and gloomy wrong, nor anything but a commonplace prosperity," he complained.

Herman Melville

In 1850, while writing *The House of the Seven Gables,* Hawthorne was introduced by his publisher to another writer in the midst of a novel. This was Herman Melville, the book *Moby Dick.* The two became good friends at once, for despite their dissimilar backgrounds, they had a great deal in common. Melville was a New Yorker, born in 1819, one of eight children of a merchant of distinguished lineage. His father, however, lost all his money and died when the boy was 12. Herman left school at 15, worked briefly as a bank clerk, and in 1837 went to sea. For 18 months, in 1841–1842, he was crewman on the whaler *Acushnet.* Then he jumped ship in the South Seas. For a time he lived among a tribe of cannibals in the Marquesas; later he made his way to Tahiti, where he idled away nearly a year. In August 1843 he secured a berth on a passing American warship, the frigate *United States.* After another year at sea he returned to America in the fall of 1844.

Although he had never before attempted serious writing, in 1846 he published *Typee,* an account of his life in the Marquesas. The book was a great success, for Melville had visited a part of the world almost unknown to Americans, and his descriptions of his bizarre experiences suited the taste of a romantic age. "The man who had lived among the cannibals" became suddenly a well-known figure. Success inspired him to write a sequel, *Omoo* (1847); other books followed quickly.

As he wrote Melville became conscious of deeper powers. He read widely, thought profoundly. In 1849 he began a systematic study of Shakespeare, pondering the bard's intuitive grasp of human nature. *Antony and Cleopatra* and *King Lear* particularly intrigued him. Like Hawthorne, Melville could not accept the prevailing optimism of his generation. Unlike his friend, he admired Emerson, seconding the Emersonian demand that Americans reject European ties and develop their own literature. "Believe me," he wrote, "men not very much inferior to Shakespeare are this day being born on the banks of the Ohio." Yet he considered Emerson's vague talk about striving and the inherent goodness of mankind complacent nonsense, his individualism "a self-conceit so intensely intellectual and calm that at first one hesitates to call it by its right name."

Experience made Melville too aware of the evil in the world to be a transcendentalist. His novel *Redburn* (1849), based on his adventures on a Liverpool packet, was, as the critic F. O. Matthiessen put it, "a study in disillusion, of innocence confronted with the world, of ideals shattered by facts." Yet Melville was no cynic; he expressed deep sympathy for the Indians and for immigrants, crowded like animals into the holds of transatlantic vessels. He denounced the brutality of discipline in the United States Navy in *White-Jacket* (1850). His essay "The Tartarus of Maids," a moving if somewhat overdrawn description of young women working in a paper factory, protested the subordination of human beings to machines.

Hawthorne, whose dark view of human nature coincided with Melville's, encouraged him to press ahead with *Moby Dick* (1851). This book, Melville said, was "broiled in hellfire." Against the background of a whaling voyage (no better account of whaling has ever been written), he dealt subtly and symbolically with the problems of good and evil, of courage and cowardice, of faith, stubbornness, pride. In Captain Ahab, driven relentlessly to hunt down the huge white whale Moby Dick, which had destroyed his leg, Melville created one of the great figures of literature; in the book as a whole, he produced one of the finest novels written by an American, comparable to the best in any language.

As Melville's work became more profound, it lost its appeal to the average reader, and its originality and symbolic meaning escaped most of the critics. *Moby Dick,* his masterpiece, received little attention and most of that unfavorable. Melville had not expected the book to be popular. "Dollars damn me," he told Hawthorne, to whom *Moby Dick* was dedicated. "What I feel most moved to write, that is banned,—it will not pay." He kept on writing until his death in 1891 but was virtually ignored. Only in the 1920s did the critics rediscover him and give him his merited place in the history of American literature. His "Billy Budd, Foretopman," now considered one of his best stories, was not published until 1924.

Criticized as undisciplined and pretentious, Walt Whitman expressed a fresh viewpoint on commonplace subjects.

Walt Whitman

Walt Whitman, whose *Leaves of Grass* (1855) was the last of the great literary works of this brief outpouring of genius, was the most romantic and by far the most distinctly American writer of his age. He was born on Long Island, outside New York City, in 1819. At 13 he left school and became a printer's devil; thereafter he held a succession of newspaper jobs in the metropolitan area. He was an ardent Jacksonian and later a Free Soiler, which got him into hot water with a number of the publishers for whom he worked.

Although genuinely a "common man," thoroughly at home among tradesmen and laborers, he was surely not an ordinary man. Deeply introspective, he read omnivorously, if in a rather disorganized fashion. He soaked up Homer, Dante, Shakespeare, Goethe, Carlyle, Scott, and many others, meanwhile working out a new, intensely personal mode of expression. During the early 1850s, while employed as a carpenter and composing the poems that made up *Leaves of Grass,* he regularly carried a book of Emerson in his lunch box. "I was simmering, simmering, simmering," he later recalled. "Emerson brought me to a boil." The transcendental idea that inspiration and aspiration are at the heart of all achievement captivated him. A poet could best express himself, he believed, by relying uncritically on his natural inclinations without regard for rigid metrical forms. In this sense Whitman was the opposite of Poe, the careful literary craftsman (whose work he characterized as "brilliant and dazzling, but with no heat").

Leaves of Grass consisted of a preface, in which Whitman made the extraordinary statement that Americans had "probably the fullest poetical nature" of any people in history, and 12 strange poems in free verse: rambling, uneven, appearing to most readers shocking both in the commonplace nature of the subject matter and the coarseness of the language. Emerson, Thoreau, and a few others saw a fresh talent in these poems, but most readers and reviewers found them offensive. Indeed, the work was so undisciplined and so much of it had no obvious meaning that it was easy to miss the many passages of great beauty and originality that were scattered throughout.

Part of Whitman's difficulty arose because there was much of the charlatan in his makeup; often his writing did not ring true. He loved to use foreign words and phrases, and since he had no more than a smattering of any foreign language, he frequently sounded pretentious and sometimes downright foolish when he did so. In reality a sensitive, effeminate person, he tried to pose as a great, rough character. (Later in his career he bragged of fathering no less than six illegitimate children, which was assuredly untrue.) He never married, and his work suggests that his strongest emotional ties were with men. He displayed a great deal of the American love of show and bombast. Thomas Carlyle once remarked shrewdly that Whitman thought he was a big man because he lived in a big country.

Whitman's work was more authentically American than that of any contemporary. His egoism—he titled one of his finest poems "Song of Myself"—was tempered by his belief that he was typical of all humanity.

I celebrate myself, and sing myself,
And what I assume you shall assume,
For every atom belonging to me as good belongs to you.

He had a remarkable ear for rendering common speech poetically, for employing slang, for catching the breezy informality of Americans and their faith in themselves.

Earth! you seem to look for something at my hands,
Say, old top-knot, what do you want?

I bequeath myself to the dirt to grow from the grass I love,
If you want me again look for me under your boot-soles.

Because of these qualities and because in his later work, especially during the Civil War, he occasionally struck a popular chord, Whitman was never as neglected as Melville. When he died in 1892, he was, if not entirely understood, at least widely appreciated.

The Wider Literary Renaissance

Emerson, Thoreau, Poe, Hawthorne, Melville, and Whitman were the great figures of American literature before the Civil War. A number of others, if they lacked genius, were leading literary lights in their own day and are still worth reading. One was Henry Wadsworth Longfellow. In 1835, while still in his 20s, Longfellow became professor of modern languages at Harvard. Although he published a fine translation of Dante's *The Divine Comedy* and was expert in many languages, his fame came from his poems: "The Village Blacksmith"; "Paul Revere's Ride"; *The Courtship of Miles Standish,* a sentimental tale of Pilgrim days; and *The Song of Hiawatha,* the romantic retelling of an Indian legend. These brought him excellent critical notices and considerable fortune; his work was widely translated and reprinted.

Though musical, polished, and full of vivid images, Longfellow's poetry lacked profundity, originality, and force, as he did himself. But it was neither cheap nor trivial. When Longfellow wrote

Life is real! life is earnest!
And the grave is not its goal . . .

he expressed the heartfelt belief of most of his generation. In this sense he captured the spirit of his times better than any of his great contemporaries, better even than Whitman.

Longfellow was the most talented of a group of minor New England writers who collectively gave that section great intellectual vitality in the decades before the Civil War. Prominent in this "flowering of New England" was John Greenleaf Whittier, a poet nearly as popular as Longfellow in his day. Whittier believed ardently in the abolition of slavery and worked actively in politics and journalism. A few of his poems can still be read with pleasure, among them "The Barefoot Boy," dealing with his rural childhood. Somewhat more weighty was the achievement of James Russell Lowell, the first editor of the *Atlantic Monthly,* founded in Boston in 1857. Lowell's humorous stories written in the New England dialect (see page 344) made an original and influential contribution to the national literature. Dr. Oliver Wendell Holmes, professor of medicine at Harvard, was widely known as a poet and essayist. A few of his poems, such as "The Chambered Nautilus" and "Old Ironsides," are interesting examples of American romantic verse, and his "Autocrat of the Breakfast-Table" series in the *Atlantic Monthly* became a regional if not a national institution.

Collectively these minor writers had a salutary effect on American culture, for if rather smug and narrow, they were serious and industrious. If they did not often soar, at least they fixed their gaze upward and encouraged their readers to do likewise.

So did the important historians of the period, all of them New Englanders. George Bancroft, one of the first Americans to study in Germany, began in 1834 to publish a ten-volume *History of the United States* based on thorough research. William Hickling Prescott, though nearly blind, wrote extensively on the history of Spain and Spain's American empire, his *Conquest of Mexico* (1843) and *Conquest of Peru* (1847) being his most important works. John Lothrop Motley, another German-trained historian, published his *Rise of the Dutch Republic* in 1856, and Francis Parkman began his great account of the struggle between France and Great Britain for the control of North America with *Conspiracy of Pontiac* in 1851.

The public read these histories avidly. They suited the taste of the times, they were written with a mass audience in mind, and they were thoroughly in the romantic tradition. As David Levin said in his important study *History as Romantic Art,* "they all shared an 'enthusiastic' attitude toward the Past, an affection for grand heroes, an affection for Nature and the 'natural.' "

Southern literature was even more markedly romantic than that of New England. John Pendleton Kennedy of Baltimore wrote several novels with regional historical themes, much in the manner of Sir Walter Scott. Kennedy was also a Whig politician of some importance who served several terms in Congress; in 1852 he became secretary of the navy in the Fillmore Cabinet. The more versatile and influential William Gilmore Simms of South Carolina wrote nearly two dozen novels, several volumes of poetry, and a number of biographies. At his peak in the 1830s he earned as much as $6,000 a year with his pen. His favorite theme was the South Carolina frontier, which he portrayed in *The Partisan* (1835), one of a series of novels dealing with the Revolution, and *The Yemassee* (1835), the story of an early 18th-century Indian war. His novels seem too melodramatic for modern tastes; the plots lack variety, the style lacks discipline. His portraits of the planter class are too bloodless and reverential to be convincing, and his female characters are nearly all pallid and fragile. Only when Simms wrote of the frontier life and its people did his work possess much power, yet along with Kennedy he contributed largely to the glamorous legend of the Old South.

Domestic Tastes

Architecture flourished in the northern cities chiefly as a result of the work of Charles Bulfinch and some of his disciples. Bulfinch, who had studied in England, was influenced by British architects, but he developed a manner all his own. Thanks to his "Federal" style, parts of Boston achieved a dignity and charm equal to the finest sections of London. The State House, many other public buildings, and, best of all, many of Bulfinch's private houses—austere yet elegant, solid yet airy and graceful—gave the town a distinction it had lacked before the Revolution. Bulfinch and a few of his followers, notably Samuel McIntire and Asher Ben-

Architect Charles Bulfinch did much to lift the face of Boston in the 1840s and 1850s with his domestic and public buildings, such as the Otis House.

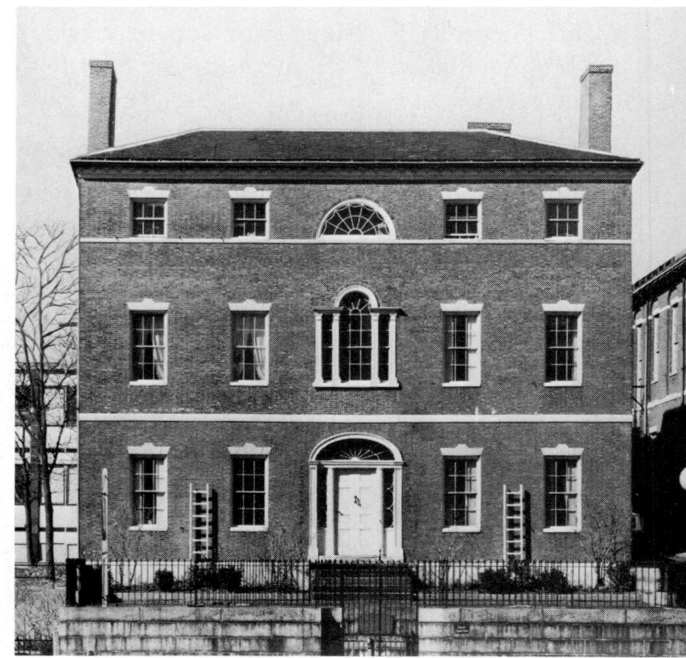

jamin, equaled the achievements of the best European architects of their day.

In the 1830s and 1840s new techniques made it possible to weave colored patterns into cloth by machine, to manufacture wallpaper printed with complicated designs, and to produce rugs and hangings that looked like tapestries. Combined with the use of machine methods in the furniture business, these inventions had a powerful impact on public taste. That impact, at least in the short run, was aesthetically unfortunate; manufacturers were carried away by the possibilities opened up by their new machinery. As Russell Lynes writes in his entertaining study *The Tastemakers,* "Styles ran riot. The new mechanical methods of making furniture gave designers a free hand to indulge their delight in ornamentation. . . . The new chairs and sofas, bedecked with fruit, flowers, and beasties and standing on twisted spindles, crowded into living rooms and parlors."

The new wood-turning machinery added to the popularity of the elaborately decorated "Gothic" style of architecture. The irregularity and uniqueness of Gothic buildings suited the prevailing romanticism, their aspiring towers, steeples, and arches and their flexibility (a new wing or extension could always be added without spoiling the effect) made them especially attractive to a people enamored of progress. The huge pile of pink masonry of the Smithsonian Institution in Washington, with its nine distinct types of towers, represents American Gothic at its most giddy and lugubrious stage. The building, which was designed in 1846 by James Renwick, confounded generations of architects, but with the passage of time it came to seem the perfect setting for the vast collection of mementoes that fill "the nation's attic." The best of the Gothic designers was probably Andrew Jackson Downing, author of *The Architecture of Country Houses* (1850). "Greek" and "Italian" styles also flourished in this period, the former particularly in the South; elsewhere the Gothic was by all odds the most popular.

Increasingly, Americans of the period were purchasing native art. George Catlin, who painted hundreds of pictures of Indians and their surroundings, all rich in authentic detail, displayed his work before admiring crowds in many cities. Outstanding genre painters (artists whose canvases told stories, usually drawn from everyday life), most notably William Sidney Mount of New York and George Caleb Bingham of Missouri, were successful with both genre paintings and portraits. Rumor had it that Mount received $1,000 for his first important canvas; Bingham's paintings commanded excellent

Machine-made consumer goods, such as this iron furniture, became widely available around 1850. They had great impact on popular taste.

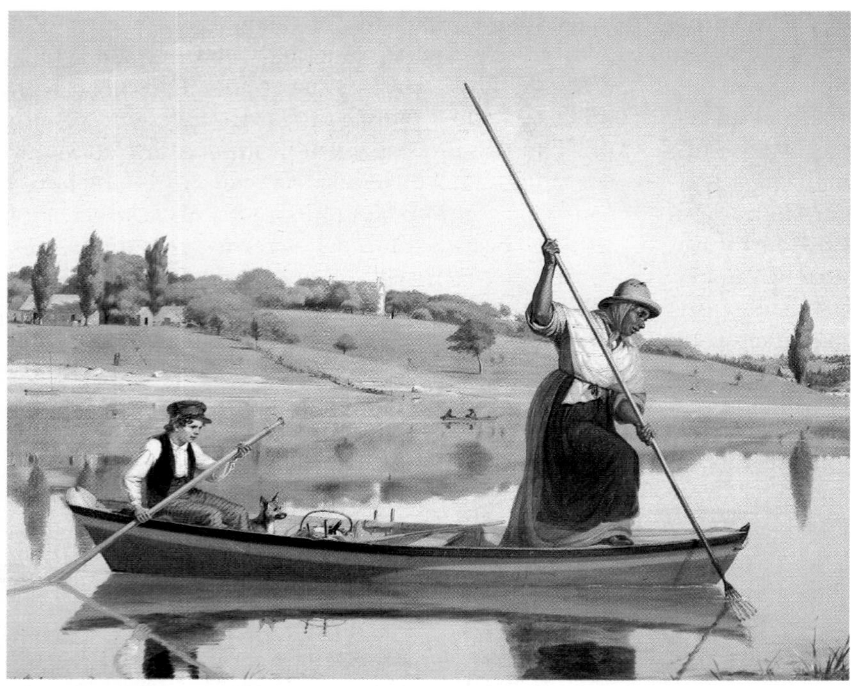

A lifelong resident of rural Long Island, William Sidney Mount took everyday life of that corner of America as his inspiration. Eel Spearing at Setauket, *1845, is one of his most characteristic canvases. Mount's subject matter had universal appeal; engravings of his work sold widely in Europe.*

prices; and the public bought engravings of the work of both men in enormous numbers.

The more academic artists of the period were popular as well. The "luminists" and members of the romantic Hudson River school specialized in grandiose pictures of wild landscapes. Their best work was distinctively American, and some of them disposed of their canvases at good prices. In the 1840s Thomas Doughty regularly collected $500 each for his paintings. The works of Asher B. Durand, John Kensett, and Thomas Cole were in demand. The collector Luman Reed commissioned five large Cole canvases for an allegorical series, *The Course of Empire,* and crowds flocked to see another of Cole's series, *The Voyage of Life,* when it was exhibited in New York.

In 1839 the American Art-Union was formed in New York to encourage native art. The Art-Union hit on the ingenious device of selling what were in effect lottery tickets and using the proceeds to purchase paintings, which became the prizes in the lottery. Annual "memberships" sold for $5; 814 subscribed in 1839, nearly 19,000 10 years later. Soon the Art-Union was giving every member an engraving of one of its principal prizes. The organization had to disband after a New York court outlawed the lottery in 1851, but in 1854 a new Cosmopolitan Art-Union was established in Ohio. In the years before the Civil War it boomed, reaching a peak of 38,000 members and paying as much as $6,000 for an individual work—the sculptor Hiram Powers's boneless female nude, *The Greek Slave.* It also distributed an art magazine and each year gave a young artist a gold medal and $2,000 for foreign study.

The art-unions made little effort to encourage innovators, but they were a boon to many artists. The American Art-Union paid out as much as $40,000 for its prizes in a single year. By distributing thousands upon thousands of engravings and colored prints, they introduced competent American works of art into middle-class homes.

Beginning in the late 1850s the prints of the firm of Currier and Ives brought a crude but charming kind of art to a still wider audience. Currier and Ives lithographs portrayed horse racing, trains, rural landscapes, and "every tender domestic moment, every sign of national progress, every regional oddity, every private or public disaster from a cut finger to a forest fire." They were issued in very large editions and sold for as little as 15 cents.

Miniature copies of Hiram Powers's The Greek Slave, *Henry James said, stood "exposed under little glass covers" in parlors from Boston to San Francisco.*

Education for Democracy

Except on the edge of the frontier and in the South, most youngsters between the ages of 5 and 10 attended a nearby school for at least a couple months of the year. These schools, however, were privately run and charged fees. Attendance was not required and fell off sharply once children learned to read and do their sums well enough to get along in day-to-day life. The teachers were usually young men waiting for something better to turn up.

All this changed with the rise of the common-school movement. At the heart of the movement was the belief, widely expressed in the first days of the Republic, that a government based on democratic rule must provide the means to, as Jefferson put it, "diffuse knowledge throughout the mass of the people." This meant free tax-supported schools, which all children were expected to attend. It also came to mean that such an educational system should be administered on a statewide basis and that teaching should become a profession which required formal training.

The two most effective leaders of the common-school movement were Henry Barnard and Horace Mann. Both were New Englanders, Whigs, trained in the law, and in other ways conservative types. They shared an unquenchable faith in the unlimited improvability of the human race through education. Barnard served in educational posts in Connecticut, Rhode Island, and New York in the 1840s and 1850s and as editor of the *American Journal of Education* from 1855 until 1882.

As a member of the Massachusetts legislature, Mann drafted the 1837 law creating a state school board, and then he became its first secretary. Over the next decade his annual reports carried the case for common schools to every corner of the land. Seldom given to understatement, Mann called common schools "the greatest discovery ever made by man." In his reports he criticized wealthy parents who sent their children to private academies rather than bring them into contact with their poorer neighbors in the local school. He encouraged young women to become teachers while commending them to school boards by claiming that they could get along on lower salaries than men. In still other reports he championed the social uses of group singing, the benefits of physical exercise, and—Mann being an ardent believer in phrenology—the therapeutic value of massaging a bump just above the right ear.

By the 1850s every state outside the South provided free elementary schools and supported institutions for training teachers. Many extended the concept of publicly financed education to include high schools, and Michigan and Iowa even established publicly supported colleges.

Historians differ in explaining the success of the common-school movement. All admit that it was the most successful reform movement of the era. Some stress the arguments Mann used to win support from employers by appealing to their need for trained and well-disciplined workers. Others see the schools as designed to "Americanize" the increasing numbers of non-English and non-Protestant immigrants who were flooding into the country. (Force is lent to this argument by the fact that Catholic bishops in New York and elsewhere op-

By the 1850s, every state outside the South provided free elementary schools. Pictured here is a "Girls' Evening School" about 1840. The studies appear to be both domestic and literary: some students are sewing; others are reading.

posed laws requiring Catholic children to attend these "Protestant" schools and set up their own parochial schools.) Still others argue that middle-class reformers favored public elementary schools on the theory that they would instill the values of hard work, punctuality, and submissiveness to authority in children of the laboring classes. According to this argument, the reformers favored the new public high schools mainly because they provided free education for their own children. Almost no working-class children attended high school, public or private, until late in the 19th century.

All these reasons played a part in advancing the cause of the common schools. Yet it remains the case, as the historians Carl F. Kaestle and Maris Vinovskis have recently shown, that the most compelling argument for common schools was cultural; more effectively than any other institution they brought Americans of different economic circumstances and ethnic backgrounds into early and mutually beneficial contact with one another. They served the two roles that Mann assigned to them: "the balance wheel of the social machinery" and "the great equalizer."

Engines of Culture

As the population grew and became more concentrated, and as society, especially in the North, was permeated by a middle-class point of view, popular concern for "culture" in the formal sense increased. A largely literate and prosperous people, committed to the idea of education but not generally well educated, set their hearts on being "refined" and "cultivated." Industrialization made it easier to satisfy this new demand for culture, though the new machines also tended to make the artifacts of culture more stereotyped.

Efficient printing techniques reduced the cost of books, magazines, and newspapers. By the 1850s one publisher sold a 50-volume set of the wildly popular Sir Walter Scott for $37.50. The first penny newspaper, as opposed to the earlier and more expensive party and mercantile papers, was the New York *Sun* (1833), but James Gordon Bennett's New York *Herald,* founded in 1835, brought the cheap new journalism to perfection. The Boston *Daily Times* and the Philadelphia *Public Ledger* soon followed. The penny newspapers depended on sensation, crime stories, and society gossip to attract readers, but they covered important national and international news too.

In the 1850s the moralistic and sentimental "domestic" novel entered its prime. The most successful writers in this genre were women, which prompted Hawthorne to complain bitterly that "a d----d mob of scribbling women" was taking over American literature. Typical were Susan Warner's *The Wide, Wide World* (1850), a sad tale about a pious, submissive girl who cried "more readily and more steadily than any other tormented child in a novel at the time," and Maria Cummins's *The Lamplighter* (1854), the story of little Gerty, an orphan rescued by a kindly lamplighter named Trueman Flint. *The Lamplighter* sold 70,000 copies within a year of publication. As the literary historian Ann Douglas has written in *The Feminization of American Culture,* such novels provided American readers of the 1840s and 1850s (most of whom were women) with the consumer pleasures that today are provided by television soaps, while making Americans "the first society in history to locate and express many personal 'unique' feelings and responses through dime-a-dozen artifacts."

Besides reading countless volumes of sentimental nonsense (the books of another novelist, Mary Jane Holmes, sold over a million copies in these years), Americans consumed reams of religious literature. In 1840 the American Tract Society distributed 3 million copies of its publications; in 1855, more than 12 million. The Society had hundreds of missionary-salesmen, called colporteurs, who fanned out across the country preaching the gospel and selling or giving away religious pamphlets and books. These publications played down denominational differences in favor of a generalized brand of evangelical Christianity. They bore titles such as *Quench Not the Spirit* (over 900,000 copies distributed by 1850) and *The Way to Heaven.* The American Bible Society issued hundreds of thousands of copies of the Old and New Testaments each year. Americans also devoured books on self-improvement, some aimed at uplifting the reader's character, others, which would today be called "how-to-do-it" books, at teaching everything from raising chickens to carving tombstones.

Rich men left large sums to charity and other good causes; Stephen Girard left $6 million for "educating poor white orphan boys" in his adopted Philadelphia; John Jacob Astor of New York and George Peabody of Massachusetts endowed libraries; John Lowell, son of the pioneer cotton manufacturer, upon his death left $500,000 to establish the Lowell Institute in Boston to sponsor free public lectures. In the late 1850s the industrialist Peter Cooper founded the Cooper Institute in New York City, where workers could take free courses in practical subjects. Mechanics' libraries sprang up in every industrial center and attracted so many readers that pressure was soon applied to grant them state funds. In 1848 Massachusetts led the way by authorizing the use of public money to back the Boston Public Library, and soon several states were encouraging local communities to found tax-supported libraries.

The desire for knowledge and culture in America is well illustrated by the success of the mutual improvement societies known as lyceums. The movement began in Great Britain; in the United States its prime mover was Josiah Holbrook, an itinerant lecturer and sometime schoolmaster from Connecticut. Holbrook founded the first lyceum in 1826 at Millbury, Massachusetts; within five years there were over a thousand scattered across the country. The lyceums conducted discussions, established libraries, and lobbied for better schools. Soon they began to sponsor lecture series on topics of every sort. Many of the nation's political and intellectual leaders, such as Webster, Emerson,

The Lyceum movement sponsored lectures on every imaginable subject in hundreds of towns. In this lively 1841 caricature, meteorologist James Pollard Espy holds forth to a mixed audience at Clinton Hall in New York City.

Melville, and Lowell, regularly graced their platforms. So did other, less famous lecturers who in the name of culture pronounced on subjects ranging from "Chemistry Applied to the Mechanic Arts" to a description of the tombs of the Egyptian pharaohs.

The State of the Colleges

Unlike common schools, with their democratic overtones, private colleges had at best a precarious place in Jacksonian America. For one thing, there were too many of them. "Colleges," President Phillip Lindsley of the University of Nashville complained in 1825, "spring up like mushrooms." Any town with pretensions of becoming a regional center felt it had to have a college of its own. Ohio had 25 different colleges in the 1850s, Tennessee 16. Many of these institutions were short-lived. Of the 14 colleges founded in Kentucky between 1800 and 1850 only 7 were still operating in 1860.

The problem of supply was compounded by a demand problem—too few students. The enrollments at the largest, Yale, never topped 400 until the mid-1840s. "Excessive multiplication," President Lindsley argued, led to "dwarfish dimensions." Higher education was beyond the means of the average family. Although most colleges charged less than half the $55 tuition required by Harvard, that still represented a substantial outlay for most families, wages being what they were (see page 384). So desperate was the shortage that colleges accepted applicants as young as 11 and 12 and as old as 30.

Once enrolled (and tuition paid), students had little worry about making the grade, not least because grades were not given. Since students were hard to come by and classwork was relatively unimportant, discipline was lax. Challenges of official authority were frequent, outbreaks of rioting over such weighty matters as the quality of meals far from unknown. A father who visited his son's college dormitory in 1818 found it inhabited by "half a dozen loungers in a state of oriental lethargy, each stretched out upon two or three chairs, with scarce any indication of life in them [other] than the feeble effort to keep up the fire of their *cigarrs*."

The typical college curriculum, dominated by the study of Latin and Greek, had almost no practical relevance except for future clergymen. The Yale faculty, most of them ministers, defended the classics as admirably providing for both "the discipline and the furniture of the mind," but these subjects commended themselves to college officials chiefly because they did not require costly equipment or a faculty that knew anything else. Professors spent most of their time in and out of the classroom trying to maintain a semblance of order, "to the exclusion of any great literary undertakings to which their choice might lead them," one explained. "Our country is yet too young for old professors," a Bostonian informed the German visitor Francis Grund in the 1830s, "and, besides, they are too poorly paid to induce first rate men to devote themselves to the business of lecturing. . . . We consider professors as secondary men."

Fortunately for the future of higher education, some college officials recognized the need for a drastic overhaul of their institutions. President Francis Wayland of Brown University used his 1842 address, "On the Present Collegiate System," to call for a thorough revamping of the curriculum to make it responsive to the economic realities of American society. This meant more courses in science, economics (where Wayland's own *Elements of Political Economy* might be used!), modern history, and applied mathematics; fewer in Hebrew, Biblical studies, Greek, and ancient history.

Yale established a separate school of science in 1847, which it hoped would attract serious-minded students and research-minded professors. At Harvard, which also opened a scientific school, students were allowed to choose some of their courses and were compelled to earn grades as a stimulus to study. Colleges in the West and South began to offer mechanical and agricultural subjects relevant to their regional economies. Oberlin enrolled four female students in 1837, and the first women's college, the Georgia Female College, opened its doors in 1839.

These reforms slowed the downward spiral of colleges; they did not restore them to the honored place they had enjoyed in the Revolutionary era. Of the first six presidents of the United States, only Washington did not graduate from college. Beginning in 1829, seven of the next eleven did not. In this, of course, Presidents Jackson, Van Buren, Harrison, Taylor, Fillmore, Lincoln, and Johnson were like 98 of every 100 white males, all blacks and Indians, and all but a handful of white women in mid-19th-century America. Going to college had yet, in Wayland's words, to "commend itself to the good sense and patriotism of the American people."

Civic Cultures

Unlike the capitals of Europe, which were also centers of art and culture, Washington was a cultural backwater, and the politicians seemed content to keep it that way. Whether the United States had *any* cultural center, and, if so, where it was, is another matter. Boston, Philadelphia, and New York vied for primacy, but many smaller cities, such as Lexington, Kentucky, the self-proclaimed "Athens of the West," set the tone for the surrounding hinterland.

In the cities members of the "learned professions," especially the lawyers, were generally accepted as the arbiters of taste in literature and art. "At the bar or the bench the American aristocracy is found," and there too resides "the most intellectual section of society," the ever-insightful Tocqueville reported. Lawyers came mostly from the upper reaches of the city's economic order, usually from families long in residence.

Emerson only half mockingly called Boston "the hub of the universe," but this was a case when local pride triumphed over his usual good judgment. Boston was indeed the home of the country's leading literary magazine, the *North American Review,* founded in 1815, but Philadelphia had *Graham's,* the country's first illustrated magazine, and *Godey's Ladies Book,* which reached 150,000 subscribers in the 1850s, an enormous number for that date. New Yorkers also had a fine magazine, *The Knickerbocker,* and several literary societies and clubs. By 1825 New York's House of Harper, organized in 1817, was the largest book publisher in the nation. By the early 1830s James Fenimore Cooper was dead and Washington Irving was living in retirement outside the city, but Melville and Whitman regarded New York as home. On the other hand, Boston was the home of the nation's leading historians, and Philadelphia, with the Pennsylvania Academy of Fine Arts (1815) and the Philadelphia Academy of Music (1857), was conceded by all but blind Bostonians and tin-eared New Yorkers to predominate in artistic and musical matters.

In the West, Cincinnati could point to its seven weekly and two daily newspapers, a literary monthly, a medical journal, and a magazine for teenagers. The first Beethoven symphony ever heard in America was performed in Cincinnati in 1817. By the 1830s such coups had enabled the

"Queen City" to replace the "Athens of the West" as the center of trans-Allegheny culture. Having quickly accomplished so much, its boosters reasoned, Cincinnati would soon assume national leadership in cultural matters, as it already had in the processing of pork bellies.

Even smaller cities like Portland, Providence, Hartford, Albany, and Pittsburgh had literary and natural history societies and were regular stops on the lyceum circuit. All in all, American cities had a vitality and diversity that foreign visitors both celebrated and decried. Life in the towns was by some standards crude; many of the people were pushy, crass, and dedicated to the accumulation of wealth. But on this last count, the English novelist Charles Dickens offered some international perspective. "The golden calf they worship," he wrote of Americans in 1841,

> is a pigmy compared with the giant effigies set up in other parts of that vast counting-house which lies beyond the Atlantic; and the almighty dollar sinks into something comparatively insignificant amidst a whole Pantheon of better gods.

Scientific Stirrings

"Few of the civilized nations of our time," Tocqueville wrote in 1835, "have made less progress than the United States in the higher sciences." Few Americans disagreed, and some historians have since suggested that American interest in science—and contributions to its advancement—had declined from the levels achieved during the Revolutionary era. Despite Jefferson's assurances in the 1780s that the United States would soon "produce her full quota of genius," a half century had gone by without a single American scientist even approaching the international recognition accorded Benjamin Franklin.

Tocqueville attributed Americans' indifference to science to their distrust of theory and abstract knowledge. "The purely practical side," he conceded, "is cultivated admirably." Some contemporaries cited more pressing needs. "We are a new country," a Boston doctor reminded his son, who wished to pursue a scientific career:

> We have, as it were, just landed on these shores; there is a vast deal to be done; and he who will not be doing, must be set down as a drone.

There was some progress. Beginning with Massachusetts's in 1830, state-sponsored geological surveys provided at least temporary livings for the European-trained geologist James Hall and the botanist Asa Gray. (Later, as a Harvard professor, Gray was the leading American advocate of his friend Charles Darwin's theory of natural selection.) Additional jobs opened up with the expansion of the United States Coastal Survey, directed by Benjamin Franklin's great-grandson, Alexander Dalles Bache, in 1843. The opening in 1846 of the Smithsonian Institution in Washington, to which the physicist Joseph Henry was appointed first secretary, helped too. Henry's researches in electromagnetism in the 1830s led to Samuel F. B. Morse's invention of the telegraph, and Bache's lobbying resulted in the founding of the American Association for the Advancement of Science in 1848.

Yet few Americans pursued science except on a part-time basis. The star sightings and tidal measurements that went into Nathaniel Bowditch's internationally recognized manual, *The New American Practical Navigator,* had to be made in his spare time. He made his living as an actuary in an insurance company. Maria Mitchell, America's best-known 19th-century woman scientist, won international celebrity and a gold medal from the King of Denmark for calculating the position of a new comet in 1847. She was employed as a librarian in Nantucket when she made the calculations.

For all the practical obstacles in the way of doing serious science in Jacksonian America, its near-wilderness circumstances sometimes provided those on the lookout with unexpected targets of opportunity. An almost literal case in point is that of Dr. William Beaumont. In 1822, while serving as an army surgeon in upstate New York, Beaumont was called to attend to one Alexis St. Martin, a 19-year-old Canadian woodsman, who had been shot by accident. The shell, fired from no more than 3 feet away, had blasted a hole in the lad's chest the size of a grapefruit; it had blown away the sixth rib, fractured the fifth, and left protruding a portion of his lung "as large as a turkey's egg." There was also something else sticking out. "What at first view I could not believe possible," Beaumont recorded in his diary, "on closer observation, I found to be actually the stomach with a puncture in the protruding portion large enough to receive my forefinger, and through which a portion of the food he had

Maria Mitchell won recognition from the King of Denmark for calculating the position of a new comet in 1847. She is shown here in her later years with a group of fellow astronomers at Vassar College, where she was on the faculty.

taken for breakfast had come out and lodged in his clothing."

Believing the patient to be a goner, Dr. Beaumont did what he could to administer relief and dress the wound. But the young man survived, exposed stomach and all. Eventually a flap formed over the opening in the stomach, but it could be pushed back, exposing the inner workings of the organ. After St. Martin recovered, Beaumont took him into his household and began studying how he digested food.

Over the next decade—except for unscheduled breaks when his houseguest took off for the Canadian woods—Beamont performed hundreds of experiments testing the relative digestibility of foods and analyzing the chemical properties of gastric juices. His *Experiments and Observations on the Gastric Juices and the Physiology of Digestion* (1833), though largely ignored in the United States, won him a reputation among European physiologists as the world's leading expert on the the human gastric system. His fame, however, did not prevent his army superiors, perhaps resenting the time he was diverting from his official duties, from forcing him to resign in 1840. St. Martin then returned to Canada, where he married, fathered four children, and died (we assume with his shirt on) at the ripe age of 83.

American Humor

The clash between the desire of a few for a "high" culture and the simpler tastes of the majority led James Fenimore Cooper to conclude that Americans would be forever "wanting in most of the high tastes, and consequently in the high enjoyments." But other writers were not so sure, and some, rather than despair over the cultural incongruities, found in them a rich source of humor.

They were hardly the first to do so. The comic potential in juxtaposing high ideals and low reality had been exploited by the Greek playwright Aristophanes; by Rabelais, the creator of *Gargantua*; and by Cervantes in *The Adventures of Don Quixote*—all, incidentally, works available in mid-century America. William Byrd and Benjamin Franklin had both used the differences between the pretensions of colonial sophisticates and the ways of common folk to good comic effect, and so did Washington Irving (see page 325). But the possibilities of this kind of humor were greatly enlarged in the Jacksonian era. Where else was there a country theoretically based upon equality whose inhabitants were so strikingly varied?

One of the first writers to exploit the comic aspects of Jacksonian democracy was Seba Smith, a newspaperman from Portland, Maine. Smith's fictional creation, Major Jack Downing, was a thoroughgoing Jackson man from a part of the country suspicious of both the General's politics and his intelligence. Smith had Major Downing accompany the president on his 1833 tour of New England, which included, among other adventures, an appearance at Harvard to receive an honorary degree. In the presence of so many learned gentlemen with political views contrary to his own, Downing advised the president "jest to say nothing, but look as knowing as any of them." Which was exactly what Jackson did, even when faced by snickering "sassy students." "The General stood it out like a hero," the Major assured his readers, "and got through very well."

A writer who turned the possibilities of "Down East" humor to more telling satirical effect was James Russell Lowell, author of the *Biglow Papers*, which began appearing in 1847. Lowell juxtaposed Hosea Biglow, a Yankee farmer of "homely common-sense heated up by conscience," and Birdofredum Sawin, a scoundrel hoping to turn a profit on his patriotism. When approached by a recruiting officer, Hosea Biglow set his opposition to the Mexican War (actually, Lowell's) to verse:

They may talk o' Freedom's airy
Till they're pupple in the face,—
It's a grand gret cemetary
For the barthrights of our race;
They jest want this Californy
So's to lug new slave-states in
To abuse ye, an' to scorn ye,
An' to plunder ye like sin.

Birdofredum, on the other hand, signed up to fight in Mexico, where he lost an eye, a leg, and his left arm. When he returned home he ran for political office. As to his platform:

Ef, wile you're 'lectioneerin round, some curus chaps should beg
To know my views o' state affairs, jest answer WOODEN LEG!
Ef they aint settisfied with thet, an' kin o' pry an' doubt
An' ax fer sutthin' deffynit, jest say ONE EYE PUT OUT!

The Old Southwest provided another locale for juxtaposing the genteel and the vulgar. Life in the region provided chroniclers with more than enough violence to capture the attention of their "gentle readers." Like their Yankee counterparts, the southwestern humorists were well educated and politically conservative. Many of their sketches first appeared in *The Spirit of the Times*, a New York sporting and theatrical journal with a largely Yankee and urban readership.

Violence figures prominently in Augustus Baldwin Longstreet's "The Fight," in which one Ransy Sniffle, "who, in his earlier days, had fed copiously upon red clay and blackberries," promoted a wrestling match between two toughs, Bill and Bob. After provoking both to do battle, Ransy sat back to enjoy the slaughter. And slaughter it was. Bob, the victor, "entirely lost his left ear and a large piece of his left cheek." As for Bill, he

> presented a hideous spectacle. About a third of his nose, at the lower extremity, was bit off, and his face so swelled and bruised that it was difficult to discover anything of the human visage, much more the fine features which he carried into the fight.

Johnson J. Hooper's creation Simon Suggs was the ultimate frontier rogue as confidence man. Whether engaged in horse swapping or faking a conversion experience at a camp meeting in order to steal the collection basket, Suggs lived by the maxim "It is good to be shifty in a new country." He was not alone in this opinion. In a new country, it made sense not to take oneself too seriously. While the outcome of the nation's experiment in combining democracy and cultural aspiration remained in doubt, most Americans took their laughs where they could find them.

SUPPLEMENTARY READING

Titles marked with an asterisk have been published in paperback.

Useful surveys of cultural and intellectual currents in this period are Merle Curti, **The Growth of American Thought** (1951), Russel B. Nye, **Society and Culture in America** * (1974), and Rush Welter, **The Mind of America, 1820–1860** * (1975). See also Richard Hofstadter, **Anti-Intellectualism in American Life** * (1963), and Stow Persons, **The Decline of American Gentility** (1975), for a more critical assessment. F. O. Mattheissen, **American Renaissance: Art and Expression in the Age of Emerson and Whitman** (1941), remains valuable.

On Transcendentalism see Perry Miller (ed.), **The American Transcendentalists** (1957). R. L. Rusk, **The Life of Ralph Waldo Emerson** (1949), and J. W. Krutch, **Henry David Thoreau** (1948), are first-rate biographies, while Joel Porte, **Emerson and Thoreau: Transcendentalists in Conflict** (1966), and **Representative Man: Ralph Waldo Emerson in His Time** * (1979), treat the transcendentalist "community." For critical appraisals, see Quentin Anderson, **The Imperial Self** (1971), and Perry Miller, **Consciousness in Concord** (1958). On Margaret Fuller, see her **Woman in the Nineteenth Century** * (1855).

On American literature, Van Wyck Brooks, **The Flowering of New England** * (1936), and Lewis Mumford, **The Golden Day** * (1926), remain readable surveys, while Alfred Kazin, **On Native Grounds** * (1942), is more critically disposed. Biographies of the leading writers of the period include Edward Wagenknecht, **Edgar Allan Poe** (1963), J. R. Mellow, **Nathaniel Hawthorne and His Times** (1980), Leon Howard, **Herman Melville** (1951), Justin Kaplan, **Walt Whitman** (1980), and Newton Arvin, **Longfellow: His Life and Work** (1963). For a comparative study, see Harry Levin, **The Power of Blackness: Hawthorne, Poe, and Melville** (1958). David Levin, **History as Romantic Art** (1959), is excellent on the era's historians and their approaches to their craft.

On the cultural life of the South, see Clement Eaton, **The Mind of the Old South** * (1964), and Drew Faust, **A Sacred Circle: The Dilemma of the Intellectual in the Old South** (1977). On education, see Lawrence A. Cremin, **American Education: The National Experience** * (1980), for a comprehensive account. Also useful is Jonathan Messerli, **Horace Mann** (1972). Michael B. Katz, **The Irony of Early School Reform** * (1968), questions the motives of the reformers, while Diane Ravitch, **The Revisionists Revised** * (1978), questions Katz. Carl F. Kaestle and Maris Vinovskis, **Education and Social Change in 19th-Century Massachusetts** (1980), is excellent.

Popular culture is discussed in Carl Bode, **The Anatomy of Popular Culture** (1959), and Russell Lynes, **The Tastemakers** * (1954). Bode's **The American Lyceum** * (1956), is also useful. Ann Douglas, **The Feminization of American Culture** (1977), is excellent on the pervasiveness and impact of sentimental literature. O. W. Larkin, **American Art and Life in America** (1949), surveys American painting and architecture, while Neil Harris, **The Artist in American Society** * (1966), puts art in its social setting. See also Barbara Novak, **Nature and Culture: American Landscape Painting** (1980).

The standard sources for the history of American colleges remain Richard Hofstadter, **Academic Freedom in the Age of the College** (1955), and Fred Rudolph, **The American College and University** (1961). But see also David Allmendinger, **Paupers and Scholars** (1975), Robert A. McCaughey, "The Transformation of American Academic Life," **Perspectives in American History** (1975), Ronald Story, **The Forging of an Aristocracy** (1980), and Colin Burke, **American Collegiate Populations: A Test of the Traditional View** (1982).

On civic cultures, in addition to the urban-history works cited above, see Digby Baltzell, **Puritan Boston and Quaker Philadelphia** (1979), Robert A. Ferguson, **Law and Letters in American Culture** (1984), Martin Green, **The Problem of Boston** (1966), and Perry Miller, **The Raven and the Whale: The War of Words in the Era of Poe and Melville** (1955).

Scientific activities are examined in George H. Daniels, **American Science in the Age of Jackson** (1968), Alexandra Oleson and Sanborn C. Brown (eds.), **The Pursuit of Knowledge in the Early American Republic** (1976), William H. Goetzmann, **Exploration and Empire: The Explorer and the Scientist in the Winning of the American West** * (1967), William Stanton, **The Great United States Exploring Expedition** (1975), and A. Hunter Dupree, **Science in the Federal Government** (1957). On Beaumont's researches, see Jesse S. Myer, **Life and Letters of Dr. William Beaumont** (1912).

On American humor before the Civil War, see Kenneth S. Lynn (ed.), **The Comic Tradition in America** * (1958), Walter Blair, **Native American Humor** * (1937), Constance Rourke, **American Humor** (1931), and Richard Dorson, **William T. Porter and the "Spirit of the Times"** (1977).

12

Expansion and Slavery

Were other reasoning wanting in favor of now elevating this question . . . it is surely to be found, found abundantly, in . . . the fulfilment of our manifest destiny to overspread the continent allotted by Providence for the free development of our yearly multiplying millions. JOHN L. O'SULLIVAN, *1845*

President John Tyler was a thin, rather delicate-appearing man with pale blue eyes and a long nose. Courteous, tactful, soft-spoken, he gave the impression of being weak, an impression reinforced by his professed belief that the president should defer to Congress in the formulation of policy. This was a false impression; John Tyler was stubborn and proud, and these characteristics combined with an almost total lack of imagination to make him worship consistency, as so many second-raters do. He had turned away from Jackson because of the aggressive way the president had used his powers of appointment and the veto, but he also disagreed with Henry Clay and the northern Whigs about the Bank, protection, and federal internal improvements. Being a states' rights southerner, he considered such measures unconstitutional. Nevertheless, he was prepared to cooperate with Clay as the leader of what he called the "more immediate representatives" of the people, the members of Congress, but not to be Clay's puppet. He asked all of Harrison's Cabinet to remain in office.

Tyler's Troubles

Tyler and Clay did not get along, and for this Clay was chiefly to blame. He behaved in an overbearing manner that was out of keeping with his nature, probably because he resented having been passed over by the Whigs in 1840. (When news of Harrison's nomination reached him in Washington he was half drunk. His face darkened. "I am the most unfortunate man in the history of parties," he said "always run . . . when sure to be defeated, and now betrayed for a nomination when I, or anyone, would be sure of an election.") He considered himself the real head of the Whig party and intended to exercise his leadership.

In Congress Clay announced a comprehensive "program" that ignored Tyler's states' rights view of the Constitution. Most important was his plan to set up a new Bank of the United States. A bill to repeal the Independent Treasury Act caused no difficulty, but when Congress passed a new Bank bill, Tyler vetoed it. The entire Cabinet except Secretary of State Webster thereupon resigned in protest.

Abandoned by the Whigs, Tyler attempted to build a party of his own. For the remainder of his term the political squabbling in Washington was continuous. Clay wanted to distribute the proceeds from land sales to the states, presumably to bolster their sagging finances but actually to reduce federal revenues in order to justify raising the tariff. To win western votes for distribution, he agreed to support a preemption bill legalizing the right of squatters to occupy unsurveyed land and to buy it later at $1.25 an acre without bidding for it at auction. The Preemption Act of 1841 put this compromise into effect. However, the southerners insisted on an amendment pledging that distribution would be stopped if the tariff were raised above the 20 percent level, and when the Whigs blithely tried to ignore this proviso by pushing a high tariff through Congress without repealing the Distribution Act, Tyler vetoed the bill. Finally, the Distribution Act was repealed and Tyler signed the new Tariff Act of 1842, raising duties to about the levels of 1832.

Webster-Ashburton Treaty

Webster's decision to remain in the Cabinet was motivated in part by his desire to complete several important negotiations with Great Britain. The unsettled boundary between Maine and New Brunswick was the most important issue. The intent of the peace treaty of 1783 had been to award the United States all land in the area drained by rivers flowing into the Atlantic rather than the St. Lawrence, but the wording was obscure and the old maps conflicting. The issue became critical in 1838 when Canadians began cutting timber in the Aroostook Valley, which was claimed by the United States. When Maine sent an agent to remonstrate with the lumberjacks, he was arrested. Maine and New Brunswick each called up militia and the Aroostook "War" followed. No one was killed, yet the danger of a real war was great. Acting with admirable restraint, Van Buren sent General Winfield Scott to the area, and Scott managed to arrange a truce. At the time that Webster took over the State Department, nothing further had been accomplished.

Slavery also caused Anglo-American friction. The British outlawed the slave trade in 1807 and in 1834 abolished slavery throughout the empire.

John Tyler posed for a daguerreotypist about 1850, after he had retired from public life. Tyler voted in favor of Virginia's secession ordinance in 1861.

While the United States also forbade the trade, it was still touchy because of British aggressiveness before 1812, and it refused to permit visit and search of American vessels by British warships under any circumstances. This cause of ill feeling was aggravated late in 1841 when the American brig *Creole,* out of Hampton Roads, Virginia, put in at Nassau in the British West Indies. *Creole* had been en route to New Orleans with a cargo of slaves (a perfectly legal voyage) when the slaves had broken loose. They seized the ship and put into Nassau to claim asylum. The British promptly arrested the ringleaders, charging them with mutiny and murder, but the bulk of the slaves were freed despite protests from the State Department.

In 1842 the British sent a new minister, Lord Ashburton, to the United States to try to settle all outstanding disputes. Ashburton, head of a London banking house that had large investments in the United States, made an ideal ambassador. He and Webster easily worked out a compromise boundary. The British cared relatively little about the Aroostook Valley timber but needed part of the territory to the north to build a military road connecting Halifax and Quebec. Webster, who thought any settlement desirable simply to eliminate a possible cause of war, willingly agreed.

The problem of placating Maine and Massachusetts, which wanted every acre of the land in dispute, Webster solved in an extraordinary manner. It was known that during the peace negotiations ending the Revolution, Franklin had marked the boundary between Maine and Canada on a map with a heavy red line, but no one could locate the Franklin map. Webster obtained an old map of the area and had someone mark off in red a line that followed the British version of the boundary. He showed this document to representatives of Maine and Massachusetts, convincing them that they had better agree to his compromise before the British got wind of it and demanded the whole region! It later came out that the British had a true copy of the Franklin map, which showed that the entire area rightfully belonged to the United States.

Webster's generosity made excellent sense. Lord Ashburton, gratified by having obtained the strategic territory, made concessions elsewhere along the Canadian and American border (see map, page 367). Through a foolish error, the United States had built a million-dollar fort at the northern end of Lake Champlain on what turned out to be Canadian soil. Ashburton agreed to cede this strip of land along the New York and Vermont border to the United States. He also yielded 6,500 square miles of wild land between Lake Superior and Lake of the Woods, which later proved to contain one of the richest deposits of iron ore in the world. Webster and Ashburton agreed to maintain separate but cooperating naval squadrons off the African coast to aid in the suppression of the slave trade.

The Senate ratified the Webster-Ashburton Treaty in August 1842. Its importance, more symbolic than practical, was nonetheless great. British dependence on foreign foodstuffs was increasing; America's need for British capital was rising. War, or even unsettled affairs, would have injured vital business relations and produced no compensating gains. This spirit of mutual concession persisted in later years. This was the most important result of the Webster-Ashburton negotiations.

The Texas Question

The settlement with Great Britain won support in every section of the United States, but the same could not be said for Tyler's attempt to annex the Republic of Texas, for this involved the question of slavery. In the Transcontinental Treaty of 1819 with Spain, the boundary of the United States had been drawn in such a way as to exclude Texas. This seemed unimportant at the time, yet within months of the ratification of the treaty in February 1821, Americans led by Stephen F. Austin had begun to settle in the area, then part of an independent Mexico. Cotton flourished on the fertile Texas plains, and the Mexican authorities offered free land to groups of settlers. By 1830 there were some 20,000 white Americans in Texas, together with about 2,000 slaves, while only a few thousand Mexicans lived there.

President John Quincy Adams had offered Mexico $1 million for Texas, and Jackson was willing to pay $5 million, but Mexico would not sell. Nevertheless the flood of American settlers alarmed the Mexican authorities. The immigrants apparently felt no loyalty to Mexico. Most were Protestants, though Mexican law required that all immigrants be Catholics; few attempted to learn more than a few words of Spanish. When Mexico outlawed slavery, they evaded the law by "freeing" their slaves and then signing them to lifetime contracts as indentured servants. In 1830 Mexico prohibited further immigration of Americans into Texas, though again the law proved impossible to enforce.

As soon as the Mexican government began to restrict them, the Texans began to seek independence. In 1835 a series of skirmishes escalated into a full-scale rebellion. The Mexican president, Antonio López de Santa Anna, marched north with 6,000 soldiers to subdue the rebels. Late in February 1836 he reached San Antonio.

A force of 187 men under Colonel William B. Travis held the city. They took refuge behind the stout walls of a former mission called the Alamo. For 10 days they beat off Santa Anna's assaults, inflicting terrible casualties on the attackers. Finally, on March 6, the Mexicans carried the walls. Once inside they killed everyone, even the wounded, then soaked the corpses in oil and burned them. Among the dead were the legendary Davy Crockett and Jim Bowie, inventor of the Bowie knife.

After the Alamo and the slaughter of another

A painting (now lost) done in 1885, after a study of available sources, is probably the most accurate view of the final storming of the Alamo. Mexican troops poured through two openings made in the walls by their artillery fire; others scaled ladders to gain the interior of the fort. The Texans made their last stand in the mission at right.

garrison at Goliad, southeast of San Antonio, peaceful settlement of the dispute between Texas and Mexico was impossible. On March 2, 1836, the Texans declared their independence. Sam Houston, a former congressman and governor of Tennessee and an experienced Indian fighter, was placed in charge of the rebel army. For a time Houston retreated before Santa Anna's troops, who greatly outnumbered his own. At the San Jacinto River he took a stand. On April 21, 1836, shouting "Forward! Charge! Remember the Alamo! Remember Goliad!" he ordered the attack. His troops routed the Mexican army, which soon retreated across the Rio Grande. In October Houston was elected president of the Republic of Texas, and a month later a plebiscite revealed that an overwhelming majority favored annexation by the United States.

President Jackson hesitated. To take Texas might lead to war with Mexico. Assuredly it would stir up the slavery controversy. On his last day in office he recognized the republic, but he made no move to accept it into the Union, nor did his successor, Van Buren. Texas thereupon went its own way, which involved developing friendly ties with Great Britain. An independent Texas suited British tastes perfectly, for it could provide an alternative supply of raw cotton and a market for manufactures unfettered by tariffs.

These events caused alarm in the United States, especially among southerners, who dreaded the possibility that a Texas dominated by Great Britain might abolish slavery. As a southerner, Tyler shared these feelings; as a beleaguered politician, spurned by the Whigs and held in contempt by most Democrats, he saw in annexation a chance to revive his fortunes. When Webster resigned as secretary of state in 1843, Tyler replaced him with a fellow Virginian, Abel P. Upshur, whom he ordered to seek a treaty of annexation. The South was eager to take Texas, and in the West and even the Northeast the patriotic urge to add such a magnificent new territory to the national domain was great. Counting noses, Upshur convinced himself that the Senate would approve annexation by the necessary two-thirds majority. He negotiated a treaty in February 1844, but before he could sign it he was killed by the accidental explosion of a cannon on U.S.S. *Princeton* during a weapons demonstration.

To insure the winning of Texas, Tyler appointed John C. Calhoun secretary of state. This was a blunder; by then Calhoun was so closely associated with the South and with slavery that his

In this 1844 cartoon a slave awaits the outcome of the "Great Prize-Fight" matching the American eagle against Spanish and British contenders, with Texas and California as the prize. The ghost of Washington encourages the Republic with "Go it, my Boy, you will beat them all!" Britain's John Bull bets Canada while Spain's Don Quixote bets Cuba.

appointment alienated thousands of northerners who might otherwise have welcomed annexation. Suddenly Texas became a hot political issue. Clay and Van Buren, who seemed assured of the 1844 Whig and Democratic presidential nominations, promptly announced that they opposed annexation, chiefly on the ground that it would probably lead to war with Mexico. With a national election in the offing, northern and western senators refused to vote for annexation, and in June the Senate rejected the treaty, 35 to 16. The Texans were angry and embarrassed, the British eager again to take advantage of the situation.

Manifest Destiny

The Senate, Clay, and Van Buren had all misinterpreted public opinion. John C. Calhoun, whose world was so far removed from that of the average citizen, in this case came much closer to comprehending the mood of the country than any of its other leaders.

For two centuries Americans had been gradually conquering a continent. While the first colonists had envisaged a domain extending from the Atlantic to the Pacific, they had not realized the immensities of the New World. By the time their descendants came to appreciate its size, they had been chastened by the experience of battling the Indians for possession of the land and then laboriously developing it. The Revolution and its aftermath of nationalism greatly stimulated expansion, and then, before the riches of trans-Appalachia had even been inventoried, Jefferson had stunned the country with Louisiana, an area so big that the mere thought of it left Americans giddy.

The westward march from the 17th century to the 1840s had seemed fraught with peril, the prize golden but attainable only through patient labor and fearful hardships. Wild animals and wild men, mighty forests and mighty foreign powers beset the path. John Adams wrote of "conquering" the West "from the trees and rocks and wild beasts." He was "enflamed" by the possibilities of "that vast scene which is opening in the West," but to win it the United States would have to "march *intrepidly* on."

Quite rapidly (as historians measure time) the atmosphere changed. Each year of national growth increased the power and confidence of the people, and every forward step revealed a wider horizon. Now the West seemed a ripe apple, to be picked almost casually. Where pioneers had once stood in awe before the majesty of the Blue Ridge, then hesitated to venture from the protective shadows of the forest into the open prairies of Illinois, they now shrugged their shoulders at great deserts and began to talk of the Rocky Mountains as "mere molehills" along the road to the Pacific. After 200 years of westward expansion had brought them as far as Missouri and Iowa, Americans perceived their destined goal. *The whole continent was to be theirs!* Theirs to exploit, and theirs to make into one mighty nation, a land of opportunity, a showcase to display the virtues of democratic institutions, living proof that Americans were indeed God's chosen people. A New York journalist, John L. O'Sullivan, captured the new mood in a sentence. Nothing must interfere, he wrote in 1845, with "the fulfilment of our *manifest destiny* to overspread the continent allotted by Providence for the free development of our yearly multiplying millions."

The politicians did not sense the new mood in 1844; even Calhoun, who saw the acquisition of Texas as part of a broader program, was thinking of balancing sectional interests rather than of national expansion. In fact, the expansion, stimulated by the natural growth of the population and by a revived flood of immigration, was going on in every section and with little regard for political boundaries. New settlers rolled westward in hordes. Between 1830 and 1835, 10,000 entered "foreign" Texas, and this was a trickle compared to what the early 1840s were to bring. By 1840 many Americans had also settled far to the west in California, which was unmistakably Mexican territory, and in the Oregon country, jointly claimed by the United States and Great Britain.

California and Oregon

California was a huge and sparsely settled land dominated by Mexican cattlemen and a network of 21 Catholic missions running north from San Diego to beyond San Francisco. The mission friars controlled more than 30,000 Indian converts who lived and worked on their properties. By the 1830s a handful of Americans had established themselves

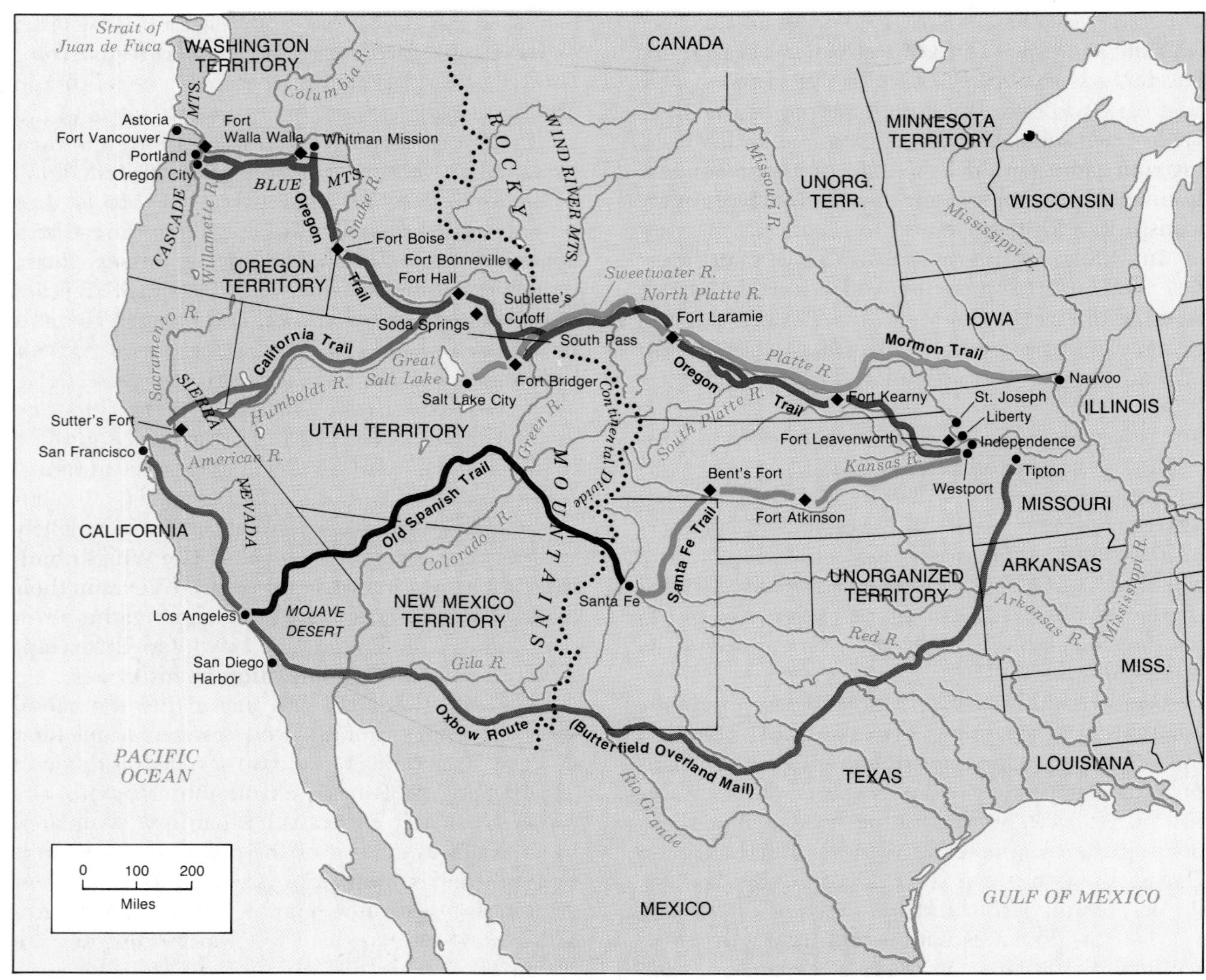

TRAILS WEST

The Old Spanish Trail was the earliest of the trails west. Part of it was mapped in 1776 by a Franciscan missionary. The Santa Fe Trail came into wide use after 1823. The Oregon Trail was pioneered by trappers and missionaries. The Mormon Trail was first traversed in 1847, while the Oxbow Route, developed under a federal mail contract, was used from 1858 to 1861.

in California. Richard Henry Dana, a Harvard College student, sailed around South America to California as an ordinary seaman on the brig *Pilgrim* in 1834. His account of that voyage in *Two Years Before the Mast* (1840) contains a fine description of what life was like for these people: "There is no working class (the Indians being practically serfs and doing all the hard work) and every rich man looks like a grandee, and every poor scamp like a broken-down gentleman."

Oregon, a vaguely defined area between California and Russian Alaska, proved still more alluring to Americans. Captain Robert Gray had sailed up the Columbia River in 1792, and Lewis and Clark had visited the region on their great expedition. In 1811 John Jacob Astor's Pacific Fur Company had established trading posts on the Columbia. Some two decades later Methodist, Presbyterian, and Catholic missionaries began to find their way into the Willamette Valley, a green land of rich soil, mild climate, and tall forests teeming with game. Gradually a small number of settlers followed, until by 1840 there were about 500 Americans in the Willamette area.

In the early 1840s, fired by the spirit of manifest destiny, the country suddenly burned with "Oregon fever." In dozens upon dozens of towns, societies were founded to collect information and organize groups to make the march to the Pacific. Land hunger (stimulated by the glowing reports of those on the scene) drew the new migrants most powerfully, but the patriotic concept of manifest destiny gave the trek across the 2,000 miles of wilderness separating Oregon from the western edge of American settlement in Missouri the character of a crusade. In 1843 nearly 1,000 pioneers made the long trip.

The Oregon Trail began at the western border of Missouri and followed the Kansas River and the perverse, muddy Platte ("a mile wide and six inches deep") past Fort Laramie to the Rockies. It crossed the Continental Divide by the relatively easy South Pass, veered south to Fort Bridger, on Mexican soil, and then ran north and west through the valley of the Snake River and eventually, by way of the Columbia, to Fort Vancouver, a British post guarding the entrance to the Willamette Valley.

Over this tortuous path wound the canvas-covered caravans with their scouts and their accompanying herds. Each group became a self-governing community on the march, with regulations democratically agreed upon "for the purpose of keeping good order and promoting civil and military discipline." For large groups Indians posed no great threat (though constant vigilance was necessary), but the five-month trip was full of labor, discomfort, and uncertainty; in the words of the historian David Lavender, a "remorseless, unending, weather-scoured, nerve-rasping plod on and on and on and on, foot by aching foot." And at the end lay the regular tasks of pioneering. The spirit of the trail-blazers is caught in an entry from the diary of James Nesmith:

> Friday, October 27.—Arrived at Oregon City at the falls of the Willamette.
>
> Saturday, October 28.—Went to work.

Behind the dreams of the Far West as an American Eden lay the commercial importance of the three major West Coast harbors: San Diego, San Francisco, and the Strait of Juan de Fuca leading into Puget Sound. Eastern merchants considered these harbors the keys to the trade of the Orient. That San Diego and San Francisco were Mexican and the Puget Sound district was claimed by Great Britain only heightened their desire to possess them. As early as 1835, Jackson tried to buy the San Francisco region. Even Calhoun called San Francisco the future New York of the Pacific and proposed buying all of California from Mexico.

The Election of 1844

In the spring of 1844 expansion did not seem likely to affect the presidential election. The Whigs nominated Clay unanimously and ignored Texas in their party platform. When the Democrats gathered in convention at Baltimore in May, Van Buren appeared to have the nomination in his pocket. He too wanted to keep Texas out of the campaign. That a politician of Van Buren's caliber, controlling the party machinery, could be upset in a national convention seemed unthinkable. But upset he was, for the southern delegates rallied round the Calhoun policy of taking Texas to save it for slavery. "I can beat Clay and Van Buren put together on this issue," Calhoun boasted. "They are behind the age." With the aid of a few northern expansionists the southerners forced through a rule requiring that the choice be by a two-thirds majority. This Van Buren could not muster. After a brief deadlock, a "dark horse," James K. Polk of Tennessee, swept the convention.

Polk was a good Jacksonian; his supporters called him "Young Hickory." He opposed high tariffs and was dead set against establishing another national bank. But he believed in taking Texas, and he favored expansion generally. To mollify the Van Burenites, the convention nominated Senator Silas Wright of New York for vice-president, but Wright was Van Buren's loyal friend and equally opposed to annexation. When the word was flashed to him in Washington over the new "magnetic telegraph" which Samuel F. B. Morse had just installed between the convention hall in Baltimore and the Capitol, he refused to run. The delegates then picked an annexationist, George M. Dallas of Penn-

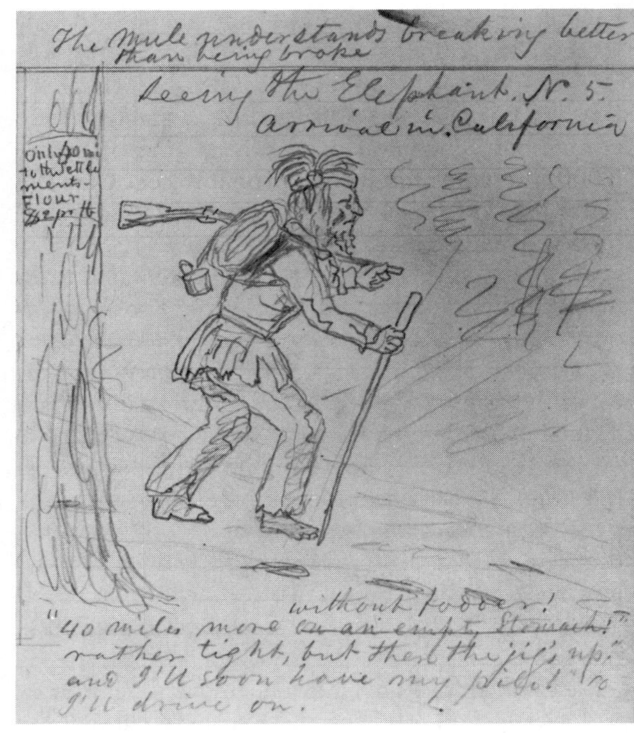

The hard road to El Dorado was sketched by J. Goldsborough Bruff, a Washington, D.C., draftsman who led a company "to see the elephant" (in the phrase of the day) in 1849. Two self-portraits from Bruff's diary neatly sum up the journey, with pencil notes reading as follows. Leaving Home (No. 1): "D——n your $3, when one can make $100 a day easy." Arrival in California (No. 5): "The mule understands breaking better than being broke. . . . 40 miles more without fodder! rather tight, but then the jig's up and I'll soon have my pile! so I'll drive on." The sign on the tree reads "Only 40 mi. to the Settlements. Flour $2.25 lb."

sylvania. The Democratic platform demanded that Texas be "reannexed" (implying that it had been part of the Louisiana Purchase) and that all of Oregon be "reoccupied" (suggesting that the joint occupation of the region with Great Britain, which had been agreed to in the Convention of 1818, be abrogated).

Texas was now in the campaign. The friends of Tyler, convening in Baltimore, had nominated the president on a "Tyler and Texas" ticket, which threatened to split the expansionist vote; old Andrew Jackson, who had nothing but contempt for "Tiler," was persuaded to write a letter professing "real regard" for him and praising his "good sense and patriotism." This, together with more flattery from Polk, convinced Tyler that he should withdraw.

When Clay sensed the new expansionist sentiment of the voters, he tried to hedge on his opposition to annexation, but he probably lost as many votes as he gained. The election was extremely close. The campaign followed the pattern established in 1840, with stress on parades, mass meetings, and slogans. Polk carried the country by only 38,000 of 2.7 million votes. In the electoral college the vote was 170 to 105.

The decisive factor in the contest was the Liberty party, an antislavery splinter group organized in 1840. Only 62,000 voters supported candidate James G. Birney, a "reformed" Kentucky slaveholder, but nearly 16,000 of them lived in New York, most in the western part of the state, a Whig stronghold. Since Polk carried New York by barely 5,000, the votes for Birney probably cost Clay the state. Had he won New York's 36 electoral votes, he would have been elected, 141 to 134.

Polk's victory was nevertheless taken as a mandate for expansion. Tyler promptly called on Congress to take Texas by joint resolution, which would avoid the necessity of obtaining a two-thirds majority in the Senate. This was done a few days before Tyler left the White House. Under the resolution Texas retained title to all public lands within its boundaries but accepted full responsibility for debts incurred while an independent republic. If the new state agreed, as many as four new states might be carved from its territory. Polk accepted this arrangement, and in December 1845 Texas became a state.

Polk as President

President Polk, a slightly built, erect, handsome man with large, grave, steel-gray eyes, was approaching 50. His mind was not of the first order, for he lacked imagination and was too tense and calculating to allow his intellect free rein. He was an efficient, hard worker with a strong will and a tough skin, qualities that stood him in good stead in the White House, and he made politics his whole life. It was typical of the man that he developed a special technique of handshaking in order better to cope with the interminable reception lines that every leader has to endure. "When I observed a strong man approaching," he once explained, "I generally took advantage of him by being a little quicker than he was and seizing him by the tip of his fingers, giving him a hearty shake, and thus preventing him from getting a full grip upon me." In four years in office he was away from his desk in Washington for a total of only six weeks.

Polk was uncommonly successful in doing what he set out to do as president. He persuaded Congress to lower the tariff of 1842 and to restore the Independent Treasury. He opposed federal internal improvements and managed to have his way. He made himself the spokesman of American expansion by committing himself to obtaining, in addition to Texas, both Oregon and the great Southwest. Here again, he succeeded.

Oregon was the first order of business. In his inaugural address Polk stated the American claim to the entire region in the plainest terms, but from the American point of view the remote northern half of the Oregon country had little value, and after allowing the British time to digest his demand for everything, he informed the British minister in Washington, Richard Pakenham, that he would accept a boundary following the 49th parallel to the Pacific.

Pakenham rejected this proposal without submitting it to London, and Polk thereupon decided to insist again on the whole area. When Congress met in December 1845, he asked for authority to give the necessary one year's notice for abrogating the 1818 treaty of joint occupation. "The only way to treat John Bull," he told one congressman, "was to look him straight in the eye." Following considerable discussion, Congress complied. It was, Representative Robert Winthrop of Massachusetts proclaimed in the debate, "our manifest destiny to spread over this whole continent." In May 1846 Polk notified Great Britain that he intended to terminate the joint occupation.

The British decided to compromise. Officials of the Hudson's Bay Company had become alarmed by the rapid growth of the American settlement in the Willamette Valley. By 1845 there were some 5,000 people there, whereas the country north of the Columbia contained no more than 750 British subjects. A clash between the groups could have but one result. The company decided to shift its base from the Columbia to Vancouver Island. And British experts outside the company reported that the Oregon country could not possibly be defended in case of war. Thus, when Polk accompanied the one-year notice with a hint that he would again consider a compromise, the British foreign secretary, Lord Aberdeen, hastened to suggest dividing the Oregon territory along the 49th parallel. Polk, abandoning his belligerent attitude, agreed. The treaty followed that line from the Rockies to Puget Sound, but Vancouver Island, which extends below the line, was left entirely to the British, so both nations retained free use of the Strait of Juan de Fuca (see map, page 352). Although some northern Democrats accused Polk of treachery because he had failed to fight for all of Oregon, the treaty so obviously accorded with the national interest that the Senate approved it by a large majority in June 1846. Polk was then free to take up the Texas question in earnest.

War with Mexico

One reason for the popularity of the Oregon compromise was that the country was already at war with Mexico and wanted no trouble with Great Britain. While the expansionist spirit and the confidence born of its overwhelming advantages of size and wealth certainly encouraged the United States to bully Mexico, the war had broken out in large measure because of the Mexicans' stubborn pride. Texas had been independent for the better part of a decade and Mexico had made no serious effort to reconquer it; nevertheless the government promptly broke off diplomatic relations when the United States annexed the republic.

This satiric 1846 cartoon reflects an anti–Mexican War bias, with its deadpan title "Volunteers for Texas" and its caricatured lineup of unsavory-looking enlistees—a black man carrying an umbrella rather than a gun, an Irishman, a drunk (possibly German)—being eyed disdainfully through the monocle of an effete officer.

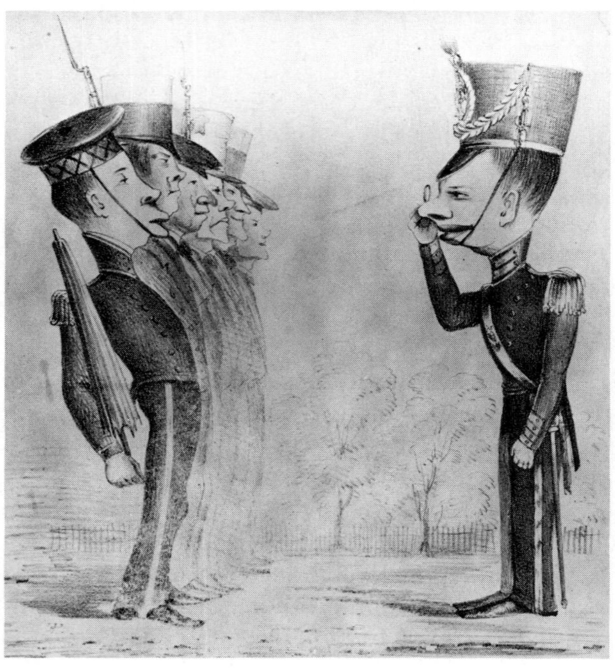

Polk, who did not want to fight if he could obtain what he wanted by negotiation, ordered General Zachary Taylor into Texas to defend the border. However, the location of that border was in dispute. Texas claimed the Rio Grande; Mexico insisted that the boundary was the Nueces River, which emptied into the Gulf about 150 miles to the north. Taylor reached the Nueces in July 1845 with about 1,500 troops and crossed into the disputed territory. He stopped on the southern bank at Corpus Christi, not wishing to provoke the Mexicans by marching to the Rio Grande.

In November Polk sent an envoy, John Slidell, on a secret mission to Mexico to try to obtain the disputed territory by negotiation. Mexico was in default on some $2 million owed American citizens for losses suffered during political upheavals in the country. Polk authorized Slidell to cancel this debt in return for recognition of the annexation of Texas and acceptance of the Rio Grande boundary. The president also empowered him to offer as much as $30 million if Mexico would sell the United States all or part of New Mexico and California.

It would have been to Mexico's long-range advantage to have made a deal with Slidell. The country could well have used the money, and the area Polk wanted, lying in the path of American expansion, was likely to be engulfed as Texas had been, without regard for the actions of the American or Mexican governments.

Polk assumed that his tough stance would compel the Mexicans to give in. But the Mexican government refused to receive Slidell. The Mexican people had little love for the undemocratic regime of President José Herrera. They loved their country, however, and their despair over local conditions exaggerated their patriotism. The mere news that Slidell was in Mexico City hastened the overthrow of Herrera, and the new president, General Mariano Paredes, promptly reaffirmed his country's claim to *all* Texas. In March 1846 Slidell returned to Washington convinced that the Mexicans could not negotiate until they had been "chastised."

Polk had already decided to fight and had ordered Taylor to advance to the Rio Grande. By March 28 his army, swelled to about 4,000, was drawn up on the north bank of the river, across

The general public obtained glimpses of the war through popular lithographs like this by Currier & Ives. The Mexican soldiers (in green) seem to be powerless, despite their cannons, against the onslaught of "Gringos" in blue.

from the Mexican town of Matamoros. When a Mexican force crossed the river on April 25 and attacked an American mounted patrol, the president had an ideal pretext. His message to Congress treated the matter as a fait accompli: "War exists," he stated flatly. He asked for authority not merely to drive the Mexicans back but to prosecute the war to "a speedy and successful termination." Congress accepted this reasoning and without actually declaring war voted to raise and supply an additional 50,000 troops. For the first time (but not the last) a president had led the nation into war without the formal declaration required by the Constitution.

From the first battle, the outcome of the Mexican War was never in doubt. At Palo Alto, north of the Rio Grande, 2,300 Americans scattered a Mexican force more than twice their number. Then, hotly pursuing, 1,700 Americans routed 7,500 Mexicans at Resaca de la Palma. Fewer than 50 United States soldiers lost their lives in these engagements, while Mexican losses in killed, wounded, and captured exceeded 1,000. Within a week of the declaration of war the Mexicans had been driven across the Rio Grande and General Taylor had his troops firmly established on the southern bank.

The Mexican army was poorly equipped and, despite a surfeit of high-ranking officers, poorly led. The well-supplied American forces had a hard core of youthful West Pointers eager to make their reputations and regulars trained in Indian warfare to provide the leadership needed to turn volunteer soldiers into first-rate fighting men. Yet Mexico was a large, rugged country with few decent roads; conquering it proved to be a formidable task.

To the Halls of Montezuma

President Polk insisted not only on directing grand strategy (he displayed real ability as a military planner) but on supervising hundreds of petty details, down to the purchase of mules and the promotion of enlisted men. But he allowed party considerations to control his choice of generals. This partisanship caused unnecessary turmoil in army ranks. He wanted, as Thomas Hart Benton said, "a small war, just large enough to require a treaty of peace, and not large enough to make military reputations dangerous for the presidency."

Unfortunately for Polk, both Taylor and Winfield Scott, the commanding general in Washington, were Whigs. Polk, who tended to suspect the motives of anyone who disagreed with him, feared that one or the other would make political capital of his popularity as a military leader. The examples of his hero, Jackson, and of General Harrison loomed large in Polk's thinking.

Polk's attitude was narrow, almost unpatriotic, but not unrealistic. Zachary Taylor was not a brilliant soldier. Polk believed that he lacked the "grasp of mind" necessary for high command, and General Scott complained of his "comfortable, laborsaving contempt for learning of every kind." But Taylor commanded the love and respect of his men (they called him Old Rough and Ready and even Zack), and he knew how to deploy them in the field. He had joined the army in 1808 and made it his whole life; he cared so little for politics that he had never bothered to cast a ballot in an election. Yet the dust had barely settled on the field of Resaca de la Palma when Whig politicians began to pay him court. "Great expectations and great consequences rest upon you," a Kentucky politician explained to him. "People everywhere begin to talk of converting you into a political leader, when the War is done."

Polk's concern was heightened because domestic opposition to the war was growing. Many northerners feared that the war would lead to the expansion of slavery. Others—among them an obscure Illinois congressman named Abraham Lincoln—felt that Polk had misled Congress about the original outbreak of fighting and that the United States was the aggressor. The farther from the Rio Grande one went in the United States, the less popular "Mr. Polk's War" became; in New England opposition was almost as widespread as it had been to "Mr. Madison's War" in 1812.

Polk's design for prosecuting the war consisted of three parts. First, he would clear the Mexicans from Texas and occupy the northern provinces of Mexico. Second, he would take possession of California and New Mexico. Finally, he would march on Mexico City. Proceeding west from the Rio Grande, Taylor swiftly overran Mexico's northern provinces. In June 1846 American settlers in the Sacramento Valley seized Sonoma and raised the "Bear Flag" of the republic of California. Another group, headed by Captain John C. Frémont, leader of an American exploring party which happened to be in the area, clashed with the Mexican authorities around Monterey, California, and then joined with the Sonoma rebels. A naval squadron under Commodore John D. Sloat captured Monterey and San Francisco in July 1846, and a squadron of cavalry joined the other American units in mopping-up operations around San Diego and Los Angeles. By February 1847 the United States had won control of nearly all of Mexico north of the capital city.

The campaign against Mexico City was the most difficult of the war. Fearful of Taylor's growing popularity and entertaining certain honest misgivings about his ability to oversee a complicated campaign, Polk put Winfield Scott in charge of the offensive. He tried to persuade Congress to make Thomas Hart Benton a lieutenant general so as to have a Democrat in nominal control, but the Senate had the good sense to vote down this absurd proposal.

About Scott's competence no one entertained a doubt. But he seemed even more of a threat to the Democrats than Taylor, because he had political ambitions as well as military ability. In 1840 the Whigs had considered running him for president. Scion of an old Virginia family, Scott was nearly six and a half feet tall; in uniform his presence was commanding. He was intelligent, even-tempered, and cultivated, if somewhat pompous. After a sound but not spectacular record in the War of 1812, he had added to his reputation by helping to modernize military administration and strengthen the professional training of officers. The vast difference between the army of 1812 and that

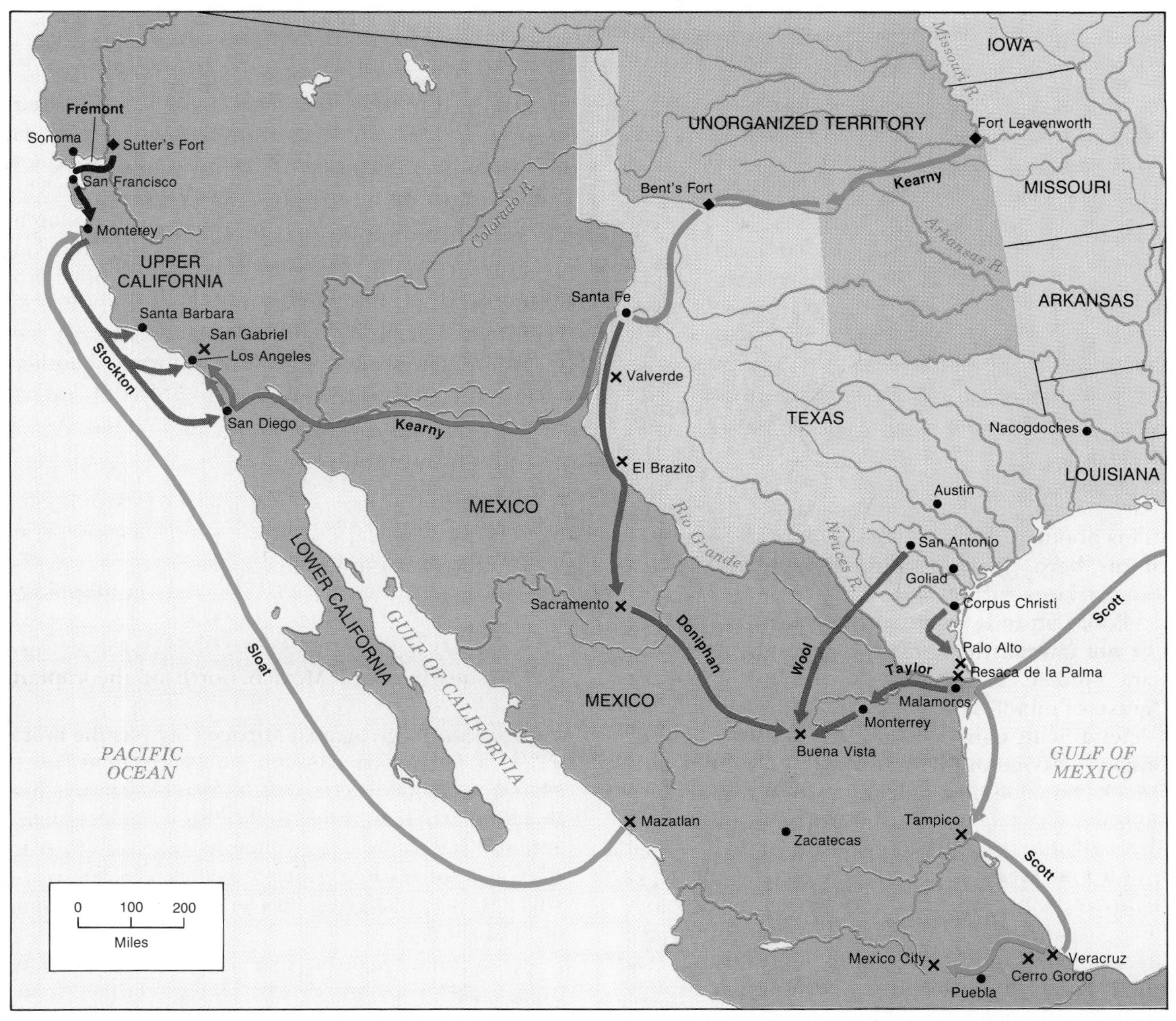

THE MEXICAN WAR, 1846–1848

American naval power proved a decisive factor in the Mexican War. The Pacific Squadron, under John D. Sloat and Robert F. Stockton, secured California, and a 200-vessel fleet conveyed Winfield Scott's army to Veracruz. The light salmon-colored area was later ceded to the United States by Texas.

of 1846 was chiefly his doing. On the record, and despite the politics of the situation, Polk had little choice but to give him this command.

Scott landed his army south of Veracruz, Mexico, on March 9, 1847, laid siege to the city, and obtained its surrender in less than three weeks with the loss of only a handful of his 10,000 men. Marching westward through hostile country, he maintained effective discipline, avoiding atrocities that might have inflamed the countryside against him.

This 1846 daguerreotype is the earliest known American war photograph. U.S. General John E. Wool poses with his staff in Saltillo, Mexico.

Finding his way blocked by well-placed artillery and a large army at Cerro Gordo, where the national road rose steeply toward the central highlands, Scott outflanked the Mexican position and then carried it by storm, capturing more than 3,000 prisoners and much equipment. By mid-May he had advanced to Puebla, only 80 miles southeast of Mexico City.

After delaying until August for the arrival of reinforcements, he pressed on, won two hard-fought victories at the outskirts of the capital, and on September 14 hammered his way into the city. In every engagement the American troops had been outnumbered, yet they always exacted a far heavier toll from the defenders than they themselves were forced to pay. In the fighting on the edge of Mexico City, for example, Scott's army sustained about 1,000 casualties, for the Mexicans defended their capital bravely. But 4,000 Mexicans were killed or wounded in the engagements, and 3,000 (including eight generals, two of them former presidents of the republic) were taken prisoner.

The Treaty of Guadalupe Hidalgo

The Mexicans were thoroughly beaten, but they refused to accept the situation. As soon as the news of the capture of Veracruz reached Washington, Polk sent Nicholas P. Trist, chief clerk of the State Department, to accompany Scott's army and to act as peace commissioner after the fall of Mexico City. Trist, a competent though pompous man, possessed impeccable credentials as a Democrat, for he had married a granddaughter of Thomas Jefferson and had served for a time as secretary to Andrew Jackson. Long residence as United States consul at Havana had given him an excellent command of Spanish.

Trist joined Scott at Veracruz in May. The two men took an instant dislike to each other. Scott considered it a "personal dishonor" to be asked to defer to what he considered a State Department flunky, and his feelings were not salved when Trist sent him an officious 30-page letter discoursing upon the nature of his assignment. However, Scott was eager to end the war and realized that a petty quarrel with the president's emissary would not advance that objective. Trist fell ill, and Scott sent him a jar of guava marmalade; after that they became good friends.

Because of the confused state of affairs following the fall of Mexico City, Trist could not commence negotiations with Mexican peace commissioners until January 1848. Polk, unable to understand the delay, became impatient. Originally he had authorized Trist to pay $30 million for New Mexico, Upper and Lower California, and the right of transit across Mexico's narrow Isthmus of Tehuantepec. Now, observing the disorganized state of Mexican affairs, he began to consider demanding more territory and paying less for it. He summoned Trist home.

Trist, with Scott's backing, ignored the order. He realized that unless a treaty was arranged soon the Mexican government might disintegrate, leaving no one in authority to sign a treaty. He dashed off a 65-page letter to the president, in effect refusing to be recalled, and proceeded to negotiate. Early in February the Treaty of Guadalupe Hidalgo was completed. By its terms Mexico accepted the Rio Grande as the boundary of Texas and ceded New Mexico and Upper California to the United States. In return the United States agreed to pay Mexico $15 million and to take on the claims of American citizens against Mexico, which by that time amounted to another $3.25 million.

Trist sent the treaty to Polk in the care of a New Orleans newspaperman. When he learned that Trist had ignored his orders, the president seethed. Trist was "contemptibly base," he thought, an "impudent and unqualified scoundrel." He ordered Trist placed under arrest and fired from his State Department job.* Yet Polk had no choice but to submit the treaty to the Senate, for to have insisted on more territory would have meant more fighting, and the war had become increasingly unpopular. The relatively easy military victory made some people ashamed that their country was crushing a weaker neighbor. Abolitionists, led by William Lloyd Garrison, called it an "invasion . . . waged solely for the detestable and horrible purpose of extending and perpetuating American slavery." The Senate, subject to the same pressures as the president, ratified the agreement by a vote of 38 to 14.

The Fruits of Victory

The Mexican War, won quickly and at relatively small cost in lives and money, brought huge territorial gains. The Pacific Coast from south of San Diego to the 49th parallel and all the land between the coast and the Continental Divide had become the property of the American people. Immense amounts of labor and capital would have to be invested before this new territory could be made to yield its bounty, but the country clearly had the capacity to accomplish the job.

In this atmosphere came what seemed a sign from the heavens. In January 1848, while Scott's veterans rested upon their victorious arms in Mexico City, a mechanic named James W. Marshall was building a sawmill on the American River in the Sacramento Valley east of San Francisco. One day, while supervising the deepening of the millrace, he noticed a few flecks of yellow in the bed of the stream. These he gathered up and tested. They were pure gold.

Other strikes had been made in California and been treated skeptically or as matters of local curiosity; since the days of Jamestown, too many pioneers had run fruitlessly in search of El Dorado, too much fool's gold had been passed off as the real thing. Yet this discovery produced an international sensation. The gold was real and plentiful—$200 million of it was extracted in four years—but equally important was the fact that everyone was ready to believe the news. The gold rush reflected the heady confidence inspired by Guadalupe Hidalgo; it seemed the ultimate justification of manifest destiny. Surely an era of continental prosperity and harmony had dawned.

Slavery: The Fire Bell in the Night Rings Again

Prosperity came in full measure but harmony did not, for once again expansion brought the nation face to face with the divisive question of slavery. This giant chunk of North America, most of it vacant, its future soon to be determined—should it be slave or free? The question, in one sense, seems hardly worth the national crisis it provoked. Slavery had little future in New Mexico, less in California, none in Oregon. Why did the South fight so hard for the *right* to bring slaves into a region so unsuited to their exploitation? Why did southern congressmen vote against barring slavery in Oregon Territory, and why, for that matter, did their northern

* Trist was retired to private life without being paid for his time in Mexico. In 1870, when he was on his deathbed, Congress finally awarded him $14,299.20.

colleagues insist that it be legally barred there, when everyone, North and South, knew that forbidden, encouraged, or ignored, the institution would never gain a foothold in the area?

The answers to these questions are complicated and tragic. Narrow partisanship provides part of the explanation. In districts where slavery was entrenched, a congressman who watched over the institution with the eyes of Argus, ever ready to defend it against the most trivial slight, usually found himself a popular hero. In the northern states, the representatives who were vigilant in what they might describe as "freedom's cause" seldom regretted it on election day. But slavery raised a moral question. Most Americans tried to avoid confronting this truth; as patriots they assumed that any sectional issue could be solved by compromise. However, while the majority of whites had little respect for blacks, slave or free, few persons, northern or southern, could look upon the ownership of one human being by another as simply an alternative form of economic organization and argue its merits as they would those of the protective tariff or a national bank. Twist the facts as they might, slavery was either right or it was wrong; being on the whole honest and moral, they could not, having faced that truth, stand by unconcerned while the question was debated.

The question could come up in Congress only indirectly, for the Constitution did not give the federal government any control over slavery in the states. But Congress had complete control in the territories. Therefore the fact that slavery had no future in the Mexican cession was unimportant—in fact, for the foes of slavery it was an advantage. By attacking slavery where it did not and probably never could exist, they could conceal from the slaveholders—and perhaps even from themselves—their hope ultimately to extinguish the institution.

Slavery had complicated the Texas problem from the start, and it beclouded the future of the Southwest even before the Mexican flag had been stripped from the staffs at Santa Fe and Los Angeles. The northern, Van Burenite wing of the Democratic party had become increasingly uneasy about the proslavery cast of Polk's policies, which were unpopular in their part of the country. Once it became likely that the war would bring new territory into the Union, these northerners felt compelled to try to check the president and to assure their constituents that they would resist the admission of further slave territory. On August 8, 1846, during the debate on a bill appropriating money for the conduct of the war, Congressman David Wilmot of Pennsylvania, normally a staunch supporter of the Polk administration, introduced an amendment that provided "as an express and fundamental condition to the acquisition of any territory from the Republic of Mexico" that "neither slavery nor involuntary servitude shall ever exist in any part of said territory, except for crime, whereof the party shall first be duly convicted."

The Wilmot Proviso passed the House, where northern congressmen outnumbered southern, but lost in the Senate, where southerners held the balance. To counter it, Calhoun, again senator from South Carolina, introduced a series of resolutions in February 1846 that argued that Congress had no right to bar slavery from any territory; since territories belonged to all the states, slave and free, all should have equal rights in them. From this position it was only a step (soon taken) to demanding that Congress guarantee the right of slaveowners to bring slaves into the territories and establish federal slave codes in the territories. Most northerners considered this proposal as repulsive as southerners found the Wilmot Proviso.

Calhoun's resolutions could never pass the House of Representatives, and Wilmot's Proviso had no chance in the Senate. Yet their very existence threatened the Union; as Senator Benton remarked, they were like the blades of a pair of scissors, ineffective separately, an efficient cutting tool taken together.

To resolve the territorial problem, two compromises were offered. One, eventually backed by President Polk, would extend the Missouri Compromise line to the Pacific. The majority of southerners were willing to go along with this scheme, but most northerners would no longer agree to the reservation of *any* new territory for slavery. The other possibility, advocated by Senator Lewis Cass of Michigan, called for organizing new territories without mention of slavery, thus leaving it to local settlers, through their territorial legislatures, to determine their own institutions. Cass's "popular sovereignty," known more vulgarly as "squatter sovereignty," had the superficial merit of appearing to be democratic. Its virtue for the members of Congress, however, was that it allowed them to escape

Two leading lights of the day, Clay and Webster, as they looked at about the time they played major roles in the Compromise of 1850. The daguerreotype of Clay dates from the late 1840s; that of Webster from 1851, a year before his death. Both are by the noted Boston firm of Southworth and Hawes.

the responsibility of deciding the question themselves.

The Election of 1848

One test of strength occurred in August, before the 1848 presidential election. After six months of acrimonious debate, Congress passed a bill barring slavery from Oregon. The test, however, proved little. If it required half a year to settle the question for Oregon, how could an answer ever be found for California and New Mexico? Plainly the time had come, in a democracy, to go to the people. The coming presidential election seemed to provide an ideal opportunity.

The opportunity was missed. The politicians of both parties hedged, fearful of losing votes in one section or another. With the issues blurred, the electorate had no real choice. That the Whigs should behave in such a manner was perhaps to be expected of the party of "Tippecanoe and Tyler too," but in 1848 they outdid even their 1840 performance, nominating Zachary Taylor for president. They chose the general despite his total lack of political sophistication and after he had flatly refused to state his opinion on any current subject. The party offered no platform. Taylor was a brave man and a fine general; the Democrats had mistreated him; he was a common, ordinary fellow, unpretentious and warmhearted. Such was the Whig "argument." Taylor's contribution to the campaign was so naive as to be pathetic. "I am a Whig, *but not an ultra Whig*. . . . If elected . . . I should feel bound to administer the government untrammeled by party schemes."

The Democratic party had little better to offer. All the drive and zeal characteristic of it in the Jackson period had gradually seeped away. Polk's espousal of Texas annexation had driven many northerners from its ranks. Individuals like James Buchanan of Pennsylvania, Polk's secretary of state, and William L. Marcy of New York, his secretary of war—cautious, cynical politicians interested chiefly in getting and holding office—now came to the fore in northern Democratic politics.

The Democratic nominee was Lewis Cass, the father of popular sovereignty, but the party did not endorse that or any other solution to the territorial question. Cass was at least an experienced politician, having been governor of Michigan Territory, secretary of war, minister to France, and senator. Nevertheless, he was vain, aloof, and conservative. His approach to life was exemplified by an annoying habit he displayed at Washington social functions: a teetotaler, he would circulate among the guests with a glass in hand, raising it to his lips repeatedly but never swallowing a drop.

The Van Buren wing of the Democratic party was known as the Barnburners to call attention to their radicalism—supposedly they would burn down the barn to get rid of the rats. The Barnburners could not stomach Cass, in part because he was willing to countenance the extension of slavery into new territories, in part because he had led the swing to Polk in the 1844 Democratic convention. Combining with the antislavery Liberty party, they formed the Free Soil party and nominated Van Buren.

Van Buren knew he could not be elected, but he believed the time had come to take a stand. "The minds of nearly all mankind have been penetrated by a conviction of the evils of slavery," the onetime "Fox" and "Magician" declared. The Free Soil party polled nearly 300,000 votes, about 10 percent of the total, in a very dull campaign. Offered a choice between the honest ignorance of Taylor and the cynical opportunism of Cass, the voters—by a narrow margin—chose the former, Taylor receiving 1.36 million votes to Cass's 1.22 million. Taylor carried 8 of the 15 slave states and 7 of the 15 free states, proof that the sectional issue had been avoided. Once again, a third party had determined the outcome, a fact that neither the Democrats nor the Whigs could ignore.

The Compromise of 1850

It was now clear that the question of slavery in the territories had to be faced. The discovery of gold had brought an army of prospectors into California. By the summer of 1848 San Francisco had become almost a ghost town, and an estimated two-thirds of the adult males of Oregon had hastened south to the gold fields. After President Polk confirmed the "extraordinary character" of the strike in his annual message of December 1848, there was no containing the gold seekers. During 1849, 25,000 Americans made their way to California from the East by ship; more than 55,000 others crossed the continent by overland routes. About 8,000 Mexicans, 5,000 South Americans, and numbers of Europeans joined the rush.

The rough limits of the gold country had been quickly marked out. For 150 miles and more along the western slope of the Sierras stretched the great mother lode. Along the expanse any stream or canyon, any ancient gravel bed might conceal a treasure in nuggets, flakes, or dust. Armed with pickaxes and shovels, with washing pans, even with knives and spoons, the eager prospectors hacked and dug and sifted, each accumulating a horde, some great, some small, of gleaming yellow metal.

The impact on the region was enormous. Almost overnight the Spanish-American population was reduced to the status of a minority. Disregarding justice and reason alike, the newcomers from the East, as one observer noted, "regarded every man but a native [North] American as an interloper." They referred to people of Latin American origin as "greasers" and sought by law and by violence to keep them from mining for gold. Even the local Californians (now American citizens) were discriminated against.

The ethnic conflict was only part of the problem. Rough, hard men, separated from women, lusting for gold in a strange wild country where fortunes could be made in a day, gambled away in an hour, or stolen in an instant—the situation demanded the establishment of a territorial government. President Taylor appreciated this, and in his gruff, simplehearted way he suggested an uncomplicated answer: admit California directly as a state, letting the Californians decide for themselves about slavery. The rest of the Mexican Cession could be formed into another state. No need for Congress, with its angry rivalries, to meddle at all, he believed. In this way the nation could avoid the divisive effects of sectional debate.

The Californians reacted favorably to Taylor's proposal. They were overwhelmingly opposed to slavery, though not for humanitarian reasons. On the contrary, they tended to look upon blacks as they did Mexicans and feared that if slavery were permitted, white gold seekers would be disadvantaged. "They would be unable," one delegate to the California constitutional convention predicted, "to compete with the bands of negroes who would be set to work under the direction of capitalists. It would become a monopoly." By October 1849 they had drawn up a constitution that outlawed slavery, and by December the new state government was functioning.

At this the South stood aghast. Taylor was the owner of a large plantation and many slaves; southerners had assumed (without bothering to ask) that he would fight to keep the territories open to slavery. To admit California would destroy the balance between free and slave states in the Senate; to allow all the new land to become free would doom the South to wither in a corner of the country, surrounded by hostile free states. Should that happen, how long could slavery sustain itself even in South Carolina? Radicals were already saying that the South would have to choose between secession and surrender. Taylor's plan played into the hands of extremists.

This was no longer a squabble over territorial governments. With the Union itself at stake, Henry Clay rose to save the day. He had been as angry and frustrated when the Whigs nominated Taylor as he was when they passed him over for Harrison. Now, well beyond 70 and in ill health, he put away his ambition and his resentment and for the last time concentrated his remarkable vision on a great, multifaceted national problem. California must be free and soon admitted to the Union, but the South must have some compensation. For that matter, why not seize the opportunity to settle every outstanding sectional conflict related to slavery? Clay pondered long and hard, drew up a plan, then consulted his old Whig rival Webster and obtained his general approval. On January 29, 1850, he laid his proposal, "founded upon mutual forbearance," before the Senate. A few days later he defended it on the floor of the Senate in the last great speech of his life.

California should be brought directly into the Union as a free state, he argued. The rest of the Southwest should be organized as a territory without mention of slavery: the southerners would retain the right to bring slaves there, while in fact none would do so. "You have got what is worth more than a thousand Wilmot Provisos," Clay pointed out to his northern colleagues. "You have nature on your side." The empty lands in dispute along the Texas border should be assigned to New Mexico Territory, Clay continued, but in exchange the United States should take over Texas's preannexation debts. The slave trade should be abolished in the District of Columbia (but not slavery itself), and a more effective federal fugitive slave law should be enacted and strictly enforced in the North.

Clay's proposals occasioned one of the most magnificent debates in the history of the Senate. Every important member had his say. Calhoun, perhaps even more than Clay, realized that the future of the nation was at stake and that his own days were numbered.* Too feeble to deliver his speech himself, he sat impassive, wrapped in a great cloak, while Senator James M. Mason of Virginia read it to the crowded Senate. Calhoun thought his plan would save the Union, but his speech was an argument for secession; he demanded that the North yield completely on every point, ceasing even to discuss the question of slavery. Clay's compromise was unsatisfactory; he himself had no other to offer. If you will not yield, he said to the northern senators, "let the States . . . agree to separate and part in peace. If you are unwilling we should part in peace, tell us so, and we shall know what to do. . . ."

Three days later, on March 7, Daniel Webster took the floor. He too had begun to fail; the brilliant volubility and the thunder were gone, and when he spoke his face was bathed in sweat and there were strange pauses in his delivery. But his argument was lucid. Clay's proposals should be adopted. Since the future of all the territories had already been fixed by geographical and economic factors, the Wilmot Proviso was unnecessary. The North's constitutional obligation to yield fugitive slaves, he said, braving the wrath of New England abolitionists, was "binding in honor and conscience." (A cynic might say that once again Webster was placing property rights above human rights.) The Union, he continued, could not be sundered without bloodshed. At the thought of the dread possibility, the old fire flared: "Peaceable secession!" Webster exclaimed, "Heaven forbid! Where is the flag of the republic to remain? Where is the eagle still to tower?"

* He died on March 31.

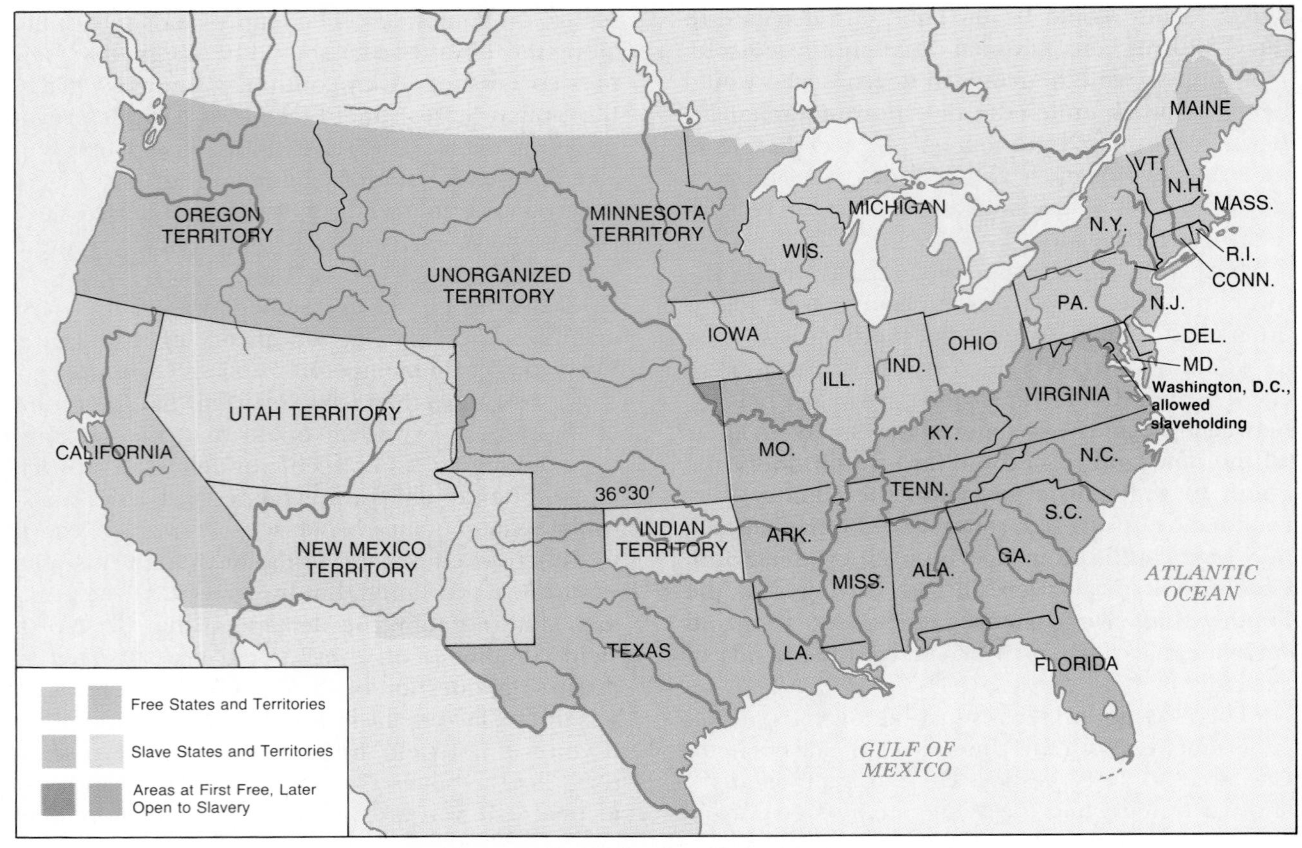

FREE AND SLAVE AREAS, 1850

This map and the map on the facing page show different aspects of the Compromise of 1850. Here, the two shades of salmon and the two shades of green show clearly the distribution of slave and free areas. The Utah and New Mexico territories were allowed to choose to be either free or slave, as their own constitutions determined.

The debate did not end with the aging giants. Every possible viewpoint was presented, argued, rebutted, rehashed. Senator William H. Seward of New York, a new Whig leader, close to Taylor's ear, caused a stir while arguing against concessions to the slave interests by saying that despite the constitutional obligation to return fugitive slaves, a "higher law" than the Constitution, the law of God, forbade anything that countenanced the evil of slavery.

The majority clearly favored some compromise, but nothing could have been accomplished without the death of President Taylor on July 9. Obstinate, probably resentful because few people paid him half the heed they paid Clay and other prominent members of Congress, he had insisted on his own plan to bring both California and New Mexico directly into the Union. When Vice-President Millard Fillmore succeeded him, the deadlock between the White House and Capitol Hill was broken. Even so, each part of the compromise had to be voted upon separately, for too many stubborn congressmen were willing to overturn the whole plan because they objected to specific parts of it. Senator Benton, for example, announced against Clay's Omnibus Bill because he objected to the fugitive slave provision and the Texas boundary settlement.

The final congressional maneuvering was managed by another relative newcomer, Senator Stephen A. Douglas of Illinois, who took over when

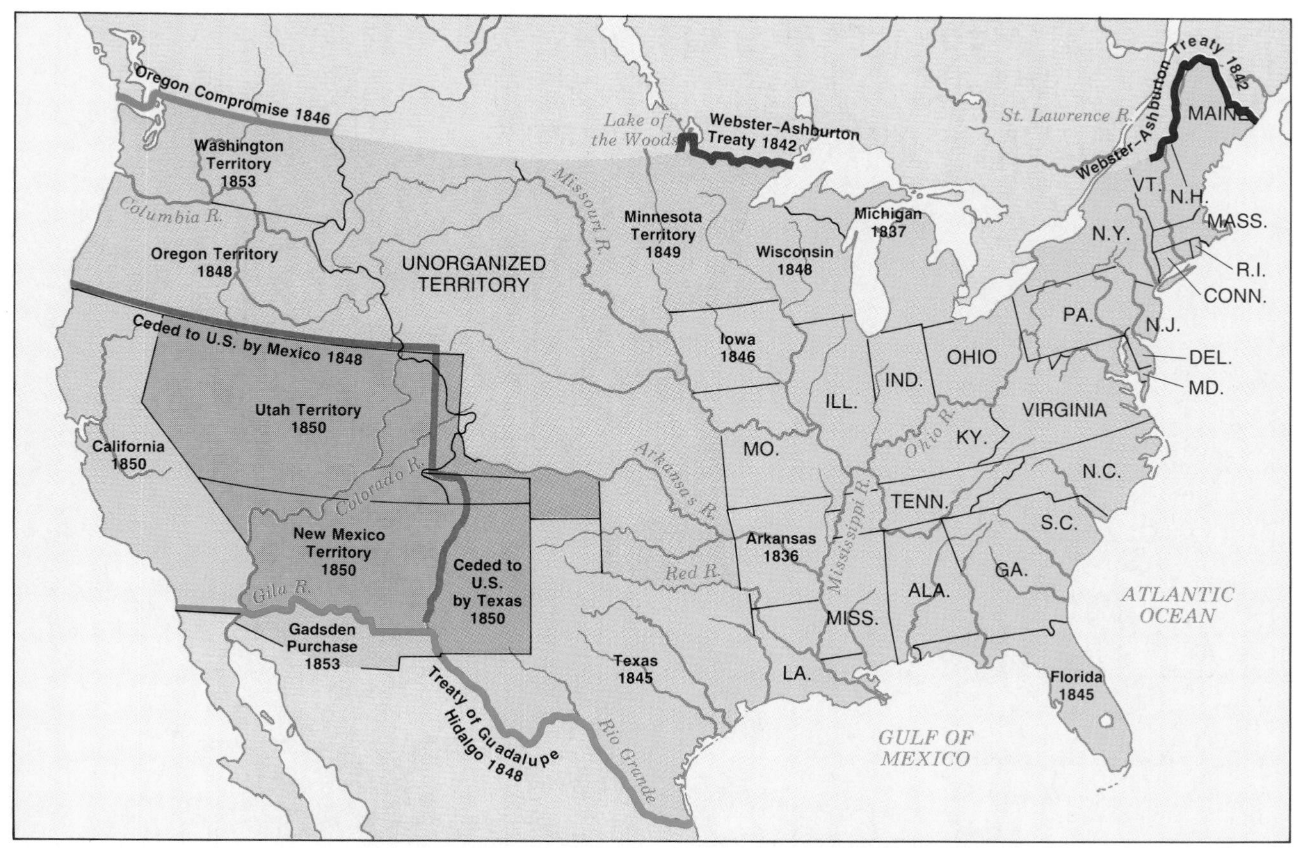

THE UNITED STATES AT MID-CENTURY

This map indicates the provisions of the Compromise of 1850 that applied to the Mexican Cession. Beginning with the annexation of Texas in 1845 and ending with the Gadsden Purchase in 1853 (to furnish a route for a southern transcontinental railroad), the United States acquired more than 869 million acres of territory. With the Gadsden Purchase, the geographical expansion of the continental United States was completed.

Washington's summer heat prostrated the exhausted Clay. Partisanship and economic interests complicated Douglas's problem. According to rumor, Clay had persuaded an important Virginia newspaper editor to back the compromise by promising him a $100,000 government printing contract. This inflamed many southerners. New York merchants, fearful of the disruption of their southern business, submitted a petition bearing 25,000 names in favor of compromise, a document that had a favorable effect in the South. The prospect of the federal government's paying the debt of Texas made ardent compromisers of a horde of speculators. Between February and September, Texas bonds rose erratically from 29 to over 60, while men like W. W. Corcoran, whose Washington bank held more than $400,000 of these securities, entertained legislators and supplied lobbyists with large amounts of cash.

In the Senate and then in the House, tangled combinations pushed through the separate measures, one by one. California became the thirty-first state. The rest of the Mexican Cession was divided into two territories, New Mexico and Utah, each to be admitted to the Union when qualified, "with or without slavery as [its] constitution may prescribe." Texas received $10 million to pay off its debt in return for accepting a narrower western boundary. The slave trade in the District of Columbia was abolished as of January 1, 1851. The Fugi-

'CONQUERING PREJUDICE,'
or
"Fulfilling a Constitutional duty with alacrity."
"My God!_ My Child!_ Will no one help!_ Is there no mercy!"
"Any man can perform an agreeable duty_ it is not every one that can perform a disagreeable duty."
"By Heaven! he exceeds my most sanguine expectation—he marks his way so clearly & treads so loyally on the track of the Constitution.— It is more than great_ it is sublime_ I feel a great sense of relief."

New Englanders severely criticized Webster for his support of the fugitive slave bill that became part of the Compromise of 1850. In this lithograph he is the central figure. "He exceeds my most sanguine expectation," cries the slave catcher running beside him.

tive Slave Act of 1793 was amended to provide for the appointment of federal commissioners with authority to issue warrants, summon posses, and compel citizens under pain of fine or imprisonment to assist in the capture of fugitives. The fugitives could not testify in their own defense. They were to be returned to the South without jury trial merely upon the submission of an affidavit by their "owner."

Only 4 senators and 28 representatives voted for all these bills. In general, the Democrats gave more support to the compromise than the Whigs, but party lines never held firmly. For example, 17 Democrats and 15 Whigs voted to admit California as a free state. A large number of congressmen absented themselves when parts of the settlement unpopular in their home districts came to a vote; 21 senators and 36 representatives failed to commit themselves on the new fugitive slave bill. Senator Jefferson Davis of Mississippi voted for the fugitive slave measure and the bill creating Utah Territory, remained silent on the New Mexico bill, and opposed the other measures. Senator Salmon P. Chase of Ohio, an abolitionist, supported only the admission of California and the abolition of the slave trade.

In this piecemeal fashion the Union was preserved. The credit belongs mostly to Clay, whose original conceptualization of the compromise enabled lesser minds to understand what they must do.

Everywhere sober and conservative citizens sighed with relief. Mass meetings throughout the country "ratified" the result. Hundreds of newspapers gave the compromise editorial approval. In Washington patriotic harmony reigned. "You would suppose that nobody had ever thought of disunion," Webster wrote. "All say they always meant to stand by the Union to the last." When Congress met again in December, it seemed that party asperities had been buried forever. "I have determined never to make another speech on the slavery question," Senator Douglas told his colleagues. "Let us cease agitating, stop the debate, and drop the subject." If this were done, he predicted, the compromise would be accepted as a "final settlement." With this bit of wishful thinking the year 1850 passed into history.

SUPPLEMENTARY READING

Titles marked with an asterisk have been published in paperback.

G. G. Van Deusen, **The Jacksonian Era*** (1959), provides a convenient summary of the period. For the Tyler administration, see O. D. Lambert, **Presidential Politics in the United States: 1841–1844** (1936), R. J. Morgan, **A Whig Embattled: The Presidency under John Tyler** (1954), G. R. Poage, **Henry Clay and the Whig Party** (1936), and Robert Seager, **And Tyler Too!** (1963), which is useful chiefly for its portrayal of Tyler's personal life.

On diplomatic affairs, see P. A. Varg, **United States Foreign Relations: 1820–1860** (1979), and D. M. Pletcher, **The Diplomacy of Annexation: Texas, Oregon, and the Mexican War** (1973). E. C. Barker, **Mexico and Texas** (1928) and **Life of Stephen F. Austin*** (1925), discuss the migration of Americans into the Texas region, while W. C. Binkley, **The Texas Revolution** (1952), and Marquis James, **The Raven*** (1929), the latter a biography of Sam Houston, are good accounts of the Texans' struggle for independence.

The new expansionism is discussed in A. K. Weinberg, **Manifest Destiny*** (1935), and in Frederick Merk, **Manifest Destiny and Mission in American History*** (1963) and **The Monroe Doctrine and American Expansionism** (1966). H. N. Smith, **Virgin Land*** (1950), is also important for an understanding of this subject. The course of western development is treated in R. A. Billington, **The Far Western Frontier*** (1956). On Oregon, see O. O. Winther, **The Great Northwest** (1947), David Lavender, **Westward Vision: The Story of the Oregon Trail*** (1963), Sandra Myres (ed.), **Ho for California! Women's Overland Diaries** (1980), and Francis Parkman's classic account, **The Oregon Trail*** (1849). The history of the American penetration of California is covered in R. G. Cleland, **From Wilderness to Empire** (1944).

For the election of 1844, see J. C. N. Paul, **Rift in the Democracy*** (1961). The best biography of Polk is C. G. Sellers's **James K. Polk** (1957–1966), but see also C. A. McCoy, **Polk and the Presidency** (1960), and Allan Nevins (ed.), **Polk: The Diary of a President** (1929). N. A. Graebner, **Empire on the Pacific** (1955), is the fullest analysis of the factors influencing the Oregon boundary compromise.

There are a number of good brief accounts of the Mexican War, including A. H. Bill, **Rehearsal for Conflict** (1947), and O. A. Singletary, **The Mexican War*** (1960). See also Holman Hamilton, **Zachary Taylor: Soldier of the Republic** (1946), and C. W. Elliott, **Winfield Scott** (1937). J. H. Schroeder, **Mr. Polk's War** (1973), discusses American opposition to the conflict. Allan Nevins's masterpiece, **The Ordeal of the Union** (1947–1960), commences with 1847 and so covers part of the Mexican conflict. For the discovery of gold in California, in addition to the work of Billington mentioned above, see R. W. Paul, **California Gold: The Beginning of Mining in the Far West*** (1947), and J. W. Caughey, **Gold Is the Cornerstone** (1948). On the treatment of Mexicans and blacks, see R. F. Heizer and A. J. Almquist, **The Other Californians*** (1971), and R. M. Lapp, **Blacks in Gold Rush California** (1977).

The fullest study of the Compromise of 1850 is Holman Hamilton, **Prologue to Conflict*** (1964). See also Allan Nevins's **Ordeal of the Union,** the biographies of Clay, Calhoun, and Webster cited in earlier chapters, C. B. Going, **David Wilmot: Free-Soiler** (1924), R. W. Johannsen, **Stephen A. Douglas** (1973), Holman Hamilton, **Zachary Taylor: Soldier in the White House** (1951), and A. O. Craven, **The Growth of Southern Nationalism** (1953).

13
The Sections Go Their Ways

It is a great mistake to suppose that disunion can be effected by a single blow. The cords which bind these states together in one common Union are far too numerous and powerful for that. Disunion must be the work of time. JOHN C. CALHOUN, *March 4, 1850*

A nation growing as rapidly as the United States in the middle decades of the 19th century changed continually in hundreds of ways. The country was developing a *national* economy marked by the dependence of each area upon all the others, the production of goods in one region for sale in all, the increased specialization of agricultural and industrial producers, and the growth in size of units of production. Basic adjustments were taking place, sometimes unnoticed. Cotton remained the most important southern crop and the major American export. However, manufacturing in the Northeast and the railroads, which revolutionized transportation and communication, became the mainsprings of economic growth. The continuing westward movement of agriculture had significant new effects. American foreign commerce changed radically, and the flood of European immigration had an impact on manufacturing, town life, and farming.

The Cotton South

The South was less affected than the other sections by urbanization, by European immigration, by the transportation revolution, and by industrialization. The region remained predominantly agricultural; cotton was still king, slavery the most distinctive southern institution. But important changes were occurring *within* southern agriculture. Cotton continued to march westward until by 1859, 1.3 million of the 4.3 million bales grown in the United States came from beyond the Mississippi. In the Upper South, Virginia held its place as the leading tobacco producer, but states beyond the Appalachians were raising more than half the crop by the 1850s. Early in that decade the introduction of Bright Yellow, a mild variety of tobacco that (miraculously) grew best in poor soil, gave a great stimulus to production. The older sections of Maryland, Virginia, and North Carolina shifted to the kind of diversified farming usually associated with the Northeast. By 1849 the wheat crop of Virginia was worth twice as much as the tobacco crop.

In the time of Washington and Jefferson, progressive Virginia planters had experimented with crop rotation and fertilizers. In the mid-19th century, pressed by the exhaustion of their soils after decades of tobacco cultivation, many Virginia farmers adopted advanced methods. Edmund Ruffin introduced the use of marl, an earth rich in calcium, to counteract the acidity of worn-out tobacco fields. Ruffin discovered that dressings of marl, combined with the use of fertilizers and with proper drainage and plowing methods, doubled and even tripled the yield of corn and wheat. In the 1840s some southerners began to import Peruvian guano, a high-nitrogen fertilizer of bird droppings, which increased yields. Others experimented with contour plowing to control erosion and with improved breeds of livestock, new types of plows, and agricultural machinery.

The Economics of Slavery

The increased importance of cotton in the South strengthened the hold of slavery on the region. The price of slaves rose until by the 1850s a prime field hand was worth as much as $1,800, roughly three times the cost in the 1820s. While the prestige value of owning this kind of property affected prices, the rise chiefly reflected the increasing value of the South's agricultural output. "Crop value per slave" jumped from less than $15 early in the century to more than $125 in 1859.

In the cotton fields of the Deep South slaves brought several hundred dollars per head more than in the older regions; thus the tendency to sell them "down the river" continued. Mississippi took in some 10,000 slaves a year throughout the period; by 1830 the black population of the state exceeded the white. Slave trading became a big business. There were about 50 dealers in Charleston in the 1850s and 200 in New Orleans. The largest traders were Isaac Franklin and John Armfield, who collected slaves from Virginia and Maryland at their "model jail" in Alexandria and shipped them by land and sea to a depot near Natchez. Each of the partners cleared half a million dollars before retiring, and some smaller operators did proportionately well.

The impact of the trade on the slaves was frequently disastrous. Husbands were often separated from wives, parents from children. This was somewhat less likely to happen on large, well-managed plantations than on small farms, but it was common enough everywhere. Because the business was so profitable, the prejudice against slave traders

This engraving of a "Sale of Estates, Pictures, and Slaves in the Rotunda, New Orleans," appeared in an 1842 book, Slave States of America *by J. S. Buckingham, published in London.*

abated as the price of slaves rose. Men of high social status became traders, and persons of humble origin who had propered in the trade had little difficulty in buying land and setting up as respectable planters.

As blacks became more expensive, the ownership of slaves became more concentrated. On the eve of the Civil War only one white southern family in four owned any at all. In 1850 only 254 persons owned 200 or more slaves. In 1860 only about 46,000 of the 8 million white residents of the slave states had as many as 20. When one calculates the cost of 20 slaves and the land to keep them profitably occupied, it is easy to understand why this figure is so small. The most efficient size of a plantation worked by gangs of slaves ranged between 1,000 and 2,000 acres. In every part of the South the majority of farmers cultivated no more than 200 acres, in many sections less than 100 acres. A few large plantations and many small farms—this was the pattern. However, the *trend* in the South was toward larger agricultural units.

There were few genuine economies of scale in southern agriculture. Small farmers grew the staple crops, and many of them owned a few slaves, often working beside them in the fields. These yeomen farmers were hardworking, self-reliant, and moderately prosperous, quite unlike the "poor white trash" of the pine barrens and the remote valleys of the Appalachians who scratched a meager subsistence from substandard soils and lived in ignorance and squalor.

Well-managed plantations yielded annual profits of 10 percent and more, and in general, money invested in southern agriculture earned at least a modest return. Considering the way the work force was exploited, this is hardly surprising. Recent estimates indicate that after allowing for the cost of land and capital, the average plantation slave "earned" cotton worth $78.78 in 1859. It cost masters about $32 a year to feed, clothe, and house a slave. In other words, almost 60 percent of the product of slave labor was expropriated by the masters.

The South failed to develop locally owned marketing and transportation facilities, and for this slavery was at least partly responsible. In 1840 *Hunt's Merchant Magazine* estimated that it cost $2.85 to move a bale of cotton from the farm to a seaport and that additional charges for storage, insurance, port fees, and freight to a European port exceeded $15. Middlemen from outside the South commonly earned most of this money. New York capitalists gradually came to control much of the South's cotton from the moment it was picked, and a large percentage of the crop found its way into New York warehouses before being sold to manufacturers. The same middlemen supplied most of the foreign goods that the planters purchased with their cotton earnings.

Southerners complained about this state of affairs but did little to correct it. Capital tied up in the ownership of labor could not be invested in anything else, and social pressures in the South militated against investment in trade and commerce. Ownership of land and slaves yielded a kind of psychic income not available to any middleman. As one British visitor pointed out, the southern blacks were "a nonconsuming class." Still more depressing, under slavery the enormous reservoir of intelligence and skill that the blacks represented was almost entirely wasted. Many slave artisans worked on the plantations, and a few free blacks made their way in the South remarkably well, but the amount of talent unused, energy misdirected, and imagination smothered can only be guessed.

Foreign observers in New England frequently noted the alertness and industriousness of ordinary laborers and attributed this, justifiably, to the high level of literacy. Nearly everyone in New England could read and write. Correspondingly, the stagnation and inefficiency of southern labor could be attributed in part to the high degree of illiteracy, for over 20 percent of *white* southerners could not read or write, another tragic squandering of human resources.

The Sociology of Slavery

It is difficult to generalize about the "peculiar institution" because so much depended on the individual master's behavior. Owners exercised power over their human possessions "as absolute . . . as the Khan of Tartary." Yet the system was fundamentally paternalistic. Most owners felt responsibilities toward their slaves, and slaves were dependent on and in some ways imitative of white values. However, powerful fears and resentments, not always recognized, existed on both sides. The plantation environment forced the two races to live in close proximity. From this circumstance could rise every sort of human relationship. One planter, using the appropriate pseudonym Clod Thumper, could write: "Africans are nothing but brutes, and they will love you better for whipping, whether they deserve it or not." Another, describing a slave named Bug, could say: "No one knows but myself what feeling I have for him. Black as he is we were raised together."

The United States was the only nation in the Western Hemisphere where the slave population grew by natural increase. After the ending of the slave trade in 1808, the black population increased at nearly the same rate as the white. Put differently, during the entire period from the founding of Jamestown to the Civil War only a little more than half a million slaves were imported into the country, about 5 percent of the number of Africans carried by slavers to the New World. Yet in 1860 there were about 4 million blacks in the United States.

Most owners provided adequate clothing, housing, and food for their slaves, for only a fool or a sadist would fail to take care of such valuable property. But the slave diet (chiefly corn and hog fat) was deficient in protein, and this could make slaves disease-prone. Vital statistics indicate that infant mortality among slaves was twice the white rate, life expectancy at least five years less. One student of this subject, Richard Sutch, concludes: "The returns from slavery were maximized by using force to extract the maximum amount of work from the slaves while providing them only with sufficient food, shelter, clothing, and health care to keep them healthy and hard working."

Slaves were without rights; they developed a distinctive way of life by attempting to resist oppression and injustice while accommodating themselves to the system. Their marriages had no legal status, but their partnerships seem to have been as loving and stable as those of their masters. Certainly they were acutely conscious of family relationships and responsibilities. Slave religion, on the surface an untutored form of Christianity tinctured with some African survivals, seemed to most slaveowners a useful instrument for teaching meekness and resignation and for providing harmless emotional release, which it sometimes was and did. However, religion also sustained the slaves' sense of their own worth as beings made in the image of God, and it taught them, therefore, that while human beings can be enslaved in body, their spirits cannot be enslaved without their consent.

These reportorial views of slavery were sketched by a young Austrian, Franz Hölzlhuber, who toured the South between 1856 and 1860. Above is a rice plantation on the Arkansas River. The slaves at right, harvesting sugar cane in Louisiana, are dressed in striped garb to discourage attempts at escape.

Nearly every white observer claimed that slaves were congenitally lazy; George Washington, for example, wrote that "when an overlooker's back is turned, the most of them will slight their work, or be idle altogether." In part this tendency can be explained as a rational response to forced, uncompensated labor. As one planter confessed, slaves "are not stimulated to care and industry as white people are, who labor for themselves." "Laziness" was also a reflection of a peasantlike view of the world, one that was a product of their surroundings, not of their servile status. The historian Eugene D. Genovese says that owners might have liked their slaves to behave like clock-punching factory workers, but plantations were not factories, and no one, least of all the masters, punched a clock. "Do as I say, not as I do," is not an effective way of teaching anything. Moreover, it must be remembered that under slavery the "overlooker's back" was rarely turned. Slaves worked long and hard, whatever their innate tendencies might have been.

Observing that slaves often seemed happy and were only rarely overtly rebellious, whites persuaded themselves that most blacks accepted the system without resentment and indeed preferred slavery to the uncertainties of freedom. There was much talk about "loyal and faithful servants." The Civil War, when slaves flocked to the Union lines once assured of freedom and fair treatment, disabused them of this illusion.

As slaves became more valuable and as northern opposition to the institution grew more vocal, the system hardened perceptibly. Southerners made much of the danger of insurrection. When a plot was uncovered or a revolt took place, instant and savage reprisals resulted. In 1822, after the conspiracy of Denmark Vesey was exposed by informers, 37 slaves were executed and another 30-odd deported, although no overt act of rebellion had occurred. After a rising in Louisiana, 16 blacks were decapitated, their heads left to rot on poles along the Mississippi as a grim warning. The Nat Turner revolt in Virginia in 1831 was the most sensational of the slave uprisings; 57 whites lost their lives before it was suppressed. Southerners treated runaways almost as brutally as rebels, though they posed no real threat to whites. The authorities tracked down fugitives with bloodhounds and subjected captives to merciless lashings.

After the Nat Turner uprising, interest in doing away with slavery vanished in the South. The southern states made it increasingly difficult, if not impossible, for masters to free their slaves. During 1859 in all the South only about 3,000 in a slave population of nearly 4 million were given their freedom, and many of them were elderly and thus of little or no economic value.

Slavery did not flourish in urban settings, and cities did not flourish in societies where slavery was important. Baltimore, the largest southern city, had a population of more than 128,000 in 1850, but its economy was geared more to the North than to the South. Most other southern cities were

SLAVERY RECORD.

INSURRECTION IN VIRGINIA!

Extract of a letter from a gentleman to his friend in Baltimore, dated

'RICHMOND, August 23d.

An express reached the governor this morning, informing him that an insurrection had broken out in Southampton, and that, by the last accounts, there were seventy whites massacred, and the militia retreating. Another express to Petersburg says that the blacks were continuing their destruction; that three hundred militia were retreating in a body, before six or eight hundred blacks. A shower of rain coming up as the militia were making an attack, wet the powder so much that they were compelled to retreat, being armed only with shot-guns. The negroes are armed with muskets, scythes, axes, &c. &c. Our volunteers are marching to the scene of action. A troop of cavalry left at four o'clock, P. M. The artillery, with four field pieces, start in the steam boat Norfolk, at 6 o'clock, to land at Smithfield. Southampton county lies 80 miles south of us, below Petersburg.'

From the Richmond Whig, of Tuesday.

Disagreeable rumors have reached this city of an insurrection of the slaves in Southampton County, with loss of life. In order to correct exaggeration, and at the same time to induce all salutary caution, we state the following particulars:

An express from the Hon. James Trezvant states that an insurrection had broken out, that several families had been murdered, and that the negroes were embodied, requiring a considerable military force to reduce them.

The names and precise numbers of the families are not mentioned. A letter to the Post Master corroborates the intelligence. Prompt and efficient measures are being taken by the Governor, to call out a sufficient force to put down the insurrection, and place lower Virginia on its guard.

Serious danger of course there is none. The deluded wretches have rushed on assured destruction.

The Fayette Artillery and the Light Dragoons will leave here this evening for Southampton; the artillery go in a steamboat, and the troop by land.

We are indebted to the kindness of our friend Lyford for the following extract of a letter from the Editors of the Norfolk Herald, containing the particulars of a most murderous insurrection among the blacks of Southampton County,* Virginia.—*Gaz.*

NORFOLK, 24th Aug. 1831.

I have a horrible, a heart rending tale to relate, and lest even its worst feature might be distorted by rumor and exaggeration, I have thought it proper to give you all and the worst information, that has as yet reached us through the best sources of intelligence which the nature of the case will admit.

A gentleman arrived here yesterday express from Suffolk, with intelligence from the upper part of Southampton county, stating that a band of insurgent slaves (some of them believed to be runaways from the neighboring Swamps,) had turned out on Sunday night last, and murdered several whole families, amounting to 40 or 50 individuals. Some of the families were named, and among them was that of Mrs. Catharine Whitehead, sister of our worthy townsman, Dr. N. C. Whitehead,—who, with her son and five daughters, fell a sacrifice to the savage ferocity of these demons in human shape.

The insurrection was represented as one of a most alarming character, though it is believed to have originated only in a design to plunder, and not a view to a more important object—as Mrs. Whitehead being a wealthy lady, was supposed to have had a large sum of money in her house. Unfortunately a large number of the effective male popu-

* Southampton is bounded by the counties of Isle of Wight on the North, and Northampton, in North Carolina, on the South.

The abolitionist Liberator *reprinted southern accounts of the Nat Turner revolt.*

small, and within them, slaves made up a small fraction of the labor force. The existence of slavery goes a long way toward explaining why the South was so rural and why it had so little industry. Blacks were much harder to supervise and control in urban settings. More important, as the historian Barbara Jeanne Fields has explained, there was a "profound basis for antagonism between slavery and urban development." Individual slaves were successfully employed in southern manufacturing plants, but they made up only an insignificant fraction of the South's small industrial labor supply. Wherever there was industrial development, the proportion of slaves in the population was declining.

Southern whites considered the existence of free blacks undesirable, no matter where they lived. The mere fact that they could support themselves disproved the notion that they were by nature childlike and shiftless, unable to work efficiently without white guidance. From the whites' point of view, free blacks set a bad example for slaves. At a minimum, the sight of "a vile and lazy free negro lolling in the sun-shine" might make slaves envious. Still worse it might encourage them to try to escape, and worst of all, the free blacks might help them to do so.

Many southern states passed laws aimed at forcing free blacks to emigrate, but these laws were not well enforced. There is ample evidence that the white people of, say, Maryland would have liked to get rid of the state's large free-black population. Free blacks were barred from occupations in which they might cause trouble—no free black could be the captain of a ship, for example—and they were required by law to find a "respectable" white person who would testify as to their "good conduct and character." But whites did not try very hard to expel them, as Professor Fields has shown, because they needed their labor.

Some unscrupulous southerners engaged in smuggling of blacks from Africa. About 54,000 slaves were brought to America illegally after the trade was outlawed in 1808, not a very large number relative to the slave population. British, French, Portuguese, and American naval vessels patrolled the African coast continuously. The American navy alone seized more than 50 suspected slavers in the two decades before 1860. However, the fast, sharklike pirate cruisers were hard to catch, the anti-slave-trade laws imperfectly worded and unevenly enforced. Many accounts tell of slaves in America long after 1808 with filed teeth, tattoos, and other signs of African origin, yet no one owning such a person was ever charged with the possession of contraband goods.

Slave traders continued to smuggle their cargoes to America long after importation was outlawed. This engraving of the deck of the Wildfire *upon the ship's capture at Key West was published in* Harper's Weekly *in June 1860.*

Psychological Effects of Slavery

The injustice of slavery needs no proof; less obvious is the fact that it had a corrosive effect on the personalities of southerners, slave and free alike. By "the making of a human being an animal without hope," the system bore heavily on all slaves' sense of their own worth. Some found the condition absolutely unbearable. They became the habitual runaways who collected whip scars like medals, the "loyal" servants who struck out in rage against a master knowing that the result would be certain death, the leaders of slave revolts.

Denmark Vesey of South Carolina, even after buying his freedom, could not stomach the subservience demanded of slaves by the system. When he saw Charleston slaves step into the gutter to make way for whites, he taunted them: "You deserve to remain slaves!" For years he preached resistance to his fellows, drawing his texts from the Declaration of Independence and the Bible and promising help from black Haiti. So vehemently did he argue that some of his followers claimed they feared Vesey more than their masters, even more than God. He planned his uprising for five years, patiently working out the details, only to see it aborted at the last moment when a few of his recruits lost their nerve and betrayed him. For Denmark Vesey, death was probably preferable to living with such rage as his soul contained.

Yet Veseys were rare. Most slaves appeared, if not contented, at least resigned to their fate. Some seemed even to accept the whites' evaluation of their inherent abilities and place in society. The historian Stanley Elkins has drawn an interesting parallel between the behavior of slaves and that of the inmates of Adolf Hitler's concentration camps, arguing that in both cases such factors as the fear of arbitrary punishment and the absence of any hope of escape led to the disintegration of the victim's personality—to childishness, petty thievery, chronic irresponsibility, and even to a degrading identification with the "master race" itself.

The comparison is overdrawn, for plantations were not concentration camps. Slaves had strong family and group attachments and a complex culture of their own, maintained, so to speak, under the noses of their masters. By a mixture of subterfuge, accommodation, and passive resistance, they erected subtle defenses against exploitation, achieving a sense of community that helped sustain the psychic integrity of individuals. And if some slaves indeed became fawning "Sambos" and "Uncle Toms," it must be remembered that the slave system was designed to make blacks submissive. It discouraged, if it did not extinguish, independence of judgment and self-reliance. These qualities are difficult enough to develop in human beings under the best circumstances; when every element in society encouraged slaves to let others do their thinking for them, to avoid questioning the status quo, to lead a simple, animal existence, many did so willingly enough. Was this not slavery's greatest shame?

Slavery warped whites perhaps even more severely than it did blacks. This subject too has attracted the attention of psychoanalytically inclined historians, who have suggested, among other things, that the system encouraged whites to conceal their animal natures from themselves by projecting on the helpless slaves their own base passions. Many planters, these historians note, took advantage of their position to avail themselves of slave women. (Estimates of the proportion of the slave population fathered by whites range from 4 to 8 percent.) To avoid facing the fact that they were rapists, the whites pictured *blacks* as lustful, superpotent, and incapable of self-restraint. In a related manner, idle slaveowners exacted labor from their slaves by brute force and justified their cruel whips by claiming that blacks were inherently lazy. The harm done to the slaves by such mental distortions is obvious. More obscure is the effect on the masters: self-indulgence is perhaps only contemptible; self-delusion is pitiable and ultimately destructive.

Such a description of master-slave relations is one-sided. Probably the large majority of owners respected the most fundamental personal rights of their slaves. Indeed, so far as sexual behavior is concerned, there are countless known cases of lasting relationships based on love and mutual respect between owners and what law and the community defined as their "property."

And the psychological injury inflicted on whites by slavery can be demonstrated without resort to Freudian insights. By associating working for others with servility, it discouraged many poor southerners from hiring out to earn a stake. It provided the weak, the shiftless, and the unsuccessful with a scapegoat that made their own miserable state easier to bear but harder to escape. A few slaveowning sadists could not resist the temptations that the possession of human beings put before them. Such types could speak of "amusing" themselves with "the old strap." Growing up in Hannibal, Missouri, Sam Clemens, the future Mark Twain, once saw an angry overseer brain a clumsy slave for some minor ineptitude. "He was dead in an hour," Clemens later recalled. "Nobody in the village approved of that murder, but of course no one said much about it. . . . Considerable sympathy was felt for the slave's owner, who had been bereft of valuable property by a worthless person who was not able to pay for it."

More typical were the countless petty cruelties that the system allowed. "I feel badly, got very angry, and whipped Lavinia," one Louisiana woman wrote in her diary. "O! for government over my temper." But for slavery, she would surely have had better self-control. Similar though more subtle was the interaction of the institution with the American tendency to brag and bluster. "You can manage ordinary niggers by lickin' 'em and by givin' 'em a taste of hot iron once in a while when they're extra ugly," one uncouth Georgian was heard to say at a slave auction shortly before the Civil War. "But if a nigger ever sets himself up against me, I can't never have any patience with him. I just get my pistol and shoot him right down; and that's the best way." With the price of slaves as high as it was, this was probably just talk, but bad talk, harmful to speaker and listener alike. Northern braggarts, perforce, were less objectionable.

Still, braggarts are inconsequential in most social situations; historians need seldom pay them much heed. However, the finest white southerners were often warped by the institution. Even those who abhorred slavery sometimes let it corrupt their thinking: "I consider the labor of a breeding woman as no object, and that a child raised every 2 years is of more profit than the crop of the best laboring man." This cold calculation came from the pen of the author of the Declaration of Independence.

Manufacturing in the South

Although the temper of southern society discouraged business and commercial activity, considerable manufacturing developed. Small flour and lumber mills flourished. Iron and coal were mined in Virginia, Kentucky, and Tennessee. In the 1850s the Tredegar Iron Works in Richmond did an annual business of about $1 million.

The availability of the raw material and the abundance of waterpower along the Appalachian slopes made it possible to manufacture textiles profitably in the South. By 1825 a thriving factory was functioning at Fayetteville, North Carolina, and soon others sprang up elsewhere in North Carolina and in adjoining states. William Gregg's factory at Graniteville, South Carolina, established in 1846, was a constant money-maker. An able propagandist as well as a good businessman, Gregg saw the textile business not only as a source of profit but as a device for improving the lot of the South's poor whites. He worked hard to weaken the southern prejudice against manufacturing and made his plant a model of benevolent paternalism similar to that of the early mills of Lowell. As with every other industry, however, southern textile manufacturing amounted to very little when compared with that of the North. Gregg employed only about 300 textile workers in 1850, the whole state of South Carolina fewer than 900. Lowell, Massachusetts, had more spindles turning in 1860 than did the entire South.

Less than 15 percent of all the good manufactured in the United States in 1860 came from the South; the region did not really develop an industrial society. Its textile manufacturers depended on the North for machinery, for skilled workers and technicians, for financing, and for insurance. When the English geologist Charles Lyell visited New Orleans in 1846, he was astounded to discover that the thriving city supported not a single book publisher. Even a local guidebook that he purchased bore a New York imprint.

The Northern Industrial Juggernaut

The most obvious change in the North in the decades before the Civil War was the rapid expansion of industry. The best estimates suggest that immediately after the War of 1812 the United States was manufacturing annually less than $200 million worth of goods. In 1859 the northeastern states alone produced $1.27 billion of the national total of almost $2 billion. The rate of growth was accelerating: in 1837 Massachusetts, a typical industrial state, turned out manufactured products worth over $86 million; in 1845, about $125 million; in 1855, nearly $300 million.

Manufacturing expanded in so many directions that it is difficult to portray or to summarize its evolution. The factory system made great strides. The development of rich anthracite coalfields in Pennsylvania was particularly important in this connection. The coal could be floated cheaply on canals to convenient sites and used to produce both heat for smelting and metalworking and steam power to drive machinery. Steam permitted greater flexibility in locating factories and in organizing work within them, and since waterpower was al-

The leading American industries as listed in the 1860 census of manufacturers are ranked here by value of product. The boot and shoe industry employed the most workers—123,000. Next were cotton goods and men's clothing, each with just under 115,000 workers.

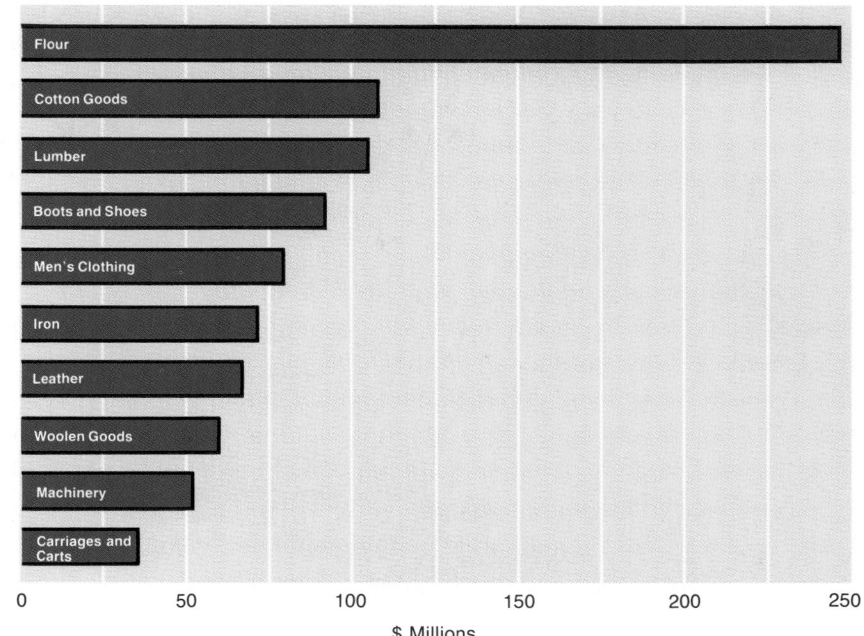

ready being used to capacity, steam was essential for the expansion of output.

American industry displayed a remarkable receptivity to technological change. In *March of the Iron Men,* Roger Burlingame provides a long list of inventions and processes developed between 1825 and 1850, including—besides such obviously important items as the sewing machine, the vulcanization of rubber, and the cylinder press—the screw-making machine, the friction match, the lead pencil, and an apparatus for making soda water. A society in flux put a premium on resourcefulness; an environment that offered so much freedom to the individual encouraged experimentation. The expanding market inspired businessmen to use new techniques. With skilled labor always in short supply, the pressure to substitute machines for trained hands was great.

In the 1820s a foreign visitor noted: "Everything new is quickly introduced here, and all the latest inventions. There is no clinging to old ways; the moment an American hears the word 'invention' he pricks up his ears." Twenty years later a Frenchman wrote: "If they continue to work with the same ardor, they will soon have nothing more to desire or to do. All the mountains will be flattened, the valleys filled, all matter rendered productive." By 1850 the United States led the world in the manufacture of goods that required the use of precision instruments, and in certain industries the country was well on the way toward modern mass production methods. American clocks, pistols, rifles, and locks were outstanding.

The American exhibits at the London Crystal Palace Exhibition of 1851 so impressed the British that they sent two special commissions to the United States to study manufacturing practices. After visiting the Springfield Arsenal, the British investigators placed a large order for gunmaking machinery and hired a number of American technicians to help organize what became the Enfield rifle factory. They were amazed by the lock and clock factories of New England and by the plants where screws, files, and similar metal objects were turned out in volume by automatic machinery. Instead of resisting new laborsaving machines, the investigators noted, "the workingmen hail with satisfaction all mechanical improvements."

Invention alone does not account for the industrial advance. Every year new natural resources

This color lithograph appeared as the frontispiece to a book published in 1854 commemorating the New York Crystal Palace Exhibition.

were discovered and made available by the westward march of settlement, and the expansion of agriculture produced an ever-larger supply of raw materials for the mills and factories. Of the ten leading industries in 1860, *eight* (flour milling, cotton textiles, lumber, shoes, men's clothing, leather, woolen goods, and liquor) relied on farm products for their raw materials.

In the 1850s the earlier prejudice against the corporation began to break down; by the end of the decade the northern and northwestern states had all passed general incorporation laws. Of course the corporate device made possible larger accumulations of capital. While the federal government did not charter business corporations, two actions of Congress illustrate the shift in public attitudes. In 1840 a group of scientists sought a federal charter for a National Institution for the Promotion of Science. They were turned down on constitutional grounds; if Congress "went on erecting corporations in this way," one legislator said, "they would come, at last, to have corporations for everything." In 1863, however, the bill creating the National Academy of Science went through both houses without debate.

Industrial growth led to a great increase in the demand for labor. The effects, however, were mixed. Skilled artisans, technicians, and toolmakers earned good wages and found it relatively easy to set themselves up first as independent craftsmen, later as small manufacturers. The expanding frontier drained off much agricultural labor that might otherwise have been attracted to industry, and the thriving new towns of the West absorbed large numbers of eastern artisans of every kind. At the same time, the pay of an unskilled worker was never enough to support a family decently, and the new machines weakened the bargaining power of artisans by making skill less important.

Many other forces acted to stimulate manufacturing. As discussed earlier (see page 295), immigration increased rapidly in the 1830s and 1840s. An avalanche of strong backs and willing hands and thousands of keen minds descended upon the country from Europe. European investors poured large sums into the booming American economy, and the savings of millions of Americans and the great hoard of new California gold added to the supply of capital. Improvements in transportation, the growth of the population, the absence of internal tariff barriers, and the relatively high per capita wealth of the people all meant an ever-expanding market for manufactured goods.

Self-generated Expansion

The *pace* of the advance is best explained by the many interactions that industrial activity produced. The cotton textile business was clearly the most important example. Samuel Slater built his first machines in his own little plant, but soon the industry spawned dozens of companies devoted to the manufacture of looms, spinning frames, and other machines. They in turn stimulated the growth of machine-tool production, metalworking companies, and eventually the mining and refining of iron. "For a considerable . . . period," George S. Gibb writes in his study *Textile Machinery Building in New England, 1813–1849,* "the manufacture of textile machinery appears to have been America's greatest heavy goods industry. . . . From the textile mills and the textile machine shops came the men who supplied most of the tools for the American Industrial Revolution. From these mills and shops sprang directly the machine-tool and locomotive industries together with a host of less basic metal fabricating trades."

Other examples abound. The invention of the sewing machine in 1846 by Elias Howe (who got his early training in a Lowell cotton-machine factory) resulted in the creation of the ready-made clothing industry. The sewing machine also revolutionized the shoe industry, speeding the trend toward factory production and triggering the same kind of secondary growth that occurred in the textile business. The new agricultural machinery business, besides stimulating other industries, made possible a huge expansion of farm production, which stimulated economic growth still more.

A Nation of Immigrants

Rapid industrialization influenced American life in countless ways, none more significant than its effect on the character of the work force and consequently on the structure of society. The jobs created by industrial expansion attracted European immigrants by the tens of thousands. It is a truism that America is a nation of immigrants—even the ancestors of the Indians came to the New World from Asia. But only with the development of nationalism, that is, with the establishment of the independent United States, did the word *immigrant,* meaning a foreign-born resident, come into existence.

The "native" population (*native* in this case meaning those whose ancestors had come from Europe rather than the only true native Americans, the Indians) tended to look down on immigrants, and many of the immigrants, in turn, developed prejudices of their own. The Irish, for example, disliked the blacks, with whom they often competed for work. One Irish leader in the old country, Daniel O'Connell, admitted that the American Irish were "among the worst enemies of the colored race." And of course blacks responded with equal bitterness. "Every hour sees us elbowed out of some employment to make room for some newly-arrived emigrant from the Emerald Isle, whose hunger and color entitle him to special favor," one of them complained. Antiblack prejudice was less noticeable among other immigrant groups but by no means absent; most immigrants adopted the views of the local majority, which was in every area unfriendly to blacks.

Social and racial rivalries aside, unskilled immigrants caused serious disruptions of economic patterns wherever they appeared. Their absorption into the factories of New England speeded the disintegration of the system of hiring young farm women. Already competition and technical ad-

BOOM AND BUST IN THE EARLY REPUBLIC, 1790–1860

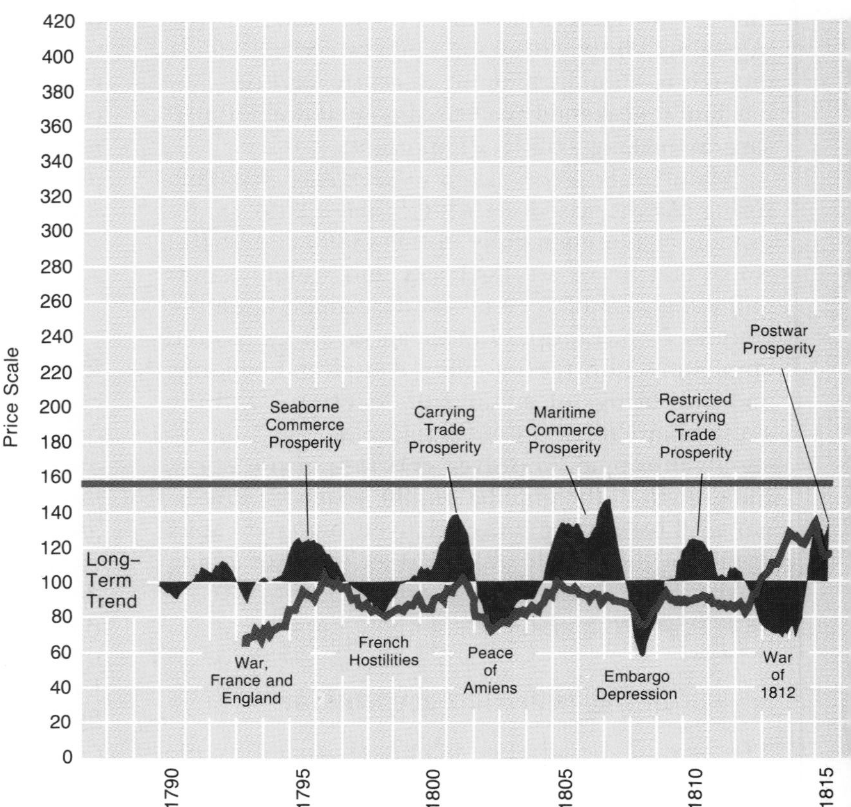

The price scale on the left axis applies to the blue line and shows changes in wholesale commodity prices as they rise above and fall below the base line of 100. During most of this era, wholesale prices were depressed. The base line of 100 is also the long-term trend line for the United States economy as a whole. The peaks and valleys above and below the long-term trend line give a general sense of boom and bust periods. The right axis and green line show, for comparison, the price of a year's tuition at Harvard College. In 1790 it was $24, but by 1860 it had risen to $104.

vances in the textile industry were increasing the pace of the machines and reducing the number of skilled workers needed to run them. Fewer young farm women were willing to work under these conditions. Recent immigrants, who required less coddling and who seemed to provide the mills with a "permanent" working force, replaced the women in large numbers. By 1860 Irish immigrants alone made up more than 50 percent of the labor force in the New England mills.

The influx of immigrants does not entirely explain the low standard of living of industrial workers during this period. Low wages and the crowding that resulted from the swift expansion of city populations produced slums that would make the most noisome modern ghetto seem a paradise. A Boston investigation in the late 1840s described one district as "a perfect hive of human beings . . . huddled together like brutes." In New York tens of thousands of the poor lived in dark, rank cellars, those in the waterfront districts often invaded by high tides. Tenement houses like great gloomy prisons rose back to back, each with many windowless rooms and often without heat or running water.

Out of doors, city life for the poor was almost equally squalid. Slum streets were littered with garbage and trash. Recreational facilities were almost nonexistent; work on Central Park in New York City, the first important urban park in the country, was not begun until the mid-1850s. Police and fire protection in the cities were pitifully inadequate. "Urban problems" were less critical than a century later only because they affected a smaller part of the population; for those who experienced them they were, all too often, crushing. In the mid-1850s

In 1855 the immigration facility at Castle Garden was completed; the millions who arrived at the port of New York in the next four decades first set foot in America here, in the round building on the left.

Annual Tuition at Harvard College, $

125
100
75
50
25
0

Harvard Tuition

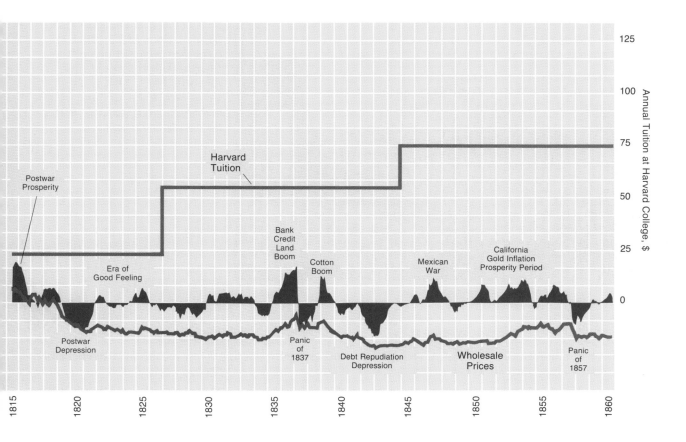

Postwar Prosperity

Era of Good Feeling

Bank Credit Land Boom

Cotton Boom

Mexican War

California Gold Inflation Prosperity Period

Postwar Depression

Panic of 1837

Debt Repudiation Depression

Wholesale Prices

Panic of 1857

1815 1820 1825 1830 1835 1840 1845 1850 1855 1860

New York's notorious Five Points District, about 1827. "Reeking everywhere with dirt and filth," Charles Dickens wrote of Five Points in 1842. "Where dogs would howl to lie, men and women and boys slink off to sleep, forcing the dislodged rats to move."

large numbers of children in New York scrounged a bare existence by begging and scavenging. They took shelter at night in coal bins and empty barrels.

In the early factory towns most working families maintained small vegetable gardens and a few chickens; low wage rates did not necessarily reflect a low standard of living. In the new industrial slums even a blade of grass was unusual. In 1851 the editor Horace Greeley's New York *Tribune* published a minimum weekly budget for a family of five. The budget, which allowed nothing for savings, medical bills, recreation, or other amenities (Greeley did include 12 cents a week for newspapers), came to $10.37. Since the weekly pay of a factory hand seldom reached $5, the wives and children of most male factory workers also had to labor in the factories merely to survive. And child labor in the 1850s differed fundamentally from child labor in the 1820s. The pace of the machines had become much faster by then, the working environment more depressing.

Relatively few workers belonged to unions. Local federations of craft unions sprang up in the major cities, and during the boom that preceded the Panic of 1837, a National Trades' Union representing a few northeastern cities managed to hold conventions. Early in the Jackson era, "workingmen's" political parties enjoyed a brief popularity, occasionally electing a few local officials. These organizations were made up mostly of skilled craftsmen, professional reformers, and even businessmen. They soon expired, destroyed by internal bickering over questions that had little or nothing to do with working conditions.

The depression of the late 1830s led to the demise of most trade unions. Nevertheless, *skilled* workers improved their lot somewhat in the 1840s and 1850s. The working day declined gradually from about 12.5 hours to 10 or 11 hours. Many states passed 10-hour laws and laws regulating child labor, but they were poorly enforced. Most states, however, enacted effective mechanic's lien laws, giving workers first call on the assets of bankrupt and defaulting employers, and the Massachusetts court's decision in the case of *Commonwealth* v. *Hunt* (1842), establishing the legality of labor unions, became a judicial landmark when other state courts followed the precedent.

The flush times of the early 1850s caused the union movement to revive. Many strikes occurred and a few new national organizations appeared. Most unions were local institutions, weak and with little control over their membership. The Panic of 1857 dealt the labor movement another body blow. Thus there was no trend toward the general unionization of labor between 1820 and the Civil War.

For this the workers themselves were partly responsible: craftsmen took little interest in unskilled workers except to keep them down. Few common laborers considered themselves part of a permanent working class with different objectives from those of their employers. The traditional individualism of Americans, the fluidity of society, the constant influx of job-hungry immigrants, and the widespread employment of women and children in unskilled jobs made labor organization difficult, for the assumption was that nearly anyone who was willing to work could eventually escape from the wage-earning class. "If any continue through life in the condition of the hired laborer," Abraham Lincoln declared in 1859, "it is . . . because of either a dependent nature which prefers it, or improvidence, folly, or singular misfortune."

Any investigation of American society before the Civil War reveals a paradox that is obvious but difficult to resolve. The United States was a land of opportunity, a democratic society with a prosperous, expanding economy and few class distinctions. Its people had a high standard of living in comparison with the citizens of European countries. Yet within this rich, confident nation there existed a class of miserably underpaid and depressed unskilled workers, mostly immigrants, who were worse off materially than nearly any southern slave. The literature is full of descriptions of needleworkers earning 12 cents a day, of women driven to prostitution because they could not earn a living decently, of hunger marches and soup kitchens, of disease and crime and people sunk into apathy by hopeless poverty. In 1848 more than 56,000 New Yorkers, about a quarter of the population, were receiving some form of public relief. A police drive in that city in 1860 brought in nearly 500 beggars.

The middle-class majority seemed indifferent to or at best unaware of these conditions. Reformers conducted investigations, published exposés, and labored to help the victims of urbanization and industrialization. They achieved little. Great fires burned in these decades to release the incredible energies of America. The poor were the ashes, sifting down silent and unnoticed beneath the dazzle and the smoke. While the industrial revolution was making the United States the richest nation in the world, it was also creating, as the historian Robert H. Bremner has said, "a poverty problem, novel in kind and alarming in size." Industrialization produced poverty (in Marxian terminology, a proletarian class) and a capitalistic aristocracy. Tenements sprang up cheek by jowl with the urban palaces of the new rich and the tree-lined streets of the prosperous middle class.

Economic opportunities were great, and taxation was minimal. Little wonder that as the generations passed, the rich got richer. Industrialization accelerated the process and, by stimulating the immigration of masses of poor workers, skewed the social balance still further. Society became more stratified, differences in wealth and status among citizens greater. But the ideology of egalitarian democracy held its own. By the mid-19th century Americans were convinced that all men were equal, and indeed all *white* men had equal political rights. Socially and economically, however, the distances between top and bottom were widening. This situation endured for the rest of the century, and in some respects it still endures.

Foreign Commerce

Changes in the pattern of foreign commerce were less noticeable than those in manufacturing but were nevertheless significant. After increasing erratically during the 1820s and 1830s, both imports and exports leaped forward in the next 20 years. The nation remained primarily an exporter of raw materials and an importer of manufactured goods, and in most years it imported more than it exported. Cotton continued to be the most valuable export, in 1860 accounting for a record $191 million of total exports of $333 million. Despite America's own thriving industry, textiles still held the lead among imports, with iron products second. As in earlier days, Great Britain was both the best customer of the United States and its leading supplier.

The success of sailing packets, those "square-riggers on schedule," greatly facilitated the movement of passengers and freight. Fifty-two packets were operating between New York and Europe by 1845, and many more plied between New York and other American ports. The packets accelerated the tendency for trade to concentrate in New York and to a lesser extent in Boston, Philadelphia, Baltimore, and New Orleans. The commerce of smaller towns like Providence and New Haven, which had flourished in earlier days, now languished.

New Bedford and a few other southern New England towns shrewdly saved their prosperity by concentrating on whaling, which boomed between 1830 and 1860. The supply of whales seemed unlimited—as indeed it was, given the primitive hunting techniques of the age of sail. By the mid-1850s, with sperm oil selling at over $1.75 a gallon and the country exporting an average of $2.7 million worth of whale oil and whalebone a year, New Bedford boasted a whaling fleet of well over 300 vessels and a population approaching 25,000. The whalers ranged the oceans of the world; they lived a hard, lonely life punctuated by moments of exhilaration when they sighted the great mammoths of the deep and drove the harpoon home. They also made magnificent profits: to clear 100 percent in a single voyage was merely routine.

The increase in the volume and value of trade and its concentration at larger ports had a marked effect on the construction of ships. By the 1850s the average vessel was three times the size of those built 30 years earlier. Startling improvements in design, culminating in the long, sleek, white-winged clipper ships, made possible speeds previously undreamed of. Appearing just in time to supply the need for fast transportation to the California gold fields, the clippers cut sailing time around the Horn to San Francisco from five or six months to three, the record of 89 days being held jointly by *Andrew Jackson* and Donald McKay's famous *Flying Cloud.* Another McKay-designed clipper, *Champion of the Seas,* once logged 465 nautical miles in 24 hours, far in excess of the best efforts of any modern yacht. To achieve such speeds, cargo capacity had to be sacrificed, making clippers uneconomical for carrying the bulky produce that was the mainstay of commerce. But for specialty goods, in their brief heyday the clippers were unsurpassed. Hong Kong merchants, never known for extravagance, willingly paid 75 cents a cubic foot to ship teas by clipper to London even though slower vessels charged only 28 cents. In the early 1850s clippers sold for as much as $150,000; with decent luck a ship might earn its full cost in a voyage or two.

Steam Conquers the Atlantic

The reign of the clipper ship was short. Like so many other things, ocean commerce was being mechanized. Steamships conquered the high seas more slowly than the rivers because early models were unsafe in rough waters and uneconomical. A river boat could take on fuel along its route, while an Atlantic steamer had to carry tons of coal across the ocean, thereby reducing its capacity for cargo. However, by the late 1840s steamers were capturing most of the passenger traffic, mail contracts, and first-class freight. These vessels could not keep up with the clippers in a heavy breeze, but their average speed was far greater, especially on the westward voyage against the prevailing winds. Steamers were soon crossing the Atlantic in less than ten days. Nevertheless, for very long voyages, such as the 15,000-mile haul around South America to California, fast sailing ships held their own for many years.

The steamship, and especially the iron ship, which had greater cargo-carrying capacity and was stronger and less costly to maintain, took away the advantages that American shipbuilders had held since colonial times. American lumber was cheap, but the British excelled in iron technology. Although the United States invested about $14.5 million in subsidies for the shipping industry, the funds were not employed intelligently and did little good. In 1858 all government effort to aid shipping was abandoned.

The combination of competition, government subsidy, and technological advance drove shipping rates down drastically. Between the mid-1820s and the mid-1850s the cost of moving a pound of cotton from New York to Liverpool fell from 1 cent to about a third of a cent. Transatlantic passengers could obtain the best accommodations on the fastest ships for under $200, good accommodations on slower packets for as little as $75.

Rates were especially low for European emigrants willing to travel to America on cargo vesels. By the 1840s at least 4,000 ships were engaged in carrying bulky American cotton and Canadian lumber to Europe. On their return trips with manufactured goods they had much unoccupied space, which they converted into rough quarters for passengers. Conditions on these ships were crowded,

By 1837, when this aquantint of New York as seen from Brooklyn Heights was made, the sailing clipper was being phased out in favor of the steamer.

gloomy, and foul. Frequently epidemics took a fearful toll among steerage passengers. On one crossing of the ship *Lark,* 158 of 440 passengers died of typhus. Some ships carried diseased passengers so habitually that American immigration officers turned them back even before they reached port.

Yet without this cheap means of transportation, thousands of poor immigrants would simply have remained at home. Bargain freight rates also help explain the clamor of American manufacturers for high tariffs, for transportation costs added relatively little to the price of European goods.

Railroads and Canals

Another dramatic change in the United States in the pre–Civil War years was the shift in the direction of the nation's internal commerce and its immense increase. From the time of the first settlers in the Mississippi Valley, the Great River had controlled the flow of goods from farm to market. The completion of the Erie Canal in 1825 heralded a shift, speeded by the feverish canal construction of the following decade.* However, even in the late 1830s the bulk of the trade of the valley still flowed down to New Orleans.

Each year saw more western produce moving to market through the canals. In 1845 the Erie was still drawing over two-thirds of its west-east traffic from within New York, but by 1847, despite the fact that this local business held steady, more than half of its traffic came from west of Buffalo, and by 1851 more than two-thirds. The volume of western commerce over the Erie in 1851 amounted to more than twenty times what it had been in 1836, while the value of western goods reaching New Orleans in this period increased only two and a half times.

The expanding traffic and New York's enormous share of it caused businessmen in other eastern cities whose canal projects had been unsuccessful to respond promptly when a new means of transport, the railroad, became available. The first railroads were built in England in the 1820s. In 1830 the first American line, the ambitiously named Baltimore and Ohio Railroad, carried in its first year 80,000 passengers over a 13-mile stretch of track. By 1833 Charleston, South Carolina, had a line reaching 136 miles to Hamburg, on the Savannah River. Two years later the first cars rolled over the Boston and Worcester Railroad. The Panic of 1837 slowed construction, but by 1840 the United States had 3,328 miles of track, equal to the canal mileage and nearly double the railroad mileage of all Europe.

The first railroads did not compete with the canals for intersectional traffic. The through connections needed to move goods economically over great distances materialized slowly. Of the 6,000 miles of track operating in 1848, nearly all lay east

* In 1830 there were 1,277 miles of canal in the United States; by 1840 there were 3,326 miles.

This scene from 1834 showing the Camden and Amboy Railroad in New Jersey was re-created in 1905 by E. L. Henry. Note the resemblance of the railroad cars to the stagecoaches of the period. The locomotive was called "Planet"; early engines were given names.

of the Appalachians, and little of it had been coordinated into railroad *systems.* The intention of most early builders had been to monopolize the trade of surrounding districts, not to establish connections with competing centers. Frequently railroads used tracks of different widths deliberately to prevent other lines from tying into their tracks.

Engineering problems held back growth. Steep grades and sharp curves—unavoidable in many parts of the country if the cost of the roads was not to be prohibitive—required more powerful and flexible engines than yet existed. Sparks from wood-burning locomotives caused fires. Wooden rails topped with strap iron wore out quickly and broke loose under the weight and vibration of heavy cars. In time, hard work and ingenuity solved these difficulties. The iron T rail and the use of crossties set in loose gravel to reduce vibration increased the durability of the tracks and made possible heavier, more efficient equipment. Modifications in the design of locomotives enabled the trains to negotiate sharp curves. Engines that could burn hard coal appeared, thereby eliminating the danger of starting fires along the right of way and reducing fuel costs.

Between 1848 and 1852 railroad mileage nearly doubled. Three years later it had doubled again and by 1860 the nation had 30,636 miles of track. During this extraordinary burst of activity, four companies drove lines of gleaming iron from the Atlantic seaboard to the great interior valley. In 1851 the Erie, longest road in the world with 537 miles of track, linked the Hudson River north of New York City with Dunkirk on Lake Erie. Late the next year the Baltimore and Ohio reached the Ohio River at Wheeling, and in 1853 a banker named Erastus Corning consolidated eight short lines connecting Albany and Buffalo to form the New York Central. Finally, in 1858 the Pennsylvania Railroad completed a line across the mountains from Philadelphia to Pittsburgh.

In the states beyond the Appalachians building went on at an even more feverish pace. In the 1850s Ohio laid more than 2,300 miles of track, Illinois more than 2,600, Wisconsin nearly 900. In the South, where construction was slower, Mississippi laid about 800 miles, Alabama over 600. By 1855 passengers could travel from Chicago or St. Louis to the East Coast entirely by railroad at a cost ranging from about $20 to $30, the trip taking, with

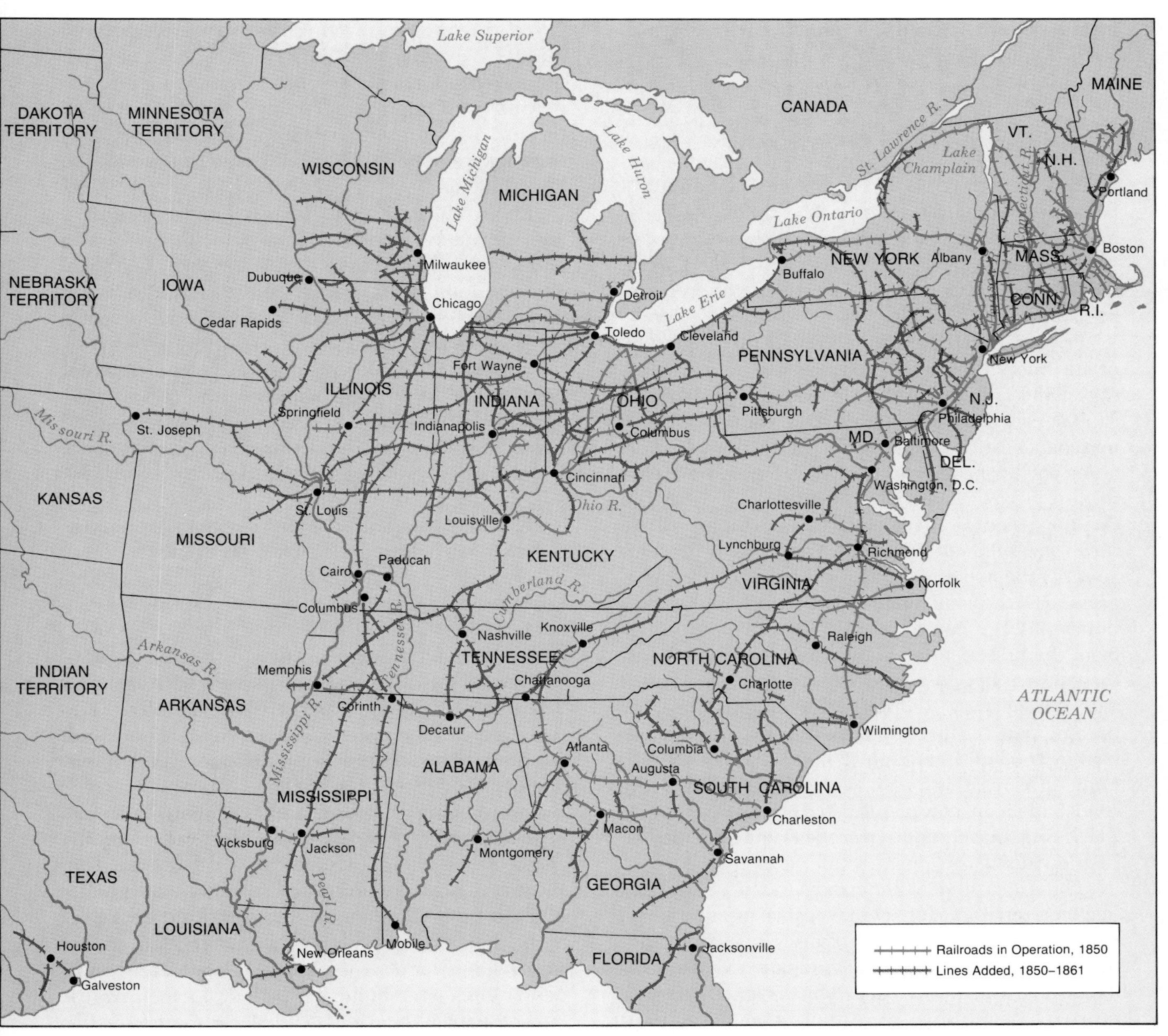

RAILROADS, 1850–1861

The great decade of railroad building is shown here in detail. Certain towns and cities owed most of their spectacularly rapid growth to the railroad, Chicago being the outstanding example. The map also suggests the strong influence of the railroads on the expansion and economic prosperity of smaller cities such as Fort Wayne, Milwaukee, and Nashville. At the outbreak of the Civil War in 1861, the relative lack of railroads in the South was a bad omen for the Confederacy.

luck, less than 48 hours. A generation earlier such a trip required two to three weeks.

Financing the Railroads

Railroad building required immense amounts of labor and capital at a time when many other demands for these resources existed. Immigrants or (in the South) slaves did most of the heavy work. Raising the necessary money proved a more complex task.

Private investors supplied about three-quarters of the money invested in railroads before 1860, over $800 million in the 1850s alone. Much of this capital, especially in the early days, came from local merchants and businessmen and from farmers along the proposed rights of way. Funds were easy to raise because subscribers seldom had to lay out the full price of their stock at one time; instead they were subject to periodic "calls" for a percentage of their commitment as construction progressed. If the road made money, much of the additional mileage could be paid for out of earnings from the first sections built, which was what investors always hoped would be the case. The Utica and Schenectady Railroad, one of the lines that became part of the New York Central, was capitalized in 1833 at $2 million (20,000 shares at $100). Only $75 per share was ever called; in 1844 the road had been completed, shares were selling at $129, and shareholders were receiving handsome cash dividends.

The Utica and Schenectady was a short road in a rich territory; for less favorably situated lines, stocks were hard to sell because their value depended on the ability of the company to earn profits. Bonds, which were backed by the land and other property of the line, were more commonly used to raise money. In the West the population was thin, the distances were great, and property values were relatively low. Outside capital had to be found. Much of it came from New England, where investors like the China merchant John Murray Forbes were increasingly active in railroad finance. They dealt mainly in bonds, using stock chiefly to maintain control of the companies whose bonds they held. Most foreign investors preferred bonds over stocks; by 1853 Europeans owned about a quarter of all American railroad bonds.

Of the lines connecting the seaboard with the Middle West, the New York Central alone needed no public aid, chiefly because it ran through prosperous, well-populated country and across level terrain. The others were all "mixed enterprises," drawing about half their capital from state and local governments.

Public aid took many forms. Towns, counties, and the states themselves lent money to railroads and invested in their stock. Special privileges, such as exemption from taxation and the right to condemn property, were often granted, and in a few cases states built and operated roads as public corporations. In all, the proportionate contribution of state and local governments to the cost of railroad building—between 25 and 30 percent—was much less than their contribution to canals, and it declined steadily as the rail network expanded and matured.

As with earlier internal improvement proposals, federal financial aid to railroads was usually blocked in Congress by a combination of eastern and southern votes. But in 1850 a scheme for granting federal lands to the states to build a line from Lake Michigan to the Gulf of Mexico won considerable southern and eastern support and passed both houses. The main beneficiary was the Illinois Central Railroad, which received a 200-foot right of way and alternate strips of land along the track 1 mile wide and 6 miles deep, a total of almost 2.6 million acres. By mortgaging this land and by selling portions of it to farmers, the Illinois Central raised nearly all the $23.4 million it spent on construction. The success of this operation led to additional grants of almost 20 million acres in the 1850s, benefiting more than 40 railroads. Far larger federal grants were made after the Civil War, when the transcontinental lines were built.

Frequently the capitalists who promoted railroads were more concerned with making money out of the *construction* of the lines than with operating them. The banker Erastus Corning was a good railroad man; his lines were well maintained and efficiently run. Yet he was also mayor of Albany, an important figure in state and national politics, and a manufacturer of iron. He accepted no salary as president of the Utica and Schenectady, "asking only that he have the privilege of supplying all the rails, running gear, tools and other iron and steel articles used." When he could not himself produce rails of the proper quality, he purchased them in England, charging the railroad a commission for his services. Corning's actions led to stockholder complaints, and a committee was appointed to investigate. He managed to control this group easily enough, but it did report that "the practice of buying articles for the use of the Railroad Company from its own officers might in time come to lead to abuses of great magnitude." The prediction proved all too accurate in the generation following the Civil War.

Corning, it must be emphasized, was honest enough; his mistake, if mistake it was, lay in overestimating his own impartiality a little. Others in the business were unashamedly crooked and avidly took advantage of the public passion for railroads. Some officials issued stock to themselves without paying for it and then sold the shares to gullible investors for hard cash. Others manipulated the books of their corporations, used inside information to make killings in the stock market, and set up special construction companies and paid them exorbitant returns out of railroad assets. These practices did not become widespread until after the Civil War, but all of them first sprang up in the period now under discussion. At the same time that the country was first developing a truly national economy it was also producing its first really big-time crooks.

Railroads and the Economy

The effects of so much railroad construction were profound. While the main reason that farmers put more land under the plow was an increase in the price of agricultural products, the railroad helped determine just what land was utilized and how profitably it could be farmed. Much of the fertile prairie through which the Illinois Central ran had been available for settlement for many years before 1850, but development had been slow because it was remote from navigable waters and had no timber. In 1840 the three counties immediately northeast of Springfield had a population of about 8,500. They produced about 59,000 bushels of wheat and 690,000 bushels of corn. In the next decade the region grew slowly by the standards of that day: the three counties had about 14,000 people in 1850 and produced 71,000 bushels of wheat and 2.2 million bushels of corn. Then came the railroad and with it an agricultural revolution. By 1860 the population of the three counties had soared to over 38,000, wheat production had topped 550,000 bushels, and corn 5.7 million bushels. "Land-grant" railroads such as the Illinois Central stimulated agricultural expansion by advertising their lands widely and selling farm sites at low rates on liberal terms.

Access to world markets gave the farmers of the upper Mississippi Valley an incentive to increase output. Land was plentiful and cheap, but farm labor was scarce; consequently agricultural wages rose sharply, especially after 1850. New tools and machines appeared in time to ease the labor shortage. First came the steel plowshare, invented by John Deere, a Vermont-born blacksmith who had moved to Illinois in 1837. The prairie sod was tough and sticky, but Deere's smooth metal plows cut through it easily. In 1839 Deere turned out ten such plows in his little shop in Moline, Illinois. By 1857 he was selling 10,000 a year. Still more important was the perfection of the mechanical reaper, for wheat production was limited more by the amount that farmers could handle during the brief harvest season than by the acreage they could plant and cultivate. Although many inventors made significant contributions and no single company monopolized production, the major figure in the development of the reaper was Cyrus Hall McCormick. McCormick's horse-drawn reaper bent the grain against the cutting knife and then deposited it neatly on a platform, whence it could easily be raked into windrows. With this machine, two workers could cut 14 times as much wheat as with scythes.

McCormick prospered, but despite his patents he could not keep other manufacturers out of the business. Competition led to continual improvement of the machines and kept prices within the reach of most farmers. Installment selling added to demand. By 1860 nearly 80,000 reapers had been sold; their efficiency helps explain why wheat output rose by nearly 75 percent in the 1850s.

The railroad had an equally powerful impact on American cities. The seaports that formed the eastern terminuses of the network benefited, and so did countless intermediate centers, such as Buffalo and Cincinnati.

No city depended more on railroads than Chi-

A pre–Civil War lithograph of Chicago's Michigan Avenue viewed from the lakefront attests to Chicago's importance as the railroad center for the Midwest.

cago. In 1850 not a single line had reached there; five years later it was terminal for 2,200 miles of track and controlled the commerce of an imperial domain. By extending half a dozen lines west to the Mississippi, it drained off nearly all the river traffic north of St. Louis. The Illinois Central sucked the expanding output of the prairies into Chicago as well. Most of this freight went eastward over the new railroads or on the Great Lakes and the Erie Canal. Nearly 350,000 tons of shipping plied the lakes by 1855.

The railroads, like the textile industry, stimulated other kinds of economic activity. They transformed agriculture, as we have seen; both real estate values and buying and selling of land increased whenever the iron horse puffed into a new district. The railroads spurred regional concentration of industry and an increase in the size of business units. Their insatiable need for capital stimulated the growth of investment banking. The complexity of their operations made them, as the historian Alfred D. Chandler, Jr., writes, "the first modern business enterprises," the first to employ large numbers of salaried managers and to develop "a large internal organizational structure with carefully defined lines of responsibility."

Although they apparently did not have a very great effect on general manufacturing before the Civil War, the roads consumed large amounts of iron, thereby helping the mining and smelting industries. New foundries sprang up to turn out locomotives. In 1860 railroads purchased nearly half the nation's output of bar and sheet iron. Railroad demands also led to technological advances that were of great importance in the iron industry. Probably more labor and more capital were occupied in economic activities resulting from the development of railroads than in the roads themselves—another way of saying that the railroads were immensely valuable internal improvements.

The proliferation of trunk lines and the competition of the canal system (for many products the slowness of canal transportation was not a serious handicap) led to a sharp decline in freight and passenger rates. Periodically, railroads engaged in "wars" to capture business. At times a person could travel from New York to Buffalo for as little as $4; anthracite was being shipped from the Pennsylvania mines to the coast for $1.50 a ton. The Erie Canal reduced its toll charges by more than two-thirds in the face of railroad competition, and the roads in turn cut rates drastically until, on the eve of the Civil War, it cost less than 1 cent per ton-mile to send produce through the canal and only slightly more than 2 cents a mile on the railroads. By that time one could ship a bushel of wheat from Chicago to New York by railroad for less than 35 cents.

Cheap transportation had a revolutionary effect on western agriculture. Farmers in Iowa could now raise grain to feed the factory workers of Lowell and even of Manchester, England. Two-thirds of the meat consumed in New York City was soon arriving by rail from beyond the Appalachians. The center of American wheat production shifted westward to Illinois, Wisconsin, and Indiana. When the

Crimean War (1853–1856) and European crop failures increased foreign demand, these regions boomed. Success bred success for farmers and for the railroads. Profits earned carrying wheat enabled the roads to build feeder lines that opened up still wider areas to commercial agriculture and made it easy to bring in lumber, farm machinery, household furnishings, and the settlers themselves at very low cost.

Railroads and the Sectional Conflict

Increased production and cheap transportation boosted the western farmer's income and standard of living. The days of isolation and self-sufficiency, even for the family on the edge of the frontier, rapidly disappeared. Frontiersmen became businessmen and, to a far greater extent than their forbears, consumers, buying all sorts of manufactured articles that their ancestors had made for themselves or done without. This had its cost. Like southern planters, they now became dependent on middlemen and lost some of their feeling of self-reliance. Overproduction became a problem. It began to take more capital to buy a farm, for as profits increased, so did the price of land. Machinery was an additional expense. The proportion of farm laborers and tenants increased.

The linking of East and West had fateful effects on politics. The increased ease of movement from section to section and the ever more complex social and economic integration of East and West stimulated nationalism and thus became a force for the preservation of the Union. Without the railroads and canals, Illinois and Iowa would scarcely have dared to side against the South in 1861. When the Mississippi ceased to be essential to them, citizens of the upper valley could afford to be more hostile to slavery and especially to its westward extension. Economic ties with the Northeast reinforced cultural connections.

The South might have preserved its influence in the Northwest if it had pressed forward its own railroad-building program. It failed to do so. There were many southern lines but nothing like a southern *system.* As late as 1856 one could get from Memphis to Richmond or Charleston only by very indirect routes. As late as 1859 the land-grant road extending the Illinois Central to Mobile, Alabama, was not complete, nor did any economical connection exist between Chicago and New Orleans. This state of affairs could be accounted for in part by

Commerce on the lower Mississippi depended heavily on steamboats, because railroads were far less extensive in the South than in the North.

the scattered population of the South, the paucity of passenger traffic, the seasonal nature of much of the freight business, and the absence of large cities. Southerners placed too much reliance on the Mississippi: the fact that traffic on the river continued heavy throughout the 1850s blinded them to the precipitous rate at which their *relative* share of the nation's trade was declining. But the fundamental cause of the South's backwardness in railroad construction was the attitude of its leaders. Southerners of means were no more interested in commerce than in industry; their capital found other outlets.

The Economy on the Eve of Civil War

Between the mid-1840s and the mid-1850s the United States experienced one of the most remarkable periods of growth in the history of the world. Manufacturing output increased an astounding 69 percent in ten years. Every economic indicator surged forward: grain and cotton production, population, gold production, sales of public land. The building of the railroads stimulated business, and by making transportation cheaper the completed lines energized the nation's economy. The "American System" that Henry Clay had dreamed of arrived with a rush just as Clay was passing from the scene.

Inevitably this growth caused dislocations, these aggravated by the boom psychology that once again infected the popular mind. In 1857 there was a serious collapse. The return of Russian wheat to the world market after the Crimean War caused grain prices to fall. This checked agricultural expansion, which hurt the railroads and cut down on the demand for manufactures.

People called this abrupt downturn the Panic of 1857 and worried about a depression. Yet the vigor of the economy was such that the bad times did not last long. The upper Mississippi Valley suffered most, for so much new land had been opened up that supplies of farm produce greatly exceeded demand, and the world situation remained unhelpful. Elsewhere conditions improved rapidly. Gold-mad California had escaped the depression entirely.

The South, somewhat out of the hectic rush to begin with, was affected very little by the collapse of 1857, for cotton prices continued high. This gave planters the false impression that their economy was immune to such violent downturns. Some began to argue that the South would be better off out of the Union.

Before a new national upward swing could become well established, however, the sectional crisis between North and South shook people's confidence in the future. Then the war came, and with it a new set of forces shaped economic development.

SUPPLEMENTARY READING

Titles marked with an asterisk have been published in paperback.

Most of the volumes dealing with economic developments mentioned in Chapter 8 continue to be useful for this period. See especially G. R. Taylor, **The Transportation Revolution*** (1951), P. W. Gates, **The Farmer's Age*** (1960), D. C. North, **The Economic Growth of the United States*** (1961), and Stuart Bruchey, **The Roots of American Economic Growth*** (1965). Allan Nevins has interesting chapters on economic developments in **The Ordeal of the Union** (1947).

An excellent survey of the antebellum South is Clement Eaton, **The Growth of Southern Civilization*** (1961). For more detailed coverage, see C. S. Sydnor, **The Development of Southern Sectionalism*** (1948), Gavin Wright, **The Political Economy of the Cotton South** (1978), and A. O. Craven, **The Growth of Southern Nationalism** (1953).

The literature on slavery is extensive and of high quality. See especially K. M. Stampp, **The Peculiar Institution*** (1956), S. M. Elkins, **Slavery*** (1959), E. D. Genovese, **Roll, Jordan, Roll*** (1975), J. W. Blassingame, **The Slave Community*** (1972), L. W. Levine, **Black Culture and Black Consciousness** (1977), N. I. Huggins, **Black Odyssey** (1977), H. G. Gutman, **Black Family in Slavery and Freedom** (1976), and Catharine Clinton, **Plantation Mistress** (1984). Among specialized volumes, Bertram Wyatt-Brown, **Southern Honor** (1982), and Ira

Berlin, **Slaves Without Masters** (1975), on free blacks, are important. On slave insurrections, E. D. Genovese, **From Rebellion to Revolution: Afro-American Slave Revolts** (1979), and S. B. Oates, **The Fires of Jubilee: Nat Turner's Fierce Rebellion** (1975), are excellent, and William Styron's novel, **The Confessions of Nat Turner*** (1967), is a fine example of how historical research can be put to effective use by a writer of fiction. R. C. Wade, **Slavery in the Cities*** (1964), contains much interesting material, as does W. K. Scarborough, **The Overseer: Plantation Management in the Old South** (1966). On southern manufacturing, see Broadus Mitchell, **William Gregg: Factory Master of the Old South** (1941).

On industrial developments, in addition to the books mentioned in Chapter 8, see A. C. Cole, **The Irrepressible Conflict*** (1934), H. J. Habbakuk, **American and British Technology in the Nineteenth Century*** (1962), and G. S. Gibb, **The Saco-Lowell Shops: Textile Machinery Building in New England** (1950). On labor history, F. R. Dulles, **Labor in America*** (1960), is a good introduction. N. J. Ware, **The Industrial Worker, 1840–1860*** (1924), and W. A. Sullivan, **The Industrial Worker in Pennsylvania** (1955), are more specialized. See also Thomas Dublin, **Women at Work** (1977), R. A. Mohl, **Poverty in New York** (1971), and B. M. Wertheimer, **We Were There** (1977). For workingmen's political activities, see Edward Pessen, **Most Uncommon Jacksonians: The Radical Leaders of the Early Labor Movement*** (1967).

Immigration is dealt with in M. A. Jones, **American Immigration*** (1960), and M. L. Hansen, **The Immigrant in American History*** (1940). More specialized works include Hansen's **The Atlantic Migration*** (1940), Oscar Handlin, **Boston's Immigrants*** (1941), and Robert Ernst, **Immigrant Life in New York City** (1949). Poverty in America is examined by R. H. Bremner, **From the Depths*** (1956), and in Mohl's **Poverty in New York.**

Taylor's **Transportation Revolution** is outstanding on developments in commerce and communication. On the age of sail, see S. E. Morison, **The Maritime History of Massachusetts*** (1921), C. C. Cutler, **Greyhounds of the Sea** (1960), and Robert Carse, **The Moonrakers** (1961). J. F. Stover, **Iron Road to the West** (1978), is a good survey of railroad building in the 1850s. Among the specialized studies of railroad development are T. C. Cochran, **Railroad Leaders** (1953), P. W. Gates, **The Illinois Central Railroad and Its Colonization Work** (1934), E. C. Kirkland, **Men, Cities, and Transportation** (1948), A. D. Chandler, Jr., **Henry Varnum Poor** (1956), R. W. Fogel, **Railroads and American Economic Growth*** (1964), and Albert Fishlow, **American Railroads and the Transformation of the Ante-Bellum Economy** (1965).

14
The Coming of the Civil War

"A house divided against itself cannot stand." I believe this government cannot endure permanently half slave and half free. I do not expect the Union to be dissolved; I do not expect the house to fall; but I do expect it will cease to be divided. It will become all one thing, or all the other. ABRAHAM LINCOLN, *June 17, 1858*

135,000 SETS, 270,000 VOLUMES SOLD.

UNCLE TOM'S CABIN

FOR SALE HERE.

AN EDITION FOR THE MILLION, COMPLETE IN 1 Vol., PRICE 37 1-2 CENTS.
" " IN GERMAN, IN 1 Vol., PRICE 50 CENTS.
" " IN 2 Vols., CLOTH, 6 PLATES, PRICE $1.50.
SUPERB ILLUSTRATED EDITION, IN 1 Vol., WITH 153 ENGRAVINGS,
PRICES FROM $2.50 TO $5.00.

The Greatest Book of the Age.

The political settlement between North and South designed by Henry Clay in 1850 lasted only four years. One specific event wrecked it, but it was probably doomed in any case. Americans continued to migrate westward by the thousands, and as long as slaveholders could carry their human property into federally controlled territories, northern resentment would smolder. Slaves continued to seek freedom in the North, and the stronger federal Fugitive Slave Act did not guarantee their capture and return. Abolitionists intensified their propaganda. With wisdom and forbearance, perhaps a real reconciliation of the sections could have been negotiated, but the historian who searches for examples of intelligent and tolerant statesmanship in the fateful 1850s seeks almost in vain.

The Slave Power Comes North

The new fugitive slave law caused a sharp increase in the efforts of southerners to recover escaped slaves. Something approaching panic reigned in the black communities of northern cities after its passage. Hundreds of former slaves fled to Canada, but many more remained. A few were arrested, generally without incident. However, not all the captives were in fact runaways, and northerners frequently refused to stand aside while these people were dragged off in chains.

Shortly after the passage of the act, a New Yorker, James Hamlet, was seized, convicted, and rushed off to slavery in Maryland without even being allowed to communicate with his wife and children. The New York black community was outraged, and with help from white neighbors it swiftly raised $800 to buy his freedom. In 1851 Euphemia Williams, who had lived for years as a free woman in Pennsylvania, was seized, her presumed owner claiming also her six children, all Pennsylvania-born. A federal judge released Mrs. Williams, but the case created alarm in the North.

Abolitionists often interfered with the enforcement of the law, even in cases where the black was unquestionably a runaway. When two Georgians came to Boston to reclaim William and Ellen Craft, admitted fugitives, an abolitionist "Vigilance Committee"' forced them to return home empty-handed. The Crafts prudently—or perhaps in disgust—decided to leave the United States for England. Early in 1851 a Virginia agent captured Frederick "Shadrach" Wilkins, a waiter in a Boston coffee house. While Wilkins was being held for deportation, a mob of blacks broke into the courthouse and freed him. That October a slave named Jerry, who had escaped from Missouri, was arrested in Syracuse, New York. Within minutes the whole town had the news. Crowds surged through the streets, and when night fell, a mob smashed into the building where Jerry was being held and spirited him away to safety.

Such incidents exacerbated feelings. Southerners accused the North of reneging on one of the main promises made in the Compromise, while the sight of harmless human beings being hustled off to a life of slavery disturbed many northerners who were not abolitionists. Although most white northerners were probably not prepared to break it, in some states the Fugitive Slave Act became virtually unenforceable. Massachusetts passed a strong personal liberty law. When a newspaperman in Wisconsin was convicted of rousing a mob to free a captured runaway, the state supreme court declared the Fugitive Slave Act unconstitutional and released him. After long delays the United States Supreme Court overruled this decision (*Ableman* v. *Booth,* 1859), but in the meantime the act was a dead letter in Wisconsin and in other states as well. In all, in the decade of the act's existence, about 300 fugitives were returned to their owners. In the process far larger numbers of white northerners got an eyewitness view of the heartlessness of slavery.

Uncle Tom's Cabin

Tremendously important in increasing sectional tensions and bringing home the evils of slavery to still more people in the North was Harriet Beecher Stowe's novel *Uncle Tom's Cabin* (1852). Mrs. Stowe was neither a professional writer nor an abolitionist, and she had almost no firsthand knowledge of slavery. But her conscience had been roused by the Fugitive Slave Act, which she called a "nightmare abomination." In gathering material for the book she depended heavily on abolitionist writers, many of whom she knew. She dashed it off quickly; as she later recalled, it seemed to write

CAUTION!!

COLORED PEOPLE

OF BOSTON, ONE & ALL,

You are hereby respectfully CAUTIONED and advised, to avoid conversing with the

Watchmen and Police Officers of Boston,

For since the recent ORDER OF THE MAYOR & ALDERMEN, they are empowered to act as

KIDNAPPERS

AND

Slave Catchers,

And they have already been actually employed in KIDNAPPING, CATCHING, AND KEEPING SLAVES. Therefore, if you value your LIBERTY, and the *Welfare of the Fugitives* among you, *Shun* them in every possible manner, as so many *HOUNDS* on the track of the most unfortunate of your race.

Keep a Sharp Look Out for KIDNAPPERS, and have TOP EYE open.

APRIL 24, 1851.

An 1851 broadside by Boston abolitionist Theodore Parker alerted the city's black community to the dangers posed by the new Fugitive Slave Act.

itself. Nevertheless, *Uncle Tom's Cabin* was an immediate success: 10,000 copies were sold in a week, 300,000 in a year. Soon it was being translated into dozens of languages. Dramatized versions were staged in countries throughout the world.

Uncle Tom's Cabin had little literary merit, for Mrs. Stowe was hardly a distinguished writer. Her approach to the subject explains the book's success. This tale of the pious, patient slave Uncle Tom, the saintly white child Eva, and the callous slave driver Simon Legree appealed to an audience far wider than that reached by the abolitionists. It avoided the self-righteous, accusatory tone of most abolitionist tracts and did not seek to convert readers to belief in racial equality. Many of the southern characters were fine, sensitive people, while the cruel Simon Legree was a transplanted Connecticut Yankee. There were many heartrending scenes of pain, self-sacrifice, and heroism. The story proved especially effective on the stage: the slave Eliza crossing the frozen Ohio River to freedom, the death of Little Eva, Eva and Tom ascending to heaven—these scenes left audiences in tears.

Southern critics pointed out, correctly enough, that Mrs. Stowe's picture of plantation life was distorted, her slaves atypical. They called her a "coarse, ugly, long-tongued woman" and accused her of trying to "awaken rancorous hatred and malignant jealousies" that would undermine national unity. Most northerners, having little basis on which to judge the accuracy of the book, tended to discount southern criticism as biased. In any case, *Uncle Tom's Cabin* raised questions in many minds that transcended the issue of accuracy. Did it matter if all slaves were not as kindly as Uncle Tom, as determined as George Harris? What if only *one* white master was as evil as Simon Legree? No earlier white American writer had looked at slaves as *people.*

The pious, patient slave Uncle Tom was patterned after the real-life Reverend Josiah Henson, who is depicted in this wood engraving that appeared in Henson's autobiography.

Uncle Tom's Cabin touched the hearts of millions. Some became abolitionists; others, still hesitating to step forward, asked themselves as they put the book down: Is slavery just?

"Young America"

Clearly a distraction was needed to help keep the lid on sectional troubles in both the North and the South. Some people hoped to find one in foreign affairs, for American diplomacy in the 1850s was active and aggressive. The spirit of manifest destiny explains this in large part; once the United States had reached the Pacific, expansionists began to seek new worlds to conquer. In the late 1840s they talked about transmitting the dynamic, democratic spirit of the United States to other countries, aiding local revolutionaries, opening up new markets, perhaps annexing foreign lands.

To an extent this "Young America" spirit was purely emotional, a mindless confidence that democracy would triumph everywhere, that public opinion was "stronger than the Bayonet." At the time of the European revolutions of 1848, Americans talked freely about helping the liberals in their struggles against autocratic governments. Horace Greeley's New York *Tribune* predicted that all Europe would soon become "one great and splendid Republic . . . and we shall all be citizens of the world." When the Austrians crushed a rebellion in Hungary, Secretary of State Daniel Webster addressed an insulting note full of vague threats to the Austrian chargé in Washington. Hungarian revolutionary hero Louis Kossuth visited the United States in search of aid in 1851–1852; President Fillmore put the U.S.S. *Mississippi* at his disposal, and great crowds turned out to cheer him.

The United States had no intention of going to war to win independence for the Hungarians, as Kossuth soon learned to his sorrow. However, the same democratic-expansionist sentiment led to dreams of conquests in the Caribbean area. In 1855 a freebooter named William Walker, backed by an American company engaged in transporting migrants to California across Central America, seized control of Nicaragua and elected himself president. He was ousted two years later but made repeated attempts to regain control until, in 1860, he died before a Honduran firing squad. Another would-be dictator, "General" George W. L. Bickley, claiming that he was disturbed by that "crookedest of all boundary lines, the Rio Grande," tried to organize an expedition to conquer Mexico.

While many northerners suspected them of engaging in dastardly plots to obtain more territory for slavery, Walker and Bickley were primarily adventurers trying to use the prevailing mood of buoyant expansionism for selfish ends. They attracted southern recruits by suggesting that slavery might follow in their wake—Bickley proposed that Mexico be divided into 25 slave states—but at the same time some northerners proposed colonizing ex-slaves in the Caribbean in order to "build up a free black power" in the area to prevent the extension of slavery there.

The rapid development of California created a need for improved communication with the West Coast. A canal across Central America would cut weeks from the sailing time between New York and San Francisco. In 1850 Secretary of State John M. Clayton and the British minister to the United States, Henry Lytton Bulwer, negotiated a treaty providing for the demilitarization and joint Anglo-American control of any canal across the isthmus. Although no canal was built at the time, the United States had officially staked out its interest in the region.

As this area began to assume strategic importance to the United States, the desire to obtain Cuba grew stronger. In 1854 President Franklin Pierce instructed his minister to Spain, Pierre Soulé of Louisiana, to offer $130 million for the island. Since Soulé was a hotheaded bungler, the administration arranged for him first to confer in Belgium with the American ministers to Great Britain and France, James Buchanan and John Y. Mason, to work out a plan for persuading Spain to sell. Out of this meeting came the Ostend Manifesto, a confidential dispatch to the State Department proposing that the United States try to buy Cuba and suggesting that if Spain refused to sell, "the great law of self-preservation" might justify "wresting" it from Spain by force.

News of the manifesto leaked out, and it had to be published. Northern opinion was outraged by this "slaveholders' plot." Europeans claimed to be shocked by such "dishonorable" and "clandestine" diplomacy. The government had to disavow the manifesto, and any hope of obtaining Cuba

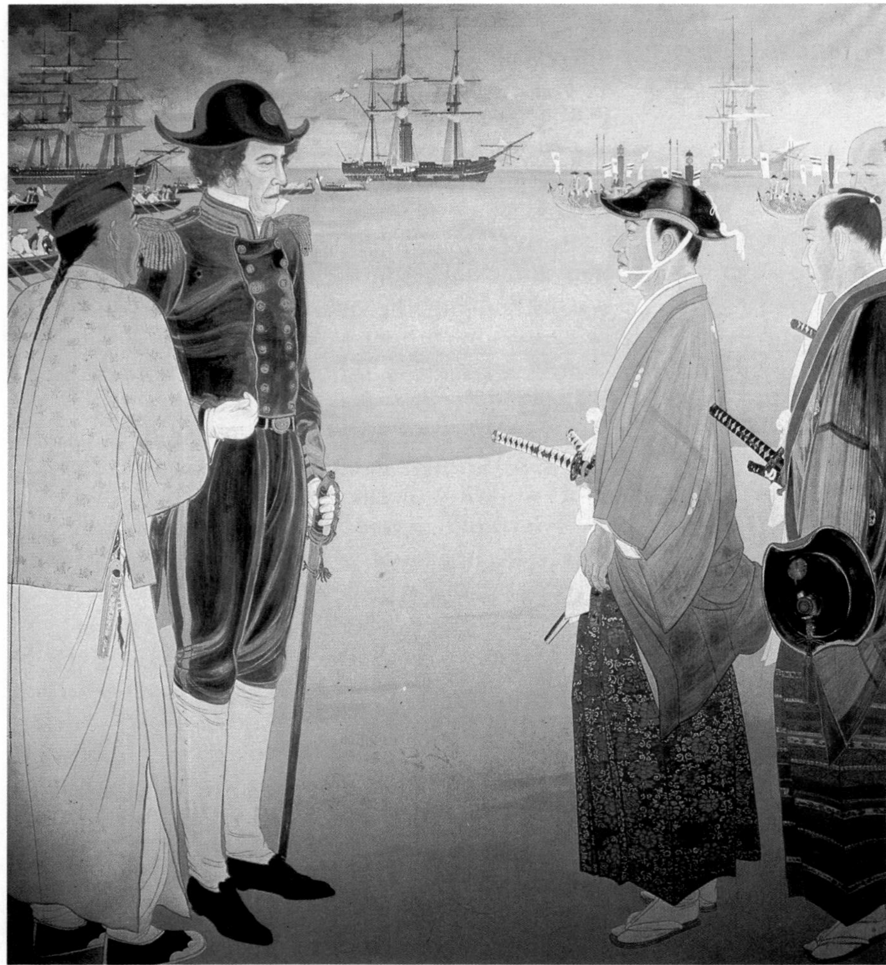

Japanese artist Gessan Ogata painted this watercolor of Commodore Perry's "First landing at Kurihama, July 14, 1853." The "black ships" of Perry's squadron are in the background.

or any other territory in the Caribbean vanished.

The expansionist mood of the moment also explains President Fillmore's dispatching an expedition under Commodore Matthew C. Perry to try for commercial concessions in the isolated kingdom of Japan in 1852. Perry's expedition was a great success. The Japanese, impressed by American naval power, agreed to establish diplomatic relations. In 1858 an American envoy, Townsend Harris, negotiated a commercial treaty that opened to American ships six Japanese ports heretofore closed to foreigners. President Pierce's negotiation of a Canadian reciprocity treaty with Great Britain in 1854 and an unsuccessful attempt, also made under Pierce, to annex the Hawaiian Islands are further illustrations of the assertive foreign policy of the period.

The Little Giant

The most prominent spokesman of the Young America movement was Stephen A. Douglas. The senator from Illinois was the Henry Clay of his generation. Like Clay at his best, Douglas was able to see the needs of the nation in the broadest perspective. He was born in Vermont in 1813 and moved to Illinois when barely 20. There he studied law and was soon deep in Democratic politics. Thereafter he held a succession of state offices before being elected to Congress in 1842. After two terms in the House, he was chosen United States senator.

Douglas succeeded at almost everything he attempted. His law practice was large and prosperous. He dabbled in Chicago real estate and made a large fortune. Politics suited him to perfection. Rarely has a man seemed so closely attuned to his time and place in history. Although very short, he had powerful shoulders, a large head, strong features, and deep-set, piercing eyes. His high forehead was made to appear even bolder by the way he wore his hair, swept back in a pompadour and draped over his collar. His appearance was so imposing that friends called him the Little Giant. "I live with my constituents," he once boasted, "drink with them, lodge with them, pray with them, laugh, hunt, dance, and work with them. I eat their corn dodgers and fried bacon and sleep two in a bed with them." Yet he was no mere backslapper. He read widely, wrote poetry, financed a number of young American artists, served as a regent of the Smithsonian Institution, and was interested in scientific farming.

The foundations of Douglas's politics were expansion and popular sovereignty. He had been willing to fight for all of Oregon in 1846, and he supported the Mexican War to the hilt, in sharp contrast to his one-term Illinois colleague in Congress, Abraham Lincoln. That local settlers should determine their own institutions was, to his way of thinking, axiomatic. Arguments over the future of slavery in the territories he believed a foolish waste of energy and time since he was convinced that natural conditions would keep the institution out of the West. The main thing, he insisted, was to get on with the development of the United States. Let the nation build railroads, acquire new territory, expand its trade. He believed slavery "a curse beyond computation" for both blacks and whites, but he refused to admit that any moral issue was involved. He cared not, he boasted, whether slavery was voted up or voted down. This was not really true, but the question was interfering with the rapid exploitation of the continent. Douglas wanted it settled so that the country could concentrate on more important matters.

Douglas's success in steering the Compromise of 1850 through Congress added to his already considerable reputation. In 1851, although only 38, he set out to win the Democratic presidential nomination. He reasoned that since he was the brightest, most imaginative, and hardest-working Democrat around, he had every right to press his claim. This brash aggressiveness proved his undoing. He expressed open contempt for James Buchanan and said of his other chief rival, Lewis Cass, who had won considerable fame while serving as minister to France, that his "reputation was beyond the C."

At the 1852 Democratic convention Douglas had no chance. Cass and Buchanan killed each other off and the delegates finally chose a dark

"By God, sir, I made James Buchanan, and by God, sir, I will unmake him!" Stephen A. Douglas remarked with characteristic exaggeration during the debate over Kansas.

horse, Franklin Pierce of New Hampshire. The Whigs, rejecting the colorless Fillmore, nominated General Winfield Scott, who was known as Old Fuss and Feathers "because of his punctiliousness in dress and decorum." In the campaign both sides supported the Compromise of 1850. The Democrats won an easy victory, 254 electoral votes to 42.

So handsome a triumph seemed to insure stability, but in fact it was a prelude to political chaos. The Whig party was crumbling fast. The "Cotton Whigs" of the South, alienated by the antislavery attitude of their northern brethren, were flocking into the Democratic fold. In the North the radical "Conscience" Whigs and the conservative "Silver Gray" faction that was undisturbed by slavery found themselves more and more at odds with each other. Congress fell overwhelmingly into the hands of proslavery southern Democrats, a development profoundly disturbing to many northern Democrats as well as to die-hard Whigs.

Kansas-Nebraska Act

Franklin Pierce was a youthful-appearing 48 when he took office. He was generally well liked by politicians. His career had included service in the New Hampshire legislature and in both houses of Congress. Alcohol had become a problem for him in Washington, however, and in 1842 he had resigned from the Senate and returned home to try to best the bottle, a struggle in which he was successful. The setback proved temporary; his New Hampshire law practice boomed, and he added to his reputation by serving as a brigadier general during the Mexican War. While his nomination for president had been a surprise, once made, it had appeared perfectly reasonable. Great things were expected of his administration, especially after he surrounded himself with men of all factions: to balance his appointment of a radical states' rights Mississippian, Jefferson Davis, as secretary of war, for example, he named a conservative Unionist, William L. Marcy of New York, as secretary of state.

Only a strong man, however, can manage a ministry of all talents, and that President Pierce was not. He followed, as Allan Nevins has written, a "policy of smiling on everybody but specially favoring both ends against the middle." The ship of state was soon drifting; Pierce seemed incapable of holding firm the helm.

This was the situation in January 1854 when Senator Douglas, chairman of the Committee on Territories, introduced what looked like a routine bill organizing the land west of Missouri and Iowa as Nebraska Territory. Since settlers were beginning to trickle into the area, the time had arrived to set up a civil administration. But Douglas also acted because a territorial government was essential to railroad development. As a director of the Illinois Central line and as a land speculator, he hoped to make Chicago the terminus of a transcontinental railroad, but construction could scarcely begin before the entire route was cleared of Indians and brought under some kind of civil control.

Southerners, wishing to bring the transcontinental line to Memphis or New Orleans, pointed out that a right of way through organized territory already existed across Texas and New Mexico Territory. In 1853 the United States minister to Mexico, James Gadsden, a prominent southern railroad executive, had engineered the purchase of more than 29,000 square miles of Mexican territory south of the Gila River, which provided an easy route (see map, page 367) through the mountains for such a railroad. Douglas, whose vision of the economic potentialities of the nation was Hamiltonian, would have been willing to support the construction of two or even three transcontinental railroads, but he knew that Congress would not go that far. In any case, he believed that the Nebraska region must be organized promptly.

The powerful southern faction in Congress would not go along with Douglas's proposal as it stood. The railroad question aside, Nebraska would presumably become a free state, for it lay north of latitude 36°30′ in a district from which slavery had been excluded since 1820 by the Missouri Compromise. To win over the southerners, Douglas agreed first to divide the region into two territories, Kansas and Nebraska, and then—a fateful concession—to repeal the part of the Missouri Compromise that excluded slavery from land north of 36°30′. Whether the new territories should become slave or free, he argued, should be left to the decision of the settlers in accordance with the democratic principle of popular sovereignty. No one, he thought, could legitimately object; the region, unsuited to plantation agriculture, would

The Gadsden Purchase was signed on July 4, 1854, at Mesilla, New Mexico Territory, in a formal ceremony attended by local residents. This painting was executed by a Mesilla native to commemorate the event on its 75th anniversary.

surely become free. The fact that he might advance his presidential ambitions by making concessions to the South must have influenced Douglas too, as must the local political situation in Missouri, where slaveholders feared being "surrounded" on three sides by free states.

Douglas's miscalculation of northern sentiment was monumental. It was one thing to apply popular sovereignty to the new territories in the Southwest as a way of avoiding a confrontation with the slave states, quite another to apply it to a region that had been part of the United States for half a century and free soil for 34 years. Word that the area was to be reopened to slavery caused an indignant outcry; many moderate opponents of slavery were radicalized. A group of abolitionist congressmen issued an "Appeal to the Independent Democrats" (actually, all were Free Soilers and Whigs) denouncing the Kansas-Nebraska bill as "a gross violation of a sacred pledge" and calling for a campaign of letter writing, petitions, and public meetings to prevent its passage. The unanimity and force of the northern public's reaction was like nothing in America since the days of the Stamp Act and the Intolerable Acts.

Protests could not defeat the bill. Southerners

in both houses backed it regardless of party. Douglas, at his best when under attack, pushed it with all his power. The authors of the "Appeal," he charged, were "the pure unadulterated representatives of Abolitionism, Free Soilism, [and] Niggerism." President Pierce added whatever force the administration could muster. As a result, the northern Democrats split and the bill became law late in May 1854. Thus the nation took the greatest single step in its blind march toward the abyss of secession and civil war.

Party Realignment

The repeal of the Missouri Compromise struck the North like a slap in the face—at once shameful and challenging. Presumably the question of slavery in the territories had been settled forever; now, without justification, it had been reopened. Two days after the Kansas-Nebraska bill passed the House of Representatives, Anthony Burns, a slave who had escaped from Virginia by stowing away on a ship, was arrested in Boston. A mob tried to free him but was thrown back by federal agents. Troops were rushed to the scene to restrain the swelling crowds. Burns was a runaway, and the federal commissioner ruled that he should be returned to his master. This was done, but, as one eyewitness scornfully pointed out, it required two companies of artillery and a thousand police and marines to take "one trembling colored man to the vessel which was to carry him to slavery." As the grim parade marched past buildings festooned with black crepe, the crowd shouted "Kidnappers! Kidnappers!" at the soldiers. Estimates of the cost of returning this single slave to his owner ran as high as $100,000. In previous cases Boston's conservative leaders, Whig to a man, had tended to hold back; after the Kansas-Nebraska Act, even they opposed the return of fugitive slaves.

The Democratic party lost heavily in the North as a result of the Kansas-Nebraska Act—there were 91 free-state Democrats in the House of Representatives when the act was passed, only 25 after the next election. With the Whig party already moribund, dissidents flocked to two new parties. The American, or "Know-Nothing," party (its members used the password "I don't know") sought to take advantage of the anxieties and frustrations generated by the slavery controversy, by the rapid social and economic changes of the time, and by the growing popular dissatisfaction with political leaders who were not solving these problems. The party denounced both abolitionists and southern fire-eaters; it appealed at once to the patriotism of the voters and to their meanest emotions. Its program was nativist—a kind of defensive nationalism that idealized the virtues of "native" Protestant Americans and denounced Catholics and recent immigrants. These "new" elements, it claimed, were undermining American values.

The argument was simplistic and wrongheaded, but for a time this "politics of impatience" achieved considerable success. Operating often in tacit alliance with the antislavery forces (dislike of slavery did not prevent many abolitionists from being prejudiced against Catholics and immigrants), the Know-Nothings won a string of local victories in 1854 and elected more than 40 congressmen.

Far more significant was the formation of the Republican party, made up of former Free Soilers, Conscience Whigs, and "Anti-Nebraska" Democrats. The Know-Nothing party at least made a pretense of being a national organization, but the Republican party was purely sectional. It sprang up spontaneously throughout the Old Northwest and caught on with a rush in New England. Republicans presented themselves as the party of freedom. They were not abolitionists (though most abolitionists were soon voting Republican), but they insisted that slavery be kept out of the territories. The heart of their reasoning was that if America was to remain a land of opportunity, free white labor must have exclusive access to the West. Thus the party appealed not only to voters who disapproved of slavery, but also to those who wished to keep blacks—free or slave—out of their states. In 1854 the Republicans won over 100 seats in the House of Representatives and control of many state governments.

Still the furor might have died down if settlement of the new territories had proceeded in an orderly manner. Almost none of the settlers who flocked to Kansas owned slaves, relatively few of them were primarily interested in the slavery question, and most had a low opinion of blacks. ("I kem to Kansas to live in a free state," one northerner explained. "I don't want niggers a-trampin' over my grave.") Like nearly all frontiersmen, they wanted land and local political office, lucrative government contracts, and other business opportunities.

When Congress opened the gates to settlement in May 1854, *none* of the land in the territory was available for sale. Treaties extinguishing Indian titles had yet to be ratified, and public lands had not been surveyed. In July Congress authorized squatters to occupy unsurveyed federal lands, but much of this property was far to the west of the frontier and practically inaccessible. The situation led to confusion over property boundaries, to graft and speculation, and to general uncertainty among settlers, thereby exacerbating the difficulty of establishing an orderly government.

The legal status of slavery in Kansas became the focus of all these conflicts. Both northern abolitionists and southern defenders of slavery were determined to have Kansas. They made of the territory first a testing ground and then a battlefield, thus exposing the fatal flaw in the Kansas-Nebraska Act and the idea of popular sovereignty. The law said that the people of Kansas were "perfectly free" to decide the slavery question. But the citizens of territories were *not* entirely free; by definition, territories were not sovereign political units. The act had created a political vacuum, which its vague statement that the settlers must establish their domestic institutions "subject . . . to the Constitution" did not begin to fill. When should the institutions be established? Was it democratic to let a handful of early arrivals make decisions that would affect the lives of the thousands soon to follow? The virtues of the time-tested system of congressional control established by the Northwest Ordinance became fully apparent only when the system was discarded.

More serious was the fact that outsiders, North and South, refused to permit Kansans to work out their own destiny. The contest for control began at once. A New England Emigrant Aid Society was formed, with grandiose plans for transporting antislavery settlers to the area. The society was mostly bluff; it transported only a handful of New Englanders to Kansas. Yet the New Englanders were very conspicuous and undoubtedly encouraged other antislavery settlers to make the move.

In doing so, they stirred southerners to fight back. The proslavery forces enjoyed several advantages in this struggle. The first inhabitants in frontier regions nearly always came from lands immediately to the east. In this case they were proslavery Missourians. When word spread that "foreigners" from New England were seeking to "steal" Kansas, many Missourians rushed to protect their "rights."

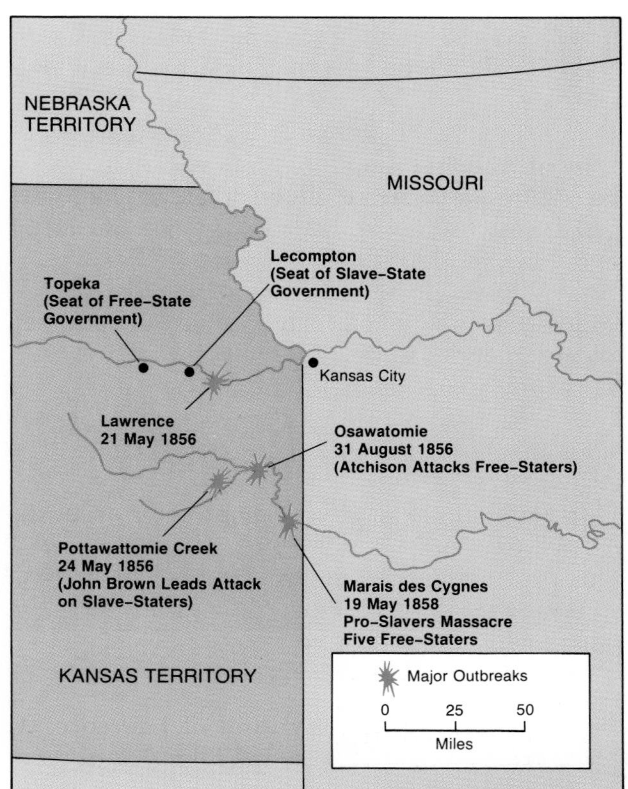

"BLEEDING KANSAS"

In November 1854 an election was held in Kansas to pick a territorial delegate to Congress. A large band of Missourians crossed over specifically to elect a proslavery man and carried it easily. In March 1855 some 5,000 "Border Ruffians" again descended upon Kansas and elected a territorial legislature. A census had recorded 2,905 elegible voters, but 6,307 votes were cast. The legislature promptly enacted a slave code and laws prohibiting abolitionist agitation. Antislavery settlers refused to recognize this regime and held elections of their own. By January 1856 two governments existed in Kansas, one based on fraud, the other extralegal.

By denouncing the free-state government located at Topeka, President Pierce encouraged the proslavery settlers to assume the offensive. In May

This daguerreotype is evidence that by 1856 force of arms was viewed as effective law in Kansas. The gun crew was protecting Topeka, the seat of the free-state government.

they sacked the antislavery town of Lawrence. A psychopathic Free Soiler named John Brown then took the law into his own hands in retaliation. In May 1856, together with six companions (four of them his sons), Brown stole into a proslavery settlement on Pottawatomie Creek in the dead of night. They dragged five unsuspecting settlers from their rude cabins and murdered them. This senseless slaughter brought men on both sides to arms by the hundreds. Brown and his followers were indicted for the murders, but as Brown's recent biographer, Stephen B. Oates, has written, "Kansas was in complete chaos." Armed bands, one led by Brown himself, "prowled the countryside, shooting at one another and looting."

Pressure from federal troops eventually forced Brown to go into hiding. He finally left Kansas in October 1856. By that time some 200 persons had lost their lives. Exaggerated accounts of "Bleeding Kansas" filled the pages of northern newspapers.

A certain amount of violence was normal in any frontier community, but it suited the political interests of the Republicans to make the situation in Kansas seem worse than it was. The Democrats were also partly to blame, for although residents of nearby states often tried to influence elections in new territories, the actions of the Missouri Border Ruffians made a mockery of the democratic process. Yet the main responsibility for the Kansas tragedy must be borne by the Pierce administration in Washington. Under popular sovereignty the national government was supposed to see that elections were orderly and honest. Instead, the president acted as a partisan. When the first governor of the territory objected to the manner in which the proslavery legislature had been elected, Pierce replaced him with a man who backed the southern group without question.

Making a Senator a Martyr

As counterpoint to the fighting in Kansas there rose an almost continuous cacophony in the halls of Congress. Every event in Kansas brought forth tirades in the Capitol. Red-faced legislators traded insults and threats. Epithets like "liar" were freely tossed about. Prominent in these angry outbursts was a new senator, Charles Sumner of Massachusetts. Brilliant, learned, and articulate, Sumner had made a name for himself in New England as a reformer interested in the peace movement, prison reform, and the abolition of slavery. He possessed great magnetism and was, according to the tastes of the day, an accomplished orator, but he suffered inner torments of a complex nature that warped his personality. He was egotistical and humorless. His unyielding devotion to his principles was less praiseworthy than it seemed on casual examination, for it resulted from his complete lack of respect for the principles of others. Reform movements evidently provided him a kind of emotional release; he became combative and totally lacking in objectivity when espousing a cause.

In the Kansas debates Sumner displayed vindictiveness and an icy disdain for his foes. Colleagues threatened him with assassination, called him a "filthy reptile" and a "leper." He was impervious to such hostility. In the spring of 1856 he loosed a dreadful blast at "the crime against Kansas." Characterizing administration policy as tyrannical, imbecilic, absurd, and infamous, he demanded that Kansas be admitted to the Union at once as a free state. Then he began a long and intemperate personal attack on both Douglas and the elderly Senator Andrew P. Butler of South Carolina, who was not present to defend himself.

Sumner described Butler as a "Don Quixote" who had taken "the harlot, slavery" as his mistress, and he spoke scornfully of "the loose expectoration" of Butler's speech. This was an inexcusable reference to the uncontrollable drooling to which the elderly senator was subject. While he was still talking, Douglas, who normally shrugged off such language as part of the game, was heard to mutter, "That damn fool will get himself killed by some other damn fool."

Such a "fool" quickly materialized in the person of Congressman Preston S. Brooks of South Carolina, a nephew of Senator Butler. Since Butler was absent from Washington, Brooks, who was probably as mentally unbalanced as Sumner, assumed the responsibility of defending his kinsman's honor. A southern romantic par excellence, he decided that caning Sumner would reflect his contempt more effectively than challenging him to a duel. Two days after the speech, Brooks entered the Senate as it adjourned. Sumner remained at his desk writing. After waiting with exquisite punctilio until a talkative woman in the lobby had left so that she would be spared the sight of violence, Brooks walked up to Sumner and rained blows upon his head with a gutta-percha cane until he fell, unconscious and bloody, upon the floor. "I . . . gave him about 30 first-rate stripes," Brooks later boasted. "Towards the last he bellowed like a calf. I wore my cane out completely but saved the head which is gold." The physical damage suffered by Sumner was relatively superficial, but the incident so affected him psychologically that he was unable to return to his seat in Congress until 1859.

Both sides made much of this disgraceful incident. When the House censured him, Brooks resigned, returned to his home district, and was triumphantly reelected. A number of well-wishers even sent him souvenir canes. Northerners viewed the affair as illustrating the brutalizing effect of slavery on southern whites and made a hero of Sumner.

A well-known contemporary drawing gives a dramatic view of Brooks caning Sumner. Beneath Sumner's left hand is a scroll inscribed "Kansas." The cartoon's title is "Southern Chivalry—Argument versus Clubs."

Buchanan Tries His Hand

Such was the atmosphere surrounding the 1856 presidential election. The Republican party now dominated much of the North, where it stood not for abolition but for restricting slavery to areas where it already existed. It nominated John C. Frémont, "the Pathfinder," one of the heroes of the conquest of California during the Mexican War. Frémont fitted the Whig tradition of presidential candidates; a popular military man with almost no political experience. Unlike Taylor and Scott, however, he was sound and articulate on the issue of slavery in the territories. Although men of diverse interests had joined the party, Republicans expressed their objectives in one simple slogan: "Free soil, free speech, and Frémont."

The Democrats cast aside the ineffectual Pierce, but they did not dare nominate Douglas because he had raised such a storm in the North. They settled on James Buchanan, chiefly because he had been out of the country serving as minister to Great Britain during the long debate over Kansas! The Know-Nothing party nominated ex-president Fillmore, a choice the remnants of the Whigs endorsed. The poet Walt Whitman had been an ardent Democrat. But the party's stand on slavery in the territories disgusted him. In 1856 he wrote a poem, "The 18th Presidency," denouncing both Buchanan and Fillmore:

Two galvanized old men, close on
the summons to depart this life
. . . relics and proofs of the little
political bargains . . .

In the campaign, the Democrats concentrated on denouncing the Republicans as a sectional party that threatened to destroy the Union. On this issue they carried the day. Buchanan won only a minority of the popular vote, but he had strength in every section. He got 174 electoral votes to Frémont's 114 and Fillmore's 8. The significant contest took place in the populous states just north of slave territory—Pennsylvania, Ohio, Indiana, and Illinois. Buchanan carried all but Ohio, though by narrow margins.

James Buchanan "never made a witty remark, never wrote a memorable sentence, and never showed a touch of distinction," according to historian Allan Nevins.

No one could say that James Buchanan lacked political experience. He had been elected to the Pennsylvania legislature in 1815 when only 24. He served for well over 20 years in Congress and had been minister to Russia, then Polk's secretary of state, then minister to Great Britain under Pierce. Personally, Buchanan was a bundle of contradictions. Dignified in bearing and by nature cautious, he could consume enormous amounts of liquor without showing the slightest sign of inebriation. A big, heavy man, he was nonetheless remarkably graceful and light on his tiny feet, of which he was inordinately proud. He wore a very high collar to conceal a scarred neck, and because of an eye defect he habitually carried his head to one side and slightly forward, which gave him, as his most recent biographer says, "a perpetual attitude of courteous deference and attentive interest" that sometimes led individuals to believe they had won a greater share of his attention and support than was actually the case. In fact he was extremely stubborn and sometimes vindictive.

Buchanan was popular with women and attracted to them as well, but although he contemplated marriage on more than one occasion, he never took the final step. Over the years many strong men in politics had, like Walt Whitman, held him in contempt. Yet he was patriotiç, conscientious, and moderate. While Republican extremists called him a "Doughface"—they believed he lacked the force of character to stand up against southern extremists—many voters in 1856 thought—or allowed themselves to think—that he had the qualities necessary to steer the nation to calmer waters.

The Court Tries Its Hand

Before Buchanan could fairly take the Kansas problem in hand, an event occurred that drove another deep wedge between North and South. Back in 1834 Dr. John Emerson of St. Louis joined the army as a surgeon and was assigned to duty at Rock Island, Illinois. Later he was transferred to Fort Snelling, in Wisconsin Territory. In 1838 he returned to Missouri. Accompanying him on these travels was his body servant, Dred Scott, a slave. In 1846, after Emerson's death, Scott, with the help of a friendly lawyer, brought suit in the Missouri courts for his liberty, arguing that residence in Illinois, where slavery was barred under the Northwest Ordinance, and in Wisconsin Territory, where the Missouri Compromise outlawed it, had made him a free man.

The future of Dred Scott mattered not at all to the country or the courts; at issue was the question of whether Congress or the local legislatures had the power to outlaw slavery in the territories. After many years of litigation, the case reached the Supreme Court. On March 6, 1857, two days after Buchanan's inauguration, the high tribunal acted. Free or slave, the Court declared, blacks were not citizens; therefore Scott could not sue in a federal court. This doubious legal logic settled Scott's fate. However, the Court went further. Since the plaintiff had returned to Missouri, the laws of Illinois no longer applied to him. His residence in Wisconsin Territory—this was the most controversial part of the decision—did not make him free because the Missouri Compromise was unconstitutional. According to the Bill of Rights (the Fifth Amendment), the federal government cannot deprive any person of life, liberty, or property without due process of law.* Therefore, Chief Justice Roger B. Taney reasoned, "an Act of Congress which deprives a person . . . of his liberty or property merely because he came himself or brought his property into a particular Territory . . . could hardly be dignified with the name of due process of law."

The Dred Scott decision has been widely criticized on legal grounds. Each justice filed his own opinion, and in several important particulars there was no line of argument that any five of the nine agreed upon. Some critics have argued that the justices should have gone beyond the minimum of argument necessary to settle the case, and many have made much of the fact that a majority of the justices were southerners. It would be going too far, however, to accuse the Court of plotting to extend slavery. The judges were trying to settle the vexing question of slavery in the territories once and for all. If this admirable objective could only be accomplished by fuzzy reasoning—well, it would not be the first or the last time in the history of jurisprudence that an important result rested on shaky logic.

In addition to invalidating the already repealed Missouri Compromise, the decision threatened Douglas's principle of popular sovereignty, for if Congress could not exclude slaves from a territory, how could a mere territorial legislature do so? Until statehood was granted, slavery seemed as inviolate as freedom of religion or speech or any other civil liberty guaranteed by the Constitution. Thus it was close to what Calhoun had argued for in 1850. Where formerly freedom (as guaranteed in the Bill of Rights) was a national institution and slavery a local one, now, according to the Court, slavery was nationwide, excluded only where states had specifically abolished it.

The irony of employing the Bill of Rights to keep blacks in chains did not escape northern critics. Now slaves could be brought into Minnesota Territory, even into Oregon. In his inaugural address Buchanan had sanctimoniously urged the people to accept the forthcoming ruling—"whatever this may be"—as a final settlement. Many assumed (indeed, it was true) that certain judges had "leaked" word of the decision to him in advance of his speech. If this "greatest crime in the judicial annals of the Republic" was allowed to stand, northerners argued, the Republican party would have no reason to exist: its program had been declared unconstitutional! The Dred Scott decision convinced thousands that the South was engaged

* Some state constitutions had similar provisions, but the slave states obviously did not. The Fourteenth Amendment to the Constitution extended the ban to the states (see pages 461–462).

in an aggressive attempt to extend the peculiar institution so far that it could no longer be considered peculiar.

The Lecompton Constitution

Kansas soon provided a test for northern suspicions. Initially Buchanan handled the problem of Kansas well by appointing Robert J. Walker as governor. Although he was from Mississippi, Walker had no desire to foist slavery on the territory against the will of its inhabitants. He was a small man but a courageous one, patriotic, vigorous, tough-minded, much like Douglas in temper and belief. A former senator and Cabinet member, he had more political stature by far than any previous governor of the territory. The proslavery leaders in Kansas had managed to convene a constitutional convention at Lecompton, but the Free Soil forces had refused to participate in the election of delegates. When this rump body drafted a proslavery constitution and then refused to submit it to a fair vote of all the settlers, Walker denounced its work and hurried back to Washington to explain the situation to Buchanan.

The president refused to face reality. His prosouthern advisers were clamoring for him to "save" Kansas. Instead of rejecting the Lecompton constitution, he asked Congress to admit Kansas to the Union with this document as its frame of government.

Buchanan's decision brought him head-on against Stephen A. Douglas, and the repercussions of their clash shattered the Democratic party. Principle and self-interest (an irresistible combination) forced Douglas to oppose the leader of his party. If he stood aside while Congress admitted Kansas, he would not only be abandoning popular sovereignty, he would be committing political suicide. He was up for reelection to the Senate in 1858. Fifty-five of the 56 newspapers in Illinois had declared editorially against the Lecompton constitution; if he supported it, defeat was certain. In a dramatic confrontation at the White House he and Buchanan argued the question at length, tempers rising. Finally, the president tried to force him into line. "Mr. Douglas," he said, "I desire you to remember that no Democrat ever yet differed from an Administration of his own choice without being crushed." "Mr. President," Douglas replied contemptuously, "I wish *you* to remember that General Jackson is dead!" And he stalked out of the room.

Buchanan then compounded his error by putting tremendous political pressure on Douglas, cutting off his Illinois patronage on the eve of his reelection campaign. Of course Douglas persisted, openly joining the Republicans in the fight. Congress rejected the bill.

Meanwhile, the extent of the fraud perpetrated at Lecompton became clear. In October 1857 a new legislature had been chosen in Kansas, the antislavery voters participating in the balloting. It ordered a referendum on the Lecompton constitution in January 1858. The constitution was overwhelmingly rejected, this time the proslavery settlers boycotting the test. When Buchanan persisted in pressing Congress to admit Kansas under the Lecompton constitution, Congress ordered another referendum. To slant the case in favor of approval, the legislators stipulated that if the constitution was voted down, Kansas could not be admitted into the Union until it had a population of 90,000. Nevertheless, the Kansans rejected it by a ratio of six to one.

More than opposition to slavery influenced this vote, for by 1858 most Kansans were totally alienated from the Democratic administration in Washington because of its bungling and corrupt management of the public lands. After delaying sales unconscionably, Buchanan suddenly put 8 million acres up for auction in 1858. Squatters on this land were faced, in the midst of a depression, with finding $200 in cash to cover the minimum price of their quarter sections or losing their improvements. Local protests forced a delay of the sales, but Kansans by the thousands were convinced that Buchanan had thrown the land on the market out of pique at their original rejection of the Lecompton constitution.

The Emergence of Lincoln

These were dark days. During the summer of 1857 a panic struck the New York stock market, heralding a sharp downturn of the economy. This depression was probably unavoidable after the feverish expansion and speculation of the previous ten years, but northerners blamed the southern-dominated Congress, which had just reduced tariff duties to the lowest levels in nearly half a century. As prices plummeted and unemployment rose, they attributed the collapse to foreign competition and accused the South of having sacrificed the prosperity of the rest of the nation for its selfish advantage. The South in turn read in the panic proof of the superiority of the slave system, for the depression had little effect on the southern economy, chiefly because the world price of cotton remained high.

Dissolution threatened the Union. To many Americans Stephen A. Douglas seemed to offer the best hope of preserving it. For this reason unusual attention was focused on his campaign for reelection to the Senate in 1858. The importance of the contest and Douglas's national prestige put great pressure on the Republicans of Illinois to nominate someone who would make a good showing against him. The man they chose was Abraham Lincoln.

After a towering figure has passed from the stage, it is always difficult to discover what he was like before his rise to prominence. This is especially true of Lincoln, who changed greatly when power and responsibility and fame came to him. Lincoln was not unknown in 1858, but his public career had not been distinguished. He was born in Kentucky in 1809, and the story of his early life can be condensed, as he once said himself, into a single line from Gray's *Elegy:* "The short and simple annals of the poor." His illiterate, ne'er-do-well father, Thomas Lincoln, was a typical frontier wanderer. When Abraham was 7 the family moved to Indiana. In 1830 they pushed west again into southern Illinois. The boy received almost no formal schooling.

However, Lincoln had a good mind, and he was extremely ambitious. He cut loose from his family, made a trip to New Orleans, and for a time managed a general store in New Salem, Illinois. In 1834, when barely 25, he won a seat in the Illinois legislature as a Whig. Meanwhile, he studied law and was admitted to the bar in 1836.

Lincoln remained in the legislature until 1842, displaying a perfect willingness to adopt the Whig position on all issues. In 1846 he was elected to Congress. While not engaged in politics he worked at the law, maintaining an office in Springfield and following the circuit, taking a variety of cases, few of much importance. He earned a decent but by no means sumptuous living. After one term in Congress, marked by his partisan opposition to Polk's Mexican policy, his political career petered out. He seemed fated to pass his remaining years as a typical small-town lawyer.

Even during this period Lincoln's personality was enormously complex. His bawdy sense of humor and his endless fund of stories and tall tales made him a legend first in Illinois and then in Washington. He was admired in Illinois as a powerful and expert axman and a champion wrestler. He was thoroughly at home with toughs like the "Clary's Grove Boys" of New Salem and in the convivial atmosphere of a party caucus. But in a society where most men drank heavily, he never touched liquor. And he was subject to periods of melancholy so profound as to appear almost psychopathic. Friends spoke of him as having "cat fits," and he wrote of himself in the early 1840s: "I am now the most miserable man living. If what I felt were equally distributed to the whole human family, there would not be one cheerful face on earth."

In a region swept by repeated waves of religious revivalism, Lincoln managed to be at once a man of calm spirituality and a skeptic without appearing offensive to conventional believers. He was a party wheelhorse, a coroporation lawyer, even a railroad lobbyist, yet his reputation for integrity was stainless.

The revival of the slavery controversy in 1854 stirred Lincoln deeply. No abolitionist, he always tried to take a "realistic" view of the problem. The Kansas-Nebraska bill led him to see the moral issue more clearly. "If slavery is not wrong, nothing is wrong." he stated with the clarity and simplicity of expression for which he later became famous. Compromises made for the sake of sectional harmony had always sought to preserve as much territory as possible for freedom. Yet unlike most northern Free Soilers, he did not blame the southerners for slavery. "They are just what we would be in their situation," he confessed.

The fairness and moderation of his position combined with its moral force won Lincoln many admirers in the great body of citizens who were trying to reconcile their generally low opinion of blacks and their patriotic desire to avoid an issue

How Lincoln aged during his term of office is evident when one compares Alexander Hesler's portrait, taken on June 3, 1860, with one by an unnamed photographer taken on April 10, 1865.

that threatened the Union with their growing conviction that slavery was sinful. *Anything* that aided slavery was wrong, Lincoln argued. But before casting the first stone, every northerner should look into his own heart: "If there be a man amongst us who is so impatient of [slavery] as a wrong as to disregard its actual presence among us and the difficulty of getting rid of it suddenly in a satisfactory way . . . that man is misplaced if he is on our platform." And Lincoln confessed:

> If all earthly power were given to me, I should not know what to do as to the existing institution. But . . . [this] furnishes no more excuse for permitting slavery to go into our free territory than it would for reviving the African slave trade.

Thus Lincoln was at once compassionate toward the slaveowner and stern toward the institution. "A house divided against itself cannot stand," he warned. "I believe this government cannot endure permanently half slave and half free." Without minimizing the difficulties or urging a hasty and ill-considered solution, Lincoln demanded that the people look toward a day, however remote, when not only Kansas but the entire country would be free.

The Lincoln-Douglas Debates

As Lincoln developed these ideas his reputation grew. In 1855 he almost won the Whig nomination for senator. He became a Republican shortly thereafter, and in June 1856, at the first Republican National Convention, he received 110 votes for the vice-presidential nomination. He seemed the logical man to pit against Douglas in 1858.

In July Lincoln challenged Douglas to a series of seven debates. The senator accepted. The debates were well attended and widely reported, for the idea of a direct confrontation between candidates for an important office captured the popular imagination.

The choice of the next senator lay, of course, in the hands of the state legislature. Technically, Douglas and Lincoln were campaigning for candidates for the legislature who were pledged to support them for the Senate seat. The candidates presented a sharp physical contrast that must have helped ordinary voters in sorting out their differing points of view. Douglas was short and stocky, Lincoln long and lean. Douglas gave the impression of irrepressible energy. While speaking, he roamed the platform; he used broad gestures and bold, exaggerated arguments. He did not hesitate to call "Honest Abe" a liar. Lincoln on his part was slow and deliberate of speech, his voice curiously high-pitched. He seldom used gestures or oratorical tricks, trying rather to create an impression of utter sincerity to add force to his remarks.

The two employed different political styles, each calculated to project a particular image. Douglas epitomized efficiency and success. He dressed in the latest fashion, favoring flashy vests and the finest broadcloth. Ordinarily he arrived in town in a private railroad car, to be met by a brass band, then to ride at the head of a parade to the appointed place. Lincoln appeared before the voters as a man of the people. He wore ill-fitting black suits and a stovepipe hat—repository for letters, bills, scribbled notes, and other scraps—that exaggerated his great height. He presented a worn and rumpled appearance, partly because he traveled from place to place on day coaches, accompanied by only a few advisers. When local supporters came to meet him at the station, he preferred to walk with them through the streets to the scene of the debate.

Lincoln and Douglas maintained a high intellectual level in their speeches, but these were *political* debates. They were seeking not to influence future historians (who have nonetheless pondered their words endlessly) but to win votes. They tended to exaggerate their differences, which were not in fact enormous. Neither wanted to see slavery in the territories or thought it economically efficient, and neither sought to abolish it by political action or force. Both believed blacks congenitally inferior to whites, though Douglas took more pleasure in expounding on racial differences than Lincoln.

Douglas's strategy was to make Lincoln look like an abolitionist. He accused the Republicans of favoring racial equality and refusing to abide by the decision of the Supreme Court in the Dred Scott case. Himself he pictured as a heroic champion of democracy, attacked on one side by the "black" Republicans and on the other by the Buchananites, yet ready to fight to his last breath for popular sovereignty.

Lincoln tried to picture Douglas as proslavery and a *defender* of the Dred Scott decision. "Slavery is an unqualified evil to the negro, to the white man, to the soil, and to the State," he said. "Judge Douglas," he also said, "is blowing out the moral lights around us, when he contends that whoever wants slaves has a right to hold them." However, Lincoln often weakened the impact of his arguments, being perhaps too eager to demonstrate his conservatism. The historian David M. Potter drew a nice distinction in Lincoln's position between "what he would do for the slave" and "what he would do for the Negro." "All men are created equal," he would say, on the authority of the Declaration of Independence, only to add: "I am not, nor ever have been, in favor of bringing about in any way the social and political equality of the white and black races." He opposed allowing blacks to vote, to sit on juries, to marry whites, even to be citizens. He predicted the "ultimate extinction" of slavery, but when pressed he predicted that it would not occur "in less than a hundred years at the least." He took a fence-sitting position on the question of abolition in the District of Columbia and stated flatly that he did not favor repeal of the Fugitive Slave Act.

In the debate at Freeport, a town northwest of Chicago near the Wisconsin line, Lincoln cleverly asked Douglas if, considering the Dred Scott decision, the people of a territory could exclude slavery *before* the territory became a state. Unhesitatingly Douglas replied that they could, simply by not passing the local laws essential for holding blacks in bondage. "It matters not what way the Supreme Court may hereafter decide as to the abstract question," he said. "The people have the lawful means to introduce or exclude it as they please, for the reason that slavery cannot exist . . . unless it is supported by local police regulations."

This argument saved Douglas in Illinois. The Democrats carried both houses of the legislature by a narrow margin, whereas it is almost certain that if Douglas had accepted the Dred Scott decision outright, the balance would have swung to the Republicans. But the "Freeport Doctrine" cost him heavily two years later when he made his bid for the Democratic presidential nomination. "It matters not what way the Supreme Court may hereafter decide"—southern extremists would not accept a man who suggested that the Dred Scott decision could be circumvented, though in fact Douglas had only stated the obvious.

Probably Lincoln had not thought beyond the senatorial election when he asked the question; he was merely hoping to keep Douglas on the defensive and perhaps injure him in southern Illinois, where considerable proslavery sentiment existed. In any case, defeat did Lincoln no harm politically. He had more than held his own against one of the most formidable debaters in politics, and his distinctive personality and point of view had impressed themselves upon thousands of minds. Indeed, the defeat revitalized his political career.

The campaign of 1858 marked Douglas's last triumph, Lincoln's last defeat. Elsewhere the elections in the North went heavily to the Republicans. When the old Congress reconvened in December, northern-sponsored economic measures (a higher tariff, the transcontinental railroad, river and harbor improvements, a free homestead bill) were all blocked by southern votes.

Whether the South could continue to prevent the passage of this legislation in the new Congress was problematical. In early 1859 even many moderate southerners were uneasy about the future. The radicals, made panicky by Republican victories and their own failure to win in Kansas, spoke openly of secession if a Republican was elected president in 1860. Lincoln's "house divided" speech was quoted out of context, while Douglas's Freeport Doctrine added to southern woes. When Senator William H. Seward of New York spoke of an "irrepressible conflict" between freedom and slavery, southerners became still more alarmed.

Naturally they struck back. Led by such self-described "fire-eaters" as William L. Yancey of Alabama and Senators Jefferson Davis of Mississippi, John Slidell of Louisiana, and James H. Hammond of South Carolina, they demanded a federal slave code for the territories and talked of annexing Cuba and reviving the African slave trade. "Issues were becoming emotionalized," the historian David Herbert Donald wrote of these unhappy times. "Slogans were reducing public sentiment to stereotyped patterns; social psychology was approaching a hair-trigger instability."

John Brown's Raid

In October 1859 John Brown, the scourge of Kansas, made his second tragic contribution to the unfolding sectional drama. Gathering a group of 18 followers, white and black, he staged an attack on Harpers Ferry, Virginia, a town on the Potomac upstream from Washington. He planned to seize the federal arsenal there; arm the slaves, who he thought would flock to his side; establish a black republic in the mountains of Virginia; and then press ahead with a sort of private war against the South.

Simply by overpowering a few night watchmen, Brown and his men occupied the arsenal and a nearby rifle factory. They captured several hostages, one of them Colonel Lewis Washington, a great-grandnephew of George Washington. But no slaves came forward to join them. Federal troops commanded by Robert E. Lee soon trapped Brown's men in an engine house of the Baltimore and Ohio Railroad. After a two-day siege in which the attackers picked off ten of his men, Brown was captured.

No incident so well illustrates the role of emotion and irrationality in the sectional crisis as John Brown's raid. Over the years before his Kansas escapade, Brown had been a drifter, horse thief, and swindler, several times a bankrupt, a failure in everything he attempted. His maternal grandmother, his mother, and five aunts and uncles were certifiably insane, as were two of his own children and many collateral relatives. After his ghastly Pottawatomie murders it should have been obvious to anyone that he was mad: some of the victims were hacked to bits. Yet numbers of supposedly high-minded northerners, including Emerson and Thoreau, had supported him and his antislavery "work" after 1856. Some—including Franklin B. Sanborn, a teacher; Thomas Wentworth Higginson, a clergyman; and the merchant George L. Stearns—contributed directly and knowingly to his Harpers Ferry enterpise. After Brown's capture, Emerson, in an essay on "Courage," called him a martyr who would "make the gallows as glorious as the cross."

Many southerners reacted to Harpers Ferry with an equal irrationality, some with a rage similar to Brown's. Dozens of hapless northerners in the southern states were arrested, beaten, or driven

The image of John Brown as martyr was memorialized in art as well as in song and story. Here is a sentimental interpretation, The Last Moments of John Brown, *painted in 1884 by American genre artist Thomas Hovenden.*

off. One, falsely suspected of being an accomplice of Brown, was lynched.

Brown's fate lay in the hands of the Virginia authorities. Ignoring his obvious derangement, they charged him with treason, conspiracy, and murder. He was speedily convicted and sentenced to death by hanging.

Yet "Old Brown" had still one more contribution to make to the developing sectional tragedy. Despite the furor he had created, cool heads everywhere called for calm and denounced his attack. Most leading Republican politicians repudiated him and tried to reassure the South that they would never condone the use of violence against slavery. Even execution would probably not have made a martyr of Brown had he behaved like a madman after his capture. Instead, an enormous dignity descended upon him as he lay in his Virginia jail awaiting death. "If it is deemed necessary that I should forfeit my life for the furtherance of the ends of justice, and mingle my blood further with the blood of . . . millions in this slave country whose rights are disregarded by wicked, cruel, and unjust enactments," he said before the judge pronounced sentence, "I say, let it be done."

This John Brown, with his patriarchal beard and sad eyes, so apparently incompatible with the bloody terrorist of Pottawatomie and Harpers Ferry, led thousands in the North to ignore his past and their own better judgment and treat him as a martyr—thus a saint. Thoreau compared his execution to Christ's crucifixion.

And so a megalomaniac became to the North a hero and to the South a symbol of northern ruthlessness. The historian C. Vann Woodward put it this way: "Paranoia continued to induce counter-paranoia, each antagonist infecting the other reciprocally, until the vicious spiral ended in war." Soon, as the popular song had it, Brown's body lay "a-mouldering in the grave," and the memory of his bloody act did indeed go "marching on."

The Election of 1860

By 1860 the nation was teetering on the brink of disunion. Radicals North and South were heedlessly provoking one another. When a disgruntled North Carolinian, Hinton Rowan Helper, published *The Impending Crisis of the South* (1857), an attempt to demonstrate statistically that slavery was ruining the South's economy and corrupting its social structure, the Republicans flooded the country with an abridged edition, though they knew that southerners considered the book an appeal for social revolution. "I have always been a fervid Union man," one southerner wrote in 1859, "but I confess the [northern] endorsement of the Harpers Ferry outrage and Helper's infernal doctrine has shaken my fidelity." In February 1860 the legislature of Alabama formally resolved that the state ought to secede if a Republican was elected president.

Extremism was more evident in the South, and to any casual observer that section must have seemed the aggressor in the crisis. Yet even in demanding the reopening of the African slave trade, southern radicals believed they were defending themselves against attack. They felt surrounded by hostility. The North was growing at a much faster rate; if nothing was done, they feared, a flood of new free states would soon be able to amend the Constitution and emancipate the slaves. The decline of slavery in border states from Maryland to Missouri seemed to be bringing that day closer, and the increasing worldwide condemnation of the institution added a further psychological burden. John Brown's raid, with its threat of black insurrection, reduced them to a state of panic.

When legislatures in state after state in the South cracked down on freedom of expression, made the manumission of slaves illegal, banished free blacks, and took other steps that northerners considered blatantly provocative, the advocates of these policies believed that they were only defending the status quo. Perhaps, by seceding from the Union, the South could raise a dike against the tide of abolitionism and preserve its way of life. Secession also provided an emotional release—a way of dissipating tension by striking back at criticism.

Stephen A. Douglas was probably the last hope of avoiding a rupture between North and South, but when the Democrats met at Charleston, South Carolina, in April 1860 to choose their presidential candidate, the southern delegates would not accept him unless he promised not to disturb slavery in the territories. Indeed, they went further in their demands. The North, William L. Yancey of Alabama insisted, must accept the proposition that slavery was not merely tolerable but *right.* Of course the northerners would not go so far. "Gentlemen of the South," said Senator George E. Pugh of Ohio in replying to Yancey, "you mistake us—you mistake us! We will not do it!" When southern proposals were voted down, most of the delegates from the Deep South walked out. Without them Douglas could not obtain the required two-thirds majority, and the convention adjourned without naming a candidate.

In June the Democrats reconvened at Baltimore. Again they failed to reach agreement. The two wings then met separately, the northerners nominating Douglas, the southerners John C. Breckinridge of Kentucky, Buchanan's vice-president. On the question of slavery in the territories, the northerners promised to "abide by the decision of the Supreme Court," which meant, in effect, that they stood for Douglas's Freeport Doctrine. The southerners announced their belief that neither Congress nor any territorial government could prevent citizens from settling "*with their property*" in any territory.

Meanwhile the Republicans, meeting in Chicago in mid-May, had drafted a platform attractive to all classes and all sections of the northern and western states. For manufacturers they proposed a high tariff, for farmers a homestead law providing free land for settlers. Internal improvements "of a National character," notably a railroad to the Pacific, should receive federal aid. No restrictions should be placed on immigration. As to slavery in the territories, the Republicans did not equivocate: "The normal condition of all the territory of the United States is that of freedom." Neither Congress nor

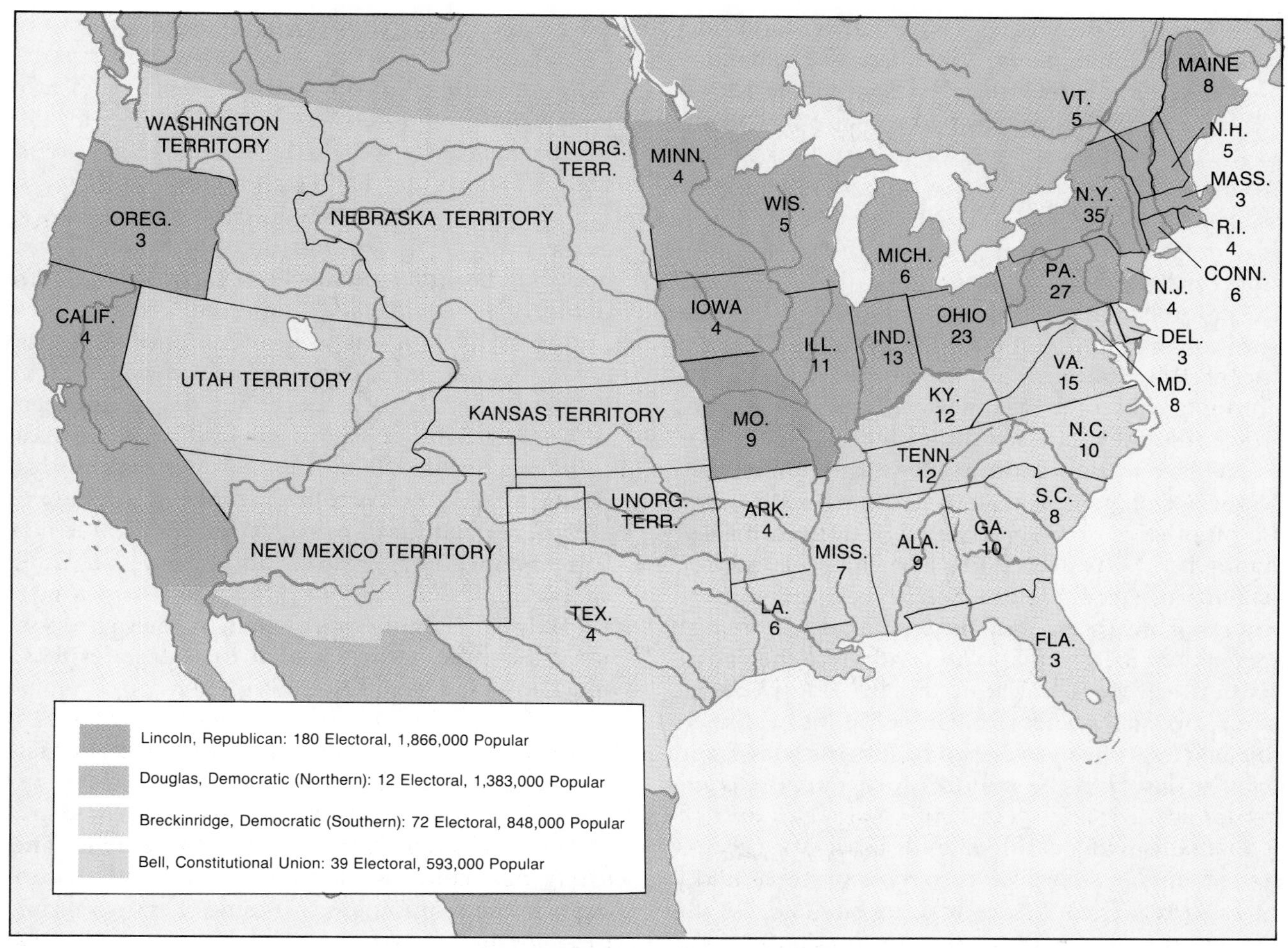

THE ELECTION OF 1860

a local legislature could "give legal existence to Slavery in any Territory."

In choosing a presidential candidate the convention displayed equally shrewd political judgment. Seward was the front-runner, but he had taken too extreme a stand and appeared unlikely to carry the crucial states Pennsylvania, Ohio, and Illinois. He led on the first ballot but could not get a majority. Then the delegates began to look closely at Abraham Lincoln. His thoughtful and moderate views on the main issue of the times attracted many, and so did his political personality. "Honest Abe," the "Railsplitter," a man of humble origins (born in a log cabin), self-educated, self-made, a common man but by no means an ordinary man—the combination seemed unbeatable.

It also helped that Lincoln had an excellent team of convention managers. Taking advantage of the fact that the convention was meeting in Lincoln's home state, they packed the gallery with leather-lunged ward heelers assigned the task of shouting for their man. They also made a series of deals with the leaders of other state delegations to win additional votes. "I authorize no bargains and will be bound by none," Lincoln telegraphed the convention. "Lincoln ain't here and don't know what we have to meet," one of his managers remarked—and proceeded to trade off two cabinet posts for the votes of key states. On the second ballot Lincoln drew shoulder to shoulder with Seward, on the third he was within two votes of victory. Before the roll could be called again, delegates began to switch their votes, and in a landslide, soon made unanimous, Lincoln was nominated.

A few days earlier the remnants of the Know-Nothing and Whig parties had formed the Constitutional Union party and nominated John Bell of Tennessee for president. "It is both the part of patriotism and of duty," they resolved, "to recognize no political principle other than the Constitution of the country, the union of the states, and the enforcement of the laws." Ostrichlike, the Constitutional Unionists ignored the conflicts rending the nation. Only in the border states, where the consequences of disunion were sure to be most tragic, did they have any following.

With four candidates in the field, no one could win a popular majority, but it soon became clear that Lincoln was going to be elected. Breckinridge had most of the slave states in his pocket and Bell would run strong in the border regions, but the populous northern and western states had a large majority of the electoral vote, and there the choice lay between the Republicans and the Douglas Democrats. In such a contest the Republicans, with their attractive economic program and their strong stand against slavery in the territories, were sure to come out on top.

Lincoln avoided campaigning and made no public statements. Douglas, recognizing the certainty of Lincoln's victory, accepted his fate and for the first time in his career rose above ambition. "We must try to save the Union," he said. "I will go South." Everywhere, even in the heart of the Cotton Kingdom, he appealed to the voters to stand by the Union whoever was elected. He was the only candidate to do so; the others refused to remind the voters that their election might result in secession and civil war.

When the votes were counted, Lincoln had 1,866,000, almost a million fewer than the combined total of his three opponents, but he swept the North and West, which gave him 180 electoral votes and the presidency. Douglas received 1,383,000 votes, so distributed that he carried only Missouri and part of New Jersey. Breckinridge, with 848,000 popular votes, won most of the South; Bell, with 593,000, carried Virginia, Tennessee, and Kentucky. Lincoln was thus a minority president, but his title to the office was unquestionable. Even if his opponents could have combined their *popular* votes in each state, Lincoln would have won.

The Secession Crisis

A few days after Lincoln's victory, the South Carolina legislature ordered an election of delegates to a convention to decide the state's future course. On December 20 the convention voted unanimously to secede, basing its action on the logic of Calhoun. "The State of South Carolina has *resumed* her position among the nations of the world," the delegates announced.

By February 1, 1861 the six other states of the Lower South had followed suit. A week later, at Montgomery, Alabama, a provisional government of the Confederate States of America was established. Virginia, Tennessee, North Carolina, and Arkansas did not leave the Union but announced that if the federal government attempted to use force against the new Confederacy, they too would secede.

Why were southerners willing to wreck the Union their grandfathers had put together with so much love and labor? No simple explanation is possible. The danger that the expanding North would overwhelm them was for neither today nor tomorrow. Lincoln had assured them that he would respect slavery where it existed. He had even offered to support a constitutional amendment to that effect. The Democrats had retained control of Congress in the election; the Supreme Court was firmly in their hands as well. If the North *did* try to destroy slavery, *then* secession was perhaps a logical tactic, but why wait until the threat materialized? To leave the Union meant abandoning the very objectives for which the South had been contending for over a decade: a share of the federal territories and an enforceable fugitive slave act.

One reason why the South rejected this line of thinking was the tremendous economic energy generated in the North, which seemed to threaten the South's independence. As one southerner complained at a commercial convention in 1855:

> From the rattle with which the nurse tickles the ear of the child born in the South to the shroud which covers the cold form of the dead, everything comes from the North. We rise from between sheets made in Northern looms, and pillows of Northern feathers, to wash in basins made in the North. . . . We eat from Northern plates and dishes; our rooms are swept with Northern brooms, our gardens dug with Northern spades . . . and the very wood which feeds our

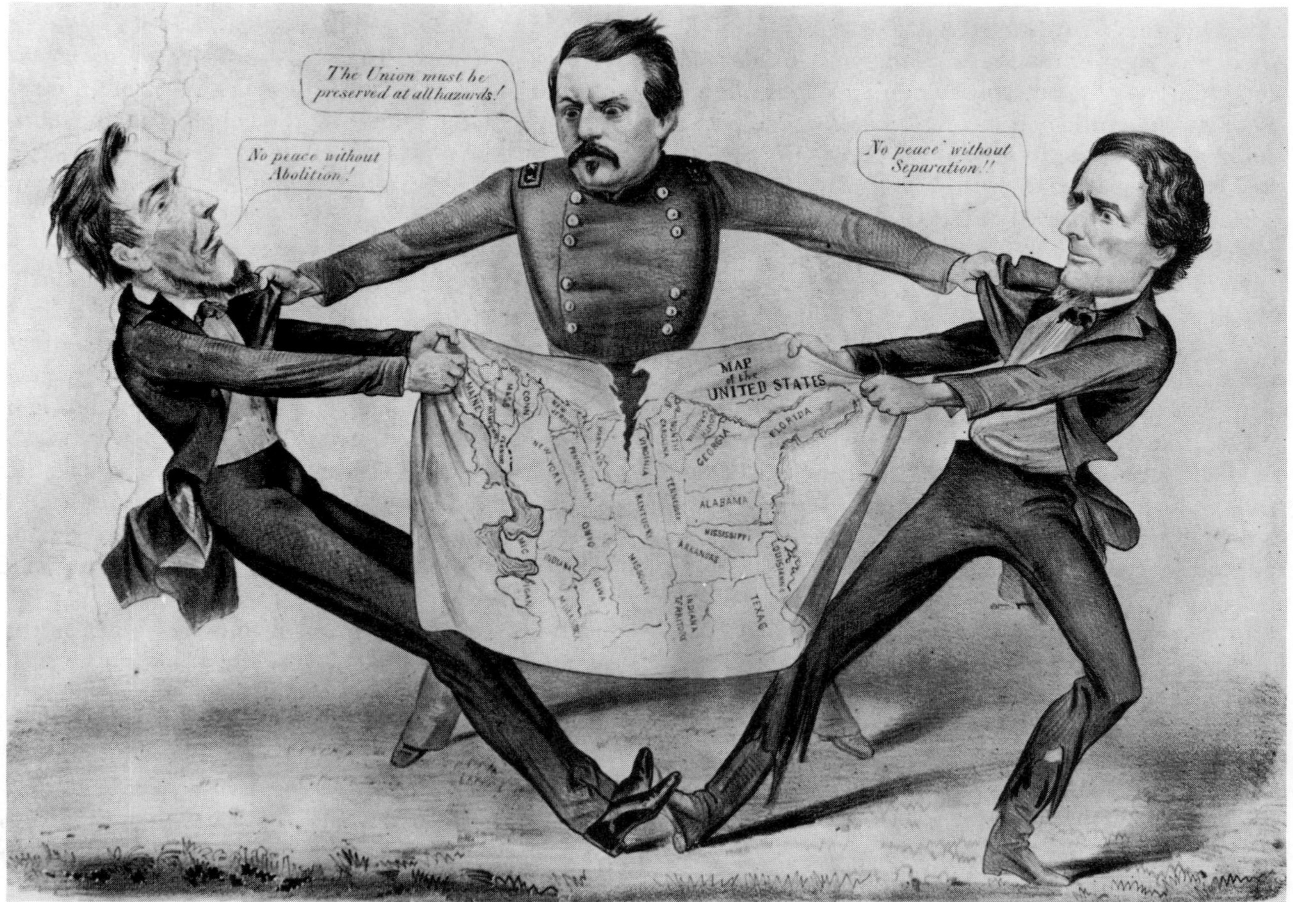

"The Union must be preserved at all hazards!" cries "General Mac" as Lincoln and Davis threaten to tear the map of the United States asunder.

fires is cut with Northern axes, helved with hickory brought from Connecticut and New York.

Secession, southerners argued, would "liberate" the South and produce the kind of balanced economy that was proving so successful in the North and so unachievable in the South. Moreover, the mere possibility of emancipation was a powerful force for secession. "We must either submit to degradation, and to the loss of property worth four billions," the Mississippi convention declared, "or we must secede."

The years of sectional conflict, the growing northern criticism of slavery, perhaps even an unconscious awareness that this criticism was well founded, had undermined and in many cases destroyed the patriotic feelings of southerners. Because of the constant clamor set up by New England antislavery groups, the South tended to identify all northerners as "Yankee abolitionists" and to resent them with increasing passion. "I look upon the whole New England race as a troublesome unquiet set of meddlers," one Georgian wrote. Moreover, a Republican president did not need the consent of Congress to flood the South with unfriendly federal officials: abolitionists and perhaps even blacks. Such a possibility most southerners found unsupportable. Fear approaching panic swept the region.

Although states' rights provided the rationale for leaving the Union, and southerners expounded the strict-constructionist interpretation of the Constitution with great ingenuity, the economic and emotional factors were far more basic. Thus the Lower South decided to go ahead with secession regardless of the cost. "Let the consequences be what they may," an Atlanta newspaper proclaimed. "Whether the Potomac is crimsoned in human gore, and Pennsylvania Avenue is paved ten fathoms in depth with mangled bodies . . . the South will never submit. . . ."

Not every slaveowner, it must be repeated, could contemplate secession with such bloodthirsty equanimity. Some believed that the risks of war and slave insurrection were too great. Others retained a profound loyalty to the United States. Many accepted secession only after the deepest examination of conscience. But almost without exception, in the end they did accept it. Lieutenant Colonel Robert E. Lee of Virginia was typical of thousands. "I see only that a fearful calamity is upon us," he wrote during the secession crisis. "There is no sacrifice I am not ready to make for the preservation of the Union save that of honour. If a disruption takes place, I shall go back in sorrow to my people & share the misery of my native state."

In the North there was a foolish but understandable reluctance to believe that the South really intended to break away permanently; in the South, an equally unrealistic expectation that the North would not resist secession forcibly. President-elect Lincoln was inclined to write off secession as a bluff designed to win concessions he was determined not to make. Lincoln also showed a lamentable political caution in refusing to announce his plans or to cooperate with the outgoing Democratic administration before taking over on March 4.

As for President Buchanan, he recognized the seriousness of the situation but professed himself powerless. Secession, he said, was illegal, but the federal government had no legal way to prevent it. He urged making concessions to the South yet lacked the forcefulness to take the situation in hand. Of course he faced unprecedented difficulties. His term was about to run out, and since he could not commit his successor, his influence was minuscule. Yet a bolder man might still have rallied the Unionists of the South by some dramatic stroke. And Buchanan ought to have denounced secession in uncompromising terms. Instead he vacillated between compromise and aimless drift. His friendly biographer, Philip Klein, has written: "Importuned, threatened, warned, begged, pushed, pulled, and shoved in every direction . . . the president at length became distraught and despaired of achieving a solution."

Appeasers, well-meaning believers in compromise, and those prepared to fight to preserve the Union were alike incapable of effective action. A group of moderates headed by Henry Clay's disciple, Senator John J. Crittenden of Kentucky, proposed a constitutional amendment in which slavery would be "recognized as existing" in all territories south of latitude 36°30′. The amendment also promised that no future amendment would tamper with the institution in the slave states and offered other guarantees to the South. But Lincoln refused to consider any arrangement that would open new territory to slavery. "On the territorial question," he wrote, "I am inflexible." The Crittenden Compromise got nowhere.

The new southern Confederacy set vigorously to work drafting a constitution, choosing Jefferson Davis as provisional president, seizing arsenals and other federal property within its boundaries, and preparing to dispatch diplomatic representatives to enlist the support of foreign powers. Buchanan bumbled helplessly in Washington. And out in Illinois, Abraham Lincoln juggled Cabinet posts and grew a beard.

SUPPLEMENTARY READING

Titles marked with an asterisk have been published in paperback.

The events leading to the Civil War have been analyzed by dozens of historians. Allan Nevins provides the fullest and most magisterial treatment in his **The Ordeal of the Union** (1947) and **The Emergence of Lincoln*** (1950). An excellent briefer summary is D. M. Potter, **The Impending Crisis*** (1976). See also W. J. Cooper, Jr., **Liberty and Slavery: Southern Politics to 1860** (1983), and Michael Holt, **The Political Crisis of the 1850s** (1978). R. F. Nichols, **The Disruption of American Democracy*** (1948), discusses the political developments of 1856–1861 exhaustively and perceptively. Eric Foner, **Free Soil, Free Labor, Free Men* (1970), is an excellent analysis of Republican ideas and policies.**

The works on the abolitionists mentioned in Chapter

10 cover the enforcement of the Fugitive Slave Act; see also Harriet Beecher Stowe, **Uncle Tom's Cabin.*** R. F. Wilson, **Crusader in Crinoline** (1941), is a satisfactory biography of Harriet Beecher Stowe. E. L. McKitrick (ed.), **Slavery Defended*** (1963), contains a typical southern review of **Uncle Tom's Cabin.** Two recent studies stress the antiblack feelings of whites in the western states and their relation to the sectional crisis: E. H. Berwanger, **The Frontier Against Slavery: Western Anti-Negro Prejudice and the Slavery Extension Controversy*** (1967), and V. J. Voegeli, **Free But Not Equal: The Midwest and the Negro During the Civil War*** (1967).

For the foreign policy of the 1850s, see Dexter Perkins, **The Monroe Doctrine: 1826–1867** (1933), D. S. Spencer, **Louis Kossuth and Young America** (1977), Basil Rauch, **American Interests in Cuba** (1948), R. F. Nichols, **Advance Agents of American Destiny** (1956), Arthur Walworth, **Black Ships Off Japan** (1946), I. D. Spencer, **The Victor and the Spoils: A Life of William L. Marcy** (1959), and P. S Klein, **President James Buchanan** (1962).

On Stephen A. Douglas, see R. W. Johannsen, **Stephen A. Douglas** (1973), and G. M. Capers's **Stephen A. Douglas*** (1959). Nevins is particularly good on the whole Kansas controversy, but see also R. F. Nichols's biography of Franklin Pierce, **Young Hickory of the Granite Hills** (1931), P. W. Gates, **Fifty Million Acres: Conflicts Over Kansas Land Policy*** (1954), H. H. Simms, **A Decade of Sectional Controversy** (1942), and J. C. Malin's **The Nebraska Question** (1953) and **John Brown and the Legend of Fifty-Six** (1942).

Sumner's role in the deepening crisis is brilliantly discussed in David Donald, **Charles Sumner and the Coming of the Civil War** (1960). Klein's life of Buchanan is careful and judicious. On the Dred Scott case, see D. E. Fehrenbacher, **The Dred Scott Case** (1978).

The best modern biographies of Lincoln are B. P. Thomas, **Abraham Lincoln** (1952), and Stephen Oates, **With Malice Toward None*** (1977). On his early career, see A. J. Beveridge, **Abraham Lincoln** (1928), and D. E. Fehrenbacher, **Prelude to Greatness*** (1962). The text of the Lincoln-Douglas debates is conveniently reprinted in R. W. Johannsen (ed.), **The Lincoln–Douglas Debates of 1858*** (1965). The best analysis of the debates is H. V. Jaffa, **Crisis of the House Divided*** (1959).

S. B. Oates, **To Purge This Land with Blood** (1970), is a good modern biography of John Brown, but Nevins's **Ordeal of the Union** provides the finest account of the raid on Harpers Ferry. C. V. Woodward's essay, "John Brown's Private War," in his **The Burden of Southern History*** (1960), is excellent on the effects of the Harpers Ferry raid. Nichols's **The Disruption of American Democracy*** describes the breakup of the Democratic party and the election of 1860. For the secession crisis and the outbreak of the Civil War, consult K. M. Stampp, **And the War Came*** (1950), D. M. Potter, **Lincoln and His Party in the Secession Crisis*** (1950), S. A. Channing, **Crisis of Fear*** (1970), and J. L. Roark, **Masters Without Slaves*** (1977).

15
The War to Save the Union

If the thing is pressed I think Lee will surrender. General Philip Sheridan *to General Ulysses S. Grant, April 6, 1865*

Let the thing be pressed. President Abraham Lincoln *to Generals Grant and Sheridan, April 7, 1865*

The nomination of Lincoln had succeeded brilliantly for the Republicans, but had his election been a good thing for the country? As the inauguration approached, many Americans had their doubts. Honest Abe was a clever politician who had spoken well about the central issue of the times, but would he act decisively in this crisis? His behavior as president-elect was not reassuring. He spent much time closeted with politicians. Was he too obtuse to understand the grave threat to the Union posed by secession? People remembered uneasily that he had never held executive office, that his congressional career had been short and undistinguished. When finally he uprooted himself from Springfield in February 1861, his occasional speeches en route to the capital were vague, almost flippant in tone. He kissed babies, shook hands, mouthed platitudes. Some thought it downright cowardly that he would let himself be spirited in the dead of night through Baltimore, where feeling against him ran high.

Cabinet Making

Everyone waited tensely to see whether Lincoln would oppose secession with force or, as many persons such as the influential Horace Greeley of the New York *Tribune* were suggesting, allow the "wayward sisters" to "depart in peace." Lincoln seemed concerned only with organizing his Cabinet. The final slate was not ready until the morning of inauguration day, and shrewd observers found it alarming, for the new president had chosen to construct a "balanced" Cabinet representing a wide range of opinion instead of putting together a group of harmonious advisers who could help him face the crisis.

William H. Seward, the secretary of state, was the ablest and best known of the appointees. Despite his reputation for radicalism, the hawk-nosed, chinless, tousle-haired Seward hoped to conciliate the South and was thus in bad odor with the radical wing of the Republican party. In time Seward proved himself Lincoln's strong right arm, but at the start he badly underestimated the president and expected to dominate him. Senator Salmon P. Chase, a bald, square-jawed antislavery leader from Ohio, whom Lincoln named secretary of the treasury, represented the radicals. Chase was humorless and vain but able; he detested Seward, agreeing with him only in thinking Lincoln a weakling. Simon Cameron of Pennsylvania, the secretary of war, was a politician of dubious integrity; Lincoln picked him to honor a deal made at the convention by his managers. Many of the president's selections worried thoughtful people.

Lincoln's inaugural address was conciliatory but firm. Southern institutions were in no danger from his administration. Secession, however, was illegal, the Union "perpetual." Federal property in the South would be held and protected. "A husband and wife may be divorced," Lincoln said, employing one of his homely and, by the Victorian standards of the day, slightly risqué metaphors, "but the different parts of our country cannot. . . . Intercourse, either amicable or hostile, must continue between them." The tone throughout was calm and warm. His concluding words catch the spirit of the inaugural perfectly:

> I am loath to close. We are not enemies, but friends. We must not be enemies. Though passion may have strained, it must not break, our bonds of affection. The mystic chords of memory, stretching from every battlefield and patriot grave to every living heart . . . will yet swell the chorus of the Union when again touched, as surely they will be, by the better angels of our nature.

Border-state moderates found the speech encouraging; so did the fiery Charles Sumner, who shared the opinion of many intellectuals that Lincoln was a dolt. The Confederates, however, read Lincoln's denial of the right of secession as justifying their decision to secede.

Fort Sumter: The First Shot

While stoutly denying the legality of secession, Lincoln had in fact taken a temporizing position. The Confederates had seized most federal property in the Deep South. Lincoln admitted frankly that he would not attempt to reclaim this property. However, two strongpoints, Fort Sumter, on an island in Charleston harbor, and Fort Pickens, at Pensacola, Florida, were still in loyal hands. Most Republicans, Lincoln included, did not want to surrender them without a show of resistance. To do so, one

ARE WE TO HAVE WAR?

Special Government Envoy Despatched to Montgomery.

The Naval and Military Preparations of the Government.

Operations at the Brooklyn, Philadelphia and Charlestown Navy Yards.

Shipments of Munitions of War on a Large Scale.

ACTIVITY AT THE TROY ARSENAL.

IMPORTANT FROM WASHINGTON.

THREATENED TROUBLE IN THE CABINET.

THE POSITION OF MR. SEWARD.

Fort Sumter Probably to be Evacuated To-Morrow.

Throughout April 1861, the New York Herald *ominously reported the events triggered by the bombardment of Fort Sumter. Lincoln based his war proclamation on an old law giving the president power to federalize state militias.*

wrote, would be to convert the American eagle into a "debilitated chicken."

Yet to reinforce the forts might mean bloodshed that would make reconciliation impossible. After weeks of indecision, Lincoln took the moderate step of sending a naval expedition to supply the beleaguered Sumter garrison with food. Unwilling to permit this, the Confederates opened fire on the fort on April 12 before the supply ships arrived. After holding out against the bombardment of shore batteries for 34 hours, Major Robert Anderson and his men surrendered.

The attack precipitated an outburst of patriotic indignation in the North. Lincoln promptly issued a call for 75,000 volunteers, and this caused Virginia, North Carolina, Arkansas, and Tennessee to secede. After years of conflict and compromise, the nation chose to settle the great quarrel between the sections by force of arms.

Southerners considered Lincoln's call for troops an act of naked aggression. When the first Union troops tried to pass through Baltimore in mid-April, they were attacked by a mob. The pro-southern chief of police telegraphed the Maryland state's attorney: "Streets red with blood. Send . . . for the riflemen to come, without delay. Fresh hordes will be down on us to-morrow." The chief and the mayor of Baltimore then ordered the railroad bridges connecting Baltimore with the northern states destroyed. Order was not restored until a large Union force commanded by a tough-minded politician soldier, Benjamin F. Butler, occupied key points in the city. The southerners were seeking to exercise what a later generation would call the right of self-determination. How, they asked, could the North square its professed belief in democratic free choice with its refusal to permit the southern states to leave the Union peaceably when a majority of their citizens wished to do so?

Lincoln took the position that secession was a *rejection* of democracy. If the South could refuse to abide by the result of an election in which it had freely participated, then everything that monarchists and other conservatives had said about the instability of republican governments would be proved true. "The central idea of secession is the essence of anarchy," he said. The United States must "demonstrate to the world" that "when ballots have been fairly and constitutionally decided, there can be no successful appeal except to ballots themselves, at succeeding elections."

This was the proper ground for Lincoln to take, both morally and politically. A war against slavery would not have been in keeping with his many pronouncements, and it would not have been supported by a majority of the people. Slavery was the root cause of secession but not of the North's determination to resist secession, which resulted from the people's commitment to the Union. Although abolition was to be one of the major results of the Civil War, the war was fought for nationalistic reasons, not to destroy slavery. Lincoln made this plain beyond argument when he wrote in response to an editorial by Horace Greeley urging immediate emancipation: "I would save the Union. . . . If I could save the Union without freeing *any* slave, I would do it; and if I could save it by freeing *all* the slaves, I would do it; and if I could do it by freeing some and leaving others alone, I would also do that." He added, however, "I intend no modification of my oft-expressed *personal* wish that all men, everywhere, could be free."

The Blue and the Gray

In any test between the United States and the 11 states of the Confederacy, the former possessed tremendous advantages. There were more than 20 million people in the northern states (excluding Kentucky and Missouri, where opinion was divided) but only 9 million in the South of whom about 3.5 million were slaves the whites hesitated to trust with arms. The North's economic capacity to wage war was even more preponderant, for it had seven times as much manufacturing and a far larger and more efficient railroad system than the South. Northern control of the merchant marine and the navy made possible a blockade of the Confederacy, a particularly potent threat to a region so dependent on foreign markets.

The Confederates discounted these advantages. Many doubted that public opinion in the North would sustain Lincoln if he attempted to meet secession with force. Northern manufacturers needed southern markets, and merchants depended heavily on southern business. Many western farmers were still sending their produce down the Mississippi. War would threaten the prosperity of all these groups, southerners maintained. Should the North try to cut Europe off from southern cotton, the powers, particularly Great Britain, would descend upon the land in their might, force open southern ports, and provide the Confederacy with the means of defending itself forever. "You do not dare to make war on cotton," Senator Hammond of South Carolina had taunted his northern colleagues in 1858. "No power on earth dares to make war upon it. Cotton is king."

The Confederacy also counted on certain military advantages. The new nation need only hold what it had; it could fight a defensive war, less costly in men and material and of great importance in maintaining morale and winning outside sympathy. Southerners would be defending not only their social institutions but their homes and families.

To some extent the South benefited from superior military leadership. Both armies relied on West Pointers for their top commanders. Since most professionals followed the decisions of their home states when the war broke out, about 300 West Pointers became northern officers, about 180 southern. Among officers of lesser rank, the southerners probably excelled in the first years of the struggle, for the military tradition was strong in the South, and many young men had attended military academies. Luck played a part too; the Confederacy quickly found a great commander, while the highest-ranking northern generals in the early stages of the war proved either bungling or indecisive. In battle after battle Union armies were defeated by forces equal or inferior in size. There was little to distinguish the enlisted men of the two sides. After reading thousands of letters written by Union and Confederate soldiers, the historian Bell I. Wiley concluded that if they were all tossed in the air and identifying marks removed, "it would be impossible to know which were written by Rebs, which by Yanks." Since northern and southern common soldiers were so much alike, superior generalship clearly made some difference.

Both sides faced massive difficulties in organizing for a war long feared but never properly anticipated. After southern defections, the regular army consisted of only 13,000 officers and men, far too few to absorb the 186,000 who had joined the colors by early summer. Recruiting was left to the

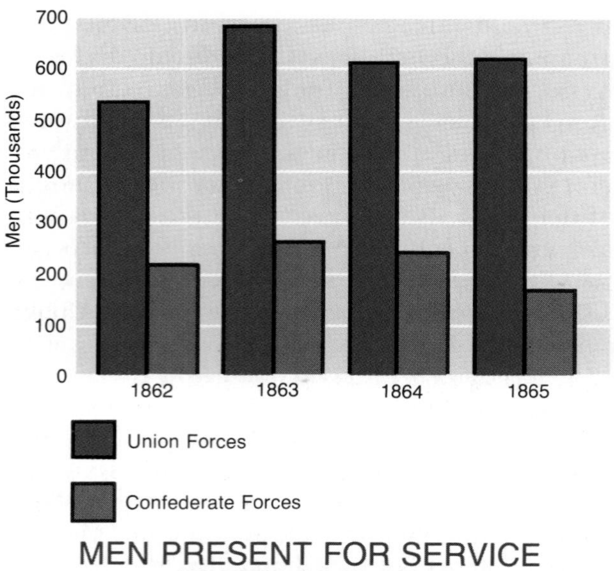

MEN PRESENT FOR SERVICE IN THE CIVIL WAR

states, each being assigned a quota; there was little central organization. Natty companies of "Fire Zouaves" and "Garibaldi Guards" in gorgeous uniforms rubbed shoulders with slovenly units composed of toughs and criminals and with regiments of farm boys from Iowa, Illinois, and Michigan. Few knew even the rudiments of soldiering. The hastily composed high command, headed by the elderly Winfield Scott, debated grand strategy endlessly while regimental commanders lacked decent maps of Virginia.

The Union mustered its military, economic, and administrative resources slowly because it had had little experience with war, none with civil war. The Whig prejudice against powerful presidents was part of Lincoln's political heritage; consequently he did not display the firmness of a Jackson or a Polk in his dealings with Congress and his Cabinet. He replaced nearly all the Democratic civil servants he could, but he failed to develop an efficient team of advisers. Fortunately, in the early stages of the war Congress proved to be cooperative. Douglas, while critical of Lincoln before the attack on Sumter, devoted all his energies to rallying the Democrats as soon as war broke out. His death in June 1861 was a great loss to the country.

Lincoln proved capable of handling heavy responsibilities. His strength lay in his ability to think problems through, to accept their implications, and then to act unflinchingly. Anything but a tyrant by nature, he boldly exceeded the conventional limits of presidential power in the emergency, expanding the army without congressional authorization, suspending the writ of habeas corpus, even emancipating the slaves when he thought military necessity demanded that action. He displayed a remarkable patience and depth of character: he would willingly accept snubs and insults from lesser men in order to advance the cause. He kept a close check on every aspect of the war effort, yet he found time for thought too. His young secretary John Nicolay reported seeing him sit sometimes for a whole hour like "a petrified image," lost in contemplation.

Gradually Lincoln's stock rose—first with men like Seward who saw him close up and experienced both his steel and his gentleness, then with the people at large, who sensed his compassion, his humility, his wisdom. He was only 52 when he became president, and already people were calling him Old Abe. Before long they would call him Father Abraham.

The Confederacy faced far greater problems than the North, for it had to create an entire administration under pressure of war, with the additional handicap of the states' rights philosophy to which it was committed. The Confederate Constitution explicitly recognized the sovereignty of the states and contained no broad authorization for laws designed to advance the general welfare. State governments repeatedly defied the central administration, located at Richmond after Virginia seceded, even with regard to military affairs.

Of course the Confederacy made heavy use of the precedents and administrative machinery taken over from the United States. The government quickly decided that all federal laws would remain in force until specifically repealed, and many former federal officials continued to perform their duties under the new auspices.

The call to arms produced a turnout in the Confederacy perhaps even more impressive than that in the North; by July 1861 about 112,000 men were under arms. As in the North, men of every type enlisted and morale was high. Ordinary militia companies sporting names like Tallapoosa Thrashers, Cherokee Lincoln Killers, and Chickasaw Desperadoes marched in step with troops of "character, blood, and social position" bearing names like

Richmond Howitzers and Louisiana Zouaves. (A "Zouave" mania swept both North and South, prospective soldiers evidently considering the broad sashes and baggy red breeches the embodiment of military splendor.)

President Jefferson Davis represented the best type of southern slaveowner. A graduate of West Point, he was a fine soldier and a successful planter, noted for his humane treatment of his slaves. In politics he had pursued a somewhat unusual course. While senator from Mississippi, he opposed the Compromise of 1850 and became a leader of the southern radicals. After Pierce made him secretary of war, however, he took a more nationalistic position, one close to that of Douglas. Davis supported the transcontinental railroad idea and spoke in favor of the annexation of Cuba and other Caribbean areas. He rejected Douglas's position during the Kansas controversy but tried to close the breach that Kansas had opened in Democratic ranks. In the crisis after the 1860 election he supported secession only reluctantly, preferring to give Lincoln a chance to prove that he meant the South no harm.

Jefferson Davis sat for this portrait in 1863 in his mansion in Richmond. It is the only wartime portrait from life of the Confederate president.

Davis was courageous, industrious, and intelligent, but he was rather too reserved and opinionated to make either a good politician or a popular leader. As president he devoted too much time to details and failed to delegate authority. He fancied himself a military expert because of his West Point training and his Mexican War service, often neglecting pressing administrative problems to concentrate on devising strategy. Unfortunately for the South, he was a mediocre military thinker. Unlike Lincoln, he quarreled frequently with his subordinates, held grudges, and allowed personal feelings to distort his judgment. "He was abnormally sensitive to disapprobation," his wife admitted. "He felt how much he was misunderstood, and the sense of mortification and injustice gave him a repellent manner." Ordinary southerners respected him for his devotion to the Confederacy, but few could feel for him the affection that Lincoln inspired.

The Test of Battle: Bull Run

As summer approached, the two nations prepared for battle, full of pride, enthusiasm, and ignorance. The tragic confrontation was beginning. "Forward to Richmond!" "On to Washington!" Such shouts propelled the troops into battle long before they were properly trained. On July 21, at Manassas Junction, Virginia, some 20 miles below Washington, on a branch of the Potomac called Bull Run, 30,000 men under General Irwin McDowell attacked a roughly equal force of Confederates commanded by the "Napoleon of the South," Pierre G. T. Beauregard. McDowell swept back the Confederate left flank. Victory seemed sure. Then a Virginia brigade under Thomas J. Jackson rushed to the field by rail from the Shenandoah Valley in the nick of time, held doggedly to a key hill, and the advance was checked. (A South Carolina general, seeking to rally his own men, pointed to the hill and shouted: "Look, there is Jackson with his Virginians, standing like a stone wall against the enemy." Thus "Stonewall" Jackson received his nickname.)

The southerners then counterattacked, driving the Union soldiers back. As often happens with green troops, retreat quickly turned to rout. McDowell's men fled toward the defenses of Washington, abandoning their weapons, stumbling through lines of supply wagons, trampling foolish sightseers

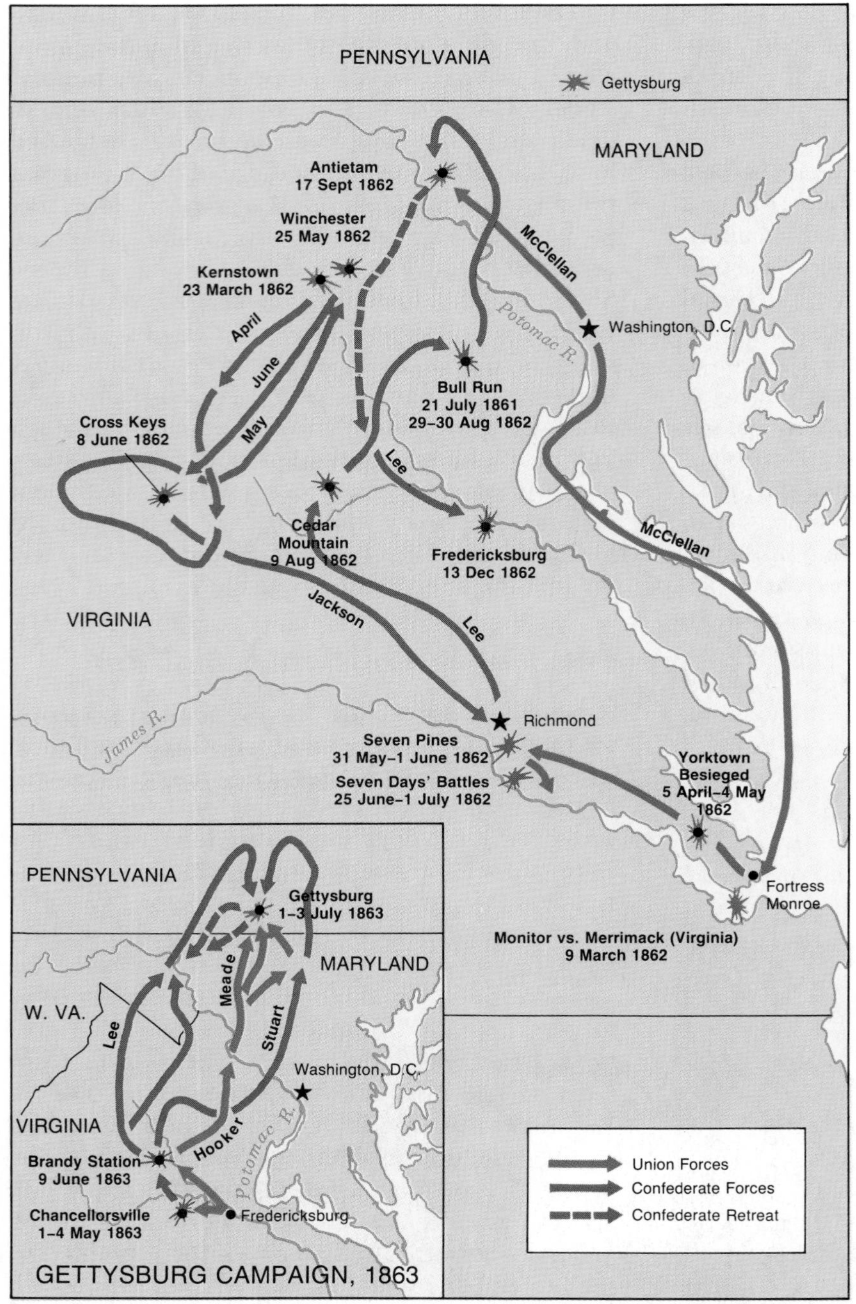

WAR IN THE EAST, 1861–1863

After the first battle at Bull Run, in July of 1861, there was little action until the following spring, when McClellan launched his Peninsula campaign. The battle of Antietam was the culmination of the fighting in the summer of 1862. Gettysburg, in July of 1863, marked the turning point of the war; after it the South never again tried to invade the North.

who had come out to watch the battle. Panic engulfed Washington and Richmond exulted, both sides expecting the northern capital to fall within hours.

The inexperienced southern troops were too disorganized to follow up their victory. Casualties on both sides were light, and the battle had little direct effect on anything but morale. Southern confidence soared, while the North began to realize how immense the task of subduing the Confederacy would be.

After Bull Run, Lincoln devised a broader, more systematic strategy for winning the war. The navy would clamp a tight blockade on all southern ports. In the West operations designed to gain control of the Mississippi would be undertaken. Most important, a new army would be mustered at Washington to invade Virginia. Congress promptly authorized the enlistment of 500,000 three-year volunteers. To lead this army and—after General Scott's retirement in November—to command the Union forces, Lincoln appointed a 34-year-old major general, George B. McClellan.

McClellan was the North's first military hero. Units under his command had driven the Confederates from the pro-Union western counties of Virginia, clearing the way for the admission of West Virginia as a separate state. The fighting had been on a small scale, but McClellan, an incurable romanticizer and something of an egomaniac, managed to inflate its importance. "You have annihilated two armies," he proclaimed in a widely publicized message to his troops. Few Americans noticed that this "annihilation claimed only about 250 lives."

Despite his penchant for self-glorification, McClellan had solid qualifications for command. One was experience. After graduation from West Point in 1846, he had served in the Mexican War. During the Crimean War he spent a year in the field, talking with British officers and studying fortifications. McClellan had a fine military bearing, a flair for the dramatic, the ability to inspire troops. He was a talented administrator and organizer. He had a sublime faith in his own destiny. He liked to concoct bold plans; dreamed of striking swiftly at the heart of the Confederacy to capture Richmond, Nashville, even New Orleans. Yet he was sensible enough to insist on massive logistical support, thorough training for the troops, iron discipline, and meticulous staff work before making a move.

A hasty pencil sketch by an unknown artist captures the panic that swept the Union ranks after the defeat at Bull Run. The scene is the main road leading through Centerville to Washington.

Paying for the War

After Bull Run, this policy was exactly right. By the fall of the year a real army was taking shape along the Potomac: disciplined, confident, adequately supplied. Northern shops and factories were producing guns, ammunition, wagons, uniforms, shoes, and the countless other supplies needed to fight a great war. Most manufacturers operated on a small scale, but with the armed forces soon wearing out 3 million pairs of shoes and 1.5 million uniforms a year, and with men leaving their jobs by the hundreds of thousands to fight, the tendency of industry to mechanize and to increase the size of the average manufacturing unit became ever more pronounced.

At the beginning of the war Secretary of the Treasury Salmon P. Chase, inexperienced in monetary matters, greatly underestimated the financial needs of the government and the probable duration of the conflict. He failed to ask Congress for enough money to fight the war properly. In August 1861 Congress passed an income tax law (3 percent on incomes over $800, later raised to a top of 10 percent on incomes over $10,000) and assessed a direct tax on the states. Loans amounting to $140 million were authorized. As the war dragged on and expenses mounted, new excise taxes on every imaginable product and service were passed, and still further borrowing was necessary. In 1863 the banking system was overhauled.

During the war the federal government borrowed a total of $2.2 billion and collected $667 million in taxes. These unprecedentedly large sums proved inadequate. Some obligations were met by printing paper money unredeemable in coin. About $431 million in "greenbacks"—the term distinguished this fiat money from the redeemable yellowback bills—were issued during the course of the war.

Printing-press money roused heated emotions; some considered it plain fraud, others a necessary way of mobilizing the national wealth in an emergency. From the modern point of view the latter position seems correct. Public confidence in all paper money vacillated with each change in the fortunes of the Union armies. Whenever the war seemed to be going badly, citizens rushed to convert this paper money into gold. Long before the first greenbacks were issued, the banks had been forced to suspend specie payments on their notes—a fortunate thing because it enabled them to ease their lending policies and thus to finance necessary industrial expansion.

On balance, the heavy emphasis on borrowing and currency inflation was expensive but not irresponsible. In a country still chiefly agricultural, people had relatively low cash incomes and therefore could not easily bear a heavy tax load. Many Americans considered it reasonable to expect future generations to pay part of the dollar cost of saving the Union when theirs was contributing so heavily in labor and blood.

Politics as Usual

Partisan politics was altered by the war but not suspended. The secession of the southern states left the Republicans with large majorities in both houses of Congress. Most Democrats supported measures necessary for the conduct of the war but objected to the way the Lincoln administration was conducting it. The sharpest conflicts came when slavery and race relations were under discussion, the Democrats adopting a conservative stance and the Republicans dividing into Moderate and Radical wings. Political divisions on economic issues such as tariffs and land policy tended to cut across party lines and—so far as the Republicans were concerned—to bear little relation to slavery and race.

As the war progressed, the Radical faction became increasingly influential. In 1861 the most prominent Radical senator was Charles Sumner, finally recovered from his caning by Preston Brooks and brimful of hatred for slaveholders. In the House, Thaddeus Stevens of Pennsylvania was the rising power. Sumner and Stevens represented the extreme left wing on all questions relating to slaves; they insisted not merely on abolition but on granting full political and civil rights to blacks. Moderate Republicans objected vehemently to treating blacks as equals and opposed making abolition a war aim, and even many of the so-called Radicals disagreed with Sumner and Stevens on race relations. Senator Benjamin Wade of Ohio, for example, was a lifelong opponent of slavery, yet he had convinced himself that blacks (he habitually called them "niggers") had a distinctive and unpleasant smell. He considered the common white prejudice against blacks perfectly understandable. But prejudice, he maintained, gave no one the right "to do injustice to anybody"; he insisted that blacks were at least as intelligent as whites and were entitled not merely to freedom but to full political equality.

At the other end of the political spectrum stood the so-called Peace Democrats. These "Copperheads" (apparently the reference was not to the poisonous snake but to an earlier time when some hard-money Democrats wore copper pennies around their necks) opposed all measures in support of the war and organized secret societies, such as the Knights of the Golden Circle, in an effort to win control of Congress and force a negotiated peace. Few were actually disloyal, but their activities at a time when thousands of men were risking their lives in battle infuriated many northerners.

Lincoln treated dissenters with a curious mixture of repression and tolerance. He suspended the writ of habeas corpus in critical areas and applied martial law freely. Over 13,000 persons were arrested and held without trial, many, as it later turned out, unjustly. The president argued that the government dared not stand on ceremony in a national emergency. His object, he insisted, was not to punish but to *prevent.* Arbitrary arrests were not made for purely political purposes, and elections were held in complete freedom throughout the war.

The federal courts compiled an admirable record in defending civil liberties, though when in conflict with the military, they could not enforce their decrees. In *Ex parte Merryman* (1861) Chief Justice Taney held General George Cadwalader in contempt for failing to produce a prisoner for trial when ordered to do so, but Cadwalader went unpunished and the prisoner continued to languish behind bars. After the war, in *Ex parte Milligan* (1866), the Supreme Court declared illegal the military trials of civilians in areas where the regular courts were functioning, but by that time the question was of only academic interest.

The most notorious domestic foe of the administration was the Peace Democrat Congressman Clement L. Vallandigham of Ohio. There were two rebellions in progress, Vallandigham claimed, "the Secessionist Rebellion" and "the Abolitionist Rebellion." "I am against both," he added. In 1863, after he had made a speech urging that the war be ended by negotiation, Vallandigham was seized by the military and thrown into jail. Of course his followers protested indignantly. Lincoln ordered him released and banished to the Confederacy. Once at liberty Vallandigham moved to Canada, from which refuge he ran unsuccessfully for governor of Ohio.

Vallandigham was a zealot who "chose to ignore expediency," as his biographer put it. "Perish offices," he once said, "perish life itself, but do the thing that is right." In 1864 he returned to Ohio. Although he campaigned against Lincoln in the presidential election, he was not molested. As the historian David Herbert Donald has written, Lincoln was not a dictator. Throughout the conflict, "the harshness of war regulations was often tempered by leniency."

Behind Confederate Lines

The South also revised its strategy after Bull Run. While it might have been wiser to risk everything on a bold invasion of the North, President Davis relied primarily on a strong defense to wear down the Union's will to fight. When volunteering slackened in 1862, the Confederate Congress passed a conscription act that contained many glaring inequities. It permitted the hiring of substitutes and exempted many classes of people (including college professors and mail carriers) whose work could hardly have been deemed essential. A provision deferring the owners of 20 or more slaves led many to grumble about "a rich man's war and a poor man's fight." In Alabama alone, nearly 1,500 planters were exempted from military service.

Although the Confederacy did not develop a two-party system, there was plenty of internal political strife. Davis made enemies easily, and his tenure was marked by bickering and needless argument. The widespread southern devotion to states' rights and individual liberty (for white men) caused endless trouble, especially when Davis found it necessary to suspend the writ of habeas corpus under certain circumstances. Throughout the war conflicts were continually erupting between Davis and southern governors jealous of their prerogatives as heads of "sovereign" states.

Finance was the Confederacy's most vexing problem. The blockade made it impossible to raise money through tariffs. The Confederate Congress

The Confederate commerce raider Nashville *(left) is towed into port by two smaller steamers. The northern navy began the war with far too few warships to effectively blockade the 3,500-mile southern coastline.*

passed an income tax together with many excise taxes, but the most effective levy was a tax in kind, amounting to one-tenth of each farmer's production. The South borrowed as much as it could ($712 million), even mortgaging cotton undeliverable because of the blockade in order to gain European credits. But it relied mainly on printing paper currency; over $1.5 billion poured from the presses during the war. Considering the amount issued, this currency held its value well until late in the war, when the military fortunes of the Confederacy began to decline. Then the bottom fell out, and by early 1865 the Confederate dollar was worth less than 2 cents in gold.

Because of the shortage of manufacturing facilities, the task of outfitting the army strained southern resources to the limit. Large supplies of small arms (some 600,000 weapons during the entire war) came from Europe through the blockade, along with other valuable materiel. As the blockade became more efficient, however, it became increasingly difficult to obtain European goods. The Confederates did manage to build a number of munitions plants, and they captured huge amounts of northern arms. No battle was lost because of a lack of guns or other military equipment, though shortages of shoes and uniforms handicapped the Confederate forces on some occasions.

Foreign policy loomed large in Confederate thinking, for the "cotton is king" theory presupposed that the great powers would break any northern blockade to get cotton for their textile mills. Southern expectations were not realized, however. The European nations would have been delighted to see the United States broken up, but none was prepared to support the Confederacy directly. The attitude of Great Britain was decisive. The cutting off of cotton did not hit the British as hard as the South had hoped. They had a large supply on hand when the war broke out, and when that was exhausted, alternative sources in India and Egypt took up part of the slack. Furthermore, British crop failures necessitated the importation of large amounts of northern wheat, providing a powerful reason for not antagonizing the United States. The fact that the mass of ordinary people in Great Britain favored the North was also of great importance in determining British policy.

Nevertheless the Civil War hurt the British economy, and the government gave serious thought to recognizing the Confederacy. Had it done so, the result would almost certainly have been war with the United States, and in that event the South might well have won its independence.

Several times the two nations came to the brink of war. In November 1861 the American warship *San Jacinto* stopped a British vessel, the *Trent,* on the high seas and forcibly arrested two Confederate envoys, James M. Mason and John Slidell, who were en route to London. This violation of international law would probably have led to war had not Lincoln decided to turn the southerners loose. In 1862 two powerful cruisers, the *Florida* and the *Alabama,* were built for the Confederates in English shipyards under the most transparent of subterfuges. Despite American protests, they were permitted to put to sea and were soon wreaking havoc among northern merchant ships. When two ironclad "rams" were also built in Britain for the Confederates, the United States made it clear that it would declare war if they were delivered. The British government then confiscated the vessels, avoiding a showdown.

The northern cause was aided by the brilliant diplomacy of Charles Francis Adams, the son of John Quincy, who served as American minister in London throughout the conflict. In the last analysis, however, the military situation determined British policy; once the North obtained a clear superiority on the battlefield, the possibility of intervention vanished.

War in the West: Shiloh

Northern superiority was achieved slowly and at enormous cost. After Bull Run no heavy fighting took place until early 1862. Then, while McClellan continued his deliberate preparations to attack Richmond, Union forces in the West, led by a shabby, cigar-smoking West Pointer named Ulysses S. Grant, invaded Tennessee from a base at Cairo, Illinois. Making effective use of armored gunboats, Grant captured forts Henry and Donelson, strongpoints on the Tennessee and Cumberland rivers in northern Tennessee, taking 14,000 prisoners. Next he marched toward Corinth, Mississippi, an important railroad junction.

To check Grant's invasion the Confederates massed 40,000 men under Albert Sidney Johnston. On April 6, while Grant slowly concentrated his forces, Johnston struck suddenly at Shiloh, 20 miles north of Corinth. Some Union soldiers were caught half-dressed, others in the midst of brewing their morning coffee. A few died in their blankets. "We

As war damage to roads and bridges worsened, military units had to improvise repairs. Here a train of three covered wagons, laden with ammunition, prepares to cross a makeshift pontoon bridge.

were more than surprised," one Illinois officer later admitted. "We were astonished." However, Grant's men stood their ground. At the end of a day of ghastly carnage the Confederates held the advantage, but fresh Union troops under General Don Carlos Buell poured in during the night, and in the course of the second day of battle the tide turned. The Confederates fell back toward Corinth, exhausted and demoralized.

Grant was too shaken by the unexpected attack and too appalled by his huge losses to apply the coup de grace; he allowed the enemy to escape. This cost him the fine reputation he had won in capturing Fort Henry and Fort Donelson. He was relieved of his command and his battle-tested army was broken up, its strength dissipated in a series of uncoordinated campaigns. Although Corinth eventually fell and New Orleans was captured by a naval force under the command of Captain David Farragut, Vicksburg, key to control of the Mississippi, remained firmly in Confederate hands. A great opportunity had been lost.

Shiloh had other results. The staggering casualties shook the confidence of both belligerents. More Americans fell there in two days than in all the battles of the Revolution, the War of 1812, and the Mexican War combined. Union losses exceeded 13,000 out of 63,000 engaged; the Confederates lost 10,699, including General Johnston. The generals began to reconsider their tactics and to experiment with field fortifications and other defensive measures. And the people, North and South, stopped thinking of the war as a romantic test of courage and military guile.

McClellan, the Reluctant Warrior

In Virginia, General McClellan, after unaccountable delays, was finally moving against Richmond. Instead of trying to advance across the difficult terrain of northern Virginia, he transported his army by water to the tip of the peninsula formed by the York and James rivers in order to attack Richmond from the southeast. After the famous battle (March 9, 1862) between U.S.S. *Monitor* and the Confederate *Merrimack,* the first fight in history between armored warships, control of these waters was securely in northern hands.

While McClellan's plan alarmed many congressmen because it seemed to leave Washington relatively unprotected, it simplified the problem of keeping the army supplied in hostile country. But McClellan now displayed the weaknesses that eventually ruined his career. To him the Civil War was not a mighty struggle over fundamental beliefs but a sort of complex game that generals played at a leisurely pace and for limited stakes. He believed it more important to capture Richmond than to destroy the army protecting it. With their capital in northern hands, surely the southerners (outwitted and outmaneuvered by a brilliant general) would abandon the contest in gentlemanly fashion and agree to return to the Union. The idea of crushing the South seemed to him wrongheaded and uncivilized.

Beyond this, McClellan was temperamentally unsuited for a position of so much responsibility. Beneath the swagger and the charm he was a profoundly insecure man. He talked like Napoleon, but he did not like to fight. Repeatedly he called for more men; when he got them, he demanded still more. He knew how to get ready, but he was never ready in his own mind. What was said of another Union general would have better been said of McClellan: he was "watching the enemy as fast as he can."

McClellan began the Peninsula campaign in mid-March. Proceeding deliberately, he floated an army of 112,000 men down the Potomac and by May 14 had established a base at White House Landing, less than 25 miles from Richmond. A swift thrust might have ended the war quickly, but McClellan delayed, despite the fact that he had 80,000 men in striking position and large reserves. As he pushed forward slowly, the Confederates caught part of his force separated from the main body by the rain-swollen Chickahominy River and attacked. The Battle of Seven Pines was indecisive yet resulted in more than 10,000 casualties.

At Seven Pines the Confederate commander, General Joseph E. Johnston, was severely wounded; leadership of the Army of Northern Virginia then fell to Robert E. Lee. Although a reluctant supporter of secession, Lee was a superb soldier. During the Mexican War his gallantry under fire inspired the most lavish praise from hardened professionals. General Scott called him the bravest

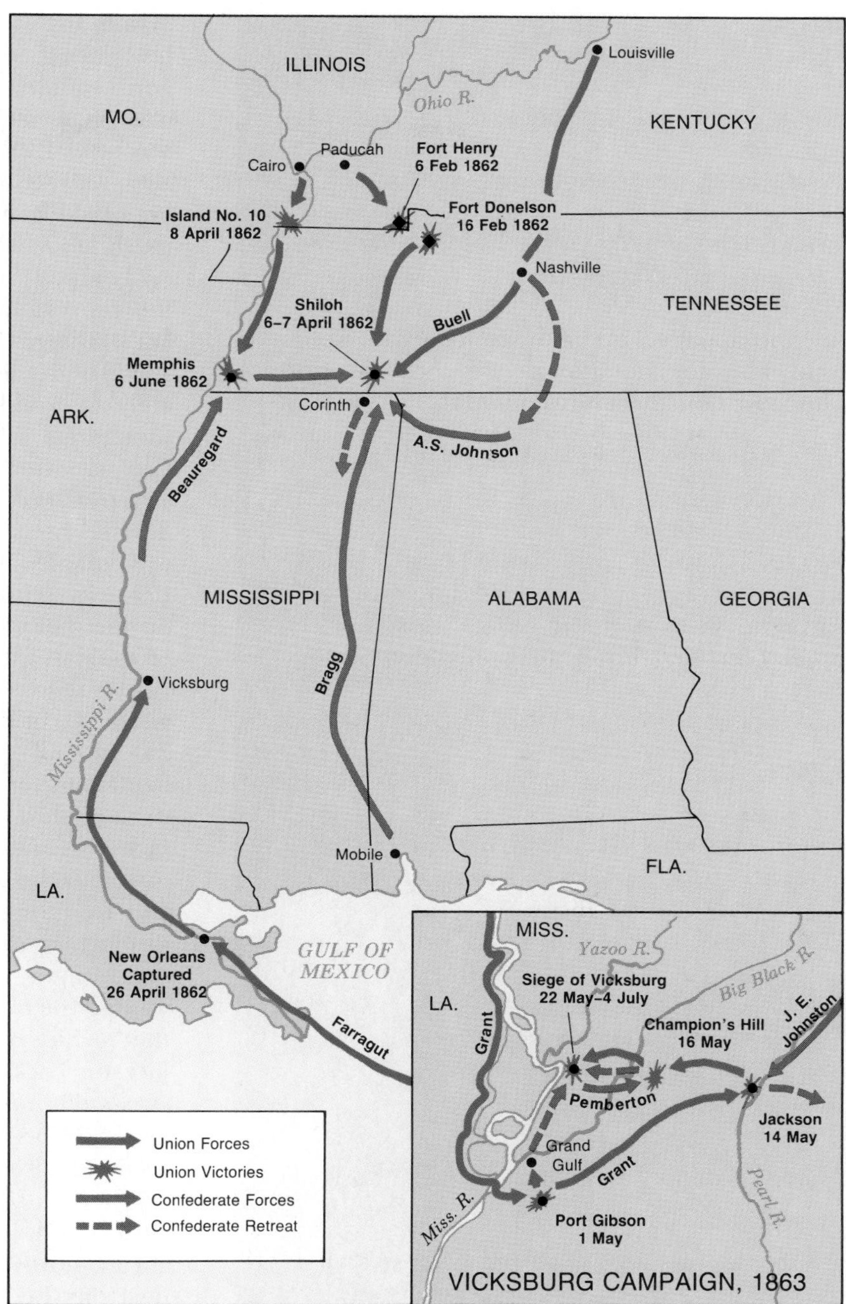

WAR IN THE WEST, 1862–1863

The bloody battle at Shiloh in April of 1862 left Vicksburg, and thus control of the Mississippi, in Southern hands. It was not until Vicksburg fell to the Union troops more than a year later—on July 4, 1863—that the river was open to the free passage of Federal forces.

Lee in 1863, by Julian Vannerson. "So great is my confidence in General Lee," Stonewall Jackson remarked, "that I am willing to follow him blind-folded."

man in the army; another officer rhapsodized over his "daring reconnaissances pushed up to the cannon's mouth." He displayed an almost instinctive mastery of tactics. Admiral Raphael Semmes, who accompanied Scott's army on the march to Mexico City, recalled in 1851 that Lee "seemed to receive impressions intuitively, which it cost other men much labor to acquire."

Lee was the antithesis of McClellan, being gentle, courtly, tactful, and entirely without McClellan's swagger and vainglorious belief that he was a man of destiny. McClellan seemed almost deliberately to avoid understanding his foes, acting as though every southern general was an Alexander. Lee, a master psychologist on the battlefield, cleverly took the measure of each Union general and devised his tactics accordingly. Where McClellan was complex, egotistical, perhaps even unbalanced, Lee was a man of almost perfect character. Yet on the battlefield Lee's boldness skirted the edge of foolhardiness.

To relieve the pressure on Richmond, Lee devised a brilliant maneuver, sending General "Stonewall" Jackson, soon to be his most trusted lieutenant, on a diversionary raid in the Shenandoah Valley, west of Richmond and Washington. Jackson struck hard and swiftly at scattered Union forces in the region, winning a number of battles and capturing vast stores of equipment. Lincoln dispatched 20,000 reserves to the Shenandoah to check him—to the dismay of McClellan, who wanted the troops to move against Richmond from the north. But after Seven Pines, Lee ordered Jackson back to Richmond. While Union armies streamed toward the valley, Jackson slipped stealthily between them. On June 25 he reached Ashland, directly north of the Confederate capital.

Before that date McClellan had possessed a clear numerical superiority yet had only inched ahead; now the advantage lay with Lee. The very next day Lee launched a massive surprise attack. For seven days the battle raged. Lee's plan was brilliant but too complicated for an army yet untested: the full weight of his force never hit the northern army at any one time. Nevertheless the shock was formidable. McClellan, who excelled in defense, fell back, his lines intact, exacting a fearful toll. Under difficult conditions he managed to transfer his troops to a new base on the James River at Harrison's Landing, where the guns of the navy could shield his position. Again the loss of life was terrible: northern casualties totaled 15,800, those of the South nearly 20,000.

Lee Counterattacks: Antietam

McClellan was still within striking distance of Richmond, in an impregnable position with secure supply lines and 86,000 soldiers ready to resume the battle. Lee had absorbed heavy losses without winning any significant advantage. Yet Lincoln was exasperated with McClellan for having surrendered the initiative and, after much deliberation, reduced his authority by placing him under General Henry W. Halleck. Halleck called off the Peninsula campaign and ordered McClellan to move his army from the James to the Potomac, near Washington. He was to join General John Pope, who was gathering a new army between Washington and Richmond.

For the president to have lost confidence in McClellan was understandable. Nevertheless, to allow Halleck to pull back the troops was a bad mistake. Had the federal army poised at Harrison's Landing made any agressive thrust, Lee would not have dared to move from the defenses of Richmond. When it withdrew, Lee seized the initiative. With typical decisiveness and daring, he marched rapidly north against Pope. Late in August, after some complex maneuvering, the Confederates drove Pope's confused troops from the field. It was the same ground, Bull Run, where the first major engagement of the war had been fought.

Thirteen months had passed since the first failure at Bull Run, and despite the expenditure of thousands of lives and millions of dollars the Union army stood as far from Richmond as ever. Dismayed by Pope's incompetence, Lincoln turned in desperation back to McClellan. When his secretary protested that McClellan had expressed contempt for the president, Lincoln replied gently: "We must use what tools we have."

While McClellan was regrouping the shaken Union Army, Lee once again took the offensive. He realized that no number of individual southern triumphs could destroy the enormous material advantages of the North. Unless some dramatic blow, delivered on northern soil, persuaded the people of the United States that military victory was impossible, the South would surely be crushed in the long run by the weight of superior resources. Lee therefore marched rapidly northwest around the defenses of Washington (see map, page 428).

Acting with even more than his usual boldness, Lee divided his army of 60,000 into a number of units. One, under Stonewall Jackson, descended upon weakly defended Harpers Ferry, capturing more than 11,000 prisoners. Another pressed as far north as Hagerstown, Maryland, nearly to the Pennsylvania line. McClellan pursued with his usual deliberation until a captured dispatch revealed to him Lee's dispositions. Then he acted more swiftly, forcing Lee to stand and fight on September 17 at Sharpsburg, Maryland, between the Potomac and Antietam Creek.* On a field that offered Lee no room to maneuver, 70,000 Union soldiers clashed with 40,000 Confederates. When darkness fell, more than 22,000 lay dead or wounded on the bloody field.

Although casualties were evenly divided and the Confederate lines intact, Lee's position was perilous. His men were exhausted. McClellan had not yet thrown in his reserves, and new federal units were arriving hourly. A bold northern general would have continued the fight without respite through the night. One of ordinary aggressiveness would have waited for first light and then struck with every soldier who could hold a rifle, for with the Potomac at his back, Lee could not retreat under fire without inviting disaster. McClellan, however, did nothing. For an entire day, while Lee scanned the field in futile search of some weakness in the Union lines, he held his fire. That night the Confederates slipped back across the Potomac into Virginia.

Lee's invasion had failed; his army had been badly mauled; the gravest threat to the Union in the war had been checked. But McClellan had let victory slip through his fingers. Soon Lee was back behind the defenses of Richmond, rebuilding his army.

Once again, this time finally, Lincoln dismissed McClellan from his command.

---

* Southerners tended to identify battles by nearby towns, northerners by bodies of water. Thus Manassas and Bull Run, Sharpsburg and Antietam, Murfreesboro and Stone's River, etc.

The "havoc effect of a 32-lb. shell" is documented by this Matthew Brady photograph. Increasingly sophisticated weapons spelled death for horses and support personnel as well as for fighting soldiers.

The Emancipation Proclamation

Antietam, though hardly the victory he had hoped for, gave Lincoln the excuse he needed to take a step that changed the character of the war. As we have seen, when the fighting started, only a few radicals wanted to free the slaves by force. The fear of alienating the border states was reason enough for not making emancipation a war aim. However, pressures to act against the South's peculiar institution mounted steadily. Slavery had divided the nation; now it was driving northerners to war within themselves. Love of country led them to fight to save the Union, but fighting roused hatreds and caused many to desire to smash the enemy. Sacrifice, pain, and grief made abolitionists of many who had no love for blacks—they sought to free the slave only to injure the master. To make abolition an object of the war might encourage the slaves to revolt.

Lincoln disclaimed this objective; nevertheless the possibility existed. Already the slaves seemed to be looking to the North for freedom: whenever Union troops invaded Confederate territory, slaves flocked into their lines. For a time Lincoln tried to check the enthusiasm of certain generals who issued proclamations freeing these slaves, but little could be done to prevent the disintegration of slavery in captured territories.

As the war progressed, the Radical faction in Congress gradually chipped away at slavery. In April 1862 they pushed through a bill abolishing it in the District of Columbia; two months later another measure outlawed it in the territories; in July a Confiscation Act "freed" all slaves owned by persons in rebellion against the United States. In fighting for these measures and in urging general emancipation, some Radicals made statements harshly critical of Lincoln; but while he carefully avoided being identified with them or with any other faction, the president was never very far from their position. He resisted emancipation because he feared it would divide the country and injure the war effort, not because he personally disapproved. Indeed, he frequently offered Radical pressure as an excuse for doing what he wished to do on his own, this being an excellent device for keeping reluctant Moderates and war Democrats in line.

Lincoln would have preferred to see slavery done away with by state law, with compensation for slaveowners and federal aid for all freedmen willing to leave the United States. He tried repeatedly to persuade the loyal slave states to adopt this policy, but without success. He moved cautiously. By the summer of 1862 he was convinced that for military reasons and to win the support of liberal opinion in Europe, the government should adopt an antislavery policy. He delayed temporarily, fearing that a statement in the face of military reverses would be taken as a sign of weakness. The "victory" at Antietam gave him his opportunity, and on September 22 he made public the Emancipation Proclamation. After January 1, 1863, it said, all slaves in areas in rebellion against the United States "shall be then, thenceforward, and forever free."

No single slave was freed directly by Lincoln's announcement, which did not apply to the border states or to those sections of the Confederacy, like New Orleans and Norfolk, Virginia, already controlled by federal troops. The Proclamation differed in philosophy, however, from the Confiscation Act in striking at the institution, not at the property of rebels. Henceforth every Union victory would speed the destruction of slavery without regard for the attitudes of individual masters.

Some of the president's advisers thought the Proclamation inexpedient and others considered it illegal. Lincoln justified it as a way to weaken the enemy. He drew on his power as commander in chief of the armed forces for the necessary authority. The Proclamation is full of phrases like "as a fit and necessary war measure" and "warranted by the Constitution upon military necessity."

Southerners considered the Proclamation an incitement to slave rebellion—as one of them put it, an "infamous attempt to incite fight, murder, and rapine . . . and convert the quiet, ignorant, dependent black son of toil into a savage incendiary and brutal murderer." Most antislavery groups approved but thought it did not go far enough. "[Lincoln] is only stopping on the edge of Niagara, to pick up a few chips," one abolitionist declared. "He and they will go over together." Foreign opinion was mixed: liberals tended to applaud, conservatives to react with alarm or contempt. "The principle is not that a human being cannot justly own another," the London *Spectator* sneered, "but that he cannot own him unless he is loyal to the United States."

As Lincoln anticipated, the Proclamation had a subtle but continuing impact in America. Its immediate effect was to aggravate racial prejudices. Millions of white Americans disapproved of slavery yet abhorred the idea of equality for blacks. David Wilmot, for example, insisted that his famous Proviso was designed to preserve the territories for whites rather than to weaken slavery, and as late as 1857 the people of Iowa rejected black suffrage by a vote of 49,000 to 8,000. To some emancipation seemed to herald an invasion of the North by blacks who would compete for jobs, drive down wages, commit crimes, spread diseases, and—eventually—destroy the "purity" of the white race. The word *miscegenation* was coined in 1863 by David G. Croly, an editor of the New York *World,* directly as a result of the Emancipation Proclamation. Its original meaning was: "The mingling of the white and black races on the continent *as a consequence of the freedom of the latter.*" Of course miscegenation in its current, more general meaning long antedated the freeing of any slave.

The Democrats spared no effort to make political capital of these fears and prejudices even before Lincoln's Emancipation Proclamation, and they made large gains in the 1862 election, especially in the Northwest. So strong was antiblack feeling that most of the Republican politicians who defended emancipation did so with racist arguments. Far from encouraging southern blacks to move north, they claimed, the ending of slavery would lead to a mass migration of northern blacks to the South.

When the Emancipation Proclamation began actually to free slaves, the government pursued a policy of "containment," that is, of keeping the ex-slaves in the South. Panicky fears of an inundation of blacks subsided in the North. Nevertheless, emancipation remained a cause of social discontent. In March 1863, volunteering having fallen off, Congress passed a conscription act. The law applied to all men between 20 and 45, but it allowed draftees to hire substitutes and even to buy exemption for $300, provisions that were patently unfair to the poor. Moreover, it represented an enormous expansion of national authority, since in effect it gave the government the power of life and death over individual citizens.

Negrophobia and the Draft Riots

After the passage of the Conscription Act, draft riots erupted in a number of cities. By far the most

The genesis of the Emancipation Proclamation seen from diametrically opposed viewpoints. The drawing above is by Adalbert Johann Volck, a Baltimore dentist and vitriolic propagandist for the Confederate cause. A satanic Lincoln, one foot on the Constitution, is inspired by a portrait of John Brown with a halo and a depiction of the alleged excesses of the Saint Domingue slave revolt of the 1790s. David Gilmour Blythe, a staunch administration supporter, left no doubt in his painting (right) that the sources of Lincoln's inspiration were of a much higher order.

serious disturbance occurred in New York City in July 1863. Many workers resented conscription in principle and were embittered by the $300 exemption fee (which represented a year's wages). The idea of being forced to risk their lives to free slaves who would then, they believed, compete with them for jobs infuriated them. On July 13 a mob attacked the office where the names of conscripts were being drawn. Most of the rioters were poor Irish laborers who resented what seemed to them the special attention blacks were suddenly receiving. For four days the city was an inferno. Public buildings,

12th MASS. BATTERY
FOR MAJ. GEN. BANKS' EXPEDITION
$138
Before You Leave the State!
75
AT THE END OF THE WAR!
Good Men are wanted for this, the most popular arm of the service. Tried officers will command.
OFFICE IN BOSTON, 11 COURT SQUARE
J. MILLER, E. M. CHAMBERLIN, C. W. WEEBER.

Volunteering for the army was advertised as a lucrative venture. A shortage of enlistees necessitated the draft, which was violently opposed in several cities.

shops, and private residences were put to the torch. What began as a protest against the draft became a campaign to exterminate blacks. Over a hundred were run down "as hounds would chase a fox" and beaten to death, some of them burned alive. It took federal troops and the temporary suspension of the draft in the city to put an end to the rioting.

The Emancipation Proclamation does not entirely account for the draft riots. The new policy neither reflected nor triggered a revolution in white thinking about the race question. Its significance was subtle but real; both the naive view that Lincoln freed the slaves on January 1, 1863, and the cynical one that his action was a meaningless propaganda trick are incorrect. Northern hostility to emancipation rose from fear of change more than from hatred of blacks, while liberal disavowals of any intention to treat blacks as equals were in large measure designed to quiet this fear. To a degree the racial backlash that the Proclamation inspired reflected the public's awareness that a change, frightening but irreversible, *had occurred.*

Most white northerners did not surrender their comforting belief in black inferiority, and Lincoln was no exception. Yet Lincoln was evolving. He talked about deporting ex-slaves to the tropics, but he did not send any there. And he began to receive black leaders in the White House and to allow black groups to hold meetings on the grounds.

Many other Americans were changing too. The brutality of the New York riots horrified many white citizens. Over $40,000 was swiftly raised to aid the victims, and some conservatives were so appalled by the Irish rioters that they began to talk of giving blacks the vote. The influential *Atlantic Monthly* commented: "It is impossible to name any standard . . . that will give a vote to the Celt and exclude the negro."

A revolutionary shift occurred in white thinking about using black men as soldiers. Although they had fought in the Revolution and in the Battle of New Orleans during the War of 1812, a law of 1792 barred blacks from the army. During the early stages of the rebellion, despite the eagerness of thousands of free blacks to enlist, the prohibition remained in force. By 1862, however, the need for manpower was creating pressure for change. In August Secretary of War Edwin M. Stanton, who had replaced the incompetent Simon Cameron, authorized the military government of the captured South Carolina sea islands to enlist slaves in the area. In January 1863 Stanton allowed the governor of Massachusetts to organize a black regiment, the famous Massachusetts 54th. Swiftly thereafter other states began to recruit black soldiers, and in May 1863 the federal government established a Bureau of Colored Troops to supervise their enlistment. By the end of the war one soldier in eight in the Union army was black.

Black soldiers were segregated and commanded by white officers. For example, the Massachusetts 54th regiment was commanded by Colonel Robert Gould Shaw of Boston, called by one admirer "the very type and flower of the Anglo-Saxon race." At first black soldiers received only $7 a month,

One company from a black regiment, formed after 1863, at Fort Lincoln, Virginia.

about half what white soldiers were paid. But they soon proved themselves in battle; 38,000 were killed, a rate of loss about 40 percent higher than that among white troops. Their bravery under fire convinced thousands of white soldiers that blacks were not by nature childish or cowardly. Even southerners were impressed. The Confederates threatened to kill or enslave black soldier-prisoners, but they almost never did. Fear of reprisals undoubtedly restrained them. So did the grudging respect that southern soldiers had to yield to men taken while charging fixed positions under fire and otherwise demonstrating their courage.

To blacks, both slave and free, the Emancipation Proclamation served as a beacon. Even if it failed immediately to liberate one slave or to lift the burdens of prejudice from one black back, it stood as a promise of future improvement. "I took the proclamation for a little more than it purported," Frederick Douglass recalled in his autobiography, "and saw in its spirit a life and power far beyond its letter." Lincoln was by modern standards a racist, but his most militant black contemporaries respected him deeply. The *Anglo-African*, an uncompromising black newspaper (the position of which is revealed in an 1862 editorial that asked: "Poor, chicken-hearted, semi-barbarous Caucasians, when will you learn that 'the earth was made for MAN?' "), referred in 1864 to Lincoln's "many noble acts" and urged his reelection. Douglass said of him: "Lincoln was not . . . either our man or our model. In his interests, in his association, in his habits of thought and in his prejudices, he was a white man." On the other hand, he spoke of Abraham Lincoln as "one whom I could love, honor, and trust without reserve or doubt."

As for the slaves of the South, after January 1, 1863, whenever the "Army of Freedom" approached, they laid down their plows and hoes and stole away in droves. "We-all knows about it," one black confided to a northern clergyman early in 1863. "Only we darsen't let on. We *pretends* not to know." Such behavior came as a shock to the owners. "[Those] who loved us best—as we thought—were the first to leave us," one planter mourned. Talk of slave "ingratitude" increased. Instead of referring to their workers as "servants" or "my black family," many owners began to describe them as "slaves" or "niggers."

Antietam to Gettysburg

It was well that Lincoln seized upon Antietam to release the Proclamation; had he waited for a more impressive victory, he would have waited nearly a year. To replace McClellan, he chose General Ambrose E. Burnside, best known to history for his magnificent side-whiskers, ever after called sideburns. Burnside, a West Pointer, had compiled a good record as a corps commander, but he lacked the self-confidence essential to anyone who takes responsibility for major decisions. He knew his limitations and tried to avoid high command, but patriotism and his sense of duty compelled him, when pressed, to accept leadership of the Army of the Potomac. He prepared to march on Richmond.

Unlike McClellan, Burnside was aggressive—too aggressive. He planned to ford the Rappahannock at Fredericksburg. Supply problems and bad weather delayed him until mid-December, giving Lee time to concentrate his army in impregnable positions behind the town. Although he had more than 120,000 men against Lee's 75,000, Burnside should have called off the attack when he saw Lee's advantage; instead he ordered the troops forward. Crossing the river over pontoon bridges, his divisions occupied Fredericksburg. Then, in wave after wave, they charged the Confederate defense line while Lee's artillery riddled them from nearby Marye's Heights. Watching the battle from his command post on the heights, General Lee was deeply moved. Turning to General James Longstreet, he said: "It is well that war is so terrible—we should grow too fond of it!"

On December 14, the day following this futile assault, General Burnside, tears streaming down his cheeks, ordered the evacuation of Fredericksburg. Shortly thereafter General Joseph Hooker replaced him.

Unlike Burnside, "Fighting Joe" Hooker was ill-tempered, vindictive, and devious. In naming him to command the Army of the Potomac, Lincoln sent him a letter, that was a measure of his desperation but is now famous for what it reveals of the president's character:

> I think that during Gen. Burnside's command of the Army, you have taken counsel of your ambition, and thwarted him as much as you could, in which you did a great wrong to the country. . . . I have heard, in such a way as to believe it, of your recently saying that both the Army and the Government need a Dictator. Of course it is not *for* this, but in spite of it, that I have given you the command. Only those generals who gain successes, can set up dictators. What I now ask of you is military success, and I will risk the dictatorship. . . . Beware of rashness, but with energy and sleepless vigilance, go forward, and give us victories.

Hooker proved no better than his predecessor, his failings more like McClellan's than Burnside's. By the spring of 1863 he had 125,000 men ready for action. Late in April he forded the Rappahannock and quickly concentrated at Chancellorsville, about 10 miles west of Fredericksburg. His army outnumbered the Confederates by more than two to one; he should have forced a battle at once. Instead he delayed, and while he did, Lee sent Stonewall Jackson's corps (28,000 men) across tangled countryside to a position directly athwart Hooker's unsuspecting flank. At 6 P.M. on May 2, Jackson attacked.

Completely surprised, the Union right crumbled, brigade after brigade overrun before it could wheel to meet Jackson's charge. At the first sound of firing, Lee had struck along the entire front to impede Union troop movements. If the battle had begun earlier in the day, the Confederates might have won a decisive victory; as it happened, nightfall brought a lull, and the next day the Union troops rallied and held their ground. Heavy fighting continued until May 5, when Hooker abandoned the field and retreated in good order behind the Rappahannock.

Chancellorsville cost the Confederates dearly, for their losses, in excess of 12,000, were almost as heavy as the North's and harder to replace. They also lost Stonewall Jackson, struck down by the bullets of his own men while returning from a reconnaissance. Nevertheless, the Union army had suffered another fearful blow to its morale.

Lee now took the offensive. He knew that time was still on the side of the North; to defend Richmond was not enough. Already federal troops in the West were closing in on Vicksburg, threatening to cut Confederate communications with Arkansas and Texas. Now was the time to strike, while the morale of the northern people was at low ebb. With 75,000 soldiers he crossed the Potomac again, a larger Union force dogging his right flank. By late June his army had fanned out across southern Pennsylvania in a 50-mile arc from Chambersburg to the Susquehanna. Gray-clad soldiers ranged 50 miles *northwest* of Baltimore, within 10 miles of Harrisburg (see map, page 428).

On July 1 Confederate troops looking for shoes in the town of Gettysburg clashed with a Union cavalry unit stationed there. Both sides sent out calls for reinforcements. Like iron filings drawn to a magnet, the two armies converged. The Confederates won control of the town, but the Union army, now commanded by General George G. Meade, took a strong position on Cemetery Ridge, a hook-shaped stretch of high ground just to the south. Lee's men occupied Seminary Ridge, a parallel position. On this field the fate of the Union was probably decided. For two days the Confederates attacked Cemetery Ridge, pounding it with the heaviest artillery barrage ever seen in America and sweeping bravely up its flanks in repeated assaults. General George E. Pickett's famous charge of 15,000 men actually carried the Union lines on the afternoon of July 3, but reserves drove them back before they could consolidate their position. By nightfall the Confederate armly was spent and bleeding, the Union lines unbroken.

The following day was the Fourth of July. The two weary forces rested on their arms. Had the Union army attacked in force, the Confederates might have been crushed, but just as McClellan had hesitated after Antietam, Meade let opportunity pass. On July 5 Lee retreated to safety. For the first time he had been clearly bested on the field of battle.

Ulysses S. Grant, photographed by Matthew Brady in 1863. Grant's strategies were sometimes bold but always realistic. His conquest of Vicksburg was as imaginative a campaign as the war produced, yet in Virginia in 1864–1865 he adjusted to different circumstances and fought a grinding war of attrition.

Lincoln Finds His General: Vicksburg

On that same Independence Day, far to the west, federal troops won another great victory. When General Halleck was called east in July 1862, Ulysses S. Grant reassumed command of the Union troops. Grant was one of the most controversial officers in the army. At West Point he had compiled an indifferent record, ranking 21st in a class of 39. During the Mexican War he served well, but when he was later assigned to a lonely post in Oregon, he took to drink and was forced to resign his commission. (His resignation was accepted by Jefferson Davis, who was Secretary of War in the Cabinet of Franklin Pierce.) Thereafter he was by turns a farmer, a real estate agent, and a clerk in a leather goods store. In 1861, approaching 40, he seemed well into a life of frustration and mediocrity.

The war gave him a second chance. Back in service, however, his reputation as a ne'er-do-well and his unmilitary bearing worked against him, as did the heavy casualties suffered by his troops at Shiloh. Yet the fact that he knew how to manage a large army and win battles did not escape Lincoln. When a gossip tried to poison the president against him by referring to his drinking, Lincoln remarked that if he knew what brand Grant favored, he would send a barrel of it to some of his other generals. Grant never used alcohol as a substitute for courage. "Old Ulysses," one of his soldiers said, "he don't scare worth a damn."

Grant's major aim was to capture Vicksburg,

a city of tremendous strategic importance. Together with Port Hudson, a bastion north of Baton Rouge, Louisiana, it guarded a 150-mile stretch of the Mississippi. The river between these points was inaccessible to federal gunboats. So long as Vicksburg remained in southern hands, the trans-Mississippi region could send men and supplies to the rest of the Confederacy (see map, page 435).

Vicksburg sits on a high bluff overlooking a sharp bend in the river. When it proved unapproachable from either west or north, Grant devised an audacious scheme for getting at it from the *east.* He descended the Mississippi from Memphis to a point a few miles north of the city. Then, leaving part of his force behind to create the impression that he planned to attack from the north, he crossed the west bank and slipped quickly southward. Recrossing the river below Vicksburg, he abandoned his communications and supply lines and struck at Jackson, the capital of Mississippi, In a series of swift engagements he captured Jackson, cutting off the army of General John C. Pemberton, defending Vicksburg, from other Confederate units. Turning next on Pemberton, he defeated him in two battles and drove him inside the Vicksburg fortifications. By mid-May the city was under siege. Grant applied relentless pressure, and on July 4 Pemberton surrendered. With Vicksburg in Union hands, federal gunboats could range the entire length of the Mississippi.* Texas and Arkansas were isolated, for all practical purposes lost to the Confederacy.

Lincoln had disliked Grant's plan for capturing Vicksburg. Now he generously confessed his error and placed Grant in command of all federal troops west of the Appalachians. Grant promptly took charge of the fighting around Chattanooga, where Confederate advances, beginning with the Battle of Chickamauga (September 19–20), were threatening to develop into a major disaster for the North. Shifting corps commanders and bringing up fresh units, he won another decisive victory at Chattanooga in a series of battles ending on November 25, 1863. This cleared the way for an invasion of Georgia. Suddenly this unkempt, stubby little man, who looked more like a tramp than a general, emerged as the military leader the North had been so desperately seeking. In March 1864 Lincoln summoned him to Washington, named him lieutenant general, and gave him supreme command of the armies of the United States.

* Port Hudson, isolated by Vicksburg's fall, surrendered on July 9.

Economic Effects, North and South

Though much blood would yet be spilled, by the end of 1863 the Confederacy was on the road to defeat. Northern military pressure, gradually increasing, was eroding the South's most precious resource, manpower. An ever-tightening naval blockade was reducing its economic strength. Shortages developed that, combined with the flood of currency pouring from the presses, led to a drastic inflation. By 1864 an officer's coat cost $2,000 in Confederate money, cigars sold for $10 each, butter was $25 a pound and flour $275 a barrel. The southern railroad network gradually wore out, the major lines maintaining operations only by cannibalizing less vital roads. Imported products such as coffee disappeared; salt became scarce. Efforts to increase manufacturing were only moderately successful because of the shortage of labor, capital, and technical knowledge. In general, southern prejudice against centralized authority prevented the Confederacy from making effective use of its scarce resources. Even blockade-running was left in private hands until 1864. Precious cargo space that should have been reserved for medical supplies and arms was often devoted to high-priced luxuries.

In the North, after a brief depression in 1861 caused by the uncertainties of the situation and the loss of southern business, the economy boomed. Government purchases greatly stimulated certain lines of manufacturing; the railroads operated at close to capacity and with increasing efficiency; a series of bad harvests in Europe boosted agricultural prices. Congress passed a number of economic measures long desired but held up in the past by southern opposition: (1) the Homestead Act (1862) gave 160 acres to any settler who would farm the land for five years; (2) the Morrill Land Grant Act of the same year provided the states with land at the rate of 30,000 acres for each member of Congress to support state agricultural colleges; (3) various tariff acts raised the duties on manufactured goods to an average rate of 47 percent in order to protect domestic manufacturers from foreign competition; (4) the Pacific Railway Act (1862) authorized subsidies in land and money for the construction of a transcontinental railroad; (5) the National Banking Act of 1863 gave the country, at last, a uniform currency. Under this last act, banks could obtain federal charters by investing at least one-third of their capital in United States bonds. They might then issue currency up to 90 percent of the value of those bonds. A 10 percent tax on the issues of state banks drove state bank notes out of circulation.

All these laws stimulated the economy and added to public confidence. Whether the overall economic effect of the Civil War was beneficial is less clear. It was fought mostly with rifles, light cannon, horses, and wagons rather than with masses of heavy artillery, tanks, and trucks. Consequently it had much less effect than later wars on heavy industry. Although production expanded, it did so more slowly during the 1860s than in the decades preceding and following. Prices soared beginning in 1862, averaging about 80 percent over the 1860 level by the end of the war. Wages, however, did not keep pace. This condition did not make for a healthy economy—nor did the fact that there were chronic shortages of labor in many fields, shortages aggravated by a sharp drop in the number of immigrants entering the country.

The war had a demoralizing effect on many businessmen. Inflation and shortages encouraged speculation and fostered a selfish, materialistic attitude toward life. "The intense desire to buy almost any kind of securities amounted almost to insanity," one observer commented in 1862. By 1864 cotton was worth $1.90 a pound in New England. It could be had for 20 cents a pound in the South. While it was illegal to traffic in the staple across the lines, unscrupulous operators did so and made huge profits. Many contractors took advantage of wartime confusion to sell the government shoddy goods and to swindle the public in other ways.

Yet the war undoubtedly helped prepare the way for modern industrial society in the United States. It posed problems of organization and planning, both military and civilian, that challenged the talents of creative persons and thus led to a more complex and efficient economy. The mechanization of industry, the growth of large corporations, the creation of a better banking system, and the emergence of business leaders attuned to these conditions would surely have occurred in any case, for industrialization was under way long before the South seceded. Nevertheless the war greatly speeded economic change.

Grant in the Wilderness

Grant's strategy as supreme commander was simple, logical, and ruthless. He would attack Lee and try to capture Richmond. General William Tecumseh Sherman would drive from Chattanooga toward Atlanta, Georgia. Like a lobster's claw, the two armies could then close to crush all resistance. Early in May 1864 Grant and Sherman commenced operations, each with more than 100,000 men.

Grant marched the Army of the Potomac directly into the tangled wilderness area south of the Rappahannock, where Hooker had been routed a year earlier. Lee, having only 60,000 men, forced the battle in the roughest possible country, where Grant found it difficult to make efficient use of his larger force. For two days (May 5–6) the Battle of the Wilderness raged. When it was over, the North had sustained another 18,000 casualties, far more than the Confederates. But unlike his predecessor, Grant did not fall back after being checked, nor did he expose his army to the kind of devastating counterattack at which Lee was so expert. Instead he shifted his troops to the southeast, attempting to outflank the Confederates. Divining his intent, Lee rushed his divisions southeastward and disposed them behind hastily thrown up earthworks in well-placed positions around Spotsylvania Court House. Grant attacked. After five more days, which cost the Union army another 12,000 men, the Confederate lines were still intact.

Grant remained undaunted. He had grasped the fundamental truth that the war could be won only by grinding the South down beneath the weight of numbers. His own losses of men and equipment could be replaced; those of Lee could not. When critics complained of the cost, he replied doggedly that he intended to fight on in the same manner if it took all summer. Once more he pressed southeastward in an effort to outflank the enemy. At Cold Harbor, 9 miles from Richmond, he found the Confederates once more in strong defenses. At dawn on June 3 he attacked. It was a battle as

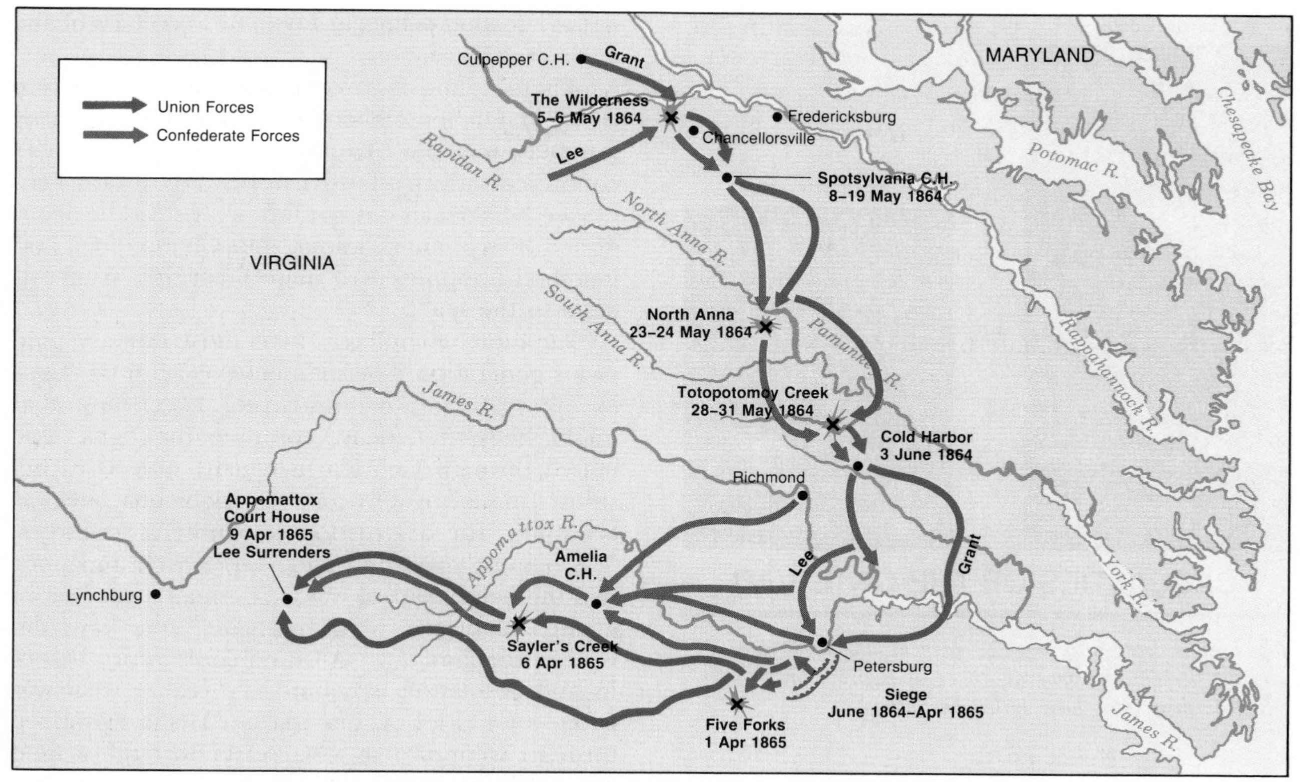

Grant's repeated and costly attempts (60,000 casualties the first month) to outflank Lee are detailed here. At Five Forks the long seige of Petersburg was broken; Richmond was evacuated. A week later, Lee surrendered.

foolish and nearly as one-sided as General Pakenham's assault on Jackson's line outside New Orleans in 1815. "At Cold Harbor," the forthright Grant confessed in his memoirs, "no advantage whatever was gained to compensate for the heavy losses we sustained."

Sixty thousand casualties in less than a month! The news sent a wave of dismay through the North. There were demands that "Butcher" Grant be removed from command. Lincoln, however, stood firm. Although the price was fearfully high, Grant was gaining his objective. At Cold Harbor, Lee had to fight without a single regiment in general reserve while Grant's army was larger than at the start of the offensive. When Grant next swung round his flank, striking south of the James River toward Petersburg, Lee had to rush his troops to that city to hold him.

As the Confederates dug in, Grant put Petersburg under siege. Soon both armies had constructed complicated lines of breastworks and trenches, running for miles in a great arc south of Petersburg, much like the fortifications that would be used so extensively in World War I in France. Methodically the Union forces extended their lines, seeking to weaken the Confederates and cut the rail connections supplying Lee's troops and the city of Richmond. Grant could not overwhelm him, but by late June, Lee was pinned to earth. Moving again would mean having to abandon Richmond—tantamount, in southern eyes, to surrender.

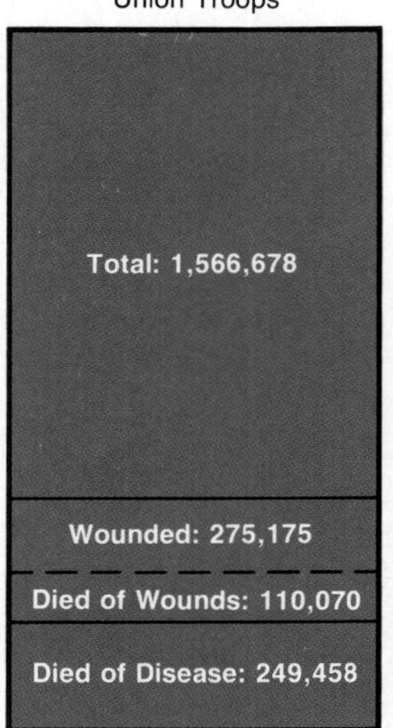

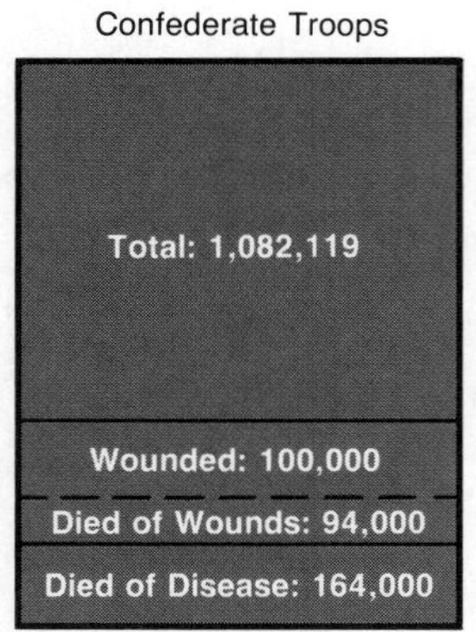

CASUALTIES OF THE CIVIL WAR

The Union death rate was 23 percent, the Confederate rate 24 percent. In general, twice as many soldiers were killed by disease as were killed by bullets.

Sherman in Georgia

The summer of 1864 saw the North submerged in pessimism. The Army of the Potomac held Lee at bay but appeared powerless to defeat him. In Georgia, General Sherman inched forward methodically against the wily Joseph E. Johnston, but when he tried a direct assault at Kennesaw Mountain on June 27, he was thrown back with heavy casualties. In July daring Confederate raiders under General Jubal Early dashed suddenly across the Potomac from the Shenandoah Valley to within 5 miles of Washington before being turned back. A draft call for 500,000 additional men did not improve the public temper. Huge losses and the absence of decisive victory were taxing the northern will to continue the fight.

In June Lincoln had been renominated on a National Union ticket, with the staunch Tennessee Unionist Andrew Johnson, a former Democrat, as his running mate. He was under attack not only from the Democrats, who nominated George B. McClellan and came out for a policy that might almost be characterized as peace at any price, but from the Radical Republicans, many of whom had wished to dump him in favor of Secretary of the Treasury Chase.

Then, almost overnight, the atmosphere changed. On September 2 General Sherman's army fought its way into Atlanta. When the Confederates countered with an offensive northward toward Tennessee,* Sherman did not follow. Instead he abandoned his communications with Chattanooga and marched unopposed through Georgia, "from Atlanta to the sea."

Far more completely than most military men of his generation, Sherman believed in total war—in appropriating or destroying everything that might help the enemy continue the fight. The march through Georgia had many objectives besides conquering territory. One obvious one was economic, the destruction of southern resources. "[We] must make old and young, rich and poor feel the hard hand of war," Sherman said. Before taking Atlanta he wrote his wife: "We have devoured the land. . . . All the people retire before us and desolation is behind. To realize what war is one should follow our tracks." His army moved through Georgia like a harvester through a field of ripe wheat. Another object of Sherman's march was psychological. "If the North can march an army right through the South," he wrote General Grant, southerners will take it "as proof positive that the North can prevail."

Sherman's victories staggered the Confederacy and the anti-Lincoln forces in the North. In November the president was easily reelected, 212 electoral votes to 21. The country was determined to carry on the struggle.

At last the South's will to resist began to crack. Sherman entered Savannah on December 22, having denuded a strip of Georgia 60 miles wide. Early in January 1865 he marched northward, leaving behind "a broad black streak of ruin and desolation—the fences all gone; lonesome smoke-stacks, surrounded by dark heaps of ashes and cinders, marking the spots where human habitations had stood." In February his troops captured Columbia, South Carolina. Soon they were in North Carolina, advancing relentlessly. In Virginia Grant's vise grew daily tighter, the Confederate lines thinner and more ragged.

* This force was crushed before Nashville in December by a Union army under General George Thomas.

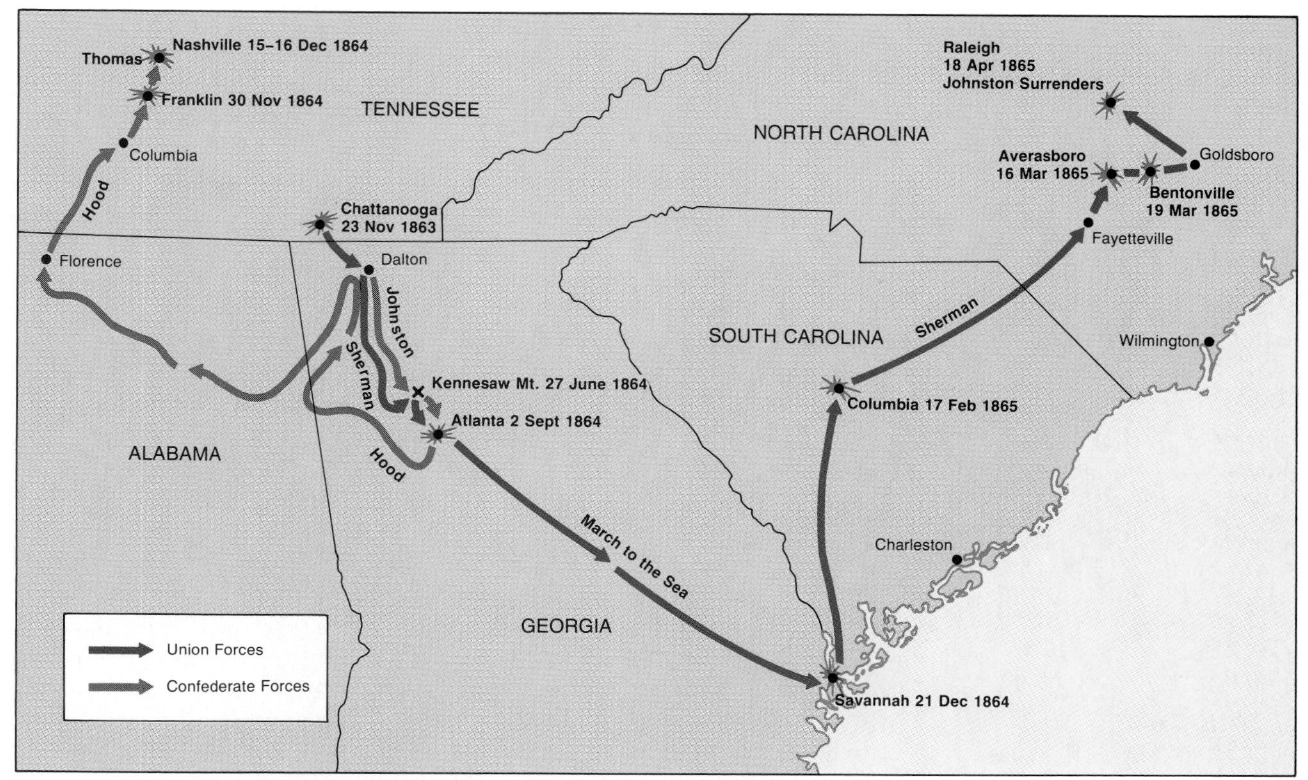

THE WAR MOVES SOUTH, 1863–1865

Confederate John B. Hood's "forlorn hope" offensive toward Nashville failed to deter Sherman from marching through Georgia. Joseph E. Johnston could offer little resistance to Sherman's drive through the Carolinas.

On March 4 Lincoln took the presidential oath and delivered his second inaugural address. Photographs taken at about this time show how four years of war had marked him. Somehow he had become both gentle and steel-tough, both haggard and inwardly calm. With victory sure, he spoke for tolerance, mercy, and reconstruction. "Let us judge not," he said after stating again his personal dislike of slavery, "that we be not judged." He urged all Americans to turn without malice to the task of mending the damage and to make a just and lasting peace between the sections.

Now the Confederate troops around Petersburg could no longer withstand the federal pressure. Desperately Lee tried to pull his forces back to the Richmond and Danville Railroad, but the swift wings of Grant's army enveloped him. Richmond fell on April 3. With fewer than 30,000 effectives to oppose Grant's 115,000, Lee recognized the futility of further resistance. On April 9 he and Grant met by prearrangement at Appomattox Court House.

It was a scene at once pathetic and inspiring. Lee was noble in defeat, Grant, despite his rough-hewn exterior, sensitive and magnanimous in victory. "I met you once before, General Lee, while we were serving in Mexico," Grant said after they had shaken hands. "I have always remembered your appearance, and I think I should have recognized you anywhere." They talked briefly of that earlier war, and then, acting upon Lincoln's instructions, with which he was in full accord, Grant outlined his terms. All that would be required was that the Confederate soldiers lay down their arms. They

This sentimental painting depicts Confederate troops furling the flag after Lee's surrender. A Federal officer wrote of the event, "On our part [there was] not a sound of trumpet . . . nor roll of drum; not a cheer . . . but an awed stillness rather. . . ."

could return to their homes in peace. When Lee hinted (he was too proud to ask outright for the concession) that his men would profit greatly if allowed to retain possession of their horses, Grant generously offered to let them do so.

Costs and Prospects

And so the war ended. It cost the nation 600,000 lives. The story of one of the lost thousands must stand for all, Union and Confederate. Jones Budbury, a tall, 19-year-old redhead, was working in a Pennsylvania textile mill when the war broke out, and he enlisted at once. His regiment first saw action at Bull Run. He took part in McClellan's Peninsula campaign. He fought at Second Bull Run, at Chancellorsville, and at Gettysburg. A few months after Gettysburg he was wounded in the foot and spent some time in an army hospital. By the spring of 1864 he had risen through the ranks to first sergeant and his hair had turned gray. In June he was captured and sent to Andersonville military prison, but he fell ill and the Confederates released him. In March 1865 he was back with his regiment in the lines besieging Richmond. On April 6, three days before Lee's surrender, Jones Budbury was killed while pursuing Confederate units near Sailor's Creek, Virginia.

The war also caused enormous property losses, especially in the Confederacy. All the human and material destruction explains the eroding hatred and bitterness that the war implanted in millions of hearts. The corruption, the gross materialism, and the selfishness generated by wartime conditions were other disagreeable by-products of the conflict. Such sores fester in any society, but the Civil War bred conditions that inflamed and multiplied them. The war produced many examples of charity, self-sacrifice, and devotion to duty as well, yet if the general moral atmosphere of the postwar generation can be said to have resulted from the experiences of 1861–1865, the effect overall was bad.

What had been obtained at this price? Slavery was dead. Paradoxically, while the war had been fought to preserve the Union, after 1865 the people tended to see the United States not as a union of states, but as a *nation.* After Appomattox, secession was almost literally inconceivable. In a strictly political sense, as Lincoln had predicted from the start, the northern victory heartened friends of republi-

The ruins of the Tredegar Iron Works in Richmond. The factory was one of the South's major manufacturing facilities before and during the war.

can government and democracy throughout the world. A better-integrated society and a more technically advanced and productive economic system also resulted from the war.

The Americans of 1865 estimated the balance between cost and profit according to their individual fortunes and prejudices. Only the wisest realized that no final accounting could be made until the people had decided what to do with the fruits of victory. That the physical damage would be repaired no one could reasonably doubt; that even the loss of human resources would be restored in short order was equally apparent. But would the nation make good use of the *opportunities* the war had made available? What would the ex-slaves do with freedom? How would whites, northern and southern, react to emancipation? To what end would the new technology and social efficiency be directed? Would the people be able to forget the recent past and fulfill the hopes for which so many brave soldiers had given their "last full measure of devotion"?

SUPPLEMENTARY READING

Titles marked with an asterisk have been published in paperback.

Allan Nevins, **Ordeal of the Union** (1947–1971), continues to be the fullest and most judicious interpretation of the period down to 1863. It excels both as an account of the fighting and as an analysis of political, social, and economic developments. J. G. Randall, **Lincoln, the President*** (1945–1955), is an excellent scholarly study; the last volume of this work was completed after Randall's death by R. N. Current. Good one-volume surveys of the period include James McPherson, **Ordeal by Fire: The Civil War and Reconstruction** (1982), and J. G. Randall and David Donald, **The Civil War and Reconstruction** (1961).

Political and constitutional problems are dealt with in J. G. Randall, **Constitutional Problems Under Lincoln** (1926). Lincoln's dealings with the Radicals have been extensively investigated. H. L. Trefousse, **The Radical Republicans: Lincoln's Vanguard for Racial Justice*** (1969), which praises Lincoln's management of the Radicals and minimizes his differences with them, is a good summary, but see also T. H. Williams, **Lincoln and the Radicals*** (1941). W. B. Hesseltine, **Lincoln and the War Governors** (1948), F. L. Klement, **The Copperheads in the Middle West** (1960), J. H. Silbey, **A Respectable Minority: The Democratic Party in the Civil War Era*** (1977), and Wood Gray, **The Hidden Civil War*** (1942), consider other aspects of the political history of the period.

For the movement to make abolition a war aim and the reaction to it, see J. M. McPherson, **The Struggle for Equality: Abolitionists and the Negro in the Civil War and Reconstruction*** (1964), G. M. Frederickson, **The Inner Civil War: Northern Intellectuals and the Crisis of the Union*** (1965), and V. J. Voegeli, **Free but Not Equal: The Midwest and the Negro During the Civil War*** (1967). The activities and attitudes of blacks during the war are summarized in D. T. Cornish, **The Sable Arm: Negro Troops in the Union Army*** (1956), Benjamin Quarles, **The Negro in the Civil War*** (1969), and B. I. Wiley, **Southern Negroes*** (1938).

For aspects of economic and social history, see P. W. Gates, **Agriculture and the Civil War** (1965), M. E. Massey, **Bonnet Brigades: American Women and the Civil War** (1966), and R. P. Sharkey, **Money, Class, and Party: An Economic Study of Civil War and Reconstruction*** (1959). E. D. Fite, **Social and Industrial Conditions in the North During the Civil War** (1910), is still useful, and so is Margaret Leech, **Reveille in Washington*** (1941).

Clement Eaton, **A History of the Southern Confederacy*** (1954), is an excellent brief account of the South during the war. E. M. Thomas, **The Confederate Nation** (1979), is a more recent treatment. The fullest biography of Jefferson Davis is Hudson Strode, **Jefferson Davis** (1955–1965). Other useful volumes on the Confederacy include C. W. Ramsdell, **Behind the Lines in the Southern Confederacy** (1944), R. W. Patrick, **Jefferson Davis and His Cabinet** (1944), and B. J. Hendrick, **Statesmen of the Lost Cause** (1939).

The voluminous literature on the military history of the Civil War can only be sampled. K. P. Williams, **Lincoln Finds a General** (1949–1952), is exhaustive and judicious. T. H. Williams, **Lincoln and His Generals*** (1952), is briefer and more lively. Bruce Catton, **The Centennial History of the Civil War** (1961–1965), is vivid and detailed, as are Catton's volumes on the war in the eastern theater, **Mr. Lincoln's Army*** (1951), **Glory Road*** (1952), and **A Stillness at Appomattox*** (1953). The famous **Battles and Leaders of the Civil War,** written during the 1880s by participants, is available in condensed form in Ned Bradford (ed.), **Battles**

and Leaders of the Civil War (1956). H. S. Commager (ed.), **The Blue and the Gray*** (1951), is an exciting collection of contemporary accounts of the fighting. R. M. Ketchum (ed.), **The American Heritage Picture History of the Civil War** (1960), is excellent. B. I. Wiley, **The Life of Billy Yank*** (1952), discusses the role of the common soldier. For the naval side of the conflict, see V. C. Jones, **The Civil War at Sea** (1960–1962), and R. S. West, Jr., **Mr. Lincoln's Navy** (1957).

For books dealing with the Confederate military effort, see Frank Vandiver, **Rebel Brass** (1956), A. B. Moore, **Conscription and Conflict in the Confederacy** (1942), D. S. Freeman, **Lee's Lieutenants** (1942–1944), and B. I. Wiley, **The Life of Johnny Reb*** (1943); see also David Donald (ed.), **Why the North Won the Civil War*** (1960).

Among the biographies of Civil War generals, northern and southern, the following are especially noteworthy: W. S. McFeely, **Grant: A Biography** (1981), W. W. Hassler, Jr., **General George B. McClellan** (1957), Lloyd Lewis, **Sherman, Fighting Prophet** (1932), D. S. Freeman, **R. E. Lee** (1934–1935), and Frank Vandiver, **Mighty Stonewall** (1957). U. S. Grant, **Personal Memoirs*** (1885–1886), should not be missed.

The diplomacy of the Civil War period is covered in H. D. Jordan and E. J. Pratt, **Europe and the American Civil War** (1931), Jay Monaghan, **Diplomat in Carpet Slippers*** (1945), E. D. Adams, **Great Britain and the American Civil War** (1925), M. B. Duberman, **Charles Francis Adams*** (1961), and F. L. Owsley, **King Cotton Diplomacy** (1931).

TIME LINE 4 ▪ The Union Disrupted and Restored, 1800–1900

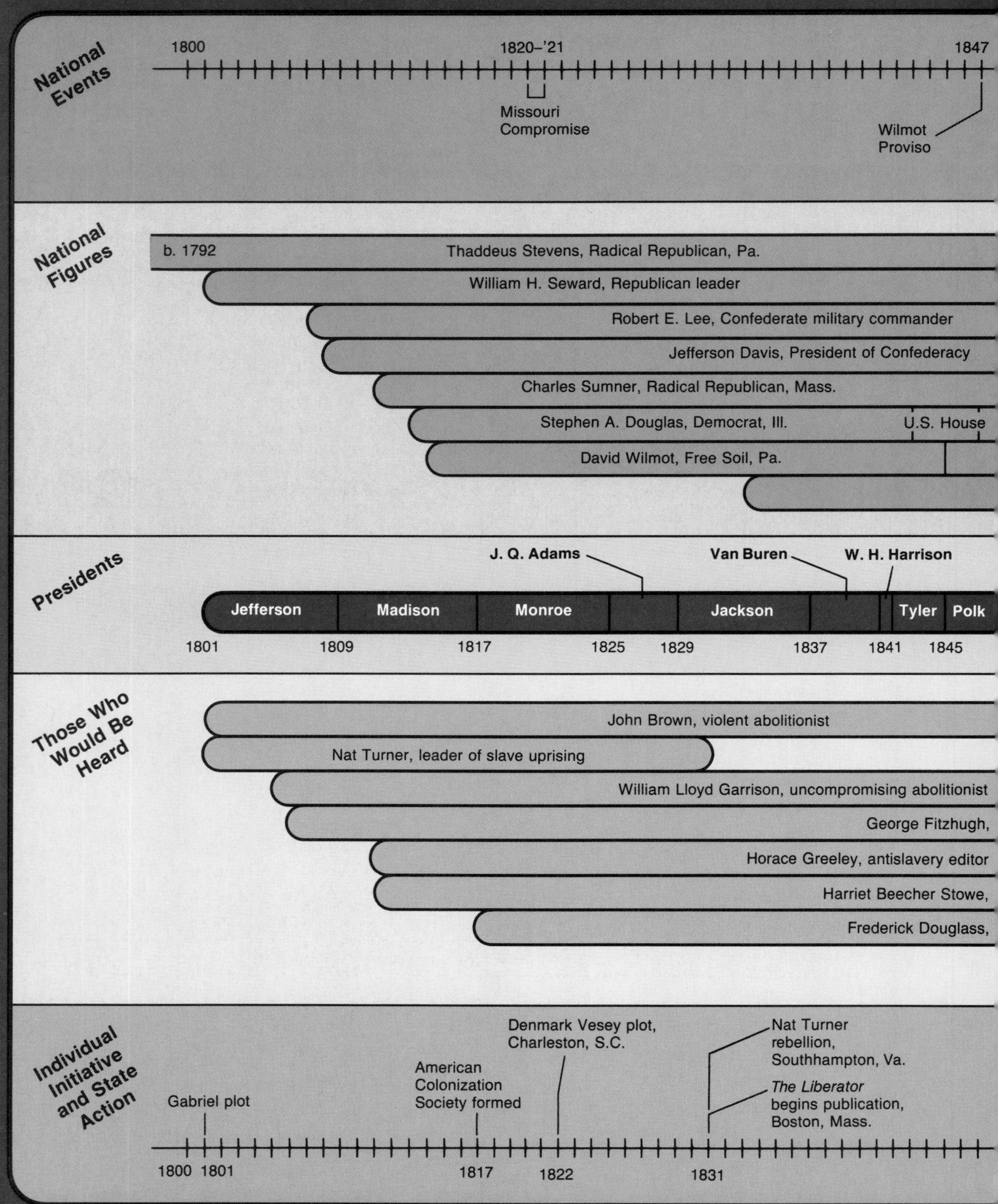

National Events
1800
1820–'21
1847
Missouri Compromise
Wilmot Proviso
National Figures
b. 1792
Thaddeus Stevens, Radical Republican, Pa.
William H. Seward, Republican leader
Robert E. Lee, Confederate military commander
Jefferson Davis, President of Confederacy
Charles Sumner, Radical Republican, Mass.
Stephen A. Douglas, Democrat, Ill.
U.S. House
David Wilmot, Free Soil, Pa.
Presidents
J. Q. Adams
Van Buren
W. H. Harrison
Jefferson
Madison
Monroe
Jackson
Tyler
Polk
1801
1809
1817
1825
1829
1837
1841
1845
Those Who Would Be Heard
John Brown, violent abolitionist
Nat Turner, leader of slave uprising
William Lloyd Garrison, uncompromising abolitionist
George Fitzhugh,
Horace Greeley, antislavery editor
Harriet Beecher Stowe,
Frederick Douglass,
Individual Initiative and State Action
Gabriel plot
American Colonization Society formed
Denmark Vesey plot, Charleston, S.C.
Nat Turner rebellion, Southhampton, Va.
The Liberator begins publication, Boston, Mass.
1800
1801
1817
1822
1831

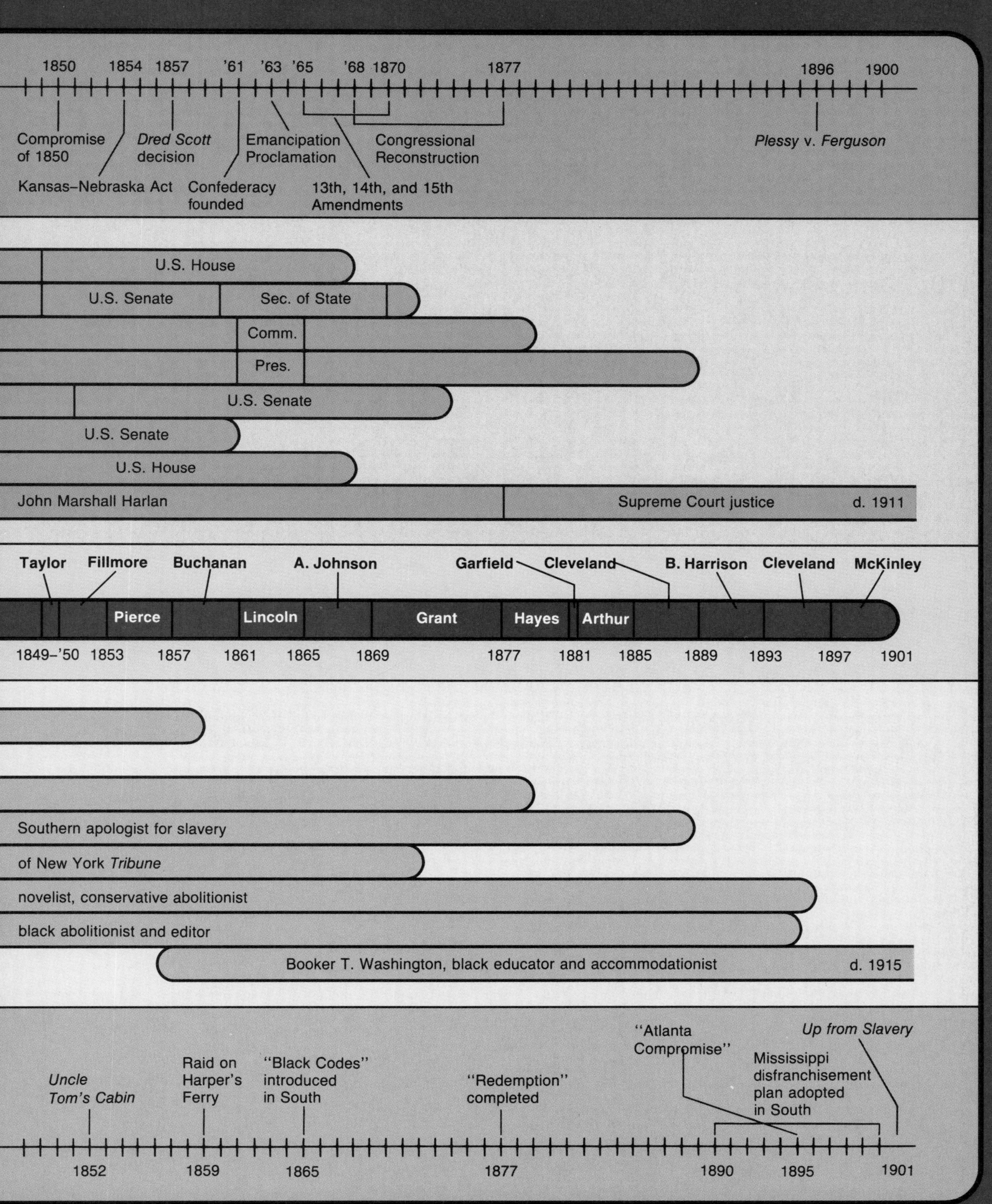

1850
1854
1857
'61
'63
'65
'68
1870
1877
1896
1900
Compromise of 1850
Dred Scott decision
Emancipation Proclamation
Congressional Reconstruction
Plessy v. Ferguson
Kansas–Nebraska Act
Confederacy founded
13th, 14th, and 15th Amendments
U.S. House
U.S. Senate
Sec. of State
Comm.
Pres.
U.S. Senate
U.S. Senate
U.S. House
John Marshall Harlan
Supreme Court justice
d. 1911
Taylor
Fillmore
Buchanan
A. Johnson
Garfield
Cleveland
B. Harrison
Cleveland
McKinley
Pierce
Lincoln
Grant
Hayes
Arthur
1849–'50
1853
1857
1861
1865
1869
1877
1881
1885
1889
1893
1897
1901
Southern apologist for slavery
of New York Tribune
novelist, conservative abolitionist
black abolitionist and editor
Booker T. Washington, black educator and accommodationist
d. 1915
"Atlanta Compromise"
Up from Slavery
Mississippi disfranchisement plan adopted in South
Uncle Tom's Cabin
Raid on Harper's Ferry
"Black Codes" introduced in South
"Redemption" completed
1852
1859
1865
1877
1890
1895
1901

16
Reconstruction and the South

No great social revolution ever took place without causing great temporary loss and inconvenience.
THE NATION, *1867*

The experiment has totally failed. THE NATION, *1871*

This is socialism. THE NATION, *1874*

Entered according to act of Congress in the year 1872 by Currier & Ives, in the Office of the Librarian of Congress at Washington.
ROBERT C. DE LARGE, M.C. of S,Carolina
JEFFERSON H. LONG, M.C. of Georgia
U.S. Senator H.R.REVELS, of Mississippi
BENJ. S. TURNER, M.C. of Alabama.
JOSIAH T. WALLS, M.C. of Florida.
JOSEPH H. RAINY, M.C. of S.Carolina.
R. BROWN ELLIOT, M.C. of S.Carolina.
THE FIRST COLORED SENATOR AND REPRESENTATIVES.
In the 41st. and 42nd. Congress of the United States.

On April 5, 1865, Abraham Lincoln visited Richmond. The fallen capital lay in ruins, sections blackened by fire, but the president was able to walk the streets unmolested and almost unattended. The townspeople seemed to have accepted defeat without resentment. A few days later, in Washington, Lincoln delivered an important speech on Reconstruction, urging compassion and open-mindedness. On April 14 he held a Cabinet meeting at which postwar readjustment was considered at length. That evening, while Lincoln was watching a performance of the play *Our American Cousin* at Ford's Theater, a half-mad actor, John Wilkes Booth, slipped into his box and shot him in the back of the head with a small pistol. Early the next morning, without having regained consciousness, Lincoln died.

The murder was part of a complicated plot organized by die-hard prosoutherners. Seldom have fanatics displayed so little understanding of their own interests, for with Lincoln perished the South's best hope for a mild peace. After his body had been taken home to Illinois, the national mood hardened. It was not a question of avenging the beloved Emancipator; rather a feeling took possession of the public mind that the time of pain and suffering was not yet over, that the awesome drama was still unfolding, that retribution and a final humbling of the South were inevitable.

Presidential Reconstruction

Despite its bloodiness, the Civil War had caused less intersectional hatred than might have been expected. Although civilian property was often seized or destroyed, the invading armies treated the southern population with remarkable forbearance, both during the war and after Appomattox. While he was ensconced in Richmond behind Lee's army, northerners boasted that they would "hang Jeff Davis to a sour apple tree," and when he was captured in Georgia in May 1865, he was at once clapped into irons preparatory to being tried for treason and murder. But feeling against Davis subsided quickly. In 1867 the military turned him over to the civil courts, which released him on bail. He was never brought to trial. A few other Confederate officials spent short periods behind bars, but the only southerner executed for war crimes was Major Henry Wirz, the commandant of Andersonville military prison.

The legal questions related to bringing the defeated states back into the Union were extremely complex. Since southerners believed that secession was legal, logic should have compelled them to argue that they were out of the Union and would thus have to be formally readmitted. Northerners should have taken the contrary position, for they had fought to prove that secession was illegal. Yet the people of both sections did just the opposite. Senator Charles Sumner and Congressman Thaddeus Stevens, in 1861 uncompromising expounders of the theory that the Union was indissoluble, now insisted that the Confederate states had "committed suicide" and should be treated like "conquered provinces." Erstwhile states' rights southerners claimed that their states were still within the Union. Lincoln believed the issue a "pernicious abstraction" and tried to ignore it.

The process of readmission began in 1862, when Lincoln appointed provisional governors for those parts of the South that had been occupied by federal troops. On December 8, 1863, he issued a proclamation setting forth a general policy. With the exception of high Confederate officials and a few other special groups, all southerners could reinstate themselves as United States citizens by taking a simple loyalty oath. When, in any state, a number equal to ten percent of those voting in the 1860 election had taken this oath, they could set up a state government. Such governments had to be republican in form, must recognize the "permanent freedom" of the slaves, and must provide for black education. The plan, however, did not require that blacks be given the right to vote.

This "ten percent plan" reflected Lincoln's lack of vindictiveness and his political wisdom. He realized that any government based on such a small minority of the population would be, as he put it, merely "a tangible nucleus which the remainder . . . may rally around as fast as it can," a sort of puppet regime, like the paper government established in those sections of Virginia under federal control.* The regimes established under this plan in Tennessee, Louisiana, and Arkansas bore, in the

* By approving the separation of the western counties that had refused to secede, this government provided a legal pretext for the creation of West Virginia.

president's mind, the same relation to finally reconstructed states that an egg bears to a chicken. "We shall sooner have the fowl by hatching it than by smashing it," he remarked. He knew that eventually representatives of the southern states would again be sitting in Congress, and he wished to lay the groundwork for a strong Republican party in the section. Yet he realized that Congress had no intention of seating representatives from the "ten percent" states at once.

The Radicals in Congress disliked the ten percent plan, partly because of its moderation and partly because it enabled Lincoln to determine Union policy toward the recaptured regions. In July 1864 they passed the Wade-Davis bill, which provided for constitutional conventions only after a *majority* of the voters in a southern state had taken a loyalty oath. Confederate officials and anyone who had "voluntarily borne arms against the United States" were barred from voting in the election or serving at the convention. Besides prohibiting slavery, the new state constitutions would have to repudiate Confederate debts. Lincoln disposed of the Wade-Davis bill with a pocket veto and thus managed to retain the initiative in Reconstruction for the remainder of the war. There matters stood when Andrew Johnson became president following the assassination.

Lincoln had picked Johnson for a running mate in 1864 because he was a border-state Unionist Democrat and something of a hero as a result of his courageous service as military governor of Tennessee. From origins even more lowly than Lincoln's, Johnson had risen to be congressman, governor of Tennessee, and United States senator. He was able and ambitious but fundamentally unsure of himself, as could be seen in his boastfulness and stubbornness. His political strength came from the poor whites and yeomen farmers of eastern Tennessee, and he was inordinately fond of extolling the common man and attacking "stuck-up aristocrats." Thaddeus Stevens called him a "rank demagogue" and a "damned scoundrel," and it is true that he was a masterful rabble-rouser. But few men of his generation labored so consistently in behalf of small farmers. Free homesteads, public education, absolute social equality—such were his objectives. The father of communism, Karl Marx, a close observer of American affairs at this time, wrote approvingly of Johnson's "deadly hatred of the oligarchy."

Andrew Johnson, as recorded by Matthew Brady's camera in 1865. Johnson, Charles Dickens reported, radiated purposefulness but no "genial sunlight."

Johnson was a Democrat, but because of his record and his reassuring penchant for excoriating southern aristocrats, the Republicans in Congress were ready to cooperate with him. "Johnson, we have faith in you," said Radical Senator Ben Wade, author of the Wade-Davis bill, the day after Lincoln's death. "By the gods, there will be no trouble now in running the government!"

Johnson's reply, "Treason must be made infamous," delighted the Radicals, but the president proved temperamentally unable to work with them. As Eric L. McKitrick has shown in *Andrew Johnson and Reconstruction,* Johnson was an "outsider," a "lone wolf" in every way. "The only role whose attributes he fully understood was that of the maverick," McKitrick writes. "For the full nourishment and maximum functioning of his mind, matters had to be so arranged that all the organized forces of society could in some sense, real or symbolic, be leagued against him." Like Randolph of Roanoke, his antithesis intellectually and socially, opposition was his specialty; he soon alienated every powerful Republican in Washington.

Radical Republicans listened to Johnson's diatribes against secessionists and the great planters and assumed that he was antisouthern. Nothing could have been further from the truth. He shared most of his poor white Tennessee constituents' prejudices against blacks. "Damn the negroes, I am fighting these traitorous aristocrats, their masters," he told a friend during the war. "I wish to God," he said on another occasion, "every head of a family in the United States had one slave to take the drudgery and menial service off his family."

The new president did not want to injure or humiliate the entire South. On May 29, 1865, he issued an amnesty proclamation only slightly more rigorous than Lincoln's. It assumed, correctly enough, that with the war over most southern voters would freely take the loyalty oath; thus it contained no ten percent clause. More classes of Confederates, including those who owned taxable property in excess of $20,000, were excluded from the general pardon. By the time Congress convened in December, all the southern states had organized governments, ratified the Thirteenth Amendment abolishing slavery, and elected senators and representatives. Johnson promptly recommended these new governments to the attention of Congress.

Republican Radicals

Peace found the Republicans in Congress no more united than they had been during the war. A small group of "ultra" Radicals were demanding immediate and absolute racial equality. Senator Sumner led this faction. A second group of Radicals, headed by Thaddeus Stevens in the House and Ben Wade in the Senate, agreed with the ultras' objectives but were prepared to accept half a loaf if necessary to win the support of less radical colleagues.

This did not reflect any ambivalence about racial equality. When Stevens died, he was buried in a black cemetery. Here is his epitaph, written by himself: "I repose in this quiet and secluded spot, not from any natural preference for solitude, but finding other cemeteries limited as to race, by charter rules, I have chosen this that I might illustrate in my death the principles which I advocated through a long life, equality of man before his Creator."

The moderate Republicans wanted to protect ex-slaves from exploitation and guarantee their ba-

Brady photographed two of the stalwart Radical Republicans, Thaddeus Stevens of Pennsylvania (top) and Benjamin Wade of Ohio (bottom). Stevens served in the House from 1859 until his death in 1868. During the Civil War, Senator "Bluff Ben" Wade chaired the Joint Committee on the Conduct of the War.

sic rights but were unprepared to push for full political and social equality. A handful of Republicans sided with the Democrats in support of Johnson's approach, but all the rest insisted at least on the minimum demands of the moderates. Thus Johnsonian Reconstruction had no chance of winning congressional approval.

Johnson's proposal that Congress accept Reconstruction as completed and admit the new southern representatives was also doomed for reasons having little to do with black rights. The Thirteenth Amendment had the effect of increasing the representation of the southern states in Congress because it made the Three-fifths Compromise (see page 156) meaningless. Henceforth those who had been slaves would be counted as whole persons in apportioning seats in the House of Representatives. If Congress seated the southerners, the balance of power might swing to the Democrats. To expect the Republicans to surrender power in such a fashion was unrealistic. Former Copperheads gushing with extravagant praise for Johnson put them instantly on guard. And northerners remained suspicious of ex-Confederates. Although most of them were ready to reenter the Union, they were not overflowing with goodwill toward their conquerors.

Some of the new state governments were less than straightforward about accepting the most obvious results of the war. South Carolina, instead of repudiating secession, merely repealed its secession ordinance. A minority of southerners would have nothing to do with amnesties and pardons:

Oh, I'm a good old rebel,
Now that's just what I am;
For the "fair land of freedom,"
I do not care a dam.
I'm glad I fit against it—
I only wish we'd won
And I don't want no pardon
For anything I done.

Southern voters had further provoked northern resentment by their choice of congressmen. Georgia elected Alexander H. Stephens, vice-president of the Confederacy, to the Senate, though he was still in a federal prison awaiting trial for treason! Several dozen men who had served in the Confederate Congress had been elected to either the House or the Senate, together with four generals and many other high officials. The southern people understandably selected locally respected and experienced leaders, but it was equally reasonable that these choices would sit poorly with northerners.

Finally, the so-called Black Codes enacted by southern governments to control former slaves alarmed the North. These varied in severity from state to state. When seen in historical perspective, even the strictest codes represented a considerable improvement over slavery. Most permitted blacks to sue and to testify in court, at least in cases involving members of their own race. Blacks were allowed to own certain kinds of property; marriages were made legal; other rights were guaranteed. However, blacks could not bear arms, be employed in occupations other than farming and domestic service, or leave their jobs without forfeiting back pay. The Louisiana code required them to sign labor contracts for the year during the first ten days of January. A similar rule was put into effect in Mississippi, where, in addition, drunkards, vagrants, beggars, "common night-walkers," and even persons who "misspend what they earn" and who could not pay the stiff fines assessed for such misbehavior were to be "hired out . . . at public outcry" to the white persons who would take them for the shortest period in return for paying the fines. Such laws, apparently designed to get around the Thirteenth Amendment, outraged even moderate northerners.

For all these reasons the Republicans in Congress rejected Johnsonian Reconstruction. Quickly they created a joint committee on Reconstruction, headed by Senator William P. Fessenden of Maine, a moderate, to study the question of readmitting the southern states.

The committee held extensive public hearings that produced much evidence of the mistreatment of blacks. Colonel George A. Custer, stationed in Texas, testified: "It is of weekly, if not of daily occurrence that Freedmen are murdered." The nurse Clara Barton told a gruesome tale about a pregnant woman who had been brutally whipped. Others described the intimidation of blacks by poor whites. The hearings played into the hands of the Radicals, who had been claiming all along that the South was perpetuating slavery under another name.

President Johnson's attitude speeded the swing

toward the Radical position. While the hearings were in progress, Congress passed a bill expanding and extending the Freedmen's Bureau, which had been established in March 1865 to care for refugees. The bureau, a branch of the War Department, was already exercising considerable coercive and supervisory power in the South. Now Congress sought to add to its authority in order to protect the black population. The bill had wide support even among moderates. Nevertheless Johnson vetoed it, arguing that it was an unconstitutional extension of military authority in peacetime. Congress then passed a Civil Rights Act that, besides declaring that blacks were citizens of the United States, denied the states the power to restrict their rights to testify in court and to hold property.

Once again the president refused to go along, though his veto was sure to drive more moderates into the arms of the Radicals. On April 9, 1866, Congress repassed the Civil Rights Act by a two-thirds majority, the first time in American history that a major piece of legislation became law over the veto of a president. This event marked a revolution in the history of Reconstruction. Thereafter Congress, not President Johnson, had the upper hand, and it placed progressively stricter controls on the South.

In the clash between the president and Congress, Johnson was his own worst enemy. His language was often intemperate, his handling of men inept, his analysis of southern conditions incorrect. He had assumed that the small southern farmers who made up the majority in the Confederacy shared his prejudices against the planter class. They did not, as their choices in the postwar elections demonstrated. In fact, Johnson's hatred of the southern aristocracy may have been based more on jealousy than on principle. Under the Reconstruction plan, persons excluded from the blanket amnesty could apply individually for the restoration of their rights. When wealthy and socially prominent southerners flocked to Washington, hat in hand, he found their flattery and humility exhilarating. He issued pardons wholesale, saying: "I did not expect to keep out all who were excluded from the amnesty. . . . I intended they should sue for pardon, and so realize the enormity of their crime."

The president misread northern opinion. He believed that Congress had no right to pass laws affecting the South before southern representatives had been readmitted to Congress. However, in the light of the refusal of most southern whites to grant any real power or responsibility to the freedmen (an attitude that Johnson did not condemn), the public would not accept this point of view. Johnson placed his own judgment over that of the overwhelming majority of northern voters, and this was a great error, morally and tactically. By encouraging southerners to resist efforts to improve the lot of blacks, Johnson played into the hands of northern extremists.

The Radicals encountered grave problems in fighting for their program. Northerners might object to the Black Codes and to seating "rebels" in Congress, but few believed in racial equality. Between 1865 and 1868 Wisconsin, Minnesota, Connecticut, Nebraska, New Jersey, Ohio, Michigan, and Pennsylvania all rejected bills granting blacks the vote.

The Radicals were in effect demanding not merely equal rights for freedmen but *extra* rights: not merely the vote but special protection of that right against the pressure that southern whites would surely apply to undermine it. This idea flew in the face of conventional American beliefs in equality before the law and individual self-reliance. Such protection would involve interference by the federal government in local affairs, a concept at variance with American practice. Events were to show that the Radicals were correct—that what amounted to a political revolution in state-federal relations was essential if blacks were to achieve real equality. But in the climate of that day their proposals encountered bitter resistance, and not only from southerners.

Thus, while the Radicals sought partisan advantage in their battle with Johnson and sometimes played on war-bred passions in achieving their ends, they were taking large political risks in defense of genuinely held principles. One historian has aptly called them the "moral trustees" of the Civil War.

The Fourteenth Amendment

In June 1866 Congress submitted to the states a new amendment to the Constitution. The Fourteenth Amendment was, in the context of the times, a truly radical measure. Never before had newly freed slaves been granted significant political rights. For example, in the British Caribbean sugar islands, where slavery had been abolished in the 1830s, stiff property qualifications and poll taxes kept freedmen from voting. The Fourteenth Amendment was also a milestone along the road to the centralization of political power in the United States because it reduced the power of *all* the states. In this sense it confirmed the great change wrought by the Civil War: the growth of a more complex, more closely integrated social and economic structure requiring closer national supervision. Few people understood this aspect of the amendment at the time.

First the amendment supplied a broad definition of American citizenship: "All persons born or naturalized in the United States, and subject to the jurisdiction thereof, are citizens of the United States and of the State wherein they reside." Obviously this included blacks. Then it struck at discriminatory legislation like the Black Codes: "No State shall make or enforce any law which shall abridge the privileges or immunities of citizens of the United States; nor shall any State deprive any person of life, liberty, or property, without due process of law." The next section attempted to force the southern states to permit blacks to vote. If a state denied the vote to any class of its adult male citizens, its representation was to be reduced proportionately. Under another clause, former federal officials who had served the Confederacy were barred from holding either state or federal office unless specifically pardoned by a two-thirds vote of Congress. Finally, the Confederate debt was repudiated.

While the amendment did not specifically outlaw segregation or prevent a state from disfranchising blacks if it was willing to see its representation in Congress reduced, the southern states would have none of it. Without them the necessary three-fourths majority of the states could not be obtained. The governor of Mississippi denounced it as "an insulting outrage" to those "who have shed glory and lustre upon our section and our race." Women's rights groups in the North objected to the implication that black men were more fitted to vote than white women. Elizabeth Cady Stanton warned that the amendment would create "an antagonism between black men and all women."

President Johnson vowed to make the choice between the Fourteenth Amendment and his own policy the main issue of the 1866 congressional elections. He embarked on "a swing around the circle" to rally the public to his cause. He failed dismally. Northern opinion had hardened; a large majority was determined that blacks must have at least formal legal equality. The Republicans won better than two-thirds of the seats in both houses, together with control of all the northern state governments. Johnson emerged from the campaign discredited, the Radicals stronger and determined to have their way. The southern states, Congressman James A. Garfield of Ohio said in February 1867, have "flung back into our teeth the magnanimous offer of a generous nation. It is now our turn to act."

The Reconstruction Acts

Had the southern states been willing to accept the Fourteenth Amendment, coercive measures might have been avoided. Their recalcitrance and continuing indications that local authorities were persecuting blacks finally led to the passage, on March 2, 1867, of the First Reconstruction Act. This law divided the former Confederacy—exclusive of Tennessee, which had ratified the Fourteenth Amendment—into five military districts, each controlled by a major general. It gave these officers almost dictatorial power to protect the civil rights of "all persons," maintain order, and supervise the administration of justice. To rid themselves of military rule, the former states were required to adopt constitutions guaranteeing blacks the right to vote and disfranchising broad classes of ex-Confederates. If the new constitutions proved satisfactory to Congress, and if the new governments ratified the Fourteenth Amendment, their representatives would be admitted to Congress and military rule ended. Johnson's veto of the act was easily overridden.

Although drastic, the Reconstruction Act was so vague that it proved unworkable. Military control was easily established. But in deference to moderate Republican views, the law had not spelled out the process by which the new constitutions were to be drawn up. Southern whites preferred the status quo, even under army control, to enfranchising blacks and retiring their own respected leaders. They made no effort to follow the steps laid down

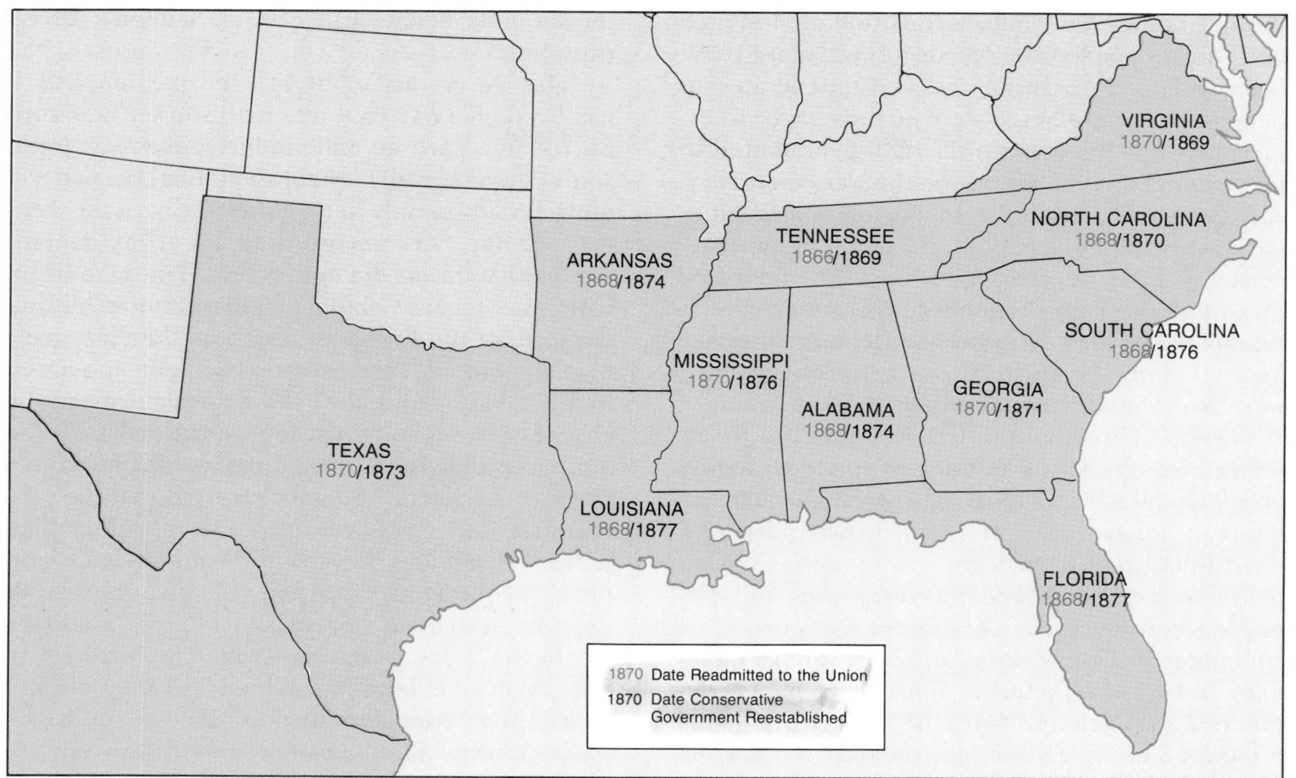

THE SOUTH RETURNS TO THE UNION

The dates printed in red are those years in which the new state constitutions were ratified by a majority of the states' voters. The dates in black show when the conservative (that is, Democratic) state governments reestablished themselves and Federal occupation troops were removed. The last three states to be "redeemed," as part of the Compromise of 1877, were Florida, Louisiana, and South Carolina.

in the law. Congress therefore passed a second act, requiring the military authorities to register voters and supervise the election of delegates to constitutional conventions. A third act further clarified procedures.

Still white southerners resisted. The laws required that the constitutions be approved by a majority of the registered voters. Simply by staying away from the polls, whites prevented ratification in state after state. At last, in March 1868, a full year after the First Reconstruction Act, Congress changed the rules again. The constitutions were to be ratified by a majority of the *voters.* In June 1868 Arkansas, having fulfilled the requirements, was readmitted to the Union, and by July a sufficient number of states had ratified the Fourteenth Amendment to make it part of the Constitution. But it was not until July 1870 that the last southern state, Georgia, qualified to the satisfaction of Congress.

Congress Takes Charge

To carry out this program in the face of determined southern resistance required a degree of single-mindedness over a long period seldom demonstrated by an American legislature. The persistence resulted in part from the suffering and frustrations of the war years. The refusal of the South to accept the spirit of even the mild reconstruction designed by Johnson goaded the North to ever more overbearing efforts to bring the ex-Confederates to heel. Most congressmen were already eager to assert their independence after having submitted to presidential dominance during the war emergency, and President Johnson's stubbornness also influenced their mood. Republican leaders became obsessed with the need to defeat him. The unsettled times and the large Republican majorities, always threatened by the possibility of a Democratic resurgence if "unreconstructed" southern congressmen were readmitted, sustained their determination.

These considerations led Republicans to attempt a kind of grand revision of the federal government, one that almost destroyed the balance between judicial, executive, and legislative power established in 1789. A series of measures passed between 1866 and 1868 increased the authority of Congress over the army, over the process of amending the Constitution, and over Cabinet members and lesser appointive officers. Even the Supreme Court felt the force of the congressional drive for power; its size was reduced, as was the range of its jurisdiction over civil rights cases. Finally, in a showdown caused by emotion more than by practical considerations, the Republicans attempted to remove President Johnson from office.

Johnson was a poor president and out of touch with public opinion, but he had done nothing to merit ejection from office. While he had a low opinion of blacks, his opinion was so widely shared by whites that it is unhistorical to condemn him as a reactionary on this ground. Johnson believed that he was fighting to preserve constitutional government. He was honest and devoted to duty, and his record easily withstood the most searching examination. When Congress passed laws taking away powers granted him by the Constitution, he refused to submit.

The chief issue was the Tenure of Office Act of 1867, which prohibited the president from removing officials who had been appointed with the consent of the Senate without first obtaining Senate approval. In February 1868 Johnson "violated" this act by dismissing Secretary of War Edwin M. Stanton, who had been openly in sympathy with the Radicals for some time. The House, acting under the procedure set up in the Constitution for removing the president, promptly impeached him before the bar of the Senate, Chief Justice Salmon P. Chase presiding.

This "great act of ill-directed passion," as it has been characterized by one historian, was conducted in a partisan and vindictive manner. Johnson's lawyers easily established that he had removed Stanton only in an effort to prove the Tenure of Office Act unconstitutional. They demonstrated that the act did not protect Stanton to begin with, since it gave Cabinet members tenure "during the term of the President by whom they may have been appointed," and Stanton had been appointed by Lincoln! Nevertheless the Radicals pressed the charges (11 separate articles) relentlessly. To the argument that Johnson had committed no crime, the learned Senator Sumner retorted that the proceedings were "political in character" rather than judicial. Thaddeus Stevens, directing the attack on behalf of the House, warned the senators that although "no corrupt or wicked motive" could be attributed to Johnson, they would "be tortured on the gibbet of everlasting obloquy" if they did not convict him. Tremendous pressure was applied to the handful of Republican senators who were unwilling to disregard the evidence.

Seven of them resisted to the end, and the Senate failed by a single vote to convict Johnson. This was probably fortunate. Had he been forced from office on such flimsy grounds, the independence of the executive might have been permanently weakened. Then the legislative branch would have become supreme.

The Fifteenth Amendment

The failure of the impeachment did not affect the course of Reconstruction. The president was acquitted on May 16, 1868. A few days later, the Republican National Convention nominated General Ulysses S. Grant for the presidency. At the Democratic convention Johnson had considerable support, but the delegates nominated Horatio Seymour, a former governor of New York. In November Grant won an easy victory in the electoral college, 214 to 80, but the popular vote was close: 3 million to 2.7 million. Although he would probably have carried the electoral college in any case, Grant's margin in the popular vote was supplied by southern blacks enfranchised under the Recon-

The Fifteenth Amendment, ratified in 1870, provides that the right to vote shall not be denied "on account of race, color, or previous condition of servitude." In this engraving, freedmen register to vote in Richmond's first municipal election after the war.

struction Acts, about 450,000 of whom supported him. A majority of white voters probably preferred Seymour. Since many citizens undoubtedly voted Republican because of personal admiration for General Grant, the election statistics suggest that a substantial white majority opposed the policies of the Radicals.

The ratification of the Fourteenth Amendment and the Reconstruction Acts achieved the purpose of enabling black southerners to vote. The Radicals, however, were not satisfied; despite the unpopularity of the idea in the North, they wished to guarantee the right of blacks to vote in every state. Another amendment seemed the only way to accomplish this objective, but passage of such an amendment appeared impossible. The Republican platform in the 1868 election had smugly distinguished between blacks voting in the South ("demanded by every consideration of public safety, of gratitude, and of justice") and in the North (where the question "properly belongs to the people").

However, after the election had demonstrated how crucial the votes of ex-slaves could be, Republican strategy shifted. Grant had carried Indiana by less than 10,000 votes and lost New York by a similar number. If blacks in these and other closely divided states had voted, Republican strength would have been greatly enhanced.

Suddenly Congress blossomed with suffrage

amendments. After considerable bickering over details, the Fifteenth Amendment was sent to the states for ratification in February 1869. It forbade *all* the states to deny the vote to anyone "on account of race, color, or previous condition of servitude." Once again nothing was said about denial of the vote on the basis of sex.

Most southern states, still under federal pressure, ratified the amendment swiftly. The same was true in most of New England and in some western states. Bitter battles were waged in Connecticut, New York, Pennsylvania, and the states immediately north of the Ohio River, but by March 1870 most of them had ratified the amendment and it became part of the Constitution. The debates occasioned by these contests show that partisan advantage was not the only reason why voters approved black suffrage at last. The unfairness of a double standard of voting, North and South, the contribution of black soldiers during the war, and the hope that by passing the amendment the strife of Reconstruction could finally be ended all played a part.

When the Fifteenth Amendment went into effect, President Grant called it "the greatest civil change and . . . the most important event that has occurred since the nation came to life." The American Anti-Slavery Society formally dissolved itself, its work apparently completed. One prominent Radical Republican called this triumph over prejudice "hardly explicable on any other theory than that God willed it."

Many of the celebrants lived to see the amendment subverted in the South. That it could be evaded by literacy tests and other restrictions was apparent at the time and may even have influenced some persons who voted for it. But a stronger amendment—one, for instance, that positively granted the right to vote to all men and put the supervision of elections under national control—could not have been ratified.

"Black Republican" Reconstruction

The Radicals had at last succeeded in imposing their will upon the South. It was, writes Eric Foner in *Nothing but Freedom,* "a stunning experiment," an "attempt by an outside power in league with the emancipated slaves to fashion an interracial democracy from the ashes of slavery." Throughout the region former slaves had real political influence; they voted, held office, and exercised the "privileges" and enjoyed the "immunities" guaranteed them by the Fourteenth Amendment. Almost to a man they voted Republican.

The spectacle of blacks not five years removed from slavery in positions of power and responsibility attracted much attention at the time and has since been examined exhaustively by historians. The subject is controversial, but certain facts are beyond argument. Black officeholders were neither numerous nor inordinately influential. None was ever elected governor of a state; fewer than a dozen and a half during the entire period served in Congress; only one (in South Carolina) rose to be a justice of a state supreme court. Blacks held many minor offices and were influential in southern legislatures, though (except in South Carolina) they never made up the majority. Certainly they did not share the spoils of office in proportion to their numbers.

The real rulers of the "black Republican" governments were white: the "scalawags"—southerners willing to cooperate with the freed slaves out of principle or to advance their own interests—and the "carpetbaggers"—northerners who went to the South as idealists to help the freed slaves, as employees of the federal government, or more commonly as settlers hoping to improve themselves. The carpetbaggers were a more varied lot. Illinois-born Henry Clay Warmoth, who became governor of Louisiana in 1868 (salary $8,000), was worth $1 million when he left office four years later. On the other hand, Adelbert Ames of Maine, who was governor of Mississippi in 1874–1875, was, in the words of historian Richard N. Current, "about as pure and incorruptible a governor as Mississippi or any other state is likely ever to have." A few scalawags were well-to-do planters and merchants who had been Whigs until the crises of the 1850s destroyed that party in the South, but most were former opponents of secession from sections that had small slave populations before the war.

That blacks should fail to dominate southern governments is certainly understandable. They lacked experience in politics and were mostly poor and uneducated. They were nearly everywhere a minority. Those blacks who held office during Reconstruction tended to be better educated and more prosperous than most southern blacks. In

Southern state legislatures, formerly controlled by white Republicans, underwent sweeping changes as black voters chose new congressmen. In this 1876 incident, newly elected black Democrats had to force their way into the South Carolina legislative chamber.

his interesting analysis of black South Carolina politicians, Thomas Holt shows that a disproportionate number of them had been free before the war. Of those freed by the Thirteenth Amendment, a large percentage had been house servants or artisans, not field hands. Mulatto politicians were also disproportionately numerous and (as a group) more conservative and economically better off than other black leaders.

In South Carolina and elsewhere, black officeholders proved in the main able and conscientious public servants: able because the best tended to rise to the top in such a fluid situation and conscientious because most of those who achieved importance sought eagerly to demonstrate the capacity of their race for self-government. Extensive studies of states such as Mississippi show that even at the local level, where the quality of officials was usually poor, there was little difference in the degree of competence displayed by white and black officeholders. In power, the blacks were not vindictive; by and large they did not seek to restrict the rights of ex-Confederates.

Not all black legislators and administrators were paragons of virtue. In South Carolina, despite their control of the legislature, they broke up into factions repeatedly and failed to press for laws that would improve the lot of poor black farm workers. In *The Prostrate South* (1874), James S. Pike, a northern newspaperman, wrote: "The rule of South Carolina should not be dignified with the name of government. It is the installation of a huge system of brigandage." Like many northern commentators, Pike exaggerated the immorality and incompetence of the blacks, but waste and corruption were common in South Carolina and in other Reconstruction governments. Legislators paid themselves large salaries and surrounded themselves with armies of useless, incompetent clerks. Half the budget of Louisiana in some years went for salaries and "mileage" for representatives and their staffs. Large sums were appropriated for imposing state capitols and other less-than-essential buildings. One Arkansas black took $9,000 from the state for repairing a bridge that had cost only $500 to build. A South Carolina legislator was voted an additional $1,000 in salary after he lost that sum betting on a horse race.

However, the corruption must be seen in perspective. The big thieves were nearly always white; blacks got mostly crumbs. Furthermore, graft and callous disregard of the public interest characterized government in every section and at every level during the decade after Appomattox. Big-city bosses in the North made off with sums that dwarfed the most brazen southern frauds. The New York City Tweed Ring probably made off with more money than all the southern thieves, black and white, combined. While the evidence does not justify the southern corruption, it suggests that the unique features of Reconstruction politics—black suffrage, military supervision, carpetbagger and scalawag influence—do not explain it.

The "black Republican" governments displayed qualities that grew directly from the ignorance and political immaturity of the former slaves. There was a tragicomic aspect to the South Carolina legislature during these years, its many black members—some dressed in old frock coats, others in rude farm clothes—rising to points of order and personal privilege without reason, discoursing ponderously on subjects they did not understand. "A wonder and a shame to modern civilization," one northern observer called this spectacle.

The country might have been better served if blacks had been enfranchised gradually, as Lincoln suggested. But those who complained about the ignorance and irresponsibility of blacks conveniently forgot that the tendency of 19th-century American democracy was away from educational, financial, or any other restrictions on the franchise. Thousands of white southerners were as illiterate and uncultured as the freedmen, yet no one suggested depriving them of the ballot.

Despite the corruption, confusion, and conflict, the Radical southern governments accomplished a great deal. They spent money freely but not entirely wastefully. Tax rates zoomed, but the money financed the repair and expansion of the South's dilapidated railroad network, rebuilt crumbling levees, and expanded social services. Before the Civil War, public education in the South had lagged far behind the rest of the country, and the education of blacks was illegal. During Reconstruction an enormous gap had to be filled, and it took a great deal of money to fill it. The Freedmen's Bureau made a start, and northern religious and philanthropic organizations did important work. Eventually, however, the state governments established and supported systems of free public education that, while segregated, greatly benefited everyone, whites as well as blacks.

The former slaves grasped eagerly at the opportunity to learn. Nearly all appreciated the immense importance of knowing how to read and write; the sight of elderly men and women poring laboriously over elementary texts beside their grandchildren was common everywhere. Schools and other institutions were supported chiefly by property taxes, and these, of course, hit well-to-do white farmers hard. Hence much of the complaining about the "extravagance" of Reconstruction governments concealed selfish objections to paying for public projects. Eventually the benefits of expanded government services to the entire population became clear, and when white supremacy was reestablished, most of the new services remained in force, and the corruption and inefficiency inherited from the carpetbagger governments continued.

The Ravaged Land

The South's grave economic problems complicated the rebuilding of its political system. The section had never been as prosperous as the North, and wartime destruction left it desperately poor by any standard. In the long run the abolition of slavery released immeasurable quantities of human energy previously stifled, but the immediate effect was to

The Freedmen's Bureau established 4,329 schools, attended by some 250,000 ex-slaves, in the postwar South. Harper's Weekly *artist Alfred Waud sketched a Freedmen's Bureau school in Vicksburg, Mississippi, in 1866. Many of the teachers were white women from the North.*

create confusion. Understandably, many former slaves at first equated legal freedom with freedom from having to earn a living, a tendency reinforced for a time by the willingness of the Freedmen's Bureau to provide rations and other forms of relief in war-devastated areas. Freedom to move about without a pass, to "see the world," was one of the most cherished benefits of emancipation. "I's want to be free man, cum when I please, and nobody say nuffin to me, nor order me roun'," one Alabama black told a northern journalist after Appomattox. Thousands flocked to southern towns and cities where there was little they could do to earn a living.

Others expected that freedom would also mean free land, and the slogan "forty acres and a mule" achieved wide popularity in the South in 1865. This idea was forcefully supported by the relentless Congressman Thaddeus Stevens, whose hatred of the planter class was pathological. "The property of the chief rebels should be seized," he stated. If the lands of the richest "70,000 proud, bloated and defiant rebels" were confiscated, the federal government would obtain 394 million acres. Every adult male ex-slave could easily be supplied with 40 acres. The beauty of his scheme, Stevens insisted, was that "nine-tenths of the [southern] people would remain untouched." Dispossessing the great planters would make the South "a safe republic," its lands cultivated by "the free labor of intelligent citizens." If the plan drove the planters into exile, "all the better."

Although Stevens's figures were faulty, many Radicals agreed with him. "We must see that the freedmen are established on the soil," Senator Sumner declared. "The great plantations, which have been so many nurseries of the rebellion, must be broken up, and the freedmen must have the pieces." Stevens, Sumner, and others who wanted to give land to the freedmen weakened their case by associating it with the idea of punishing the former rebels; the average American had too much respect for property rights to support a policy of confiscation.

Aside from its vindictiveness, the extremists' view was simplistic. Land without tools, seed, and other necessities would have done the freedmen little good. Congress did throw open 46 million acres of poor-quality federal land in the South to blacks under the Homestead Act, but few settled upon it. Establishing former slaves on small farms with adequate financial aid would have been of incalculable benefit to them and to the nation. This would have been practicable, but it was not done.

The freedmen therefore had to work out their destiny within the established framework of southern agriculture. White planters, influenced by the

Homesteading in the newly opened territories in the West, rather than sharecropping in the South, was an attractive alternative for many black families. The Shores family was photographed in Custer County, Nebraska, in 1887.

precipitous decline of sugar production in Jamaica and other Caribbean islands that had followed the abolition of slavery there, expected the ex-slaves to be incapable of self-directed effort. If allowed to become independent farmers, they would either starve to death or descend into barbarism. Of course the blacks did neither. True, the output of cotton and other southern staples declined precipitously after slavery was abolished. Observers soon came to the conclusion that a free black produced no more than half as much as a slave had produced, and modern econometric studies indicate that this estimate was not far off.

However, the decline in productivity was not caused by the *inability* of free blacks to work independently. What happened was that since they now held, in the pithy phrase of the economist Robert Higgs, "property rights over their own bodies," they chose no longer to work like slaves. They let their children play instead of forcing them into the fields. Mothers devoted more time to child care and housework, less to farm labor. Elderly blacks worked less.

Noting these changes, white critics spoke scornfully of black laziness and shiftlessness. "You cannot make the negro work without physical compulsion," was the common view. As the economic historians Roger Ransom and Richard Sutch have said, the perfectly reasonable desire of ex-slaves to devote more time to leisure was "taken as 'evidence' to support racist characterizations of blacks as lazy, incompetent, and unwilling to work." A leading southern magazine complained in 1866 that black women now expected their husbands "to support them in idleness." It would never have made such a comment about white housewives. Ransom and Sutch also point out that, while working less, emancipated blacks were far better off materially than under slavery. Their earnings brought them almost 30 percent more than the value of the subsistence provided by their former masters.

Before the passage of the Reconstruction Acts, plantation owners tried to farm their land with gang labor, the same system as before, only now paying wages to the ex-slaves. This method did not work well for two entirely different reasons. Money was scarce, and capital, never adequate even before the collapse of the Confederacy, accumulated slowly. Interest rates were extremely high. This situation made it difficult for landowners to pay their laborers in cash. More important, blacks did not like working for wages because it kept them under the direction of whites and thus reminded them of slavery. They wanted to be independent, to manage not merely their free time but their entire lives for themselves. Since the voluntary withdrawal of so much black labor from the work force had produced a shortage, the blacks had their way.

Quite swiftly, a new agricultural system known as sharecropping emerged. Instead of cultivating the land by gang labor as in antebellum times, planters broke up their estates into small units and established on each a black family. The planter provided housing, agricultural implements, draft animals, seed, and other supplies, and the family provided labor. The crop was divided between them, usually on a fifty-fifty basis. If the landlord supplied only land and housing, the laborer got a larger share. This was called share tenancy.

Sharecropping gave blacks the day-to-day control of their lives that they craved and at least the hope of earning enough to buy a small farm. But few achieved this ambition because whites resisted their efforts adamantly. As late as 1880 blacks owned less than 10 percent of the agricultural land in the South, though they made up more than half of the region's farm population. Mississippi actually prohibited the purchase of farmland by blacks.

Many white farmers in the South were also trapped by the sharecropping system and by white efforts to keep blacks in a subordinate position. New fencing laws kept them from grazing livestock on undeveloped land, a practice common before the Civil War. But the main cause of southern rural poverty for whites as well as blacks was the lack of enough capital to finance the sharecropping system. Like their colonial ancestors, the landowners had to borrow against October's harvest to pay for April's seed. Thus the crop-lien system developed, and to protect their investments, lenders tended to insist that the grower concentrate on readily marketable cash crops: tobacco, sugar, and especially cotton.

The system injured everyone. Diversified farming would have reduced the farmers' need for cash, preserved the fertility of the soil, and, by placing a premium on imagination and shrewdness, aided

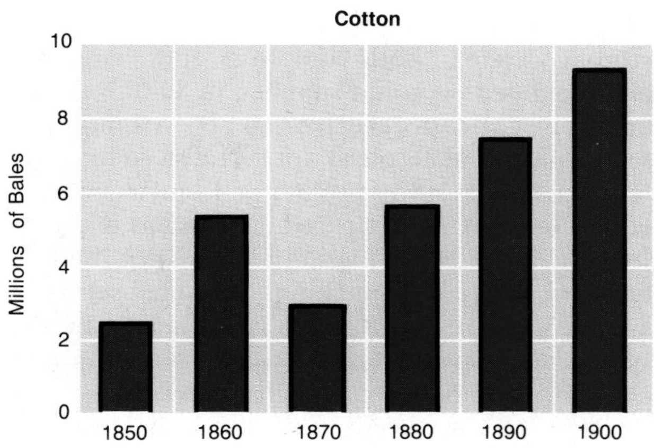

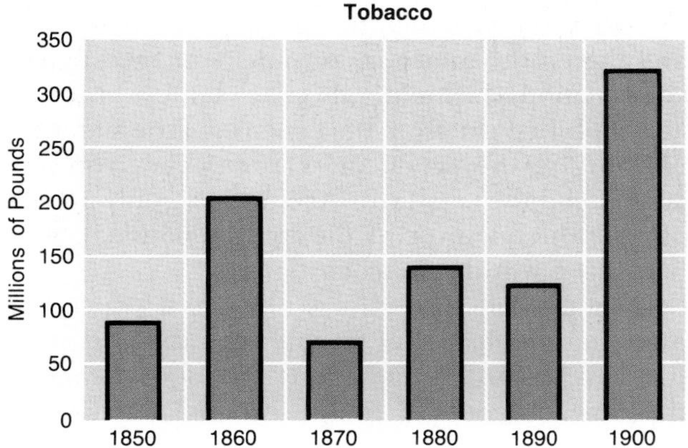

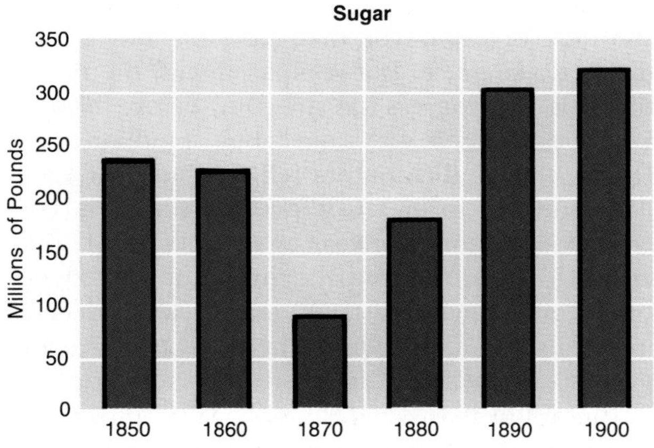

SOUTHERN AGRICULTURE, 1850–1900

Cotton production recovered to its prewar level by 1880, but tobacco and sugar production lagged. Not until 1900 did tobacco growers have a better year than they had in 1860. The years following 1870 saw a general downward trend in wholesale prices for farm commodities. (*Statistics are for the 11 states of the Confederacy.*)

the best of them to rise in the world. Under the crop-lien system, both landowner and sharecropper depended on credit supplied by local bankers, merchants, and storekeepers for everything from seed, tools, and fertilizer to overalls, coffee, and salt. Crossroads stores proliferated, and a new class of small merchants appeared. The prices of goods sold on credit were high, adding to the burden borne by the rural population. The small southern merchants were almost equally victimized by the system, for they also lacked capital, bought goods on credit, and had to pay high interest rates.

Seen in broad perspective, the situation is not difficult to understand. The South, drained of every resource by the war, was competing for funds with the North and West, both vigorous and expanding and therefore voracious consumers of capital. Reconstruction, in the literal sense of the word, was accomplished chiefly at the expense of the standard of living of the producing classes. The crop-lien system and the small storekeeper were only agents of an economic process dictated by national, perhaps even worldwide, conditions.

Commercial agriculture, the rural aspect of modern capitalism, was putting an end to the independent, self-sufficient farmer. This does not mean that small farmers of both races did not lust for material gain as avidly as the bankers and merchants who exploited their labor. Nor does it mean that the South's economy was paralyzed by the shortage of capital or that recovery and growth did not take place. But compared with the rest of the country, progress was slow. Just before the Civil War cotton harvests averaged about 4 million bales. During the conflict, output fell to about half a million, and the former Confederate states did not enjoy a 4-million-bale year again until 1870. Only after 1874 did the crop begin to top that figure consistently. In contrast, national wheat production in 1859 was 175 million bushels and in 1878, 449 million. About 7,000 miles of railroad were built in the South between 1865 and 1879; in the rest of the nation nearly 45,000 miles of track were laid.

In manufacturing the South made important gains after the war. The tobacco industry, stimulated by the sudden popularity of the cigarette, expanded rapidly. The town of Durham, North Carolina, home of the famous Bull Durham pipe and cigarette tobacco, flourished. So did Virginia tobacco towns like Richmond, Lynchburg, and Petersburg. The exploitation of the coal and iron deposits of northeastern Alabama in the early 1870s made a boom town of Birmingham. The manufacture of cotton cloth increased, productive capacity nearly doubling between 1865 and 1880. Yet the mills of Massachusetts alone had eight times the capacity of the entire South in 1880. Despite the increases, the South's share of the national output of manufactured goods declined sharply during the Reconstruction era.

The White Counterrevolution

Radical southern governments could sustain themselves only so long as they had the support of a significant proportion of the white population, for except in South Carolina and Louisiana, the blacks were not numerous enough to win elections alone. The key to Radical survival lay in the hands of the wealthy merchants and planters, mostly former Whigs. People of this sort had nothing to fear from black economic competition. Taking a broad view, they could see that improving the lot of the former slaves would benefit all classes.

These southerners exercised a restraining influence on the rest of the white population. Poor white farmers, the most "unreconstructed" of all southerners, bitterly resented blacks, whose every forward step seemed to weaken their own precarious economic and social position. When the Republicans began to organize and manipulate the new voters in much the way big-city bosses were managing voters in the North, the poor whites seethed with resentment.

Southern Republicans used the Union League of America, a patriotic club founded during the war, to control the black vote. Employing secret rituals, exotic symbols, and other paraphernalia calculated to impress unsophisticated people, they enrolled the freedmen in droves, made them swear to support the League list of candidates at elections, and then marched them to the polls en masse.

Powerless to check the League by open methods, dissident southerners established a number of secret terrorist societies, bearing such names as the Ku Klux Klan, the Knights of the White Camelia, and the Pale Faces. The most notorious of these organizations was the Klan, which organized in Tennessee in 1866. At first it was purely a social club, but by 1868 it had been taken over by vigilante types dedicated to driving blacks out of politics, and it was spreading rapidly across the South. Sheet-clad night riders roamed the countryside, frightening the impressionable and chastising the defiant. Klansmen, using a weird mumbo jumbo and claiming to be the ghosts of Confederate soldiers, spread horrendous rumors and published broadsides designed to persuade the freedmen that it was unhealthy for them to participate in politics:

> *Niggers and Leaguers, get out of the way,*
> *We're born of the night and we vanish by day.*
> *No rations have we, but the flesh of man—*
> *And love niggers best—the Ku Klux Klan;*
> *We catch 'em alive and roast 'em whole,*
> *Then hand 'em around with a sharpened pole.*
> *Whole Leagues have been eaten, not leaving a man,*
> *And went away hungry—the Ku Klux Klan. . . .*

When intimidation failed, the Klansmen beat their victims and in hundreds of cases murdered them, often in the most gruesome manner. Congress struck at the Klan with three Force Acts (1870–1871), which placed elections under federal jurisdiction and imposed fines and prison sentences on persons convicted of interfering with any citizen's exercise of the franchise. Troops were dispatched to areas where the Klan was strong, and by 1872 the federal authorities had arrested enough Klansmen to break up the organization.

Nevertheless the Klan contributed substantially to the destruction of Radical regimes in the South. Its depredations weakened the will of white Republicans (few of whom really believed in racial equality), and it intimidated many blacks, who gave up trying to exercise their rights.

Gradually it became respectable to intimidate black voters. Beginning in Mississippi in 1874, a number of terrorist movements spread through the South. Instead of hiding behind masks and operating in the dark, these terrorists donned red shirts, organized into military companies, and paraded openly. The Mississippi redshirts seized militant blacks and whipped them publicly. Killings were frequent. When blacks dared to fight back, the well-organized whites easily put them to rout. In other states similar organizations sprang up, and the same tragic results followed.

Terrorism fed on fear, fear on terrorism. White violence led to fear of black retaliation and thus to even more brutal attacks. The slightest sign of resistance came to be seen as the beginning of race war, and when the blacks suffered indignities and persecutions in silence, the awareness of how much they must resent the mistreatment made them appear more dangerous still. Thus self-hatred was displaced, guilt suppressed, aggression justified as

A graphic warning by the Alabama Klan "of the fate in store for" scalawags and carpetbaggers, "those great pests of Southern society," from the Tuscaloosa Independent Monitor, *September 1, 1868.*

self-defense, individual conscience submerged in the animality of the mob.

Before long the blacks learned to stay home on election day. One by one, "Conservative" parties—Democratic in national affairs—took over southern state governments. Angry northern Radicals attributed the Democratic victories entirely to intimidation, but intimidation was only a partial explanation. The increasing solidarity of whites, northern and southern, was equally significant.

The North had subjected the South to outside control while sustaining the federal system and preserving state sovereignty in the North itself. In the long run this discrimination proved unworkable. Many northerners had supported the Radical policy only out of irritation with President Johnson. After his retirement their enthusiasm waned. The war was fading into the past and with it the worst of the bad feeling it had generated. Northern voters could still be stirred by references to the sacrifices Republicans had made to save the Union and by reminders that the Democratic party was the organization of rebels, Copperheads, and the Ku Klux Klan. Yet emotional appeals could not push legislation through Congress or convince northerners that it was still necessary to maintain a large army in the South. In 1869 the occupying forces were down to 11,000 men. After Klan disruption and intimidation had made a farce of the 1874 elections in Mississippi, Governor Ames appealed to Washington for help. President Grant's attorney general, Edwards Pierrepont, refused to act. "The whole public are tired out with these autumnal outbreaks in the South," he explained. "Preserve the peace by the forces of your own state."

Nationalism was reasserting itself. Had not Washington and Jefferson been Virginians? Was not Andrew Jackson Carolina-born? Since most northerners had little real love or respect for blacks, their interest in racial equality flagged once they felt reasonably certain that blacks would not be reenslaved if left to their own devices in the South.

Another, much subtler force was also at work. The prewar Republican party had stressed the common interest of workers, manufacturers, and farmers in a free and mobile society, a land of equal opportunity where all could work in harmony. Southern whites had insisted that laborers must be disciplined if large enterprises were to be run efficiently. By the 1870s, as large industrial enterprises developed in the northern states, the thinking of business leaders changed—the southern argument began to make sense to them, and they became more sympathetic to the southern demand for more control over "their" labor force.

Grant as President

Other matters occupied the attention of northern voters. The expansion of industry and the rapid development of the West, stimulated by a new wave of railroad building, loomed more important to many than the fortunes of ex-slaves. Beginning in 1873, when a stock market panic struck at public confidence, economic difficulties plagued the country for nearly a decade. Heated controversies arose over tariff policy, with western agricultural interests seeking to force reductions from the high levels established during the war, and over the handling of the wartime greenback paper money, with debtor groups and many manufacturers favoring further expansion of the supply of dollars and conservative merchants and bankers arguing for retiring the greenbacks in order to return to a "sound" currency. These controversies tended to divert attention from conditions in the South.

More damaging to the Republicans was the failure of Ulysses S. Grant to live up to expectations as president. Qualities that had made Grant a fine military leader for a democracy—his dislike of political maneuvering and his simple belief that the popular will could best be observed in the actions of Congress—made him a poor chief executive. When Congress failed to act on his suggestion that the quality of the civil service needed improvement, he announced meekly that if Congress did nothing, he would assume the country did not want anything done, and he dropped the subject. Grant was honest, but his honesty was of the naive type that made him the dupe of unscrupulous friends and schemers. In fact he disliked being president and avoided the responsibilities of the office whenever he could.

His most serious weakness as president was his failure to deal effectively with economic and social problems, but the one that injured him and the Republicans most was his inability to cope with government corruption. Grant did not cause the corruption, nor did he participate in the remotest way in the rush to "fatten at the public trough,"

At first glance this colorful lithograph, in which the panels show Grant performing many useful tasks, seems admiring, but on a closer second look it reveals a definite satirical tone. For example, the lower panel, second from left, showing Grant serving as a broker, is titled "I Fleece You All."

as the reformers of the day might have put it. But he did nothing to prevent the scandals that disgraced his administration. Out of a misplaced belief in the sanctity of friendship, he protected some of the worst culprits and allowed calculating tricksters to use his good name and the prestige of his office to advance their own interests at the country's expense.

The worst of the scandals—such as the Whiskey Ring affair, which implicated Grant's private secretary, Orville E. Babcock, and cost the government millions in tax revenue, and the defalcations of Secretary of War William W. Belknap in the management of Indian affairs—did not become public knowledge during Grant's first term. However, in 1872 a reform group in the Republican party, alarmed by rumors of corruption and disappointed by Grant's failure to press for civil service reform, organized the Liberal Republican party and nominated Horace Greeley, the able but eccentric editor of the New York *Tribune,* for president. The Democrats also nominated Greeley, though he had devoted his political life to flailing the Democratic party in the *Tribune.* That surrender to expediency, together with Greeley's temperamental unsuitability for the presidency, made the campaign a fiasco for the reformers. Grant triumphed easily, with a popular majority of nearly 800,000.

Nevertheless, the defection of the Liberal Republicans hurt the Republican party in Congress. In the 1874 elections, no longer hampered as in the presidential contest by Greeley's notoriety and Grant's fame, the Democrats carried the House of Representatives. It was clear that the days of military rule in the South were ending. By the end of 1875 only three southern states—South Carolina, Florida, and Louisiana—were still under Republican control. The Republican party in the South was "dead as a doornail," a reporter noted. He reflected the opinion of thousands when he added: "We ought to have a sound sensible republican . . . for the next President as a measure of safety; but only on the condition of absolute noninterference in Southern local affairs, for which there is no further need or excuse."

The Disputed Election of 1876

Against this background the presidential election of 1876 took place. Since corruption in government was the most widely discussed issue, the Republicans passed over their most attractive political personality, the dynamic James G. Blaine, Speaker of the House of Representatives, who had been connected with some chicanery involving railroad securities. Instead they nominated Governor Rutherford B. Hayes of Ohio, a former general with an unsmirched reputation. The Democrats picked Governor Samuel J. Tilden of New York, who had attracted national attention for his part in breaking up the Tweed Ring in New York City.

In November Tilden triumphed easily in all the southern states from which the Radical regimes had been ejected. He also carried New York, New Jersey, Connecticut, and Indiana. In the three "Unredeemed" southern states, Florida, South Carolina, and Louisiana, he won apparent majorities. This seemed to give him 203 electoral votes to Hayes's 165, with a popular plurality in the neighborhood of 250,000 out of more than 8 million votes cast.

Republican leaders had anticipated the possible loss of Florida, South Carolina, and Louisiana and were prepared to use their control of the election machinery in those states to throw out sufficient Democratic ballots to alter the results if doing so would change the national outcome. Realizing that the 19 electoral votes of those states were exactly enough to elect their man, they telegraphed their henchmen on the scene, ordering them to go into action. The board of canvassers in each of the states invalidated Democratic ballots in wholesale lots and filed returns showing Hayes the winner. Naturally the local Democrats protested vigorously and filed their own returns.

The Constitution provides that presidential electors must meet in their respective states to vote and forward the results to "the Seat of the Government." There, it adds, "the President of the Senate shall, in the Presence of the Senate and House of Representatives, open all the Certificates, *and the Votes shall then be counted.*" But who was to do the counting? The House was Democratic, the Senate Republican; neither would agree to allow the other to do the job. On January 29, 1877, scarcely a month before inauguration day, Congress created an electoral commission to decide the disputed cases. The commission consisted of five senators (three Republicans and two Democrats), five representatives (three Democrats and two Republicans), and five justices of the Supreme Court (two Democrats, two Republicans, and one "independent" judge, David Davis). Since it was a foregone conclusion that the others would vote for their party no matter what the evidence, Davis would resumably swing the balance in the interest of fairness.

But before the commission met, the Illinois legislature elected Davis senator! He had to resign from the Court and the commission. Since independents were rare even on the Supreme Court, no neutral was available to replace him. The vacancy went to Associate Justice Joseph P. Bradley of New Jersey, a Republican.

Evidence presented before the commission revealed a disgraceful picture of election shenanigans. On the one hand, in all three disputed states Democrats had clearly cast a majority of the votes; on the other, it was unquestionable that many blacks had been forcibly prevented from voting.

The sordid truth was that both sides had been shamefully corrupt. Lew Wallace, a northern politician later famous as the author of the novel *Ben Hur,* visited Louisiana and Florida shortly after the election. "It is terrible to see the extent to which all classes go in their determination to win," he wrote his wife from Florida. "Money and intimidation can obtain the oath of white men as well as black to any required statement. . . . If we win, our methods are subject to impeachment for possible fraud. If the enemy win, it is the same thing." The governor of Louisiana was reported willing to sell his state's electoral votes for $200,000. The Florida election board was supposed to have offered itself to Tilden for the same price. "That seems to be the standard figure," Tilden remarked ruefully.

Most modern authorities take the view that in a fair election the Republicans would have carried South Carolina and Louisiana but that Florida would have gone to Tilden, giving him the election, 188 electoral votes to 181. In the last analysis, this opinion has been arrived at simply by counting white and black noses: blacks were in the majority in South Carolina and Louisiana. Amid the tension and confusion of early 1877, however, even a Solomon would have been hard pressed to judge rightly amid the rumors, lies, and contradictory statements, and the electoral commission was not composed of Solomons. The Democrats had some hopes that Justice Bradley would be sympathetic to their case, for he was known to be opposed to harsh Reconstruction policies. On the eve of the commission's decision in the Florida controversy, he was apparently ready to vote in favor of Tilden. But the Republicans subjected him to tremendous political pressure. When he read his opinion on February 8, it was for Hayes. Thus, by a vote of 8 to 7, the commission awarded Florida's electoral votes to the Republicans.

The rest of the proceedings were routine. The atmosphere of judicial inquiry and deliberation was a façade. With the spitefulness common to rejected suitors, the Democrats assailed Bradley until, as the New York *Times* put it, he seemed like "a middle-aged St. Sebastian, stuck full of Democratic darts." Unlike Sebastian, however, Bradley was protected from the arrows by the armor of his Republican faith. The commission assigned all the disputed electoral votes (including one in Oregon, where the Democratic governor had seized on a technicality to replace a single Republican elector with a Democrat) to Hayes.

To such a level had the republic of Jefferson and John Adams descended. Democratic institutions, shaken by the South's refusal to go along with the majority in 1860 and by the suppression of civil rights during the rebellion, and further weakened by military intervention and the intimidation of blacks in the South during Reconstruction, seemed now a farce. According to Tilden's campaign manager, angry Democrats in 15 states, chiefly war veterans, were readying themselves to march on Washington to force the inauguration of Tilden. Tempers flared in Congress, where some spoke ominously of a filibuster that would prevent the recording of the electoral vote and leave the country, on March 4, with no president at all.

The Compromise of 1877

Fortunately, forces for compromise had been at work behind the scenes in Washington for some time. Although northern Democrats threatened to fight to the last ditch, many southern Democrats were willing to accept Hayes if they could gain something in exchange. If Hayes would promise to remove the troops and allow the southern states to manage their internal affairs by themselves, they would be sorely tempted to go along with his election. A more specialized but extremely important group consisted of the ex-Whig planters and merchants who had reluctantly abandoned the carpetbag governments and who were always uncomfortable in alliance with poor whites. If Hayes would agree to let the South alone and perhaps appoint a conservative southerner to his Cabinet, these men would support him willingly, hoping eventually to restore the two-party system that had been destroyed in the South during the 1850s.

Other southerners favored Republican policies because of their economic interests. The Texas and Pacific Railway Company, chartered to build a line from Marshall, Texas, to San Diego, had many southern backers, and supporters of Hayes were quick to point out that a Republican administration would be more likely to help the Texas and Pacific than a retrenchment-minded Democratic one. Ohio Congressman James A. Garfield urged Hayes to find "some discreet way" of showing these southerners that he favored "internal improvements." Hayes replied: "Your views are so nearly the same as mine that I need not say a word."

Tradition has it that a great compromise between the sections was worked out during a dramatic meeting at the Wormley Hotel in Washington on February 26. Actually, as C. Vann Woodward has demonstrated in his important book *Reunion and Reaction,* the negotiations were long-drawn-out and informal, and the Wormley conference was but one of many. With the tacit support of many Democrats, the electoral vote was counted by the president of the Senate on March 2, and Hayes was declared elected, 185 votes to 184.

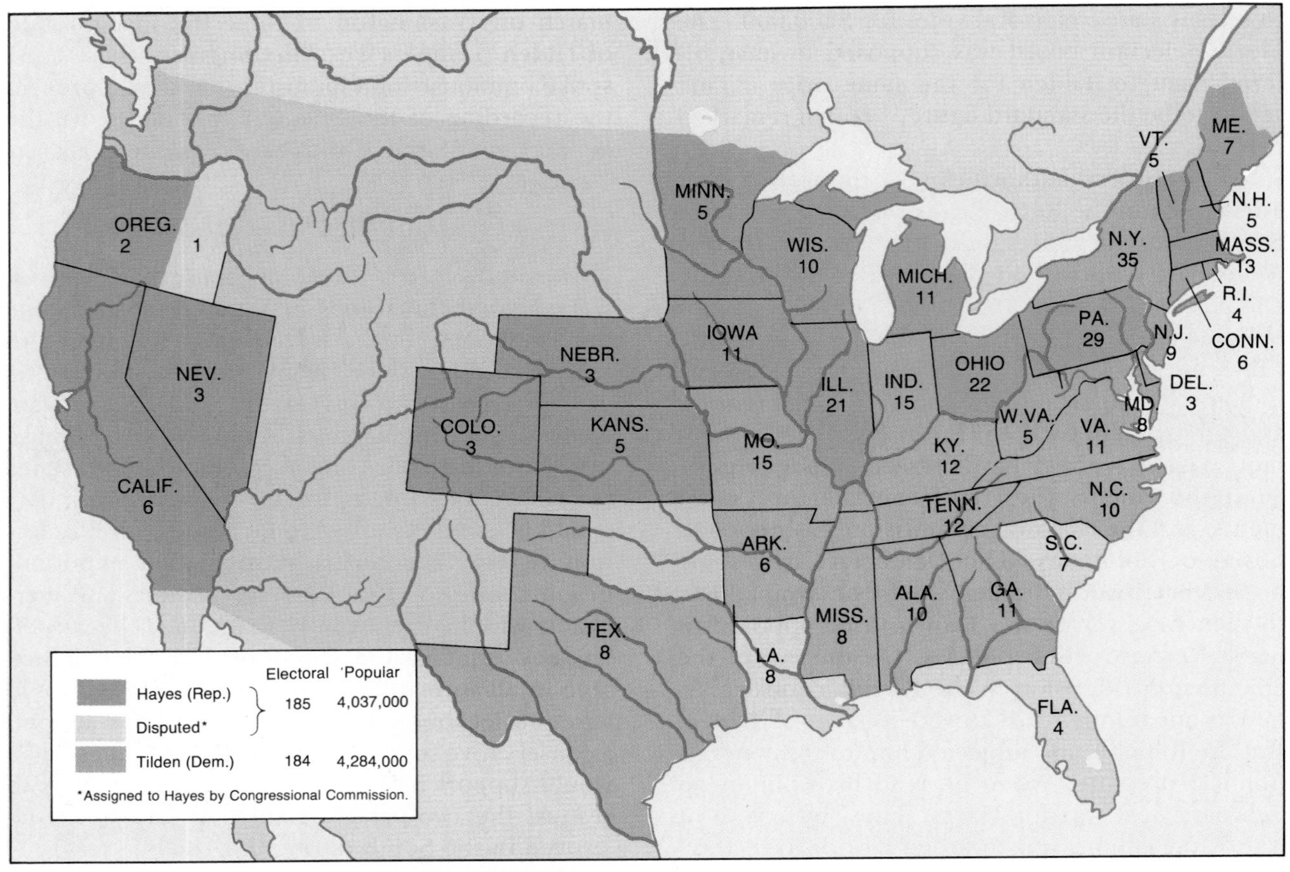

THE COMPROMISE OF 1877

Like all compromises, this agreement was not entirely satisfactory; like most, it was not honored in every detail. Hayes recalled the last troops from South Carolina and Louisiana in April. He appointed a former Confederate general, David M. Key of Tennessee, postmaster general and delegated to him the congenial task of finding southerners willing to serve their country as officials of a Republican administration. The new alliance of ex-Whigs and northern Republicans did not flourish, however, and the South remained solidly Democratic. The hoped-for federal aid for the Texas and Pacific did not materialize. The major significance of the compromise, one of the great intersectional political accommodations of American history, has been well summarized by Professor Woodward:

> The Compromise of 1877 marked the abandonment of principles and force and a return to the traditional ways of expediency and concession. The compromise laid the political foundation for reunion. It established a new sectional truce that proved more enduring than any previous one and provided a settlement for an issue that had troubled American politics for more than a generation. It wrote an end to Reconstruction and recognized a new regime in the South. More profoundly than Constitutional amendments and wordy statutes it shaped the future of four million freedmen and their progeny for generations to come.

For most of the former slaves, this future was to be bleak. Forgotten in the North, manipulated and then callously rejected by the South, rebuffed by the Supreme Court, voiceless in national affairs, they and their descendants were condemned in the interests of sectional harmony to lives of poverty, indignity, and little hope. Meanwhile, the rest of the United States continued its golden march toward wealth and power.

SUPPLEMENTARY READING

Titles marked with an asterisk have been published in paperback.

J. G. Randall and David Donald, **The Civil War and Reconstruction** (1961), is as excellent on postwar readjustments as it is on the war years. K. M. Stampp, **The Era of Reconstruction*** (1964), and J. H. Franklin, **Reconstruction: After the Civil War*** (1961), are outstanding. E. M. Coulter, **The South During Reconstruction** (1947), presents a prosouthern point of view and is strong on economic developments. The older approach to the period, stressing the excesses of black-influenced governments and criticizing the Radicals, derives from the seminal work of W. A. Dunning, **Reconstruction, Political and Economic*** (1907), W. E. B. Du Bois, **Black Reconstruction in America*** (1935), militantly problack, was the pioneering counterattack against the Dunning view. See also Eric Foner, **Politics and Ideology in the Age of the Civil War** (1980), and Foner's **Nothing But Freedom*** (1984).

Lincoln's ideas about Reconstruction are analyzed in W. B. Hesseltine, **Lincoln's Plan of Reconstruction*** (1960), and in many of the Lincoln volumes mentioned in earlier chapters. There is no satisfactory biography of Andrew Johnson, but Albert Castel, **The Presidency of Andrew Johnson** (1979), is a balanced recent account. Of the special studies of Johnson's battle with the congressional Radicals, H. K. Beale, **The Critical Year** (1930), takes Johnson's side, but later studies have been critical of the president. See H. L. Trefousse, **The Radical Republicans: Lincoln's Vanguard for Racial Justice*** (1969), E. L. McKitrick, **Andrew Johnson and Reconstruction*** (1960), and W. R. Brock, **An American Crisis: Congress and Reconstruction*** (1963), the last a particularly thoughtful analysis of the era.

A number of biographies provide information helpful in understanding the Radicals. These include B. P. Thomas and H. M. Hyman, **Stanton** (1962), F. M. Brodie, **Thaddeus Stevens*** (1959), R. N. Current, **Old Thad Stevens** (1942), and H. L. Trefousse, **Benjamin Franklin Wade** (1963); J. M. McPherson, **The Struggle for Equality: Abolitionists and the Negro in the Civil War and Reconstruction*** (1964), is also valuable. On the Fourteenth Amendment, see Joseph James, **The Framing of the Fourteenth Amendment*** (1956); on the Fifteenth Amendment, see William Gillette, **The Right to Vote: Politics and the Passage of the Fifteenth Amendment*** (1965).

Conditions in the South during Reconstruction are discussed in all the works cited in the first paragraph. Jean Litvack, **Been in the Storm Too Long** (1979), discusses the transition of blacks from slavery to freedom. Of state studies, see V. L. Wharton, **The Negro in Mississippi*** (1947), C. E. Wynes, **Race Relations in Virginia** (1961), W. L. Rose, **Rehearsal for Reconstruction: The Port Royal Experiment*** (1964), Thomas Holt, **Black over White: Negro Political Leadership in South Carolina** (1977), and Joel Williamson, **After Slavery: The Negro in South Carolina During Reconstruction*** (1965). See also Joel Williamson, **The Crucible of Race: Black-White Relations in the American South Since Emancipation** (1984), a psychoanalytical interpretation of racism. G. R. Bentley, **A History of the Freedmen's Bureau** (1955), discusses the work of that important organization, but see also W. S. McFeely, **Yankee Stepfather: General O. O. Howard and the Freedmen*** (1968). On the Ku Klux Klan, see G. C. Rable, **But There Was No Peace*** (1984), and A. W. Trelease, **White Terror: The Ku Klux Klan Conspiracy and Southern Reconstruction** (1971).

On the economic and social effects of Reconstruction, see R. L. Ransom and Richard Sutch, **One Kind of Freedom: The Economic Consequences of Emancipation*** (1977), Robert Higgs, **Competition and Coercion: Blacks in the American Economy, 1865–1914** (1977), and C. F. Oubre, **Forty Acres and a Mule** (1978). F. A. Shannon, **The Farmer's Last Frontier*** (1945), is also useful on southern agriculture. For the growth of industry, see Broadus Mitchell, **The Rise of Cotton Mills in the South** (1921), and J. F. Stover, **The Railroads of the South** (1955).

On Grant's presidency, see W. S. McFeely, **Grant** (1981), but Allan Nevins, **Hamilton Fish: The Inner History of the Grant Administration** (1936), and Matthew Josephson, **The Politicos*** (1938), contain much additional information. On the election of 1868, see C. H. Coleman, **The Election of 1868** (1933), and Stewart Mitchell, **Horatio Seymour** (1938); on the reform movement of the period within the Republican party, see J. G. Sproat, **"The Best Men": Liberal Reformers in the Gilded Age*** (1968), and M. B. Duberman, **Charles Francis Adams*** (1961). For the disputed election of 1876 and the compromise following it, consult C. V. Woodward, **Reunion and Reaction*** (1951), Harry Barnard, **Rutherford B. Hayes and His America** (1954), K. I. Polakoff, **The Politics of Inertia: The Election of 1876 and the End of Reconstruction** (1973), and Allan Nevins, **Abram S. Hewitt** (1935). P. H. Buck, **The Road to Reunion*** (1937), traces the gradual reconciliation of North and South after 1865. William Gillette, **Retreat from Reconstruction** (1980), is an important recent study.

PORTFOLIO FIVE

Blacks in Slavery and Freedom

It is much easier to generalize about what life was like for American blacks under slavery than for free people of that time. Indeed, the fact that the restrictions imposed upon slaves reduced drastically their possibilities for individual development and self-expression was the basic injustice of the slave system. Nevertheless, as these illustrations show, the institution affected its victims in many different ways. Seen from this perspective, the ending of slavery expanded the ability of individual blacks to "be themselves." Even after more than a century, however, the possibilities open to the average black are still more limited than those available to the average white. Finally ending this discrimination is one of the major tasks our society faces today.

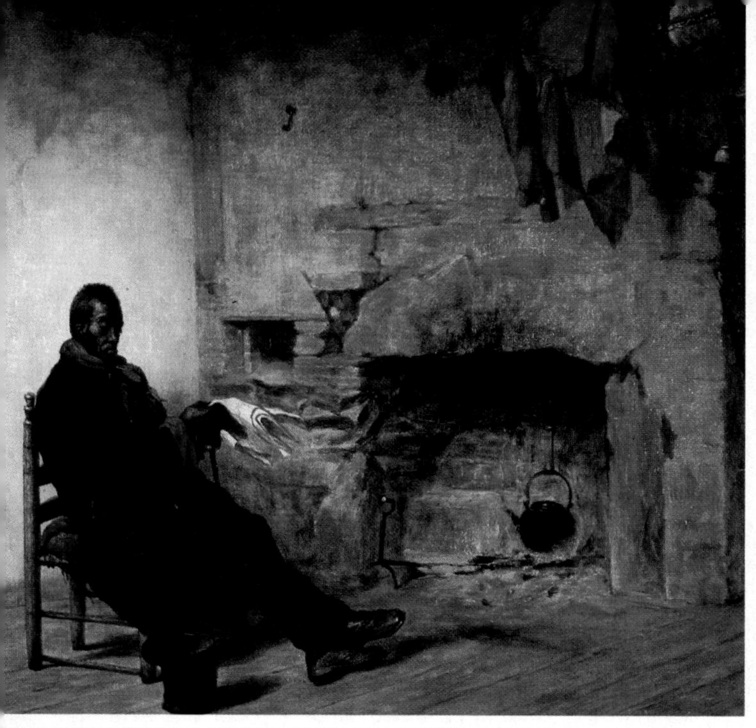

The three views of slave life on this page throw different lights on "the peculiar institution." Edwin White, an academic painter, titled his carefully humble yet dignified portrayal of a quiet moment *Thoughts of Liberia.* Actually, few blacks ever returned to Africa in spite of colonization efforts by well-meaning groups.

In 1862, T. H. O'Sullivan made this extraordinary photograph of five generations of a slave family. All were born on the plantation of J. J. Smith in Beaufort, South Carolina.

A Northern visitor, George Fuller, traveled through Alabama in 1858 to observe the conditions under which slaves lived. He sketched this woman, her skirts hitched up and the reins of a plantation mule looped around her neck, plowing a field. In the background are a cotton gin (the building on stilts) and a cotton press, which was used to compress the ginned cotton into bales for shipping.

Before 1860, many of the free blacks of the northern states lived in cities and towns. For most, the church was the center of community life. This 1853 scene from *Frank Leslie's Illustrated Newspaper* shows a prayer meeting in the African Church of Cincinnati, Ohio.

Thomas "Daddy" Rice was a popular vaudeville star in the pre–Civil War years. He introduced the character "Jim Crow" in a song-and-dance blackface act ("Wheel a-bout and turn a-bout/And jump . . . Jim Crow") based on the antics of a black stable boy he claimed to have seen. His "Jump Jim Crow" act help launch the popular minstrel shows of the 19th century. Unfortunately, they also promoted the stereotype of the shiftless black man. The term *Jim Crow* later came to be applied to the system of Southern segregation laws and customs in the late 19th century.

Slaves, of course, could be bought and sold at their owners' discretion, like any piece of property. Edwin Taylor's 1852 painting *American Slave Market* catches a sense of the mundane way that most owners viewed the trade in human beings. With the slave went a bill of sale. Below is a receipt covering the sale of "a Negro man by the name of Ned about 38 or 40 years of age which negro I warrant to be a slave for life" for $800. The note in the upper right corner, added by the buyer's great-grandson, comments that Ned was reputed to be a good cabinet maker.

My Great Grand Father Jas. Benson Zachry
Old Henry County Present Newton County
This slave was reputed to be a good Cabinet maker.

Columbus 25th May 1842

Received of James B Zachry by the hands of John Morton Eight Hundred dollars in full consideration for a Negro Man by the name of Ned about 38 or 40 years of age which negro I warrant to be a Slave for life & to be sound & well both in body & mind & I also warrant him against the Claims of myself my heirs or against the Claims of any other person or persons whomsoever given under my hand and seal this day and year above written

Henry Morton
Ivis Boswell

Stephen Wall

When the Civil War broke out, blacks in the Union army were not allowed to serve in combat units. But by 1863 heavy white casualties caused the government to change its policy. By the end of the war, about 10 percent of the Union troops were black. These men fought in segregated units and were led by white officers. A Currier & Ives lithograph romantically depicts "the charge of the 54th Massachusetts Regiment on the Rebel works at Fort Wagner, Morris Island, near Charleston" in July of 1863.

54th
Mass.

Reconstruction meant a new set of accommodations to freedom within an older social order. Winslow Homer's tense painting, "A Visit from the Old Mistress," conveys a feeling of the complex relationships that developed between newly freed blacks and their former owners.

For most former slaves, day-to-day activity in the rural South remained a round of planting, cultivating, and harvesting. For example, the way that hogs were slaughtered and the meat cured or made into sausage did not change. Some blacks, however, did not stay on the land, but instead worked in industrial settings, such as this tobacco-processing plant in Danville, Virginia, where men, women, and children were employed stripping tobacco.

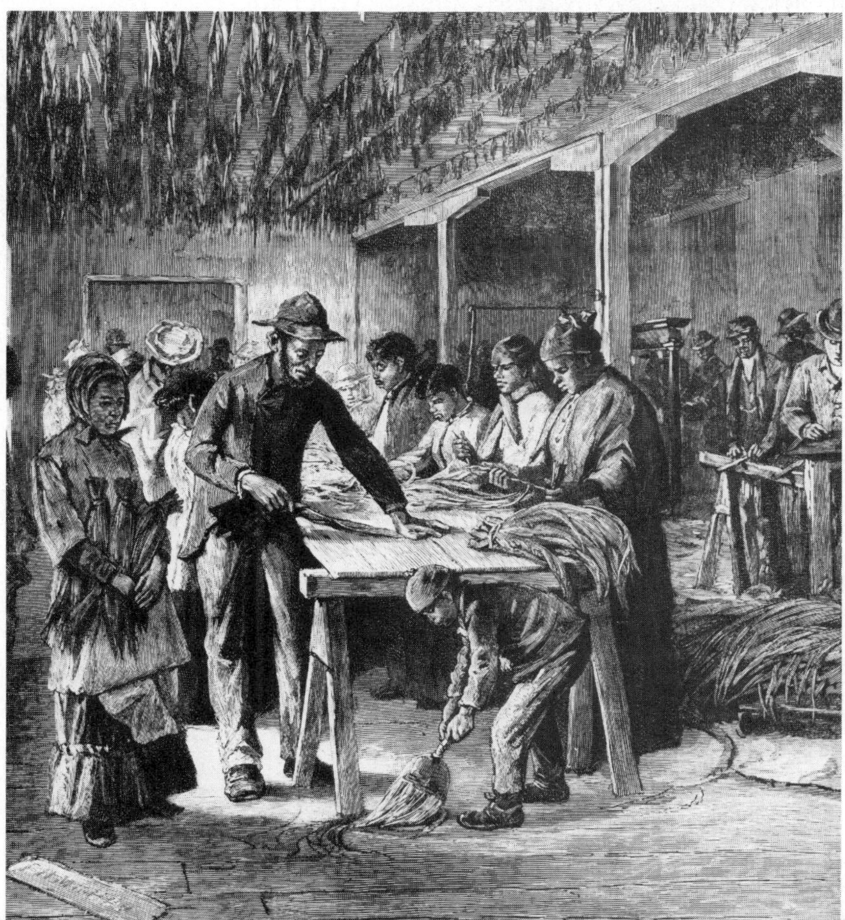

17
An Age of Exploitation

It may be metaphorically said that natural selection is daily and hourly scrutinizing, throughout the world, the slightest variations; rejecting those that are bad, preserving and adding up all that are good; silently and insensibly working, whenever and wherever opportunity offers. CHARLES DARWIN, The Origin of Species, *1859*

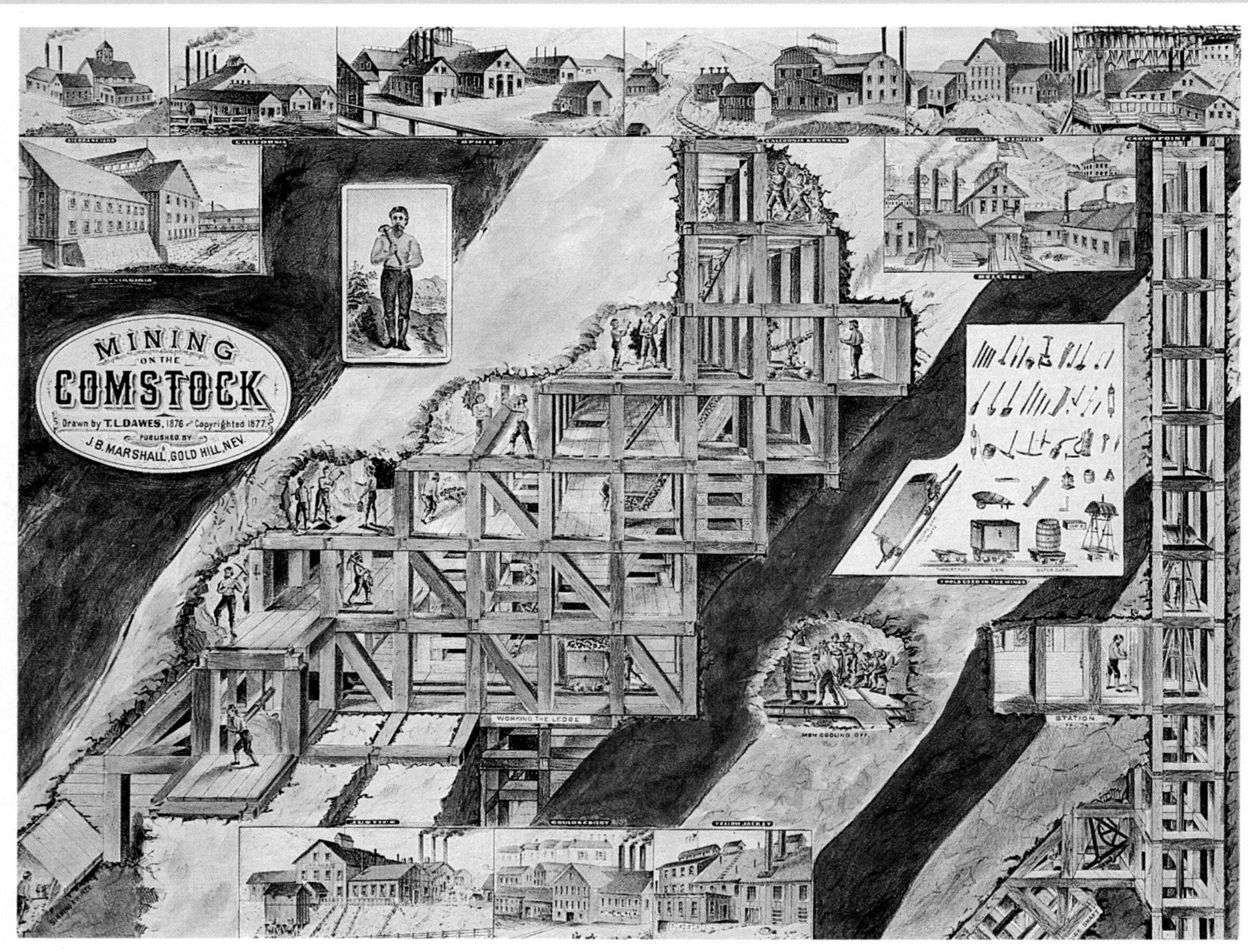

When Americans turned from fighting and making weapons to more constructive occupations, they transformed their agriculture, trade, manufacturing, mining, and means of communication. Immigration increased rapidly. Cities grew in size and number, exerting on every aspect of life an influence at least as pervasive as that exercised on earlier generations by the frontier. More and more Americans were flocking to the towns and cities, supporting themselves by laboring at machines or by scratching accounts in ledgers. Yet such was the expansive force of the time that farm production rose to new heights, invigorated by new marketing methods and the increased use of machinery. Railroad construction stimulated and unified the economy, helping to make possible still larger and more efficient industrial and agricultural enterprises. The flow of gold and silver from western mines excited people's imaginations and their avarice, while petroleum, the "black gold" discovered in Pennsylvania shortly before the war, gave rise to a new industry soon to become one of the most important in the nation. These developments amounted to more than a mere change of scale; they altered the structure of the economy and the society.

"Root, Hog, or Die"

After Appomattox, boom conditions existed everywhere outside the South. Americans seemed to have abandoned all restraint in a mad race for personal gain. The immense resources of the United States, combined with certain aspects of the American character, such as the high value assigned to work and achievement, made the people strongly materialistic. From colonial times they had assumed that prosperity was the natural state of things, and they had shown an inordinate respect for wealth. The Civil War further encouraged the glorification of money and the things it could buy. The North's capacity to produce the tools of war had helped preserve the Union; the role of businessmen and manufacturers in winning the struggle was clear to every soldier from General Grant to the lowliest private.

During the emotional letdown that followed the war, Americans seemed even more enamored of material values. They were tired of sacrifice, eager to act for themselves. Except in their attitude toward the South, still psychologically "outside" the United States, they professed to believe strongly in a government policy of noninterference, or laissez faire. " 'Things regulate themselves' . . . means, of course, that God regulates them by his general laws," Professor Francis Bowen of Harvard wrote in his *American Political Economy* (1870). "The progress of the country," another economist said, "is independent of legislation."

Impressed by such logic and never especially noted for their sophistication, taste, or interest in preserving the resources of the country, the people now tolerated the grossest kind of waste and seemed to care little about corruption in high places, so long as no one interfered with their personal pursuit of profit. Mark Twain, raised in an earlier era, called this a Gilded Age, dazzling on the surface, base metal below. A later writer, Vernon Parrington, named the period the Great Barbecue, a time when everyone rushed to gobble up the national inheritance like hungry picnickers crowding around the savory roast at one of the big political outings common in those years. Twain and other critics took too dark a view of the era. Never, perhaps, did Americans display more vigor, more imagination, or greater confidence in themselves and the future of the country. In his novel, *The Gilded Age,* written with Charles Dudley Warner, Twain portrayed this aspect of the period along with its cheapness and corruption.

Certain intellectual currents encouraged the exploitative drives of the people. Charles Darwin's *The Origin of Species* was published in 1859, and by the 1870s his theory of evolution was beginning to influence opinion in the United States. That nature had ordained a kind of inevitable progress, governed by the natural selection of those individual organisms best adapted to survive in a particular environment, seemed eminently reasonable to most Americans, for it fitted well with their own experiences. "Let the buyer beware; that covers the whole business," the sugar magnate Henry O. Havemeyer explained to an investigating committee. "You cannot wet-nurse people from the time they are born until the time they die. They have to wade and get stuck, and that is the way men are educated."

This reasoning was similar to that of the classical economists and was thus at least as old as Adam

Smith's *Wealth of Nations* (1776). But it appeared to supply a hard scientific substitute for Smith's somewhat vague "invisible hand" as an explanation of why free competition advanced the common good. Yale professor William Graham Sumner, an ardent advocate of laissez faire economics in the 1870s, sometimes used the survival-of-the-fittest analogy in teaching undergraduates. "Professor," one student asked Sumner, "don't you believe in any government aid to industries?" "No!" Sumner replied, "It's root, hog, or die." The student persisted: "Suppose some professor of political science came along and took your job away from you. Wouldn't you be sore?" "Any other professor is welcome to try," Sumner answered promptly. "If he gets my job, it is my fault. My business is to teach the subject so well that no one can take the job away from me."

Few men of practical affairs were directly influenced by Darwin's ideas. Most eagerly accepted any aid they could get from the government, many were active in philanthropy, some felt a deep sense of social responsibility. Nevertheless, most were sincere individualists. They believed in competition, being convinced that the nation would best prosper if all people were free to seek their personal fortunes by their own methods. With such ideas ascendant, exploitation and complacency became the hallmarks of the postwar decades.

An Oglala Sioux named Kills Two painted this portrayal of "An Indian Horse Dance." Horses were vital to survival for the Sioux, as their inclusion in such ceremonies demonstrates.

The Plains Indians

For 250 years the Indians had been driven back steadily, yet on the eve of the Civil War they still inhabited roughly half the United States. By the time of Hayes's inauguration, however, the Indians had been shattered as independent peoples, and in another decade the survivors were penned up on reservations, the government committed to a policy of extinguishing their way of life.

In 1860 the survivors of most of the eastern tribes were living peacefully in what is now Oklahoma. In California the forty-niners had made short work of the local tribes. Elsewhere in the West—in the deserts of the Great Basin between the Sierras and the Rockies, in the mountains themselves, and on the semiarid, grass-covered plains between the Rockies and the edge of white civilization in eastern Kansas and Nebraska—nearly a quarter of a million Indians dominated the land.

By far the most important lived on the High Plains. From the Blackfeet of southwestern Canada and the Sioux of Minnesota and the Dakotas to the Cheyenne of Colorado and Wyoming and the Comanche of northern Texas, the plains tribes possessed a generally uniform culture. All lived by hunting the hulking American bison, or buffalo, which ranged over the plains by the millions. The buffalo provided the Indians with food, clothing, even shelter, for the famous Indian tepee was covered with hides. On the treeless plains, dried buffalo dung was used for fuel. The buffalo was also an important symbol in Indian religion.

Although they seemed the epitome of freedom, pride, and self-reliance, the plains Indians had begun to fall under the sway of white power. They eagerly adopted the products of the more technically advanced culture—cloth, metal tools, weapons, cheap decorations. However, the most important thing the whites gave them had nothing to do with technology: it was the horse.

The geological record shows that the genus *Equus* was native to America, but it had become extinct in the Western Hemisphere long before Cortés brought the first modern horses to America in the 16th century. Multiplying rapidly thereafter, the animals soon roamed wild from Texas to the Argentine. By the 18th century the Indians of the plains had made them a vital part of their culture. Horses thrived on the plains and so did their masters. Mounted Indians could run down buffalo instead of stalking them on foot. They could move more easily over the country and fight more effectively too. They could acquire and transport more possessions and increase the size of their tepees, for horses could drag heavy loads heaped on A-shaped frames (called travois by the French), where earlier Indians had only dogs to depend on as pack animals. The frames of the travois, when disassembled, served as poles for tepees. The Indians also adopted modern weapons: the cavalry sword, which they particularly admired, and the rifle. Both added to their effectiveness as hunters and fighters. However, like the whites' liquor and diseases, horses and guns caused problems. The buffalo herds began to diminish, and warfare became bloodier and more frequent.

In a familiar and tragic pattern, the majority of the western tribes greeted the first whites to enter their domains in a friendly fashion. As late as the 1830s, white hunters and trappers ranged freely over most of the West, trading with the Indians and often marrying Indian women. Settlers pushing cross-country toward Oregon in the 1840s met with relatively little trouble, though at times bands of braves on the warpath molested small groups or indulged in petty thievery that the migrants found annoying.

After the start of the gold rush the need to link the East with California meant that the tribes were pushed aside. Deliberately the government in Washington prepared the way. In 1851 Thomas Fitzpatrick, an experienced mountain man, a founder of the Rocky Mountain Fur Company, scout for the first large group of settlers to Oregon in 1841 and for American soldiers in California during the Mexican War, and now an Indian agent, summoned a great "council" of the tribes. About 10,000 Indians, representing nearly all the plains tribes, gathered that September at Horse Creek, 37 miles east of Fort Laramie, in what is now Wyoming.

The Indians respected Fitzpatrick, who was an intelligent and sensible man. He had recently married a woman who was half Indian. At Horse Creek he persuaded each tribe to accept definite limits to its hunting grounds. For example, the Sioux nations were to keep north of the Platte River, and the Cheyenne and Arapaho were to confine themselves to the Colorado foothills. In return the Indians were promised gifts and annual payments. This policy, known as "concentration," was designed to cut down on intertribal warfare and—far more important—to enable the government to negotiate separately with each tribe. It was the classic strategy of divide and conquer.

Although it made a mockery of diplomacy to treat with Indian tribes as though they were European powers, the United States maintained that each tribe was a sovereign nation, to be dealt with as an equal in solemn treaties. Both sides knew that this was not the case. When Indians agreed to meet in council, they were tacitly admitting defeat. They seldom drove hard bargains or broke off negotiations. Moreover, tribal chiefs had only limited power; young braves frequently refused to respect agreements made by their elders.

Indian Wars

The government showed little interest in honoring agreements with Indians. "Treaties," the historian Wilcomb E. Washburn writes, "were often made, often modified, often ignored, and often broken." No sooner had the Kansas-Nebraska bill become law than the Kansas, Omaha, Pawnee, and Yankton Sioux tribes began to feel pressure for further concessions of territory. By 1860 most of Kansas and Nebraska had been cleared; the Indians had lost all but 1.5 million of the 19-odd million acres. A gold rush into Colorado in 1859 sent thousands of greedy prospectors across the plains to drive the Cheyenne and Arapaho from land guaranteed them in 1851. Other trouble developed in the Sioux country. Thus it happened that in 1862, after federal troops had been pulled out of the West for service against the Confederacy, most of the plains Indians rose up against the whites. For five years intermittent but bloody clashes kept the entire area in a state of alarm.

This was guerrilla warfare, with all its horror and treachery. In 1864 a party of Colorado militia fell upon an unsuspecting Cheyenne community at Sand Creek and killed an estimated 450. "Kill and scalp all, big and little," Colonel J. M. Chivington, a minister in private life, told his men. "Nits make lice." A white observer described the scene: "They were scalped, their brains knocked out; the men used their knives, ripped open women, clubbed little children, knocked them in the head with their guns, beat their brains out, mutilated their bodies in every sense of the word." General Nelson A. Miles called this "Chivington Massacre" the "foulest and most unjustifiable crime in the annals of America," but it was no worse than many incidents in earlier conflicts with Indians and not very different from what was later to occur in guerrilla wars involving American troops in the Philippines and (more recently) in Vietnam.

In turn the Indians slaughtered dozens of isolated white families, ambushed small parties, and fought many successful skirmishes against troops and militia. They achieved their most notable triumph in December 1866, when the Oglala Sioux, under their great chief Red Cloud, wiped out a party of 82 soldiers under Captain W. J. Fetterman. Red Cloud fought ruthlessly, but only when goaded by the construction of the Bozeman Trail, a road through the heart of the Sioux hunting grounds in southern Montana.

In 1867 the government tried a new strategy. The "concentration" policy had evidently not gone far enough. All the plains Indians would be confined to two small reservations, one in the Black Hills of Dakota Territory, the other in Oklahoma, and forced to become farmers. At two great conclaves held in 1867 and 1868 at Medicine Lodge Creek and Fort Laramie, the principal chiefs yielded to the government's demands.

Many Indians refused to abide by these agreements. With their whole way of life at stake, they raged across the plains like a prairie fire—and were almost as destructive. General Philip Sheridan, Grant's cavalry commander, explained the situation accurately: "We took away their country and their means of support, broke up their mode of living, their habits of life, introduced disease and decay among them, and it was for this and against this that they made war. Could anyone expect less?"

That a relative handful of "savages," without central leadership or plan, could hold off the cream of the army, battle-hardened in the Civil War, can be explained by the character of the vast, trackless country and the ineptness of most American military commanders. Indian leadership was also poor in that few chiefs were capable of organizing a campaign or following up an advantage. But the Indians made superb guerrillas. Every observer called them the best cavalry soldiers in the world. Armed with stubby, powerful bows capable of driving an arrow clear through a bull buffalo, they were a fair match for troops equipped with carbines and Colt revolv-

General Sherman and the United States commissioners in council with the Sioux chiefs at Fort Laramie in 1868.

ers. Expertly they led pursuers into traps, swept down on unsuspecting supply details, stole up on small parties the way a mountain lion stalks a grazing lamb. They could sometimes be rounded up, as Sheridan herded the tribes of the Southwest into Indian Territory in 1869, but once the troops withdrew, braves began to melt away into the emptiness of the surrounding grasslands. The distinction between "treaty" Indians, who had agreed to live on the new reservations, and the "nontreaty" variety shifted almost from day to day. Trouble flared here one week, next week somewhere else, perhaps 500 miles away. No less an authority than General William Tecumseh Sherman testified that a mere 50 Indians could often "checkmate" 3,000 soldiers.

If one concedes that no one could reverse the direction of history or stop the invasion of Indian lands, then some version of the "small reservation" policy would probably have been best for the Indians. Had they been given a reasonable amount of land and adequate subsidies and allowed to maintain their way of life, they might have accepted the situation and ceased to harry the whites.

Whatever chance that policy had was greatly weakened by the government's maladministration of Indian affairs. In dealing with Indians, 19th-century Americans displayed a grave lack of talent for administration. After 1849 the Department of the Interior supposedly had charge of tribal affairs. Most of its agents systematically cheated the Indians. One, heavily involved in mining operations on the side, diverted goods intended for his charges to his private ventures. When an inspector looked into his records, he sold him shares in a mine. That worthy in turn protected himself by sharing some of the loot with the son of the commissioner of Indian affairs. Army officers squabbled frequently with Indian agents over policy, while an "Indian Ring" in the Department of the Interior systematically stole funds and supplies intended for the reservation Indians. "No branch of the national government is so spotted with fraud, so tainted with corruption, so utterly unworthy of a free and enlightened government, as this Indian Bureau," Republican Congressman James A. Garfield charged in 1869.

At about this time a Yale paleontologist, Professor Othniel C. Marsh, who wished to dig for fossils on the Sioux reservation, asked Red Cloud for permission to enter his domain. The chief agreed on condition that Marsh, whom the Indians called Big Bone Chief, take back with him samples of the moldy flour and beef that government agents were supplying to his people. Appalled by what he saw on the reservation, Marsh took the rotten supplies directly to President Grant and prepared a list of charges against the agents. General Sherman, in overall command of the Indian country, claimed in 1875: "We could settle Indian troubles in an hour, but Congress wants the patronage of the Indian bureau, and the bureau wants the appropriations without any of the trouble of the Indians themselves."

Grant wished to place the reservations under army control, but the Indians opposed this. In areas around army camps Indians fared no better than on the reservations. A quartermaster in the Apache country in New Mexico made off with 12,000 pounds of corn from the meager supplies set aside for Indian relief. According to one late-19th-century historian, "officers at those camps where the Indians were fed habitually used their official position to break the chastity of Indian women."

In 1869 Congress created a nonpolitical Board of Indian Commissioners to oversee Indian affairs, but the bureaucrats in Washington stymied the commissioners at every turn. "Their recommendations were ignored . . . gross breaking of the law was winked at, and . . . many matters were not submitted to them at all," the biographer of one commissioner has written. "They decided that their task was as useless as it was irritating."

In time the Indians might have submitted had they been allowed to hold the lands granted them under the "small reservation" policy, for they knew they could never eject the whites from their country. This was not to be. Gold was discovered in the Black Hills in 1874. By the next winter thousands of miners had invaded the reserved area. Already alarmed by the approach of crews building the Northern Pacific Railroad, the Sioux once again went on the warpath. Joining with nontreaty tribes to the west, they concentrated in the region of the Bighorn River, in southern Montana Territory.

The summer of 1876 saw three columns of troops in the field against them. The commander of one column, General Alfred H. Terry, sent ahead a small detachment of the Seventh Cavalry under Colonel George A. Custer with orders to locate the Indians' camp and then block their escape route into the inaccessible Bighorn Mountains. Custer was vain and rash, and vanity and rashness were grave handicaps in Indian fighting. Grossly underestimating the number of the Indians, he decided to attack directly with his tiny force of 264 men. At the Little Bighorn late in June he found himself surrounded by 2,500 Sioux under Rain-in-the-Face, Crazy Horse, and Sitting Bull. He and his men fought bravely, but every one of them died on the field.

Because it was so one-sided, "Custer's Last Stand" was not a typical battle, though it may be taken as symbolic of the Indian warfare of the period in the sense that it was characterized by bravery, foolhardiness, and a tragic waste of life. The battle greatly heartened the Indians, but it did not gain them their cause. That autumn, short of rations and hard pressed by overwhelming numbers of soldiers, they surrendered and returned to the reservation.

Destruction of Tribal Life

Thereafter, the plains fighting slackened. For this the building of transcontinental railroads and the destruction of the buffalo were chiefly responsible. An estimated 13 to 15 million head had roamed the plains in the mid-1860s. Then the slaughter began. Thousands were butchered to feed the gangs of laborers engaged in building the Union Pacific Railroad. Thousands more fell before the guns of sportsmen. Buffalo hunting became a fad, and a brisk demand developed for buffalo rugs and mounted buffalo heads. Railroads ran excursion trains for hunters; even the shameful practice of gunning down the beasts directly from the cars was allowed. In 1871–1872 the Grand Duke Alexis of Russia headed a gigantic hunt, supported by "Buffalo Bill" Cody, most famous of the professional buffalo killers, by the Seventh United States Cavalry under General Sheridan, and by hundreds of Indians.

SIXTEENTH ANNUAL CIRCULAR.

BUFFALO ROBES!

HART, TAYLOR & CO.

BOSTON.

COLLECTION OF

BUFFALO ROBES 1876.

UNLINED ROBES.

No. 1 Seasonable, Sewed Robes,	$9.00
" 2 " " "	8.00
" 3 " " "	7.00
" 1 " XX whole "	12.00
" 1 " " "	10.50
" 2 " " "	9.00
" 3 " " "	8.00
Calf, according to size,	4.00 to 8.00
Choice Whole and Split Robes,	12.00 to 15.00

LINED BUFFALO ROBES.

Medium and Small Lined Buffalo, $8, and	$9.00
" Lined "	11.00
" X " "	12.00
Large " "	13.50
" X " "	15.00
" XX " "	16.50
Extra Lined Robes, with superior Linings and Trimmings,	18.00 to 24.00

WE HAVE PAID SPECIAL ATTENTION TO LINING ROBES, AND CALL PARTICULAR ATTENTION TO OUR $12.00 TO $18.00 GRADES.

BUFFALO COATS.

Buffalo Overcoats, Buffalo Trimmings,	$13.50
" " Nutria,	15.00
" " Beaver Collar,	16.50
" " Beaver Collar and Facings,	18.50

Extra Length and Quality, $1.50 to 5.00 Extra.

WE HAVE REDUCED THE PRICE OF OUR COATS $1.50 EACH FROM LAST SEASON PRICES AND *HAVE NOT REDUCED* THE QUALITY.

Coon Coats,	33.00 to 45.00
Beaver "	75.00 " 100.00

WOLF AND OTHER FUR ROBES.

Black Bear Robes,	$35.00 to $100.00
Russia " "	25.00
Wolverine,	40.00 to 75.00
Beaver,	60.00 " 80.00
Raccoon,	18.00 " 30.00
Genet,	12.00 " 20.00
"Japanese" Wolf Robes,	20.00 " 25.00
Hudson Bay " 6 skins,	35.00 " 45.00
" " " 4 "	25.00 " 35.00
" " Medium Grade,	21.00 " 25.00
Prairie Wolf,	15.00 " 21.00

THE SUCCESS WE HAD WITH JAPANESE WOLF ROBES LAST SEASON, WARRANTS US IN PLACING THESE GOODS BEFORE OUR CUSTOMERS THE COMING SEASON. THE FACT THAT WE "*IMPORT*" THESE GOODS ENABLES US TO GIVE FULL VALUE TO OUR CUSTOMERS IN THIS ARTICLE. HUDSON BAY WOLF ARE SCARCE AND HIGH AS LAST SEASON, THE CATCH BEING SMALLER THAN USUAL.

Buffalo robes for carriages and sleighs were enormously popular in the eastern states, as were buffalo overcoats (which sold for less than $20). Strips of the tough hides were widely used as belts on power-driven machinery.

Preparing to surrender to General Crook, Geronimo (mounted, left) and Natiche stand with their respective sons and Geronimo's grandson; the sons wear ceremonial paint. This photograph was taken in the Sierra Madre mountains of Mexico in 1886, just before the surrender.

The discovery in 1871 of a way to make commercial use of buffalo hides completed the tragedy. In the next three years about 9 million head were killed; after another decade the animals were almost extinct. No more efficient way could have been found for destroying the plains Indians. The disappearance of the bison left them starving, homeless, purposeless.

By 1887 the tribes of the mountains and deserts beyond the plains had also given up the fight. Typical of the heartlessness of the government's treatment of these peoples was that afforded the Nez Percé of Oregon and Idaho, who were led by the remarkable Chief Joseph. After outwitting federal troops in a campaign across more than 1,000 miles of rough country, Joseph finally surrendered in October 1877. The Nez Percé were then settled on "the malarial bottoms of the Indian Territory" in far-off Oklahoma. The last Indians to abandon the unequal battle were the bitter, relentless Apaches of the Southwest, who finally yielded upon the capture of their leader, Geronimo, in 1886.

By the 1880s, the advance of whites into the plains had become, in the words of one congressman, as irresistible "as that of Sherman's to the sea." Greed for land lay behind the pressure, but large numbers of disinterested people, including most of those who deplored the way the Indians had been treated in the past, believed that the only practical way to solve the "Indian problem" was to persuade the Indians to abandon their tribal culture and live on family farms. The "wild" Indian must be changed into a "civilized" member of "American" society.

To accomplish this goal Congress passed the Dawes Severalty Act of 1887. Tribal lands were to be split up into individual allotments. To keep speculators from wresting the allotments from the Indians while they were adjusting to their new way of life, the land could not be disposed of for 25 years. Funds were to be appropriated for educating and training the Indians, and those who accepted allotments, took up residence "separate from any tribe," and "adopted the habits of civilized life" were to be granted United States citizenship.

The sponsors of the Severalty Act thought they were effecting a fine humanitarian reform. "We must throw some protection over [the Indian]," Senator Henry L. Dawes declared. "We must hold up his hand." But no one expected all the Indians to accept allotments at once, and for some years little pressure was put on any to do so. The law was a statement of policy rather than a set of specific rules and orders. "Too great haste . . . should be avoided," Indian Commissioner John Atkins explained. "The public must not be impatient. . . . Character, habits, and antecedents cannot be changed by enactment." For a decade or more after 1887, relatively little effort was made to get Indians to accept allotments.

Despite the intentions of its sponsors, the Dawes Act had disastrous results in the long run. Devised in an age that knew almost nothing about anthropology or social structure, it assumed that Indians could be transformed into small agricultural capitalists by an act of Congress. It shattered what was left of the Indians' culture without enabling them to adapt to white ways. Moreover, unscrupulous white men systematically tricked many Indians into leasing their allotments for a pittance, and local authorities often taxed Indian lands at excessive rates. In 1934, after about 86 million of the 138 million acres assigned under the Dawes Act had passed into white hands, the government returned to a policy of encouraging tribal ownership of Indian lands.

Blacks After Reconstruction

Americans shunted the Indians aside merely because they stood in their way. Other minorities were treated with equal callousness and contempt in the postwar decades. That the South would deal harshly with the former slaves once federal control was relaxed probably should have been expected. Men like Governor Wade Hampton of South Carolina had previously promised to respect black civil rights. "We . . . will secure to every citizen, the lowest as well as the highest, black as well as white, full and equal protection in the enjoyment of all his rights under the Constitution," Hampton said in 1877. This pledge was not kept.

President Hayes had urged blacks to trust the southern whites. A new Era of Good Feelings had dawned, he announced after making a goodwill tour of the South shortly after his inauguration. By December 1877 he had been sadly disillusioned. "By state legislation, by frauds, by intimidation, and by violence of the most atrocious character, colored citizens have been deprived of the right of suffrage," he wrote in his diary. However, though he had written earlier, "My task was to wipe out the color line," he did nothing to remedy the situation except, as his biographer Harry Barnard says, "to scold the South and threaten action." Frederick Douglass called Hayes's policy "sickly conciliation."

Hayes's successors in the 1880s did no better. "Time is the only cure," President Garfield said, thereby confessing that he had no policy at all. President Arthur gave federal patronage to anti-black groups in an effort to split the Democratic South. In President Cleveland's day blacks had scarcely a friend in high places, North or South. In 1887 Cleveland explained to a correspondent why he opposed "mixed schools." Expert opinion, the president said, believed "that separate schools were of much more benefit for the colored people." Hayes, Garfield, and Arthur were Republicans, Cleveland a Democrat; party made little difference. Both parties subscribed to hypocritical statements about equality and constitutional rights, and neither did anything to implement them.

For a time blacks were not totally disfranchised in the South. Rival white factions tried to manipulate them, and corruption flourished as widely as in the machine-dominated wards of the northern cities. In the 1890s, however, the southern states, led by Mississippi, began to deprive blacks of the vote despite the Fifteenth Amendment. Poll taxes, often cumulative, raised a formidable economic barrier, one that also disfranchised many poor whites. Literacy tests completed the work; a number of states provided a loophole for illiterate whites by including an "understanding" clause whereby an illiterate person could qualify by demonstrating an ability to explain the meaning of a section of the state constitution when an election official read it to him. Blacks who attempted to take the test were uniformly declared to have failed it.

In Louisiana, 130,000 blacks voted in the election of 1896. Then the law was changed. In 1900 only 5,000 votes were cast by blacks. With unctuous hypocrisy, white southerners insisted that they loved "their" blacks dearly and wished only to protect them from "the machinations of those who would use them only to further their own base ends." "We take away the Negroes' votes," a Louisiana politician explained, "to protect them just as we would protect a little child and prevent it from injuring itself with sharp-edged tools."

Practically every Supreme Court decision after 1877 that affected blacks somehow "nullified or curtailed" their rights, Professor Rayford W. Logan writes. In *Hall* v. *De Cuir* (1878) the Court even threw out a state law *forbidding* segregation on river boats, arguing that it was an unjustifiable interference with interstate commerce. The *Civil Rights Cases* (1883) declared unconstitutional the Civil Rights Act of 1875, which had barred segregation in public facilities. Blacks who were refused equal accommodations or privileges by hotels, theaters, and other privately owned facilities had no recourse at law, the Court announced. The Fourteenth Amendment guaranteed their civil rights against invasion by the states, not by individuals.

Finally, in *Plessy* v. *Ferguson* (1896), the Court ruled that even in places of public accommodation, such as railroads and, by implication, schools, segregation was legal so long as "separate but equal" facilities were provided. "If one race be inferior to the other socially, the Constitution of the United States cannot put them upon the same plane." In a noble dissent in the Plessy case, Justice John Marshall Harlan protested this line of argument. "Our Constitution is color-blind," he said. "The arbitrary separation of citizens, on the basis of race . . . is a badge of servitude wholly inconsistent with civil freedom and the equality before the law established by the Constitution." Alas, more than half a century was to pass before the Court came around to Harlan's reasoning and reversed the Plessy decision. Meanwhile, total segregation was imposed throughout the South. Separate schools, prisons, hospitals, recreational facilities, and even cemeteries were provided for blacks, and these were almost never equal to those available to whites.

Most northerners supported the government and the Court. Nearly all the newspapers commented favorably on the decision in the *Civil Rights Cases.* In news stories, papers presented a stereotyped, derogatory picture of blacks, no matter what the circumstances. Northern magazines, even high-quality publications such as *Harper's, Scribner's,* and the *Century,* repeatedly made blacks the butt of crude jokes. "The Negro's day is over," the tough-minded William Graham Sumner explained. "He is out of fashion."

The Atlanta Compromise

Since nearly all contemporary biologists, physicians, and other supposed experts on race were convinced that blacks were inferior beings, educated northerners generally accepted black inferiority as fact. James Bryce, an Englishman whose study of the United States at this time, *The American Commonwealth,* has become a classic, saw much of Americans of this type and often absorbed their point of view. Negroes, Bryce wrote, were docile, pliable, submissive, lustful, childish, impressionable, emotional, heedless, and "unthrifty." They had "no capacity for abstract thinking, for scientific inquiry, or for any kind of invention." Being "unspeakably inferior," they were "unfit to cope with a superior race."

Like Bryce, most Americans did not especially wish blacks ill; they simply refused to consider them quite human and consigned them complacently to oblivion, along with the Indians. A vicious circle was established. By denying blacks decent educational opportunities and good jobs, the dominant race could use the blacks' resultant ignorance and poverty to justify the inferior facilities offered them.

Southern blacks reacted to this deplorable situation in a variety of ways. Some sought redress in racial pride and what would later be called black nationalism. Such persons founded a number of all-black communities in Oklahoma Territory and led the great "exodus" of 1879, when, to the consternation of southern whites, thousands of blacks suddenly migrated to Kansas.* Some became so disaffected with American life that they tried to revive the African colonization movement. "Africa is our home," insisted Bishop Henry M. Turner, a huge, plainspoken man who had served as an army chaplain during the war and as a member of the Georgia legislature during Reconstruction. "Every man that has the sense of an animal must see there is no future in this country for the Negro." Another militant, T. Thomas Fortune, editor of the New York *Age* and founder of the Afro-American League (1887), called on blacks to demand full civil rights, better schools, and fair wages and to fight against discrimination of every sort. "Let us stand up like men in our own organization," he urged. "If others use . . . violence to combat our peaceful arguments, it is not for us to run away from violence."

* When a congressman asked Henry Adams, a leader of the exodus, why he and his followers had left the South, Adams replied: "We seed there was no way on earth . . . that we could better our condition there. . . . The white people . . . treat our people so bad in many respects that it is impossible for them to stand it."

Booker T. Washington's autobiography, Up from Slavery, *was published in 1901. Washington wrote his memoirs in hope of gaining aid for Tuskegee Institute.*

Militancy and black separatism won few adherents among southern blacks. For one thing, life was better than it had been under slavery. According to the most conservative estimates, the living standard of the average southern black more than doubled between 1865 and 1900. On the other hand, the forces of repression were extremely powerful. The late 19th century saw more lynchings in the South than any other period of American history. This helps explain the tactics of Booker T. Washington, one of the most extraordinary Americans of that generation.

Washington had been born a slave in Virginia in 1856. Laboriously he obtained an education, supporting himself while a student by working as a janitor. In 1881, with the financial help of northern philanthropists, he founded Tuskegee Institute in Alabama, which specialized in vocational training. His experiences convinced Washington that blacks must lift themselves by their own bootstraps but that they must also accommodate themselves to white prejudices. A persuasive speaker and a brilliant fund-raiser, he soon developed a national reputation as a "reasonable" champion of his race. (In 1891 Harvard awarded him an honorary degree.)

Washington's greatest fame and influence followed his speech to a mixed white and black audience in Atlanta in 1895. To the blacks he said: "Cast down your bucket where you are," by which he meant stop fighting segregation and second-class citizenship and concentrate on learning useful skills. "Dignify and glorify common labor," he urged. "Agitation of questions of racial equality is the extremest folly." Progress up the social and economic ladder would come not from "artificial forcing" but from self-improvement. "There is as much dignity in tilling a field as in writing a poem."

Washington asked the whites of what he called "our beloved South" to lend the blacks a hand in their efforts to advance themselves. If you will do so, he promised, you will be "surrounded by the most patient, faithful, law-abiding, and unresentful people that the world has seen."

This "Atlanta Compromise" delighted white southerners and won Washington financial support in every section of the country. He became one of the most powerful men in the United States, consulted by presidents, in close touch with business and philanthropic leaders, and capable of influencing in countless unobtrusive ways the fate of millions of blacks.

Blacks responded to the Compromise with mixed feelings. Accepting Washington's approach would relieve them of many burdens and dangers and bring them considerable material assistance. After all, being obsequious seemed, like discretion, the better part of valor. But the cost was high in surrendered personal dignity and lost hopes of obtaining real justice.

Washington's career illustrates the terrible dilemma that American blacks have always faced: the choice between confrontation and accommodation. This choice was particularly difficult in the late 19th century.

Washington chose accommodation. It is easy to condemn him as a toady but difficult to see how, at that time, a more aggressive policy could have succeeded. One can even interpret the Atlanta Compromise as a subtle form of black nationalism; in a way, Washington was urging his people not to *accept* inferiority and racial slurs but to *ignore* them. His own behavior lends force to this view, for his method of operating was indeed subtle, even devious. In his public speeches he minimized the importance of civil and political rights and accepted separate but equal facilities—if they were truly equal. Behind the scenes he lobbied against restrictive measures, marshaled large sums of money to fight test cases in the courts, and worked hard in northern states to organize the black vote and make sure that black political leaders got a share of the spoils of office. As one black militant put it, Washington knew the virtue of "sagacious silence." He was perhaps not personally an admirable man, but he was a useful one. His defects point up more the unlovely aspects of the age than those of his own character.

"The Yellow Peril"

Other disadvantaged groups also suffered during this period. Beginning in the mid-1850s a steady flow of Chinese migrated to the United States, most of them finding work in the California gold fields. About four or five thousand a year came until the negotiation of the Burlingame Treaty of 1868, the purpose of which was to provide cheap labor to fill out the construction crews building the Central Pacific Railroad. Thereafter the annual influx more than doubled, though before 1882 it exceeded 20,000 only twice. When the railroads were completed and the Chinese began to compete with native workers, a great cry of resentment went up on the West Coast. Riots broke out in San Francisco in 1877. Chinese workers were called "groveling worms," "more slavish and brutish than the beasts that roam the fields." When the migration suddenly increased in 1882 to nearly 40,000,* the protests reached such a peak that Congress passed a law prohibiting all Chinese immigration for ten years. Later legislation extended the ban indefinitely.

Chinese immigrants created genuine social problems. Most did not intend to remain in the United States and therefore made little effort to accommodate themselves to American ways. Their supposed attachment to gambling, opium, and prostitutes—over 90 percent of the Chinese in America in the 1880s were males—alarmed respectable citizens. But the westerners' attitude toward the Chinese differed only in degree from their attitude toward the Mexicans who flocked into the Southwest to work as farm laborers and to help build the railroads of the region, or from that of the rest of the country toward the European immigrants who were flooding into the country in the 1880s. While industrialists wished to keep the gates wide open in order to obtain plentiful supplies of cheap labor, organized workers and many middle-class Americans were beginning to display antiforeign attitudes reminiscent of the 1850s, when Know-Nothingism was at its height. During economic depressions and in periods of social unrest, the underlying intolerance of the majority burst forth. The Chicago Haymarket bombing of 1886, supposedly the work of foreign anarchists, produced a wave of denunciations of "long-haired, wild-eyed, bad-smelling, atheistic, reckless foreign wretches."

Women also felt the sting of discrimination in these years. Their efforts to win the vote through the Fifteenth Amendment failed, as did similar attempts in the states, seven of which rejected female suffrage proposals between 1867 and 1877. In *Minor* v. *Happersett* (1875) the Supreme Court unanimously rejected the argument that women could vote because they were citizens. Although Congress passed a law allowing women lawyers to practice in federal courts, some states barred them from the profession and the Supreme Court upheld such laws. "The natural and proper timidity and delicacy which belongs to the female sex," one justice proclaimed, "unfits it for many . . . occupations." Women, he added, should stick to "the noble and benign offices of wife and mother." Thus women too received short shrift in post–Civil War America.

Exploiting Mineral Wealth in the West

The natural resources of the nation were exploited in these decades even more ruthlessly and thoughtlessly than were its human resources. Americans had long regarded the West as a limitless treasure to be grasped as rapidly as possible, and after 1865 they engrossed its riches still faster and in a wider variety of ways. Miners had invaded the western

* This was still only about 5 percent of the total immigration of that year. From Germany alone, in 1882, over 250,000 people came to the United States.

The first piece of music published in California (that's what this cover says) was appropriately titled "The California Pioneers."

mountains long before the Civil War. From the mid-1850s to the mid-1870s thousands of gold-crazed prospectors fanned out through the Rockies, panning every stream and hacking furiously at every likely outcropping from the Fraser River country of British Columbia to Tucson in southern Arizona, from the eastern slopes of the Sierras to the Great Plains.

Gold and silver were scattered throughout the area, though usually too thinly to make mining profitable. Whenever anyone made a "strike," prospectors flocked to the site, drawn by rumors of streambeds gleaming with auriferous gravel and of nuggets the size of men's fists. For a few months the area teemed with activity. Towns of 5,000 or more sprang up overnight; improvised roads were crowded with people and supply wagons. Claims were staked out along every stream and gully. Then, usually, expectations faded in the light of reality: high prices, low yields, hardship, violence, and deception. The boom collapsed and the towns died as quickly as they had risen. A few would have found wealth, the rest only backbreaking labor and disappointment—until tales of another strike sent them dashing feverishly across the land on another golden chase.

In the spring of 1858 it was upon the Fraser River in Canada that the horde descended, 30,000 Californians in the van. The following spring, Pikes Peak in Colorado attracted the pack, experienced California prospectors ("yonder siders") mixing with "greenhorns" from every corner of the globe. In June 1859 came the finds in Nevada, where the famous Comstock Lode yielded ores worth nearly $4,000 a ton. In 1861, while men in the settled areas were laying down their tools to take up arms, the miners were racing to the Idaho panhandle, hoping to become millionaires overnight. The next year the rush was to the Snake River valley, then in 1863 and 1864 to Montana. In 1874–1876 the Black Hills in the heart of the Sioux lands were inundated.

In a sense the Denvers, Aurarias, Virginia Cities, Orofinos, and Gold Creeks of the West during the war years were harbingers of the view that flourished in the East in the age of President Grant and his immediate successors. The miners enthusiastically adopted the get-rich-quick philosophy, willingly enduring privations and laboring hard, always with the object of striking it rich. The idea of reserving any part of the West for future generations never entered their heads.

The sudden prosperity of the mining towns attracted every kind of shady character. The mines, one forty-niner wrote, were "loaded to the muzzle" with "rascals from Oregon, pickpockets from New York, accomplished gentlemen from Europe, interlopers from Lima and Chile, Mexican thieves, gamblers from no particular spot, and assassins manufactured in Hell." Gambling dens, dance halls, saloons, and brothels mushroomed wherever precious metal was found. Law enforcement was a constant problem, but sooner or later the "better element" in every mining community formed a "vigilance committee" and by a few summary hangings drove the outlaws out of town. Much of the difficulty lay in the antisocial attitudes of the miners themselves. "They were hardened individualists who paid little attention to community affairs unless their own interests were threatened," Ray Allen

Billington, a historian of the frontier, has written.

Gold and silver dominated people's thoughts and dreams, and few paid much attention to the means employed in accumulating this wealth. Storekeepers charged outrageous prices; claim holders "salted" worthless properties with nuggets in order to swindle gullible investors. Ostentation characterized the successful, braggadocio those who failed. During the administration of President Grant, Virginia City, Nevada, was at the peak of its vulgar prosperity, producing an average of $12 million a year in ore. Built upon the richness of the Comstock Lode ($306 million in gold and silver was extracted from the Comstock in 20 years), it had 25 saloons before it had 4,000 people. By the 1870s its mountainside site was disfigured by ugly, ornate mansions where successful mine operators ate from fine china and swilled champagne as though it were water.

In 1873, after the discovery of the Big Bonanza, a seam of rich ore more than 50 feet thick, the future of Virginia City seemed boundless. Other discoveries shortly thereafter indicated to optimists that the mining boom in the West would continue indefinitely. The finds in the Black Hills district in 1875 and 1876, heralding deposits yielding eventually $100 million, led to the mushroom growth of Deadwood, home of Wild Bill Hickok, Deadwood Dick, Calamity Jane, and such lesser-known characters as California Jack and Poker Alice. In Deadwood, according to Professor Billington, "the faro games were wilder, the hurdy-gurdy dance halls noisier, the street brawls more common, than in any other western town." New strikes in Colorado in 1876 and 1877 caused the town of Leadville to boom; in 1880 there were 30,000 people in the area. However, this was the last important flurry to ruffle the mining frontier. The West continued to yield much gold and silver, especially silver, but big corporations produced nearly all of it. The mines around Deadwood were soon controlled by one large company, Homestake Mining.

This is the culminating irony of the history of the mining frontier: Shoestring prospectors, independent and enterprising, made the key discoveries. They established local institutions and supplied the West with much of its color and folklore. But the stockholders of large corporations, many of whom had never seen a mine, made off with the lion's share of the wealth. Those whose worship of gold was direct and incessant, the prospectors who peopled the mining towns and gave the frontier its character, mostly died poor, still seeking a prize as elusive if not as illusory as the pot of gold at the end of the rainbow.

For the mining of gold and silver is not essentially different from the mining of coal and iron. To operate profitably, large capital investments, heavy machinery, railroads, and hundreds of hired hands are required. Henry Comstock, the prospector who gave his name to the Comstock Lode, was luckier than most, but he sold his claims to the lode for a pittance, disposing of what became one valuable mine for $40 and receiving only $10,000 for his share of the fabulous Ophir, the richest concentration of gold and silver ever found. His greatest financial gain from the Comstock came some years later when the owners of the Ophir paid him well to testify in their corporation's behalf in an important lawsuit. More typical of the successful mine owner was George Hearst, senator from California and father of the newspaper tycoon William Randolph Hearst, who, by shrewd speculations, obtained large blocks of stock in mining properties scattered from Montana to Mexico.

Though marked by violence, fraud, greed, and lost hopes, the gold rushes had valuable results. The most obvious was the new metal itself, which bolstered the financial position of the United States during and after the Civil War. Quantities of European goods needed for the war effort and for postwar economic development were paid for with the yield of the new mines. Gold and silver also caused a great increase of interest in the West. A valuable literature appeared, part imaginative, part reportorial, describing the mining camps and the life of the prospectors. These works fascinated contemporaries (as they have continued to fascinate succeeding generations when adapted to the motion picture and to television). Mark Twain's *Roughing It* (1872), based in part on his experiences in the Nevada mining country, is the most famous example of this literature.

Each new strike and rush, no matter how ephemeral, brought permanent settlers along with the prospectors: farmers, cattlemen, storekeepers, teamsters, lawyers, and ministers. Some saw from the start that a better living could be made supplying the needs of the gold seekers than looking for the elusive metal. Others, failing to find mineral wealth, took up whatever occupation they could rather than starve or return home empty-handed. In every mining town—along with the saloons and brothels—schools, churches, and newspaper offices sprang up.

The philosopher Josiah Royce (1855–1916), the son of forty-niners, grew up in a California mining town and in San Francisco. Many years later, while teaching at Harvard, he wrote a book about life in the camps. "The romantic degradation of the early mining life, with its . . . inevitable brutality and its resulting loathsome corruption, gave place to the commonplace industries of the later mining days," he recalled. "That a community of Americans could sin as fearfully as, in the early years, the mining community did sin, and could yet live to purify itself within so short a time," he explained, was due to "the moral elasticity" and "social vitality" of the people.

The mines also speeded the political organization of the West. Colorado and Nevada became territories in 1861, Arizona and Idaho in 1863, Montana in 1864. Although Nevada was admitted before it had 60,000 residents (in 1864, to ratify the Thirteenth Amendment and help reelect Lincoln), most of these territories did not become states for decades. But because of the miners, the framework for future development was early established.

The Land Bonanza

While the miners were engrossing the mineral wealth of the West, other interests were snapping up the region's choice farmland. Presumably the Homestead Act of 1862 had ended the reign of the speculator and the large landholder. An early amendment to the act even prevented husbands and wives from filing separate claims. The West, land reformers had assumed, would soon be dotted with 160-acre family farms.

They were doomed to disappointment. Most landless Americans were too poor to become farmers even when they could obtain land without cost. The expense of moving a family to the ever-receding frontier exceeded the means of many, and the costs of hoes and scythes, harvesting machines, fencing, and housing presented a formidable barrier. As for the industrial workers for whom the free land was supposed to provide a "safety valve," they had neither the skills nor the inclination to become farmers. Homesteaders usually came from districts not far removed from frontier conditions. And despite the intent of the law, speculators often managed to obtain large tracts. They hired men to stake out claims, falsely swear that they had fulfilled the conditions laid down in the law for obtaining legal title, and then deed the land over to their employers.

Furthermore, 160 acres was not enough for raising livestock or for the kind of commercial agriculture that was developing west of the Mississippi. Congress made a feeble attempt to make larger holdings available to homesteaders by passing the Timber Culture Act of 1873, which permitted individuals to claim an additional 160 acres if they would agree to plant a quarter of it in trees within 10 years. This law proved helpful to some farmers in the tier of states from North Dakota to Kansas. Nevertheless, fewer than 25 percent of the 245,000 who took up land under it obtained final title to the property. Raising large numbers of seedling trees on the plains was a difficult task.

While futilely attempting to make a forest of parts of the treeless plains, the government permitted private interests to gobble up and destroy many of the great forests that clothed the slopes of the Rockies and the Sierras. The Timber and Stone Act of 1878 allowed anyone to claim a quarter section of forest land for $2.50 an acre if it was "unfit for civilization." This laxly drawn measure enabled lumber companies to obtain thousands of acres by hiring dummy entrymen, whom they marched in gangs to the land offices, paying them a few dollars for their time after they had signed over their claims. "In many instances whole townships have been entered under this law in the interest of one person or firm, to whom the lands have been conveyed as soon as receipts for the purchase price were issued," the commissioner of the General Land Office complained in 1901.

Had the land laws been better drafted and more honestly enforced, it is still unlikely that the policy of granting free land to small homesteaders would have succeeded. Aside from the built-in difficulties faced by small-scale agriculturalists in the West, too many people in every section were eager to exploit the nation's land for their own profit, without regard for the general interest. Immediately

The crews of five combines stopped during the wheat harvest on a bonanza farm in northern California to have their picture taken. Combines such as these reaped, threshed, cleaned, and bagged grain in a single operation.

after the war, for example, Congress reserved 47.7 million acres of public land in the South for homesteaders, stopping all cash sales in the region. But in 1876 this policy was reversed and the land thrown open. Speculators flocked to the feast in such numbers that the Illinois Central Railroad ran special trains from Chicago to Mississippi and Louisiana. Between 1877 and 1888 over 5.6 million acres were sold; much of the land covered with valuable pine and cypress.

However they attained their acres, frontier farmers of the 1870s and 1880s grappled with novel problems as they pushed across the grasslands of Kansas, Nebraska, and the Dakotas with their families. The first settlers took up land along the rivers and creeks, where they found enough timber for home building, fuel, and fencing. Later arrivals had to build houses of the tough prairie sod and depend on hay, dried sunflower stalks, and even buffalo dung for fuel. The soil was rich, but the climate, especially in the semiarid regions beyond the 98th meridian of longitude, made agriculture frequently difficult and often impossible. Blizzards, floods, grasshopper plagues, and prairie fires caused repeated heartaches, but periodic drought and searing summer heat were the worst hazards, destroying the hopes and fortunes of thousands.

At the same time, the flat immensity of the land, combined with newly available farm machinery and the development of rail connections with the East, encouraged the growth of corporation-controlled "bonanza" farms, some of them tens of thousands of acres in size. One such organization was the railroad-owned empire managed by Oliver Dalrymple in Dakota Territory, which cultivated 25,000 acres of wheat in 1880. Dalrymple employed 200 pairs of harrows to prepare his soil, 125 seeders to sow his seed, and 155 binders to harvest his crop. Bonanza farmers could buy supplies wholesale and obtain concessions from railroads and processors, which added to their profits.

Even the biggest organizations could not cope with prolonged drought, however, and most of the bonanza outfits failed in the dry years of the late 1880s. Those wise farmers who diversified their crops and cultivated their land intensively fared better in the long run, though even they could not hope to earn a profit in really dry years.

Despite the hazards of plains agriculture, the region became the breadbasket of America in the decades following the Civil War. By 1889 Minnesota topped the nation in wheat production, and ten years later four of the five leading wheat states lay west of the Mississippi. The plains also accounted for heavy percentages of the nation's other cereal crops, together with immense quantities of beef, pork, and mutton.

Like other exploiters of the nation's resources, farmers took whatever they could from the soil with little heed for preserving its fertility and preventing erosion. The consequent national loss was less apparent because it was diffuse and slow to assume drastic proportions, but it was very real.

Western Railroad Building

Further exploitation of land resources by private interests resulted from the government's policy of subsidizing western railroads. Here was a clear illustration of the conflict between the idea of the West as a national heritage to be disposed of to deserving citizens and the concept of the region as a cornucopia pouring forth riches to be gathered up and carted off by anyone powerful and determined enough to take them. When it came to a choice between giving a particular tract to railroads or to homesteaders, the homesteaders nearly always lost out. To serve the valuable national purpose of the linking of the sections by rail, the land of the West was dispensed wholesale as a substitute for cash subsidies.

Federal land grants to railroads began in 1850 with those allotted the Illinois Central. Over the next two decades about 49 million acres were given to various lines indirectly in the form of grants to the states, but the most lavish gifts of the public domain were those made directly to builders of intersectional trunk lines. These roads received more than 155 million acres in this fashion, although about 25 million acres reverted to the government when certain companies failed to construct the required miles of track. About 75 percent of this land went to aid the construction of four transcontinental railroads: the Union Pacific–Central Pacific line, running from Nebraska to San Francisco, completed in 1869; the Atchison, Topeka and Santa Fe, running from Kansas City to Los Angeles by way of Santa Fe and Albuquerque, completed in 1883; the Southern Pacific line, running from San Francisco to New Orleans by way of Yuma and El Paso, completed in 1883; and the Northern Pacific, running from Duluth, Minnesota, to Portland, Oregon, completed in 1883.

Unless the government had been willing to build the transcontinental lines itself—and this was

Railroads expanded using bridges and trestles to cross inhospitable terrain that had presented problems for horse and wagon. This bridge east of Santa Fe, New Mexico, was completed in 1880.

unthinkable in an age dominated by belief in individual exploitation and wary of any activity that entrusted the spending of large sums to politicians—some system of subsidy was essential. For private investors would not hazard the huge sums needed to lay tracks across hundreds of miles of rugged, empty country when traffic over the road could not possibly produce profits for many years. Grants of land seemed a sensible way of financing construction. The method avoided direct outlays of public funds, for the companies could pledge the land as security for bond issues or sell it directly for cash. Moreover, land and railroad values were intimately linked in contemporary thinking. "The occupation of new land and the building of new mileage go hand in hand," the *Commercial and Financial Chronicle* explained in 1886.

> There could be no great or continuous opening up of new territory without the necessary facilities in the way of railroads. On the other hand, most new mileage on the borders of our Western territory is prosecuted with the idea and expectation that it is to pave the way for an accession of new settlers and an extension of the area of land devoted to their uses.

In many cases the value of the land granted might be recovered by the government when it sold other lands in the vicinity, for such properties would certainly be worth more after transportation facilities to eastern markets had been constructed. "Why," the governor of one eastern state asked in 1867, "should private individuals be called upon to make a useless sacrifice of their means, when railroads can be constructed by the unity of public and private interests, and made profitable to all?"

The Pacific Railway Act of 1862 established the pattern for these grants. It gave the builders of the Union Pacific and Central Pacific railroads 5 square miles of public land on each side of their right of way for each mile of track laid. The land was allotted in alternate sections, forming a pattern like a checkerboard, the squares of one color representing railroad property, the other government property. Presumably this arrangement benefited the entire nation since half the land close to the railroad remained in public hands.

However, whenever grants were made to railroads, the adjacent government lands were not opened to homesteaders—on the theory that free land in the immediate vicinity of a line would prevent the road from disposing of its properties at good prices. Since, in addition to the land granted the railroads, a wide zone of "indemnity" lands was reserved to allow the roads to choose alternative sites to make up for lands that settlers had already taken up within the checkerboard, homesteading was in fact prohibited near land-grant railroads. Grants per mile of track ranged from five alternate sections on each side of the track to the Union and Central Pacific to 40 sections to the Northern Pacific, authorized in 1864. In the latter case, when the indemnity zone was included, homesteaders were barred from an area 100 miles wide, all the way from Lake Superior to the Pacific. More than 20 years after receiving its immense grant, the Northern Pacific was still attempting to keep homesteaders from filing in the indemnity zone. President Cleveland finally put a stop to this in 1887, saying that he could find "no evidence" that "this vast tract is necessary for the fulfillment of the grant."

Historians have argued at length about the fairness of the land-grant system. No railroad corporation waxed fat directly from the sale of its lands, which were sold at prices averaging between $2 and $5 an acre. Collectively the roads have taken in between $400 million and $500 million from this source, but only over the course of a century. Land-grant lines did a great deal to encourage the growth of the West by advertising their property widely and providing cheap transportation for prospective settlers and efficient shipping services for farmers. They were required by law to carry troops and handle government business free or at reduced rates, which saved the government many millions over the years. At the same time, the system imposed no effective restraints on how the railroads used the funds raised with federal aid. Building their lines largely with money obtained from land grants, the operators tended to be extravagant and often downright corrupt.

The Union Pacific was built by a construction company, the Crédit Mobilier, which was owned by the promoters. These men awarded themselves contracts at prices that assured the Crédit Mobilier fat profits. When Congress threatened to investigate the Union Pacific in 1868, Oakes Ames, a stockholder in both companies who was also a member of Congress, sold key congressmen and

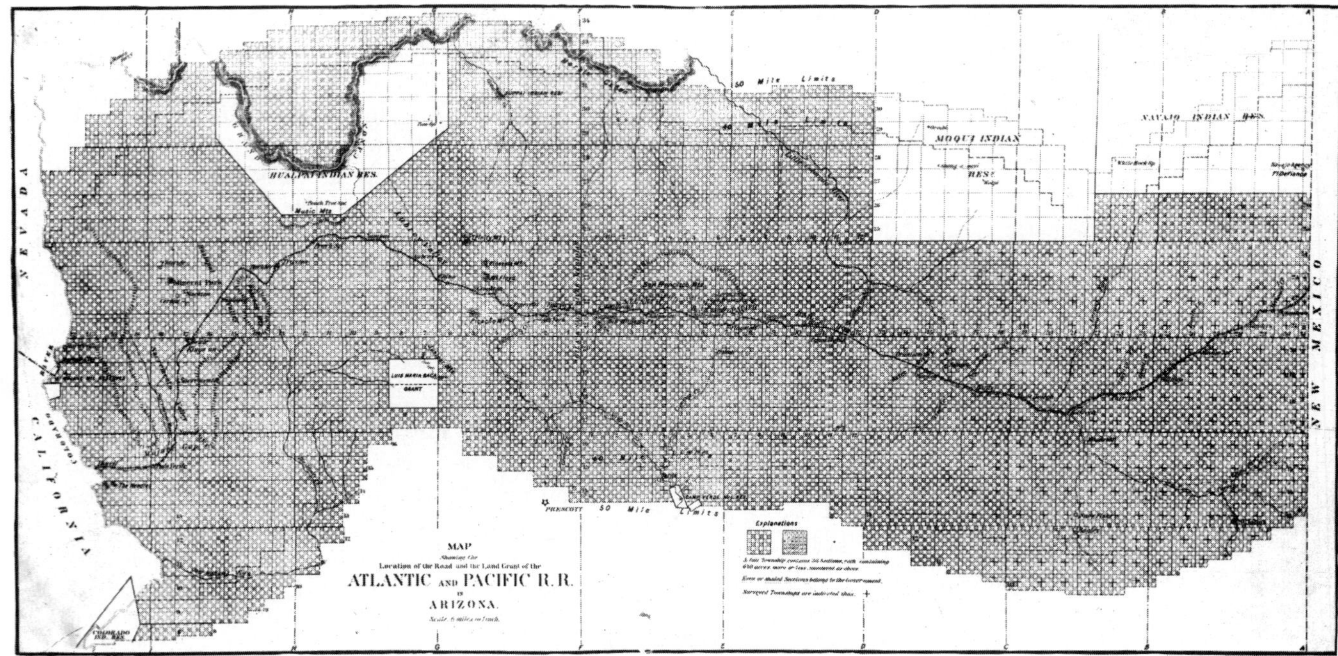

On the contemporary map above, the Atlantic and Pacific Railroad land grant in Arizona appears as shaded squares on a checkerboard. The grant cut a 100-mile-wide swath across the entire territory (below).

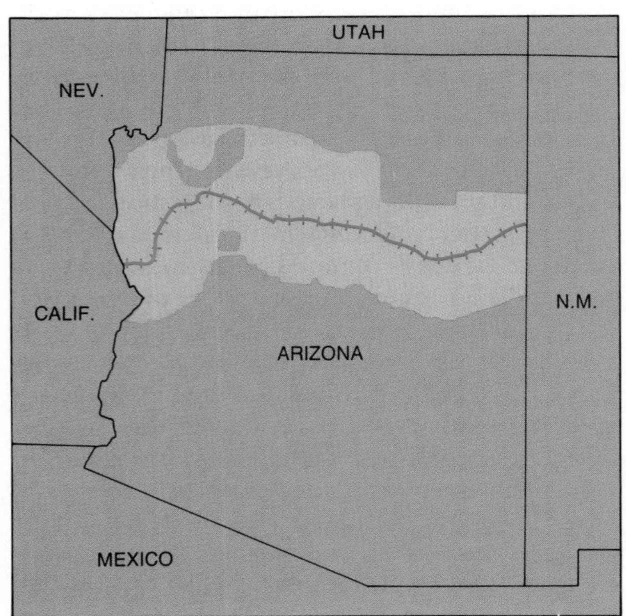

government officials over 300 shares of Crédit Mobilier stock at a price far below its real value. The shares were placed "where they will do the most good," Ames said. "I have found," he also said, "there is no difficulty in inducing men to look after their own property."

When these transactions were exposed, the House of Representatives censured Ames, but such was the temper of the times that neither he nor most of his associates believed he had done anything immoral. According to the president of one western railroad, congressmen frequently tried to use their influence to get railroad land at bargain prices. "Isn't there a discount?" they would ask. "Surely you can give the land cheaper to a friend. . . ." The railroads seldom resisted this type of pressure.

The construction of the Central Pacific in the 1860s illustrates how the system encouraged extravagance. In addition to land grants, the Central Pacific and the Union Pacific were given loans in the form of government bonds—from \$16,000 to \$48,000 for each mile of track laid, depending on the difficulty of the terrain. The two competed with each other for the subsidies, the Central Pacific building eastward from Sacramento, the Union Pa-

The meeting of the rails at Promontory Point, Utah, on May 10, 1869. The Central Pacific's engine, "Jupiter," moved slowly toward the Union Pacific's No. 119. Dignitaries gathered for the ceremonial driving of the golden spike by rail magnate Leland Stanford. Stanford swung and missed.

cific westward from Nebraska. They put huge crews to work grading and laying track, bringing up supplies over the already completed road. The Union Pacific employed Civil War veterans and Irish immigrants, the Central Chinese immigrants.

This plan favored the Union Pacific. While the Central Pacific was inching upward through the gorges and granite of the mighty Sierras, the Union Pacific was racing across the level plains. Once beyond the Sierras, the Central Pacific would have easy going across the Nevada-Utah plateau country, but by then it might be too late to prevent the Union Pacific from making off with most of the government aid.

The Central Pacific construction crews were managed by Charles Crocker, a hulking, relentless driver of men who had come to California during the gold rush and made a small fortune as a merchant in Sacramento. Crocker wasted huge sums by working through the winter in the High Sierras. Often the men labored in tunnels dug through 40-foot snowdrifts to get at the frozen ground. To speed construction of the Summit Tunnel, Crocker had a shaft cut down from above so that crews could work out from the middle as well as in from each end. In 1866, over the most difficult terrain, he laid 28 miles of track—at a cost of more than $280,000 a mile. Experts later estimated that 70 percent of this sum could have been saved had speed not been a factor. Such prodigality made economic sense to the "Big Four" (Collis P. Huntington, Leland Stanford, Mark Hopkins, and Crocker) who controlled the Central Pacific because of the fat profits they were making through its construction company and because of the gains they could count on once they reached the flat country beyond the Sierras, where construction costs would amount to only half the federal aid.

Crocker's herculean efforts paid off. The mountains were conquered, and then the crews raced across the Great Basin to Salt Lake City and beyond. The meeting of the rails—the occasion of a national celebration—took place at Promontory, north of Ogden, Utah, on May 10, 1869. Leland Stanford drove the final ceremonial golden spike with a silver hammer.* The Union Pacific had built 1,086 miles of track, the Central 689 miles.

In the long run the wasteful way in which the

* A mysterious "San Francisco jeweler" passed among the onlookers, taking orders for souvenir watch chains that he proposed to make from the spike at $5 each.

Central Pacific was built hurt the road severely. It was ill constructed, over grades too steep and around curves too sharp, and burdened with debts that were too heavy. Such was the fate of nearly all the railroads constructed with the help of government subsidies. The likely alternative to the land-grant system, government construction and ownership, attracted little support. The only transcontinental built without land grants was the Great Northern, running from St. Paul, Minnesota, to the Pacific. Spending private capital, its guiding genius, James J. Hill, was compelled to build economically and to plan carefully. As a result, his was the only transcontinental line to weather the depression of the 1890s without going into bankruptcy.

The Cattle Kingdom

While miners were digging out the mineral wealth of the West and railroaders were taking possession of much of its land, another group was avidly acquiring its endless acres of grass. For 20 years after the Civil War cattlemen and sheep raisers dominated huge areas of the High Plains, making millions of dollars by grazing their herds on lands they did not own.

Columbus brought the first cattle to the New World in 1493, on his second voyage, and later *conquistadores* took them to every corner of Spain's American empire. Mexico proved to be so well suited to cattle raising that many were allowed to roam loose. They multiplied rapidly, and by the late 18th century what is now southern Texas harbored enormous herds. The beasts interbred with nondescript "English" cattle, brought into the area by American settlers, to produce the Texas longhorn. Hardy, wiry, ill-tempered, and fleet, with horns often attaining a spread of 6 feet, these animals were far from ideal as beef cattle and almost as hard to capture as wild horses, but they existed in southern Texas by the million, most of them unowned.

The lack of markets and transportation explains why Texas cattle were so lightly regarded. But conditions were changing. Industrial growth in the East was causing an increase in the urban population and a consequent rise in the demand for food. At the same time, the expansion of the railroad network made it possible to move cattle cheaply over long distances. As the iron rails inched across the plains, astute cattlemen began to do some elementary figuring. Longhorns could be had locally for $3 and $4 a head. In the northern cities they would bring ten times that much, perhaps even more. Why not round them up and herd them northward to the railroads, allowing them to feed along the way on the abundant grasses of the plains?

In 1866 a number of Texans drove large herds northward toward Sedalia, Missouri, railhead of the Missouri Pacific. This route took the herds through wooded and settled country and across Indian reservations, which provoked many difficulties. The next year the drovers, inspired by a clever young Illinois cattle dealer named Joseph G. McCoy and other entrepreneurs, led their herds north by a more westerly route, across unsettled grasslands, to Abilene, Kansas, on the Kansas Pacific line. They earned excellent profits, and during the next five years about 1.5 million head made the "long drive" over the Chisholm Trail to Abilene, where they were sold to ranchers, feedlot operators, and the agents of eastern meat packers. Other shipping points sprang up as the railroads pushed westward.

The technique of the long drive, which involved guiding herds of two or three thousand cattle slowly across as much as a thousand miles of country, produced the American cowboy, renowned in song, story, and on film. Half a dozen of these men could control several thousand steers. Mounted on wiry ponies, they would range alongside the herd, keeping the animals on the move but preventing stampedes, allowing them time to rest yet steadily pressing them toward the yards of Abilene.

Although the cowboy's life was far more prosaic than it appears in modern legend, consisting mainly of endless hours on the trail surrounded by thousands of bellowing beasts, he was indeed an interesting type, perfectly adapted to his environment. Cowboys virtually lived on horseback, for their work kept them far from human habitation for months on end. Most, accustomed to solitude, were indeed "strong, silent men." They were courageous—and expert marksmen, too, for they lived amid many dangers and had to know how to protect themselves. Few grew rich, yet like the miners they were true representatives of their time—determinedly individualistic, contemptuous of authority, crude, devoted to coarse pleasures.

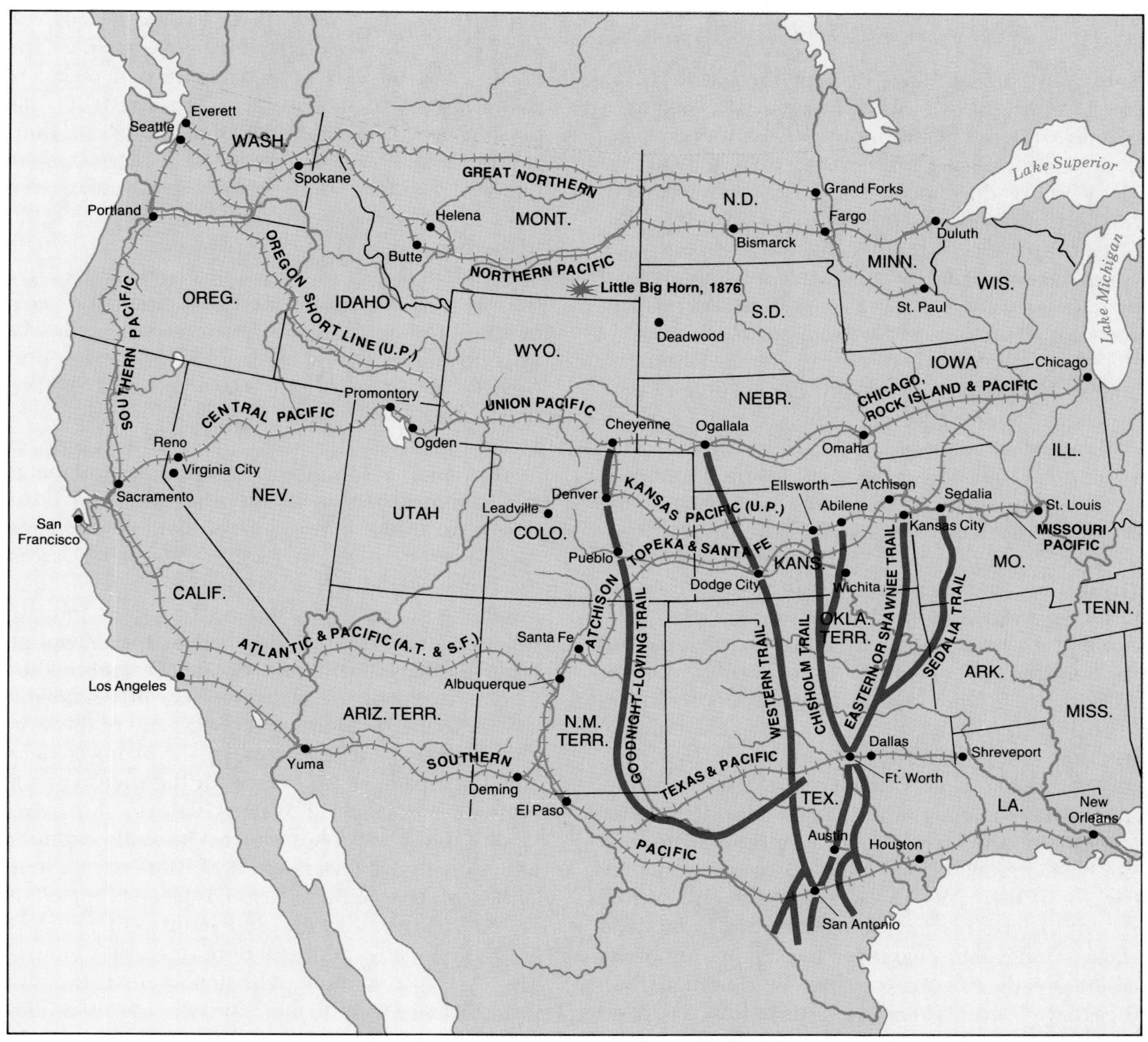

THE WEST: CATTLE, RAILROADS, AND MINING, 1850–1893

The major "cattle towns," Abilene, Wichita, Ellsworth, Dodge City, and Caldwell, had their full share of saloons, gambling dens, and "dance houses" patronized by cowboys and other transients bent on having a good time. Most were young, male, and single. Violence punctuated their activities, but not nearly as frequently as legend suggests. Stories of individual desperadoes and gangs of outlaws "shooting up" towns and terrorizing honest citizens are fictitious. Police forces were well organized. Indeed, the "respectable" town residents tended to urge leniency for lawbreakers because of the money they and their fellows brought to the towns. A careful check of the records by the historian Robert Dykstra revealed that between 1870 and 1885 there were only 45 homicides in these five towns, and some of them had nothing to do with the cattle trade.

Open-Range Ranching

Soon cattlemen discovered that the hardy Texas stock could survive the winters of the northern plains. Attracted by the apparently limitless forage, they began to bring up herds to stock the vast regions where the buffalo had so recently roamed. Introducing pedigreed Hereford bulls, they improved the stock without weakening its resistance to harsh conditions. By 1880 some 4.5 million head had spread across the sea of grass that ran from Kansas to Montana and west to the Rockies.

The prairie grasses offered cattlemen a bonanza almost as valuable as the gold mines. Open-range ranching required actual ownership of no more than a few acres along some watercourse. In this semiarid region, control of water enabled a rancher to dominate all the surrounding area back to the divide separating his range from the next stream without investing a cent in the purchase of land. His cattle, wandering freely on the public domain, fattened on grass owned by all the people, to be turned into beefsteak and leather for the profit of the rancher. Theoretically, anyone could pasture stock on the open range, but without access to water it was impossible to do so. "I have 2 miles of running water," a cattleman said in testifying before the Public Land Commission. "That accounts for my ranch being where it is. The next water from me in one direction is 23 miles; now no man can have a ranch between these two places. I have control of the grass, the same as though I owned it." By having his cowhands take out homestead claims along watercourses in his region, a rancher could greatly expand the area he dominated. In the late 1870s one Colorado cattle baron controlled an area roughly the size of Connecticut and Rhode Island even though he owned only 105 small parcels that totaled about 15,500 acres.

Generally a group of ranchers acted together, obtaining legal title to the lands along the bank of a stream and grazing their cattle over the area drained by it. The herds became thoroughly intermixed, each owner's being identified by his individual brand mark. Every spring and fall the ranchers staged a great roundup, driving in all the cattle to a central place, separating them by brand marks, culling steers for shipment to market, and branding new calves.

With the demand for meat rising and transportation cheap, a princely fortune could be made in a few years with a relatively small investment. Capitalists from the East and from Europe began to pour funds into the business. Attracted by what one writer called the "Beef Bonanza"—in a book subtitled *How to Get Rich on the Plains*—Eastern "dudes" like Theodore Roosevelt, a young New York assemblyman who sank over $50,000 in his Elkhorn Ranch in Dakota Territory in 1883, bought up cattle as a sort of profitable hobby. Roosevelt, clad in buckskin and armed with a small armory of rifles and six-shooters, made quite a splash in Dakota, but not as a rancher. Soon large outfits such as the Prairie Cattle Company and the Nebraska Land and Cattle Company, controlled by British investors, and the Union Cattle Company of Wyoming, a $3 million corporation, dominated the business, just as large companies had taken over most of the important gold and silver mines.

Unlike other exploiters of the West's resources, the ranchers did not at first injure or reduce any public resource. Grass eaten by their stock annually renewed itself, the soil enriched by the droppings of the animals. Furthermore, ranchers poached on the public domain because there was no reasonable way for them to obtain legal possession of the large areas necessary to raise cattle on the plains. Federal land laws made no allowance for the special conditions of the semiarid West. "Title to the public lands [of the West] cannot be honestly acquired under the homestead laws," S. E. Burdett, commissioner of the General Land Office, reported in 1875. "That cultivation and improvement which are required . . . in the place of price, are impossible. . . . A system of sale should be authorized in accordance with the necessities of the situation."

Such a system was soon devised by Major John Wesley Powell, later the director of the United States Geological Survey. His *Report on the Lands of the Arid Region of the United States* (1879) suggested that western lands be divided into three classes: irrigable lands, timber lands, and "pasturage" lands. On the pasturage lands the "farm unit" ought to be at least 2,560 acres (four sections), Powell urged. Groups of these units should be organized into "pasturage districts" in which the ranchers "should have the right to make their own regulations for the division of lands, the use of the water . . . and for the pasturage of lands in common or in severalty."

Barbed-Wire Warfare

Congress refused to change the land laws in any basic way, and this had two harmful effects. First, it encouraged fraud: those who could not get title to enough land honestly turned to subterfuge. The Desert Land Act (1877) allowed anyone to obtain 640 acres in the arid states for $1.25 an acre provided the owner irrigated part of it within three years. Since the original claimant could transfer the holding, the ranchers set their cowboys and other hands to filing claims, which were then signed over to them. Over 2.6 million acres were taken up under the act, and according to the best estimate, about 95 percent of the claims were fraudulent—no sincere effort was made to irrigate the land.

Second, overcrowding became a problem that led to serious conflicts, even killings, because no one had uncontestable title to the land. The leading ranchers banded together in cattlemen's associations to deal with overcrowding and with such problems as quarantine regulations, water rights, and thievery. In most cases these associations devised effective and sensible rules, but their functions would better have been performed by the government, as such matters usually are.

To keep other ranchers' cattle from those sections of the public domain they considered their own, the associations and many individuals began to fence huge areas. This was possible only because of the invention in 1874 of barbed wire by Joseph F. Glidden, an Illinois farmer. By the 1880s thousands of miles of the new fencing had been strung across the plains, often across roads and in a few cases around entire communities. "Barbed-wire wars" resulted, fought by rancher against rancher, cattleman against sheepman, herder against farmer. The associations tried to police their fences and to punish anyone who cut their wire. Signs posted along lonely stretches gave dire warnings to trespassers. "The Son of a Bitch who opens this

In 1885 masked Nebraskans seeking access to water posed for photographer S. D. Butcher, who captioned the picture "Settlers taking the law in their own hands: cutting 15 miles of the Brighton Ranch fence."

fence had better look out for his scalp," one such sign announced, a perfect statement of the philosophy of the age.

By installing fences the cattlemen were unwittingly destroying their own way of doing business. On a truly open range, cattle could fend for themselves, instinctively finding water during droughts, drifting safely downwind before blizzards. Barbed wire prevented their free movement. During winter storms these slender strands became as lethal as high-tension wires: the drifting cattle piled up against them and died by the thousands. "The advent of barbed wire," Walter Prescott Webb wrote in his classic study *The Great Plains* (1931), "brought about the disappearance of the open, free range and converted the range country into the big-pasture country."

The boom times were ending. Overproduction was driving down the price of beef; expenses were on the rise; many sections of the range were badly overgrazed. The dry summer of 1886 left the stock in such poor condition as winter approached that the *Rocky Mountain Husbandman* urged its readers to sell their cattle despite the prevailing low prices rather than "endanger the whole herd by having the range overstocked."

Some ranchers took this advice; those who did not made a fatal error. Winter that year arrived early and with unparalleled fury. Blizzards raged and temperatures plummeted far below zero. Cattle crowded into low places only to be engulfed in giant snowdrifts; barbed wire took a fearful toll. When spring finally came, the streams were choked with rotting carcasses. Between 80 and 90 percent of all cattle on the range were dead. "We have had a perfect smashup all through the cattle country," Theodore Roosevelt wrote sadly in April 1887 from Elkhorn Ranch.

After that cruel winter, open-range cattle raising was finished. The large companies were bankrupt; many independent operators, like Roosevelt, became discouraged and sold out. When the industry revived, it was on a smaller, more efficiently organized scale. The fencing movement continued, but now each stockman enclosed land he actually owned. It then became possible to bring in pedigreed bulls to improve the breed. Cattle raising, like mining before it, ceased to be an adventure in rollicking individualism and reckless greed and became a business.

By the late 1880s the bonanza days of the West were over. No previous frontier had caught the imagination of Americans so completely as the Great West, with its wealth, its heroic size, its awesome emptiness, its massive, sculptured beauty. Now the frontier was no more. Most of what Professor Webb called the "primary windfalls" of the region—the furs, the precious metals, the forests, the cattle, and the grass—had been snatched up by firstcomers and by individuals already wealthy. Big companies were taking over all the West's resources. The nation was becoming more powerful, richer, larger, and its economic structure more complex and diversified as the West yielded its treasures. But the East, and especially eastern industrialists and financiers, were increasingly dominating the economy of the entire nation.

SUPPLEMENTARY READING

Titles marked with an asterisk have been published in paperback.

The economic, political, and legal ideas current in this period are covered in Sidney Fine, **Laissez Faire and the General Welfare State*** (1956), and J. W. Hurst, **Law and the Conditions of Freedom in the Nineteenth-Century United States*** (1956). C. D. Warner and Mark Twain, **The Gilded Age*** (1873), is a useful and entertaining contemporary impression. On Social Darwinism, Richard Hofstadter's **Social Darwinism in American Thought*** (1945) should be supplemented by R. C. Bannister, **Social Darwinism** (1979). On the views of businessmen, see E. C. Kirkland, **Dream and Thought in the Business Community*** (1956), Kirkland's edition of Andrew Carnegie's writings, **The Gospel of Wealth** (1962), R. G. McCloskey, **American Conservatism in the Age of Enterprise*** (1951), T. C. Cochran, **Railroad Leaders** (1953), and J. D. Rockefeller, **Random Reminiscences of Men and Events** (1909).

R. A. Billington, **Westward Expansion** (1967), is the best introduction to the history of the exploitation of the West. On the Indians, general works include W. E.

Washburn, **The Indian in America*** (1975), and W. T. Hagan, **American Indians*** (1961). Of more specialized books, the following are useful: F. G. Roe, **The Indian and the Horse** (1955), R. W. Mardock, **The Reformers and the American Indian** (1971), R. M. Utley, **Frontier Regulars: The United States Army and the Indian*** (1973), L. R. Hafen and W. J. Ghent, **Broken Hand: The Life Story of Thomas Fitzpatrick** (1931), and R. G. Athearn, **William Tecumseh Sherman and the Settlement of the West** (1956). The destruction of the buffalo is described in vivid if highly imaginative terms in Mari Sandoz, **The Buffalo Hunters*** (1954). H. H. Jackson, **A Century of Dishonor*** (1881), is a powerful contemporary indictment of United States Indian policy.

For the fate of other minority groups, see J. H. Franklin, **From Slavery to Freedom*** (1956), R. W. Logan, **The Negro in American Life and Thought: The Nadir*** (1954), Joel Williamson, **The Crucible of Race** (1984), L. R. Harlan, **Booker T. Washington*** (1972), S. P. Hirshson, **Farewell to the Bloody Shirt*** (1962), V. P. De Santis, **Republicans Face the Southern Question** (1959), C. V. Woodward, **The Strange Career of Jim Crow*** (1966), J. A. Garraty (ed.), **Quarrels That Have Shaped the Constitution*** (1964), Gunther Barth, **Bitter Strength: A History of the Chinese in the United States** (1964), R. A. Billington, **The Protestant Crusade*** (1938), and John Higham, **Strangers in the Land*** (1955).

For the mining frontier, consult R. W. Paul, **Mining Frontiers of the Far West*** (1963), W. T. Jackson, **Treasure Hill: Portrait of a Silver Mining Camp*** (1963), D. A. Smith, **Rocky Mountain Mining Camps: The Urban Frontier*** (1967), and W. J. Trimble, **The Mining Advance into the Inland Empire** (1914). Mark Twain, **Roughing It*** (1872), is a classic contemporary account, and W. H. Goetzmann, **Exploration and Empire** (1966), throws much light on all aspects of western development. For federal land policy, see R. M. Robbins, **Our Landed Heritage*** (1942), P. W. Gates, **Fifty Million Acres*** (1954), and F. A. Shannon, **The Farmer's Last Frontier*** (1945), which is excellent on all questions relating to post–Civil War agriculture. Everett Dick, **The Sod-House Frontier** (1937), presents a graphic picture of farm life on the treeless plains. Bonanza farming is described in H. M. Drache, **The Day of the Bonanza** (1964).

The development of transcontinental railroads is discussed in R. E. Riegel, **The Story of the Western Railroads*** (1926), Julius Grodinsky, **Transcontinental Railway Strategy** (1962), O. O. Winther, **The Transportation Frontier*** (1964), and G. R. Taylor and I. D. Neu, **The American Railroad Network** (1956). For a sampling of the literature on specific roads, see Oscar Lewis, **The Big Four** (1938), J. B. Hedges, **Henry Villard and the Railroads of the Northwest** (1930), Albro Martin, **James J. Hill and the Opening of the Northwest** (1976), R. G. Athearn, **Union Pacific Country*** (1971), and L. L. Waters, **Steel Rails to Santa Fe** (1950). Matthew Josephson, **The Robber Barons*** (1934), discusses the chicanery connected with railroad construction at length.

On cattle ranching on the plains, a good account is Lewis Atherton, **The Cattle Kings*** (1961), but see also Don Worcester, **The Chisholm Trail** (1980), E. S. Osgood, **The Day of the Cattleman*** (1929), and Louis Pelzer, **The Cattlemen's Frontier** (1936). For the cowboy and his life, see J. B. Frantz and J. E. Choate, **The American Cowboy: The Myth and Reality** (1955), and R. R. Dykstra, **The Cattle Towns*** (1968). W. P. Webb, **The Great Plains*** (1931), is a fascinating analysis of the development of a unique civilization on the plains.

18
An Industrial Giant

You know how often I had not an unbroken night's sleep, worrying about how it was all coming out. All the fortune I have made has not served to compensate for the anxiety of that period. . . . If I had foreseen the future I doubt whether I would have had the courage to go on. John D. Rockefeller

When the Civil War began, the country's industrial output, while important and increasing, did not approach that of major European powers. By the end of the century the United States had become far and away the colossus among world manufacturers, dwarfing the production of Great Britain and Germany. The world had never seen such a remarkable example of rapid economic growth. The value of American manufactured products rose from $1.8 billion in 1859 to over $13 billion in 1899. Modern economists estimate that the output of goods and services in the country (the gross national product, or GNP) increased by 44 percent between 1874 and 1883 and continued to expand in succeeding years. This growth was not confined to the Northeast. Wisconsin, for example, underwent what the historian Robert C. Nesbit calls "a major transformation" between 1873 and 1893. "An extractive frontier economy producing primarily grain and lumber . . . emerged as a mainly urban-centered economy operating on the leading edge of contemporary industrial technology."

Industrial Growth: An Overview

American manufacturing flourished for many reasons. New natural resources were discovered and exploited steadily, thereby increasing opportunities. These opportunties, in turn, attracted the brightest and most energetic of a vigorous and expanding population. The growth of the country added constantly to the size of the national market, and protective tariffs shielded that market from foreign competition. Yet foreign capital entered the market freely, in part because tariffs kept out so many foreign goods. The dominant spirit of the time encouraged businessmen to maximum effort by emphasizing progress, glorifying material wealth, and justifying aggressiveness. European immigrants provided the additional labor needed by expanding industry; 2.5 million arrived in the 1870s, twice that number in the 1880s.

It was a period of rapid advance in basic science, and technicians created a bountiful harvest of new machines, processes, and power sources that increased productivity in many industries and created new industries as well. In agriculture there were what one contemporary expert called "an endless variety of cultivators," better harvesters and binding machines, and combines capable of threshing and bagging 450 pounds of grain a minute. An 1886 report of the Illinois Bureau of Labor Statistics claimed that "new machinery has displaced fully 50 percent of the muscular labor formerly required to do a given amount of work in the manufacture of agricultural implements." As a result of improvements in the milling of grain, packaged cereals appeared on the American breakfast table. The commercial canning of food, spurred by the "automatic line" canning factory, expanded so rapidly that by 1887 a writer in *Good Housekeeping* magazine could say: "Housekeeping is getting to be ready made, as well as clothing." The Bonsack cigarette-rolling machine created a new industry that changed the habits of millions. George B. Eastman created still another with his development of mass-produced roll photographic film and the simple but efficient Kodak camera. The perfection of the typewriter by the Remington company in the 1880s revolutionized the way office work was performed.

Railroads: The First Big Business

In 1866, returning from his honeymoon in Europe, 30-year-old Charles Francis Adams, Jr., grandson and great-grandson of presidents, full of ambition and ready, as he put it, to confront the world "face to face," looked about in search of a career. "Surveying the whole field," he later explained, "I fixed on the railroad system as the most developing force and the largest field of the day, and determined to attach myself to it." Adams's judgment was acute: for the next 25 years the railroads were probably the most significant element in American economic development, railroad executives the most powerful people in the country.

Railroads were important first as an industry in themselves. Less than 35,000 miles of track existed when Lee laid down his sword at Appomattox. In 1875 railroad mileage exceeded 74,000 and the skeleton of the network was complete. Over the next two decades the skeleton was fleshed out. In 1890 the mature but still-growing system took in over $1 billion in passenger and freight revenues. (The federal government's income in 1890 was only $403 million.) The value of railroad properties and equipment was more than $8.7 billion. The

Links in the nation's increasingly complex and interdependent transportation network can be glimpsed in this 1878 painting by a primitive artist, Herman Decker. The scene is the bustling Lonsdale Wharf in Providence, Rhode Island.

national *railroad* debt of $5.1 billion was almost five times the national debt of $1.1 billion! By 1900 the nation had 193,000 miles of track.

The emphasis in railroad construction after 1865 was on organizing integrated systems. The lines had high fixed costs: taxes, interest on their bonds, maintenance of track and rolling stock, salaries of office personnel. A short train with half-empty cars required almost as many workers and as much fuel to operate as a long one jammed with freight or passengers. In order to earn profits the railroads had to carry as much traffic as possible. They therefore spread out feeder lines to draw business to their main lines the way the root network of a tree draws water into its trunk.

Before the Civil War, as we have seen, passengers and freight could travel by rail from beyond Chicago and St. Louis to the Atlantic Coast, but only after the war did true interregional trunk lines appear. In 1861, for example, the New York Central ran from Albany to Buffalo. One could proceed from Buffalo to Chicago, but on a different company's trains. In 1867 the Central passed into the hands of "Commodore" Cornelius Vanderbilt, who had made a large fortune in the shipping business. Vanderbilt already controlled lines running from Albany to New York City; now he merged these properties with the Central. In 1873 he integrated the Lake Shore and Michigan Southern into his empire and two years later the Michigan Central. The Commodore spent large sums improving his properties and buying feeder lines. At his death in 1877 the Central operated a network of over 4,500 miles of track between New York City and most of the principal cities of the Middle West.

While Vanderbilt was putting together the New York Central complex, Thomas A. Scott was fusing roads to Cincinnati, Indianapolis, St. Louis, and Chicago to his Pennsylvania Railroad, which linked Pittsburgh and Philadelphia. In 1871 the Pennsylvania obtained access to New York; soon it reached Baltimore and Washington. By 1869 another important system, the Erie, controlled by a triumvirate of railroad freebooters, Daniel Drew, Jay Gould, and Jim Fisk, had extended itself from New York to Cleveland, Cincinnati, and St. Louis. Soon thereafter it too tapped the markets of Chicago and other principal cities. In 1874 the Baltimore and Ohio also obtained access to Chicago.

The transcontinentals were trunk lines from the start; the emptiness of the western country would have made short lines unprofitable, and builders quickly grasped the need for direct connections to eastern markets and thorough integration of feeder lines.

The dominant system builder of the Southwest was Jay Gould, a soft-spoken, unostentatious man who looked, according to one witness, "like an insignificant pigmy." Gould was in fact ruthless, cynical, and aggressive. His mere appearance in Wall Street, one Texas newspaper reported in 1890, made "millionaires tremble like innocent sparrows . . . when a hungry hawk swoops down upon them." (A railroad president used a better image when he called Gould a "perfect eel.") With millions acquired in shady railroad and stock market ventures, Gould invaded the West in the 1870s, buying 370,000 shares of Union Pacific stock. He took over the Kansas Pacific, running from Denver to Kansas City, which he consolidated with the Union Pacific, and the Missouri Pacific, a line from Kansas City to St. Louis, which he expanded through mergers and purchases into a 5,300-mile system. Often Gould put together such properties merely to unload them on other railroads at a profit, but his grasp of the importance of integration was sound.

In the Northwest, Henry Villard, a German-born ex-newspaperman, constructed another great complex based on his control of the Northern Pacific and properties in Oregon and California. James J. Hill's expansion of the St. Paul and Pacific Railroad into the Great Northern system, absorbing a number of other lines in addition to laying track all the way to Seattle, produced still another western network.

The Civil War had highlighted the need for through railroad connections in the South. Shortly after the conflict, northern capital began to flow into southern railroad construction. The Chesapeake and Ohio, organized in 1868, opened a direct line from Norfolk, Virginia, to Cincinnati. The Richmond and Danville absorbed some 26 lines after the war, forming a system that ran from Washington to the Mississippi. It in turn became part of the Richmond and West Point Terminal Company, which by the late 1880s controlled an 8,558-mile network. Like other southern trunk lines such as the Louisville and Nashville and the Atlantic Coast Line, this system was largely controlled by northern capitalists.

The trunk lines interconnected and thus had to standardize many of their activities. This, in turn, led to the standardization of other aspects of life. The present system of time zones was developed in 1883 by the roads. The standard track gauge (4 feet $8\frac{1}{2}$ inches) was established in 1886. Standardized car coupling and braking mechanisms, standard signal systems, even standard methods of accounting were essential to the effective functioning of the network.

The lines sought to work out fixed rates for carrying different types of freight, charging more for valuable manufactured goods than for bulky products like coal or wheat, and they agreed to permit rate concessions to shippers when necessary to avoid hauling empty cars. In other words, they charged what the traffic would bear. However, by the 1880s the men who ran the railroads had come to recognize the advantages of cooperating with one another in order to avoid "senseless" competition. Railroad management was becoming a kind of profession, with certain standard ways of doing things, even with its own professional journals and with regional organizations such as the Eastern Trunk Line Association and the Western Traffic Association.

The railroads stimulated the economy indirectly. Like foreign commerce and the textile industry in earlier times, they were a "multiplier" speeding development. In 1869 they bought $41.6 million worth of cars and locomotives, in 1889 $90.8 million. The roads in 1881 used about 94 percent of all the rolled steel manufactured in the United States. Such purchases created thousands of jobs and led to countless technological advances.

Because of their voracious appetite for traffic, railroads in sparsely settled regions and in areas with undeveloped resources devoted much money and effort to stimulating local economic growth. The Louisville and Nashville, for instance, was a prime mover in the expansion of the iron industry

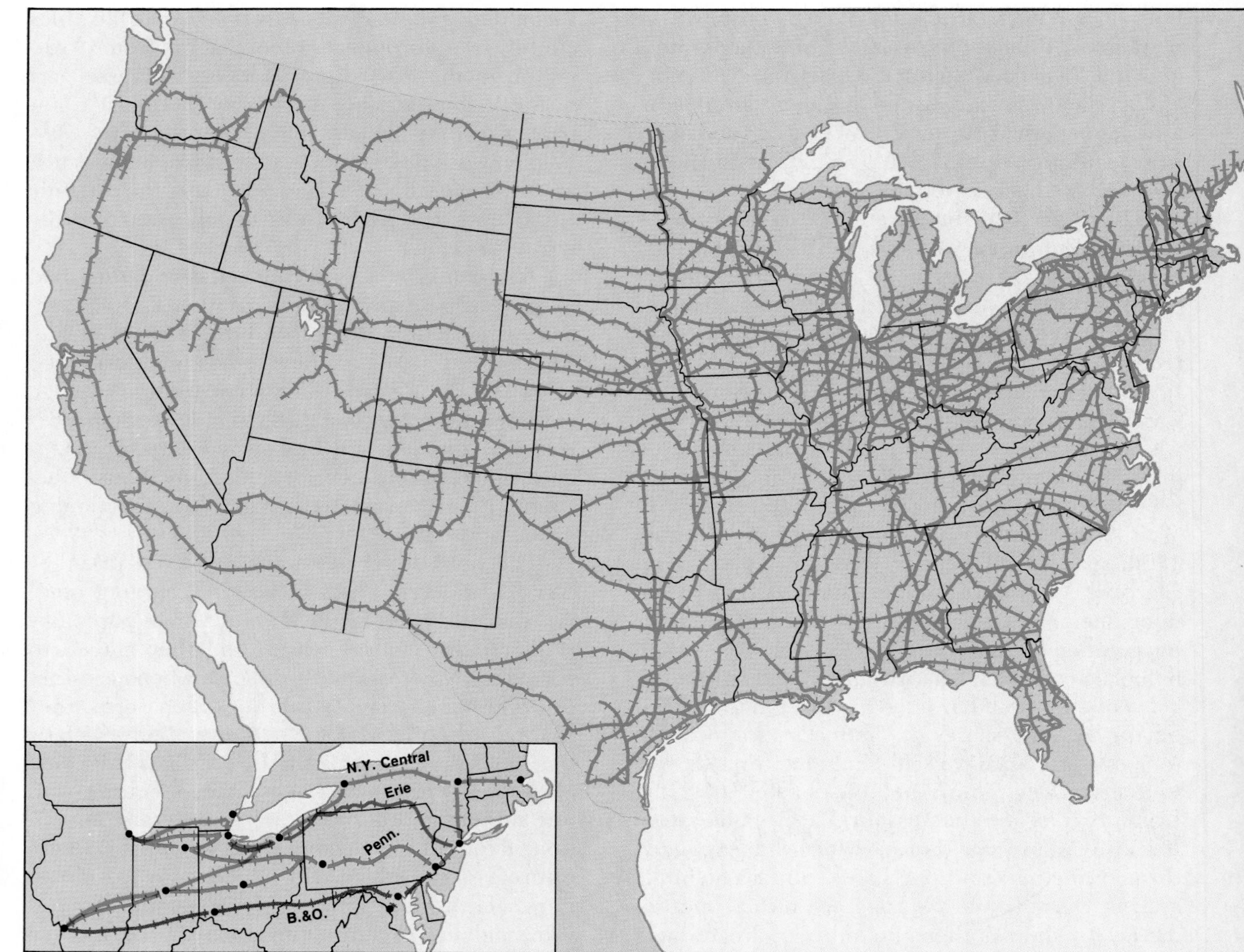

PRIMARY RAILROADS, 1890

In the map inset is a sketch of the four northeast trunk lines, which linked up with the western railroads through Chicago and St. Louis. A trunk line is generally defined as a system handling long-distance through traffic.

in Alabama in the 1880s. The state's output of iron increased tenfold between 1880 and 1889, in considerable part because of the railroad's activities in building spur lines to mines and furnaces and attracting capital into the industry.

To speed the settlement of new regions, the land-grant railroads sold land cheaply and on easy terms, for sales meant future business as well as current income. Roads like the Northern Pacific offered reduced rates to travelers interested in buying farms, and they entertained potential customers with a free hand. Land-grant lines set up "bureaus of immigration" that distributed elaborate brochures describing the wonders of the new country. Their agents greeted immigrants at the great eastern ports and tried to steer them to railroad prop-

A Northern Pacific poster offers its land as the "best and cheapest" available. By 1917 this railroad had realized $136 million on its land grants.

erty. They sent agents who were usually themselves immigrants—often ministers—all over Europe to recruit prospective settlers, many of whom could be expected to buy railroad land. Occasionally entire colonies migrated to America under railroad auspices, such as the 1,900 Mennonites who came to Kansas from Russia in 1874 to settle on the land of the Atchison, Topeka and Santa Fe.

Technological advances in railroading accelerated economic development in complex ways. In 1869 George Westinghouse invented the air brake. By enabling an engineer to apply the brakes to all cars simultaneously (formerly each car had to be braked separately by its own conductor or brakeman) this invention made possible revolutionary increases in the size of trains and the speed at which they could safely operate. The sleeping car, invented in 1864 by George Pullman, now came into its own.

To pull the heavier trains, more powerful locomotives were needed. They in turn produced a call for stronger and more durable rails to bear the additional weight. Steel, itself reduced in cost because of technological developments, supplied the answer, for steel rails outlasted iron many times despite the use of much heavier equipment. "Steel rails," one expert said in the 1880s, "form the very 'cornerstone' of the great improvements which have taken place in railroad efficiency." In 1880 only 50 percent of the nation's rails were of steel; by 1890 less than 1 percent were not.

A close tie developed between the railroads and the nation's telegraph network, dominated by the Western Union Company. Commonly the roads allowed Western Union to string wires along their rights of way, and they transported telegraphers and their equipment without charge. In return they received free telegraphic service, important for efficiency and safety. It is no coincidence that the early 1880s, a period of booming railroad construction, saw a fantastic expansion of Western Union. By 1883 the company was transmitting 40 million messages a year over 400,000 miles of wire. The two industries, as Jay Gould put it, went "hand in hand, . . . integral parts" of American civilization.

Iron, Oil, and Electricity

The transformation of iron manufacturing affected the nation almost as much as railroad development. Output rose from 920,000 tons in 1860 to 10.3 million tons in 1900, but the big change came in the development of ways to mass-produce steel. In its pure form (wrought iron) the metal is tough but relatively soft. Ordinary cast iron, which contains large amounts of carbon and other impurities, is hard but brittle. Steel, which contains 1 or 2 percent carbon, combines the hardness of cast iron with the toughness of wrought iron. For nearly every purpose—structural girders for bridges and buildings, railroad track, machine tools, boiler plate, barbed wire—steel is immensely superior to other kinds of iron.

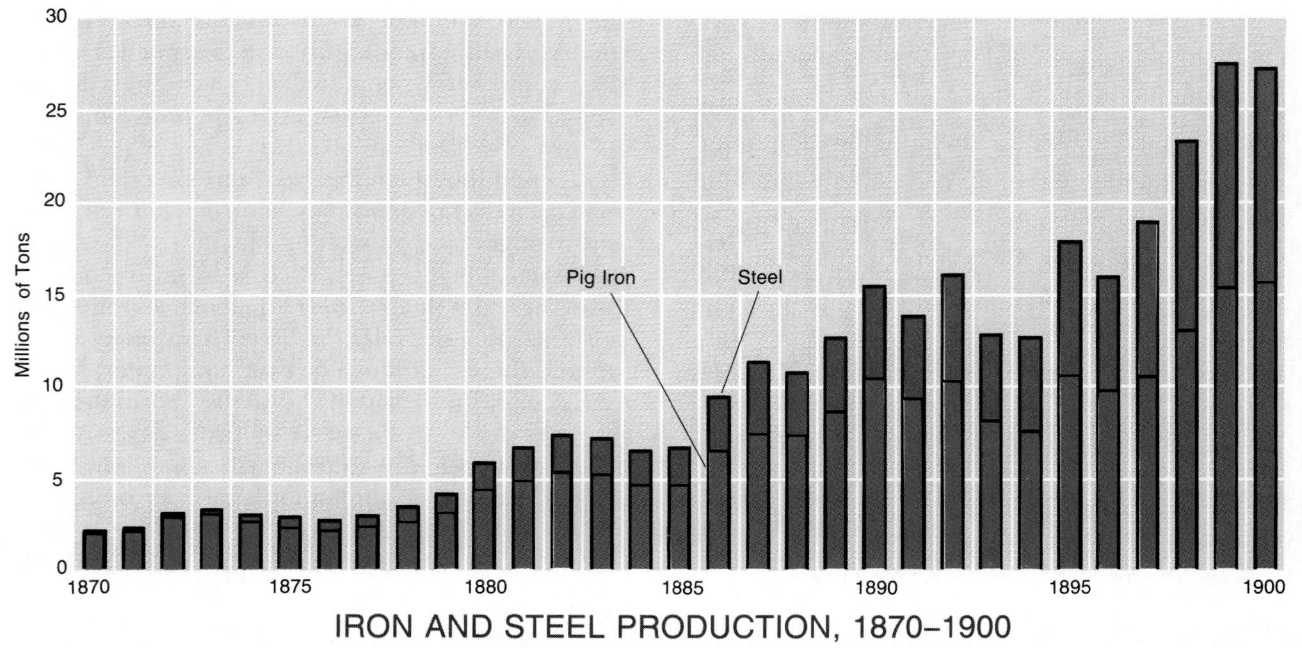

IRON AND STEEL PRODUCTION, 1870–1900

Minnesota's Mesabi Range (shown in 1899) was developed largely with Rockefeller money. It shipped 4,000 tons of iron ore in 1892 and within a decade tripled that amount—an increase reflected in the graph.

But steel was so expensive to manufacture that it could not be used for bulky products until the invention in the 1850s of the Bessemer process, perfected independently by Henry Bessemer, an Englishman, and William Kelly of Kentucky. Bessemer and Kelly discovered that a stream of air directed into a mass of molten iron caused the carbon and other impurities to combine with oxygen and burn off. When measured amounts of carbon, silicon, and manganese were then added, the brew became steel. What had been a rare metal could now be produced by the hundreds and thousands of tons. The Bessemer process and the open-hearth method, a slower but more precise technique that enabled producers to sample the molten mass and thus control quality closely, were introduced commercially in the 1860s. In 1870, 77,000 tons of steel were manufactured, less than 4 percent of the volume of pig iron. By 1880, however, 1.39 million tons were pouring annually from the converters, and by 1900 nearly 11.4 million tons.

Such growth would have been impossible but for the huge supplies of iron ore in the United States and the coal necessary to fire the furnaces that refined it. In the 1870s the great iron fields rimming Lake Superior began to yield their treasures. The Menominee range in Michigan began production in 1877, followed in 1884 by the Gogebic range, on the Michigan-Wisconsin border. In each case the completion of rail connections to the fields had been necessary before large-scale mining could take place—another illustration of the importance of railroads in the economic history of the era. The Vermilion range, in the northeast corner of Minnesota, was opened up at about the same time, and somewhat later the magnificent Mesabi region, where the enormous iron concentrations made a compass needle spin like a top. Mesabi ores could be mined with steam shovels, almost like gravel.

Pittsburgh, surrounded by vast coal deposits, became the iron and steel capital of the country, the Minnesota ores reaching it by way of steamers on the Great Lakes and rail lines from Cleveland. Other cities in Pennsylvania and Ohio were important producers, and a separate complex, centering on Birmingham, Alabama, developed to exploit local iron and coal fields.

The petroleum industry expanded even more spectacularly than iron and steel. Edwin L. Drake drilled the first successful well in Pennsylvania in 1859. During the Civil War, production ranged between 2 million and 3 million barrels a year. In 1873 almost 10 million barrels were produced, and in the early 1880s annual output averaged over 20 million barrels. A decade later the figure had leaped to about 50 million barrels.

Before the invention of the gasoline engine and the automobile, the most important petroleum product was kerosene, which was burned in lamps. In the early years in Pennsylvania hundreds of tiny refineries, often reminiscent of the ramshackle stills of nearby moonshiners, were engaged in making kerosene. The refiners heated crude oil in large kettles and, after the volatile elements had escaped, condensed the kerosene in coils cooled by water. The heavier petroleum tars were discarded.

Technological advances came rapidly. By the

A scene on the Oil Creek Railroad in western Pennsylvania in the 1860s. Initially, crude oil was shipped to refineries in barrels by barge or on railroad flatcars, as shown here. The familiar "boiler-shaped" tank car was invented in 1869, and by the 1870s a network of pipelines was laid to handle the growing oil output.

early 1870s, refiners had learned how to "crack" petroleum by applying high temperatures to the crude in order to rearrange its molecular structure, thereby increasing the percentage of kerosene yielded. By-products such as naphtha, gasoline (used in vaporized form as an illuminating gas), rhigolene (a local anesthetic), cymogene (a coolant for refrigerating machines), and many lubricants and waxes began to appear on the market. At the same time a great increase in the supply of crude oil—especially after the German-born chemist Herman Frasch perfected a method for removing sulfur from low-quality petroleum—drove prices down.

These circumstances put a premium on refining efficiency. Larger plants utilizing expensive machinery and employing skilled technicians became more important. In the mid-1860s only three refineries in the country could process 2,000 barrels of crude a week; a decade later plants capable of handling 1,000 barrels a day were common.

Two other important new industries were the telephone and electric light businesses. Both were typical of the period, being products of technical advances and intimately related to the growth of a high-speed, urban civilization that put great stress on communication. The telephone was invented in 1876 by Alexander Graham Bell, who had been led to the study of acoustics through his interest in the education of the deaf. Bell's work with a device for transcribing tone vibrations electrically to help deaf-mutes learn to speak encouraged him to experiment with a "speaking telegraph" that used electrified metal disks, acting like the drum of the human ear, to convert sound waves into electrical impulses and electrical impulses back into sound waves.

Although considered little more than a clever gadget at first—the Western Union Company passed up an opportunity to buy the invention for $100,000, its president calling the telephone an "electrical toy"—Bell's invention soon proved its practical value. By 1880, 85 towns and cities had local telephone networks. In 1895 there were more than 300,000 phones in the country, in 1900 almost 800,000, twice the total for all Europe. By that date the American Telephone and Telegraph Company, a consolidation of over 100 local systems, dominated the business.

When Western Union realized the importance of the telephone, it tried for a time to compete with Bell by developing a machine of its own. The man it commissioned to devise this machine was Thomas A. Edison. Bell's patents proved unassailable, and Western Union abandoned the effort to maintain a competing system, but Edison vastly improved telephonic transmission. Not yet 30 when he turned to the telephone problem, Edison had already made a number of contributions toward solving what he called the "mysteries of electrical force," including a multiplex telegraph capable of sending four messages over a single wire at the same time. At Menlo Park, New Jersey, he built the prototype of the modern research laboratory, where specific problems could be attacked on a mass scale by a team of trained specialists. During his lifetime he took out more than 1,000 patents, dealing with machines as varied as the phonograph, the motion-picture projector, the storage battery, and the mimeograph. He also contributed substantially to the development of the electric dynamo, ore-separating machinery, and railroad signal equipment.

Edison's most significant achievement was unquestionably his perfection of the incandescent lamp, or electric light bulb. Others before Edison had experimented with the idea of producing light by passing electricity through a filament in a vacuum. Always, however, the filaments quickly burned out. Edison tried hundreds of fibers before producing, in 1879, a carbonized filament that would glow brightly in a vacuum tube for as long as 170 hours without crumbling. At Christmastime he decorated the grounds about his laboratory with a few dozen of the new lights. People flocked by the thousands to see this miracle of the "Wizard of Menlo Park." To the admirers of his "bright, beautiful light, like the mellow sunset of an Italian autumn," the inventor boasted that soon he would be able to illuminate entire towns, even great cities like New York.

He was true to his promise. In 1882 his Edison Illuminating Company opened a power station in New York and began to supply current for lighting to 85 consumers, including the New York *Times* and the banking house of J. P. Morgan and Company. Soon central stations were springing up everywhere until, by 1898, there were about 3,000 in the country. Edison's manufacturing subsidiaries flourished equally: in 1885 they turned out 139,000 incandescent lamps, by the end of the decade nearly a million a year.

The Edison system employed direct current at

Edison patented the phonograph in 1878, budgeting $18 for its invention. He was photographed in his laboratory on June 16, 1888, at 5:30 A.M., working on a wax-cylinder model.

low voltages, which limited the distance that power could be transmitted to about 2 miles. Technicians soon demonstrated that by using alternating current, stepped up to high voltages by tranformers, power could be transported over great distances economically and then reduced to safe levels for use by consumers. This encouraged George Westinghouse, inventor of the air brake, to found the Westinghouse Electric Company in 1886.

Edison stubbornly refused to accept the superiority of high-voltage alternating current. "Just as certain as death Westinghouse will kill a customer within 6 months," he predicted. For a time the language was graced with the term "to Westinghouse," meaning to electrocute. But the Westinghouse system quickly proved itself safe as well as efficient, and alternating current became standard.

The substitution of electric for steam power in

Revolving overhead belts were a common means of driving factory machinery; they also represented a grave hazard for workers. In this National Biscuit Company packing plant, probably photographed about 1915, the belts are encased in wire "cages" affording some protection.

factories was as liberating as that of steam for waterpower before the Civil War. Small, safe electric motors replaced dangerous and cumbersome mazes of belts and wheels. The electric power industry expanded rapidly. By the early years of the 20th century almost 6 billion kilowatt-hours of electricity were being produced annually. Yet this was only the beginning.

Competition and Monopoly: The Railroads

During the post–Civil War era, expansion in industry went hand in hand with concentration. With each passing decade, fewer and larger firms controlled an increasing share of the business. The principal cause of this trend, aside from the obvious economics resulting from large-scale production and the growing importance of expensive machinery, was the downward trend of prices after 1873. The deflation, which resulted mainly from the failure of the money supply to keep pace with the rapid increase in the volume of goods produced, affected agricultural goods as well as manufactures, and it lasted until 1896 or 1897.

Contemporaries believed they were living through a "great depression." That label is misleading, for output expanded almost continuously, and at a rapid rate, until 1893, when production slumped and a true depression struck the country. Falling prices, however, kept a steady pressure on profit margins, and this led to increased production and thus to intense competition for markets. Rival concerns battled for business, the strongest, most efficient, and most unscrupulous destroying or absorbing their foes. If no clear victor emerged, the exhausted contenders frequently ended the warfare by combining voluntarily. For a time the government did little about laying down rules for either the fighting or the consolidations that seemed to result from it.

According to the classical economists (see page 582), competition advanced the public interest by keeping prices low and assuring the most efficient producer the largest profit. Up to a point it accomplished these purposes in the years after 1865, but it also caused side effects that injured both the economy and society as a whole. Railroad managers, for instance, found it impossible to enforce "official" rate schedules and maintain their regional associations once competitive pressures mounted. In 1865 it had cost from 96 cents to $2.15 per 100 pounds, depending on the class of freight, to ship goods from New York to Chicago. In 1888 rates ranged from 35 cents to 75 cents. A decade later the cost of shipping 100 pounds of wheat from Chicago to New York had dropped to 20 cents.

Competition cut deeply into railroad profits, causing the lines to seek desperately to increase volume. They did so chiefly by reducing rates still more, on a selective basis. They gave rebates (secret reductions below the published rates) to large shippers in order to capture their business. The granting of discounts to those who shipped in volume made economic sense: it was easier to handle freight in carload lots than in smaller units. So intense was the battle for business, however, that the roads often made concessions to big customers far beyond what the economics of bulk shipment justified. In the 1870s the New York Central regularly reduced the rates charged important shippers by 50 to 80 percent. One large Utica dry-goods merchant received a rate of 9 cents while others paid 33 cents. Two big New York City grain merchants paid so little that they soon controlled the grain business of the entire city.

Railroad officials disliked rebating but found no way to avoid the practice. "Notwithstanding my horror of rebates," the president of a New England trunk line told one of his executives in discussing the case of a brick manufacturer, "bill at the usual rate, and rebate Mr. Cole 25 cents a thousand." In extreme cases the railroads even gave large shippers drawbacks, which were rebates on the business of the shippers' competitors!

Besides rebating, railroads issued passes to favored shippers, built sidings at the plants of important companies without charge, and gave freely of their landholdings to attract businesses to their territory. Railroads also battled directly with one another in ways damaging both to themselves and to the public. Unscrupulous operators like Jay Gould often threw together roundabout, inefficient trunk lines merely to blackmail established roads, forcing them to buy up the essentially useless properties at inflated prices. Others tried to win control of competing lines in the stock market. Between 1866 and 1868 Vanderbilt of the New York Central waged a futile campaign to win control of the Erie. The raffish Erie directors fought back by issuing themselves thousands of shares of new stock without paying for them, thereby grossly inflating the capitalization of the line. Both roads stooped to bribery in an effort to obtain favorable action in the New York legislature, and there were pitched battles between the hirelings of each side.

"The force of competition," a railroad man explained, "is one that no carrying corporation can withstand and before which the managing officers of a corporation are helpless." James F. Joy of the Chicago, Burlington, and Quincy made the same point more bluntly: "Unless you prepare to defend yourselves," he advised the president of the Michigan Central, "you will be boarded by pirates in all quarters." Railroad executives are "hardly better than a race of horse-jockeys," Charles Francis Adams, Jr., wrote in *Railroads: Their Origin and Problems* (1879). A person trying to run a railroad honestly, Adams also said, would be like Don Quixote tilting at a windmill.

To make up for losses forced upon them by competitive pressures, railroads charged higher rates at way points along their tracks where no competition existed. Frequently it cost more to ship a product a short distance than a longer one. Rochester, New York, was served only by the New York Central. In the 1870s it cost 30 cents to transport a barrel of flour from Rochester to New York City, a distance of 350 miles. At the same time flour could be shipped from Minneapolis to New York, a distance of well over 1,000 miles, for only 20 cents a barrel. One Rochester businessman told a state investigating committee that he could save 18 cents a hundredweight by sending goods to St. Louis by way of New York, where several carriers competed for the traffic, even though, in fact, the goods might come back through Rochester over the same tracks on the way to St. Louis!

Although cheap transportation stimulated the economy, few people benefited from cutthroat competition. Small shippers—and all businessmen in cities and towns with limited rail outlets—suffered heavily; railroad discrimination speeded the concentration of industry in large corporations located in major centers. The instability of rates even troubled interests like the middle western flour millers who benefited from the competitive situation, for it hampered planning. Nor could manufacturers who received rebates be entirely happy, since few could be sure that some other producer was not getting a larger reduction.

Probably the worst sufferers were the roads themselves. The loss of revenue resulting from rate cutting, combined with inflated debts, put most of them in grave difficulty when faced with a downturn in the business cycle. In 1876 two-fifths of all railroad bonds were in default; three years later 65 lines were bankrupt. Since the public would not countenance bankrupt railroads going out of business, these companies were placed in the hands of court-appointed receivers. The receivers, however, seldom provided efficient management and had no funds at their disposal for new equipment.

During the 1880s the major roads responded to these pressures by building or buying lines in order to create interregional systems. These were the first giant corporations, capitalized in the hundreds of millions of dollars. The enormous cost of these systems led to another wave of bankruptcies when a true depression struck in the 1890s.

The consequent reorganizations brought most of the big systems under the control of financiers, notably J. Pierpont Morgan, head of a powerful firm of New York bankers, and such other private bankers as Kuhn, Loeb of New York and Lee, Higginson of Boston. The economic historian A. D. Noyes described in 1904 what the bankers did:

> Bondholders were requested to scale down interest charges, receiving new stock in compensation, while the shareholders were invited to pay a cash assessment, thus providing a working fund. [The bankers] combined to guarantee that the requisite money should be raised. They too were paid in new stock. . . . Though the total capital issues were increased, fixed charges were diminished and a sufficient fund for road improvement and new equipment was provided.

The reorganizations—critics called them Morganizations—put the bankrupt trunk lines back on their feet. Representatives of the bankers sat on the board of every line they saved. While they generally took no part in the everyday affairs of the roads, their influence was predominant. They consistently opposed rate wars, rebating, and other competitive practices. In effect, control of the railroad network became centralized, even though the companies maintained their separate existences

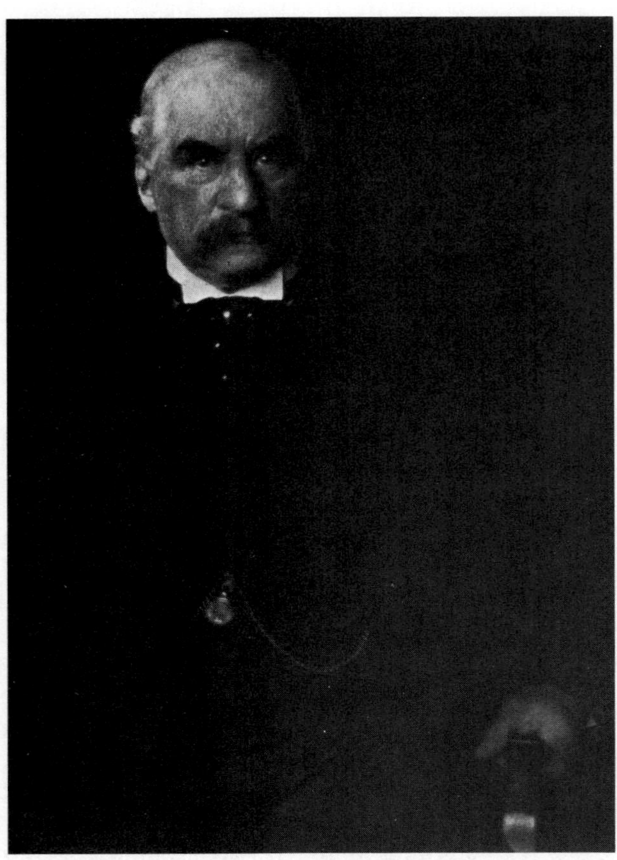

Edward Steichen's memorable photograph of J. Pierpont Morgan, taken in 1906. Looking the formidable Morgan in the eye, Steichen said, was like facing the headlights of an onrushing express train.

and operated in a seemingly independent manner. When Morgan died in 1913, "Morgan men" dominated the boards of the New York Central; the Erie; the New York, New Haven and Hartford; the Southern; the Pere Marquette; the Atchison, Topeka and Santa Fe; and many other lines.

The Steel Industry: Carnegie

The iron and steel industry was also intensely competitive. Despite the trend toward higher production, demand varied erratically from year to year, even from month to month. In good times producers built new facilities, only to suffer heavy losses when demand declined and much of their capacity lay idle. The forward rush of technology put a tremendous emphasis on efficiency; expensive plants quickly became obsolete. Improved transportation facilities allowed manufacturers in widely separated places to compete with one another; despite the importance of the Pittsburgh region, in the early 1890s multimillion-dollar mills existed in Alabama, Colorado, Illinois, and elsewhere.

The kingpin of the industry was Andrew Carnegie. Carnegie was born in Dunfermline, Scotland, and came to the United States in 1848 at the age of 12. His first job, as a bobbin boy in a cotton mill, brought him $1.20 a week, but his talents perfectly fitted the times, and he rose rapidly: to Western Union messenger boy, to telegrapher, to private secretary, to railroad manager. He saved his money, made some shrewd investments, and by 1868 had an income of $50,000 a year.

At about this time he decided to specialize in the iron business. Carnegie possessed great talent as a salesman, boundless faith in the future of the country, an uncanny knack of choosing topflight subordinates, and enough ruthlessness to survive in the iron and steel jungle. Where other steelmen built new plants in good times, he preferred to expand in bad times, when it cost far less to do so. During the 1870s, he later recalled, "many of my friends needed money. . . . I . . . bought out five or six of them. That is what gave me my leading interest in this steel business."

Carnegie grasped the importance of technological improvements in his industry. Slightly skeptical of the Bessemer process at first, once he became convinced of its practicality he adopted it enthusiastically. In 1875 he built the J. Edgar Thomson Steel Works, named after a president of the Pennsylvania Railroad, his biggest customer. He employed chemists and other specialists and was soon making steel from iron oxides that other manufacturers had discarded as waste. He was a merciless competitor. When a plant manager announced: "We broke all records for making steel last week," Carnegie replied: "Congratulations! *Why not do it every week?*" Carnegie sold rails by paying "commissions" to railroad purchasing agents, and he was not above reneging on a contract if he thought it profitable and safe to do so.

By 1890 the Carnegie Steel Company dominated the industry, and its output increased nearly tenfold during the next decade. Profits mounted from $3 million in 1893 to $6 million in 1896 and then soared to $40 million in 1900. Alarmed by his increasing control of the industry, the makers of finished steel products such as barbed wire and tubing began to combine and to consider entering the primary field. Carnegie, his competitive temper aroused, threatened to turn to finished products himself. A colossal steel war seemed imminent.

However, Carnegie longed to retire in order to devote himself to philanthropic work. He believed that great wealth entailed social responsibilities and that it was a disgrace to die rich. When J. P. Morgan approached him through an intermediary with an offer to buy him out, he assented readily. In 1901 Morgan put together United States Steel, the "world's first billion-dollar corporation." This combination included all the Carnegie properties, the Federal Steel Company (Carnegie's largest competitor), and such important fabricators of finished products as the American Steel and Wire Company, the American Tin Plate Company, and the National Tube Company. Vast reserves of Minnesota iron ore and a fleet of Great Lakes ore steamers were also included. U.S. Steel was capitalized at $1.4 billion, about twice the value of its component properties but not necessarily an overestimation of its profit-earning capacity. The owners of Carnegie Steel received $492 million, of which $250 million went to Carnegie himself.

Andrew Carnegie in later life. His phenomenal rags-to-riches career was one of the real-life models for Horatio Alger's dime novels on the theme "poor boy makes good."

The Standard Oil Trust: Rockefeller

The pattern of fierce competition leading to combination and monopoly is well illustrated by the history of the petroleum industry. Irresistible pressures pushed the refiners into a brutal struggle to dominate the business. Production of crude oil, subject to the uncertainties of prospecting and drilling, fluctuated constantly and without regard for need. In general, output surged far ahead of demand.

By the 1870s the chief oil-refining centers were Cleveland, Pittsburgh, Baltimore, and the New York City area. Of these Cleveland was the fastest growing, chiefly because the New York Central and Erie railroads competed fiercely for its oil trade and the Erie Canal offered an alternative route. Pittsburgh depended entirely on the Pennsylvania Railroad, and New York and Baltimore suffered from being far removed from the oil fields.

The Standard Oil Company of Cleveland, founded in 1870 by a 31-year-old merchant named John D. Rockefeller, emerged as the giant among the refiners. Rockefeller exploited every possible technical advance and employed fair means and foul to persuade competitors first in the Cleveland area and then elsewhere either to sell out or to join forces. By 1879 he controlled 90 percent of the nation's oil-refining capacity along with a network of oil pipelines and large reserves of petroleum in the ground. The existence of this monopoly, together with the remarkable expansion of the entire industry, caused Standard Oil to attract far more attention than its importance warranted in the late 19th century. The period of its greatest growth and economic influence did not come until later.

Standard Oil emerged victorious from the competitive wars because Rockefeller and his associates were the toughest and most imaginative fighters as well as the most efficient refiners in the business. In addition to obtaining from the railroads a 10 percent rebate and drawbacks on its competitors' shipments, Standard Oil cut prices locally to force small independents to sell out or face ruin. One Massachusetts refiner testified that Standard drove down the price of kerosene in his district from $9\frac{1}{4}$ cents to $5\frac{1}{4}$ cents simply to destroy his business. Since kerosene was sold in grocery stores, Standard supplied its own outlets with meat, sugar, and other products at artifically low prices to help crush the stores that handled other brands of kerosene. The company employed spies to track down the customers of independents and offer them oil at bargain prices. Bribery was also a Standard practice; the reformer Henry Demarest Lloyd quipped that the company had done everything to the Pennsylvania legislature except refine it. Rockefeller's sympathetic biographer, Allan Nevins, admitted that Standard Oil "committed acts against competitors which could not be defended."

John D. Rockefeller carried his passion for perfection onto the golf course, hiring a boy to do nothing but intone "keep your head down" on each shot.

Although a bold planner and a daring taker of necessary risks, Rockefeller was far too orderly and astute to enjoy the free-swinging battles that plagued his industry. Born in an upstate New York village in 1839, he settled in Cleveland in 1855 and became a produce merchant. During the Civil War he invested in a local refinery and by 1865 was engaged full time in the oil business.

Like Carnegie, Rockefeller was an organizer; he knew little about the technology of petroleum. He sought efficiency, order, and stability. His forte was meticulous attention to detail: stories are told of his ordering the number of drops of solder used to seal oil cans reduced from 40 to 39 and of his insisting that the manager of one of his refineries account for 750 missing barrel bungs. Not miserliness but a profound grasp of the economies of large-scale production explain this behavior.

Rockefeller competed ruthlessly not primarily to crush other refiners but to persuade them to join with him, to share the business peaceably and rationally so that all could profit. Competition was obsolescent, he argued, though no more effective competitor than he ever lived. In truth most of the independent refiners that Standard Oil destroyed by unfair competition had previously turned down offers to merge or sell out on terms that modern students consider generous.

Having achieved his monopoly, Rockefeller stabilized and structured it by creating a new type of business organization, the trust. Standard Oil was an Ohio corporation, prohibited by local law from owning plants in other states or holding stock in out-of-state corporations. As Rockefeller and his associates took over dozens of companies with facilities scattered across the country, serious legal and managerial difficulties arose. How could these many organizations be integrated with Standard Oil of Ohio?

A rotund, genial little Pennsylvania lawyer named Samuel C. T. Dodd came up with an answer to this question in 1879.* The stock of Standard of Ohio and of all the other companies that the Rockefeller interests had swallowed up was turned over to nine trustees, who were empowered to "exercise general supervision" over all the properties. Stockholders received in exchange trust certificates, on which dividends were paid. This seem-

* The trust formula was not "perfected" until 1882.

ingly simple device brought order to the petroleum business. Competition almost disappeared; prices steadied; profits skyrocketed. By 1892 John D. Rockefeller was worth over $800 million.

The Standard Oil Trust was not a corporation. It had no charter, indeed no legal existence at all. For many years few people outside the organization knew that it existed. The form they chose persuaded Rockefeller and other Standard Oil officials that without violating their consciences, they could deny under oath that Standard Oil of Ohio owned or controlled other corporations "directly or indirectly through its officers or agents." The *trustees* controlled these organizations—and Standard of Ohio too!

After Standard Oil's duplicity was revealed during a New York investigation in 1888, the word *trust,* formerly signifying a fiduciary arrangement for the protection of the interests of individuals incompetent or unwilling to guard them themselves, immediately became a synonym for monopoly. Standard Oil became the most hated and feared company in the United States. However, from the company's point of view, monopoly was not the purpose of the trust—that had been achieved before the device was invented. Centralization of the management of diverse and far-flung operations in the interest of efficiency was its chief function. Standard Oil headquarters in New York became the brain of a complex network where information from salaried managers in the field was collected and digested, where top managerial decisions were made, and whence orders went out to armies of drillers, refiners, scientists, and salesmen.

Utilities and Retailing

That utilities such as the telephone and electric lighting industries tended to form monopolies is not difficult to explain, for in such fields competition involved costly duplication of equipment and, particularly in the case of the telephone, loss of service efficiency. However, competitive pressures were strong in the early stages of their development. Since these industries depended on patents, Bell and Edison had to fight mighty battles in the courts with rivals seeking to infringe upon their rights. Few quibbled over means when so much money hung in the balance. After Western Union employed Edison to invent a device that would enable it to circumvent Bell's rights, the Bell interests challenged Edison's improved telephone transmitter, claiming that it infringed on patents issued to one Emile Berliner, which they had bought up. Western Union was the victor in this particular battle, but in the end the telegraph company became convinced that the courts would uphold Bell's claims and abandoned the field.

Much of Edison's own time was taken up with legal battles to protect his many patents. When he first announced his electric light, capitalists, engineers, and inventors flocked to Menlo Park. Edison proudly revealed to them the secrets of his marvelous lamp. Many hurried away to turn this information to their own advantage, thinking the "Wizard" a naive fool. When they invaded the field, the law provided Edison with far less protection than he had expected. He had to fight a "Seven Years' War" with Westinghouse over the carbon-filament incandescent lamp. Although he won, his legal fees exceeded $2 million, and when the courts finally decided in his favor, only two years remained before the patent expired. "My electric light inventions have brought me no profits, only forty years of litigation," Edison later complained. A patent, he said bitterly, was "simply an invitation to a lawsuit."

The attitude of businessmen toward the rights of inventors and industrial pioneers is illustrated by an early advertisement of the Westinghouse Company:

> We regard it as fortunate that we have deferred entering the electrical field until the present moment. Having thus profited by the public experience of others, we enter ourselves for competition, hampered by a minimum of expense for experimental outlay. . . . In short, our organization is free, in large measure, of the load with which [other] electrical enterprises seem to be encumbered. The fruit of this . . . we propose to share with the customer.

Competition in the electric lighting business raged for some years among Edison, Westinghouse, and another corporation, the Thomson-Houston Electric Company, which was operating 870 central lighting stations by 1890. In 1892 the Edison and Thomson-Houston companies merged, forming General Electric, a $35 million corporation. Thereafter, General Electric and Westinghouse main-

F. W. Woolworth's five-and-ten-cent stores numbered over 1,000 by 1911, when this photograph was probably taken. Note the happy mix of merchandise, from baby bibs to greeting cards, sewing notions to hair ornaments; CHINA IN THE BASEMENT *reads the sign on the post.*

tained their dominance in the manufacture of bulbs and electrical equipment as well as in the distribution of electrical power.

The pattern of competition leading to dominance by a few great companies was repeated in many businesses. In life insurance an immense expansion took place after the Civil War, stimulated by the development of a new type of group policy, the "tontine," by Henry B. Hyde of the Equitable Life Company.* High-pressure salesmanship prevailed; agents gave rebates to customers by shaving their own commissions; companies stole crack agents from their rivals and raided new territories. They sometimes invested as mush as 96 percent of the first year's premiums in obtaining new business. By 1900, after three decades of fierce competition, three giants dominated the industry—Equitable, New York Life, and Mutual Life, each with approximately $1 billion of insurance in force.

In retailing, the period saw the growth of huge urban department stores. In 1862 Alexander T. Stewart had built an eight-story emporium in New York City that covered an entire block and employed 2,000 persons. John Wanamaker in Philadelphia and Marshall Field in Chicago headed similar establishments by the 1880s, and there were others. These department stores were run like factories. They advertised heavily, stressing low prices, efficient service, and money-back guarantees. High volume made for large profits. Here is how one of Field's biographers described his methods:

> His was a one-price store, with the price plainly marked on the merchandise. Goods were not misrepresented, and a reputation for quality merchandise and for fair and honest dealing was built up. . . . Courtesy toward customers was an unfailing rule. Stocks of goods were bought at wholesale for cash in anticipation of consumer demand and then a demand for them was created.

Americans React to Big Business

The expansion of industry and its concentration in fewer and fewer hands changed the way many people felt about the role of government in eco-

* A tontine policy paid no dividends for a stated period of years. The heirs of a policyholder who died received the face value but no dividends. At the end of the tontine period, survivors collected not only their own dividends but those of the unfortunates who had died or permitted their policies to lapse. This was psychologically appealing, since it stressed living rather than dying and added an element of gambling to insurance.

nomic and social affairs. The fact that Americans disliked powerful governments in general and strict regulation of the economy in particular had never meant that they objected to *all* government activity in the economic sphere. Banking laws, tariffs, internal-improvement legislation, and the granting of public land to railroads are only the most obvious of the conomic regulations enforced in the 19th century by both the federal government and the states. Americans saw no contradiction between government activities of this type and the free enterprise philosophy, for such laws were intended to release human energy and thus *increase* the area in which freedom could operate. Tariffs stimulated industry and created new jobs, railroad grants opened up new regions for development, and so on. As J. W. Hurst has written in a thought-provoking study, *Law and the Conditions of Freedom in the Nineteenth-Century United States,* the people "resort[ed] to law to enlarge the options open to private individual and group energy."

The growth of huge industrial and financial organizations and the increasing complexity of economic relations frightened people yet made them at the same time greedy for more of the goods and services the new society was turning out. To many, the great new corporations and trusts resembled Frankenstein's monster—marvelous and powerful but a grave threat to society. The astute James Bryce described the changes clearly in *The American Commonwealth* (1888):

> New causes are at work. . . . Modern civilization . . . has become more exacting. It discerns more benefits which the organized power of government can secure, and grows more anxious to attain them. Men live fast, and are impatient of the slow working of natural laws. . . . There are benefits which the law of supply and demand do not procure. Unlimited competition seems to press too hard on the weak. The power of groups of men organized by incorporation as joint-stock companies, or of small knots of rich men acting in combination, has developed with unexpected strength in unexpected ways, overshadowing individuals and even communities, and showing that the very freedom of association which men sought to secure by law . . . may, under the shelter of the law, ripen into a new form of tyranny.

To some extent public fear of the industrial giants reflected concern about monopoly. If Standard Oil dominated oil refining, it might raise prices inordinately at vast cost to consumers. Charles Francis Adams, Jr., expressed this feeling in the 1870s: "In the minds of the great majority, and not without reason, the idea of any industrial combination is closely connected with that of monopoly, and monopoly with extortion."

Although in isolated cases monopolists did raise prices unreasonably, generally they did not. On the contrary, prices tended to fall until by the 1890s a veritable "consumer's millennium" had arrived. Far more important in causing resentment was the fear that the monopolists were destroying economic opportunity and threatening democratic institutions. It was not the *wealth* of tycoons like Carnegie and Rockefeller and Morgan so much as their *influence* that worried people. In the face of the growing disparity between rich and poor, could republican institutions survive? "The belief is common," wrote Charles Francis Adams's brother Henry as early as 1870, "that the day is at hand when corporations . . . swaying power such as has never in the world's history been trusted in the hands of mere private citizens . . . will ultimately succeed in directing government itself."

Some observers believed either autocracy or a form of revolutionary socialism to be almost inevitable. In 1890 former president Hayes pondered "the wrong and evils of the money-piling tendency of our country, which is changing laws, government, and morals and giving all power to the rich" and decided that he was going to become a "nihilist." Campaigning for the governorship of Texas in 1890, James S. Hogg, a staunch conservative, said: "Within a few years, unless something is done, most of the wealth and talent of our country will be on one side, while arrayed on the other will be the great mass of the people, composing the bone and sinew of this government." John Boyle O'Reilly, a liberal Catholic journalist, wrote in 1886: "There is something worse than Anarchy, bad as that is; and it is irresponsible power in the hands of mere wealth." William Cook, a New York lawyer, warned in *The Corporation Problem* (1891) that "colossal aggregations of capital" were "dangerous to the republic."

These were typical reactions of responsible citizens to the rise of industrial combinations. Less thoughtful Americans sometimes went much further in their hatred of entrenched wealth. In 1900

THE AGE OF GIANT ENTERPRISE, 1861–1920

This is the second of three price graphs; the first appeared in Chapter 13, pages 382–383. The price scale on the left axis applies to the blue line. It shows changes in wholesale commodity prices as they vary around the base line/trend line of 100. In the 45 years after 1870, wholesale prices were consistently below par, regardless of the periods of relative prosperity and depression shown by the solid peaks and valleys. The green line, scaled to the right axis, shows as a contrast what the retail price of a dozen eggs was between 1870 and 1920. This line reflects the wholesale price line.

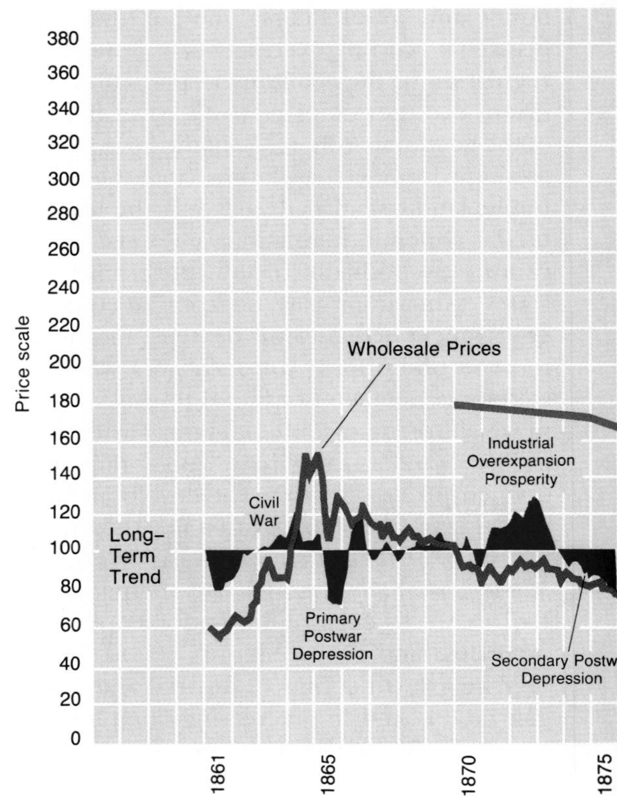

Eddie Cudahy, son of a prominent member of the Beef Trust, was kidnapped. His captor, Pat Crowe, received $25,000 ransom but was apprehended. Crowe's guilt was clear: "I want to start right by confessing in plain English that I was guilty of the kidnapping," he wrote. Yet a jury acquitted him, presumably on the theory that it was all right to rob a member of the Beef Trust.

As criticism mounted, business leaders rose to their own defense. Rockefeller described in graphic terms the chaotic conditions that plagued the oil industry before the rise of Standard Oil: "It seemed absolutely necessary to extend the market for oil . . . and also greatly improve the process of refining so that oil could be made and sold cheaply, yet with a profit. We proceeded to buy the largest and best refining concerns and centralized the administration of them with a view to securing greater economy and efficiency." Carnegie, in an essay published in 1889, insisted that the concentration of wealth was necessary if humanity was to progress, softening this "Gospel of Wealth" by insisting that the rich must use their money "in the manner which . . . is best calculated to produce the most beneficial results for the community." The rich man was merely a trustee for his "poorer brethren," Carnegie said, "bringing to their service his superior wisdom, experience, and ability to administer." Lesser tycoons echoed these arguments.

The voices of the critics were louder if not necessarily more influential. Many clergymen denounced unrestrained competition, which they considered un-Christian. The new class of professional economists (the American Economic Association was founded in 1885) tended to repudiate laissez faire. State aid, Richard T. Ely of Johns Hopkins University wrote, "is an indispensable condition of human progress."

The Radical Reformers

The popularity of a number of radical theorists reflects public feeling in the period. In 1879 Henry George, a California newspaperman, published *Progress and Poverty,* a forthright attack on the maldistribution of wealth in the United States. George argued that labor was the true and only source of capital. Observing the speculative fever of the West, which enabled landowners to reap profits merely by holding property while population increased, George proposed a property tax that would confiscate this "unearned increment." The value of land depended on society and should belong to society; allowing individuals to keep this

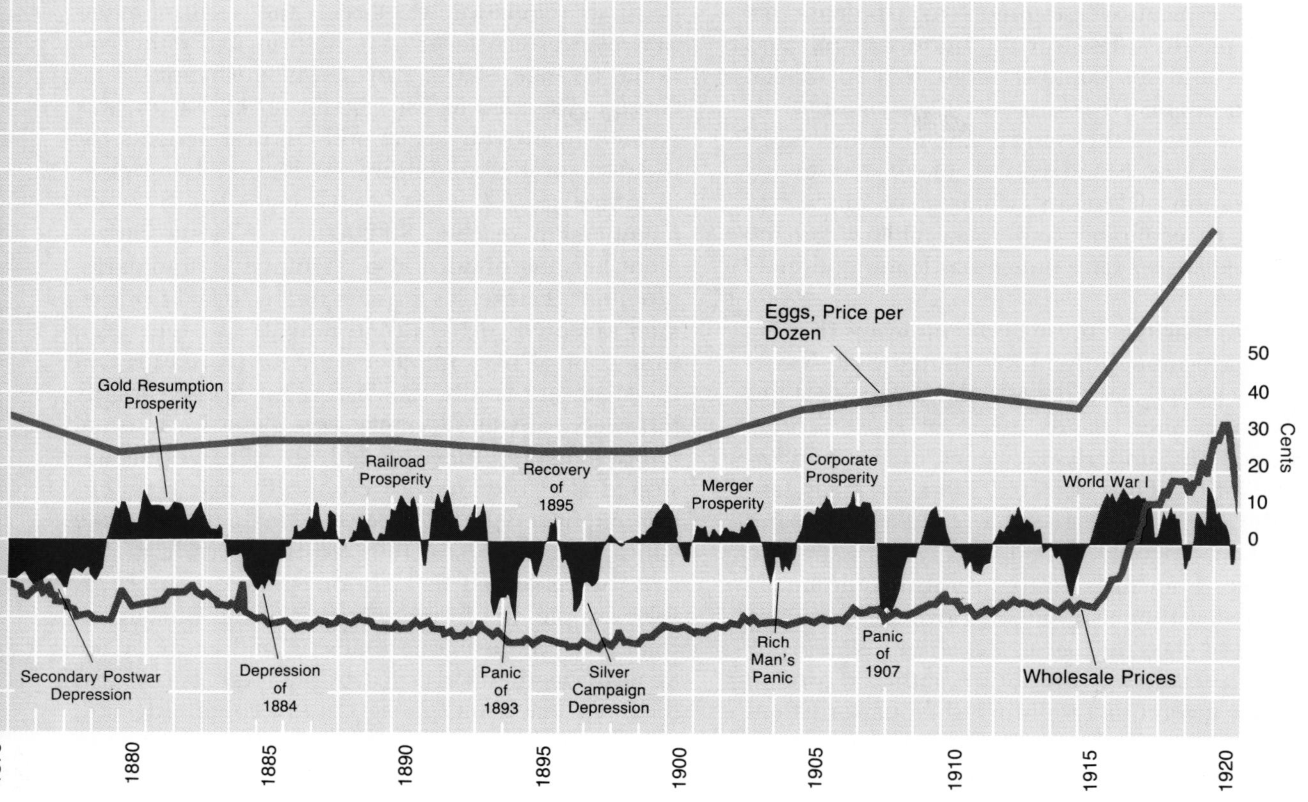

wealth was the major cause of the growing disparity between rich and poor, George believed.

George's "Single Tax," as others called it, would bring in so much money that no other taxes would be necessary, and the government would have plenty of funds to establish new schools, museums, theaters, and other badly needed social and cultural services. While the Single Tax was never adopted, George's ideas attracted enthusiastic attention. Single Tax clubs sprang up throughout the nation, and *Progress and Poverty* became a best-seller.

Even more spectacular was the reception afforded *Looking Backward, 2000–1887,* a utopian novel written in 1888 by Edward Bellamy. This book, which sold over a million copies in its first few years, described a future America that was completely socialized, all economic activity carefully planned. Bellamy compared 19th-century society to a lumbering stagecoach upon which the favored few rode in comfort while the mass of the people hauled them along life's route. Occasionally one of the toilers managed to fight his way onto the coach; whenever a rider fell from it, he had to join the multitude dragging it along.

Such, Bellamy wrote, was the working of the vaunted American competitive system. He suggested that the ideal socialist state, in which all citizens shared equally, would arrive without revolution or violence. The trend toward consolidation would continue, he predicted, until one monster trust controlled *all* economic activity. At this point everyone would realize that nationalization was essential.

A third influential attack on monopoly was that of Henry Demarest Lloyd, whose *Wealth Against Commonwealth* appeared in 1894. Lloyd, a journalist of independent means, devoted years to preparing a denunciation of the Standard Oil Company. Marshaling masses of facts and vivid examples of Standard's evildoing, he assaulted the trust at every point. Although in his zeal Lloyd sometimes distorted and exaggerated the evidence to make his indictment more effective—"Every important man in the oil, coal and many other trusts ought today to be in some one of our penitentiaries," he wrote in a typical overstatment—as a polemic his book was peerless. His forceful but uncomplicated arguments and his copious references to official documents made *Wealth Against Commonwealth* utterly convincing to thousands. The book was more than an attack on Standard Oil. Lloyd denounced the application of Darwin's concept of survival of the fittest to economic and social affairs, and he condemned laissez faire policies as leading directly to monopoly.

The popularity of these books indicates that the trend toward monopoly in the United States worried many people. But despite the drastic changes suggested in their pages, none of these writers questioned the underlying values of the middle-class majority. They rejected Marxian ideas, abjured the use of force to achieve their goals, and assumed that people were basically altruistic and reasonable. They insisted that reform could be accomplished without serious inconvenience to any individual or class. In *Looking Backward* Bellamy pictured the socialists of the future gathered around a radiolike gadget in a well-furnished parlor listening to a minister delivering an inspiring sermon.

Nor did most of their millions of readers seriously consider trying to apply the reformers' ideas. Henry George ran for mayor of New York City in 1886 and lost narrowly to Abram S. Hewitt, a wealthy iron manufacturer, but even if he had won, he would have been powerless to apply the Single Tax to metropolitan property. The national discontent was apparently not as profound as the popularity of these works might suggest. If John D. Rockefeller became the bogeyman of American industry because of Lloyd's attack, no one prevented him from also becoming the richest man in the United States.

Early Railroad Regulation

Political action came first on the state level and dealt chiefly with the regulation of railroads. Even before the Civil War, a number of New England states established railroad commissions to supervise lines within their borders; by the end of the century, 28 states had such boards. The New England type held mere advisory powers; those set up in the Middle West were true regulatory bodies with authority to fix rates and control other railroad activities.

Strict regulation was largely the result of agitation by western farm groups, principally the National Grange of the Patrons of Husbandry. The Grange, founded in 1867 by Oliver H. Kelley, was created to provide social and cultural benefits for isolated rural communities. As it spread and grew in influence—14 states had Granges by 1872 and membership reached 800,000 in 1874–the movement became political too. "Granger" candidates, often not themselves farmers (many local businessmen resented such railroad practices as rebating), won control of a number of state legislatures in the West and South. Railroad regulation invariably followed, for while farmers were eager for internal improvements, they tended to become disillusioned after the lines were built. Intense competition might reduce rates between major centers like Chicago and the East, but most western farm districts were served by only one railroad. In 1877, for example, the freight charges of the Burlington road were almost four times as high west of the Missouri as they were east of the river. It cost less to ship wheat from Chicago to Liverpool, England, than from some parts of the Dakotas to Minneapolis.

Granger-controlled legislatures tried to eliminate this kind of discrimination. The Illinois Granger laws were typical. The revised state constitution of 1870 declared railroads to be public highways and authorized the legislature to "pass laws establishing reasonable maximum rates" and to "prevent unjust discrimination." The legislature did so and set up a commission to enforce the laws and punish violators. The railroads protested, insisting that they were being deprived of property without due process of law. In *Munn* v. *Illinois* (1877), a case that involved a grain elevator whose owner had refused to comply with a state warehouse act, the Supreme Court upheld the constitutionality of this kind of act in very broad terms. Any business that served a public interest, such as a railroad or a grain warehouse, was subject to state control, the justices ruled. Legislatures might fix maximum charges; if the charges seemed unreasonable to the parties concerned, they should direct their complaints to the legislatures or to the voters, not to the courts.

Regulation of the railroad network by the individual states was inefficient, and in some cases the commissions were incompetent and even corrupt. When the Supreme Court, in the *Wabash* case

Railroad interests strangle commerce, agriculture, and manufacturing in this parody of the classical Greek statue of Laocoön.

(1886), declared unconstitutional an Illinois regulation outlawing the long-and-short-haul evil (see p. 525), federal action became necessary. (The Wabash, St. Louis and Pacific Railroad had charged 25 cents per 100 pounds for shipping goods from Gilman, Illinois, to New York City and only 15 cents from Peoria, which was 86 miles farther from New York.) Illinois judges had held this to be illegal, but the Supreme Court decided that Illinois could not regulate interstate shipments.

Congress had been considering federal railroad regulation for years, so the legislators were prepared to fill the gap created by the Wabash decision. In February 1887 the Interstate Commerce Act was passed. All charges made by railroads "shall be reasonable and just," the act stated. Rebates, drawbacks, the long-and-short-haul evil, and other competitive practices were declared unlawful, and so were their monopolistic counterparts—pools and traffic-sharing agreements. Railroads were required to publish schedules of rates and forbidden to change them without due public notice. Most important, the law established an Interstate Commerce Commission (ICC), the first federal regulatory board, to supervise the affairs of railroads, investigate complaints, and issue cease and desist orders when the roads acted illegally.

The Interstate Commerce Act broke new ground, yet it was neither a radical nor a particularly effective measure. Its terms contradicted one another, some being designed to stimulate, others to penalize competition. The chairman of the commission soon characterized the law as an "anomaly." It sought, he said, to "enforce competition" at the same time that it outlawed "the acts and inducements by which competition is ordinarily effected." The commission had less power than the law seemed to give it. It could not fix rates, only bring the roads to court when it considered rates unreasonably high. Such cases could be extremely complicated; applying the law "was like cutting a path through a jungle." With the truth so hard to determine and the burden of proof on the commission, the courts in nearly every instance decided in favor of the railroads. "This commission," the ICC reported in 1903, "has no power to determine what rate is reasonable, and such orders as it can make have no binding effect."

State regulatory commissions fared poorly in the Supreme Court in the last years of the century. Overruling part of their decision in *Munn* v. *Illinois,* the justices declared in *Chicago, Milwaukee and St. Paul Railroad Company* v. *Minnesota* (1890) that the reasonableness of rates was "eminently a question for *judicial* investigation." In a Texas case, *Reagan* v. *Farmers' Loan and Trust Company* (1894), the Court held that it had the "power and duty" to decide if rates were "unjust and unreasonable" even when the state legislature itself had established them. Nevertheless, by describing so clearly the right of Congress to regulate private corporations engaged in interstate commerce, the Interstate Commerce Act challenged the philosophy of laissez faire. Later legislation made the commission more effective. The commission also served as the model for a host of similar federal administrative authorities, such as the Federal Communications Commission (1934).

The Sherman Antitrust Act

As with railroad legislation, the first antitrust laws originated in the states, but they were southern and western states with relatively little industry, and most of the statutes were vaguely worded and ill enforced. Federal action came in 1890 with the passage of the Sherman Antitrust Act. Any combination "in the form of trust or otherwise" that was "in restraint of trade or commerce among the several states, or with foreign nations" was declared illegal. Persons forming such combinations were subject to fines of $5,000 and a year in jail. Individuals and businesses suffering losses because of actions that violated the law were authorized to sue in the federal courts for triple damages.

Where the Interstate Commerce Act sought to outlaw the excesses of competition, the Sherman Act was supposed to restore competition. If businessmen joined together to "restrain" (monopolize) trade in a particular field, they should be punished and their deeds undone. Monopoly was already illegal under the common law, but as Senator George Frisbie Hoar of Massachusetts pointed out during the antitrust debates, no *federal* common law existed.

"The great thing this bill does," Senator Hoar explained, "is to extend the common-law principle . . . to international and interstate commerce." This was important because the states ran into legal difficulties when they tried to use the common law to restrict corporations engaged in interstate activities. The Sherman Act was rather loosely worded—Thurman Arnold, a modern authority, once said that it made it "a crime to violate a vaguely stated economic policy." Critics have argued that the congressmen were more interested in quieting the public clamor for action against the trusts than in actually breaking up any of the new combinations. Quieting the clamor was certainly one of their objectives. No politician likes having to cope with indignant voters, especially in an election year. Yet Congress was trying to solve a new problem and was not sure how to proceed. A law with teeth too sharp might do more harm than good. Most Americans assumed that the courts would deal with the details, as they always had in common-law matters.

In fact the Supreme Court quickly emasculated the Sherman Act. In *United States* v. *E. C. Knight Company* (1895) it held that the American Sugar Refining Company had not violated the law by taking over a number of important competitors. Although the Sugar Trust now controlled about 98 percent of all sugar refining in the United States, it was not restraining *trade.* "Doubtless the power to control the manufacture of a given thing involves in a certain sense the control of its disposition," the Court said in one of the greatest feats of judicial understatement of all time. "Although the exercise of that power may result in bringing the operation of commerce into play, it does not control it, and affects it only incidentally and indirectly."

If the creation of the Sugar Trust did not violate the Sherman Act, it seemed unlikely that any other combination of manufacturers could be convicted under the law. In *The History of the Last Quarter-Century in the United States* (1896), E. Benjamin Andrews, president of Brown University, delivered a strong indictment of trusts. "The crimes to which some of them resorted to crush out competition were unworthy of civilization," he wrote. Yet he referred only obliquely to the Sherman Act, dismissing it as "obviously ineffectual" and "of little avail."

But in a series of cases in 1898 and 1899 the Supreme Court ruled that agreements to fix prices or divide markets violated the Sherman Act. These decisions precipitated a wave of outright mergers in which a handful of large companies swallowed up hundreds of smaller ones. Presumably mergers were not illegal. When, some years after his retirement, Andrew Carnegie was asked by a committee of the House of Representatives to explain how he had dared participate in the formation of the U.S. Steel Corporation, he replied: "Nobody ever mentioned the Sherman Act to me, that I remember."

American industry was flourishing, but each year more of it seemed to fall into fewer hands. As with the railroads, other industries were coming to be strongly influenced, if not completely dominated, by bankers—the Money Trust seemed fated to become the ultimate monopoly. The firm of J. P. Morgan and Company controlled many railroads; the largest steel, electrical, agricultural machinery, rubber, and shipping companies in the nation; two life insurance companies; and a number of banks. By 1913 Morgan and the Rockefeller–National City Bank group between them could name 341 directors to 112 corporations worth over $22.2 billion.

Centralization unquestionably increased efficiency, at least in industries that used a great deal of expensive machinery to turn out goods for the mass market, and in those where close coordination of output, distribution, and sales was important. The public benefited immensely from the productive efficiency and the rapid growth of the new empires. Living standards rose. But the trend toward giantism raised doubts. With ownership falling into fewer hands, what would be the ultimate effect of big business on American democracy?

SUPPLEMENTARY READING

Titles marked with an asterisk have been published in paperback.

Of works dealing with industrial growth, E. C. Kirkland, **Industry Comes of Age*** (1961), is the best general introduction, but see also V. S. Clark's detailed **History of Manufactures in the United States** (1929), Allan Nevins, **The Emergence of Modern America*** (1927), I. M. Tarbell, **Nationalizing Big Business*** (1936), and T. C. Cochran and William Miller, **The Age of Enterprise*** (1942). Matthew Josephson, **The Robber Barons*** (1934), is highly critical but provocative. Rendigs Fels, **American Business Cycles** (1959), is technical but valuable. A. D. Chandler, Jr., **The Visible Hand** (1977), covers the way businesses were organized and managed. On technological developments, see H. J. Habakkuk, **American and British Technology in the Nineteenth Century*** (1962), W. P. Strassmann, **Risk and Technological Innovation: American Manufacturing Methods During the Nineteenth Century** (1959), and Lewis Mumford, **Technics and Civilization*** (1934).

For the railroad industry, consult G. R. Taylor and I. D. Neu, **The American Railroad Network** (1956), J. F. Stover, **American Railroads*** (1961), T. C. Cochran, **Railroad Leaders** (1953), Julius Grodinsky, **Transcontinental Railway Strategy** (1962) and **Jay Gould** (1957). C. F. Adams, Jr., **Railroads: Their Origin and Problems** (1879), is a valuable contemporary analysis.

The iron and steel business is discussed in detail in J. F. Wall, **Andrew Carnegie** (1970), Peter Temin, **Iron and Steel in Nineteenth-Century America** (1964), an economic analysis, J. H. Bridge, **The Inside History of the Carnegie Steel Company** (1903), and in Carnegie's **Autobiography** (1920); there is no solid scholarly history of the industry. For the oil industry, however, a number of excellent volumes exist. See Carl Solberg, **Oil Power*** (1976), a good survey, H. F. Williamson and A. R. Daum, **The American Petroleum Industry: Age of Illumination** (1959), Allan Nevins, **Study in Power: John D. Rockefeller** (1953), and R. W. and M. E. Hidy, **Pioneering in Big Business** (1955), the first volume of their **History of Standard Oil Company (New Jersey)** (1955–1956).

The electrical industry is discussed in an excellent study, H. C. Passer, **The Electrical Manufacturers** (1953), and in an equally good biography, Matthew Josephson, **Edison*** (1959). H. G. Prout, **A Life of George Westinghouse** (1921), is also useful. On the telephone, see John Brooks, **Telephone: The First Hundred Years** (1976), and R. V. Bruce, **Alexander Graham Bell and the Conquest of Solitude** (1973).

Many of these volumes deal with the problems of competition and monopoly. See also, however, E. G. Campbell, **The Reorganization of the American Railroad System** (1938), Gabriel Kolko, **Railroads and Regulation*** (1965), which is critical of both railroad leaders and of government policy, J. D. Rockefeller, **Random Reminiscences of Men and Events** (1909), H. D. Lloyd, **Wealth Against Commonwealth** (1894), Lewis Corey, **The House of Morgan** (1930), H. W. Laidler, **Concentration of Control in American Industry** (1931), and J. W. Jenks, **The Trust Problem** (1905).

For contemporary discussions of the monopoly problem, see Lloyd's **Wealth Against Commonwealth,** Henry George, **Progress and Poverty*** (1879), and Edward Bellamy, **Looking Backward*** (1888). The background of government regulation of industry is treated in Sidney Fine, **Laissez Faire and the General-Welfare State*** (1956), J. W. Hurst, **Law and the Conditions of Freedom in the Nineteenth-Century United States*** (1956), J. A. Garraty, **The New Commonwealth*** (1968), and Lee Benson, **Merchants, Farmers, and Railroads** (1955). Other useful volumes include Ari and Olive Hoogenboom, **A History of the ICC*** (1976), H. B. Thorelli, **The Federal Antitrust Policy** (1954), S. J. Buck, **The Granger Movement*** (1913), and G. W. Miller, **Railroads and the Granger Laws** (1971).

19
The Response to Industrialism

Power seemed to have outgrown its servitude and to have asserted its freedom. . . . The city had the air and movement of hysteria, and the citizens were crying, in every accent of anger and alarm, that the new forces must at any cost be brought under control. HENRY ADAMS

The industrialization that followed the Civil War profoundly affected every aspect of American life. New machines, improvements in transportation and communication, the appearance of the great corporation with its uncertain implications for the future—all made deep impressions on the economy and on the social and cultural development of the nation. Indeed, the history of the period may be treated, historian Samuel P. Hays suggests, as a "response to industrialism," the "story of the impact of industrialism on every phase of human life."

The American Worker

Wage earners felt the full force of the tide, being affected in countless ways—some beneficial, others unfortunate. As industry became more important, the number of industrial workers multiplied rapidly: from 885,000 in 1860 to more than 3.2 million in 1890. While workers lacked much sense of solidarity, they exerted a far larger influence on society at the turn of the century than they had in the years before the Civil War. More efficient methods of production enabled them to increase their output, making possible a rise in their standard of living.

This generalization, however, conceals some important differences. Skilled industrial workers—such types as railroad engineers and conductors, machinists, and iron molders—were quite well off in most cases. But it was still true that unskilled laborers could not earn enough to maintain a family decently by their own efforts alone. James H. Ducker's *Men of the Steel Rails,* a study of the work force of the Atchison, Topeka and Santa Fe Railroad, throws much light on working conditions and workers' attitudes at this time. Ordinary track laborers were paid from $1 to $1.25 a day, whereas engineers received three times that amount or more. In addition, many of the better-paid workers picked up additional sums, some by legitimate means, such as renting spare rooms to other workers, some by practices ranging from shady to flagrantly criminal.

Mangement tried to discipline the labor force by establishing rules for each job category, but it had difficulty enforcing them. "There were many schemes to avoid work and evade regulations," Ducker reports. Drunkenness on the job was a constant problem. Many conductors were said to be "color blind," the term indicating that they could not tell the difference between the road's money and their own. Baggage and freight handlers frequently made off with goods ranging from a few cigars or a bottle of whiskey to entire shipments of merchandise. According to Ducker, transient workers, called "boomers," had "a deserved reputation as rowdies who cared more for drink than decorum, cards than church, lust than love." Other workers, of course, were law-abiding, hardworking family men.

Industrialization created problems for workers beyond the obvious one of earning enough money to support themselves. When machines took the place of human skills, jobs became monotonous. Mechanization undermined both the artisans' pride and their bargaining power vis-à-vis their employers. As expensive machinery became more important, the worker seemed of necessity less important. Machines more than workers controlled the pace of work and its duration. The time clock regulated the labor force more rigidly than the most exacting foreman. As businesses grew larger, personal contact between employer and hired hand tended to disappear. Relations between them became less human, more businesslike and ruthless. On the other hand, large enterprises usually employed a higher percentage of managerial and clerical workers than smaller companies, thus providing opportunities for more workers to rise in the industrial hierarchy.

The trend toward bigness seemed to make it more difficult for workers to rise from the ranks of labor to become themselves manufacturers, as Andrew Carnegie, for example, had done during the Civil War era. Careful studies of large numbers of late-19th-century business leaders show that most came from comfortably-off families. They were better educated than the average person of that day and belonged to one or another of the leading Protestant churches.

Another problem for workers was that industrialization tended to accentuate swings of the business cycle. On the upswing something approaching full employment existed, but in periods of depression unemployment became a problem that affected workers without regard for their individual abilities. It is significant that the word *unemployment* (though not, of course, the condition itself) was a late-19th-century invention.

By and large, skilled workers, always better off than the unskilled, improved their positions relatively, despite the increased use of machinery. Women and children continued to supply a significant percentage of the industrial working force, always receiving lower wages than adult male workers. But now many more women were working outside their homes; the factory had almost completely replaced the household as the seat of manufacturing.

Women found new types of work in these years. They made up the overwhelming majority of salespersons and cashiers in the new department stores. Managers considered women more polite, easier to control, and more honest than male workers, all qualities especially valuable in the huge emporiums. Women also replaced men in business offices. They operated the new typewriters, mastery of which demanded a sound knowledge of spelling and grammar. Most men with these skills had better opportunities and were uninterested in office work, so women high school graduates, of whom there was an increasing number, filled the gap. Both department store clerks and "typewriters" (as they were called) earned more money than unskilled factory workers, and working conditions were more pleasant. Opportunities for promotion, however, were rare; managerial posts in these fields remained almost exclusively in the hands of men.

Early social workers who visited the homes of industrial laborers in this period reported enormous differences in the standard of living of people engaged in the same line of work, differences related to such variables as the wife's ability as a homemaker and the degree of the family's commitment to middle-class values. Some families spent most of their income on food; others saved substantial sums even when earning no more than $400 or $500 a year. Family incomes varied greatly among workers who received similar hourly wages, depending on the steadiness of employment and on the number of family members holding jobs.

For most laborers the working day still tended to approximate the hours of daylight, but it was shortening perceptibly by the 1880s. In 1860 the average was 11 hours; by 1880 only one worker in four labored more than 10 hours, and radicals were beginning to talk about 8 hours as a fair day's work. To some extent the exhausting pace of the new factories made longer hours uneconomical, but employers realized this only slowly, and until they did, many workers suffered.

Despite the improvement in living standards, there was a great deal of dissatisfaction among industrial workers. Writing in 1885, the labor leader Terence V. Powderly reported that "a deep-rooted feeling of discontent pervades the masses." A few years later a Connecticut official conducted an informal survey of labor opinion in the state and found a "feeling of bitterness' and "distrust of employers" endemic.

The discontent had many causes. For some, poverty was still the chief problem, but for others, rising aspirations triggered discontent. Workers were confused about their destiny; the tradition that no one of ability need remain a hired hand died hard. They wanted to believe their bosses and the politicians when those worthies voiced the old slogans about a classless society and the community of interest of capital and labor. "Our men," William Vanderbilt of the New York Central said in 1877, "feel that, although I . . . may have my millions and they the rewards of their daily toil, still we are about equal in the end. If they suffer, I suffer, and if I suffer, they cannot escape." "The poor," another conservative spokesman said a decade later, "are not poor because the rich are rich." Instead "the service of capital" softened their lot and gave them many benefits.

Statements such as these, though self-serving, were essentially correct. The rich were growing richer and more people were growing rich, but ordinary workers were better off too. However, the gap between the very rich and the ordinary citizen was widening. "The tendency . . . is toward centralization and aggregation," the Illinois Bureau of Labor Statistics reported in 1886. "This involves a separation of the people into classes, and the permanently subordinate status of large numbers of them."

To study social and economic mobility in a large industrial country is extraordinarily difficult. Americans in the late 19th century believed their society offered great opportunities for individual advancement, and to prove it they pointed to men like Andrew Carnegie and to other poor boys who accumulated large fortunes. How general was the rise from rags to riches (or even to modest comfort) is another question.

Fascinating studies of census records, the most

important being those of Stephan Thernstrom, show that there was considerable geographical mobility in urban areas throughout the last half of the 19th century and into the 20th. Most investigations reveal that only about half the people recorded in one census were still in the same place ten years later; as Thernstrom puts it, "transiency was part of the American way of life. . . . The country had an enormous reservoir of footloose men, who could be lured to new destinations when opportunity beckoned."

In most of the cities studied, mobility was accompanied by some economic and social improvement. On the average, about a quarter of the manual laborers traced rose to middle-class status during their lifetimes, and the sons of manual laborers were still more likely to improve their place in society. In New York City about a third of the Italian and Jewish immigrants of the 1890s had risen from unskilled to skilled jobs a decade later. Even in Newburyport, Massachusetts, a town that was something of an economic backwater, most laborers made some progress, though far fewer rose to skilled or white-collar positions than in more prosperous cities.

There is no evidence, however, that progress from rags to real riches was common. The Carnegies, clearly, were rare exceptions. The dashing of unrealistic hopes inspired by such cases more than the absence of real opportunity probably explains why so many workers, even when expressing dissatisfaction with life as it was, continued to subscribe to such middle-class values as hard work and thrift—that is, they continued to hope. Thernstrom notes that hundreds of poor people in Newburyport, by practicing what he calls "ruthless underconsumption," gradually accumulated enough money to buy their own homes and provide for themselves in their old age.

Labor Organizations

Discontent and class consciousness led some workers to join unions, but only a small percentage of the work force was organized, and most of this consisted of cigarmakers, printers, carpenters, and other skilled workers rather than factory hands. Aside from ironworkers, railroad workers, and miners, few industrial laborers belonged to unions. Nevertheless the union was the worker's response to the big corporation: a combination designed to eliminate competition for jobs and to provide efficient organization for labor.

After 1865 the growth of national craft unions similar to those of the iron molders, the printers, and the cigarmakers, which had been organized in the 1850s, quickened perceptibly. By the early 1870s about 300,000 workers belonged to such organizations, and many new trades, notably in railroading, had been unionized. A federation of such unions, the National Labor Union, was created in 1866, but it remained chiefly a paper organization. Most of its leaders were visionaries who were out of touch with the practical needs and aspirations of workers. They opposed the wage system, strikes, and anything that increased the laborers' sense of being members of the working class. A major objective was the formation of worker-owned cooperatives.

Far more remarkable was the Knights of Labor, a curious organization founded in 1869 by a group of Philadelphia garment workers headed by Uriah

A black delegate introduces Terence V. Powderly at a Knights of Labor convention held in Richmond. At one point the union had some 60,000 black members.

S. Stephens. Like so many labor organizers of the period, Stephens was a reformer of wide interests rather than a man dedicated to the specific problems of industrial workers. He, his successor Terence V. Powderly, and many other leaders of the Knights would have been thoroughly at home in the labor organizations of the Jacksonian era. Like the Jacksonians, they supported political objectives that had no direct connection with working conditions, such as currency reform and the curbing of land speculation. They rejected the idea that workers must resign themselves to remaining wage earners. By pooling their resources, workingmen could advance up the economic ladder and enter the capitalist class. "There is no good reason," Powderly wrote in his autobiography, *The Path I Trod,* "why labor cannot, through cooperation, own and operate mines, factories, and railroads." The leading Knights saw no contradiction between their denunciation of "soulless" monopolies and "drones" like bankers and lawyers and their talk of "combining all branches of trade in one common brotherhood." Such muddled thinking led the Knights to attack the wage system and to frown on strikes as "acts of private warfare."

If the Knights had one foot in the past, they also had one foot in the future. They supported some startlingly advanced ideas. Rejecting the traditional grouping of workers by crafts, they developed a concept closely resembling modern industrial unionism. They welcomed blacks (though mostly in segregated locals), women, and immigrants, and they accepted unskilled workers as well as artisans. The eight-hour day was one of their basic demands, their argument being that increased leisure would give workers time to develop more cultivated tastes and higher aspirations. Higher pay would inevitably follow.

The growth of the union, however, had little to do with ideology. Stephens had made the Knights a secret organization with an elaborate ritual. Under his leadership, as late as 1879 it had fewer than 10,000 members. Under Powderly, secrecy was discarded. Between 1882 and 1886 successful strikes by local "assemblies" against western railroads, including one against the hated Jay Gould's Missouri Pacific, brought recruits by the thousands. The membership passed 42,000 in 1882, 110,000 in 1885; and in 1886 it soared beyond the 700,000 mark. Alas, sudden prosperity was too much for the Knights. Its national leadership was unable to control local groups. A number of poorly planned strikes failed dismally, and the public was alienated by sporadic acts of violence and intimidation. Disillusioned recruits began to drift away.

Circumstances largely fortuitous caused the collapse of the organization. By 1886 the movement for the eight-hour day had gained wide support among workers. Several hundred thousand (estimates vary) were on strike in various parts of the country by May of that year. In Chicago, a center of the eight-hour movement, about 80,000 workers were involved, and a small group of anarchists was trying to take advantage of the excitement to win support.

When a striker was killed in a fracas at the McCormick Harvesting Machine Company, the anarchists called a protest meeting on May 4, at Haymarket Square. Police intervened to break up the meeting, and someone—his identity was never established—hurled a bomb into their ranks. Seven policemen were killed and many others injured.

While the anarchists were the immediate victims of the resulting public indignation and hysteria—seven were condemned to death and four eventually executed—organized labor, especially the Knights, suffered heavily. No tie between the Knights and the bombing could be established, but the union had been closely connected with the eight-hour agitation, and the public tended to associate it with violence and radicalism. Its membership declined as suddenly as it had risen, and soon it ceased to exist as a force in the labor movement.

The Knights' place was taken by the American Federation of Labor, a combination of national craft unions established in 1886. In a sense the AFL was a reactionary organization. Its principal leaders, Adolph Strasser and Samuel Gompers of the Cigarmakers Union, were, like the founders of the Knights of Labor, originally interested in utopian social reforms. They even toyed with the idea of forming a workingmen's political party. Experience, however, soon led them to concentrate on organizing skilled workers and fighting for "bread-and-butter" issues such as higher wages and shorter hours. "Our organization does not consist of idealists," Strasser explained to a congressional

An anarchist group printed 20,000 of these bilingual handbills on the day of the Haymarket bombing in Chicago in 1886.

committee. "We do not control the production of the world. That is controlled by the employers. . . . I look first to cigars."

The AFL was modern in its attitude toward industrial trends. It accepted the fact that most workers would remain wage earners all their lives and tried to develop in them a sense of common purpose and pride in their skills and station. Strasser and Gompers paid great attention to building a strong organization of dues-paying members committed to unionism as a way of improving their lot. Rank-and-file AFL members were naturally eager to win wage increases and other benefits, but most also valued their unions for the companionship they provided, the sense of belonging to a group. In other words, despite statements such as Strasser's, unions, in and out of the AFL, were a kind of club as well as a means of defending and advancing their members' material interests.

The chief weapon of the federation was the strike, which it used to win concessions from employers and to attract recruits. Gompers, president of the AFL almost continuously from 1886 until his death in 1924, encouraged workers to make "an intelligent use of the ballot" in order to advance their own interests. The federation adopted a "legislative platform" that demanded such things as eight-hour, employers' liability, and mine-safety laws, but it avoided direct involvement in politics. "I have my own philosophy and my own dreams," Gompers once told a left-wing French politician, "but first and foremost I want to increase the workingman's welfare year by year. . . . The French workers waste their economic force by their political divisions." Gompers's approach to labor problems produced solid, if unspectacular, growth for the AFL. Unions with a total of about 150,000 members formed the federation in 1886. By 1892 the membership had reached 250,000, and in 1901 it passed the million mark.

Labor Militancy Rebuffed

The stress of the AFL on the strike weapon reflected rather than caused the increasing militancy of labor. Workers felt themselves threatened from all sides: the growing size and power of their corporate employers, the substitution of machines for human skills, the invasion of foreign workers willing to accept substandard wages. At the same time they had tasted some of the material benefits of industrialization and had learned the advantages of concerted action.

The average employer behaved like a tyrant when dealing with his workers. He discharged them arbitrarily when they tried to organize unions; he hired scabs to break strikes; he frequently failed to provide the most rudimentary protections against injury on the job. Some employers, Carnegie for example, professed to approve of unions, but almost none would bargain with labor collectively. To do so, they argued, would be to deprive workers of their freedom to contract for their own labor in any way they saw fit.

The industrialists of the period were not all ogres; they were as alarmed by the rapid changes of the times as their workers, and since they had more at stake materially, they were probably more frightened by the uncertainties. Deflation, technological change, and intense competition kept even the most successful under constant pressure.

The thinking of most employers was remarkably confused. They considered workers who joined unions "disloyal," and at the same time they treated labor as a commodity to be purchased as cheaply as possible. "If I wanted boiler iron," Henry B. Stone, a railroad official, explained, "I would go out on the market and buy it where I could get it cheapest, and if I wanted to employ men, I would do the same." Yet Stone was furious when the men he had "bought" joined a union. When labor was scarce, employers resisted demands for higher wages by arguing that the price of labor was controlled by its productivity; when it was plentiful, they justified reducing wages by referring to the law of supply and demand.

Thus capital and labor were often spoiling for a fight, frequently without fully understanding why. When labor troubles developed, they tended to be bitter, even violent. In 1877 a great railroad strike convulsed much of the nation. It began on the Baltimore and Ohio system in response to a wage cut and spread to other eastern lines and then throughout the West until about two-thirds of the railroad mileage of the country had been shut down. Violence broke out, rail yards were put to the torch, dismayed and frightened businessmen formed militia companies to patrol the streets of Chicago and other cities. Eventually President Hayes sent federal troops to the trouble spots to restore order, and the strike collapsed. There had been no real danger of revolution, but the violence and destruction of the strike had been without precedent in America.

The disturbances of 1877 were a response to a business slump, those of the next decade a response to good times. Twice as many strikes occurred in 1886 as in any previous year. Even before the Haymarket bombing centered the country's attention on labor problems, the situation had become so disturbing that President Cleveland, in the first presidential message devoted to labor problems, had urged Congress to create a voluntary arbitration board to aid in settling labor disputes—a remarkable suggestion for a man of Cleveland's conservative, laissez faire approach to economic issues.

In 1892 a violent strike broke out among silver miners at Coeur d'Alene, Idaho, and a far more important clash shook Andrew Carnegie's Homestead steel plant near Pittsburgh when strikers attacked 300 private guards brought in to protect strikebreakers. Seven guards were killed and the rest forced to "surrender" and march off ignominiously. The Homestead affair was part of a harsh struggle between capital and labor in the steel industry. The steelmen insisted that the workers were holding back progress by resisting technological advances, while the workers believed that the company was refusing to share the fruits of more efficient operation fairly. The strike was precipitated by the decision of company officials to crush the union at all costs. The final defeat, after a five-month walkout, of the 24,000-member Amalgamated Association of Iron and Steel Workers, one of the most important elements in the AFL, destroyed unionism as an effective force in the steel industry and set back the progress of organized labor all over the country.

As in the case of the Haymarket bombing, the activities of radicals on the fringe of the dispute turned the public against the steelworkers. The boss of Homestead was Henry Clay Frick, a tough-minded foe of unions who was determined to "teach our employees a lesson." Frick made the decision to bring in strikebreakers and to employ Pinkerton detectives to protect them. During the course of the strike, Alexander Berkman, an anarchist, burst into Frick's office and attempted to assassinate him. Frick was only slightly wounded, but the attack brought him much sympathy and unjustly discredited the strikers.

The most important strike of the period took place in 1894. It began when the workers at George Pullman's Palace Car factory outside Chicago walked out in protest against wage cuts. (While reducing wages, Pullman insisted on holding the line on rents in the company town of Pullman; when a delegation called on him to remonstrate, he refused to give in and had three of the leaders fired.) Some Pullman workers belonged to the American Railway Union, headed by Eugene V. Debs. After

A periodical's dramatic depiction of an episode during the 1894 Pullman strike, in which National Guard troops, using railroad work cars as a barricade, fired into a mob of strikers.

the strike had dragged along for weeks, the union voted to refuse to handle trains with Pullman cars. The union was perfectly willing to handle mail trains, but the owners refused to run trains unless they were made up of a full complement of cars. When Pullman cars were added to mail trains, the workers refused to move them. The resulting railroad strike tied up trunk lines running in and out of Chicago.

Bypassing Governor John Peter Altgeld of Illinois because of his prolabor views, the railroad owners appealed to President Cleveland to send troops to preserve order. On the pretext that the soldiers were needed to ensure the movement of the mails, Cleveland agreed. When Debs defied a federal injunction, he was jailed for contempt and the strike was broken.

The crushing of the Pullman strike demonstrated the power of the courts to break strikes by issuing injunctions. Even more ominous for organized labor was the fact that the government based its request for the injunction on the Sherman Antitrust Act, arguing that the American Railway Union was a combination in restraint of trade. Another result of the strike was that Eugene V. Debs became a national figure. While serving his sen-

After the collapse of his American Railway Union in 1897, Eugene V. Debs (shown here addressing a Socialist party gathering) devoted himself to politics.

tence for contempt, he was visited by a number of prominent socialists who sought to convert him to their cause. One gave him a copy of Karl Marx's *Capital,* which he found too dull to finish, but he did read *Looking Backward* and *Wealth Against Commonwealth.* In 1897 he became a socialist. Later he ran for president five times on the Socialist party ticket.

The "New" Immigration

Industrial expansion increased the need for labor, and this in turn powerfully stimulated immigration. Between 1866 and 1915 about 25 million foreigners entered the United States. Industrial growth alone does not explain the influx. The Atlantic crossing, once so hazardous and uncomfortable, became safe and speedy with the perfection of the steamship. Competition between the great packet lines such as Cunard, North German Lloyd, and Holland-America drove down the cost of the passage, and advertising by the lines further stimulated traffic. Improved transportation wrought changes in the economies of many European countries that caused an increase in the flow of people to America. Cheap wheat from the United States, Russia, and other parts of the world could now be imported into western Europe, bringing disaster to farmers in England, Germany, and the Scandinavian countries. The spreading industrial revolution led to the collapse of the peasant economy of central and southern Europe. For rural inhabitants this meant the loss of self-sufficiency, the fragmentation of landholdings, poverty, and for many the decision to make a new start in the New World. Political and religious persecutions pushed still others into the migrating stream. However, the main reason for immigration remained the desire for economic betterment. "In America," a British immigrant said, "you get pies and puddings."

While immigrants continued to people the farms of America, industry absorbed an ever-increasing number of them. In 1870 one industrial worker in three was foreign-born. When congressional investigators examined 21 major industries early in the new century, they discovered that well over half of the labor force was foreign-born.

Most of the new millions came into the United States by way of New York City. A Serbian immigrant, Michael Pupin, later a distinguished physicist at Columbia University, has left a moving description of what it was like to enter. He arrived in 1874 on the Hamburg-American liner *Westphalia* amid a horde of newcomers. Disembarking at Hoboken, he was taken by tug to the immigration reception center at Castle Garden on the southern tip of Manhattan. He confessed to the authorities that he had only 5 cents to his name and knew no Americans except—by reputation—Franklin, Lincoln, and Harriet Beecher Stowe. But he explained in eloquent phrases why he wanted to live in the land of liberty rather than in the Austro-Hungarian empire. The officials conferred briefly, then admitted him. After a good breakfast, supplied by the immigration authorities, the Castle Garden Labor Bureau offered him a job as a farmhand in Delaware. Within 24 hours of his arrival he had reached his destination, ready to work.

Before 1882, when—in addition to the Chinese—criminals, idiots, lunatics, and persons liable to become public charges were excluded, entry into the United States was almost unrestricted. Indeed,

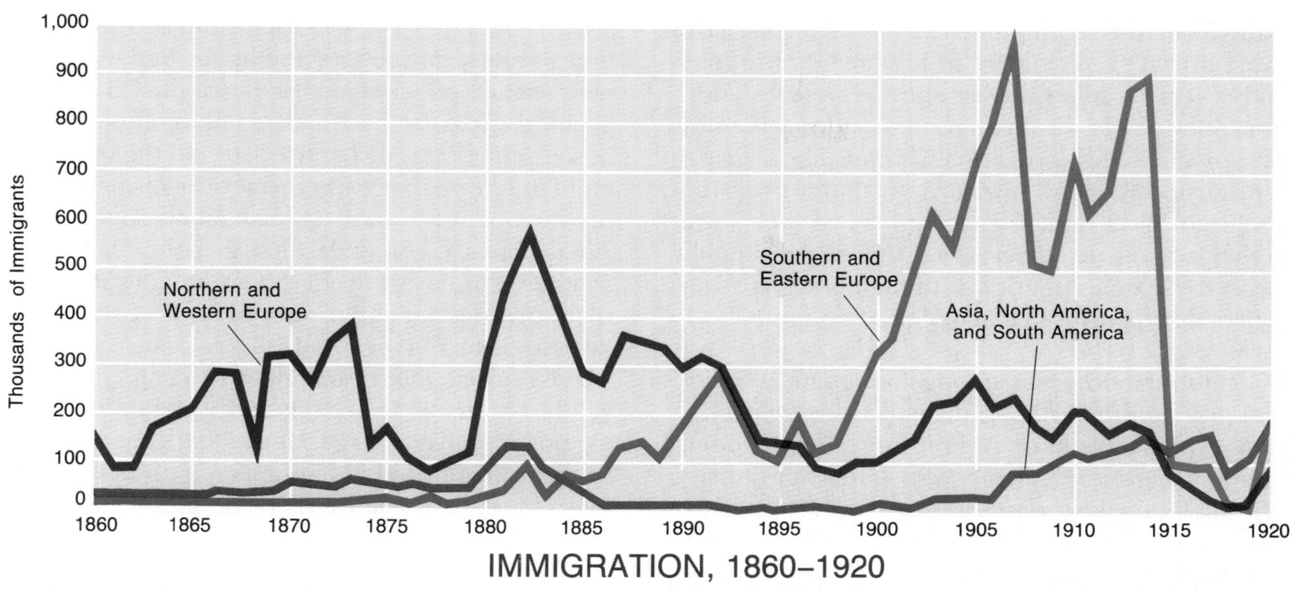

In this graph Germany is counted as a part of northern and western Europe. Note the tide of "new" immigration from southern and eastern Europe in the early 1900s, and how it plummeted during World War I.

until 1891 the Atlantic Coast states, not the federal government, exercised whatever controls were imposed on newcomers. Private agencies, philanthropic and commercial, served as a link between the new arrivals and employers looking for labor. Until the Foran Act of 1885 outlawed the practice, a few companies brought in skilled workers under contract, advancing them passage money and collecting it in installments from their paychecks. Numerous nationality groups assisted (and sometimes exploited) their compatriots by organizing "immigrant banks" that recruited labor in the old country, arranged transportation, and then housed the newcomers in boardinghouses in the United States while finding them jobs. The *padrone* system of the Italians and Greeks was typical. The *padrone,* a sort of contractor who agreed to supply gangs of unskilled workers to companies for a lump sum, usually signed on immigrants unfamiliar with American wage levels at rates that assured him a fat profit.

Beginning in the 1880s, the spreading effects of industrialization in Europe caused a shift in the sources of American immigration from northern and western to southern and eastern sections of the Continent. In 1882, 789,000 immigrants entered the United States; more than 350,000 of them came from Great Britain and Germany, only 32,000 from Italy, and fewer than 17,000 from Russia. In 1907—the all-time peak year, with 1,285,000 immigrants—Great Britain and Germany supplied fewer than half as many as they had 25 years earlier, while Russia and Italy were supplying eleven times as many as then.*

The "new" immigrants, like the "old" Irish of the 1840s and 1850s, were mostly poor and uneducated. They also seemed more than ordinarily clannish; southern Italians typically called all people outside their families *forestieri,* foreigners. Old-stock Americans thought them harder to assimilate, and in fact many were. Some Italian immigrants, for example, were unmarried men who had come to the United States to earn enough money to buy a farm back home. Such people made hard and willing workers but were not much concerned with rising in an American community.

The "birds of passage" were a substantial mi-

* Up to 1880, only about 200,000 southern and eastern Europeans had migrated to America. Between 1880 and 1910, approximately 8.4 million arrived.

nority, but the immigrant who saved in order to bring his wife and children or his younger brothers and sisters to America was more typical. In addition, thousands of immigrants came as family groups and intended to remain. Some, like the eastern European Jewish migrants, were refugees who could not have returned to the land of their birth if they wanted to. They were almost desperately eager to become Americans, though of course they retained and nurtured much of their traditional culture.

Cultural differences among immigrants were often large and had important effects on their relations with native-born Americans and with other immigrant groups. Italians who settled in the city of Buffalo, the historian Virginia Yans-McLaughlin has shown, adjusted relatively smoothly to urban industrial life because of their close family and kinship ties. Poverty, unemployment, female job holding outside the home, and other traumas that might have been expected to disrupt family relationships apparently had little effect. Polish immigrants in Buffalo, having different traditions, found adjustment more difficult. German-American and Irish-American Catholics had different attitudes that caused them to clash over such matters as the policies of the Catholic University in Washington. Although (or perhaps because) the Haymarket anarchists were German-born, in 1887 one prominent German-American denounced the Knights of Labor as a hotbed of radicalism—and was said to have claimed that it was dominated by "Irish ignoramuses." Controversies erupted between Catholic and Protestant German-Americans, between Greek-American groups supporting various political factions in their homeland, and so on.

Confused by such differences and conflicts, many "older" Americans concluded, wrongly but understandably, that the new immigrants were incapable of becoming good citizens and should be kept out. During the 1880s large numbers of social workers, economists, and church leaders, worried by the social problems that arose when so many poor immigrants flocked into cities already bursting at the seams, began to believe that some restriction should be placed on the incoming human tide. The directors of charitable organizations, which bore the burden of aiding the most unfortunate immigrants, complained that their resources were being exhausted by the needs of the flood.

Pseudoscientific thinkers obsessed with ideas about "racial purity" also found the new immigration alarming. Misunderstanding the findings of the new science of genetics, they attributed the social problems associated with mass immigration to supposed physiological characteristics of the newcomers. Forgetting that earlier Americans had accused pre–Civil War Irish and German immigrants of similar deficiencies, they decided that the peoples of southern and eastern Europe were racially (and therefore permanently) inferior to "Nordic" and "Anglo-Saxon" types and ought to be kept out.

Organized labor, fearing the competition of workers with low living standards and no bargaining power, spoke out against the "enticing of penniless and unapprised immigrants . . . to undermine our wages and social welfare." Some corporations, especially in fields like mining, which employed large numbers of unskilled workers, made use of immigrants as strikebreakers, and this particularly angered union members. "The Poles, Slavs, Huns and Italians," a labor paper editorialized in 1909, "come over without any ambition to live as Americans live and . . . accept work at any wages at all, thereby lowering the tone of American labor as a whole." David Brody, historian of the steelworkers, describes an "unbridgeable gulf" in the steel industry between native and foreign laborers.

Employers were not disturbed by the influx of people with strong backs willing to work hard for low wages. Nevertheless, by the late 1880s many of them were alarmed about the supposed radicalism of the immigrants. The Haymarket bombing focused attention on the handful of foreign-born extremists in the country and loosed a flood of unjustified charges that "anarchists and communists" were dominating the labor movement. Nativism, which had waxed in the 1850s under the Know-Nothing banner and waned during the Civil War, now flared up again. Denunciations of "long-haired, wild-eyed, bad-smelling, atheistic, reckless foreign wretches," of "Europe's human and inhuman rubbish," of the "cutthroats of Beelzebub from the Rhine, the Danube, the Vistula and the Elbe" crowded the pages of the nation's press. The Grand Army of the Republic, an organization of Civil War veterans, grumbled about foreign-born radicals.

The nativists denounced Catholics and other minority groups more than immigrants as such. The largest nativist organization of the period, the American Protective Association, founded in 1887,

Contemporary cartoonists reflected the "new nativist" attitude toward unrestricted immigration. Frank Beard's 1885 drawing shows anarachists, socialists, and members of the Mafia arriving from the sewers of Europe and being resisted by Columbia and her watchdogs "Law" and "Order."

existed primarily to resist what its members called "the Catholic menace." But nowhere in America did prejudice lead to interference with religious freedom in the narrow sense. The Protestant majority treated "new" immigrants as underlings, tried to keep them out of the best jobs, and discouraged their efforts to climb the social ladder. This prejudice functioned only at the social and economic level. And neither labor leaders nor important industrialists, despite their misgivings about immigration, took a broadly antiforeign position.

After the Exclusion Act of 1882 and the almost meaningless 1885 ban on importing contract labor, no further restrictions were imposed on immigration until the 20th century. Strong support for a literacy test for admission developed in the 1890s, pushed by a new organization, the Immigration Restriction League. Since there was much more illiteracy in the southeastern quarter of Europe than in the northwestern, such a test would discriminate without seeming to do so on national or racial grounds. A literacy test bill passed both houses of Congress in 1897, but President Cleveland vetoed it. Such a "radical departure" from the "generous and free-handed policy" of the past, Cleveland said, was unjustified. He added, perhaps with tongue in cheek, that a literacy requirement would not keep out "unruly agitators," who were only too adept at reading and writing.

The Expanding City and Its Problems

Americans who favored restricting immigration made much of the fact that so many of the newcomers crowded into the cities, aggravating problems

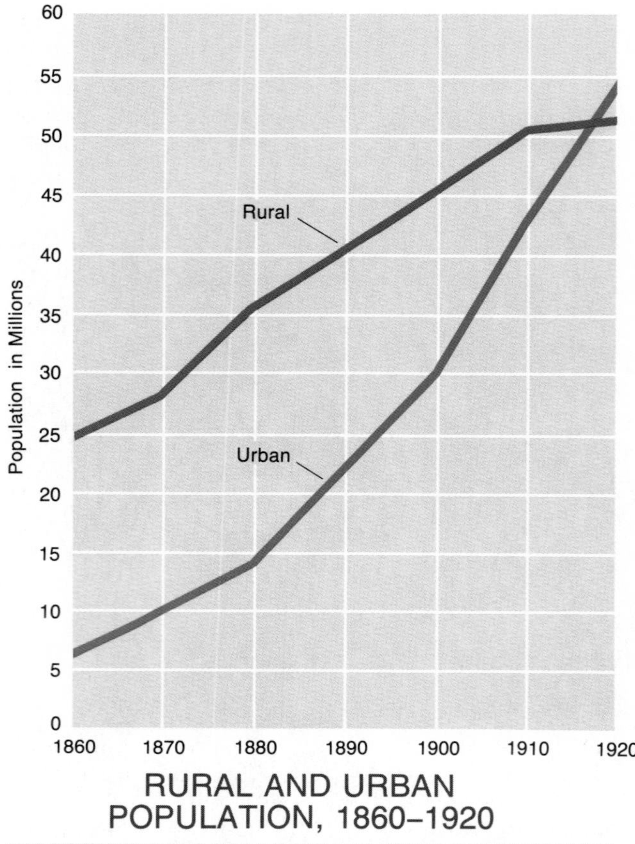

RURAL AND URBAN POPULATION, 1860–1920

of housing, public health, crime, and immorality. Immigrants concentrated in the cities because the jobs created by expanding industry were located there. So, of course, did native Americans; the proportion of urban dwellers had been steadily increasing since about 1820.

It is important to keep in mind that population density is not necessarily related to the existence of large cities. In the late 19th century there were areas in Asia as large as the United States that were as densely populated as Belgium and England yet were overwhelmingly rural. The United States by any standard was sparsely populated, but well before the Civil War it had become one of the most urban nations in the world. Industrialization does not entirely explain the growth of 19th-century cities. All the large American cities began as commercial centers, and the development of huge metropolises like New York and Chicago would have been impossible without the national transportation network. But by the final decades of the century, the expansion of industry had become the chief cause of city growth. Thus the urban concentration continued; in 1890 one person in three lived in a city, by 1910 nearly one in two.

A steadily increasing proportion of the urban population was made up of immigrants. In 1890 the foreign-born population of Chicago almost equaled the *total* population of Chicago in 1880; a third of all Bostonians and a quarter of all Philadelphians were immigrants; and four out of five residents of New York City were either foreign-born or the children of immigrants.

After 1890 the immigrant concentration became even more dense. The "new" migrants from eastern and southern Europe lacked the resources to travel to the agriculturally developing regions (to say nothing of the sums necessary to acquire land and farm equipment). As the concentration progressed it fed upon itself, for all the eastern cities developed many ethnic neighborhoods, in each of which immigrants of one nationality congregated. Lonely, confused, often unable to speak English, the Italians, the Greeks, the Polish and Russian Jews, and other immigrants tended to settle where their predecessors had settled. Eager to maintain their traditional culture, they supported "national" churches and schools. Newspapers in their native languages flourished, as did social organizations of all sorts. Each great American city became a Europe in microcosm where it sometimes seemed that every language in the world but English could be heard. New York, the great entrepôt, had a Little Italy, Polish, Greek, Jewish, and Bohemian quarters, even a Chinatown.

Although "ethnic" neighborhoods were crowded, unhealthy, and crime-ridden and many of the residents were desperately poor, they were not ghettos in the European sense, for those who lived there were not compelled by law to remain. Thousands "escaped" yearly to better districts. The ghettos were places where hopes and ambitions were fulfilled, where people worked hard and endured hardships in order to improve their own and their children's lot.

Observing the immigrants' attachment to "foreign" values and institutions, numbers of "natives" accused the newcomers of resisting Americanization and blamed them for urban problems. The immigrants were involved in these problems, but the rapidity of urban expansion explains the troubles associated with city life far more fully than the high percentage of foreigners. The cities were suffering from growing pains. Sewer and water facilities frequently could not keep pace with skyrocketing needs. By the 1890s the tremendous growth of Chicago had put such a strain on its sanitation system that the Chicago River had become virtually an open sewer, and the city's drinking water contained such a high concentration of germ-killing chemicals that it tasted like creosote. In the 1880s all the sewers of Baltimore emptied into the sluggish Back Basin, and, according to the journalist H. L. Mencken, every summer the city smelled "like a billion polecats."

Fire protection became increasingly inadequate; garbage piled up in the streets faster than it could be carted away; and the streets themselves crumbled beneath the pounding of heavy traffic. Urban growth proceeded with such speed that new streets were laid out more rapidly than they could be paved. Chicago had more than 1,400 miles of dirt streets in 1890.

People poured into the great cities faster than housing could be built to accommodate them. The influx into areas already densely packed in the 1840s became unbearable as rising property values and the absence of zoning laws conspired to make builders utilize every possible foot of space, squeezing out light and air ruthlessly in order to wedge in a few additional family units. Substandard living quarters aggravated other evils such as disease and the disintegration of family life with its attendant mental anguish, crime, and juvenile delinquency. The bloody New York riots of 1863, though sparked by dislike of the Civil War draft and blacks, reflected the bitterness and frustration of thousands jammed together amid filth and threatened by disease. A citizens' committee seeking to discover the causes of the riots expressed its amazement after visiting the slums "that so much misery, disease, and wretchedness can be huddled together and hidden . . . unvisited and unthought of, so near our own abodes."

New York City created a Metropolitan Health Board in 1866, and a state tenement house law the following year made a feeble beginning at regulating city housing. Another law in 1879 placed a limit on the percentage of lot space that could be covered by *new* construction and established minimal standards of plumbing and ventilation. The magazine *Plumber and Sanitary Engineer* sponsored a contest to pick the best design for a tenement that met these specifications. The winner of the competition was James E. Ware, whose plan for a "dumbbell" apartment house managed to crowd from 24 to 32 four-room apartments on a plot of ground only 25 by 100 feet.

> The feat was accomplished [writes Oscar Handlin in *The Uprooted*] by narrowing the building at its middle so that it took on the shape of a dumbbell. The indentation was only two-and-a-half feet wide and varied in length from five to fifty feet; but, added to the similar indentations on the adjoining houses, it created on each side an air-shaft five feet wide. . . . The stairs, halls, and common water closets were cramped into the narrow center of the building so that almost the whole of its surface was available for living quarters.

An alley known as "Bandit's Roost," on New York's Lower East Side, photographed for the New York Sun *in 1887 by police reporter Jacob Riis, himself an immigrant. "What sort of an answer, think you, would come from these tenements to the question 'Is life worth living?' " Riis asked in his book* How the Other Half Lives.

Despite these efforts at reform, in 1890 more than 1.4 million persons were living on Manhattan Island, and in some sections the population density exceeded 900 persons per acre. Jacob Riis, a reporter, captured the horror of the crowded warrens in his classic study of life in the slums, *How the Other Half Lives* (1890):

> Be a little careful, please! The hall is dark and you might stumble. . . . Here where the hall turns and dives into utter darkness is . . . a flight of stairs. You can feel your way, if you cannot see it. Close? Yes! What would you have? All the fresh air that enters these stairs comes from the hall-door that is forever slamming. . . . The sinks are in the hallway, that all the tenants may have access—and all be poisoned alike by their summer stenches. . . . Here is a door. Listen! That short, hacking cough, that tiny, helpless wail—what do they mean? . . . The child is dying of measles. With half a chance it might have lived; but it had none. That dark bedroom killed it.

The unhealthiness of the tenements was notorious; one noxious corner of New York became known as the "lung block" because of the prevalence of tuberculosis among its inhabitants. In 1900 three out of five babies born in one poor district of Chicago died before their first birthday. Equally frightening was the impact of overcrowding on the morals of the tenement dweller. The number of prison inmates in the United States increased by 50 percent in the 1880s, and the homicide rate nearly tripled, most of the rise occurring in cities. Driven into the streets by the squalor of their homes, slum youths formed gangs bearing names like Alley Gang, Rock Gang, and Hell's Kitchen Gang. From petty thievery and shoplifting they graduated to housebreaking, bank robbery, and murder. According to Jacob Riis, when the leader of the infamous Whyo Gang, convicted of murder, confessed his sins to a prison chaplain, "his father confessor turned pale . . . though many years of labor as chaplain of the Tombs had hardened him to such rehearsals."

Slums bred criminals—the wonder was that they bred so few. They also drove well-to-do residents into exclusive sections and to the suburbs. From Boston's Beacon Hill and Back Bay to San Francisco's Nob Hill, the rich retired into great cluttered mansions and ignored conditions in the poorer parts of town.

City Government

The big-city political bosses, with their corrupt yet useful "machines," filled the vacuum created by upper-class abdication of responsibility. The immigrants, largely of peasant stock, had no experience with representative government, and the tendency of urban workers to move frequently lessened the likelihood that they would develop political influence independently. Furthermore, the difficulties of life in the slums bewildered and often overwhelmed newcomers, both native and foreign-born. Hopeful, passive, naive, they could hardly be expected to take a broad view of social problems when so harassed by personal ones. Shrewd urban politicians, most of them of Irish origin—the Irish being the firstcomers among the migrants and, according to mobility studies, more likely to stay put—took command of the city masses and marched them in obedient phalanxes to the polls.

Most city machines were loose-knit neighborhood organizations headed by ward bosses, not tightly geared hierarchical bureaucracies ruled by a single leader. "Big Tim" Sullivan of New York's lower east side and "Hinky Dink" Kenna of Chicago were typical of the breed. They found jobs for new arrivals and distributed food and other help to all in bad times. Anyone in trouble with the law could obtain at least a hearing from the ward boss, and often, if the crime was venial or due to ignorance, the difficulty was quietly "fixed" and the culprit sent off with a word of caution. Sullivan provided turkey dinners for 5,000 or more derelicts each Christmas, distributed new shoes to the poor children of his district on his birthday, arranged summer boat rides and picnics for young and old alike. At any time of year the victim of some sudden disaster could turn to the local clubhouse for help. Informally, probably without consciously intending to do so, the bosses educated the immigrants in the complexities of American civilization, helping them to leap the gulf between the almost medieval society of their origins and the modern industrial world.

The price of such aid—the bosses were no altruists—was unquestioning political support, which the bosses converted into cash. In New York Sullivan levied tribute on gambling, had a hand in the liquor business, and controlled the issuance of peddlers' licenses. When he died in 1913, he was reputedly worth a million dollars. Yet he and others like him were immensely popular; 25,000 grieving constituents followed Big Tim's coffin to the grave.

While he served a useful social function, the typical boss was not a reformer. Surveying the role of the Irish in New York City politics, Daniel P. Moynihan notes that despite their successes, "they did not know what to do with power. . . . They never thought of politics as an instrument of social change." The more visible and better-known "city" bosses played even less socially justifiable roles than the ward bosses. Their principal technique for extracting money from the public till was the "kickback." In order to get city contracts, suppliers were made to pad their bills and turn over the excess to the politicians. Similarly, operators of streetcar lines, gas and electricity companies, and other public utilities were compelled to pay huge bribes to obtain favorable franchises.

The most notorious—and probably the most despicable—of the major 19th-century city bosses was William Marcy Tweed, whose "Ring" extracted tens of millions of dollars from New York City during the brief period 1869–1871. Tweed was swiftly lodged in jail. More typical of the city bosses was Richard Croker, who ruled New York's Tammany Hall organization from the mid-1880s to the end of the century. Croker held a number of local offices, but his power rested on his position as chairman of the Tammany Hall finance committee. Although more concerned than Tweed with the social and economic services that machines provided, Croker was primarily a corrupt political manipulator; he accumulated a large fortune and owned a $200,000 mansion and a stable of racehorses, one of which was good enough to win the English Derby.

Despite their welfare work and their popularity, most bosses were essentially thieves. Efforts to romanticize them as the Robin Hoods of industrial society grossly distort the facts. However, the system developed and survived because too many middle-class city dwellers were indifferent to the fate of the poor. Except during occasional "reform waves," few tried to check the rapaciousness of the politicos. Many substantial citizens shared at least indirectly in the corruption. The owners of tenements were interested in crowding as many rent payers as possible into their buildings. Utility companies seeking franchises preferred a system that enabled them to buy favors. Honest citizens who had no selfish stake in the system and who were repelled by the sordidness of city government were seldom sufficiently concerned to do anything about it. When young Theodore Roosevelt decided to seek a political career in 1880, his New York socialite friends laughed in his face. "[They] told me," Roosevelt wrote in his autobiography, "that politics were 'low'; that the organizations were not controlled by 'gentlemen'; that I would find them run by saloon-keepers, horse-car conductors, and the like."

Many so-called urban reformers resented the boss system mainly because it gave political power to those who were not "gentlemen," or as one re-

Thomas Nast's devastating assaults on the Tweed ring, printed in Harper's Weekly, *helped bring about the ring's demise. In this cartoon Tweed and his fellow vultures cower under the storm against them. Tweed offered Nast a $500,000 bribe to stop the cartoon.*

former put it, to a "proletarian mob" of "illiterate peasants, freshly raked from Irish bogs, or Bohemian mines, or Italian robber nests." A British visitor in Chicago struck at the root of the urban problem of the era. "Everybody is fighting to be rich," he said, "and nobody can attend to making the city fit to live in."

The Cities Modernize

As American cities grew larger and more crowded, thereby aggravating a host of social problems, practical forces operated to bring about improvements. Once the relationship between polluted water and disease was fully understood, everyone saw the need for decent water and sewage systems. While some businessmen profited from corrupt dealings with the city machines, more of them wanted efficient and honest government in order to reduce their tax bills. City dwellers of all classes resented dirt, noise, and ugliness, and in many communities public-spirited groups formed societies to plant trees, clean up littered areas, and develop recreational facilities. When one city undertook improvements, others tended to follow suit, spurred on by local pride and the booster spirit.

Gradually the basic facilities of urban living were improved. Streets were paved, first with cobblestones and wood blocks and then with smoother, quieter asphalt. Gaslight, then electric arc lights, and finally Edison's incandescent lamps brightened the cities after dark, making law enforcement easier, stimulating night life, and permitting factories and shops to operate after sunset.

Urban transportation underwent enormous changes. Until the 1880s, horse-drawn cars running on tracks set flush with the street were the main means of urban public transportation. In 1860, New York City's horsecars were carrying about 100,000 passengers a day. But horsecars had serious drawbacks. Enormous numbers of horses were needed, and feeding and stabling the animals was costly. Their droppings (ten pounds per day per horse) became a major source of urban pollution. That is why the invention of the electric trolley car in the 1880s put an end to horsecar transportation. Trolleys were cheaper and less unsightly than horsecars and quieter than steam-powered trains.

A retired naval officer, Frank J. Sprague, in-

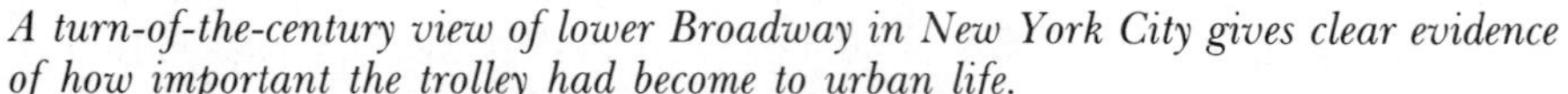

A turn-of-the-century view of lower Broadway in New York City gives clear evidence of how important the trolley had become to urban life.

stalled the first practical electric trolley line in Richmond, Virginia, in 1887–1888. At once other cities seized upon the trolley. Trolley lines soon radiated outward from the city centers, bringing commuters and shoppers from the residential districts to the business district. Without them the big-city department stores could not have flourished as they did. By 1895 some 850 lines were busily hauling city dwellers over 10,000 miles of track, and mileage tripled in the following decade. As with other new enterprises, control of street railways quickly became centralized until a few big operators controlled the trolleys of more than 100 eastern cities and towns.

Streetcars changed the character of big-city life. Before their introduction urban communities were limited by the distances people could conveniently walk to work. The "walking city" could not easily extend more than $2\frac{1}{2}$ miles from its center. Streetcars increased this radius to 6 miles or more, which meant that the *area* of the city expanded enormously. Dramatic population shifts resulted as the better-off moved away from the center in search of air and space, abandoning the crumbling, jampacked older neighborhoods to the poor. Thus economic segregation speeded the growth of ghettos. Older peripheral towns that had maintained some of the self-contained qualities of village life were swallowed up, becoming metropolitan centers. The village of Medford, Massachusetts, outside Boston, had 11,000 residents in 1890 when the first trolley line from the city center reached it. By 1905 its population had reached 23,000. As time passed, each new area, originally peopled by rising economic groups, tended to become crowded and then to deteriorate. The middle class pushed steadily outward—which helps to explain why this group abandoned its interest in city government. By extending their tracks *beyond* the developed areas, the streetcar companies further speeded suburban growth because they assured developers, bankers, builders, and prospective home buyers of efficient transport to the center of town. By keeping fares low (5 cents a ride was standard) the lines enabled poor people to "escape" to the countryside on holidays. "The pattern was as follows," Kenneth T. Jackson writes in *Crabgrass Frontier.* "First, streetcar lines were built out to existing villages. . . . These areas subsequently developed into large communities. Second, the tracks actually created residential neighborhoods where none had existed before."

Los Angeles, according to Jackson, "provides the premier example of the confluence of street railway entrepreneurs and real-estate development." Henry E. Huntington, a nephew of the railroad baron Collis P. Huntington, built his Pacific Electric Railway into a vast network of lines primarily to aid in selling homesites on lands he had purchased cheaply before the tracks were laid.

The combined activities of real estate developers, trolley operators, and efficient builders made home ownership possible for people of modest means. "For the first time in the history of the world," Professor Jackson writes, "middle-class families . . . could reasonably expect to buy a detached home on an accessible lot in a safe and sanitary environment."

Advances in bridge design, notably the perfection of the steel-cable suspension bridge by John A. Roebling, aided the ebb and flow of metropolitan populations. The Brooklyn Bridge—"a weird metallic Apparition under a metallic sky, out of proportion with the winged lightness of its arch, traced for the conjunction of worlds . . . the cables, like divine messages from above . . . cutting and dividing into innumerable musical spaces the nude immensity of the sky"—was Roebling's triumph. Completed in 1883 at a cost of $15 million, it was soon carrying more than 33 million passengers a year over the East River between Manhattan and Brooklyn.

Even the high cost of urban real estate, which spawned the tenement, produced some beneficial results in the long run. Instead of crowding squat structures cheek by jowl on 25-foot lots, architects began to build upward. The introduction of the iron-skeleton type of construction, which freed the walls from bearing the immense weight of a tall building, was the work of a group of Chicago architects who had been attracted to the metropolis of the Midwest by opportunities to be found amid the ashes of the great fire of 1871. The group included William Le Baron Jenney, John A. Holabird, Martin Roche, John W. Root, and Louis H. Sullivan. Jenney's Home Insurance Building, completed in 1885, was the first metal-frame edifice. Height alone, however, did not satisfy these innovators; they sought a form that would reflect the structure and purpose of their buildings.

Their leader was Louis Sullivan. Builders must

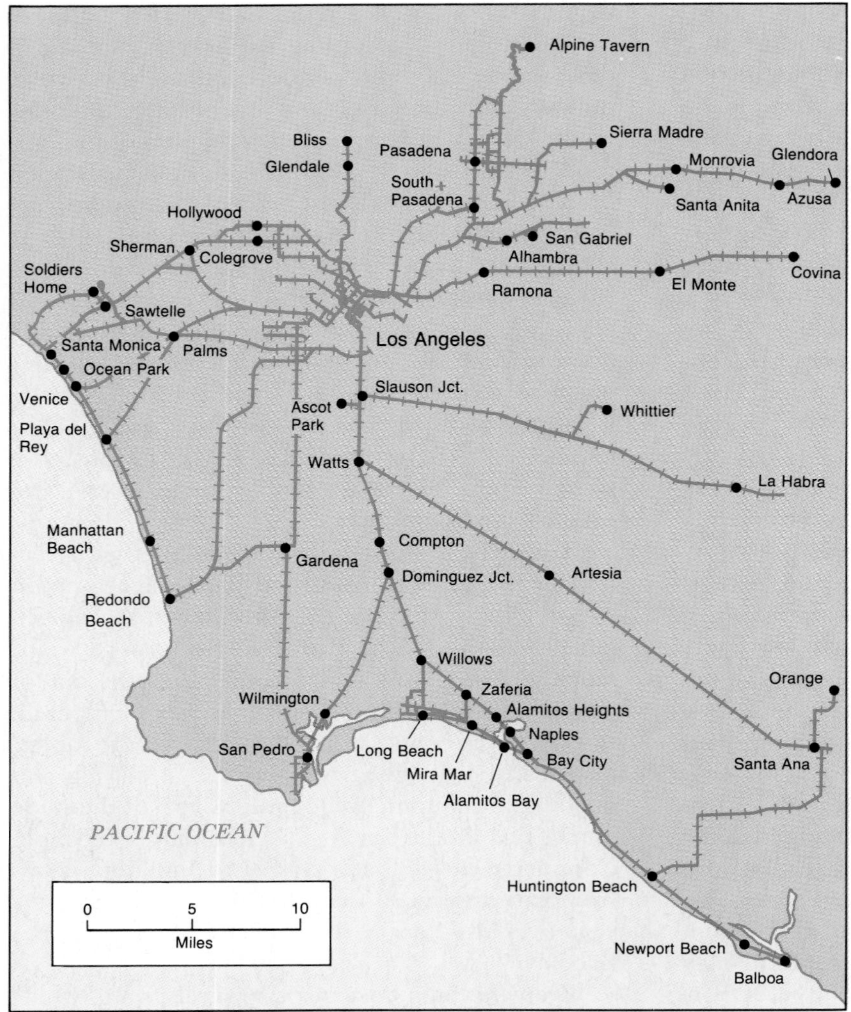

By the early 1900s, a street railway network radiated from the settled parts of central Los Angeles for 30 miles and more. Henry Huntington claimed that the Los Angeles and Pacific Electric system "extended into the open country, ahead of, and not behind, the population. . . ." Data from Fogelson, The Fragmented Metropolis.

discard "books, rules, precedents, or any such educational impedimenta" and design functional buildings, he argued. A tall building "must be every inch a proud and soaring thing, rising in sheer exultation . . . from bottom to top . . . a unit without a single dissenting line." Sullivan's Wainwright Building in St. Louis and his Prudential Building in Buffalo, both completed in the early 1890s, combined beauty, modest construction costs, and efficient use of space in pathbreaking ways. Soon a "race to the skies" was on in the great cities of America, and the words *skyscraper* and *skyline* entered the language.

Efforts to redesign American cities, stimulated by the remarkable "White City" built for the Chicago World's Fair of 1893 by Daniel H. Burnham, with its broad vistas and acres of open space, resulted in a "City Beautiful" movement, the most lasting result of which was the development of many public parks. The landscape architect Frederick Law Olmsted, designer of New York's Central Park, was a leading figure in the movement.

Efforts to relieve the congestion in slum districts made little headway. In Brooklyn Alfred T. White established Home Buildings, a 40-family model tenement, in 1877; eventually he expanded the experiment to include 267 apartments. Each unit had plenty of light and air and contained its own sink and toilet. Ellen Collins developed a smaller project in Manhattan's Fourth Ward in the 1890s. These model tenements were self-sustaining, but of necessity they yielded only modest returns. The landlords were essentially philanthropists; their work had no significant impact on urban housing in the 19th century.

The Churches Respond to Industrialism

The modernization of the great cities was not solving most of the social problems of the slums. As this fact became clear, a number of urban religious leaders began to take a hard look at the situation. Traditionally, American churchmen had insisted that where sin was concerned there were no extenuating circumstances. To the well-to-do they preached the virtues of thrift and hard work; to the poor they extended the possibility of a better existence in the next world; to all they stressed one's responsibility for one's own behavior—and thus for one's own salvation. Such a point of view brought meager comfort to residents of slums. Consequently the churches lost influence in the poorer sections. Furthermore, as better-off citizens followed the streetcar lines out from the city centers, their church leaders followed them.

In New York, 17 Protestant congregations abandoned the depressed areas of Lower Manhattan between 1868 and 1888. Catering thereafter almost entirely to middle-class and upper-class worshipers, the pastors tended to become even more conservative. No more strident defender of reactionary ideas existed than the pastor of Brooklyn's fashionable Plymouth Congregational Church, Henry Ward Beecher. Beecher, a younger brother of Harriet Beecher Stowe, the author of *Uncle Tom's Cabin,* attributed poverty to the improvidence of laborers who, he claimed, squandered their wages on liquor and tobacco. "No man in this land suffers from poverty," he said, "unless it be more than his fault—unless it be his *sin.*" The best check on labor unrest was a plentiful supply of cheap immigrant labor, he told President Hayes. Unions were "the worst form of despotism and tyranny in the history of Christendom."

An increasing proportion of the residents of the blighted districts were Catholics, and the Roman church devoted much effort to distributing alms, maintaining homes for orphans and old people, and other forms of social welfare. But church leaders seemed unconcerned with the social causes of the blight; they were deeply committed to the idea that sin and vice were personal, poverty an act of God. They deplored the rising tide of crime, disease, and destitution among their coreligionists, yet they failed to see the connection between these evils and the squalor of the slums. "Intemperance is the great evil we have to overcome," wrote the president of the leading Catholic charitable organization, the Society of St. Vincent de Paul. "It is the source of the misery for at least three-fourths of the families we are called upon to visit and relieve." The church, according to the historian Aaron I. Abell, "seemed oblivious to the bearing of civil legislation on the course of moral and social reform." Instead it invested much money and energy in chimerical attempts to colonize poor city dwellers in the West.

Like conservative Protestant clergymen, the Catholic hierarchy tended to be at best neutral toward organized labor. Cardinal James Gibbons spoke favorably of the Knights of Labor in 1886 after the Haymarket bombing, but even he took a dim view of strikes. The clergy's attitude changed somewhat after Pope Leo XIII issued his encyclical *Rerum novarum* (1891). This statement criticized the excesses of capitalism, including the "greed of unchecked competition"; it defended the right of labor to form unions and stressed the duty of government to care for the poor. Workers were entitled to wages that would guarantee their families a reasonable and frugal comfort, Leo declared, and they committed no sin by seeking government aid to get it. Concrete action by American Catholics, however, was slow in coming. One leading authority notes "the isolation of Catholics from the reform movements of the 19th century," which he attributes to the conservatism of the clergy and the parochial concerns of lay leaders.

The conservatism of most Protestant and Catholic clergymen did not prevent some earnest preachers from working directly to improve the lot of the city poor. Some followed the path blazed by Dwight L. Moody, who became famous throughout America and Great Britain as a lay evangelist in the 1870s. A gargantuan figure weighing nearly 300 pounds, Moody conducted a vigorous campaign to persuade the denizens of the slums to cast aside their sinful ways. He went among them full of enthusiasm and God's love and made an impact no less powerful than that of George Whitefield during the Great Awakening of the 18th century or Charles Grandison Finney in the first part of the 19th. The evangelists founded mission schools in the slums and tried to provide spiritual and recreational facilities for the unfortunate. They were prominent in the establishment of American branches of the Young Men's Christian Association (1851) and the Salvation Army (1880).

However, the evangelists paid little heed to the causes of urban poverty and vice, believing that faith in God would enable the poor to transcend the material difficulties of life. For a number of Protestant clergymen who had become familiar with the slums, a different approach seemed called for. Slum conditions caused the sins and crimes of the cities; the wretched human beings who committed them could not be blamed, these ministers argued. They began to preach a "Social Gospel" that focused on improving living conditions rather than on saving souls. If people were to lead pure lives, they must have enough to eat, decent homes, and opportunities to develop their talents. Social Gospelers advocated civil service reform to break the power of the machines, child labor legislation, the regulation of big corporations, and heavy taxes on incomes and inheritances.

The most influential preacher of the Social Gospel was probably Washington Gladden. At first, Gladden, who was raised on a Massachusetts farm, had opposed all government interference in social and economic affairs, but his experiences as a minister in Springfield, Massachusetts, and Columbus, Ohio, exposed him to the realities of life in industrial cities, and his views changed. In *Applied Christianity* (1886) and in other works he defended labor's right to organize and strike and denounced the idea that supply and demand should control wage rates. He favored factory inspection laws, strict regulation of public utilities, and other reforms.

Gladden never questioned the basic values of capitalism. By the 1890s a number of ministers had gone all the way to socialism. The Reverend William D. P. Bliss of Boston, for example, believed in the kind of welfare state envisioned by Edward Bellamy in *Looking Backward.* He founded the Society of Christian Socialists (1889) and edited a radical journal, *The Dawn.* In addition to nationalizing industry, Bliss and other Christian Socialists advocated government unemployment relief programs, public housing and slum clearance projects, and other measures designed to aid the city poor.

Nothing so well reveals the receptivity of the public to the Social Gospel as the popularity of Charles M. Sheldon's novel *In His Steps* (1896), one of America's all-time best-sellers. Sheldon, a minister in Topeka, Kansas, described what happened in the mythical city of Raymond when a group of leading citizens decided to live truly Christian lives, asking themselves "What would Jesus do?" before adopting any course of action. Naturally the tone of Raymond's society was immensely improved, but basic social reforms followed quickly. The "Rectangle," a terrible slum area, "too dirty, too coarse, too sinful, too awful for close contact," became the center of a great reform effort. One of Raymond's "leading society heiresses" undertook a slum clearance project, and a concerted attack was made on drunkenness and immorality. The moral regeneration of the entire community was soon accomplished.

The Settlement Houses

Although millions read *In His Steps,* its effect, and that of other Social Gospel literature, was merely inspirational. On the practical level, a number of earnest souls began to grapple with slum problems by organizing what were known as settlement houses. These were community centers located in poor districts which provided guidance and services to all who would use them. The settlement workers, most of them idealistic, well-to-do young people, lived in the houses and were active in neighborhood affairs.

The prototype of the settlement house was London's Toynbee Hall, founded in the early 1880s; the first American example was the Neighborhood Guild, opened on the Lower East Side of New York in 1886 by Dr. Stanton Coit. By the turn of the century 100 had been established, the most famous being Jane Addams's Hull House in Chicago (1889), Robert A. Woods's South End House in

Boston (1892), and Lillian Wald's Henry Street Settlement in New York (1893).

While some men were active in the movement, the most important settlement house workers were women fresh from college—the first generation of young women to experience the trauma of having developed their capacities only to find that society offered them few opportunities to use them (see pages 580–581). The settlements provided an outlet for their hopes and energies, and they seized upon it avidly. An English social reformer who visited Hull House around the turn of the century described the residents as "strong-minded energetic women, bustling about their various enterprises" and "earnest-faced self-subordinating and mild-mannered men who slide from room to room apologetically."

The settlement workers tried to interpret American ways to the new immigrants and to create a community spirit in order to teach, in the words of one of them, "right living through social relations." Unlike most charity workers, who acted out of a sense of upper-class responsibility toward the unfortunate, they expected to benefit morally and intellectually themselves by experiencing a way of life far different from their own and by obtaining "the first-hand knowledge the college classroom cannot give." Lillian Wald, a nurse by training, explained the concept succinctly in *The House on Henry Street* (1915): "We were to live in the neighborhood . . . identify ourselves with it socially, and, in brief, contribute to it our citizenship."

Lillian Wald and other leaders soon discovered that practical problems occupied most of their energies. They agitated for tenement house laws, the regulation of the labor of women and children, and better schools. They employed private resources to establish playgrounds in the slums, along with libraries, classes in arts and crafts, social clubs, and day nurseries. In Boston Robert A. Woods organized clubs to get the youngsters of the South End off the streets, helped establish a restaurant where a meal could be had for 5 cents, acted as an arbitrator in labor disputes, and lobbied for laws tightening up the franchises of public utility companies. In Chicago Jane Addams developed an outstanding cultural program that included classes in music and art and an excellent "little theater" group. Hull House soon boasted a gymnasium, a day nursery, and several social clubs. Addams also worked tirelessly and effectively for improved public services and for social legislation of all kinds. She even got herself appointed garbage inspector in her ward and hounded local landlords and the garbage contractor until something approaching decent service was established.

This portrait of Jane Addams was completed in 1896 by Alice Kellog Tyler, who worked as an artist at Hull House.

A few critics considered the settlement houses mere devices to socialize the unruly poor by teaching them the "punctilios of upper-class propriety," but almost everyone appreciated their virtues. By the end of the century even the Catholics, laggard in entering the arena of practical social reform, were joining the movement, partly because they were losing many communicants to socially minded Protestant churches. The first Catholic-run settlement house was founded in 1898 in an Italian district of New York. Two years later Brownson House in Los Angeles, catering chiefly to Mexican immigrants, threw open its doors.

With all their accomplishments, the settlement houses seemed to be fighting a losing battle. "Private beneficence," Jane Addams wrote of Hull House, "is totally inadequate to deal with the vast numbers of the city's disinherited." As a tropical forest grows faster than a handful of men armed with machetes can cut it down, so the slums, fed by an annual influx of hundreds of thousands, blighted new areas more rapidly than the intrepid settlement house workers could clean up old ones. It became increasingly apparent that the wealth and authority of the state must be brought to bear in order to keep abreast of the problem.

Social Legislation

The first state laws aimed at the social problems resulting from industrialism and urbanization date from before the Civil War, but the early ones were either so imprecise as to be unenforceable or—like the Georgia law "limiting" textile workers to 11 hours a day—so weak as to be ineffective. As time passed, however, a scattering of workable laws was enacted. In 1874 Massachusetts restricted the working hours of women and children to 10 per day, and by the 1890s many other states, mostly in the East and Middle West, had followed suit. Illinois passed an eight-hour law for women workers in 1893. A New York law of 1882 struck at the sweatshops of the slums by prohibiting the manufacture of cigars on premises "occupied as a house or residence."

As part of this trend, some states established special rules for workers in hazardous industries. In the 1890s Ohio and several other states began to regulate the hours of railroad workers on the ground that fatigue sometimes caused railroad accidents. New York set a ten-hour-per-day limit for brickyard workers (1893) and bakers (1897). Utah restricted miners to eight hours in 1896. California in 1881 made it illegal for women to work as waitresses in saloons. In 1901 New York finally enacted an effective tenement house law, greatly increasing the area of open space on building lots and requiring toilets for each apartment, better ventilation systems, and more adequate fireproofing. Many other states soon passed laws modeled on acts of these types.

The collective impact of such legislation was not impressive. Powerful interests, such as manufacturers and landlords, threw their weight against many kinds of social legislation and often succeeded in defeating the bills or rendering them innocuous. Many of the early laws limiting hours, for example, were made to apply only "in the absence of agreements" to work longer hours.

The federal system itself complicated the task of obtaining effective legislation. Throughout the 19th century few authorities contested the right of government to protect society and individuals from anything that threatened the general welfare, but these authorities assumed that such problems would be dealt with by the states, not the national government.* As a rule, this "police power" of the states was broadly interpreted; the courts even upheld laws prohibiting the manufacture and sale of liquor on the ground that drunkenness was a social as well as an individual problem, affecting nonimbibers as well as drinkers.

The development of a truly national economy after the Civil War complicated the problem of coping with social and industrial problems at the state level. Once producers throughout the country could compete effectively with one another, it became difficult, for example, to persuade legislators in one state to prohibit child labor when others refused to do so. If they did, they would injure their own manufacturers by giving firms in other states an unfair advantage. Yet a federal child labor law seemed out of the question on constitutional grounds.

The enemies of state social legislation discovered still another weapon: the Fourteenth Amendment to the Constitution. Although enacted to protect the civil rights of blacks, the amendment imposed a revolutionary restriction on state power, for it forbade the states to "deprive any person of life, liberty, or property without due process of law." Since state tenement house laws, child labor laws, and other social legislation represented new uses of police power that conservative judges considered dangerous and unwise, the Fourteenth

* Congress enacted an eight-hour law for government workers in 1892.

Amendment gave them an excuse to overturn the laws on the ground that they deprived someone of liberty or property. Both state and federal courts began to draw lines beyond which the states could not go in this area.

Some measures seemed unexceptionable; the courts did not interfere with laws requiring fire escapes on tall buildings, though these regulations certainly deprived builders of property (by increasing their costs) and of the liberty to erect any kind of structure they pleased. Laws regulating the hours and conditions of labor, however, met mixed fates, depending on the wording of the acts and the prejudices of particular judges.

Where women and children were concerned, and in dangerous and unhealthy occupations like mining, the new legislation fared better than where it involved the laboring population as a whole. But it is difficult to generalize. The pioneering Massachusetts ten-hour law of 1874, restricting the working day of women and children, was upheld as a valid exercise of the police power by the Massachusetts courts. The Illinois law of 1893 limiting the hours of women employed in manufacturing to eight per day was declared unconstitutional. "The mere fact of sex will not justify the legislature in putting forth the police power," the Illinois court declared in *Ritchie* v. *People.* "There is no reasonable ground . . . for fixing upon eight hours in one day as the limit within which woman can work without injury to her physique." The New York Court of Appeals threw out the sweatshop law of 1882 on similar grounds. "It cannot be perceived," Justice Earl wrote in a decision so unrealistic that it appears preposterous to anyone who knows even a little about slum conditions in the 1880s, "how the cigar maker is to be improved in his health or his morals by forcing him from his home with its hallowed associations and beneficent influences, to ply his trade elsewhere."

As stricter and more far-reaching laws were enacted, conservative judges, sensing what they took to be a trend toward socialism and regimentation, adopted an increasingly narrow interpretation of state police power. The United States Supreme Court upheld the Utah mining law of 1896 (*Holden* v. *Hardy,* 1898), but in 1905 it declared a piece of state social legislation unconstitutional for the first time. New York's ten-hour act for bakers, the Court declared in *Lochner* v. *New York,* deprived bakers of the liberty of working as long as they wished and thus violated the Fourteenth Amendment. Justice Oliver Wendell Holmes, Jr., wrote a famous dissenting opinion in this case. If the people of New York believed that the public health was endangered by bakers working long hours, he reasoned, it was not the Court's job to overrule them. "A constitution is not intended to embody a particular economic theory, whether of paternalism . . . or of *laissez faire,*" Holmes said. "The word 'liberty,' in the Fourteenth Amendment, is perverted when it is held to prevent the natural outcome of a dominant opinion." Of course Holmes's dissent did not alter the decision, which was deplored by all those who hoped to limit the hours of labor through legislation.

Civilization and Its Discontents

As the 19th century died, the majority of the American people, especially those comfortably well off, the residents of small towns, the shopkeepers, many farmers, some skilled workers, remained confirmed optimists and uncritical admirers of their civilization. However, blacks, immigrants, and others who failed to share equitably in the good things of life, along with a growing number of humanitarian reformers, found little to cheer about and much to lament in their increasingly industrialized society. Giant monopolies flourished despite federal restrictions. The gap between rich and poor appeared to be widening, while the slum spread its poison and the materially successful made a god of their success. Human values seemed in grave danger of being crushed by impersonal forces typified by the great corporations.

In 1871 Walt Whitman, usually so full of extravagant praise for the American way of life, called his fellow countrymen the "most materialistic and money-making people ever known":

> I say we had best look our times and lands searchingly in the face, like a physician diagnosing some deep disease. Never was there, perhaps, more hollowness of heart than at present, and here in the United States.

By the late 1880s a well-known journalist could write to a friend: "The wheel of progress is to be run over the whole human race and smash us all."

Others noted an alarming jump in the national divorce rate and an increasing taste for all kinds of luxury. "People are made slaves by a desperate struggle to keep up appearances," a Massachusetts commentator declared, and the economist David A. Wells expressed concern over statistics showing that heart disease and mental illness were on the rise. These "diseases of civilization," Wells explained, were "one result of the continuous mental and nervous activity which modern high-tension methods of business have necessitated."

Wells was a prominent liberal, but pessimism was no monopoly of liberals. A little later, Senator Henry Cabot Lodge of Massachusetts, himself a millionaire, complained of the "lawlessness" of "the modern and recent plutocrat" and his "disregard of the rights of others." Lodge spoke of "the enormous contrast between the sanguine mental attitude prevalent in my youth and that, perhaps wiser, but certainly darker view, so general today." His onetime Harvard professor, Henry Adams, was still more critical of the way his contemporaries had become moneygrubbers. "All one's friends," he complained, along with church and university leaders and other educated people, "had joined the banks to force submission to capitalism."

Of course intellectuals often tend to be critical of the world they live in, whatever its nature; Thoreau denounced materialism and the worship of progress in the 1840s as vigorously as any late-19th-century prophet of gloom. But the voices of the dissatisfied were rising. Despite the many benefits that industrialization had made possible, it was by no means clear around 1900 that the American people were really better off under the new dispensation.

SUPPLEMENTARY READING

Titles marked with an asterisk have been published in paperback.

The idea of interpreting social and economic history in the post–Civil War decades as a broad reaction to the growth of industry is presented in S. P. Hays, **The Response to Industrialism*** (1957). Other general treatments of the period include R. H. Wiebe, **The Search for Order*** (1968), and Ray Ginger, **The Age of Excess*** (1965). J. A. Garraty, **The New Commonwealth*** (1968), treats all subjects covered in this chapter; A. M. Schlesinger, **The Rise of the City*** (1933), stresses the importance of urban developments and provides a wealth of information about social trends. Both H. U. Faulkner, **Politics, Reform, and Expansion*** (1959), and Blake McKelvey, **The Urbanization of America** (1962), contain useful information. Henry Adams, **The Education of Henry Adams*** (1918), is a fascinating if highly personal view of the period. James Bryce, **The American Commonwealth*** (1888), while primarily a political analysis, contains a great deal of information about social conditions, as does D. A. Wells, **Recent Economic Changes** (1889).

On industrial workers, see David Montgomery, **Beyond Equality*** (1967), J. E. Drucker, **Men of the Steel Rails** (1983), Walter Licht, **Working on the Railroad** (1984), and H. G. Gutman, **Work, Culture, and Society in Industrializing America*** (1977). J. A. Garraty (ed.), **Labor and Capital in the Gilded Age*** (1968), provides a convenient selection of testimony from the great 1883 Senate investigation of that subject, while David Brody, **Steelworkers in America*** (1960), and Stephan Thernstrom, **Poverty and Progress: Social Mobility in a Nineteenth-Century City*** (1964), throw much light on the lives of workingmen. S. M. Rothman, **Woman's Proper Place** (1978), discusses the new job opportunities for women. Thernstrom's **The Other Bostonians: Poverty and Progress in the American Metropolis*** (1973), is a brilliant analysis of social and geographical mobility and an excellent summary of work on these important topics. Businessmen's attitudes are covered in T. C. Cochran, **Railroad Leaders** (1953), and E. C. Kirkland, **Dream and Thought in the Business Community*** (1956). On the growth of unions, see Montgomery's **Beyond Equality,** Philip Taft, **The A.F. of L. in the Time of Gompers** (1957), G. N. Grob, **Workers and Utopia*** (1961), Samuel Gompers, **Seventy Years of Life and Labor** (1925), and T. V. Powderly, **Thirty Years of Labor** (1889). The important strikes and labor violence of the period are described in R. V. Bruce, **1877: Year of Violence*** (1959), Paul Arvich, **The Haymarket Tragedy** (1984), Leon Wolff, **Lockout** (1965), Almont Lindsey, **The Pullman Strike*** (1942), and W. G. Broehl, Jr., **The Molly Maguires*** (1964).

On immigration, see M. A. Jones, **American Immigration*** (1960), John Higham, **Send These to Me*** (1975), M. L. Hansen, **The Immigrant in American His-**

tory* (1940), and I. S. Hourwich, **Immigration and Labor** (1923). Oscar Handlin, **The Uprooted*** (1951), describes the life of the new immigrants somewhat romantically but with sensitivity, while John Higham, **Strangers in the Land*** (1955), and B. M. Solomon, **Ancestors and Immigrants*** (1956), stress the reactions of native Americans to successive waves of immigration. Moses Rischin, **The Promised City: New York's Jews*** (1962), Thomas Kessner. **The Golden Door: Italian and Jewish Immigrant Mobility** (1977), Humbert Nelli, **The Italians of Chicago*** (1970), Virginia Yans-McLaughlin, **Family and Community: Italian Immigrants in Buffalo** (1977), T. N. Brown, **Irish-American Nationalism*** (1966), Charlotte Erickson, **American Industry and the European Immigrant** (1957), and R. T. Berthoff, **British Immigrants in Industrial America: 1790–1950** (1953), are important monographs.

A brief interpretive history of urban development is C. N. Glaab and A. T. Brown, **A History of Urban America*** (1967). K. T. Jackson, **Crabgrass Frontier** (1985), is a pioneering history of suburban development, and J. C. Teaford, **The Unheralded Triumph: City Government in America** (1984), gives weight to the accomplishments of the cities as well as their inadequacies. For the growing pains of American cities, consult the volumes by Schlesinger and McKelvey mentioned above, and R. H. Bremner, **From the Depths*** (1956), Jacob Riis, **How the Other Half Lives*** (1890), and R. Lubove, **The Progressives and the Slums: Tenement House Reform in New York City** (1962). For urban government, see the classic criticisms in Bryce's **American Commonwealth,** and also F. W. Patton. **The Battle for Municipal Reform: Mobilization and Attack** (1940). Urban architecture is discussed in O. W. Larkin, **Art and Life in America** (1949), Lewis Mumford, **The Brown Decades*** (1931), and J. E. Burchard and Albert Bush-Brown, **The Architecture of America*** (1961). S. B. Warner, Jr., **Streetcar Suburbs*** (1962), is an interesting study of Boston's development that is full of suggestive ideas about late-19th-century growth.

The response of religion to industrialism is discussed in H. F. May, **Protestant Churches and Industrial America*** (1949), in two books by A. I. Abell, **The Urban Impact on American Protestantism** (1943) and **American Catholicism and Social Action*** (1960), Arthur Mann, **Yankee Reformers in the Urban Age*** (1954), and C. H. Hopkins, **The Rise of the Social Gospel in American Protestantism*** (1940). See also Washington Gladden, **Applied Christianity** (1886), and R. T. Ely, **Social Aspects of Christianity** (1889). For the settlement house movement, see A. F. Davis, **Spearheads for Reform*** (1967), Davis's life of Jane Addams, **American Heroine*** (1973), and two classic personal accounts, Jane Addams, **Twenty Years at Hull House*** (1910), and Lillian Wald, **The House on Henry Street*** (1915).

Sidney Fine, **Laissez Faire and the General-Welfare State*** (1956), deals with both social and economic thought and with state and federal social legislation, but see also C. G. Groat, **Attitude of American Courts in Labor Cases** (1911), A. M. Paul, **Conservative Crisis and the Rule of Law: Attitudes of Bar and Bench*** (1960), and R. G. McCloskey, **American Conservatism in the Age of Enterprise*** (1951).

PORTFOLIO SIX
The New Immigrants

A great many immigrants in the late 1800s and early 1900s settled in large East Coast cities, especially New York. This 1886 watercolor of Baxter Street is a reasonably realistic sketch of an area in New York's infamous Five Points slum. The sketch was done for a stage set used in a comedy about Irish immigrants.

The immigrants came by boat. The photographer Alfred Stieglitz captured their patience and endurance under the dirty, crowded conditions of the immigrant crossing in this photo called *The Steerage.* After 1886, immigrants arriving in New York Harbor saw from shipboard the inspiring monumental statue *Liberty Enlightening the World.*

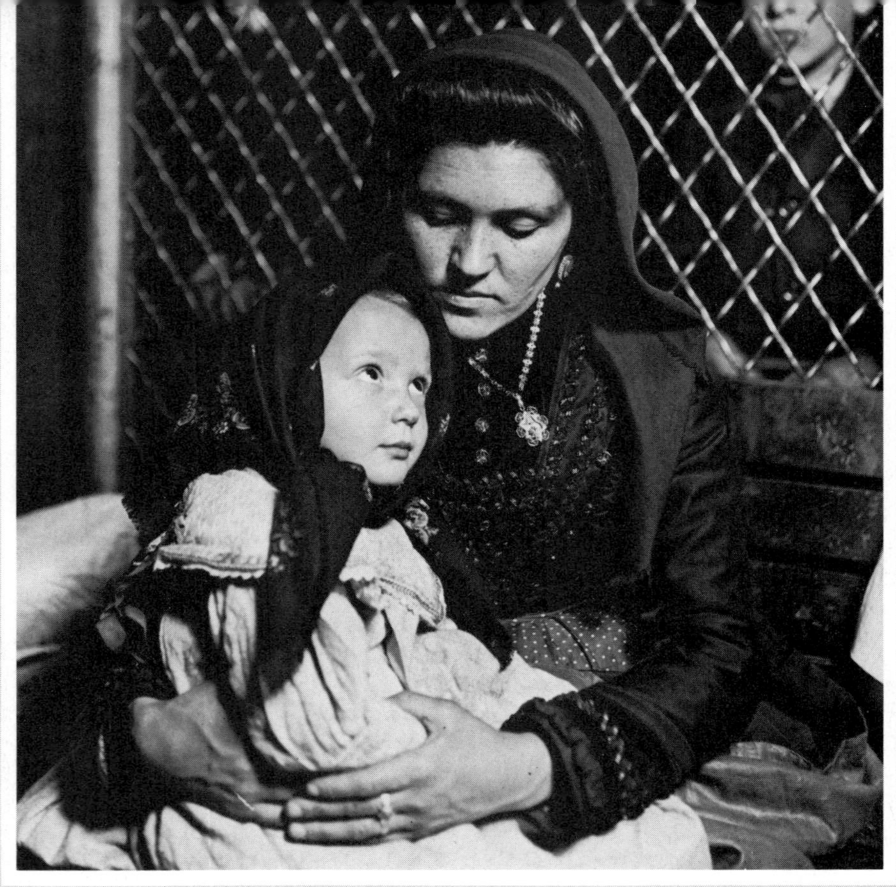

Starting in 1892, Ellis Island in New York Harbor was the processing center for immigrants. The newcomers often had to wait hours before being cleared for entry into the United States. Many were from southern and eastern Europe. Lewis Hine photographed this Italian mother and child waiting to be admitted.

Part of the processing was a medical examination. Here a doctor checks a group of women with her stethoscope. The eye chart on the back wall is in Cyrillic (the Russian alphabet).

Once cleared at Ellis Island, the immigrants often found their way to neighborhoods in New York City where people from their mother country had already settled. Orchard St. (upper left) in Manhattan was a bustling shopping area for the eastern European Jewish community, with food and clothing sold out of storefronts and off pushcarts in the street. Mulberry Bend (right) was in the heart of the Italian district of Manhattan's Lower East Side.

Living conditions in the tenements that lined these streets could be appalling. The boy at upper right fills a basin at a communal faucet, which was the tenants' only source of water for cooking, laundry, and bathing.

Getting a job was the first priority for immigrants, since most arrived with little money or other resources. This New York employment agency, photographed by Lewis Hine in 1910, posted available jobs in construction and coal mining in places as far away as West Virginia.

For some families the workplace was the same tenement room in which they ate and slept. The garment industry, employing a largely Jewish immigrant work force, relied on "home work" and paid workers by the garment (the piece) rather than by the hour.

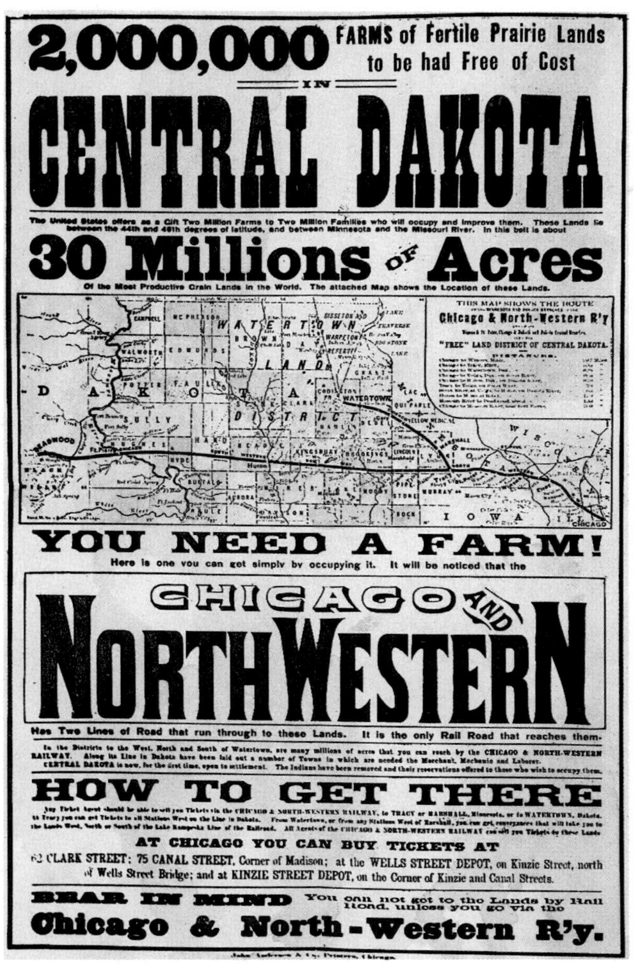

Some immigrants bypassed the cities to settle on land in the Midwest and Far West. To encourage the economic growth of the sparsely populated areas over which the land-grant railroads had been built, the railroads made glowing promises of free or cheap land.

A settler in northern Wisconsin in 1893: Nels Wickstrom, his wife and children, and the family dog posed in front of their log home. Note the small garden plot, fenced and bordered by rocks.

Levi Strauss (1830–1902) was not a "new" immigrant, having emigrated to New York from Bavaria in 1847. He peddled clothing and household items until 1853, when he booked passage on a clipper ship bound for San Francisco. He had planned to sell dry goods to the gold prospectors, including canvas for tents and wagon covers, but he found that what the miners needed most was sturdy work clothes. So he hired a tailor to sew the canvas into trousers—he later switched to blue-dyed denim—and soon "those pants of Levi's" became famous. By the 1870s Strauss's copper-riveted Model 501 Double X blue jeans and denim overalls were an established American institution, as this ad from the period shows.

Levi Strauss's success was repeated by many of the "new" immigrants. A sampling of people who achieved their ambitions in various fields in their adopted country appears on the facing page.

Jacob Riis (1849–1914)
**From Denmark in 1870.
Journalist and photographer. Author of *How the Other Half Lives* (1890), an exposé of immigrant life in the slums.**

Mother Frances Xavier Cabrini (1850–1917)
**From Italy in 1889.
Roman Catholic saint, canonized in 1946. Founded convents, schools, orphanages, and hospitals.**

Nikola Tesla (1856–1943)
**From Croatia, part of the Austro-Hungarian Empire, in 1884.
Inventor. Pioneered in high-tension electricity and large generators; invented the AC motor and the Tesla coil transformer.**

Felix Frankfurter (1882–1965)
**From Austria in 1894.
Supreme Court justice, 1939–1962.
Harvard law professor, 1914–1939.
A founder of the American Civil Liberties Union.**

Sidney Hillman (1887–1946)
**From Lithuania in 1907.
Labor leader. President of Amalgamated Clothing Workers of America, 1914–1946. Active in Roosevelt's New Deal.**

Irving Berlin (1888–   )
**From Russia in 1893.
Songwriter. Composed nearly one thousand songs, including "God Bless America," "White Christmas," and "Alexander's Ragtime Band," his first big hit in 1911.**

20
Intellectual and Cultural Trends

These natural ordermakers, whether amateurs or officials, came to the front immediately. There seemed to be no possibility which there was not some one there to think of, or which within twenty-four hours was not in some way provided for. . . . California education has, of course, made the thought of all possible recuperation easy. WILLIAM JAMES, *eyewitness account of the San Francisco earthquake, 1906*

Industrialization altered the way Americans thought at the same time that it transformed their ways of making a living. Technological advances revolutionized the communication of ideas more drastically than they did the transportation of goods or the manufacture of steel. The materialism that permeated American attitudes toward business also affected contemporary education and literature, while Charles Darwin's theory of evolution influenced American philosophers, lawyers, and historians profoundly. At the same time, the older ideologies of romantic individualism and faith in democracy continued to affect American thinking. No dominant pattern emerged; the American mind, like the people themselves, was too diverse—one might say confused, even incoherent—to be neatly delimited.

Public Education

The history of American education after about 1870 reflects the impact of many social and economic forces. While Horace Mann, Henry Barnard, and others had laid the foundations for state-supported school systems in the Age of Jackson, these systems became compulsory only after the Civil War, when the growth of cities provided the concentrated populations necessary for economical mass education. Only then did the spurt of human productivity resulting from industrialization produce the huge sums that universal education required. In the 1860s about half the children in the country received some formal education, but this did not mean that half the children were attending school at any one time. Sessions were short, and many students dropped out after only two or three years of classes; as late as 1870 the average American had received only four years of schooling.

Thereafter, steady growth and improvement took place. Attendance in the public schools increased from 6.8 million in 1870 to 15.5 million in 1900, a remarkable expansion even when allowance is made for the growth of the population. Public expenditures for education rose from $63 million in 1870 to $234 million in 1902. The national rate of illiteracy declined from 20 percent in 1870 to 10.7 percent in 1900.* Nearly all the states outside the South had compulsory education laws by 1900, and over the years the laws were gradually extended to cover broader age groups and longer school sessions. The number of high schools jumped from perhaps 100 in 1860 to 6,000 at the end of the century. At the other extreme, the kindergarten, developed in Germany in the 1830s by Friedrich Froebel, caught on rapidly. The first public kindergarten was opened in St. Louis in 1873, and by the 1890s most systems of any size had adopted the idea.

Southern schools lagged behind the rest of the nation, in part because the section was poor and still predominantly rural. The restoration of white rule abruptly halted the progress in public education for blacks that the reconstruction governments had made. Church groups and private foundations such as the Peabody Fund and the Slater Fund, financed chiefly by northern philanthropists, supported black schools after 1877, among them two important experiments in vocational training, Hampton Institute (1868) and Booker T. Washington's Tuskegee Institute (1881).

These schools had to overcome considerable resistance and suspicion in the white community; they survived only because they taught a docile, essentially subservient philosophy, preparing students to accept second-class citizenship and become farmers and craftsmen. Since proficiency in academic subjects might have given the lie to the southern belief that blacks were intellectually inferior to whites, such subjects were avoided. The southern insistence on segregating the public schools, buttressed by the "separate but equal" decision of the Supreme Court in *Plessy* v. *Ferguson*, imposed a crushing financial burden on sparsely settled communities, and the dominant opinion that blacks were not really educable did not encourage communities to make special efforts in their behalf.

An industrial society created demands for vocational and technical training. Science courses appeared in the new high schools. In 1880 Calvin M. Woodward opened his Manual Training School in St. Louis, and soon a number of institutions were offering courses in carpentry, metalwork, sewing, and other crafts. By 1890, 36 American cities had public vocational high schools. Woodward thought of vocational training as part of a broad general education rather than as preparation for

* At present the rate is about 2 percent.

Frances Benjamin Johnston, the first black woman photographer of note, documented Tuskegee Institute's activities in the early years of the century. Here students help with building construction about 1900.

a specific occupation, but manual training attracted the backing of industrialists with more practical objectives. Their support in turn made organized labor suspicious of the new trend. One union leader called the trade schools "breeding schools for scabs and rats." Fortunately, the usefulness of such training soon became evident to the unions; by 1910 the AFL was lobbying side by side with the National Association of Manufacturers for more trade schools.

Foreign influences also caused a revolution in teaching methods. Traditionally, American teachers had emphasized the three Rs and relied on strict discipline and rote learning. Typical of the pedagogues of the period was the Chicago teacher, described by a reformer in the 1890s, who told her students firmly: "Don't stop to think, tell me what you know!" Yet the ideas of early 19th-century German educators, notably Johann Friedrich Herbart, were attracting attention in the United States. According to Herbart, teachers could best arouse the interest of their students by relating new information to what they already knew; good teaching called for professional training, psychological insight, enthusiasm, and imagination, not merely facts and a birch rod. At the same time, evolutionists were pressing for a kind of education that would help children to "survive" by adapting to the demands of their environment.

Forward-looking educators seized upon these ideas because dynamic social changes were making the old system increasingly inadequate. Settlement house workers discovered that slum children needed training in handicrafts, good citizenship, and personal hygiene as much as in reading and writing. They were appalled by the local schools, which suffered from the same diseases—filth, overcrowding, rickety construction—that plagued the tenements, and by the school systems, most of which were controlled by machine politicians who doled out teaching positions to party hacks and other untrained persons. They recognized the value of school playgrounds, kindergartens, adult education programs, and extracurricular clubs. Gradually they came to regard educational reform as central to the problem of improving society. "We are impatient with the schools which lay all stress on reading and writing," Jane Addams declared. This type of education "fails to give the child any clew to the life about him."

The philosopher who summarized and gave direction to these forces was John Dewey, a professor at the University of Chicago. Dewey was concerned with the implications of evolution—indeed, of all

science—for education. Essentially his approach was ethical. Was the nation's youth being properly prepared for the tasks it faced in the modern world? He became interested in Francis W. Parker's remarkable experimental school in Chicago, which was organized as "a model home, a complete community and embryonic democracy." In 1896, together with his wife, Dewey founded the Laboratory School to put his educational ideas to the test. Three years later he published *The School and Society*, describing and defending his theories.

"Education," Dewey insisted, was "the fundamental method of social progress and reform." To seek to improve conditions merely by passing laws was "futile." Moreover, in an industrial society the family no longer performed many of the educational functions it had carried out in an agrarian society. Farm children learn about nature, about work, about human character in countless ways denied to children in cities. The school can fill the gap by becoming "an embryonic community . . . with types of occupations that reflect the life of the larger society." At the same time, education should center on the child, and new information should be related to what the child already knows. Children's imagination, energy, and curosity are tools for broadening their outlook and increasing their store of information. Finally, the school should become an instrument for social reform, "saturating [the child] with the spirit of service" and helping to produce a "society which is worthy, lovely, and harmonious." Education, in other words, ought to build character and teach good citizenship as well as transmit knowledge.

The School and Society created a stir, and Dewey immediately assumed leadership of what in the next generation was called progressive education. Although the gains made in public education before 1900 were more quantitative than qualitative and the philosophy dominant in most schools was not very different at the end of the century from that prevailing in Horace Mann's day, change was in the air. The best educators of the period were full of optimism, convinced that the future was theirs.

Keeping the People Informed

The inadequacy of so much of their schooling left many Americans with a hunger for knowledge. Nothing so well illustrates the mass desire for information as the rise of the Chautauqua movement, founded by John H. Vincent, a Methodist minister, and Lewis Miller, an Ohio manufacturer of farm machinery. Vincent had charge of Sunday schools for the Methodist church. In 1874 he and Miller organized a two-week summer course for Sunday school teachers on the shores of Lake Chautauqua in New York. Besides instruction, they offered good meals, evening songfests around the campfire, and a relaxing atmosphere—all for $6 for the two weeks.

The 40 young teachers who attended were delighted with the program, and soon the leafy shore of Lake Chautauqua became a city of tents each summer as thousands poured into the region from all over the country. The founders expanded their offerings to include instruction in literature, science, government, and economics. Famous authorities, including, over the years, six presidents of the United States, came to lecture to open-air audiences on every subject imaginable. Eventually Chautauqua supplied speakers to Reading Circles throughout the country; it even offered correspondence courses leading over a four-year period to a diploma, the program designed, in Vincent's words, to give "the college outlook" to persons who had not had the opportunity to obtain a higher education. Books were written specifically for the program, and a monthly magazine, the *Chautauquan,* was published.

Such success provoked imitation, and by 1900 there were about 200 Chautauqua-type organizations. Intellectual standards in these programs varied greatly; in general they were very low. Entertainment was as important an objective as enlightenment. Musicians (good and bad), homespun humorists, inspirational lecturers, and assorted quacks shared the platform with prominent divines and scholars. Moneymaking undoubtedly motivated many of the entrepreneurs who operated the centers, all of which, including the original Chautauqua, reflected the prevailing tastes of the American people—diverse, enthusiastic, uncritical, and shallow. Nevertheless the movement provided opportunities for thousands seeking stimulation and intellectual improvement.

Still larger numbers profited from the proliferation of public libraries. By the end of the century nearly all the states supported libraries. Private do-

nors, led by the ironmaster Andrew Carnegie, contributed millions to the cause. In 1900 over 1,700 libraries in the United States had collections of more than 5,000 volumes.

Newspapers and magazines were important means for disseminating information and educating the masses. Here new technology supplied the major incentive for change. The development by Richard Hoe and Stephen Tucker of the web press (1871), which printed simultaneously on both sides of paper fed into it from large rolls, and Ottmar Mergenthaler's linotype machine (1886), which cast rows of type as needed directly from molten metal, cut printing costs dramatically. Machines for making paper out of wood pulp reduced the cost of newsprint to a quarter of what it had been in the 1860s. By 1895 machines were printing, cutting, and folding 32-page newspapers at a rate of 24,000 an hour.

The telegraph and transoceanic cables wrought a similar transformation in the gathering of news. Press associations, led by the New York Associated Press, flourished; the syndicated article appeared; and a few publishers—Edward W. Scripps was the first—began to acquire chains of newspapers.

Population growth and better education created an ever-larger demand for printed matter. At the same time, the integration of the economy enabled manufacturers to sell their goods all over the country. Advertising became important, and sellers soon learned that newspapers and magazines were excellent means of placing their products before millions of eyes. Advertising revenues soared just when new machines and general expansion were making publishing an expensive business. The day of the journeyman printer-editor ended; magazine publishing and newspaper publishing were becoming big business. Rich men such as the railroad magnates Jay Gould, Henry Villard, and Tom Scott and the mining tycoon George Hearst invested heavily in important newspapers in the postwar decades. These publishers tended to be conservative, a tendency increased by the prejudices of their businessmen-advertisers. On the other hand, reaching the masses meant lowering intellectual and cultural standards, appealing to emotions, and adopting popular, sometimes radical, causes.

Cheap, mass-circulation papers had first appeared in the 1830s and 1840s, the most successful being the *Sun*, the *Herald*, and the *Tribune* in New York, the Philadelphia *Public Ledger*, and the Baltimore *Sun* (see page 339). None of them much exceeded a circulation of 50,000 before the Civil War. The first publisher to reach a truly massive audience was Joseph Pulitzer, a Hungarian-born immigrant who made a first-rate paper of the St. Louis *Post-Dispatch*. In 1883 Pulitzer bought the New York *World*, a sheet with a circulation of perhaps 20,000. Within a year he was selling 100,000 copies daily, and by the late 1890s the *World*'s circulation regularly exceeded 1 million.

Pulitzer achieved this brilliant success by casting a wide net. To the masses he offered bold, black headlines devoted to crime (ANOTHER MURDERER TO HANG), scandal (VICE ADMIRAL'S SON IN JAIL), catastrophe (TWENTY-FOUR MINERS KILLED), society and the theater (LILY LANGTRY'S NEW ADMIRER), together with feature stories, political cartoons, comics, and pictures. For the educated and affluent he provided better political and financial coverage than the most respectable New York journals. Pulitzer made the *World* a crusader for civic improvement by attacking political corruption, monopoly, and slum problems. His energetic reporters literally made news, masquerading as criminals and poor workers in order to write graphic accounts of conditions in New York's jails and sweatshops.

"The *World* is the people's newspaper," Pulitzer boasted, and in the sense that it interested men and women of every sort, he was correct. Pulitzer's methods were quickly copied by competitors, especially William Randolph Hearst, who purchased the New York *Journal* in 1895 and soon outdid the *World* in sensationalism. But no other newspaperman of the era approached Pulitzer in originality, boldness, and the knack of reaching the masses without abandoning seriousness of purpose and basic integrity.

Growth and ferment also characterized the magazine world. In 1865 there were about 700 magazines in the country, by the turn of the century more than 5,000. Until the mid-1880s, few of the new magazines were in any way unusual. A handful of serious periodicals, such as the *Atlantic Monthly*, *Harper's*, and the *Century* among the monthlies and the *Nation* among the weeklies, dominated the field. They were staid in tone and conservative in political caste. Articles on current affairs, a good deal of fiction and poetry, historical and biographical studies, and similar material filled their pages,

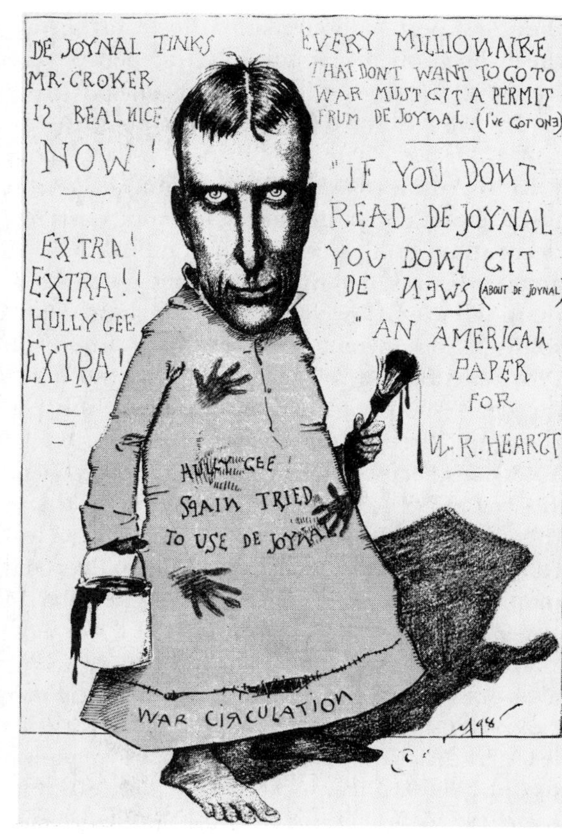

John Singer Sargent's 1905 portrait of Joseph Pulitzer and an opposition paper's caricature of Hearst as the Yellow Kid, a sleazy comic strip character and inspiration for the phase "yellow journalism."

and many of them justly prided themselves on the quality of their illustrations. Although they had great influence, none approached a mass circulation because of the limited size of the upper-middle-class audience they aimed at. The *Century* touched a peak in the 1880s of about 250,000 when it published a series of articles on Civil War battles by famous commanders, but it could not sustain that level. A circulation of 100,000 was considered good for such magazines; the *Nation,* though extremely influential, seldom sold more than 8,000 copies.

Magazines directed at the average citizen were of low quality. The leading publisher of this type in the 1860s and 1870s was Frank Leslie, whose periodicals bore such titles as *Frank Leslie's Chimney Corner, Frank Leslie's Illustrated Newspaper,* and *Frank Leslie's Jolly Joker.* Leslie specialized in illustrations of current events (he put as many as 34 engravers to work on a single picture in order to bring it out quickly) and on providing what he frankly admitted was "mental pabulum"—a combination of cheap romantic fiction, old-fashioned poetry, jokes, and advice columns. Some of his magazines sold as many as 300,000 copies per issue.

After about 1885 vast changes began to take place. New magazines such as the *Forum* (1886) and the *Arena* (1889) emphasized hard-hitting articles on controversial subjects by leading experts. The weekly *Literary Digest* (1890) offered summaries of press opinion on current events, and the *Review of Reviews* (1891) provided monthly commentary on the news. Even more startling changes revolutionized the mass-circulation field. Between 1883 and 1893 the *Ladies' Home Journal, Cosmopolitan, Munsey's,* and *McClure's* appeared on the scene. Although superficially similar to the Frank Leslie type, these magazines maintained a far higher intellectual level.

In 1889 Edward W. Bok became editor of the *Ladies' Home Journal.* Besides advice columns ("Ruth Ashmore's Side Talks with Girls"), he offered articles on child care, gardening, and interior decorating, published fine contemporary novelists, and commissioned public figures, such as presidents Grover Cleveland and Benjamin Harrison, to discuss important questions. He printed colored reproductions of art masterpieces—the invention of cheap photoengraving was of enormous significance in the success of mass-circulation magazines—and crusaded for women's suffrage, conservation, and other reforms. Bok did more than cater to public tastes; he created new tastes. He even refused to accept patent medicine advertising, a major source of revenue for many popular magazines.

Samuel S. McClure and Frank A. Munsey were also masters of popular journalism. *McClure's* specialized in first-class fiction, serious historical studies, and articles attacking political corruption, monopoly, and other social evils. *Munsey's* adopted the same formula but pitched its appeal somewhat lower.

Bok, McClure, Munsey, and a number of their competitors reached millions of readers. Like Pulitzer in the newspaper field, they found ways of interesting rich and poor, the cultivated and the ignorant. Utilizing the new printing technology to cut costs and drawing heavily on advertising revenues, they sold their magazines for 10 or 15 cents a copy and still made fortunes. Under Bok the *Journal* reached a circulation of 2 million. Between 1894 and 1907, Munsey cleared over $7.8 million from his numerous publications. All had an acute sensitivity to the shifting interests of the masses. "I want to know if you enjoy a story," McClure once told his star reporter, Lincoln Steffens. "If you do, then I know that, say, ten thousand readers will like it. . . . But I go most by myself. For if I like a thing, then I know that millions will like it. My mind and my taste are so common that I'm the best editor."*

* McClure added ruefully: "There's only one better editor than I am, and that's Frank Munsey. If *he* likes a thing, then *everybody* will like it."

Colleges and Universities

Improvements in public education and the needs of an increasingly complex society for every type of intellectual skill led to advances in higher education and professional training. The number of colleges rose from about 350 to 500 between 1878 and 1898, and the student body roughly tripled. Less than 2 percent of the population attended college, but the aspirations of the nation's youth were rising, and more and more parents had the financial means necessary for fulfilling them.

More significant than the expansion of the colleges were the alterations in their curricula and in the atmosphere permeating the average campus. In 1870 most colleges were much as they had been in the 1830s: small, limited in their offerings, intellectually stagnant. The ill-paid professors were seldom scholars of stature. Thereafter, change came like a flood tide. State universities proliferated; the federal government's land-grant program in support of training in "agriculture and the mechanic arts," established under the Morrill Act of 1862, came into its own; wealthy philanthropists poured fortunes into old institutions and founded new ones; educators introduced new courses and adopted new teaching methods; professional schools of law, medicine, education, business, journalism, and other specialties increased in number.

In the forefront of reform was Harvard, the oldest and most prestigious college in the country. In the 1860s it possessed an excellent faculty, but teaching methods were antiquated and the curriculum had remained almost unchanged since the colonial period. In 1869, however, a dynamic president, the chemist Charles W. Eliot, undertook a transformation of the college. Eliot introduced the elective system, gradually eliminating required courses and expanding offerings in such areas as modern languages, economics, and the laboratory sciences. He encouraged the faculty to experiment with new teaching methods, and he brought in professors with original minds and new ideas. One was Henry Adams, grandson of John Quincy Adams, who made the study of medieval history a true intellectual experience. "Mr. Adams roused the spirit of inquiry and controversy in me," one student later wrote. Another, the historian Edward Channing, called Adams "the greatest teacher that I ever encountered."

Under Eliot's guidance the standards of the medical school were raised and the case method was introduced in the law school. For the first time, students were allowed to borrow books from the library! In some respects Eliot went too far—the elective system encouraged superficality and laxness in many students—but on balance he transformed Harvard from a college, "a place to which a young man *is sent,*" to a university, a place "to which he *goes.*"

An even more important development in higher education was the founding of Johns Hopkins in 1876. This university was one of many established in the period by wealthy industrialists; its benefactor, the Baltimore merchant Johns Hopkins, had made his fortune in the Baltimore and Ohio Railroad. Its distinctiveness, however, was due to the vision of Daniel Coit Gilman, its first president. Gilman modeled Johns Hopkins on the German universities, where meticulous research and absolute freedom of inquiry were the guiding principles. In staffing the institution, he sought scholars of the highest reputation, scouring Europe as well as America in his search for talent and offering outstanding men high salaries for that time—up to $5,000 for a professor. At the same time, he employed a number of relatively unknown but brilliant younger scholars, such as the physicist Henry A. Rowland and Herbert Baxter Adams, whom he made an associate in history on the strength of his excellent doctoral dissertation at the University of Heidelberg. Gilman promised his teachers good students and ample opportunity to pursue their own research (which explains why so many Hopkins professors repeatedly turned down attractive offers from other universities).

Johns Hopkins specialized in graduate education. In the generation after its founding, it turned out a remarkable percentage of the most important scholars in the nation, including Woodrow Wilson in political science, John Dewey in philosophy, Frederick Jackson Turner in history, and John R. Commons in economics. The seminar conducted by Herbert Baxter Adams was particularly productive: the Adams-edited *Johns Hopkins Studies in Historical and Political Science,* consisting of the doctoral dissertations of his students, was both voluminous and influential—"the mother of similar studies in every part of the United States." At Johns Hopkins, the reformer Frederick C. Howe recalled, "my life really began. . . . I felt a sense of responsibility to the world. I wanted to change things."

The success of Johns Hopkins did not stop the migration of American scholars to Europe; more than 2,000 matriculated at German universities during the 1880s. But as Hopkins graduates took up professorships at other institutions and as scholars trained elsewhere adopted the Hopkins methods, true graduate education became possible in most sections of the country.

The example of Johns Hopkins encouraged other wealthy individuals to endow universities offering advanced work. Clark University in Worcester, Massachusetts, founded by Jonas Clark, a merchant and real estate speculator, opened its doors in 1889. Its president, G. Stanley Hall, had been a professor of psychology at Hopkins, and he built the new university in that institution's image. More important was John D. Rockefeller's creation, the University of Chicago (1892). The president of Chicago, William Rainey Harper, was a brilliant biblical scholar—he received his Ph.D. from Yale at the age of 18—and an energetic and imaginative administrator. The new university, he told Rockefeller, should be designed "with the example of Johns Hopkins before our eyes."

Like Daniel Coit Gilman, Harper sought top-flight scholars for his faculty. He offered such high salaries that he was besieged with over 1,000 applications. Armed with Rockefeller dollars, he "raided" the best institutions in the nation. He decimated the faculty of the new Clark University—"an act of wreckage," the indignant President Hall complained, "comparable to anything that the worst trust ever attempted against its competitors." Chicago offered first-class graduate and undergraduate education. During its first year there were 120 instructors for fewer than 600 students, and despite fears that the mighty tycoon Rockefeller would enforce his social and economic views on the institution, academic freedom was the rule.

State and federal aid to higher education expanded rapidly. The Morrill Act, granting land to each state at a rate of 30,000 acres for each senator and representative, provided the endowments that gave many important modern universities, such as Illinois, Michigan State, and Ohio State, their start. While the federal assistance was earmarked for specific subjects, the land-grant colleges offered a full range of courses, and all received additional state

A geology field trip in the 1880s sets out from the administration building of Smith College. Along with their picks and hammers, the young women carry baskets which look as though they might contain lunch.

funds. Other state institutions benefited, for the public was displaying an increasing willingness to support their activities.

The land-grant universities adopted new ideas quickly. They were coeducational from the start, and most developed professional schools and experimented with extension work and summer programs. Typical of the better state institutions was the University of Michigan, which reached the top rank among the nation's universities during the presidency of James B. Angell (1871–1909). Like Eliot at Harvard, Angell expanded the undergraduate curriculum and strengthened the law and medical schools. He encouraged graduate studies, seeking to make Michigan "part of the great world of scholars," and sought ways in which the university could serve the general community.

Important advances were made in women's education. Beginning with Vassar College, which opened its doors to 300 women students in 1865, the opportunity for young women to pursue serious academic work gradually expanded. Wellesley and Smith, both founded in 1875, completed the so-called Big Three women's colleges. Together with the already established Mount Holyoke, and with Bryn Mawr (1885), Barnard (1889), and Radcliffe (1893), they became known as the Seven Sisters.

Opportunities for women graduates were severely limited. The only career easily available to them was teaching; of the first 815 graduates of

Vassar, all but 10 taught at some time in their lives. Nevertheless, the remarkable women that these institutions trained were conscious of their uniqueness and determined to demonstrate their capabilities. "Sending a daughter to college," the historian William H. Chafe writes, was "like letting the genie out of the bottle."

Not all the changes in higher education were beneficial. The elective system led to superficiality; students gained a smattering of knowledge of many subjects and mastered none. Intensive graduate work often produced narrowness of outlook and research monographs on trivial subjects. Attempts to apply the scientific method in fields such as history and economics often enticed students into making smug claims to objectivity and definitiveness which from the nature of the subjects they could not even approach in their work.

The gifts of rich industrialists sometimes came with strings, and college boards of trustees tended to be dominated by businessmen who sometimes attempted to impose their own social and economic beliefs on faculty members. While few professors lost their positions because their views offended trustees, at many institutions trustees exerted constant nagging pressures that limited academic freedom and scholarly objectivity. At state colleges, politicans often interfered in academic affairs, even treating professorships as part of the patronage system.

Thorstein Veblen pointed out in his caustic study of *The Higher Learning in America* (1918) that "the intrusion of businesslike ideals, aims and methods" harmed the universities in countless subtle ways. Size alone—the verbose Veblen called it "an executive weakness for spectacular magnitude"—became an end in itself, and the practical values of education were exalted over the humanistic. When universities grew bigger, administration became more complicated and the prestige of administrators rose inordinately. At many institutions professors came to be regarded as mere employees of the governing boards. In 1893 the members of the faculty of Stanford University were officially classified as personal servants of Mrs. Leland Stanford, widow of the founder. This was done in good cause—the Stanford estate was tied up in probate court and the ruling made it possible to pay professors out of Mrs. Stanford's allowance for household expenses—but that such a procedure was even conceivable must have appalled the scholarly world.

As the number of college graduates increased, and as colleges ceased being primarily training institutions for clergymen, the influence of alumni on educational policies began to make itself felt, not always happily. Campus social activities became more important. Fraternities proliferated. Interest in organized sports first appeared as a laudable outgrowth of the general expansion of the curriculum, but soon athletic contests were playing a role all out of proportion to their significance. Football evolved as the leading intercollegiate sport, especially after Walter Camp, coach of the Yale team, began selecting "All American" squads in 1889. By the early 1890s important games were attracting huge crowds (over 50,000 attended the Yale-Princeton game in 1893). Football became a source of revenue that many colleges dared not neglect. Since students, alumni, and the public demanded winning teams, college administrators stooped to subsidizing student athletes, in extreme cases employing players who were not students at all. One exasperated college president quipped that the B.A. degree was coming to mean Bachelor of Athletics.

Thus higher education reflected American values, with all their strengths and weaknesses. A complex society required a more professional and specialized education for its youth; the coarseness and the rampant materialism and competitiveness of the era inevitably found expression in the colleges and universities.

Scientific Advances

Much has been made of the crassness of late-19th-century American life, yet the period produced intellectual achievements of the highest quality. If the business mentality dominated society, and if the great barons of industry, exalting practicality over theory, tended to look down on the life of the mind, intellectuals, quietly pondering the problems of their generation, nonetheless created works that affected the country as profoundly as the achievements of industrial organizers like Rockefeller and Carnegie and technicians like Edison and Bell.

In pure science America produced a number of outstanding figures in these years. The giant among them, whose contributions some experts rank with those of Newton, Darwin, and Einstein, was Josiah Willard Gibbs, professor of mathematical physics at Yale from 1871 to 1903. Gibbs created an entirely new science, physical chemistry, and made possible the study of how complex substances respond to changes in temperature and pressure. Purely theoretical at the time, Gibbs's ideas led to vital advances in metallurgy and in the manufacutre of plastics, drugs, and other products. Gibbs is often used to illustrate the supposed indifference of the age to its great minds, but this is hardly fair; he was a shy, self-effacing man who cared little for the spotlight or for collecting disciples. He published his major papers in the obscure *Transactions of the Connecticut Academy of Arts and Sciences.* Furthermore, he was so far ahead of his time that only a handful of specialists had a glimmering of the importance of his work. The editors of *Transactions* admitted that they did not understand his papers.

Of lesser but still major significance was the work of Henry A. Rowland, the first professor of physics at Johns Hopkins University. President Gilman, with characteristic insight, had plucked the youthful Rowland from the faculty of Rensselaer Polytechnic Institute, where his brilliance was not fully appreciated. Rowland conducted research in spectrum analysis and contributed to the development of electron theory. His work led to the improvement of transformers and dynamos and laid the basis for the modern electric power industry. Still another important American physicist was Albert A. Michelson of the University of Chicago, who made the first accurate measurements of the speed of light. Michelson's researches in the 1870s and 1880s helped prepare the way for Einstein's theory of relativity; in 1907 he became the first American scientist to win a Nobel prize.

Many scientists of the period deserve mention: the astronomer Edward C. Pickering, director of the Harvard Observatory, a pioneer in the field of astrophysics; Samuel P. Langley of the Smithsonian Institution, an expert on solar radiation who contributed to the development of the airplane; the paleontologist Othniel C. Marsh, whose study of fossil horses provided a convincing demonstration of evolution; John Wesley Powell, director of the U.S. Geological Survey, noted for his studies of the Grand Canyon and for his work on the uses of water in arid regions (see page 510). These and others of only slightly lesser stature give the lie to the myth that late-19th-century Americans were interested only in applied science.

The New Social Sciences

In the social sciences a close connection existed between the practical issues of the age and the achievements of the leading thinkers. The application of the theory of evolution to every aspect of human relations, the impact of industrialization on society—such topics were of intense concern to American economists, sociologists, and historians. An understanding of Darwin increased the already strong interest in studying the *development* of institutions and their interactions one with another. Controversies over trusts, slum conditions, and other problems drew scholars out of their towers and into practical affairs. Social scientists were impressed by the progress being made in the physical and biological sciences. They eagerly applied the scientific method to their own specialties, hoping thereby to arrive at objective truths in fields that by nature were essentially subjective.

Among the economists something approaching a revolution took place in the 1880s. The classical school, which maintained that immutable natural laws governed all human behavior, and which used the insights of Darwin only to justify unrestrained competition and laissez faire, was challenged by a group of young economists who argued that as times changed, economic theories and laws must be modified in order to remain relevant. Richard T. Ely, another of the scholars who made Johns Hopkins a font of new ideas in the 1880s, summarized the thinking of this group in 1885. "The state [is] an educational and ethical agency whose positive aid is an indispensable condition of human progress," Ely proclaimed. Laissez faire was outmoded and dangerous. Economic problems were basically moral problems; their solution required "the united efforts of Church, state and science." The proper way to study these problems was by analyzing actual conditions, not by applying abstract laws or principles.

This approach led Henry Carter Adams (Ph.D., Johns Hopkins, 1878) to analyze the circumstances under which the government might regulate competition and even, in certain industries, establish monopolies under public control. Simon Patten of the University of Pennsylvania offered a theory justifying state economic planning. Such ideas gave birth to the so-called institutionalist school of economics, whose members made detailed, on-the-spot investigations of sweatshops, factories, and mines, studied the history of the labor movement, and conducted similar research activities of a concrete nature. The study of institutions would lead both to theoretical insights and to practical social reform, they believed. John R. Commons, one of Ely's students at Johns Hopkins and later professor of economics at the University of Wisconsin, was the outstanding member of this school. His ten-volume *Documentary History of American Industrial Society* (1910–1911) reveals the institutionalist approach at its best.

A similar revolution struck sociology in the mid-1880s. Prevailing opinion up to that time rejected the idea of government interference with the organization of society. The influence of the Englishman Herbert Spencer, who objected even to public schools and the postal system, was immense. Spencer and his American disciples, among them Edward L. Youmans, editor of *Popular Science Monthly,* twisted the ideas of Darwin to mean that society could be changed only by the force of evolution, which moved with cosmic slowness. "You and I can do nothing at all," Youmans told the reformer Henry George. "It's all a matter of evolution. Perhaps in four or five thousand years evolution may have carried men beyond this state of things."

Such a point of view made little sense in America, where society was changing rapidly and the range of government social and economic activity was expanding. It was first challenged by an obscure scholar employed by the U.S. Geological Survey, Lester Frank Ward, whose *Dynamic Sociology* was published in 1883. Ward assailed the Spencerians for ignoring the possibility of "the improvement of society by cold calculation." In *The Psychic Factors of Civilization* (1893) he blasted the "law of competition." Human progress, he argued, consisted of "triumphing little by little over this law,"—for example, by interfering with biological processes through the use of medicines to kill harmful bacteria. Government regulation of the economy offered another illustration of how people could control the environment. "Nothing is more obvious today," Ward wrote in the *Forum* in 1895, "than the signal inability of capital and private enterprise to take care of themselves unaided by the state." Society must indeed evolve, but it would evolve through careful social planning.

Like the new economists, Ward emphasized the practical and ethical sides of his subject. Sociologists should seek "the betterment of society," he said, "Dynamic Sociology aims at the organization of happiness." He had little direct influence because his writings were highly technical. In six years only 500-odd copies of *Dynamic Sociology* were sold. However, a handful of specialists, including the economist Ely, President Andrew D. White of Cornell, the Social Gospel preacher Washington Gladden, and the sociologists Albion W. Small and Edward A. Ross—two more products of Johns Hopkins—carried his ideas to a wider audience. Their arguments yielded few concrete results before 1900, but they effectively demolished the Spencerians and laid the theoretical basis for the modern welfare state.

Similar currents of thought influenced other social sciences. In *Systems of Consanguinity* (1871) the pioneer anthropologist Lewis Henry Morgan developed a theory of social evolution and showed how kinship relationships reflected and affected tribal institutions. Morgan's *Ancient Society* (1877–1878) stressed the mutability of social and cultural patterns and the need to adjust these patterns to meet altered conditions. Applying his knowledge of primitive societies to modern life, he warned against overemphasizing the importance of property. "Since the advent of civilization, the outgrowth of property has been so immense . . . that it has become, on the part of the people, an unmanageable power," he wrote. "The time will come, nevertheless, when human intelligence will rise to the mastery over property, and define the relations of the state to the property it protects.

The new political scientists were also evolutionists and institutionalists. The Founding Fathers, living in a world dominated by Newton's concept of the universe as an immense, orderly machine, had conceived of the political system as an impersonal set of institutions and principles—a government of laws rather than of men. Nineteenth-century thinkers (John C. Calhoun is the best example) concerned themselves with abstractions, such as states' rights, and ignored the extralegal aspects of politics, such as parties and pressure groups. In the 1880s political scientists began to employ a different approach. In his doctoral dissertation at Johns Hopkins, *Congressional Government* (1885), Woodrow Wilson analyzed the American political system. He concluded that the real locus of authority lay in the committees of Congress, which had no constitutional basis at all. Wilson was by no means a radical—he idolized the great English conservative Edmund Burke. Nevertheless, he viewed politics as a dynamic process and offered no theoretical objection to the expansion of the state power. In *The State* (1889) he distinguished between essential functions of government, such as the protection of property and the punishment of crime, and the "ministrant" functions, such as education, the regulation of corporations, and social welfare legislation. The desirability of any particular state action of the latter type was simply a matter of expediency. "Every means," he wrote, "by which society may be perfected through the instrumentality of government . . . ought certainly to be diligently sought."

Law and History

Even jurisprudence, by its nature conservative and rooted in tradition, felt the pressure of evolutionary thought and the new emphasis on studying institutions as they actually are. In 1881 Oliver Wendell Holmes, Jr., published *The Common Law.* Rejecting the ideas that judges should limit themselves to the mechanical explication of statutes and that law consisted only of what was written in law books, Holmes argued that "the felt necessities of the time" rather than precedent should determine the rules by which people are governed. "The life of the law has not been logic; it has been experience," he wrote. "It is revolting," he added on another occasion, "to have no better reason for a rule of law than that so it was laid down in the time of Henry IV."

Holmes went on to a long and brilliant judicial career, during which he repeatedly stressed the right of the people, through their elected representatives, to deal with contemporary problems in any reasonable way, unfettered by outmoded conceptions of the proper limits of government authority. Like the societies they regulated, laws should evolve as times and conditions changed, he said.

This way of reasoning caused no sudden reversal of judicial practice. Holmes's most notable opinions as a judge tended, as in the Lochner bakeshop case (see page 561), to be dissenting opinions. But his philosophy reflected the advanced thinking of the late 19th century, and his influence grew with every decade of the 20th.

The new approach to knowledge did not always advance the cause of liberal reform. Historians in the graduate schools became intensely interested in studying the origins and evolution of political institutions. They concluded, after much "scientific" study of old charters and law codes, that the roots of democracy were to be found in the customs of the ancient tribes of northern Europe. This theory of the "Teutonic origins" of democracy, which has since been thoroughly discredited, fitted well with the prejudices of people of British stock, and it provided ammunition for those who favored restricting immigration and for those who argued that blacks were inferior beings.

Out of this work came the frontier thesis of Frederick Jackson Turner, still another scholar trained at Johns Hopkins. Turner's essay "The Significance of the Frontier in American History" (1893) argued that the frontier experience, through which every section of the country had passed, had affected the thinking of the people and the shape of American institutions. The isolation of the frontier and the need during each successive westward advance to create civilization anew account, Turner wrote, for the individualism of Americans and the democratic character of their society. Nearly everything unique in our culture could be traced to the existence of the frontier, he claimed.

Turner, and still more his many disciples, made too much of his basic insights. Life on the frontier was not as democratic as Turner believed, and it certainly does not "explain" American development as completely as he said it did. Nevertheless, his work showed how important it was to investigate the evolution of institutions, and it encouraged historians to study social and economic, as well as purely political, subjects. If the claims of the new historians to objectivity and definitiveness were absurdly overstated, their emphasis on thoroughness, exactitude, and impartiality did much to raise standards in the profession. Perhaps the finest product of the new scientific school, a happy combination of meticulous scholarship and literary artistry, was Henry Adams's nine-volume *History of the United States During the Administrations of Jefferson and Madison.*

Realism in Literature

When what Mark Twain called the Gilded Age began, American literature was dominated by the romantic mood. All the important writers of the 1840s and 1850s except Hawthorne, Thoreau, and Poe were still living. Longfellow stood at the height of his fame, and the lachrymose Susan Warner—"tears on almost every page"—continued to turn out stories in the style of her popular *The Wide, Wide World.* Romanticism, however, had lost its creative force; most writing in the decade after 1865 was sentimental trash pandering to the preconceptions of middle-class readers. Magazines like the *Atlantic Monthly* overflowed with stories about fair ladies worshiped from afar by stainless heroes, women coping selflessly with drunken husbands, and poor but honest youths rising through various combinations of virtue and assiduity to positions of wealth and influence. Most writers of fiction tended to ignore the eternal conflicts inherent in human nature and the social problems of the age; polite entertainment and pious moralizing appeared to be their only objectives.

The patent unreality, even dishonesty of contemporary fiction eventually caused a reaction. In the mid 1860s Thomas Wentworth Higginson, essayist, historian, abolitionst, Civil War commander of a black regiment, attacked the sentimentality of American literature and urged writers to concern themselves with "real human life." New antiromantic foreign influences—Emile Zola's first novels appeared in the 1860s—began to affect American interests and tastes. But the most important forces giving rise to the Age of Realism were those that were transforming every other aspect of American life: industrialism, with its associated complexities and social problems; the theory of evolution, which made people more aware of the force of the environment and the basic conflicts of existence; the new science, which taught dispassionate, empirical observation.

The 1870s saw a gradual shift in styles; by the 1880s realism was beginning to flower. Novelists undertook the examination of social problems such as slum life, the conflict between capital and labor, and political corruption. They created multidimensional characters, depicted persons of every social class, used dialect and slang to capture the flavor of particular types, and fashioned painstaking descriptions of the surroundings into which they placed their subjects.*

One early sign of the new realism was the "local color" school, for writers seeking to describe real situations turned to the regions they knew best for material. In 1880 Joel Chandler Harris began to publish his Uncle Remus stories, faithfully reproducing the dialect of Georgia blacks and incidentally creating a remarkably realistic literary character. The novels of Edward Eggleston, from *The Hoosier Schoolmaster* (1871) to *The Graysons* (1888), drew vivid pictures of middle western life. Sarah Orne Jewett's carefully constructed tales of life in Maine, first published in the *Atlantic Monthly* in the mid-1870s, caught the spirit of that region. Most local colorists could not rise above the conventional sentimentality of the era. By concentrating, as most did, on depicting rural life, they were retreating from current reality. Yet their concern for precise description and their fascination with local types reflected a growing interest in realism.

Mark Twain

While it was easy to romanticize the West, that region also lent itself to the realistic approach. Almost of necessity, novelists writing about the West employed dialect, described coarse characters from the lower levels of society, and dealt with crime and violence. It would have been difficult indeed to write a genteel romance about a mining camp. The outstanding figure of western literature, the first great American realist, was Mark Twain. Born Samuel L. Clemens in 1835, he grew up in Hannibal, Missouri, on the banks of the Mississippi. After mastering the printer's trade and working as a riverboat pilot, he went west to Nevada in 1861. The

* The romantic novel did not disappear. General Lew Wallace's *Ben Hur* (1880) and Frances Hodgson Burnett's *Little Lord Fauntleroy* (1886) were best-sellers. Francis Marion Crawford's shamelessly romantic tales, published in wholesale lots between 1883 and his death in 1909, were very popular. In the 1890s a spate of historical romances made the realists fume.

Mark Twain is caricatured riding his "Celebrated Jumping Frog of Calaveras County" in this 1872 cartoon by English artist Frederick Waddy.

wild, rough life of Virginia City fascinated him, but prospecting got him nowhere, and he became a reporter for the *Territorial Enterprise.* Soon he was publishing humorous stories about the local life under the nom de plume Mark Twain. In 1865, while working in California, he wrote "The Celebrated Jumping Frog of Calaveras County," a story that brought him national recognition. A tour of Europe and the Holy Land in 1867–1868 led to the writing of *The Innocents Abroad* (1869), which made him famous.

Twain's greatness stemmed from his acute reportorial eye and ear, his eagerness to live life to the full, his marvelous sense of humor, his ability to be at once "in" society and outside it, to love humanity yet be repelled by human vanity and perversity. He epitomized the zest and adaptability of his age and also its materialism. No contemporary pursued the almighty dollar more assiduously. An inveterate speculator, he made a fortune with his pen and lost it in foolish business ventures. He wrote tirelessly and endlessly about America and

Europe, his own times and the feudal past, about tourists, slaves, tycoons, cracker-barrel philosophers—and human destiny. He was equally at home and equally successful on the Great River of his childhood, in the mining camps, and in the eastern bourgeois society of his mature years. But every prize slipped through his fingers. Twain died a dark pessimist, surrounded by adulation yet alone, an alien and a stranger in the land he loved and knew so well.

Twain excelled every contemporary in the portrayal of character. In his biting satire *The Gilded Age* (1873) he created that magnificent mountebank Colonel Beriah Sellers, purveyor of eyewash ("the Infallible Imperial Oriental Optic Liniment") and false hopes, ridiculous, unscrupulous, but lovable. In *Huckleberry Finn* (1884), his masterpiece, his portrait of the slave Jim, loyal, patient, naive, yet withal a man, is unforgettable. When Huck takes advantage of Jim's credulity merely for his own amusement, the slave turns from him coldly and says: "Dat truck dah is *trash;* en trash is what people is dat puts dirt on de head er dey fren's en makes 'em ashamed." And there is Huck Finn himself, one of the great figures of literature, full of deviltry, romantic, amoral—up to a point—and at bottom the complete realist. When Miss Watson tells him he can get anything he wants by praying for it, he makes the effort, is disillusioned, and concludes: "If a body can get anything they pray for, why don't Deacon Winn get back the money he lost on pork? . . . Why can't Miss Watson fat up? No, I says to myself, there ain't nothing in it."

Whether directly, as in *The Innocents Abroad* and in his fascinating account of the world of the river pilot, *Life on the Mississippi* (1883), or when transformed by his imagination in works of fiction such as *Tom Sawyer* (1876) and *A Connecticut Yankee in King Arthur's Court* (1889), Mark Twain always put much of his own experience and feeling into his work. "The truth is," he wrote in 1886, "my books are mainly autobiographies." A story, he told a fellow author, "must be written with the blood out of a man's heart." His innermost confusions, the clash between his recognition of the pretentiousness and meanness of human beings and his wish to be accepted by society, added depths and overtones to his writing that together with his comic genius give it lasting appeal. He could not rise above the sentimentality and prudery of his generation entirely, for these qualities were part of his nature. He never dealt effectively with sexual love, for example, and often—even in *Huckleberry Finn*—he contrived to end his tales on absurdly optimistic notes that ring false after so many brilliant pages portraying life as it is. On balance Twain's achievement was magnificent. Rough and uneven like the man himself, his works catch more of the spirit of the age he named than those of any other writer.

William Dean Howells

Mark Twain's realism was far less self-conscious than that of his longtime friend William Dean Howells. Like Twain, Howells, who was born in Ohio in 1837, had little formal education. He learned the printer's trade from his father and became a reporter for the *Ohio State Journal.* In 1860 he wrote a campaign biography of Lincoln and was rewarded with an appointment as consul in Venice. His sketches in *Venetian Life* (1866) were a product of this experience. After the Civil War he worked briefly for the *Nation* in New York and then moved to Boston, where he became editor of the *Atlantic Monthly.* In 1886 he returned to New York as editor of *Harper's.*

A long series of novels and much literary criticism poured from Howells's pen over the next 34 years. While he insisted on treating his material honestly, he was not at first a critic of society, being content to write about what he called "the smiling aspects" of life. Realism to Howells meant concern for the complexities of individual personalities and faithful description of the genteel, middle-class world he knew best. Nevertheless, he did not hesitate to discuss what prudish critics called "sordid" and "revolting" subjects, such as the unhappy marriage of respectable people, which he treated sensitively in *A Modern Instance* (1882).

Besides a sharp eye and an open mind, Howells had a real social conscience. Gradually he became aware of the problems that industrialization had created. In 1885, in *The Rise of Silas Lapham,* he dealt with some of the ethical conflicts faced by businessmen in a competitive society. The harsh public reaction to the Haymarket bombing in 1886 stirred him, and he threw himself into a futile campaign to prevent the execution of the anarchist suspects. Thereafter he moved rapidly toward the left;

soon he was calling himself a socialist. "After fifty years of optimistic content with 'civilization' . . . I now abhor it, and feel that it is coming out all wrong in the end, unless it bases itself anew on a real equality," he wrote.* *A Hazard of New Fortunes* (1890), in which Howells put his own ideas in the mouth of a magazine editor, Basil March, contained a broad criticism of industrial America—of the slums, of the callous treatment of workers, of the false values of the promoter and the new-rich tycoon.

Howells was more than a reformer, more than an inventor of utopias like Edward Bellamy, though he admired Bellamy and wrote a utopian novel of his own, *A Traveller from Altruria* (1894). *A Hazard of New Fortunes* attempted to portray the whole range of metropolitan life, its plot weaving the destinies of a dozen interesting personalities from diverse sections and social classes. The book represents a triumph of realism in its careful descriptions of various sections of New York and the ways of life of rich and poor, in the intracacy of its characters, and in its rejection of sentimentality and romantic love. "A man knows that he can love and wholly cease to love, not once merely, but several times," the narrator says, "but in regard to women he cherishes the superstition of the romances that love is once for all, and forever." Basil March, himself happily married, tells his wife: "Why shouldn't we rejoice as much at a nonmarriage as a marriage? . . . In reality, marriage is dog cheap, and anyone can have it for the asking—if he keeps asking enough people."

His own works were widely read, and Howells was also the most influential critic of his time. He helped bring the best contemporary foreign writers, including Tolstoy, Dostoevsky, Ibsen, and Zola, to the attention of readers in the United States, and he encouraged many important young American novelists, among them Stephen Crane, Theodore Dreiser, Frank Norris, and Hamlin Garland.

Some of these writers went far beyond Howells's realism to what they called naturalism. Many, like Twain and Howells, began as newspaper reporters. Working for a big-city daily in the 1890s was sure to teach anyone a great deal about the dark side of life. Naturalist writers believed that the human being was essentially an animal, a helpless creature whose fate was determined by environment. Their world was Darwin's world—mindless, without mercy or justice. They wrote chiefly about the most primitive emotions—lust, hate, greed. In *Maggie, A Girl of the Streets* (1893) Stephen Crane described the seduction, degradation, and eventual suicide of a young woman, all set against the background of a sordid slum; in *The Red Badge of Courage* (1895) he captured the pain and humor of war. In *McTeague* (1899) Frank Norris told the story of a brutal, dull-witted dentist who murdered his greed-crazed wife with his bare fists.

Such stuff was too strong for Howells, yet he recognized its importance and befriended the younger writers in many ways. He found a publisher for *Maggie* after it had been rejected many times, and he wrote appreciative reviews of the work of Garland and Norris. Even Theodore Dreiser, who was contemptuous of Howells's writings and considered him hopelessly middle class in point of view, appreciated his aid and praised his influence on American literature. Dreiser's first novel, *Sister Carrie* (1900), treated sex so forthrightly that it was withdrawn after publication.

Henry James

Henry James was very different in spirit and background from the tempestuous naturalists. Born to wealth, reared in a cosmopolitan atmosphere, twisted in some strange way while still a child and unable to achieve satisfactory relationships with women, James spent most of his mature life in Europe, writing novels, short stories, plays, and volumes of criticism. Although far removed from the world of practical affairs, he was preeminently a realist, determined, as he once said, "to leave a multitude of pictures of my time" for the future to contemplate. He admired the European realists and denounced the "floods of tepid soap and water which under the name of novels are being vomited forth" by the romancers. "All life belongs to you," he told his fellow novelists. "There is no impression of life, no manner of seeing it and feeling it, to which the plan of the novelist may not offer a place."

* With remarkable self-insight he added immediately: "Meanwhile I wear a fur-lined overcoat, and live in all the luxury my money can buy." Like nearly all American reformers of the era, he was not really very radical.

An 1897 drawing from the comic weekly Life, *titled "Our Popular but Over-advertised Authors," features (from left) William Dean Howells, George W. Cable, John K. Bangs, James Whitcomb Riley, Mark Twain, Mary Freeman, Richard Harding Davis, F. Marion Crawford, Frances Burnett, and Joel Chandler Harris.*

While he preferred living in the cultivated surroundings of London high society, James yearned for the recognition of his fellow Americans almost as avidly as Mark Twain. However, he was incapable of modifying his rarefied, overly subtle manner of writing. Most serious writers of the time admired his books, and he received many honors, but he never achieved widespread popularity. His major theme was the clash of American and European cultures, his primary interest the close-up examination of wealthy, sensitive, yet often corrupt persons in a cultivated but far-from-polite society.

James dealt with social issues such as feminism and the difficulties faced by artists in the modern world, but he subordinated them to his interest in his subjects as individuals. *The American* (1877) told the story of the love of a wealthy American in Paris for a French noblewoman who rejected him because her family disapproved of his "commercial" background. *The Portrait of a Lady* (1881) described the disillusionment of an intelligent woman married to a charming but morally bankrupt man and her eventual decision to remain with him nonetheless. *The Bostonians* (1886) was a complicated and psychologically sensitive study of the varieties of female behavior in a seemingly uniform social situation.

James's reputation, greater today than in his lifetime, rests more on his highly refined accounts of the interactions of individuals and their environment and his masterful commentaries on the novel as a literary form than on his ability as a storyteller. Few major writers have been more long-winded, more prone to circumlocution. Yet few have been so dedicated to their art, possessed of such psychological penetration, or so successful in producing a large body of important work.

Realism in Art

American painters responded to the times as writers did, but with this difference: despite the new concern for realism, the romantic tradition retained its vitality. Preeminent among the realists was Thomas Eakins, who was born in Philadelphia in 1844. Eakins studied in Europe in the late 1860s and was influenced by the great realists of the 17th century, Velásquez and Rembrandt. Returning to America in 1870, he passed the remainder of his life teaching and painting in Philadelphia.

The scientific spirit of the age suited Eakins perfectly. He mastered human anatomy; some of his finest paintings, such as *The Gross Clinic* (1875), are graphic illustrations of surgical operations. He was an early experimenter with motion pictures, using the camera to capture exactly the attitudes of human beings and animals in action. Like his friend Walt Whitman, whose portrait is one of his greatest achievements, Eakins gloried in the ordinary. But he had none of Whitman's weakness for sham and self-delusion. His portraits are monuments to his integrity and craftsmanship: never would he touch up or soften a likeness to please his sitter. When the Union League of Philadelphia commissioned a canvas of Rutherford B. Hayes, Eakins showed the president working in his shirt sleeves, which scandalized the club fathers. His work was no mere mirror reflecting surface values. His study of six men bathing (*The Swimming Hole*) is a stark portrayal of nakedness; his surgical scenes catch the tenseness of a situation without descending into sensationalism.

Winslow Homer, a Boston-born painter best

Thomas Eakins's interest in science was as great as his interest in art. In the early 1880s he collaborated with the photographer Eadweard Muybridge in serial-action photographic experiments and later devised a special camera for his anatomical studies; this is one of his pictures taken with the Marey wheel.

The impact of Eakins's photographic experiments can be seen in The Swimming Hole, *painted in 1883. Eakins was then director of the Pennsylvania Academy's art school.*

known for his brilliant watercolors, was also influenced by realist ideas. Homer was a lithographer as well as a master of the watercolor medium, yet he had had almost no formal training. Indeed, he had contempt for academicians and refused to go abroad to study. Aesthetics seemed not to concern him at all; he liked to shock people by referring to his profession as "the picture line." His concern for accuracy was so intense that in preparation for painting *The Life Line* (1884) he made a trip to Atlantic City to observe the handling of a breeches buoy. "When I have selected [a subject]," he said, "I paint it exactly as it appears."

During the Civil War, Homer worked as an artist-reporter for *Harper's Weekly,* and he continued to do magazine illustrations for some years thereafter. He roamed America, painting scenes of southern farm life, Adirondack campers, and, after about 1880, magnificent seascapes and studies of fishermen and sailors. For years he made his home in a cottage at Prout's Neck, in Maine, though he traveled extensively in the Caribbean region, where some of his best watercolors were executed.

In some ways Homer resembled the local colorists of American literature. Like the work of many members of that group, Homer's work contains romantic elements. His *Gulf Stream* (1899), showing a sailor on a small, broken boat menaced by an approaching waterspout and a school of sharks, and his *Fox Hunt* (1893), in which huge, ominous crows hover over a fox at bay, express his interest in the violence and drama of raw nature, a distinctly romantic theme. However, his approach, even in these works, was utterly prosaic. When some silly women complained about the fate of the black sailor in *Gulf Stream,* Homer wrote his dealer sarcastically: "Tell these ladies that the unfortunate Negro . . . will be rescued and returned to his friends and home, and live happily ever after."

The outstanding romantic painter of the period was Albert Pinkham Ryder, a strange, neurotic genius haunted by the mystery and poetry of the sea. Ryder was born in New Bedford, Massachusetts, in 1847, during that city's heyday as a whaling port, and spent most of his mature years in New York City, living and working in a dirty, cluttered attic studio. He typified the solitary romantic—brooding, eccentric, otherworldly, mystical. His heavily glazed paintings of dark seas and small boats "bathed in an atmosphere of golden luminosity" beneath a pale moon, weird canvases like *The Race Track* (*Death on a Pale Horse*), which shows a specter carrying a scythe riding on an empty track under an ominous sky, radiate a strange magic. Yet they are masterpieces of design.

The careers of Eakins, Homer, and Ryder show that the late-19th-century American environment was not uncongenial to first-rate artists. Nevertheless, at least two major American painters abandoned native shores for Europe. One was James A. McNeill Whistler, whose portrait of his mother, which he called *Arrangement in Grey and Black,* is probably the most famous canvas ever painted by an American. Whistler left the United States in 1855 when he was 21 and spent most of his life in Paris and London. "I shall come to America," he announced grandly, "when the duty on works of art is abolished!" Whistler made a profession of eccentricity, but he was a remarkably talented and versatile artist. Some of his portraits are triumphs of realism, while his misty studies of the London waterfront—which the critic John Ruskin characterized as pots of paint flung in the face of the beholder, and which Whistler conceived as visual expressions of poetry—are thoroughly romantic in conception. Paintings such as "Whistler's Mother" represent still another expression of his talent. Spare and muted in tone, they are more interesting as precise arrangements of color and space than as images of particular objects; they had a tremendous influence on the course of modern art.

The second important expatriate artist was Mary Cassatt, daughter of a wealthy Pittsburgh banker and sister of Alexander J. Cassatt, who was president of the Pennsylvania Railroad around the turn of the century. She went to Paris as a tourist and dabbled in art like many conventional young socialites, then was caught up in the impressionist movement and decided to become a serious painter. Her work is more French than American and was little appreciated in the United States before the First World War. When once she returned to America for a visit, the Philadelphia *Public Ledger* reported: "Mary Cassatt, sister of Mr. Cassatt, president of the Pennsylvania Railroad, returned from

Now widely recognized as one of America's finest impressionist painters, Mary Cassatt found her talent ignored in this country during her lifetime. She portrayed mothers and children with a grace and tenderness that (some would say) only a woman artist could convey.

Europe yesterday. She has been studying painting in Paris, and owns the smallest Pekinese dog in the world."

If Mary Cassatt was unappreciated and if Whistler had reasons for considering Americans uncultured, it remains true that interest in art was considerable. Museums and art schools increased in number and settlement house workers put on exhibitions that attracted enthusiastic crowds. Wealthy patrons gave countless commissions to portrait painters, the most fashionable of whom, a fine craftsman if not a great artist, was John Singer Sargent. Millionaries poured fortunes into collecting, and if some were interested only in display and others had execrable taste, some were discriminating collectors. Martin A. Ryerson, with a fortune made in lumber, bought the works of the French impressionists when few Americans understood their importance. Charles L. Freer of the American Car and Foundry Company, a friend and admirer of Whistler, was a specialist in oriental art. John G. Johnson, a successful corporation lawyer, covered the walls of his Philadelphia mansion with a carefully chosen collection of Italian primitives, accumulated before anyone else appreciated them.

Other enthusiasts, notably the banker J. P. Morgan, employed experts to help them put together their collections. Nor were the advanced painters of the day rejected by all wealthy patrons. Only a handful of his contemporaries recognized the talent of the weird, avant-garde Ryder. But while Eakins's work was undervalued, he received many important commissions. Some of Homer's canvases commanded thousands of dollars, and so did those of the radical Whistler.

The Pragmatic Approach

It would have been remarkable indeed if the intellectual ferment of the late 19th century had not affected contemporary ideas about the meaning of life, the truth of revealed religion, moral values, and similar fundamental problems. In particular the theory of evolution, so important in altering contemporary views of science, history, and social relations, produced significant changes in American thinking about religious and philosophical questions.

Evolution posed an immediate challenge to religion: if Darwin was correct, the Biblical account of the creation was obviously untrue and the idea that the human race had been formed in God's image was highly unlikely. A bitter controversy erupted, described by President Andrew D. White of Cornell in *The Warfare of Science with Theology in Christendom* (1896). While millions continued to believe in the literal truth of the Bible, among intellectuals, lay and clerical, victory went to the evolutionists because in addition to the arguments of the geologists and the biologists, scholars were throwing light on the historical origins of the Bible, showing it to be of human rather than divine inspiration.

Evolution did not undermine the faith of any large percentage of the population. If the account of the creation in Genesis could not be taken literally, the Bible remained a repository of wisdom and inspiration. Such books as John Fiske's *The Outlines of Cosmic Philosophy* (1874) provided religious persons with the comforting thesis that evolution, while true, was merely God's way of ordering the universe—as the liberal preacher Washington Gladden put it, "a most impressive demonstration of the presence of God in the world."

The effects of Darwinism on philosophy were less dramatic but in the end more significant. Fixed systems and eternal verities were difficult to justify in a world that was constantly evolving. By the early 1870s a few philosophers had begun to reason that ideas and theories mattered little except when applied to specifics. "Nothing justifies the development of abstract principles but their utility in enlarging our concrete knowledge of nature," wrote Chauncey Wright, secretary of the American Academy of Arts and Sciences. In "How to Make Our Ideas Clear" (1878), Wright's friend Charles S. Peirce, an amazingly versatile and talented albeit obscure thinker, argued that concepts could be fairly understood only in terms of their practical effects. Once the mind accepted the truth of evolution, Peirce believed, logic required that it accept the impermanence even of scientific laws. There was, he wrote, "an element of indeterminacy, spontaniety, or absolute chance in nature."

This startling philosophy, which Peirce called pragmatism, was presented in more understandable language by William James, brother of the novelist. James was one of the most remarkable persons of his generation. Educated in London, Paris, Bonn, and Geneva—as well as at Harvard—he studied painting, participated in a zoological expedition

William James (with the beard) and his novelist brother Henry James in a warm photographic portrait taken around 1900.

to South America, took a medical degree, and was professor at Harvard successively of comparative anatomy, psychology, and finally philosophy. His *Principles of Psychology* (1890) may be said to have established that discipline as a modern science. His *Varieties of Religious Experience* (1902), which treated the subject from both psychological and philosophical points of view, helped thousands of readers to reconcile their religious faith with their increasing knowledge of psychology and the physical universe.

Although he was less rigorous a logician than Peirce, James's wide range and his verve and imagination as a writer made him by far the most influential philosopher of his times. He rejected the deterministic interpretation of Darwinism and all other one-idea explanations of existence. Belief in free will was one of his axioms; environment might influence survival, but so did the *desire* to survive, which existed independent of surrounding circumstances. Even truth was relative; it did not exist in the abstract; it *happened* under particular circumstances. What a person thought helped to make thought occur, or come true. The mind, James wrote in a typically vivid phrase, has "a vote" in determining truth. Religion was true, for example, because people were religious.

The pragmatic approach inspired much of the reform spirit of the late 19th century and even more of that of the early 20th. James's hammer blows shattered the laissez faire extremism of Herbert Spencer. In "Great Men and Their Environment" (1880) he argued that social changes were brought about by the actions of geniuses whom society had selected and raised to positions of power, rather than by the impersonal force of the environment. Such reasoning fitted the preconceptions of rugged individualists yet encouraged those dissatisfied with society to work for change. Educational reformers like John Dewey, the institutionalist school of economists, settlement house workers, and other reformers adopted pragmatism eagerly. James's philosophy did much to revive the buoyant optimism that had characterized the pre–Civil War reform movement.

Yet pragmatism brought Americans face to face with somber problems. While relativism made them optimistic, it bred insecurity, for there could be no certainty, no comforting reliance on any eternal value in the absence of absolute truth. Pragmatism also seemed to suggest that the end justified the means, that what worked was more important than what ought to be. At the time of James's death in 1910, the *Commercial Financial Chronicle* pointed out that the pragmatic philosophy was helpful to businessmen in making decisions. By emphasizing practice at the expense of theory, the new philosophy encouraged materialism, anti-intellectualism, and other unlovely aspects of the American character. And what place had conventional morality in such a system? Perhaps pragmatism placed too much reliance on the free will of human beings, ignoring their capacity for selfishness and self-delusion.

The people of the new century found pragmatism a heady wine. They would quaff it freely and enthsiastically—down to the bitter dregs.

SUPPLEMENTARY READING

Titles marked with an asterisk have been published in paperback.

All the surveys of American intellectual history deal extensively with this period. See, for example, Merle Curti, **The Growth of American Thought** (1943), Louis Hartz, **The Liberal Tradition in America*** (1955), and Clinton Rossiter, **Conservatism in America: The Thankless Persuasion*** (1962). P. A. Carter, **The Spiritual Crisis of the Gilded Age** (1971), H. S. Commager, **The American Mind*** (1950), and A. M. Schlesinger, **The Rise of the City*** (1933), contain much interesting information, and there are useful essays on some aspects of the subject in H. W. Morgan (ed.), **The Gilded Age: A Reappraisal*** (1970). Ray Ginger, **The Age of Excess*** (1965), is also stimulating.

L. A. Cremin, **The Transformation of the School: Progressivism in American Education*** (1961), is an excellent introduction to the subject. On education in the South, see C. W. Dabney, **Universal Education in the South** (1936). For the work of Dewey, consult Sidney Hook, **John Dewey** (1939). The best treatment of the Chautauqua movement is Victoria and R. O. Case, **We Called It Culture** (1948). Trends in the history of journalism are discussed in J. M. Lee, **History of American Journalism** (1923), B. A. Weisberger, **The American Newspaperman** (1961), and F. L. Mott, **A History of American Magazines** (1938–1957). George Juergens, **Joseph Pulitzer and the New York World** (1966), W. A. Swanberg, **Citizen Hearst*** (1961), and Peter Lyon, **Success Story: The Life and Times of S. S. McClure** (1963), are useful biographies.

On higher education, see L. R. Veysey, **The Emergence of the American University*** (1965), Richard Hofstadter and W. P. Metzger, **The Development of Academic Freedom in the United States*** (1955), and E. A. Green, **Mary Lyon and Mount Holyoke** (1979). Of the many histories of particular universities, S. E. Morison, **Three Centuries of Harvard** (1936), and Hugh Hawkins, **Pioneer: A History of the Johns Hopkins University** (1960), are particularly important for this period. E. D. Ross, **Democracy's College** (1942), deals with the land-grant institutions. Hugh Hawkins, **Between Harvard and America: The Educational Leadership of Charles W. Eliot** (1972), and Allan Nevins, **John D. Rockefeller: The Heroic Age of American Enterprise** (1940), also contain valuable information. Thorstein Veblen, **The Higher Learning in America*** (1918), is full of stimulating opinions.

For developments in American science, see the excellent essay by P. F. Boller, Jr., in H. W. Morgan (ed.), **The Gilded Age*** (1970), and Bernard Jaffe, **Men of Science in America** (1944). Muriel Rukeyser, **Willard Gibbs*** (1942), is a good biography. A good general introduction to the work of the social scientists is Sidney Fine, **Laissez Faire and the General-Welfare State*** (1957), but H. S. Commager's **American Mind** is also useful, as are Richard Hofstadter, **Social Darwinsim in American Thought*** (1944), and Jurgen Herbst, **The German Historical School in American Scholarship** (1965). Biographies of prominent figures include P. G. Rader, **The Academic Mind and Reform: The Influence of Richard T. Ely in American Life** (1967), H. W. Bragdon, **Woodrow Wilson: The Academic Years** (1967), Samuel Chugerman, **Lester F. Ward: The American Aristotle** (1939), Carl Resek, **Lewis Henry Morgan*** (1960), M. DeW. Howe, **Justice Oliver Wendell Holmes: The Proving Years** (1963), and W. H. Jordy, **Henry Adams: Scientific Historian*** (1952).

The great literary figures of the age are discussed in Everett Carter, **Howells and the Age of Realism** (1954), Alfred Kazin, **On Native Grounds*** (1942), Larzer Ziff, **The American 1890s*** (1966), and Van Wyck Brooks, **New England: Indian Summer, 1865–1915*** (1940) and **The Confident Years: 1885–1915** (1952). See also, on Twain, Bernard De Voto, **Mark Twain's America*** (1932), and Justin Kaplan, **Mr. Clemens and Mark Twain*** (1966); on Howells, E. H. Cady, **The Realist at War** (1958); on James, Leon Edel, **Henry James*** (1953–1962).

American painting is discussed in O. W. Larkin, **Art and Life in America** (1949). On pragmatism, see Hofstadter's **Social Darwinism***, Commager's **American Mind***, R. B. Perry, **The Thought and Character of William James*** (1935), and Bruce Kuklick, **The Rise of American Philosophy** (1977).

TIME LINE 5 ▪ The Arts and Sciences in America, 1820–1920

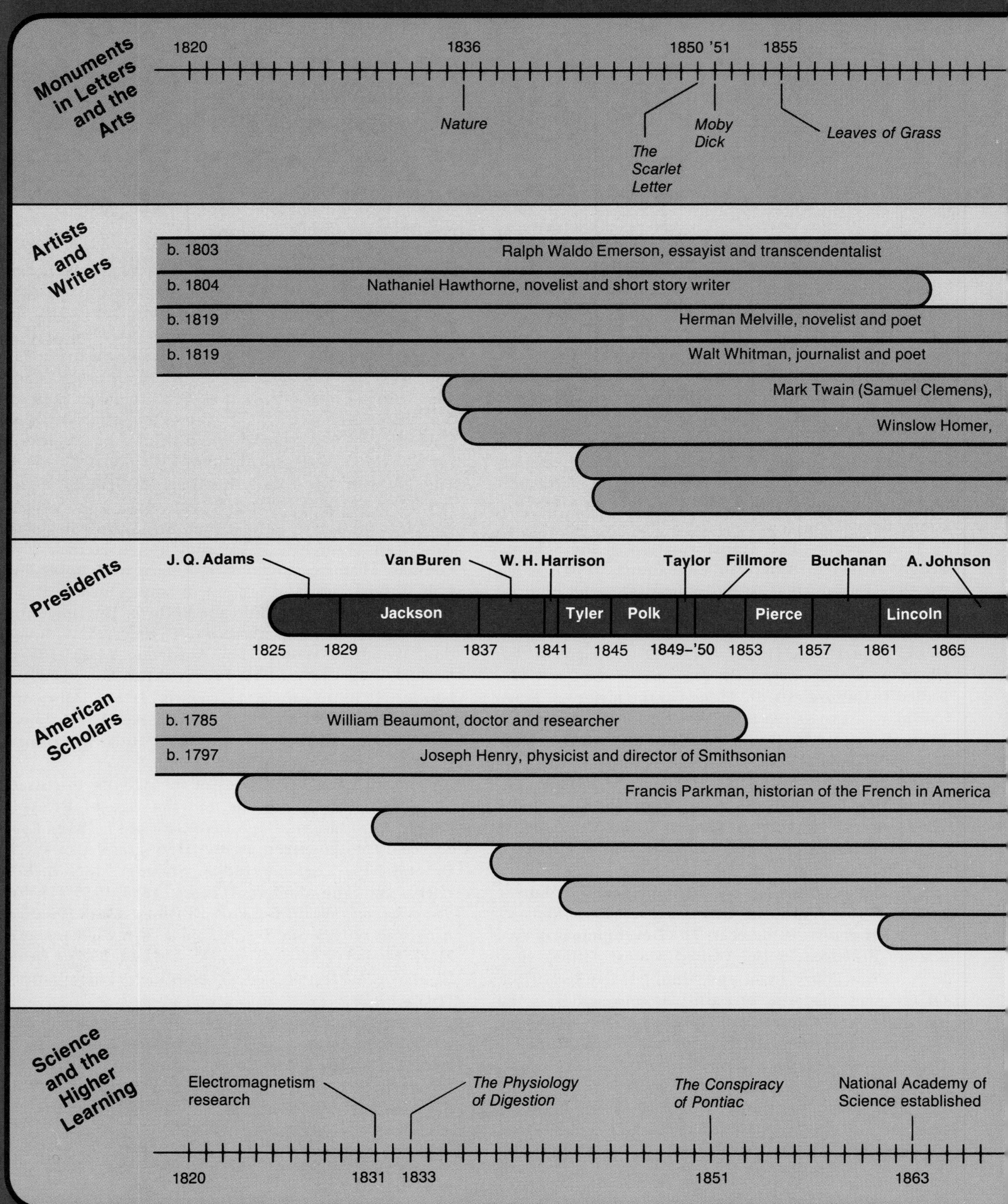

Monuments in Letters and the Arts
1820
1836
1850 '51
1855
Nature
The Scarlet Letter
Moby Dick
Leaves of Grass
Artists and Writers
b. 1803 Ralph Waldo Emerson, essayist and transcendentalist
b. 1804 Nathaniel Hawthorne, novelist and short story writer
b. 1819 Herman Melville, novelist and poet
b. 1819 Walt Whitman, journalist and poet
Mark Twain (Samuel Clemens),
Winslow Homer,
Presidents
J. Q. Adams
Van Buren
W. H. Harrison
Taylor
Fillmore
Buchanan
A. Johnson
Jackson
Tyler
Polk
Pierce
Lincoln
1825
1829
1837
1841
1845
1849–'50
1853
1857
1861
1865
American Scholars
b. 1785 William Beaumont, doctor and researcher
b. 1797 Joseph Henry, physicist and director of Smithsonian
Francis Parkman, historian of the French in America
Science and the Higher Learning
Electromagnetism research
The Physiology of Digestion
The Conspiracy of Pontiac
National Academy of Science established
1820
1831
1833
1851
1863

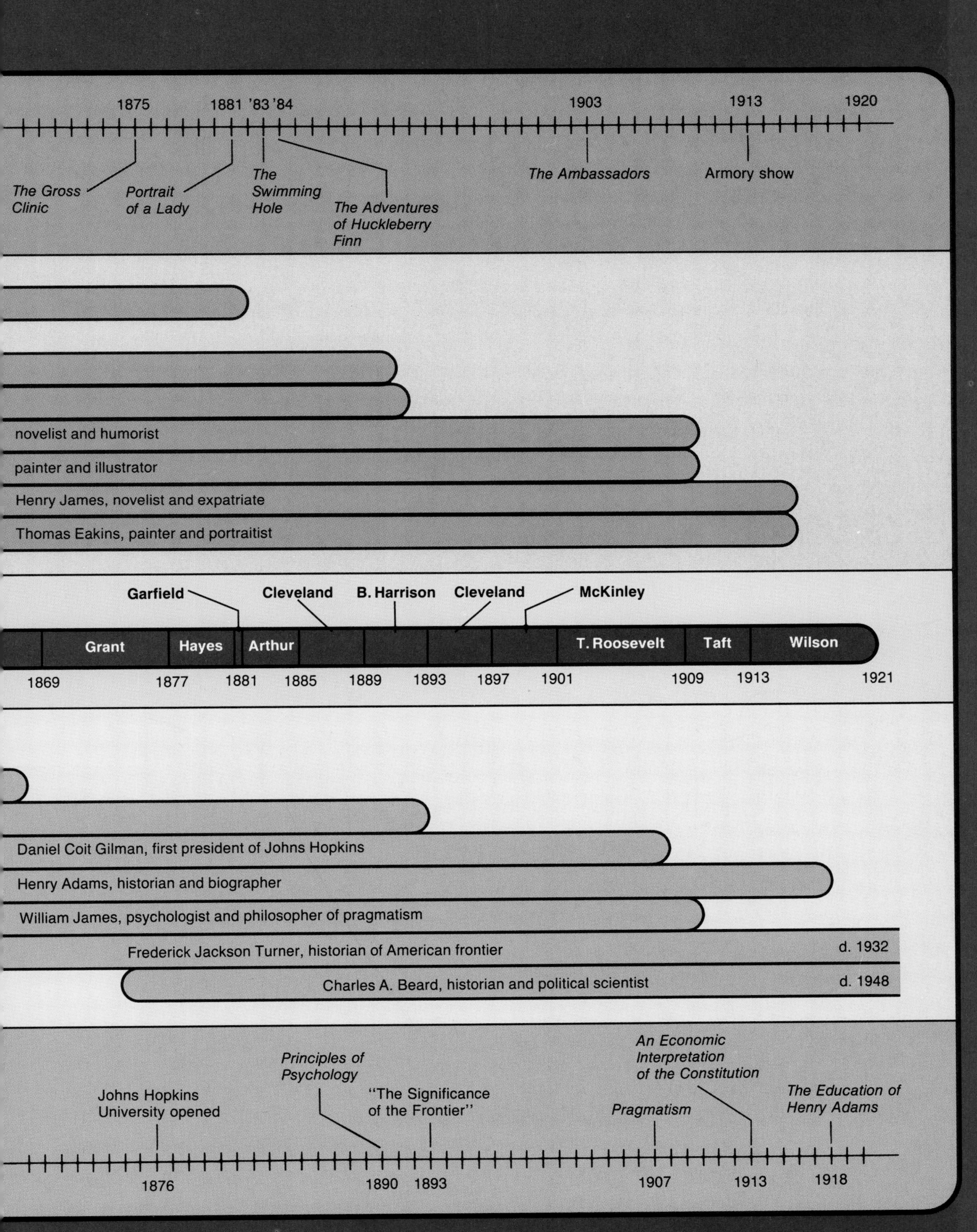
1875
1881
'83
'84
1903
1913
1920
The Gross Clinic
Portrait of a Lady
The Swimming Hole
The Adventures of Huckleberry Finn
The Ambassadors
Armory show
novelist and humorist
painter and illustrator
Henry James, novelist and expatriate
Thomas Eakins, painter and portraitist
Garfield
Cleveland
B. Harrison
Cleveland
McKinley
Grant
Hayes
Arthur
T. Roosevelt
Taft
Wilson
1869
1877
1881
1885
1889
1893
1897
1901
1909
1913
1921
Daniel Coit Gilman, first president of Johns Hopkins
Henry Adams, historian and biographer
William James, psychologist and philosopher of pragmatism
Frederick Jackson Turner, historian of American frontier
d. 1932
Charles A. Beard, historian and political scientist
d. 1948
Johns Hopkins University opened
Principles of Psychology
"The Significance of the Frontier"
Pragmatism
An Economic Interpretation of the Constitution
The Education of Henry Adams
1876
1890
1893
1907
1913
1918

21
National Politics, 1877-1896

"What a pity he is so dreadfully senatorial," said Mrs. Lee. "Otherwise I rather admire him."

"Now he is settling down to his work," continued Carrington. "See how he dodges all the sharp issues. . . . What a genius the fellow has for leading a party." HENRY ADAMS, Democracy, *1880*

Most students of the subject have concluded that the political history of the United States in the last quarter of the 19th century was singularly divorced from the meaningful issues of that day. On the rare occasions that important, supposedly controversial measures such as the Sherman Antitrust Act, the Interstate Commerce Act, the Pendleton Civil Service Act, and the Dawes Severalty Act were debated, they excited far less argument than they merited.

A graduated income tax, the greatest instrument for orderly economic and social change that a democratic society has devised, was enacted during the Civil War, repealed after that conflict, reenacted in 1894 as part of the maneuvering over tariff reform, and then declared unconstitutional in 1895 without causing much more than a ripple in the world of partisan politics. Proponents of the tax argued only that it offered a fairer way of distributing the costs of government, its foes that it penalized efficiency and encouraged government extravagance. Almost no one saw it as a means of redistributing wealth. This was typical; as the English observer James Bryce noted in the late 1880s, the politicians were "clinging too long to outworn issues" and "neglecting to discover and work out new principles capable of solving the problems which now perplex the country." Congress, another critic wrote, "does not solve the problems, the solution of which is demanded by the life of the nation."

Yet the public remained intensely interested in politics. Huge crowds gathered to hear orators mouth hackneyed slogans and meaningless generalities. Most elections were closely contested; millions of voters turned out enthusiastically to choose, essentially, between Tweedledum and Tweedledee.

The American Commonwealth

A succession of weak presidents presided over the White House. Although the impeachment proceedings against Andrew Johnson had failed, Congress dominated the government. "There has not been a single presidential candidate since Abraham Lincoln," Bryce wrote in 1888, "of whom his friends could say that he had done anything to command the gratitude of the nation."

Within Congress, the Senate generally overshadowed the House of Representatives. In his novel *Democracy* (1880), the cynical Henry Adams wrote that the United States had a "government of the people, by the people, for the benefit of Senators." Critics called the Senate a "rich man's club," and it did contain many millionaires, among them Leland Stanford, founder of the Central Pacific Railroad; James G. "Bonanza" Fair of Nevada, who extracted a fortune of $30 million from the Comstock Lode; Philetus Sawyer, a self-made Wisconsin lumberman; and Nelson Aldrich of Rhode Island, whose wealth derived from banking and a host of corporate connections. However, the true sources of the Senate's influence lay in the long tenure of many of its members (which enabled them to master the craft of politics), in the fact that it was small enough to encourage real debate, and in its long-established reputation for wisdom, intelligence, and statesmanship.

The House of Representatives, on the other hand, was one of the most disorderly and inefficient legislative bodies in the world. "As I make my notes," a reporter wrote in 1882 while sitting in the House gallery, "I see a dozen men reading newspapers with their feet on their desks. . . . 'Pig-Iron' Kelley of Pennsylvania has dropped his newspaper and is paring his fingernails. . . . The vile odor of . . . tobacco . . . rises from the two-for-five-cents cigars in the mouths of the so-called gentlemen below. . . . They chew, too! Every desk has a spittoon of pink and gold china beside it to catch the filth from the statesman's mouth."

An infernal din rose from the crowded chamber. Desks slammed; members held private conversations, hailed pages, shuffled from place to place, clamored for the attention of the Speaker—and all the while some poor orator tried to discuss the question of the moment. Speaking in the House, one writer said, was like trying to address the crowd on a passing Broadway bus from the curb in front of the Astor House in New York. On one occasion in 1878 the adjournment of the House was held up for more than 12 hours because most of the members of an important committee were too drunk to prepare a vital appropriations bill for final passage. President Hayes was furious. "*It should be investigated,*" he wrote in his diary.

The great political parties professed undying enmity to each other, but they seldom took clearly

Joseph Keppler's 1890 Puck *cartoon, "None but Millionaires Need Apply—The Coming Style of Presidential Election," comments acidly on the low status of the presidency. The tag* EIGHT PIECES WITH THIS SET *on the chief executive's chair refers to the Cabinet. As the examples in this chapter show, the late 19th century was a heyday for political cartoonists.*

opposing positions on the questions of the day. Democrats were separated from Republicans more by accidents of geography, religious affiliation, ethnic background, and emotion than by economic issues. Questions of state and local importance, unrelated to national politics, often determined the outcome of congressional elections and thus who controlled the federal government.

The fundamental division between Democrats and Republicans was sectional, a result of the Civil War. The South, after the political rights of blacks had been drastically circumscribed, became heavily Democratic. Most of New England was solidly Republican. Elsewhere the two parties stood in fair balance, though the Republicans tended to have the advantage. A preponderance of the well-to-do, cultured northerners were Republicans. Perhaps in reaction to this concentration, immigrants, Catholics, and—except for blacks—other minority groups tended to vote Democratic. But there were so many exceptions that these generalizations are of little practical importance. German and Scandinavian immigrants usually voted Republican; many powerful business leaders supported the Democrats.

The personalities of political leaders often dictated the voting patterns of individuals and groups. In 1884 J. P. Morgan voted Democratic because he admired Grover Cleveland, while Irish-Americans, traditionally Democrats, cast thousands of ballots for Republican James G. Blaine. In 1892, when Cleveland defeated Benjamin Harrison, a prominent steel manufacturer wrote to Andrew Carnegie: "I am very sorry for President Harrison, but I cannot see that our interests are going to be affected one way or the other." And Carnegie replied: "We have nothing to fear. . . . Cleveland is [a] pretty good fellow. Off for Venice tomorrow."

The bulk of the people—farmers, laborers, shopkeepers, white-collar workers—distributed their ballots fairly evenly between the two parties in most elections; the balance of political power after 1876 was almost perfect—"the most spectacular degree of equilibrium in American history." Between 1856 and 1912 the Democrats elected a president only twice (1884 and 1892), but most contests were extremely close. Majorities in both the Senate and the House fluctuated continually. Between 1876 and 1896, the "dominant" Republican party controlled both houses of Congress and the presidency at the same time for only one two-year period.

Issues of the Gilded Age

Four questions obsessed politicians in these years. One was the "bloody shirt." The term, which became part of the language after a Massachusetts congressman dramatically displayed to his colleagues in the House the bloodstained shirt of an Ohio carpetbagger who had been flogged by terrorists in Mississippi, referred to the tactic of reminding the electorate of the northern states that the men who had taken the South out of the Union and precipitated the Civil War had been Democrats and that they and their descendants were still Democrats. Should their party regain power, former rebels would run the government and undo all the work accomplished at such sacrifice during the war. "Every man that endeavored to tear down the old flag," a Republican orator proclaimed in 1876, "was a Democrat. Every man that tried to destroy this nation was a Democrat. . . . The man that assassinated Abraham Lincoln was a Democrat. . . . Soldiers, every scar you have on your heroic bodies was given you by a Democrat."

Every scoundrel or incompetent who sought office under the Republican banner waved the bloody shirt in order to divert the attention of northern voters from his own shortcomings, and the technique worked so well that many decent candidates could not resist the temptation to employ it in close races. Nothing, of course, so effectively obscured the real issues of the day.

Waving the bloody shirt was related intimately to the issue of the rights of blacks. Throughout this period Republicans vacillated between trying to build up their organization in the South by appealing to black voters—which required them to make sure that blacks in the South could vote—and trying to win conservative white support by stressing economic issues such as the tariff. When the former strategy seemed wise, they waved the bloody shirt with vigor; in the latter case, they piously announced that the blacks' future was "as safe in the hands of one party as it is in the other."

The question of veterans' pensions also bore a close relationship to the bloody shirt. Following the Civil War, Union soldiers founded the Grand Army of the Republic. By 1890 the organization had a membership of 409,000. The GAR put immense pressure on Congress, first for aid to veterans with service-connected disabilities, then for those with *any* disability, and eventually for all former Union soldiers. Republican politicians played on the emotions of the ex-soldiers by waving the bloody shirt, but the tough-minded leaders of the GAR demanded that they prove their sincerity by treating in openhanded fashion the warriors whose blood had stained the shirt.

The tariff was another perennial issue in post–Civil War politics. Despite considerable loose talk about free trade, almost no one in the United States except for a handful of professional economists, most of them college professors, believed in eliminating duties on imports. Manufacturers desired protective tariffs to keep out competing products, and a majority of their workers were convinced that wage levels would fall if goods produced by cheap foreign labor entered the United States untaxed. Many farmers supported protection, though almost no competing agricultural products were being imported. Congressman William McKinley of Ohio, who reputedly could make a tariff schedule sound like poetry, stated the majority opinion in the clearest terms: high tariffs foster the growth of industry and thus create jobs. "Reduce the tariff and labor is the first to suffer," he said. Whatever the professors may say about the virtues of free trade, "the school of experience" teaches that protection is necessary if America is to prosper.

Voters found this reasoning irrefutable. Duties had been raised during the Civil War to an average of about 50 percent ad valorem. Some slight reduc-

Uncle Sam walks the floor with a fretful "Infant Industries," saying "I guess he won't stop howling till I give him enough Protection Soothing Syrup to burst him!" An 1896 Puck *cartoon by Louis Dalrymple.*

tions were made in the 1870s and 1880s, but in 1890 the McKinley tariff restored these cuts. This law even granted protection to a nonexistent industry, the manufacture of tin plate, and to agricultural products, such as eggs and potatoes, that would not have been imported under free trade. When the legislators decided to remove the duty on raw sugar in order to get rid of an embarrassing revenue surplus, they compensated domestic sugar raisers by awarding them a subsidy of 2 cents a pound on their product.

The tariff could have been a real political issue because American technology was advancing so rapidly that many industries no longer required protection from foreign competitors. A powerful argument could have been made for scientific rate making that would adjust duties to actual conditions and avoid overprotection. The Democrats professed to believe in moderation, yet whenever party leaders tried to revise the tariff downward, Democratic congressmen from industrial states like Pennsylvania and New York sided with the Republicans. Many Republicans endorsed tariff reform in principle, but when particular schedules came up for discussion, most of them demanded the highest rates for industries in their own districts and traded votes shamelessly with colleagues representing other interests in order to get what they wanted. Every new tariff bill became an occasion for logrolling, lobbying, and outrageous politicking rather than for sane discussion and careful evaluation of the public interest.

A third political question in this period was currency reform. During the Civil War, it will be recalled, the government, faced with obligations it could not meet by taxing or borrowing, suspended specie payments and issued about $450 million in paper money. The greenbacks did not command the full confidence of a people accustomed to money readily convertible into gold or silver. Greenbacks seemed to threaten inflation, for how could one trust the government not to issue them in wholesale lots to avoid passing unpopular tax laws? Thus, when the war ended, strong sentiment developed for withdrawing the greenbacks from circulation and returning to a bullion standard. "By a law resting on the concurring judgment . . . of mankind in all ages and countries, the precious metals have been the measure of value," one politician wrote. "That law can no more be repealed by act of Congress than the law of gravitation."

At the same time, the nation's burgeoning population and the rapid expansion of every kind of economic activity increased the need for currency. In fact, prices declined sharply after Appomattox. The deflation increased the real income of bondholders and other creditors but injured debtors. Farmers were particularly hard hit, for many of them had borrowed heavily during the wartime boom to finance expansion.

Here was a question of great significance. Many groups supported some kind of currency inflation. A National Greenback party nominated Peter Cooper, an iron manufacturer, for president in 1876. Cooper received only 81,000 votes, but a new Greenback Labor party polled over a million in 1878, electing 14 congressmen. However, the major parties refused to confront each other over the currency question. While Republicans professed to be the party of sound money, most western Republicans favored expansion of the currency. And while one wing of the Democrats flirted with the Greenbackers, the conservative, or "Bourbon" Democrats favored deflation as much as Republicans did.

In 1874 a bill to increase the supply of greenbacks was defeated in a Republican-dominated Congress only by the veto of President Grant. The next year Congress voted to resume specie payments, but in order to avoid a party split on the question, the Republicans agreed to allow $300 million in greenbacks to remain in circulation and to postpone actual resumption of specie payments until 1879.

Spurred on by the silver miners and by those advocating any measure that would increase the volume of money in circulation, numbers of congressmen introduced proposals to coin large amounts of silver. Neither party took a clear-cut stand on silver. Under various administrations steps were taken to increase or decrease the amount of money in circulation, but the net effect on the economy was not significant. Few politicians before 1890 considered fiscal policy as a device for influencing economic development. The effect of all the controversy, in the words of the economist Joseph Schumpeter, was "so light as to justify exclusion from the general analysis of the determining factors of the economic process."

The final major political issue of these years was civil service reform. That the federal bureaucracy needed overhauling nearly everyone agreed.

As American society grew larger and more complex in an industrial age, the government necessarily took on more functions. The need for professional administration increased. The number of federal employees rose from 53,000 in 1871 to 256,000 at the end of the century. Corruption flourished; waste and inefficiency were the normal state of affairs. The collection of tariff duties offered perhaps the greatest opportunity for venality. The New York Custom House, one observer wrote in 1872, teemed with "corrupting merchants and their clerks and runners, who think that all men can be bought, and . . . corrupt swarms [of clerks], who shamelessly seek their price."

With a succession of relatively ineffective presidents and a Congress that squandered its energies on private bills, pork-barrel projects, and other trivia, the administration of the government was monumentally inefficient. "The federal system from Grant through McKinley was generally undistinguished," the historian Leonard D. White concluded after an exhaustive study of the period. "Nobody, whether in Congress or in the executive departments, seemed able to rise much above the handicraft office methods that were cumbersome even in the simpler days of the Jacksonians."

Every honest observer could see the need for reform, but the politicians refused to surrender the power of dispensing government jobs to their lieutenants without regard for their qualifications. They argued that patronage was the lifeblood of politics, that parties could not function without armies of loyal political workers, and that the workers expected and deserved the rewards of office when their efforts were crowned with victory at the polls. Typical was the attitude of the New York assemblyman who, according to Theodore Roosevelt, had "the same idea about Public Life and the Civil Service that a vulture has of a dead sheep." When reformers suggested establishing the most modest kind of professional, nonpartisan civil service, politicians of both parties subjected them to every kind of insult and ridicule even though both the Democratic and Republican parties regularly wrote civil service reform planks into their platforms.

Political Strategy and Tactics

The major American parties have nearly always avoided clear-cut stands on controversial questions in order to appeal to as wide a segment of the electorate as possible, but in the last quarter of the 19th century their equivocations assumed abnormal proportions. This was due in part to the precarious balance of power between them: neither dared declare itself too clearly on any question lest it drive away more voters than it attracted. The rapid pace of social and economic change also militated against political decisiveness. No one in or out of politics had as yet devised effective solutions for many current problems. When party leaders tried to deal with the money question, they discovered that the bankers and the professional economists were as confused as the public at large. "We dabble in theories of our own and clutch convulsively at the doctrines of others," a Philadelphia banker confessed. "From the vast tract of mire by which the subject is surrounded, overlaid, and besmeared, it is almost impossible to arrive at anything like a fair estimate of its real nature." How could mere politicians act rationally or consistently in such circumstances?

The parties stumbled badly when they confronted the tariff problem because tariffs in a complex industrial economy are not susceptible to determination by counting noses. Modern experience has shown that they are better arrived at by impartial boards of experts, once broad policies have been laid down by Congress, but in the 19th century specialists had not yet arrived at this conclusion. Reformers could thunder self-righteously against the spoils system, but how could political parties exist without it? They could denounce laissez faire, but who had devised instruments for social and economic control that could be centrally administered with intelligence and efficiency? The embryonic social sciences had not devised the techniques or even collected the statistical information necessary for efficient social management.

If the politicians steered clear of the "real" issues, they did so as much out of a healthy respect for their own ignorance as out of any desire to avoid controversy. Unable to provide answers to the meaningful questions, they turned to simpler issues that they and their constituents could understand in order to provide the political system with a semblance of purposefulness. Meanwhile, society blindly but steadily accumulated the experience and skills required for dealing with the results of the industrial revolution.

With the Democrats invincible in the South and

the Republicans predominant in New England and most of the states beyond the Mississippi, the outcome of presidential elections was usually determined in a handful of populous states: New York (together with its satellites, New Jersey and Connecticut), Ohio, Indiana, and Illinois. The fact that opinion in these states on important questions such as the tariff and monetary policy was divided goes far to explain why the parties hesitated to commit themselves on issues. In every presidential election Democrats and Republicans concentrated their heaviest guns on these states.

Campaigns were conducted in a carnival atmosphere, entertainment being substituted for serious debate. Large sums were spent on brass bands, barbecues, uniforms, and banners. Speakers of national reputation were imported to attract crowds, and spellbinders noted for their leather lungs—this was before the day of the loudspeaker—and their ability to rouse popular emotions were brought in to address mass meetings. With so much depending on so few, the level of political morality was abysmal. Mudslinging, character assassination, and plain lying were standard practice, bribery routine. Drifters and other dissolute citizens were paid in cash—or more often in free drinks—to vote the party ticket. The names of persons long dead were solemnly inscribed in voting registers, their suffrages exercised by impostors. Since both parties indulged in these tactics, their efforts often canceled one another, yet in some instances presidents were made and unmade in this sordid fashion.

The Men in the White House

The leading statesmen of the period showed as little interest in important contemporary questions as the party hacks who made up the rank and file of their organizations. Consider the presidents.

Rutherford B. Hayes, president from 1877 to 1881, came to office with a distinguished record. Born in Delaware, Ohio, in 1822, he attended Kenyon College and the Harvard Law School before settling down to practice in Cincinnati. Although he had a family to support, he volunteered for service within weeks after the first shell fell on Fort Sumter. "This [is] a just and necessary war," he wrote in his diary. "I would prefer to go into it if I knew I was to die . . . than to live through and after it without taking any part."

Hayes fought bravely, even recklessly, through nearly four years of war. He was wounded at South Mountain on the eve of Antietam, and later he served under Sheridan in the Shenandoah Valley campaign of 1864. Entering the army as a major, he emerged a major general. In 1864 he was elected to Congress; four years later he became governor of Ohio, serving three terms altogether. The Republicans nominated him for president in 1876 because of his reputation for honesty and moderation, and his election, made possible by the Compromise of 1877, seemed to presage an era of sectional harmony and political probity.

Hayes was a long-faced man with deep-set blue eyes, a large nose, a broad, smooth forehead, and a full beard. Outwardly he had a sunny disposition; inwardly, in his own words, he was sometimes "nervous to the point of disaster." Despite his geniality, he was utterly without political glamour. Politically temperate and cautious, he had never been a vigorous waver of the bloody shirt, though in the heat of a hard campaign he was not above urging others to stress the dangers of "rebel rule" should the Democrats win. He played down the tariff issue whenever possible, favoring protection in principle but refusing to become a mere spokesman for local interests. On the money question he was conservative. He cheerfully approved the resumption of gold payments in 1879 and vetoed bills to expand the currency by coining silver. He accounted himself a civil service reformer, appointing Carl Schurz, a leader of the movement, to his Cabinet. He opposed the collection of political contributions from federal officeholders and issued an order forbidding them "to take part in the management of political organizations, caucuses, conventions, or election campaigns."

Hayes was a president in the Whig tradition. He saw himself more as a caretaker than a leader and believed that Congress should assume the main responsibility for solving national problems. According to a recent biographer, "he had no intention of . . . trying to be a President in the heroic mold," and another historian writes that he showed "no capacity for such large-minded leadership as might have tamed the political hordes and aroused the enthusiasm, or at least the interest, of the public."

In this 1880 campaign lithograph by Currier & Ives, "Farmer Garfield" uses a scythe made of honesty, ability, and patriotism to cut a swath to the White House through brush infested by snakes with names like Falsehood and Malice. One snake bears the countenance of Garfield's predecessor, Hayes.

Hayes hated having to make decisions on controversial questions. He complained about the South's failure to treat blacks decently after the withdrawal of federal troops, but he took no action. He worked harder for civil service reform yet failed to achieve the "thorough, rapid and complete" change he had promised. In this as in most other matters, he was content to "let the record show that he had made the requests."

In the eyes of contemporaries the Hayes administration was a failure. Neither he nor they seriously considered him for a second term. "I am not liked as President," he confessed to his diary, and the Republican minority leader of the House admitted that the president was "almost without a friend" in Congress.

Hayes's successor, James A. Garfield, was cut down by an assassin's bullet four months after his inauguration. Even in that short time, however, his ineffectiveness had been demonstrated. Garfield grew up in poverty on an Ohio farm. He was only 29 when the Civil War broke out, but he helped organize a volunteer regiment and soon proved himself a fine disciplinarian and an excellent battlefield commander. He fought at Shiloh and later at Chickamauga, where he was General William S. Rosecrans's chief of staff. He rose in two years from lieutenant colonel to major general. In 1863 he won a seat in Congress, where his oratorical and managerial skills brought him to prominence in the affairs of the Republican party.

Garfield was a big, broad-shouldered man, balding, with sharp eyes, an aquiline nose, and a full beard. Studious, industrious, with a wide-ranging, well-stocked mind, he was called by one friend "the ideal self-made man." His great weakness was indecisiveness—what another of his admirers described as a "want of certainty" and a "deference for other men's opinions." As President Hayes put it, Garfield "could not face a frowning world. . . . His course at various times when trouble came betrayed weakness."

Like many ex-soldiers, including Hayes and even General Ulysses S. Grant, Garfield did not enjoy waving the bloody shirt, but when hard pressed politically—as when his name was linked with the Crédit Mobilier railroad scandal—he would lash out at the South in an effort to distract the voters. In theory he was inclined toward low tariffs. "The scholarship of modern times," he said in 1870, "is . . . leading in the direction of what is called free trade." Nevertheless, he would not sacrifice the interests of Ohio manufacturers for a mere principle. "I shall not admit to a considerable reduction of a few leading articles in which my constituents are deeply interested when many others of a similar character are left untouched," he declared. Similarly, though eager to improve the efficiency of the government and resentful of the "intellectual dissipation" resulting from time wasted listening to the countless appeals of office seekers, he often wilted under pressure from the spoilsmen. Only on fiscal policy did he take a firm stand: he opposed categorically all inflationary schemes.

Political patronage proved to be Garfield's undoing. The Republican party in 1880 was split into two factions, the "Stalwarts" and the "Half-Breeds." The Stalwarts, led by the New York politico Senator Roscoe Conkling, believed in the blatant pursuit of the spoils of office. The Half-Breeds did not disagree but behaved more circumspectly, hoping to attract the support of independents. Competition for office was the main reason for their rivalry.

Garfield had been a compromise choice at the 1880 Republican convention. His election precipitated a great battle over patronage, the new president standing in a sort of no-man's-land between the factions. "I am considering all day whether A or B shall be appointed to this or that office," he moaned. "Once or twice I felt like crying out in the agony of my soul against the greed for office and its consumption of my time." Soon he was complaining to his secretary of state: "My God! What is there in this place that a man should ever want to get into it?"

Garfield did stand up to the most grasping politicians, resisting in particular the demands of Senator Conkling. By backing the investigation of a post office scandal, and by appointing a Half-Breed collector of the Port of New York, he infuriated the Stalwarts. In July 1881 an unbalanced Stalwart lawyer named Charles J. Guiteau, who had been haunting Washington offices in search of a consulship or some other post, shot Garfield in the Washington railroad station. After lingering for weeks, the president died on September 19.

The assassination of Garfield elevated Chester A. Arthur to the presidency. Arthur was born in Vermont in 1829. After graduating from Union College, he studied law and settled in New York City. An abolitionist, he became an early convert to the Republican party and rose rapidly in its local councils. In 1871 Grant gave him the juiciest political plum in the country, the collectorship of the Port of New York, which he held until removed by Hayes in 1878 for refusing to keep his hands out of party politics.

The only elective position that Arthur had ever held was the vice-presidency. Before Garfield's death he had paid little attention to questions like the tariff and monetary policy, being content to take in fees ranging upward of $50,000 a year as collector of the port and to oversee the operations of the New York customs office, with its hordes of clerks and laborers. (During Arthur's tenure, the novelist Herman Melville was employed as an "outdoor inspector" by the Custom House.) Of course Arthur was an unblushing defender of the spoils system, though in fairness it must be said that he was personally honest and an excellent administrator.

The tragic circumstances of his elevation to the presidency sobered Arthur considerably. Although he was a genial, convivial man, perhaps overly fond of good food and flashy clothes, he comported himself with great dignity as president. He did not cut his ties with the Stalwart faction, but he handled patronage matters with restraint. He continued the investigation of the post office scandals over the objections of important Republican politicians who were involved in them, and he gave at least nominal support to the movement for civil service reform, which had been strengthened by the public indignation following the assassination of Garfield. In 1883 Congress passed the Pendleton Act, "classifying" about 10 percent of all government jobs and creating a bipartisan Civil Service Commission to prepare and administer competitive examinations for these positions. The law made it illegal to force officeholders to make political contributions and empowered the president to expand the list of classified positions at his discretion.

While many politicians resented the new system—one senator denounced it as "un-American"—the Pendleton Act opened a new era in government administration. The results have been summed up by the historian Ari Hoogenboom: "An unprofessional civil service became more professionalized. Better-educated civil servants were recruited and society accorded them a higher place. . . . Local political considerations gave way in civil servants' minds to the national concerns of a federal office. Business influence and ideals replaced those of the politician."

Arthur also took a moderate position on the tariff. He urged the appointment of a nonpartisan commission to study existing rates and to suggest rational reductions; when such a commission was created, he urged Congress to adopt its recommendations. He came out for federal regulation of railroads several years before the passage of the Interstate Commerce Act. "Congress should protect the people . . . against acts of injustice which the State governments are powerless to prevent," he said. He vetoed pork-barrel legislation and pushed for the much-needed construction of a modern navy.

As an administrator Arthur was systematic, thoughtful, businesslike, and at the same time cheerful and considerate. Just the same, he too was a political failure. He made no real attempt to push his program through Congress, instead devoting most of his energies to a futile effort to build up his personal following in the Republican party by distributing favors. But the Stalwarts would not forgive his "desertion," and the reform element could not forget his past. At the 1884 convention the politicos shunted him aside.

The election of 1884 brought the Democrat Grover Cleveland to the White House. Born in New Jersey in 1837, Cleveland grew up in western New York. After studying law, he settled in Buffalo. While somewhat lacking in the social graces and in intellectual pretensions, he had a basic integrity that everyone recognized; when a group of reformers sought a candidate for mayor in 1881, he was a natural choice. His success in Buffalo led to his election as governor of New York in 1882. In the governor's chair his no-nonsense attitude toward public administration endeared him to civil service reformers at the same time that his basic conservatism pleased businessmen. When he vetoed a popular bill to force a reduction of the fares charged by the New York City elevated railway on the ground that it was an unconstitutional violation of the company's franchise, his stock soared. Here was a man who cared more for principle than the adulation of the multitude, a man of courage, honest, hardworking, and eminently sound. The Democrats nominated him for president in 1884.

The election revolved around personal issues, for the platforms of the parties were almost identical. The Republican candidate, the dynamic James G. Blaine, had an immense following, but his reputation had been soiled by the publication of the "Mulligan letters," which connected him with the corrupt granting of congressional favors to the Little Rock and Fort Smith Railroad. On the other hand, it came out during the campaign that Cleveland, a bachelor, had fathered an illegitimate child. Instead of debating public issues, the Republicans chanted the ditty

Ma! Ma! Where's my pa?
Gone to the White House,
Ha! Ha! Ha!

to which the Democrats countered

Blaine, Blaine, James G. Blaine,
The continental liar from the State of Maine.

Blaine lost more heavily in the mudslinging than Cleveland, whose quiet courage in saying "Tell the truth" when his past was brought to light contrasted favorably with Blaine's glib and unconvincing denials. A significant group of distinguished eastern Republicans, known as Mugwumps, campaigned for the Democrats.* However, Blaine ran a strong race against a general pro-Democratic trend; Cleveland won the election by fewer than 25,000 votes. The change of 600 ballots in New York would have given that state, and the presidency, to his opponent.

* The Mugwumps considered themselves reformers, but on social and economic questions nearly all of them were very conservative. They were sound-money proponents and advocates of laissez faire. Reform to them consisted almost entirely of doing away with corruption and making the government more efficient.

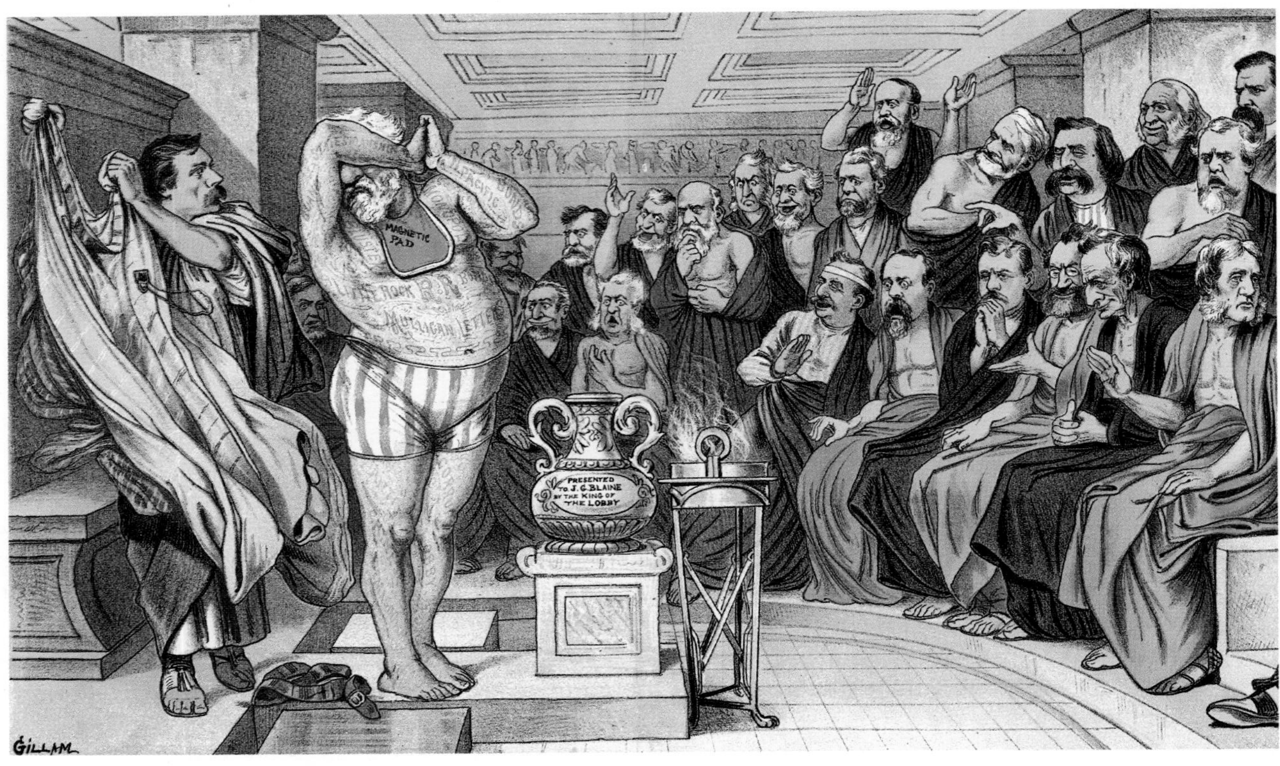

Parodying a popular painting of the day depicting a beautiful Greek courtesan being unveiled before Athenian statesmen, Puck's *Bernhard Gillam drew James G. Blaine revealed to Republican leaders in 1884. The "Mulligan letters" receive prominent display among the tattoos, and Blaine's renowned personal magnetism is labeled as a fraud.*

As a Democrat, Cleveland had no stomach for refighting the Civil War in every campaign. He did not overly favor the South when in office, thereby quieting Republican fears that a Democratic administration would fill Washington with unreconstructed rebels. Civil service reformers overestimated his commitment to their cause, for he believed in rotation in office, being as convinced as Andrew Jackson that anyone of "reasonable intelligence" could handle most government jobs. He would not summarily dismiss Republicans, but he thought that when they had served four years, they "should as a rule give way to good men of our party." He did, however, insist on honesty and efficiency regardless of party. As a result, he made few poor appointments.

Probably no president could have handled patronage problems much better, considering the times. The Democrats had been out of the White House since before the Civil War. They clamored for the spoils of victory. The Mugwumps, who had contributed considerably to Cleveland's election, were dead set against politicking with government jobs. Steering a middle course, Cleveland failed to satisfy either group.

Cleveland had little imagination and too narrow a conception of his powers and duties to be a successful president. His appearance perfectly reflected his character: a squat, burly man weighing well over 200 pounds, he could defend a position against heavy odds, yet his mind lacked flexibility and he provided little effective leadership. He took a fairly broad view of the powers of the federal government—he supported the Interstate Commerce Act and agricultural research, and he even came out for federal arbitration of labor disputes—

but he thought it unseemly to put pressure on Congress, believing in "the entire independence of the executive and legislative branches."

As a mayor and a governor, Cleveland had been best known for his vetoes. Little wonder that he found being president a burdensome duty. Scarcely a year after his inauguration he was complaining of the "cursed constant grind." Later he grumbled about "the want of rest" and "the terrible nagging" he had to submit to. One of his biographers says that he "approached the presidency as though he were a martyr."

Toward the end of his term, Cleveland bestirred himself and tried to provide constructive leadership on the tariff question. The government was embarrassed by a large surplus revenue, which Cleveland hoped to reduce by cutting the duties on necessities and on raw materials used in manufacturing. He devoted his entire annual message of December 1887 to the tariff, thereby focusing public attention on the subject. When worried Democrats reminded him that an election was coming up and that the tariff might cause a rift in the organization, he replied simply: "What is the use of being elected or re-elected, unless you stand for something?"

The House of Representatives, dominated by southern Democrats, passed a bill reducing many duties, but the measure, known as the Mills bill, was flagrantly partisan: it slashed the rates on iron products, glass, wool, and other items made in the North and left those on southern goods almost untouched. The Republican-controlled Senate rejected the Mills bill, and the issue was left to be settled by the voters at the 1888 election. However, in a fashion typical of the period, it did not work out this way. The Democrats hedged by nominating a protectionist, 75-year-old Allen G. Thurman, for vice-president and putting another high-tariff man at the head of the Democratic National Committee. Cleveland toned down his attacks on the important protected industries.

Other issues attracted attention. In the "Murchison letter," Sir Lionel Sackville-West, the British minister at Washington, was tricked into expressing the opinion that the reelection of Cleveland would best advance the interests of Great Britain. This undoubtedly cost the Democrats the votes of many Irish-Americans, who were rabidly anti-British. Corruption was perhaps more flagrant than in any other presidential election. Cleveland obtained a plurality of the popular vote, but his opponent, Benjamin Harrison, grandson of President William Henry Harrison, carried most of the key northeastern industrial states by narrow margins, thereby obtaining a comfortable majority in the electoral college, 233 to 168.

The new president was a short, rather rotund but erect man with a full, graying beard, narrow blue eyes, and a broad forehead. Although intelligent and able, he was too reserved to make a good politician. He did not suffer fools gladly and kept even his most important advisers at arm's length. One observer called him a "human iceberg." Nevertheless, his career, like his ancestry, had been distinguished. After graduating from Miami University in 1852 at the age of 18, he studied law. He settled in Indiana, where for a number of years

A portrait of Grover Cleveland by the artist Anders Zorn. The well-fed look was the trademark of most politicians of that era.

he was Indiana Supreme Court reporter, editing five volumes of *Reports* with considerable skill. During the Civil War he rose to command a brigade. He fought under Sherman at Atlanta and won a reputation as a stern, effective disciplinarian. In 1876 he ran unsuccessfully for governor of Indiana, but in 1881 he was elected to the Senate.

Harrison believed ardently in the principle of protection, stating firmly if illogically that he was against "cheaper costs" because cheaper costs seemed "necessarily to involve a cheaper man and woman under the coat." His approach to fiscal policy was conservative, though he was freehanded in the matter of veterans' pensions. He would not use "an apothecary's scale," he said, "to weigh the rewards of men who saved the country." No more flamboyant waver of the bloody shirt existed. "I would a thousand times rather march under the bloody shirt, stained with the lifeblood of a Union soldier," he said in 1883, "than to march under the black flag of treason or the white flag of cowardly compromise."

Harrison professed to favor civil service reform, but his biographer, Father Harry J. Sievers, admits that he fashioned a "singularly unimpressive" record on the question. He objected to the law forbidding the solicitation of campaign funds from officeholders. He appointed the vigorous young reformer Theodore Roosevelt to the Civil Service Commission and then proceeded to undercut him systematically. Before long the frustrated Roosevelt was calling the president a "cold blooded, narrow minded, prejudiced, obstinate, timid old psalm singing Indianapolis politician."

Under Harrison, Congress distinguished itself by expending, for the first time in a period of peace, more than $1 billion in a single session. It raised the tariff to an all-time high. The Sherman Antitrust Act was passed; so was a Silver Purchase Act authorizing the government to coin large amounts of that metal, a measure much desired by mining interests and those favoring inflation. A Federal Elections, or "Force" bill, providing for federal control of elections as a means of protecting the right of southern blacks to vote, a right increasingly under attack, passed the House only to be filibustered to death in the Senate.

Harrison had little to do with the fate of any of these measures. By and large he failed, as one historian has said, to give the people "magnetic and responsive leadership." The Republicans lost control of Congress in 1890, and two years later Grover Cleveland swept back into power, defeating Harrison by more than 350,000 votes.

Congressional Leaders

Among the lesser politicians of the period, the most outstanding was unquestionably James G. Blaine of Maine, who served in Congress from 1863 to 1881, first in the House and then in the Senate. Blaine had many of the qualities that mark a great leader: personal dynamism, imagination, political intuition, oratorical ability, and a broad view of the national interest. President Lincoln spotted him when he was a freshman congressman, calling him "one of the brightest men in the House" and "one of the coming men of the country."

Blaine was essentially a reasonable man. He favored sound money without opposing inflexibly every suggestion for increasing the volume of the currency. He supported the protective system yet advocated reciprocity agreements to increase trade. He adopted a moderate and tolerant attitude toward the South. Almost alone among the men of his generation, he was deeply interested in foreign affairs. His personal warmth captivated thousands. He never forgot a name. His handshake—he would grasp a visitor's hand firmly at a reception and often hold it throughout a brief conversation with unaffected, open friendliness—won him hundreds of adherents. This was perhaps calculated, yet he was capable of impulsive acts of generosity and kindness too.

That Blaine, though perennially an aspirant, never became president was in part a reflection of his very abilities and his participation in so many controversial affairs. Naturally, he aroused jealousies and made many enemies. But some inexplicable flaw marred his character. He had a streak of recklessness entirely out of keeping with his reasonable position on most issues. He waved the bloody shirt with cynical vigor, heedless of the effect on the nation as a whole. He showered contempt on civil service reformers, characterizing them as "noisy but not numerous . . . ambitious but not wise, pretentious but not powerful." The scandal of the Mulligan letters made a dark blot on his record, and there is reason to doubt his general honesty, for, as one historian has pointed out, he "became wealthy without visible means of support." Sometimes he seemed almost deliberately to injure himself by needlessly antagonizing powerful colleagues. Blaine moved though history amid cheers and won a host of spectacular if petty triumphs, yet his career was barren, essentially tragic.

Roscoe Conkling's was another remarkable but empty career. Handsome, colorful, companionable, and dignified, Conkling served in Congress almost continuously from 1859 to 1881 and was a great power, dominating the complex politics of New York for many years. Such was his prestige that two presidents offered him a seat on the Supreme Court. Yet no measure of importance was attached to his name; he squandered his energies in acrimonious personal quarrels, caring only for partisan advantage. While he wanted very much to be president, he had no conception of what a president must be, and in the end even his own hack followers deserted him.

Dozens of other figures might be mentioned; the following are representative types.

Congressman William McKinley of Ohio was the most personally attractive. He was a man of simple honesty, nobility of character, quiet warmth—and a politician to the core. The tariff was McKinley's special competence, the principle of protection his guiding star. The peak of his career still lay in the future in the early 1890s.

Another Ohioan, John Sherman, brother of the famous Civil War general, accomplished the remarkable feat of holding national office continuously for nearly half a century, from 1855 to 1898. Three times a prominent candidate for the Republican presidential nomination, he had a deserved reputation for expertise in financial matters. However, he was colorless and stiff—he was called the Ohio Icicle—and altogether too willing to compromise his beliefs for political advantage. He admired Andrew Johnson and sympathized with his attitude toward reconstructing the South, yet he voted to convict him at the impeachment trial. Repeatedly he made concessions to the inflationists despite his belief in sound money. Sherman gave his name (and not much else) to the Antitrust Act of 1890 and to other important legislation, but in retrospect he left little mark on the history of the country despite his long service.

Thomas B. Reed, Republican congressman from Maine, was a witty, widely read man but ultraconservative and cursed with a sharp tongue that he could never curb. Reed coined the famous definition of a statesman: "a politician who is dead." When one pompous politico said in his presence that he would rather be right than president, Reed advised him not to worry, since he would never be either. In 1890 Reed was elected Speaker of the House and quickly won the nickname Czar because of his autocratic way of expediting business. Since the Republicans had only a paper-thin majority, the Democrats attempted to block action on partisan measures by refusing to answer to their names on quorum calls. Reed coolly ordered the clerk to record them as present and proceeded to carry on the business of the House. His control became so absolute that Washington jokesters said that representatives dared not breathe without his permission. Reed had large ambitions and the courage of his convictions, but his vindictiveness kept him from exercising a constructive influence on his times.

One of the most attractive Democratic politicians of the era was Richard P. "Silver Dick" Bland of Missouri, congressman from 1873 until the late 1890s. While a young man Bland had spent ten years as a prospector and miner, and he devoted most of his energies in politics to fighting for the free coinage of silver. Although almost fanatical on this question, he was no mere mouthpiece for special interests; he fought monopolies and consistently opposed the protective tariff. He lived simply and was immune to the temptations that led so many colleagues to use their political influence to line their pockets. Yet he never became a truly national leader.

More colorful yet utterly sterile was the career of Benjamin F. Butler of Massachusetts. Butler was a political chameleon. A states' rights Democrat before the Civil War, he supported Jefferson Davis for the Democratic presidential nomination in 1860. During the conflict he served as a Union general, during reconstruction as a Radical Republican congressman. In 1878 he came out for currency inflation and won a seat in Congress as a Greenbacker. In 1882 he was elected governor of Massachusetts, this time as a Democrat! Butler had a sharp wit, a vivid imagination, and a real feeling for the interests of industrial workers. He detested sham and pretense. He was also a brutal, corrupt demagogue, almost universally hated by persons of culture and public spirit. By no means a typical politician, Butler typified many aspects of the age—its shaky morality, its extremism, its intense interest in meaningless political controversy.

Agricultural Discontent

The vacuity of American politics may well have stemmed from the complacency of the middle-class majority. The country was growing; no foreign enemy threatened it; the poor were mostly recent immigrants, blacks, and others with little influence, who were easily ignored by those in comfortable circumstances. However, one important group in society suffered increasingly as the years rolled by: the farmers. Out of their travail came the force that finally, in the 1890s, brought American politics face-to-face with the problems of the age.

Long the backbone of American society, the farmer was rapidly being left behind in the race for wealth and status. The number of farmers and the volume of agricultural production continued to rise, but agriculture's relative place in the national economy was declining. Between 1860 and 1890 the number of farms rose from 2 million to 4.5 million; wheat output leaped from 173 million bushels to 449 million, cotton from 5.3 million bales to 8.5 million. The rural population increased from 25 million to 40.8 million. Yet industry was expanding far faster, and the urban population, quadrupling in the period, would soon overtake and pass that of the countryside. Immediately after the Civil War, wheat sold at nearly $1.50 a bushel, and in the early 1870s it was still worth well over a dollar. By the mid-1890s the average price stood in the neighborhood of 60 cents. Cotton, the great southern staple, which sold for more than 30 cents a pound in 1866 and 15 cents in the early 1870s, at times in the 1890s fell below 6 cents.

The tariff on manufactured goods appeared to aggravate the farmers' predicament, and so did the domestic marketing system, which enabled a multitude of middlemen to gobble up a large share of the profits of agriculture. The shortage of credit, particularly in the South, was an additional burden. Furthermore, the improvements in transportation that made it practicable for farmers in Australia, Canada, Russia, and Argentina to sell their produce in western European markets increased the competition faced by Americans seeking to dispose of surplus produce abroad.

Along with declining income, farmers suffered a decline in status. Compared to city dwellers, they seemed provincial and behind the times. Rural educational standards did not keep pace; modern concepts such as evolution were either ignored or rejected, and religious fundamentalism, cast aside by eastern sophisticates, maintained its hold in the countryside. People in the cities began to refer to farmers as "rubes," "hicks," and "hayseeds" and to view them with amused tolerance or even contempt.

This combination of circumstances angered and frustrated farmers. Waves of radicalism swept the agricultural regions, giving rise to demands for social and economic experiments that played a major role in breaking down rural laissez faire prejudices. As we have seen, in the 1870s pressure from the Patrons of Husbandry produced legislation regulating railroads and warehouses. This Granger movement also led to many cooperative experiments in the marketing of farm products and in the purchase of machinery, fertilizers, and other goods.

Farmers were not all affected by economic developments in the same way. Because of the steady decline of the price level, those in newly settled regions were usually worse off than those in older areas, since they had to borrow money to get started and were therefore burdened with fixed interest charges that became harder to meet each year. In the 1870s farmers in Illinois and Iowa suffered most—which accounts for the strength of the Granger movement in that region. Except as a purely social organization, the Grange had little importance in eastern states where farmers were relatively prosperous. However, by the late 1880s farmers in the old Middle West had become better established. When prices dipped and a general depression gripped the country, they were able to weather the bad times nicely, as Allan G. Bogue has shown. Illinois farmers took advantage of the new technology to increase output, shifting from wheat to the production of corn, oats, hogs, and cattle, which did not decline so drastically in price.

On the agricultural frontier from Texas to the Dakotas, and through the states of the old Confederacy, farmers were less fortunate. The burdens of the crop-lien system (see pages 471–472) kept

The western land boom reached a climax on April 22, 1889, when parts of Oklahoma were opened to settlers. Within a few hours, nearly 2 million acres were claimed by hordes of "boomers." This photograph was taken a few weeks later in the boom town of Guthrie, whose sign painter was working overtime.

thousands of southern farmers in penury. On the plains life was a succession of hardships—the back-breaking labor; the hazards of storm, drought, and insect plagues; and isolation and loneliness. Hamlin Garland, a writer of the naturalist school who grew up in the region, described conditions in graphic and moving terms in his autobiography, *A Son of the Middle Border* (1890), and in *Main-Travelled Roads* (1891). Life was particularly hard for farm women, who in addition to endless heavy chores were forced to endure drab, cheerless surroundings without the companionship of neighbors or the respites and stimulations of social life. After Garland's mother read the grim discussions of women's lot in *Main-Travelled Roads,* she wrote him: "You might have said more, but I'm glad you didn't. Farmers' wives have enought to bear as it is."

Throughout the mid-1880s farmers on the plains experienced boom conditions. Adequate rainfall produced bountiful harvests, credit was available, and property values rose rapidly. In the 1880s the population of Kansas increased by 43 percent, that of Nebraska by 134 percent, that of the Dakotas by 278 percent. This agricultural expansion contributed to the destruction of open-range cattle raising and changed the economy of cattle towns like Dodge City, which came to depend more on farmers than on cowboys and ranchers for business.

Speculative booms occur periodically in every frontier district; like all others, this one collapsed when settlers and investors took a more realistic look at the prospects of the region. In this case special circumstances turned the slump into a catastrophe. A succession of dry years shattered the hopes of the farmers. Then the downward swing of the business cycle in the early 1890s completed the devastation. Settlers who had paid more for their lands than they were worth and borrowed money at high interest rates to do so found themselves squeezed relentlessly. Thousands lost their farms and returned eastward, penniless and dispirited. The population of Nebraska increased by fewer than 4,000 persons in the entire decade of the 1890s.

The Populist Movement

The agricultural depression triggered a new outburst of farm radicalism, the Alliance movement. Alliances were organizations of farmers' clubs, most of which had sprung up during the bad times of the late 1870s. The first "Knights of Reliance" was founded in 1877 in Lampasas County, Texas. Under the name The Farmers Alliance this organization gradually expanded in northeastern Texas, and after 1885 it spread rapidly throughout the cotton states. Alliance leaders stressed cooperation. Their co-ops bought fertilizer and other supplies in bulk and sold them at fair prices to members. They sought to market their crops cooperatively but could not raise the necessary capital from banks—with the result that some of them began to question the workings of the American financial and monetary system. They became economic and social radicals in the process. In the northern regions a similar though less influential alliance movement developed.

The alliances adopted somewhat differing policies, but all agreed that agricultural prices were too low, that transportation costs were too high, and that something was radically wrong with the nation's financial system. "There are three great crops raised in Nebraska," an angry rural editor proclaimed in 1890. "One is a crop of corn, one is a crop of freight rates, and one a crop of interest. One is produced by farmers who by sweat and toil farm the land. The other two are produced by men who sit in their offices and behind their bank counters and farm the farmers." All agreed on the need for political action if the lot of the agriculturalist was to be improved.

Although the state alliances of the Dakotas and Kansas joined the Southern Alliance in 1889, for a time local prejudices and conflicting interests prevented the formation of a single national organization. Northern farmers mostly voted Republican, southerners Democratic, and resentments created during the Civil War lingered in all sections. Cotton-producing southerners opposed the protective tariff; most northerners, fearing the competition of foreign grain producers, favored it. Railroad regulation and federal land policy seemed vital questions to northerners; financial reform loomed most important in southern eyes. Northerners were receptive to the idea of forming a third party, while southerners, wedded to the one-party system, preferred working to capture local Democratic machines.

The farm groups entered local politics in the 1890 elections. Convinced of the righteousness of their cause, they campaigned with tremendous fervor. The results were encouraging. In the South, Alliance-sponsored gubernatorial candidates won in Georgia, Tennessee, South Carolina, and Texas; 8 southern legislatures fell under Alliance control; 44 congressmen and 3 senators committed to Alliance objectives were sent to Washington. In the West, Alliance candidates swept Kansas and captured a majority in the Nebraska legislature and enough seats in Minnesota and South Dakota to hold the balance of power between the major parties.

Such success, coupled with the reluctance of the Republicans and Democrats to make concessions to their demands, encouraged Alliance leaders to create a new national party. By uniting southern and western farmers, they succeeded in breaking the sectional barrier erected by the Civil War. If they could recruit industrial workers, perhaps a real political revolution could be accomplished. In February 1892, farm leaders, representatives of the Knights of Labor, and various professional reformers, some 800 in all, met at St. Louis, organized the People's, or Populist party, and issued a call for a national convention to meet at Omaha in July.

That convention nominated General James B. Weaver of Iowa for president (with a one-legged Confederate veteran as his running mate) and drafted a platform that called for a graduated income tax and national ownership of railroads and the telegraph and telephone systems. A "subtreasury" plan that would permit farmers to hold nonperishable crops off the market when prices were low was also advocated. Under this proposal the government would make loans in the form of greenbacks to farmers, secured by crops held in storage in federal warehouses. When prices rose, the farmers could sell their crops and repay the loans. To further combat deflation, the platform demanded the unlimited coinage of silver and an increase in the money supply "to no less than $50 per capita." To make the government more responsive to public opinion, it urged the adoption of the initiative and referendum procedures and the election of United States senators by popular vote. To win the support of industrial workers the platform denounced the use of Pinkerton detectives in labor disputes and backed the eight-hour day and the restriction of "undesirable" immigration.

The Populists created, in the phrase of the historian Lawrence Goodwyn, "a multi-sectional institution of reform." They were not, however, revolutionaries. They saw themselves not as a persecuted minority but as a victimized majority betrayed by what would now be called the establishment. They were at most ambivalent about the free enterprise system, and they tended to attribute social and economic injustices not to built-in inequities in the system but to nefarious conspiracies organized by selfish interests in order to subvert the system.

The appearance of the new party was the most exciting and significant aspect of the presidential campaign of 1892, which saw Harrison and Cleveland refighting the election of 1888. The Populists put forth a host of colorful spellbinders: Tom Watson, a Georgia congressman whose temper was such that on one occasion he administered a beating to a local planter with the man's own riding crop; William A. Peffer, a senator from Kansas whose long beard and grave demeanor gave him the look of a Hebrew prophet; "Sockless Jerry" Simpson of Kansas, unlettered but full of grassroots shrewdness and wit, a former Greenbacker and an admirer of the Single Tax Doctrine of Henry George; Ignatius Donnelly, "the Minnesota Sage," who claimed to be an authority on science, Shakespeare (he believed that Francis Bacon wrote the plays), and economics, and whose widely read novel, *Caesar's Column* (1891), pictured an America of the future wherein a handful of plutocrats tyrannized masses of downtrodden workers and serfs.

In the one-party South, Populist strategists sought to wean black farmers away from the ruling Democratic organization. Their competition forced the "subsidies" paid for black votes up to as much as a dollar—two days' wages. Southern black farmers had their own Colored Alliance, and even before 1892 their leaders had worked closely with the white alliances. Nearly 100 black delegates had attended the Populist convention at St. Louis. Of course the blacks would be useless to the party if they could not vote; therefore white Populist leaders opposed the southern trend toward disfranchising blacks and called for full civil rights for all.

Mary Elizabeth Lease was a prominent Populist noted for her rallying cry to "raise less corn and more hell."

In the Northwest the Populists assailed the "bankers' conspiracy" in unbridled terms. Ignatius Donnelly, running for governor of Minnesota, wrote another futuristic political novel, *The Golden Bottle,* made 150 speeches, and talked personally with 10,000 voters, vowing to make the campaign "the liveliest ever seen" in the state.

The results proved disappointing. Tom Watson lost his seat in Congress, and Donnelly ran a poor third in the Minnesota gubernatorial race. The Populists did sweep Kansas. They elected numbers of local officials in other western states and cast over a million votes for Weaver. But the effort to unite white and black farmers in the South failed miserably. Conservative Democrats, while continuing with considerable success to attract black voters, played on racial fears cruelly, insisting that the Populists sought to undermine white supremacy. Since most white Populists saw the alliance with blacks as at most a marriage of convenience—they did not really believe in racial equality or propose to do anything for black sharecroppers—this argument had a deadly effect. Elsewhere, even in the old centers of the Granger movement, the party made no significant impression. Urban workers remained aloof.

By standing firmly for conservative financial policies, Cleveland attracted considerable Republican support and won a solid victory over Harrison in the electoral college, 277 to 145. Weaver's electoral vote was 22.

Showdown on Silver

One conclusion that politicians reached on analyzing the 1892 returns was that the money question, particularly the controversy over the coinage of silver, was of paramount interest to the voters. Despite the wide-ranging appeal of the Populist platform, most of Weaver's strength came from the silver-mining states. On the other hand, Cleveland's strong stand for gold proved popular in the Northwest.

In truth, the issue of gold versus silver was superficial; the important question was what, if anything, should be done to check the deflationary spiral. The declining price level benefited bondholders and others with fixed incomes, and injured debtors. Industrial workers profited from deflation except during periods of depression, when unemployment rose—which helps explain why the Populists made little headway among them. Southern farmers, who were prisoners of the crop-lien system, and farmers in the plains states were hit hard by the downward trend.

By the early 1890s, discussion of federal monetary policy revolved around the coinage of silver. Traditionally the United States had been on a bimetallic standard. Both gold and silver were coined, the number of grains of each in the dollar being adjusted periodically to reflect the commercial value of the two metals. An act of 1792 established a 15:1 ratio—371.25 grains of silver and 24.75 grains of gold were each worth one dollar at the Mint. In 1834 the ratio was changed to 16:1, and in 1853 to 14.8:1, the latter reduction in the value of gold reflecting the new discoveries in California. This ratio slightly undervalued silver. In 1861, for example, the amount of silver bullion in a dollar was worth $1.03 in the open market, so no one took silver to the Mint for coinage. However, an avalanche of silver from the mines of Nevada and Colorado gradually depressed the price until, around 1874, it again became profitable for miners to coin their bullion. Alas, when they tried to do so, they discovered that the Coinage Act of 1873, taking account of the fact that no silver had been presented to the Mint in years, had demonetized the metal.

The silver mines denounced this "Crime of 1873," and inflationists, who wanted more money put into circulation regardless of its base, joined them in demanding a return to bimetallism. Conservatives, still fighting the battle against greenback paper money, resisted strongly. The result was a series of compromises. In 1878 the Bland-Allison Act authorized the purchase of $2 million to $4 million of silver a month at the market price, but this had little inflationary effect because the government consistently purchased the minimum amount. The commercial price of silver continued to fall; in 1890 its ratio to gold was 20:1. In that year the Sherman Silver Purchase Act required the government to buy 4.5 million *ounces* of silver monthly, but in the face of increasing supplies the price of silver fell still further. The ratio reached 26:1 in 1893 and 32:1 in 1894.

The compromises satisfied no one. Silver miners grumbled because their bullion brought in only half what it had in the early 1870s. Debtors noted angrily that because of the general decline of prices, the dollars they used to meet their obligations were worth more than twice as much as in 1865. Advocates of the gold standard feared that unlimited silver coinage would be authorized, "destroying the value of the dollar." When a financial panic brought on by the collapse of the London banking house of Baring Brothers ushered in a severe industrial

Mutiny aboard the good ship Democracy, *as seen by W. A. Rogers of* Harper's Weekly *in 1894. Civil service and tariff reform (along with one of their advocates) are about to be thrown overboard, the Tammany tiger gorges himself, and, at the stern, Captain Grover Cleveland cuts loose mutineers promoting a silver purchase bill.*

depression, the confidence of both silverites and "gold bugs" was further eroded.

President Cleveland believed that the controversy over silver had caused the depression by shaking the confidence of the business community and that all would be well if the country returned to a single gold standard. He summoned a special session of Congress, and by exerting immense political pressure obtained the repeal of the Sherman Silver Purchase Act in October 1893. All that this accomplished was to split the Democratic party, its southern and western wings deserting him almost to a man.

During 1894 and 1895, while the nation floundered in the worst depression it had ever experienced, a series of events further undermined public confidence. In the spring of 1894 an "army" of unemployed led by Jacob S. Coxey, an eccentric Ohio businessman, marched on Washington to demand relief. Coxey wanted the government to undertake a program of federal public works and to authorize local communities to exchange noninterest-bearing bonds with the Treasury for $500 million in paper money, the funds to be used to hire unemployed workers to build roads. The scheme, Coxey claimed, would pump money into the economy, provide work for the jobless, and benefit the entire nation by improving transportation facilities.

When Coxey's group of demonstrators, perhaps 500 in all, reached Washington, he and two other leaders were arrested for trespassing on the grounds of the Capitol. Their followers were dispersed by club-wielding policemen. This callous treatment convinced many Americans that the government had little interest in the suffering of the people, an opinion strengthened when Cleveland, in July 1894, used federal troops to crush the Pullman strike.

The next year the Supreme Court handed down several reactionary decisions. In *United States* v. *E. C. Knight Company* it refused to employ the Sherman Antitrust Act to break up the Sugar Trust. In *Pollock* v. *Farmers' Loan and Trust Company* it invalidated a federal income tax law despite the fact that a similar measure levied during the Civil War had been upheld by the Court in *Springer* v. *United States* (1881). Finally, the Court denied a writ of habeas corpus to Eugene V. Debs of the American Railway Union, who had been imprisoned for disobeying a federal injunction during the Pullman strike.

On top of these indications of official conservatism came a desperate financial crisis. Throughout 1894 the Treasury's supply of gold dwindled as worried citizens exchanged greenbacks (now convertible into gold) for hard money and foreign investors cashed in large amounts of American securities. The government tried to sell bonds for gold to bolster the reserve, but since most investors purchased the bonds with gold-backed paper money, in effect withdrawing gold from the Treasury and then returning it for the bonds, the gold reserve continued to melt away. Early in 1895 it touched a low point of $41 million. At this juncture a syndicate of bankers headed by J. P. Morgan turned the tide by underwriting a $62 million bond issue, guaranteeing that half the gold would come from Europe. This caused a great public outcry; the spectacle of the nation being saved from bankruptcy by a private banker infuriated millions.

These events, together with the continuing depression, discredited the Cleveland administration. "I haven't got words to say what I think of that old bag of beef," Governor "Pitchfork Ben" Tillman of South Carolina, who had resolutely resisted the Populists in 1892, told a local audience two years later. "If you send me to the Senate, I promise I won't be bulldozed by him."

As the presidential election of 1896 approached, with the Populists demanding unlimited coinage of silver at a ratio of 16:1, the major parties found it impossible to continue straddling the money question. The Populist vote had increased by 42 percent in the 1894 congressional elections. Southern and western Democratic leaders feared that they would lose their entire following unless Cleveland was repudiated. Western Republicans, led by Senator Henry M. Teller of Colorado, were threatening to bolt to the Populists unless their party came out for silver coinage. After a generation of political equivocation, the major parties had to face an important issue squarely.

The Republicans, meeting to choose a candidate at St. Louis in June 1896, announced for the gold standard. "We are unalterably opposed to every measure calculated to debase our currency or impair the credit of our country," the platform declared. "We are therefore opposed to the free coinage of silver. . . . The existing gold standard must be maintained." The party then nominated Ohio's William McKinley for president. McKinley, best known for his staunch advocacy of the protective tariff yet highly regarded by labor, was expected to run strongly in the Middle West and the East.

The Democratic convention met in July at Chicago. The pro-gold Cleveland element made a hard fight, but the silverites swept them aside. The high point came when a youthful Nebraskan named William Jennings Bryan spoke for silver against gold, for western farmers against the industrial East. Bryan's every sentence provoked ear-shattering applause.

> We have petitioned and our petitions have been scorned; we have entreated, and our entreaties have been disregarded; we have begged, and they have mocked when our calamity came. We beg no longer; we entreat no more; we petition no more. *We defy them!*

The crowd responded like a great choir to Bryan's oratorical cues. "Burn down your cities and leave our farms," he said, "and your cities will spring up again as if by magic; but destroy our farms and the grass will grow in the streets of every city in the country." He ended with a marvelous figure of speech that set the tone for the coming campaign. "You shall not press down upon the brow of labor this crown of thorns," he warned, bringing

Portraits of William Jennings Bryan with his wife and children, along with the text of the "cross of gold" speech, appeared on this typically colorful campaign poster for the 1896 campaign.

his hands down suggestively to his temples. "You shall not crucify mankind upon a cross of gold!" Dramatically, he extended his arms to the side, the very figure of the crucified Christ.

The convention promptly adopted a platform calling for "the free and unlimited coinage of both silver and gold at the present legal ratio of 16 to 1" and went on to nominate Bryan, who was barely 36, for president.

This action put tremendous pressure on the Populists. If they supported Bryan, they risked losing their party identity; if they nominated another man, they would insure McKinley's election. Those more concerned with immediate political advantage, especially holders of and seekers after office, took the former position. Those (mostly old Alliance members raised in the cooperative movement) who considered free silver a minor issue and a poor substitute for the subtreasury plan as an approach to the deflation problem, rejected "fusion" with the Democrats. "The Democratic idea of fusion," Tom Watson complained, is "that we play Jonah while they play whale." In part because the delegates could not find a person of stature willing to become a candidate against him, the Populist convention nominated Bryan, seeking to preserve the party identity by substituting Watson for the Democratic vice-presidential nominee, Arthur Sewall of Maine.

The Election of 1896

Never did a presidential campaign raise such intense emotions or produce such drastic political realignments. The Republicans from the silver-mining states swung solidly behind Bryan. The gold Democrats refused to accept the decision of the Chicago convention. Cleveland professed to be "so dazed by the political situation that I am in no condition for speech or thought on the subject." Many others adopted the policy of Governor David B. Hill of New York, who said, "I am a Democrat still—very still." The extreme gold bugs, calling themselves National Democrats, nominated their own candidate, 79-year-old Senator John M. Palmer of Illinois. Palmer ran only to injure Bryan. "Fellow Democrats," he announced, "I will not consider it any great fault if you decide to cast your vote for William McKinley."

At the start the Republicans seemed to have everything in their favor. Bryan's youth and relative lack of political experience—two terms in the House—contrasted unfavorably with McKinley's distinguished war record, his long service in Congress and as governor of Ohio, and his reputation for honesty and good judgment. The severe depression operated in favor of the party out of power, although by repudiating Cleveland, the Democrats escaped much of the burden of explaining away his errors. The newspapers came out almost unanimously for the Republicans. Important Democratic papers such as the New York *World*, the Boston *Herald*, the Baltimore *Sun*, the Chicago *Chronicle*, and the Richmond *Times* supported McKinley editorially and even slanted news stories against the Democrats. The New York *Times* accused Bryan of being insane, his affliction being variously classified as "paranoia querulenta," "graphomania," and "oratorical monomania." The Democrats had very little money and few well-known speakers to fight the campaign.

But Bryan proved a formidable opponent. Casting aside tradition, he took to the stump personally, traveling 18,000 miles and making over 600 speeches. He was one of the greatest of orators. A big, handsome man with a voice capable of carrying without strain to the far corners of a great hall yet equally effective before a cluster of auditors at a rural crossroads, he projected an image of absolute sincerity without appearing fanatical or argumentative. At every major stop on his tour, huge crowds assembled. In Minnesota he packed the 10,000-seat St. Paul Auditorium, while thousands more milled in the streets outside. His energy was amazing, his charm and good humor unfailing. At one whistle stop, while he was shaving in his compartment, a small group outside the train began clamoring for a glimpse of him. Flinging open the window and beaming through the lather, he shook hands cheerfully with each of the admirers. Everywhere he hammered away at the money question. Yet he did not totally neglect other issues. He was defending, he said, "all the people who suffer from the operations of trusts, syndicates, and combines."

McKinley's campaign was managed by a new type of politician, Marcus Alonzo Hanna, an Ohio businessman. In a sense Hanna was a product of the Pendleton Civil Service Act. When deprived of the contributions of officeholders, the parties turned to business for funds, and Hanna was one of the first leaders with a foot in both camps. Politics fascinated him, and despite his wealth and wide interests he was willing to labor endlessly at the routine work of political organization.

Hanna aspired to be a kingmaker and early fastened upon McKinley, whose charm he found irresistible, as the vehicle for satisfying his ambition. He spent about $100,000 of his own money on the preconvention campaign. His attitude toward the candidate, one mutual friend observed, was "that of a big, bashful boy toward the girl he loves."

Before most Republicans realized how effective Bryan was on the stump, Hanna perceived the danger and sprang into action. Since the late 1880s the character of political organization had been changing. The Civil Service Act was also cutting down on the number of jobs available to reward campaign workers. At the same time, the new mass-circulation newspapers and the nationwide press associations were increasing the pressure on candidates to speak openly and often on national issues. This trend put a premium on party organization and consistency—the old political trick of speaking out of one side of the mouth to one audience, out the other to another, no longer worked very well. The old military metaphors of political discourse, the terms *campaign* and *spoils* and *standard bearer,* remained, but others more businesslike became popular: *boss, machine, lobbyist.*

As the federal government became more involved in economic issues, business interests found more reason to be concerned about national elections and were more willing to spend money in behalf of candidates whose views they approved. In the campaign of 1888 the Republicans had set up a businessman's "advisory board" to raise money and stir up enthusiasm for Benjamin Harrison.

Hanna understood what was happening to politics. Certain that money was the key to political power, he raised an enormous campaign fund. When businessmen hesitated to contribute, he pried open their purses by a combination of persuasiveness and intimidation. Banks and insurance companies were "assessed" a percentage of their assets, big corporations a share of their receipts, until some $3.5 million had been collected. Hanna disbursed these funds with efficiency and imagination. He sent 1,500 speakers into the doubtful districts and blanketed the land with 250 million pieces of campaign literature, printed in a dozen languages. "He has advertised McKinley as if he were a patent medicine," Theodore Roosevelt exclaimed.

Incapable of competing with Bryan as a swayer of mass audiences, McKinley conducted a "front-porch campaign." This technique dated from the first Harrison-Cleveland election, when Harrison regularly delivered off-the-cuff speeches to groups of visitors representing special interests or regions in his hometown of Indianapolis. The system conserved the candidate's energies and enabled him to avoid the appearance of seeking the presidency too openly—which was still considered bad form—and at the same time allowed him to make headlines throughout the country.

Beginning with his acceptance of the Presidential nomination, William McKinley mounted his campaign from his front porch in Canton, Ohio.

Guided by the masterful Hanna, McKinley brought the front-porch method to perfection. Superficially the proceedings were delightfully informal. From every corner of the land, groups representing various regions, occupations, and interests descended on McKinley's unpretentious frame house in Canton, Ohio. Gathering on the lawn—the grass was soon reduced to mud, the fence stripped of pickets by souvenir hunters—the visitors paid their compliments to the candidate and heard him deliver a brief speech, while beside him on the porch his aged mother and adoring invalid wife listened with rapt attention. Then there was a small reception, during which the delegates were given an opportunity to shake their host's hand.

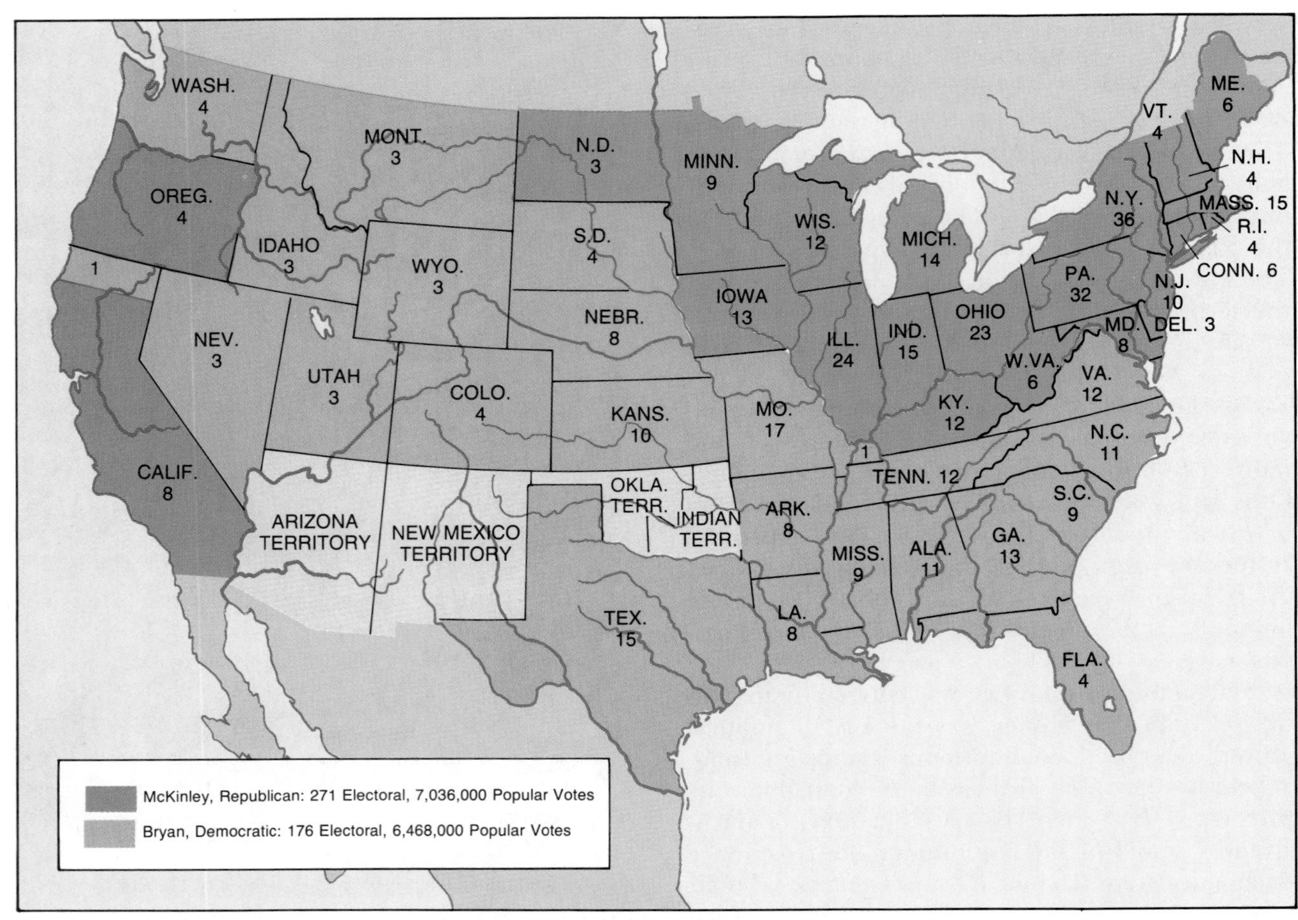

THE ELECTION OF 1896

Despite the air of informality, these performances were carefully staged. The delegations arrived on a tightly coordinated schedule worked out by McKinley's staff and the railroads, which operated cut-rate excursion trains to Canton from all over the nation. McKinley was fully briefed on the special interests and attitudes of each group, and the speeches of delegation leaders were submitted in advance. Often his secretary amended these remarks, and on occasion McKinley wrote the visitors' speeches himself. His own talks were carefully prepared in advance, each calculated to make a particular point. All were reported fully in the newspapers. Thus, without moving from his doorstep, McKinley met thousands of people from every section.

These tactics worked admirably. On election day McKinley carried the East; the Middle West, including even Iowa, Minnesota, and North Dakota; and the Pacific Coast states of Oregon and California. Bryan won in the South, the plains states, and the Rocky Mountain region. McKinley collected 271 electoral votes to Bryan's 176, the popular vote being 7,036,000 to 6,468,000.

The sharp sectional division marked the failure of the Populist effort to unite northern and southern farmers and also the triumph of the industrial part of the country over the agricultural. Business and financial interests voted solidly for the Republicans, fearing that Democratic victory would bring economic chaos. When a Nebraska landowner tried to float a mortgage during the campaign, a loan company official wrote him: "If McKinley is elected, we think we will be in the market, but we do not care to make any investments while there is an uncertainty as to what kind of money a person will be paid back in."

Other social and economic interests were far from being united. Many thousands of farmers voted for McKinley, as his success in states such as North Dakota, Iowa, and Minnesota proved. In the East and in the states bordering the Great Lakes, the agricultural depression was not severe and farm radicalism was almost nonexistent.

A preponderance of the labor vote went to the Republicans. In part this resulted from the tremendous pressures that many industrialists applied to their workers. "Men," one manufacturer announced, "vote as you please, but if Bryan is elected . . . the whistle will not blow Wednesday morning." Some companies placed orders for materials subject to cancellation if the Democrats won. Yet coercion was not a major factor, for McKinley was highly regarded in labor circles. While governor of Ohio, he had advocated the arbitration of industrial disputes and backed a law fining employers who refused to permit workers to join unions. During the Pullman strike he had sent his brother to try to persuade George Pullman to deal fairly with the strikers. He had invariably based his advocacy of high tariffs on the argument that American wage levels would be depressed if foreign goods could enter the country untaxed. Mark Hanna too had the reputation of always giving his employees a square deal. The Republicans carried nearly all the large cities, and in critical states such as Illinois and Ohio this made the difference between victory and defeat.

During the campaign, some frightened Republicans had laid plans for fleeing the country if Bryan were elected, and belligerent ones, such as Theodore Roosevelt, then police commissioner of New York City, readied themselves to meet the "social revolutionaries" on the battlefield. Victory sent such people into transports of joy. Most conservatives concluded that the way of life they so fervently admired had been saved for all time.

However heartfelt, such sentiments were not founded on fact. With workers standing beside capitalists and with the farmers divided, it cannot be said that the election divided the nation class against class or that McKinley's victory saved the country from revolution.

Far from representing a triumph for the status quo, the election marked the coming of age of modern America. The battle between gold and silver, which everyone had considered so vital, had little real significance. The inflationists seemed to have been beaten, but new gold discoveries in Alaska and South Africa and improved methods of extracting gold from low-grade ores soon led to a great expansion of the money supply. In any case, within two decades the system of basing the volume of currency on bullion had been abandoned. Bryan and the "political" Populists who supported him, supposedly the advance agents of revolution, were oriented more toward the past than the future; their ideal was the rural America of Jefferson and Jackson.

McKinley, for all his innate conservatism, was capable of looking ahead toward the new century. His approach was national where Bryan's was basically parochial. While never daring and seldom imaginative, he was able to deal pragmatically with current problems. Before long, as the United States became increasingly an exporter of manufactures, he would even modify his position on the tariff. And no one better reflected the spirit of the age than Mark Hanna, the outstanding political realist of his generation. Far from preventing change, the outcome of the election of 1896 made possible still greater changes as the United States moved into the 20th century.

SUPPLEMENTARY READING

Titles marked with an asterisk have been published in paperback.

The political history of this period is covered in lively and controversial fashion by Matthew Josephson, **The Politicos*** (1938), in briefer but equally controversial style by Ray Ginger, **Age of Excess*** (1965), and more solidly and sympathetically in H. W. Morgan, **From Hayes to McKinley** (1969). Both H. U. Faulkner, **Politics, Reform, and Expansion*** (1959), and J. R. Hollingsworth, **The Whirligig of Politics** (1963), treat the politics of the 1890s in some detail, while H. S. Merrill, **Bourbon Democracy of the Middle West*** (1953), Samuel McSeveney, **The Politics of Depression: Political Behavior in the Northeast** (1972), and C. V. Woodward, **Origins of the New South*** (1951), are important regional studies. J. A. Garraty, **The New Commonwealth*** (1968), attempts to trace the changing character of the political system after 1877. See also R. D. Marcus, **Grand Old Party: Political Structure in the Gilded Age** (1971).

There are three superb analyses of the political system of the period written by men who studied it firsthand: James Bryce, **The American Commonwealth*** (1888), Woodrow Wilson, **Congressional Government*** (1886), and Moisei Ostrogorski, **Democracy and the Organization of Political Parties*** (1902). Morton Keller, **Affairs of State** (1977), is an interesting analysis of "public life" in the period. L. D. White, **The Republican Era*** (1958), is an excellent study of the government in that period. D. J. Rothman, **Politics and Power: The United States Senate, 1869–1901*** (1966), analyzes the shifting structure of the upper house. R. J. Jensen, **The Winning of the Midwest** (1971), and Paul Kleppner, **The Cross of Culture: A Social Analysis of Midwestern Politics** (1970), are important studies based on modern computer techniques.

The issues of postreconstruction politics are discussed in P. H. Buck, **The Road to Reunion*** (1937), S. P. Hirshson, **Farewell to the Bloody Shirt*** (1962), J. W. Oliver, **History of the Civil War Military Pensions** (1917), F. W. Taussig, **The Tariff History of the United States*** (1914), D. R. Dewey, **Financial History of the United States** (1918), Allen Weinstein, **Prelude to Populism: Origins of the Silver Issue** (1970), Irwin Unger, **The Greenback Era*** (1964), Milton Friedman and A. J. Schwartz, **A Monetary History of the United States*** (1963), W. T. K. Nugent, **Money and American Society** (1968), Geoffrey Blodgett, **The Gentle Reformers: Massachusetts Democracy in the Cleveland Era** (1966), J. G. Sproat, **"The Best Men": Liberal Reformers in the Gilded Age** (1968), Ari Hoogenboom, **Outlawing the Spoils** (1961), and in several essays in H. W. Morgan (ed.), **The Gilded Age*** (1970).

Among biographies of political leaders, the following are especially worth consulting: Harry Barnard, **Rutherford B. Hayes and His America** (1954), R. G. Caldwell, **James A. Garfield** (1931), G. F. Howe, **Chester A. Arthur** (1934), Allan Nevins, **Grover Cleveland** (1932), H. S. Merrill, **Bourbon Leader: Grover Cleveland and the Democratic Party*** (1957), H. J. Sievers, **Benjamin Harrison** (1952–1968), H. W. Morgan, **William McKinley and His America** (1963), D. S. Muzzey, **James G. Blaine** (1934), and D. M. Jordan, **Roscoe Conkling** (1971).

For the farmers' problems, see F. A. Shannon, **The Farmer's Last Frontier*** (1945), S. J. Buck, **The Granger Movement*** (1913), J. D. Hicks, **The Populist Revolt*** (1931), and Theodore Saloutos, **Farmer Movements in the South*** (1960). Populism has been the subject in recent years of intensive reexamination. Richard Hofstadter, **The Age of Reform*** (1955), takes a dim view of Populism as a reform movement, while Norman Pollack, **The Populist Response to Industrial America*** (1962), pictures it as a radical one. W. T. K. Nugent, **The Tolerant Populists** (1963), leans in Pollack's direction but is more restrained. Lawrence Goodwyn, **Democratic Promise: The Populist Movement in America** (1976), rejects both positions, calling it "a people's movement of mass democratic aspiration." Both it and R. W. Cherny, **Populism, Progressivism, and the Transformation of Nebraska Politics** (1981), treat the differences between populism and early-20th-century reform. Sheldon Hackney's **Populism to Progressivism in Alabama** (1969) is more than a merely local study. C. V. Woodward, **Tom Watson: Agrarian Rebel*** (1938), and Martin Ridge, **Ignatius Donnelly: Portrait of a Politician** (1962), are excellent biographies of Populist leaders. F. E. Haynes, **James Baird Weaver** (1919), is also useful.

On the depression of the 1890s, consult Rendigs Fels, **American Business Cycles** (1959). The political and social disturbances connected with the depression are discussed in G. H. Knoles, **The Presidential Campaign and Election of 1892** (1942), Allan Nevins, **Grover Cleveland,** D. L. McMurry, **Coxey's Army** (1929), Almont Lindsey, **The Pullman Strike*** (1942), Ray Ginger, **The Bending Cross: Eugene V. Debs*** (1949) and **Altgeld's America*** (1958), and F. L. Allen, **The Great Pierpont Morgan*** (1949).

For the election of 1896, in addition to the books on Populism, see S. L. Jones, **The Presidential Election of 1896** (1964), R. F. Durden, **The Climax of Populism: The Election of 1896*** (1965), and P. W. Glad, **McKinley, Bryan, and the People*** (1964). On Bryan, consult Glad's **The Trumpet Soundeth*** (1960), and P. E. Coletta, **William Jennings Bryan** (1964); on McKinley, consult L. L. Gould, **The Presidency of William McKinley** (1980), and Herbert Croly, **Marcus Alonzo Hanna** (1912), the best life of Hanna.

22

From Isolation to Empire

I walked the floor of the White House night after night until midnight; and I am not ashamed to tell you, gentlemen, that I went down on my knees and prayed Almighty God for light and guidance more than one night. And one night late it came to me this way—I don't know how it was, but it came: (1) That we could not give them back to Spain—that would be cowardly and dishonorable; (2) that we could not turn them over to France or Germany—our commercial rivals in the Orient—that would be bad business and discreditable; (3) that we could not leave them to themselves—they were unfit for self-government—and they would soon have anarchy and misrule over there worse than Spain's was; and (4) that there was nothing left for us to do but to take them all, and to educate the Filipinos, and uplift and Christianize them, and by God's grace do the very best we could by them, as our fellow-men for whom Christ also died. PRESIDENT MCKINLEY *explaining to Methodist churchmen his decision to favor annexation of the Philippine Islands, 1899*

Americans have always been somewhat ambivalent in their attitudes toward other nations, and at no time was this more clearly the case than in the decades following the Civil War. Occupied with exploiting the West and building their great industrial machine, they gave little thought to foreign affairs. Benjamin Harrison reflected a widely held belief when he said during the 1888 presidential campaign that the United States was "an apart nation" and so it should remain. James Bryce made the same point in *The American Commonwealth.* "Happy America," he wrote, stood "apart in a world of her own . . . safe even from menace."

The historian David W. Pletcher has called the period "the awkward age" of American diplomacy, a time when the foreign service was "amateurish" and "spoils-ridden," when policy was either nonexistent or poorly planned, when treaties were clumsily drafted and state secrets ill kept. "The general idea of the diplomatic service," one reporter commented at this time, "is that it is a soft berth for wealthy young men who enjoy court society." An important New York newspaper, the *Sun,* suggested in the 1880s that the State Department had "outgrown its usefulness" and ought to be abolished.

America's Divided View of the World

Late-19th-century Americans never ignored world affairs entirely. They had little direct concern for what went on in Europe, but their interest in Latin America was great and growing, in the Far East only somewhat less so. Economic developments, especially shifts in foreign commerce resulting from industrialization, strengthened this interest with every passing year. Whether one sees isolation or expansion as the hallmark of American foreign policy after 1865 depends on what part of the world one looks at.

The disdain of the people of the United States for Europe rested on several historical foundations. Faith in the unique character of American civilization—and the converse of that belief, suspicion of Europe's supposedly aristocratic and decadent society—formed the chief basis of this isolation. Bitter memories of indignities suffered during the Revolution and the Napoleonic wars and anger at the hostile attitude of the great powers toward the United States during the Civil War strengthened it, as did the dislike of Americans for the pomp and punctilio of European monarchies. Also important was the undeniable truth that the United States was practically invulnerable to European attack and at the same time incapable of mounting an offensive against any European power. In turning their backs on Europe, Americans were taking no risk and passing up few opportunities—hence their indifference.

When occasional conflicts with one or another of the great powers erupted, the United States pressed its claims hard. It insisted, for example, that Great Britain pay for the loss of some 100,000 tons of American shipping sunk by Confederate cruisers that had been built in British yards during the rebellion. Some politicians even demanded that the British pay for the entire cost of the war after the Battle of Gettysburg—some $2 billion—on the ground that without British backing the Confederacy would have collapsed at about that point. However, the controversy never became critical, and in 1871 the two nations signed the Treaty of Washington, agreeing to arbitrate the so-called *Alabama* claims. The next year the judges awarded the United States $15.5 million for the ships and cargoes that had been destroyed.

In the 1880s a squabble developed with Germany, France, and a number of other countries over their banning of American pork products, ostensibly because some uninspected American pork was discovered to be diseased. The affair produced a great deal of windy oratory denouncing European autocracy and led to threats of economic retaliation. Congress eventually provided for the inspection of meat destined for export, and in 1891 the European nations lifted the ban. Similarly, there were repeated alarms and outbursts of anti-British feeling in the United States in connection with Great Britain's treatment of Ireland—all motivated chiefly by the desire of politicans to appeal to Irish-American voters. None of the incidents amounted to much.

The nation's interests elsewhere in the world gradually increased. During the Civil War France had established a protectorate over Mexico, installing the Archduke Maximilian of Austria as emperor. In 1866 Secretary of State William H. Seward demanded that the French withdraw, and the government moved 50,000 soldiers to the Rio

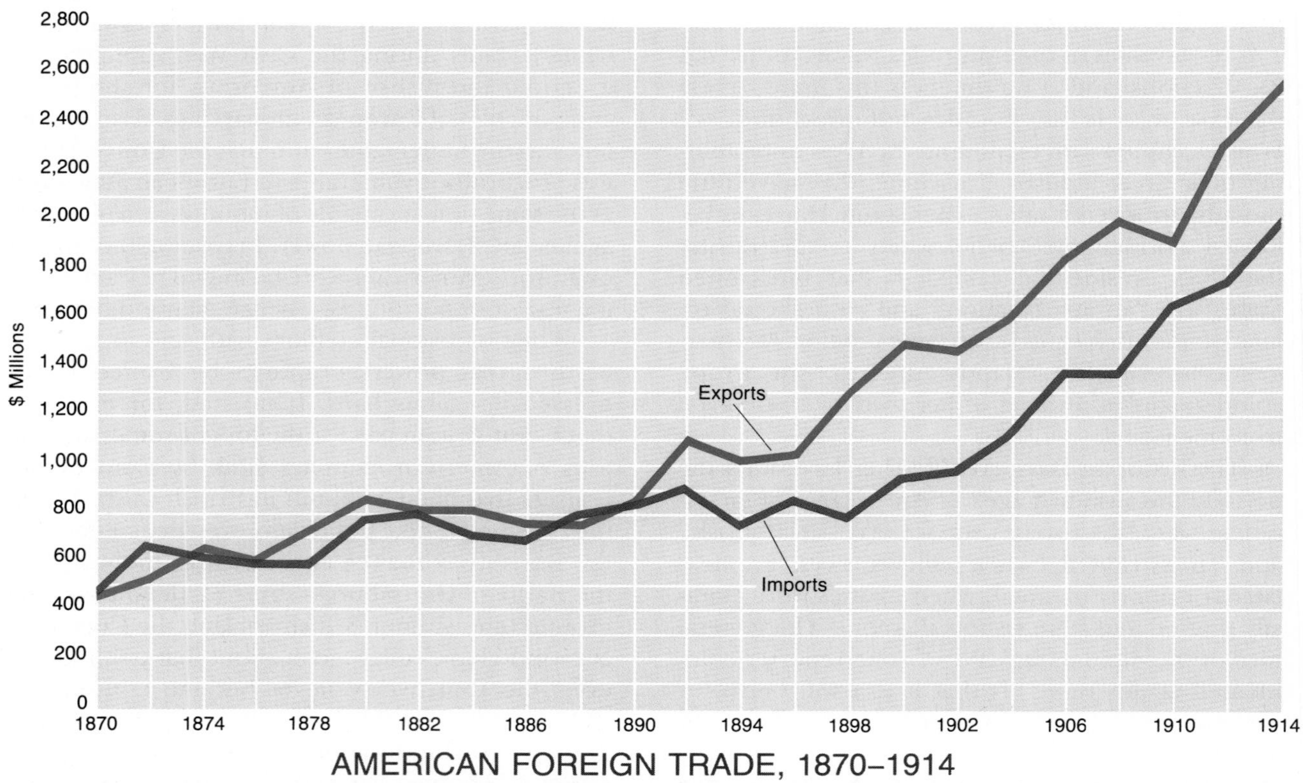

AMERICAN FOREIGN TRADE, 1870–1914

Grande. While fear of American intervention was only one of many reasons for their action, the French pulled their troops out of Mexico during the winter of 1866–1867. Nationalist rebels promptly seized and executed Maximilian. In 1867, at the instigation of Seward, the United States purchased Alaska from Russia for $7.2 million, thereby ridding the continent of another foreign power.

In 1867 the aggressive Seward acquired the Midway Islands in the western Pacific, which had been discovered in 1859 by an American naval officer, N. C. Brooks. Seward also made overtures toward annexing the Hawaiian Islands, and he looked longingly at Cuba. In 1870 President Grant submitted to the Senate a treaty annexing the Dominican Republic. He applied tremendous pressure in an effort to obtain ratification, thus forcing a "great debate" on extracontinental expansion. Expansionists stressed the wealth and resources of the country, the markets it would provide, even its "salubrious climate." But the arguments of the opposition proved more persuasive. The distance of the Dominican Republic from the continent, its crowded, dark-skinned population of what one congressman called "semi-civilized, semi-barbarous men who cannot speak our language," made annexation appear unattractive. The treaty was rejected. Seward had to admit that there was no significant support in the country for his expansionist plans. Prevailing opinion was well summarized by a Philadelphia newspaper: "The true interests of the American people will be better served . . . by a thorough and complete development of the immense resources of our existing territory than by any rash attempts to increase it."

The internal growth that preoccupied Americans eventually led them to look outward. By the late 1880s the country was exporting a steadily increasing share of its agricultural and industrial output. Exports, only $450 million in 1870, passed the billion-dollar mark early in the 1890s. Imports increased at a rate only slightly less spectacular.

The character of foreign trade was also changing: manufactures loomed ever more important among exports until in 1898 the country shipped abroad more manufactured goods than it imported.

By this time American steelmakers could compete with British producers anywhere in the world. In 1900 one American firm received a large order for steel plates from a Glasgow shipbuilder, and another won contracts for structural steel to be used in constructing bridges for the Uganda Railroad in British East Africa. When a member of Parliament questioned the colonial secretary about the latter deal, the secretary replied: "Tenders [bids] were invited in the United Kingdom . . . [but] one of the American tenders was found to be considerably the lowest in every respect and was therefore accepted." When American industrialists became conscious of their ability to compete with Europeans in far-off markets, they took more interest in world affairs, particularly during periods of depression, when domestic consumption fell.

Shifting intellectual currents further altered the attitudes of Americans. Darwin's theories, applicable by analogy to international relations, gave the concept of manifest destiny a new plausibility. Darwinists like the historian John Fiske argued that the American democratic system of government was so clearly the world's "fittest" that it was destined to spread peacefully over "every land on the earth's surface." In *Our Country* Josiah Strong found racist and religious justifications for American expansionism, again based on the theory of evolution. The Anglo-Saxon race, centered now in the United States, possessed "an instinct or genius for colonization," Strong claimed. "God, with infinite wisdom and skill is training the Anglo-Saxon race for . . . *the final competition of races.*" Christianity, he added, had developed "aggressive traits calculated to impress its institutions upon mankind." Soon American civilization would "move down upon" Mexico and all Latin America, and "out upon the islands of the sea, over upon Africa and beyond." "Can anyone doubt," Strong asked, "that the result of this . . . will be 'the survival of the fittest'?"*

The completion of the conquest of the American West encouraged Americans to consider expansion beyond the seas. "For nearly 300 years the dominant fact in American life has been expansion," declared Frederick Jackson Turner, propounder of the frontier thesis. "That these energies of expansion will no longer operate would be a rash prediction." Turner and writers who advanced other expansionist arguments were much influenced by foreign thinking. European liberals had tended to disapprove of colonial ventures, but in the 1870s and 1880s many of them were changing their minds. English liberals in particular began to talk and write about the "superiority" of English culture, to describe the virtues of the "Anglo-Saxon race," to stress a "duty" to spread Christianity among the heathen, and to advance economic arguments for overseas expansion.

European ideas were reinforced for Americans by their observations of the imperialist activities of the European powers in what would today be called underdeveloped areas. By swallowing up most of Africa and biting off bits and pieces of the crumbling empire of China, the French, British, Germans, and other colonizers inspired some patriots in the United States to advocate joining the feast before all the choice morsels had been digested. "While the great powers of Europe are steadily enlarging their colonial domination in Asia and Africa," James G. Blaine said in 1884, "it is the especial province of this country to improve and expand its trade with the nations of America." While Blaine emphasized commerce, the excitement and adventure of overseas enterprises appealed to many people even more than the economic possibilities or any sense of obligation to fulfill a supposed national, religious, or racial destiny.

Finally, military and strategic arguments were advanced to justify adopting a "large" policy. The powerful Union army had been demobilized rapidly after Appomattox; in the 1880s only about 25,000 men were under arms, their chief occupation fighting Indians in the West. Half the navy had been scrapped after the war, and the remaining ships were obsolete. While other nations were building steam-powered iron warships, the United States depended on wooden sailing vessels. In 1867 a British naval publication accurately described the American fleet as "hapless, broken-down, tattered [and] forlorn."

Although no foreign power menaced the country, the decrepit state of the navy vexed many of its officers and led one of them, Captain Alfred Thayer Mahan, to develop a startling theory about the importance of sea power. He explained his theory in two important books, *The Influence of Sea Power*

* In later writings Strong insisted that by "fittest" he meant "social efficiency," not "mere strength."

upon History (1890) and *The Influence of Sea Power upon the French Revolution and Empire* (1892). According to Mahan, history proved that a nation with a powerful navy and the overseas bases necessary to maintain it would be invulnerable in war and prosperous in time of peace. Applied to the current American situation, this meant that in addition to building a modern fleet, the United States should obtain a string of coaling stations and bases in the Caribbean, annex the Hawaiian Islands, and cut a canal across Central America. A more extensive colonial empire might follow, but these bases and the canal they would protect were essential first steps to insure America's future as a great power.

Writing at a time when the imperialist-minded European nations showed signs of extending their influence in South America and the Pacific islands, Mahan attracted many influential disciples. One was Congressman Henry Cabot Lodge of Massachusetts, a prominent member of the Naval Affairs Committee. Lodge had married into a navy family and was intimate with the head of the new Naval War College, Commodore Stephen B. Luce. He helped push through Congress in 1883 an act authorizing the building of three steel warships, and he consistently advocated expanding and modernizing the fleet. Elevated to the Senate in 1893, Lodge pressed for expansionist policies, basing his arguments on the strategic concepts of Mahan. "Sea power," he proclaimed, "is essential to the greatness of every splendid people."

Another important follower of Mahan was Benjamin F. Tracy, President Harrison's secretary of the navy, who improved the administration of his department and helped persuade Congress to increase naval appropriations. Lodge's friend Theodore Roosevelt was another ardent supporter of the "large" policy, but he had little influence until McKinley appointed him assistant secretary of the navy in 1897.

The Course of Empire

The interest of the United States in the Pacific and the Far East began in the late 18th century, when the first American merchant ship dropped anchor in Canton harbor. After the Treaty of Wanghia (1844), American merchants in China enjoyed many privileges and trade expanded rapidly. Missionaries began to flock into the country—in the late 1880s, over 500 were living there.

The Hawaiian Islands were an important way station on the route to China, and by 1820 merchants and missionaries were making contacts there. As early as 1854 a movement to annex the islands existed, though it foundered because Hawaii insisted on being admitted to the Union as a state. Commodore Perry's expedition to Japan led to the signing of a commercial treaty (1858) that opened several Japanese ports to American traders.

The United States pursued a policy of cooperating with the European powers in expanding commercial opportunities in the Far East. In Hawaii the tendency was to claim a special position but to accept the fact that Europeans also had interests in the islands. This state of affairs did not change radically following the Civil War. Despite Chinese protests over the exclusion of their nationals from the United States after 1882, American commercial privileges in China were not disturbed. American influence in Hawaii increased; the descendants of missionary families, most of them engaged in raising sugar, dominated the Hawaiian monarchy. In 1875 a reciprocity treaty admitted Hawaiian sugar to the United States free of duty in return for a promise to yield no territory to a foreign power. When this treaty was renewed in 1887, the United States obtained the right to establish a naval base at Pearl Harbor. In addition to occupying Midway, America obtained a foothold in the Samoan Islands in the South Pacific.

During the 1890s American interest in the Pacific area steadily intensified. Conditions in Hawaii had much to do with this. The McKinley Tariff Act of 1890, discontinuing the duty on raw sugar and compensating American producers of cane and beet sugar by granting them a bounty of 2 cents a pound, struck Hawaiian sugar growers hard, for it destroyed the advantage they had gained in the reciprocity treaty. The following year the death of the complaisant King Kalakaua brought Queen Liliuokalani, a determined nationalist, to the throne. Placing herself at the head of a "Hawaii for the Hawaiians" movement, she abolished the existing constitution under which the white minority had pretty much controlled the islands and attempted to rule as an absolute monarch. The resident Americans then staged a coup. In January 1893, with the connivance of the United States minister, John

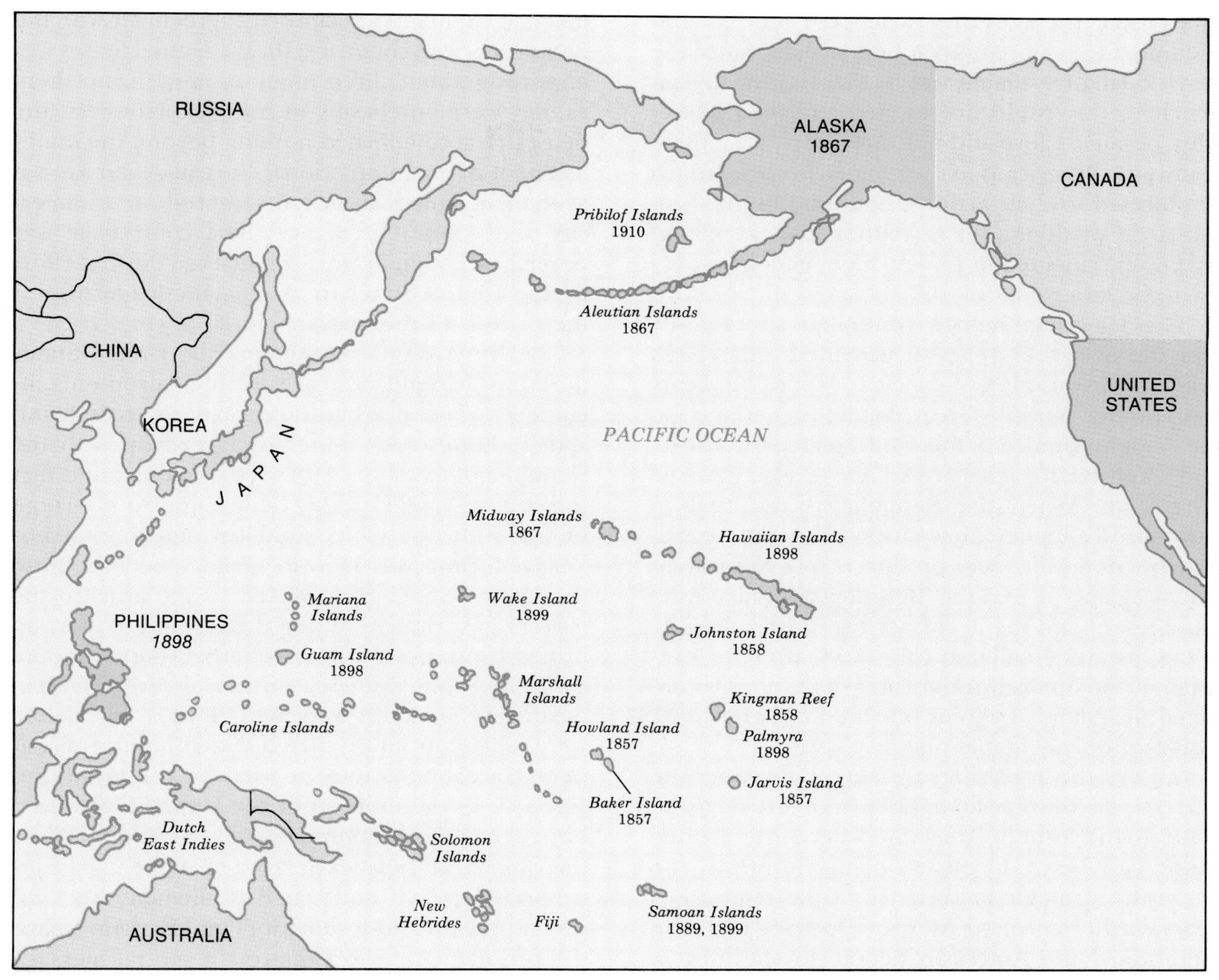

THE UNITED STATES IN THE PACIFIC

The color green on this map shows territory held or acquired by the United States in the late 19th and early 20th centuries. The two dates under the Samoan Islands at the bottom indicate a special situation. In 1889 these islands were made a tripartite protectorate under the United States, Germany, and Great Britain. Later, in 1899, they were divided between the United States and Germany.

L. Stevens, who ordered 150 marines from the cruiser *Boston* into Honolulu, they deposed Queen Liliuokalani and set up a provisional government. Stevens recognized their regime at once, and the new government sent a delegation to Washington to seek a treaty of annexation.

In the closing days of the Harrison administration such a treaty was negotiated and sent to the Senate, but when Cleveland took office in March, he withdrew it. The new president disapproved of the way American troops had been used to overthrow the monarchy. He sent a special commissioner, James H. Blount, to Hawaii to investigate. When Blount reported that the Hawaiians opposed annexation, the president dismissed Stevens and attempted to restore Queen Liliuokalani. Since the provisional government was by that time firmly entrenched, this could not be accomplished peacefully. Because Cleveland was unwilling to use force against the Americans in the islands, however much he objected to their actions, he found himself unable to do anything. The revolutionary government of Hawaii remained in power, independent yet eager to be annexed.

The Hawaiian debate continued sporadically over the next four years. It provided a thorough airing of the question of overseas expansion. Fears that another power—Great Britain or perhaps Japan—might step into the void created by Cleveland's refusal to act alarmed those who favored annexation. When the Republicans returned to power in 1897, a new annexation treaty was negotiated, but domestic sugar producers now threw their weight against it, and the McKinley administration could not obtain the necessary two-thirds majority in the Senate. Finally, in July 1898, after the outbreak of the Spanish-American War, Congress annexed the islands by joint resolution, a procedure requiring only a simple majority vote.

Most of the arguments for extending American influence in the Pacific applied more strongly to Central and South America, where the United States had much larger economic interests and where the strategic importance of the region was clear. Furthermore, the Monroe Doctrine had long conditioned the American people to the idea of acting to protect national interests in the Western Hemisphere.

As early as 1869 President Grant had come out for an American-owned canal across the Isthmus of Panama, in spite of the fact that the United States had agreed in the Clayton-Bulwer Treaty with Great Britain (1850) that neither nation would "obtain or maintain for itself any exclusive control" over an interoceanic canal. In 1880, when the French engineer Ferdinand de Lesseps organized a company to build a canal across the isthmus, President Hayes announced that the United States would not permit a European power to control such a waterway. "The policy of the country is a canal under American control," he announced, another blithe disregard of the Clayton-Bulwer agreement.

In 1889 a Pan-American Conference met in Washington to discuss hemisphere problems. Secretary of State James G. Blaine hoped to use this meeting to obtain a reciprocity agreement with the Latin American countries, for the United States was importing about three times as much from them as they were purchasing in America. However, the delegates accomplished nothing beyond the establishment of an International Bureau—later known as the Pan-American Union—to promote commercial and cultural exchange. The conference was nevertheless significant, for it marked the first effort by the United States to assume the leadership of the nations of the hemisphere.

At the Washington meeting the United States posed as a friend of peace; Blaine's proposals included a general arbitration treaty to settle hemisphere disputes. A minor disagreement with the Republic of Chile in 1891 soon demonstrated that the country could quickly be brought to the verge of war with one of its southern neighbors. Anti-*Yanqui* feeling was high in Chile, chiefly because the United States had refused to sell arms to the current government during the revolution that had brought it to power. In October a group of sailors from the U.S.S. *Baltimore* on shore leave in Valparaiso were set upon by a mob. Two of the sailors were killed and more than a dozen injured. President Harrison, furious at what he called an "insult . . . to the uniform of the United States sailors," demanded "prompt and full reparation." When the Chilean authorities delayed in supplying an appropriate apology and issued a statement that "imputed untruth and insincerity" on Harrison's part, the president sent to Congress a special message virtually inviting it to declare war. Faced with this threat, Chile backed down, offering the required apology and agreeing to pay damages to the sailors. Chile's humiliation destroyed much of the goodwill engendered by the Pan-American Conference.

When Cleveland returned to power in 1893, the possibility of trouble in Latin America seemed remote, for he had always opposed imperialistic ventures. The Latin American diplomatic colony in Washington greeted him warmly after its experience with Harrison. Yet scarcely two years later the United States was again on the verge of war in South America as a result of a crisis in Venezuela, and before this issue was settled Cleveland had made the most powerful claim to American hegemony in the hemisphere ever uttered.

The tangled borderland between Venezuela and British Guiana had long been in dispute, Venezuela demanding more of the region than it was entitled to and Great Britain submitting exaggerated claims and imperiously refusing to submit the question to arbitration. What made a crisis of the controversy was the political situation in the United States. A minor incident in Nicaragua, where the British had temporarily occupied the port of Corinto to force compensation for injuries done British subjects in that country, had alarmed American supporters of the Monroe Doctrine. Cleveland had avoided involvement, and along with his refusal to take Hawaii, the incident had angered expansionists. With his party rapidly deserting him because of his stand on the silver question, and with the election of 1896 approaching, the president desperately needed a popular issue.

There was considerable latent anti-British feeling in the United States. By taking the Venezuelan side in the boundary dispute, Cleveland would be defending a weak neighbor against a great power, a position certain to evoke a popular response. "Turn this Venezuela question up or down, North, South, East or West, and it is a 'winner,' " one Democrat advised the president.

Since he believed that Venezuela's cause was just, Cleveland did not resist the temptation to intervene. In July 1895 he ordered Secretary of State Richard Olney to send a near-ultimatum to the British. By occupying the disputed territory, Olney insisted, Great Britain was invading Venezuela and violating the Monroe Doctrine. Quite gratuitously, he went on to boast: "To-day the United States is practically sovereign on this continent, and its fiat is law upon the subjects to which it confines its interposition." Unless Great Britain responded promptly by agreeing to arbitration, the president would call the question to the attention of Congress.

The note threatened war, but the British ignored it for months. They did not take the United States seriously as a world power, and with reason, for the American navy, although expanding, could not hope to stand up against the British, who had 50 battleships, 25 armored cruisers, and many smaller vessels. When Lord Salisbury, the prime minister and foreign secretary, finally replied, he rejected outright the argument that the Monroe Doctrine had any status under international law and refused to arbitrate what he called the "exaggerated pretentions" of the Venezuelans.

If Olney's note had been belligerent, this reply was supercilious and sharp to the point of asperity. Cleveland was furious. On December 17, 1895, he asked Congress for authority to appoint an American commission to determine the correct line between British Guiana and Venezuela. When that had been done, he added, the United States should

Waiter McKinley stands ready to take Uncle Sam's order in this cartoon from the Boston Globe, *May 28, 1898. Menu selections include Cuba Steak, Porto Rico Pig, Philippine Floating Islands, and Sandwich Islands.*

"resist by every means in its power" the appropriation by Great Britain of any territory "we have determined of right belongs to Venezuela." Congress responded at once, unanimously appropriating $100,000 for the boundary commission. Popular enthusiasm was almost universal.

In Great Britain government and people suddenly awoke to the seriousness of the situation. No one wanted a war with the United States over a remote patch of tropical real estate. In Europe, Britain was concerned about German economic competition and the increased military power of that nation. In addition Canada would be terribly vulnerable to American attack in the event of war. The immense *potential* strength of the United States could no longer be ignored. Why make an enemy of a nation of 70 million, already the richest industrial power in the world? To fight with the United States, the British colonial secretary realized, "would be an absurdity as well as a crime."

Great Britain agreed to arbitrate the boundary. The war scare subsided; soon Olney was talking about "our inborn and instinctive English sympathies" and offering "to stand side by side and shoulder to shoulder with England in . . . the defence of human rights." When the boundary tribunal awarded nearly all the disputed region to Great Britain, whatever ill feeling the surrender may have occasioned in that country faded away. Instead of leading to war, the affair marked the beginning of an era of Anglo-American friendship. It had the unfortunate effect, however, of adding to the long-held American conviction that the nation could get what it wanted in international affairs by threat and bluster—a dangerous illusion.

Cuba and the War with Spain

On February 10, 1896, scarcely a week after Venezuela and Great Britain had signed the treaty ending their dispute, General Valeriano Weyler arrived in Havana from Spain to take up his duties as governor of Cuba. His assignment to this post was occasioned by the guerrilla warfare that Cuban nationalist rebels had been waging for almost a year. Weyler, a tough and ruthless soldier, set out to administer Cuba with "a salutary rigor." He began herding the rural population into wretched "reconcentration" camps in order to deprive the rebels of food and recruits. Resistance in Cuba hardened. The conflict, already bitter, became a cruel, bloody struggle that could not help affecting the American people.

The United States had been interested in Cuba since the time of John Quincy Adams and, were it not for northern opposition to adding more slave territory, might well have obtained the island one way or another before 1860. When the Cubans revolted against Spain in 1868, considerable support for intervening on their behalf developed. Hamilton Fish, Grant's secretary of state, resisted this sentiment, and Spain managed to pacify the rebels in 1878 by promising reforms. But change was slow in coming—slavery was not abolished until 1886. The worldwide depression of the 1890s hit the Cuban economy hard, and when an American tariff act in 1894 jacked up the rate on Cuban sugar by 40 percent, thus cutting off Cuban growers from the American market, the resulting distress precipitated another revolt.

Public sympathy in the United States went to the Cubans, who seemed to be fighting for liberty and democracy against an autocratic Old World power. Most American newspapers supported the Cubans; labor unions, veterans' organizations, many Protestant clergymen, and important politicians in both major parties demanded that the United States aid the rebel cause. Rapidly increasing American investments in Cuban sugar plantations, now approaching $50 million, were endangered by the fighting and by the social chaos sweeping across the island. Cuban propagandists in the United States played on American sentiments cleverly. When reports, often exaggerated, of the cruelty of "Butcher" Weyler and the horrors of his reconcentration camps filtered into America, the cry for action intensified. In April 1896 Congress adopted a resolution suggesting that the revolutionaries be granted the rights of belligerents. Since this would have been akin to formal recognition, Cleveland would not go that far, but he did exert diplomatic pressure on Spain to remove the causes of the rebels' complaints, and he offered the services of his government as mediator. The Spanish rejected the suggestion.

For a time the issue subsided. The election of 1896 deflected American attention from Cuba, and then McKinley refused to take any action that might disturb Spanish-American relations. Business inter-

Instability in Latin American led many to speculate that the U.S. would play an increasingly dominant role in the region. In Louis Dalrymple's 1895 cartoon, Uncle Sam wins the affections of the damsel Cuba as Spanish misrule and native insurgency lay waste to each other.

ests—except those with holdings in Cuba—backed McKinley, for they feared that a crisis would upset the economy, which was just beginning to pick up after the depression. In Cuba General Weyler made some progress toward stifling rebel resistance.

American expansionists, however, continued to demand intervention, and the press, especially Joseph Pulitzer's New York *World* and William Randolph Hearst's New York *Journal,* competing fiercely to increase circulation, kept resentment alive with tales of Spanish atrocities. McKinley remained adamant. Although he warned Spain that Cuba must be pacified, and soon, his tone was friendly and he issued no ultimatum. A new government in Spain relieved the situation by recalling Weyler and promising partial self-government to the Cubans. In a message to Congress in December 1897, McKinley urged that Spain be given "a reasonable chance to realize her expectations" in the island. McKinley was not insensible to Cuba's plight—while far from being a rich man, he made an anonymous contribution of $5,000 to the Red Cross Cuban relief fund—but he genuinely desired to avoid intervention.

His hopes were doomed, primarily because Spain failed to "realize her expectations." The fighting in Cuba continued. When riots broke out in Havana in January 1898, McKinley ordered the battleship *Maine* to Havana harbor to protect American citizens.

Shortly thereafter Hearst's New York *Journal* printed a letter written to a friend in Cuba by the Spanish minister in Washington, Dupuy de Lôme. The letter had been stolen by a spy. De Lôme, an experienced but arrogant diplomat, failed to appreciate McKinley's efforts to avoid intervening in

Cuba. In the letter he characterized the president as a *politicastro,* or "small-time politician," which was a gross error, and a "bidder for the admiration of the crowd," which was equally insulting though somewhat closer to the truth. Americans were outraged, and de Lôme's hasty resignation did little to soothe their feelings.

Then, on February 15, the *Maine* exploded and sank in Havana harbor, 260 of her crew perishing in the disaster. Interventionists in the United States accused Spain of having destroyed the ship and clamored for war. The willingness of Americans to blame Spain indicates the extent of anti-Spanish opinion in the United States by 1898. No one has ever discovered what actually happened. A naval court of inquiry decided that the vessel had been sunk by a submarine mine, but it now seems more likely that an internal explosion destroyed the *Maine.* The Spanish government would never have been foolish enough to commit an act that would probably bring American troops into Cuba.

With admirable courage, McKinley refused to panic; but he could not resist the wishes of millions of citizens that something be done to stop the fighting and allow the Cubans to determine their own fate. Spanish pride and Cuban patriotism had taken the issue of peace or war out of the president's hands. Spain could not put down the rebellion, and it would not yield to the nationalists' increasingly extreme demands. To have granted independence to Cuba might have caused the Madrid government to fall, might even have led to the collapse of the monarchy, for the Spanish public was in no mood to surrender. The Cubans, sensing that the continuing bloodshed aided their cause, refused to give the Spanish regime room to maneuver. After the *Maine* disaster, Spain might have agreed

This cartoon appeared in the Sacramento Bee *after Dewey's Manila Bay victory but before the destruction of Spain's Caribbean squadron (the* New York *was one of the vessels blockading Santiago); thus its label, "Prophescopic-Scoopagraph," is appropriate, if improbable. The rowboat is a swipe at editor Hearst's reporting from Cuba.*

to an armistice had the rebels asked for one, and in the resulting negotiations it might well have given up the island. The rebels refused to make the first move. The fighting continued, bringing the United States every day closer to intervention.

The president faced a dilemma. Most of the business interests of the country, to which he was particularly sensitive, opposed intervention. His personal feelings were equally firm. "I have been through one war," he told a friend. "I have seen the dead piled up, and I do not want to see another." Congress, however, seemed determined to act. When he submitted a restrained report on the sinking of the *Maine,* the Democrats in Congress, even most of those who had supported Cleveland's policies, gleefully accused him of timidity. Vice-President Garret A. Hobart warned him that the Senate could not be held in check for long; should Congress declare war on its own, the administration would be discredited. McKinley spent a succession of sleepless nights; sedatives brought him no repose. Finally, early in April, the president drafted a message asking for authority to use the armed forces "to secure a full and final termination of hostilities" in Cuba.

At the last moment the Spanish government seemed to yield; it ordered its troops in Cuba to cease hostilities. McKinley passed this information on to Congress along with his war message, but he gave it no emphasis and did not try to check the march toward war. To seek further delay would have been courageous but not necessarily wiser. Merely to stop fighting was not enough. The Cuban nationalists now insisted on full independence, and the Spanish politicians were unprepared to abandon the last remnant of their once-great American empire. If the United States took Cuba by force, the Spanish leaders might save their political skins; if they meekly surrendered the island, they were done for.

On April 20 Congress, by joint resolution, recognized the independence of Cuba and authorized the use of the armed forces to drive out the Spanish. An amendment proposed by Senator Henry M. Teller disclaiming any intention of adding Cuban territory to the United States passed without opposition. Four days later Spain declared war on the United States.

The Spanish-American War was fought to free Cuba, but the first action took place on the other side of the globe, in the Philippine Islands. Weeks earlier, Assistant Secretary of the Navy Theodore Roosevelt had alerted Commodore George Dewey, who was in command of the United States Asiatic Squadron located at Hong Kong, to move against the Spanish base at Manila if war came. Dewey had acted promptly, drilling his gun crews, taking on supplies, giving his gleaming white ships a coat of battle-gray paint, and establishing secret contacts with the Filipino nationalist leader, Emilio Aguinaldo. When word of the declaration of war reached him, he steamed from Hong Kong across the South China Sea with four cruisers and two gunboats. On the night of April 30 he entered Manila Bay, and at daybreak he opened fire on the Spanish fleet at 5,000 yards. His squadron made five passes, each time reducing the range; when the smoke had cleared, all ten of Admiral Montojo's ships had been destroyed. Not a single American was killed in the engagement.

Dewey immediately asked for troops to take and hold Manila, for now that war had been declared, he could not return to Hong Kong or put in at any other neutral port. McKinley took the fateful step of dispatching some 11,000 soldiers and additional naval support. On August 13 these forces, assisted by Filipino irregulars under Aguinaldo, captured Manila.

Meanwhile, in the main theater of operations, the United States had won a swift and total victory, though more because of the feebleness of the Spanish than because of the power or efficiency of American arms. When the war began, the regular army consisted of about 28,000 men. This tiny force was bolstered by 200,000 hastily enlisted volunteers. In May an expeditionary force gathered at Tampa, Florida. That hamlet was inundated by the masses of men and supplies that descended upon it. Entire regiments sat without uniforms or weapons while hundreds of freight cars jammed with equipment lay forgotten on sidings. Army management was abominable, rivalry between commanders a serious problem. Aggressive units like the regiment of "Rough Riders" raised by Theodore Roosevelt, now a lieutenant colonel of volunteers, scrambled for space and supplies, shouldering aside other units to get what they needed. "No words could describe . . . the confusion and lack of system and the general mismanagement of affairs here," the angry Roosevelt complained.

Scenes of the war in the Caribbean were recorded by William Glackens, a painter who later became famous as a pioneer of American realism (see page 657). One drawing shows American troop transport ships anchored in Santiago Bay, and the other the grim aftermath of the storming of San Juan Hill.

Since a Spanish fleet under Admiral Pascual Cervera was known to be in Caribbean waters, no invading army could safely embark until the fleet could be located. On May 29 American ships found Cervera at Santiago harbor, on the eastern end of Cuba, and established a blockade. In June a 17,000-man expeditionary force commanded by General William Shafter landed at Daiquiri, east of Santiago, and pressed quickly toward the city, handicapped more by its own bad staff work than by the enemy, though the Spanish troops resisted bravely. The Americans sweated through Cuba's torrid summer in heavy wool winter uniforms, ate "embalmed beef" out of cans, and fought mostly with old-fashioned rifles using black powder cartridges that marked the position of each soldier with a puff of smoke whenever he pulled the trigger. On July 1 they broke through undermanned Spanish defenses and stormed San Juan Hill, the intrepid Roosevelt in the van. ("Are you afraid to stand up while I am on horseback?" Roosevelt demanded of one soldier.)

With Santiago harbor in range of American artillery, Admiral Cervera had to run the blockade. On July 3 his black-hulled ships, flags proudly flying, steamed forth from the harbor and fled westward along the coast. Like hounds after rabbits, five American battleships and two cruisers, commanded by Rear Admiral William T. Sampson and Commodore Winfield Scott Schley, ran them down.

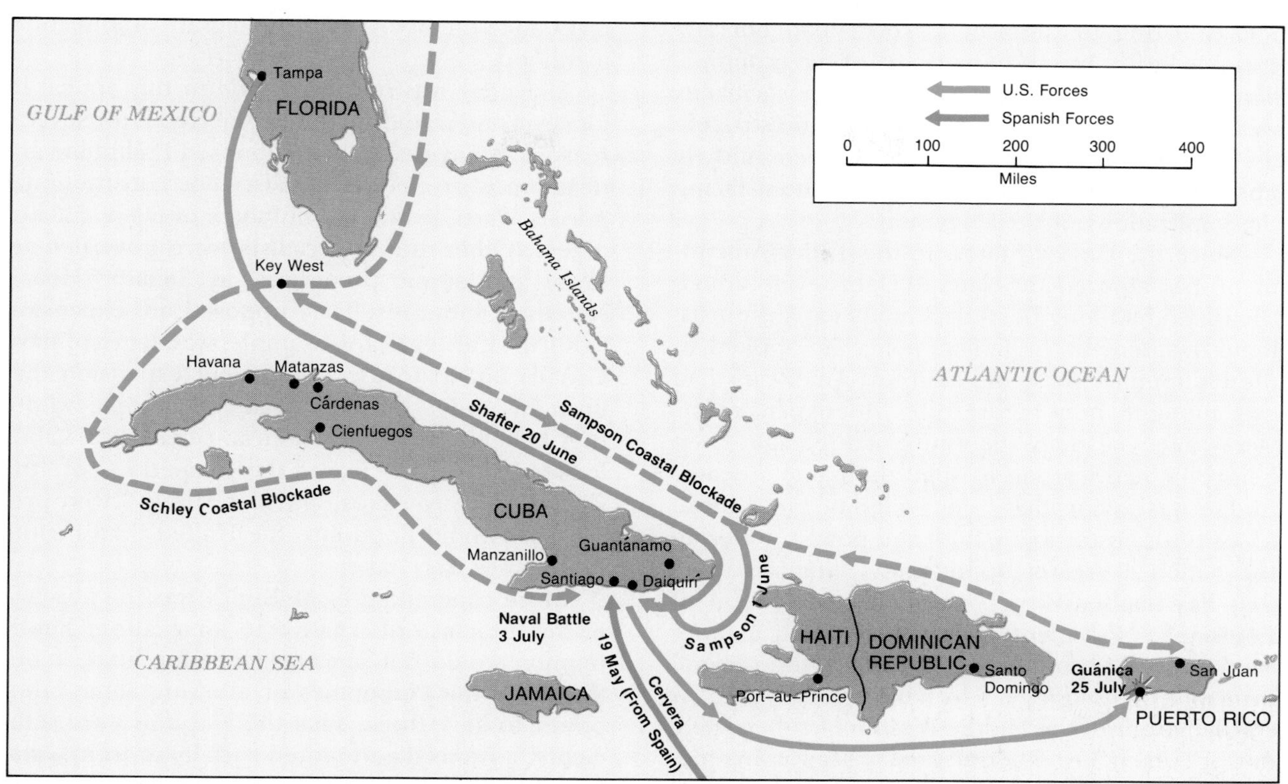

THE SPANISH–AMERICAN WAR IN THE CARIBBEAN, 1898

In four hours the entire Spanish force was destroyed by a hail of 8-inch and 13-inch projectiles. Damage to the American ships was superficial; only one seaman lost his life in the engagement.

The end then came abruptly. Santiago surrendered on July 17. A few days later, other United States troops completed the occupation of Puerto Rico. On August 12, one day before the fall of Manila, Spain agreed to get out of Cuba and to cede Puerto Rico and an island in the Marianas (Guam) to the United States. The future of the Philippines was to be settled at a formal peace conference, convening in Paris on October 1.

Developing a Colonial Policy

Although the Spanish resisted surrendering the Philippines at Paris, they had been so thoroughly defeated that they had no choice. The decision hung rather upon the outcome of a conflict over policy within the United States. The war, won at so little cost militarily, produced problems far larger than those it solved.* The nation had become a great power in the world's eyes. As a French diplomat wrote a few years later, "[The United States] is seated at the table where the great game is played, and it cannot leave it." European leaders had been impressed by the forcefulness of Cleveland's diplomacy in the Venezuela boundary dispute and by the efficiency displayed by the navy in the war. The annexation of Hawaii and other overseas bases intensified their conviction that the United States was determined to become a major force in international affairs.

But were the American *people* determined to exercise that force? The debate over taking the Philippine Islands throws much light on their attitudes. The imagination of Americans had been captured by the *trappings* of empire, not by its essence. It

* More than 5,000 Americans died as a result of the conflict, but fewer than 400 fell in combat. The others were mostly victims of yellow fever, typhoid, and other diseases.

was titillating to think of a world map liberally sprinkled with American flags and of the economic benefits that colonies might bring, but most citizens were not prepared to join in a worldwide struggle for power and influence. They entered blithely upon adventures in far-off regions without facing the implications of their decision.

Since the United States (in the Teller Amendment) had abjured any claim to Cuba, even though the island had long been desired by expansionists, logic dictated that a similar policy be applied to the Philippines, a remote land few Americans had ever thought about before 1898. But expansionists were eager to annex the entire archipelago. Even before he had learned to spell the name, Senator Lodge was saying that "the Phillipines [*sic*] mean a vast future trade and wealth and power," offering the nation a greater opportunity "than anything that has happened . . . since the annexation of Louisiana." President McKinley adopted a more cautious stance, but he too favored "the general principle of holding on to what we can get." A speaking tour of the Middle West in October 1898, during which he experimented with varying degrees of commitment to expansionism, convinced him that the public wanted the islands. Business opinion had shifted dramatically during the war. Business leaders were now calling the Philippines the gateway to the markets of the Far East.

An important minority objected strongly to the United States' acquiring overseas possessions. Persons as different in interest and philosophy as the tycoon Andrew Carnegie and the labor leader Samuel Gompers, as the venerable Republican Senator George Frisbie Hoar of Massachusetts and "Pitchfork Ben" Tillman, the southern Democratic firebrand, together with the writers Mark Twain and William Dean Howells, the reformers Lincoln Steffens and Jane Addams, and the educators Charles W. Eliot of Harvard and David Starr Jordan of Stanford united in opposing the annexation of the Philippines. These anti-imperialists insisted that since no one would even consider statehood for the Philippines, it would be unconstitutional to annex them. It was a violation of the spirit of the Declaration of Independence to govern a foreign territory without the consent of its inhabitants, Senator Hoar argued; by taking over "vassal states" in "barbarous archipelagoes" the United States was "trampling . . . on our own great Charter, which recognizes alike the liberty and the dignity of individual manhood."

McKinley was not insensitive to this appeal to idealism and tradition, but he rejected it for several reasons. Many people who opposed Philippine annexation were neither idealists nor constitutional purists. Partisanship led numbers of Democrats to object. Other anti-imperialists were governed by racial and ethnic prejudices, as Senator Hoar's statement indicates. They opposed not expansion as such—Carnegie, for example, was eager to have Canada added to the Union—but expansion that brought under the American flag people whom they believed unfit for American citizenship. Labor leaders particularly feared the competition of "the Chinese, the Negritos, and the Malays" who presumably would flood into the United States if the Philippines were taken.

More compelling to McKinley was the absence of any practical alternative to annexation. Public opinion would not sanction restoring Spanish authority in the Philippines or allowing some other power to have them. That the Filipinos were sufficiently advanced and united socially to form a stable government if granted independence seemed unlikely. Senator Hoar believed that "for years and for generations, and perhaps for centuries, there would have been turbulence, disorder and revolution" in the islands if they were left to their own devices. Strangely—for he was a kind and gentle man—Hoar faced this possibility with equanimity. McKinley was unable to do so. The president searched the depths of his soul and could find no solution but annexation. Of course the state of public feeling made the decision easier. And he probably found the idea of presiding over an empire appealing. Certainly the commercial possibilities did not escape him. In the end it was with a heavy sense of responsibility that he ordered the American peace commissioners to insist on acquiring the Philippines. To salve the feelings of the Spanish, the United States agreed to pay $20 million for the archipelago, but it was a forced sale, accepted by Spain under duress.

The peace treaty faced a hard battle in the United States Senate, where a combination of partisan politics and anticolonialism made it difficult to amass the two-thirds majority necessary for ratification. McKinley had shrewdly appointed three senators, including one Democrat, to the peace

A photograph taken in 1899 shows guerrilla troops captured during the Philippine Insurrection. Although the guerrilla leader, Emilio Aguinaldo, was seized in March 1901, fighting in the islands did not end until mid-1902.

commission. This predisposed many members of the upper house to approve the treaty, but the vote was close. William Jennings Bryan, titular head of the Democratic party, could probably have prevented ratification had he urged his supporters to vote nay. Although he was opposed to taking the Philippines, he did not do so. To reject the treaty would leave the United States technically at war with Spain and the fate of the Philippines undetermined; better to accept the islands and then grant them independence. The question should be decided, Bryan said, "not by a *minority* of the Senate but by a *majority* of the people" at the next presidential election. Perplexed by Bryan's stand, a number of Democrats allowed themselves to be persuaded by the expansionists' arguments and by McKinley's judicious use of patronage; the treaty was ratified in February 1899 by a vote of 57 to 27.

The national referendum that Bryan had hoped for never materialized. Bryan himself confused the issue in 1900 by making free silver a major plank in his platform, thereby driving conservative anti-imperialists into McKinley's arms. Moreover, early in 1899 the Filipino nationalists under Aguinaldo, furious because the United States would not withdraw, rose in rebellion. A savage guerrilla war resulted, one that cost far more in lives and money than the "splendid little" Spanish-American conflict.

Like all conflicts waged in tangled country chiefly by small, isolated units surrounded by a hostile civilian population that had little regard for the "rules" of war, this one produced many atrocities. Goaded by sneak attacks and instances of cruelty to captives, American soldiers, most of whom had little respect for Filipinos to begin with, responded in kind. Horrible tales of rape, arson, and murder by United States troops filtered into the country, providing ammunition for the anti-imperialists. "You seem to have about finished your work of civilizing the Filipinos," Andrew Carnegie wrote angrily to one of the American peace commissioners. "About 8,000 of them have been completely civilized and sent to Heaven. I hope you like it."

So long as the fighting continued it was politically impossible for the United States to withdraw from the islands. A commission appointed by McKinley in 1899 attributed the revolt to the ambitions of the nationalist leaders and recommended that the Philippines be granted independence at an indefinite future date. This seems to have been the wish of most Americans.

The reelection of McKinley in 1900 settled the

Philippine question, though it took the efforts of 70,000 American soldiers and three years of guerrilla warfare before peace was restored. Meanwhile, McKinley sent a second commission, headed by William Howard Taft, an Ohio judge, to establish civil government in the islands. Taft, a warm-hearted, affable man, took an instant liking to the Filipinos, and his policy of encouraging them to participate in the territorial government attracted many converts. In July 1901 he became the first civilian governor of the Philippines.

Anti-imperialists claimed that it was unconstitutional to take over territories without the consent of the local population. Their reasoning, while certainly not specious, was unhistorical. No American government had seriously considered the wishes of the American Indians, or those of the French and Spanish settlers in Louisiana, or those of the Eskimos of Alaska when it had seemed in the national interest to annex new lands.

Cuba and the Caribbean

Grave constitutional questions arose as a result of the acquisitions that followed the Spanish-American War. McKinley acted with remarkable independence in handling the problems involved in expansion. He set up military governments in Cuba, Puerto Rico, and the Philippines without specific congressional authority. Eventually both Congress and the Supreme Court took a hand in shaping colonial policy. In 1900 Congress passed the Foraker Act, establishing a civil government for Puerto Rico. It did not give the Puerto Ricans either American citizenship or full local self-government, and it placed a tariff on Puerto Rican products imported into the United States.

The tariff provision was promptly challenged in the courts on the ground that Puerto Rico was part of the United States, but in *Downes* v. *Bidwell* (1901) the Supreme Court upheld the legality of the duties. In this and other "insular cases" the reasoning of the judges was more than ordinarily difficult to follow. ("We suggest, without intending to decide, that there may be a distinction between certain natural rights enforced in the Constitution . . . and what may be termed artificial or remedial rights," the *Downes* opinion held.) The effect, however, was clear: the Constitution did not follow the flag; Congress could act toward the colonies almost as it pleased. A colony, one dissenting justice said, could be kept "like a disembodied shade, in an indeterminate state of ambiguous existence for an indefinite period."

While the most heated arguments raged over Philippine policy, the most difficult colonial problems concerned the relationship between the United States and Cuba, for there idealism and self-interest clashed painfully. Despite the desire of most Americans to free Cuba, an independent government could not easily be created. Order and prosperity did not automatically appear when the red and gold ensigns of Spain were hauled down from the flagstaffs of Havana and Santiago. The insurgent government was feeble, corrupt, and oligarchic, the Cuban economy in a state of collapse, life chaotic. The first Americans entering Havana found the streets littered with garbage and the corpses of horses and dogs. All public services were at a standstill; it seemed essential for the United States, as McKinley said, to give "aid and direction" until "tranquillity" could be restored.

As soon as American troops landed in Cuba, trouble broke out between them and the populace. Most American soldiers viewed the ragged, half-starved insurgents as "thieving dagoes" and displayed an unfortunate race prejudice against their dark-skinned allies. The novelist Stephen Crane, who covered the war for Pulitzer's *World,* reported: "Both officers and privates have the most lively contempt for the Cubans. They despise them." General Shafter did not help matters. He believed the Cubans "no more fit for self-government than gun-powder is for hell," and he used the insurgents chiefly as labor troops. After the fall of Santiago, he refused to let rebel leaders participate in the formal surrender of the city. This infuriated the proud and idealistic Cuban commander, General Calixto García. When McKinley established a military government for Cuba late in 1898, it was soon embroiled with local leaders. Then an eager horde of American promoters descended on Cuba in search of profitable franchises and concessions. Congress put a stop to this exploitation by forbidding all such grants as long as the occupation continued.

The problems were indeed knotty, for no strong local leader capable of uniting Cuba appeared. Even Senator Teller, father of the Teller Amend-

As the Monroe Doctrine became more significant around the turn of the century, chauvinistic cartoonists used it to taunt European powers. In this example, from a 1901 issue of Puck, *the European chickens complain, "You're not the only rooster in South America!" to which Uncle Sam retorts, "I was aware of that when I cooped you up!"*

ment, expressed concern lest "unstable and unsafe" elements gain control of the country. European leaders expected that the United States would eventually annex Cuba, and many Americans, including General Leonard Wood, who became military governor in December 1899, considered this the best solution. The desperate state of the people, the heavy economic stake of Americans in the region, and its strategic importance militated against withdrawal.

In the end the United States did withdraw, after doing a great deal to modernize sugar production, improve sanitary conditions, establish schools, and restore orderly administration. In November 1900 a Cuban constitutional convention met at Havana and proceeded without substantial American interference or direction to draft a frame of government. The chief restrictions imposed by this document on Cuba's freedom concerned foreign relations; at the insistence of the United States, it authorized American intervention whenever necessary "for the preservation of Cuban independence" and "the maintenance of a government adequate for the protection of life, property, and individual liberty." Cuba had to promise to make no treaty with a foreign power compromising its independence and to grant naval bases on its soil to the United States.

This arrangement, known as the Platt Amendment, was accepted, after some grumbling, by the Cubans. It had the support of most American opponents of imperialism. The amendment was a true compromise; as David F. Healy, a leading student of Cuban-American relations, has said, "it promised to give the Cubans real internal self government . . . and at the same time to safeguard American interests." In May 1902 the United States turned over the reins of government to the new republic. The next year the two countries signed a reciprocity treaty tightening the economic bonds between them.

True friendship did not result. Although American troops occupied Cuba only once, in 1906, and then at the specific request of Cuban authorities, the United States repeatedly used the threat of intervention to coerce the Cuban government. American economic penetration proceeded rapidly and without regard for the well-being of the Cuban peasants, many of whom lived in a state of peonage on great sugar plantations. Nor did their good intentions make up for the tendency of Americans to consider themselves innately superior to the Cubans and to overlook the fact that Cubans did not always wish to adopt American customs and culture. The reform program instituted during the occupation was marred by attempts to apply American standards at every step. The new schools used American textbooks that had been translated into Spanish without adapting the material to the experience of Cuban children. General Wood considered the Cubans "inert" because they showed little interest in his plans to grant a large measure of self-government to municipal authorities. He failed to understand that the people were accustomed to a centralized system with decision making concentrated in Havana. Wood complained that the Cubans were mired in "old ruts," yet the same charge might well have been leveled at him, though he was an efficient and energetic administrator.

If the purpose of the Spanish-American War had been to bring peace and order to Cuba, the Platt Amendment was a logical step. The same purpose soon necessitated a further extension of the principle, for once the United States accepted the role of protector and stabilizer in part of the Caribbean, it seemed desirable, for the same economic, strategic, and humanitarian reasons, to supervise the entire region.

The Caribbean countries were economically underdeveloped, socially backward, politically unstable, and desperately poor. Everywhere a few families owned most of the land and dominated social and political life. The mass of the people were uneducated peasants, many of them little better off than slaves. Rival cliques of wealthy families struggled for power, force being the usual method of effecting a change in government. Most of the meager income of the average Caribbean state was swallowed up by the military or diverted into the pockets of the current rulers.

Cynicism and fraud poisoned the relations of most of these nations with the great powers. European merchants and bankers systematically cheated their Latin American customers, who in turn frequently refused to honor their obligations. Foreign bankers floated Caribbean bond issues on outrageous terms, while revolutionary Caribbean governments annulled concessions and repudiated debts with equal disdain for honest business dealing.

Because these countries were weak, the powers tended to intervene whenever their nationals were cheated or when chaotic conditions endangered the lives and property of foreigners. In one notorious instance Germany sent two warships to Port-au-Prince, Haiti, and by threatening to bombard the town compelled the Haitian government to pay $30,000 in damages to a German citizen who had been arrested and fined for allegedly assaulting a local policeman. Such actions as this aroused the concern of the United States government.

In 1902, shortly after the United States had pulled out of Cuba, trouble erupted in Venezuela, where a dictator, Cipriano Castro, was refusing to honor debts owed the citizens of European nations. To force Castro to pay up, Germany and Great Britain established a blockade of Venezuelan ports and destroyed a number of Venezuelan gunboats and harbor defenses. Under American pressure the Europeans agreed to arbitrate the dispute. At last the great powers were coming to accept the broad implications of the Monroe Doctrine. The British prime minister, Arthur Balfour, went so far as to state publicly that "it would be a great gain to civilization if the United States were more actively to interest themselves in making arrangements by which these constantly recurring difficulties . . . could be avoided."

By this time Theodore Roosevelt had become president of the United States, and he quickly capitalized on the new European attitude. In 1903 the Dominican Republic defaulted on bonds totaling some $40 million. When European investors urged their governments to intervene, Roosevelt announced that under the Monroe Doctrine the

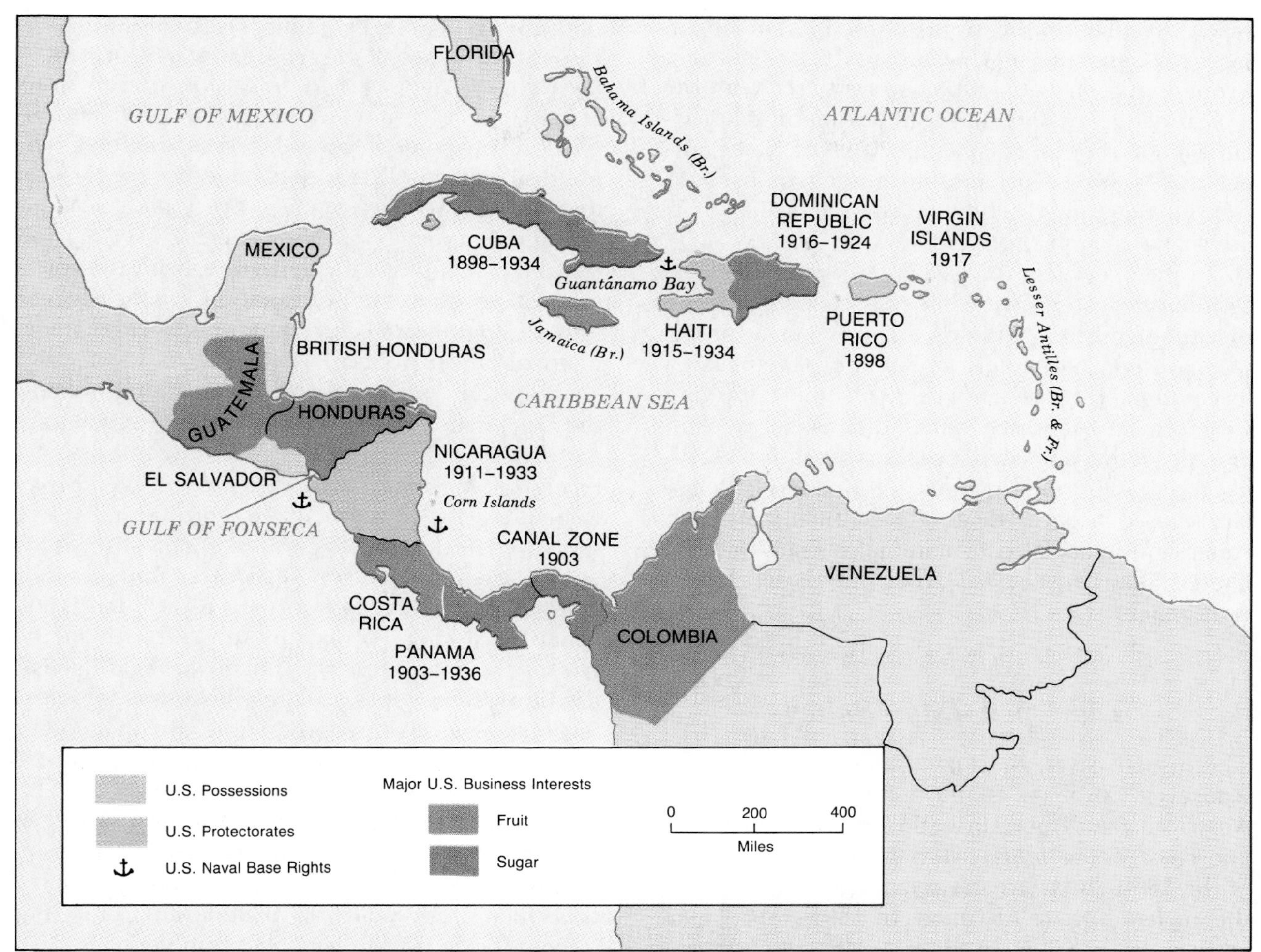

THE UNITED STATES IN THE CARIBBEAN

Puerto Rico was ceded by Spain after the Spanish-American War; the Virgin Islands were bought from Denmark; and the Canal Zone was leased from Panama. The ranges of dates following Cuba, Dominican Republic, Haiti, Nicaragua, and Panama cover those years during which the United States either had troops in occupation or, in some other way (such as financial), had a protectorate relationship with that country.

United States could not permit foreign nations to intervene in Latin America. But, he added, Latin American nations should not be allowed to escape their obligations. "If we intend to say 'Hands off' . . . sooner or later we must keep order ourselves," he told Secretary of War Elihu Root.

The president did not want to make a colony of the Dominican Republic. "I have about the same desire to annex it as a gorged boa constrictor might have to swallow a porcupine wrong-end-to," he said. He therefore arranged for the United States to take charge of the Dominican customs service—the one reliable source of revenue in that poverty-stricken country. Fifty-five percent of the customs duties would be devoted to debt payment, the remainder turned over to the Dominican government to care for its internal needs.

Roosevelt defined his policy, known as the Roosevelt Corollary to the Monroe Doctrine, in a message to Congress in December 1904. "Chronic wrongdoing" in Latin America, he stated with his typical disregard for the subtleties of complex affairs, might require outside intervention. Since, under the Monroe Doctrine, no other nation could step in, the United States must "exercise . . . an international police power."

In the short run this policy worked admirably. Dominican customs were honestly collected for the first time and the country's finances put in order. The presence of American warships in the area discouraged revolutionary elements (most of whom were cynical spoilsmen rather than social reformers), providing a needed measure of political stability. In the long run, however, the Roosevelt Corollary caused a great deal of resentment in Latin America, for it added to nationalist fears that the United States wished to exploit the region for its own benefit.

The Open Door Policy

The insular cases, the Platt Amendment, and the Roosevelt Corollary established the framework for American policy both in Latin America and in the Far East. Coincidental with the Cuban rebellion of the 1890s, a far greater upheaval had convulsed the ancient empire of China. In 1894–1895 Japan easily defeated China in a war over Korea. Alarmed by Japan's aggressiveness, the European powers hastened to carve out for themselves new spheres of influence along China's coast. After the annexation of the Philippines, McKinley's secretary of state, John Hay, urged on by businessmen fearful of losing out in the scramble to exploit the Chinese market, tried to prevent the further absorption of China by the great powers. For the United States to join in the dismemberment of China was politically impossible because of anti-imperialist feeling, so Hay sought to protect American interests by clever diplomacy. In a series of "Open Door" notes (1899) he asked the powers to agree to respect the trading rights of all countries and to impose no discriminatory duties within their spheres of influence. Chinese tariffs should continue to be collected in these areas and by Chinese officials.

The replies to the Open Door notes were at best noncommittal, yet Hay blandly announced in March 1900 that the powers had "accepted" his suggestions! Thus he could claim to have prevented the breakup of the empire and protected the right of Americans to do business freely in its territories. In reality nothing had been accomplished; the imperialist nations did not extend their political control of China only because they feared that by doing so they might precipitate a major war among themselves. Nevertheless, Hay's action marked a revolutionary departure from the traditional American policy of isolation, a bold advance into the complicated and dangerous world of international power politics.

Within a few months of Hay's announcement the Open Door policy was put to the test. Chinese nationalists, angered by the spreading influence of foreign governments, launched the so-called Boxer Rebellion. They swarmed into Peking and drove foreigners within the walls of their legations, which were placed under siege. For weeks, until an international rescue expedition (which included 2,500 American soldiers) broke through to free them, the fate of the foreigners was unknown. Fearing that the Europeans would use the rebellion as a pretext for further expropriations, Hay sent off another round of Open Door notes announcing that the United States believed in the preservation of "Chinese territorial and administrative entity" and in "the principle of equal and impartial trade with all parts of the Chinese Empire." This broadened the Open Door policy to include all China, not merely the European spheres of influence.

Hay's diplomacy was superficially successful. While the United States maintained no important military force in the Far East, American business and commercial interests there were free to develop and to compete with Europeans. But once again European jealousies and fears rather than American cleverness were responsible. When the Japanese, mistrusting Russian intentions in Manchuria, asked Hay how he intended to implement his policy, he replied meekly that the United States was "not prepared . . . to enforce these views on the east by any demonstration which could present a character of hostility to any other power." The United States was being caught up in the power struggle in the Far East without having faced the implications of its actions.

In time the country would pay a heavy price for this unrealistic attitude, but in the decade following 1900 its policy of diplomatic meddling unbacked by bayonets worked fairly well. Japan at-

In August 1900 an international expeditionary force—including American, British, French, German, Japanese, and Russian troops—succeeded in breaking the siege of Peking. Here the soldiers prepare to make their formal entrance into the Forbidden City.

tacked Russia in a quarrel over Manchuria, smashing the Russian fleet in 1905 and winning a series of battles on the mainland. Japan was not prepared for a long war, however, and suggested to President Roosevelt that an American offer to mediate would be favorably received.

Eager to preserve the nice balance in the Far East, which enabled the United States to exert influence without any significant commitment of force, Roosevelt accepted the hint. In June 1905 he invited the belligerents to a conference at Portsmouth, New Hampshire. At the conference the Japanese won title to Russia's sphere around Port Arthur and a free hand in Korea, but when they demanded Sakhalin Island and a large money indemnity, the Russians balked. Unwilling to resume the war, the Japanese settled for half of Sakhalin and no money.

The Treaty of Portsmouth was unpopular in Japan, and the government managed to place the blame on Roosevelt, who had supported the compromise. Ill feeling against Americans increased in 1906 when the San Francisco school board, responding to local opposition to the influx of cheap labor from Japan, instituted a policy of segregating oriental children in a special school. Japan protested, and President Roosevelt persuaded the San Franciscans to abandon segregation in exchange for his pledge to cut off further Japanese immigration. He accomplished this through a "Gentlemen's Agreement" (1907) in which the Japanese promised not to issue passports to laborers seeking to come to America. Discriminatory legislation based specifically on race was thus avoided. However, the atmosphere between the two countries remained charged. Japanese resentment at American race prejudice was great; many Americans talked fearfully of the "yellow peril."

Theodore Roosevelt was preeminently a realist in foreign relations. "Don't bluster," he once said. "Don't flourish a revolver, and never draw unless you intend to shoot." In the Far East he failed to follow his own advice. He considered the situation in that part of the world fraught with peril. The Philippines, he said, were "our heel of Achilles," indefensible in case of a Japanese attack. He suggested privately that the United States ought to "be prepared for giving the islands independence . . . much sooner than I think advisable from their own standpoint." Yet he did not increase appreciably American naval and military strength in the Orient, he did not stop trying to influence the course of events in the area, and he took no step toward withdrawing from the Philippines. He sent the fleet on a world cruise to demonstrate its might to Japan but knew well that this was mere bluff. "The 'Open Door' policy," he warned his successor, "completely disappears as soon as a powerful nation determines to disregard it." Nevertheless he allowed the belief to persist in the United States that the nation could influence the course of Far Eastern history without risk or real involvement.

Caribbean Diplomacy

In the Caribbean region American policy centered on building an interoceanic canal across Central America. Expanding interests in Latin America and the Far East made a canal necessary, a truth pointed up during the war with Spain by the two-month voyage of the U.S.S. *Oregon* around South America from California waters to participate in the action against Admiral Cervera's fleet at Santiago. The first step was to get rid of the old Clayton-Bulwer Treaty with Great Britain, which barred the United States from building a canal on its own. In 1901

Lord Pauncefote, the British ambassador, and Secretary of State John Hay negotiated an agreement abrogating the Clayton-Bulwer pact and giving America the right to build, and by implication fortify, a transisthmian waterway. The United States agreed in turn to maintain any such canal "free and open to the vessels of commerce and of war of all nations."

One possible canal route lay across the Colombian province of Panama, where the French-controlled New Panama Canal Company had taken over the franchise of the old De Lesseps company (see page 632). Only 50 miles separated the oceans in Panama. The terrain, however, was rugged and unhealthy. While the French company had sunk much money into the project, it had little to show for its efforts aside from some rough excavations. A second possible route ran across Nicaragua. This route was about 200 miles long but was relatively easy, since much of it traversed Lake Nicaragua and other natural waterways.

President McKinley appointed a commission to study the alternatives. It reported that the Panamanian route was technically superior but recommended building in Nicaragua because the New Panama Canal Company was asking $109 million for its assets, which the commission valued at only $40 million. Lacking another potential purchaser, the French company lowered its price to $40 million, and after a great deal of clever propagandizing by Philippe Bunau-Varilla, a French engineer with heavy investments in the company, President Roosevelt settled on the Panamanian route.

In January 1903 Secretary of State Hay negotiated a treaty with Tomás Herrán, the Colombian chargé in Washington. In return for a 99-year lease on a zone across Panama 6 miles wide, the United States agreed to pay Colombia $10 million and an annual rent of $250,000. The Colombian senate, however, unanimously rejected this treaty, in part because it did not adequately protect Colombian sovereignty over Panama and in part because it hardly seemed fair that the New Panama Canal Company should receive $40 million for its frozen assets and Colombia only $10 million. The government demanded $15 million directly from the United States, plus $10 million of the company's share.

A little more patience might have produced a mutually satisfactory settlement, but Roosevelt looked upon the Colombians as highwaymen who were "mad to get hold of the $40,000,000 of the Frenchmen." ("You could no more make an agreement with the Colombian rulers," Roosevelt later remarked, "than you could nail currant jelly to a wall.") When Panamanians, egged on by the French company, staged a revolution in November 1903, he ordered the cruiser *Nashville* to Panama. Colombian government forces found themselves looking down the barrels of the guns of the *Nashville* and shortly thereafter eight other American warships. The revolution succeeded.

Roosevelt instantly recognized the new Republic of Panama. Secretary Hay and the new Panamanian minister, Bunau-Varilla, then negotiated a treaty granting the United States a zone *10* miles wide *in perpetuity,* on the same terms as those rejected by Colombia. Within the Canal Zone the United States could act as "the sovereign of the territory . . . to the entire exclusion of . . . the Republic of Panama." The United States guaranteed the independence of the republic. The New Panama Canal Company then received its $40 million.

Historians have condemned Roosevelt for his actions in this shabby affair, and with good reason. It was not that he fomented the revolution, for he did not. Separated from the government at Bogotá by an impenetrable jungle, the people of Panama province had long wanted to be free of Colombian rule. Since an American-built canal would bring a flood of dollars and jobs to the area, they were prepared to take any necessary steps to avoid having the United States shift to the Nicaraguan route. Nor was it that Roosevelt prevented Colombia from suppressing the revolution. He sinned, rather, in his disregard of Latin American sensibilities. He referred to the Colombians as "dagoes" and insisted smugly that he was defending "the interests of collective civilization" when he overrode their opposition to his plans. "They cut their own throats," he said. "They tried to hold us up; and too late they have discovered their criminal error."

If uncharitable, Roosevelt's analysis was not entirely inaccurate, yet it did not justify his haste in taking Panama under his wing. "Have I defended myself?" Roosevelt asked Secretary of War Elihu Root. "You certainly have, Mr. President," Root retorted. "You were accused of seduction and you have conclusively proved that you were guilty of rape." Throughout Latin America, especially as na-

A New York Times *cartoonist did not approve of Roosevelt's handling of the Panamanian affair. When Bunau-Varilla asked the president to send a warship to Panama "to protect American lives and interests," he got no answer. "But his look was enough for me," Bunau-Varilla recalled.*

tionalist sentiments grew stronger, Roosevelt's intolerance and aggressiveness in the canal incident bred resentment and fear.

In 1921 the United States made amends by giving Colombia \$25 million. Colombia in turn recognized the independence of the Republic of Panama.* Meanwhile, the first vessels passed through the canal in 1914—and American hegemony in the Caribbean expanded. Yet even in that strategically vital area there was more show than substance to American strength. The navy ruled Caribbean waters largely by default, for it lacked adequate bases in the region. In 1903, as authorized by the Cuban constitution, the United States obtained an excellent site for a base at Guantanamo Bay, but before 1914 Congress appropriated only \$89,000 to develop it.

The tendency was to try to influence outlying areas without actually controlling them. Roosevelt's successor, William Howard Taft, called this policy dollar diplomacy, his reasoning being that economic penetration would bring stability to underdeveloped areas and power and profit to the United States without the government's having to commit troops or spend public funds.

Under Taft the State Department won a place for American bankers in an international syndicate engaged in financing railroads in Manchuria. When Nicaragua defaulted on its foreign debt in 1911, the department arranged for American bankers to reorganize Nicaraguan finances and manage the customs service. Although the government truthfully insisted that it did not "covet an inch of territory south of the Rio Grande," dollar diplomacy provoked further apprehension in Latin America. Efforts to establish similar arrangements in Honduras, Costa Rica, and Guatemala all failed. In Nicaragua orderly administration of the finances did not bring internal peace. In 1912, 2,500 American marines and sailors had to be landed to put down a revolution.

Economic penetration proceeded briskly. American investments in Cuba reached \$500 million by 1920, and smaller but significant investments were made in the Dominican Republic and in Haiti. In Central America the United Fruit Company accumulated large holdings in banana plantations, railroads, and other ventures. Other firms plunged heavily in Mexico's rich mineral resources.

---

* Panama was independent only in name because of American control of the canal. In 1978 the United States and Panama agreed to a treaty turning the entire Canal Zone over to Panama in the year 2000 (see page 923).

"Non-Colonial Imperial Expansion"

The United States deserves fair marks for effort in its foreign relations following the Spanish-American War, barely passable marks for performance, and failing marks for results. If one defines imperialism narrowly as a policy of occupying and governing foreign lands, American imperialism lasted for an extremely short time. With trivial exceptions, all the American colonies—Hawaii, the Philippines, Guam, Puerto Rico, the Guantanamo base, and the Canal Zone—were obtained between 1898 and 1903. In retrospect it seems clear that the urge to own colonies was only fleeting; the legitimate questions raised by the anti-imperialists and the headaches connected with the management of overseas possessions soon produced a change of policy.

The objections of protectionists to the lowering of tariff barriers, the shock of the Philippine insurrection, and a growing conviction that the costs of colonial administration outweighed the profits affected American thinking. Hay's Open Door notes (which anti-imperialists praised highly) marked the beginning of the retreat from imperialism as thus defined, while the Roosevelt Corollary and dollar diplomacy signaled the consolidation of a new policy. Elihu Root summarized this policy as it applied to the Caribbean nations (and by implication to the rest of the underdeveloped world) in 1905: "We do not want to take them for ourselves. We do not want any foreign nations to take them for themselves. We want to help them."

Yet imperialism can be given a broader definition. The historian William Appleman Williams, a sharp critic, has described 20th-century American foreign policy as one of "non-colonial imperial expansion." Its object was to obtain profitable American economic penetration of underdeveloped areas without the trouble of owning and controlling them. Its subsidiary aim was to encourage these countries to "modernize," that is, to remake themselves in the image of the United States. The Open Door policy, in Williams's view, was not unrealistic and by no means a failure—indeed, it was *too* successful. He criticizes American policy not because it did not work or because it led to trouble with the powers but because of its harmful effects on underdeveloped countries.

Examined from this perspective, the Open Door policy, the Roosevelt Corollary, and dollar diplomacy make a single pattern of exploitation, "tragic" rather than evil, according to Williams, because its creators were not evil but only of limited vision. They did not recognize the contradictions in their ideas and values. They saw American expansion as beneficial to all concerned—and not exclusively in materialistic terms. They genuinely believed that they were exporting democracy along with capitalism and industrialization.

Williams probably goes too far in arguing that American statesmen consciously planned their foreign policy in these terms. American economic interests in foreign nations expanded enormously in the 20th century, but diplomacy had relatively little to do with this. Western industrial society (not merely American) was engulfing the rest of the world, as it continues to engulf it. Yet he is correct in pointing out that western economic penetration has had many unfortunate results for the nonindustrial nations. It is also true that Americans were particularly, though not uniquely, unimpressed by the different social and cultural patterns of people in far-off lands and insensitive to the wishes of such people to develop in their own way.

Both the United States government and American businessmen showed little interest in finding out what the people of Cuba wanted from life. They assumed that the Cubans wanted what *everybody* (read "Americans") wanted and, if by some strange chance this was not the case, that it was best to give it to them anyway. Dollar diplomacy had as its objectives the avoidance of violence and the economic development of Latin America; it paid small heed to how peace was maintained and how the fruits of development were distributed. The policy was self-defeating, for in the long run stability depended on the support of the people, and this was seldom forthcoming.

By the eve of World War I the United States had become a world power and had assumed what it saw as a duty to guide the development of many countries with traditions far different from its own. The American people, however, did not understand what these changes involved. While they stood ready to extend their influence into distant lands, they did so blithely, with little awareness of the implications of their behavior for themselves or for other peoples. The national psychology, if such a term has any meaning, remained fundamentally isolationist. Americans understood that their wealth and numbers made their nation strong and that geography made it practically invulnerable. Thus they proceeded to do what they wanted to do in foreign affairs, limited more by their humanly flexible consciences than by any rational analysis of the probable consequences. This policy seemed safe enough—in 1914.

SUPPLEMENTARY READING

Titles marked with an asterisk have been published in paperback.

Among the many general diplomatic histories, Alexander De Conde, **A History of American Foreign Policy*** (1963), is the most detailed, and R. W. Leopold, **The Growth of American Foreign Policy** (1962), is the most thoughtful and interpretative. Milton Plesur, **America's Outward Thrust*** (1971), offers fuller detail, while J. A. S. Grenville and G. B. Young, **Politics, Strategy, and American Diplomacy: Studies in Foreign Policy** (1966), throws new light on many aspects of the period. Post–Civil War expansionism is treated in Dexter Perkins, **The Monroe Doctrine: 1867–1907*** (1937), and Allan Nevins, **Hamilton Fish** (1936). W. LaFeber, **The New Empire** (1963), presents a forceful but somewhat overstated argument on the extent of expansionist sentiment, especially on the part of American businessmen.

The new expansionism is also discussed in A. K. Weinberg, **Manifest Destiny*** (1935), J. W. Pratt, **Expansionists of 1898*** (1936), and Harold and Margaret Sprout, **The Rise of American Naval Power*** (1939). Contemporary attitudes are reflected in Josiah Strong, **Our Country** (1885), while A. T. Mahan, **The Influence of Sea Power upon History: 1660–1783*** (1890), provides the clearest presentation of Mahan's thesis. W. D. Puleston, **Mahan** (1939), is a good biography.

D. W. Pletcher, **The Awkward Years: American Foreign Relations Under Garfield and Arthur** (1962), is definitive. Other useful studies include A. F. Tyler, **The Foreign Policy of James G. Blaine** (1927), S. K. Stevens, **American Expansion in Hawaii** (1945), Allan Nevins, **Grover Cleveland** (1932) and **Henry White** (1930), L. M. Gelber, **The Rise of Anglo-American Friendship** (1938), and Henry James, **Richard Olney** (1923).

On the Spanish-American War, a good brief summary is H. W. Morgan, **America's Road to Empire*** (1965). For greater detail, consult E. R. May, **Imperial Democracy*** (1961), L. L. Gould, **The Presidency of William McKinley** (1980), and Orestes Ferrara, **The Last Spanish War** (1937).

On imperialism, see David Healy, **U.S. Expansionism: The Imperialist Urge in the 1890's** (1970), E. R. May, **American Imperialism: A Speculative Essay** (1968), and W. A. Williams, **The Tragedy of American Diplomacy*** (1962). R. L. Beisner, **Twelve Against Empire: The Anti-Imperialists*** (1968), contains lively and thoughtful sketches of leading foes of expansion. See also E. B. Thompkins, **Anti-Imperialism in the United States** (1970). For colonial problems, see Leon Wolff, **Little Brown Brother** (1961), on the Philippines, D. F. Healy, **The United States in Cuba: 1898–1902** (1963), and D. G. Munro, **Intervention and Dollar Diplomacy in the Caribbean: 1900–1921** (1964). S. F. Bemis, **The Latin American Policy of the United States*** (1943), is an excellent general account of the subject. Other useful volumes include D. C. Miner, **The Fight for the Panama Route** (1940), David McCullough, **The Path Between the Seas** (1977), H. K. Beale, **Theodore Roosevelt and the Rise of America to World Power*** (1956), A. W. Griswold, **The Far Eastern Policy of the United States*** (1938), Tyler Dennett, **John Hay** (1938), C. S. Campbell, Jr., **Special Business Interests and the Open Door Policy** (1951), Thomas McCormick, **China Market*** (1967), and H. C. Hill, **Roosevelt and the Caribbean** (1927). R. E. Osgood, **Ideals and Self-Interest in America's Foreign Relations*** (1953), and G. F. Kennan, **American Diplomacy: 1900–1950*** (1951), are important interpretations of early-20th-century United States policy, more general in scope than May's **American Imperialism** and Williams's **Tragedy of American Diplomacy.***

23
The Progressive Era

The true friend of property, the true conservative, is he who insists that property shall be the servant and not the master of the commonwealth. . . . The citizens of the United States must effectively control the mighty commercial forces which they have themselves called into being. THEODORE ROOSEVELT, *1910*

The period bounded roughly by the end of the Spanish-American War and American entry into World War I is usually called the Progressive Era. Like all such generalizations about complex subjects, this title involves a great simplification. Whether *progressive* is taken to mean "tending toward change" or "improvement" or is merely used to suggest an attitude of mind, it was neither a unique nor a universal characteristic of the early years of the 20th century. Progressive elements had existed in earlier periods and did not disappear when the first American soldiers took ship for France. In important ways the progressivism of the time was a continuation of the response to industrialism that began after the Civil War, a response which has not ended. Historians have scoured the sources trying to define and explain the Progressive Era without devising an interpretation of the period satisfactory to all. Nevertheless the term *progressive* provides a useful description of this exciting and significant period of American history.

Roots of Progressivism

The progressives were never a single group seeking a single objective. The movement sprang from many sources. One was the fight against corruption and inefficiency in government, which dated at least to the Grant era. The struggle for civil service reform was only the first skirmish in this battle; the continuing power of corrupt political machines and the growing influence of large corporations and their lobbyists on municipal and state governments outraged thousands of citizens and led them to seek ways of purifying politics and making the machinery of government responsive to the majority rather than to special interest groups.

Progressivism also had roots in the effort to regulate and control big business, which characterized the Granger and Populist agitation of the 1870s and 1890s. The failure of the Interstate Commerce Act to end railroad abuses and of the Sherman Antitrust Act to check the growth of monopolies became increasingly apparent after 1900. The return of prosperity after the depression of the 1890s aggravated these problems by strengthening the big corporations. It encouraged the opposition by removing the inhibiting fear, so influential in the 1896 presidential campaign, that an assault on the industrial giants might lead to the collapse of the economy.

Between 1897 and 1904 the trend toward concentration in industry accelerated. Such new giants as Amalgamated Copper (1899), U. S. Steel (1901), and International Harvester (1902) attracted most of the attention, but even more alarming were the overall statistics. In a single year (1899) more than 1,200 firms were absorbed in mergers, the resulting combinations being capitalized at $2.2 billion. By 1904 there were 318 industrial combinations with an aggregate capital of $7.5 billion in the country. Those who considered bigness inherently evil demanded that the huge new "trusts" be broken up or at least strictly controlled.

Settlement house workers and other reformers concerned about the welfare of the urban poor made up a third battalion in the progressive army. The working and living conditions of slum dwellers remained abominable. The child labor problem was particularly acute; in 1900 about 1.7 million children under the age of 16 were working full time—more than the membership of the American Federation of Labor. Laws regulating the hours and working conditions of women in industry were far from adequate, and almost nothing had been done, despite the increased use of dangerous machinery in the factories, to enforce safety rules or to provide compensation or insurance for workers injured on the job. As the number of professionally competent social workers grew, the movement for social welfare legislation gained momentum.

All these tendencies may be summed up in Robert H. Wiebe's phrase, "the search for order." America was becoming more urban, more industrial, more mechanized, more centralized—in short, more complex. This trend put a premium on efficiency and cooperation. It seemed obvious to the progressives that people must become more socially minded, the economy more carefully organized.

By attracting additional thousands of sympathizers to the general cause of reform, the return of prosperity after 1896 produced the progressive movement. Good times made the average person more tolerant and generous. So long as his own profits were on the rise, the average businessman did not object if labor improved its position too. Middle-class Americans who had been prepared to go to the barricades in the event of a Bryan victory

The impact of The Silent War, *a 1906 novel by John Ames Mitchell that dealt with the growing class struggle in America, was enhanced by William Balfour-Ker's graphic illustration,* From the Depths.

in 1896 became conscience-stricken when they compared their own comfortable circumstances with those of the "huddled masses" of immigrants and native poor. Nonmaterialistic, humanitarian motives governed their behavior; they were reformers more "of the heart and the head than of the stomach."

Giant industrial and commercial corporations threatened not so much the economic well-being as the ambitions and sense of importance of the middle class. What owner of a small mill or shop could now hope to rise to the heights attained by Carnegie or merchants like John Wanamaker and Marshall Field? The growth of large labor organizations worried such types. Union membership tripled between 1896 and 1910; bargaining became a clash of organized interests; individual relationships between employer and worker no longer counted for much. In general, character and moral values seemed less influential; organizations—cold, impersonal, heartless—were coming to control business, politics, and too many other aspects of life.

The historian Richard Hofstadter suggested still another explanation of the progressive movement. Numbers of moderately prosperous businessmen, together with members of the professions and other educated people, felt threatened by the increasing power and status of the new tycoons, many of them coarse, domineering, and fond of vulgar display. The antics of machine politicians who made a mockery of the traditions of duty, service, and patriotism associated with statesmanship also troubled them. Comfortably well-off, middle-level businessmen lived in what seemed like genteel poverty compared to a Rockefeller or a Morgan, and they often found that the influence in the community that they considered their birthright had been usurped by a cynical local boss.

Protestant pastors accustomed to the respect and deference of their flocks found their moral leadership challenged by materialistic vestrymen who did not even pay them decent salaries. College professors worried about their institutions falling under the sway of wealthy trustees who had little interest in or respect for learning. Lawyers had been "the aristocracy of the United States," James Bryce recalled in 1905; they were now merely "a part of the great organized system of industrial and financial enterprise."

Such people could support reform measures without feeling that they were being very radical because the intellectual currents of the time harmonized with their ideas of social improvement and the welfare state. The new doctrines of the social scientists, the Social Gospel religious leaders, and the philosophers of pragmatism provided a salubrious climate for progressivism. Many of the thinkers who formulated these doctrines in the 1880s and 1890s turned to the task of putting them into practice in the new century. Their number included the economist Richard T. Ely, the philosopher John Dewey, and the Baptist clergyman Walter Rauschenbusch, who, in addition to his many books extolling the Social Gospel, was active in civic reform movements in Rochester, New York.

The Muckrakers

As the diffuse progressive army gradually formed its battalions, a new journalistic fad brought the movement into focus. For many years the magazines *Forum, Arena, McClure's,* and even the staid *Atlantic Monthly* had been publishing articles discussing current political, social, and economic problems. Henry Demarest Lloyd's first blast at the Standard Oil monopoly appeared in the *Atlantic Monthly* in 1881; the radicals Henry George and Eugene V. Debs discussed a variety of problems in the pages of *Arena* in the early 1890s; Josiah Flynt exposed the corrupt relationship between criminals and the New York police for *McClure's* in 1900.

Over the years the tempo and forcefulness of this type of literature increased. Then, in the fall of 1902, *McClure's* began two particularly hard-hitting series of articles, one on Standard Oil by Ida Tarbell, the other on big-city political machines by Lincoln Steffens. These articles evoked much comment. When S. S. McClure decided to include in the January 1903 issue an attack on labor gangsterism in the coalfields along with installments of the Tarbell and Steffens series, he called attention to the circumstance in a striking editorial. Something was radically wrong with the "American character," he wrote. These articles showed that large numbers of American employers, workers, and politicians were fundamentally immoral. Lawyers were becoming tools of big business, judges were permitting evildoers to escape justice, the churches were materialistic, the colleges were incapable of understanding what was happening. "There is no one left; none but all of us," McClure concluded. "We have to pay in the end."

McClure's editorial, one of the most influential ever published in an American magazine, loosed a chain reaction. The issue sold out quickly. Thousands of readers found their own vague apprehensions brought into focus, some becoming active in progressive movements, more lending passive support.

Other editors jumped to adopt the McClure formula. A small army of professional writers soon flooded the periodical press with denunciations of the insurance business, the drug business, college athletics, prostitution, sweatshop labor, political corruption, and dozens of other subjects. The intellectual level and the essential honesty of their work varied greatly. Much of it was lurid, distorted, designed to titillate and scandalize rather than to inform. This type of article inspired Theodore Roosevelt, with his gift for vivid language, to compare the journalists to "the Man with the Muck-Rake" in John Bunyan's *Pilgrim's Progress,* whose attention was so fixed on the filth at his feet that he could not notice the "celestial crown" that was offered him in exchange. Roosevelt's characterization grossly misrepresented the more worthy literature of exposure, but the label *muckraking* was thereafter permanently affixed to the type. Despite the connotations, *muckraker* became a term of honor.

"The Smile That Won't Come Off": a caricature of muckraker Ida M. Tarbell, the nemesis of Standard Oil, reproduced in the New York Telegram, *May 5, 1906.*

The Progressive Mind

Progressives were essentially middle-class moralists seeking to arouse the conscience of "the people" in order to purify American life. They were convinced that human beings were by nature decent, well-intentioned, and kind. (After all, the words *human* and *humane* have the same root.) More deeply than earlier reformers they believed that the source of society's evils lay in the structure of its institutions, not in the weaknesses or sinfulness of individuals.

Therefore the solution to social problems lay in changing faulty institutions. Local, state, and national government must be made more responsive to the will of decent citizens who stood for the traditional virtues. Then the government (once purified) must *act.* Whatever its virtues, laissez faire was obsolete. Businessmen, especially big businessmen, must be compelled to behave fairly, their acquisitive drives curbed in the interests of justice and equal opportunity for all. The weaker elements in society—women, children, the poor, the infirm—must be protected against unscrupulous power. The people, by which (whether they realized it or not) most progressives meant the middle class, must assume new responsibilities toward the unfortunate.

Despite its fervor and democratic rhetoric, progressivism was paternalistic, moderate, and often softheaded. Typical reformers of the period oversimplified complicated issues and treated their personal values as absolute standards of truth and morality. Thus progressives often acted at cross-purposes; at times some were even at war with themselves. This accounts for the diffuseness of the movement. Cutthroat business practices were criticized by great tycoons seeking to preserve their own positions and by small operators trying to protect themselves against the tycoons. But the former wanted federal regulation of big business and the latter strict enforcement of the antitrust laws. Political reforms like the direct primary election appealed to rural progressives but found few adherents among progressive businessmen.

Many progressives who desired to improve the living standards of industrial workers rejected the proposition that workers could best help themselves by organizing powerful national unions. They found it difficult to cooperate with actual working people, who seemed to them unrefined and narrow-minded. Union leaders favored government action to outlaw child labor and restrict immigration but adopted a laissez faire attitude toward wages-and-hours legislation; they preferred to win these objectives through collective bargaining, thereby justifying their own existence. Many who favored "municipal socialism" (public ownership of streetcar lines, waterworks, and other local utilities) adamantly opposed the national ownership of railroads. Progressives stressed individual freedom yet gave strong backing to the drive to deprive the public of its right to drink alcoholic beverages. Few progressives worked more assiduously than Congressman George W. Norris of rural Nebraska for reforms that would increase the power of the ordinary voter, such as the direct primary and popular election of senators, yet Norris characterized the mass of urban voters as "the mob."

The progressives never challenged the fundamental principles of capitalism, nor did they attempt a basic reorganization of society. They would have little to do with the socialist brand of reform. Wisconsin was the most progressive of states, but its leaders never cooperated with the Socialist party of Milwaukee. When socialists threatened to win control of Los Angeles in 1911, California progressives made common cause with reactionary groups in order to defeat them. Many progressives were anti-immigrant and only a handful had anything to offer blacks, surely the most exploited group in American society.

"Progressive" Artists

A good example of the relatively limited radicalism of progressives is offered by the experiences of progressive artists. Early in the century a number of painters, including Robert Henri, John Sloan, and George Luks, tried to develop a distinctively American style. They turned to city streets and the people of the slums for their models, and they depended more on inspiration and inner conviction than careful craftsmanship to achieve their effects. These "ashcan" artists were individualists, yet they supported social reform and were caught up in the progressive movement. Their idols were socially conscious painters such as Hogarth, Goya, and Daumier; they thought of themselves as rebels.

In 1912 they formed the Association of American Painters and Sculptors. The following year they organized a big showing of their work in New

American realists like William Glackens (see also page 638) earned the collective name "The Ashcan School" for their frank portrayals of working-class life. In The Green Car, *1910, Glackens includes muddy streets and curbside piles of slush in the everyday scene of a woman waiting for a streetcar.*

York's 69th Regiment Armory. Almost incidentally they decided to include a sampling of recent and current European art to add another dimension to the exhibition.

Artistically the ashcan painters were not very advanced, being uninfluenced by (if not ignorant of) the outburst of Postimpressionist activity then taking place in Europe. The Europeans stole the show. For the first time Americans—well over 250,000 of them—were offered a comprehensive view of "modern" art, from Manet and Cézanne to Matisse and Picasso. Most found the dazzling color and weird distortions of the European "madmen" shocking but fascinating. A relatively unimportant cubist painting, Marcel Duchamp's *Nude Descending a Staircase,* became the focal point of the exhibition, attracting the scorn of conservative critics and the snickers of unschooled observers. One critic proposed renaming it "Explosion in a Shingle Factory"; another wit suggested "Rush Hour at the Subway"; Theodore Roosevelt, reviewing the exhibition for *Outlook,* compared it unfavorably with a Navaho rug in his bathroom.

Amid the furor, the work of the Americans was

European paintings, notably Marcel Duchamp's Nude Descending a Staircase, No. 2, *1912, stole the Armory show away from the American hosts.*

virtually ignored. As a means of demonstrating their daring and originality, the show was an almost total failure. Even Roosevelt, who praised the ashcan painters while laughing off the cubist "Knights of the Isosceles Triangle" and other members of the "lunatic fringe," believed that the association had arranged the Armory Show "primarily . . . to give the public a chance to see what has recently been going on abroad." Most of the ashcan painters were confused and disheartened by their show; their hopes for creating a new American style died.

Political Reform: Cities First

To most progressives, political corruption and inefficiency lay at the root of the evils plaguing American society, and nowhere were corruption and inefficiency more obvious than in the nation's cities. Two characteristics of urban life are its anonymity and its complexity. These qualities help explain why slavery did not flourish in cities, which was undoubtedly a good thing, but also why the above-named vices did flourish, which was not good at all. Despite the efforts of the late-19th-century urban reformers, they persisted into the Progressive Era and (alas) beyond. As the cities grew, their antiquated and boss-ridden administrations became more and more disgraceful. Consider the example of San Francisco. After 1901, a shrewd lawyer named Abe Ruef ruled one of the most powerful and dissolute political machines in the nation. Only one kind of paving material was used on San Francisco's steets, and Ruef was the lawyer for the company that supplied it. When the gas company asked for a rate increase of 10 cents per 100 cubic feet, Ruef, who was already collecting $1,000 a month from the company as a "retainer," demanded and got an outright bribe of $20,000. A streetcar company needed city authorization to install overhead trolley wires; Ruef's approval cost the company $85,000. Prostitution flourished, with Ruef and his henchmen sharing in the profits. There was a brisk illegal trade in liquor licenses and other favors.

Similar conditions existed in dozens of communities. For his famous muckraking series for *McClure's,* Lincoln Steffens visited St. Louis, Minneapolis, Pittsburgh, New York, Chicago, and Philadelphia and found them all riddled with corruption.

Beginning in the late 1890s progressives mounted a massive assault on dishonest and inefficient urban governments. In San Francisco a group headed by the newspaperman Fremont Older and Rudolph Spreckels, a wealthy sugar manufacturer, broke the machine and lodged Ruef in jail. In Toledo, Ohio, Samuel M. "Golden Rule" Jones won election as mayor in 1897 and succeeded in arousing the citizenry against the corruptionists. The signs that Jones placed on the lawns of Toledo's parks reflected the spirit of his administration. Instead of "Keep Off the Grass," they read: "Citizens, Protect Your Property." Other important progressive mayors were Tom L. Johnson of Cleveland, whose administration Lincoln Steffens called the best in the United States; Seth Low and later John P. Mitchell of New York; and Hazen S. Pingree of Detroit. In St. Louis the prosecutor Joseph W. Folk led a major reform drive.

City reformers could seldom destroy the machines without changing urban political institutions. Some cities obtained "home rule" charters that gave them greater freedom from state control in dealing with local matters. Many created research bureaus that investigated government problems in a scientific and nonpartisan manner. A number of middle-sized communities (Galveston, Texas, was the prototype) experimented with a system that integrated executive and legislative powers in the hands of a small elected commission, thereby concentrating responsibility and making it easier to coordinate complex activities. Out of this experiment came the city manager system, under which the commissioners appointed a professional manager to administer city affairs on a nonpartisan basis. Dayton, Ohio, which adopted the plan after the town was devastated by a flood in 1913, offers the best illustration of the city manager system in the Progressive Era.

Political Reform: The States

To carry out this kind of change required the support of state legislatures, since all municipal government depends on the authority of a sovereign state. Such approval was often difficult to obtain—local bosses were usually entrenched in powerful state machines, and most legislatures were controlled by rural majorities insensitive to urban needs. Therefore the progressives had to strike at inefficiency and corruption at the state level too.

During the first decade of the new century, Wisconsin, the progressive state par excellence, was transformed by Robert M. La Follette, one of the most remarkable figures of the age. La Follette was born in Primrose, Wisconsin, in 1855. He had served three terms as a Republican congressman (1885–1891) and developed a reputation as an uncompromising foe of corruption before being elected governor in 1900. That the people would do the right thing in any situation if properly informed and inspired was the fundamental article of his political faith. "Machine control is based upon misrepresentation and ignorance," La Follette said. "Democracy is based upon knowledge. . . . The only way to beat the boss and ring rule [is] to keep the people thoroughly informed." His own career seemed to prove his point, for in his repeated clashes with the conservative Wisconsin Republican machine, he won battle after battle by vigorous grass-roots campaigning.

La Follette overhauled the political structure of Wisconsin. Over the opposition of conservative

Robert M. La Follette speaking to Wisconsin farmers in 1897. After six years as governor of the state, he won election to the Senate, serving four terms.

Republicans subservient to railroad and lumbering interests, he obtained a direct primary system for nominating candidates, a corrupt practices act, and laws limiting campaign expenditures and lobbying activities. In power he became something of a boss himself. He made ruthless use of patronage, demanded absolute loyalty of his subordinates, and often stretched, or at least oversimplified, the truth when presenting complex issues to the voters.

La Follette was a consummate showman who never rose entirely above rural prejudices. He was prone to scent a nefarious "conspiracy" organized by "the interests" behind even the mildest opposition to his proposals. But he was devoted to the cause of honest government. Realizing that some state functions called for specialized technical knowledge, he used commissions and agencies to handle such matters as railroad regulation, tax assessment, conservation, and highway construction. Wisconsin established a legislative reference library to assist lawmakers in drafting bills. For work of this kind, La Follette called on the faculty of the University of Wisconsin, enticing such scholars as the economist Balthasar H. Meyer and the political scientist Thomas S. Adams into the public service and drawing freely on the advice of such outstanding social scientists as Richard T. Ely, John R. Commons, and E. A. Ross.

The success of what became known as the Wisconsin Idea led other states to adopt similar programs. Reform administrations swept into office in Iowa and Arkansas (1901), Oregon (1902), Minnesota, Kansas, and Mississippi (1904), New York and Georgia (1906), Nebraska (1909), New Jersey and Colorado (1910). In some cases the reformers were Republicans, in others Democrats, but in all these states and in many others, the example of Wisconsin was influential. By 1910, 15 states had established legislative reference services, most of them staffed by personnel trained in Wisconsin. The direct primary system became almost universal.

Some states went beyond Wisconsin in striving to make their governments responsive to the popular will. In 1902 Oregon began to experiment with the initiative, a system by which a bill could be forced on the attention of the legislature by popular petition, and the referendum, a method for allowing the electorate to approve measures rejected by their representatives and to repeal measures that the legislature had passed. Eleven states, most of them in the West, had legalized these devices by 1914.

Political Reform in Washington

On the national level the Progressive Era saw the culmination of the struggle for women's suffrage. The shock occasioned by the failure of the Thirteenth and Fourteenth Amendments to give women the vote resulted in a split among feminists. One group, the American Women's Suffrage Association, focused on the vote question alone. The more radical National Women's Suffrage Association, led by Elizabeth Cady Stanton and Susan B. Anthony, concerned itself with many issues of importance to women as well as the suffrage. The NWSA took an exceedingly partisan stance, placing the immediate interests of women ahead of everything else. It was deeply involved in efforts to unionize women workers, yet it did not hesitate to urge women to be strikebreakers if they could get better jobs by doing so.

Aside from the weaknesses resulting from their lack of unity, feminists were handicapped in the late 19th century by Victorian sexual inhibitions, which most of their leaders shared. Dislike of male-dominated society was hard enough to separate from dislike of men under the best of circumstances. At a time when sex was an unmentionable topic in polite society and sexual feelings were often deeply repressed, some of the most militant advocates of women's rights probably did not understand their own feelings. Most feminists, for example, opposed contraception, insisting that birth control by any means other than continence would encourage what they called masculine lust. The Victorian idealization of female "purity" and the popular image of women as the revered guardians of home and family further confused many reformers. And the trend of 19th-century scientific thinking, influenced by the Darwinian concept of biological adaptation, led to the conclusion that the female personality was fundamentally different from the male and that the differences were inherent, not culturally determined.

These ideas and prejudices enticed feminists into a logical trap. If women were morally superior to men—a tempting conclusion—feminists could advance a practical argument for giving women the suffrage; it would improve the character of the electorate. Society would benefit in dozens of ways—politics would become less corrupt, war would become a thing of the past, and so on. "City housekeeping has failed," said Jane Addams of Hull House in arguing for the reform of municipal government, "partly because women, the traditional housekeepers, have not been consulted."

The trouble with this argument (aside from the fact that opponents could easily demonstrate that in states where women did vote, governments were no better or worse than elsewhere) was that it surrendered the principle of equality. In the long run this was to have serious consequences for the women's movement, though the immediate effect of the "purity" argument probably was to advance the suffragists' cause.

By the early 20th century there were signs of progress. In 1890 the two major women's groups combined as the National American Women's Suffrage Association. While Stanton and Anthony were the first two presidents of the association, new leaders were emerging, the most notable being Carrie Chapman Catt, a woman who combined superb organizing abilities and political skills with commitment to broad social reform. The NAWSA made winning the right to vote its main objective and concentrated on a state-by-state approach.

In the 1890s it won some minor victories; by 1896 Wyoming, Utah, Colorado, and Idaho had been won over to women's suffrage. The burgeoning of the progressive movement helped as middle-class recruits of both sexes adopted the cause. California voted for women's suffrage in 1911 after having defeated the proposal some years earlier, and several other states fell in line. For the first time, large numbers of working-class women began to agitate for the vote.

The suffragists then shifted the campaign back to the national level, the lead taken by a new organization, the Congressional Union, headed by Alice Paul. After some hesitation the NAWSA began to campaign for a constitutional amendment, which won congressional approval in 1918. By 1920 the necessary three-quarters of the states had approved the Nineteenth Amendment; the long fight was over.

The progressive drive for political democracy also found expression in the Seventeenth Amendment to the Constitution, ratified in 1913, which required the popular election of senators. And a group of "insurgent" congressmen managed to reform the House of Representatives by limiting the power of the Speaker. During the early years of the century, operating under the system established in the 1890s by "Czar" Thomas B. Reed, Speaker Joseph G. Cannon exercised tyrannical authority, appointing the members of all committees and controlling the course of legislation. Representatives could seldom obtain the floor without first explaining their purpose to Cannon and obtaining the Speaker's consent. In 1910 the insurgents, led by George W. Norris of Nebraska, stripped Cannon of his control over the House Rules Committee. Thereafter, appointments to committees were determined by the entire membership, acting through party caucuses. This change was thoroughly progressive. "We want the House to be representative of the people and each individual member to have his ideas presented and passed on," Norris explained.

No other important alterations of the national political system were made during the Progressive Era. Although some 20 states passed presidential primary laws, no change in the cumbersome and undemocratic method of electing presidents was accomplished. An attempt to improve the efficiency of the federal bureaucracy led Congress to create a Commission on Efficiency and Economy in 1911, but it did not act on the commission's recommendations. Congress did pass a law in 1911 requiring its members to file statements of their campaign expenses.

Social and Economic Reforms

Political reform was only a means to an end; once the system had been made responsive to the desires of the people, the progressives hoped to use it to improve society itself. Many cities experimented with "gas and water socialism," taking over public utility companies and operating them as departments of the municipal government. Under "Golden Rule" Jones, Toledo established a minimum wage for city employees, built playgrounds and golf courses, and moderated its harsh penal code. Mayor Seth Low improved New York's public transportation system and obtained the passage of

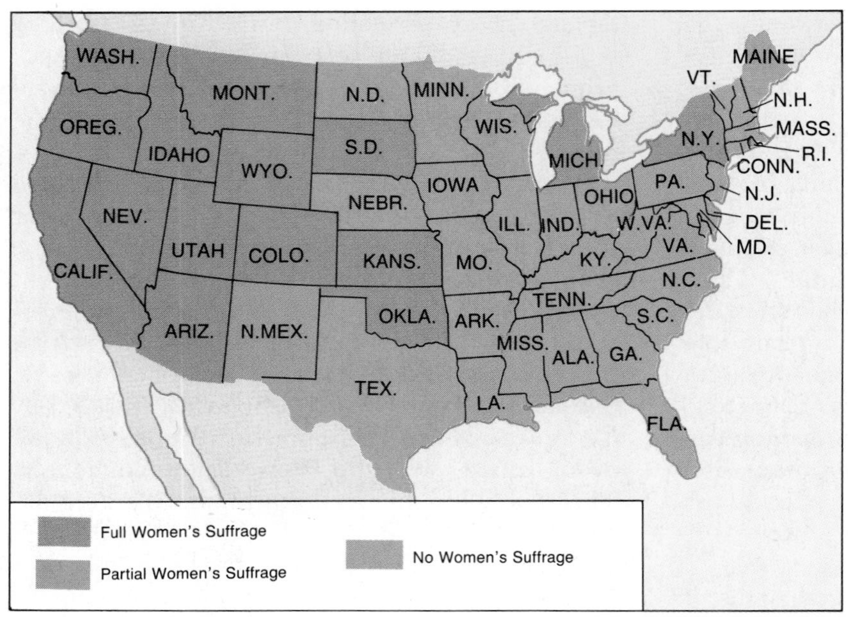

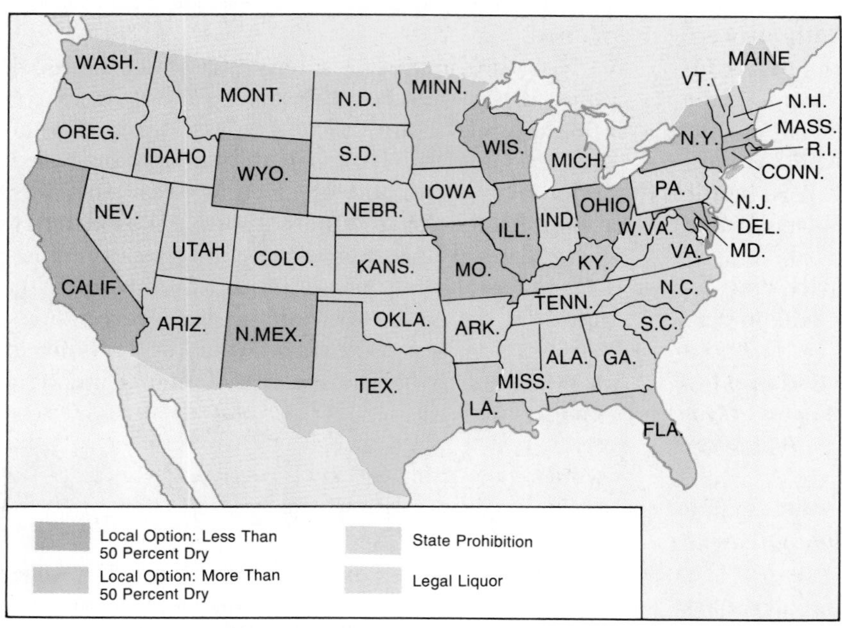

SUFFRAGE AND PROHIBITION, 1917

These maps give a sense of the state-by-state progress of women's suffrage and prohibition by 1917. The Eighteenth Amendment, enforcing national prohibition, passed in 1919; the Nineteenth Amendment, allowing women the right to vote, in 1920. Both amendments were a culmination of reform efforts before and during the Progressive Era. The original 1917 version of the temperance map referred to the three "wet" states—New Jersey, Pennsylvania, and Nevada—as "Booze States."

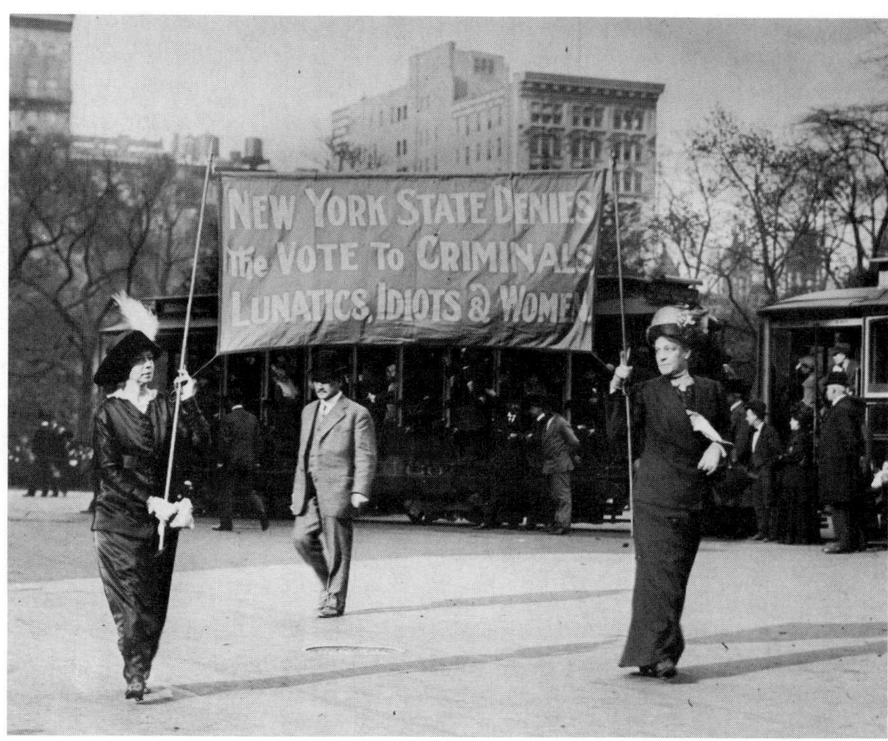

A banner in a 1911 women's suffrage parade carries one of the longest-standing arguments in favor of women getting the vote.

the tenement house law of 1901. Mayor Tom Johnson forced a fare cut to 3 cents on the Cleveland street railways.

At the state level, progressives continued to battle for legislation based on the police power, despite restrictions imposed by the courts under the Fourteenth Amendment. Women played a particularly important part in these struggles; their campaign for the right to vote was part of a larger commitment to reform.

Industrial workers improved their position mainly because good times kept unemployment down. Real wages rose only slightly in spite of the rapid increase in labor productivity, and the length of the workweek declined slowly. However, government action forced a significant decline in the employment of children. Sparked by the National Child Labor Committee, organized in 1904, reformers over the next ten years obtained laws in nearly every state banning the employment of young children (the minimum age varied from 12 to 16). Many states also limited the hours of older children to eight or ten per day and outlawed night work and labor in dangerous occupations by minors. These laws fixed no uniform standards and many were poorly enforced, yet when Congress passed a federal child labor law in 1916, the Supreme Court, in *Hammer* v. *Dagenhart* (1918), declared it unconstitutional.*

By 1917 nearly all the states had placed limitations on the hours of women industrial workers, and about ten states had set minimum wage standards for women. Once again federal action that would have extended such regulation to the entire country did not materialize. Even a ten-hour law for women workers in the District of Columbia was thrown out by the Court in *Adkins* v. *Children's Hospital* (1923).

Laws protecting workers against on-the-job accidents were enacted by many states. Disasters like the 1911 Triangle fire in New York City, in which nearly 150 women perished because the Triangle shirtwaist factory had no fire escapes, led to the passage of stricter municipal building codes and

* A second child labor law, passed in 1919, was also thrown out by the Court, and a child labor amendment, submitted in 1924, failed to achieve ratification by the necessary three-quarters of the states.

many state factory inspection acts. By 1910 most states had modified the common-law principle that a worker accepted the risk of accident as a condition of employment and was not entitled to compensation if injured unless it could be proved that the employer had been negligent. Gradually the states adopted accident insurance plans, and some began to grant pensions to widows with small children. Most manufacturers favored such measures, if for no other reason than that they regularized procedures and avoided costly lawsuits.

The passage of so much state social legislation sent conservatives scurrying to the Supreme Court for redress. Such persons believed, quite sincerely in most instances, that *no* government had the power to deprive either workers or employers of the right to negotiate any kind of labor contract they wished. The decision of the Supreme Court in the Lochner bakeshop case (1905) seemed to indicate that the justices would adopt this point of view. But when an Oregon law limiting women laundry workers to ten hours a day was challenged in *Muller* v. *Oregon* (1908), Florence Kelley and Josephine Goldmark of the Consumers' League persuaded Louis D. Brandeis to defend the statute before the Court.

The Consumers' League, whose slogan was "investigate, agitate, legislate," was probably the most effective women's organization of the period. With the aid of League researchers Brandeis prepared a remarkable brief stuffed with economic and sociological evidence indicating that *in fact* long hours damaged both the health of individual women and the health of society. This nonlegal evidence greatly impressed the judges. "It may not be amiss," they declared, "to notice . . . expressions of opinion from other than judicial sources" in determining the constitutionality of such laws. "Woman's physical structure, and the functions she performs in consequence thereof, justify special legislation," they concluded. "The limitations which this statute places upon her contractual powers . . . are not imposed solely for her benefit, but also largely for the benefit of all."

The fact that the Oregon law applied only to women reduced the importance of the Muller decision. In some later cases the Court threw out labor laws based on the police power. Nevertheless, after 1908 the right of states to protect women, children, and workers performing dangerous and unhealthy tasks by special legislation was widely accepted. The use of the "Brandeis brief" technique to demonstrate the need for such legislation became standard practice.

Progressives also launched a massive if ill-coordinated attack on problems related to monopoly. When the evils of the boss system could be connected to the threat posed by "monopolistic" big business, the impact on public opinion, and thus on legislation, could be formidable. The variety of regulatory legislation passed by the states between 1900 and 1917 was almost infinite. In Wisconsin the progressives created a powerful railroad commission staffed with nonpartisan experts; they enacted a graduated income tax and strengthened the state tax commission, which then proceeded to force corporations to bear a larger share of the cost of government; they overhauled the laws regulating insurance companies and set up a small state-owned life insurance company to serve as a yardstick for evaluating the rates of private companies. In 1911, besides creating an industrial commission to enforce the state's labor and factory legislation, they established a conservation commission, headed by Charles R. Van Hise, president of the University of Wisconsin.

A similar spate of legislation characterized the brief reign of Woodrow Wilson as governor of New Jersey (1911–1913). Urged on by the relentless Wilson, the legislature created a strong public utility commission with authority to evaluate the properties of railroad, gas, electric, telephone, and express companies and to fix rates and set standards for these corporations. The legislature enacted storage and food inspection laws, and in 1913, after Wilson had moved on to the presidency, it passed seven bills (the "Seven Sisters" laws) tightening the state's loose controls over corporations, which had won New Jersey the unenviable reputation of being "the mother of trusts."

Economic reforms in other states were less spectacular but impressive in the mass. In New York an investigation of the big life insurance companies led to comprehensive changes in the insurance laws and put Charles Evans Hughes, who had conducted the investigation, in the governor's chair, where he achieved other progressive reforms. In Iowa stiff laws regulating railroads were passed in 1906. In Nebraska the legislature created a system of bank deposit insurance in 1909. Minnesota levied an inheritance tax and built a harvesting machine factory to compete with the harvester trust. Georgia raised the taxes on corporations.

These are examples plucked almost at random from among hundreds of laws passed by states in every part of the nation. However, as in the area of social legislation, piecemeal state regulation failed to solve the problems of an economy growing yearly more integrated and complex. It was on the national level that the most significant battles for economic reform were fought.

Theodore Roosevelt: Cowboy in the White House

On September 6, 1901, an anarchist named Leon Czolgosz shot President McKinley during a public reception at the Pan-American Exposition at Buffalo, New York. Eight days later McKinley died and Theodore Roosevelt became president of the United States. The new president hastened to assure the country that he intended to carry on in his predecessor's footsteps, but his ascension to the presidency marked the beginning of a new era in national politics.

Although only 42, by far the youngest president in the nation's history up to that time, Roosevelt brought solid qualifications to his high office. Son of a well-to-do New York merchant of Dutch ancestry, he had graduated from Harvard in 1880 and studied law briefly at Columbia, though he did not complete his degree. In addition to political experience that included three terms in the New York assembly, six years on the United States Civil Service Commission, two years as police commissioner of New York City, another as assistant secretary of the navy, and a term as governor of New York, he had been a rancher in Dakota Territory and a soldier in the Spanish-American War. He was also a well-known historian: his *Naval War of 1812* (1882), begun during his undergraduate days at Harvard, and his four-volume *Winning of the West* (1889–1896) were valuable works of scholarship, and he had written two popular biographies and other books as well. Politically, he had always been a loyal Republican. He rejected the Mugwump heresy in 1884, despite his distaste for Blaine, and during the tempestuous 1890s he vigorously denounced Populism, Bryanism, and "labor agitators."

Nevertheless Roosevelt's elevation to the presidency alarmed many conservatives, and not without reason. He did not fit their conception, based on a composite image of the chief executives from Hayes to McKinley, of what a president should be like. He seemed too undignified, too energetic, too outspoken, too unconventional. It was one thing to have operated a cattle ranch, another to have captured a gang of rustlers at gunpoint; one thing to have run a metropolitan police force, another to have roamed New York slums in the small hours in order to catch patrolmen fraternizing with thieves and prostitutes; one thing to have commanded a regiment, another to have killed a Spaniard personally.

Roosevelt had been a sickly child, plagued by asthma and poor eyesight, and he seems to have spent much of his adult life compensating for the sense of inadequacy that these troubles bred in him. He repeatedly carried his displays of physical stamina and personal courage, and his love of athletics and big-game hunting, to preternatural lengths. Henry Adams, who watched Roosevelt's development over the years with a mixture of fear and amusement, once said that he possessed "the singular primitive quality that belongs to ultimate matter . . . —he was pure act." Once, while fox hunting, he fell from his horse, cutting his face severely and breaking his left arm. Instead of waiting for help or struggling to some nearby house to summon a doctor, Roosevelt clambered back on his horse and resumed the chase. "I was in at the death," he wrote next day. "I looked pretty gay, with one arm dangling, and my face and clothes like the walls of a slaughter house." That evening, after his arm had been set and put in splints, he attended a dinner party.

Roosevelt worshiped aggressiveness and was extremely sensitive to any threat to his honor as a gentleman. When another young man showed some slight interest in Roosevelt's fiancée, he sent for a set of French dueling pistols. His teachers found him an interesting student, for he was intelligent and imaginative if rather annoyingly argumentative. "Now look here, Roosevelt," one Harvard professor finally said to him, "let me talk. I'm running this course."

Few individuals have rationalized or sublimated their feelings of inferiority as effectively as Roosevelt and to such good purpose. And few have been more genuinely warmhearted, more full of spontaneity, more committed to the ideals of public service and national greatness. As a political leader he was energetic and hard-driving. Conservatives and timid souls, sensing his aggressiveness even when he held it in check, distrusted Roosevelt's judgment, fearing he might go off half-cocked in some crisis. In fact his judgment was nearly always sound; responsibility usually tempered his aggressiveness.

When Roosevelt was first mentioned as a running mate for McKinley in 1900, he wrote: "The Vice Presidency is a most honorable office, but for a young man there is not much to do." It would have been unthinkable for him to preside over a caretaker administration devoted to maintaining the status quo. However, the reigning Republican politicos, basking in the sunshine of the prosperity that had contributed so much to their victory in 1900, distrusted anything suggestive of change. Mark Hanna reflected the mood of most of his fellow senators when he urged the country to "stand pat and continue Republican prosperity." The same sentiment pervaded the House, where Speaker Cannon said that his philosophy could be summed up in the phrase "Stand by the status."

Had Roosevelt been the impetuous hothead that conservatives feared, he would have plunged ahead without regard for their feelings and influence. Instead he moved slowly and often got what he wanted by using his executive power rather than by persuading Congress to pass new laws. His domestic program, ill defined at first, included some measure of control of big corporations, more power for the Interstate Commerce Commission, and the conservation of natural resources. By consulting congressional leaders and following their advice not to bring up controversial matters like the tariff and currency reform, with which he was not deeply concerned in any case, he obtained a modest budget of new laws.

The Newlands Act (1902) funneled the proceeds from land sales in the West into federal irrigation projects. The Expedition Act (1903) speeded the handling of antitrust suits in the courts. Another 1903 law created a Department of Commerce and Labor, which was to include a Bureau of Corporations with authority to investigate industrial combines and issue reports. The Elkins Railroad Act of 1903 strengthened the Interstate Commerce Commission's hand against the railroads by making the receiving as well as the granting of rebates illegal and by forbidding the roads to deviate in any way from their published rates.

Roosevelt and Big Business

Roosevelt soon became known as a trustbuster, and in the sense that he considered the monopoly problem the most pressing issue of the times, the term has some meaning. But he did not believe in breaking up big corporations indiscriminately. "Much of the legislation . . . enacted against trusts," he said in 1900 while governor of New York, "is not one whit more intelligent than the mediaeval bull against the comet, and has not been one particle more effective." Regulation, rather than disruption, seemed the best way to deal with the big corporations because industrial giantism "could not be eliminated unless we were willing to turn back the wheels of modern progress."

With Congress unwilling to pass a stiff regulatory law—even the bill creating the relatively innocuous Bureau of Corporations ran into much opposition—Roosevelt resorted to the Sherman Act to get at the problem. Although the Supreme Court decision in the Sugar Trust case seemed to have emasculated that law, in 1902 he ordered the Justice Department to bring suit against the Northern Securities Company.

He chose his target wisely. The Northern Securities Company controlled the Great Northern, the Northern Pacific, and the Chicago, Burlington and Quincy railroads. It had been created in 1901 after a titanic battle on the New York Stock Exchange between the forces of J. P. Morgan and James J. Hill and those of E. H. Harriman, who was associated with the Rockefeller interests. In their efforts to obtain control of the Northern Pacific, the rivals had forced its stock up to $1,000 a share, ruining many speculators and threatening to cause a panic. Neither side could win a clear-cut victory, so they decided to put the stock of all three railroads in a holding company owned by the two groups. Since Harriman already controlled the Union Pacific and the Southern Pacific, a virtual monopoly of western railroads was effected. The public had been alarmed, for the merger seemed to typify the rapa-

Roosevelt, the trust-busting lion tamer, whips beef, oil, steel, and other trusts into shape as they emerge from their Wall Street den.

ciousness of the tycoons. Few big corporations had more enemies; thus Roosevelt's attack won wide support.

The announcement of the suit caused consternation in the business world. Morgan rushed to the White House. "If we have done anything wrong," he said to the president, "send your man to my man and they can fix it up." Roosevelt was not fundamentally opposed to this sort of agreement, but it was too late to compromise in this instance. Attorney General Philander C. Knox pressed the case vigorously, and in 1904 the Court ordered the dissolution of the Northern Securities Company. The decision served notice on the great corporations that they could no longer ignore the Sherman Act. Roosevelt ordered suits against the meat packers, the Standard Oil Trust, and the American Tobacco Company. His stock among progressives rose, yet he had not embarrassed the conservatives in Congress by demanding new antitrust legislation.

The president went out of his way to assure *cooperative* corporation magnates that he had no intention of attacking them. He saw no basic conflict between capital and labor and was not against size per se. "In our industrial and social system," he explained, "the interests of all men are so closely intertwined that in the immense majority of cases a straight-dealing man who by his efficiency, by his ingenuity and industry, benefits himself must also benefit others." His Bureau of Corporations followed a policy of "obtaining hearty co-operation rather than arousing [the] antagonism of business and industrial interests." At a White House conference in 1905, Roosevelt and Elbert H. Gary, chairman of the board of U.S. Steel, reached a "gentlemen's agreement" whereby Gary promised "to co-operate with the Government in every possible way." The Bureau of Corporations would conduct an investigation of U.S. Steel, Gary allowing it full access to company records. Roosevelt in turn promised that if the investigation revealed any corporate malpractices, he would allow Gary to set matters right voluntarily, thereby avoiding an antitrust suit. He reached a similar agreement with the International Harvester Company two years later.

There were limits to the effectiveness of such arrangements. Standard Oil agreed to a similar détente and then reneged, refusing to turn over vital records to the bureau. The Justice Department brought suit against the company under the Sherman Act of 1890, and eventually it was broken up at the order of the Supreme Court. Roosevelt would have preferred a more binding kind of regulation, but when he asked for laws giving the government supervisory authority over big combinations, Congress refused to act. Given this situation, gentlemen's agreements seemed the best alternative. Trusts that conformed to Roosevelt's somewhat subjective standards could remain as they were; others must take their chances with the Supreme Court.

Square Dealing

Roosevelt made remarkable use of his executive power during the anthracite coal strike of 1902. In June the United Mine Workers, led by John Mitchell, laid down their picks and demanded higher wages, an eight-hour day, and recognition of the union. Most of the anthracite mines were owned by railroads. Two years earlier the miners had won a 10 percent wage increase in a similar strike, chiefly because the owners feared that labor unrest might endanger the election of McKinley. Now the coal companies were dead set against further concessions; when the men walked out, they shut down their properties and prepared to starve the strikers into submission.

The strike dragged on through summer and early fall. The miners conducted themselves with great restraint, avoiding violence and offering to submit their claims to arbitration. As the price of anthracite soared with the approach of winter, sentiment in their behalf mounted. The fact that railroad corporations allied with Wall Street controlled most of the mines and that the operators refused even to negotiate with the union predisposed the public in the workers' favor.

The owners' spokesman, George F. Baer of the Reading Railroad, proved particularly inept at public relations. Baer stated categorically that God was on the side of management, but when someone suggested asking an important Roman Catholic prelate to arbitrate the dispute, he replied icily: "Anthracite mining is a business and not a religious, sentimental or academic proposition."

Roosevelt shared the public's sympathy for the miners, and the threat of a coal shortage alarmed him. For months he could think of no legal way to intervene. Early in October he summoned both sides to a conference in Washington. He urged them as patriotic Americans to sacrifice "personal consideration[s]" for the "general good." His action enraged the coal operators, for they believed he was trying to force them to recognize the union. They refused even to speak to the UMW representatives at the conference and demanded that Roosevelt end the strike by force and bring suit against the union under the Sherman Act. Mitchell, aware of the immense prestige that Roosevelt had conferred on the union by calling the conference, cooperated fully with the president.

The attitudes of management and the union strengthened public support for the miners. Even former president Grover Cleveland, who had used federal troops to break the Pullman strike, said that he was "disturbed and vexed by the tone and substance of the operators' deliverances." Encouraged by this state of affairs, Roosevelt took a bold step: he announced that unless a settlement was reached promptly, he would order federal troops into the anthracite regions, not to break the strike but to seize and operate the mines.

The threat of government intervention brought the owners to terms. A Cabinet member, Elihu Root, worked out the details with J. P. Morgan, whose firm had major interests in the Reading and other railroads, while cruising the Hudson River on Morgan's yacht. The miners would return to the pits and all issues between them and the coal companies would be submitted for settlement to a commission appointed by Roosevelt. After a last-minute crisis over the inclusion of a union representative on the commission—solved by Roosevelt's appointing the president of one of the railroad brotherhoods but classifying him as an "eminent sociologist" to save the faces of the owners—both sides accepted the arrangement and the men went back to work. In March 1903 the commission granted the miners a 10 percent wage increase and a nine-hour day.

To the public the incident seemed a perfect illustration of the progressive spirit—in Roosevelt's words, everyone had received a "square deal." In fact the results were by no means so clear-cut. The miners gained relatively little and the companies lost still less, for they were not required to recognize the United Mine Workers and the commission also recommended a 10 percent increase in the price of coal, ample compensation for the increased wage costs. The president was the main winner. The public acclaimed him as a fearless, imaginative, public-spirited leader.

Construing the powers of his office broadly, Roosevelt had interjected the federal government into a labor dispute, forced both sides to accept his leadership, and established an extralegal committee of neutrals representing the national interest to arbitrate the questions at issue. Without calling on Congress for support, he had expanded his own authority and hence that of the federal government in order to protect the public interest. His action marked a major forward step in the evolution of the modern presidency.

TR: In His Own Right

By reviving the Sherman Act, settling the coal strike, and pushing moderate reforms through

A silent procession of striking coal miners makes an orderly demonstration at Shenandoah, Pennsylvania, during the 1902 coal strike.

Congress, Roosevelt insured that he would be reelected president in 1904. Progressives were pleased by his performance if not yet captivated. Conservative Republicans offered no serious objection to his renomination and supported him during the campaign. Sensing that Roosevelt had won over the liberals, the Democrats nominated a conservative, Judge Alton B. Parker of New York, and bid for the support of eastern industrialists.

This strategy failed, for businessmen continued to eye the party of Bryan with intense suspicion. They preferred, as the New York *Sun* put it, "the impulsive candidate of the party of conservatism to the conservative candidate of the party which the business interests regard as permanently and dangerously impulsive." Despite his resentment at Roosevelt's attack on the Northern Securities Company, J. P. Morgan contributed $150,000 to the Republican campaign. Other tycoons gave with equal generosity. Roosevelt swept the country, carrying even the normally Democratic border states of Maryland and Missouri. According to one wit, "Parker ran for the presidency against Theodore Roosevelt and was defeated by acclamation."

Encouraged by the landslide and the increasing militancy of progressives, Roosevelt pressed for more reform legislation. His most imaginative proposal was a plan to make the District of Columbia a model progressive community. He suggested child labor and factory inspection laws and a slum clearance program, but Congress refused to act. Likewise, his request for a minimum wage for railroad workers was rejected.

He had greater success when he proposed still another increase in the power of the Interstate Commerce Commission. The Elkins Railroad Act had proved a disappointment, for the courts continued to favor the railroads in most cases. Rebating remained a serious problem. With progressive state governors demanding federal action and with farmers and manufacturers, especially in the Middle West, clamoring for relief against discriminatory rates, Roosevelt was ready by 1905 to make railroad legislation his major objective. The ICC should be empowered to fix rates, not merely to challenge unreasonable ones. It should have the right to inspect the private records of the railroads, since fair rates could not be determined unless the true financial condition of the roads was known.

Because these proposals struck at rights that businessmen considered sacrosanct, many congressmen balked. But Roosevelt applied presidential pressure, and that, combined with broad public support for stiffer regulation, caused a majority to fall in line.

In June 1906 the Hepburn bill became law. It gave the commission the power to inspect the books of railroad companies, to set maximum rates (once a complaint had been filed by a shipper), and to control sleeping car companies, owners of oil pipelines, and other firms engaged in transportation. Railroads could no longer issue passes freely—an important check on their political influence. In all, the Hepburn Act made the ICC a more powerful and more active body. While it did not outlaw judicial review of ICC decisions, thereafter those decisions were seldom overturned by the courts. The staff of the commission grew from fewer than 200 in 1905 to more than 500 in 1909. The number of complaints filed by shippers jumped from 65 to 1,097 in the same years.

How the commission exercised its power was another question. Some authorities claim that it adopted an "archaic" view of the public interest (one based on conditions in the railroad business that were long out of date) and became "a standpat body that ignored inflation and refused rate increases" almost automatically. With their costs rising, the railroads were soon again in financial difficulties. Profits slumped and capital investment declined.

Congress also passed meat inspection and pure food and drug legislation in 1906. The question of federal regulation of slaughterhouses dated back to the "pork controversy" with the European powers in the 1880s. Feelings about meat inspection in the business world were mixed. The major packers tended to favor inspection because of their interest in the export market; most local packers objected. Other businessmen were divided, some objecting in principle to any extension of government regulation. In 1906 the president of the National Association of Manufacturers opposed regulating the packers, but the NAM board of directors voted not to campaign against inspection.

The publication in 1906 of Upton Sinclair's novel *The Jungle,* a devastating exposé of the filthy conditions in the Chicago slaughterhouses, focused attention on the issue. Sinclair was more interested in writing a socialist tract than he was in meat inspection, but his book, a best-seller, raised a storm against the packers. After Roosevelt read *The Jungle* he sent two officials to Chicago to investigate. Their report was so shocking, he said, that its publication would "be well-nigh ruinous to our export trade in meat." He threatened to release the report, however, unless Congress acted. After a hot fight, the meat inspection bill passed. A Pure Food and Drug Act, forbidding the manufacture and sale of adulterated and fraudulently labeled products, rode through Congress on the coattails of this measure.

Roosevelt has probably received more credit than he deserves for these laws. He had never been deeply interested in pure food legislation, and he considered Dr. Harvey W. Wiley, chief chemist of the Department of Agriculture and the leader of the fight for this reform, something of a crank. He compromised with opponents of meat inspection cheerfully, despite his loud denunciations of the evils under attack. "As now carried on the [meat-packing] business is both a menace to health and an outrage on decency," he said. "No legislation that is not drastic and thoroughgoing will be of avail." Yet he went along with the packers' demand that the government pay the costs of inspection, though he believed that "the only way to secure efficiency is by the imposition upon the packers of a fee." Nevertheless the end results were positive

Before the passage of the Pure Food and Drug Act in 1906, manufacturers were free to use any ingredients they chose. Many "tonics" kept their promises of increased vigor by delivering doses of cocaine, alcohol, or other narcotics.

and in line with his conception of the public good.

To advanced liberals Roosevelt's achievements seemed limited when placed beside his professed objectives and his smug evaluations of what he had done. How could he be a reformer and a defender of established interests at the same time? Roosevelt found no difficulty in holding such a position. As one historian has said, "he stood close to the center and bared his teeth at the conservatives of the right and the liberals of the extreme left."

Tilting Left

As the progressive movement advanced, Roosevelt advanced with it. He never accepted all the ideas of what he called its "lunatic fringe," but he took steadily more liberal positions. He always insisted that he was not hostile to business interests, but when those interests sought to exploit the national domain, they had no more implacable foe. He placed some 150 million acres of forest lands in federal reserves, and he strictly enforced the laws governing grazing, mining, and lumbering. When his opponents attached to an important appropriations bill a rider prohibiting the creation of further reserves without the approval of Congress, Roosevelt, in a typical example of his broad use of executive power, transferred an additional 17 million acres to the reserve before signing the bill. In 1908 he organized a National Conservation Conference, attended by 44 governors and 500 others, to discuss conservation matters. As a result of this meeting, most states created conservation commissions.

As Roosevelt became more liberal, conservative Republicans began to balk at following his lead. The sudden panic that struck the financial world in October 1907 speeded the trend. Government policies had no direct bearing on the panic, which began with a run on several important New York trust companies and spread to the Stock Exchange when speculators found themselves unable to borrow money to meet their obligations. In the emergency Roosevelt authorized the deposit of large amounts of government cash in New York banks. He informally agreed to the acquisition of the Tennessee Coal and Iron Company by U.S. Steel when the bankers told him that the purchase was necessary to end the panic. In spite of his efforts, conservatives insisted on referring to the financial collapse as "Roosevelt's Panic," and they blamed the president for the depression that followed on its heels.

Roosevelt, however, turned left rather than right. In 1908 he came out for federal income and inheritance taxes, for stricter regulation of interstate corporations, and for reforms designed to help industrial workers. He denounced "the speculative folly and the flagrant dishonesty" of "malefactors of great wealth," further alienating conservative, or Old Guard Republicans, who believed that economic reform had gone far enough and that political reforms like the direct primary were undermining their power. They resented the attacks on their integrity implicit in many of Roosevelt's statements. When the president began criticizing the courts, the last bastion of conservatism, he lost all chance of obtaining further reform legislation. As he said himself, during his last months in office "the period of stagnation continued to rage with uninterrupted violence."

Taft was the first presidential golfer, playing enthusiastically despite his bulk. He ended his career happily as a chief justice of the Supreme Court.

William Howard Taft: The Listless Progressive

Roosevelt remained popular and politically powerful; before his term ended, he chose William Howard Taft, his secretary of war, to succeed him and easily obtained his nomination. William Jennings Bryan was again the Democratic candidate. Campaigning on Roosevelt's record, Taft carried the country by well over a million votes, defeating Bryan 321 to 162 in the electoral college.

Taft was intelligent, experienced, and public-spirited; he seemed ideally suited to carry out Roosevelt's policies. Born in Cincinnati in 1857, educated at Yale, he had served as an Ohio judge, as solicitor general of the United States under Harrison, and then as a federal circuit court judge before accepting McKinley's assignment to head the Philippine Commission in 1900. His success as civil governor of the Philippines led Roosevelt to make him secretary of war in 1904. He supported the Square Deal loyally. This, together with his mentor's ardent endorsement, won him the backing of most progressive Republicans. Yet the conservative Old Guard liked him too; although outgoing, he had none of the Roosevelt impetuosity and aggressiveness. His antilabor opinions voiced while on the bench raised his status among conservatives. His genial personality and his obvious desire to avoid conflict appealed to moderates.

However, Taft lacked the physical and mental stamina required of a modern chief executive. While he was not lazy, he weighed over 300 pounds and needed to rest this vast bulk more than the job allowed. He liked to eat in leisurely fashion, to idle away mornings on the golf course, to take an afternoon nap. Campaigning bored him; speech-making seemed a needless chore. The judicial life was his real love; intense partisanship dismayed and confused him. He was too reasonable to control a coalition and not ambitious enough to impose his will on others. He found extremists irritating, persistent people (such as his wife) difficult to resist. He supported many progressive measures, but he never absorbed the progressive spirit.

Taft honestly desired to carry out most of Roosevelt's policies. He enforced the Sherman Act vigorously and continued to add land to the national forest reserves. He signed the Mann-Elkins Act of 1910, which empowered the Interstate Commerce Commission to suspend rate increases without waiting for a shipper to complain and established a Commerce Court to speed the settlement of railroad rate cases. An eight-hour day for all persons engaged in work on government contracts, mine safety legislation, and several other reform measures received his approval. He even summoned Congress into special session specifically to reduce tariff duties—something Roosevelt had not dared to attempt.

But Taft had been disturbed by Roosevelt's sweeping use of executive power. "We have got to work out our problems on the basis of law," he insisted. Where Roosevelt had excelled at maneuvering around congressional opposition and in finding ways to accomplish his objectives without waiting for Congress to act, Taft adamantly refused to use such tactics. His restraint was in many ways admirable, but it reduced his effectiveness.

In case after case Taft's lack of vigor and his political ineptness led to trouble. He had an uncanny ability to alienate politicians with views substantially like his own. In the matter of the tariff, he favored downward revision. When the special session met in 1909, the House promptly passed a bill that was in line with his desires. But Senate protectionists restored the high rates of the Act of 1897 on most items. A group of insurgent senators, led by Robert La Follette of Wisconsin, Jonathan Dolliver of Iowa, and Albert J. Beveridge of Indiana, fought these changes desperately, producing masses of statistics to show that the proposed schedules on cotton goods, woolens, and other products were unreasonably high. They were fighting the president's battle, yet Taft did little to help them. He signed the final Payne-Aldrich measure and called it "the best [tariff] bill that the Republican party ever passed." He had some justification for this faint praise, since the act did make important reductions in the duties on cotton goods, hides, shoes, and iron ore. But his attitude dumbfounded the progressives.

In 1910 Taft got into difficulty with the conservationists. While he believed in husbanding natural resources carefully, he did not like the way Roosevelt had circumvented Congress in adding to the forest reserves. He demanded, and eventually obtained, specific legislation to accomplish this purpose. The issue that roused the conservationists concerned the integrity of his secretary of the interior, Richard A. Ballinger. A less-than-ardent conservationist, Ballinger returned to the public domain certain waterpower sites that his predecessor in the Roosevelt administration had withdrawn on the legally questionable ground that they were to become ranger stations. Ballinger's action alarmed Chief Forester Gifford Pinchot, the darling of the conservationists. When Pinchot learned that Ballinger intended to validate the shaky claim of powerful mining interests to a large tract of coal-rich land in Alaska, he launched an intemperate attack on the secretary.

In the Ballinger-Pinchot controversy Taft felt obliged to support his own man. The coal lands dispute was complex, and Pinchot's charges were exaggerated and in poor taste. It was certainly unfair to call Ballinger "the most effective opponent the conservation policies have yet had." When Pinchot, whose own motives were partly political, persisted in criticizing Ballinger, Taft dismissed him, bringing down upon himself the wrath of the conservationists. He had no choice under the circumstances, but a more adept politician would have found some way of avoiding a showdown.

Breakup of the Republican Party

One ominous aspect of the Ballinger-Pinchot affair was that Pinchot was a close friend of Theodore Roosevelt. After Taft's inauguration, Roosevelt had gone off to hunt big game in Africa, bearing in his baggage an autographed photograph of his protégé and a touching letter of appreciation, in which the new president said: "I can never forget that the power I now exercise was a voluntary transfer from you to me." For months, as he trudged across Africa, guns blazing, Roosevelt was out of touch with affairs in the United States. As soon as he emerged from the wilderness in March 1910, bearing more than 3,000 trophies, including 9 lions, 5 elephants, and 13 rhinos, he was caught up in the squabble between the progressive members of his party and its titular head. Pinchot met him in Italy, laden with injured innocence and a packet of angry letters from various progressives. His intimate friend Senator Lodge, essentially a conservative, barraged him with messages, the gist of which was that Taft was lazy and inept and that Roosevelt should prepare to become the "Moses" who would guide the party "out of the wilderness of doubt and discontent" into which Taft had led it.

Roosevelt hoped to steer a middle course, but Pinchot's complaints impressed him. Taft had decided to strike out on his own, he concluded. "No man must render such a service as that I rendered Taft and expect the individual . . . not in the end to become uncomfortable and resentful," he wrote

Lodge sadly. No immediate break took place, but Taft sensed the former president's coolness and was offended. He was egged on by his ambitious wife, who wanted him to stand clear of the Roosevelt shadow and establish his own reputation.

Perhaps the resulting rupture was inevitable. The Republican party was dividing into two factions, the progressives and the Old Guard. Forced to choose between them, Taft threw in his lot with the Old Guard. When House progressives revolted against the domination of Speaker Cannon, Taft deprived them of patronage, practically reading them out of the party.

Roosevelt backed the progressives. Speaking at Osawatomie, Kansas, in August 1910, he came out for a comprehensive program of social legislation, which he called the New Nationalism. Besides attacking "special privilege" and the "unfair money-getting" practices of "lawbreakers of great wealth," he called for a broad expansion of federal power. "The betterment we seek must be accomplished," he said, "mainly through the National Government."

The final break came in October 1911, when the president ordered an antitrust suit against U.S. Steel. Roosevelt, of course, opposed breaking up large corporations. "The effort at prohibiting all combination has substantially failed," he said in his New Nationalism speech. "The way out lies . . . in completely controlling them." Taft was prepared "to enforce [the Sherman] law or die in the attempt." What angered Roosevelt was Taft's emphasis in the steel suit on U.S. Steel's absorption of the Tennessee Coal and Iron Company, which Roosevelt had unofficially authorized during the panic of 1907. The government's antitrust brief made Roosevelt appear to have been either an abettor of monopoly or—far worse—a fool who had been duped by the steel corporation. He began to criticize Taft publicly, and early in 1912 he declared himself a candidate for the Republican presidential nomination.

The dramatic split between the nation's two leading Republicans intensified the conflict within the party. In January 1911 the liberal faction had organized a National Progressive Republican League, which was pushing Senator La Follette for the Republican nomination. Roosevelt's entry into the race encouraged the progressives to strike more boldly against the administration. Although some, particularly those from the Middle West, found Roosevelt's position on the Sherman Act unpalatable, the fact that he stood a better chance than La Follette of being elected president led most of them to swing to his support.

Roosevelt plunged into the preconvention campaign with typical energy. He was almost uniformly victorious in states that held presidential primaries, carrying even Ohio, Taft's home state. However, the president controlled the party machinery and entered the national convention with a small majority of the delegates. Since some Taft delegates had been chosen under questionable circumstances, the Roosevelt forces challenged the right of 254 of them to their seats. The Taft-controlled credentials committee, paying little attention to the evidence, gave all but a few of the disputed seats to the president, who then won the nomination on the first ballot.

Had Roosevelt swallowed his resentment and

Cartoonists had a field day with Roosevelt as a Bull Moose; in this cartoon from Harper's, *T.R. enters the political zoo.*

bided his time, Taft would almost certainly have been defeated in the election and the 1916 Republican nomination would have been Roosevelt's for the asking. But he was understandably outraged by the ruthless manner in which the Taft "steamroller" had overridden his forces. When his leading supporters urged him to organize a third party, and when two of them, George W. Perkins, formerly a partner of the banker J. P. Morgan, and the publisher Frank Munsey, offered to finance the campaign, Roosevelt agreed to make the race. In August, amid scenes of hysterical enthusiasm, the first convention of the Progressive party met at Chicago and nominated him for president. Announcing that he felt "as strong as a bull moose," Roosevelt delivered a stirring "confession of faith," calling for strict regulation of corporations, a tariff commission, national presidential primaries, minimum wage and workers' compensation laws, the elimination of child labor, and many other reforms.

The Election of 1912

The Democrats made the most of the opportunity offered by the Republican schism. Had they nominated a conservative or allowed Bryan a fourth chance, they would probably have insured Roosevelt's election. Instead, after battling through 46 ballots at their convention in Baltimore, they nominated Woodrow Wilson, who had achieved a remarkable liberal record as governor of New Jersey.

Although as a political scientist Wilson had sharply criticized the status quo and had taken a pragmatic approach to the idea of government regulation of the economy, he had objected strongly to the Bryan brand of politics. In 1896 he voted for the Gold Democratic party candidate for president. But by 1912, influenced partly by ambition and partly by the spirit of the times, he had been converted to progressivism. He called his brand of reform the New Freedom.

The federal government could best advance the cause of social justice, Wilson reasoned, by eradicating the special privileges that enabled the "interests" to flourish. Where Roosevelt had lost faith in competition as a way of protecting the public against monopolies, Wilson insisted that competition could be restored. The government must break up the great trusts and establish fair rules for doing business, subjecting violators to stiff punishments. Thereafter, the checks of the free enterprise system would protect the public from exploitation without destroying individual initiative and opportunity. "If America is not to have free enterprise, then she can have freedom of no sort whatever," he said. Although rather vague, this argument appealed to thousands of voters who found the growing power of large corporations frightening but who hesitated to make the thoroughgoing commitment to government control of business that Roosevelt was advocating.

Roosevelt's reasoning was perhaps theoretically sound. Fear of a powerful national government was an inheritance from the 18th century, when political power had been equated with monarchy and tyranny and when America had been sparsely settled and decentralized. In the early 20th century, with democratic institutions firmly established and with a closely integrated economy, citizens had less reason to fear political centralization and economic regulation. As Herbert Croly insisted in *The Promise of American Life* (1909), the time had come to employ Hamiltonian means to achieve Jeffersonian ends. Laissez faire made less sense than it had in earlier times. Philosophers and scientists had undermined the old view of an orderly society designed by a divine watchmaker and capable of running itself. The complexities of the modern world seemed to call for a positive approach, a plan, the close application of human intelligence to social and economic problems.

Roosevelt dismissed Wilson's New Freedom as "rural toryism," but being less drastic and more in line with American experience than the New Nationalism, it had much to recommend it. The danger that selfish individuals would use the power of the state for their own ends had certainly not disappeared, despite the efforts of progressives to make government more responsive to popular opinion. Any considerable expansion of national power would increase the danger and probably create new difficulties. Managing so complicated an enterprise as an industrialized nation was sure to be a formidable task. Furthermore, individual freedom of opportunity merited the toleration of a certain amount of inefficiency.

To choose between the New Nationalism and the New Freedom, between the dynamic Roosevelt and the idealistic Wilson, was indeed difficult.

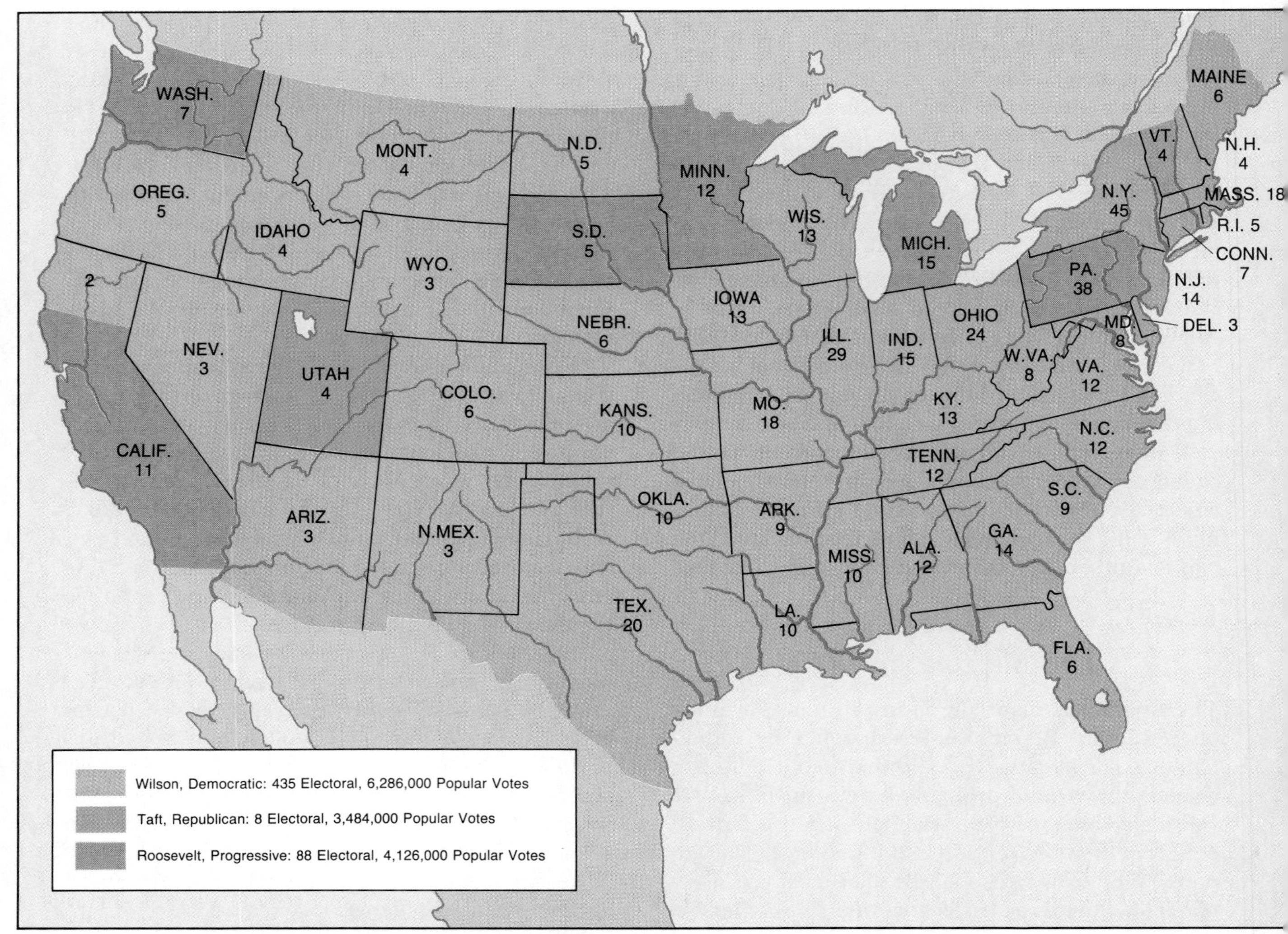

THE ELECTION OF 1912

The fourth largest vote getter in the election of 1912 was Eugene V. Debs of the Socialist party, who gained about 900,000 popular votes (or approximately 6 percent of the total popular vote), but no electoral vote.

Thousands grappled with this problem before going to the polls, but partisan politics determined the outcome of the election. Taft got the hard-core Republican vote but lost the progressive wing of the GOP to Roosevelt. Wilson had the solid support of both conservative and liberal Democrats. As a result, Wilson won an easy victory in the electoral college, receiving 435 votes to Roosevelt's 88 and Taft's 8. The popular vote was Wilson, 6,286,000; Roosevelt, 4,126,000; and Taft, 3,484,000.

If partisan politics had determined the winner, the election was nonetheless an overwhelming endorsement of progressivism. The temper of the times was shown by the 897,000 votes given Eugene V. Debs, the Socialist candidate. Altogether, professed liberals amassed over 11 million of the 15 million ballots cast. Wilson was a minority president, but he took office with a clear mandate to press forward with further reforms.

Wilson: The New Freedom

No man ever rose more suddenly and spectacularly in American politics than Woodrow Wilson. In the spring of 1910 he was president of Princeton University; he had never held or even run for public office. In the fall of 1912 he was president-elect of the United States. Yet if his rise was meteoric, in a very real sense he had devoted his life to preparing for it. He was born in Staunton, Virginia, in 1856, the son of a Presbyterian minister. As a student he became deeply interested in political theory, developing a profound admiration for the British parliamentary system and for such British statesmen as Edmund Burke and William Gladstone. While still in college he dreamed of representing his state in the Senate. He studied law solely because he thought it the best avenue to public office, and when he discovered that he did not like legal work, he took a doctorate at Johns Hopkins in political science.

For years Wilson's political ambitions appeared doomed to frustration. He taught at Bryn Mawr, then at Wesleyan, finally at his alma mater, Princeton. He wrote several influential books, among them *Congressional Government* and *The State,* and achieved an outstanding reputation as a teacher and lecturer. In 1902 he was chosen president of Princeton and soon won a place among the nation's leading educators. He revised the curriculum, introducing many new subjects and insisting that students pursue an organized and integrated course of study. He instituted the preceptorial system, which placed the students in close intellectual and social contact with their teachers. He attracted many outstanding young scholars to the Princeton faculty.

In time, Wilson's educational ideas and his overbearing manner of applying them got him in trouble with some of Princeton's alumni and trustees. Though his university career was wrecked, the controversies, in which he appeared to be championing democracy and progress in the face of reactionary opponents, especially his opposition to Princeton's elite undergraduate eating clubs, brought him at last to the attention of the politicians. Then, in a great rush, came power and fame.

Wilson was an immediate success as president. Since Roosevelt's last year in office Congress had been almost continually at war with the executive branch and with itself. Legislative achievements had been relatively few. Now a small avalanche of important measures received the approval of the lawmakers. In October 1913 the Underwood Tariff brought the first significant reduction of duties since before the Civil War. Food products, wool, iron and steel, shoes, agricultural machinery, and other items that could be produced more cheaply in the United States than abroad were placed on the free list. Rates on most other goods were cut substantially, the object being to equalize foreign and domestic costs. To compensate for the expected loss of revenue, the act provided for a graduated tax on personal incomes.*

Two months later the Federal Reserve Act gave the country a central banking system for the first time since Jackson destroyed the Bank of the United States. The measure divided the nation into 12 banking districts, each under the supervision of a Federal Reserve Bank, a sort of bank for bankers. All national banks in each district and those state banks that wished to participate had to invest 6 percent of their capital and surplus in the Reserve Bank, which was empowered to exchange (the technical term is *rediscount*) paper money, called Federal Reserve notes, for the commercial and agricultural paper that member banks took in as security from borrowers. The volume of currency was no longer at the mercy of the supply of gold or any other particular commodity.

The crown and nerve center of the system was a Federal Reserve Board in Washington, which appointed a majority of the directors of the Federal Reserve Banks and had some control over rediscount rates (the commission charged by the Reserve Banks for performing the rediscounting function). The board provided a modicum of public control over the banks, but the effort to weaken the power of the great New York banks by decentralizing the system proved ineffective. Nevertheless a true central banking system was created.

---

* The Sixteenth Amendment, ratified in February 1913, authorized the imposition of a federal income tax.

In a clever parody of Nude Descending a Staircase *(see page 658), John T. McCutcheon caricatures Woodrow Wilson as a futurist painter. Underwood gloomily regards the tariff's demise.*

When inflation threatened, the Reserve Banks could raise the rediscount rate, discouraging borrowing and thus reducing the amount of money in circulation. In bad times it could lower the rate, making it easier to borrow and injecting new dollars into the economy. Much remained to be learned about the proper management of the money supply, but the nation finally had a flexible yet safe currency.

In 1914 Congress passed two important laws affecting corporations. One created a Federal Trade Commission to replace Roosevelt's Bureau of Corporations. In addition to investigating interstate corporations and publishing reports, this nonpartisan board could issue cease and desist orders against "unfair" trade practices brought to light through its researches. The law did not define the term *unfair,* and the commission's rulings could be taken on appeal to the federal courts, but the FTC was nonetheless a powerful instrument for protecting the public against the trusts.

The second measure, the Clayton Antitrust Act, made certain specific business practices illegal, including price discrimination that tended to foster monopoly, "tying" agreements—which forbade retailers from handling the products of a firm's competitors—and the creation of interlocking directorates as a means of controlling competing companies. The act exempted labor unions and agricultural organizations from the antitrust laws and curtailed the use of injunctions in labor disputes. The officers of corporations could be held individually responsible when their companies violated the antitrust laws.

While Wilson was not in sympathy with all the terms of these laws, the laws reflected his desires. The Democrats controlled both houses of Congress for the first time since 1890 and were eager to make a good record, but Wilson's imaginative and aggressive use of presidential power was decisive. He entered office determined, like a British prime minister, to play an active part in the formulation of legislation and the management of Congress.

Wilson called the legislators into special session in April 1913 and appeared before them to lay out his program; he was the first president to address Congress in person since John Adams. Then he followed the course of administration bills closely. He had a private telephone line installed between the Capitol and the White House. Administration representatives haunted the cloakrooms and lobbies of both houses. Cooperative congressmen began to receive notes of praise and encouragement, recalcitrant ones stern demands for support, often pecked out on the president's own portable typewriter. When lobbyists tried to frustrate his plans for tariff reform by bringing pressure to bear on key senators, he made a dramatic appeal to the people. "The public ought to know the extraordinary exertions being made by the lobby in Washington," he told reporters. "Only public opinion can check and destroy it." The voters responded so strongly that the Senate passed the tariff bill substantially as Wilson desired it.

Despite his lack of political experience, Wilson proved to be a masterful politician and an inspiring leader. He explained his success by saying, only half humorously, that running the government was child's play for anyone who had managed the faculty of a university. Responsible *party* government was his objective; he expected individual Democrats to support the decisions of the party majority, and his idealism never prevented him from awarding the spoils of office to city bosses and conservative congressmen, so long as they supported his program.

Nor did his career as a political theorist make him rigid and doctrinaire. In practice the differences between his New Freedom and Roosevelt's New Nationalism tended to disappear. The Underwood Tariff and the Clayton Antitrust Act fitted the philosophy Wilson had expounded during the campaign, but the Federal Trade Commission represented a step toward the kind of regulated economy that Roosevelt advocated. So did the Federal Reserve system.

There were limits to Wilson's progressivism, limits imposed partly by his temperament and partly by his philosophy. He disliked all forms of privilege, and objected as strenuously to laws granting special favors to farmers and workers as to those benefiting the tycoons. When a bill was introduced in 1914 making low-interest loans available to farmers, he refused to support it. "It is unwise and unjustifiable to extend the credit of the Government to a single class of the community," he said. He considered the provision exempting unions from the antitrust laws equally unsound. Nor would he push for a federal law prohibiting child labor; such a measure would be unconstitutional, he believed. Wilson refused to back the constitutional amendment giving the vote to women. Perhaps he thought it improper for women to mix in politics, but he argued publicly that it was wrong to deprive the states of their control of the suffrage.

Wilson proved far more sympathetic to big business than some of his campaign pronouncements had led observers to expect. He appointed persons friendly to the corporations to the FTC and conducted no trustbusting crusade. When the business cycle took a turn downward in the fall of 1913, he adopted the Roosevelt policy of allowing corporation leaders to work out informal agreements with the Justice Department protecting them against antitrust actions. Delegations of businessmen and bankers were soon trooping through the White House, and the president went out of his way to insist that he had no quarrel with bigness per se.

By the end of 1914 the Wilsonian record, on balance, was positive but distinctly limited. The president believed that the major progressive goals had been achieved; he had no plans for further reform. Many other progressives thought that a great deal more remained to be done.

The Progressives and Minority Rights

On one important issue Wilson was distinctly reactionary. This was the question of race relations. With a mere handful of exceptions the progressives exhibited strong prejudices against nonwhite people, and against certain categories of whites as well. Many were as unsympathetic to immigrants from Asia and eastern and southern Europe as any of the "conservative" opponents of immigration in the 1880s and 1890s. The Gentlemen's Agreement excluding Japanese immigrants was reached in 1907 at the height of the progressive movement. In the same year Congress appointed a commission headed by Senator William Dillingham of Vermont to study the immigration question. The Dillingham Commission labored for more than two years and brought forth a 41-volume report that led in 1913 to a bill restricting the number of newcomers to be admitted and reducing especially the influx from eastern and southern Europe. Only the outbreak of war in Europe in 1914, which cut immigration to a trickle, prevented the passage of this measure.

American Indians were also affected by the progressives' racial attitudes. Where the sponsors of the Dawes Act had assumed that Indians were inherently capable of adopting the ways of "civilized" people, in the progressive period the tendency was to write Indians off as fundamentally inferior and to assume that they would make second-class citizens at best. A leading muckraker, Ray Stannard Baker, who was far more sympathetic to blacks than most progressives, dismissed Indians as pathetic beings, "eating, sleeping, idling, with no more thought of the future than a white man's child." Theodore Roosevelt knew from his experiences as a rancher in Dakota territory that Indians could be as energetic and capable as whites, but he considered these "exceptional" types. As for the rest, it would be many generations before they could be expected to "move forward" enough to become "ordinary citizens," Roosevelt believed. "The Indian stirred little controversy among the leading political warriors of the progressive era," a recent scholar writes.

To say that blacks did not fare well at the hands of progressives would be a gross understatement. Populist efforts to unite white and black farmers in the southern states had led to the imposition of further repressive measures. Segregation became more rigid, white opposition to black voting more monolithic. In 1900 the body of a Mississippi black was dug up by order of the state legislature and reburied in a segregated cemetery; in Virginia in 1902 the daughter of Robert E. Lee was arrested for riding in the black section of a railroad car. "Insult is being added to injury continually," a black journalist in Alabama complained. "Have those in power forgotten that there is a God?"

Many progressive women, still smarting from the insult to their sex entailed in the Fourteenth and Fifteenth Amendments and eager to attract southern support for their campaign for the vote, adopted racist arguments. They contrasted the supposed corruption and incompetence of black voters with their own "purity" and intelligence. Southern progressives of both sexes argued that disenfranchising blacks would reduce corruption by removing from unscrupulous white politicians the temptation to purchase black votes!

The typical southern attitude toward the education of blacks was summed up in the folk proverb "When you educate a Negro, you spoil a good field hand." In 1910, only about 8,000 black children in the entire South were attending high schools. Despite the almost total suppression of black rights, lynchings continued to occur; between 1900 and 1914 more than 1,100 blacks were murdered by mobs, most (but not all) in the southern states. In the rare cases where local prosecutors brought the lynchers to trial, juries almost without exception brought in verdicts of not guilty.

Booker T. Washington was shaken by this trend, but he could find no way to combat it. The times were passing him by. He appealed to his white southern "friends" for help but got nowhere. Increasingly he talked about the virtues of rural life, the evils of big cities, and the uselessness of higher education for black people. By the turn of the century a number of young, well-educated blacks, most of them northerners, were breaking away from his accommodationist leadership.

Black Militancy

William E. B. Du Bois was the most prominent of the militants. Du Bois was born in Great Barrington, Massachusetts, in 1868. His father, a restless wanderer of Negro and French Huguenot stock, abandoned the family, and young William grew up on the edge of poverty. Neither accepted nor openly rejected by the overwhelmingly white community, he devoted himself to his studies, showing such brilliance that his future education was assured by scholarships: to Fisk University, then to Harvard, then to the University of Berlin. In 1895 Du Bois became the first American black to earn a Ph.D. from Harvard; his dissertation, *The Suppression of the African Slave Trade to the U.S.A., 1638–1870* (1896), remains a standard reference.

Personal success and "acceptance" by whites did not make the proud and sensitive Du Bois complacent. Outraged by white racism and the willingness of many blacks to settle for second-class citizenship, he set out to make American blacks proud of their color—"beauty is black," he said—and of their African origins and culture. American blacks must organize themselves. They must establish their own businesses, run their own newspapers and colleges, write their own literature; they must preserve their identity rather than seek to amalgamate themselves into a society that offered them only crumbs and contempt.

Like Washington, Du Bois wanted blacks to lift themselves by their own bootstraps, and for a time he cooperated with the head of Tuskegee Institute. But in time he rejected Washington's limited goals and his accommodating approach to white prejudices. In 1903, in an essay, "Of Mr. Booker T. Washington and Others," published in his book *Souls of Black Folk,* he subjected Washington's "attitude of adjustment and submission" to polite but searching criticism. Washington had asked blacks to give up political power, civil rights, and the hope of higher education, not realizing that "voting is necessary to modern manhood, that . . . discrimination is barbarism, and that black boys need education as well as white boys." Washington "apologizes for injustice," Du Bois charged. "He belittles the emasculating effects of caste distinctions, and opposes the higher training and ambitions of our brightest minds." This was totally wrong. "The way

A striking likeness of W.E.B. Du Bois drawn by Winold Reiss when Du Bois was in his fifties.

for a people to gain their reasonable rights is not by voluntarily throwing them away."

Du Bois was not an uncritical admirer of the ordinary American black. He believed that "immorality, crime, and laziness" were common vices. Quite properly he blamed the weaknesses of blacks on the treatment afforded them by whites, but his approach to the solution of racial problems was frankly elitist. "The Negro race," he wrote, "is going to be saved by its exceptional men," what he called the "talented tenth" of the black population. As the historian Benjamin Quarles has said, Du Bois was "uncomfortable in the presence of the rank and file." After describing in vivid detail how white mistreatment had corrupted his people, Du Bois added loftily: "A saving remnant continually survives and persists, continually aspires, continually shows itself in thrift and ability and character."

Whatever his prejudices, Du Bois exposed both the weaknesses of Washington's strategy and the callousness of white American attitudes. "Accommodation" was not working. Washington was praised, even lionized by prominent southern whites, yet when Theodore Roosevelt invited him to a meal at the White House they exploded with indignation, and Roosevelt, although not personally prejudiced, meekly backtracked, never repeating his "mistake." He defended his record by saying, "I have stood as valiantly for the rights of the negro as any president since Lincoln," which, sad to relate, was true enough.

Not mere impatience but despair led Du Bois and a few like-minded blacks to meet at Niagara Falls in July 1905 and to issue a stirring list of demands: the unrestricted right to vote; an end to every kind of segregation; equality of economic opportunity; higher education for the talented; equal justice in the courts; an end to trade-union discrimination. This Niagara Movement did not attract mass support, but it did stir the consciences of some whites, many of them the descendants of abolitionists, who were also becoming disenchanted by the failure of accommodation to provide blacks with real opportunity.

In 1909, the centennial of the birth of Abraham Lincoln, a group of these liberals, including the newspaperman Oswald Garrison Villard (grandson of William Lloyd Garrison), the social worker Jane Addams, the philosopher John Dewey, and the novelist William Dean Howells, founded the National Association for the Advancement of Colored People (NAACP). The organization was dedicated to the eradication of racial discrimination. Its leadership was predominantly white in the early years, but Du Bois became a national officer and the editor of its journal, *The Crisis.*

A turning point had been reached: after 1909 virtually every important leader of the blacks, white and black alike, rejected the Washington approach. More and more, blacks turned to the study of their past in an effort to stimulate pride in their heritage. In 1915 Carter G. Woodson founded the Association for the Study of Negro Life and History; the following year he began editing the *Journal of Negro History,* which became the major organ for the publishing of scholarly studies of the subject.

This militancy produced few results in the Progressive Era. Theodore Roosevelt behaved no differently than earlier Republican presidents: he courted blacks when he thought it advantageous, turned his back when he did not. When he ran for president on the Progressive ticket in 1912, he pursued a "lily-white" policy, hoping to break the Democrats' monopoly in the South. By trusting in "[white] men of justice and of vision," Roosevelt argued in the face of decades of experience to the contrary, "the colored men of the South will ultimately get justice."

The southern-born Wilson was actively antipathetic to blacks. During the 1912 campaign he appealed to them for support and promised to "assist in advancing the interest of their race" in every possible way. Once elected, he refused even to appoint a privately financed commission to study the race problem. Southerners dominated his administration and the Congress; as a result, blacks were further degraded. No less than 35 blacks in the Atlanta Post Office lost their jobs. In Washington employees in many government offices were rigidly segregated, those who objected being summarily discharged.

These actions roused such a storm that Wilson backtracked a little, but he never abandoned his belief that segregation was in the best interests of both races. "Wilson . . . promised a 'new freedom,' " one newspaperman complained. "On the contrary we are given a stone instead of a loaf of bread." Even Booker T. Washington admitted that his people were more "discouraged and bitter" than at any time in his memory.

Du Bois, who had supported Wilson in 1912, attacked administration policy in *The Crisis*. In November 1914 the militant editor of the Boston *Guardian*, William Monroe Trotter, a classmate of Du Bois at Harvard and a far more caustic critic of the Washington approach, led a delegation to the White House to protest the segregation policy of the government. When Wilson accused him of blackmail, Trotter lost his temper and an ugly confrontation resulted. The mood of black leaders had changed completely.

By this time the Great War had broken out in Europe. Soon its effects would be felt by every American, by blacks perhaps more than by any other group. In November 1915, a year almost to the day after Trotter's clash with Wilson, Booker T. Washington died. One era had ended; a new one was beginning.

SUPPLEMENTARY READING

Titles marked with an asterisk have been published in paperback.

Two excellent volumes trace the political history of the Progressive Era: G. E. Mowry, **The Era of Theodore Roosevelt*** (1958), and A. S. Link, **Woodrow Wilson and the Progressive Era*** (1954). A number of historians have offered new interpretations of progressivism in recent years. Richard Hofstadter, **The Age of Reform*** (1955), stresses the idea of the status revolution. Gabriel Kolko, **The Triumph of Conservatism*** (1963), sees the period as dominated by the efforts of big business to attain its objectives with the aid of the government. Other interesting studies include R. B. Nye, **Midwestern Progressive Politics** (1951), J. M. Cooper, Jr., **The Warrior and the Priest: Theodore Roosevelt and Woodrow Wilson** (1983), D. W. Grantham, **Southern Progressivism** (1983), and R. H. Wiebe, **Businessmen and Reform*** (1962). D. P. Thelen, **The New Citizenship** (1972), is good on the origins of progressivism, though confined to the study of one state, Wisconsin.

The role of muckraking journalism is considered in C. C. Regier, **The Era of the Muckrakers** (1932), Louis Filler, **Crusaders for American Liberalism*** (1939), D. M. Chalmers, **The Social and Political Ideas of the Muckrakers*** (1964), and Peter Lyon, **Success Story: The Life and Times of S. S. McClure** (1963). Arthur and Lila Weinberg (eds.), **The Muckrakers*** (1961), is a convenient collection of writings by the muckrakers. Also useful are Lincoln Steffens, **Autobiography*** (1931), and I. M. Tarbell, **All in the Day's Work** (1939).

State and local progressivism are considered in G. E. Mowry, **The California Progressives*** (1951), R. S. Maxwell, **La Follette and the Rise of Progressivism in Wisconsin** (1956), R. E. Noble, **New Jersey Progressivism Before Wilson** (1946), R. M. Abrams, **Conservatism in a Progressive Era** (1964), H. L. Warner, **Progressivism in Ohio** (1964), Sheldon Hackney, **Populism to Progressivism in Alabama** (1969), Z. L. Miller, **Boss Cox's Cincinnati: Urban Politics in the Progressive Era*** (1968), J. D. Buenker, **Urban Liberalism and Progressive Reform** (1973), G. B. Tindall, **The Emergence of the New South** (1967), and C. V. Woodward, **Origins of the New South*** (1951). The story of the fight for reform in San Francisco is told in W. E. Bean, **Boss Ruef's San Francisco*** (1952).

The struggle for women's suffrage is described in

A. S. Kraditor, **The Ideas of the Woman Suffrage Movement*** (1965), and in Eleanor Flexner, **Century of Struggle*** (1959). See also W. L. O'Neill, **Everyone Was Brave: The Rise and Fall of Feminism in America*** (1969). Books treating special aspects of progressivism include A. F. Davis, **Spearheads for Reform: The Social Settlements and the Progressive Movement*** ((1967), Melvin Dubofsky, **When Workers Organize** (1968), Irwin Yellowitz, **Labor and the Progressive Movement in New York State** (1965), Samuel Haber, **Efficiency and Uplift** (1964), J. P. Felt, **Hostages of Fortune** (1965), J. H. Timberlake, **Prohibition and the Progressive Movement*** (1963), Albro Martin, **Enterprise Denied: Origins of the Decline of American Railroads** (1971), and W. L. O'Neill, **Divorce in the Progressive Era** (1967). On blacks in this period, see C. F. Kellogg, **NAACP: A History of the National Association for the Advancement of Colored People*** (1970), E. M. Rudwick, **W. E. B. Du Bois: Propagandist of the Negro Protest*** (1960), W. E. B. Du Bois, **The Souls of Black Folk*** (1903), J. T. Kirby, **Darkness at the Dawning: Race and Reform in the Progressive South** (1972), and August Meier, **Negro Thought in America: 1880–1915*** (1963). On the treatment of Indians, consult F. E. Hoxie, **A Final Promise: The Campaign to Assimilate the Indians** (1984).

Many progressives have written autobiographical accounts of their work. See especially Theodore Roosevelt, **Autobiography** (1913), R. M. La Follette, **Autobiography*** (1913), W. A. White, **Autobiography** (1946), and G. W. Norris, **Fighting Liberal*** (1945).

W. H. Harbaugh, **Power and Responsibility: The Life and Times of Theodore Roosevelt*** (1961), is the soundest scholarly treatment of Roosevelt's career. G. W. Chessman, **Theodore Roosevelt and the Politics of Power*** (1969), is a good brief account, while Chessman's **Governor Theodore Roosevelt: The Albany Apprenticeship** (1965), throws much light on the development of Roosevelt's ideas before 1901. J. M. Blum, **The Republican Roosevelt*** (1954), is a brilliant analysis of his political philosophy and his management of the presidency. The essays on Roosevelt—and on Wilson—in Richard Hofstadter, **The American Political Tradition*** (1948), merit close reading.

For specific events during Roosevelt's presidency, consult R. J. Cornell, **The Anthracite Coal Strike of 1902** (1957), the essay on the Northern Securities case in J. A. Garraty (ed.), **Quarrels That Have Shaped the Constitution*** (1964), S. P. Hays, **Conservation and the Gospel of Efficiency*** (1959), and J. R. Hollingsworth, **The Whirligig of Politics** (1963).

On Taft, see D. F. Anderson, **William Howard Taft: A Conservative's Conception of the Presidency** (1973), and P. E. Coletta, **The Presidency of William Howard Taft** (1973). On the Ballinger-Pinchot controversy, see M. N. McGeary, **Gifford Pinchot** (1960). The breakup of the Republican party and the history of the Progressive party are discussed in G. E. Mowry, **Theodore Roosevelt and the Progressive Movement*** (1946), and J. A. Garraty, **Right-Hand Man: The Life of George W. Perkins** (1960).

The standard biography of Wilson, still incomplete, is A. S. Link, **Wilson** (1947–). Two brief biographies are J. M. Blum, **Woodrow Wilson and the Politics of Morality*** (1956), and J. A. Garraty, **Woodrow Wilson*** (1956).

Among the many biographies of political leaders in the period are J. M. Blum, **Joe Tumulty and the Wilson Era** (1951), C. G. Bowers, **Beveridge and the Progressive Era** (1932), R. M. Lowitt, **George W. Norris** (1963), B. C. and Fola La Follette, **Robert M. La Follette** (1953), P. C. Jessup, **Elihu Root** (1938), J. A. Garraty, **Henry Cabot Lodge** (1953), A. T. Mason, **Brandeis** (1946), and M. J. Pusey, **Charles Evans Hughes** (1951).

The student should sample some of the political writings of the progressives themselves. See especially Theodore Roosevelt, **The New Nationalism*** (1910), Woodrow Wilson, **The New Freedom*** (1913), Herbert Croly, **The Promise of American Life*** (1909), Walter Weyl, **The New Democracy*** (1912), and Walter Lippmann, **Drift and Mastery*** (1914).

"Look! the boss has a WOMAN
to write his letters"

Women in the Workplace

It used to be argued that the "liberation" of American women occurred in the 1920s with the emergence of the "flapper," with her short skirts, bobbed hair, and fondness for cigarettes, alcohol, and other forms of what was quaintly described as "making whoopee." The flapper phenomenon was explained by referring to the disillusionment that affected people after the World War, and to the passage of the women's suffrage amendment, which, by giving women political power, was thought to have opened the way for the achievement of full equality.

It is now clear that flappers were the exception rather than the rule in the 1920s, that they were by no means as liberated as they and others thought, and that, in any case, the struggle for true equality of the sexes was far from over. Furthermore, much more significant changes in the lives of women were taking place at that time than those associated with what the flappers were doing, or even with the right to vote.

None of these changes was more important than the fact that increasing numbers of women were holding down full-time jobs. The trend toward taking up work outside the home began to accelerate in the prewar years and has, of course, continued into the present day. But what happened to working women in the 1920s marked a kind of turning point.

In the 1890s, a new female secretary in an office might be the butt of wisecracks from the male help (see opposite page), but more and more educated middle-class women were venturing into the world of work outside the home. This 1908 visiting nurse, climbing over the tenement rooftops of New York's Lower East Side on her way to see patients who were too sick to visit a clinic, was perhaps more venturesome than most.

Women had, of course, worked in mills and factories and as domestics for a very long time. Working children, like this little girl tending textile machinery, were common. Their plight was a serious concern to muckraking writers and photographers like Lewis Hine. Black women often found it impossible even to get industrial jobs, and had to settle for domestic work as maids and cooks.

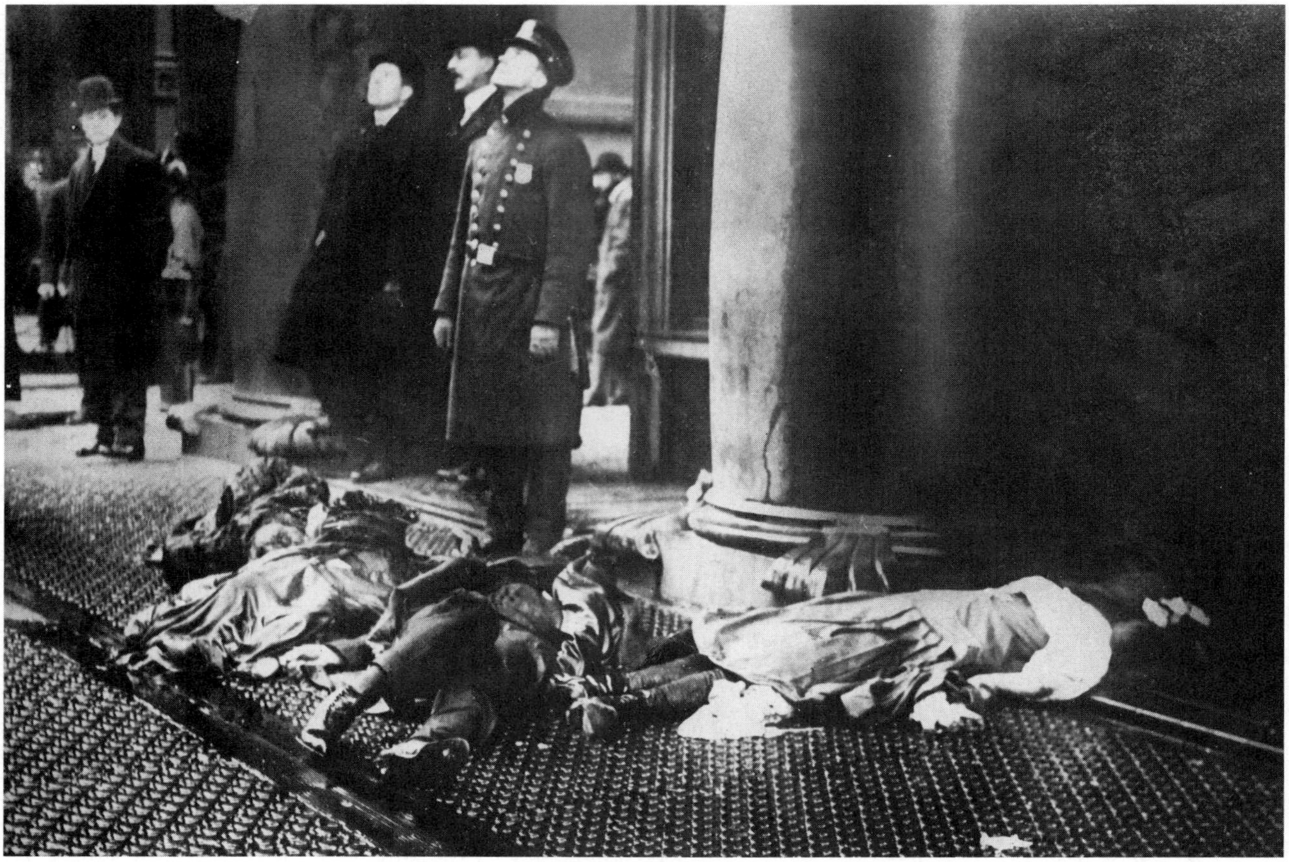

WE CONDEMN CHILD LABOR.
Unity is Strength ORGANIZE.
Demand the Union Label stop. Supporting Scabs.
Independence is Achieved by Unity. ORGANIZE
Girls get togethe and ORGANIZ
Do you want Fair Treatment? ORGANIZE
Do you want Fire Protection? ORGANIZE.
TRADE UNION LEAGUE
THE EIGHT HOUR DAY
OF NEW YORK

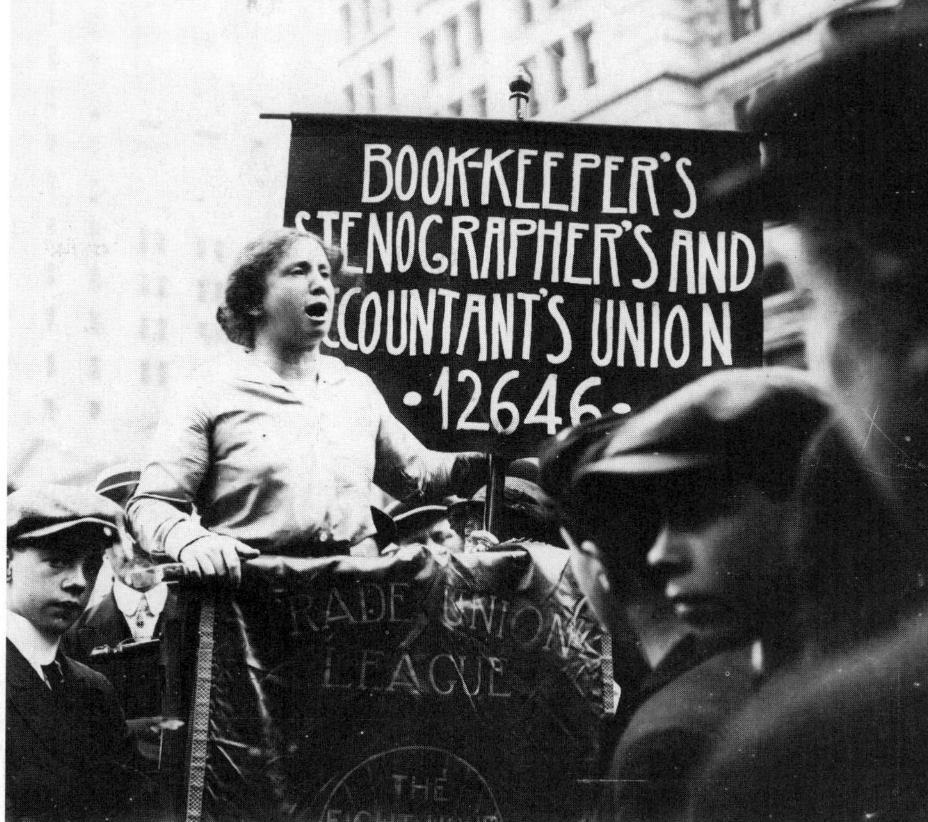

Many immigrant women worked in garment industry sweatshops. In 1911, the tragic fire at the Triangle Shirtwaist Co. (see Chapter 23), which caused these workers to leap to their deaths, gave impetus to labor organizations such as the Women's Trade Union League and the International Ladies' Garment Workers Union (ILGWU). The Women's League sponsored demonstrations (note the sign on the right of the photo at lower left: "Do You Want Fire Protection? Organize") and pushed for better pay and conditions for women workers. Among the League's most effective leaders was Rose Schneiderman (upper right), later a good friend of Eleanor Roosevelt. The ILGWU was equally active in trying to organize the garment trades. This bilingual poster, in English and Polish, urges "waist, dress, skirt, & white goods workers" to attend a mass meeting.

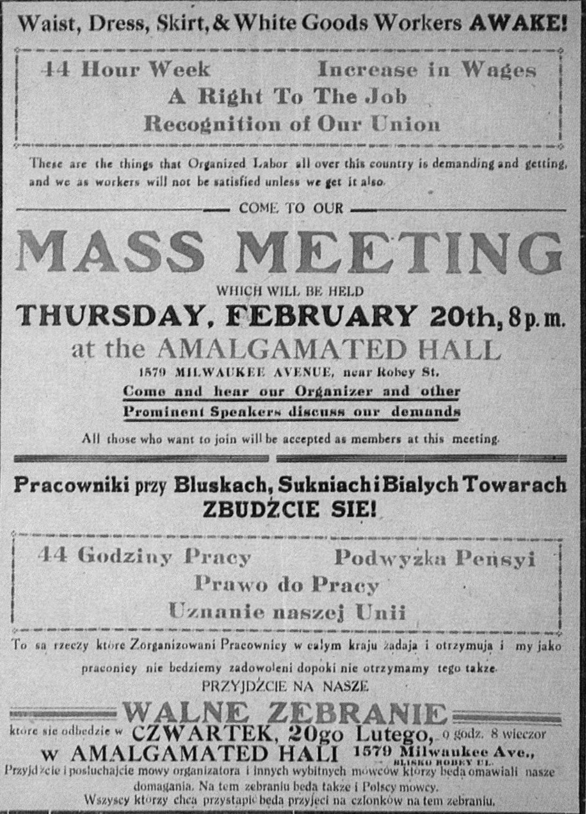

Waist, Dress, Skirt, & White Goods Workers **AWAKE!**

44 Hour Week **Increase in Wages**
A Right To The Job
Recognition of Our Union

These are the things that Organized Labor all over this country is demanding and getting, and we as workers will not be satisfied unless we get it also.

COME TO OUR

MASS MEETING

WHICH WILL BE HELD

THURSDAY, FEBRUARY 20th, 8 p.m.

at the AMALGAMATED HALL

1579 MILWAUKEE AVENUE, near Robey St.

Come and hear our Organizer and other Prominent Speakers discuss our demands

All those who want to join will be accepted as members at this meeting.

Pracowniki przy **Bluskach, Sukniach i Bialych Towarach**
ZBUDŹCIE SIE!

44 Godziny Pracy **Podwyżka Pensyi**
Prawo do Pracy
Uznanie naszej Unii

To sa rzeczy które Zorganizowani Pracownicy w calym kraju żadaja i otrzymuja i my jako praconicy nie bedziemy zadowoleni dopoki nie otrzymamy tego także.

PRZYJDŹCIE NA NASZE

WALNE ZEBRANIE

które sie odbedzie w **CZWARTEK, 20go Lutego,** o godz. 8 wieczor
w AMALGAMATED HALI **1579 Milwaukee Ave.,** BLISKO ROBEY UL.

Przyjdźcie i posluchajcie mowy organizatora i innych wybitnych mówców którzy beda omawiali nasze domagania. Na tem zebraniu beda także i Polscy mówcy.
Wszyscy którzy chca przystapić beda przyjeci na czlonków na tem zebraniu.

Y.M.C.A.

ONE OF THE THOUSAND Y.M.C.A. GIRLS IN FRANCE

United War Work Campaign Nov. 11th to 18th

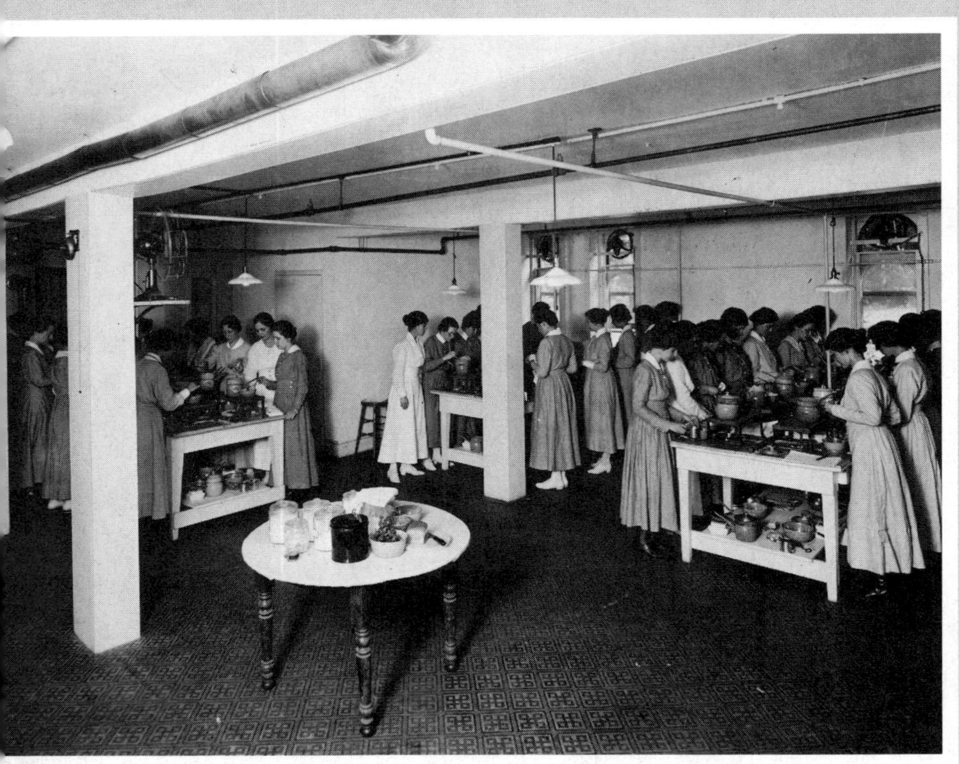

American entry in World War I brought great changes to the lives of women workers. A few went to France with YMCA units and other service organizations that ran field kitchens, hospitals, and recreation programs for American troops. Many more took jobs formerly held by men who had joined the army. For example (see opposite page), they served as welders in munitions plants, as streetcar conductors, and as car cleaners on the Northern Pacific Railroad. Even privileged young women such as the Vassar College group at left took cooking lessons in a patriotic spirit, to help on the home front.

3560
3278
3274
1262

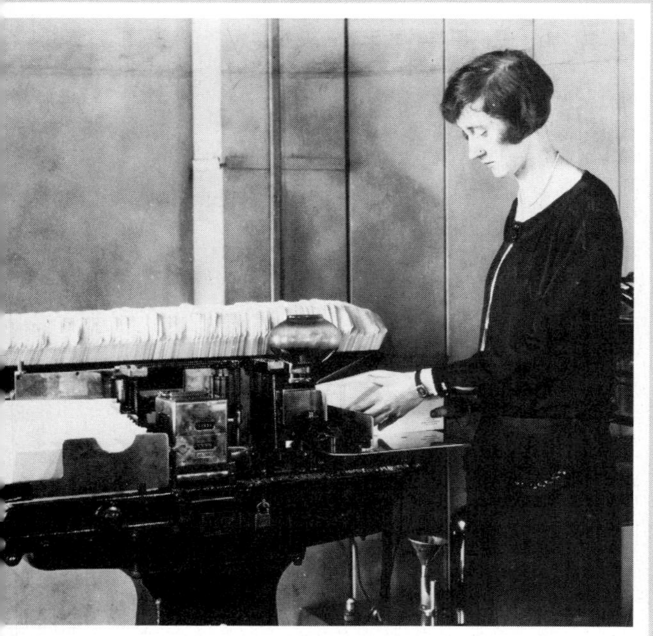

Though they were usually laid off from wartime jobs when the servicemen returned to civilian life, in the 1920s women had access to a wider choice of occupations than before the war. Schoolteaching, as had been true for decades, continued to be a common, respectable career choice for educated women. But there were also new opportunities for employment in businesses such as Eastman Kodak; here a secretary meters the mail. Factory jobs, however, were usually more grueling, as can be seen in the lower left photo of women operatives, supervised by men, tending automatic corn-husking machines while perched on uncomfortable-looking benches.

Reginald Marsh's painting *Subway, 14th St.* (1930) catches the turbulent, competitive spirit of rush-hour New York in which women were no longer "protected," in the Victorian sense, from the realities of working life.

24

Woodrow Wilson and the Great War

It is a fearful thing to lead this great people into war, into the most terrible and disastrous of all wars, civilization itself seeming to be in the balance. But the right is more precious than peace, and we shall fight for the things which we have always carried nearest our hearts—for democracy. WOODROW WILSON, *War Message to Congress, April 2, 1917*

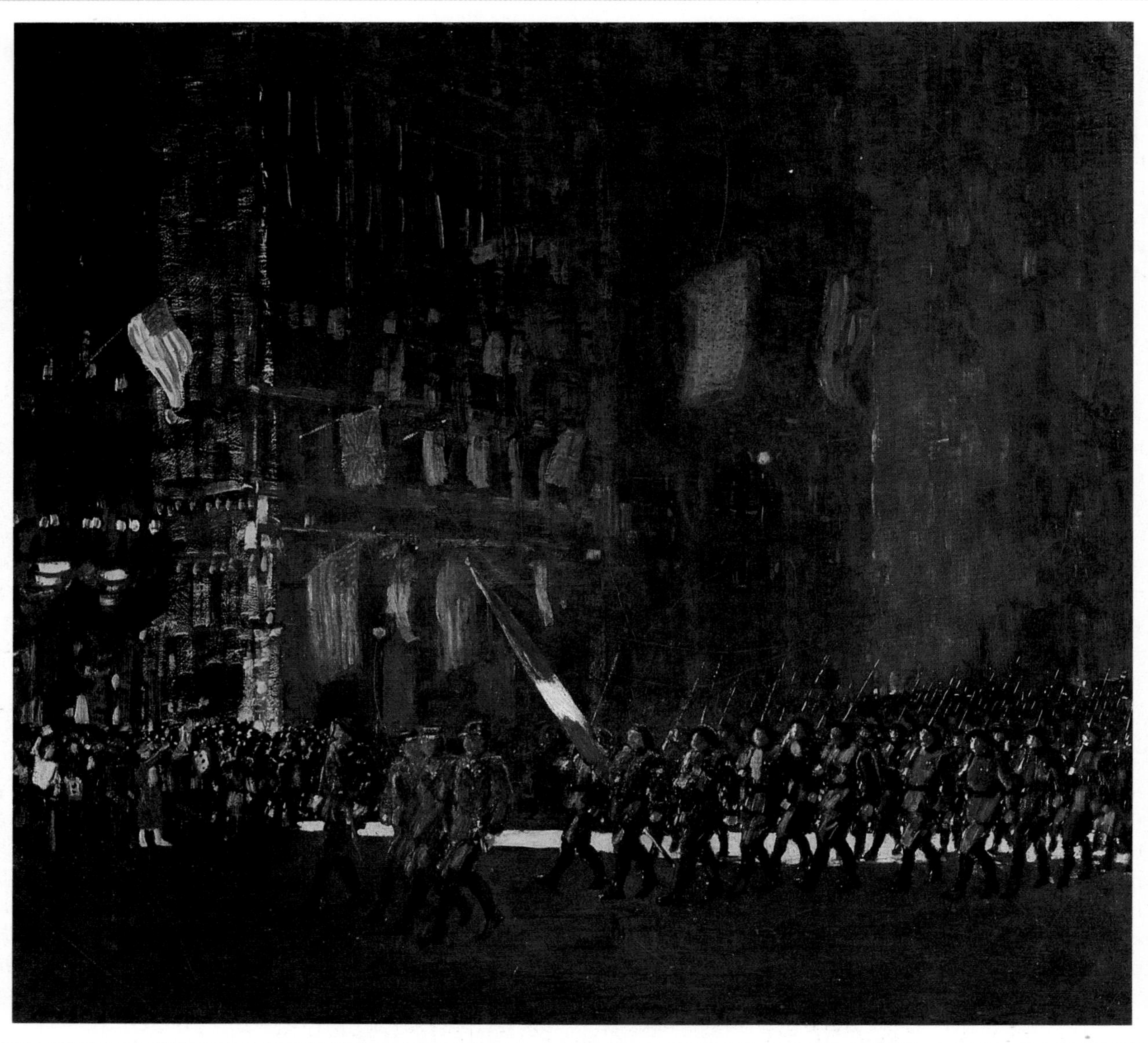

Woodrow Wilson's approach to foreign relations was well intentioned and idealistic but somewhat confused. He knew that the United States had no wish to injure any foreign state and assumed that all nations would recognize this fact and cooperate. He wanted to help other countries, especially the republics of Latin America, achieve stable democratic governments and improve the living conditions of their people. Imperialism was in his eyes immoral. At the same time he felt obliged to sustain and protect American interests abroad. The maintenance of the Open Door in China and the completion of the Panama Canal were as important to him as they had been to Theodore Roosevelt.

Wilson's view of nations with traditions different from those of the United States was shortsighted and provincial. His attitude resembled that of 19th-century Christian missionaries: he wanted to spread the gospel of American democracy, to lift and enlighten the unfortunate and the ignorant—but in his own way. "I am going to teach the South American republics to elect good men!" he told one British diplomat.

Missionary Diplomacy

Wilson set out to raise the moral tone of American foreign policy by denouncing dollar diplomacy. Encouraging bankers to lend money to countries like China, he said, implied the possibility of "forcible interference" if the loans were not repaid, and that would be "obnoxious to the principles upon which the government of our people rests." To seek special economic concessions in Latin America was "unfair" and "degrading." The United States would deal with Latin American nations "upon terms of equality and honor."

In certain small matters Wilson succeeded in conducting American diplomacy on this idealistic basis. He withdrew the government's support of the international consortium that was arranging a loan to develop Chinese railroads, and American bankers pulled out. When the Japanese attempted, in the notorious Twenty-one Demands (1915), to reduce China almost to the status of a Japanese protectorate, he persuaded them to modify their conditions slightly. Congress had passed a law in 1912 exempting American coastal shipping from the payment of tolls on the Panama Canal in spite of a provision in the Hay-Pauncefote Treaty with Great Britain guaranteeing that the canal would be available to the vessels of all nations "on terms of entire equality." Wilson insisted that Congress repeal the law. He also permitted Secretary of State William Jennings Bryan to negotiate conciliation treaties with 21 nations. The distinctive feature of these agreements was the provision for a "cooling-off" period of one year, during which signatories agreed, in the event of a dispute, not to engage in hostilities.

Where more vital interests of the United States were concerned, Wilson sometimes failed to live up to his promises. Because of the strategic importance of the Panama Canal, he was unwilling to tolerate "unrest" anywhere in the Caribbean. Within months of his inauguration he was pursuing the same tactics that circumstances had forced on Roosevelt and Taft. The Bryan-Chamorro Treaty of 1914, which gave the United States an option to build a canal across Nicaragua, made that country virtually an American protectorate and served to maintain in power an unpopular dictator, Adolfo Díaz. When a revolution broke out in the Dominican Republic in 1916, United States marines occupied the country. American troops also took over in revolution-torn Haiti and installed a puppet president. By a treaty of September 1915, Haiti became a United States protectorate.

A much more serious example of missionary diplomacy occurred in Mexico. In 1911 a liberal coalition overthrew the dictator Porfirio Díaz, who had been exploiting the resources and people of Mexico for the benefit of a small class of wealthy landowners, clerics, and military men since the 1870s. Francisco Madero became president.

Madero, a wealthy landowner apparently influenced by the progressive movement in the United States, was committed to economic reform and the drafting of a democratic constitution. Unfortunately, he was both weak-willed and a terrible administrator. Conditions in Mexico deteriorated rapidly, and less than a month before Wilson's inauguration one of Madero's generals, Victoriano Huerta, treacherously seized power and had his former chief murdered. Huerta was an unabashed reactionary, but he was committed to maintaining

THE UNITED STATES IN MEXICO, 1914–1917

the stability that foreign investors desired. Most of the European powers promptly recognized his government.

The American ambassador in Mexico City, together with important American financial and business interests in Mexico and in the United States, urged Wilson to do so too, but he refused. His sympathies were all with the government of Madero, whose murder had horrified him. "I will not recognize a government of butchers," he said. This was unconventional; nations do not ordinarily consider the means by which a foreign regime has come to power before deciding to establish diplomatic relations.

Wilson brought enormous pressure to bear against Huerta. He dragooned the British into withdrawing recognition. He dickered with other Mexican factions. He demanded that Huerta hold free elections as the price of American mediation in the continuing civil war. Huerta would not yield an inch. Indeed, he drew strength from Wilson's effort to oust him, for even his enemies resented American interference in Mexican affairs. Frustration, added to his moral outrage, weakened Wilson's judgment. He subordinated his wish to let the Mexicans solve their own problems to his personal desire to destroy Huerta.

The tense situation exploded in April 1914, when a small party of American sailors was arrested in the port of Tampico, Mexico. When the Mexican government refused to supply the apology demanded by the sailors' commander, Wilson fastened on the affair as an excuse for sending troops into Mexico.

The invasion took place at Veracruz, whence Winfield Scott had launched the assault on Mexico City in 1847. Instead of meekly surrendering the city, the Mexicans resisted tenaciously, suffering 400 casualties before falling back. This bloodshed caused dismay throughout Latin America and failed to unseat Huerta.

At this point, Argentina, Brazil, and Chile offered to mediate the dispute. Wilson accepted, Huerta also agreed, and the conferees met at Niagara Falls, Ontario, in May. Although no settlement was reached, Huerta, hard pressed by Mexican opponents, abdicated. On August 20, 1914, General Venustiano Carranza entered Mexico City in triumph.

Carranza favored representative government, but he proved scarcely more successful than the tyrant Huerta in controlling the country. One of his own generals, Francisco "Pancho" Villa, rose against him and seized control of Mexico City.

Wilson now made a monumental blunder. Villa professed to be willing to cooperate with the United States, and Wilson, taking him at his word, gave him his support. However, Villa was little more than an ambitious bandit with no other objective than personal power. Carranza, while no radical, was committed to social reform. Fighting back, he drove the Villistas into the northern provinces.

Wilson finally realized the extent of Carranza's influence in Mexico, and in October 1915 he recognized the Carranza government. Still his Mexican troubles were not over; Villa, seeking to undermine Carranza by forcing the United States to intervene, began a series of unprovoked attacks on Americans. Early in 1916 he stopped a train in northern Mexico and killed 16 American passengers in cold blood. Then he crossed into New Mexico and burned the town of Columbus, killing 19. Having learned his lesson, Wilson would have preferred to bear even this assault in silence, but public opinion forced him to send American troops under General John

The American camp at Colonia Dublan, Mexico, photographed in 1916 during Pershing's pursuit of Villa. Pershing was an advocate of black troops; hence his nickname, "Black Jack."

J. Pershing across the border in pursuit of Villa.

Villa proved impossible to catch. Cleverly he drew Pershing deeper and deeper into Mexico, and this alarmed Carranza, who insisted that the Americans withdraw. Several clashes occurred between Pershing's men and Mexican regulars, and for a brief period in June 1916 war seemed imminent. Wilson now acted bravely and wisely. Early in 1917 he recalled Pershing's force, leaving the Mexicans to work out their own destiny.

Missionary diplomacy in Mexico had produced mixed but in the long run beneficial results. By opposing Huerta, Wilson had surrendered to his prejudices, yet he had also helped the real revolutionaries even though they opposed his acts. His bungling bred anti-Americanism in Mexico, but by his later restraint in the face of stinging provocations, he permitted the constitutionalists to consolidate their power.

Outbreak of the Great War

On June 28, 1914, in the Austro-Hungarian provincial capital of Sarajevo, Gavrilo Princip, a young student, assassinated the Archduke Franz Ferdinand, heir to the imperial throne. Princip was a member of the Black Hand, a Serbian terrorist organization. He was seeking to further the cause of Serbian nationalism. Instead his rash act precipitated a general European war. Within little more than a month, following a complex series of diplomatic challenges and responses, two great coalitions, the Central Powers (chiefly Germany and Austria-Hungary) and the Allied Powers (chiefly Great Britain, France, and Russia), were locked in a brutal struggle that brought one era in world history to a close and inaugurated another.

The outbreak of what contemporaries were soon to call the Great War caught Americans psychologically unprepared; few understood the significance of what had happened. President Wilson promptly issued a proclamation of neutrality and asked the nation to be "impartial in thought." While no one, including the president, had the superhuman self-control that this request called for, the almost unanimous reaction of Americans, aside from dismay, was that the conflict did not concern them. They were wrong, for this was a world war and Americans were sure to be affected by its outcome.

There were good reasons, aside from a failure to understand the significance of the struggle, why the United States sought to remain neutral. Over a third of its 92 million inhabitants were either foreign-born or the children of immigrants. Sentimental ties bound former Europeans to the lands of their ancestors. American involvement would create new internal stresses in a society already strained by the task of assimilating so many diverse groups. War was also an affront to the prevailing progressive spirit, which assumed that human beings were reasonable, high-minded, and capable of settling disputes peaceably. Along with the traditional American fear of entanglement in European affairs, these were ample reasons for remaining aloof.

While most Americans hoped to keep out of the war, nearly everyone was partial to one side or the other. People of German or Austrian descent, about 8 million in number, and the nation's 4.5 million Irish-Americans, motivated chiefly by hatred of the British, sympathized with the Central Powers. The majority of the people, however, influenced by bonds of language and culture, preferred an Allied victory, and when the Germans launched a mighty assault across neutral Belgium in an effort to outflank the French armies, this unprovoked attack on a tiny nation whose neutrality the Germans had previously agreed to respect caused a great deal of anti-German feeling.

As the war progressed the Allies cleverly exploited American prejudices by such devices as publishing exaggerated tales of German atrocities against Belgian civilians. A supposedly impartial study of these charges by the widely respected James Bryce, author of *The American Commonwealth,* portrayed the Germans as ruthless and cruel barbarians. The Germans also conducted a shrewd and extensive propaganda campaign in the United States, but they labored under severe handicaps and won few converts.

Freedom of the Seas

Propaganda did not basically alter American attitudes; far more important were questions rising out of trade and commerce. All the warring nations wanted to draw on American resources. Under international law neutrals could trade freely with any belligerent. Americans were prepared to do so, but because the British fleet dominated the North Atlantic, they could not. While the specific issues differed somewhat, the situation was similar to that which had prevailed during the Napoleonic wars. The British declared nearly all commodities, even foodstuffs, to be contraband of war. They set limits on exports to neutral nations such as Denmark and the Netherlands so that those countries could not transship supplies to Germany. They forced neutral merchant ships into Allied ports in order to search them for goods headed for the enemy. Many cargoes were confiscated, often without payment. American firms that traded with the Central Powers were "blacklisted," which meant that no British subject could deal with them. When these policies caused protests in America, the British answered that in a battle for survival they dared not adhere to old-fashioned rules of international law.

Had the United States insisted that Great Britain abandon these "illegal" practices, as the Germans demanded, no doubt it could have had its way. The British foreign secretary, Sir Edward Grey, later admitted: "The ill-will of the United States meant certain defeat. The object of diplomacy, therefore, was to secure the maximum of blockade that could be enforced without a rupture with the United States." It is ironic that an embargo, which failed so ignominiously in Jefferson's day, would have been almost instantly effective if applied at any time after 1914, for American supplies were vital to the Allies.

While British tactics frequently exasperated Wilson, he never considered taking such a drastic step. He faced a dilemma. To allow the British to make the rules meant siding against the Central Powers. Yet to insist on the old rules (which had never been obeyed in wartime) meant siding against the Allies because that would have deprived them of much of the value of their naval superiority. *Nothing* the United States might do would be truly impartial.

Wilson's own sentiments made it doubly difficult for him to object strenuously to British practices. No American admired British institutions and culture more extravagantly. "Everything I love most in the world is at stake," he confessed privately to the British ambassador. A German victory "would be fatal to our form of Government and American ideals."

In any event, the immense expansion of American trade with the Allies made an embargo unthinkable. While commerce with the Central Powers fell to a trickle, that with the Allies soared from $825 million in 1914 to over $3.2 billion in 1916. An attempt to limit this commerce would have raised a storm; to have eliminated it would have caused a catastrophe. Munitions makers and other businessmen did not want the United States to enter the war. Neutrality suited their purposes admirably. Despite British harassments, they profited from the war and wished to continue to do so.

The Allies soon exhausted their ready cash and had to borrow in order to continue their purchases. Wilson first refused to let American bankers lend them money, then reversed himself. By early 1917 Britain and France had borrowed well over $2 billion. While these loans violated no principle of international law, they fastened the United States more closely to the Allies' cause.

During the first months of the Great War the Germans were not especially concerned about neutral trade or American goods because they expected to crush the Allied armies quickly. When their first swift thrust was blunted along the Marne and the war became a bloody stalemate, they began to challenge the Allies' control of the seas. Unwilling to risk their battleships and cruisers against the much larger British fleet, they resorted to a new weapon, the submarine, commonly known as the U-boat (*Unterseeboot*).

German submarines played a role in World War I not unlike that of American privateers in the Revolution and the War of 1812: they ranged the seas stealthily in search of merchant ships. However, submarines could not operate under the ordinary rules of war, which required that a raider stop its prey, examine its papers and cargo, and give the crew and passengers time to get off in lifeboats before sending it to the bottom. When surfaced, U-boats were vulnerable to the deck guns that many merchant ships carried; they could even be sunk by ramming, once they had stopped and put out a boarding party. Therefore they commonly launched their torpedoes from below the surface without warning. The result was often a heavy loss of life on the torpedoed ships.

In February 1915 the Germans declared the waters surrounding the British Isles a zone of war and announced that they would sink without warning all enemy merchant ships encountered in the area. Since Allied vessels sometimes flew neutral flags to disguise their identity, neutral ships entering the zone would do so at their own risk. This statement was largely bluff, for the Germans had only a handful of submarines at sea; but they were feverishly building more.

Wilson—perhaps too hurriedly, considering the importance of the question—warned the Germans that he would hold them to "strict accountability" for any loss of American life or property resulting from violations of "acknowledged [neutral] rights on the high seas." He did not distinguish clearly between losses incurred through the destruction of *American* ships and those resulting from the sinking of other vessels. If he meant to hold the Germans responsible for injuries to Americans on *belligerent* vessels, he was changing international law as arbitrarily as the Germans were. Secretary of State Bryan, who opposed Wilson vigorously on this point, took sound legal ground when he said: "A ship carrying contraband should not rely upon passengers to protect her from attack—it would be like putting women and children in front of an army." "Strict accountability" ultimately meant war unless the Germans backed down. Yet Wilson was not prepared to fight; he refused even to ask Congress for increased military appropriations, saying that he did not want to "turn America into a military camp."

Wise or unwise, Wilson's position reflected the attitude of most Americans. It seemed barbaric to them that defenseless civilians should be killed without warning, and they refused to surrender their "rights" as neutrals to cross the North Atlantic on any ship they wished. The depth of their feeling was demonstrated when, on May 7, 1915, the submarine *U-20* sank the British liner *Lusitania* off the Irish coast. Nearly 1,200 persons, including 128 Americans, lost their lives in this catastrophe.

The torpedoing of the *Lusitania* caused as profound and emotional a reaction in the United States as that following the destruction of the *Maine* in Havana harbor. Wilson, like McKinley in 1898, was shocked, but he kept his head. He demanded that Germany disavow the sinking, indemnify the victims, and promise to stop attacking passenger vessels. When the Germans quibbled about these points, he responded with further diplomatic correspondence rather than with an ultimatum.

NOTICE!

TRAVELLERS intending to embark on the Atlantic voyage are reminded that a state of war exists between Germany and her allies and Great Britain and her allies; that the zone of war includes the waters adjacent to the British Isles; that, in accordance with formal notice given by the Imperial German Government, vessels flying the flag of Great Britain, or of any of her allies, are liable to destruction in those waters and that travellers sailing in the war zone on ships of Great Britain or her allies do so at their own risk.

IMPERIAL GERMAN EMBASSY
WASHINGTON, D. C., APRIL 22, 1915.

Three weeks before the Lusitania *was torpedoed this notice appeared in the classified sections of Washington newspapers.*

In one sense this was sound policy. The Germans pointed out that they had published warnings in American newspapers saying they considered the *Lusitania* subject to attack, that the liner was carrying munitions, and that on past voyages it had flown the American flag as a *ruse de guerre.* It would have been difficult politically for the German government to have backed down before an American ultimatum; however, after dragging the controversy out for nearly a year, it apologized and agreed to pay an indemnity. After the torpedoing of the French channel steamer *Sussex* in March 1916 had produced another stiff American protest, the Germans at last promised—the *Sussex* pledge—to stop sinking merchant ships without warning.

Had Wilson forced a showdown in 1915, he would have alienated a large segment of American opinion. Even his relatively mild notes resulted in the resignation of Secretary of State Bryan, who believed it unneutral to treat German violations of international law differently than Allied violations—and Bryan reflected the feelings of thousands.*

On the other hand, if Wilson had sought a declaration of war over the *Lusitania,* a majority of Congress and the country would probably have gone along, and in that event the dreadful carnage in Europe would have been ended much sooner. This is the reasoning of hindsight, yet such a policy would have been logical, given Wilson's assumptions about the justice of the Allied cause and America's stake in an Allied victory.

The president and most Americans were not clearheaded enough in 1915 to act entirely logically. In November 1915 Wilson at last began to press for increased military and naval expenditures. Nevertheless he continued to vacillate. He dispatched a sharp note protesting Allied blacklisting of American firms, and he told his confidant, Colonel Edward M. House, that the British were "poor boobs!" His position on preparedness remained so equivocal that his secretary of war, Lindley M. Garrison, resigned in protest.

The Election of 1916

Part of Wilson's confusion in 1916 resulted from the political difficulties he faced in his fight for reelection. He had won the presidency in 1912 only because the Republican party had split in two. Now Theodore Roosevelt, the chief defector, had become so incensed by Wilson's refusal to commit the United States to the Allied cause that he was ready to support almost any Republican in order to guarantee the president's defeat. At the same time, many progressives were complaining about Wilson's unwillingness to work for further domestic reforms. Unless he could find additional support, he seemed likely to be defeated.

* Wilson appointed Robert Lansing, counselor of the State Department, to succeed Bryan.

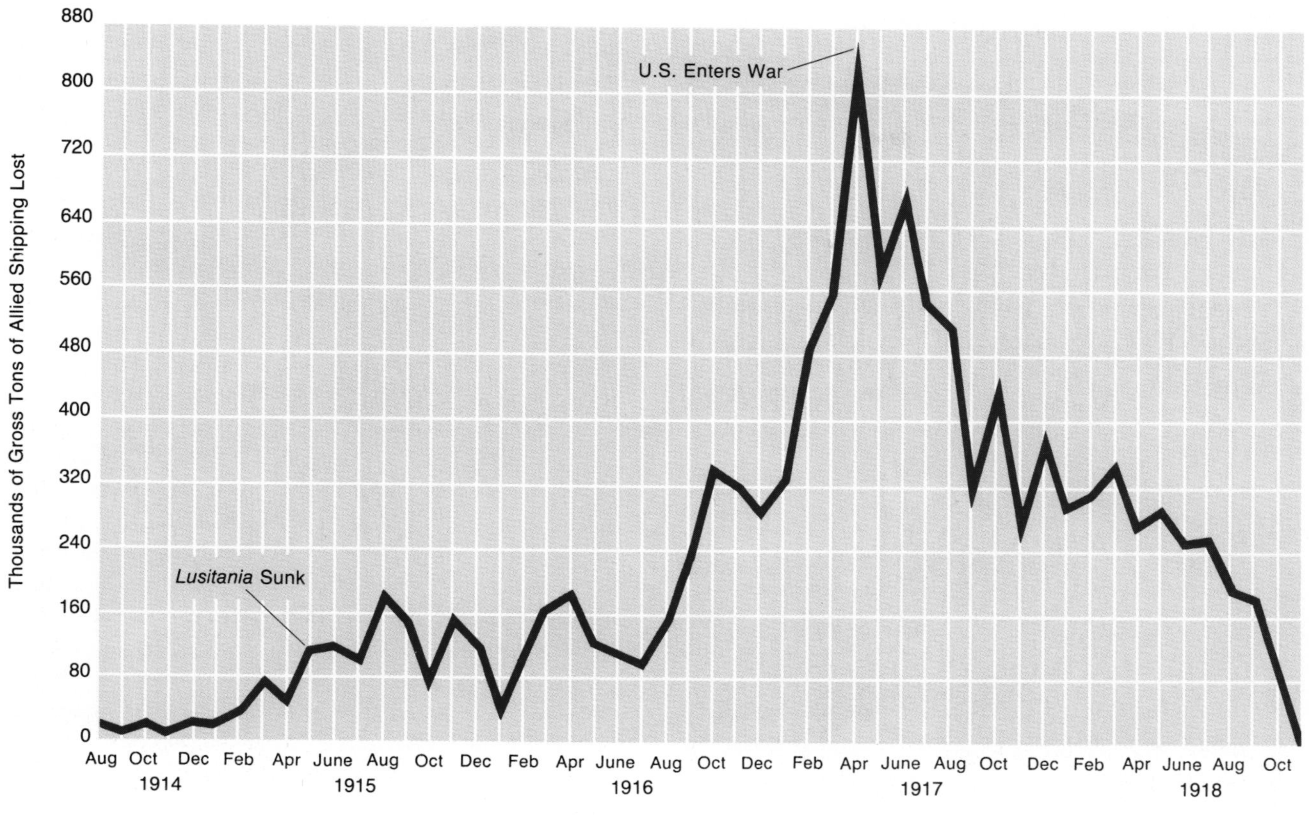

U–BOAT CAMPAIGN, 1914–1918

He attacked the problem by wooing the progressives. In January 1916 he appointed Louis D. Brandeis to the Supreme Court. In addition to being an advanced progressive, Brandeis was Jewish, the first American of that religion appointed to the Court. Wilson's action won him many friends among people who favored fair treatment for minority groups. In July he bid for the farm vote by signing the Farm Loan Act to provide low-cost loans based on agricultural credit. Shortly thereafter he approved the Keating-Owen Child Labor Act, barring goods manufactured by the labor of children under 16 from interstate commerce, and a workers' compensation act for federal employees. He persuaded Congress to pass the Adamson Act, establishing an eight-hour day for railroad workers, and he modified his position on the tariff by approving the creation of a tariff commission and accepting "antidumping" legislation designed to protect American industry from cutthroat foreign competition after the war.

Each of these actions represented a sharp reversal. In 1913 Wilson had considered Brandeis too radical even for a Cabinet post. The new farm, labor, and tariff laws were all examples of the kind of "class legislation" he had refused to countenance in 1913 and 1914. As Arthur S. Link has pointed out, Wilson was putting into effect "almost every important plank of the Progressive platform of 1912." It would be uncharitable to conclude that he did so only to win votes, but his actions paid spectacular political dividends when Roosevelt refused to run as a Progressive and came out for the Republican nominee, Associate Justice Charles Evans Hughes. The Progressive convention then endorsed Hughes, who had compiled a fine liberal record as governor of New York, but many of Roosevelt's 1912 supporters felt he had betrayed them and voted for Wilson in 1916.

The key issue in the campaign was American policy toward the warring powers. Wilson intended to stress preparedness, which he was now whole

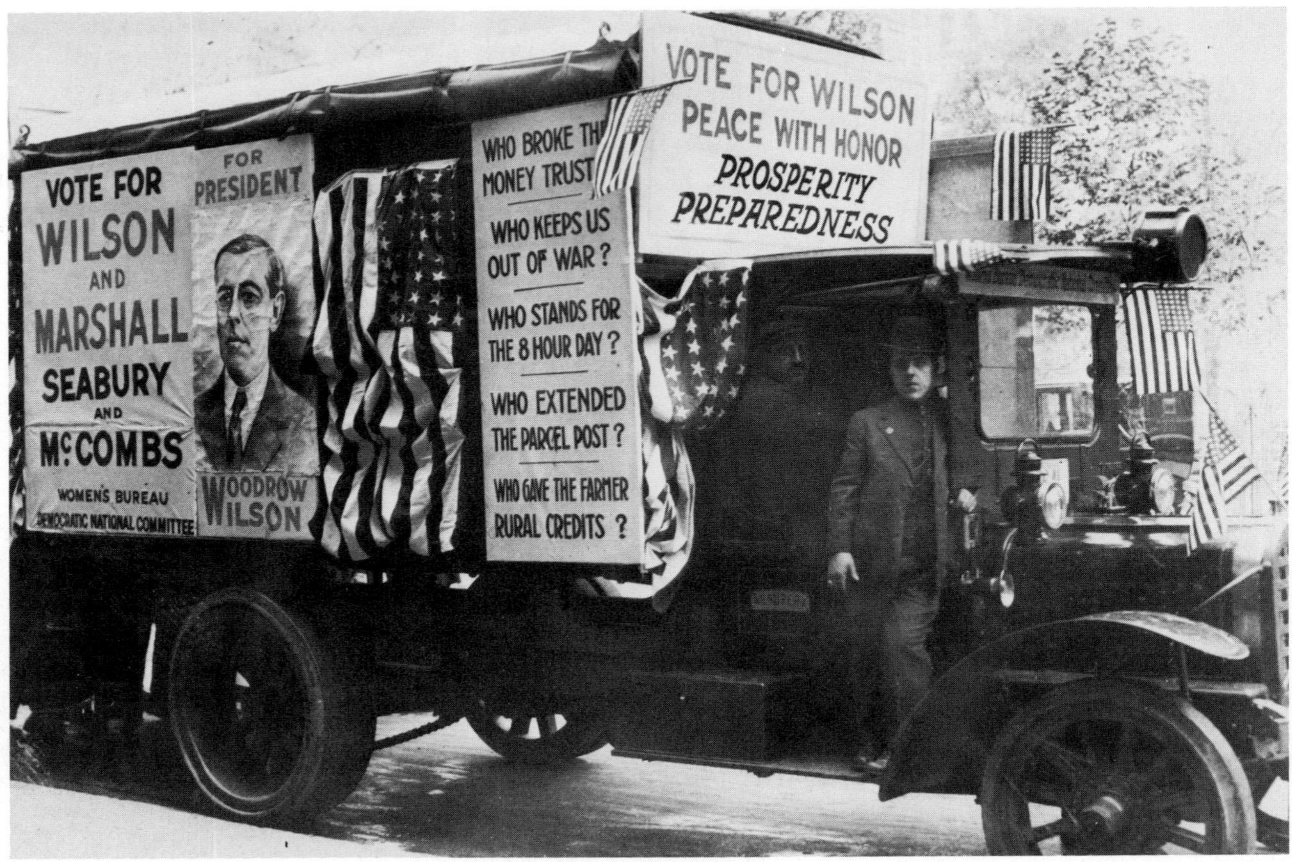

A Wilson campaign truck offered New York City voters a convenient summary of the 1916 Democratic platform. The eight-hour-day plank refers to the president's support of a federal law for railroad workers.

heartedly supporting. However, during the Democratic convention the delegates shook the hall with cheers whenever orators referred to the president's success in keeping the country out of the war. One spellbinder, referring to the *Sussex* pledge, announced that the president had "wrung from the most militant spirit that ever brooded above a battlefield an acknowledgement of American rights and an agreement to American demands," and the convention erupted in a demonstration that lasted more than 20 minutes. Thus "He Kept Us Out of War" became the Democratic slogan.

To his credit, Wilson made no promises. "I can't keep the country out of war," he told one member of his Cabinet. "Any little German lieutenant can put us into the war at any time by some calculated outrage." His attitude undoubtedly cost him the votes of extremists on both sides, but it won the backing of thousands of moderates.

The combination of progressivism and the peace issue placed the Democrats on substantially equal terms with the Republicans; thereafter personal factors probably tipped the balance. Hughes was very stiff and an ineffective speaker; he offended a number of important politicians, especially in crucial California, where he inadvertently snubbed the popular progressive governor, Hiram Johnson; and he equivocated on a number of issues. Nevertheless, on election night he appeared to have won, having carried nearly all the East and Middle West. Late returns gave Wilson California, however, and with it victory by the narrow margin of 277 to 254 in the electoral college. He led Hughes in the popular vote, 9.1 million to 8.5 million.

The Road to War

Encouraged by his triumph, appalled by the continuing slaughter on the battlefields, fearful that the United States would be dragged into the holocaust, Wilson made one last effort to end the war by negotiation. In 1915 he had sent his friend Colonel House on a secret mission to London, Paris, and Berlin to try to mediate between the belligerents. House had been received cordially, but he made little progress and his negotiations were disrupted by the *Lusitania* crisis. A second House mission (January–February 1916) had proved equally fruitless. Now, after another long season of bloodshed, perhaps the powers would listen to reason.

Wilson's own feelings were more genuinely neutral than at any other time during the war, for the Germans had stopped sinking merchant ships without warning and the British had irritated him repeatedly by their arbitrary restrictions on neutral trade. He drafted a note to the belligerents asking them to state the terms on which they would agree to lay down their arms. Unless the fighting ended soon, he warned, neutrals and belligerents alike would be so ruined that peace would be meaningless. When neither side responded encouragingly, Wilson, on January 22, 1917, delivered a moving, prophetic speech aimed, as he admitted, at "the *people* of the countries now at war" more than at their governments. Any settlement imposed by a victor, he declared, would breed hatred and more wars. There must be a "peace without victory" based on the principles that all nations were equal and that every nationality group should determine its own form of government. He mentioned, albeit vaguely, disarmament and freedom of the seas, and he suggested the creation of some kind of international organization to preserve world peace. "There must be not a balance of power, but a community of power," he said, and he added, "I am speaking for the silent mass of mankind everywhere."

This noble appeal met a tragic fate. The Germans had already decided to renounce the *Sussex* pledge and unleash their submarines against *all* vessels headed for Allied ports. After February 1 any ship in the war zone would be attacked without warning. Possessed now of more than 100 U-boats, the German military leaders had convinced themselves that they could starve the British people into submission and reduce the Allied armies to impotence by cutting off the flow of American supplies. The United States would probably declare war, but the Germans believed they could overwhelm the Allies before the Americans could get to the battlefields in force. "The United States . . . can neither inflict material damage upon us, nor can it be of material benefit to our enemies," Admiral von Holtzendorff boasted. "I guarantee that for its part the U-boat war will lead to victory."

In *Tiger at the Gates* the French playwright Jean Giraudoux makes Ulysses say, while attempting to stave off what he considers an inevitable war with the Trojans: "The privilege of great men is to view catastrophe from a terrace." This is not always true, but in 1917, after the German military leaders had

"U-Boote Heraus!" (*"U-boats go home!"*) *proclaims an anti-German poster apparently designed to be seen by submarine captains.*

made their decision, events moved relentlessly, almost uninfluenced by the actors who presumably controlled the fate of the world:

> *February 3: S.S. Housatonic* torpedoed. Wilson announces to Congress that he has severed diplomatic relations with Germany. Secretary of State Lansing hands the German ambassador, Count von Bernstorff, his passport. *February 24:* Walter Hines Page, United States ambassador to Great Britain, transmits to the State Department an intercepted German dispatch (the "Zimmermann Telegram") revealing that Germany has proposed a secret alliance with Mexico, Mexico to receive, in the event of war with the United States, "the lost territory in Texas, New Mexico, and Arizona." *February 25:* Cunard liner *Laconia* torpedoed, two American women perish. *February 26:* Wilson asks Congress for authority to arm American merchant ships. *March 1:* Zimmermann Telegram released to the press. *March 4:* President Wilson takes oath of office, beginning his second term. Congress adjourns without passing the Armed Ship bill, the measure having been filibustered to death by antiwar senators. Wilson characterizes the filibusterers, led by Senator Robert M. La Follette, as "a little group of willful men, representing no opinion but their own." *March 9:* Wilson, acting under his executive powers, orders the arming of American merchantmen. *March 12:* Revolutionary provisional government established in Russia. *Algonquin* torpedoed. *March 15:* Czar Nicholas II of Russia abdicates. *March 16: City of Memphis, Illinois, Vigilancia* torpedoed. *March 21:* New York *World,* a leading Democratic newspaper, calls for declaration of war on Germany. Wilson summons Congress to convene in special session on April 2. *March 25:* Wilson calls up the National Guard. *April 2:* Wilson asks Congress to declare war. Germany is guilty of "throwing to the winds all scruples of humanity," he says. America must fight, not to conquer, but for "peace and justice. . . . The world must be made safe for democracy." *April 4, 6:* Congress declares war—the vote, 82–6 in the Senate, 373–50 in the House.

The bare record conceals Wilson's agonizing search for an honorable alternative to war. To admit that Germany posed a threat to the United States meant confessing that interventionists had been right all along. To go to war meant, besides sending innocent Americans to their deaths, unleashing the forces of hatred and intolerance in the United States and allowing "the spirit of ruthless brutality [to] enter into the very fibre of our national life." The president's Presbyterian conscience tortured him relentlessly. He lost sleep, appeared gray and drawn. When someone asked him which side he hoped would win, he answered petulantly, "Neither." "He was resisting," Secretary of State Lansing recorded, "the irresistible logic of events." In the end Wilson could satisfy himself only by giving intervention an idealistic purpose. The war had become a threat to humanity. Unless the United States threw its weight into the balance, western civilization itself might be destroyed. Out of the long bloodbath must come a new and better world. The war must be fought to end, for all time, war itself. Thus, in the name not of vengeance and victory but of justice and humanity, he sent his people into battle.

The Home Front

America's entry into the World War determined its outcome. The Allies were running out of money and supplies; their troops, decimated by nearly three years in the trenches, were disheartened and rebellious. In February and March 1917 U-boats sent over a million tons of Allied shipping to the bottom of the Atlantic. The outbreak of the Russian Revolution in March 1917, at first lifting the spirits of the western democracies, led to the Bolshevik takeover under Lenin. The Russian armies collapsed; by December 1917 Russia was out of the war and the Germans were moving masses of men and equipment from the eastern front to France. Without the aid of the United States, it is likely that the war would have ended in 1918 on terms dictated from Berlin. Instead American men and supplies helped contain the Germans' last drives and then push them back to final defeat.

It was a close thing, for the United States entered the war little better prepared to fight than it had been in 1898. For this Wilson was partly to blame. Because of his devotion to peace he had not tried hard enough to ready the country for war.

The conversion of American industry to war production had to be organized and carried out without prearrangement. What the historian Harvey A. DeWeerd has called "absurdly large" goals were set, far beyond what the army could use. Confusion and waste resulted. The hurriedly designed shipbuilding program was an almost total fiasco.

The gigantic Hog Island yard, which cost $65 million and employed at its peak over 34,000 workers, completed its first vessel after the war ended. The nation's railroads, strained by immensely increased traffic, became progressively less efficient. A monumental tie-up in December and January 1917–1918 finally persuaded Wilson to appoint Secretary of the Treasury William G. McAdoo director-general of the railroads, with power to run the roads as a single system.

Airplane, tank, and artillery construction programs, all too large to begin with, developed too slowly to affect the war. The big guns that backed up American soldiers in 1918 were made in France and Great Britain; of the 8.8 million rounds of artillery ammunition fired by American troops, only about 8,000 were manufactured in the United States. In 1917 the Army had only 50-odd airplanes, all obsolete. Congress authorized the manufacture of 20,000, but only a handful, mostly British-designed planes made in America, got to France.

"America," writes David M. Kennedy in *Over Here*, "was no 'arsenal of democracy' in World War I; the American doughboy in France was typically transported in a British ship; wore a steel helmet modeled on the British Tommy's, and fought with French ordnance." American pilots such as the great "ace" Captain Eddie Rickenbacker flew British Sopwiths and De Havillands or French Spads and Nieuports. Theodore Roosevelt's son Quentin was shot down while flying a Spad over Château-Thierry in July 1918.

The problem of mobilization was complicated. It took Congress six weeks of hot debate merely to decide on conscription. Only in September 1917, nearly six months after the declaration of war, did the first draftees reach the training camps, and it is hard to see how Wilson could have speeded this process appreciably. He wisely supported the professional soldiers, who insisted that he resist the appeals of politicians who wanted to raise volunteer units, even rejecting, at considerable political cost, Theodore Roosevelt's offer to raise an entire army division.

Wilson was a forceful and inspiring war leader once he grasped what needed to be done. Waste there was, and inefficiency, but no one in the country worked harder or displayed such unfailing patience in the face of frustration and criticism. Raising an army was only a small part of the job. The Allies had to be supplied with food and munitions, and immense amounts of money had to be collected.

Wilson placed the task in the hands of a Council of National Defense, consisting of six Cabinet officers and a seven-member advisory commission. The council attempted to coordinate the manufacture of munitions and other war goods, but it lacked the authority to do the job properly. After a series of experiments, it created (July 1917) the War Industries Board (WIB) to oversee all aspects of industrial production and distribution. The head of the board, Bernard Baruch, a Wall Street speculator by trade, was given almost dictatorial power to allocate scarce materials, standardize production, fix prices, and coordinate American and Allied purchasing.

Evaluating the mobilization effort raises interesting historical questions. The antitrust laws were suspended and producers were encouraged, even compelled, to cooperate with one another. Government regulation went far beyond what the New Nationalists had envisaged in 1912. As for the New Freedom variety of laissez faire, it had no place in a wartime economy. McAdoo's Railroad Administration pooled all railroad equipment, centralized purchasing, standardized accounting practices, and raised wages and passenger rates. Under difficult conditions it ran the railroads effectively. Wilson accepted the kind of government-industry agreement developed under Theodore Roosevelt that he had denounced in 1912. Prices were set by the WIB at levels that allowed large profits—U.S. Steel, for example, despite high taxes, cleared over half a billion dollars in two years. Baruch justified these returns with what seemed to him irrefutable logic: "You could be forgiven if you paid too much to get the stuff, but you could never be forgiven if you did not get it, and lost the war." It is at least arguable that producers would have turned out just as much even though compelled to charge lower prices.

At the start of the war, army procurement was decentralized and inefficient—as many as eight bureaus were purchasing material in competition with one another. One official bought 1,200 typewriters, stacked them in the basement of a government building, and announced proudly to his superior: "There is going to be the greatest competition for typewriters around here, and I have them all."

Wartime belt-tightening inspired new business ventures for a few entrepreneurs. GET ACQUAINTED—CUT DOWN YOUR MEAT BILLS AND BUY HORSE MEAT, *urges the sign at right.*

The army chief of staff when the war began was General Hugh L. Scott, a veteran of the Indian wars. According to one of his subordinates, "General Scott was a man who knew very little about the war, and he spent most of his time asleep." By January 1918 the supply system was in a condition approaching chaos. At this point Secretary of War Newton D. Baker made General Peyton C. March Army chief of staff. March was a first-rate administrator. He got rid of incompetents and promoted talented officers without regard for seniority.

Mobilization required close cooperation between business and the military. However, the army resisted cooperating with civilian agencies, being, as the historian Paul Koistiner writes, "suspicious of, and hostile toward civilian institutions." Wilson finally compelled the War Department to place officers on WIB committees, and when the army discovered that its interests were not injured by the system, the foundation was laid for what was later to be known as the "industrial-military complex," the alliance between business and military leaders that was to cause so much controversy after World War II.

The history of industrial mobilization was the history of the entire home-front effort in microcosm: prodigies were performed, but the task was so gigantic and unprecedented that a full year passed before an efficient system had been devised, and many unforeseen results occurred.

The problem of mobilizing agricultural resources was solved more quickly, and this was fortunate because in April 1917 the British had on hand only a six-weeks supply of food. Wilson named Herbert Hoover, a mining engineer who had headed the Belgian Relief Commission earlier in the war, food administrator. Acting under powers granted by the Lever Act of August 1917, Hoover set the price of wheat at $2.20 a bushel in order to encourage production. He established a government corporation to purchase the entire American and Cuban sugar crop, which he then doled out to American and British refiners. To avoid rationing, he organized a campaign to persuade consumers to conserve food voluntarily. One slogan ran "If U fast U beat U boats," another "Serve beans by all means." "Wheatless Mondays" and "Meatless Tuesdays" were the rule, and although no law compelled their observance, the public responded patriotically. Boy Scouts dug up backyards and vacant lots to plant vegetable gardens; chefs devised new recipes to save on scarce items; restaurants added horsemeat, rabbit, and whale steak to their menus and doled out butter and sugar to customers in minuscule amounts. Mothers pressured their children to "Hooverize" their plates. Chicago residents were so successful in making use of leftovers that the volume of raw garbage in the city declined from 12,862 tons to 8,386 tons per month. Without subjecting its own citizens to serious inconvenience, the United States increased food exports from 12.3 million tons to 18.6 million tons. Farmers, of course, profited greatly: their real income went up nearly 30 percent between 1915 and 1918.

With the army siphoning so many men from the labor market and with immigration reduced to a trickle, unemployment disappeared and wages rose. Although the cost of living soared, imposing hardships on those with fixed incomes, the boom produced unprecedented opportunities. Americans, always a mobile people, pulled up their roots in unprecedented numbers. Disadvantaged groups, especially blacks, were particularly attracted by jobs in big-city factories. The movement of blacks from the former slave states began with emancipation, but the mass exodus that many people had expected did not materialize. Between 1870 and 1890 only about 80,000 blacks moved to the North, most settling in the cities. Compared with the urban influx from Europe and from northern farms, this was a trivial number; the percentage of blacks in New York City, for example, fell from over 10 percent in 1800 to under 2 percent in 1900.

Around the turn of the century, as the first post-slavery generation reached maturity and as southern repression increased, the northward movement quickened—about 200,000 blacks migrated between 1890 and 1910. Then, after 1914, the war boom drew blacks north in a flood, half a million in five years. The black population of New York rose from 92,000 to 152,000, that of Chicago from 44,000 to 109,000, that of Detroit from 5,700 to 41,000.

Early in the conflict the government began regulating the wages and hours of workers building army camps and manufacturing uniforms. In April 1918, Wilson created a National War Labor Board, headed by former president Taft and Frank P. Walsh, a prominent lawyer, to settle labor disputes. The board considered more than 1,200 cases and prevented many strikes. A War Labor Policies Board, chaired by Professor Felix Frankfurter of the Harvard Law School, set wages-and-hours standards for each major war industry. Since these were determined in consultation with employers and representatives of labor, the WLPB helped speed the unionization of workers by compelling management, even in antiunion industries like steel, to deal with labor leaders. Union membership rose by 2.3 million during the war; in 1920 the American Federation of Labor could boast a membership of more than 3.2 million.

On the other hand, the wartime emergency roused the public against strikers; some conservatives even demanded that war workers be conscripted just as soldiers were. While he opposed strikes that impeded the war effort, Wilson set great store in preserving the individual worker's freedom of action. It would be "most unfortunate . . . to relax the laws by which safeguards have been thrown about labor," he said. "We must accomplish the results we desire by organized effort rather than compulsion."

Trends in the steel industry reflect the improvement of the lot of labor in wartime. Wages of unskilled steelworkers more than doubled. Thousands of southern blacks flocked into the steel towns. Union organizers made inroads in many plants, especially after a War Labor Board decision forbade the companies to interfere with their activities. By the summer of 1918 they were preparing an all-out effort to unionize the industry. If the world was to be made safe for democracy, they argued, there must be "economic democracy [along] with political democracy."

Wilson managed the task of financing the war effectively. The struggle cost the United States about $33.5 billion, not counting pensions and other postwar expenses. About $7 billion of this was lent to the Allies,* but since this money was largely spent in America, it contributed to the national prosperity.

Over two-thirds of the cost of the war was met by borrowing. Five Liberty and Victory Loan drives, spurred by advertising, parading, and appeals to patriotism, persuaded the people to open their purses. Industrialists, eager to inculcate in their employees a sense of personal involvement in the war effort, conducted campaigns in their plants. Some went so far as to threaten "A Bond or Your Job," but more typical was the appeal of the managers of the Gary, Indiana, plant of U.S. Steel, who

* In 1914 Americans owed foreigners about $3.8 billion. By 1919 Americans *were owed* $12.5 billion by Europeans alone.

The nation's advertising and entertainment industries were mobilized to promote war bond drives.

published bond advertisements in six languages in order to reach their immigrant workers.

In addition to borrowing, the government collected about $10.5 billion in taxes during the war. A steeply graduated income tax took more than 75 percent of the incomes of the wealthiest citizens. A 65 percent excess-profits tax and a 25 percent inheritance tax were also enacted. Thus, while many individuals made fortunes out of the war, its cost was distributed far more equitably than was that of the Civil War. Americans also contributed generously to philanthropic agencies engaged in war work. Most notable, perhaps, was the great 1918 drive of the United War Work Council, an interfaith religious group, which raised over $200 million mainly to finance recreational programs for the troops overseas.

Propaganda and Civil Liberties

Wilson was preeminently a teacher and preacher, a specialist in the transmission of ideas and ideals. He excelled at mobilizing public opinion and inspiring Americans to work for the better world he hoped would emerge from the war. In April 1917 he created a Committee on Public Information (CPI) headed by the journalist George Creel. Soon 75,000 speakers were deluging the country with propaganda prepared by hundreds of CPI writers. They pictured the war as a crusade for freedom and democracy, the Germans as a bestial people bent on world domination.

A large majority of the nation supported the war enthusiastically. But thousands of persons—German-Americans and Irish-Americans, for example; people of pacifist leanings such as Jane Addams, the founder of Hull House; and some who thought both sides in the war were wrong—bitterly opposed American involvement. Creel's committee, and a number of unofficial "patriotic" groups, allowed their enthusiasm for the conversion of the hesitant to become suppression of dissent. Persons who refused to buy war bonds were often exposed to public ridicule and even to assault. People with German names were persecuted without regard for their views; some school boards outlawed the teaching of the German language; sauerkraut was renamed "liberty cabbage." Opponents of the war of unquestionable patriotism were subjected to coarse abuse. The cartoonist Rollin Kirby pictured Senator Robert La Follette receiving an Iron Cross from the German militarists, and the faculty of his own University of Wisconsin voted to censure La Follette.*

Wilson, "a friend of free speech in theory," the historian David M. Kennedy has written, "was its foe in fact." He signed the Espionage Act of 1917, which imposed fines of up to $10,000 and jail sentences ranging to 20 years on persons convicted of aiding the enemy or obstructing recruiting, and authorized the postmaster general to ban from the mails any material which he considered treasonable or seditious.

In May 1918, again with Wilson's approval, Congress passed the Sedition Act, which made it a crime even to speak against the purchase of war

* Kirby later expressed deep regret for having defamed La Follette.

bonds or to "utter, print, write, or publish any disloyal, profane, scurrilous, or abusive language" about the government, the Constitution, or the uniform of the army or navy. Socialist periodials such as *The Masses* were suppressed, and Eugene V. Debs was sentenced to 10 years in prison for making an antiwar speech. Ricardo Flores Magon, an anarchist, was sentenced to 20 years in jail for publishing a statement criticizing Wilson's Mexican policy, an issue that had nothing to do with the war.

While legislation to prevent sabotage and control subversives was justifiable, these laws went far beyond what was necessary to protect the national interest. Some local officials used them to muzzle liberal opinion. Citizens were jailed for suggesting that the draft law was unconstitutional and for criticizing private organizations like the Red Cross and the YMCA. One woman was sent to prison for writing: "I am for the people, and the government is for the profiteers."

In 1917 the Germania Life Insurance Building in St. Paul was renamed the Guardian Building; since Germania herself could not be disguised, down she came.

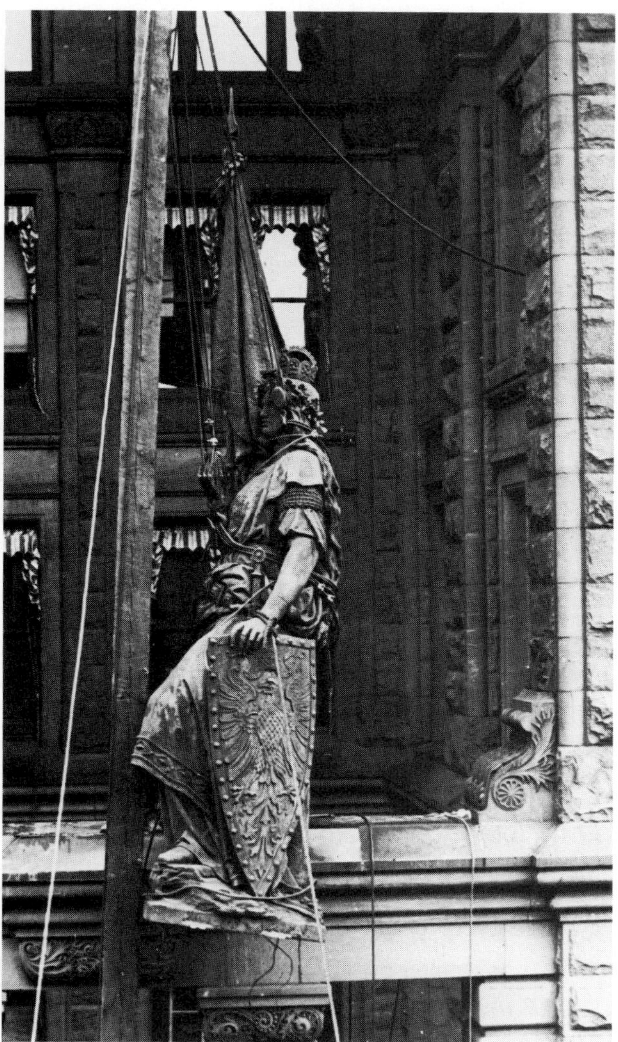

The Supreme Court upheld the constitutionality of the Espionage Act in *Schenck* v. *United States* (1919), a case involving a man who had mailed circulars to draftees urging them to refuse to report for induction into the army. Free speech has its limits, Justice Oliver Wendell Holmes, Jr., explained. No one has the right to cry *Fire!* in a crowded theater. When there is a "clear and present danger" that a particular statement would threaten the national interest, it can be repressed by law. In peacetime Schenck's circulars would be permissible, but not in time of war.

The "clear and present danger" doctrine did not prevent judges and juries from interpreting the Espionage and Sedition acts broadly, and while in many instances their decisions were overturned by higher courts, this usually did not occur until after the war. The wartime hysteria far exceeded anything that happened in Great Britain and France. In 1916 the French novelist Henri Barbusse published *Le Feu* (*Under Fire*), a graphic account of the horrors and purposelessness of trench warfare. In one chapter Barbusse described a pilot flying over the trenches on a Sunday, observing French and German soldiers at Mass in the open fields, each worshiping the same God. Yet *Le Feu* circulated freely in France and even won the coveted Prix Goncourt.

Wartime Reform

The American mobilization experience was part and product of the Progressive Era. The work of the progressives at the national and state levels in expanding government functions in order to deal with social and economic problems provided precedents and conditioned the people for the all-out effort of 1917–1918. This effort in turn had a great influence on national policy in later crises, notably during the New Deal period and in World War II. Social and economic planning and the management of huge business operations by public boards and committees got their first large-scale practical tests. College professors, technicians, and others with complex skills entered government service en masse. Congress imposed steeply graduated income taxes on the wealthy. The federal government for the first time entered actively such fields as housing and labor relations.

Many progressives believed that the war was creating the sense of common purpose that would stimulate the people to act unselfishly to benefit the poor and to eradicate social evils. As one reformer said, "enthusiasm for social service is epidemic." Patriotism and public service seemed at last united. Secretary of War Baker, a prewar urban reformer, expressed this attitude in supporting a federal child labor law: "We cannot afford, when we are losing boys in France to lose children in the United States." Men and women of this sort worked for a dozen causes only remotely related to the war effort. The women's suffrage movement was brought to fruition, as was the campaign against alcohol. Reformers began to talk about health insurance. A national campaign against prostitution and venereal disease was mounted.*

War-inspired cooperation brought social benefits to black Americans to supplement their new economic opportunities. Despite some terrible race riots in a number of cities, triggered by white resentment of the thousands of migrants who were crowding in to fill war jobs, significant forward steps were taken. The draft law applied to blacks and whites equally, and while it is possible to view this cynically, most blacks saw it as an important gain because it implicitly recognized their bravery and patriotism.

Although 75,000 black soldiers served in the army, only 1,200 were officers. Most blacks were assigned to labor battalions; only a relative handful saw combat. There were black Red Cross nurses, and some blacks held relatively high posts in government agencies.

W. E. B. Du Bois supported the war wholeheartedly. He praised Wilson for making, at last, a strong statement against lynching. He even went along with the fact that black officer candidates were trained in segregated camps. "Let us," he wrote in *The Crisis,* "while the war lasts, forget our special grievances and close ranks shoulder to shoulder with our fellow citizens and the allied nations that are fighting for democracy." Many blacks condemned Du Bois's accommodationism (which he promptly abandoned when the war ended), but for the moment the prevailing mood was one of optimism. "We may expect to see the walls of prejudice gradually crumble"—this was the common attitude of blacks in 1917–1918. If winning the war would make *the world* safe for democracy, surely blacks in the United States would be better off when it was won.

"Over There"

All activity on the home front had one ultimate objective: defeating the Central Powers on the battlefield. This was accomplished. The navy performed with special distinction. In April 1917, German submarines sank more than 870,000 tons of Allied shipping; after April 1918, monthly losses never reached 300,000 tons. The decision to send merchant ships across the Atlantic in convoys screened by destroyers made the reduction possible. Checking the U-boats was essential because of the need to transport American troops to Europe. Slightly more than 2 million soldiers made the voyage safely. Those who crossed on fast ocean liners were in little danger so long as the vessels maintained high speed and followed a zigzag course. Those who traveled on slower troop transports benefited from the protection of destroyers and also from the fact that the Germans concentrated on attacking supply ships. They continued to believe that inexperienced American soldiers would not be a major factor in the war.

The first units of the American Expeditionary Force (AEF), elements of the regular army commanded by General John J. Pershing, reached Paris on Independence Day 1917. They took up positions on the front near Verdun in October. Not until the spring of 1918, however, did the doughboys play a significant role in the fighting—except insofar as their mere presence boosted French and British morale.

* The effort to wipe out prostitution around military installations was a cause of some misunderstanding with the Allies, who provided licensed facilities for their troops as a matter of course. When the premier of France graciously offered to supply prostitutes for American units in his country, Secretary Baker is said to have remarked: "For God's sake . . . don't show this to the President or he'll stop the war."

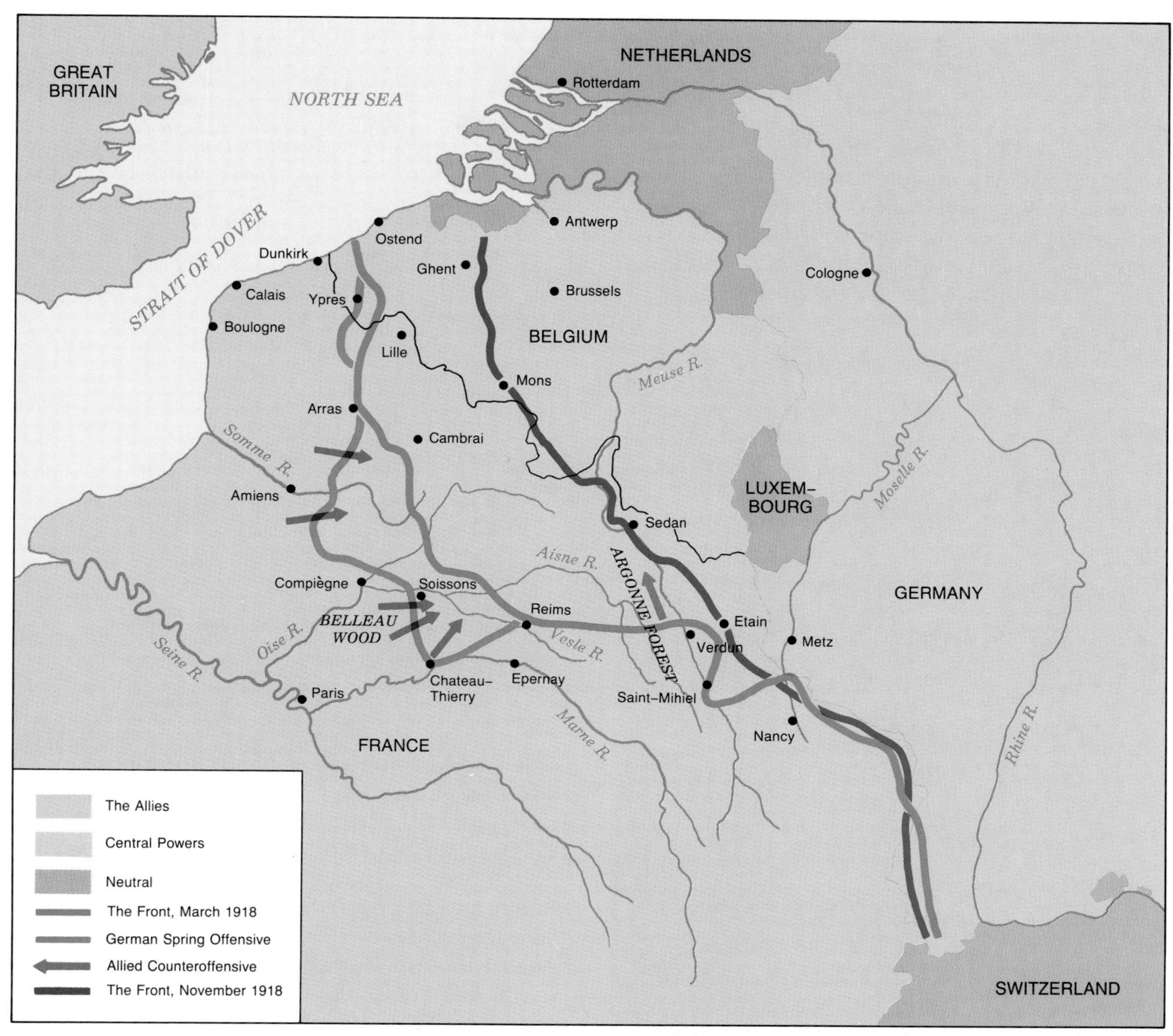

THE WESTERN FRONT, 1918

Pershing, as commander of the AEF, insisted on maintaining his troops as independent units; he would not allow them to be filtered into the Allied armies as reinforcements. This was part of a perhaps unfortunate general policy that reflected America's isolationism and suspicion of Europeans: its refusal to accept full membership in the Allied coalition. (Wilson always referred to the other nations fighting Germany as "associates," not as "allies.")

In March 1918 the Germans launched a great spring offensive, their armies strengthened by thousands of veterans from the Russian front. By late May they had reached a point on the Marne River near the town of Château-Thierry, only 50 miles from Paris. Early in June the AEF fought its first major engagements, driving the Germans back from Château-Thierry and Belleau Wood.

In this fighting only about 27,500 Americans saw action and they suffered appalling losses. Nev-

Aerial reconnaissance, a new innovation, and trench warfare, an older strategy now pushed to its limits, were mainstays of fighting in World War I. Both photographs were taken in France's Argonne region in 1918.

ertheless, when the Germans advanced again in the direction of the Marne in mid-July, 85,000 Americans were in the lines that withstood their charge. Then, in the major turning point of the war, the Allied armies counterattacked. Some 270,000 Americans participated, helping to flatten the German bulge between Reims and Soissons. By late August the American First Army, 500,000 strong, was poised before the Saint-Mihiel salient, a deep extension of the German lines southeast of Verdun. On September 12 this army, buttressed by French troops, struck and in two days wiped out the salient.

Late in September began the greatest American engagement of the war. No fewer than 1.2 million doughboys drove forward west of Verdun into the Argonne Forest. For over a month of indescribable horror they inched ahead through the tangle of the Argonne and the formidable defenses of the Hindenburg Line, while to the west French and British armies staged similar drives. In this one offensive the AEF suffered 120,000 casualties. Finally, on November 1, they broke the German center and raced toward the vital Sedan-Mézières railroad. On November 11, with Allied armies advancing on all fronts, the Germans signed the Armistice, ending the fighting.* Beyond question, the victory could not have been achieved without the AEF.

Preparing for Peace

On November 11, 1918, western civilization stood at a turning point. The fighting had ended, but the shape of the postwar world remained to be determined. European society had been shaken to its foundations. Confusion reigned. People wanted peace yet burned for revenge. Millions faced starvation. Other millions were disillusioned by the seemingly purposeless sacrifices of four years of horrible war. Communism—to some an idealistic promise of human betterment, to others a commitment to rational economic and social planning, to still others a danger to individual freedom, toleration, and democracy—having conquered Russia, threatened to envelop Germany and much of the defunct Austro-Hungarian empire, perhaps even the victorious Allies. How could stability be restored? How could victory be made worth its enormous cost?

Woodrow Wilson had grasped the significance of the war while most statesmen still thought that triumph on the battlefield would settle everything automatically. He faced the future on November 11 with determination and sober confidence. As early as January 1917 he had realized that victory would be wasted if the winners permitted themselves the luxury of vengeance. Such a policy would disrupt the balance of power and lead to economic and social chaos. American participation in the struggle had not blurred his vision. The victors must build a better society, not punish those they believed had destroyed the old.

Long before the war ended, in a speech to Congress on January 8, 1918, Wilson outlined a plan, known as the Fourteen Points, designed to make the world "fit and safe to live in." The peace treaty should be negotiated in full view of world opinion, not in secret. It should guarantee the freedom of the seas to all nations, in war as in peacetime. It should tear down barriers to international trade, provide for a drastic reduction of armaments, and establish a colonial system that would take proper account of the interests of the native peoples concerned. European boundaries should be redrawn so that no substantial group would have to live under a government not of its own choosing. More specifically, captured Russian territory should be restored, Belgium evacuated, Alsace-Lorraine returned to France, the heterogeneous nationalities of Austria-Hungary accorded autonomy. Italy's frontiers should be adjusted "along clearly recognizable lines of nationality," the Balkans made free, Turkey divested of its subject peoples, an independent Polish state (with access to the Baltic) created. To oversee the new system, Wilson insisted, "a general association of nations must be formed under specific covenants for the purpose of affording mutual guarantees of political independence and territorial integrity to great and small states alike."

Wilson's Fourteen Points for a fair peace lifted the hopes of people everywhere. After the guns fell silent, however, the vagueness and inconsistencies in the Points became apparent. Complete national self-determination was impossible in polyglot Europe; there were too many regions of mixed population for every group to be satisfied. Self-determination, like the war itself, fostered the spirit of nationalism that Wilson's dream of international organization, a league of nations, was designed to deemphasize. Furthermore, the Allies had made territorial commitments to one another in secret treaties that ran counter to the principle of self-determination, and they were not ready to give up all claim to Germany's sprawling colonial empire. Freedom of the seas in wartime posed another problem; the British flatly refused to accept the idea. In every Allied country millions rejected the idea of a peace without indemnities. They expected to make the enemy pay for the war, hoping, as Sir Eric Geddes, first lord of the Admiralty said, to squeeze Germany "as a lemon is squeezed—until the pips squeak."

Wilson assumed that the practical benefits of his program would compel opponents to fall in line. He had the immense advantage of seeking nothing for his own country and the additional

* American losses in the war amounted to 112,432 dead and 230,074 wounded. More than half of the deaths, however, resulted from disease. While severe, these casualties were trivial compared with those of the other belligerents. British Commonwealth deaths amounted to 947,000, French to 1.38 million, Russian to 1.7 million, Italian to 460,000. Among the Central Powers, Germany lost 1.8 million men, Austria-Hungary 1.2 million, Turkey 325,000. In addition, about 20 million were wounded.

strength of being leader of the one important nation to emerge from the war richer and more powerful than it had been in 1914. Yet this combination of altruism, idealism, and power was his undoing; it intensified his tendency to be overbearing and undermined his judgment. He had never found it easy to compromise. Once, at Princeton, he got into an argument over some abstract question with a professor while shooting a game of pool. To avoid acrimony, the professor finally said: "Well, Doctor Wilson, there are two sides to every question." "Yes," Wilson answered, "a right side and a wrong side." Now, believing that the fate of humanity hung on his actions, he was unyielding. Always a preacher, he became in his own mind a prophet—almost, one fears, a kind of god.

In the last weeks of the war Wilson proved to be a brilliant diplomat, first dangling the Fourteen Points before the German people to encourage them to overthrow Kaiser Wilhelm II and sue for an armistice, then sending Colonel House to Paris to persuade Allied leaders to accept the points as the basis for the peace. When the Allies raised objections, House made small concessions, but by hinting that the United States might make a separate peace with Germany, he forced them to agree. Under the Armistice, Germany had to withdraw behind the Rhine River and surrender its submarines, together with quantities of munitions and other materials. In return it received the assurance of the Allies that the Wilsonian principles would prevail at the peace conference.

Wilson then came to a daring decision: he would personally attend the conference, which convened on January 12, 1919, at Paris, as a member of the United States Peace Commission. This was a precedent-shattering step, for no previous president had left American territory while in office. (Taft, who had a summer home on the St. Lawrence River in Canada, never vacationed there during his term, believing that to do so would be unconstitutional.)

Wilson probably erred in going to Paris, but not because of the novelty or possible illegality of the act. In leaving the country he was turning his back on obvious domestic problems. Western farmers believed they had been discriminated against during the war, since wheat prices had been controlled while southern cotton had been allowed to rise unchecked from 7 cents a pound in 1914 to 35 cents in 1919. The administration's drastic tax program had angered many businessmen. Labor, despite its gains, was restive in the face of reconversion to peacetime conditions.

Wilson had increased his political difficulties by making a partisan appeal for the election of a Democratic Congress in 1918. Republicans, who had in many instances supported his war program more loyally than the Democrats, considered the action a gross affront. The appeal failed; the Republicans won majorities in both houses. Wilson appeared to have been repudiated at home at the very moment that he set forth to represent the nation abroad. Most important, Wilson intended to break with the isolationist tradition and bring the United States into a league of nations. Such a revolutionary change would require explanation; he should have undertaken a major campaign to convince the people of the wisdom of this step.

Wilson also erred in his choice of the other commissioners. He selected Colonel House, Secretary of State Lansing, General Tasker H. Bliss, and Henry White, a career diplomat. These men were thoroughly competent, but only White was a Republican, and he had no stature as a politician. Since the peace treaty would have to be ratified by the Senate, Wilson should have given that body some representation on the commission, and since the Republicans would have a majority in the new Senate, a Republican senator, or someone who had the full confidence of the Republican leadership, should have been appointed. (The wily McKinley named *three* senators to the American delegation to the peace conference after the Spanish-American War.)

The Paris Peace Conference

Wilson arrived in Europe a world hero. He toured England, France, and Italy briefly and was greeted ecstatically almost everywhere. The reception tended to increase his sense of mission and to convince him, in the fashion of a typical progressive, that whatever the European politicians might say about it, "the people" were behind his program.

When the conference settled down to its work, control quickly fell into the hands of the so-called Big Four: Wilson, Prime Minister David Lloyd George of Great Britain, Premier Georges Clemenceau of France, and Prime Minister Vittorio Orlando of Italy. Wilson stood out in this group but did not dominate it. His principal advantage in the negotiations was his untiring industry. He alone

The "Big Four" at the Hotel Crillon in Paris. First row, from the left: Orlando of Italy, Lloyd George of Great Britain, Clemenceau of France, and Wilson of the United States.

of the leaders tried to master all the complex details of the task.

The 78-year-old Clemenceau cared only for one thing: French security. He viewed Wilson cynically, saying that since mankind had been unable to keep God's Ten Commandments, it was unlikely to do better with Wilson's Fourteen Points. Lloyd George's approach was pragmatic and almost cavalier. He sympathized with much that Wilson was trying to accomplish but found the president's frequent sermonettes about "right being more important than might, and justice being more eternal than force" incomprehensible. "If you want to succeed in politics," Lloyd George advised a British statesman, "you must keep your conscience well under control." Orlando, clever, cultured, a believer in international cooperation but inflexible where Italian national interests were concerned, was not the equal of his three colleagues in influence. He left the conference in a huff when they failed to meet all his demands.

The conference labored from January to May 1919 and finally brought forth the Versailles Treaty. American liberals whose hopes had soared at the thought of a peace based on the Fourteen Points found the document abysmally disappointing. The peace settlement failed to carry out the principle of self-determination completely. It gave Italy a large section of the Austrian Tyrol, though the area contained 200,000 people who considered themselves Austrians. Other German-speaking groups were incorporated into the new states of Poland and Czechoslovakia. Japan was allowed to take over the Chinese province of Shantung, and one or another of the Allies swallowed up all the German colonies in Africa and the Far East.

The victors forced Germany to accept responsibility for having caused the war—an act of senseless vindictiveness as well as a gross oversimplification—and to sign a "blank check," agreeing to pay for all damage to civilian properties and even future pensions and other indirect war costs. This reparations bill, as finally determined, amounted to $33 billion, a sum far beyond Germany's ability to pay. Instead of attacking imperialism, the treaty attacked *German* imperialism; instead of seeking a new international social order based on liberty and democracy, it created a great-power entente designed to crush Germany and to exclude Bolshevist Russia from the family of nations. It said nothing about freedom of the seas, the reduction of tariffs, or disarmament. To those who had taken Wilson's "peace without victory" speech and the Fourteen Points literally, the Versailles Treaty seemed an abomination.

The complaints of the critics were individually

reasonable, yet their conclusions were not entirely fair. The new map of Europe left fewer people on "foreign" soil than in any earlier period of history. While the Allies seized the German colonies, they were required, under the mandate system, to render the League of Nations annual accounts of their stewardship and to prepare the inhabitants for eventual independence. Above all, Wilson persuaded the powers to incorporate the League of Nations in the treaty.

Wilson expected the League of Nations to make up for all the inadequacies of the Versailles Treaty. Once the League had begun to function, problems like freedom of the seas and disarmament would solve themselves, he argued, and the relaxation of trade barriers would surely follow. The League would arbitrate international disputes, act as a central body for registering treaties, and employ military and economic sanctions against aggressor nations. Each member promised (Article X) to protect the "territorial integrity" and "political independence" of all other members. No great power could be made to go to war against its will, but—and this Wilson emphasized—all were *morally* obligated to carry out League decisions. Liberal critics of the League were correct in saying that Wilson was seeking to prop up the existing social and economic system. He was gravely concerned lest communism or even democratic socialism gain the upper hand in central Europe. He hoped, unrealistically as it turned out, to see Europe develop a capitalist-laborer consensus like that which existed in the United States.

By any standard, Wilson had achieved a remarkably moderate peace, one full of hope for the future. Except for the war-guilt clause and the crushing reparations imposed on Germany, he could be justly proud of his work.

The Senate and the League of Nations

When Wilson returned from France, he finally directed his attention to the task of winning public approval of his handiwork. A large majority of the people probably favored the League of Nations in principle, though few understood all its implications or were entirely happy with every detail. Wilson had persuaded the Allies to accept certain changes in the original draft to mollify American opposition. One provided that no nation could be forced to accept a colonial mandate, another that "domestic questions" such as tariffs and the control of immigration did not fall within the competence of the League. The Monroe Doctrine was excluded from League control to satisfy American opinion, and a clause was added permitting members to withdraw from the organization on two years' notice.

Many senators found the modifications insufficient. Even before the peace conference ended, 37 Republican senators signed a Round Robin, devised by Henry Cabot Lodge of Massachusetts, opposing Wilson's League and demanding that the question of an international organization be put off until "the urgent business of negotiating peace terms with Germany" had been completed. Wilson rejected this suggestion icily. The Allies had already exacted major concessions in return for the changes he had requested; further alterations were out of the question. "Anyone who opposes me . . . I'll crush!" he told one Democratic senator. "I shall consent to nothing. *The Senate must take its medicine.*" Thus the stage was set for a monumental test of strength between the president and the Republican majority in the Senate.

Partisanship, principle, and prejudice clashed mightily in this contest. A presidential election loomed. Should the League prove a success, the Republicans wanted to be able to claim a share of the credit, but Wilson had refused to allow them to participate in drafting the document. This predisposed all of them to favor changes. Politics aside, genuine alarm at the possible sacrifice of American sovereignty to an international authority led many Republicans to urge modification of the League Covenant, or constitution. Personal dislike of Wilson and his high-handed methods motivated others. Yet the noble purpose of the League made many reluctant to reject it entirely. The intense desire of the people to have an end to the long war made GOP leaders hesitate before voting down the Versailles Treaty, and they could not reject the League without rejecting the treaty.

Wilson could count on the Democratic senators almost to a man, but he had to win over many Republicans to obtain the two-thirds majority necessary for ratification. Republican opinion divided roughly into three segments. At one extreme were some dozen "irreconcilables," led by the shaggy-browed William E. Borah of Idaho, an able and kindly person of progressive leanings but an uncompromising isolationist. Borah claimed that he would vote against the League even if Jesus Christ returned to earth to argue in its behalf, and most of his followers were equally inflexible. At the other extreme stood another dozen "mild" reservationists who were in favor of the League but who hoped to alter it in minor ways, chiefly for political purposes. In the middle were the "strong" reservationists, senators willing to go along with the League only if American sovereignty were fully protected and it was made clear that their party had played a major role in fashioning the final document.

Senator Lodge, the leader of the Republican opposition, was a haughty, rather cynical, intensely partisan individual. He possessed a keen intelligence, a mastery of parliamentary procedure, and, as chairman of the Senate Foreign Relations Committee, a great deal of power. Although not an isolationist, he had little faith in the League. He also had a profound distrust of Democrats, especially Wilson, whom he considered a hypocrite and a coward. The president's pious idealism left him cold. While perfectly ready to see the country participate actively in world affairs, Lodge insisted that its right to determine its own best interests in every situation be preserved. He had been a senator since 1893 and an admirer of senatorial independence since early manhood. When a Democratic president tried to ram the Versailles Treaty down the Senate's throat, he fought him with every weapon he could muster.

Lodge belonged to the strong reservationist faction. His own proposals, known as the Lodge Reservations, 14 in number to match Wilson's Fourteen Points, limited the United States' obligations to the League and stated in unmistakable terms the right of Congress to decide when to honor these obligations. Some of the reservations were mere quibbles. Others, such as the provision that the United States would not endorse Japan's seizure of Chinese territory, were included mainly to embarrass Wilson by pointing up compromises he had made at Versailles. The most important reservation applied to Article X of the League Covenant, which committed signatories to protect the political independence and territorial integrity of all member nations. Wilson had rightly called Article X "the heart of the Covenant." Lodge's reservation made it inoperable so far as the United States was concerned "unless in any particular case the Congress . . . shall by act or joint resolution so provide."

Lodge performed brilliantly if somewhat unscrupulously in uniting the three Republican factions behind the reservations. He got the irreconcilables to agree to them by conceding their right to vote against the final version in any event, and he held the mild reservationists in line by modifying some of his demands and stressing the importance of party unity. Reservations—as distinct from amendments—would not have to win the formal approval of other League members. In addition, the Lodge proposals dealt forthrightly with the problem of reconciling traditional concepts of national sovereignty with the new idea of world cooperation. Supporters of the League could accept them without sacrifice of principle. Wilson, however, refused to agree. "Accept the Treaty with the *Lodge* reservations," the president snorted when a friendly senator warned him that he must accept a compromise. "Never! Never!"

This foolish intransigence seems almost incomprehensible in a man of Wilson's intelligence and political experience. In part his hatred of Lodge accounts for it, in part his faith in his League. His physical condition in 1919 also played a role. At Paris he had suffered a violent attack of indigestion that was probably a symptom of a minor stroke. Thereafter many observers noted small changes in his personality, particularly an increased stub-

A skeptical view of the League of Nations in London's Punch. *The dove of peace looks askance at Wilson's hefty olive branch, asking "Isn't this a bit thick?"*

bornness and a loss of good judgment. Instead of making concessions, the president set out early in September on a nationwide speaking tour to rally support for the League. While some of his speeches were brilliant, they had little effect on senatorial opinion, and the effort drained his last physical reserves. On September 25, after an address in Pueblo, Colorado, he collapsed. The rest of the trip had to be canceled. A few days later, in Washington, he suffered a severe stroke that partially paralyzed his left side.

For nearly two months as he slowly recovered, the president was almost totally cut off from affairs of state, leaving supporters of the League leaderless while Lodge maneuvered the reservations through the Senate. Gradually, popular attitudes toward the League shifted. Organized groups of Italian-, Irish-, and German-Americans, angered by what they considered unfair treatment of their native lands in the Versailles Treaty, clamored for outright rejection. The arguments of the irreconcilables persuaded many citizens that Wilson had made too sharp a break with America's isolationist past and that the Lodge Reservations were therefore necessary. Other issues connected with the reconversion of society to a peacetime basis increasingly occupied the public mind.

A coalition of Democratic and moderate Republican senators could easily have carried the treaty. That no such coalition was organized was Wilson's fault. Lodge obtained the simple majority necessary to add his reservations to the treaty merely by keeping his own party united. When the time came for the final roll call on November 19, Wilson, bitter and emotionally distraught, urged the Democrats to vote for rejection. "Better a thousand times to go down fighting than to dip your colours to dishonourable compromise," he explained to his wife. Thus the amended treaty failed, 35 to 55, the irreconcilables and the Democrats voting against it. Lodge then allowed the original draft without his reservations to come to a vote. Again the result was defeat, 38 to 53. Only one Republican cast a ballot for ratification.

Dismayed but not yet crushed, friends of the League in both parties forced reconsideration of the treaty early in 1920. Neither Lodge nor Wilson would yield an inch. Lodge, who had little confidence in the effectiveness of any league of nations, was under no compulsion to compromise. Wilson, who believed that the League was the world's best hope, did have such a compulsion. Yet he would not compromise either. As the British historian Robert Skidelsky has written, "the architect of the Treaty's defeat in Congress was Wilson himself." His behavior is further evidence of his physical and mental decline. Probably he was incompetent to perform the duties of his office. Had he died or stepped down, the treaty, with reservations, would almost certainly have been ratified. When the Senate balloted again in March, half the Democrats violated Wilson's orders and voted for the treaty with the Lodge Reservations. The others, mostly southern party regulars, joined the irreconcilables. Together they mustered 35 votes, 7 more than the one-third that meant defeat.

The Election of 1920

Wilson still hoped for vindication at the polls in the presidential election, which he sought to make a "great and solemn referendum" on the League. He would have liked to run for a third term, but in his enfeebled condition, he attracted no support among Democratic leaders. The party nominated James M. Cox of Ohio. Cox favored joining the League, but the election did not produce the referendum on the new organization that Wilson desired. The Republicans, whose candidate was another Ohioan, Senator Warren G. Harding, equivocated shamelessly on the issue. The election turned on other matters, largely emotional. Disillusioned by the results of the war, many Americans had had their fill of idealism. They wanted, apparently, to end the long period of moral uplift and reform agitation that had begun under Theodore Roosevelt and return to what Harding called "normalcy."

To the extent that the voters were expressing opinions on Wilson's League, their response was overwhelmingly negative. Senator Harding had been a strong reservationist, yet he swept the country, winning over 16.1 million votes to Cox's 9.1 million. In July 1921 Congress formally ended the war with the Central Powers by passing a joint resolution.

The defeat of the League was a tragedy both for Wilson, whose crusade for a world order based on peace and justice ended in failure, and for the world, which was condemned by the result to endure another still more horrible and costly war. Perhaps this dreadful outcome could not have been avoided. The United States in 1919–1920 was not ready to assume the responsibility of preserving peace in other lands. Had Wilson compromised and Lodge behaved like a statesman instead of a politician, America would have joined the League, but it might well have failed to respond when called on to meet its obligations. As events soon demonstrated, the League powers acted pusillanimously and even dishonorably when challenged by aggressor nations.

Perhaps it would have been different had the Senate ratified the Versailles Treaty; America's retreat from international cooperation discouraged supporters of the League in other countries. The western democracies might have drawn closer together and become more firm of heart if *all* had been committed to the League. What was lost when the treaty failed in the Senate was not peace but the *possibility* of peace, a tragic loss indeed.

SUPPLEMENTARY READING

Titles marked with an asterisk have been published in paperback.

Wilson's handling of foreign relations is discussed in several volumes by A. S. Link: **Wilson** (1947–), **Woodrow Wilson and the Progressive Era*** (1954), and **Wilson the Diplomatist*** (1957), as well as in the Wilson biographies listed in the preceding chapter. R. H. Ferrell, **Woodrow Wilson and World War I*** (1985), is an up-to-date survey of the period. See also N. G. Levin, Jr., **Woodrow Wilson and World Politics: America's Response to War and Revolution*** (1968). Latin American affairs under Wilson are treated in S. F. Bemis, **The Latin American Policy of the United States*** (1943), H. F. Cline, **The United States and Mexico*** (1953), and D. G. Munro, **Intervention and Dollar Diplomacy in the Caribbean** (1964). R. E. Quirk, **An Affair of Honor: Woodrow Wilson and the Occupation of Veracruz*** (1962), is an admirable monograph, and C. C. Clendenen, **The United States and Pancho Villa** (1961), is also interesting.

For American entry into the Great War, see, in addition to the Link volumes mentioned above, E. R. May, **The World War and American Isolation*** (1959), E. H. Buehrig, **Woodrow Wilson and the Balance of Power** (1955), Charles Seymour, **American Diplomacy During the World War** (1934) and **American Neutrality** (1935), all essentially favorable to Wilson. For contrary views, see Walter Millis, **The Road to War** (1935), and C. C. Tansill, **America Goes to War** (1938).

The war on the home front is covered in D. M. Kennedy, **Over Here: The First World War and American Society** (1980), and more briefly in W. E. Leuchtenburg, **The Perils of Prosperity*** (1958). A good account of military preparation is H. A. DeWeerd, **President Wilson Fights His War** (1968). Other useful volumes include R. D. Cuff, **The War Industries Board** (1973), S. L. Vaughn, **Holding Fast the Inner Lines** (1980), which deals with the Committee on Public Information, M. I. Urofsky, **Big Steel and the Wilson Administration** (1969), Zechariah Chafee, **Free Speech in the United States*** (1941), Donald Johnson, **The Challenge to American Freedoms** (1963), David Brody, **Steelworkers in America*** (1960), Herbert Stein, **Government Price Policy During the World War** (1939), D. R. Beaver, **Newton D. Baker and the American War Effort** (1966), and S. W. Livermore, **Politics Is Adjourned: Woodrow Wilson and the War Congress*** (1966).

On American military participation, consult DeWeerd, **President Wilson Fights His War.** Laurence Stallings, **The Doughboys*** (1963), is a good popular account of the American army in France. See also F. E. Vandiver, **Black Jack: The Life and Times of John J. Pershing** (1977), J. J. Pershing, **My Experiences in the World War** (1931), E. E. Morison, **Admiral Sims and the Modern American Navy** (1942), and T. G. Frothingham, **The Naval History of the World War** (1924–1926). On blacks in the army, see A. E. Barbeau and F. Henri, **The Unknown Soldiers** (1974).

On the peace settlement, in addition to the biographies of Wilson, consult A. J. Mayer, **Politics and Diplomacy of Peacemaking** (1967), Paul Birdsall, **Versailles Twenty Years After** (1941), Harold Nicolson, **Peacemaking, 1919*** (1939), T. A. Bailey, **Woodrow Wilson and the Lost Peace*** (1944) and **Woodrow Wilson and the Great Betrayal*** (1945), J. A. Garraty, **Henry Cabot Lodge** (1953), H. C. Lodge, **The Senate and the League of Nations** (1925), Allan Nevins, **Henry White** (1930), Ralph Stone, **The Irreconcilables*** (1970), J. M. Keynes, **The Economic Consequences of the Peace** (1919), and Robert Lansing, **The Peace Negotiations: A Personal Narrative** (1921). On the election of 1920, see Wesley Bagby, **The Road to Normalcy*** (1962), and R. K. Murray, **The Harding Era** (1969).

25

The Twenties: The Aftermath of the Great War

In the spring of '27 something bright and alien flashed across the sky. A young Minnesotan who seemed to have nothing to do with his generation did a heroic thing and for a moment people set down their glasses in the country clubs and speakeasies and thought of their old best dreams. F. SCOTT FITZGERALD *on Lindbergh's flight to Paris*

The Armistice of 1918 ended the fighting, but the Great War had so shaken the world that for a whole generation most of the human race lived in its shadow. Americans sought desperately to escape from its influence, tried almost to deny that it had occurred. Yet every aspect of their lives in the postwar years reflected its baneful impact. Convinced that they had made a terrible mistake by going to war, a great many Americans rejected the values that had led them to do so. Idealism gave way to materialism, naiveté to cynicism, moral purposefulness to irresponsibility, faith to iconoclasm. This reaction, like so many defense mechanisms, was neurotic, based on unreal and conflicting assumptions.

Demobilization

To win the war the nation had accepted drastic regulation of the economy in order to increase production and improve social efficiency. When the war ended, the government, in Wilson's words, "took the harness off" at once, blithely assuming that the economy could readjust itself without direction. The army was hastily demobilized, pouring millions of veterans into the job market without plan. All society seemed in flux. When the War Department sent letters to the next of kin of 30,000 soldiers buried in France, 12,000 of the letters were returned by the Post Office as undeliverable. No person of the name on the envelope lived at the indicated address. Nearly all controls established by the War Industries Board and other agencies were dropped overnight. Billions of dollars worth of war contracts were canceled. Despite the obvious benefits that government operation of the railroads had brought and the fact that the Plumb plan for government ownership had the support of the railroad unions, the roads were returned to private management.*

Business boomed in 1919 as consumers spent wartime savings on automobiles, homes, and other goods that had been in short supply during the conflict. But termporary shortages caused inflation; by 1920 the cost of living stood at more than twice the level of 1913.

Inflation in turn produced labor trouble. The unions, grown strong during the war, struck for wage increases in order to hold their gains. Over 4 million workers, one out of five in the labor force, were on strike at some time during 1919. Work stoppages aggravated shortages, triggering further inflation and more strikes. Then came one of the most precipitous economic declines in American history. Between July 1920 and March 1922, prices, especially agricultural prices, plummeted. Unemployment soared. Thus the unrealistic attitude of the Wilson government toward the complexities of economic readjustment caused considerable unnecessary strife.

The Red Scare

Far more serious than the economic losses were the social effects of these difficulties. Everyone wanted peace, but wartime tensions did not subside; apparently people continued to need some release for the aggressive drives they had formerly focused on the Germans. Most Americans recognized the services that industrial workers had contributed to the war effort and sympathized with their aspirations for a better way of life, but they found strikes frustrating and drew invidious comparisons between the lot of the unemployed soldier who had risked his life for a dollar a day and that of the striker who had drawn fat wages during the war in perfect safety.

The activities of radicals in the labor movement led millions of Americans to associate unionism and strikes with the new threat of communist world revolution. Although there were only a relative handful of communists in the United States, Russia's experience persuaded many people that a tiny minority of ruthless revolutionaries could take over a nation of millions if conditions were right. Communists appointed themselves the champions of workers; labor unrest attracted them magnetically. When a wave of strikes broke out, some accompanied by violence, many people interpreted them as communist inspired preludes to revolution. One businessman wrote the attorney general in 1919:

* In 1920 the Esch-Cummins Transportation Act strengthened the Interstate Commerce Commission's power to set rates and oversee railroad financing and created a Railroad Labor Board to handle labor problems. Reversing previous efforts to encourage competition, the commission in the 1920s favored consolidation and authorized the pooling of traffic in the interest of efficiency.

"There is hardly a respectable citizen of my acquaintance who does not believe that we are on the verge of armed conflict in this country." Louis Wiley, an experienced New York *Times* reporter, told a friend at this time that anarchists, socialists, and radical labor leaders were "joining together with the object of overthrowing the American Government through a bloody revolution and establishing a Bolshevist republic."

Organized labor in America had seldom been truly radical. The Industrial Workers of the World (IWW), influential in western mining and among migratory workers in the Progressive Era, had advocated violence and the abolition of the wage system but had made little impression in most industries. Some labor leaders, among them Eugene V. Debs, had been attracted to socialism, and many Americans failed to distinguish between the common ends sought by communists and socialists and the entirely different methods by which they proposed to achieve those ends. When a general strike paralyzed Seattle in February 1919, the fact that a procommunist had helped organize it sent shivers down countless conservative spines. When the radical William Z. Foster began a drive to organize the steel industry at about this time, the fears became more intense. In September 1919, 343,000 steelworkers walked off their jobs, and in the same month the Boston police struck. Violence marked the steel strike, and the suspension of police protection in Boston led to looting and fighting that ended only when Governor Calvin Coolidge (who might have prevented the strike had he acted earlier) called out the National Guard.

During the same period a handful of terrorists caused widespread alarm by attempting to murder various prominent persons, including John D. Rockefeller, Justice Oliver Wendell Holmes, Jr., and Attorney General A. Mitchell Palmer. Although the terrorists were anarchists and anarchism had little in common with communism, many citizens lumped all extremists together and associated them with a monstrous assault on society.

What aroused the public even more was the fact that most radicals were not American citizens. Wartime fear of alien saboteurs easily transformed itself into peacetime terror of foreign radicals. In place of Germany, the enemy became the lowly immigrant, usually an Italian or a Jew or a Slav and usually an industrial worker. In this muddled way, radicalism, unionism, and questions of racial and national origins combined to make many Americans believe that their way of life was in imminent danger. That few immigrants were radicals, that most workers had no interest in communism, that the extremists themselves were faction-ridden and irresolute did not affect conservative thinking. From all over the country came demands that radicals be ruthlessly suppressed. Thus the "Red Scare" was born.

Attorney General Palmer was the key figure in the resulting purge. He had been a typical progressive, a supporter of the League of Nations and such reforms as women's suffrage and child labor legislation. When the clamor against alien radicals began, he tried to resist it. Continued pressure from Congress and the press and his growing conviction that the communists really were a menace led him to change his mind. When he did, he joined the "red hunt" with the enthusiasm of the typical convert. Soon he was saying of the radicals: "Out of the sly and crafty eyes of many of them leap cupidity, cruelty, insanity, and crime; from their lopsided faces, sloping brows, and misshapen features may be recognized the unmistakable criminal type."

In August 1919 Palmer established within the Department of Justice a General Intelligence Division, headed by J. Edgar Hoover, to collect information about clandestine radical activities. In November Justice Department agents swooped down upon the meeting places in a dozen cities of an anarchist organization known as the Union of Russian Workers. More than 650 persons, many of them unconnected with the union, were arrested, but in only 43 cases could evidence be found to justify deportation. Nevertheless the public reacted so favorably that Palmer, thinking now of winning the 1920 Democratic presidential nomination, planned an immense roundup of communists. He obtained 3,000 warrants, and on January 2, 1920, his agents, reinforced by local police and self-appointed vigilantes, struck simultaneously in 33 cities.

Palmer's biographer, Stanley Coben, has described the "Palmer raids" vividly:

> There was a knock on the door, the rush of police. In meeting houses, all were lined up to be searched; those who resisted often suffered brutal treat-

During the Red Scare, radical cartoonist William Gropper sharply criticized the tactics of Attorney General Palmer. These drawings appeared in The Liberator *early in 1920. At left, Palmer's agents warn, "Clear the road there, boys—we got a dangerous Red." At right, a suspect faces a loutish, unsympathetic audience.*

> ment. . . . Prisoners were put in overcrowded jails or detention centers where they remained, frequently under the most abominable conditions. . . . Police searched the homes of many of those arrested; books and papers, as well as many people found in these residences, were carried off to headquarters. Policemen also sought those whose names appeared on seized membership lists; they captured many of these suspects in bed or at work, searching their homes, confiscating their possessions, almost always without warrants.

About 6,000 persons were taken into custody, many of them citizens and therefore not subject to the deportation laws, many others unconnected with any radical cause. Some were held incommunicado for weeks while the authorities searched for evidence against them. In a number of cases, individuals who went to visit prisoners were themselves thrown behind bars on the theory that they too must be communists. Hundreds of suspects were jammed into filthy "bullpens," beaten, forced to sign "confessions."

The public tolerated these wholesale violations of civil liberties because of the supposed menace of communism. Gradually, however, protests began to be heard, first from lawyers and liberal magazines, then from a wider segment of the population. No revolutionary outbreak had taken place. Of 6,000 seized in the Palmer raids, only 556 proved liable to deportation. The widespread ransacking of communists' homes and meeting places produced mountains of inflammatory literature but only three pistols.

Palmer, attempting to maintain the crusade, announced that the radicals planned a gigantic terrorist demonstration for May Day 1920. In New York and other cities thousands of police were placed on round-the-clock duty; federal troops stood by anxiously. But the day passed without even a rowdy meeting. Suddenly Palmer appeared ridiculous. His presidential boom collapsed and the Red Scare swiftly subsided.

Closing the Gates

The ending of the Red Scare did not herald the disappearance of xenophobia. It was perhaps inevitable and possibly wise that some limitation be placed on the entry of immigrants into the United States after the war. An immense backlog of prospective migrants had piled up during the conflict, and the desperate postwar economic condition of Europe led hundreds of thousands to seek better circumstances in the United States. Immigration increased from 110,000 in 1919 to 430,000 in 1920 and 805,000 in 1921, with every prospect of continuing to rise.

In 1921 Congress, reflecting a widespread prejudice against eastern and southern Europeans, passed an emergency act establishing a quota system. Each year 3 percent of the number of foreign-born residents of the United States in 1910 (about 350,000 persons) might enter the country. Each country's quota was based on the number of its nationals in the United States in 1910. This meant that only a relative handful of the total would be from southern and eastern Europe. In 1924 the quota was reduced to 2 percent and the base year shifted to 1890, thereby lowering further the proportion of southern and eastern Europeans admitted.

In 1929 Congress established a system that allowed only 150,000 immigrants a year to enter the country. Each national quota was based on the supposed origins of the entire white population of the United States in 1920, not merely on the foreign-born. Here is an example of how the system worked:

$$\frac{\text{Italian quota}}{150{,}000} = \frac{\text{Italian-origin population, 1920}}{\text{White population, 1920}}$$

$$\frac{\text{Italian quota}}{150{,}000} = \frac{3{,}800{,}000}{95{,}500{,}000}$$

$$\text{Italian quota} = 6{,}000 \text{ (approximately)}$$

Presumably this method would preserve the status quo; in fact it heavily favored immigrants from Great Britain. The system was complicated and unscientific, for no one could determine with accuracy the "origins" of millions of citizens.

The law reduced actual immigration to far below 150,000 a year. British immigration between 1931 and 1939, for example, amounted to only 23,000 even though the *annual* British quota was over 65,000. Meanwhile, hundreds of thousands of southern and eastern Europeans waited for admission.

The United States had closed the gates. Instead of an open, cosmopolitan society eager to accept, in Emma Lazarus's stirring line, the "huddled masses yearning to breathe free," America now became committed to preserving a homogeneous, "Anglo-Saxon" population. Anglo-Saxon and homogeneous it did not become, but the foreign-born percentage of the population fell from about 13 percent in 1920 to 4.7 percent in 1970.

Urban-Rural Conflict

The war-born tensions and hostilities of the 1920s also found expression in ways related to an older rift in American society—the conflict between the urban and the rural ways of life. The census of 1920 revealed that for the first time a majority of Americans (54 million in a total population of 106 million) lived in "urban" rather than "rural" places. These figures are somewhat misleading when applied to the study of social attitudes because the census classified anyone in a community of 2,500 or more as urban. Of the 54 million "urban" residents in 1920, over 16 million lived in villages and towns of fewer than 25,000 persons, and the evidence suggests strongly that a large majority of them held ideas and values more like those of rural citizens than like those of city dwellers. But the truly urban Americans, the one person in four who lived in a city of 100,000 or more—and particularly the nearly 16.4 million who lived in metropolises of at least half a million—were increasing steadily in number and influence. More than 19 million persons moved from farms to cities in the 1920s, and the population living in centers of 100,000 or more increased by about a third.

To both the scattered millions who tilled the soil and the millions who lived in towns and small cities, the new city-oriented culture seemed sinful, overly materialistic, and unhealthy. Yet there was no denying its fascination. Made even more aware of the appeal of the city by such modern improvements as radio and the automobile, farmers and townspeople coveted the comfort and excitement of city life at the same time that they condemned its vices.

Out of this ambivalence developed strange social phenomena, all exacerbated by the backlash of wartime emotions. Rural society proclaimed the superiority of its ways, as much to protect itself from temptation as to denounce urban life. Change, omnipresent in the postwar world, must be resisted even at the cost of individualism and freedom. The fact that those who held such views were in the majority, yet were conscious that their majority was rapidly disappearing, explains their desperation and thus their intolerance.

One expression of this intolerance was the resurgence of religious fundamentalism. Although it was especially prevalent in certain Protestant sects, such as the Baptists and Methodists, fundamental

In Baptism in Kansas *(1928), John Steuart Curry viewed sympathetically the sincerity and depth of feeling that marked the revival of religious fundamentalism in much of rural America during the 1920s. Curry was a leader of the rural regionalist painters, seeking, he said, to show the "struggle of man against nature."*

ism was primarily an attitude of mind, profoundly conservative, rather than a religious idea. Fundamentalists rejected the theory of evolution, indeed all knowledge about the origins of the universe and the human race that had been discovered during the 19th century. Urban sophisticates tended to dismiss the fundamentalists as boors and hayseed fanatics, yet the persistence of old-fashioned ideas was understandable. In rural areas where educational standards were low and culture relatively static, old ideas remained unchallenged. The power of reason, so obvious in a technologically advanced society, seemed much less obvious to rural people. Farmers, living in close contact with the capricious, elemental power of nature, tended to have more respect for the force of divine providence than city folk. Beyond this, the majesty and beauty of the King James translation of the Bible, the only book in countless rural homes, made it extraordinarily difficult for many persons to abandon their belief in its literal truth.

What made crusaders of the fundamentalists,

however, was their resentment of modern urban culture. While in some cases they harassed liberal ministers, their religious attitudes had little public significance; their efforts to impose their views on public education were another matter. The teaching of evolution must be prohibited, they insisted. Throughout the early twenties they campaigned vigorously for laws banning discussion of Darwin's theory in textbooks and classrooms.

Their greatest asset in this unfortunate crusade was William Jennings Bryan. Age had not improved the "Peerless Leader." Never a profound thinker, after leaving Wilson's Cabinet in 1915 he devoted much time to religious and moral issues without applying himself conscientiously to the study of these difficult questions. He went about the country charging that "they"—meaning the mass of educated Americans—had "taken the Lord away from the schools." He denounced the use of public money to undermine Christian principles, and he offered $100 to anyone who would admit to being descended from an ape. His immense popularity in rural areas assured him a wide audience, and no one came forward to take his money.

The fundamentalists won a minor victory in 1925, when Tennessee passed a law forbidding instructors in the state's schools and colleges to teach "any theory that denies the story of the Divine Creation of man as taught in the Bible." Although the bill passed both houses by big majorities, few legislators really approved of it. They voted aye only because they dared not expose themselves to charges that they disbelieved the Bible. Educators in the state, hoping to obtain larger school appropriations from the legislature, hesitated to protest. Governor Austin Peay, an intelligent and liberal-minded man, feared to veto the bill lest he jeopardize other measures he was backing. "Probably the law will never be applied," he predicted when he signed it. Even Bryan, who used his influence to obtain passage of the measure, urged—unsuccessfully—that it include no penalties.

Upon learning of the passage of this act, the American Civil Liberties Union announced that it would finance a test case challenging its constitutionality if a Tennessee teacher would deliberately violate the statute. Urged on by friends, John T. Scopes, a young biology teacher in Dayton, reluctantly agreed to do so. He was arrested. A battery of nationally known lawyers came forward to defend him, while the state obtained the services of Bryan himself. The Dayton "Monkey Trial" became an overnight sensation.

Clarence Darrow, chief counsel for the defendant, stated the issue clearly. "Scopes isn't on trial," he said, "civilization is on trial. The prosecution is opening the doors for a reign of bigotry equal to anything in the Middle Ages. No man's belief will be safe if they win." The comic aspects of the trial obscured this issue. Big-city reporters like H. L. Mencken of the Baltimore *Evening Sun* flocked to Dayton to make sport of the fundamentalists. The judge, John Raulston, was strongly prejudiced against the defendant, refusing even to permit expert testimony on the validity of evolutionary theory. The conviction of Scopes was a foregone conclusion; after the jury rendered its verdict, Judge Raulston fined him $100.

Nevertheless the trial exposed both the stupidity and the danger of the fundamentalist position. The high point came when Bryan agreed to testify as an expert witness on the Bible. In a sweltering courtroom, both men in shirt sleeves, the lanky, rough-hewn Darrow cross-examined the aging champion of fundamentalism, mercilessly exposing his childlike faith and his abysmal ignorance. Bryan admitted to believing that the earth had been created in 4004 B.C., that Eve had been created from Adam's rib, and that a whale had swallowed Jonah. "I believe in a God that can make a whale and can make a man and make both do what He pleases," he explained.

The Monkey Trial ended badly for nearly everyone concerned. Scopes moved away from Dayton. Judge Raulston was defeated when he sought reelection to the bench. Bryan departed amid the cheers of his disciples only to die in his sleep a few days later. In retrospect the heroes of the Scopes trial—science, tolerance, freedom of thought—seem somewhat less stainless than they did to liberals at the time. The account of evolution in the textbook used by Scopes was far from satisfactory, yet it was advanced as unassailable fact. The book also contained statements that to the modern mind seem at least as bigoted as anything that Bryan said at Dayton. In a section on "the Races of Man," for example, it described Caucasians as "the highest type of all . . . represented by the civilized white inhabitants of Europe and America."

Prohibition: The Noble Experiment

The conflict between the countryside and the city was fought on many fronts, and in one sector the rural forces achieved a quick victory. This was the prohibition of the manufacture, transportation, and sale of alcoholic beverages by the Eighteenth Amendment, ratified in 1919. Although there were some big-city advocates of prohibition, on no issue did urban and rural views divide more clearly. The Eighteenth Amendment, in the words of the historian Andrew Sinclair, marked a triumph of the "Corn Belt over the conveyor belt."

The temperance movement had been important since the age of Jackson; by the time of the Progressive Era many reformers were eager to prohibit drinking entirely. Indeed, prohibition was a typical progressive reform, moralistic, backed by the middle class, aimed at frustrating "the interests"—in this case the distillers. It was also expected to reduce political corruption since the liquor interests contributed heavily to big-city political machines.

The war aided the prohibitionists by increasing the nation's need for food. The Lever Act of 1917 outlawed the use of grain in the manufacture of alcoholic beverages, primarily as a conservation measure. The prevailing dislike of foreigners helped the dry cause still more: beer drinking was associated with Germans, wine consumption with Italians. State and local laws had made a large part of the country dry by 1917. National prohibition became official in January 1920.

This "experiment noble in purpose," as Herbert Hoover called it, achieved a number of socially desirable results. It reduced the national consumption of alcohol from 2.6 gallons per capita in the period just before the war to under one gallon in the early thirties. Arrests for drunkenness fell off sharply, as did deaths from alcoholism. Fewer workers squandered their wages on drink. If the drys had been more reasonable—if they had permitted, for example, the use of beer and wine—the experiment might have worked. Instead, by insisting on total abstinence, they drove moderates to violation of the law. In such circumstances strict enforcement became impossible, especially in the cities.

The Prohibition Bureau had only between 1,500 and 3,000 agents to police the illicit liquor trade, and many of them were inefficient and corrupt. In areas where sentiment favored prohibition strongly, liquor remained difficult to find. Elsewhere, anyone with sufficient money could obtain it easily. Smuggling became a major business, *bootlegger* a household word. Private individuals busied themselves learning how to manufacture "bathtub gin." Many druggists issued prescriptions for alcohol with a free hand. The manufacture of wine for religious ceremonies was legal—consumption of sacramental wine jumped by 800,000 gallons during the first two years of prohibition. The saloon disappeared, replaced by the speakeasy, a supposedly secret bar or club, operating under the benevolent eye of the local police.

That the law was often violated does not mean that it was ineffective any more than violations of laws against theft and murder mean that those laws are ineffective. Although gangsters such as Alphonse "Scarface Al" Capone of Chicago were engaged in the liquor traffic, hijacking one another's shipments, gunning down their enemies in broad daylight, and bombing rival distilleries and warehouses without regard for passing innocents, they and their "organizations" existed before the passage of the Eighteenth Amendment.

In any case, prohibition widened already serious rifts in the social fabric of the country. Besides undermining public morality by encouraging hypocrisy, its repressive spirit pitted city against farm, native against immigrant, race against race. In the South, where the dominant whites had argued that prohibition would improve the morals of the blacks, it was the blacks who became the chief bootleggers. Prohibition almost destroyed the Democratic party as a national organization; Democratic immigrants in the cities hated it, but southern Democrats sang its praises (often while continuing to drink). The humorist Will Rogers quipped that Mississippi would vote dry "as long as the voters could stagger to the polls."

The hypocrisy of prohibition had a particularly deleterious effect on politicians, a class seldom famous for candor. Congressmen catered to the demands of the powerful lobby of the Anti-Saloon League yet failed to grant adequate funds to the Prohibition Bureau. Nearly all the prominent leaders, Democrat and Republican, from Wilson and La Follette to Hoover and Franklin D. Roosevelt, equivocated shamelessly on the liquor question. By the end of the decade almost every competent

Ben Shahn's Prohibition Alley *is a richly symbolic summary of the seamier side of the "noble experiment." Under a diagram of the workings of a still, bootleggers stack whiskey smuggled in by ship, an operation eyed by Chicago gangster Al Capone. At lower left is a victim of gang warfare; at lower right, patrons outside a speak-easy.*

observer recognized that prohibition at least needed to be overhauled, but the well-organized and powerful dry forces rejected all proposals for modifying it.

The Ku Klux Klan

The most horrible manifestation of the social malaise of the 1920s was the revival of the Ku Klux Klan. Like its predecessor of Reconstruction days, the new Klan began as an instrument for oppressing southern blacks. In the reactionary postwar period lynchings increased in number. In the summer and fall of 1919 race riots broke out in a dozen cities. The new Klan, founded in 1915 by William J. Simmons, a former preacher, expanded rapidly in this atmosphere.

Simmons gave his society the kinds of trappings and mystery calculated to attract gullible and bigoted persons who yearned to express their frustrations and hostilities without personal risk. Klansmen masked themselves in white robes and hoods and enjoyed a childish mumbo jumbo of magnificent-sounding titles and dogmas (kleagle, klaliff, kludd; kloxology, kloran). They burned crosses in the night, organized mass demonstrations to intimidate people they disliked, put pressure on businessmen to fire black workers from better-paying jobs. When its enemies resisted, the Klan frequently employed brutal means to achieve its ends.

The Klan admitted only native-born white Protestants. The distrust of foreigners, Catholics, and Jews implicit in this regulation explains why the Klan flourished in the social climate that spawned religious fundamentalism, immigration restriction, and prohibition. In 1920 two unscrupulous publicity agents, Edward Y. Clarke and Elizabeth Tyler, got control of the movement and organized a massive membership drive, diverting a major share of the initiation fees into their own pockets. In a little over a year they enrolled 100,000 recruits, and by 1923 they claimed the astonishing total of 5 million.

The Klan had relatively little appeal in the Northeast or in metropolitan centers in other parts of the country, but it found many members in middle-sized cities and in the small towns and villages of middle western and western states like Indiana, Ohio, and Oregon. The scapegoats in such regions were immigrants, Jews, and especially Catholics. The rationale was an urge to return to an older, supposedly finer America and a desire to stamp out all varieties of nonconformity. Klansmen "watched everybody," themselves safe from observation behind their masks and robes. Posing as guardians of public and private morality, they persecuted gamblers, "loose" women, violators of the prohibition laws, and anyone who happened to differ from them on religious questions or who belonged to a "foreign race."

Klan leaders claimed that the pope intended to move his court from Rome to the United States, that American bishops were stockpiling guns in their cathedrals, that Catholic traitors had entrenched themselves in many branches of the government. Since a considerable percentage of Klan members were secret libertines and corruptionists, the dark, unconscious drives leading men to join the organization are not hard to imagine.

The very success of the Klan led to its undoing. Factionalism sprang up and rival leaders squabbled over the large sums that had been collected from the membership. The cruel and outrageous behavior of the organization roused both liberals and conservatives in every part of the country. And of course its victims joined forces against their tor-

A Ku Klux Klan initiation ceremony, photographed in Kansas in the 1920s. During its peak influence at mid-decade, Klan endorsement was essential to political candidates in many areas of the West and Midwest. Campaigning for reelection in 1924, an Indiana congressman testified, "I was told to join the Klan, or else."

mentors. When the powerful leader of the Indiana Klan, a middle-aged reprobate named David C. Stephenson, was convicted of assaulting and causing the death of a young woman, the rank and file abandoned the organization in droves. The Klan remained influential for a number of years, contributing to the defeat of the Catholic Alfred E. Smith in the 1928 presidential election, but it ceased to be a dynamic force after 1924. By 1930 it had only some 9,000 members.

The "New" Woman

The malaise of postwar society also produced dissatisfactions among urban sophisticates and among others who looked to the future rather than to the past. To many young people the narrowness and prudery of the fundamentalists and the stuffy conservatism of the politicans seemed not merely old-fashioned but ludicrous. The repressiveness of red-baiters and Klansmen made such people place an exaggerated importance on their right to express themselves in bizarre ways, and the casual attitude of drinkers toward the prohibition laws encouraged them to flout other institutions as well. The new psychology of Sigmund Freud, with its stress on the importance of sex, persuaded many who had never read Freud to adopt what they called "emancipated" standards of behavior that Freud, himself a staid, highly moral man, had neither advocated nor practiced.

This was the "Jazz Age," the era of "flaming youth." Young people danced to syncopated "African" rhythms, swilled bootleg liquor from pocket flasks, careened about the countryside in automobiles in search of pleasure and forgetfulness, made gods of movie stars and professional athletes. "Younger people," one shrewd observer noted as early as 1922, had only "contempt . . . for their elders." They were attempting "to create a way of life free from the bondage of an authority that has lost all meaning."

Conservatives bemoaned the breakdown of moral standards, the increasing popularity of divorce, the fragmentation of the family, and the decline of parental authority—all with some reason. Nevertheless, society was not collapsing. Much of the rebelliousness was faddish in nature, in a sense a kind of youthful conformity. It soon petered out.

The twenties proved disillusioning to feminists, who now paid a price for their single-minded pursuit of the right to vote in the Progressive Era. Superficially, sex-based restrictions and limitations seemed to be breaking down. Women discarded bulky, uncomfortable undergarments and put on short skirts; they could smoke and drink in public places without fear of being considered prostitutes or wantons. The birth control movement, led by Margaret Sanger, was making progress. The divorce laws had been modified in most states. Moreover, more women were finding jobs; over 10.6 million were working by the end of the decade, in contrast with 8.4 million in 1920.

Most of these gains were illusory. Relaxation of the strict standards of sexual morality did not eliminate the double standard. More women worked, but most of the jobs they held were menial or of a kind that few men wanted: domestic service, elementary school teaching, clerical work, selling behind a counter. Where they competed for jobs with men, women usually received much lower wages. Educational opportunities for women expanded, but the colleges placed more emphasis on subjects like home economics. As one Vassar College administrator (a woman!) said, colleges should provide "education for women along the lines of their chief interests and responsibilities, motherhood and the home."

The prosperity of the postwar years and the abandonment of taboos improved the economic position of women, but these gains did not end discrimination based on sex. This helps to explain why many women remained dissatisfied with their position in society. So does the confusion resulting from the passage of the Nineteenth Amendment. After its ratification, Carrie Chapman Catt was exultant, "We are no longer petitioners," she announced, "but free and equal citizens." Many activists, assuming the battle won, lost interest in agitating for change and sat back smugly to enjoy the benefits of their new position.

Others believed that the suffrage amendment had given them the one weapon needed to achieve whatever women still lacked. In fact, being able to vote reduced rather than strengthened the influence of women, for it soon became apparent that women did not vote as a bloc. Many, perhaps most, married women voted for the candidates their husbands supported. The Amendment increased the size of the electorate but did not add to the power of any particular party or interest group.

When radical women discovered that voting did not automatically bring true equality, they founded the Women's party and began campaigning for an equal rights amendment. Their leader, Alice Paul, a dynamic if somewhat fanatical person, disdained specific goals such as disarmament, ending child labor, and liberalized birth control. Total equality for women was the one objective. The party considered protective legislation governing the hours and working conditions of women discriminatory.

The Women's party never attracted a wide following. Many more women joined the more moderate League of Women Voters, which attempted to mobilize support for a broad spectrum of reforms, some of which had no specific connection with the interests of women as such. Feminists also split on generational lines, the younger ones tending to adopt more liberal attitudes toward sexual relations, the older still bound by Victorian inhibitions. The entire women's movement lost momentum. The battle for the equal rights amendment persisted through the 1930s, but it was lost. By the end of that decade the women's movement was amost dead.

Sacco and Vanzetti

The excesses of the fundamentalists, the xenophobes, the Klan, the red-baiters, and the prohibitionists disturbed American intellectuals profoundly. More and more they became alienated, bitter, and contemptuous of those who appeared to control the country. Yet their alienation came at the very time that society was growing more dependent on brains and sophistication. This compounded the confusion and disillusionment characteristic of the period.

Nothing demonstrates this fact so clearly as the Sacco-Vanzetti case. In April 1920 two men in South Braintree, Massachusetts, killed a paymaster and a guard in a daring daylight robbery of a shoe

Vanzetti (left) and Sacco were led into court handcuffed in April 1927 to hear the death sentence pronounced. They were electrocuted in August of that year, six years after their conviction.

factory. Shortly thereafter Nicola Sacco and Bartolomeo Vanzetti were charged with the crime, and in 1921 they were convicted of murder. Sacco and Vanzetti were anarchists and Italian immigrants. Their trial was a travesty of justice. The presiding judge, Webster Thayer, conducted the proceedings like a prosecuting attorney; privately he referred to the defendants as "those anarchist bastards."

The case became a cause célèbre. Prominent persons throughout the world protested, and for years Sacco and Vanzetti were kept alive by efforts to obtain a new trial. Vanzetti's quiet dignity and courage in the face of death wrung the hearts of millions. "You see me before you, not trembling," he told the court. "I never commit a crime in my life. . . . I am so convinced to be right that if you could execute me two times, and if I could be reborn two other times, I would live again and do what I have done already." When, in August 1927, the two were at last electrocuted, the disillusionment of American intellectuals with current values was profound. Some historians, impressed by modern ballistic studies of Sacco's gun, now suspect that he, at least, may have been guilty. Nevertheless, the truth and the shame remain: Sacco and Vanzetti paid with their lives for being radicals and aliens, not for any crime.

Literary Trends

The literature of the twenties reflects the disillusionment of the intellectuals. For example, among the many writers shaken by the execution of Sacco and Vanzetti were the poet Edna St. Vincent Millay, the playwright Maxwell Anderson, and the novelists Upton Sinclair and John Dos Passos. The prewar period had been an age of hopeful experimentation in the world of letters. Writers, applying the spirit of progressivism to the realism they had inherited from Howells and the naturalists, had been predominantly optimistic. Ezra Pound, for example, talked grandly of an American Renaissance and fashioned a new kind of poetry called Imagism, which, while not appearing to be realistic, abjured all abstract generalizations and concentrated on concrete word pictures to convey meaning. "Little" magazines and experimental theatrical companies sprang to life by the dozen, each convinced that it would revolutionize its art. New York's Greenwich Village teemed with youthful Bohemians contemptuous of middle-class values yet too fundamentally cheerful to reject the modern world. The poet Carl Sandburg, the best-known representative of the "Chicago school," denounced the local plutocrats but sang the praises of the city they had made: "Hog Butcher for the World . . . City of the Big Shoulders." Most writers eagerly adopted Freudian psychology without understanding it. Freud's teachings seemed only to mean that they should cast off the senseless restrictions of Victorian prudery; they ignored his essentially dark view of human nature. Theirs was an "innocent rebellion," exuberant—and rather muddleheaded.

The historian Henry F. May has shown that writers, along with most other intellectuals, began to abandon this view about 1912. World War I and then the antics of the fundamentalists, the cruelty of the red-baiters, and the philistinism of the dull politicos of the 1920s turned them into critics of society. Ezra Pound dropped his talk of an American Renaissance and wrote instead of a "botched civilization." The soldiers, he said,

walked eye-deep in hell
believing in old men's lies, then unbelieving
came home, home to a lie,
home to deceits,
home to old lies and new infamy . . .

Out of this negativism came a literary flowering of major importance. The herald of the new day was Henry Adams, whose autobiography, *The Education of Henry Adams,* was published posthumously in 1918. Adams's disillusionment long antedated the war, but his description of late-19th-century corruption and materialism and his warning that industrialism was crushing the human spirit beneath the weight of its machines appealed powerfully to those whose pessimism was newborn. Soon hundreds of bright young men and women were referring to themselves, with a self-pity almost maudlin, as the "lost generation."

The symbol of the lost generation, in his own mind as well as to his contemporaries and to later critics, was F. Scott Fitzgerald. Born to modest wealth in St. Paul, Minnesota, in 1896, Fitzgerald attended Princeton and served in the army during the World War. He rose to sudden fame in 1920 when he published *This Side of Paradise,* a somewhat sophomoric novel that captured the fears and confusions of the lost generation and the façade of frenetic gaiety that concealed them. In *The Great Gatsby* (1925), a more mature work, Fitzgerald dissected a modern millionaire—coarse, unscrupulous, jaded, in love with another man's wife. Gatsby's tragedy lay in his dedication to a woman who, Fitzgerald made clear, did not merit his passion. He lived in "the service of a vast, vulgar, meretricious beauty," and in the end he understood this himself.

The tragedy of *The Great Gatsby* was related to Fitzgerald's own. Pleasure-loving and extravagant, he squandered the money earned by *This Side of Paradise.* When *The Great Gatsby* failed to sell as well, he turned to writing potboilers. "I really worked hard as hell last winter," he told the critic Edmund Wilson, "but it was all trash and it nearly broke my heart." While some of his later work, particularly *Tender Is the Night* (1934), was first-class, he descended into the despair of alcoholism and ended his days as a Hollywood scriptwriter.

Many young American writers and artists became expatriates in the twenties. They flocked to Rome, Berlin, and especially Paris, where they could live cheaply and escape what seemed to them the "conspiracy against the individual" prevalent in their own country. The *quartier latin* along the left bank of the Seine was a large-scale Greenwich Village in those days. Writers, artists, and eccentrics of every sort lived there. Some made meager livings as journalists, translators, and editors, perhaps turning an extra dollar from time to time by selling a story or a poem to an American magazine, a painting to a tourist. Others idled away the days, dreaming of fame and fortune rather than earning them.

Ernest Hemingway was the most talented of the expatriates. Born in 1898 in Illinois, Hemingway first worked as a reporter for the Kansas City *Star.*

Contrasting images of two literary stars of the "lost generation": (left) F. Scott Fitzgerald as the thoughtful, introspective artist, and (right) Ernest Hemingway, sportsman and man of action.

He served in the Italian army during the war, was grievously wounded (in spirit as well as in body), and then, after further newspaper experience, settled in Paris in 1922 to write. His first novel, *The Sun Also Rises* (1926), portrayed the café world of the expatriate and the rootless desperation, amorality, and sense of outrage at life's meaninglessness that obsessed so many in those years. In *A Farewell to Arms* (1929) he drew on his military experiences to describe the confusion and horror of war.

Hemingway's books were best-sellers and he became a legend in his own time, but his style rather than his ideas explains his towering reputation. Few novelists have been such self-conscious craftsmen or capable of suggesting powerful emotions and action in so few words. Mark Twain and Stephen Crane were his models, Gertrude Stein, a queer, revolutionary genius, his teacher, but his style was his own, direct, simple, taut, sparse:

> I went out the door and down the hall to the room where Catherine was to be after the baby came. I sat in a chair there and looked at the room. I had the paper in my coat that I had bought when I went out for lunch and I read it. . . . After a while I stopped reading and turned off the light and watched it get dark outside. (*A Farewell to Arms*)

This kind of writing, evoking rather than describing emotion, fascinated readers and inspired hundreds of imitators; it has made a permanent mark on world literature. What Hemingway had to say was of less universal interest—he was an unabashed, rather muddled romantic, an adolescent emotionally. He wrote about bullfights, hunting and fishing, violence; while he did so with masterful penetration, these themes placed limits on his work that he never transcended. The critic Alfred Kazin summed Hemingway up in a sentence: "He brought a major art to a minor vision of life."

Although neither was the equal of Hemingway or Fitzgerald, two other writers of the twenties deserve mention: H. L. Mencken and Sinclair Lewis. Each reflected the distaste of intellectuals for the climate of the times. Mencken, a Baltimore newspaperman and founder of one of the great magazines of the era, the *American Mercury*, was a thoroughgoing cynic. He coined the world *booboisie* to define the complacent, middle-class majority, and he fired superbly witty broadsides at fundamentalists, prohibitionists, and "Puritans." "Doing Good," he once said, "is in bad taste."

But Mencken was never indifferent to the many aspects of American life that roused his contempt. Politics at once fascinated and repelled him, and he assailed the statesmen of his generation with magnificent impartiality:

> BRYAN: "If the fellow was sincere, then so was P. T. Barnum. . . . He was, in fact, a charlatan, a mountebank, a zany without sense or dignity."
>
> WILSON: "The bogus Liberal. . . . A pedagogue thrown up to 1000 diameters by a magic lantern."
>
> HARDING: "The numskull, Gamaliel. . . . the Marion stonehead. . . . The operations of his medulla oblongata . . . resemble the rattlings of a colossal linotype charged with rubber stamps."
>
> COOLIDGE: "A cheap and trashy fellow, deficient in sense and almost devoid of any notion of honor—in brief, a dreadful little cad."
>
> HOOVER: "Lord Hoover is no more than a pious old woman, a fat Coolidge. . . . He would have made a good bishop."

As these examples demonstrate, Mencken's diatribes, while amusing, were not profound. In perspective he seems more a professional iconoclast than a constructive critic; like both Fitzgerald and Hemingway, he was something of a perennial adolescent. However, he consistently supported freedom of expression of every sort.

Sinclair Lewis was probably the most popular American novelist of the twenties. Like Fitzgerald, his first major work brought him instant fame and notoriety—and for the same reason. *Main Street* (1920) portrayed the smug ignorance and bigotry of the American small town so accurately that even Lewis's victims recognized themselves; his title became a symbol for provinciality and middle-class meanness of spirit. Next he created, in *Babbitt* (1922), an image of the businessman of the twenties. George Babbitt, gregarious, a "booster," was blindly orthodox in his political and social opinions, a slave to every cliché, and full of loud self-confidence. Underneath the surface Babbitt was a bumbling, rather timid fellow who would have liked to be better than he was but dared not try.

Lewis went on to dissect a variety of American attitudes and occupations: the medical profession in *Arrowsmith* (1925), religion in *Elmer Gantry*

(1927), fascism in *It Can't Happen Here* (1935), and many others. Although his indictment of contemporary society rivaled Mencken's in savagery, Lewis was not a cynic. Superficially as objective as an anthropologist, he remained at heart committed to the way of life he was assaulting. His remarkable powers of observation depended on his identification with the society he described. He was frustrated by the fact that his victims, recognizing themselves in his pages, accepted his criticisms with remarkable good temper and, displaying the very absence of intellectual rigor that he decried, cheerfully sought to reform.

At the same time, lacking Mencken's ability to remain aloof, Lewis tended to value his own work in terms of its popular reception. He craved the good opinion and praise of his fellows. When he was awarded the Pulitzer prize for *Arrowsmith,* he petulantly refused it because it had not been offered earlier. He politicked shamelessly for a Nobel prize, which he received in 1930, the first American author to win this honor.

Lewis was preeminently a product of the twenties. When times changed, he could no longer portray society with such striking verisimilitude; none of his later novels approached the level of *Main Street* and *Babbitt.* When critics noticed this, Lewis became bewildered, almost disoriented. He died in 1951 a desperately unhappy man.

Popular Culture: Movies and Radio

The postwar decade saw immense changes in popular culture. Unlike the literary flowering of the era, those changes seemed in tune with the times, not a reaction against them. This was true in part because they were products as much of technology as of human imagination.

The first motion pictures were made around 1900, but the medium only came into its own after the Great War. The early films, such as the eight-minute epic *The Great Train Robbery* (1903), were brief, action-packed, and unpretentious. Professional actors viewed them with contempt. But their success was instantaneous. In 1912 there were nearly 13,000 movie houses in the United States, more than 500 in New York City alone. Many of these places were converted stores called nickelodeons because the admission charge was 5 cents.

In the beginning the mere recording of movement seemed to satisfy the public, but success led to rapid technical and artistic improvements. David W. Griffith's 12-reel *Birth of a Nation* 1915) was a particularly important breakthrough in both areas, though Griffith's sympathetic treatment of the Ku Klux Klan of Reconstruction days angered blacks and white liberals.

By the mid-twenties the industry, centered in Hollywood, California, was the fourth largest in the nation in capital investment. Films moved from the nickelodeons to converted theaters. So large was the audience that movie "palaces" seating several thousand people sprang up in the major cities. They counted yearly ticket sales in the tens of millions. With the introduction of talking movies, beginning with *The Jazz Singer* (1927), and color films a few years later, the motion picture reached technological maturity. Costs and profits mounted: by the thirties million-dollar productions were common.

Many movies were tasteless trash catering to the prejudices of the multitude. Sex, crime, war, romantic adventure, broad comedy, and luxurious living were the main themes, endlessly repeated in predictable patterns. Popular actors and actresses tended to be either handsome, talentless sticks or so-called character actors who were typecast over and over again as heroes, villains, comedians. The stars attracted armies of adoring fans and received thousands of dollars a week for their services. Critics charged that the movies were destroying the legitimate stage (which underwent a sharp decline), corrupting the morals of youth, and glorifying the materialistic aspects of life.

Nevertheless the motion picture made positive contributions to American culture. Beginning with the work of Griffith, filmmakers created an entirely new theatrical art, using close-ups to portray character and heighten tension, broad panoramic shots to transcend the limits of the stage. They employed, with remarkable results, special lighting effects, the fade-out, and other techniques impossible in the live theater. Movies enabled dozens of established actors to reach wider audiences and developed many first-rate new ones. In Charlie Chaplin, whose characterization of the sad little tramp with his toothbrush moustache and his cane, tight frock coat, and baggy trousers became famous throughout the world, the new form found perhaps the

Man against machine: Charlie Chaplin duels a folding Murphy bed in the film One A.M.

supreme comic artist of all time. The animated cartoon, perfected by Walt Disney, was a lesser but significant achievement that gave endless delight to millions of children. And as the medium matured, it produced many dramatic works of high quality. At its best the motion picture offered a breadth and power of impact superior to anything on the traditional stage.

Even more pervasive in its effects on the American people was radio. Wireless transmission of sound was developed in the late 19th century by many scientists in Europe and the United States. An American, Lee De Forest, working in the decade before the Great War, devised the key improvements that made long-distance broadcasting possible. During the war radio was put to important military uses and was strictly controlled; immediately thereafter the airwaves were thrown open to everybody.

Radio was briefly the domain of hobbyists, thousands of "hams" chatting in indiscriminate fashion. Even under these conditions, the manufacture of radio equipment became a big business. In 1920 the first commercial station (KDKA in Pittsburgh) began broadcasting, and by the end of 1922 over 500 stations were in operation.

It took little time for broadcasters to discover the power of the new medium. When one pioneer interrupted a music program to ask listeners to phone in requests, the station received 3,000 calls in an hour. The immediacy of radio explained its tremendous impact. As a means of communicating the latest news, it had no peer; beginning with the broadcast of the 1924 presidential nominating conventions, all major public events were covered "live."

Advertisers seized on radio too; it proved to be as useful for selling soap as for transmitting news. Advertising had mixed effects on broadcasting. The sums paid by business for air time made possible elaborate entertainments performed by the finest actors and musicians, all without cost to listeners. However, advertisers hungered for mass markets. They preferred to sponsor programs of little intellectual content, aimed at the lowest tastes and utterly uncontroversial. And good and bad alike, programs were constantly interrupted by irritating pronouncements extolling the supposed virtues of one commercial product or another.

In 1927 Congress limited the number of stations and parceled out wavelengths to prevent interference. Further legislation in 1934 established the Federal Communications Commission, with power to revoke the licenses of stations that failed to operate in the public interest. But the FCC placed no effective controls on programming or on advertising practices. The general level remained lamentably inferior to that of government-owned European systems.

The "New Negro"

Even more than for white liberals, the postwar reaction had brought despair for many blacks. Aside from the barbarities of the Klan, they suffered from the postwar middle-class hostility to labor (and from the persistent reluctance of organized labor to admit black workers to its ranks). The increasing presence of southern blacks in northern cities also caused conflict. Some 393,000 settled in New York, Pennsylvania, and Illinois in the twenties, most of them in New York City, Philadelphia, and Chicago. The black population of New York City more than doubled between 1920 and 1930.

In earlier periods blacks in northern cities had tended to live together but in small neighborhoods scattered over large areas. Now the tendency was toward concentration in what came to be called ghettos. Harlem, a white middle-class residential section of New York City as late as 1910, had 50,000 blacks in 1914, 73,000 in 1920, and nearly 165,000 in 1930.

The restrictions of ghetto life produced a vi-

Beginning in the late 1930s black artist Jacob Lawrence painted a series of powerful "picture-narratives" dealing with the black experience in America. This painting, of Southern blacks crowding onto northbound trains during World War I, is the first of a 60-panel narrative that Lawrence titled The Migration of the Negro.

cious circle of degradation. Population growth and segregation caused a desperate housing shortage; rents in Harlem doubled between 1919 and 1927. Since the average black worker was unskilled and ill paid, tenants were forced to take in boarders. Landlords converted private homes into rooming houses and allowed their properties to fall into disrepair. The process of decay was speeded by the influx of what the black sociologist E. Franklin Frazier called "ignorant and unsophisticated peasant people" from the rural South, who were inexperienced in city living. These conditions caused disease and crime rates to rise sharply.

Even in small northern cities where they made up only a tiny proportion of the population, blacks were badly treated. When Robert S. and Helen M. Lynd made their classic sociological analysis of *Middletown* (Muncie, Indiana), they discovered that although black and white children attended the same schools, the churches, the larger movie houses, and other places of public accommodation were segregated. The local YMCA had a gymnasium where high school basketball was played, but the secretary refused to allow any team with a black player to use it. Even the news in Muncie was segregated. Local papers chronicled the affairs of the black community—roughly 5 percent of the population—under the heading "In Colored Circles."

Coming after the hopes inspired by wartime gains, the disappointments of the 1920s produced a new militancy among many blacks. In 1919 W. E. B. Du Bois wrote in *The Crisis:* "We are cowards and jackasses if . . . we do not marshal every ounce of our brain and brawn to fight . . . against the forces of hell in our own land." He increased his commitment to black nationalism, organizing a series of Pan African Conferences in an effort—futile, as it turned out—to create an international black movement.

Du Bois never made up his mind whether to work for integration or black separatism. Such ambivalence never troubled Marcus Garvey, a West Indian whose Universal Negro Improvement Association attracted hundreds of thousands of followers in the early twenties. Garvey had nothing but contempt for whites, for light-skinned blacks like Du Bois, and for organizations such as the NAACP, which sought to bring whites and blacks together to fight segregation and other forms of prejudice. "Back to Africa" was his slogan; the black man must "work out his salvation in his motherland." (Paradoxically, Garvey's ideas won the enthusiastic support of the Ku Klux Klan and other white racist groups.)

Garvey's message was naive, but it served to build racial pride among the masses of poor and unschooled blacks. He dressed in elaborate braided uniforms, wore a plumed hat, drove about in a limousine. Both God and Christ were black, he insisted. He organized black businesses of many sorts, including a company that manufactured black dolls. He established a corps of Black Cross nurses and a Black Star Line Steamship Company to transport blacks back to Africa. More sophisticated black leaders like Du Bois detested Garvey, whom they thought something of a charlatan. His motives are at this distance unclear, and part of his troubles resulted only from his being a terrible businessman. In 1923 his steamship line went into bankruptcy. He was convicted of defrauding the thousands of his supporters who had invested in its stock and was sent to prison. Nevertheless, his message, if not his methods, helped to create the "New Negro," proud of being black and prepared to resist both white mistreatment and white ideas. "Up, you mighty race, you can accomplish what you will!"

The ghettos produced compensating advantages for blacks. One effect, not fully utilized until later, was to increase their political power by enabling them to elect representatives to state legislatures and to Congress and to exert considerable influence in closely contested elections. More immediately, city life stimulated self-confidence; despite their horrors, the ghettos offered economic opportunity, political rights, and freedom from the everyday debasements of life in the South. The ghetto was a black world where black men and women could be themselves.

Black writers, musicians, and artists found in the ghettos both an audience and the "spiritual emancipation" that unleashed their capacities. Jazz, the great popular music of the age, was largely the creation of black musicians working in New Orleans before the turn of the century. By the 1920s it had spread throughout the country and to most of the rest of the world. White musicians and white audiences took it up—in a way, it became a force for racial tolerance and understanding. Jazz meant improvisation, and both players and audiences experienced in it a kind of liberation. Jazz was the music of the 1920s in part because it expressed the desire of so many people to break with tradition and throw off conventional restraints. Surely this helps to explain why it was so important to blacks.

Harlem, the largest black city in the world, became in the 1920s a cultural capital, center of the "Harlem Renaissance." Black newspapers and magazines flourished along with theatrical companies and libraries. Du Bois opened *The Crisis* to young writers and artists, and a dozen "little" magazines sprang up. Langston Hughes, one of the best poets of the era, described the exhilaration of his first arrival in this city within a city, a "magnet" for every black intellectual and artist. "Harlem! I . . . dropped my bags, took a deep breath, and felt happy again."

With some exceptions, black writers like Hughes did not share in the disillusionment that afflicted so many white intellectuals. The persistence of prejudice angered them and made them militant. But to be militant, one must be at some level hopeful, and this they were. Sociologists and psychologists (for whom the ghettos were indispensable social laboratories) were demonstrating that environment rather than heredity was preventing black economic progress. Together with the achievements of creative blacks, which for the first time were being appreciated by large numbers of white intellectuals, these discoveries seemed to herald the eventual disappearance of race prejudice. The black, Alain Locke wrote in *The New Negro* (1925), "lays aside the status of beneficiary and ward for that of a collaborator and participant in American civilization." Alas, as Locke and other black intellectuals were soon to discover, this prediction, like so many made in the 1920s, did not come to pass.

The Era of "Normalcy"

The men who presided over the government of the United States during this era were Warren G. Harding of Ohio and Calvin Coolidge of Massachusetts. Harding was a newspaperman by trade, publisher of the Marion *Star,* with previous political experience as a legislator and lieutenant governor in his home state and as a United States senator. No president, before or since, looked more like a statesman; few were less suited for running the country. Coolidge was a taciturn, extremely conservative New England type with a long record in Massachusetts politics climaxed by his inept but much-admired suppression of the Boston police strike while governor. Harding referred to him as "that little fellow from Massachusetts." Coolidge preferred to follow public opinion and hope for the best. "Mr. Coolidge's genius for inactivity is developed to a very high point," the correspondent Walter Lippmann wrote. "It is a grim, determined, alert inactivity, which keeps Mr. Coolidge occupied constantly."*

Harding won the 1920 Republican nomination because the party convention could not decide between General Leonard Wood, who represented the Roosevelt faction, and Frank Lowden, governor of Illinois. His genial nature and lack of strong convictions made him attractive to many of the politicos after eight years of the headstrong Wilson. During the campaign he exasperated sophisticates by his ignorance and imprecision. He coined the famous vulgarism *normalcy* as a substitute for the word *normality,* referred, during a speech before a group of actors, to Shakespeare's play "Charles the Fifth," and committed numerous other blunders. "Why does he not get a private secretary who can clothe . . . his 'ideas' in the language customarily used by educated men?" one Boston gentleman demanded of Senator Lodge, who was strongly supporting Harding. Lodge, ordinarily a stickler for linguistic exactitude, replied acidly that he found Harding a paragon by comparison with Wilson, "a man who wrote English very well without ever saying anything." A large majority of the voters, untroubled by the candidate's lack of erudition, shared Lodge's confidence that he would be a vast improvement over Wilson.

Harding has often been characterized as lazy and incompetent. In fact, he was hardworking and politically shrewd; his major weaknesses were indecisiveness and an unwillingness to offend. He turned the most important government departments over to efficient administrators of impeccable reputation: Charles Evans Hughes, the secretary of state; Herbert Hoover in the Commerce

---

* Coolidge was physically delicate, being plagued by chronic stomach trouble. He required 10 or 11 hours of sleep a day.

Many said that Warren G. Harding was elected largely because of his good looks; his was the first presidential election after women got to vote.

Department; Andrew Mellon in the Treasury; and Henry C. Wallace in Agriculture. Harding kept track of what these men did but seldom initiated policy in their areas. However, many lesser offices, and a few of major importance, Harding gave to the unsavory "Ohio Gang" headed by Harry M. Daugherty, whom he made attorney general.

The president was too kindly, too well-intentioned, and too unambitious to be dishonest. He appointed corruptionists like Daugherty, Secretary of the Interior Albert B. Fall, Director of the Mint "Ed" Scobey, and Charles R. Forbes, head of the new Veterans Bureau, out of a sense of personal obligation or because they were old friends who shared his taste for poker and liquor. Before 1921 he had enjoyed officeholding; he was adept at mouthing platitudes, a loyal party man who seldom questioned the decisions of his superiors. In the lonely eminence of the White House, whence, as President Harry Truman later said, the buck cannot be passed, he found only misery. "The White House is a prison," he complained. "I can't get away from the men who dog my footsteps. I am in jail."

"Regulating" Business

In domestic affairs Secretary of the Treasury Mellon, multimillionaire banker and master of the aluminum industry, dominated the Harding administration. Mellon set out to lower the taxes of the rich, reverse the low-tariff policies of the Wilson period, return to the laissez faire philosophy of McKinley, and reduce the national debt by cutting expenses and administrating the government more efficiently. In principle his program had considerable merit. Tax rates designed to check consumer spending in time of war and to raise the huge sums needed to defeat the Central Powers were undoubtedly hampering economic expansion in the early twenties. Certain industries that had sprung up in the United States during the Great War were suffering from German and Japanese competition now that the fighting had ended. Rigid regulations necessary during a national crisis could well be dispensed with in peacetime. And efficiency and economy in government are always desirable.

Yet Mellon carried his policies to unreasonable extremes. He proposed eliminating inheritance taxes and reducing the tax on high incomes by two-thirds in order to stimulate investment, but he opposed lower rates for taxpayers earning less than $66,000 a year, apparently not realizing that economic expansion required greater mass consumption as well. Freeing the rich from "oppressive" taxation, he argued, would enable them to invest more in potentially productive enterprises, the success of which would create jobs for ordinary people. Little wonder that Mellon's admirers called him the greatest secretary of the treasury since Alexander Hamilton.

Although the Republicans had large majorities in both houses of Congress, Mellon's proposals were too reactionary to win unqualified approval. Congress passed a Budget and Accounting Act (1921), creating a director of the budget to assist the president in preparing a unified budget for the government and a comptroller general to audit all government accounts. A general budget had long been needed; previously Congress had dealt with the requirements of each department separately, trusting largely to luck that income and expenditures would balance at year's end. The appointment of a comptroller general enabled Congress to check up on how the departments used the sums granted them.

Mellon's tax and tariff program ran into stiff opposition from middle western Republicans and southern Democrats, who combined to form the so-called Farm Bloc. The revival of European agriculture cut the demand for American farm produce just when the increased use of fertilizers and machinery was boosting output. As in the era after the Civil War, farmers found themselves burdened with heavy debts while their income dwindled. In the decade after 1919 their share of the national income fell by nearly 50 percent. The Farm Bloc represented a kind of conservative populism, economic grievances combining with a general prejudice against "Wall Street financiers" and rich industrialists to unite agriculture against "the interests."

Mellon epitomized everything the Farm Bloc disliked. Rejecting his more extreme suggestions, it pushed through the Revenue Act of 1921, which abolished the excess-profits tax and cut the top income tax rate from 73 percent to 50 percent but raised the tax on corporate profits slightly and left inheritance taxes untouched. Three years later Congress cut the maximum income tax to 40 percent, reduced taxes on lower incomes significantly, and raised inheritance levies. The Farm Bloc also overhauled Mellon's tariff proposals. It placed heavy duties on agricultural products in 1921. The Fordney-McCumber Tariff of 1922 granted more-than-adequate protection to the "infant industries" (rayon, china, toys, and chemicals) yet held to the Wilsonian principle of moderate protection for most industrial products. Agricultural machinery and other items used by farmers remained on the free list.

Mellon nevertheless succeeded in balancing the budget and reducing the national debt by an average of over $500 million a year. So committed were the Republican leaders to retrenchment that they even resisted the demands of veterans, organized in the politically potent American Legion, for an "adjusted compensation" bonus. Arguing not entirely without reason that they had served for a pittance while war workers had been drawing down high wages, the veterans sought grants equal to a dollar a day for their period in uniform ($1.25 for time overseas). Congress responded sympathetically, but Harding and Coolidge both vetoed bonus bills in the name of economy. Finally, in 1924, a compromise bill granting the veterans paid-up life insurance policies was passed over Coolidge's veto.

That the business community heartily approved the policies of Harding and Coolidge is not surprising. Both presidents were uncritical advocates of the business point of view. "We want less government in business and more business in government," Harding pontificated, to which Coolidge added, "The business of the United States is business." Harding and Coolidge used their power of appointment to convert regulatory bodies like the Interstate Commerce Commission and the Federal Reserve Board into probusiness agencies that ceased almost entirely to restrict the activities of the industries they were supposed to be controlling. The ICC became almost the reverse of what it had been in the Progressive Era. The Federal Trade Commission, in the words of one bemused academic, seemed to be trying to commit hara-kiri.

The Harding Scandals

At least Mellon was honest. The Ohio Gang used its power in the most corrupt way imaginable. Jesse Smith, a crony of Attorney General Daugherty, was what today would be called an influence peddler. When he was exposed in 1923, he committed suicide. Charles R. Forbes of the Veterans Bureau siphoned millions of dollars appropriated for the construction of hospitals into his own pocket. When he was found out, he fled to Europe. Later he returned, stood trial, and was sentenced to two years in prison. His assistant, Charles F. Cramer, committed suicide. Daugherty himself was implicated in the fraudulent return of German assets seized by the alien property custodian to their original owners. He escaped imprisonment only by refusing to testify on the ground that he might incriminate himself. Thomas W. Miller, the alien property custodian, was sent to jail for accepting a bribe.

The worst scandal involved Secretary of the Interior Albert B. Fall, a former senator. In 1921 Fall arranged with the complaisant Secretary of the Navy Edwin Denby for the transfer to the Interior

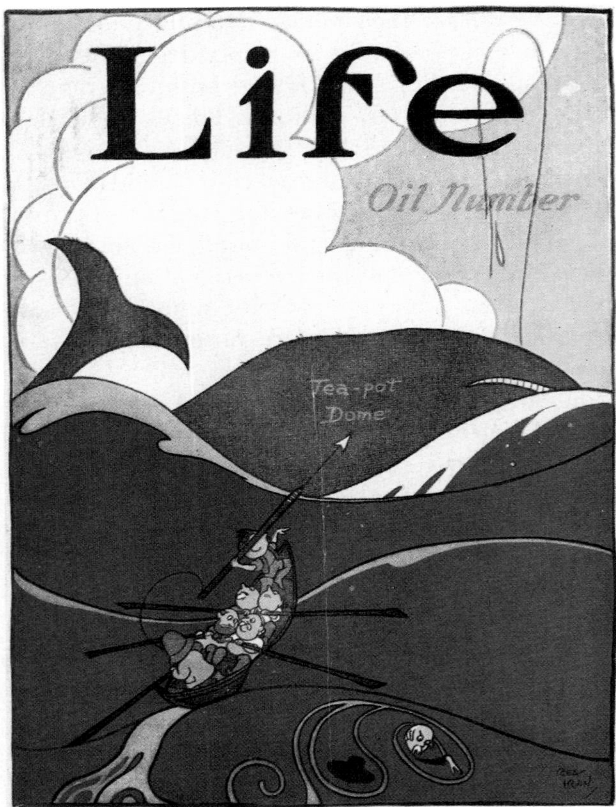

"Thar she blows!!" proclaims the cover of the humor magazine Life*'s "oil number" in March 1924, as an honest citizen prepares to harpoon the Teapot Dome conspiracy. A guilty-looking politician has bailed out and is trying to swim clear of the impending fracas.*

Department of government oil reserves being held for the future use of the navy. He then leased these properties to private oil companies. Edward L. Doheny's Pan-American Petroleum Company got the Elk Hills reserve in California; the Teapot Dome reserve in Wyoming was turned over to Harry F. Sinclair's Mammoth Oil Company. When critics protested, Fall explained that it was necessary to develop the Elk Hills and Teapot Dome properties because adjoining private drillers were draining off the navy's oil. Nevertheless, in 1923 the Senate ordered a full-scale investigation, conducted by Senator Thomas J. Walsh of Montana. It soon came out that Doheny had "lent" Fall $100,000 in hard cash, handed over secretly in a "little black bag." Sinclair had given Fall over $300,000 in cash and negotiable securities.

Although the three culprits escaped conviction on the charge of conspiring to defraud the government, Sinclair was sentenced to nine months in jail for contempt of the Senate and for tampering with a jury, and Fall was fined $100,000 and given a year in prison for accepting a bribe. In 1927 the Supreme Court revoked the leases and the two reserves were returned to the government.

The public still knew little of the scandals when, in June 1923, Harding left Washington on a speaking tour that included a visit to Alaska. His health was poor, his spirits low, for he had begun to understand how his "Goddamn friends" had betrayed him. On the return trip from Alaska, he came down with what his physician, an incompetent crony whom he had made surgeon general of the United States, diagnosed as ptomaine poisoning resulting from his having eaten a tainted Japanese crab. In fact the president had suffered a heart attack. He died in San Francisco on August 2.

Few presidents have been more deeply mourned by the people at the moment of their passing. Harding's kindly nature, his very ordinariness, increased his human appeal. Three million people viewed his coffin as it passed across the country. When the scandals came to light, sadness turned to scorn and contempt. The poet e. e. cummings came closer to catching the final judgment of Harding's contemporaries than has any historian:

the first president to be loved by his
bitterest enemies" is dead
the only man woman or child who wrote
a simple declarative sentence with seven grammatical
errors "is dead"
beautiful Warren Gamaliel Harding
"is" dead
he's
"dead"
if he wouldn't have eaten them Yapanese Craps
somebody might hardly never not have been
unsorry, perhaps

Coolidge Prosperity

Had he lived, Harding might well have been defeated in 1924 because of the scandals. Vice-President Coolidge, unconnected with the troubles and not the type to surround himself with cronies of any kind, seemed the ideal person to clean out the corruptionists. After he had replaced Attorney General Daugherty with Harlan Fiske Stone, dean of the Columbia Law School, the scandals ceased to be a serious political handicap for the Republicans.

Coolidge soon became the darling of the conservatives. His admiration for businessmen and his devotion to laissez faire knew no limit. "The man who builds a factory builds a temple," he said in all seriousness. "The Government can do more to remedy the economic ills of the people by a system of rigid economy in public expenditures than can be accomplished through any other action." Andrew Mellon, whom he kept on as secretary of the treasury, became his mentor in economic affairs.

Coolidge won the 1924 Republican nomination easily. The Democrats, badly split, required 103 ballots to choose a candidate. The southern wing, dry, anti-immigrant, pro-Klan, had fixed on William G. McAdoo, Wilson's secretary of the treasury. The eastern, urban, wet element supported Governor Alfred E. Smith of New York, child of the slums, a Catholic who had compiled a distinguished record in the field of social welfare legislation. After days of futile politicking, the party compromised on John W. Davis, a conservative corporation lawyer closely allied with the Morgan banking interests.

Dismayed by the conservatism of Coolidge and Davis, Robert M. La Follette, backed by the Farm Bloc, the Socialist party, the American Federation of Labor, and numbers of intellectuals, entered the race as the candidate of a new Progressive party. The Progressives adopted a neopopulist platform calling for the nationalization of railroads, the direct election of the president, the protection of labor's right to bargin collectively, and other reforms.

The situation was almost exactly the opposite of 1912, when one conservative had run against two liberals and had been swamped. Coolidge received 15.7 million votes, Davis 8.4 million, La Follette 4.8 million. In the electoral college LaFollette won only his native Wisconsin; Coolidge defeated Davis, 382 to 136. Conservatism was clearly the dominant mood of the country.

The glorification of the sluggish Coolidge and of the "New Era" over which he presided had its origin in the unprecedented prosperity that the nation enjoyed during his reign. Business boomed, real wages rose, unemployment declined. The United States was as rich as all Europe; perhaps 40 percent of the world's total wealth lay in American hands. Little wonder that thousands came to believe that no one should tamper with the marvelous economic machine that was yielding such bounty. At the end of Coolidge's term in 1929, the Boston merchant Frank W. Stearns claimed that except for Lincoln's, Coolidge's had been "the greatest administration since that of George Washington from the point of view of what it had done for the country."

Prosperity rested on many bases, one of which was the friendly, hands-off attitude of the government, which bolstered the confidence of the business community. The Federal Reserve Board kept interest rates low, a further stimulus to economic growth. Pent-up wartime demand helped to power the boom; the construction business in particular profited from a series of extremely busy years. The continuing mechanization and rationalization of industry provided a more fundamental stimulus to the economy. From heavy road-grading equipment and concrete mixers to devices for making cigars and glass tubes, from pneumatic tools to the dial telephone, machinery was replacing human hands at an ever more rapid rate. Industrial output almost doubled between 1921 and 1929 without any substantial increase in the industrial labor force. Greater use of power, especially of electricity, also encouraged expansion—by 1929 the United States was producing more electricity than the rest of the world combined.

Most important, American manufacturing was experiencing a remarkable improvement in efficiency. The method of breaking down the complex processes of production into many simple operations and the use of interchangeable parts were 19th-century innovations; in the 1920s they were adopted on an almost universal scale. The moving assembly line, which carried the product to the worker, first devised by Henry Ford in his automobile plant in the decade before World War I, speeded production and reduced costs. In ten years the hourly output of Ford workers quadrupled. The time-and-motion studies of Frederick W. Taylor, developed early in the century, were applied in hundreds of factories after the war. Taylor's method was to make careful analyses of each step and movement in the manufacturing process. Then workers would be taught exactly how best to perform each function. Taylor described his system as "*enforced* standardization" made possible by the "*enforced* cooperation" of workers. "Taylorism" alarmed some union leaders, but no one could deny the effectiveness of "scientific shop management" methods.

The growing ability of manufacturers to create new consumer demands also stimulated the economy. Advertising and salesmanship were raised almost to the status of fine arts. Bruce Barton, one of the advertising "geniuses" of the era, wrote a best-selling book, *The Man Nobody Knows* (1925), in which he described Jesus as the "founder of modern business," the man who "picked up twelve men from the bottom ranks . . . and forged them into an organization that conquered the world." In 1930 no less a personage than Eleanor Roosevelt, wife of the governor of New York, gave a testimonial for a leading breakfast cereal, which had, she said, "undoubtedly played its part" in building the "robust physique" of her teenage son, John. Producers concentrated on making their goods more attractive and on changing models frequently to entice buyers into the market. The practice of selling goods on the installment plan helped bring expensive items within the reach of the masses. Inventions and technological advances created new or improved products: radios, automobiles, electric appliances such as vacuum cleaners and refrigerators, gadgets like cigarette lighters, new forms of entertainment like motion pictures.

These influences interacted in much the way the textile industry in the early 19th century and the railroad industry after the Civil War had been the "multipliers" of their times. Undoubtedly the automobile had the single most important impact on the nation's economy in the twenties. Although well over a million cars a year were being regularly produced by 1916, the real expansion of the industry came after 1921. Output reached 3.6 million in 1923 and fell below that figure only twice during the remainder of the decade. By 1929, 23 million private cars clogged the highways, an average of nearly one per family.

The auto industry created industries that manufactured tires and spark plugs and other products. It consumed immense quantities of rubber, paint, glass, nickel, and petroleum products. It triggered a gigantic road-building program: there were 387,000 miles of paved roads in the United States in 1921, 662,000 miles in 1929. Thousands of persons found employment in filling stations, roadside stands, and other businesses catering to the motoring public. The tourist industry profited, and the shift of population from the cities to the suburbs was accelerated. The automobile made life more mobile yet also more encapsulated. It changed recreational patterns and family life. It created a generation of tinkerers and amateur mechanics and explorers. In addition, it profoundly affected the way Americans thought. It gave them a freedom never before imagined. The owner of the most rickety jalopy could travel further, faster, and far more comfortably than a monarch of old with his blooded steeds and gilded coaches.

These benefits were real and priceless. But cars came to have a symbolic significance that was equally important; they gave their owners a feeling of power and status similar to that which owning a horse gave to a medieval knight. According to some authorities the typical American cared more about owning an automobile than a home.

In time there were undesirable, even dangerous results of the automotive revolution: roadside scenery disfigured by billboards, gas stations, and other enterprises aimed at satisfying the traveler's needs; horrendous traffic jams; soaring accident rates; air pollution; the deterioration of inner cities. All these disadvantages were noticed during the 1920s, but in the springtime of the new industry they were discounted. The automobile seemed an unalloyed blessing—part toy, part tool, part symbol of American freedom, prosperity, and individualism.

Henry Ford

The person most directly responsible for the growth of the automobile industry was Henry Ford, a self-taught mechanic from Greenfield, Michigan. Ford was not a great inventor or one of the true automobile pioneers. He was not even the first person to manufacture a good low-priced car (that being the achievement of Ransom E. Olds, producer of the "Merry Oldsmobile"). He had two brilliant insights. The first was, in his words, "Get the prices down to the buying power." Through mass production, cars could be made cheaply enough to put them within reach of the ordinary citizen. In 1908 he designed the Model T Ford, a simple, tough box on wheels, powered by a light, durable, easily repaired engine. In a year he proved his point by selling 11,000 Model Ts. Thereafter, relentlessly cutting costs and increasing efficiency by installing the assembly-line system, he expanded production at an unbelievable rate. By 1925 he was turning out more than 9,000 cars a day, one approximately every 10 seconds, and the price of the Model T had been reduced to below $300.

Ford grasped the importance of high wages in stimulating output (and selling more automobiles). This was his second insight. The assembly line simplified the laborer's task and increased the pace of work; at the same time it made each worker much more productive. Jobs became boring and fatiguing, absenteeism and labor turnover serious problems. To combat this difficulty, in 1914 Ford established the $5 day, an increase of about $2 over prevailing wages. The rate of turnover in his plant fell 90 percent, and although critics charged that he recaptured his additional labor costs by speeding up the line, his policy had a revolutionary effect on wage rates. Later he raised the minimum to $6 and then to $7 a day.

Ford's profits soared along with sales; since he owned the entire company, he became a billionaire. Throughout the twenties he cleared an average of about $25,000 *a day.* He also became an authentic folk hero: his homespun simplicity, his dislike of bankers and sophisticated society, his intense individualism endeared him to millions. He stood as a symbol of the wonders of the American system—he had given the nation a marvelous convenience at a low price, at the same time enriching himself and raising the living standards of his thousands of employees.

Unfortunately, Ford had the defects of his virtues in full measure. He paid high wages but tyrannized over his workers. He refused to deal with any union and employed spies to investigate the private lives of his help and gangsters and bully boys to enforce plant discipline. When he discovered a worker driving any car but a Ford, he had him dismissed. So close was the supervision in the factory that workers devised the "Ford whisper," a means of talking without moving the lips.

Success made Ford stubborn. The Model T remained essentially unchanged for nearly 20 years. Other companies, notably General Motors, were soon turning out better vehicles for very little more money. Customers, increasingly affluent and style-conscious, began to shift to Chevrolets and Chryslers. Finally, in 1927, Ford shut down all operations for 18 months in order to retool for the Model A. His competitors rushed in during this period

According to his biographer, Allan Nevins, Henry Ford's complex personality included the characteristics of "a wry, cross-grained, brilliant adolescent." Here, on a summer outing, Ford poses as a western badman.

to fill the vacuum. Although his company continued to make a great deal of money, Ford never regained the dominant position he had held for so long.

Ford was enormously uninformed, yet—because of his success and the praise the world heaped upon him—he did not hesitate to speak out on subjects far outside his area of competence, from the evils of drink and tobacco to medicine and international affairs. He developed political ambitions and published virulent anti-Semitic propaganda. He said he would not give 5 cents for all the art in the world.

While praising his talents as a manufacturer, historians have not dealt kindly with Ford the man, in part no doubt because he once said, "History is more or less the bunk."

The Airplane

Henry Ford was also an early manufacturer of airplanes, and while the airplane industry was not economically important in the 1920s, its development in that decade laid the basis for changes in lifestyles and attitudes at least as momentous as those produced by the automobile. The invention of the internal combustion gasoline engine, with its extremely high ratio of power to weight, made the airplane possible, which explains why the early experiments with "flying machines" took place at about the same time that the prototypes of the modern automobile were being manufactured. Wilbur and Orville Wright made their famous flight at Kitty Hawk, North Carolina, in 1903, five years before Ford produced his Model T. Another pair of brothers, Malcolm and Haimes Lockheed, built their Model G, one of the earliest commercial planes (commercial in the sense that they used it to take passengers up at 5 dollars a ride) in 1913.

The World War speeded the advance of airplane technology, and most of the planes built in the twenties were intended for military use. Practical commercial air travel was long delayed. Aerial acrobats, parachute jumpers, wing walkers, and other "daredevils" who put on shows at county fairs and similar places where crowds gathered were the principal civilian aviators of the 1920s. They "barnstormed" from town to town, living the same kind of inbred, encapsulated lives that circus people did, their chief rewards being the sense of independence and pride that the successful performance of their highly skilled but risky trade provided.

The great event of the decade for aviation, still an achievement that must strike awe in the hearts of reflective persons, was Charles A. Lindbergh's nonstop flight from New York to Paris in May 1927. It took more than 33 hours for Lindbergh's single-engine *Spirit of St. Louis* to cross the Atlantic, a formidable physical achievement for the pilot as well as an example of skill and courage. When the public learned that the interpid "Lucky Lindy" was handsome, modest, uninterested in converting his new fame into cash, and a model of propriety (he neither drank nor smoked), his role as American hero was assured. It was a role Lindbergh detested—one biographer has described him as "by nature solitary"—but could not avoid.

Lindbergh's flight enormously increased public interest in flying, but it was a landmark in aviation technology as well. The day of routine passenger flights was at last about to dawn. In July 1927, a mere two months after the *Spirit of St. Louis* touched down at Le Bourget Field in France, William E. Boeing of Boeing Air Transport began flying passengers and mail between San Francisco and Chicago, using the M-40, a plane of his own design and manufacture. Early in 1928 he changed the company name to United Aircraft and Transport. Two years later Boeing produced the first all-metal, low-wing plane, and in 1933 the twin-engine 247, called by the historian John B. Rae "the first genuinely modern transport airplane."

Economic Problems

Like Ford, its outstanding success, the American economic system of the twenties had grave flaws. Certain industries did not share in the good times. The coal business, suffering from the competition of petroleum, entered a period of decline. The production of cotton and woolen cloth also lagged because of the competition of new synthetics, principally rayon. The industry began to be plagued by falling profit margins and chronic unemployment.

The movement toward consolidation in indus-

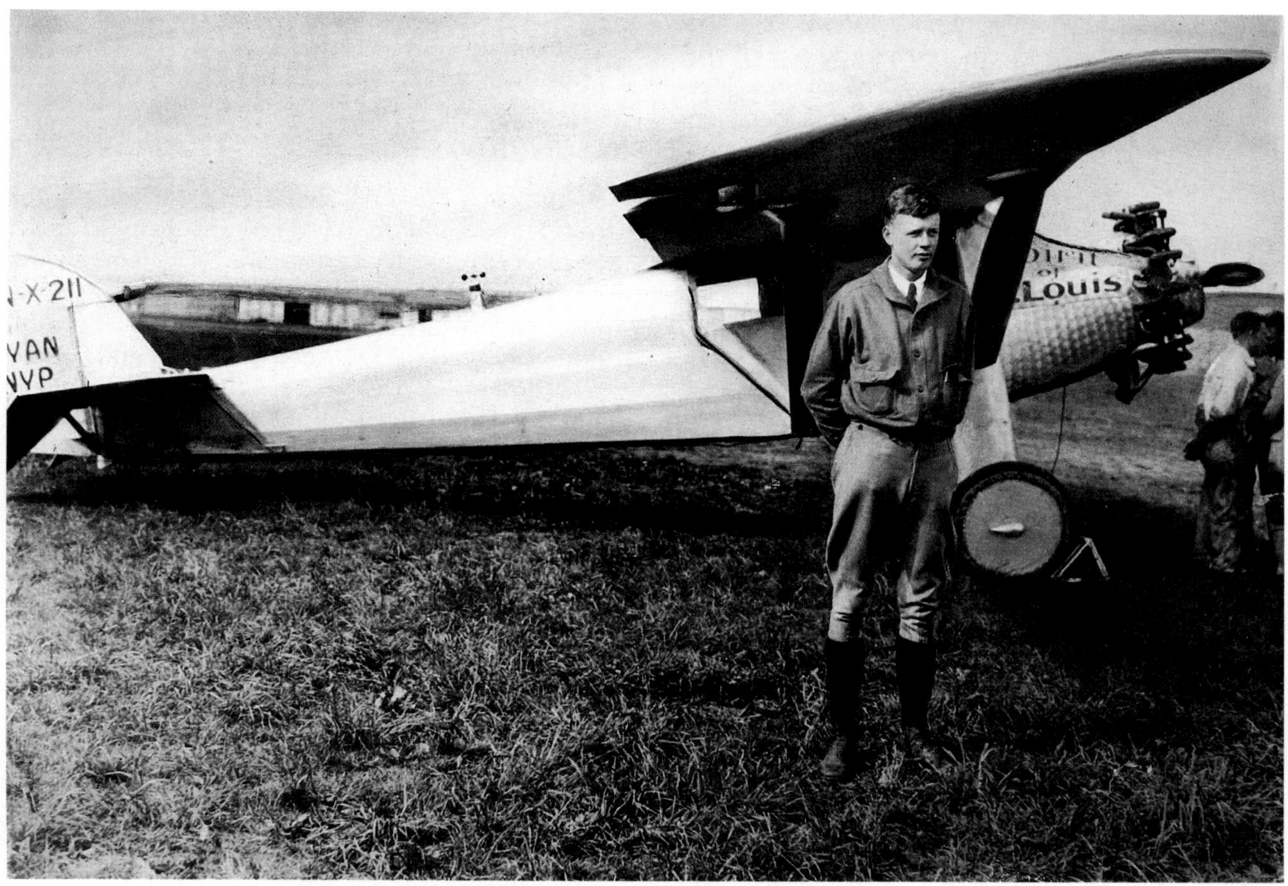

Charles Lindbergh beside The Spirit of St. Louis *shortly before he took off for Paris from Roosevelt Field, Long Island, on May 20, 1927.*

try, somewhat checked during the latter part of the Progressive Era, resumed; by 1929, 200 corporations controlled nearly half the nation's corporate assets. General Motors, Ford, and Chrysler turned out nearly 90 percent of all American cars and trucks. Four tobacco companies produced over 90 percent of the cigarettes. One percent of all financial institutions controlled 46 percent of the nation's banking business. Even retail merchandising, traditionally the domain of the small shopkeeper, reflected the trend. The A & P food chain expanded from 400 stores in 1912 to 17,500 in 1928. The Woolworth chain of five-and-ten-cent stores experienced similar growth.

Most large manufacturers, aware that bad public relations resulting from the unbridled use of monopolistic power outweighed any immediate economic gain, sought stability and "fair" prices rather than the maximum profit possible at the moment. "Regulated" competition was the order of the day, oligopoly the typical situation. The trade association movement flourished; producers formed voluntary organizations to exchange information, discuss policies toward government and the public, and "administer" prices in their industry. Usually the largest corporation, such as U.S. Steel in the iron and steel business, became the "price leader," its competitors, some themselves giants, following slavishly.

The success of the trade associations depended in part on the attitude of the federal government, for such organizations might well have been attacked under the antitrust laws. Their defenders argued that the associations made business more efficient and prevented violent gyrations of prices and production. President Harding accepted this line of reasoning. His secretary of commerce, Herbert Hoover, put the facilities of his department at the disposal of the associations. "We are passing from a period of extremely individualistic action into a period of associational activities," Hoover stated. After Coolidge became president, the Antitrust Division of the Justice Department itself encouraged the trade associations to cooperate in ways that had previously been considered violations of the Sherman Act.

Even more important to the trade associations were the good times. With profits high and markets expanding, the most powerful producers could afford to share the bounty with smaller, less efficient competitors.

The weakest element in the economy was agriculture. Farm prices slumped and farmers' costs mounted. Besides having to purchase expensive machinery in order to compete, farmers were confronted by high foreign tariffs and in some cases quotas on the importation of foodstuffs. As crop yields per acre rose, chiefly because of the increased use of chemical fertilizers, agricultural prices fell further.

Despite the efforts of the Farm Bloc, the government did little to improve the situation. President Harding opposed direct aid to agriculture as a matter of principle. "Every farmer is a captain of industry," he declared. "The elimination of competition among them would be impossible without sacrificing that fine individualism that still keeps the farm the real reservoir from which the nation draws so many of the finest elements of its citizenship." During his administration Congress strengthened the laws regulating railroad rates and grain exchanges and made it easier for farmers to borrow money, but it did nothing to increase agricultural income. Nor did the high tariffs on agricultural produce have much effect. Being forced to sell their surpluses abroad, farmers found that world prices depressed domestic prices despite the tariff wall.

The attitude of Claude R. Wickard, a "master farmer" from Carroll County, Indiana, and later secretary of agriculture under Franklin D. Roosevelt, typifies the feelings of American farmers during the twenties:

> I was disturbed—genuinely disturbed—by the trend of things, and I think, what was most important of all, my hope began to vanish. I became discouraged with agriculture. We didn't know where we were going.

In 1921 George N. Peek, a plow manufacturer from Moline, Illinois, advanced a scheme to "make the tariff effective for agriculture." The federal government, Peek suggested in "Equality for Agriculture," should buy up the surplus American production of wheat.* This additional demand would cause domestic prices to rise. Then the government could sell the wheat abroad at the lower world price. It could recover its losses by assessing an "equalization fee" on the wheat farmers.

Peek's plan had flaws. If the price of staples rose, farmers would tend to increase their output. Yet this problem might have been solved by imposing production controls. It was certainly a promising idea; hundreds of organizations in the farm belt endorsed it. Farm Bloc congressmen took it up and in 1927 the McNary-Haugen bill was passed, only to be vetoed by President Coolidge. Although he raised a number of practical objections, Coolidge based his opposition chiefly on constitutional and philosophical grounds. "A healthy economic condition is best maintained through a free play of competition," he insisted, ignoring the fact that the scheme had been devised precisely because competition was proving unhealthy for American farmers. Congress passed a similar bill in 1928, and again Coolidge rejected it.

Thus, while most economic indicators reflected an unprecedented prosperity, the boom times rested on unstable foundations. The problem was mainly one of maldistribution of resources. Productive capacity raced ahead of buying power. Too large a share of the profits went into too few pockets. The 27,000 families with the highest annual incomes in 1929 received as much money as the 11 million with annual incomes of under $1,500, which was the minimum sum required at that time to maintain a family decently. High earnings and low taxes permitted huge sums to pile up in the hands of individuals who did not invest the money

* He soon extended his plan to cover cotton and other staples.

productively. A good deal of it went into stock market speculation, which led to the "big bull market" and eventually to the Great Depression.

While Coolidge reigned, few realized the danger. Complacency was the order of the day. "The country," Coolidge told Congress in 1928, "can regard the present with satisfaction, and anticipate the future with optimism."

The Election of 1928

The climax of Coolidge's New Era came in 1928. The president—somewhat cryptically, as was his wont—decided not to run again, and Herbert Hoover, whom he detested, easily won the Republican nomination. Hoover was the intellectual leader, almost the philosopher, of the New Era. He spoke and wrote of "progressive individualism." American capitalists, he believed, had learned to curb their selfish instincts. Voluntary trade associations could create "codes of business practice and ethics that would eliminate abuses and make for higher standards."

Although stiff and uncommunicative and entirely without experience in elective office, Hoover made an admirable candidate in 1928. His roots in the Middle West and West (Iowa-born, he was raised in Oregon and educated at Stanford University in California) neatly balanced his outstanding reputation among eastern business tycoons. He took a "modern" approach to both capital and labor; businessmen should cooperate with one another and with their workers too. He opposed both union busting and trustbusting. His career as a mining engineer had given him a wide knowledge of the world, yet he had become highly critical of Europe—which disarmed the isolationists, who might otherwise have suspected that his long years abroad had made him an effete cosmopolite.

The Democrats, having had their fill of factionalism in 1924, could no longer deny the nomination to Governor Al Smith. Superficially, Smith was Hoover's antithesis. Born and raised in New York's Lower East Side slums, affable, witty, determinedly casual of manner, he had been schooled in machine politics by Tammany Hall. He was a Catholic, Hoover a Quaker, a wet where Hoover supported prohibition; he dealt easily with people of every race and nationality, while Hoover had little interest in and less knowledge of blacks and immigrants. However, like Hoover, Smith managed to combine a basic conservatism with humanitarian concern for the underprivileged. As adept in administration as Hoover, he was equally uncritical of the American capitalist system.

Unwilling to challenge the public's complacent view of Coolidge prosperity, the Democrats adopted a conservative platform. Smith appointed John J. Raskob, a wealthy automobile executive, to manage his campaign. Franklin D. Roosevelt, who ran for governor of New York at Smith's urging in 1928, charged that Hoover's expansion of the functions of the Department of Commerce had been at least mildly socialistic. This strategy failed miserably. Nothing Smith could do or say was capable of convincing Republican businessmen that he was a better choice than Hoover. His Catholicism, his brashness, his criticism of prohibition, his machine connections, and his urban background hurt him in rural areas, especially in the South.

In the election Hoover won a smashing triumph, 444 to 87 in the electoral college, 21.4 million to 14 million in the popular vote. All the usually Democratic border states and even North Carolina, Florida, and Texas went to the Republicans, along with the entire West and Northeast save for Massachusetts and Rhode Island.

After this defeat the Democratic party appeared on the verge of extinction. Nothing could have been further from the truth. The religious question and his big-city roots had hurt Smith, but the chief reason he lost was prosperity—and the good times were soon to end. Hoover's overwhelming victory also concealed a political realignment that was taking place. Working-class voters in the cities, largely Catholic and unimpressed by Coolidge prosperity, had swung heavily to the Democrats. In 1924 the 12 largest cities had been solidly Republican; in 1928 all went Democratic. In agricultural states like Iowa, Smith ran far better than Davis had in 1924, for Coolidge's vetoes of the McNary-Haugen bills had caused considerable resentment.

A new coalition of urban workers and dissatisfied farmers was in the making. Prosperity held the Republican edifice together in 1928; when the good times ended, it crumbled, suddenly but completely, in one of the greatest political reversals in the nation's history.

SUPPLEMENTARY READING

Titles marked with an asterisk have been published in paperback.

A comprehensive survey of the twenties is J. D. Hicks, **Republican Ascendancy*** (1960), but W. E. Leuchtenburg, **The Perils of Prosperity*** (1958), is equally broad in coverage and more interpretive. Other interesting volumes are Roderick Nash, **The Nervous Generation** (1970), and R. H. Elias, **Entangling Alliances with None** (1973). F. L. Allen, **Only Yesterday*** (1931), is an excellent popular account, a modern classic, oriented especially toward social history. R. K. Murray, **The Politics of Normalcy*** (1973), is a good brief survey, and the essays in P. A. Carter, **Another Part of the Twenties** (1977), and in John Braeman et al. (eds.), **Change and Continuity: The Twenties** (1968), are also helpful. The economic history of the period is covered in George Soule, **Prosperity Decade*** (1947), but see also E. W. Hawley, **The Great War and the Search for a Modern Order*** (1979), and Robert Sobel, **The Great Bull Market: Wall Street in the 1920's*** (1968).

The labor history of the postwar decade is discussed in Irving Bernstein, **The Lean Years*** (1960), and R. H. Zieger, **Republicans and Labor** (1969). David Brody, **The Steel Strike of 1919*** (1965), and R. L. Friedheim, **The Seattle General Strike** (1965), are useful special studies. On the Red Scare, see R. K. Murray, **Red Scare*** (1955), Zechariah Chafee, **Free Speech in the United States*** (1941), and Stanley Coben, **A. Mitchell Palmer** (1963). Nativism and immigration restriction are covered in M. A. Jones, **American Immigration*** (1960), and John Higham, **Strangers in the Land*** (1955). Fundamentalism is treated in N. F. Furniss, **The Fundamentalist Controversy** (1954), the Monkey Trial in Ray Ginger, **Six Days or Forever?*** (1958). The fullest and most thoughtful history of prohibition is Andrew Sinclair, **Prohibition: The Era of Excess*** (1962), but see also J. R. Gusfield, **Symbolic Crusade** (1963), and N. H. Clark, **Deliver Us from Evil*** (1976), the latter quite sympathetic toward the Amendment. On the Klan, consult D. M. Chalmers, **Hooded Americanism: The History of the Ku Klux Klan*** (1965), K. T. Jackson, **The Ku Klux Klan in the City*** (1967), and A. S. Rice, **The Ku Klux Klan in American Politics** (1961). On women, see W. H. Chafe, **The American Woman: Her Changing Social, Economic, and Political Roles*** (1972), and L. W. Tentler, **Wage-Earning Women: 1900–1930** (1979). Sacco and Vanzetti are dealt with sympathetically in Felix Frankfurter, **The Case of Sacco and Vanzetti*** (1927), but Francis Russell, **Tragedy in Dedham** (1962), casts doubt on their innocence.

The literature of the prewar period is discussed in H. F. May, **The End of American Innocence*** (1959), that of the twenties in Alfred Kazin, **On Native Grounds*** (1942), and F. J. Hoffman, **The Twenties*** (1955), On Fitzgerald, see Arthur Mizener, **The Far Side of Paradise*** (1951); on Hemingway, C. H. Baker, **Hemingway: The Writer as Artist*** (1956); on Mencken, W. R. Manchester, **Disturber of the Peace: The Life of H. L. Mencken*** (1951); on Lewis, Mark Schorer, **Sinclair Lewis*** (1961). P. S. Fass, **The Damned and the Beautiful: American Youth in the 1920's** (1977), is a useful corrective to the "flaming youth" stereotype. On popular culture, see Russell Lynes, **The Tastemakers*** (1954), Lewis Jacobs, **The Rise of the American Film*** (1939), Hortense Powdermaker, **Hollywood*** (1950), C. H. Sterling and J. M. Kittross, **Stay Tuned: A Concise History of American Broadcasting** (1978), and P. T. Rosen, **The Modern Stentors: Radio Broadcasting and the Federal Government** (1980).

For the history of blacks, see, besides the sociologist Gunnar Myrdal's classic **An American Dilemma*** (1944), Gilbert Osofsky, **Harlem: The Making of a Ghetto*** (1965), E. M. Rudwick, **W. E. B. Du Bois: Propagandist of the Negro Protest*** (1960), E. D. Cronon, **Black Moses: The Story of Marcus Garvey*** (1955), Alain Locke, **The New Negro: An Interpretation*** (1925), and Nathan Huggins, **Harlem Renaissance*** (1971).

The best brief biography of Harding is Andrew Sinclair, **The Available Man*** (1965), the fullest analysis of his presidency, R. K. Murray, **The Harding Era** (1969). D. R. McCoy, **Calvin Coolidge: The Quiet President** (1967), is the best life of Coolidge, but see also W. A. White, **A Puritan in Babylon*** (1938). Other useful political biographies include Richard Lowitt, **George W. Norris** (1963–1978), Oscar Handlin, **Al Smith and His America*** (1958), Frank Freidel, **Franklin D. Roosevelt: The Ordeal** (1954), and Arthur Mann, **La Guardia: A Fighter Against His Time*** (1959). David Burner, **The Politics of Provincialism: The Democratic Party in Transition*** (1968), discusses the evolution of the Democratic party in the 1920s. R. F. Himmelberg, **The Origins of the National Recovery Act*** (1976), is good on the trade associations.

On Henry Ford, see Allan Nevins and F. E. Hill, **Ford** (1954–1957), and Keith Sward, **The Legend of Henry Ford*** (1948). J. B. Rae, **The American Automobile Industry** (1984), and D. L. Lewis and Lawrence Goldstein (eds.), **The Automobile and American Culture** (1984), are full of interesting material. Morrell Heald, **The Social Responsibilities of Business** (1970), covers a broader period but is particularly useful for the 1920s. Farm discontent is covered in Theodore Saloutos and J. D. Hicks, **Twentieth Century Populism: Agricultural Discontent in the Middle West*** (1951), and G. C. Fite, **George N. Peek and the Fight for Farm Parity** (1954). On the election of 1928, see E. A. Moore, **A Catholic Runs for President** (1956).

PORTFOLIO EIGHT

EDWARD HOPPER *Early Sunday Morning* (1930)

American Painting, 1920–1960

JOHN MARIN *Sun Spots* (1920)

John Marin's watercolor *Sun Spots* shows the influence of modern French artists such as Monet and Picasso. In his cityscapes and landscapes, Marin used simplified, scattered shapes to paint nature's "warring, pushing, pulling" forces.

Edward Hopper's aim as an artist was "the most exact transcription" of his "most intimate impressions." With concentrated simplicity, he painted an essence of the American scene, conveying an eerie sense of loneliness. He displayed little interest in foreign artistic trends.

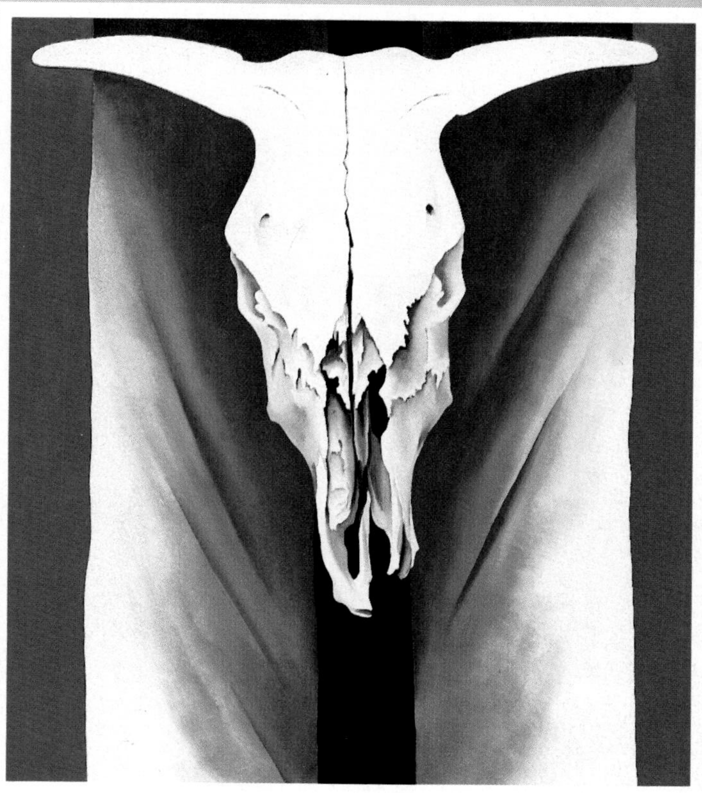

GEORGIA O'KEEFFE *Cow Skull: Red, White, and Blue* (1931)

In the 1920s Georgia O'Keeffe, America's premier woman painter, moved to the Southwest. Like Hopper, she ignored European influences and found her way to artistic abstraction through observation of her desert surroundings.

THOMAS HART BENTON *Romance* (1931/32)

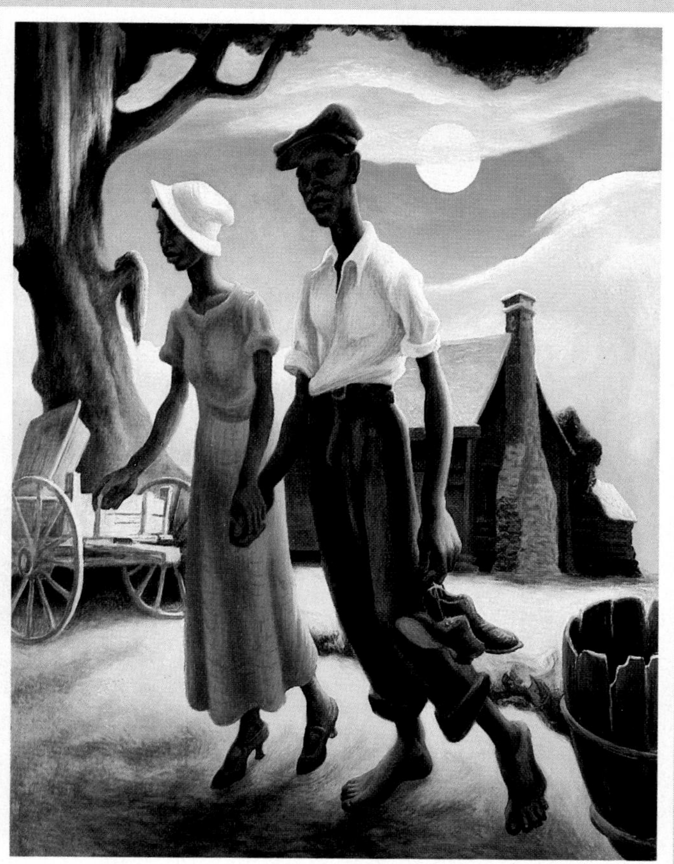

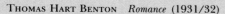

The most controversial and probably the most influential of the so-called regional painters was Thomas Hart Benton. A violently opinionated Populist, Benton denounced the entire modern movement in painting as "dirt." His main subject was his native Missouri, as exemplified in this touching 1931 scene.

In the 1930s a group of artists now known as social realists used their work to probe into the lives of ordinary people. Reginald Marsh haunted run-down New York neighborhoods during the depression to record his impressions of bums, honky-tonks, and subways. In *Twenty Cent Movie* (left) the front of a seedy movie house pulses with color and action. Louis Bouché also painted New York area scenes, here (below left) the cabin of a New Jersey ferry unloading passengers. Ben Shahn is well-known for his powerfully sympathetic portrayals of the abandoned, the homeless, the crippled, and the derelict (below).

During the New Deal, unemployed artists, along with writers and musicians and actors, were treated as a national resource that deserved public help. At its peak, the Federal Art Project employed some 5,000 artists. They produced an amazing number of works: 108,099 easel paintings; 2,566 murals; and 17,744 sculptures.

REGINALD MARSH *Twenty Cent Movie* (1936)

LOUIS BOUCHÉ *Ten Cents a Ride* (1942)

BEN SHAHN *Willis Avenue Bridge* (1940)

John Steuart Curry *Comedy* (1937)

John Steuart Curry did two murals, *Comedy* and *Tragedy*, for a Westport, Connecticut, school. *Comedy* portrays many of the comic strip characters of the thirties, including Mutt and Jeff, Popeye and Olive Oyl, and Mickey Mouse. Below Charlie Chaplin (with roller skates and cane) are Amos and Andy of radio fame, dancers Vernon and Irene Castle, Will Rogers (in the cowboy hat), and, on either side of the curtain, Curry and his wife, Kathleen.

ARSHILE GORKY *Agony* (1947)

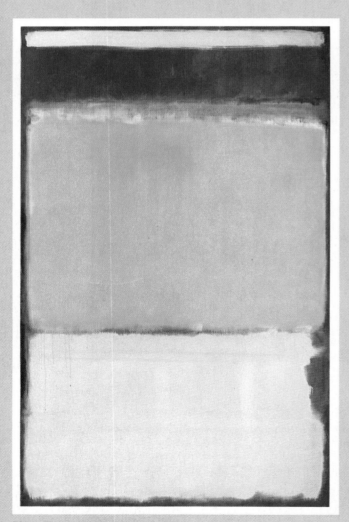

MARK ROTHKO *Number 10* (1950)

FRANZ KLINE *New York, N.Y.* (1953)

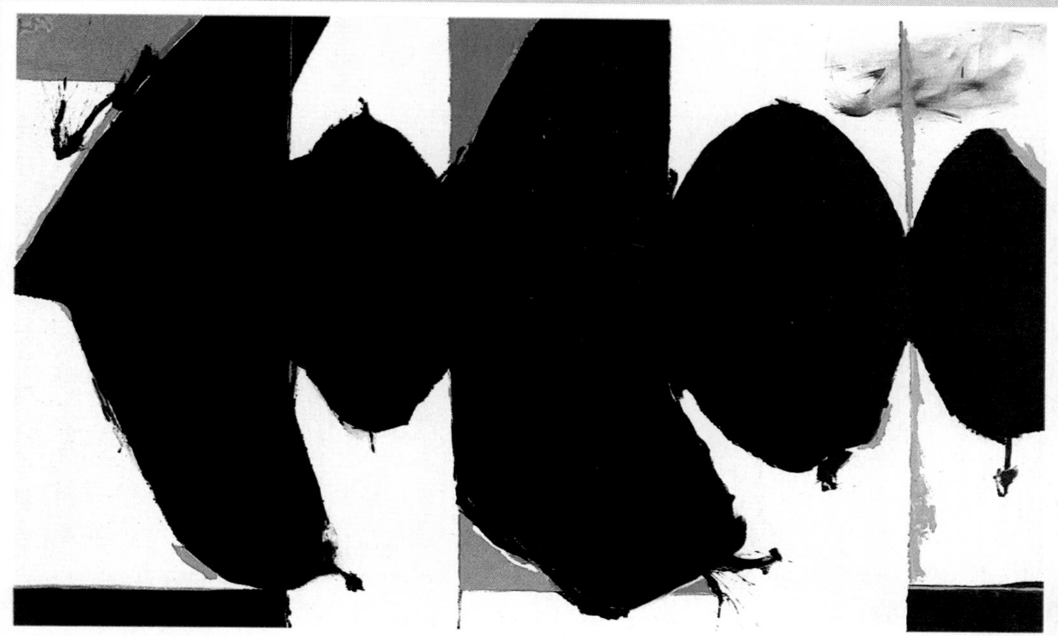

ROBERT MOTHERWELL
Elegy to the Spanish Republic 108 (1965/67)

Abstract expressionism burst on the art scene in the decade following 1945. The five artists whose work appears on these two pages were key figures in the "New York School" that developed the form..

Arshile Gorky's *Agony* (upper left) represents not a person in pain, but pain itself. Franz Kline's *New York, N.Y.* (immediate left) and Robert Motherwell's "Elegy to the Spanish Republic" (above) used actual places and events as a starting point for abstract comment. Mark Rothko pioneered "color-field abstraction," the subtle interaction of areas of color (far left). Willem de Kooning, an action painter like Jackson Pollock (see page 872), did a famous series of canvases on the theme of women (right).

WILLEM DE KOONING
Women and Bicycle (1952/53)

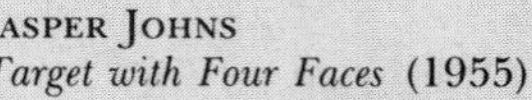

JASPER JOHNS
Target with Four Faces (1955)

Op and pop artists turned from the emotionalism of most abstract expressionism to a cool and more detached approach. Josef Albers's *Homage to the Square: Apparition* (lower left) was one of his long series of canvases studying the variations of color and dimension possible within one simple design. Jasper Johns, in *Target with Four Faces* (upper left), a precursor of pop art, used a repetitively simple and easily identified symbol, the target.

Whatever the art fashion of the moment, representational art is always in demand. The commercial uses of such work are everywhere. And serious easel painting retains a durable human appeal. The modern persistence of the realist tradition is best demonstrated by the work of Andrew Wyeth, whose paintings portray in careful detail the people and places he knows best.

JOSEF ALBERS
Homage to the Square: Apparition (1959)

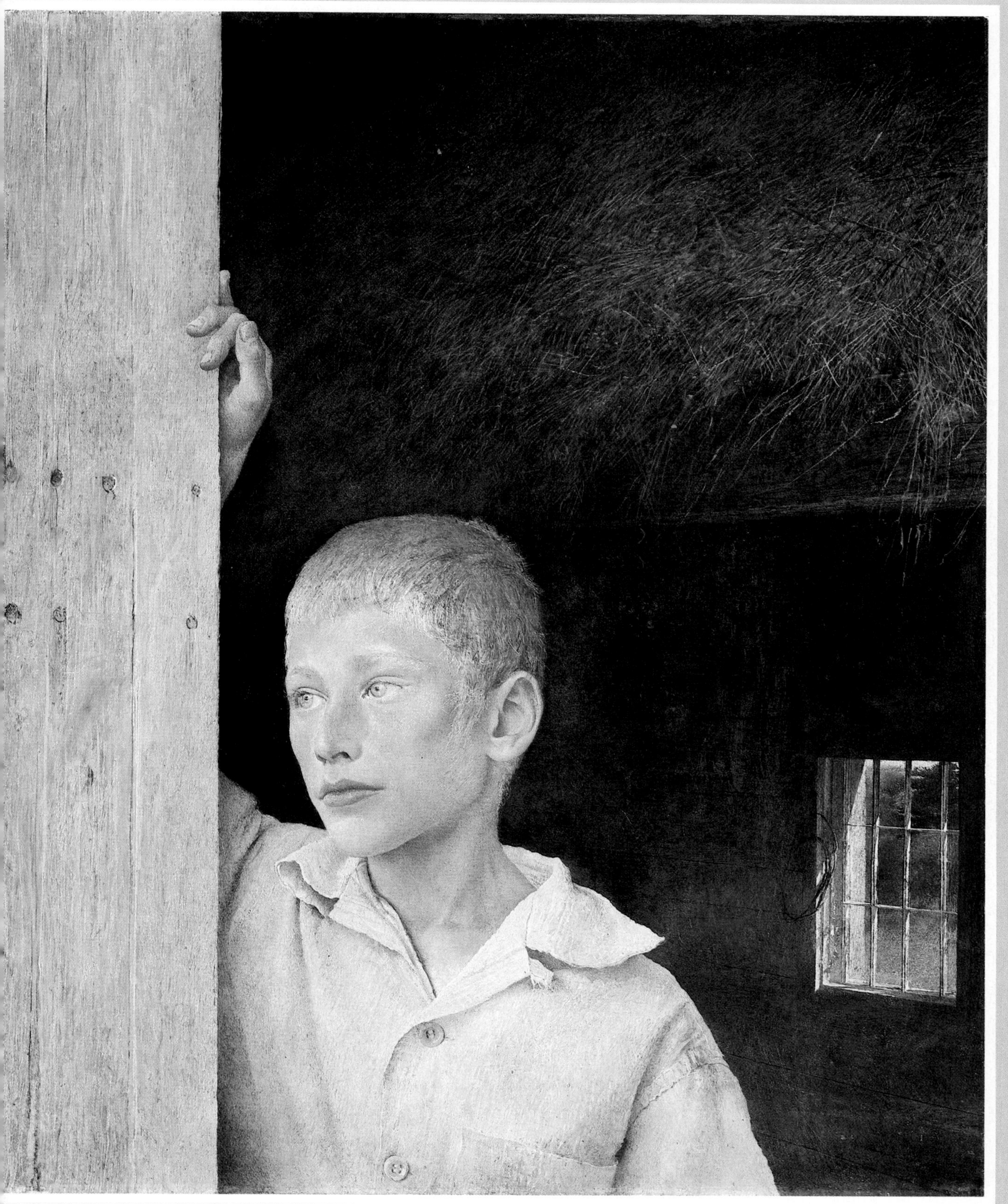

ANDREW WYETH *Albert's Son* (1959)

26
The Great Depression: 1929-1939

I have been having an interesting time here. . . . Washington seems much more intelligent and cheerful than under any recent Administration, but . . . nothing really makes much sense, because Roosevelt has no real policy. EDMUND WILSON, *critic, 1934*

In the spring of 1928, prices on the New York Stock Exchange, already at a historic high, began to surge ahead. As the presidential campaign gathered momentum, the market increased its upward pace, stimulated by the candidates' efforts to outdo each other in praising the marvels of the American economic system. "Glamour" stocks skyrocketed—Radio Corporation of America rose from under 100 to 400 between March and November. A few conservative brokers expressed alarm, warning that most stocks were grossly overpriced. The majority scoffed at such talk. "Be a bull on America," they urged. "Never sell the United States short."

During the first half of 1929 stock prices climbed still higher. A mania for speculation swept the country, thousands of small investors putting their savings in common stocks.

In September the market wavered. Amid volatile fluctuations stock averages eased downward. Most analysts contended that the Exchange was "digesting" previous gains. A prominent Harvard economist expressed the prevailing view when he said that stock prices had reached a "permanently high plateau" and would soon resume their advance.

On October 24 a wave of selling sent prices spinning. Nearly 13 million shares changed hands—a record. Bankers and politicans rallied to check the decline, as they had during the Panic of 1907 (see page 671). J. P. Morgan, Jr., rivaled the efforts of his father in that earlier crisis. President Hoover assured the people that "the business of the country . . . is on a sound and prosperous basis." But on October 29, the bottom seemed to drop out. More than 16 million shares were sold, prices plummeting. The boom was over.

Hoover and the Depression

The collapse of the stock market did not cause the depression; stocks rallied late in the year, and business activity did not begin to decline significantly until the spring of 1930. The Great Depression was a worldwide phenomenon caused chiefly by economic imbalances resulting from the chaos of the Great War. In the United States too much wealth had fallen into too few hands, with the result that consumers were unable to buy all the goods produced. The trouble came to a head mainly because of the easy-credit policies of the Federal Reserve Board and the Mellon tax structure, which favored the rich. Its effects were so profound and prolonged because the politicians (and for that matter the professional economists) did not fully understand what was happening or what to do about it.

The chronic problem of underconsumption operated to speed the downward spiral. Unable to rid themselves of mounting inventories, manufacturers closed plants and laid off workers, thereby causing demand to shrink further. Automobile output fell from 4.5 million units in 1929 to 1.1 million in 1932. When Ford closed his Detroit plants in 1931, some 75,000 workers lost their jobs, and the decline in auto production affected a host of suppliers and middlemen as well.

The financial system cracked under the strain. More than 1,300 banks closed their doors in 1930, 3,700 more during the next two years. Each failure deprived thousands of persons of funds that might have been used to buy goods; when the Bank of the United States in New York City became insolvent in December 1930, 400,000 depositors found their savings immobilized. And of course the industrial depression worsened the depression in agriculture by further reducing the demand for American foodstuffs. Every economic indicator reflected the collapse. New investments declined from $10 billion in 1929 to $1 billion in 1932, and the national income fell from over $80 billion to under $50 billion in the same brief period. Unemployment, under 1 million at the height of the boom, rose to at least 13 million.

President Hoover was an intelligent man, experienced in business matters and knowledgeable in economics. Secretary of the Treasury Mellon insisted that the economy be allowed to slide unchecked until the cycle had found its bottom. "Let the slump liquidate itself," Mellon urged. "Liquidate labor, liquidate stocks, liquidate the farmers. . . . People will work harder, live a more moral life. Values will be adjusted, and enterprising people will pick up the wrecks from less competent people." Hoover realized that such a policy would cause unbearable hardship for millions. He rejected Mellon's advice to let the depression run its course.

Hoover's program for ending the depression evolved gradually between 1929 and 1932. It called

James Rosenberg, an attorney and amateur artist, sketched this grim view of the Wall Street financial district, October 29, 1929 ("Black Tuesday"), as a Day of Judgment.

for cooperative action by businessmen, free from fear of antitrust prosection, to maintain prices and wages; for tax cuts to increase consumers' spendable income; for public works programs to stimulate production and create jobs for the unemployed; for lower interest rates to make it easier for businesses to borrow in order to expand; for federal loans to banks and industrial corporations threatened with collapse; and for aid to homeowners unable to meet mortgage payments. The president proposed measures making it easier for farmers to borrow money, and he suggested that cooperative farm marketing schemes designed to solve the problem of overproduction be supported by the government. He called for an expansion of state and local relief programs and urged all who could afford it to give more to charity. Above all he tried to restore public confidence. The economy was basically healthy; the depression was only a minor downturn; prosperity was "just around the corner."

In other words, Hoover rejected classical economics. Indeed, many laissez faire theorists attacked his handling of the depression. The English economist Lionel Robbins, writing in 1934, criticized Hoover's "grandiose buying organizations" and his efforts to maintain consumer income "at all costs." Numbers of "liberal" economists, on the other hand, praised the Hoover program.

While Hoover's plans were theoretically sound, they failed to check the economic slide, in part because of curious limitations in his conception of how they should be implemented. He placed far too much reliance on his powers of persuasion and the willingness of citizens to act in the public interest without legal compulsion. He urged manufacturers to maintain wages and keep their factories in operation, but the manufacturers, under the harsh pressure of economic realities, soon slashed wages and curtailed output sharply. He permitted the Federal Farm Board (created under the Agricultural Marketing Act of 1929) to establish semipublic stabilization corporations with authority to buy up surplus wheat and cotton, but he refused to countenance crop or acreage controls. These corporations poured out hundreds of millions of dollars without checking falling agricultural prices because farmers increased production faster than the corporations could buy up the excess for disposal abroad.

Hoover resisted proposals to shift responsibility from state and local agencies to the federal government, despite the fact—soon obvious—that the lesser government bodies lacked the resources to cope with the emergency. By 1932 the federal government, with Hoover's approval, was spending $500 million a year on public works projects, but because of the decline in state and municipal construction, the total public outlay fell nearly $1 billion below what it had been in 1930. More serious was his refusal, on constitutional grounds, to allow federal funds to be used for the relief of individuals. State and municipal agencies and private charities must take care of the needy.

Unfortunately the depression was drying up the sources of private charities just as the demands on these organizations were expanding. State and municipal agencies were swamped at a time when their capacities to tax and borrow were shrinking. By 1932 more than 40,600 Boston families were on relief (compared with 7,400 families in 1929); in Chicago 700,000 persons—40 percent of the work force—were unemployed. Only the national government possessed the power and the credit to deal adequately with the crisis. Yet Hoover would not act. He set up a committee to coordinate local relief activities but insisted on preserving what he called "the principles of individual and local responsibility." For the federal government to take over relief would "lead to the super-state where every man becomes the servant of the state and real liberty is lost."

Federal loans to businessmen were constitutional, he believed, because the money could be put to productive use and eventually repaid. When drought destroyed the crops of farmers in the South and Southwest in 1930, the government lent them money to buy seed and even food for their livestock, but Hoover would permit no direct relief for the farmers themselves. In 1932 he approved the creation of the Reconstruction Finance Corporation to lend money to banks, railroads, and insurance companies. The RFC represented an important extension of national authority, yet it was thoroughly in line with Hoover's philosophy. Its loans, secured by solid collateral, were commercial transactions, not gifts; the agency did almost nothing for individuals in need of relief. The same could be said of the Glass-Steagall Banking Act of 1932, which eased the tight credit situation by permitting Federal Reserve banks to accept a wider variety of commercial paper as security for loans. The public grew increasingly resentful of the president's doctrinaire adherence to principle while breadlines lengthened and millions of willing workers searched fruitlessly for jobs.

Hoover stressed the importance of balancing the federal budget, reasoning that since citizens had to live within their limited means in hard times, the government should set a good example. This policy was made impossible to carry out. Since the government's income fell precipitously, there was a good deal of what the economist Herbert Stein has called "fiscal stimulation by inadvertence"—by June 1931 the budget was nearly $500 million in the red. Efforts to balance the budget were also counterproductive; by reducing its expenditures the government made the depression worse.

Hoover understood the value of pumping money into a stagnant economy. He might have made a virtue of necessity. The difficulty lay in the fact that nearly all "informed" opinion believed that a balanced budget was essential to recovery. The most prestigious economists insisted on it; so did business leaders, labor leaders, and even most socialists. In 1932, when the House of Representatives refused to vote a tax increase, the Democratic Speaker compelled reconsideration of the bill by asking those "who do not want to balance the budget to rise." Not a single member did so. As late as 1939 a public opinion poll revealed that over 60 percent of the people (even 57.5 percent of the unemployed) favored reducing government expenditures in order to balance the budget. When Hoover said, "prosperity cannot be restored by raids on the public Treasury," he was wrong, but it is also wrong to criticize him for failing to understand what almost no one understood in the 1930s.

Hoover can, however, be faulted for allowing his anti-European prejudices to interfere with the implementation of his program. In 1930 Congress passed the Hawley-Smoot Tariff Act, which raised duties on most manufactured products to prohibitive levels. While more than a thousand economists joined in urging Hoover to veto this measure on the grounds that it would encourage inefficiency and stifle world trade, he signed it cheerfully. The new tariff made it impossible for European nations to earn the dollars they needed to continue making payments on their World War I debts to the United States, and it helped bring on a financial collapse in Europe in 1931. In that year Hoover wisely proposed a one-year "moratorium" on all international obligations. But the efforts of Great Britain and many other countries to save their own skins by devaluing their currencies in order to encourage foreigners to buy their goods led him to blame them for the depression itself. He seemed unable to grasp what should have been obvious to a person of his intelligence: that high American tariffs made currency devaluation almost inevitable in Europe and that the curtailment of American investment on the Continent as a result of the depression had dealt a staggering blow to the economies of all the European nations.

Much of the contemporary criticism of Hoover and a good deal of that heaped upon him by later historians was unfair. Yet his record as president shows that he was too rigid and doctrinaire, too wedded to a particular theory of government to cope effectively with the problems of the day. Since these problems were in a sense insoluble—no one possessed enough knowledge and intelligence to understand entirely what was wrong or enough authority to enforce the proper corrective measures—flexibility and a willingness to experiment were essential to any program aimed at restoring prosperity. Hoover lacked these qualities. He was his own worst enemy, being too uncompromising to get on well with the politicians and too aloof to win the confidence and affection of oridinary people. As Joan Hoff Wilson has noted, he refused "to backslap, fraternize with local supporters, kiss babies." He had too much faith in himself and his plans. When he failed to achieve the results he anticpated, he attracted, despite his devotion to duty and his concern for the welfare of the country, not sympathy but scorn.

The Economy Hits Bottom

During the spring of 1932, as the economy sounded the depths, thousands of Americans faced starvation. In Philadelphia during an 11-day period when no relief funds were available, hundreds of families existed on stale bread, thin soup, and garbage. In the nation as a whole, only about one-quarter of the unemployed were receiving any public aid. In Birmingham, Alabama, landlords in poor districts gave up trying to collect rents, preferring, one Alabama congressman told a Senate committee, "to have somebody living there free of charge rather than to have the house . . . burned up for fuel [by scavengers]." Many people were evicted, and they often gathered in ramshackle communities constructed of packing boxes, rusty sheet metal, and similar refuse on swamps, garbage dumps, and other wasteland. People began to call these places "Hoovervilles."

Thousands of tramps roamed the countryside begging for food. At the same time, food prices fell so low that farmers burned corn for fuel. In Iowa and Nebraska farmers organized Farm Holiday movements, refusing to ship their crops to market in protest against the 31-cent-a-bushel corn and 38-cent wheat. They blocked roads and rail lines, dumped milk, overturned trucks, and established picket lines to enforce their boycott. The world seemed to have been turned upside down. Professor Felix Frankfurter of the Harvard Law School remarked only half humorously that henceforth the terms B.C. and A.D. would mean "Before Crash" and "After Depression."

A bread line in Chicago. The Great Depression, an English observer said, "outraged and baffled" the nation that took it as "an article of faith . . . that America, somehow, was different from the rest of the world."

The national mood ranged from apathy to resentment. In 1931 federal immigration agents and local groups in the Southwest began rounding up Mexican-Americans and deporting them. Some of those returned to Mexico had entered the United States illegally; others had come in properly. Unemployed Mexicans were ejected because they might become public charges, those with jobs because they were presumably taking bread from the mouths of citizens. "Capitolism is dying," the philosopher Reinhold Niebuhr remarked in 1932, "and . . . it ought to die."

In June and July 1932, 20,000 veterans marched on Washington to demand immediate payment of their "adjusted compensation" bonuses. When Congress rejected their appeal, some 2,000 refused to leave, settling with their families in a jerry-built camp of shacks and tents at Anacostia Flats, a swamp bordering the Potomac. President Hoover, alarmed, charged incorrectly that the "Bonus Army" was largely composed of criminals and radicals and sent troops into the Flats to disperse it with bayonets, tear gas, and tanks. The task was accomplished amid much confusion; fortunately no one was killed. The protest had been aimless and not entirely justified, yet the spectacle of the United States government chasing unarmed veterans with tanks appalled the nation.

The unprecedented severity of the depression led some persons to favor radical economic and political changes. The disparity between the lots of the rich and the poor, always a challenge to democracy, became more striking and engendered considerable bitterness. "Unless something is done to provide employment," two labor leaders warned Hoover, "disorder . . . is sure to arise. . . . There is a growing demand that the entire business and social structure be changed because of the general dissatisfaction with the present system."

The Communist party gained few converts among farmers and industrial workers, but a considerable number of intellectuals, alienated by the trends of the twenties, responded positively to the communists' emphasis on economic planning and the total mobilization of the state to achieve social goals. Even the popular cracker-barrel humorist Will Rogers was impressed by reports of the absence of serious unemployment in Russia. "All roads lead to Moscow," the former muckraker Lincoln Steffens wrote.

Literature in the Depression

Some American novelists found Soviet communism attractive and wrote "proletarian" novels in which ordinary workers were the heroes, and stylistic niceties gave way to the rough language of the street and the factory. Most of these books were of little artistic merit and none achieved great commercial success. The best of the depression writers avoided the party line, though they were critical of many aspects of American life. One was John Dos Passos, author of the trilogy *U.S.A.* (1930–1936).

Dos Passos came from a well-to-do family of Portuguese descent. He was educated at Harvard and drove an ambulance in France during the Great War. *U.S.A.* was a massive work, rich in detail and intricately constructed, that advanced a fundamentally anticapitalist and deeply pessimistic point of view. It portrayed American society between 1900 and 1930 in broad perspective, interweaving the stories of five major characters and a galaxy of lesser figures. Throughout the narrative Dos Passos scattered capsule sketches of famous people, ranging from Andrew Carnegie and William Jennings Bryan to the movie idol Rudolph Valentino and the architect Frank Lloyd Wright. He included "newsreel" sections recounting events of the period and "camera eye" sections in which he revealed his personal reactions to the passing parade.

Dos Passos's method was relentless, cold, methodical—utterly realistic. He displayed immense craftsmanship but no sympathy for his characters or their world. *U.S.A.* was a monument to the despair and anger of liberals confronted with the Great Depression. After the depression, however, Dos Passos rapidly abandoned his radical views.

James T. Farrell, a novelist in the naturalist tradition of Theodore Dreiser, also wrote a trilogy in the thirties, the saga of *Studs Lonigan* (1932–1935). It described the squalid life of Chicago's Irish slums. Farrell's overly literal realism was full of anger and conviction and was therefore powerful. Unlike Dos Passos, he remained a radical in later, more prosperous times.

The novel that best portrayed the desperate plight of the millions impoverished by the depression was John Steinbeck's *The Grapes of Wrath* (1939), which described the fate of the Joads, an Oklahoma farm family driven by drought and bad times to abandon their land and become migratory laborers in California. Steinbeck captured the patient bewilderment of the downtrodden, the brutality bred of fear that characterized their exploiters, and the furious resentments of the radicals of the thirties. He depicted the parching blackness of the Oklahoma dust bowl, the grandeur of California, the backbreaking toil of the migrant fruit pickers, and the ultimate indignation of a people repeatedly degraded. "In the eyes of the hungry there is a growing wrath. In the souls of the people the grapes of wrath are filling and growing heavy, growing heavy for the vintage."

Like so many other writers of the thirties, Steinbeck was an angry man. "There is a crime here that goes beyond denunciation," he wrote. He had the compassion that Dos Passos and Farrell lacked, and this quality raised *The Grapes of Wrath* to the level of great tragedy. In other works, such as *Tortilla Flat* (1935) and *The Long Valley* (1938), Steinbeck described the life of California cannery workers and ranchers with moving warmth without becoming overly sentimental.

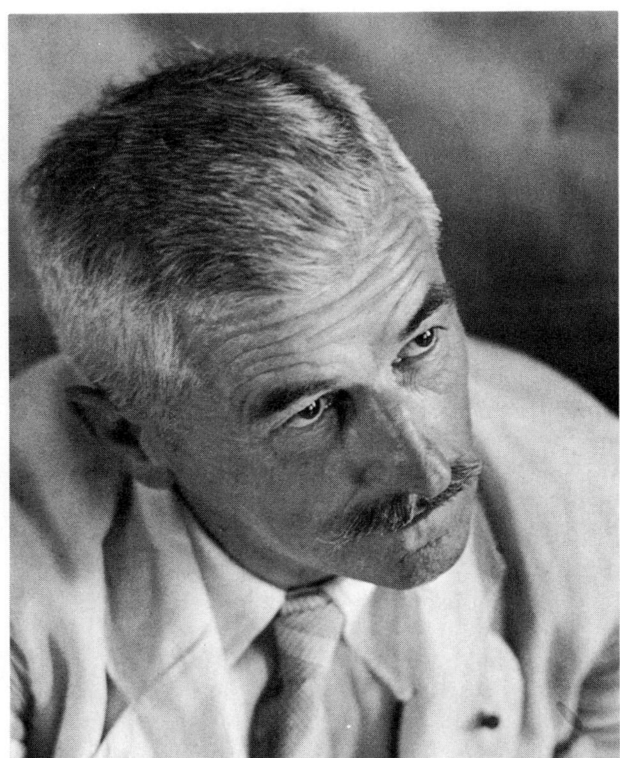

Accepting the Nobel Prize in literature, Faulkner spoke of a lifelong attempt "to create out of the materials of the human spirit something which did not exist before."

"I am completely partisan," Steinbeck wrote. "Every effort I can bring to bear is . . . at the call of the common working people."

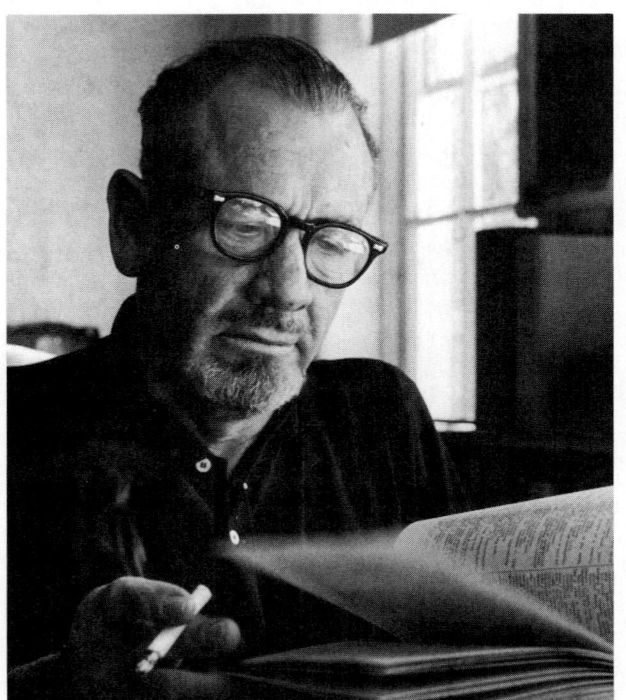

Although his work was less political than that of Dos Passos or Farrell or Steinbeck, Thomas Wolfe was another major interpreter of his times. Wolfe was born in Asheville, North Carolina, in 1900 and educated at the state university and at Harvard. A passionate, intensely troubled young man of vast but undisciplined talents, he sought to describe the kaleidoscopic character of American life, the limitless variety of the nation. "I will know this country when I am through as I know the palm of my hand, and I will put it on paper and make it true and beautiful," he boasted.

During the last ten years of his short life (he died in 1938), Wolfe wrote four novels: *Look Homeward, Angel* (1929), *Of Time and the River* (1935), and two published posthumously, *The Web and the Rock* (1939) and *You Can't Go Home Again* (1940). All were autobiographical and to some extent repetitious, for he was an unabashed egoist. Nevertheless he was a superb interpreter of contemporary society. He crammed his pages with unforgettable vignettes—a train hurtling across the Jersey meadows in the dark, a young woman clutching her skirts on a windswept corner, a group of derelicts huddled for shelter in a public toilet on a frigid night. And no writer caught more clearly the frantic pace and confusion of the great cities, the despair of the depression, the divided nature of human beings, their fears and hopes, their undirected, uncontrollable energy.

William Faulkner, probably the finest of modern American novelists, responded to the era in still another way. Born in 1897, within a year of Fitzgerald and Hemingway, like Wolfe he attained literary maturity only in the thirties. After service in the Canadian air force in World War I, he returned to his native Mississippi, working at a series of odd jobs and publishing relatively inconsequential poetry and fiction. Suddenly, between 1929 and 1932, he burst into prominence with four major novels: *The Sound and the Fury, As I Lay Dying, Sanctuary,* and *Light in August.*

Faulkner created a local world, Yoknapatawpha County, and peopled it with some of the most remarkable characters in American fiction—the Sartoris family, typical of the old southern aristocracy worn down at the heels; the Snopes clan, shrewd, unscrupulous, boorish respresentatives of the new day; and many others. He pictured vividly the South's poverty and its pride, its dreadful racial problem, the guilt and obscure passions plaguing white and black alike. He also dealt effectively with the clash of urban and rural values. Yet Faulkner was far more than a local colorist. No contemporary excelled him as a commentator on the multiple dilemmas of modern life. His characters are possessed, driven to pursue high ideals yet weighted down with their awareness of their inadequacies and their sinfulness. They are imprisoned in their surroundings however they may strive to escape them. The French novelist Simone de Beauvoir caught this aspect of Faulkner's work when she wrote that he "offered us a glimpse of fascinating depths . . . in those secret, shameless fires that rage in the bellies of men and women alike."

Although capable of humor and full of the joy of life, Faulkner was essentially a pessimist. His weakness as a writer, aside from a sometimes exasperating obscurity and verbosity, resulted from his somewhat confused view of himself and the world he described. Much of his work was passion imprisoned in words without discernible meaning; his characters continually experienced emotions too intense to be bearable, often too profound and too subtle for the natures he had given them. Nevertheless his stature was beyond question, and unlike so many other novelists of the period he maintained a high level in his later years with *The Hamlet* (1940), *Intruder in the Dust* (1948), *A Fable* (1954), and *The Reivers* (1962). He was awarded the 1949 Nobel Prize for literature.

The Election of 1932

As the end of his term approached, President Hoover seemed to grow daily more petulant and pessimistic. The depression, coming after 12 years of Republican rule, probably insured a Democratic victory in any case, but his attitude as the election neared alienated many voters and turned defeat into rout.

Confident of victory, the Democrats chose Governor Franklin Delano Roosevelt of New York as their presidential candidate. Roosevelt owed his nomination chiefly to his success as governor. Under his administration, New York had led the nation in providing relief for the needy and had enacted an impressive program of old-age pensions, unemployment insurance, and conservation and public power projects. In 1928, while Hoover was carrying New York against Smith by a wide margin, Roosevelt won election by 25,000 votes. In 1930 he swept the state by a 700,000-vote majority, double the previous record. He also had the advantage of the Roosevelt name (he was a distant cousin of the inimitable T.R.), and his sunny, magnetic personality contrasted favorably with that of the glum and colorless Hoover.

Roosevelt was far from being a radical. Although he had supported the League of Nations while campaigning for the vice-presidency in 1920, during the twenties he had not seriously challenged the basic tenets of Coolidge prosperity. He never had much difficulty adjusting his views to prevailing attitudes. For a time he even served as head of the American Construction Council, a trade association. Indeed, his life before the depression gave little indication that he understood the aspirations of ordinary people or had any deep commitment to social reform.

Roosevelt was born to wealth and social status in Dutchess County, New York, in 1882. Pampered in childhood by a doting yet domineering mother, he was educated at the exclusive Groton School and then at Harvard, where he proceeded, as his biographer Frank Freidel has written, "from one extracurricular triumph to another." Ambition as much as the desire to render public service motivated his career in politics; even after an attack of polio in 1921 left him badly crippled in both legs, he refused to abandon his hopes for high office. During the 1920s he was a hardworking member of the liberal wing of his party. He supported Smith for president in 1924 and 1928.

To some observers Roosevelt seemed rather a lightweight intellectually. When he ran for the vice-presidency, the Chicago *Tribune* commented: "If he is Theodore Roosevelt, Elihu Root is Gene Debs, and Bryan is a brewer." Twelve years later many critics judged him too irresolute, too amiable, too eager to please all factions to be a forceful leader. Herbert Hoover thought he was "ignorant but well-meaning," and the political analyst Walter Lippmann, in a now-famous observation, called him "a pleasant man who, without any important qualifications for the job, would very much like to be President."

Despite his physical handicap—he could walk only a few steps, and then only with the aid of steel braces and two canes—Roosevelt was a brilliant campaigner. He traveled back and forth across the country, radiating confidence and good humor even when directing his sharpest barbs at the Republicans. Like every great political leader, he took as much from the people as he gave them, understanding the causes of their confusion, sensing their needs. "I have looked into the faces of thousands of Americans," he told a friend. "They have the fightened look of lost children. . . . They are saying: 'We're caught in something we don't understand; perhaps this fellow can help us out.' "

Voters responded in a similar manner. "The people," one member of the Hoover administration noted, "seem to be lifting eager faces to Franklin Roosevelt, having the impression that he is talking intimately to them." But this man then added: "I am glad of his enthusiasm and buoyance but I cannot escape the sense that he really does not

Well-wishers greet the president at Warm Springs, Georgia, in 1933. The Roosevelt "magic," unfeigned and inexhaustible, amazed his associates. "I have never had contact with a man who was loved as he is," reported Secretary of the Interior Harold L. Ickes.

understand the full meaning of his own recitations."

Roosevelt soaked up information and ideas from a thousand sources—from professors like Raymond Moley and Rexford Tugwell of Columbia, from politicans like the Texan vice-presidential candidate John N. Garner, from social workers, businessmen, and lawyers. To those seeking specific answers to the questions of the day, he was seldom satisfying. On such vital matters as farm policy, the tariff, and government spending, he equivocated, contradicted himself, or remained silent.

Aided by hindsight, historians have discovered portents of much of his later program in his campaign speeches. These pronouncements, buried among dozens of conflicting generalities, often passed unnoticed at the time. He said, for example, "If starvation and dire need on the part of any of our citizens make necessary the appropriation of additional funds which would keep the budget out of balance, I shall not hesitate to . . . ask the people to authorize the expenditure of that additional amount." In the same speech he called for sharp cuts in federal spending and a balanced budget, and he castigated Hoover for presiding over "the greatest spending administration in peace time in our history."

Nevertheless Roosevelt's basic position was unmistakable. There must be a "re-appraisal of values," a "New Deal." Instead of adhering to conventional limits on the extent of federal power, the government should do whatever was necessary to protect the unfortunate and advance the public good. Lacking concrete answers, Roosevelt advocated a point of view rather than a plan: "The country needs bold, persistent experimentation. It is common sense to take a method and try it. If it fails, admit it frankly and try another. But above all, try something."

The popularity of this approach was demonstrated in November. Hoover, who had lost only eight states in 1928, won only six, all in the Northeast, in 1932. Roosevelt amassed 22.8 million votes to Hoover's 15.8 million and carried the electoral college, 472 to 59.

During the interval between the election and Roosevelt's inauguration in March 1933, the Great Depression reached its nadir. The holdover "lame duck" Congress, last of its kind, proved incapable of effective action.* President Hoover, perhaps understandably, hesitated to institute changes without the cooperation of his successor. Roosevelt, for equally plausible reasons, refused to accept responsibility before assuming power officially. The nation, curiously apathetic in the face of so much suffering, drifted aimlessly, like a sailboat in a flat calm.

Then the banking system disintegrated—no word less strong portrays the extent of the collapse. Starting in the rural West and spreading to major cities like Detroit and Baltimore, a financial panic swept the land. Depositors lined up before the doors of even the soundest institutions, desperate to withdraw their savings. Hundreds of banks were forced to close. In February, to check the panic, the governor of Michigan declared a "bank holiday," shutting every bank in the state for eight days. Maryland, Kentucky, California, and a number of other states followed suit; by inauguration day four-fifths of the states had suspended all banking operations. So great was the fear and confusion that the New York Stock Exchange was closed on March 4.

The Hundred Days

Something drastic had to be done. The most conservative business leaders were as ready for government intervention as the most advanced radicals. Partisanship, while not disappearing, was for once subordinated to broad national needs. A sign of this change came in February, even before Roosevelt took office, when Congress submitted the Twenty-first Amendment, putting an end to prohibition, to the states. Before the year was out the necessary three-quarters of the states had ratified it. The prohibition era was over.

But it was unquestionably Franklin D. Roosevelt who provided the spark that reenergized the American people. His inaugural address, delivered in a raw mist beneath dark March skies, reassured the country and at the same time stirred it to action: "The only thing we have to fear is fear itself. . . .

---

* The Twentieth Amendment (1933) provided for convening new Congresses in January instead of the following December. It also advanced the date of the president's inauguration from March 4 to January 20.

Our true destiny is not to be ministered unto but to minister to ourselves and to our fellow men. . . . This Nation asks for action, and action now. . . . I assume unhesitatingly the leadership of this great army of our people. . . ." Many such lines punctuated the brief address, which concluded with a stern pledge: "In the event that Congress shall fail . . . I shall not evade the clear course of duty that will then confront me. I shall ask the Congress for the one remaining instrument to meet the crisis—broad Executive power to wage a war against the emergency."

The inaugural captured the heart of the country; almost half a million letters of congratulation poured into the White House. When Roosevelt summoned Congress into special session on March 9, the legislators outdid one another to enact his proposals into law. "I had as soon start a mutiny in the face of a foreign foe as . . . against the program of the President," one representative declared. In the following "Hundred Days" (Congress adjourned on June 16), an impressive body of legislation was placed on the statute books. Opposition, in the sense of an organized group committed to resisting the administration, simply did not exist.

Roosevelt had the power and the will to act but no comprehensive plan of action. He and his eager congressional collaborators proceeded in a dozen directions at once, sometimes wisely, sometimes not, often at cross-purposes with themselves and one another. One of the first administration measures was the Economy Act, which reduced the salaries of federal employees by 15 percent and cut various veterans' benefits. Such belt-tightening measures could only make the depression worse.

Although Roosevelt never entirely got over the urge to economize in hard times, most of the New Deal programs were designed to stimulate the economy. Untangling the national financial mess was the most immediate task. On March 5 Roosevelt declared a nationwide bank holiday and placed an embargo on the exportation of gold. Within hours after it convened, Congress passed an emergency banking bill confirming these measures, outlawing the hoarding of gold, and giving the president broad power over the operations of the Federal Reserve system.

To explain the complexities of the banking problem to the public, Roosevelt delivered the first of his "fireside chats" over a national radio network. "I want to talk for a few minutes with the people of the United States about banking," he explained. His warmth and steadiness reassured millions of listeners. A plan for reopening the banks under Treasury Department licenses was devised, and soon most of them were functioning again, public confidence in their solvency restored. In April, Roosevelt took the country off the gold standard, hoping thereby to cause prices to rise. Before the session ended, Congress established the Federal Deposit Insurance Corporation to guarantee bank deposits. It also forced the separation of investment banking and commercial banking concerns while extending the power of the Federal Reserve Board over both types of institutions, and it created the Home Owners Loan Corporation to refinance mortgages and prevent foreclosures. It passed a Federal Securities Act requiring promoters to make public full financial information about new stock issues and giving the Federal Trade Commission the right to regulate such transactions.*

After the adjournment of Congress, the government began buying gold on the open market. When this policy failed to push up the price of gold, Congress, in January 1934, passed the Gold Reserve Act, which gave the president the power to fix the price of gold by proclamation. Roosevelt promptly set the price at $35 an ounce, an increase of about 40 percent.

Problems of unemployment and industrial stagnation had high priority during the Hundred Days. Congress appropriated $500 million for relief of the needy, and it created the Civilian Conservation Corps to provide jobs for men between the ages of 18 and 25 in reforestation and other conservation projects. To stimulate industry, Congress passed one of its most controversial measures, the National Industrial Recovery Act (NIRA). Besides establishing the Public Works Administration with authority to spend $3.3 billion, this law permitted manufacturers to draw up industrywide codes of "fair business practices." Under the law producers could agree to raise prices and limit production without violating the antitrust laws. The law gave

* In 1934 this task was transferred to the new Securities and Exchange Commission, which was given broad authority over the activities of stock exchanges.

workers the protection of minimum wage and maximum hours regulations and guaranteed them the right "to organize and bargain collectively through representatives of their own choosing," an immense stimulus to the union movement.

The NIRA was a variant on the idea of the corporate state. This concept envisaged a system of industrywide organizations of capitalists and workers (supervised by the government) that would resolve conflicts internally, thereby avoiding wasteful economic competition and dangerous social clashes. It was an outgrowth of the trade association idea, although Hoover, who had supported *voluntary* associations, denounced it because of its compulsory aspects. It was also similar to experiments being carried out by the fascist dictator Benito Mussolini in Italy and by the Nazis in Adolf Hitler's Germany. It did not, of course, turn America into a fascist state, but it did herald an increasing concentration of economic power in the hands of interest groups, both industrialists' organizations and labor unions.

The act created a government agency, the National Recovery Administration (NRA), to supervise the drafting and operation of the business codes. Drafting posed difficult problems, first because each industry insisted on tailoring the agreements to its special needs and second because most manufacturers were unwilling to accept all the provisions of Section 7a of the law dealing with the rights of labor. While thousands of employers agreed to the pledge "We Do Our Part" in order to receive the Blue Eagle symbol of NRA, many were more interested in the monopolistic aspects of the act than in boosting wages and encouraging unionization. In practice, the codes were drawn up by the largest manufacturers in each industry. General Hugh Johnson, the head of NRA, was soon fulminating against "chiselers." His impetuosity and his violent tongue did much to destroy whatever spirit of cooperation the manufacturers possessed. After Johnson had been a year in office, President Roosevelt forced his resignation.

The effects of NIRA were both more and less than the designers of the system had intended. In a sense it tried to accomplish the impossible—to change the very nature of business ethics and control the everyday activities of millions of individual enterprises. At the practical level, it did not end the depression. There was a brief upturn in the spring of 1933, but the expected revival of industry did not take place; in nearly every case the dominant producers in each industry used their power to raise prices and limit production rather than to hire more workers and increase output.

Beginning with the cotton textile code, however, the agreements succeeded in doing away with the centuries-old problem of child labor in industry. They established the principle of federal regulation of wages and hours and led to the organization of thousands of workers, even in industries where unions had seldom been significant. Within a year John L. Lewis's United Mine Workers expanded from 150,000 members to a half a million. About 100,000 automobile workers joined unions, as did a comparable number of steelworkers.

Labor leaders cleverly used the NIRA to persuade workers that the popular President Roosevelt *wanted* them to join unions—which was something of an overstatement. In 1935, because the conservative and craft-oriented AFL had displayed little enthusiasm for enrolling unskilled workers on an industrywide basis, John L. Lewis, together with officials of the garment trade unions, formed the Committee for Industrial Organization (CIO) and set out to rally workers in each of these mass-production industries into one union without regard for craft lines, a far more effective method of organization. The AFL expelled these unions, however, and in 1938 the CIO became the Congress of Industrial Organizations. Soon it rivaled the AFL in size and importance.

Roosevelt was more concerned about the plight of the farmers than that of any other group in the country because he believed that the nation was becoming overcommitted to industry. The New Deal farm program, incorporated in the Agricultural Adjustment Act of May 1933, combined compulsory restrictions on production with government subsidies to growers of wheat, cotton, tobacco, pork, and a few other staple crops. The money for these payments was raised by levying processing taxes on middlemen such as flour millers. The object was to lift agricultural prices to "parity" with industrial prices, the ratio in most cases being based on the levels of 1909–1914, when farmers had been reasonably prosperous. In return for withdrawing part of their land from cultivation, farmers received "rental" payments from the Agricultural Adjustment Administration (AAA).

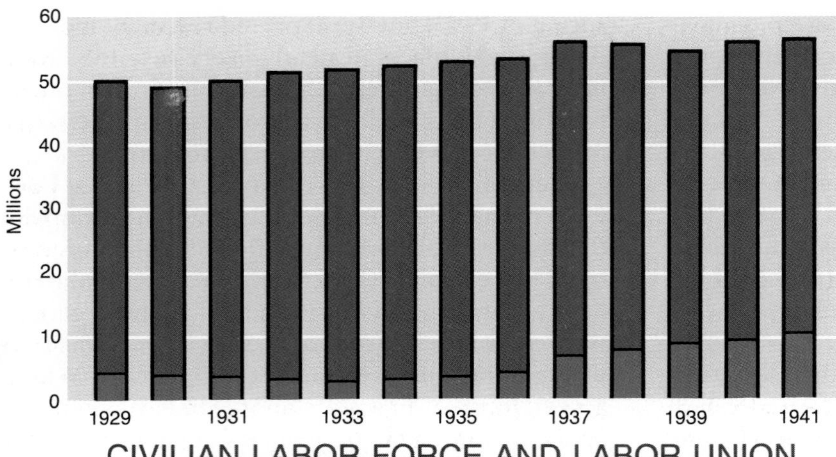

The green portion of the vertical bars represents the number of civilian labor force workers in unions, as against the total work force. Union membership more than doubled in the years from 1937 to 1941, from less than 5 million to more than 10.

Since the 1933 crops were growing when the law was passed, Secretary of Agriculture Henry A. Wallace, son of Harding's secretary of agriculture and himself an experienced farmer and plant geneticist, decided to pay farmers to destroy the crops in the field. Cotton planters plowed up 10 million acres, receiving $100 million in return. Six million baby pigs and 200,000 pregnant sows were slaughtered. Such ruthlessness appalled observers, particularly when they thought of the millions of hungry Americans who could have eaten all that pork.

Thereafter, limitation of acreage proved sufficient to raise some agricultural prices considerably. Tobacco farmers benefited and so did those who raised corn and hogs. The price of wheat also rose, though more because of bad harvests than the AAA program. But dairy farmers and cattlemen were hurt by the law, as were the railroads (which had less freight to haul) and of course consumers. Many farmers insisted that NRA was raising the cost of manufactured goods more than AAA was raising the prices they received for their crops. "While the farmer is losing his pants to his creditors," one Iowan complained, "NRA is rolling up his shirt. [Soon] we'll have a nudist colony." A far more serious weakness of the program was its failure to assist tenant farmers and sharecroppers, many of whom lost their livelihoods completely when owners took land out of production to obtain AAA payments. Yet acreage restrictions and mortgage relief helped thousands. In addition, the farm program was a remarkable attempt to bring order to the chaotic agricultural economy. One New Deal official described the AAA as "the greatest single experiment in economic planning under capitalist conditions ever attempted by a democracy in times of peace." This was an overstatement. The AAA was a drastic change of *American* policy, but foreign producers of coffee, sugar, tea, rubber, and other staples had adopted the same techniques of restricting output and subsidizing growers well before the United States did.

Another striking achievement of the Hundred Days was the creation of the Tennessee Valley Authority (TVA). During World War I the government had constructed a hydroelectric plant at Muscle Shoals, Alabama, where the Tennessee River plunges 130 feet in a 40-mile stretch, to provide power for factories manufacturing synthetic nitrate explosives. After 1920 farm groups and public power enthusiasts, led by Senator George W. Norris of Nebraska, had blocked administration plans to turn these facilities over to private capitalists. Their efforts to have the site operated by the government had been defeated by presidential vetoes.

Roosevelt wanted to have the entire Tennessee Valley area incorporated into a broad experiment in social planning. Besides expanding the hydroelectric plants at Muscle Shoals and developing nitrate manufacturing in order to produce cheap fertilizers, he envisioned a coordinated program of soil conservation, reforestation, and industrialization. Since the Tennessee River flowed through seven states, national control of the project was essential.

Over the objections of private power companies, led by Wendell L. Willkie of the Commonwealth and Southern Corporation, Congress passed the TVA Act in May 1933. This law created a board authorized to build dams, power plants, and transmission lines and sell fertilizers and electricity to individuals and local communities. The board could undertake flood control, soil conservation, and reforestation projects and improve the navigation of the river. While TVA never became the comprehensive regional planning organization some of its sponsors had anticipated, it improved the standard of living of millions of inhabitants of the valley. In addition to producing electricity and fertilizers and providing a "yardstick" whereby the efficiency—and thus the rates—of private power companies could be tested, it took on other functions ranging from the eradication of malaria to the development of recreational facilities.

The New Deal Spirit

By the end of the Hundred Days the country had made up its mind about Roosevelt's New Deal, and despite the vicissitudes of the next decade, it never really changed it. A large majority labeled the New Deal a solid success. Considerable recovery had taken place, but more basic was the fact that Roosevelt, recruiting an army of forceful officials to staff the new government agencies, had infused his administration with a spirit of bustle and optimism. The director of the presidential Secret Service unit, returning to the White House on inauguration day after escorting Herbert Hoover to the railroad station, found the executive mansion "transformed during my absence into a gay place, full of people who oozed confidence." Washington was changed, one observer noted, "from a placid leisurely Southern town . . . into a gay, breezy, sophisticated and metropolitan center."

Dozens of people who lived through those stirring times have left records that reveal the New Deal spirit. "Come at once to Washington," Senator Robert La Follette, Jr., son of "Fighting Bob," telegraphed Donald Richberg, an old Theodore Roosevelt progressive. "Great things are under way." When Richberg arrived, he found his friends "seething with excitement and anticipation." I have

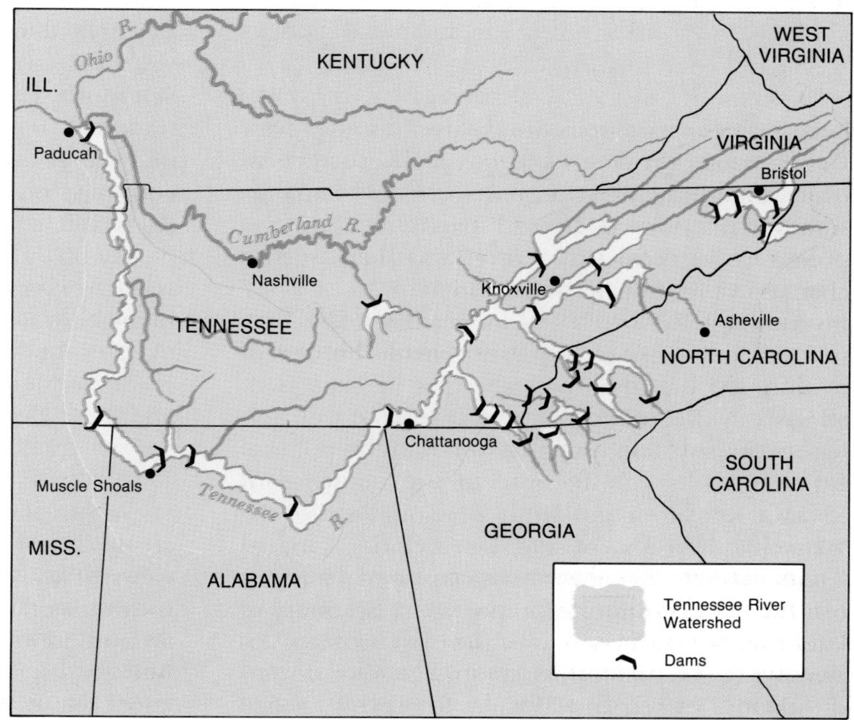

THE TENNESSEE VALLEY AUTHORITY

Workers at the Carnegie Steel Company plant in Pittsburgh give a warm welcome to Frances Perkins, FDR's secretary of labor. She had been a prominent social worker and reformer in the Progressive Era.

been in a constant spin of activity," another New Dealer wrote a friend. "I feel as if I were alive all over, and that this cockeyed world is taking us somewhere." Justice Harlan Fiske Stone of the Supreme Court recorded: "Never was there such a change in the transfer of government."

Although Roosevelt was not much of an intellectual, his openness to suggestion made him eager to draw on the ideas and energies of experts of all sorts. New Deal agencies soon teemed with college professors and young lawyers without political experience. Largely because of the influence of Eleanor Roosevelt and Molly Dewson, head of the Women's Division of the Democratic National Committee, the administration employed a number of women in positions of importance. Secretary of Labor Frances Perkins was the first woman appointed to a Cabinet post, and there were dozens of others; Dewson and Eleanor Roosevelt headed an informal but effective "network"—women in key posts who kept in touch constantly, always seeking to place reform-minded women in government jobs. (According to the historian William H. Chafe, "Washington seemed like a perpetual convention of social workers as women . . . [took] on government assignments.") Molly Dewson, a close friend of the Roosevelts, became a major force in the Democratic party. She won a larger influence for women in conventions and campaigns and a larger share of the "spoils" that came with victory. Between 1932 and 1938 the number of women postmasters increased 50 percent.

Roosevelt himself seemed to have been "transfigured," one reporter said, "from a man of charm and buoyancy to one of dynamic aggressiveness." During the first days of the New Deal the financial expert Norman H. Davis, who had known Roosevelt since the time of their joint service under Woodrow Wilson, encountered a mutual friend on the White House steps. "That fellow in there is not the fellow we used to know," he said. "There's been a miracle here."

The New Deal lacked any consistent ideological base. While the so-called Brains Trust (a group of college professors headed by Raymond Moley, a Columbia political scientist, that included Columbia economists Rexford G. Tugwell and Adolf A. Berle, Jr., and a number of others) attracted a great deal of attention, theorists never impressed Roosevelt much. His New Deal drew on the old populist tradition, as seen in its antipathy to bankers and its willingness to adopt schemes for inflating the currency; on the New Nationalism of Theodore Roosevelt in its dislike of competition and its deemphasis of the antitrust laws; and on the ideas of social workers trained in the Progressive Era. Techniques developed by the Wilsonians also found a place in the system: Louis D. Brandeis had considerable influence on Roosevelt's financial reforms, and New Deal labor policy grew directly out of the experience of the War Labor Board of 1917–1918.

Within the administrative maze that Roosevelt created, rival bureaucrats battled to enforce their views. The "spenders," led by Tugwell, clashed with those favoring strict economy, who gathered around Lewis Douglas, director of the budget. Blithely disregarding logically irreconcilable differences, Roosevelt mediated between the factions, deciding this time in favor of one, next in favor of the other. Washington became a battleground for dozens of special interest groups: the Farm Bureau Federation, the unions, the trade associations, the silver miners. William E. Leuchtenburg has described New Deal policy as "interest-group democracy"; another historian, Ellis W. Hawley, called it "counterorganization" policy aimed at creating "monopoly power" among groups previously unorganized, such as farmers and industrial workers. While, as Leuchtenburg says, the system was superior to that of Roosevelt's predecessors—who had allowed one interest, big business, to predominate—it slighted the unorganized majority. NRA aimed frankly at raising the prices paid by consumers of manufactured goods; the AAA processing tax came ultimately from the pocketbooks of ordinary citizens. Yet the public assumed that Roosevelt's objective was to improve the lot of all classes of society and that he was laboring imaginatively in pursuit of this goal.

The Unemployed

At least 9 million persons were still without work in 1934, yet the Democrats confounded the political experts, including their own, by increasing their already large majorities in both houses of Congress in the 1934 elections. All the evidence indicates that most of the jobless continued to support the administration. Their loyalty can best be explained by Roosevelt's unemployment policies.

In May 1933 Congress had established the Federal Emergency Relief Administration and given it $500 million to be dispensed through state relief organizations. Roosevelt appointed Harry L. Hopkins, an eccentric but brilliant and dedicated social worker, to direct FERA. Hopkins insisted that the unemployed needed jobs, not handouts. In November he persuaded Roosevelt to create a Civil Works Administration, and within a month he put more than 4 million persons to work building and repairing roads and public buildings, teaching, decorating the walls of post offices with murals, and utilizing their special skills in dozens of other ways.

The cost of this program frightened Roosevelt—Hopkins spent about $1 billion in less than five months—and he soon abolished the CWA. But an extensive public works program was continued throughout 1934 under FERA. Despite charges that many of the projects were "boondoggles," thousands of roads, bridges, schools, and other valuable structures were built or refurbished, and the morale of several million otherwise jobless workers was immeasurably raised. Even those who did not benefit directly took the program as an indication of

Unemployment of non–farm workers reached nearly 40 percent by early 1933. The Federal Employment Relief Act (FERA) of May 1933 was followed by the Civil Works Administration (CWA) later that year, and in turn by the Works Progress Administration (WPA) in April of 1935.

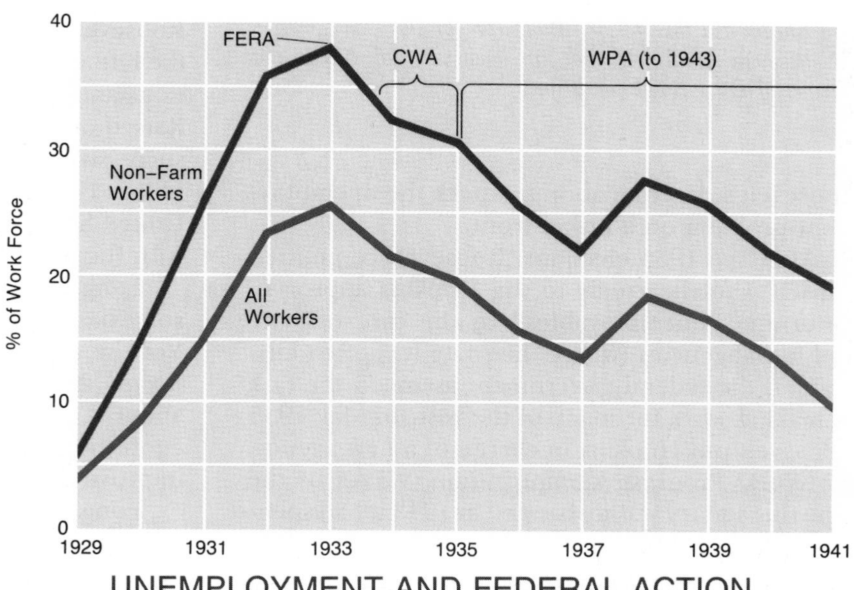

UNEMPLOYMENT AND FEDERAL ACTION, 1929–1941

YEARS OF DUST
DUST STORM
RESETTLEMENT ADMINISTRATION
Rescues Victims
Restores Land to Proper Use

Ben Shahn did this 1937 lithograph for the government's Resettlement Administration, an agency established to aid victims of Dust Bowl conditions.

Roosevelt's determination to attack the unemployment problem on a broad front.

After the 1934 elections, Roosevelt committed himself wholeheartedly to the Hopkins approach. Returning "unemployables" to the care of state and local agencies (where their fate was often miserable), the federal government assumed the task of making work for many of the rest. In May 1935 Roosevelt put Hopkins in charge of a new agency, the Works Progress Administration (WPA). By the time this agency was disbanded in 1943 it had spent $11 billion and found employment for 8.5 million persons. Besides building public works, WPA developed the Federal Theatre Project, which put thousands of actors, directors, and stagehands to work; the Federal Writers' Project, which turned out valuable guidebooks, collected local lore, and published about 1,000 books and pamphlets; and the Federal Art Project, which employed needy painters and sculptors. In addition, the National Youth Administration created part-time jobs for more than 2 million high school and college students and a larger number of other youths who could not technically be classified as unemployed but who needed financial help.

WPA did not reach all the unemployed. At no time during the New Deal years did unemployment fall below 10 percent of the work force, and in some places it was much higher. Unemployment in Boston, for instance, ranged between 20 and 30 percent throughout the 1930s. Like so many New Deal programs, WPA did not go far enough, chiefly because Roosevelt could not escape his fear of unbalancing the budget drastically. Halfway measures did not provide the massive stimulus the economy needed. The president also hesitated to pay adequate wages to WPA workers and to undertake projects that might compete with private enterprises for fear of offending business. Yet his caution did him no good politically; the business interests he sought to placate were becoming increasingly hostile to the New Deal.

The Extremists

Roosevelt's moderation roused extremists both on the left and on the right. The most formidable was Lousiana's Senator Huey Long, the "Kingfish." Raised on a farm in northern Louisiana, Long was successively a traveling salesman, a lawyer, state railroad commissioner, governor, and, after 1930, United States senator. By 1933 he ruled Louisiana with the absolutism of an oriental monarch.

Long was a controversial figure in his day and so he has remained. He was certainly a demagogue. Yet the plight of all poor people concerned him deeply. More important, he tried to do something about it. His record in Louisiana is a mixture of egotism, sordid politicking, and genuine efforts to improve the lot of the poor, black as well as white.

Long did not question segregation or white supremacy, nor did he suggest that Louisiana blacks should be allowed to vote. He used the word *nigger* with total unself-consciousness, even when addressing northern black leaders. But he treated black-baiters with scathing contempt. When Hiram W. Evans, imperial wizard of the Ku Klux Klan, announced his intention to campaign against him in Louisiana, Long told reporters; "Quote me as saying that that Imperial bastard will never set foot in Louisiana, and that when I call him a sonofabitch I am not using profanity, but am referring to the circumstances of his birth."

As a reformer, Long stood in the populist tradition; he hated bankers and "the interests." He believed that poor people, regardless of color, should have a chance to earn a decent living and get an education. His arguments were simplistic, patronizing, possibly insincere, but effective. "Don't say I'm working for niggers," he told one northern journalist. "I'm for the poor man—all poor men. Black and white, they all gotta have a chance. . . . 'Every Man a King'—that's my slogan."

Raffish, totally unrestrained, yet shrewd—a fellow southern politican called him "the smartest lunatic I ever saw"—Long had supported the New Deal at the start, but partly because he thought Roosevelt too conservative and partly because of his own ambition, he soon broke with the administration. While Roosevelt was probably more hostile to the big financiers than to any other interest, Long denounced him as "a phoney" and a stooge of Wall Street. "I can take him," he boasted in a typical sally. "His mother's watching him, and she won't let him go too far, but I ain't got no mother left, and if I had, she'd think anything I said was all right."

By 1935 Long's "Share-Our-Wealth" movement had a membership of over 4.6 million. His program called for the confiscation of family fortunes of more than $5 million and a tax of 100 percent on incomes of over $1 million a year. The money thus collected would be enough to buy every family a "homestead" (a house, a car, and other necessities) and provide an annual family income of $2,000 to $3,000, plus old-age pensions, educational benefits, and veterans' pensions. In addition Long proposed that the hours of labor be limited in order to make more jobs and that a farm price-support program be established. As the 1936 election approached, he planned to organize a third party to split the liberal vote. He assumed that the Republicans would win the election and so botch the job of fighting the depression that he could sweep the country in 1940.

Less powerful than Long but more widely influential was Father Charles E. Coughlin, the "Radio Priest." A big, genial Irishman of Canadian birth, Coughlin in 1926 began braodcasting a weekly religious message over station WJR in Detroit. His mellifluous voice and orotund rhetoric won him a huge national audience, and the depression gave him a secular cause. In 1933 he had been an eager New Dealer, but his dislike of New Deal financial policies—he believed that inflating the currency drastically would end the depression—and his need for ever more sensational ideas to hold his radio audience from week to week led him to turn against the New Deal. By 1935 he was calling Roosevelt a "great betrayer and liar."

Although Coughlin's National Union for Social Justice was especially appealing to Catholics, it attracted people of every faith, particularly in the lower-middle-class districts of the big cities. Some of his sensational radio talks caused more than a million people to send him messages of congratulation; contributions amounting to perhaps $500,000 a year flooded his headquarters. Coughlin attacked bankers, New Deal planners, Roosevelt's farm program, and the alleged sympathy of the administration for communists and Jews. His program resembled fascism more than any leftist philosophy, but he posed a threat, especially in combination with Long, to the continuation of Democratic rule.

Another rapidly growing movement alarmed the Democrats in 1934–1935: Dr. Francis E. Townsend's campaign for "Old-Age Revolving Pensions." Townsend, a retired California physician, who was colorless and low-keyed, had an oversimplified and therefore appealing "solution" to the nation's troubles. The pitiful state of thousands of elderly persons, whose job prospects were even dimmer than those of the mass of the unemployed, he found shocking. "We owe a decent living to the older people," he insisted. He advocated paying every person 60 and over a pension of $200 a month, the only conditions being that the pensioners not hold jobs and that they spend the entire sum within 30 days. Their purchases, he argued, would stimulate production, thereby creating new jobs and revitalizing the economy. A stiff transactions tax, collected whenever any commodity changed hands, would pay for the program.

Economists quickly pointed out that with about 10 million persons eligible for the Townsend pen-

Senator Huey Long in a typical energetic speaking pose. Father Charles Coughlin, the "Radio Priest," was photographed in Detroit as he promoted his National Union for Social Justice.

sions, the cost would amount to $24 billion a year, roughly half the national income. But among the elderly the scheme proved exrtremely popular. Townsend Clubs, their proceedings conducted in the spirit of revivalist camp meetings, flourished everywhere, and the *Townsend National Weekly* reached a circulation of over 200,000. Although most Townsendites were anything but radical politically, their plan, like Long's Share-Our-Wealth scheme, would have revolutionized the distribution of wealth in the country. On the one hand, the movement reflected a reactionary spirit like that of religious fundamentalists, on the other, the emergence of a new force in American society. With medical advances lengthening the average life span, the percentage of old people in the population was rising. The breakdown of close family ties in an increasingly mobile society now caused many of these citizens to be cast adrift to live out their last years poor, sick, idle, and alone. Dr. Townsend's program focused the attention of the country on a new problem—one it has not yet resolved.

With the possible exception of Long, the extremists had little understanding of practical affairs. (It could be said that Townsend knew what to do with money but not how to get it and Coughlin knew how to get money but not what to do with it.) Collectively they represented a threat to Roosevelt; their success helped to make the president see that he must move boldly to restore good times or face serious political trouble in 1936.

Political imperatives had much to do with his decision, and the influence of Justice Brandeis and his disciples, notably Felix Frankfurter, was great. They urged Roosevelt to abandon his probusiness programs, especially NRA, and stress restoring competition and taxing corporations more heavily. The fact that most businessmen were turning away from him encouraged the president to accept this advice; so did the Supreme Court's decision in *Schecter* v. *United States* (May 1935), which declared the National Industrial Recovery Act unconstitutional. (The case involved the provisions of the NRA Live Poultry Code; the Court voided the act on the grounds that Congress had delegated too much legislative power to the code authorities and that the defendants, four brothers engaged in slaughtering chickens in New York City, were not engaged in interstate commerce.)

The Second New Deal

Existing laws had failed to end the depression; extremists were luring away some of Roosevelt's supporters; conservatives had failed to appreciate his moderation; the Supreme Court was undermining his achievements. For these many reasons, Roosevelt, in June, launched what historians call the Second New Deal.

The Second Hundred Days was one of the most productive periods in the history of American legislation. The National Labor Relations Act—commonly known as the Wagner Act—restored the labor guarantees wiped out by the Schechter decision. It gave workers the right to bargain collectively and prohibited employers from interfering with union organizational activities in their factories. A National Labor Relations Board (NLRB) was established to supervise plant elections and designate successful unions as official bargaining agents when a majority of the workes approved. It was difficult to force some big corporations to bargain "in good faith," as the law required, but the NLRB could conduct investigations of employer practices and issue cease and desist orders when "unfair" activities came to light. Repeatedly the NLRB forced corporations to rehire workers discharged for union activities. The law gave union leaders great control over the rank and file, and while in the long run this produced serious problems, its immediate effect was to make labor more powerful.

The Social Security Act of August 1935 set up a system of old-age insurance, financed partly by a tax on wages (paid by workers) and partly by a tax on payrolls (paid by employers). It created a state-federal system of unemployment insurance, similarly financed. Liberal critics considered this social security system inadequate because it did not cover agricultural workers, domestics, self-employed persons, and some other groups particularly in need of its benefits. Health insurance was not included, and because the size of pensions depended on the amount earned, the lowest-paid workers could not count on much support after reaching 65. Yet the law was of major significance. Over the years the pension payments were increased and the classes of workers covered expanded.

Among other important laws enacted at this time were a new banking act and a Public Utility Holding Company Act. The former strengthened the control of the Federal Reserve Board (renamed the Board of Governors) over member banks and over commercial credit and interest rates. The latter outlawed the pyramiding of control of gas and electricity companies through the use of holding companies and gave federal commissions the power to regulate the rates and financial practices of these companies. The hotly debated "death sentence" clause of the holding company law provided for the dismemberment of all utility complexes more than twice removed from the actual operating companies and authorized the Securities and Exchange Commission to break up smaller ones that could not demonstrate that their existence served some socially useful purpose.

The Rural Electrification Administration (REA), created by executive order, also began to function during this remarkable period. REA lent money at low interest rates to utility companies and to farmer cooperatives interested in bringing electricity to rural areas. When REA went into operation, only one farm in ten had electricity; by 1950 only one in ten did not.

Another important measure was the Wealth Tax Act of August 1935, which, while not the "soak-the-rich" measure both its supporters and its opponents claimed, raised taxes on large incomes considerably. Estate and gift taxes were increased. Stiffer taxes on corporate profits reflected the Brandeis group's desire to penalize corporate giantism. Much of the opposition to other New Deal legislation rose from the fact that after these changes in the tax laws were made, the well-to-do had to bear a larger share of the cost of *all* government activities.

Whether the Second New Deal was more radical than the First depends largely on the vantage point from which it is considered. Measures like the Social Security Act had greater long-range effect on American life than the legislation of the first Hundred Days but were fundamentally less revolutionary than laws like the National Industrial Recovery Act and the Agricultural Adjustment Act, which

The proliferation of federal agencies during the New Deal inspired cartoonists. In this example, from Vanity Fair, *Uncle Sam becomes Swift's Gulliver, tied down by the Lilliputian Brain Trusters.*

attempted to establish a planned economy. "Where the First New Deal contemplated government, business, and labor marching hand in hand toward a brave new society," Arthur M. Schlesinger, Jr., has written, "the Second New Deal proposed to revitalize the tired old society. . . . The First New Deal characteristically told business what it must do. The Second New Deal characteristically told business what it must *not* do."

This distinction escaped most of Roosevelt's critics, particularly the businessmen, who felt the impact of his assault on existing conditions most directly. If in theory NIRA threatened the free enterprise system, it was less objectionable to manufacturers than laws that increased their taxes and forced them to contribute to old-age pensions for their workers.

Herbert Hoover epitomized the attitude of conservatives when he called the New Deal "the most stupendous invasion of the whole spirit of Liberty that the nation has witnessed." Undoubtedly many opponents of the New Deal sincerely believed that it was undermining the foundations of American freedom. The cost of the New Deal also alarmed them. By 1936 some members of the administration had fallen under the influence of the British economist John Maynard Keynes, who argued that the world depression could be conquered if governments would deliberately unbalance their budgets by reducing interest rates and taxes and increasing expenditures in order to stimulate consumption and investment. Roosevelt never accepted Keynes's theories; he conferred with the economist in 1934 but could not grasp the "rigmarole of figures" with which Keynes deluged him.

Nevertheless the imperatives of the depression forced Roosevelt to spend more than the government was collecting in taxes; thus he adopted in part the Keynesian approach. Conservative businessmen considered him financially irresponsible, and the fact that deficit spending seemed to be good politics—one cynical New Dealer reputedly said that the administration would "spend, spend, spend" and "elect, elect, elect" until doomsday—made them seethe with rage.

The Election of 1936

The election of 1936 loomed as a showdown. "America is in peril," the Republican platform declared. The GOP candidate, Governor Alfred M.

The gap between the blue (income) line and the red (spending) line shows the deficit each year for the ten years between 1932 and 1941, and the bars show how the total debt increased to almost $43 billion by 1941. According to Keynes, such deficits help to stimulate a lagging economy.

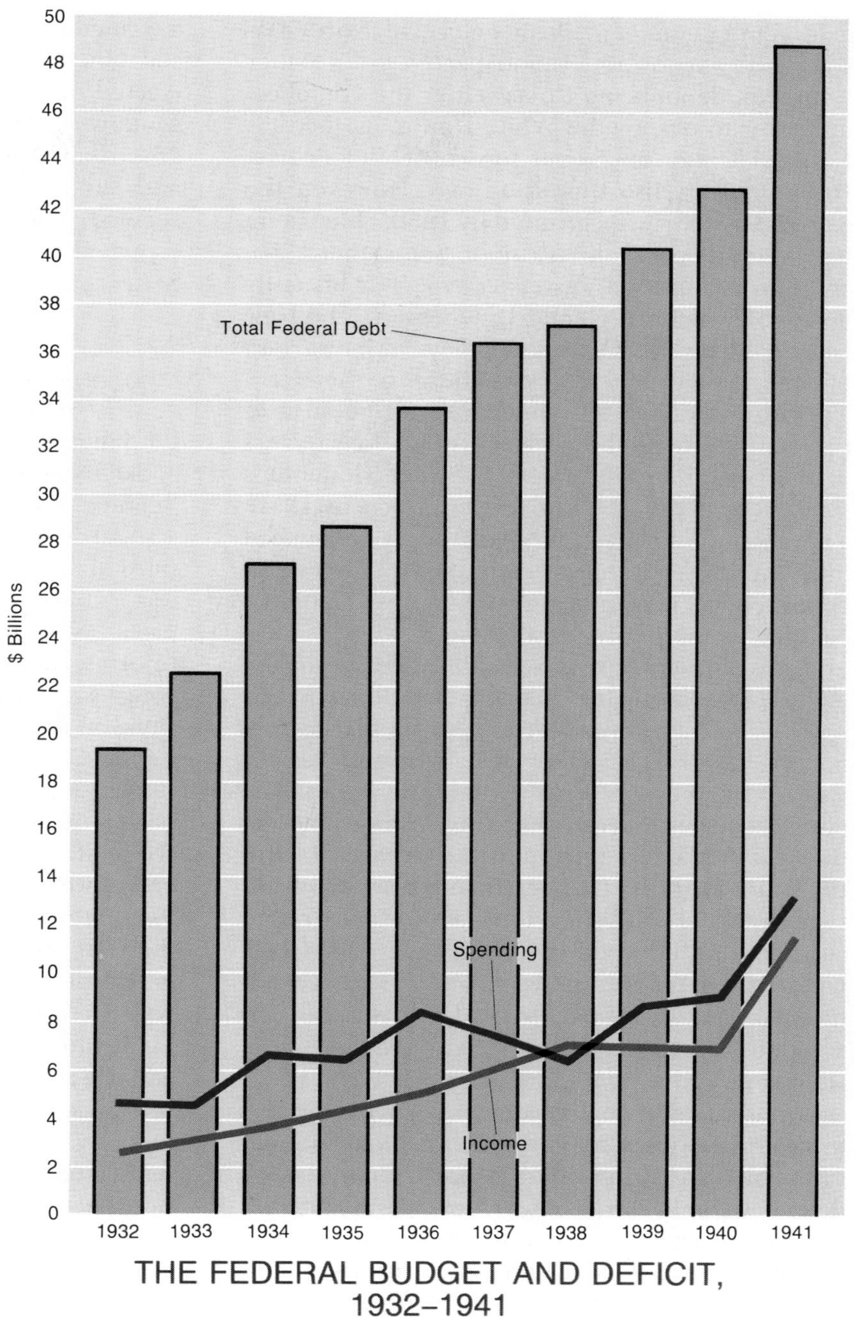

THE FEDERAL BUDGET AND DEFICIT, 1932–1941

Landon of Kansas, was reasonably liberal, a former follower of Theodore Roosevelt, a foe of the Ku Klux Klan in the twenties, and a believer in government regulation of business. But he was a poor speaker, colorless, and handicapped by the reactionary views of many of his backers. Against the charm and political astuteness of Roosevelt, Landon's arguments—chiefly that he could administer the government more efficiently than the president—made little impression. He won the support of some anti–New Deal Democrats, among them two former presidential candidates, Al Smith and John W. Davis, but this was not enough.

The radical fringe put a third candidate in the

field, Congressman William Lemke of North Dakota, who ran on the Union party ticket. Father Coughlin, denouncing Roosevelt as the "dumbest man ever to occupy the White House," rallied his National Union for Social Justice behind Lemke; Dr. Townsend also supported him. However, the extremists were losing ground by 1936. Huey Long had fallen victim of an assassin in September 1935, and his organization was taken over by a blatantly demagogic rightist, Gerald L. K. Smith. The New Deal, Smith said in 1936, was led by "a slimy group of men culled from the pink campuses of America." The Townsendites fell under a cloud because of rumors that some of their leaders had their fingers in the organization's treasury. Father Coughlin's slanderous assaults on Roosevelt caused a backlash; a number of American Catholic prelates denounced him, and the Vatican issued an unofficial but influential rebuke. Lemke made little impression on the country, polling only 892,000 votes.

Roosevelt did not win in 1936 because of the inadequacies of his foes. Having abandoned his efforts to hold the businessmen, whom he now denounced as "economic royalists," he appealed for the votes of workers and the underprivileged. The new labor unions gratefully poured thousands of dollars into the campaign to reelect him. Black voters switched to the Democrats in record numbers.

Farmers liked Roosevelt because of his evident concern for their welfare: when the Supreme Court declared the Agricultural Adjustment Act unconstitutional (*United States* v. *Butler,* 1936), he immediately rushed through a new law, the Soil Conservation and Domestic Allotment Act, which accomplished the same objective by paying farmers to divert land from commercial crops to soil-building plants like clover and soybeans. Countless elderly persons backed Roosevelt out of gratitude for the Social Security Act. Homeowners were grateful for his program guaranteeing mortgages—eventually about 20 percent of all urban private dwellings were refinanced by the Home Owners Loan Corporation—and for the Federal Housing Administration, which, beginning in 1934, made available low-cost, long-term loans for modernizing old buildings and constructing new ones. A modest upturn, which raised industrial output to the levels of 1930, played into Roosevelt's hands. For the first time since 1931 U.S. Steel was showing a profit.

On election day the country gave the president a tremendous vote of confidence. He carried every state but Maine and Vermont. The Republicans elected only 89 members of the House of Representatives and their strength in the Senate fell to 16, an all-time low. Both Roosevelt's personality and his program had captivated the land. He seemed irresistible, the most powerfully entrenched president in the history of the United States.

Roosevelt and the "Nine Old Men"

On January 20, in his second inaugural, Roosevelt spoke feelingly of the plight of millions of citizens "denied the greater part of what the very lowest standards of today call the necessities of life." A third of the nation, he added without exaggeration, was "ill-housed, ill-clad, ill-nourished." He interpreted his landslide victory as a mandate for further reforms, and with his prestige and his immense congressional majorities, nothing appeared to stand in his way. Nothing, that is, except the Supreme Court.

Throughout Roosevelt's first term the Court had stood almost immovable against increasing the scope of federal authority and broadening the general power of government, state as well as national, to cope with the exigencies of the depression. Of the nine justices, only Louis Brandeis, Benjamin N. Cardozo, and Harlan Fiske Stone viewed the New Deal sympathetically. Four others—James C. McReynolds, Willis Van Devanter, Pierce Butler, and George Sutherland—were intransigent reactionaries. Chief Justice Charles Evans Hughes and Justice Owen J. Roberts, while more open-minded, tended to side with the reactionaries on many questions.

Much of the early New Deal legislation, pushed through Congress at top speed during the Hundred Days, had been drafted without proper regard for the Constitution. Even the liberal justices considered the National Industrial Recovery Act unconstitutional (the Schechter decision was a unanimous one). The Court had also voided the federal Guffey-Snyder Act, establishing minimum wages in the coal industry, and a New York minimium wage law, thereby creating, as Roosevelt remarked, a "no man's land" where neither national nor state government could act. The conservative majority had adopted what Roosevelt called a "horse-and-buggy" interpretation of the commerce clause of the Constitution, closing off one of the most important avenues for expanding federal power. Worse, the reactionaries on the Court seemed governed by no consistent constitutional philosophy; they tended to limit the police power of the states when wages-and-hours laws came before them and to interpret it broadly when state laws restricting civil liberties were under consideration. In 1937 all the major measures of the Second Hundred Days appeared doomed. The Wagner Act had little chance of winning approval, experts predicted. Lawyers were advising employers to ignore the Social Security Act, so confident were they that the Court would declare it unconstitutional.

Faced with this situation, Roosevelt decided to ask Congress to shift the balance on the Court by increasing the number of justices, thinly disguising the purpose of his plan by making it part of a general reorganization of the judiciary. A member of the Court reaching the age of 70 would have the option of retiring at full pay. Should such a justice choose not to retire, the president was to appoint an additional justice, up to a maximum of six, in order to ease the burden of work for the aged jurists who remained on the bench.

Roosevelt knew that this measure would run into strenuous resistance, but he expected that the huge Democratic majorities in Congress could override any opposition and that the public would back him solidly. No astute politician had erred so badly in estimating the effects of an action since Stephen A. Douglas introduced the Kansas-Nebraska bill in 1854.

Although polls showed the public fairly evenly divided on the "court-packing" bill, the opposition was vocal and influential. To the expected denunciations of conservatives were added the complaints of liberals fearful that the principle of court packing might in the future be used to subvert civil liberties. What, Senator Norris asked, would have been the reaction if a man like Harding had proposed such a measure? Opposition in Congress was immediate and intense; many who had cheerfully supported every New Deal bill came out against the plan. The press denounced it, and so did most local bar associations. Chief Justice Hughes released a devastating critique; even the liberal Brandeis—the oldest judge on the court—rejected the bill out of hand.

In a New York Herald Tribune *cartoon titled "No Boost for the Administration Make-Up Department," a court-packing wolf in the sheep's clothing of a court "reform" bill acts surprised when halted by a gun-toting Senate.*

And many voters felt that Roosevelt had tried to trick them. The 1936 Democratic platform had spoken only of a possible amendment "clarifying" the Court's power, and Roosevelt had studiously avoided the issue during the campaign.

For months Roosevelt stubbornly refused to concede defeat, thus tying up the rest of his legislative program while Congress wrangled over the court reform bill. Finally, in July 1937, he had to yield. Minor administrative reforms of the judiciary were enacted, but the size of the Court remained unchanged.

The struggle did result in saving the legislation of the Second New Deal. Alarmed by the threat to the Court, Justices Hughes and Roberts, never entirely committed to the conservative position, beat a strategic retreat on a series of specific issues.

While the debate was raging in Congress, they sided with the liberals in upholding first a minimum wage law of the state of Washington that was little different from the New York act the Court had recently rejected, then the Wagner Act, then the Social Security Act. In May Justice Van Devanter retired, and Roosevelt replaced him with Senator Hugo Black of Alabama, an advanced New Dealer. The conservative justices thereupon gave up the fight, and soon Roosevelt was able to appoint enough new judges to give the Court a large pro–New Deal majority. No further measure of significance was declared unconstitutional during his presidency.

The Court fight hurt Roosevelt severely. His prestige never fully recovered. Conservative Democrats who had feared to oppose him because of his supposedly invulnerable popularity took heart and began to join with the Republicans on key issues. When the president summoned a special session of Congress in November 1937 and submitted a program of "must" legislation, not one of his bills was passed.

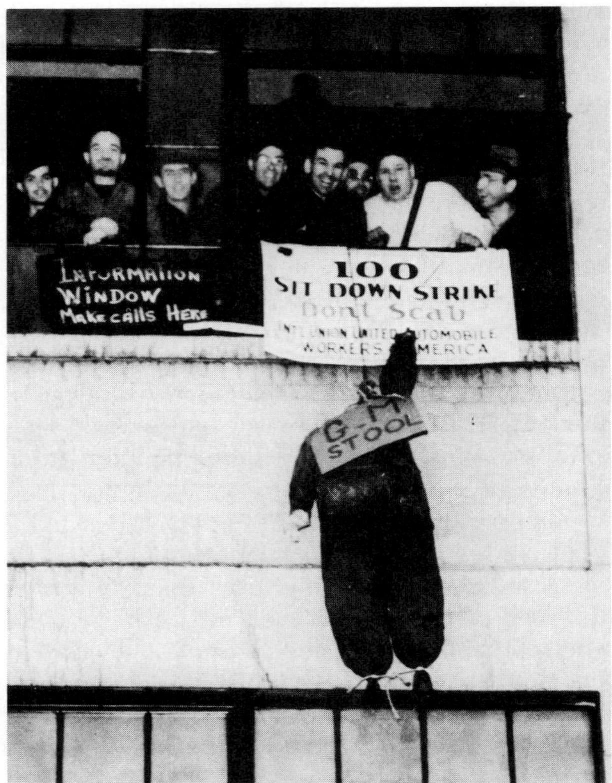

A group of sit-down strikers inside the Chevrolet plant in Flint, Michigan, looking out. They are hanging a "G-M stool" in effigy. The sign directly above the dummy reminds fellow workers: "Don't Scab."

The New Deal Winds Down

The Court fight marked the beginning of the end of the New Deal. Social and economic developments contributed to its decline, and the final blow originated in the area of foreign affairs. With unemployment high, wages low, and workers relatively powerless against their employers, most Americans had liked New Deal labor legislation and sympathized with the industrial unions whose growth it stimulated. Strength made the unions ambitious and aggressive; their organizational drives in industries like steel and automobiles changed the power structure within the economy. This gave many members of the middle class second thoughts concerning labor's demands.

In 1937 a series of "sit-down strikes" broke out, beginning at the General Motors plant in Flint, Michigan. Striking workers barricaded themselves *inside* the factories; when police and strikebreakers tried to dislodge them, they drove them off with barrages of soda bottles, tools, spare parts, and crockery. The tolerant attitude of the Roosevelt administration insured the strikers against government intervention. "It is illegal," Roosevelt said of the General Motors strike, "but shooting it out . . . [is not] the answer. . . . Why can't those fellows in General Motors meet with the committee of workers?" Fearful that all-out efforts to clear their plants would result in the destruction of expensive machinery, most employers capitulated to the workers' demands. All the automobile manufacturers but Henry Ford quickly came to terms with the United Automobile Workers.

The major steel companies, led by U.S. Steel, recognized the CIO and granted higher wages and a 40-hour week. The auto and steel unions alone boasted more than 725,000 members by late 1937; other CIO units conquered the rubber industry, the electrical industry, the textile industry, and many more. Together with the seizures of property in sit-down strikes, the disregard of unions for the "rights" of nonunion workers, and the violence that accompanied some strikes, the rapid growth alarmed many moderates. The enthusiasm of such people for all reform cooled rapidly.

While the sit-down strikes and the Court fight were going on, the New Deal suffered another heavy blow. Business conditions had been gradually improving since 1933. Heartened by the trend, Roosevelt, who had never fully grasped the importance of government spending in stimulating recovery, cut back sharply on the relief program in June 1937—with disastrous results. Between August and October the economy slipped downward like sand through a chute. Stock prices plummeted; unemployment rose by 2 million; industrial production slumped. This "Roosevelt recession" further damaged the president's reputation, and for many months he aggravated the situation by adopting an almost Hoover-like attitude. "Everything will work out all right if we just sit tight and keep quiet," he actually said.

While the president hesitated, rival theorists within his administration warred. The Keynesians, led by WPA head Harry Hopkins, Marriner Eccles of the Federal Reserve, and Secretary of the Interior Harold Ickes, clamored for stepped-up government spending. The conservatives, led by Treasury Secretary Henry Morgenthau, Jr., advocated retrenchment. Perhaps confused by the conflict, Roosevelt seemed incapable of decisive action. When Keynes offered him "some bird's eye impressions" of the recession in February 1938, urging "large scale recourse to . . . public works and other investments aided by Government funds," Roosevelt sent him only a routine acknowledgment drafted by Morgenthau.

In April 1938 Roosevelt finally committed himself to heavy deficit spending. At his urging Congress passed a $3.75 billion public works bill. Two major pieces of legislation were also enacted at about this time. A new AAA program (February 1938) set marketing quotas and acreage limitations for growers of staples like wheat, cotton, and tobacco and authorized the Commodity Credit Corporation to lend money to farmers on their surplus crops. The surpluses were to be stored by the government; when prices rose, farmers could repay the loans, reclaim their produce, and sell it on the open market, thereby maintaining an "ever-normal granary."

The second measure, the Fair Labor Standards Act, abolished child labor and established a national minimum wage of 40 cents an hour and a maximum workweek of 40 hours, with time and a half for overtime. Although the law failed to cover many of the poorest-paid types of labor, its passage meant wage increases for 750,000 workers. In later years many more classes of workers were brought within its protection and the minimum wage was repeatedly increased.

These measures further alienated conservatives without dramatically improving economic conditions. The resistance of many Democratic congressmen to additional economic and social "experiments" hardened. As the 1938 elections approached, Roosevelt decided to go to the voters in an effort to strengthen party discipline and reenergize the New Deal. He singled out a number of conservative Democratic senators, notably Walter F. George of Georgia, Millard F. Tydings of Maryland, and "Cotton Ed" Smith of South Carolina, and tried to "purge" them by backing other Democrats in the primaries.

The purge failed. Southern voters liked Roosevelt but resented his interference in local politics. Smith dodged the issue of liberalism by stressing the question of white supremacy in South Carolina; Tydings emphasized Roosevelt's "invasion" of Maryland; in Georgia the president's enemies compared his campaign against George to General Sherman's march across the state during the Civil War. All three senators were easily renominated and then reelected in November. In the nation at large the Republicans made important gains for the first time since Roosevelt had taken office. The Democrats maintained nominal control of both houses of Congress, but the conservative coalition, while unable to muster the votes to do away with accomplished reforms, succeeded in blocking additional legislation.*

Significance of the New Deal

By 1939 Roosevelt was ready to abandon further efforts at reform. The mounting danger of war in

* The so-called conservative coalition was never a well-organized group. Its membership shifted from issue to issue; it had no real leaders and certainly no long-range plans. If any common policy united its adherents, it was opposition to the New Deal's "overconcern" for the interests of unions, the unemployed, and underprivileged urban minorities.

Europe as a result of the aggressions of the German dictator, Adolf Hitler, dominated his thinking. After war broke out in 1939, the Great Depression was swept away on a wave of orders from the beleaguered European democracies. For this prosperity, Roosevelt received much undeserved credit. His New Deal had not returned the country to full employment. It is a truth still ominous for the future that no convincing reply has been devised to the argument that modern capitalism cannot flourish without the stimulus of massive military expenditures.

The perspective of time reveals other inadequacies of the New Deal. Despite the aid given the jobless, the generation of workers born between 1900 and 1910 who entered the 1930s as unskilled laborers had their careers permanently stunted by the depression. Far fewer rose to middle-class status than at any time since the 1830s and 1840s. Roosevelt's willingness to experiment with different means of combating the depression made sense because no one really knew what to do; however, his uncertainty about the ultimate objectives of the New Deal was counterproductive. He vacillated between seeking to stimulate the economy by deficit spending and trying to balance the budget; between a narrow "America First" economic nationalism and a broad-gauged international approach; between regulating monopolies and trustbusting; between helping the underprivileged and bolstering those already strong. At times he acted on the assumptions that the United States had a "mature" economy and that the major problem was overproduction. At other times he appeared to think that the answer to the depression was more production. He could never make up his mind whether to try to rally liberals to his cause without regard for party or to run the government as a partisan leader, conciliating the conservative Democrats.

Roosevelt's fondness for establishing new agencies to deal with specific problems vastly increased the federal bureaucracy, indirectly added to the influence of lobbyists, and made it more difficult to monitor government activities. His cavalier attitude toward constitutional limitations on executive power, which he justified as being necessary in a national emergency, set in motion trends that so increased the prestige and authority of the presidency that the balance between the executive, legislative, and judicial branches was threatened.

Yet these are criticisms after the fact; they ignore what one historian has called the "sense of urgency and haste" that made the New Deal "a mixture of accomplishment, frustration, and misdirected effort." On balance, the New Deal had an immense constructive impact. By 1939 the country was committed to the idea that the federal government should accept responsibility for the national welfare and act to meet specific problems in every necessary way. What was most significant was not the proliferation of new agencies or the expansion of federal power. These were continuations of trends already a century old when the New Deal began. The importance of the "Roosevelt revolution" was that it removed the issue from politics. "Never again," the Republican presidential candidate was to say in 1952, "shall we *allow* a depression in the United States."

Because of New Deal decisions, many formerly unregulated areas of American life became subject to federal authority: the stock exchange, agricultural prices and production, labor relations, old-age pensions, relief of the needy. After the New Deal the federal government accepted its obligation to try to provide all the people with a decent standard of living and to pay some attention to achieving the Jeffersonian goal of happiness for all. If the New Deal failed to end the depression, it effected changes that have—so far, at least—prevented later economic declines from becoming catastrophes. By encouraging the growth of unions the New Deal probably helped workers obtain a larger share of the profits of industry. By putting a floor under the income of many farmers it checked the decline of agricultural living standards, though not that of the agricultural population. The social security program, with all its inadequacies, lessened the impact of bad times on an increasingly large proportion of the population and provided immense psychological benefits to all.

The New Deal hastened other major changes in the United States. One of the most dramatic was the movement of black voters from the Republican to the Democratic party. In 1932 fewer blacks defected from the Republican party than the members of any other traditionally Republican group. Four years later blacks voted for Roosevelt in overwhelming numbers. Blacks supported the New Deal for the same reasons that whites did, but how the New Deal affected blacks in general and racial attitudes specifically are more complicated questions. Claiming that he dared not antagonize southern congressmen, whose votes he needed for his recovery programs, Roosevelt did nothing about civil rights before 1941 and little thereafter. Many of the early New Deal programs treated blacks as second-class citizens. They were often paid at lower rates than whites under NRA codes (and so joked sardonically that NRA stood for "Negro Run Around" and "Negroes Ruined Again"). The early farm programs shortchanged black tenants and sharecroppers. Blacks got far fewer appointments in the Civilian Conservation Corps than their numbers warranted, and those who were accepted were assigned to all-black camps. TVA developments were rigidly segregated, and almost no blacks got jobs in TVA offices. New Deal urban housing projects inadvertently but nonetheless effectively increased the concentration of blacks in particular neighborhoods. The Social Security Act, by excluding agricultural laborers and domestic servants, did nothing for hundreds of thousands of poor black workers or for Mexican-American farmhands in the Southwest. In 1939 unemployment was twice as high among blacks as among whites, and whites' wages were double the level of blacks' wages.

The fact that members of racial minorities got less than they deserved did not keep most of them from becoming New Dealers: half a loaf was more than any American government had given blacks since the time of U. S. Grant. As one black minister explained, "[Negroes] have never been so crazy as to wait for things to be perfect." Moreover, aside from the direct benefits, blacks profited in other ways. Secretary of the Interior Harold L. Ickes appointed Charles Forman as a special assistant as-

Black sharecroppers evicted from their tenant farms were photographed by Arthur Rothstein along a Missouri road in 1939. Rothstein was one of a group of outstanding photographers who created a unique "sociological and economic survey" of the nation between 1936 and 1942 under the aegis of the Farm Security Administration.

signed "to keep the government honest when it came to race." Eleanor Roosevelt, truly the first lady of the land in this respect as in so many others, worked steadily for the cause. The *Chicago Defender*, an influential black newspaper, noted that she "stood like the Rock of Gibraltar against pernicious encroachments on the rights of minorities." (A disgruntled southerner made the same point differently: "She goes around telling the Negroes they are as good as anyone else.") Her influence on the president in these matters was subtle but significant. Her championing of racial justice encouraged some New Deal administrators to hire more blacks in professional posts, not merely as laborers and clerks.

In the labor movement the new CIO unions accepted black members, and this was particularly significant because these unions were organizing industries—steel, automobiles, and mining among others—that employed large numbers of blacks. Thus, while black Americans suffered horribly during the depression, New Deal efforts to counteract its effects brought them some relief and a measure of hope. And this became increasingly true with the passage of time. During Roosevelt's second term, blacks found far less to criticize than had been the case earlier.

Among other important social changes, the TVA and the New Deal rural electrification program made farm life literally more civilized. Urban public housing, while never undertaken on a massive scale, helped rehabilitate some of the nation's worst slums. Government public power projects, such as the giant Bonneville and Grand Coulee dams in the Pacific Northwest, were only the most spectacular part of a comprehensive New Deal program to develop the natural resources of the country. Exploitation of the natural resources of the West was checked, and a start was made toward the proper national management of the land and water of the region, along with its petroleum, lumber, and other resources. The NIRA and later labor legislation forced businessmen to reexamine their role in American life and to become more socially conscious. The WPA art and theater programs widened the horizons of millions. All in all, the spirit of the New Deal heightened the people's sense of community, revitalized national energies, and stimulated the imagination and creative instincts of countless citizens.

A New Deal for Indians

In 1924 Congress finally granted citizenship to all Indians, but this did not end their special "protected" status. It was generally agreed by whites that Indians were their racial inferiors and should be treated as wards of the state. By that date, the historian Frederick E. Hoxie writes, "a version of federal guardianship had been applied to Native Americans that protected them . . . by limiting their freedom." Despite the "protection" supposedly afforded by the Dawes Act, much of the land allotted to individual Indians under the 1887 law had, by the early 1930s, passed in one way or another into the hands of whites. Assimilation had failed; indeed, tribal cultures had proved remarkably enduring. Indian languages and religious practices, patterns of family life, Indian arts and crafts—all had resisted generations of efforts to "civilize" the tribes.

Government policy took a new direction in 1933, when John Collier became commissioner of Indian affairs. In the 1920s Collier had studied the Indians of the Southwest and edited the magazine *American Indian Life.* By the time he was appointed commissioner, the depression had reduced perhaps a third of the 320,000 Indians living on reservations to penury. Collier was convinced that something should be done to revive the spirits of these downtrodden and discouraged people. He wanted to do away with "the cruel and stupid laws that rob them and crush their family lives." He favored a pluralistic approach, seeking to help the Indians preserve their ancient cultures but also (somewhat contradictorily) to help them earn more money and make use of modern medical advances and modern techniques of soil conservation. He was particularly eager to encourage the revival of tribal governments that could represent the Indians in dealings with the U.S. government and function as community service centers.

In part because of Collier's urging, Congress passed the Indian Reorganization Act of 1934. This law enabled Indians to establish tribal governments with powers like those of cities, and it encouraged Indians to return individually owned lands to tribal control. In addition, Harry Hopkins made special efforts to see that needy Indians who were not living on reservations got relief aid. There was also a special Indian division of the Civilian Conserva-

"Jicarilla [Apache] older person's home," says the caption of this telling photograph taken by H. Hospers in the late 1930s.

tion Corps which organized work for Indians right on their reservations.

New Deal Indian policy was controversial— among Indians as well as among white groups. Some critics charged Collier with trying to turn back the clock. Others objected to his employing numerous professional anthropologists with supposedly "advanced" ideas. Indians who owned profitable allotments, such as those in Oklahoma who held valuable oil and mineral rights, did not relish turning their land over to tribal control. In New Mexico, the Navajos, whose lands had relatively little commercial value, nonetheless voted decisively against going back to the communal system. All told, 77 of 269 tribes voted not to go back to communal holdings. Nevertheless, like so many of its programs, the New Deal's Indian policy marked an important and necessary shift of perspective, a bold effort to deal constructively with a long-standing national problem.

How much of the credit for these achievements belongs personally to Franklin D. Roosevelt is debatable. He had little to do with many of the details and some of the broad principles behind the New Deal. His knowledge of economics was skimpy, his understanding of many social problems superficial, his political philosophy distressingly vague. The British leader Anthony Eden described him as "a conjuror, skillfully juggling with balls of dynamite, whose nature he failed to understand," and the historian David Brody writes shrewdly of Roosevelt's "unreflective acceptance" of the basic structure of American society.

Nevertheless, every aspect of the New Deal bears the brand of Roosevelt's remarkable personality. Brain Truster Rexford Tugwell has left one of the best-balanced judgments of the president. "Roosevelt was not really very much at home with ideas," Tugwell explains. He preferred to stick with what he already knew. But he was always open to new facts, and something within him "forbade inaction when there was something to be done." Roosevelt's political genius constructed the coalition that made the program possible; his humanitarianism made it a reform movement of major significance. Although considered by many a terrible administrator because he encouraged rivalry among his subordinates, assigned different agencies overlapping responsibilities, failed to discharge many incompetents, and frequently put off making difficult decisions, he was in fact one of the most effective chief executives in the nation's history. His seemingly haphazard practice of dividing authority among competing administrators unleashed the energies and sparked the imaginations of his aides, which gave the ponderous federal bureaucracy a remarkable flexibility and *élan.*

Like Wilson, Roosevelt was almost a prime minister, taking charge of the administration forces in Congress, drafting bills, buttonholing legislators, deluging the lawmakers with special messages. Like Jackson, he maximized his role as leader of all the people. His informal biweekly press conferences proved a matchless means of keeping the public in touch with developments and himself in tune with popular thinking. He made the radio an instrument for communicating with the masses in the most direct way imaginable: his "fireside chats" convinced millions that he was personally interested in each citizen's life and welfare, as in a way he was. At a time when the size and complexity of the government made it impossible for any one person to direct the nation's destiny, Roosevelt managed the minor miracle of personifying that government to 130 million people. "There was a real dialogue between Franklin and the people," Eleanor Roosevelt said after the president's death, and she did not exaggerate. Under Hoover, a single clerk was able to handle the routine mail that flowed into the office of the president from ordinary citizens. Under Roosevelt, the task required a staff of 50.

While the New Deal was still evolving, contemporaries recognized Roosevelt's right to a place beside Washington, Jefferson, and Lincoln among the great presidents. The years have not altered their judgment. Yet as his second term drew toward its close, some of his most important work still lay in the future.

SUPPLEMENTARY READING

Titles marked with an asterisk have been published in paperback.

The Great Depression and the New Deal are covered briefly in J. D. Hicks, **Republican Ascendancy*** (1960), and W. E. Leuchtenburg, **Franklin Roosevelt and the New Deal*** (1963). The first three volumes of A. M. Schlesinger, Jr.'s still incomplete **The Age of Roosevelt*** (1957–1960) treat the period to 1936 in vivid fashion. L. V. Chandler, **America's Greatest Depression*** (1970), is also important. Broadus Mitchell, **Depression Decade*** (1947), is a good economic history. O. L. Graham, Jr., **An Encore for Reform*** (1967), compares the New Deal and Progressive ideologies, and R. H. Pells, **Radical Visions and American Dreams*** (1973), is an excellent study of intellectual currents.

For the stock market crash, consult Robert Sobel, **The Great Bull Market: Wall Street in the 1920's*** (1968), which is highly analytical; John Brooks, **Once in Golconda: A True Drama of Wall Street** (1969), a more lively account; and J. K. Galbraith, **The Great Crash*** (1955). The Hoover administration is discussed in A. U. Romasco, **The Poverty of Abundance*** (1965), M. L. Fausold, **The Presidency of Herbert Hoover** (1985), J. H. Wilson, **Herbert Hoover: Forgotten Progressive*** (1975), and in Herbert Hoover's **Memoirs: The Great Depression** (1951–1952). Roger Daniels, **The Bonus March: An Episode of the Great Depression** (1971), is fascinating and insightful. Robert Bendiner, **Just Around the Corner*** (1968), is full of interesting details. Irving Bernstein, **The Lean Years*** (1960), contains an excellent account of the early years of the depression but is too critical of Hoover. Abraham Hoffman, **Unwanted Mexican Americans in the Great Depression*** (1974), is useful for the entire decade.

On literature in the 1930s, see Alfred Kazin, **On Native Grounds*** (1942) and **Contemporaries*** (1962), Daniel Hoffman (ed.), **Harvard Guide to Contemporary American Writing** (1979), Townsend Ludington, **John Dos Passos** (1981), and Joseph Blotner, **Faulkner** (1974).

Franklin D. Roosevelt's early career is treated exhaustively in Frank Freidel, **Franklin D. Roosevelt*** (1952–1973), but see also Bernard Bellush, **Franklin D. Roosevelt as Governor of New York** (1955). Of the many biographies of Roosevelt, see especially J. M. Burns, **Roosevelt: The Lion and the Fox*** (1956). Daniel Fusfeld, **The Economic Thought of Franklin D. Roosevelt and the Origins of the New Deal** (1958), is important. Richard Hofstadter has interesting essays on Hoover and Roosevelt in **The American Political Tradition*** (1948). On Eleanor Roosevelt, see J. P. Lash, **Eleanor and Franklin*** (1971) and **Eleanor: The Years Alone** (1972). J. T. Patterson, **Congressional Conservatism and the New Deal*** (1967), is a solid study of congressional politics. On the Brains Trust, see E. A. Rosen, **Hoover, Roosevelt, and the Brains Trust** (1977).

Useful special studies of the New Deal include J. M. Blum, **From the Diaries of Henry Morgenthau, Jr.** (1959–1964), M. H. Leff, **The Limits of Symbolic Reform: The New Deal and Taxation** (1984), Richard Lowitt, **The New Deal in the West** (1984), V. L. Perkins, **Crisis in Agriculture: The AAA and the New Deal** (1969), Donald Wooster, **Dust Bowl** (1979), D. E. Conrad, **The Forgotten Farmers: The Story of Sharecroppers in the New Deal** (1965), S. F. Charles, **Minister of Relief: Harry Hopkins and the Depression** (1963), E. W. Hawley, **The New Deal and the Problem of Monopoly*** (1966), Bernard Bellush, **The Failure of NRA*** (1975), Roy Lubove, **The Struggle for Social Security** (1968), J. D. Matthews, **The Federal Theatre** (1967), M. N. Penkower, **The Federal Writers' Project** (1977), C. H. Trout, **Boston, the Great Depression, and the New Deal** (1977), Barbara Blumberg, **The New Deal and the Unemployed** (1979), B. F. Schwartz, **The Civil Works Administration** (1984), Irving Bernstein, **Turbulent Years** (1970), and two books by Sidney Fine, **The Automobile Under the Blue Eagle** (1963) and **Sit Down: The General Motors Strike of 1936–1937** (1969). On constitutional questions, see P. L. Murphy, **The Constitution in Crisis Times*** (1972).

For the activities of the "radical fringe," consult D. R. McCoy, **Angry Voices: Left-of-Center Politics in the New Deal Era** (1958), and D. H. Bennett, **Demagogues in the Depression: American Radicalism and the Union Party** (1969). On Huey Long, see T. H. Williams, **Huey Long: A Biography** (1969). On blacks during the 1930s, see Raymond Wolters, **Negroes and the Great Depression*** (1970), N. J. Weiss, **Farewell to the Party of Lincoln** (1983), and Harvard Sitkoff, **A New Deal for Blacks*** (1978); on women, W. H. Chafe, **The American Woman*** (1972), and Susan Ware, **Beyond Suffrage: Women in the New Deal** (1981); on Indians, K. R. Philip, **John Collier's Crusade for Indian Reform** (1977).

Of the many published memoirs and diaries of New Deal figures, the following are oustanding: Raymond Moley, **After Seven Years*** (1939), Frances Perkins, **The Roosevelt I Knew*** (1946), Eleanor Roosevelt, **This I Remember*** (1949), H. L. Ickes, **The Secret Diary of Harold L. Ickes** (1953–1954), Marriner Eccles, **Beckoning Frontiers** (1951), and D. E. Lilienthal, **Journals: The TVA Years: 1939–1945** (1964).

TIME LINE 6 ▪ The Age of Reform, 1880–1940

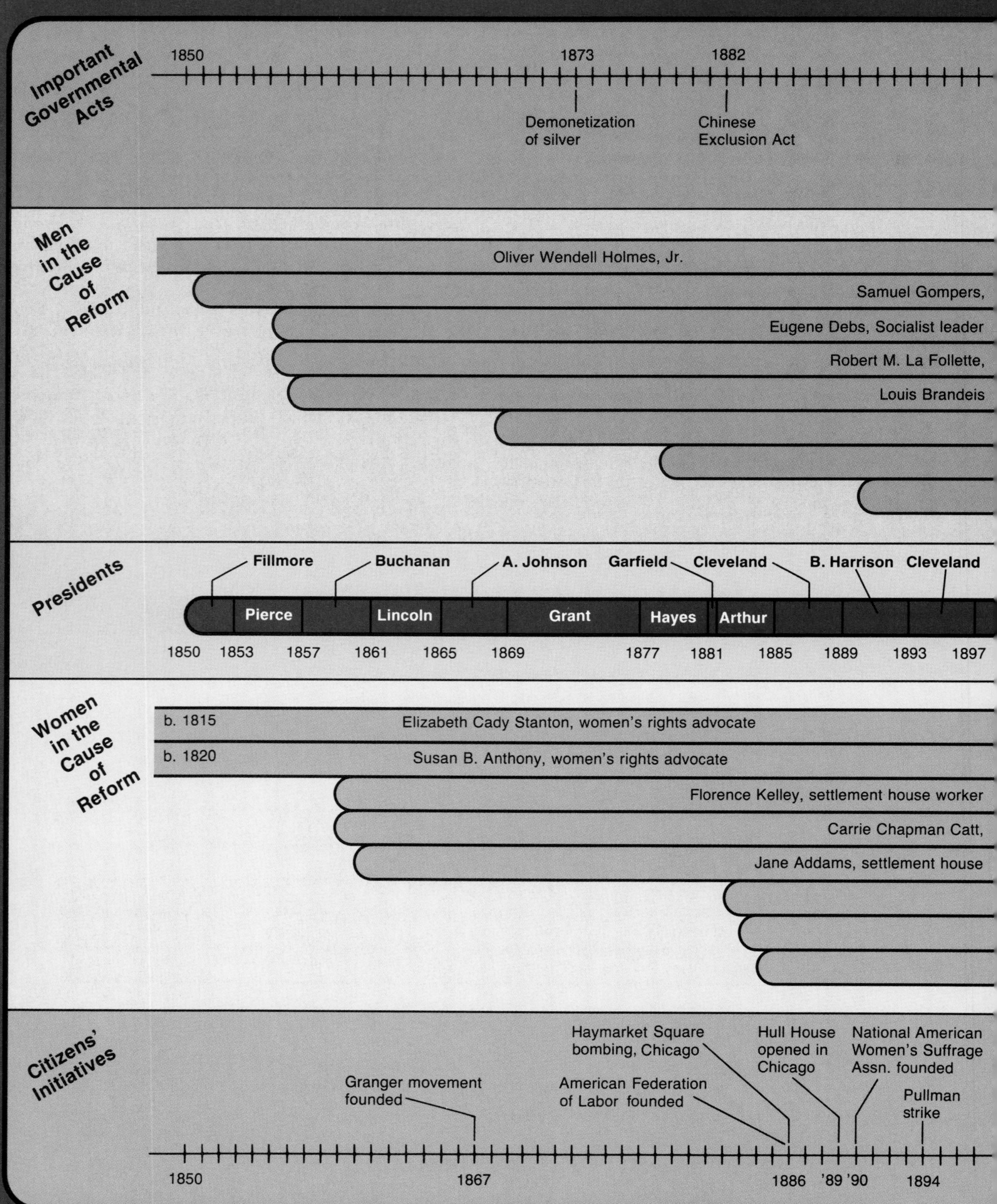

Important Governmental Acts
1850
1873
1882
Demonetization of silver
Chinese Exclusion Act
Men in the Cause of Reform
Oliver Wendell Holmes, Jr.
Samuel Gompers,
Eugene Debs, Socialist leader
Robert M. La Follette,
Louis Brandeis
Presidents
Fillmore
Buchanan
A. Johnson
Garfield
Cleveland
B. Harrison
Cleveland
Pierce
Lincoln
Grant
Hayes
Arthur
1850
1853
1857
1861
1865
1869
1877
1881
1885
1889
1893
1897
Women in the Cause of Reform
b. 1815
Elizabeth Cady Stanton, women's rights advocate
b. 1820
Susan B. Anthony, women's rights advocate
Florence Kelley, settlement house worker
Carrie Chapman Catt,
Jane Addams, settlement house
Citizens' Initiatives
Granger movement founded
American Federation of Labor founded
Haymarket Square bombing, Chicago
Hull House opened in Chicago
National American Women's Suffrage Assn. founded
Pullman strike
1850
1867
1886
'89
'90
1894

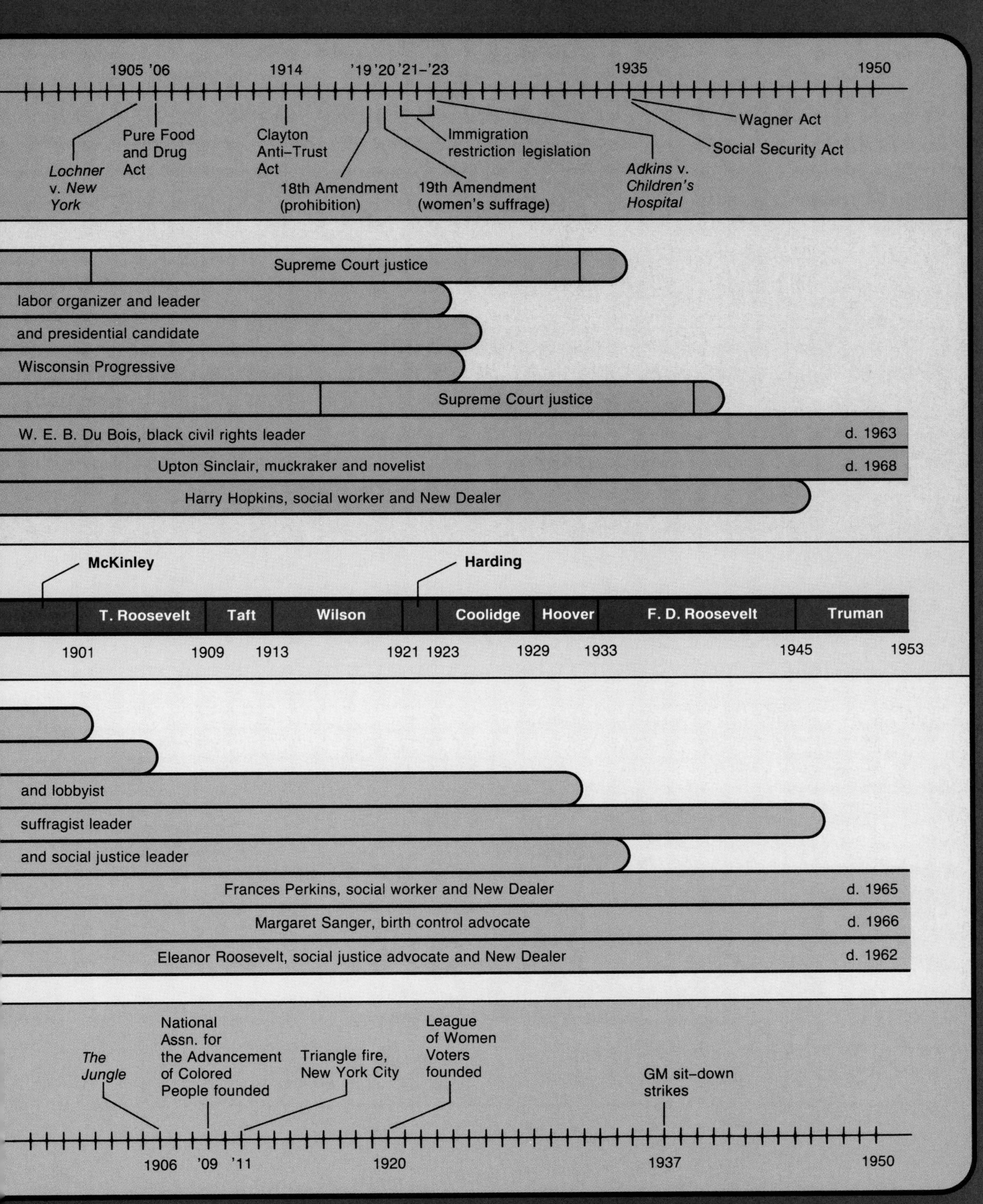

1905
'06
1914
'19
'20
'21–'23
1935
1950
Lochner v. *New York*
Pure Food and Drug Act
Clayton Anti–Trust Act
18th Amendment (prohibition)
19th Amendment (women's suffrage)
Immigration restriction legislation
Adkins v. *Children's Hospital*
Wagner Act
Social Security Act
Supreme Court justice
labor organizer and leader
and presidential candidate
Wisconsin Progressive
Supreme Court justice
W. E. B. Du Bois, black civil rights leader
d. 1963
Upton Sinclair, muckraker and novelist
d. 1968
Harry Hopkins, social worker and New Dealer
McKinley
Harding
T. Roosevelt
Taft
Wilson
Coolidge
Hoover
F. D. Roosevelt
Truman
1901
1909
1913
1921
1923
1929
1933
1945
1953
and lobbyist
suffragist leader
and social justice leader
Frances Perkins, social worker and New Dealer
d. 1965
Margaret Sanger, birth control advocate
d. 1966
Eleanor Roosevelt, social justice advocate and New Dealer
d. 1962
The Jungle
National Assn. for the Advancement of Colored People founded
Triangle fire, New York City
League of Women Voters founded
GM sit–down strikes
1906
'09
'11
1920
1937
1950

27

Disengagement, Isolationism, and War: 1921-1945

War is a contagion, whether it is declared or undeclared. . . . Yes, we are determined to keep out of war, yet we cannot insure ourselves against the disastrous effects of war and the dangers of involvement. FRANKLIN D. ROOSEVELT, *1937*

IN THESE GARDENS ARE RECORDED
THE NAMES OF AMERICANS
WHO GAVE THEIR LIVES
IN THE SERVICE
THEIR COUNTRY
AND WHOSE
RESTING PLACE
IS
LY TO GOD
Indicates
HONOR Award

Presidents Harding, Coolidge, and Hoover handled foreign relations in much the same way they managed domestic affairs. Harding deferred to senatorial prejudice against executive domination in the area and let his secretary of state, Charles Evans Hughes, make policy. Coolidge adopted a similar course. Hoover understood his diplomatic problems clearly and devised intelligent plans for dealing with them but was perhaps excessively cautious. In directing foreign relations, all three faced the obstacle of a resurgent isolationism. The same forces of war-bred hatred, postwar disillusion, and fear of communist subversion that produced the Red Scare at home led Americans to back away from close involvement in world affairs. The bloodiness and apparent senselessness of the Great War, combined with an awareness that war was the ultimate method of settling international controversies, convinced millions that the only way to be sure it would not happen again was to "steer clear" of "entanglements." That these famous words had been used by Washington and Jefferson in vastly different contexts did not deter the isolationists of the 1920s from attributing to them the same authority they gave to Scripture.

Americans were so suspicious of internationalism that the Harding administration treated the League of Nations with what the historian Richard W. Leopold calls "studied hostility." For a time the State Department refused even to answer letters from the League Secretariat in Geneva.

Peace Without a Sword

The presidents of the twenties often allowed domestic questions to control American relations with other countries. Their interest in disarmament flowed chiefly from their desire to cut taxes; tariffs were adjusted to satisfy American manufacturers without regard for how they affected the world political situation.

The first important diplomatic event of the period revealed a great deal about American foreign policy after World War I. In November 1921 delegates representing the United States, Great Britain, Japan, France, Italy, China, and three other nations gathered at Washington to discuss disarmament and the problems of the Far East. By the following February the Washington Armament Conference had drafted three major treaties and a number of lesser agreements.

The Four-Power Treaty, signed by the United States, Great Britain, Japan, and France, committed these nations to respect one another's interests in the islands of the Pacific and to confer in the event that any other country launched an attack in the area. The Five-Power Treaty, in which Italy joined the four, committed the signatories to stop building battleships for ten years and to reduce their fleets of capital ships to a fixed ratio, with Great Britain and the United States limited to 525,000 tons, Japan to 315,000 tons, and France and Italy to 175,000 tons. All conferees signed the Nine-Power Treaty, agreeing to respect China's independence and to maintain the Open Door. In a separate pact they permitted China to raise its tariffs on imports.

For the first time in history, the major powers accepted limitations on their right to arm themselves. The Open Door, never before more than a pious expression of American hopes, received the formal endorsement of all nations with far eastern interests except Russia. Japan agreed to restrict its ambitions in the Pacific area. By taking the lead in drafting the agreements, the United States regained some of the moral influence it had lost by not joining the League of Nations.

These gains masked grave weaknesses. The treaties were uniformly toothless. The signers of the Four-Power pact agreed only to consult in case of aggression in the Pacific; they made no promises to help one another or to restrict their own freedom of action. As President Harding assured the Senate, "There [was] no commitment to armed force, no alliance, no written or moral obligation to join in defense." The naval disarmament treaty said nothing about the number of other warships that the powers might build, about the far more important question of land and air forces, or about the underlying industrial and financial structures that controlled the ability of the nations to make war.* Nor did the signers of the Nine-Power Treaty intend to surrender their special privileges in China.

The United States entered into these agreements without realizing their full implications, not really prepared to play an active part in far eastern

* A second disarmament conference, held at London in 1930, attempted to place limits on smaller warships, but no agreement could be reached.

affairs. Congress failed to provide enough money to maintain the navy even at the limit set by the Five-Power pact. While stressing the fact that they had won overall naval equality with Great Britain, American diplomats failed to make clear that the 5:5:3 ratio permitted the Japanese to dominate the western Pacific. This ratio left the Philippine Islands undefendable and exposed Hawaii to possible attack. In a sense these American bases became hostages of Japan. Yet Congress was so unconcerned about Japanese sensibilities that it refused to grant *any* immigration quota to Japan under the National Origins Act of 1924, even though the formula applied to other nations would have allowed only 100 Japanese a year to enter the country. The Harding administration boasted of having been able to "force" the powers to "recognize" the Open Door principle in China, but it was unprepared to keep the door open if a more determined nation slammed it shut.

The Americans of the twenties wanted peace but would neither surrender their prejudices and dislikes nor build the defenses necessary to make it safe to indulge these passions. "The people have had all the war, all the taxation, and all the military service that they want," President Coolidge announced in 1925.

Peace societies flourished, among them the Carnegie Endowment for International Peace, designed "to hasten the abolition of war, the foulest blot upon our civilization," and the Woodrow Wilson Foundation, aimed at helping "the liberal forces of mankind throughout the world . . . who intend to promote peace by the means of justice."

Leaders of the Women's International League for Peace and Freedom assembled at the end of World War I to argue in favor of U.S. participation in a worldwide peace organization such as the League of Nations. Jane Addams is in front, fourth from left; at her left is Mrs. Robert La Follette, wife of the Wisconsin senator.

In 1923 Edward W. Bok, retired editor of the *Ladies' Home Journal,* offered a prize of $100,000 for the best workable plan for preserving international peace, and he was flooded with suggestions. Franklin D. Roosevelt drafted one while recovering from his attack of infantile paralysis. Such was the temper of the times that he felt constrained to include in the preamble this statement:

> We seek not to become involved as a nation in the purely regional affairs of groups of other nations, nor to give to the representatives of other peoples the right to compel us to enter upon undertakings calling for a leading up to the use of armed force without our full and free consent, given through our constitutional procedure.

So great was the opposition to international cooperation that the United States refused to accept membership on the World Court, although this tribunal could settle disputes only when the nations involved agreed. Probably a majority of the American people favored joining the Court, but its advocates were never able to persuade two-thirds of the Senate to ratify the necessary treaty. Too many peace lovers believed that their goal could be attained simply by pointing out the moral and practical disadvantages of war.

The culmination of this illusory faith in preventing war by criticizing it came with the signing of the Kellogg-Briand Pact in 1928. The treaty was born in the fertile brain of French Foreign Minister Aristide Briand, who was eager to collect allies against possible attack by a resurgent Germany. In 1927 Briand proposed to Secretary of State Frank B. Kellogg that their countries agree never to go to war with each other. Kellogg found the idea as repugnant as any conventional alliance, but American isolationists and pacifists found the suggestion fascinating. They plagued Kellogg with demands that he negotiate such a treaty.

To extricate himself from this situation, Kellogg cleverly suggested that the pact be broadened to include *all* nations. Now Briand was angry. Like Kellogg, he saw how meaningless such a treaty would be, especially when Kellogg insisted that it be hedged with a proviso that "every nation is free at all times . . . to defend its territory from attack and it alone is competent to decide when circumstances require war in self-defense." Nevertheless, Briand too found public pressures irresistible. In August 1928, at Paris, diplomats from 15 nations bestowed upon one another an "international kiss," condemning "recourse to war for the solution of international controversies" and renouncing war "as an instrument of national policy." Seldom has so unrealistic a promise been made by so many intelligent people. Yet most Americans considered the Kellogg-Briand Pact a milestone in the history of civilization: the Senate, habitually so suspicious of international commitments, ratified it 85 to 1.

The Good Neighbor Policy

Isolationism did not deter the government from seeking to advance American economic interests abroad. The Open Door concept remained predominant; the State Department worked to obtain opportunities in underdeveloped countries for exporters and investors, hoping both to stimulate the American economy and to bring stability to "backward" nations in the interests of world peace.

While this policy sometimes roused local resentments because of the tendency of the United States to cooperate with conservative forces abroad, it resulted in a further retreat from active interventionism. The pattern is well illustrated by events in Latin America. "Yankeephobia" had long been a chronic condition south of the Rio Grande. The continued presence of marines in Central America fed this ill feeling, as did the failure of the United States to enter the League of Nations (which all but four Latin American nations had joined). Basic, of course, was the immense wealth and power of the "Colossus of the North" and the feeling of Latin Americans that the wielders of this strength had little respect for the needs and values of their southern neighbors. However, the evident desire of the United States to limit its international involvements had a gradually mollifying effect on Latin American opinion.

In dealing with this part of the world, Harding and Coolidge performed neither better nor worse than Wilson. In the face of continued radicalism and instability in Mexico, which caused Americans with interests in land and oil rights to suffer heavy losses, President Coolidge acted with forbearance. His appointment of Dwight W. Morrow, a patient, sympathetic ambassador, resulted in an improvement in Mexican-American relations. The Mexicans were able to complete their social and economic revolution in the twenties without significant interference by the United States.

Under Herbert Hoover the United States began at last to treat Latin American nations as equals. Hoover reversed Wilson's policy of trying to teach them "to elect good men." The Clark Memorandum (1930), written by Undersecretary of State J. Reuben Clark, disassociated the right on intervention in Latin America from the Roosevelt Corollary. The corollary had been an improper extension of the Monroe Doctrine, Clark declared. The right of the United States to intervene depended rather on "the doctrine of self-preservation."

The distinction seemed slight to Latin Americans, but the underlying reasoning was important. Obviously any nation capable of doing so will intervene in the affairs of another when its own existence is at stake. But the long-established "right" of the United States under the Monroe Doctrine to keep *other* nations out of Latin America as a matter of principle did not give it a similarly broad authority to intervene there itself.

Hoover's policies were taken over and advanced by Franklin Roosevelt. At the Montevideo Pan-American Conference (December 1933) his secretary of state, Cordell Hull, voted in the affirmative on a resolution that "no state has the right to intervene in the internal or external affairs of another," a statement scarcely more meaningful than the Kellogg-Briand denunciation of war yet gratifying to sensitive Latin Americans. By 1934 the marines had been withdrawn from Nicaragua, the Dominican Republic, and Haiti. In 1934 the United States renounced the right to intervene in Cuban affairs, thereby abrogating the Platt Amendment to the Cuban constitution.

Beyond doubt the Good Neighbor Policy of Hoover and Roosevelt* persuaded many Latin Americans that the United States had no aggressive intentions south of the Rio Grande. Unfortunately, the United States did little to try to improve social and economic conditions in the region, so the underlying envy and resentment of "rich Uncle Sam" did not disappear.

* Hoover coined this term, but it was typical of the relative political effectiveness of the two presidents that Roosevelt got most of the credit.

The Totalitarian Challenge

The futility and danger of isolationism were exposed in September 1931 when the Japanese invaded Chinese Manchuria. China had been torn by revolution since 1911. By the twenties the nationalists, led by Chiang Kai-shek, had adopted a policy of driving all "foreign devils" from their country. The Japanese, however, were not satisfied merely to protect rights already held. They overran Manchuria and converted it into a puppet state called Manchukuo. This action violated both the Kellogg-Briand and the Nine-Power pacts.

China appealed to the League of Nations and to the United States for help. Neither would intervene. When League officials asked about the possibility of American cooperation in some kind of police action, President Hoover refused to consider either economic or military reprisals. The United States was not a world policeman, he said. The Nine-Power and Kellogg-Briand treaties were "solely moral instruments."

The League sent a commission to Manchuria to investigate. Henry L. Stimson, Hoover's secretary of state, announced (the Stimson Doctrine) that the United States would never recognize the legality of seizures made in violation of American treaty rights. This served only to irritate the Japanese.

In January 1932 Japan attacked Shanghai, the bloody battle marked by the indiscriminate bombing of residential districts. When the League at last officially condemned their aggressions, the Japanese withdrew from the organization and extended their control of northern China. The lesson of Manchuria was not lost on Adolf Hitler, who became chancellor of Germany on January 30, 1933.

It is easy, in surveying the diplomatic events of 1920–1939, to condemn the western democracies for their unwillingness to stand up for principles, their refusal to resist when Germany, Italy, and Japan embarked on the aggressions that led to World War II and cost the world millions of lives and billions of dollars. The democracies failed, until it was almost too late, to realize that a new ideology, totalitarianism, had arisen and that unless they resisted it forcefully, it would destroy them. It is also proper to place some of the blame for the troubles of that era on the same powers:

they controlled much of the world's resources and were far more interested in holding on to what they had than in righting past wrongs or helping other nations to improve the lives of their citizens.

Nevertheless the totalitarian states were the aggressors. Their system, which involved subordination of the individual to the state, the concentration of political power in the hands of a dictator, and the forceful suppression of all dissent, was made possible by the industrial revolution, which had produced tightly integrated national economies and the instruments of power and communication needed to control masses of people. The social and economic dislocations that followed World War I created the desperate conditions that led millions of Europeans to adopt totalitarian ideas.

The doctrine first assumed importance in 1922 in Italy, when Benito Mussolini seized power. Over the next few years Mussolini abolished universal suffrage, crushed everyone who dared speak out against him, and established a kind of dictatorial socialism which he called fascism (*fascismo*), the term referring to the Roman *fasces,* a symbol of governmental authority consisting of a bundle of rods bound around an ax. Mussolini blamed all the ills plaguing the Italian people on foreign sources, a convenient way to avoid the responsibilities that should have accompanied power.

Mussolini was an absurd poseur and mountebank whose power in world affairs remained relatively slight. Western leaders could perhaps be excused for failing to take him seriously. But the German dictator Hitler presented a threat that the democracies ignored at their peril. Besides ruthlessly persecuting innocent Jews, whom he blamed for all Germany's troubles, Hitler established a monolithic police state that crushed every form of dissent, every humane value. He announced plainly that he intended to extend his control over all German-speaking peoples. He dismissed the international agreements made by his predecessors with contempt. Germany possessed a potential for war far greater than Italy's, yet to Hitler's cruelest and most flagrantly aggressive actions, the western nations responded only by making concession after concession in the vain hope of "appeasing" him.

In a way the democracies failed to resist totalitarianism because of their very virtues: their faith in humanity, their willingness to see the other side of complicated questions, their horror of war. Any history of the period that treats the leading figures as fools or cowards grossly distorts the truth. Nevertheless, an unbiased account must conclude that western diplomats should have acted more courageously than they did. This statement applies as fully to the Americans as to the Europeans.

War Debts and Reparations

The western democracies did not stand together against the aggressors in part because they disagreed among themselves. Particularly divisive was the controversy over war debts—those of Germany to the Allies and those of the Allies to the United States. The United States had lent more than $10 billion to its comrades in arms. Since most of this money had been spent on weapons and other supplies in the United States, it might well have been considered part of America's contribution to the war effort. The public, however, demanded full repayment—with interest. "These were loans, not contributions," Secretary of the Treasury Mellon firmly declared. Even when the Foreign Debt Commission scaled down the interest rate from 5 percent to about 2 percent, the total, to be repaid over a period of 62 years, amounted to more than $22 billion.

Repayment of such a colossal sum was virtually impossible. In the first place, the money had not been put to productive use. Dollars lent to build factories or roads might be expected to earn profits for the borrower, but those devoted to the purchase of shells only destroyed wealth. Furthermore, the American protective tariff reduced the ability of the Allies to earn the dollars needed to pay the debts.

The Allies tried to load their obligations to the United States, along with the other costs of the war, on the backs of the Germans. They demanded reparations amounting to $33 billion. If this sum were collected, they declared, they could rebuild their economies and obtain the international exchange needed to pay their debts to the United States. But Germany was reluctant even to try to pay such huge reparations, and when Germany defaulted, so did the Allies.

Everyone was bitterly resentful: the Germans because they felt they were being bled white; the Americans, as Senator Hiram Johnson of California would have it, because the wily Europeans were

A merciless France demands war reparations from Germany in this Los Angeles Times *cartoon from 1922. American aid to the German economy had little effect in the face of Germany's enormous reparations costs.*

treating the United States as "an international sucker"; the Allies because (as the French said) *"l'oncle Shylock"* (a reference to Shylock, the moneylender in Shakespeare's *Merchant of Venice*) was demanding his pound of flesh with interest. "If nations were only business firms," Clemenceau wrote Calvin Coolidge in 1926, "bank notes would determine the fate of the world. . . . Come see the endless lists of dead in our villages."

Everyone shared the blame: the Germans because they resorted to a runaway inflation that reduced the mark to less than one *trillionth* of its prewar value, at least in part in hopes of avoiding their international obligations; the Americans because they refused to recognize the connection between the tariff and the debt question; the Allies because they made little effort to pay even a reasonable proportion of their obligations.

In 1924 an international agreement, the Dawes Plan, provided Germany with a $200 million loan designed to stabilize its currency. Germany agreed to pay about $250 million a year in reparations. In 1929 the Young Plan further scaled down the reparations bill. In practice, the Allies paid the United States about what they collected from Germany. Since Germany got the money largely from private American loans, the United States would have served itself and the rest of the world far better had it written off the war debts at the start. In any case, in the late 1920s Americans stopped lending money to Germany, the Great Depression struck, Germany defaulted on its reparations payments, and the Allies then gave up all pretense of meeting their obligations to the United States.

In 1931 President Hoover arranged a one-year moratorium on all international obligations. When the period of grace expired, the question of reparations and debts expired with it—the last token payments were made in 1933. All that remained was a heritage of mistrust and hostility. In 1934 Congress passed the Johnson Debt Default Act, banning loans to nations that had not paid their war debts.

Franklin Roosevelt was at heart an internationalist. He believed that for the United States to recover from the depression, the rest of the world must also recover and that world prosperity was the best insurance against fascism and the threat of another world war. However, he was unwilling to buck the isolationist trend or to rely on international cooperation alone to end the depression. In April 1933 he took the United States off the gold standard, hoping that devaluing the dollar would make it easier to sell American goods abroad.

The following month a World Economic Conference met in London. Delegates from 64 nations sought ways to increase world trade, perhaps by a general reduction of tariffs and the stabilization of currencies. After flirting with the idea of currency stabilization, Roosevelt threw a bombshell into the conference by announcing that the United States would not return to the gold standard. Like most world leaders, he now placed revival of his own nation's limping economy ahead of general world recovery. His decision increased international ill feeling, and the conference collapsed amid anti-American recrimination. In every country, narrow-minded nationalists increased their strength. The German financier Hjalmar Schacht announced smugly that Roosevelt was adopting the maxim of the great *Führer,* Adolf Hitler: "Take your economic fate in your own hands."

European dependence on the American economy is highlighted in this Jim Berryman cartoon from the early months of Roosevelt's administration.

The Triumph of Isolationism

Against this background of depression and international tension, vital changes in American foreign policy took place. Unable to persuade the country to take positive action against aggressors, internationalists like Secretary of State Stimson had begun in 1931 to work for a *discretionary* arms embargo law, to be applied by the president in time of war against whichever side had broken the peace. By early 1933 Stimson had obtained Hoover's backing for an embargo bill, as well as the support of president-elect Roosevelt. First the munitions manufacturers and then the isolationists pounced on it, and in the resulting debate it was amended to make the embargo apply impartially to *all* belligerents.

The amendment would have reversed the impact of any embargo. Instead of providing an effective if essentially negative weapon for influencing international affairs, a blanket embargo would intensify America's ostrichlike isolationism. Stimson's original idea would have permitted arms shipments to China but not to Japan, which might have discouraged the Japanese from attacking. As amended, the embargo would have automatically applied to both sides, thus removing the United States as an influence in the conflict. While Roosevelt accepted the change, the internationalists in Congress did not, and when they withdrew their support the measure died.

The attitude of the munitions makers, who opposed both forms of the embargo, led to a series of studies of the industry. The most important was a Senate investigation (1934–1936) headed by Gerald P. Nye of North Dakota. Nye was convinced that "the interests" had conspired to drag America into World War I; his investigation was more an inquisition than an honest effort to discover what American bankers and munitions makers had been doing between 1914 and 1918. The committee's staff, ferreting into subpoenaed records, uncovered sensational facts about the lobbying activities and profits of various concerns. The Du Pont company's earnings, for example, had soared from $5 million in 1914 to $82 million in 1916. When one senator suggested to Irénée Du Pont that he was displaying a somewhat different attitude toward war than most citizens, Du Pont replied coolly: "Yes; perhaps. You were not in the game, or you might have a different viewpoint."

Popular 1930s cartoonist Daniel Fitzpatrick did many daily drawings on the theme of the munitions industry. The caption reads: "Fellow diplomats—."

Munitions makers had profited far more from neutrality than from American participation in the war, but Nye, abetted by the press, exaggerated the significance of his findings. Millions of citizens became convinced that the bankers who had lent the Allies money and the "merchants of death" who had sold them arms had tricked the country into war and that the "mistake" of 1917 must never be repeated.

While the Nye committee labored, Walter Millis published *The Road to War: America, 1914–1917* (1935). In this best-seller Millis advanced the thesis that British propaganda, the heavy purchases of American supplies by the Allies, and Wilson's differing reactions to violations of neutral rights by Germany and Great Britain had drawn the United States into a war it could and should have steered clear of. Thousands found Millis's logic convincing. International lawyers, notably Charles Warren, a former assistant attorney general, argued that modern warfare had made the idea of freedom of the seas for neutrals meaningless. The United States could stay out of wars, Warren claimed, only by abandoning the seas, clamping an embargo on arms shipments, closing American ports to belligerent vessels, and placing quotas based on prewar sales on the exportation of all contraband. "Under modern conditions there is no reason why the United States Government should run the risk of becoming involved in a war simply to preserve and protect . . . [the] excessive profits to be made out of war trading by some of its citizens," Warren wrote.

These developments led in 1935 to what the historian Robert A. Divine has called "the triumph of isolation." The danger of another world war mounted steadily as Germany, Italy, and Japan repeatedly resorted to force to achieve their expansionist aims. In March 1935 Hitler instituted universal military training and began to raise an army of half a million. In May Mussolini massed troops in Italian Somaliland, using a trivial border clash as pretext for threatening the ancient kingdom of Ethiopia.

Each aggression drove the United States deeper into its shell. Congress responded by passing the Neutrality Act of 1935, which forbade the sale of munitions to *all* belligerents whenever the president should proclaim that a state of war existed. Americans who took passage on belligerent ships after such a proclamation had been issued would do so at their own risk. Roosevelt would have preferred a discretionary embargo or no new legislation at all, but he dared not rouse the ire of the isolationists by vetoing the bill.

In October 1935 Italy invaded Ethiopia and Roosevelt invoked the new neutrality law. Secretary of State Hull asked American exporters to support a "moral embargo" on the sale of oil and other products not covered by the act. His plea was ignored; oil shipments to Italy tripled between October and January. Italy quickly overran and annexed Ethiopia. In February 1936 Congress passed a second neutrality act forbidding all loans to belligerents.

Then, in the summer of 1936, civil war broke out in Spain. The rebels, led by the reactionary General Francisco Franco and strongly backed by Italy and Germany, sought to overthrow the somewhat leftist Spanish Republic. Here, clearly, was a clash between democracy and fascism, and the neutrality laws did not apply to civil wars. However,

Roosevelt now became more fearful of involvement than some isolationists. (Senator Nye, for example, favored selling arms to the legitimate Spanish government despite the fact that it was being supported by the Soviet Union.) The president believed that American interference might cause the conflict in Spain to become a global war, and he was wary of antagonizing the substantial number of American Catholics who were sympathetic to the Franco regime. He warned the Glenn L. Martin aircraft company that selling warplanes to the Spanish Republic "would not be in line with the policy of this government," and at his urging Congress passed another neutrality act broadening the arms embargo to cover civil wars.

Isolationism now reached its peak. A public opinion poll revealed in March 1937 that 94 percent of the people thought American policy should be directed at keeping out of all foreign wars rather than trying to prevent wars from breaking out. In April Congress passed still another neutrality law. It continued the embargo on munitions and loans, *forbade* Americans to travel on belligerent ships, and gave the president discretionary authority to place the sale of other goods to belligerents on a cash-and-carry basis. In theory this would preserve the nation's profitable foreign trade without the risk of war; in fact it played into the hands of the aggressors. While German planes and cannons were turning the tide in Spain, the United States was denying the hard-pressed Spanish loyalists even a case of cartridges.

"With every surrender the prospects of a European war grow darker," Claude G. Bowers, the American ambassador to Spain, warned. The New York *Herald Tribune* pointed out that the neutrality legislation was literally reactionary—designed to keep the United States out of the war of 1914–1918, not the new conflict looming on the horizon. President Roosevelt, in part because of domestic problems such as the Supreme Court packing struggle and the wave of sit-down strikes, and in part because of his own vacillation, seemed to have lost control over the formulation of American foreign policy. The American people, like wild creatures before a forest fire, were rushing in blind panic from the conflagration.

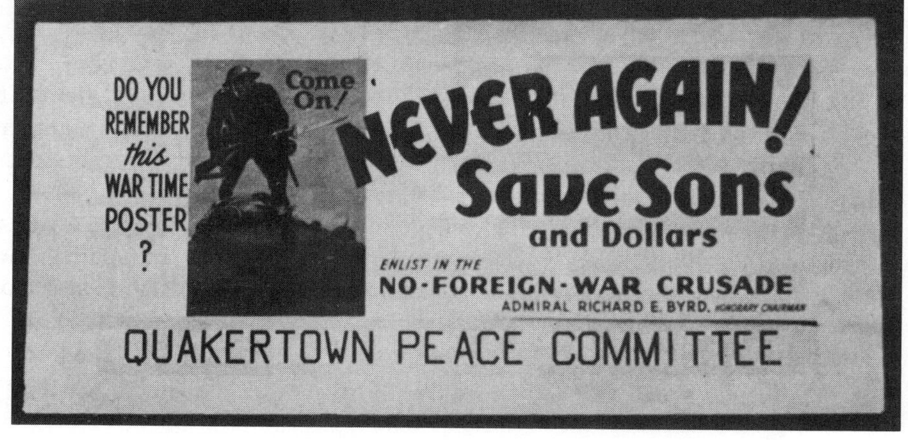

"Never again!" ("Nie wieder Krieg!") *is the message in German and English as citizens on both sides of the Atlantic spoke out against war. The German peace rally took place in the early 1920s; the American billboard dates from a decade later.*

War Again in Europe

There were limits beyond which Americans would not go. In July 1937 the Japanese again attacked China. Peiping fell and the invaders pressed ahead on a broad front. Roosevelt believed that invoking the neutrality law would only help the well-armed Japanese. Taking advantage of the fact that neither side had formally declared war, he allowed the shipment of arms and supplies to both sides.

Then the president went further. Speaking at Chicago in October, he condemned the nations—he mentioned none by name—who were "creating a state of international anarchy and instability *from which there is no escape through mere isolation or neutrality.*" He proposed that "peace-loving nations" have nothing to do with the aggressors. The way to deal with "the epidemic of world lawlessness" was to "quarantine" it. Evidently Roosevelt had no specific plan in mind; nevertheless the "quarantine speech" produced a windy burst of isolationist rhetoric that forced him to back down. "It's a terrible thing," he said, "to look over your shoulder when you are trying to lead—and to find no one there."

Roosevelt came gradually to the conclusion that resisting aggression was more important than keeping out of war; when he did, the need to keep the country united led him at times to be less than candid in his public statements. Hitler's annexation of Austria in March 1938 caused him deep concern. The Nazis' vicious anti-Semitism had caused many of Germany's 500,000 Jewish citizens to seek refuge abroad. Now 190,000 Austrian Jews were under Nazi control. When Roosevelt learned that the Germans were burning synagogues, expelling Jewish children from schools, and otherwise mistreating innocent people, he said that he "could scarcely believe that such things could occur." But public opinion opposed changing the immigration law so that more refugees could be admitted, and the president did nothing.

In September 1938 Hitler demanded that Czechoslovakia cede the German-speaking Sudetenland region to the Reich. British Prime Minister Neville Chamberlain and French Premier Edouard Deladier, in a conference with Hitler at Munich, yielded to Hitler's threats and promises and persuaded the Czechs to surrender the Sudetenland. Roosevelt, though he found this example of appeasement disturbing, did not speak out. Then, when the Nazis seized the rest of Czechoslovakia in March 1939, no one could any longer doubt their aggressive purposes. In a memorable address to Congress, Roosevelt said: "Acts of aggression against sister nations . . . automatically undermine all of us." He called for "methods short of war" to demonstrate America's determination to defend its institutions.

When Hitler threatened Poland in the spring of 1939, demanding the free city of Danzig and the Polish Corridor separating East Prussia from the rest of Germany, and when Mussolini invaded Albania, Roosevelt sent both dictators urgent appeals to keep the peace, but he also urged Congress to repeal the 1937 neutrality act so that the United States could sell arms to Britain and France in the event of war.

Congress refused. "Captain," Vice-President Garner told Roosevelt after counting noses in the Senate, "you haven't got the votes," and the president, perhaps unwisely, accepted this judgment and did not press the issue.

In August 1939 Germany and Russia signed a nonaggression pact, prelude to their joint assault on Poland. On September 1 Hitler's troops invaded Poland, at last provoking Great Britain and France to declare war. Roosevelt immediately summoned Congress into special session and again asked for repeal of the arms embargo. In November, in a vote that followed party lines closely, the Democratic majority pushed through a law permitting the sale of arms and other contraband on a cash-and-carry basis. Short-term loans were authorized, but American vessels were forbidden to carry any products to the belligerents. Since the Allies controlled the seas, cash-and-carry gave them a tremendous advantage.

The German attack on Poland effected a basic change in American thinking. Keeping out of the war remained an almost universal hope, but preventing a Nazi victory became the ultimate, if not always conscious, objective of many citizens. In Roosevelt's case it was perfectly conscious, though he dared not express his feelings candidly because of isolationist strength in Congress and the country. He moved slowly, responding to rather than directing the course of events.

Cash-and-carry did not stop the Nazis. Poland fell in less than a month; then, after a winter lull that cynics called the "phony war," Hitler loosed

A 1938 German poster glorifying Adolf Hitler. The slogan: "One people, one nation, one leader."

his armored divisions against the western powers. Between April 9 and June 22 he taught the world the awful meaning of *Blitzkrieg*—lightning war. Denmark, Norway, the Netherlands, Belgium, and France were successively overwhelmed. The British army, pinned against the sea at Dunkirk, saved itself from annihilation only by fleeing across the English Channel. After the French submitted to his harsh terms on June 22, Hitler controlled nearly all of western Europe.

Roosevelt responded to these disasters in a number of ways. In the fall of 1939, reacting to warnings from Albert Einstein and other scientists that the Germans were trying to develop an atomic bomb, he committed federal funds to a top secret atomic energy program. Even as the British and French were falling back, he sold them, without legal authority, surplus government arms. When Italy entered the war against France while that nation was reeling before Hitler's divisions, the president called the invasion a stab in the back. He froze the American assets of the conquered nations to keep them out of German hands. During the first five months of 1940 he asked Congress to appropriate over $4 billion for national defense. To strengthen national unity he named Henry L. Stimson secretary of war* and another Republican, Frank Knox, secretary of the navy. The United States had abandoned neutrality for nonbelligerency.

After the fall of France, Hitler attempted to bomb and starve the British into submission. The epic air battles over England during the summer of 1940 ended in a decisive defeat for the Nazis, but the Royal Navy, which had only about 100 destroyers, could not control German submarine attacks on shipping. Far more destroyers were needed. In this desperate hour, Prime Minister Winston Churchill, who had replaced Chamberlain in May 1940, asked Roosevelt for 50 old American destroyers to fill the gap.

The navy had 240 destroyers in commission and more than 50 under construction. But direct loan or sale of the vessels would have violated both international and American laws. Any attempt to obtain new legislation would have roused fears that the United States was going down the path that had led it into World War I. Long delay if not outright defeat would have resulted. Roosevelt therefore arranged to "trade" the destroyers for six British naval bases in the Caribbean. In addition, Great Britain leased bases in Bermuda and Newfoundland to the United States.

The destroyers-for-bases deal was one of Roosevelt's masterful achievements as a statesman and as a politician. It helped save Great Britain, and at the same time it circumvented isolationist prejudices, since the president could present it as a shrewd bargain that bolstered America's defenses. A string of island bastions in the Atlantic was more valuable than 50 old destroyers.

Lines were hardening throughout the world. In September 1940, despite last-ditch isolationist resistance, Congress enacted the first peacetime draft

---

* Stimson had held this post from 1911 to 1913 in the Taft Cabinet!

in American history. Some 1.2 million draftees were summoned for one year of service, and 800,000 reservists were called to active duty. That same month Japan signed a mutual-assistance pact with Germany and Italy. This Rome-Berlin-Tokyo axis fused the conflicts in Europe and Asia, turning the struggle into a global war.

A Third Term for FDR

In the midst of these events the 1940 presidential election took place. Why Roosevelt decided to run for a third term is a much-debated question. Partisanship had something to do with it, for no other Democrat seemed so likely to carry the country. Nor would the president have been human had he not been tempted to hold on to power, especially in such critical times. His conviction that no one else could keep a rein on the isolationists was probably decisive. In any case, he used his authority as party chief to control the Democratic convention and was easily renominated. Vice-President Garner, who had become disenchanted with Roosevelt and the New Deal, did not seek a third term; at Roosevelt's dictation, the party chose Secretary of Agriculture Henry A. Wallace for the second spot on the ticket.

The leading Republican candidates were Senator Robert A. Taft of Ohio, son of the former president, and District Attorney Thomas E. Dewey of New York, who had won fame as a "racket buster" and political reformer. Taft was considered conservative and lacking in political glamour; Dewey, barely 38, seemed too young and inexperienced. Instead the Republicans nominated the darkest of dark horses, Wendell L. Willkie of Indiana, the utility magnate who had led the fight against the TVA in 1933.

Despite his political inexperience and Wall Street connections, Willkie made an appealing candidate. He was an energetic, charming, openhearted man capable of inspiring deep loyalties. His rough-hewn rural manner (one Democrat called him "a simple, barefoot Wall Street lawyer") won him wide support in farm districts. Willkie had difficulty, however, finding issues on which to oppose Roosevelt. Good times were at last returning. The New Deal reforms were too popular and too much in line with his own thinking to invite attack.

"Here's the way I look at it. Would it be wise to get rid of Mrs. Roosevelt at a time like this?"

A different slant on FDR's campaign for a third term is expressed in this New Yorker *cartoon from July of 1940.*

He believed as strongly as the president that America could no longer ignore the Nazi threat.

In the end Willkie focused his campaign on Roosevelt's conduct of foreign relations. A preponderance of the Democrats favored all-out aid to Britain, while most Republicans still wished to avoid foreign "entanglements." But the crisis was causing many persons to shift sides. Among interventionists, organizations like the Committee to Defend America by Aiding the Allies, headed by Republican William Allen White, and the small but influential Century Group contained members of both parties. So did the isolationist America First Committee, led by Robert E. Wood of Sears Roebuck and the famous aviator, Charles A. Lindbergh.

While rejecting the isolationist position, Willkie charged that Roosevelt intended to make the United States a participant in the war. "If you reelect him," he told one audience, "you may expect war in April 1941," to which Roosevelt retorted disingenuously since he knew he was not a free agent in the situation, "I have said this before, but I shall say it again and again and again: Your boys are not going to be sent into any foreign wars." In November Roosevelt carried the country handily, though by a smaller majority than in 1932 or 1936. The popular vote was 27 million to 22 million, the electoral count 449 to 82.

The Undeclared War

The election indicated the direction in which public opinion was moving and encouraged Roosevelt to act more boldly. When Churchill informed him that the cash-and-carry system would no longer suffice because Great Britain was rapidly exhausting its financial resources, he decided at once to provide the British with whatever they needed. Instead of proposing to lend them money, a step certain to rouse memories of the vexatious war debt controversies, he devised the "lend-lease" program, one of his most ingenious and imaginative creations.

First he spoke directly to the people in a "fireside chat" that stressed the evil intentions of the Nazis and the dangers that a German victory would create for America. Aiding Britain should be looked at simply as a form of self-defense. "As planes and ships and guns and shells are produced," he said, American defense experts would decide "how much shall be sent abroad and how much shall remain at home." When the radio talk provoked a favorable public response, Roosevelt went to Congress in January 1941 with a plan calling for the expenditure of $7 billion for war materials that the president could sell, lend, lease, exchange, or transfer to any country whose defense he deemed vital to that of the United States. After two months of debate, Congress gave him what he had asked for.

Although the wording of the Lend-Lease Act obscured its immediate purpose, the saving of Great Britain, the president was frank in explaining his plan. He did not minimize the dangers involved. "If we are to be completely honest with ourselves," he said in his radio speech, "we must admit that there is risk in any course we may take." Yet his mastery of practical politics was never more in evidence. To counter Irish-American prejudices against the English, he pointed out that the Irish Republic would surely fall under Nazi domination if Hitler won the war. He coupled his demand for heavy military expenditures with his enunciation of the idealistic "Four Freedoms"—freedom of speech, freedom of religion, freedom from want, and freedom from fear—for which, he said, the war was being fought.

After the enactment of lend-lease, aid short of war was no longer seriously debated. The American navy began to patrol the North Atlantic, shadowing German submarines and radioing their locations to British warships and planes. In April 1941 United States forces occupied Greenland; in May the president declared a state of unlimited national emergency. After Hitler invaded the Soviet Union in June, Roosevelt moved slowly, for anti-Soviet feeling in the United States was intense.* But it was obviously to the nation's advantage to help any country that was resisting Hitler's armies. In November $1 billion in lend-lease aid was put at the disposal of the Russians.

Meanwhile, Iceland was occupied in July 1941, and the draft law was extended in August—by the margin of a single vote in the House of Representatives. In September the German submarine *U-652* fired a torpedo at the destroyer *Greer* in the North Atlantic. The *Greer,* which had provoked the attack by tracking *U-652* and flashing its position to a British plane, avoided the torpedo and dropped 19 depth charges in an effort to sink the submarine.

Roosevelt (nothing he ever did provided more ammunition for his critics) announced that the *Greer* had been innocently "carrying mail to Iceland." He called the U-boats "the rattlesnakes of the Atlantic" and ordered the navy to "shoot on sight" any German craft in the waters south and west of Iceland and to convoy merchant vessels as far as that island. After the sinking of the destroyer *Reuben James* on October 30, Congress voted to allow the arming of American merchant ships, and to permit them to carry cargoes to Allied ports.

* During the 1930s Russia took a far firmer stand against the fascists than any other power, but after joining Hitler in swallowing up Poland, it attacked and defeated Finland during the winter of 1939–1940 and annexed the Baltic states. These acts practically destroyed the small communist movement in the United States.

The Road to Pearl Harbor

By December 1941 the United States was in fact at war, but it is hard to see how a formal declaration could have come about or how American soldiers could have been committed to the fray had it not been for Japan. Japanese-American relations had worsened steadily after Japan resumed its war on China in 1937. As they extended their control, the invaders systematically froze out American and other foreign business interests. They declared that the Open Door policy was obsolete. Roosevelt retaliated by lending money to China and asking American manufacturers not to sell airplanes to Japan. In July 1940, with Japanese troops threatening French Indochina, Congress placed exports of aviation gasoline and certain types of scrap iron to Japan under a licensing system; in September all sales of scrap were banned and loans to China increased. After the creation of the Rome-Berlin-Tokyo axis, Roosevelt extended the embargo to include machine tools and other items. The Japanese, determined to create what they euphemistically called a Greater East Asia Co-Prosperity Sphere, pushed ahead relentlessly despite the economic pressures.

Neither the United States nor Japan wanted war. In the spring of 1941 Secretary of State Cordell Hull conferred in Washington with the Japanese ambassador, Kichisaburo Nomura, in an effort to resolve their differences. Hull's approach, while morally irreproachable, showed little appreciation of the political and military situation in the Far East. He demanded that Japan withdraw from China and promise not to attack the Dutch and French colonies in southeast Asia, which were ripe for the plucking after Hitler's victories in Europe. How Hull expected to get Japan to give up its conquests without either making concessions or going to war is not clear. He refused to recognize that the old balance of power that had enabled the United States to attain its modest objectives in the Far East without the use of force had ceased to exist.

Japan might well have accepted limited annexations in the area in return for the removal of American trade restrictions, but Hull seemed bent on converting the Japanese to pacifism by exhortation. He insisted on total withdrawal, to which even the moderates in Japan would not agree. When Hitler invaded the Soviet Union, thereby removing the threat of Russian intervention in the Far East, Japan decided to occupy Indochina even at the risk of war with the United States. Roosevelt retaliated (July 1941) by freezing Japanese assets in the United States and clamping an embargo on oil.

Now the war party in Japan assumed control. Nomura was instructed to tell Hull that his country would refrain from further expansion if the United States and Great Britain would cut off all aid to China and lift the economic blockade. Japan promised to pull out of Indochina once "a just peace" had been established with China. When the United States rejected these demands and repeated (November 26) its insistence that Japan "withdraw all military, naval, air, and police forces" from China and Indochina, the Japanese prepared to assault the Dutch East Indies, British Malaya, and the Philippines. To immobilize the United States Pacific Fleet, they planned a surprise aerial raid on the Hawaiian naval base at Pearl Harbor.

An American cryptanalyst, Colonel William F. Friedman, had "cracked" the Japanese diplomatic code; the government therefore had good reason to believe that war was imminent. On November 17 Hull warned an American general, "Those fellows mean to fight and you will have to watch out." The code breakers had also made it possible to keep close tabs on the movements of Japanese navy units. But in the hectic rush of events, both military and civilian authorities failed to make effective use of the information collected. They expected the blow to fall somewhere in southeast Asia, possibly in the Philippines.

The garrison at Pearl Harbor was alerted against "a surprise aggressive move in any direction." The commanders there, Admiral Husband E. Kimmel and General Walter C. Short, believing an attack impossible, took precautions only against Japanese sabotage. Thus when planes from Japanese aircraft carriers swooped down upon Pearl Harbor on the morning of December 7, they found easy targets. In less than two hours they reduced the Pacific Fleet to a smoking ruin: two battleships destroyed, six others heavily battered, nearly a dozen lesser vessels put out of action. More than 150 planes were wrecked; over 2,300 servicemen were killed and 1,100 wounded.

Never had American arms suffered a more devastating or shameful defeat and seldom has an

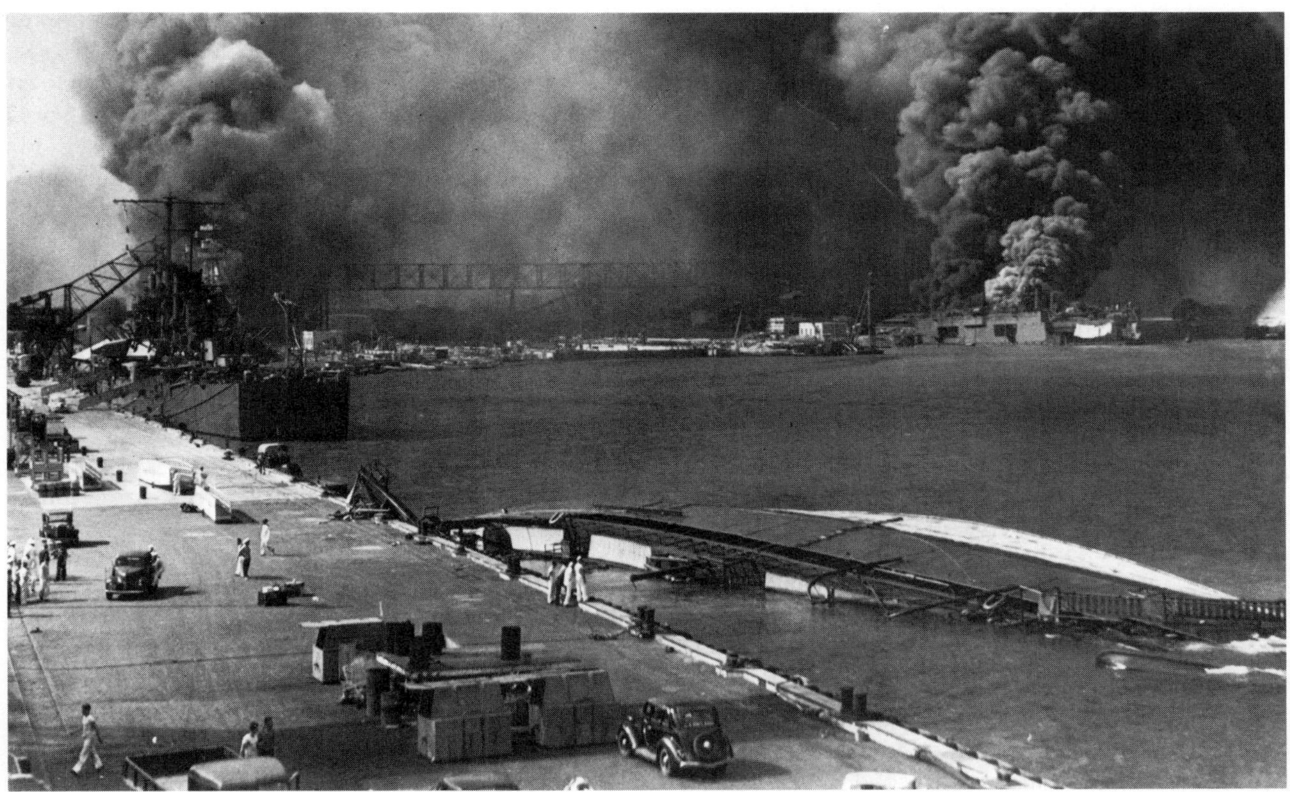

A general view of just part of the havoc wreaked by the Japanese planes at Pearl Harbor. Starting from the bottom of the photo and moving clockwise: the capsized minelayer Ogala, *the bomb-damaged 10,000-ton cruiser* Helena, *the battleship* Pennsylvania *(whose superstructure shows in back of the* Helena*), the destroyer* Shaw *on fire in drydock (right center), and the battleship* Maryland *burning at far right.*

event roused so much controversy or produced such intensive historical study. The official blame was placed chiefly on Admiral Kimmel and General Short. They might well have been more alert, but responsibility for the disaster was widespread. Military and civilian officials in Washington had failed to pass on all that they knew to Hawaii or even to one another. On the other hand, the crucial intelligence about the coming attack that the code breakers provided was mixed with masses of other information and was extremely difficult to evaluate. Certainly the argument that President Roosevelt knew of the attack before it came and held back the information in order to justify going to war is without substance.

On December 8 Congress declared war on Japan. Formal war with Germany and Italy was still not inevitable—isolationists were far more ready to resist the "yellow peril" in Asia than to fight in Europe. The Axis powers, however, honored their treaty obligations to Japan and on December 11 declared war on the United States. America was now fully engaged in the great world conflict.

Mobilizing the Home Front

War placed immense strains on the American economy and produced immense results. About 15 million men and women entered the armed services; they, and in part the millions more in Allied uniforms, had to be fed, clothed, housed, and supplied with equipment ranging from typewriters and paper clips to rifles and grenades, tanks and airplanes.

Congress granted wide emergency powers to the president. It refrained from excessive meddling in administrative problems and in military strategy. However, while the Democrats retained control of both houses throughout the war, their margins were relatively narrow. A coalition of conservatives in both parties frequently prevented the president from having his way and exercised close control over expenditures.

Roosevelt was an inspiring war leader but not a very good administrator. Any honest account of the war on the home front must reveal glaring examples of confusion, inefficiency, and pointless bickering. The squabbling and waste characteristic of the early New Deal period made relatively little difference—what mattered then was raising the nation's spirits and keeping people occupied; efficiency was less than essential, however desirable. In wartime the nation's fate, perhaps that of the entire free world, depended on delivering weapons and supplies to the battlefronts.

The confusion attending economic mobilization can easily be overstressed. Nearly all Roosevelt's basic decisions were sensible and humane: to pay a large part of the cost of the war by collecting taxes rather than by borrowing and to base taxation on ability to pay; to ration scarce raw materials and consumer goods; to regulate prices and wages. If these decisions were not always translated into action with perfect effectiveness, they always operated in the direction of efficiency and the public good.

Roosevelt's greatest accomplishment was his inspiring of businessmen, workers, and farmers with a sense of national purpose. In this respect his function duplicated his earlier role in fighting the depression, and he performed it with even greater success.

A sense of tremendous economic expansion caused by the demands of war can most easily be captured by reference to official statistics of production. In 1939 the United States was still mired in the Great Depression. The gross national product amounted to about $91.3 billion. In 1945, after allowing for changes in the price level, it was $166.6 billion. More specifically, manufacturing output nearly doubled and agricultural output rose 22 percent. In 1939 the United States turned out fewer than 6,000 airplanes, in 1944 more than 96,000. Shipyards produced 237,000 tons of vessels in 1939, 10 million tons in 1943. The index of iron and steel production leaped from 87 in 1938 to

Roosevelt's ability to reassure and inspire the public is attested to in this cheerful caricature by Justin Murray, in which the president is tagged with the mock scientific name "Unitus Andguidus."

258 in 1944, that of rubber goods from 113 to 238 in the same years. Petroleum output rose from 1.2 billion barrels in 1939 to 1.7 billion in 1945, iron ore from 28 million tons in 1938 to 105 million in 1942, copper from 562,000 tons in 1938 to over 1 million in 1942, aluminum from 286 million pounds in 1938 to 1.8 billion in 1943.

Wartime experience proved that the Keynesian economists were correct in saying that government spending would spark economic growth. About 8 million people were unemployed in June 1940. After Pearl Harbor, unemployment declined swiftly and by 1945 the *civilian* work force had increased by nearly 7 million. Millions of women flocked into defense industries, a trend memorialized in the popular song "Rosie the Riveter."

Mobilization had begun well before December 1941, when 1.6 million men were already under arms. Economic mobilization got under way in August 1939, when the president created a War Resources Board to plan for possible conversion of industry to war production. This board became the Office of Production Management (January 1941) under William S. Knudsen, president of General Motors. In April 1941 Roosevelt set up an Office of Price Administration (OPA), headed by the economist Leon Henderson, in an attempt to check profiteering and control consumer prices, and in August a Supplies Priorities and Allocation Board, directed by Donald M. Nelson, to coordinate the requests of military purchasers for scarce materials with those of industry.

These prewar efforts worked poorly, mainly because the president refused to centralize authority. The separation of the responsibility for dispensing materials from the control of the prices paid for materials practically hamstrung both Nelson's and Henderson's organizations. For months after Pearl Harbor the civilian boards squabbled with the military over everything from the allocation of scarce raw materials to the technical specifications of weapons. Roosevelt refused to settle these conflicts as only he could have.

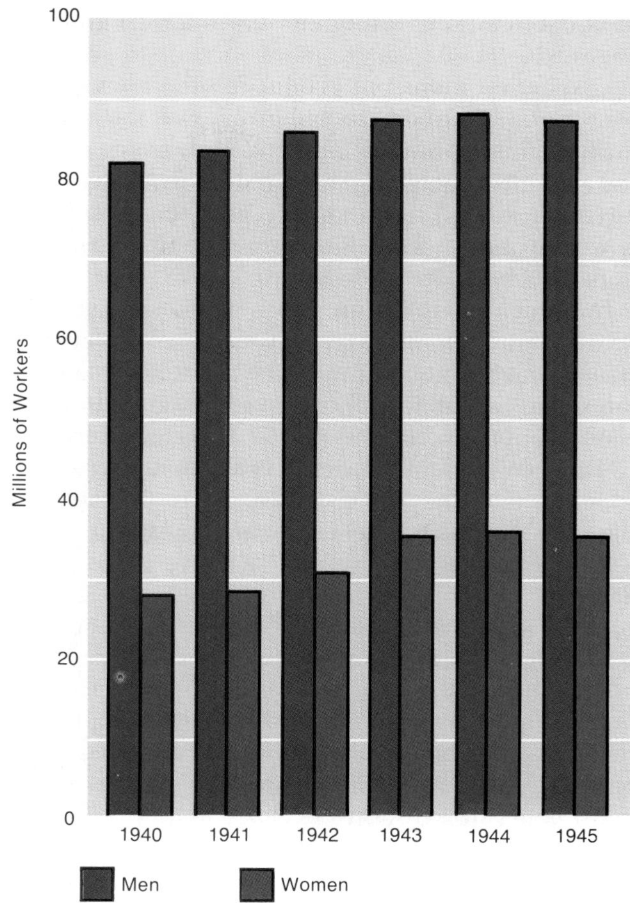

MEN AND WOMEN IN THE LABOR FORCE, 1940–1945

In 1940, about 75 percent of workers in the labor force—82 million—were men, and the other 25 percent—28 million—were women. By the end of World War II, in 1945, nearly 8 million more women had entered the work force, as against 5 million more men. The balance of the labor force had shifted to roughly 70 percent men, 30 percent women.

The War Economy

Yet by early 1943 the nation's economic machinery had been converted to a wartime footing and was functioning smoothly. Supreme Court Justice James F. Byrnes, a former senator from South Carolina, resigned from the Court to become a sort of "economic czar." His Office of War Mobilization had complete control over the issuance of priorities and over prices. Rents, food prices, and wages were strictly regulated, and items in short supply were rationed to consumers. While wages and prices had soared during 1942, after April 1943 they leveled off. Thereafter the cost of living scarcely changed until controls were lifted after the war (see graph, pages 916–917).

Expanded industrial production together with conscription caused a labor shortage that increased the bargaining power of workers. At the same time, the national emergency required some limitation on the workers' right to take advantage of this power. In March 1941 Roosevelt appointed a National Defense Mediation Board to assist labor and management in avoiding work stoppages. After Pearl Harbor he created a National War Labor Board to arbitrate disputes and "stabilize" wage rates, and he banned all changes in wages without NWLB approval. In the "Little Steel" case (July 1942), NWLB laid down the rule that wage increases should not normally exceed 15 percent of the rates of January 1941, a figure roughly in line with the increase in the cost of living since that date.

Prosperity and stiffer government controls added significantly to the strength of organized labor; indeed, the war had more to do with institutionalizing industrywide collective bargaining than the New Deal period. As workers recognized the benefits of union membership, they flocked into the organizations. Strikes declined sharply at first: 23 million hours of labor had been lost in 1941 because of strikes; only 4.18 million were lost in 1942.

Some crippling work stoppages did occur. In May 1943 the government seized the coal mines after John L. Lewis's United Mine Workers walked out of the pits. This strike led Congress to pass, over Roosevelt's veto, the Smith-Connally War Labor Disputes Act (June 1943), which gave the president the power to take over any war plant threatened by a strike. The act declared strikes against seized plants illegal and imposed stiff penalties on violators. Although strikes continued to occur—the loss in hours of labor zoomed to 38 million in 1945—when Roosevelt asked for a labor draft law, Congress refused to go along.

Wages and prices remained in fair balance. Overtime work fattened paychecks, and a new stress in labor contracts on fringe benefits such as paid vacations, premium pay for night work, and various forms of employer-subsidized health insurance added to the prosperity of labor. The war effort had almost no adverse effect on the standard of living of the average citizen, a vivid demonstration of the productivity of the American economy. The manufacture of automobiles ceased and pleasure driving became next to impossible because of gasoline rationing, but most civilian activities went on much as they had before Pearl Harbor. Because of the need to conserve cloth, skirts were shortened, cuffs disappeared from men's trousers, and the vest passed out of style. Plastics replaced metals in toys, containers, and other products. While items such as meat, sugar, and shoes were rationed, they were doled out in amounts adequate for the needs of most persons. Americans had both guns *and* butter; belt-tightening of the type experienced by the other belligerents was unheard of.

The federal government spent twice as much money between 1941 and 1945 as in its entire previous history. This made heavy borrowing necessary. The national debt, which stood at less than $49 billion in 1941, increased by more than that amount *each year* between 1942 and 1945 and totaled nearly $260 billion when the war ended. However, Roosevelt insisted that as much of the cost of the war as possible be paid for at the time: over 40 percent of the total was met by taxation, a far larger proportion than in any earlier war.

This policy helped to check inflation by siphoning off money that would otherwise have competed for scarce consumer goods. Heavy excise taxes on amusements and luxuries further discouraged spending, as did the government's war bond campaigns, which persuaded patriotic citizens to lend part of their income to Uncle Sam. The tax program also helped to maintain public morale. High taxes on incomes (up to 94 percent) and on excess profits (95 percent), together with a limit of $25,000 a year after taxes on salaries, convinced the people that no one was profiting inordinately from the war effort.

The income tax, which had never before touched the mass of white-collar and industrial workers, was extended downward until nearly everyone had to pay it. To collect efficiently the relatively small sums paid by most persons, Congress adopted the payroll-deduction system proposed by Beardsley Ruml, chairman of the Federal Reserve Bank of New York. Employers withheld the taxes owed by workers from their paychecks and turned the money over to the government.

The steeply graduated tax rates combined with a general increase in the income of workers and

Women welders beveling armor plate on tank bodies, photographed in 1943 by Margaret Bourke-White of Life.

farmers effected a substantial shift in the distribution of wealth in the United States. The poor became richer, while the rich, if not actually poorer, collected a smaller proportion of the national income. The wealthiest 1 percent of the population had received 13.4 percent of the national income in 1935 and 11.5 percent in 1941. In 1944 this group received 6.7 percent.

War and Social Change

Enormous social effects stemmed from this shift, but World War II altered the patterns of American life in so many ways that it would be wrong to ascribe the transformations to any single source. Never was the population more fluid. The millions who put on uniforms found themselves transported first to training camps in every section of the country and then to battlefields scattered from Europe and Africa to the far reaches of the Pacific. Burgeoning new defense plants drew other millions to places like Hanford, Washington, and Oak Ridge, Tennessee, where great atomic energy installations were constructed, and to the aircraft factories of California and other states. As in earlier periods the trend was from east to west, from south to north, and from countryside to the cities. The population of California increased by more than 50 percent in the forties, that of other far western states almost as much.

The war affected blacks in many ways. Several factors operated to improve their lot. One was their growing tendency to demand fair treatment. Another was the reaction of Americans to Hitler's senseless murder of millions of Jews, an outgrowth of his doctrine of "Aryan" superiority. These barbarities compelled millions of white citizens to reexamine their views about race. If the nation expected blacks to risk their lives for the common good, how could it continue to treat them as second-class citizens? Black leaders pointed out the inconsistency between fighting for democracy abroad and ignoring it at home. "We want democracy in Alabama," the NAACP announced, and this argument too had some effect on white thinking.

Blacks in the armed forces were treated a good deal more fairly than they had been in World War I. Although segregation did not end, blacks were enlisted for the first time in the air force and the marines, and they were given more responsible positions in the army and navy. The army commissioned its first black general. Some 600 black pilots won their wings. Altogether about a million served, about half of them overseas. The extensive and honorable performance of many of these units could not be ignored by the white majority.

Economic realities operated significantly to the advantage of blacks. More of them had been unemployed in proportion to their numbers than any other group; now the labor shortage brought employment for all. The CIO industrial unions continued to enroll blacks by the thousands.

These gains failed to satisfy black leaders. The NAACP, which increased its membership from 50,000 in 1940 to almost 405,000 in 1946, adopted a more militant stance than in World War I. Discrimination in defense plants seemed far less tolerable than it had in 1917–1918. Even before Pearl Harbor, A. Philip Randolph, president of the Brotherhood of Sleeping Car Porters, organized a march of blacks on Washington to demand equal opportunity for black workers. To prevent this march from taking place at a time of national crisis, President Roosevelt agreed to issue an order prohibiting discrimination in plants with defense contracts, and he set up a Fair Employment Practices Committee to see that the order was carried out. Executive Order 8802 was not perfectly enforced, but it opened up better jobs to black workers and led many employers to change their hiring practices.

Prejudice and mistreatment did not cease. Race riots erupted in many cities; black soldiers were often provided with inferior recreational facilities and otherwise discriminated against in and around army camps. Blood plasma from blacks and whites was kept separately even though the two "varieties" were indistinguishable and the process of storing plasma had been devised by a black doctor, Charles Drew. Blacks, therefore, became increasingly embittered. Roy Wilkins, head of the NAACP, put it this way in 1942: "No Negro leader with a constituency can face his members today and ask full support for the war in the light of the atmosphere the government has created." Many black newspaper editors were so critical of the administration that conservatives demanded they be indicted for sedition.

Roosevelt would have none of this, but the militants annoyed him; he felt that they should hold their demands in abeyance until the war had been won. Apparently he failed to realize the depth of black anger, and in this he was no different from the majority of whites. A revolution was in the making, yet in 1942 a poll revealed that a solid majority of whites still believed that black Americans were "satisfied" with their place in society.

While World War II affected the American people far more drastically than World War I had, it produced much less intolerance and fewer examples of the repression of individual freedom of opinion. The people seemed able to distinguish between the Nazis and Americans of German descent in a way that had escaped their parents. The fact that nearly all German-Americans were vigorously anti-Nazi helps explain this, but the underlying public attitude was more important. Americans went to war in 1941 without illusions and without enthusiasm, determined to win but expecting only to preserve what they had. They therefore found it easier to tolerate dissent, to view the dangers they faced realistically, and to concentrate on the real foreign enemy without venting their feelings on domestic scapegoats. The nation's 100,000 conscientious objectors met with little hostility.

The one flagrant example of intolerance was the relocation of the West Coast Japanese in internment camps in the interior of the country. About 110,000 Americans of Japanese ancestry were rounded up and sent off against their will. The excuse was fear that they might be disloyal, but frustration at not being able to strike a quick blow at Japan had much to do with the unjustified and callous act. The Supreme Court upheld the relocation order in *Korematsu* v. *United States* (1944), but in *Ex parte Endo* it forbade the internment of loyal Japanese-American citizens. Unfortunately the latter decision was not handed down until December 1944.

Other social changes that occurred during the war included a sharp increase in marriage and birthrates, a response both to prosperity and to the natural desire of young men going off to risk death in distant lands to establish roots before departing. The population of the United States had increased by only 3 million during the depression decade of the thirties; during the next five years it rose by 6.5 million. So many hasty marriages, followed by long periods of separation, also brought a rise

Identification tags hung from the collars of the Mochida children as they posed with their parents for photographer Dorothea Lange. The date was May 8, 1942, and the family was awaiting transportation to a detention camp from their home in Hayward, California.

in divorces from about 170 per thousand marriages in 1941 to 310 per thousand in 1945.

Allied Strategy: Europe First

Only days after Pearl Harbor, Prime Minister Churchill and his military chiefs met in Washington with Roosevelt and his advisers. In every quarter of the globe, disaster threatened. The Japanese were gobbling up the Far East. Hitler's armies, checked outside Leningrad and Moscow, were preparing for a massive attack in the direction of Stalingrad, on the Volga River. German divisions under General Erwin Rommel were beginning a drive across North Africa toward the Suez Canal. U-boats were taking a heavy toll in the North Atlantic. British and American leaders believed that eventually they could muster enough force to smash their enemies, but whether or not the troops already in action could hold out until this force arrived was an open question.

The decision of the strategists was to concentrate first against the Germans. Japan's conquests were in remote and, from the Allied point of view, relatively unimportant regions. If Russia surrendered, Hitler might well be able to invade Great Britain, thus making his position in Europe impregnable by depriving the United States of a base for a counterattack.

But how to strike at Hitler? American leaders wanted a second front in France, and the harried Russians backed them up. The British, however, believed that this would require more power than the Allies could presently command. They advocated instead air bombardment of German industry combined with peripheral attacks by land forces to harass the enemy while armies and supplies were being massed. The British were probably right. When the invasion of France did come against a greatly weakened Germany in 1944, the difficulties were still enormous. A landing in 1942 would almost certainly have been repulsed.

During the summer of 1942 Allied planes began

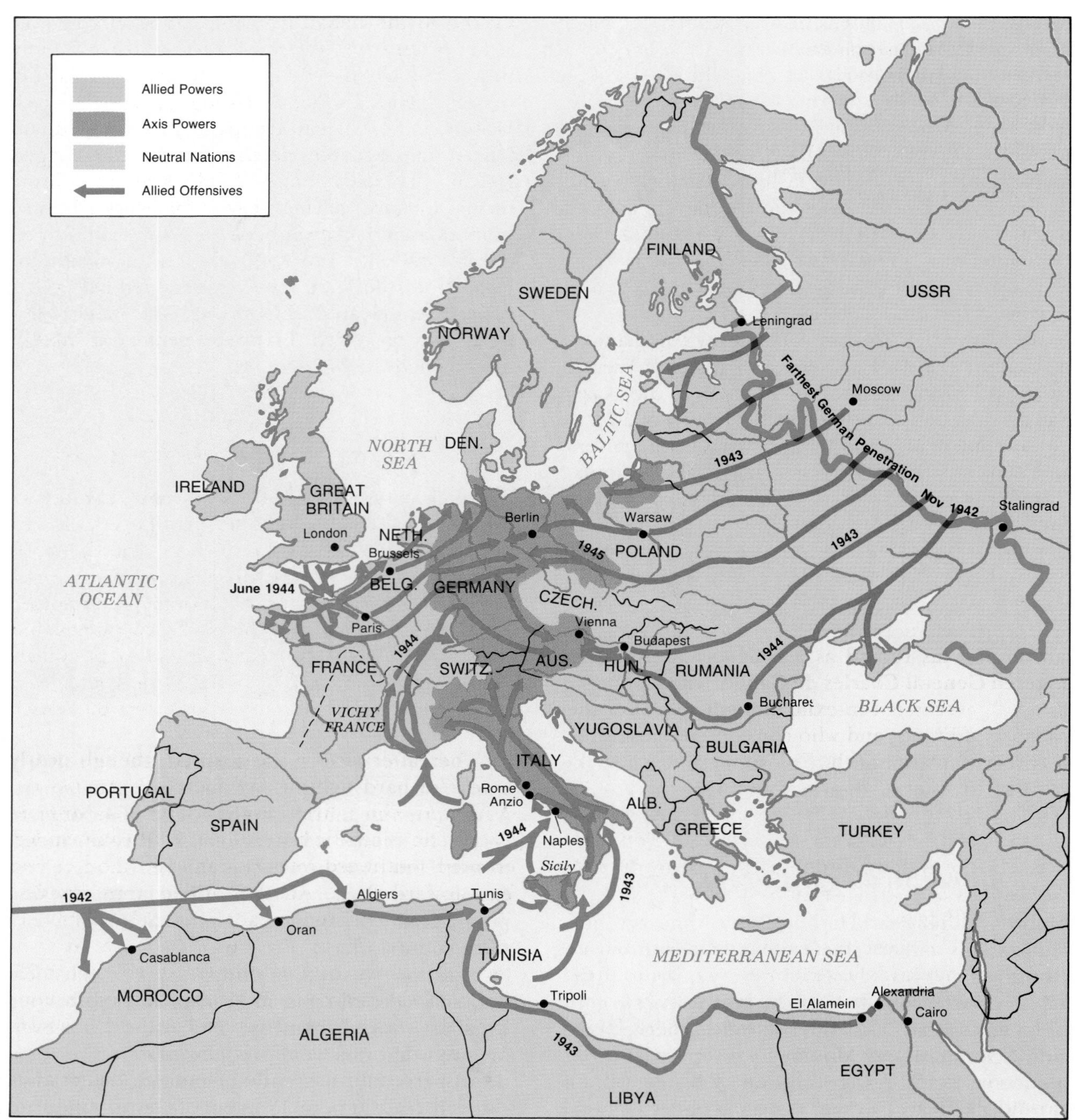

WORLD WAR II, EUROPEAN THEATER

to bomb German cities. In a crescendo through 1943 and 1944, British and American bombers pulverized the centers of Nazi might. While air attacks did not destroy the German armies' capacity to fight, they hampered war production, tangled communications, and brought the war home to the German people in awesome fashion. Humanitarians deplored the heavy loss of life among the civilian population, but the response of the realists was that Hitler had begun indiscriminate bombing, and Allied survival depended on smashing the German war machine.

In November 1942 an Allied army commanded by General Dwight D. Eisenhower struck at French North Africa. After the fall of France, the Nazis had set up a puppet regime in those parts of France not occupied by their troops, with headquarters at Vichy in central France. This collaborationist Vichy government controlled French North Africa. But the North African commandant, Admiral Jean Darlan, promptly switched sides when Eisenhower's forces landed. After a brief show of resistance, the French surrendered.

The Allies were willing to do business with Darlan despite his record as a collaborationist. This angered General Charles de Gaulle, who had organized a government-in-exile immediately after the collapse of France and who considered himself the true representative of the French people. Many liberals in the United States agreed with de Gaulle. Darlan was assassinated in December, and eventually the Free French obtained control of North Africa, but the Allied attitude had much to do with de Gaulle's postwar suspicion of both Britain and the United States.

In 1942, however, the arrangement with Darlan paid large dividends. Eisenhower was able to press forward quickly against the Germans. In February 1943 at Kasserine Pass in the desert south of Tunis, American tanks met Rommel's *Afrika Korps.* The battle ended in a standoff, but with British troops closing in from their Egyptian bases to the east, the Germans were soon trapped and crushed. In May, after Rommel had been recalled to Germany, his army surrendered.

In July 1943, while air attacks on Germany continued and the Russians slowly pushed the Germans back from the gates of Stalingrad, the Allies invaded Sicily from Africa. In September they advanced to the Italian mainland. Mussolini had already fallen from power (in April of 1945 he was caught and killed by Italian partisans), and his successor, Marshal Pietro Badoglio, surrendered. However, the German troops in Italy threw up an almost impregnable defense across the rugged Italian peninsula. The Anglo-American army inched forward, paying heavily for every advance. Monte Cassino, halfway between Naples and Rome, did not fall until May 1944, the capital itself until June; months of hard fighting remained before the country was cleared of Germans. The Italian campaign was an Allied disappointment even though it weakened the enemy.

Germany Overwhelmed

By the time the Allies had taken Rome, the mighty army needed to invade France had been collected in England under Eisenhower's command. On D-Day, June 6, the assault forces stormed ashore at five points along the coast of Normandy, supported by a great armada and thousands of planes and paratroops. Against fierce but ill-coordinated German resistance, they established a beachhead: within a few weeks a million troops were on French soil.

Thereafter victory was assured, though nearly a year of hard fighting lay ahead. In August the American Third Army under General George S. Patton, an eccentric but brilliant field commander, erupted southward into Brittany and then veered east toward Paris. Another Allied army invaded France from the Mediterranean in mid-August and advanced rapidly north. Free French troops were given the honor of liberating Paris on August 25. Belgium was cleared by British and Canadian units a few days later. By mid-September the Allies were fighting on the edge of Germany itself.

The front now stretched from the Netherlands along the borders of Belgium, Luxembourg, and France all the way to Switzerland. If the Allies had mounted a massive assault at any one point, as the British commander, Field Marshal Bernard Montgomery, urged, the struggle might have been brought to a quick conclusion. While the two armies were roughly equal in size, the Allies had complete control of the air and twenty times as many

". . . forever, Amen. Hit the dirt."

Bill Mauldin's Willie and Joe and buddies have their trenchside prayer meeting abruptly halted when the chaplain hears incoming fire.

tanks as the foe. The pressure of the advancing Russians on the eastern front made it difficult for the Germans to reinforce their troops in the west. But General Eisenhower believed a concentrated attack too risky. His supply and communications problems were fantastically complex, and the defenses of Hitler's Siegfried Line, in some regions three miles deep, presented a formidable obstacle. He prepared instead for a general advance.

While he was regrouping, the Germans on December 16 launched a counterattack, planned by Hitler himself, against the Allied center in the Ardennes Forest. The Germans hoped to break through to the Belgian port of Antwerp, thereby splitting the Allied armies in two. The plan was foolhardy and therefore unexpected, and it almost succeeded. The Germans drove a salient ("the bulge") about 50 miles into Belgium, but once the element of surprise had been overcome, their chance of breaking through to the sea was lost. Eisenhower concentrated first on preventing them from broadening the break in his lines and then on blunting the point of their advance. By late January 1945 the old line had been reestablished. The "Battle of the Bulge" cost the United States 77,000 casualties and delayed Eisenhower's offensive, but it exhausted the Germans' last reserves.

American GI's suffered the rigors of a bitter European winter in the Battle of the Bulge, 1944–1945.

The Allies pressed forward to the Rhine, winning a bridgehead on the far bank of the river on March 7. Thereafter, another German city fell almost daily. With the Russians racing westward against crumbling resistance, the end could not be long delayed. In April American and Russian forces made contact at the Elbe River. A few days later, with Russian shells reducing his capital to rubble, Hitler, by then probably insane, took his own life in his Berlin air raid shelter. On May 8 Germany surrendered.

The Naval War in the Pacific

Defeating Germany first had not meant abandoning the Pacific region entirely to the Japanese. While armies were being trained and material accumulated for the European struggle, much of the available American strength was diverted to maintaining vital communications in the Far East and preventing further Japanese expansion. The navy's aircraft carriers had escaped destruction at Pearl Harbor, a stroke of immense good fortune. Without most tacticians realizing it, the airplane had revolutionized naval warfare. Commanders discovered that carrier-based planes were far more effective against warships than the heaviest naval artillery because of their greater range and more concentrated firepower. Battleships made excellent gun platforms from which to pound shore installations and support land operations, but against other vessels aircraft were of prime importance.

This truth was demonstrated in May 1942 in the Battle of the Coral Sea. Having captured an empire in a few months without the loss of any warship larger than a destroyer, the Japanese believed the war already won. They were suffering from what one of their admirals who knew better called the "victory disease." This led them to overextend themselves.

The Coral Sea lies northeast of Australia and south of New Guinea and the Solomon Islands. Mastery of these waters would cut Australia off from Hawaii and thus from American aid. Admiral Isoroku Yamamoto, believing that he could range freely over the waters west of Pearl Harbor, had dispatched a large fleet of troop ships screened by many warships to attack Port Moresby, on the southern New Guinea coast. On May 7–8 planes from the American carriers *Lexington* and *Yorktown* struck the convoy's screen, sinking a small carrier and damaging a large one. Superficially, the battle seemed a victory for the Japanese, for their planes mortally wounded the *Lexington* and sank two other ships, but the troop transports had been forced to turn back—Port Moresby was saved. Although large numbers of cruisers and destroyers took part in the action, none came within sight or gun range of an enemy ship. All the destruction was wrought by carrier aircraft.

Encouraged by the Coral sea "victory," Yamamoto decided to force the American fleet into a showdown battle by assaulting Midway Island, west of Hawaii. His armada never reached its destination. Between June 4 and 7 control of the Central Pacific was decided entirely by air power. American dive bombers sent four large carriers to the bottom. About 300 Japanese planes were destroyed. The United States lost only the *Yorktown* and a destroyer. The powerful Japanese battleships played no role in the action, and when deprived of air cover, they had to withdraw ignominiously. Thereafter the initiative in the Pacific war shifted to the Americans.

American successes in the Pacific were in part the result of the breaking of the Japanese codes. But even with advance knowledge of Japanese intentions, victory came slowly and at painful cost. American land forces were under the command of Douglas MacArthur, a brilliant but egocentric general whose judgment was sometimes distorted by his intense concern for his own reputation. Son of General Arthur MacArthur, who had played a major role in the original conquest of the Philippines, MacArthur was in command of American troops in the islands when the Japanese struck in December 1941. After his heroic but hopeless defense of Manila and the Bataan peninsula, President Roosevelt had him evacuated by PT boat to escape capture.

Thereafter MacArthur was obsessed with the idea of personally leading an American army back to the Philippines. Although many strategists believed that the islands should be bypassed in the drive on the Japanese homeland, in the end MacArthur convinced the Joint Chiefs of Staff, who determined strategy. Two separate drives were undertaken, one from New Guinea toward the Philippines under MacArthur, the other through the Cen-

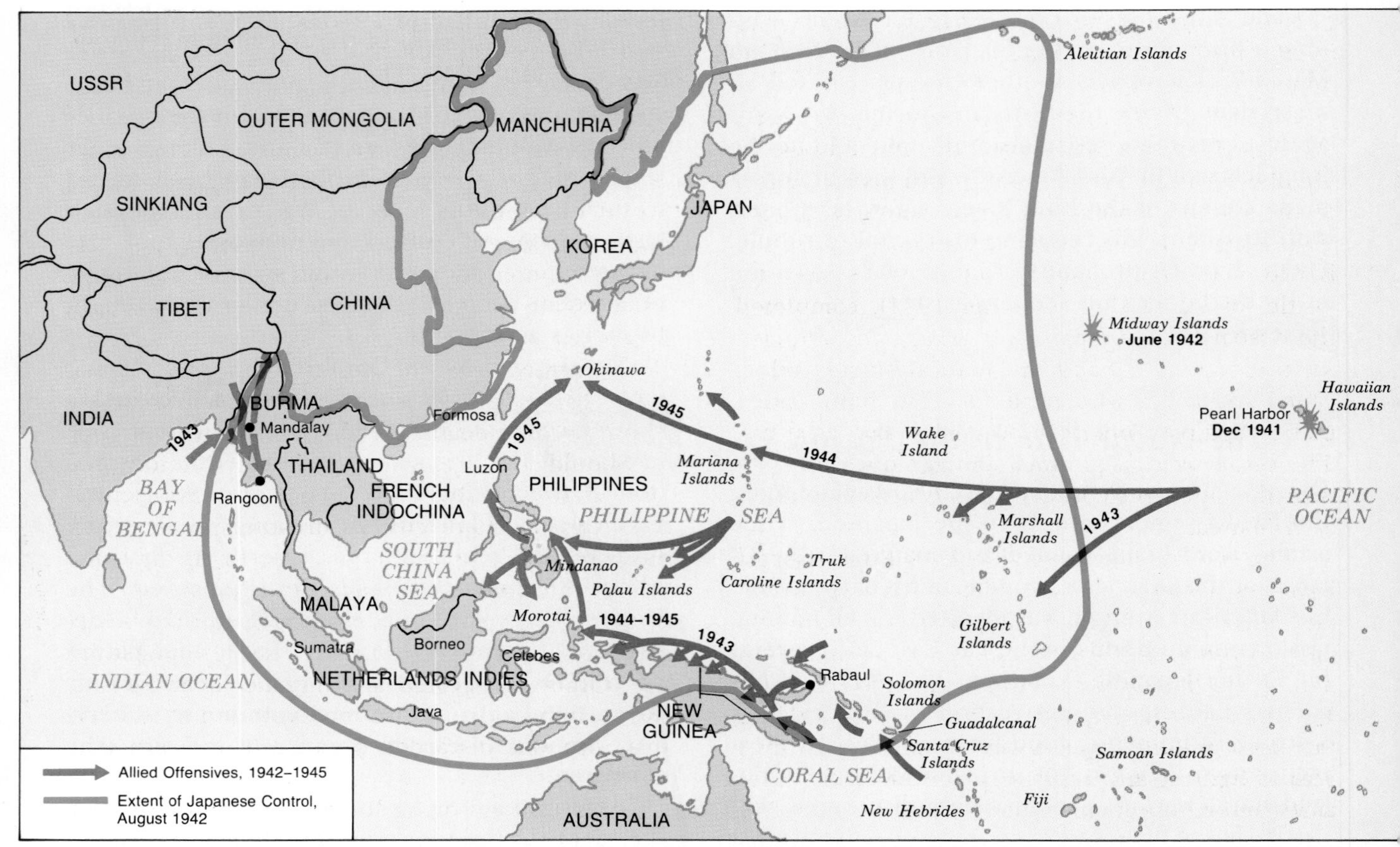

WORLD WAR II, PACIFIC THEATER

tral Pacific toward Tokyo, under Admiral Chester W. Nimitz.

Island Hopping

Before commencing this two-pronged advance, the Americans had to eject the Japanese from the Solomon Islands in order to protect Australia from a flank attack. Beginning in August 1942, a series of land, sea, and air battles raged around Guadalcanal Island in this archipelago. Once again American air power was decisive, though the bravery and skill of the ground forces that actually won the island must not be underemphasized. American pilots, better trained and with tougher planes, had a relatively easier task. They inflicted losses five to six times heavier on the enemy than they sustained themselves. Japanese air power disintegrated progressively during the long battle, and this in turn helped the fleet to take a heavy toll of the Japanese navy. By February 1943 Guadalcanal had been secured.

In the autumn of 1943 the American drives toward Japan and the Philippines got under way at last. In the Central Pacific campaign the Guadalcanal action was repeated on a smaller but equally bloody scale from Tarawa in the Gilbert Islands to Kwajelein and Eniwetok in the Marshalls, islets theretofore unknown to history. The Japanese soldiers fought like the Spartans at Thermopylae for every foot of ground. They had to be blasted and burned from tunnels and concrete pillboxes with hand grenades, flamethrowers, and dynamite. They almost never surrendered. But Admiral Nimitz's forces were in every case victorious. By midsummer of 1944 this arm of the American advance had taken Saipan and Guam in the Marianas. Now land-based bombers were within range of Tokyo.

Meanwhile, MacArthur was leapfrogging along the New Guinea coast toward the Philippines. In October 1944 he made good his promise to return to the islands, landing on Leyte, south of Luzon. Two great naval clashes in Philippine waters, the Battle of the Philippine Sea (June 1944) and the Battle for Leyte Gulf (October 1944), completed the destruction of Japan's sea power and reduced its air force to a band of fanatical suicide pilots called *kamikazes,* who tried to crash bomb-laden planes against American warships and airstrips. The *kamikazes* caused much damage but could not turn the tide. In February 1945 MacArthur liberated Manila.

The end was now inevitable. B-29 Superfortress bombers from the Marianas rained high explosives and firebombs on Japan. The islands of Iwo Jima and Okinawa, only a few hundred miles from Tokyo, fell to the Americans in March and June 1945. But such was the tenacity of the Japanese soldiers that most military experts were predicting another year of fighting and a million more American casualties before the main islands could be subdued.

"The Shatterer of Worlds"

At this point came the most controversial decision of the entire war, and it was made by a newcomer on the world scene. In November 1944 Roosevelt had been elected to a fourth term, easily defeating Thomas E. Dewey. Instead of renominating Henry A. Wallace for vice-president, the Democrats had picked Senator Harry S Truman of Missouri. The conservative Democratic politicos had considered Wallace too radical and too unstable; Truman was a reliable party man well liked by professional politicians. Then, in April 1945, Roosevelt died of a cerebral hemorrhage. Thus it was Truman, a man painfully conscious of his inferiority to his great predecessor yet equally aware of the power and responsibility of his office, who had to decide what to do when, in July 1945, American scientists placed in his hands a new and awful weapon, the atomic bomb.

After Roosevelt had responded to Albert Einstein's warning in 1939, government-sponsored atomic research had proceeded rapidly, especially after the establishment of the so-called Manhattan Project in May 1943. The manufacture of the element plutonium at Hanford, Washington, and of uranium 235 at Oak Ridge, Tennessee, continued along with the design and construction of a transportable atomic bomb at Los Alamos, New Mexico, under the direction of J. Robert Oppenheimer. Almost $2 billion was spent before a successful bomb was exploded at Alamogordo, in the New Mexican desert, on July 16, 1945. As that first mushroom cloud formed over the desert, Oppenheimer recalled the prophetic words of *The Bhagavad Gita:* "I am become death, the shatterer of worlds."

Should a bomb with the destructive force of 20,000 tons of TNT be employed against Japan? By striking a major city, its dreadful power could be demonstrated convincingly, yet doing so would bring death to tens of thousands of Japanese civilians. Many of the scientists who had made the bomb now somewhat inconsistently argued against its use. Others suggested alerting the Japanese and then staging a demonstration explosion at sea, but that idea was discarded because of concern that the bomb might fail to explode.

Truman was torn between his awareness that the bomb was "the most terrible thing ever discovered" and his hope that using it "would bring the war to an end." Every experience indicated that the Japanese army intended to fight to the last man,* but the bomb might cause a revolution in Japan, might lead the emperor to intervene, might even persuade the military to give up. Considering the hundreds of thousands of Americans who would surely die in any conventional invasion of Japan, and influenced by a desire to end the Pacific war before the Soviet Union could intervene effectively and thus claim a role in the peacemaking, the president chose to go ahead. In this decision he had the full support of Churchill and British military leaders.

The moral soundness of Truman's decision has been debated ever since. What is often forgotten by those who deplore the decision is the fact that while the immediate result was the death of many thousands of innocent Japanese civilians, far more Japanese would have died—many more than the

---

* In recapturing Guam, for example, the Americans killed 17,238 Japanese and took only 438 prisoners.

Hiroshima's Museum of Science and Industry was reduced to a skeleton in the atomic bomb blast. City officials decided to preserve the wreckage as a memorial.

Americans who would have perished—if Japan had had to be invaded.

In any case, on August 6 the Superfortress *Enola Gay* dropped an atomic bomb on Hiroshima, killing about 78,000 persons (including 20 American prisoners of war) and injuring nearly 100,000 more out of a population of 344,000. Over 96 percent of the buildings in the city were destroyed or damaged. Three days later, while the stunned Japanese still hesitated, a second atomic bomb, the only other one that had so far been assembled, blasted Nagasaki. This second drop was far less defensible morally, but it had the desired result. On August 15 Japan surrendered.

Thus ended the greatest war in history. Its cost was beyond calculation. No accurate count could be made even of the dead; we know only that the total was in the neighborhood of 20 million. As in World War I, American casualties—291,000 battle deaths and 671,000 wounded—were smaller than those of the other major belligerents. About 7.5 million Russians died in battle, 3.5 million Germans, 1.2 million Japanese, and 2.2 million Chinese; Britain and France, despite much smaller populations, suffered losses almost as large as did the United States. And far more than in World War I, American resources, human and material, had made victory possible.

No one could account the war a benefit to humanity, but in the late summer of 1945 the future looked bright. Fascism was dead. Successful wartime diplomatic dealings between Roosevelt, Churchill, and Joseph Stalin, the Soviet dictator, encouraged many to hope that the communists were ready to cooperate in rebuilding Europe. In the United States isolationism had disappeared; the message of Wendell Willkie's best-selling *One World,* written after a globe-circling tour made by the 1940 Republican presidential candidate at the behest of President Roosevelt in 1942, appeared to have been absorbed by the majority of the people. Out of the death and destruction had come technological developments that seemed to herald a better world as well as a peaceful one. Enormous advances in the design of airplanes and the development of radar (which some authorities think was more important than any weapons system in winning the war) were about to revolutionize travel and the transportation of goods. Improvements in surgery and other medical advances gave promise of saving millions of lives.

Above all, there was the power of the atom. The force that seared Hiroshima and Nagasaki could be harnessed to serve peaceful needs, the scientists promised, with results that might free humanity forever from poverty and toil. Great strides in transportation and communication lay ahead, products of wartime research in electronics, airplane design, and rocketry. The development of penicillin and other antibiotics, which had greatly reduced the death rate among troops, would perhaps banish all infectious disease.

The period of reconstruction would be prolonged, but with all the great powers adhering to the new United Nations charter, drafted at San Francisco in June 1945, international cooperation could be counted on to ease the burdens of the victims of war and help the poor and underdeveloped parts of the world toward economic and political independence. And although in some respects a less powerful organization than the defunct League of Nations, the UN would stand guard over the peace of the world. Such at least was the hope of millions in the victorious summer of 1945.

SUPPLEMENTARY READING

Titles marked with an asterisk have been published in paperback.

There are good summaries of diplomatic developments in Selig Adler, **The Uncertain Giant: American Foreign Policy Between the Wars*** (1965), and F. R. Dulles, **America's Rise to World Power*** (1955). J. C. Vinson, **The Parchment Peace** (1955), is the standard account of the Washington Armament Conference. R. H. Ferrell, **Peace in Their Time*** (1952), is excellent on the Kellogg-Briand Pact. Other important works on the diplomacy of the twenties include A. W. Griswold, **The Far Eastern Policy of the United States*** (1938), J. H. Wilson, **American Business and Foreign Policy*** (1971), E. E. Morison, **Turmoil and Tradition: A Study of the Life and Times of Henry L. Stimson*** (1960), and R. N. Current, **Secretary Stimson** (1954). R. H. Ferrell, **American Diplomacy and the Great Depression*** (1957), and Alexander De Conde, **Herbert Hoover's Latin American Policy** (1951), are also useful. Robert Dallek, **Franklin D. Roosevelt and American Foreign Policy*** (1979), is judicious and up-to-date.

On isolationism and the events leading to Pearl Harbor, see R. A. Divine, **The Reluctant Belligerent*** (1965), brief but comprehensive, and **The Illusion of Neutrality*** (1962), Manfred Jonas, **Isolationism in America*** (1966), T. R. Fehrenbach, **F.D.R.'s Undeclared War** (1967), W. S. Cole, **Senator Gerald P. Nye and American Foreign Relations** (1962) and **Roosevelt and the Isolationists** (1983), W. F. Kimball, **The Most Unsordid Act** (1969), on lend-lease, Herbert Feis, **The Road to Pearl Harbor*** (1962), Roberta Wohlstetter, **Pearl Harbor: Warning and Decision*** (1962), and J. W. Pratt, **Cordell Hull** (1964). C. C. Tansill, **Back Door to War** (1952), C. A. Beard, **American Foreign Policy in the Making** (1946) and **President Roosevelt and the Coming of the War** (1948), are interesting interpretations by isolationists, while L. C. Gardner, **Economic Aspects of New Deal Diplomacy*** (1971), is a critical scholarly analysis. Akira Iriye, **Power and Culture: The Japanese-American War** (1981), looks at the war in the Pacific from both sides and argues that the conflict was merely a break in the long history of cordial relations between the two nations.

The home front is discussed in Richard Polenberg, **War and Society*** (1972). Special aspects of the subject are covered in Bruce Catton, **War Lords of Washington** (1948), Eliot Janeway, **The Struggle for Survival** (1951), David Novik et al., **Wartime Production Controls** (1949), David Brody, **Workers in Industrial America*** (1980), Joel Seidman, **American Labor from Defense to Reconversion** (1953), W. W. Wilcox, **The Farmer in the Second World War** (1947), Roland Young, **Congressional Politics in the Second World War** (1956), and J. P. Baxter, **Scientists Against Time*** (1946). Social trends are covered in Jack Goodman (ed.), **While You Were Gone** (1946). On the treatment of conscientious objectors, see P. E. Jacob and M. Q. Sibley, **Conscription of Conscience** (1952); on the relocation of the Japanese, see Roger Daniels, **Concentration Camps USA: Japanese Americans and World War II*** (1971). The effect of the war on blacks is discussed in Ulysses Lee, **The Employment of Negro Troops** (1966), and N. A. Wynn, **The Afro-American and the Second World War** (1976).

A. R. Buchanan, **The United States in World War II*** (1964), provides an excellent overall survey of the military side of the conflict. S. E. Morison, **The Two-Ocean War*** (1963), is exciting reading.

28
The American Century: 1945-1960

BRUTUS: *I do believe that these applauses are*
For some new honours that are heaped on Caesar.

CASSIUS: *Why, man, he doth bestride the narrow world*
Like a Colossus . . .

WILLIAM SHAKESPEARE, Julius Caesar

ONE GI: *Now we have the world by the tail.*

ANOTHER: *Now we are all sons of bitches.*

A-bomb test site blockhouse, Alamogordo, N.M., July 16, 1945

On Christmas Eve 1943 Franklin D. Roosevelt reported to the nation on his first meeting with Soviet Premier Joseph Stalin at Teheran, Iran. "I 'got along fine' with Marshal Stalin," he said, "and I believe that we are going to get along very well with him and the Russian people—very well indeed." A little over a year later, describing to Congress his second meeting with Stalin, at Yalta in the Crimea, the president stressed again the good feeling that existed between the two nations and their leaders. "We argued freely and frankly across the table," he explained. "But at the end, on every point, unanimous agreement was reached. I may say we achieved a unity of thought and a way of getting along together." Privately Roosevelt characterized Stalin as "a very interesting man" whose rough exterior clothed an "old-fashioned elegant European manner." He referred to him almost affectionately as "that old buzzard" and on one occasion called him "Uncle Joe" to his face. At Yalta, Stalin gave Roosevelt a portrait photograph, with a long Cyrillic inscription in his small, tightly written hand.

Two months later Roosevelt was writing to Stalin of his "astonishment," "anxiety," and "bitter resentment" over the Soviet Union's "discouraging lack of application" of the agreements made at Yalta. A few days after dictating these words Roosevelt was dead. Before the end of the month, his successor, Harry S Truman, was complaining that "our agreements with the Soviet Union had so far been a one-way street" and telling Foreign Minister V. M. Molotov bluntly that Stalin must learn to keep his promises. "I have never been talked to like that in my life," Molotov said. "Carry out your agreements," Truman retorted, "and you won't get talked to like that!" Thus ended the brief period of Russo-American amity born of the struggle against Hitler.

Wartime Diplomacy

During the course of World War II every instrument of mass persuasion in the country was directed at convincing the people that the Russians were fighting America's battle as well as their own. Even before Pearl Harbor, former Ambassador Joseph E. Davies wrote in his best-selling *Mission to Moscow* (1941) that the communist leaders were "a group of able, strong men" with "honest convictions and integrity of purposes" who were "devoted to the cause of peace for both ideological and practical reasons." Communism was based "on the same principle of the 'brotherhood of man' which Jesus preached." Stalin possessed great dignity and charm, combined with much wisdom and strength of character, Davies said. "His brown eye is exceedingly kind and gentle. A child would like to sit in his lap and a dog would sidle up to him." In another book published in 1941 the journalist Walter Duranty described Stalin (who had ruthlessly executed hundreds of his former comrades) as "remarkably long-suffering in his treatment of various oppositions."

During the war Americans with as different points of view as General Douglas MacArthur and Vice-President Henry A. Wallace took strongly pro-Soviet positions, and American newspapers and magazines published many laudatory articles about Russia. *Life* reported that Russians "think like Americans." In 1943 *Time* named Stalin its Man of the Year. The film *Mission to Moscow,* a whitewash of the dreadful Moscow treason trials of the thirties based on Ambassador Davies' book, portrayed Stalin as a wise, grandfatherly type, puffing comfortably on an old pipe. In *One World* (1943) Wendell Willkie wrote glowingly of the Russian people, their "effective society," and their simple, warm-hearted leader. When he suggested jokingly to Stalin that if he continued to make progress in improving the education of his people he might educate himself out of a job, the dictator "threw his head back and laughed and laughed," Willkie recorded. "Mr. Willkie, you know I grew up a Georgian peasant. I am unschooled in pretty talk. All I can say is I like you very much."

These views of the character of Joseph Stalin were naive, to say the least, but the identity of interest of the United States and the Soviet Union was very real during the war. Russian military leaders conferred regularly with their British and American counterparts and fulfilled their obligations scrupulously. In October 1943 Foreign Minister Molotov committed his country to joining in the war against Japan as soon as the Germans were defeated, a promise confirmed the following month by Stalin at his meeting with Churchill and Roosevelt at Teheran.

The Soviets repeatedly expressed a willingness

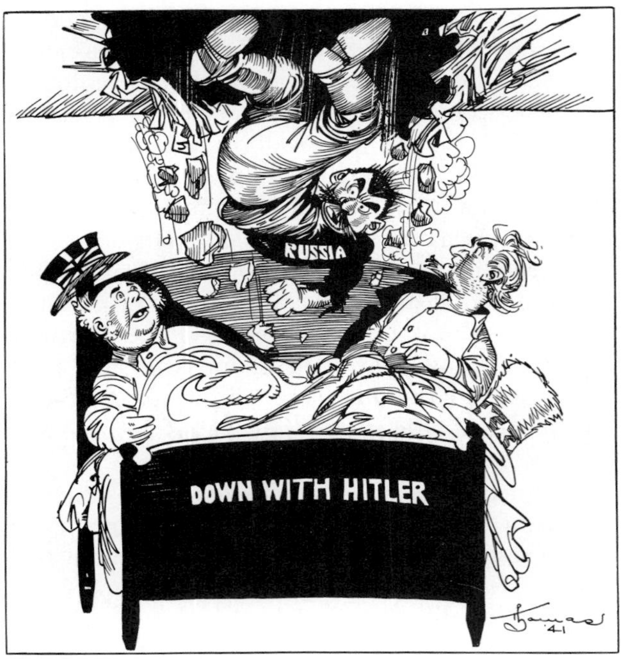

The entry of Russia into the war in 1941 meant the surprise addition of a scruffy-looking Joe Stalin to the cosy pair of Britain's John Bull and Uncle Sam.

to cooperate with the Allies in dealing with postwar problems. Russia was one of the 26 signers of the Declaration of the United Nations (January 1942), in which the Allies promised to eschew territorial aggrandizement after the war, to respect the right of all peoples to determine their own form of government, to work for freer trade and international economic cooperation, and to force the disarmament of the aggressor nations.*

In May 1943 Russia dissolved the Comintern, its official agency for the promulgation of world revolution. The following October, during a conference in Moscow with Secretary of State Cordell Hull and British Foreign Minister Anthony Eden, Molotov joined in setting up a European Advisory Commission to divide Germany into occupation zones after the war. At the Teheran Conference Stalin willingly discussed plans for a new league of nations. When Roosevelt described the kind of world organization he envisaged, the Russian dictator offered a number of constructive suggestions.

Between August and October 1944, Allied representatives met at Dumbarton Oaks, outside Washington. The chief Russian delegate, Andrei A. Gromyko, opposed limiting the use of the veto by the great powers on the future UN Security Council, but he did not take a deliberately obstructionist position. At the Yalta Conference in February 1945 Stalin joined in the call for a conference to be held in April at San Francisco to draft a charter for the United Nations, incidentally modifying the Soviet position on the veto slightly by agreeing that no power might veto Security Council *discussion* of a controversy in which it had a stake.

While the powers argued at length over the form of that charter at the 50-nation San Francisco Conference, they conducted the debates in an atmosphere of optimism and international amity. Each UN member received a seat in the General Assembly, a body designed for discussion rather than action. The locus of authority in the new organization resided in the Security Council, "the castle of the great powers." This consisted of five permanent members (the United States, the Soviet Union, Great Britain, France, and China) and six others elected for two-year terms.

The Council was charged with responsibility for maintaining world peace. It could apply diplomatic, economic, or military sanctions against any nation threatening that peace, but any great power could block UN action whenever it wished to do so. The United States insisted on this veto power as strongly as the Soviet Union did. In effect the charter paid lip service to the Wilsonian deal of a powerful international police force, but to assure Senate ratification it incorporated the limitations that Henry Cabot Lodge had proposed in his 1919 reservations (see page 715). The big-power veto represented Lodge's reservation to Article X of the League Covenant, which would have relieved the United States from the obligation of enforcing collective security without the approval of Congress.

The UN charter also provided for a Secretariat to handle routine administration, headed by a secretary general who was in addition the chief executive officer of the entire organization; a Trusteeship Council to supervise dependent areas much in the fashion of the mandate system of the League; and an International Court of Justice. An Economic and

* These were the principles first laid down in the so-called Atlantic Charter, drafted by Roosevelt and Churchill at a dramatic meeting on the U.S.S. *Augusta* off Newfoundland in August 1941.

Oscar Berger made this sketch during the 1945 UN conference in San Francisco at a cocktail party given by Soviet Foreign Minister Molotov (right). Others, from the left, are Pearson of Canada, Senator Vandenberg of Michigan, Senator Connally of Texas, Velloso of Brazil, Prime Minister Soong of China, Spaak of Belgium, Representative Bloom of New York, Foreign Minister Masaryk of Czechoslovakia, General Romulo of the Philippines, Prime Minister King of Canada, U.S. Secretary of State Stettinius, and Prince Faisal of Saudi Arabia.

Social Council was created to supervise such UN agencies as the International Labor Organization, the International Bank for Reconstruction and Development, the International Monetary Fund, the World Health Organization, and the United Nations Educational, Scientific, and Cultural Organization (UNESCO), which was assigned the task of "promoting collaboration among the nations through education, science, and culture."

The Cold War Under Way

Long before the war in Europe ended, the Allies had clashed over important policy matters. Since later world tensions developed from decisions made at this time, an understanding of the disagreements is essential for evaluating entire decades of history. Unfortunately, complete understanding is not yet possible, if it ever will be, which explains why the subject remains controversial.

Much depends on one's view of the Soviet system. If the Soviet government under Stalin was bent on world domination, events of the so-called Cold War fall readily into one pattern of interpretation. If Russia, having bravely and at enormous cost endured an unprovoked assault by the Nazis, was seeking only to protect itself against the possibility of another invasion, these events are best explained differently. Because the United States has opened nearly all its diplomatic records to scholars, we know a great deal about how American foreign policy was formulated and about the mixed motives and mistaken judgments of American leaders. This helps explain why many students have been critical of American policy and the "cold warriors" who made and directed it. The Soviet Union on the other hand has excluded historians from its archives, and consequently we know little about the motivations and inner workings of Soviet policy. Was Russia "committed to overturning the international system and to endless expansion in pursuit of world dominance?" Daniel Yergin asks in *Shattered Peace.* Only access to Soviet records can provide an answer to this vitally important question.

The Russians resented the British-American delay in opening up a second front. They were fighting for survival against the full power of the German armies; any invasion, even an unsuccessful one, would have relieved some of the pressure. Roosevelt and Churchill would not move until they were ready, and the Russians had to accept their decision. At the same time, the Russians never concealed their determination to protect themselves against future attack by extending their western frontier after the war. Stalin warned the Allies repeatedly that he would not tolerate any anti-Soviet government along Russia's western boundary.

Most Allied leaders, including Roosevelt, admitted privately during the war that the Soviet Union would annex territory and possess preponderant power in eastern Europe after the defeat of Germany, but they never said this publicly. They believed that free governments could somehow be created in countries like Poland and Bulgaria that the Soviets would trust enough to leave to their own devices. "The Poles," Winston Churchill said early in 1945, "will have their future in their own hands, with the single limitation that they must honestly follow . . . a policy friendly to Russia. This is surely reasonable."

However reasonable, Churchill's statement was impractical. The Polish question was a terribly difficult one. The war, after all, had been triggered by the German attack on Poland; the British in particular felt a moral obligation to restore that nation to its prewar independence. During the war a Polish government-in-exile was set up in London, and its leaders were determined—especially after the discovery in 1943 of the murder of some 5,000 Polish officers several years earlier at Katyn, in Russia, presumably by the Soviet secret police—to make no concessions to Soviet territorial demands. Public opinion in Poland (and indeed in all the states along Russia's western frontier) was strongly anti-Soviet. Yet Russia's legitimate interests (to say nothing of its power in the area) could not be ignored.

Stalin apparently could not understand why his allies were so concerned about the fate of a small country so remote from their strategic spheres. That they professed to be concerned seemed to him an indication that they had some secret, devious purpose. He could see no difference (and "revisionist" American historians agree with him) between the Soviet Union's dominating Poland and maintaining a government there that did not reflect the wishes of a majority of the Polish people, and the United States' dominating many Latin American nations and supporting unpopular regimes within them. Roosevelt, however, was worried about the political effects that Russian control of Poland might have in the United States. Polish-Americans would be furious if the communists took over their homeland.

At the Yalta Conference, Roosevelt and Churchill agreed to Soviet annexation of large sections of eastern Poland. In return they demanded that free elections be held in Poland itself. "I want this election to be . . . beyond question," Roosevelt told Stalin. "It should be like Caesar's wife." In a feeble attempt at a joke he added: "I did not know her but they said she was pure." Stalin agreed, almost certainly without intending to keep his promise. The elections were never held; Poland was run by a pro-Russian puppet regime.

Thus the West "lost" Poland. How it might have "won" the country when it was already occupied by the Red Army has never been explained, but had Roosevelt described the difficulties to the American people more frankly, their reaction might have been less angry. Part of the problem was that Roosevelt believed he could charm Stalin into modifying his demands. "Stalin hates the guts of all your top people," he told Prime Minister Churchill in 1942. "I think I can personally handle Stalin better than either your Foreign Office or my State Department."

President Truman, being at first somewhat unsure of himself in foreign affairs, had no such illusion and perhaps for that reason took a much tougher stand. In July 1945, following the surrender of Germany, he, Stalin, and Churchill met at Potsdam, outside Berlin.* They agreed to try the Nazi leaders as war criminals, made plans for exact-

* Clement R. Attlee replaced Churchill during the conference after his Labour party won the British elections.

Churchill, Roosevelt, and Stalin photographed at the week-long Yalta Conference in February 1945. By April 1945, Roosevelt was dead.

ing reparations from Germany, and confirmed the division of the country into four zones to be occupied separately by American, Russian, British, and French troops. Berlin, deep in the Soviet zone, had itself been split into four sectors. Stalin rejected all arguments that he loosen his hold on eastern Europe, and Truman (who received news of the successful testing of the atom bomb while at Potsdam) made no concessions. On both sides suspicions were mounting, positions hardening.

Yet all the advantages seemed to be with the United States. Was this not, as Henry Luce, the publisher of *Time* had declared, "the American Century," an era when American power and American ideals would shape the course of events the world over? Besides its army, navy, and air force and its immense industrial potential, alone among the nations the United States possessed the atomic bomb. When Stalin's actions made it clear that he intended to control all eastern Europe and to exert an important influence elsewhere in the world, most Americans first reacted somewhat in the manner of a mastiff being worried by a yapping terrier: their resentment was tempered by amazement. They refused to believe that the Russians could honestly suspect their motives.

The war had caused a fundamental change in international politics. The United States might be the strongest country in the world, but the western European nations, victor and vanquished alike, were reduced to the status of second-class powers. The Soviet Union, on the other hand, had regained the influence it had held under the czars and lost as a result of World War I and the Communist Revolution.

The Postwar Economy

In late 1945 most Americans were probably more concerned with what was happening at home than with foreign developments, and no one was more aware of this than Harry Truman. When Roosevelt died in April 1945 Truman claimed that he felt as though "the moon, the stars, and all the planets" had suddenly fallen upon him. Although he could not have been quite as surprised as he indicated (Roosevelt was known to be in extremely poor health), he was acutely conscious of his own limitations.

Truman was born in Missouri in 1884. After service with a World War I artillery unit, he opened a men's clothing store in Kansas City. The store failed in the postwar depression. Truman then became a minor cog in the political machine of Democratic boss Tom Pendergast. In 1934 he was elected to the United States Senate, where he proved to be a loyal but obscure New Dealer. He first attracted national attention during World War II when his "watchdog" committee on defense spending, working with devotion and efficiency, had saved the government immense sums. This led to his nomination and election as vice-president.

As president, Truman sought to carry on in the Roosevelt tradition. Curiously, he was at the same time humble and cocky, idealistic and cold-bloodedly political. He had an immense fund of information about American history, but like most amateurs he lacked historical judgment and was prone to interpret past events in whatever manner best suited his current convenience. He read books but distrusted ideas; he adopted liberal objectives only to pursue them sometimes by rash, even repressive means.

Truman was his own worst enemy. Too often he insulted opponents instead of convincing or conciliating them. Complications tended to confuse him, in which case he either dug in his heels or struck out blindly, usually with unfortunate results. On balance, however, he was a strong and in many ways a successful chief executive. Like Jackson, Wilson, and the two Roosevelts, he effectively epitomized the national will and projected a sense of dedication in his management of national affairs.

Nearly all the postwar leaders accepted the necessity of employing federal authority to stabilize the economy and speed national development. The Great Depression and the successful application of the theories of John Maynard Keynes during the war had convinced Democrats and Republicans alike that it was possible to prevent sharp swings in the business cycle and therefore to do away with serious unemployment. The new orthodoxy was written into law in the Employment Act of 1946, which made it government policy "to promote maximum employment, production, and purchasing power" and created a Council of Economic Advisers to assist the president in working out the technical details. In its first report the council described how stabilization could be achieved by "control of the public purse," that is, by monetary and fiscal manipulation: "The agents of government must . . . put a brake at certain points where boom forces develop . . . and support purchasing power when it becomes unduly depressed."

Despite this commitment to Keynesian economics—a commitment shared by all western nations—regulating the economy remained a source of political controversy. The rejection of laissez faire did not mean that all citizens would always agree as to what should be done. When World War II ended, nearly everyone wanted to demobilize the armed forces, remove wartime controls, and reduce taxes. Yet everyone also hoped to prevent any sudden economic dislocation, to check inflation, and to make sure that goods in short supply were fairly distributed.

Neither the politicians nor the public were able to reconcile these conflicting objectives. No group seemed willing to limit its own demands in the general interest. Labor wanted price controls retained but wage controls lifted; industrialists wished to raise prices and to keep the lid on wages. Farmers wanted subsidies but opposed price controls and the extension of social security benefits to agricultural workers.

In this difficult situation President Truman failed to win either the confidence of the people or the support of Congress. He asked for too much and demanded it too vociferously—and this despite his obvious uncertainty as to what should be done. On the one hand he proposed a comprehensive program of new legislation that included a public housing scheme, aid to education, medical insurance, civil rights guarantees, a higher minimum wage, broader social security coverage, additional conservation and public power projects patterned after TVA, increased aid to agriculture, and the retention of anti-inflationary controls. The proposal of so many new ventures at a time when millions hoped to relax now that the war was over was sure to arouse strong resistance. On the other hand he ended rationing and other controls and in November 1945 signed a bill cutting taxes by some $6 billion. He speeded the sale of government war plants and surplus goods to private interests. Whenever opposition to his plans developed, he vacillated between compromise and inflexibility.

Yet the country weathered the reconversion period with remarkable ease. The pent-up demand for homes, automobiles, clothing, washing machines, and countless other products, backed by the war-enforced savings of millions, kept factories operating at capacity. The GI Bill of Rights, passed in 1944, provided demobilized veterans with loans to start new businesses and subsidies to continue their educations or acquire new skills. However, the absence of uniform price and wage policies caused resentment and frustration, and late in 1946 all controls except those on rents were abandoned.

A period of rapid inflation followed. Food prices rose more than 25 percent between 1945 and 1947. Labor had already won large wage increases; these contributed to the rise of prices, which led to demands for still higher wages. As the historian David Montgomery has written, "workers' determination to catch up with inflation" clashed with "management's determination to tighten up its control," which had been relaxed during the hectic prosperity of wartime. The result was a wave of strikes—nearly 5,000 in 1946 alone.

Inflation and labor unrest, together with concern about the activities of the Soviet Union, helped the Republicans to win control of Congress in 1946. High on the Republican agenda was the passage of a new labor relations act.

Labor leaders tended to support the Democrats, for they remembered gratefully the Wagner Act and other help given them by the Roosevelt administration during the labor-management struggles of the 1930s. In 1943 the CIO had created a Political Action Committee to mobilize the labor vote.

Martin in The Houston Chronicle

"Let him out—I can hold him."

Cartoonist Ferman Martin of the Houston Chronicle *drew President Truman in a cowboy pose, with lasso ready to subdue the bull of national emergency strikes.*

Labor's political importance was highlighted at the democratic National Convention of 1944, when Roosevelt, debating the question of a replacement for Vice-President Henry Wallace, allegedly instructed his lieutenants to "clear it with Sidney," referring to Sidney Hillman of the Amalgamated Clothing Workers, a power in the PAC.

Yet the strikes of 1946 had alienated many citizens because they delayed the satisfaction of the demand for consumer goods. The strikes led President Truman, normally sympathetic to organized labor, to seize the coal mines, threaten to draft railroad workers, and ask Congress for other special powers to prevent national tie-ups.

This was the climate when in June 1947 the Republican-controlled Congress passed the Taft-Hartley Act over the veto of President Truman. The measure outlawed the closed shop (a provision written into many labor contracts requiring new workers to join the union before they could be employed) and declared illegal certain "unfair labor practices" such as secondary boycotts and strikes called as a result of disputes between unions over the right to represent workers. It compelled unions to register and file financial reports with the secretary of labor and, most important, it authorized the president to seek court injunctions to prevent strikes that in his opinion endangered the national interest. The injunctions would hold for 80 days—a "cooling-off" period during which a presidential fact-finding board could investigate and make recommendations. If the dispute remained unresolved after 80 days, the president was to recommend "appropriate action" to Congress.

The Taft-Hartley Act, which they called a "slave labor law," alarmed labor leaders. They resented in particular a provision that made union officers state under oath that they were not communists, a gratuitously insulting and largely ineffective requirement. The law made the task of unionizing unorganized industries more difficult, but it did not seriously hamper existing unions. While it outlawed the closed shop, it permitted union shop contracts, which forced new workers to join the union *after* accepting employment. And the provision requiring unions to file financial statements, together with other regulations aimed at protecting individual members against union officials, had only salutary effects.

The Containment Policy

Foreign policy issues continued to vex the Truman presidency. American and Russian attitudes stood in sharp confrontation when the control of atomic energy came up for discussion in the UN. Everyone recognized the threat to human survival posed by the atomic bomb. In November 1945 the United States suggested allowing the UN to supervise all nuclear energy production, and the General Assembly promptly created an Atomic Energy Commission to study the question. In June 1946 Commissioner Bernard Baruch offered a plan for the eventual outlawing of atomic weapons. A system would be set up under which UN inspectors could operate without restriction anywhere in the world to make sure that no country was making bombs clandestinely. When, at an unspecified date, the system had been established, the United States would destroy its stockpile of bombs.

Most Americans thought the Baruch plan magnanimous and some considered it positively foolhardy, but the Soviets rejected it. That no timetable for destroying the American bombs had been established, and that the American atomic monopoly would continue until one was, made the Russians suspicious. They stated flatly that they would neither permit UN inspectors in the Soviet Union nor surrender their veto power over Security Council actions dealing with atomic energy. They demanded that the United States destroy its bombs at once. Unwilling to trust the Russians or to surrender what they considered their "winning weapon," the American leaders refused to agree. The resulting stalemate increased international tension.

Postwar cooperation had failed. At the end of 1945, besides dominating most of eastern Europe, the Soviet Union controlled Outer Mongolia, parts of Manchuria, and northern Korea. It had annexed the Kurile Islands, regained the southern half of Sakhalin Island from Japan, and was fomenting trouble in Iran. The United States reacted to Russia's moves first by direct diplomatic appeals and threats and then by strenous objections in the UN, where American influence was great.

By early 1946 a new policy was emerging. Many minds contributed to its development, but the key ideas were provided by George F. Kennan, a scholarly Foreign Service officer. Kennan had been stationed for five years in Russia and had been a close student of Soviet history since his student days at Princeton in the early 1920s. He believed that the Soviet leaders were prisoners of their own ideology. They saw the world as divided into socialist and capitalist camps separated by irreconcilable differences. Nothing the United States might do, however conciliatory, would reduce Soviet hostility, Kennan claimed. Therefore the nation should accept this hostility as a fact of life and either resist Russian aggression firmly wherever it appeared or wait for time to bring about some change in Soviet policy.

Kennan's second alternative seemed both irresponsible and dangerous, whereas "getting tough with Russia" would find wide popular support; according to polls, a substantial majority considered American policy "too soft." At the same time the public was reluctant to maintain a powerful military force and to aid nations threatened by the Soviets. During 1946 the Truman administration gradually adopted a tougher stance.

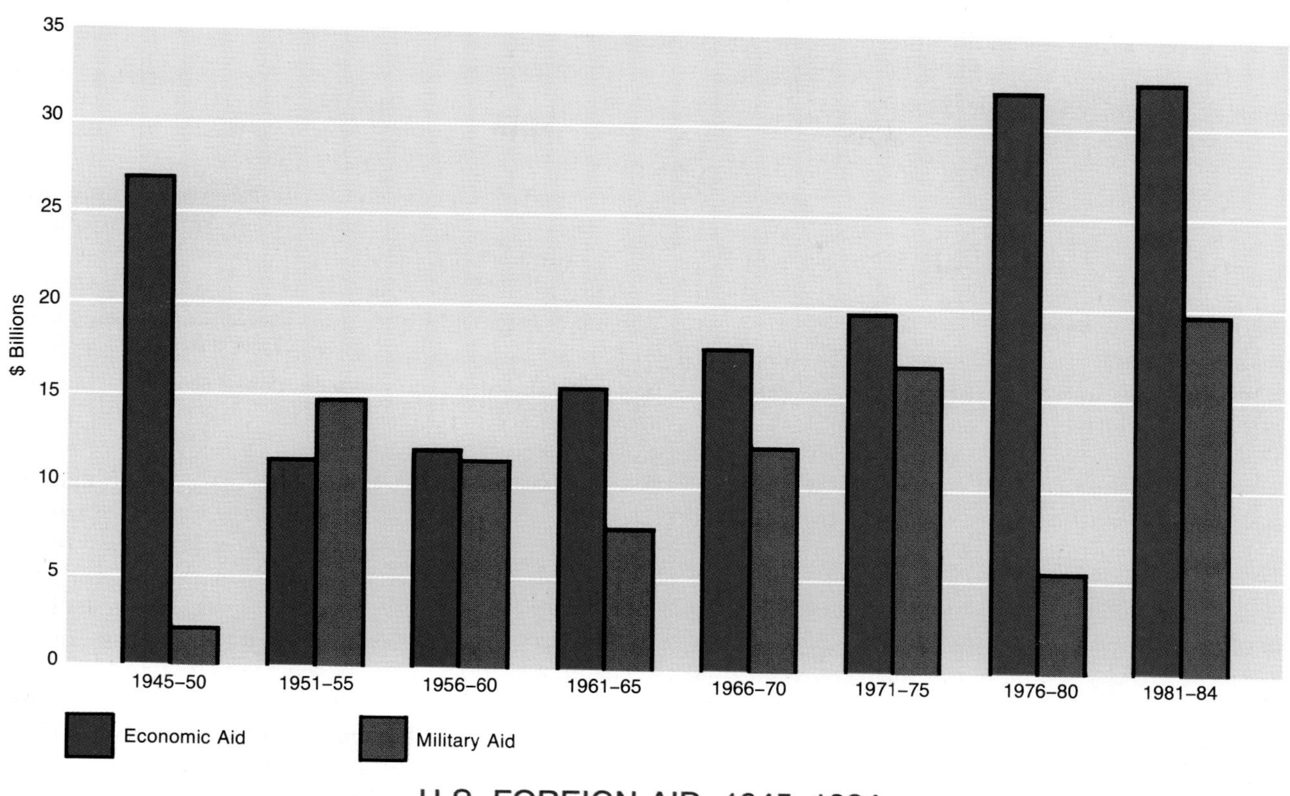

U.S. FOREIGN AID, 1945–1984

In 1945 the dollar was worth over four times its value in 1984, so in uninflated dollars United States foreign aid has lessened over the years, especially during the decade 1971–1980. Even so, the total amount of U.S. foreign assistance from 1945 to 1984 was more than $280 billion.

The decisive shift came early in 1947 as a result of a crisis in Greece. Local Greek communists, waging a guerrilla war against the monarchy, were receiving aid from Russian-dominated Yugoslavia and Bulgaria. Great Britain was assisting the monarchists. For more than a year an inconclusive civil war had wracked the country. However, Britian, its economy shaken by World War II, could not long afford this drain on its resources. In February 1947 the British informed President Truman that they would have to cut off further aid to Greece.

To American policymakers, Russia's "Iron Curtain" (a phrase invented by Winston Churchill) seemed about to ring down on another nation. That the Greek government was reactionary appeared to them less important than that it was threatened by communist forces. On March 12 President Truman went before a joint session of Congress and enunciated what became known as the Truman Doctrine. If Greece or Turkey fell to the communists, he said, all the Middle East might be lost. This in turn might shake the morale of anticommunist elements throughout western Europe. To prevent this "unspeakable tragedy," he asked Congress to appropriate $400 million for military and economic aid for Greece and Turkey. "It must be the policy of the United States to support free peoples who are resisting attempted subjugation by armed minorities or by outside pressures," he said. By exaggerating the consequences of inaction and justifying his request on ideological grounds, Truman obtained his objective. Congress appropriated the funds by margins approaching three to one in both houses.

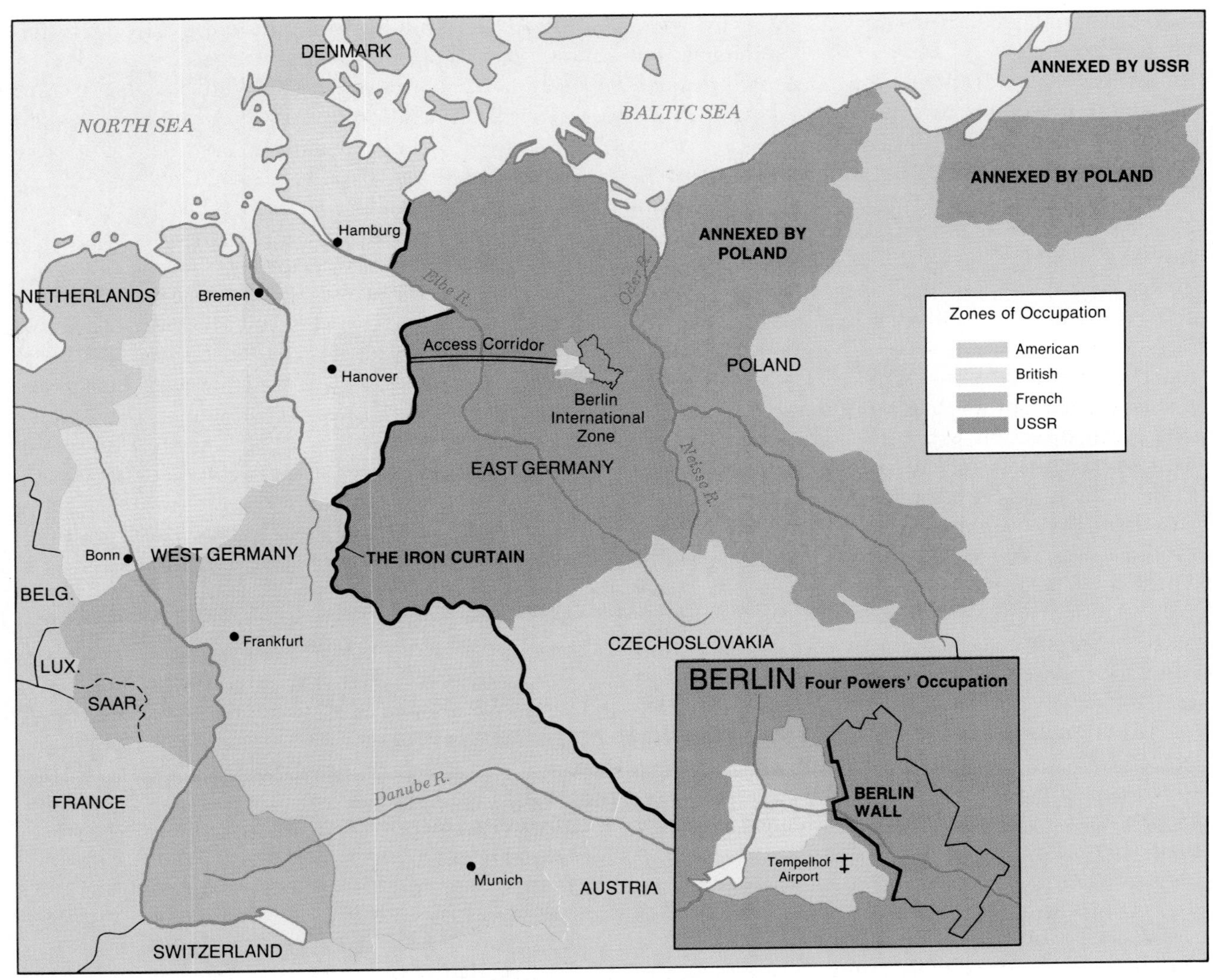

GERMANY AFTER WORLD WAR II

West Germany was created out of the merged French, British, and U.S. zones in 1947, as was West Berlin. The Russian zone became East Germany. The Berlin Wall was built later, in 1961, to keep an estimated 700 people a day from fleeing from East to West Germany.

Once official sanction was given to the communism-versus-democracy approach to foreign relations, foreign policy began to dominate domestic policy and to become more rigid. Compromise became more difficult, even when Soviet attitudes began to change. The communist threat loomed large. In May 1947 the American ambassador in Moscow reported confidentially: "There are no limits to the Soviet objectives. Statements . . . that a great struggle between Communism and capitalism will take place and that one or the other must go down are still being reiterated by Stalin. They have no inhibitions."

Meanwhile western Europe, in the words of Winston Churchill (the great phrasemaker of the era), was "a rubble-heap, a charnel house, a breeding-ground of pestilence and hate." There was a food shortage in France and something approaching a famine in occupied Germany. All of western Europe seemed in danger of falling into communist hands without the Soviet Union raising a finger to speed the process. For humane reasons as well as for political advantage the United States felt obliged to help these nations regain some measure of economic stability.

How might this be done without appearing to be as expansionist as the Russians? George Kennan provided an answer in an anonymous article in the July 1947 issue of *Foreign Affiars,* "The Sources of Soviet Conduct." The article gave public expression to the argument Kennan had advanced in his diplomatic reports. Russian diplomacy, he wrote, moves inexorably along a prescribed path, like a persistent toy automobile wound up and headed in a given direction, stopping only when it meets with some unmoveable force." A policy of "long-term, patient but firm and vigilant containment" based on the "application of counter-force" was the best means of dealing with Soviet pressures. The Cold War might be "a duel of infinite duration," Kennan admitted. It could be won if, without bluster, America maintained its own strength and convinced the communists that it would resist aggression firmly in any quarter of the globe.

Although he approved its purpose, Kennan disagreed with the *psychology* of the Truman Doctrine, which seemed to him essentially defensive as well as vulnerable to criticism by anti-imperialists. He proposed a broad program to finance European recovery, the aid to be offered even to Russia if the Soviets would contribute some of their own resources to the cause. The Europeans themselves should work out the details, America providing the money, materials, and technical advice.

George C. Marshall, army chief of staff during World War II and now secretary of state, formally suggested this program, which became known as the Marshall Plan, in a Harvard commencement speech on June 5, 1947. "Hunger, poverty, desperation, and chaos" were the real enemies of freedom and democracy, Marshall said. The need was to restore "the confidence of the European people in the economic future of their own countries." But it would be "neither fitting nor efficacious" to impose an aid plan on any country. "This is the business of the Europeans. . . . The program should be a joint one, agreed to by a number, if not all European nations."

The Marshall Plan succeeded brilliantly. Led by Great Britain and France, the European powers seized eagerly upon Marshall's suggestion. They set up a 16-nation Committee for European Economic Cooperation, which soon submitted plans calling for up to $22.4 billion in American aid. After protracted debate, much influenced by a communist coup in Czechoslovakia in February 1948, which drew still another country behind the Iron Curtain, Congress appropriated over $13 billion for the program. Results exceeded all expectations. By 1951 western Europe was booming.

Whether the policymakers realized it or not, containment and the Marshall Plan were America's response to the power vacuum created in Europe by the debilitating effects of the war. Just as the Soviet Union extended its influence over the eastern half of the Continent, the United States extended its influence in the west. Yet there was a vital difference: in the east *influence* meant domination; in the west it meant what the dictionaries say it means—"power independent of force or authority."

The Marshall Plan formed the basis for European political cooperation. In March 1948 Great Britain, France, Belgium, the Netherlands, and Luxembourg signed an alliance aimed at social, cultural, and economic collaboration. The western nations abandoned their understandable but counterproductive policy of crushing Germany economically. They instituted currency reforms in their zones and announced plans for creating a single West German Republic with a large degree of autonomy.

These decisions alarmed the Russians. In June they retaliated by closing off Allied surface access to Berlin. For a time it seemed that the Allies must either fight their way into the city or abandon it to the communists. Unwilling to adopt either alternative, Truman decided to fly supplies through the air corridors leading to the capital from Frankfurt, Hanover, and Hamburg. American C-47 and C-54 transports shuttled back and forth in weather fair and foul, carrying enough food, fuel, and other goods necessary to maintain more than 2 million West Berliners. The "Berlin Airlift" put the Soviets in an uncomfortable position; if they were determined to keep supplies from West Berlin, they would have to begin the fighting. They were not prepared to do so. In May 1949 they lifted the blockade.

Containment, some of its advocates argued, required the development of a powerful military force. In May 1948 Republican Senator Arthur H.

Vandenberg of Michigan, a prewar leader of the isolationists who had been converted to internationalism largely by President Roosevelt's solicitous attention to his views, introduced a resolution stating the "determination" of the United States "to exercise the right of individual *or collective* self-defense . . . should any armed attack occur affecting its national security." The Senate approved this resolution by a vote of 64 to 4, proof that isolationism had ceased to be an important force in American politics.

Containment worked well in Europe, at least in the short run; in the Far East, where the United States lacked powerful and determined allies, it was both more expensive and less effective. V-J Day found the Far East a shambles. Much of Japan was a smoking ruin. In China social chaos was complicated by a disorganized political situation. The nationalists under Chiang Kai-shek dominated the south, the communists under Mao Tse-tung controlled the northern countryside, and Japanese troops still held most northern cities.

President Truman acted decisively and effectively with regard to Japan, unsurely and with unfortunate results where China was concerned. Even before the Japanese surrendered, he had decided not to allow the Soviet Union any significant role in the occupation of Japan. A four-power Allied Control Council was established, but American troops commanded by General MacArthur governed the country. MacArthur displayed exactly the proper combination of imperiousness, tact, and intelligence needed to accomplish his purposes. The Japanese, revealing the same remarkable adaptability that had made possible their swift westernization in the latter half of the 19th century, accepted political and social changes that involved universal suffrage and parliamentary government, the encouragement of labor unions, the breakup of large estates and big industrial combines, and the deemphasis of the importance of the emperor. Japan lost its far-flung island empire and all claim to Korea and the Chinese mainland. Efforts to restrict economic development were abandoned in order to build up the country as a Far Eastern bastion against communism. Japan emerged economically strong, politically stable, and firmly allied with the United States.

The difficulties in China were probably insurmountable. Few Americans appreciated the latent power of the Chinese communists. When the war ended, the United States tried to install Chiang in control of all China. The Japanese were allowed to hold key north Chinese sectors until Chiang could take them over. At the same time Truman tried to bring Chiang's nationalists and Mao's communists together. He sent General Marshall to China to seek a settlement, but neither Chiang nor Mao would make significant concessions. Mao was convinced—correctly, as time soon proved—that he could win all China by force, while Chiang, presiding over a corrupt and incredibly incompetent regime, grossly exaggerated his popularity among the Chinese people. In January 1947 Truman re-

The Berlin airlift, also known as "Operation Vittles," delivered fuel and other goods, as well as food, to the isolated American sector of Berlin. Here woman "gleaners" sweep up spilled bits of coal after a delivery; every nugget was as valuable as gold.

called Marshall and named him secretary of state. Soon thereafter civil war erupted in China.

The Election of 1948

In the spring of 1948 President Truman's fortunes were at low ebb. Public opinion polls suggested that a majority of the people considered him incompetent or worse. The Republicans were in control of Congress and had rejected his legislative proposals. They seemed sure to win the 1948 presidential election, especially if Truman was the Democratic candidate. The Republican candidate, Governor Thomas E. Dewey of New York, ran confidently, even complacently, certain that he would carry the country with ease.

Truman's position seemed hopeless because he had alienated both southern conservatives and northern liberals. The southerners were particularly distressed because in 1946 the president had established a Committee on Civil Rights, which had recommended antilynching and anti-poll-tax legislation and the creation of a permanent Fair Employment Practices Commission. They founded the States' Rights ("Dixiecrat") party and nominated J. Strom Thurmond of South Carolina for president.

As for the liberals, in 1947 a group of them had founded Americans for Democratic Action (ADA) and sought an alternative candidate for the 1948 election. A faction led by former vice-president Henry A. Wallace, which believed Truman's containment policy a threat to world peace, favored greater cooperation with the Soviet Union. This group organized a new Progressive party and nominated Wallace. Most members of ADA, however, thought Wallace too pro-Soviet; in the end the organization supported Truman. Yet with two minor candidates sure to cut into the Democratic vote, the president's chances seemed minuscule.

Truman launched an aggressive "whistle-stop" campaign, making hundreds of informal but hard-hitting speeches. He excoriated the "do-nothing" Republican Congress, which had rejected his program and passed the Taft-Hartley Act, and he warned labor, farmers, and consumers that a Republican victory would undermine all the gains of the New Deal years.

Millions were moved by his arguments and by his courageous fight against great odds. The success of the Berlin Airlift during the presidential campaign helped him considerably. The Progressive party fell increasingly into the hands of communist sympathizers, driving away many liber-

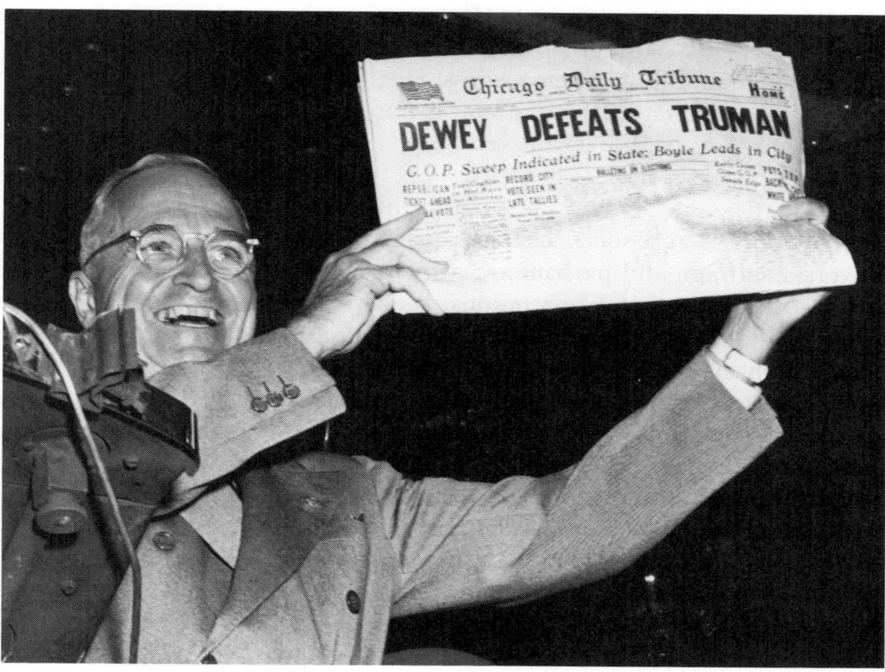

In 1948 the strongly Republican Chicago Daily Tribune *guessed disastrously wrongly in headlining its post-election editions before all the returns were in. For Truman, it was the perfect climax to his hard-won victory.*

als who might otherwise have supported Wallace. Dewey's smug, lackluster campaign failed to attract independents. The president, therefore, was able to reinvigorate the New Deal coalition, and he won an amazing upset victory on election day. He collected 24.1 million votes to Dewey's 21.9 million, the two minor candidates being held to about 2.3 million. In the electoral college his margin was a thumping 303 to 189. In his speech conceding defeat, Dewey, a man not noted for wit, remarked ruefully: "Thought I heard the voice of the people. Must have been some other noise."

Truman's victory gave the ADA considerable influence over what the president called his Fair Deal program. ADA leaders took a middle-of-the-road approach, well described in Arthur M. Schlesinger, Jr.'s *The Vital Center* (1949), which left room for both individualism and social welfare, government regulation of the economy and the encouragement of private enterprise. The approach fitted well with Cold War conditions, which favored both massive military output and continued expansion of the supply of civilian goods. Economic growth would solve all problems, social as well as material. Through growth the poor could be helped without taking from the rich. The way to check inflation, for example, was not by freezing prices, profits, or wages but by expanding production. However, relatively little of Truman's Fair Deal was enacted into law. Congress approved a federal housing program and measures increasing the minimum wage and social security benefits, but these were merely extensions of New Deal legislation.

Containing Communism Abroad

During Truman's second term the confrontation between the United States and the Soviet Union, and more broadly between what was seen as "democracy" and "communism," dominated the headlines and occupied a major part of the attention of the president and most other government officials. To strengthen ties with the European democracies, in April 1949 the North Atlantic Treaty was signed in Washington. The United States, Great Britain, France, Italy, Belgium, the Netherlands, Luxembourg, Denmark, Norway, Portugal, Iceland, and Canada* agreed "that an armed attack against one or more of them in Europe or North America shall be considered an attack against them all" and that in the event of such an attack each would take "individually and in concert with the other Parties, such action as it deems necessary, including the use of armed force." No more entangling alliance could be imagined, yet the Senate ratified this treaty by a vote of 82 to 13. The pact established the North Atlantic Treaty Organization (NATO). Disturbed by the news, released in September 1949, that the Soviet Union had produced an atomic bomb, Congress appropriated $1.5 billion to arm NATO. In 1951 General Eisenhower was recalled to active duty and placed in command of NATO forces.

The success of containment was not without price; every move evoked a Russian response. The Marshall Plan led to the seizure of Czechoslovakia, the buildup of Germany to the Berlin blockade, the creation of NATO to the multilateral military alliance known as the Warsaw Pact. George Kennan, the "father" of containment, now downplayed the Soviet military threat. He thought the stress on rearming Europe a "regrettable diversion" from the task of economic reconstruction. In any case, both sides contributed by their actions and their continuing suspicions to the heightening of Cold War tensions.

In Asia the effort to contain communism exploded into war. By the end of 1949 Mao Tse-tung's communist armies had administered a crushing defeat to the nationalists. The remnants of Chiang Kai-shek's forces fled to the island of Formosa, now called Taiwan. The "loss" of China to communism divided the American people. It strengthened right-wing opponents of internationalism in the Republican party. They and other critics charged that Truman had not backed the nationalists strongly enough and that he had stupidly underestimated Mao's dedication to the cause of world revolution.

Despite a superficial plausibility, neither charge made much sense. Nothing short of massive American military aid, including the commitment of American troops, could have prevented the communist victory. American opinion would not have supported military intervention, and such intervention would unquestionably have alienated the Chinese people, who were fed up with foreign meddling in their affairs. That *any* American action could have changed the outcome in China is un-

* In 1952 Greece and Turkey joined the alliance, and in 1954 West Germany was admitted.

likely, given the unpopularity of Chiang's repressive government and the ruthless zeal of the communists. The United States probably gave the nationlists too much aid rather than too little.

The attacks of his critics roused Truman's combativeness and led him into serious miscalculations elsewhere in Asia. After the war the province of Korea was taken from Japan and divided along the 38th parallel, the Russians controlling the northern half of the country, the Americans the southern. The occupying powers agreed to set up a unified and independent Korean republic at some future date, but in the highly charged atmosphere of the postwar years they could not agree on how this should be done. By September 1948 there were two "independent" governments in Korea, the Democratic People's Republic, backed by the Soviet Union, and the Republic of Korea, backed by the United States and the UN. Both powers withdrew their troops from the peninsula, the Russians leaving behind a well-armed local force while the Republic of Korea's army was small and ill trained.

American military strategists had decided that South Korea was not worth defending. In January 1950 Dean Acheson, who had succeeded Marshall as secretary of state, deliberately excluded Korea from the "defensive perimeter" of the United States in the Far East. It was up to the republic, backed by the UN, to protect itself from attack, he said. This the republic was unable to do; when North Korean armored divisions struck suddenly across the 38th parallel in June 1950, they quickly routed the defenders.

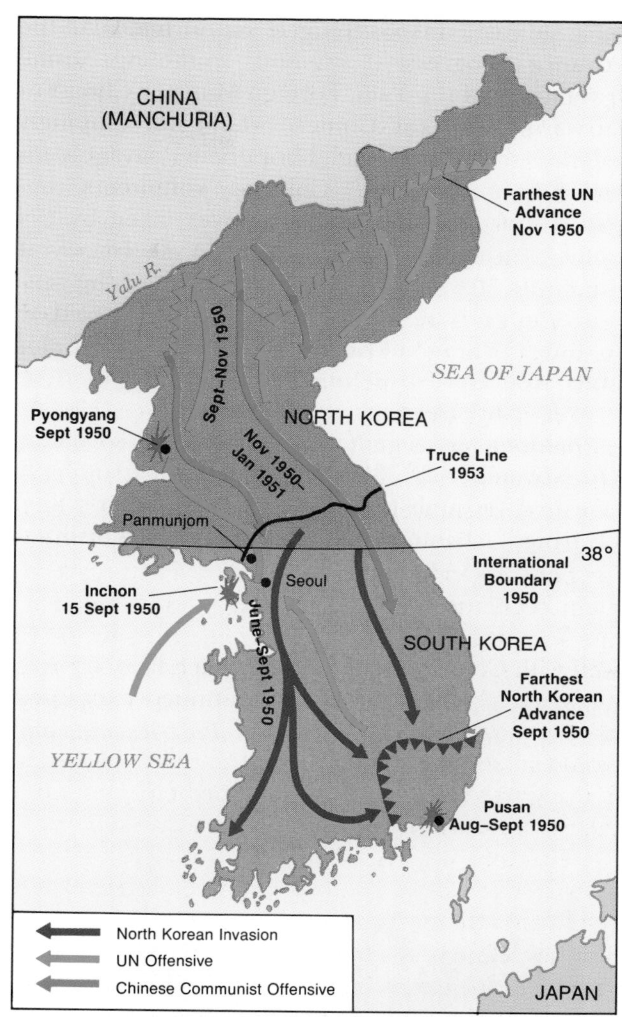

THE KOREAN WAR, 1950–1953

At this point Truman exhibited his finest qualities: decisiveness and courage. Recalling the dire results that had followed when earlier acts of aggression—beginning with the Japanese assault on Manchuria—had been allowed to pass unchecked, he decided to defend South Korea. With the backing of the UN Security Council (but without asking Congress to declare war), he sent American planes into battle.* Ground troops soon followed.

Nominally the Korean War was a struggle between the invaders and the United Nations. General MacArthur, placed in command, flew the blue UN flag over his headquarters, and 16 nations supplied troops for his army. However, more than 90 percent of the forces employed were American. At first the North Koreans pushed them back rapidly, but by the beginning of September a front was stabilized around the port of Pusan, at the southern tip of Korea. Then MacArthur executed a brilliant amphibious flanking maneuver, striking at the west coast city of Inchon, about 50 miles south of the 38th parallel. Outflanked, the North Koreans fled northward, losing thousands of men and much equipment. By October the battlefront had moved *north* of the old boundary.

Truman now permitted MacArthur to advance toward the Yalu River, the boundary between North Korea and China. It was a momentous and unfortunate decision, an example of how power,

* Russia, which could have vetoed this action, was at the moment boycotting the Security Council because the UN had refused to give the Mao Tse-tung regime China's seat on that body.

once unleashed, so often gets out of hand. As the advance progressed, ominous rumblings came from north of the Yalu. Foreign Minister Chou En-lai warned that the Chinese would not "supinely tolerate seeing their neighbors being savagely invaded by imperialists." Chinese "volunteers" began to turn up among the captives taken by UN units. Alarmed, Truman flew to Wake Island, in the Pacific, to confer with MacArthur, but the general assured him that the Chinese would not dare to intervene. If they did, MacArthur added, his army would crush them easily; the war would be over by Christmas.

Seldom has a general miscalculated so badly. On November 26, 33 Chinese divisions suddenly smashed through the center of MacArthur's line. Overnight a triumphant advance became a disorganized retreat. MacArthur now spoke of the "bottomless well of Chinese manpower" and justified his earlier confidence by claiming, not without reason, that he was fighting "an entirely new war."

The UN army rallied south of the 38th parallel and even managed to battle its way back across that line in the eastern sector. By the spring of 1951 the front had been stabilized. MacArthur then urged that he be permitted to bomb Chinese installations north of the Yalu. He also suggested a naval blockade of the coast of China and the use of Chinese nationalist troops in Korea. When Truman rejected these proposals on the ground that they would lead to a third world war, MacArthur, who tended to ignore the larger political aspects of the conflict, attempted to rouse Congress and the public against the president by criticizing administra-

Photographer David Douglas Duncan was with the First Marine Division in Korea when it was virtually isolated by the sudden Red Chinese offensive in November 1950. Conducting in frigid weather what the military historian S.L.A. Marshall called "the greatest fighting withdrawal of modern history," the marines broke out to safety.

tion policy openly. Truman ordered him to be silent, and when the general persisted, he removed him from command.

This unpopular but necessary step (a fundamental principle of democracy, civilian control over the military, was at stake) brought down a storm of abuse on the president. At first the Korean "police action" had been popular in the United States, but as the months passed and the casualties mounted many citizens became disillusioned and angry. The war had brought into the open a basic political (or better, psychological) disadvantage of the containment policy: its object was not victory but balance; it involved apparently unending tension without the satisfying release of an action completed. To Americans accustomed to triumph and fond of oversimplifying complex questions, containment seemed, as its costs in blood and dollars mounted, a monumentally frustrating policy. MacArthur's simple if dangerous strategy offered at least the hope of victory; all the president seemed to offer was a further loss of American lives and money. MacArthur returned home to launch what he called a "crusade" to rally opinion to his cause.

In time the fundamental correctness of both Truman's policy and his decision to remove MacArthur became apparent. As he reminded the country, an all-out war with Communist China, besides costing thousands of lives, would alarm America's allies and weaken the nation while the Soviet Union watched from the sidelines unscathed. Military men backed the president almost unanimously. General Omar N. Bradley, chairman of the Joint Chiefs of Staff, said that a showdown with the Chinese "would involve us in the wrong war, at the wrong place, at the wrong time and with the wrong enemy." In June 1951 the communists agreed to discuss an armistice in Korea, and though the negotiations dragged on, with interruptions, for two years while thousands more died along the static battlefront, both MacArthur and talk of bombing China subsided.

The Communist Issue at Home: McCarthyism

The frustrating Korean War highlighted the paradox that at the pinnacle of its power, the influence of the United States in world affairs was declining. Its monopoly of nuclear weapons had been lost. China had passed into the communist orbit. Elsewhere in Asia and throughout Africa, new nations, formerly colonial possessions of the western powers, were adopting a "neutralist" position in the Cold War. Despite the billions poured into armaments and foreign aid, the safety and even the survival of the country seemed far from assured.

Internal as well as external dangers appeared to threaten the nation. Alarming examples of communist espionage in Canada, in Great Britain, and in America itself convinced many citizens that clever conspirators were everywhere at work undermining American security. Republican critics of Truman's domestic policies were prominent among those charging that he was "soft" on communists. In 1947, responding to these pressures, Truman established a Loyalty Review Board to check up on government employees. He hoped to defuse the communists-in-government issue by being even more zealous in pursuit of spies than his critics, but the investigators found no significant trace of subversion.

In 1948 Whittaker Chambers, an editor of *Time* who had formerly been a communist, charged that Alger Hiss, president of the Carnegie Endowment for International Peace and a former State Department official, had been a communist in the thirties. Hiss denied the charge and sued Chambers for libel. Chambers then produced microfilms purporting to show that Hiss had copied classified documents for dispatch to Moscow. Hiss could not be indicted for espionage because of the statute of limitations; instead he was charged with perjury. His first trial resulted in a hung jury, his second, ending in January 1950, in conviction and a five-year jail term.

While many people considered Hiss the innocent victim of anticommunist hysteria, the case fed the fears of those who believed in the existence of a powerful communist underground in the United States. The disclosure in February 1950 that a respected British scientist, Klaus Fuchs, had betrayed atomic secrets to the Russians heightened these fears, as did the arrest and conviction of his American associate, Harry Gold, and two other American traitors, Julius and Ethel Rosenberg, on the same charge.

Although they were obviously not major spies and the information they revealed was not very

Senator Joseph McCarthy testifying before the Senate Foreign Relations Committee, March 9, 1950. McCarthy continued his attacks on alleged communists until he was "condemned" by the Senate by a vote of 67–22 in December 1954.

important, the Rosenbergs were executed, to the consternation of many liberals in the United States and elsewhere. However, information gathered by other spies had speeded the Soviet development of nuclear weapons. This fact encouraged some Republicans to press hard the communists-in-government issue.

On February 9, 1950, an obscure senator, Joseph R. McCarthy of Wisconsin, casually introduced this theme in a speech before the Women's Republican Club of Wheeling, West Virginia. "The reason we find ourselves in a position of impotency," he stated, "is not because our only powerful potential enemy has sent men to invade our shores, but rather because of the traitorous actions of those who have been treated so well by this nation." The State Department, he added, was "infested" with communists. "I have here in my hand a list of 205—a list of names that were known to the Secretary of State as being members of the Communist Party and who nevertheless are *still working and shaping . . . policy.*"*

* McCarthy was speaking from rough notes, and no one made an accurate record of his words. The exact number mentioned has long been in dispute. On other occasions he said there were 57 and 81 "card-carrying communists" in the State Department.

McCarthy had no shred of evidence to back up these statements, and a Senate committee headed by the conservative Democrat Millard Tydings of Maryland soon exposed his mendacity. But thousands of people were too eager to believe him to listen to reason. Within a few weeks he was the most talked-of man in Congress. Inhibited neither by scruples nor by logic, he lashed out in every direction, attacking international experts like Professor Owen Lattimore of Johns Hopkins and professional diplomats such as John S. Service and John Carter Vincent, who were already under attack for having courageously pointed out the deficiencies of the Chiang Kai-shek regime during the Chinese civil war.

When McCarthy's victims indignantly denied his charges, he distracted the public by striking out with still more sensational accusations directed at other innocents. Even General Marshall, a man of the highest character and patriotism, was subject to McCarthy's abuse. The general, he said, was "steeped in falsehood," part of a "conspiracy so immense and an infamy so black as to dwarf any previous venture in the history of man."

McCarthy was a totally unscrupulous demagogue. The "big lie" was his most effective weapon: the enormity of his charges and the status of his targets convinced thousands that there must be *some* truth to what he was saying. Nevertheless, his crude tactics would have failed if the public had not been so worried about communism. The worries were caused by the reality of Soviet military power, the attack on Korea, the loss of the nuclear monopoly, and the stories about spies. The bitter disappointment of having been plunged again into the tensions of international conflicts so soon after World War II, when they had expected to relax and enjoy life, heightened the concern of many citizens and added an irrational element to their fears. By the fall of 1950 McCarthy had become a major force and the word *McCarthyism* had entered the lexicon of politics.

In the 1950 election campaign McCarthy "invaded" Maryland and contributed mightily to the defeat of Senator Tydings; two years later William Benton of Connecticut, who had introduced a resolution calling for McCarthy's expulsion from the Senate, failed of reelection when McCarthy campaigned against him. Thereafter many congressmen who detested him dared not incur his wrath, and large numbers of Republicans found the temptation to take advantage of his voter appeal irresistible.

The Problem of Agricultural Abundance

Another of President Truman's many problems during his second term was what to do with surplus agricultural commodities. While the number of farms in the nation was declining, their output was increasing, mainly because a veritable technological revolution was taking place. Just as the Civil War had speeded the switch from human to animal power in agriculture, World War II speeded the switch from animals to the gasoline engine. Besides using more machines, farmers stepped up their consumption of fertilizers. New chemicals controlled weeds and reduced the ravages of insect pests and plant diseases. Geneticists developed more productive varieties of food plants. Better feeds made for meatier cattle and hogs; new antibiotics checked animal diseases.

Efficiency and expansion did not bring prosperity to most farmers. Conditions roughly resembled those after the Civil War and after World War I; overproduction and declining foreign markets caught agriculturalists in a price squeeze. Their relative share of the national income declined.

No significant group suggested abandoning the New Deal policy of subsidizing agriculture; the controversy concerned how much aid and what kind. The New Deal system of maintaining the price of staple crops like wheat and cotton at or near "parity" with the prices paid by farmers for manufactured goods left much to be desired in practice. First, declining farm income did not mean cheaper food for consumers; prices in groceries and butcher shops kept pace with those of other goods, since the cost of distributing and processing food rose steadily. By boosting food prices still higher, the support program aggravated the problem of the rising cost of living.

Second, acreage controls proved an ineffective way to curtail production. When farmers withdrew land from cultivation, they plowed more fertilizer into their remaining acres and continued to increase output. Potatoes were a glut on the market principally because per-acre yields rose from 155 to 215 bushels in three years. Third, Henry Wallace's "ever-normal granary" concept resulted in the piling up of huge reserves in government elevators and warehouses at great expense to the public. Finally, the system had never helped small farmers or those who raised perishable commodities. It was accelerating the trend toward large-scale agriculture, thus stimulating the movement of people from farm to city.

Despite these flaws, thousands of rural voters had supported Truman in 1948 largely because of his somewhat demagogic argument that a return to Republican rule would mean scrapping the price-support program. His own farm policy was developed by Secretary of Agriculture Charles F. Brannan, a former administrator of New Deal agricultural programs. In 1949 Brannan drafted a new approach to the problem. While continuing to support the prices of storable crops, the government, he suggested, should guarantee fixed minimum incomes to farmers raising perishable crops. The products could then seek their own price levels in the marketplace. Consumers would benefit, but not at the expense of farmers.

This scheme ran into a wall of resistance. Big farmers objected to its upper limit on guaranteed income, and even smaller operators disapproved of extending social security and minimum wage legislation to farm workers, which Brannan also advocated. Conservatives charged that the Brannan plan was both too costly and socialistic, "a controlled economy with a vengeance." Most economists thought the plan overly complicated. After much debate, Congress rejected it—along with most of President Truman's other suggestions.

The Korean War eased the situation for farmers temporarily; after it ended, surplus crops began to pile up alarmingly. Soon the government was storing grain in the holds of idle merchant ships. In June 1952 there was $1.4 billion worth of crops in storage; by June 1956 this figure had risen to $8.3 billion. Yet food prices continued to rise.

Dwight D. Eisenhower

As the 1952 presidential election approached, Truman's popularity was again at a low ebb. Senator McCarthy attacked him relentlessly for his handling of the Korean conflict and his "mistreatment" of General MacArthur. In choosing their candidate, the Republicans passed over the twice-defeated Dewey and their most prominent leader, Senator Robert A. Taft of Ohio, an outspoken conservative, and nominated General Dwight D. Eisenhower.

Eisenhower's popularity did not grow merely out of his achievements in World War II. Although a West Pointer (class of 1915), he struck most persons as anything but warlike. After the bristly, combative Truman, his genial tolerance and evident desire to avoid controversy proved widely appealing. Eisenhower's reluctance to seek political office reminded the country of Washington, while his seeming ignorance of current political issues was no more a handicap to his campaign than the similar ignorance of Jackson and Grant in their times. People "liked Ike" because of his personality—he radiated warmth and sincerity—and because his management of the allied armies promised that he would be equally competent as head of the complex federal government.

The Democrats nominated Governor Adlai E. Stevenson of Illinois, whose grandfather had been vice-president under Cleveland. Stevenson's lucid, witty, urbane speeches captivated intellectuals. His common sense and genuine humility led large numbers of young people to become active in the Democratic party at a time when it was much in need of new blood. In retrospect, however, it is clear that Stevenson had not the remotest chance of defeating the popular Eisenhower. Disillusionment with the Korean War and a widespread belief that the Democrats had been too long in power were added handicaps. His foes turned his strongest assets against him, denouncing his humor as frivolity, characterizing his appreciation of the complexities of life as self-doubt, and tagging his intellectual followers "eggheads," an appellation that effectively caricatured the balding, slope-shouldered, somewhat endomorphic candidate. "The eggheads are for Stevenson," one Republican pointed out, "but how many eggheads are there?" There were far too few to carry the country, as the election revealed.

McCarthy's attacks helped to defeat the Democrats, as did Eisenhower's promise to go to Korea himself if elected to try to bring the long conflict to an end. The result was a Republican landslide: Eisenhower received almost 34 million votes to Stevenson's 27 million, and in the electoral college his margin was 442 to 89.

In office, Eisenhower was the antithesis of Truman. The Republicans had charged the Democratic administration with being wasteful and extravagant. Eisenhower planned to run his administration on sound business principles and to eschew increases in the activities of the federal government. He spoke scornfully of "creeping socialism," called for more local control of government affairs, and promised to reduce federal spending in order to balance the budget and cut taxes. He believed that under Roosevelt and Truman the presidency had lost much of its essential dignity. By battling with Congress and pressure groups over the details of legislation, his immediate predecessors had sacrificed part of their status as chief representative of the American people. His natural wish to preserve his great popularity reinforced his conviction in this regard. Like Washington, he tried to avoid being caught up in narrow partisan conflicts. Like Washington, he was not always able to do so.

Having successfully managed the complexities of military administration, Eisenhower used the same kind of staff system as president. He appointed Sherman Adams, a former governor of New Hampshire, as his personal assistant, a role similar to that of chief of staff in the army. Adams

Dwight Eisenhower posed for a portrait in battle dress several years before he was elected to office.

had a great deal of influence over whom the President saw and what reports he read. Eisenhower also gave his Cabinet officers more responsibility than many modern presidents. He did not like to waste time and energy on administrative routine. This did not mean that he was lazy or politically naive. He knew that if he left too many small decisions to others, they would soon be controlling, if not actually making, the large decisions as well.

Although conservative, Eisenhower was neither a reactionary nor a fool. He hoped to balance the federal budget and lower taxes, but he was unwilling to do away with existing social and economic legislation or to cut back on military expenditures. Some economists claimed that he reacted too slowly in dealing with business recessions and that he showed insufficient concern for speeding the rate of national economic growth. Yet he adopted a Rooseveltian, almost a Keynesian approach to economic problems; that is, he tried to check downturns in the business cycle by stimulating the economy. In his memoir *Mandate for Change* (1963) he wrote of resorting to "preventative action to arrest the downturn [of 1954] before it might become severe" and of being ready to use "any and all weapons in the federal arsenal, including changes in monetary and credit policy, modifications of the tax structure, and a speed-up in the construction of . . . public works" to accomplish this end.

Eisenhower approved the extension of social security to an additional 10 million persons; created a new Department of Health, Education, and Welfare; and in 1955 came out for federal support of school and highway construction. But his somewhat doctrinaire belief in decentralization and private enterprise reduced the effectiveness of his social welfare measures. When Dr. Jonas Salk's polio vaccine was introduced in 1955, Secretary of Health,

Education, and Welfare Oveta Culp Hobby opposed its free distribution by the government. To do so, she said, would lead to socialized medicine "by the back door."

Just as Woodrow Wilson's exposure to faculty politics at Princeton had prepared him for running the federal government (see page 677), so Eisenhower's experience with military politics in World War II made him an excellent politician when he moved into the White House. He knew how to be flexible without compromising his basic values. His "conservatism" became first "dynamic conservatism" and then "progressive moderation." He summarized his attitude by saying that he was liberal in dealing with individuals but conservative "when talking about . . . the individual's pocketbook." But the main reason so many Americans loved Eisenhower was that he epitomized what they wished the world was like. This helps to explain why he never succeeded in forging an effective political coalition.

The Eisenhower-Dulles Foreign Policy

After the 1952 election Eisenhower kept his pledge to go to Korea. His trip produced no immediate result, but the truce talks, suspended before the election, were resumed. In July 1953, perhaps influenced by a hint that the United States might use "tactical" atomic bombs in Korea, the communists agreed to an armistice. Korea remained divided. Containment had proved extremely expensive; the United States had suffered more that 135,000 casualties, including 33,000 dead. Yet aggression had been confronted and fought to a standstill.

The American people, troubled and uncertain, counted on Eisenhower to find a way to employ the nation's immense strength constructively. The new president shared the general feeling that a change of tactics in foreign affairs was needed. He counted on Congress and his secretary of state to solve the practical problems.

Given this attitude, his choice of John Foster Dulles as secretary of state seemed inspired. Dulles's experience in diplomacy dated to 1907, when he had served as secretary to the Chinese delegation at the Second Hague Conference.* Later he had a small place among the army of experts advising Wilson at the Versailles Conference. More recently he had been an adviser to the American delegation to the San Francisco Conference and a representative of the United States in the UN General Assembly. Since 1948 he had been recognized as one of the Republican party's chief foreign policy experts, by no one more unquestioningly than himself. "With my understanding of the intricate relationships between the peoples of the world and your sensitiveness to the political considerations involved," he told Eisenhower, "we will make the most successful team in history."

Like Eisenhower, Dulles believed in change within the framework of internationalism. "What we need to do," he said, "is to recapture the kind of crusading spirit of the early days of the Republic." Dulles combined amazing energy and strong moral convictions—"there is no way to solve the great perplexing international problems except by bringing to bear on them the force of Christianity," he insisted. His objectives were magnificent, his strategy grandiose. Instead of waiting for the communists to attack and then "containing" them, the United States should warn them that "massive retaliation" directed at Moscow or Peking would be the fate of all aggressors. With the communists immobilized by this threat, positive measures aimed at "liberating" eastern Europe and "unleashing" Chiang Kai-shek against the Chinese mainland would follow. Dulles professed great faith in NATO, but he believed that if America's allies lacked the courage to follow its lead, the nation would have to undertake an "agonizing reappraisal" of its commitments to them.

Thus Dulles envisioned a policy broader, more idealistic, and more aggressive than Truman's. Not the least of its virtues, he claimed, was that it would save money—"more bang for the buck" was the way less pompous advocates of the policy than Dulles put it. By concentrating on nuclear deterrents and avoiding "brushfire" wars in remote regions, the country could dramatically reduce the cost of defense.

* The delegation was headed by Dulles's grandfather John W. Foster, who had been secretary of state under Benjamin Harrison.

Dulles during a 1956 press conference at which he rejected suggestions by Russia and India that the United States suspend further hydrogen bomb tests. His stance and gesture project his "hard line" approach.

Despite his determination, energy, and high ideals, Dulles failed to make the United States a more effective force in world affairs. Massive retaliation made little sense when the Soviet Union possessed nuclear weapons as powerful as those of the United States. In November 1952 America had won the race to make a hydrogen bomb, but the Russians duplicated this feat the following August. Thereafter the only threat behind massive retaliation was the threat of human extinction.

Brinkmanship: Asia

Most of Dulles's other schemes were equally unrealistic. "Unleashing" Chiang Kai-shek would have been like matching a Pekingese against a tiger. "Liberating" Russia's European satellites would of necessity have involved a third world war. "You can count on us," Dulles told the peoples of eastern Europe in a radio address in January 1953. But when East German workers rioted in June of that year and when the Hungarians revolted in 1956, no help was forthcoming from America. Dulles certainly did not err in refusing to prevent the Russians from crushing these rebellions, but his earlier statements had roused hopes behind the Iron Curtain that now were shattered.

Dulles's saber-rattling tactics were badly timed. While he was planning to avert future Koreas, the Soviet Union was shifting its approach. Stalin died in March 1953, and after a period of internal conflict within the Kremlin, Nikita Khrushchev emerged as the new master of Russia. Khrushchev set out to obtain communist objectives by indirection. He appealed to the antiwestern prejudices of the underdeveloped countries just emerging from the yoke of colonialism, offering them economic aid and pointing to Soviet achievements in science and technology, such as the launching of *Sputnik,* the first earth satellite (1957), as proof that communism would soon "bury" the capitalist system without troubling to destroy it by force. The Soviet Union was the friend of all peace-loving nations, he insisted.

Khrushchev was a master hypocrite, yet he was a realist too. While Dulles, product of a system that made a virtue of compromise and tolerance, insisted that the world must choose between American good and Russian evil, Khrushchev, trained to believe in the incompatibility of communism and capitalism, began to talk of "peaceful coexistence."

Dulles failed to win the confidence of America's allies or even that of his own department. Senator McCarthy moderated his attacks on the State Department not a jot when it came under the control of his own party. In 1953 its overseas information program received his special attention. He denounced Voice of America broadcasters for quoting the works of "controversial" authors and sent Roy M. Cohn, youthful special counsel of his Committee on Governmental Operations, on a mission to Europe to ferret out subversives in the United States Information Service.

Dulles did not come to the defense of his people. Instead he seemed determined to out-McCar-

The Washington Post's *Herblock was a sharp critic of the Eisenhower administration. In a comment on John Foster Dulles's "brinkmanship" diplomacy, Dulles in a Superman outfit assures Uncle Sam, "Don't be afraid—I can always pull you back."*

thy McCarthy in his zeal to get rid of "undesirables" of all sorts. He sanctioned the discharge of nearly 500 State Department employees, not one of whom was proved to have engaged in subversive activities. People were let go merely because they were suspected of being homosexuals, the argument being that they might be blackmailed into giving state secrets to the communists. By making such "concessions" to McCarthy, Dulles hoped to end attacks on the administration's foreign policy. The tactic failed; its only result was to undermine the morale of career Foreign Service officers.

But McCarthy finally overreached himself. Early in 1954 he turned his guns on the army. After a series of charges and countercharges, he accused army officials of trying to blackmail his committee and announced a broad investigation. The resulting Army-McCarthy Hearings, televised before the country, proved the senator's undoing. For weeks his dark scowl, his blind combativeness and disregard for every human value stood exposed for millions to see. When the hearings ended in June 1954 after some million words of testimony, his spell had been broken. The Senate, with President Eisenhower quietly applying pressure behind the scene, at last moved to censure him in December 1954. This reproof completed the destruction of his influence. Although he continued to issue statements and wild charges, the country no longer listened. In 1957 he died, victim of cirrhosis of the liver.

While the final truce talks were taking place in Korea, new trouble was erupting far to the south in French Indochina. Since December 1946 nationalist rebels led by the communist Ho Chi Minh had been harassing the French in Vietnam, one of three puppet kingdoms (the others were Laos and Cambodia) fashioned by France in Indochina after the defeat of the Japanese. When Communist China began supplying arms to the rebels, who were known as the Vietminh, Truman, applying the containment policy, countered with economic and military assistance to the French. When Eisenhower succeeded to the presidency, he continued and expanded this assistance.

Early in 1954 Ho Chi Minh's troops trapped and beseiged a French army in the remote stronghold of Dien Bien Phu. Faced with the loss of 20,000 soldiers, France asked the United States to commit its air force to the battle. Eisenhower, after long deliberation, decided against doing anything. Although the possibility of communist control of Vietnam worried him deeply, he did not seriously consider sending troops into the arena. Any idea of air strikes, he believed, was "just silly." The communists were "secreted all around in the jungle. How are we, in a few air strikes, to defeat them?"

In May the French garrison at Dien Bien Phu surrendered, and in July, while Dulles watched from the sidelines, France, Great Britain, Russia, and China signed an agreement at Geneva dividing Vietnam along the 17th parallel. France withdrew from the area. The northern sector became the Democratic Republic of Vietnam, controlled by Ho Chi Minh; the southern remained in the hands of the emperor, Bao Dai. An election to settle the future of all Vietnam was scheduled for 1956.

When it seemed likely that the communists would win that election, Ngo Dinh Diem, a conservative anticommunist, overthrew Bao Dai and became president of South Vietnam. The United States supplied his government liberally with aid. The planned election was never held, and Vietnam remained divided into two nations.

Dulles responded to the diplomatic setback in Vietnam by establishing the Southeast Asia Treaty Organization (September 1954), but only three Asian nations—the Philippine Republic, Thailand, and Pakistan—joined this alliance.* At the same time, the unleashed Chiang Kai-shek was engaging in a meaningless artillery duel with the Chinese communists from the tiny nationalist-held islands of Quemoy and Matsu, which lay in the shadow of the mainland. When it was suggested that the United States join in the fight, Eisenhower refused on the ground, sensible but inconsistent with Dulles's rhetoric, that intervention might set off an atomic war. The United States would not protect the offshore islands, Dulles announced, but it would defend Taiwan at all costs.

The Middle East Cauldron

Yet within a year the world teetered once again on the brink of conflict. This time trouble erupted in the Middle East. American policy in that region, aside from the ubiquitous question of restraining Russian expansion, was influenced by the huge oil resources of Iran, Iraq, Kuwait, and Saudi Arabia—about 60 percent of the world's known reserves—and by the conflict between the new Jewish state of Israel (formerly the British mandate of Palestine) and its Arab neighbors. Although he tried to woo the Arabs, President Truman had consistently placed support for Israel before other considerations in the Middle East. When Israel formally declared its independence in 1948, he recognized it even more quickly than Theodore Roosevelt had recognized Panama in 1903.

Angered by the creation of Israel, the surrounding Arab nations tried to smash the country by force. (The Israeli question had the same impact on Arab emotions that the "bloody shirt" had on Republicans after the Civil War.) While badly outnumbered, the Israelis were better organized and better armed than the Arabs and drove them off with relative ease. With them departed nearly a million Palestinian Arabs, thereby creating a desperate refugee problem in nearby countries. Truman's support of Israel and the millions of dollars contributed to the new state by American Jews produced much Arab resentment of the United States.

Dulles and Eisenhower, worried by the growing influence of the Soviet Union in the Arab world, tried to redress the balance by deemphasizing American support of Israel. In 1952 a revolution in Egypt had overthrown the dissolute King Farouk. Colonel Gamal Abdel Nasser emerged as the strongman of Egypt.

The United States was prepared to lend Nasser money to build a huge dam on the Nile at Aswan. The dam was to be the key to an Egyptian irrigation program to expand agricultural development, and it would be a source of electric power. However, the Eisenhower administration would not sell Egypt arms. The communists would. For this reason, while he accepted American economic assistance, Nasser drifted toward the communist orbit. In May 1956 he established diplomatic relations with Red China.

Eisenhower then decided not to finance the Aswan Dam. In July Dulles informed the Egyptian ambassador that the deal was off. Nasser responded a week later by nationalizing the Suez Canal. This move galvanized the British and French. Influenced by Dulles's argument that Egypt could be made an ally by cajolery, the British had acceded in 1954 to Nasser's demand that they evacuate their miltary base at Suez. Now their traditional "lifeline" to the Orient was at Egypt's mercy. In conjunction with the French, and without consulting the United States, the British decided to take back the canal by force. The Israelis, alarmed by repeated Arab hit-and-run raids along their borders, also attacked Egypt.

Events moved swiftly. Israeli armored columns crushed the Egyptian army in the Sinai Peninsula in a matter of days. France and Britain occupied Port Said, at the northern end of the canal. Nasser blocked the canal by sinking ships in the channel. In the UN the Soviet Union and the United States introduced resolutions calling for a cease-fire. Both were vetoed by Britain and France.

Then Khrushchev thundered a warning from Moscow that he might send "volunteers" to Egypt

* The other signatories were Great Britain, France, the United States, Australia, and New Zealand.

A Russian freighter edges past a couple of sunken vessels at the northern end of the Suez Canal. In 1956 the Egyptians sank 47 ships to make the waterway useless, in response to British and French threats to seize the canal.

and launch atomic missiles against France and Great Britain if they did not withdraw. Eisenhower also demanded that the invaders pull out of Egypt. In London large crowds demonstrated against their own government. On November 6, only nine days after the first Israeli units invaded Egypt, Prime Minister Eden, haggard and shaken, announced a cease-fire. Israel withdrew its troops. The crisis subsided as rapidly as it had arisen.

The United States had adhered to its principles and thus won a measure of respect in the Arab countries. But at what cost! Its major allies had been humiliated. Their ill-timed attack had enabled Russia to recover much of the prestige lost as a result of its brutal suppression of a Hungarian revolt which had broken out a week before the Suez fiasco. Eden and French Premier Guy Mollet were claiming with considerable plausibility that Dulles's futile attempt to win Arab friendship without abandoning Israel had placed them in a dilemma and that the secretary had behaved dishonorably or at least disingenuously in handling the Egyptian problem. In fact Dulles was only carrying out Eisenhower's orders, though his self-righteous, moralizing criticisms of Egyptian dealings with Russia and of the allies' attack on Egypt made the situation worse. "Mr. Dulles kicked Nasser in the teeth, with a missionary twist," one observer noted.

The bad feeling within the western alliance soon passed. When Russia seemed likely to profit from its "defense" of Egypt in the crisis, the president announced the "Eisenhower Doctrine" (January 1957), which stated that the United States was "prepared to use armed force" anywhere in the Middle East against "aggression from any country controlled by international communism." The Eisenhower Doctrine amounted to little more than a restatement of the containment policy. No sudden shift in the Middle Eastern balance of power resulted.

Eisenhower and the Russians

In Europe the Eisenhower and Dulles policies differed little from those of Truman. When Eisenhower announced his plan to rely more heavily on nuclear deterrents, the Europeans drew back in alarm, believing that in any atomic showdown they were sure to be destroyed. Khrushchev's talk of peaceful coexistence found many receptive ears, especially in France.

The president therefore yielded to European pressures for a diplomatic "summit" conference with the Russians. In July 1955 Eisenhower, Prime Minister Anthony Eden of Great Britain, and French Premier Edgar Faure met at Geneva with Khrushchev and his then coleader, Nikolai Bulganin, to discuss disarmament and the reunification of West and East Germany. The meeting produced no specific agreement, but with the Russians beaming cheerfully for the cameramen and talking of peaceful coexistence and with Eisenhower pouring martinis and projecting his famous charm, observers noted a softening of tensions that was dubbed "the spirit of Geneva."

In 1956 Eisenhower was reelected, defeating Adlai Stevenson even more decisively than he had in 1952. Despite their evident satisfaction with their leader, however, the mood of the American people was one of sober, restrained determination. Hopes of pushing back the Soviet Union with clever stratagems and moral fervor were fading. America's first successful earth satellite, launched in January 1958, brought cold comfort, for it was much smaller than the earth-circling Russian Sputniks.

In 1957 Dulles underwent surgery for an abdominal cancer, and in April 1959 he had to resign. The next month he was dead. Although Christian A. Herter, a former congressman and governor of Massachusetts, became the new secretary of state, President Eisenhower personally took over much of the task of conducting foreign relations.

Eisenhower had never avoided making decisions in the foreign policy area. The key to his approach was restraint; he exercised commendable caution in every crisis. Like U. S. Grant, he was a soldier who hated war. From Korea through the crises over Indochina, Hungary, and Suez, he avoided risky new commitments. His behavior, like his temperament, contrasted sharply with that of the aggressive, oratorically perfervid Dulles. While Dulles ran the State Department, the difference between the rhetoric of American foreign policy and its underlying philosophy was confusing. This brought the administration much unnecessary criticism.

Amid the tension that followed the Suez crisis, the belief persisted in many quarters that the "spirit of Geneva" could be revived if only a new summit meeting could be arranged. World opinion was insistent that the great powers stop making and testing nuclear weapons, for every test explosion was contaminating the atmosphere with radioactive debris that threatened the future of all life. Unresolved controversies, especially the argument over divided Germany, might erupt at any moment into a globe-shattering war.

Neither the United States nor the Soviet Union dared ignore these dangers; each therefore adopted a more accommodating attitude. In the summer of 1959 Vice-President Richard M. Nixon visited the Soviet Union and his opposite number, Vice Premier Anastas I. Mikoyan, toured the United States. Although Nixon's visit was marred by a heated argument with Khrushchev, conducted before a gaping crowd in the kitchen of a model American home that had been set up at a Moscow fair, the results of the exchanges raised hopes that a summit conference would prove profitable.

In September Khrushchev came to America. His cross-country tour had its full share of comic contretemps—when denied permission to visit Disneyland because authorities feared they could not protect him properly on the grounds, the heavy-handed Khrushchev accused the United States, only half humorously, of concealing rocket launching pads there. But the general effect of his visit seemed salutary. At the end of his stay, he and President Eisenhower agreed to convene a new four-power summit conference.

The meeting never took place. On May 1, 1960, high over Sverdlovsk, an industrial center deep in the Soviet Union, an American U-2 reconnaissance plane was shot down by antiaircraft fire. The pilot of the plane, Francis Gary Powers, survived the crash, and he confessed to being a spy. His cameras contained aerial photographs of Soviet military installations. When Eisenhower assumed full responsibility for the mission, Khrushchev accused the United States of "piratical" and "cowardly" acts of agression. The summit conference collapsed.

Latin America Aroused

Events in Latin America compounded Eisenhower's difficulties. During World War II the United States, needing Latin American raw materials, had supplied its southern neighbors liberally with economic aid. In the period following victory an era of amity and prosperity seemed assured. A hemispheric mutual defense pact was signed at Rio de Janeiro in September 1947, and the following year the Organization of American States (OAS) came into being. The United States appeared to have committed itself to a policy of true cooperation with Latin America. In the OAS, decisions were reached by a two-thirds vote; the United States had neither a veto nor any special position.

The United States tended to neglect Latin America during the Cold War years. Economic problems plagued the region, and in most nations reactionary governments did little to improve the lot of their peoples. Radical Latin Americans accused the United States of supporting cliques of wealthy tyrants, while conservatives tended to use the United States as a scapegoat, blaming lack of sufficient American economic aid for the plight of the poor.

Eisenhower, eager to improve relations, sent his brother Dr. Milton Eisenhower on a South American tour, and when Dr. Eisenhower recommended stepped-up economic assistance, the president concurred. Resistance to communism nonetheless continued to receive first priority. In 1954 the government of Jacobo Arbenz Guzmán in Guatemala began to import Soviet weapons. The United States promptly dispatched arms to the neighboring state of Honduras. Within a month an army led by an exiled Guatemalan officer marched into the country from Honduras and overthrew Arbenz. Elsewhere in Latin America, Eisenhower, as Truman had before him, continued to support conservative regimes that were often kept in power by the bayonets of the local military. He did so because the alternative seemed to be communist revolution and social chaos.

The depth of Latin American resentment of the United States became clear in the spring of 1958, when Vice-President Nixon went to South America on an eight-nation goodwill tour. Everywhere he was met with hostility. In Lima, Peru, he was mobbed; in Caracas, Venezuela, students kicked his shiny Cadillac and pelted him with eggs and stones. He had to abandon the remainder of his trip. For the first time the American people gained some inkling of Latin American opinion and the social and economic troubles that lay behind this opinion.

That there was no easy solution to Latin American problems was made clear by the course of events in Cuba. In 1959 a revolutionary movement headed by Dr. Fidel Castro overthrew Fulgencio Batista, one of the most noxious of the Latin American dictators. Eisenhower recognized the Castro government at once, but the Cuban leader soon began to criticize the United States in highly colored speeches. He ordered American property in Cuba confiscated without providing adequate compensation. Castro suppressed civil liberties, entered into close relations with the Soviet Union, and drove many of his original supporters into exile. After he negotiated a trade agreement with the Soviet Union in February 1960, which enabled the Russians to obtain Cuban sugar at bargain rates, the United States retaliated by prohibiting the importation of Cuban sugar into America. Khrushchev then announced that if the United States intervened in Cuba, he would defend the country with atomic weapons. "The Monroe Doctrine has outlived its time," Khrushchev warned. With the Castro movement—called *Fidelismo*—making inroads in many Latin American countries, Eisenhower, shortly before the end of his second term, broke off diplomatic relations with Cuba.

The Politics of Civil Rights

During Eisenhower's presidency a major change occurred in the legal status of American blacks. Eisenhower had relatively little to do with the change himself; indeed, one might say that it occurred in spite of the president more than because of him. For the change was part of a broad shift in attitudes toward the rights of minorities in democracies, where as a matter of principle, majorities were supposed to rule.

After 1945 the question of racial equality took on special importance because of the ideological competition with communism. Evidence of color prejudice in the United States damaged the nation's image, particularly in Asia and Africa, where the United States and Russia were competing for influence, trade, and strategic bases. An awareness of foreign criticism of American racial attitudes, along with resentment that almost a century after the Emancipation Proclamation they were still second-class citizens, produced a growing militancy among American blacks. At the same time, fears of communist subversion in the United States led to the repression of the rights of many whites, culminating in the excesses of McCarthyism. Both these aspects of the civil rights question divided Americans along liberal and conservative lines and shook the political structure of the country.

As we have seen, the World War II record of the federal government on civil rights was mixed. Except for the treatment of the Japanese in California there was no hysterical pursuit of imaginary spies and subversives. Yet as early as 1940, in the Smith Act, Congress made it illegal to advocate or teach the overthrow of the government by force or to belong to an organization with this objective. A dead letter during the era of Soviet-American cooperation, the law was used in the Truman era to jail the leaders of the American Communist party. The Supreme Court upheld its constitutionality in *Dennis et al.* v. *United States* (1951), in effect modifying the "clear and present danger" test established in the Schenck case of 1919 (see page 707).

In 1950 Congress passed the McCarran Internal Security Act, which made it unlawful "to combine, conspire or agree with any other person to perform any act that would substantially contribute to the establishment . . . of a totalitarian dictatorship." The law required every "Communist-front organization" to register with the attorney general. Members of "front" organizations were barred from defense work and from travel abroad. Aliens who had even been members of any "totalitarian party" were denied admission to the United States, a foolish provision that prevented many anticommunists behind the Iron Curtain from fleeing to America; even a person who had belonged to a communist youth organization was kept out by its terms.

Although his own loyalty program was administered without sufficient regard for individual rights, Truman vetoed the McCarran Act, saying that it would "put the Government into the business of thought control." Congress overrode the veto by a voice vote. As for blacks, besides setting up the Committee on Civil Rights and pressing for the desegragation of the armed forces, Truman favored anti-poll-tax and antilynching legislation. These proposals were filibustered to death in the Senate, and Congress refused Truman's request for a permanent Fair Employment Practices Commission.

Under Eisenhower, while the McCarthy hysteria reached its peak and declined, the government compiled a spotty record on civil rights. The search for subversive federal employees continued. While only a handful were charged with disloyalty, nearly 7,000 were declared "security risks" and fired. The refusal to grant security clearance to J. Robert Oppenheimer, one of the fathers of the atomic bomb, on the ground that he had associated with communists and communist sympathizers, was the most glaring instance of the administration's catering to anticommunist extremists, for it was based on the supposition that Oppenheimer could be denied access to discoveries he had helped to make possible.

Eisenhower completed the formal integration of the armed forces and appointed a Civil Rights Commission, but he was temperamentally incapable of making a frontal assault on the racial problem. This was done by the Supreme Court, which interjected itself into the civil rights controversy in dramatic fashion in 1954.

Under pressure of litigation sponsored by the National Association for the Advancement of Colored People, the Court had been gradually undermining the "separate but equal" principle laid down in *Plessy* v. *Ferguson* (see page 497). First it ruled that in graduate education segregated facilities must be truly equal. In 1938 it ordered a black admitted to the University of Missouri law school because no law school for blacks existed in the state. This decision gradually forced some southern states to admit blacks to advanced programs. "You can't build a cyclotron for one student," the president of the University of Oklahoma confessed when the Court, in 1948, ordered Oklahoma to provide equal facilities. Two years later, when Texas actually attempted to fit out a separate law school for a single black applicant, the Court ruled that truly equal education could not be provided under such circumstances.

In 1953 President Eisenhower appointed California's Governor Earl Warren chief justice of the Supreme Court.* Convinced that the Court must take the offensive in the cause of civil rights, Warren succeeded in welding his associates into a unit on the question. In 1954 an NAACP-sponsored case, *Brown* v. *Board of Education of Topeka,* came up for decision. The NAACP lawyer, Thurgood Marshall, challenged the "separate but equal" doctrine even at the elementary school level. He submitted a mass of sociological evidence to show that the mere fact of segregation made equal education impossible and did serious psychological damage to both black children and white. Speaking for a unanimous Court, Warren reversed the Plessy decision. "In the field of public education, the doctrine of 'separate but equal' has no place," he declared. "Separate educational facilities are inherently unequal." The next year the Court ordered the states to proceed "with all deliberate speed" in integrating their schools.

* Eisenhower first offered the post to John Foster Dulles, but he declined on the ground that he was too old to start a new career.

Angry jeers from whites rain down on Elizabeth Eckford, one of the first black students to arrive for registration at Little Rock's Central High School in 1957. State troops turned black students away from the school until President Eisenhower overruled the state decision and called in the National Guard to enforce integration.

Despite these decisions, few districts in the 17 southern and border states seriously tried to integrate their schools. Two months after the ruling, White Citizens Councils dedicated to all-out opposition had sprung up throughout the South. When the school board of Clinton, Tennessee, integrated the local high school in September 1956, a mob roused by a northern fanatic rioted in protest, shouting "Kill the niggers!" and destroying the property of blacks. The school was kept open with the help of the National Guard until segregationists blew up the building with dynamite. In Virginia the governor announced a plan for "massive resistance" to integration that denied state aid to local school systems that wished to desegregate. When the University of Alabama admitted a single black woman in 1956, riots broke out. University officials forced the student to withdraw and then expelled her when she complained more forcefully than they deemed proper.

President Eisenhower thought equality for blacks could not be obtained by government edict. "I am convinced that the Supreme Court decision *set back* progress in the South *at least fifteen years,*" he remarked to one of his advisers. "The fellow who tries to tell me you can do these things by *force* is just plain *nuts.*" In 1957 events compelled him to act. That September the school board of Little Rock, Arkansas, opened Central High School to a handful of black students. However, the governor of the state, Orval M. Faubus, called out the National Guard to prevent them from attending. Unruly crowds taunted the students and their parents.

Eisenhower could not ignore the direct flouting of federal authority. After the mayor of Little Rock sent him a telegram saying, in part, "SITUATION IS OUT OF CONTROL AND POLICE CANNOT DISPERSE THE MOB," he dispatched 1,000 paratroopers to Little Rock and summoned 10,000 National Guardsmen to federal duty. The black students then began to attend class. A token force of soldiers was stationed at Central High for the entire school year to protect them.

Extremist resistance strengthened the determination of blacks and many northern whites to make the South comply with the desegregation decision. Besides pressing cases in the federal courts, leaders of the movement organized a voter registration drive among southern blacks. In the Civil Rights Act of September 1957 Congress authorized the attorney general to obtain injunctions to stop southern registrars and election officials from interfering with blacks seeking to register and vote. The law also established a Civil Rights Commission with broad investigatory powers and a Civil Rights Division in the Department of Justice. Enforcing this Civil Rights Act was another matter. A later study of a typical county in Alabama revealed that between 1957 and 1960 more than 700 blacks with high school diplomas were rejected as unqualified by white election officials when they sought to register.

The Election of 1960

As the end of his second term approached, Eisenhower somewhat reluctantly endorsed Vice-President Nixon as the Republican candidate to succeed him. Richard Nixon had skyrocketed to national prominence by exploiting the public fear of communist subversion. "Traitors in the high councils of our government," he charged in 1950, "have made sure that the deck is stacked on the Soviet side of the diplomatic tables." In 1947 he was an obscure young congressman from California; in 1950 he won a seat in the Senate; two years later Eisenhower chose him as his running mate.

Whether Nixon believed what he said at this period of his career is not easily discovered; with his "instinct for omnidirectional placation," he seemed wedded to the theory that politicians should slavishly represent their constituents' opinions rather than hold to their own views. Frequently he appeared to count noses before deciding what he thought. He projected an image of almost frantic earnestness, yet he pursued a flexible course more suggestive of calculation than sincerity.

Reporters generally had a low opinion of Nixon, and independent voters seldom found him attractive. He was always controversial, distrusted by liberals even when he supported liberal measures. But his defense of American values in his confrontation with Khrushchev at the Moscow Fair had won him much praise. In any case, no prominent Republican rose to oppose his nomination.

The Democrats nominated Senator John F. Kennedy of Massachusetts, with Lyndon B. Johnson, the Senate majority leader, as his running mate. Kennedy was the son of Joseph P. Kennedy, a wealthy businessman and promoter who had served as ambassador to Great Britain under Franklin Roosevelt. As a PT boat commander in World War II, John Kennedy was severely injured in action. In 1946 he was elected to Congress. Besides wealth, intelligence, good looks, and charm, Kennedy had the advantage of his war record and his Irish-Catholic ancestry, the latter a particularly valuable asset in heavily Catholic Massachusetts. After three terms in the House, he moved on to the Senate in 1952 by defeating Henry Cabot Lodge, Jr. (Lodge's grandfather, Wilson's inveterate foe, had beaten Kennedy's maternal grandfather and namesake for the Senate in 1916). After his landslide reelection in 1958, only Kennedy's religion seemed to limit his political future. No Catholic had ever been elected president, and the defeat of Alfred E. Smith in 1928 had convinced most students of politics (including Smith) that none ever would be elected. Nevertheless, influenced by Kennedy's victories in the Wisconsin and West Virginia primaries—the latter establishing him as an effective campaigner in a predominantly Protestant region—the Democratic convention nominated him.

Early in his congressional career Kennedy had been quite conservative. He was friendly with Richard Nixon and privately delighted when Nixon defeated a liberal Democrat for a Senate seat in 1950. At that time Kennedy admitted frankly that he liked Senator Joseph McCarthy and thought that "he may have something" in his campaign against supposed communists in government. However, he had gradually become more liberal as his career developed.

In the presidential campaign Kennedy stressed his youth and "vigor" (a favorite word). He promised an imaginative, forward-looking administration that would open a "New Frontier" for the country. Nixon ran on the Eisenhower record, which he promised to extend in liberal directions. A series of television debates between the candidates, observed by some 70 million viewers, helped Kennedy by enabling him to demonstrate his warmth, maturity, and mastery of the issues. Where Nixon appeared to lecture the unseen audience like an ill-at-ease schoolmaster, Kennedy seemed relaxed, thoughtful, and confident of his powers. Although both candidates laudably avoided it, the religious issue was important. His Catholicism helped Kennedy in eastern urban areas but injured him in many farm districts and throughout the West. Kennedy's victory, 303 to 219 in the electoral college, was paper-thin in the popular vote, 34,227,000 to 34,109,000.

SUPPLEMENTARY READING

Titles marked with an asterisk have been published in paperback.

For well-balanced treatments of wartime diplomacy, see Robert Dallek, **Franklin D. Roosevelt and American Foreign Policy*** (1979), and J. L. Gaddis, **The United States and the Origins of the Cold War*** (1972). Other important books on the subject include W. H. McNeill, **America, Britain and Russia: Their Cooperation and Conflict** (1953), Gar Alperovitz, **Atomic Diplomacy*** (1965), Gaddis Smith, **American Diplomacy During the Second World War*** (1965), Herbert Feis, **Churchill, Roosevelt, Stalin*** (1957) and **Between War and Peace: The Potsdam Conference*** (1960), R. E. Sherwood, **Roosevelt and Hopkins*** (1948), and Winston Churchill, **The Second World War*** (1948–1953).

A good summary of the Cold War is T. G. Paterson, **On Every Front: The Making of the Cold War*** (1979), which makes an effort to explain Soviet motives and tactics objectively. See also L. J. Halle, **The Cold War as History*** (1967), and, more critical of American policy, Walter La Feber, **America, Russia and the Cold War*** (1968), Daniel Yergin, **Shattered Peace** (1977), and Carl Solberg, **Riding High: America in the Cold War** (1973). Harry S Truman's **Memoirs*** (1955–1956) contain much useful information.

Postwar domestic politics is treated in A. L. Hamby, **The Imperial Years** (1976), E. F. Goldman, **The Crucial Decade—And After*** (1961), and G. E. Mowry, **The Urban Nation*** (1965). Interpretive works useful for understanding the period include Samuel Lubell, **The Future of American Politics*** (1952) and **Revolt of the Moderates** (1956), A. M. Schlesinger, Jr., **The Vital Center*** (1949), R. E. Neustadt, **Presidential Power*** (1960), J. M. Burns, **The Deadlock of Democracy*** (1963), Daniel Bell, **The End of Ideology*** (1959), C. Wright Mills, **The Power Elite*** (1962), and R. H. Rovere, **The American Establishment*** (1962).

Biographical material on postwar political leaders is voluminous. On Truman, see D. R. McCoy, **The Presidency of Harry S Truman** (1984), Truman's **Memoirs,** R. J. Donovan, **Conflict and Crisis** (1977), and A. L. Hamby, **Beyond the New Deal: Harry S Truman and American Liberalism*** (1973). S. E. Ambrose's two-volume biography, **Eisenhower** (1983, 1984), is the fullest scholarly treatment of Dwight Eisenhower.

Among many analyses and evaluations of American foreign policy, the following are important: W. W. Rostow, **The United States in the World Arena*** (1960), Norman Graebner, **New Isolationism** (1956), and H. A. Kissinger, **Nuclear Weapons and Foreign Policy***

(1957). G. F. Kennan's writings on the subject are both primary sources and important secondary interpretations. See his **Memoirs*** (1969, 1972), **Realities of American Foreign Policy*** (1954), and **Russia and the West under Lenin and Stalin*** (1961).

On Truman's foreign policy, see Donovan's **Conflict and Crisis** and on the Truman Doctrine, J. M. Jones, **The Fifteen Weeks*** (1955); on the Marshall Plan, H. B. Price, **The Marshall Plan and its Meaning** (1955). R. E. Osgood, **NATO: The Entangling Alliance** (1962), is excellent. See also W. P. Davison, **The Berlin Blockade** (1958).

American relations with China are covered in Herbert Feis, **The China Tangle*** (1953), Tang Tsou, **America's Failure in China*** (1963), and A. D. Barnett, **Communist China and Asia: Challenge to American Policy*** (1960); for Japan, see E. O. Reischauer, **The United States and Japan*** (1957). On the Korean War, consult David Rees, **Korea: The Limited War** (1964), and J. W. Spanier, **The Truman-MacArthur Controversy and the Korean War*** (1959).

McCarthyism and the Hiss case are covered in Earl Latham, **The Communist Conspiracy in Washington** (1966), Alistair Cooke, **A Generation on Trial: *USA* v. *Alger Hiss**** (1950), Whittaker Chambers, **Witness*** (1952), Robert Griffith, **The Politics of Fear*** (1970), and R. H. Rovere, **Senator Joe McCarthy*** (1959).

Economic trends are considered in A. A. Berle, **The 20th Century Capitalist Revolution*** (1954) and **Power Without Property*** (1959), Herbert Stein, **The Fiscal Revolution in America*** (1969), J. K. Galbraith, **American Capitalism*** (1952) and **The Affluent Society*** (1958), H. G. Vatter, **The U. S. Economy in the 1950s** (1963), and Walter Adams and H. M. Gray, **Monopoly in America** (1955). On the 1946 Employment Act, see S. K. Bailey, **Congress Makes a Law** (1950).

On labor, consult Philip Taft, **Organized Labor in American History** (1964), Joel Seidman, **American Labor from Defense to Reconversion** (1953), E. L. Dayton, **Walter Reuther** (1958), Melvin Dubofsky and Warren Van Tine, **John L. Lewis** (1977), W. M. Leiserson, **American Trade Union Democracy** (1959), and P. A. Brinker, **The Taft-Hartley Act After Ten Years** (1958). On agriculture, see A. J. Matusow, **Farm Policies & Politics in the Truman Years*** (1970), M. R. Benedict and O. C. Stine, **The Agricultural Commodity Programs** (1956), and Lauren Soth, **Farm Trouble in an Age of Plenty** (1957).

Eisenhower's own view of his terms can be found in D. D. Eisenhower, **Mandate for Change*** (1963) and **Waging Peace** (1965). Herbert Parmet, **Eisenhower and the American Crusades** (1972), is a balanced account of his two administrations. See also C. C. Alexander, **Holding the Line: The Eisenhower Era** (1975), and J. L. Sundquist, **Politics and Policy** (1968). Of the biographies, R. J. Donovan, **Eisenhower: The Inside Story** (1956), and M. J. Pusey, **Eisenhower: The President** (1956), are favorable, while Marquis Childs, **Eisenhower: Captive Hero** (1958), is critical. See also Dean Albertson (ed.), **Eisenhower as President*** (1963). Sherman Adams, **Firsthand Report*** (1961), is a pro-Eisenhower memoir, E. J. Hughes, **The Ordeal of Power*** (1963), an anti-Eisenhower one.

John Foster Dulles's views are discussed in M. A. Guhin, **John Foster Dulles** (1972), and in Dulles's own **War or Peace** (1950). For developments in the Far East, see R. H. Fifield, **The Diplomacy of Southeast Asia** (1958); for the Middle East, see J. C. Campbell, **Defense of the Middle East*** (1960), and Herman Finer, **Dulles over Suez** (1964), which is extremely critical of the secretary. The diplomacy of the Eisenhower era is also discussed in R. A. Divine, **Eisenhower and the Cold War*** (1981), and J. E. Smith, **The Defense of Berlin** (1963) and **The United States and Cuba*** (1960).

For postwar constitutional issues, see P. L. Murphy, **The Constitution in Crisis Times*** (1972), and on racial issues in particular, B. M. Ziegler, **Desegregation and the Supreme Court*** (1958), W. C. Berman, **Politics of Civil Rights in the Truman Administration** (1970), and Anthony Lewis et al., **Portrait of a Decade*** (1964). Richard Kluger, **Simple Justice*** (1976), is an excellent account of the Brown case.

29
Affluence and Its Discontents

There's a time when the operation of the machine becomes so odious, makes you so sick at heart, that you can't take part. . . . You've got to indicate to the people that run it, the people who own it, that unless you're free, the machine will be prevented from working at all. MARIO SAVIO, *student, University of California, 1964*

John F. Kennedy made a striking and popular president. He projected an image of originality and imaginativeness combined with moderation and good sense. He appointed two Republicans to his Cabinet. He further flouted convention by making his younger brother Robert F. Kennedy attorney general. (When critics objected to this appointment, the president responded with a quip, saying that he had "always thought it was a good thing for a young attorney to get some government experience before going out into private practice.")

Kennedy had a genuinely inquiring mind. Unlike Eisenhower, he waded eagerly through long technical reports. He kept up with dozens of magazines and newspapers and consumed books of all sorts voraciously. He invited leading scientists, artists, writers, and musicians to the White House. On one occasion when he had invited a number of Nobel Prize winners to the White House, he called the group "the most extraordinary collection of talent . . . that has ever been gathered together at the White House with the possible exception of when Thomas Jefferson dined alone." This was a typical piece of political bunkum, but just as Jefferson had sought to teach Americans to value the individual regardless of status, Kennedy seemed intent on teaching the country to respect its most talented minds.

Kennedy seemed bent on being a strong president; he was determined to change the direction in which the nation was moving. He hoped to revitalize the economy and extend the influence of the United States abroad. His inaugural address was a call for commitment: "Ask not what your country can do for you," he said. "Ask what you can do for your country." In 1962 he brought the weight of his entire administration, even that of the FBI, to bear on the steel corporations when they attempted to raise prices after having made what he considered a tacit promise not to do so in return for government help in persuading the steelworkers to forgo substantial wage increases. Faced with such a potent display of presidential disapproval, including the threat of an antitrust suit, the steelmen backed down. Kennedy lavished much energy on Congress, showering the legislators with special messages and keeping himself closely informed about their doings, even to the extent of assigning to one of his aides the unenviable task of wading through the *Congressional Record* every day.

Kennedy's New Frontier

But the president was not opposed to big business. Neither was he a Wilson or Franklin Roosevelt when it came to bending Congress to his will. Perhaps he was too reasonable, too amiable, too diffident and conciliatory in his approach. A coalition of Republicans and conservative southern Democrats resisted his plans for federal aid to education, for urban renewal, for a higher minimum wage, for medical care for the aged.

The president reacted mildly, almost ruefully, when his opponents in Congress blocked proposals that in his view were reasonable and moderate. He seemed to doubt at times that the cumbersome machinery of the federal government could be made to work. Even to some of his warmest supporters he sometimes appeared strangely paralyzed, unwilling either to exert strong pressure on Congress or to appeal to public opinion. Pundits talked of a "deadlock of democracy" in which party discipline had crumbled and positive legislative action had become next to impossible.

During the presidential campaign Kennedy had promised "to get the country moving again." The slow growth of the economy in the Eisenhower years had troubled liberal economists. American output was increasing year by year, but at a much slower rate than the economies of other industrial nations. Three recessions occurred between 1953 and 1961, each marked by increases in unemployment. During the declines of 1958 and 1961, almost 7 percent of the work force was unemployed. Moreover, in the latter years of Eisenhower's presidency the rate of inflation began to rise.

Despite Eisenhower's concern for balancing the budget, during the recessions his administration reacted in the orthodox Keynesian manner, cutting taxes, easing credit, and expanding public works programs. However, liberal economists argued that he was not employing the Keynesian medicine in large enough doses. Kennedy had fewer inhibitions about federal spending and was much influenced by the liberals' ideas. The lagging growth rate and the persistence of unemployment alarmed him. But because he was worried about the continuing inflation, he rejected proposals for cutting taxes in order to stimulate consumer spending. He was afraid that tax cuts would throw the federal budget further out of balance.

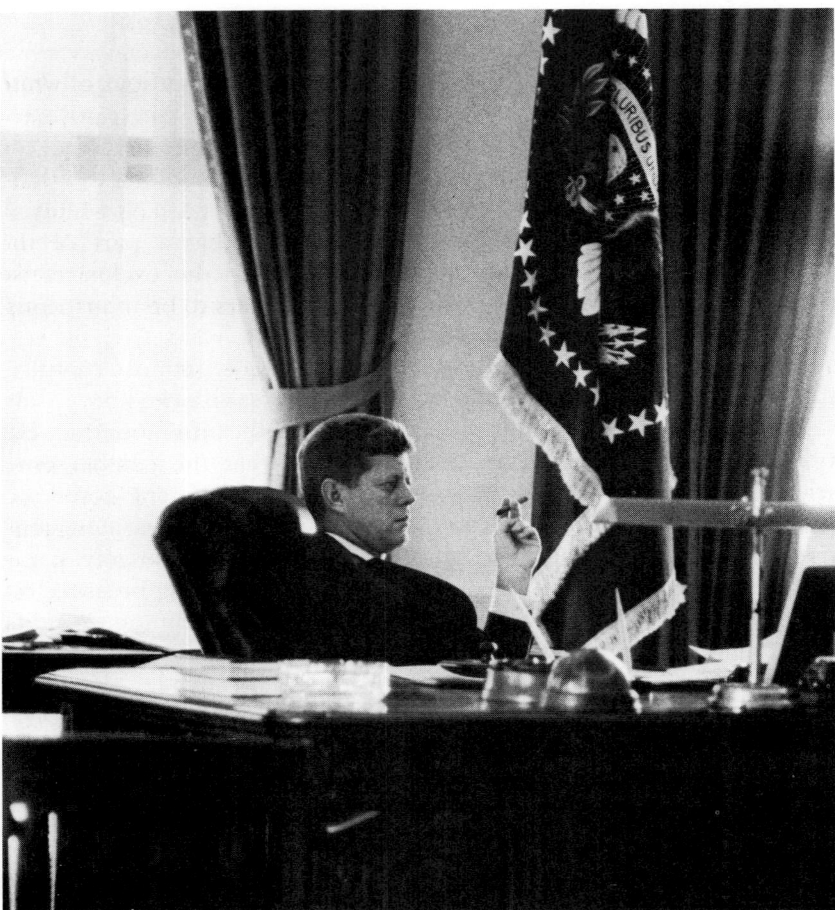

John F. Kennedy was among the most photogenic of modern chief executives. Cornell Capa snapped him in a thoughtful mood behind the presidential desk.

Economic growth remained sluggish. In January 1963 the economist Walter Heller persuaded Kennedy to try a different (but still Keynesian) approach. Any considerable increase in federal spending, Heller argued, would either require higher taxes that would drain money from the private sector of the economy and thus tend to be self-defeating or spark a new inflationary explosion. On the other hand, if personal and corporate income taxes were lowered, the public would have more money to spend on consumer goods and corporations could invest in new facilities for producing these goods. Federal expenditures need not be cut because the increase in economic activity would raise private and corporate incomes so much that tax revenues would rise even as the tax rate was falling.

Although the prospect of lower taxes was tempting, Kennedy's call for reductions of $13.5 billion ran into strong opposition. Republicans and conservative Democrats thought the reasoning behind the scheme too complex and theoretical to be practicable. It went nowhere.

"We Shall Overcome"

Kennedy's original approach to the race question was a cautious one. He did not integrate the National Guard, for example, because he was afraid that if he did, southern Guard units would withdraw. His lack of full commitment dismayed many who were concerned about the persistence of racial discrimination in the country. Seemingly without plan, a grass-roots drive for equal treatment sprang up among southern blacks.

It began in the tightly segregated city of Montgomery, Alabama. On the evening of December 1, 1955, Rosa Parks boarded a bus on her way home from work. She dutifully took a seat toward the rear as law and custom required. After white workers and shoppers had filled the forward section the driver ordered her to give up her place. She refused. She had suddenly made up her mind, she later recalled, "never to move again."

Rosa Parks was arrested. The blacks of Montgomery, led by a young Baptist clergyman, Martin Luther King, Jr., promptly organized a boycott of the buses. For a full year they refused to ride until finally, after a Supreme Court ruling in their favor, Montgomery desegregated its public transportation system.

This success encouraged blacks elsewhere in the South to band together against the caste system. It made King, who preached civil (nonviolent) disobedience as the best way to destroy segregation, a national figure. His organization, the Southern Christian Leadership Conference, moved to the forefront of the civil rights movement, and in 1964 his work won him the Nobel Peace Prize. Other organizations joined the struggle, notably the Congress of Racial Equality (CORE), which had been founded in 1942.

In February 1960 four black students in Greensboro, North Carolina, sat down at a lunch counter in a Woolworth five-and-ten and refused to leave when they were denied service. Their "sit-in" sparked a national movement; students in dozens of other southern towns and cities copied the Greensboro blacks' example. By the end of 1961 over 70,000 persons had participated in sit-ins. A new organization, the Student Nonviolent Coordinating Committee (SNCC), was founded by black college students to provide a focus for the sit-in movement and conduct voter registration drives in the South.

In May 1961 black and white foes of segregation organized a "freedom ride" to test the effectiveness of federal regulations prohibiting discrimination in interstate transportation. Boarding buses in Washington, they traveled across the South, heading for New Orleans. In Alabama they ran into bad trouble: at Anniston racists set fire to their bus, and in Birmingham they were assaulted by a mob. But violence did not stop the freedom riders. Other groups descended on the South, many deliberately seeking arrest in order to test local segregation ordinances in the courts. Repeatedly these actions resulted in the breaking down of racial barriers.

Integrationists like King attracted an enormous following, but some blacks, contemptuous of white prejudices, urged their fellows to reject "American" society and all it stood for. Black nationalism became a potent force. Elijah Muhammad, leader of the Black Muslim movement, disliked whites so intensely that he demanded that a part of the United States be set aside for the exclusive use of blacks. He urged his followers to be industrious, thrifty, and abstemious—and to view all whites with suspicion and hatred.

"This white government has ruled us and given us plenty hell, but the time has arrived that you taste a little of your own hell," Elijah Muhammad said. "There are many of my poor black ignorant brothers . . . preaching the ignorant and lying stuff that you should love your enemy. What fool can love his enemy?" Another important Black Muslim,

In Selma, Alabama, in 1965 Dr. Martin Luther King, Jr., knelt with his followers to offer a prayer. They had been arrested and were on their way to jail after committing an act of civil disobedience.

Calling for black separatism, Malcolm X told an interviewer in 1964, "The Negro [must] develop his character and his culture in accord with his own nature."

Malcolm X, put it this way in a 1960 speech: "For the white man to ask the black man if he hates him is just like the rapist asking the *raped,* or the wolf asking the *sheep,* 'Do you hate me?' " "If someone puts a hand on you," he advised blacks on another occasion, "send him to the cemetery."

Pushed by all these developments, President Kennedy gradually changed his policy. Under the direction of his brother Robert, the Justice Department acted to force the desegregation of interstate transportation facilities in the South, to compel southern election officials to obey the civil rights laws, and to override resistance to school integration. In 1962, when Mississippi authorities led by Governor Ross Barnett blocked the admission of a black to the University of Mississippi, the president called the Mississippi National Guard to federal duty and, despite bloody riots, made the university accept the student.

In 1963 Kennedy came out for a comprehensive new civil rights bill. It made racial discrimination in hotels, restaurants, and other places of public accommodation illegal, and it gave the attorney general the power to bring suits on behalf of individuals in order to speed up the lagging school desegregation movement. The measure also authorized agencies of the federal government to withhold federal funds from state-administered programs that failed to treat people of all races equally. This bill ran into stiff opposition in Congress.

Blacks organized a demonstration in Washington, attended by 200,000 people, to rally support for the measure. At this gathering, Martin Luther King, Jr., delivered his "I Have a Dream" address, looking forward to a time when racial prejudice no longer existed and people of all religions and colors could join hands and say, "Free at last! Free at last!" Kennedy sympathized with the purpose of the Washington gathering, but he feared it would make passage of the civil rights bill more difficult rather than easier. As in other areas, he was not a forceful advocate of his own proposals.

The Cuban Crises

His curious lack of determined leadership also marred Kennedy's management of foreign affairs, particularly during his first year in office. He hoped to reverse the Truman-Eisenhower policy of backing reactionary regimes merely because they were anticommunist. Recognizing that American economic aid could accomplish little in Latin America unless accompanied by internal reforms, he organized the Alliance for Progress, which committed the Latin Americans to land reform and economic development projects with the assistance of the United States. At the first sign of pro-Soviet activity in any Latin American country, however, he tended to overreact. Critics have described his behavior toward Latin America as a mixture of "overambitious idealism" and "pointless obsessiveness" about security.

His most serious blunder involved Cuba. Anti-Castro exiles were eager to organize an invasion of their homeland, reasoning that the Cuban masses would rise up against Castro as soon as "democratic" forces provided a standard they could rally to. Under Eisenhower the Central Intelligence Agency had begun training some 2,000 of these men in Central America. Kennedy, after much soul-searching, authorized the attack. The exiles were given American weapons, but no planes or warships were committed to the operation. The invaders struck on April 17, 1961, landing at the Bay of Pigs, on Cuba's southern coast.

The Cuban people failed to flock to their lines, and they were soon pinned down and forced to surrender. Since America's involvement could not be disguised, the affair exposed the country to all the criticism that a straightforward assault would have produced, without accomplishing the overthrow of Castro. Worse, it made Kennedy appear impulsive as well as unprincipled. Castro soon acknowledged that he was a Marxist and tightened his connections with the Soviet Union.

In June, Kennedy met with Premier Khrushchev in Vienna. During their discussions he evidently failed to convince the Russian that he would resist pressure with determination. In August Khrushchev abruptly closed the border between East and West Berlin and erected an ugly wall of concrete blocks and barbed wire across the city to check the exodus of dissident East Germans. When Kennedy did not order American forces in Berlin to tear down the wall, the Soviet leader found further reason to believe he could pursue aggressive tactics with impunity. Resuming the testing of nuclear weapons, he exploded a series of gigantic hydrogen bombs, one with a power three thousand times that of the bomb which had devastated Hiroshima.

When the Russians resumed nuclear testing, Kennedy followed suit. He expanded the American space program,* vowing that an American would land on the moon within ten years, and called on Congress for a large increase in military spending. At the same time, he pressed forward along more constructive lines. He visited Latin America in an effort to counteract the bad impression resulting from the Bay of Pigs incident. He established the Agency for International Development to administer American economic aid throughout the world and the Peace Corps, an organization that effectively mobilized American idealism and technical skills to help developing nations.

These actions had no observable effect on the Russians. In 1962 Khrushchev devised the boldest and most reckless challenge of the Cold War, one that brought the world to the verge of nuclear disaster. During the summer months he moved military equipment and thousands of Soviet technicians into Cuba. American intelligence reports revealed that, in addition to planes and conventional weapons, guided missiles were being imported and launching pads were being constructed on Cuban soil. Kennedy ordered U-2 reconnaissance planes to photograph these sites, and by mid-October he had proof that intermediate-range missile sites capable of delivering hydrogen warheads to points as widely dispersed as Quebec, Minneapolis, Denver, and Lima, Peru, were rapidly being completed.

The president faced a dreadful decision. To blast these sites before they became operational might result in a third world war. To delay would be to expose the United States to great danger and increase the Russians' ability to obtain their objectives elsewhere in the world by threat. At a meeting with Soviet Foreign Minister Andrei Gromyko, Kennedy, without revealing what he knew, asked for an explanation of Soviet activity in Cuba. Gromyko told him that only "defensive" (antiaircraft) missiles were being installed.

Gromyko's duplicity strengthened Kennedy's conviction that he must take strong action at once. On October 22 he went before the nation on television. The Soviet buildup was "a deliberately provocative and unjustified change in the status quo," he said. The navy would stop and search all vessels headed for Cuba and turn back any containing "offensive" weapons. Kennedy called on Khrushchev to dismantle the missile bases and remove from the island all weapons capable of striking the United States. Any Cuban-based nuclear attack would result, he warned, in "a full retaliatory response upon the Soviet Union."

For days, while the world held its breath, work on the missile bases continued. Then Khrushchev backed down. He withdrew the missiles and cut back his military establishment in Cuba to modest proportions. Kennedy then lifted the blockade.

Critics have argued that Kennedy overreacted to the Soviet missiles. There was no evidence that

* Russian superiority in space was gradually reduced. In April 1961 the "cosmonaut" Yuri Gagarin orbited the earth; in August another Russian circled the globe 17 times. The first American to orbit the earth, John Glenn, made his voyage in February 1962. In 1965 the United States kept a two-man Gemini craft in orbit two weeks, effecting a rendezvous between it and a second Gemini.

Wheeling his protégé Castro to safety, nursemaid Khrushchev snarls "Bully!" at President Kennedy. A comment in the Toronto Star *on the Bay of Pigs affair.*

the Russians were planning an attack; the missiles might be seen as a deterrent against a possible attack on the Soviet Union by United States missiles in Europe. By demanding their withdrawal Kennedy risked triggering a nuclear holocaust. Yet he probably had no choice once the existence of the sites was known to the public. (In some respects this is the most frightening aspect of the crisis.)

For better or worse, Kennedy's firmness in the missile crisis repaired the damage done his reputation by the Bay of Pigs affair. It also led to a lessening of Soviet-American tensions. At last, it seemed, the Russians were beginning to realize what all-out nuclear war would mean. Khrushchev agreed to the installation of a "hot line" telephone between the White House and the Kremlin so that in any future crisis leaders of the two nations could be in instant communication. In July 1963 all the powers except France and China signed a treaty banning the testing of nuclear weapons in the atmosphere. Peaceful coexistence seemed more and more inevitable. The Soviet Union, the United States, and all the major nations appeared to be realizing that no power could shape the earth in its own exclusive image, that the planet's teeming, diverse billions must live together in mutual tolerance if they would live at all.

LBJ and the Kennedy Agenda

Although his domestic policies were making little progress in Congress and the economy remained in rather poor shape, Kennedy retained his hold on public opinion. In the fall of 1963 most observers believed he would easily win a second term. Then, while visiting Dallas, Texas, on November 22, he was shot in the head by an assassin, Lee Harvey Oswald, and died almost instantly.

This senseless murder shocked the world and

precipitated an extraordinary series of events. Oswald had fired on the president with a rifle from an upper story of a warehouse. No one saw him pull the trigger. He was apprehended largely because, in his demented state, he killed a policeman later in the day in another part of the city. He denied his guilt, but a mass of evidence connected him with the crime. Before he could be brought to trial, he was himself murdered by one Jack Ruby, the owner of a Dallas nightclub, while being transferred, in the full view of television cameras, from one place of detention to another.

This amazing incident, together with the fact that Oswald had defected to Russia in 1959 and then returned to the United States, convinced many people that some nefarious conspiracy lay at the root of the tragedy. Oswald, the argument ran, was a pawn, his murder designed to keep him from exposing the masterminds who had engineered the assassination. An investigation by a special commission headed by Chief Justice Earl Warren came to the conclusion that Oswald acted alone, yet doubts persisted in many minds.

Kennedy's death made Lyndon B. Johnson president. A 55-year-old Texan, the first southerner to reach the White House since Woodrow Wilson, Johnson could draw on a bottomless supply of political experience, having served in Congress almost continuously since 1937. From 1949 until his election as vice-president he had been a senator and, for most of that time, Senate Democratic leader. As a lawmaker he preferred to move with contemporary currents rather than flail fruitlessly against them in search of perfection; as a legislative leader he employed "the Johnson Treatment" to influence his colleagues. He could be heavy-handed—and also devious, domineering, persistent, and at the same time obliging. Many people swore by him; few had the fortitude to swear at him. "The (Johnson) Treatment was an almost hypnotic experience and rendered the target stunned and helpless," the journalists Rowland Evans and Robert Novak explained.

Early in his career Johnson had voted against a bill making lynching a federal crime and had opposed bills outlawing state poll taxes and establishing a federal Fair Employment Practices Commission, but after he became important in national affairs he consistently championed racial equality. During the Eisenhower years he cooperated with the administration better than many Republicans; Ike's unaggressive social and economic policies seemed to suit him perfectly.

On taking office as president, Johnson benefited from the sympathy of the world and from the shame felt by many who had opposed Kennedy's proposals for political or selfish reasons. Sensing the public mood, he took advantage of it by pushing hard for Kennedy's economic and civil rights programs. Bills that had long been buried in committee now sailed through Congress. Early in 1964 Kennedy's tax cut was passed, and the resulting economic stimulus caused a boom of major dimensions. A few months later the Civil Rights Act of 1964 became law. This measure broke down the last barriers to black voting in the southern states and outlawed formal racial segregation of all sorts. Racial discrimination by employers and unions was de-

A shot of President Johnson using his hands to emphasize a point while speaking to reporters conveys the talkative, intense, persuasive nature of the man.

clared illegal, and an Equal Employment Opportunity Commission was created to enforce this provision.

Johnson could claim considerable credit for these accomplishments. He lobbied members of Congress relentlessly. He was on the telephone day and night, taking about a hundred calls a day. His energy, his earthy humor, and his almost poetic appeals for social and racial justice carried everything before him. Congressmen whom Kennedy had failed to budge succumbed to Johnson's combination of bullying and pleading and political back-scratching. One member of his Cabinet called him "a combination of Boccaccio and Machiavelli and John Keats."

The Great Society

Johnson's early successes and the sobering impact of his sudden accession to the presidency convinced him that he could be a reformer in the tradition of Franklin Roosevelt. He declared war on poverty and set out to create a "Great Society" in which poverty no longer existed. During the New Deal, Franklin Roosevelt was accused of exaggeration when he said that one-third of the nation was "ill-housed, ill-clad, ill-nourished." In fact Roosevelt had underestimated the extent of poverty when he made that statement in 1937. Wartime economic growth reduced the percentage of poor people in the country substantially, but in 1960 between 20 and 25 percent of all American families—about 40 million persons—were living below the poverty line, a government standard of minimum subsistence based on income and family size.

That so many millions could be poor in an "affluent" society was deplorable but not difficult to explain. In any community a certain number of persons cannot support themselves because of physical incapacity, low intelligence, or psychological difficulties. There were also in the United States entire regions, the best known being the Appalachian area, that had been bypassed by economic development and no longer provided their inhabitants with adequate economic opportunities.

More specific to the postwar situation was the fact that general prosperity and advancing technology had changed the definition of poverty. Things like radios and electric refrigerators, unknown to the most affluent Americans of the 1860s, were necessities a hundred years later. But as living standards rose, so did job requirements. A strong back and a willingness to work no longer guaranteed that the possessor could earn a decent living. Technology was changing the labor market. Educated workers with special skills and good verbal abilities could easily find well-paid jobs. Persons who had no special skills or were poorly educated could often find nothing.

Certain less obvious influences were at work too. Poverty tends to be more prevalent among the old and the young than among those in the prime of life; in the postwar decades these two groups were growing more rapidly than any other. Social security payments amounted to less than the elderly needed to maintain themselves decently, and some of the poorest workers, such as agricultural laborers, were not covered by the system at all. Unemployment was twice as high among youths in their late teens as in the nation as a whole and far higher among young blacks than young whites.

With the movement of the middle class to the suburbs, poverty became, in the words of Michael Harrington, whose book *The Other America* (1962) did much to call attention to the problem, "less visible" to those well-meaning citizens whose energies had to be mobilized if it was to be eradicated. Many poor people were becoming alienated from society. In earlier times most of the poor were recent immigrants, believers in the American dream of rags to riches, strivers who accepted their low status as temporary. The modern poor, many studies indicated, tended to lack motivation; they felt trapped by their condition and gave up.

Poverty exacted a heavy price, both from its victims and from society. Statistics reflected the relationship between low income and bad health. Only about 4 percent of people from middle-income families were chronically ill, whereas more than 16 percent of families with less than $2,000 were so afflicted. Mental illness varied inversely with income, as did alcoholism, drug addiction, and crime.

Johnson's war on poverty had two objectives: to give poor people the opportunity to improve themselves, and to provide them with direct assistance of various kinds. The first took the form of the Economic Opportunity Act of 1964. This law created a mélange of programs, among them a Job

Corps similar to the New Deal Civilian Conservation Corps, a community action program to finance local efforts; an educational program for small children; a work-study program for college students; and a system for training the unskilled unemployed and for lending money to small business in poor areas. The Economic Opportunity Act perfectly reflected Johnson's social philosophy. It combined the progressive concept of the welfare state with the conservative idea of individual responsibility. The government would support the weak and disadvantaged by giving them a fair chance to make it on their own.

Buttressed by this and other legislative triumphs, Johnson sought election as president in his own right in 1964. He achieved this ambition in unparalleled fashion. His championing of civil rights won him the almost unanimous support of blacks; his economy drive attracted the well-to-do and the business interests; his war on poverty held the allegiance of labor and other elements traditionally Democratic. His southern antecedents counterbalanced his liberalism on the race question in the eyes of many white southerners.

The Republicans played into his hands by nominating a conservative, Senator Barry M. Goldwater of Arizona. A large majority of the voters found Goldwater out of date on economic questions and dangerously aggressive on foreign affairs. During the campaign Democrats told a joke that went something like this:

(*Goldwater is president. An aide rushes into his office.*)

AIDE: Mr. President, the Russians have just launched an all-out nuclear attack on us. Their missiles will strike in 15 minutes. What shall we do?

GOLDWATER: Have all the wagons form a circle.

In November Johnson won a sweeping victory, collecting over 61 percent of the popular vote and carrying all the country except Goldwater's Arizona and five states in the Deep South. Quickly he pressed ahead with his Great Society program. In January 1965 he proposed a compulsory hospital insurance system for all persons over the age of 65, known as Medicare. As amended by Congress, the Medicare Act combined hospital insurance for retired people (funded by social security taxes) with a voluntary plan to cover doctors' bills (paid for in part by the government). The law also provided for grants to the states to help pay the medical expenses of poor people below the retirement age of 65. This part of the system was called Medicaid.

Next Congress passed the Elementary and Secondary Education Act. This measure supplied federal funds to school districts, the money to be devoted to improving the education of poor children. The theory was that children from city slums and impoverished rural areas tended to be "educationally deprived" and thus in need of extra help. The act was especially close to President Johnson's heart, he having taught school in a Mexican-American district after graduating from college. To focus attention on it (and for obvious political purposes), he went back to his Texas birthplace to sign it, delivering upon the occasion a homily on education as the stepping-stone to fame and fortune. Related to the Education Act was a program for poor preschool children, known as Head Start. This program was designed to prepare the children for elementary school. It also contributed incidentally to improving the health of the children by providing medical examinations and good meals.

Other laws passed at Johnson's urging in 1965 and 1966 dealt with support for scientific research, highway safety, crime control, slum clearance, clean air, and the preservation of historic sites. Of particular significance was the Immigration Act of 1965, which did away with the national-origin system of admitting newcomers. Instead, 290,000 persons a year were to be admitted, priorities being based on such grounds as skill and the need for political asylum. The law also placed a limit of 120,000 persons a year on immigration from countries in the Western Hemisphere. Previously, immigration from these countries had been unrestricted.

The Great Society program was one of the most remarkable outpourings of important legislation in American history. The results, however, were mixed. Head Start and a related program to help students in secondary schools prepare for college were unqualified successes. But the 1965 Education Act proved a disappointment. Too many local school districts found ways of using the federal money to cover their ordinary expenses, and the sums actually devoted to programs for the poor failed to improve most students' performances significantly. Medicare and Medicaid certainly provided good medical treatment for millions of people, but since the patients no longer paid most

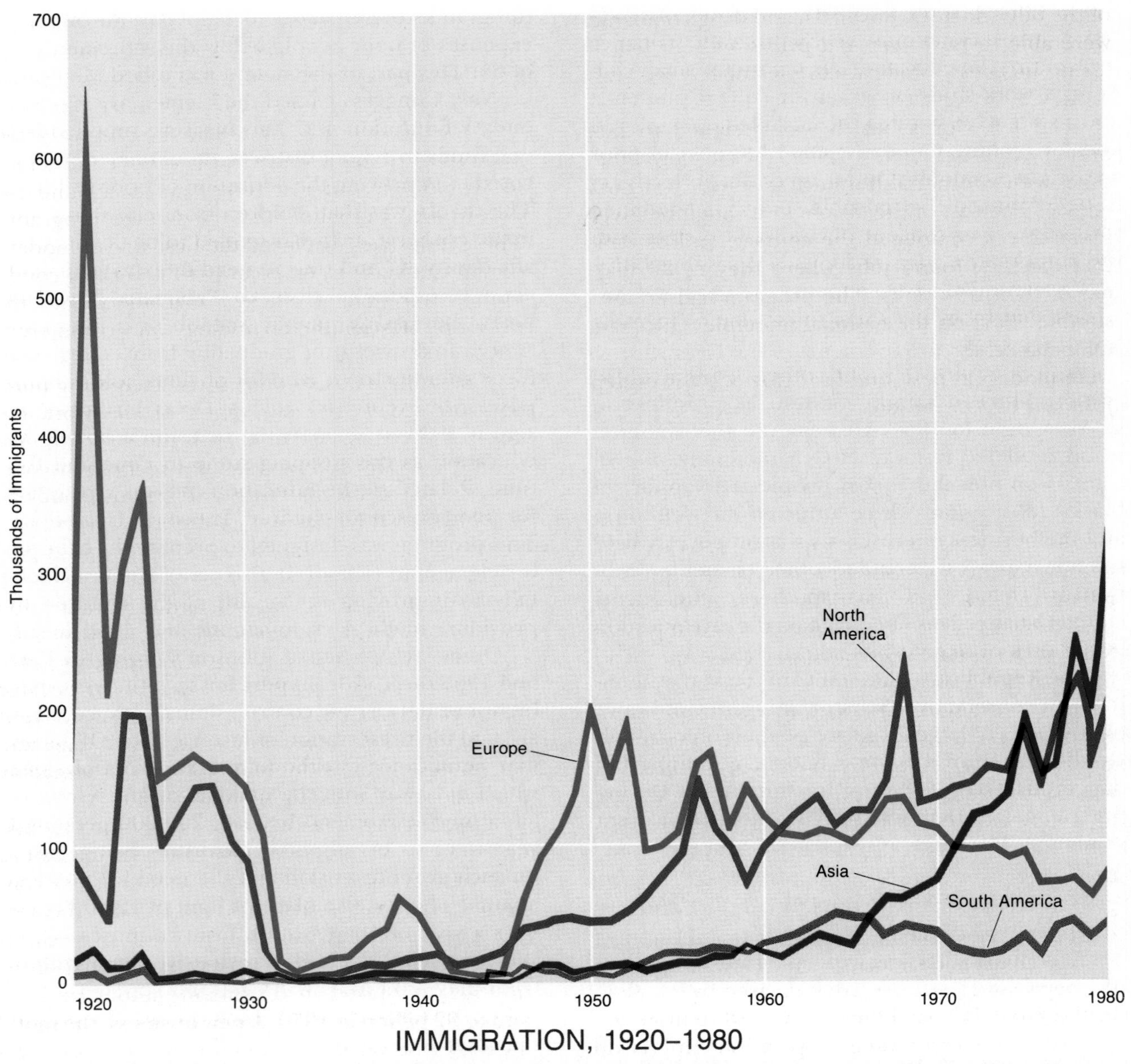

Immigration quotas imposed in the 1920s, together with the dampening effect of the depression years and World War II, meant that up to 1980 immigration had still not reached its pre–World War I levels, in spite of the post-1960 influx from Asia and North America. Canada, Mexico, Central America, and the West Indies are included in the North America category.

of the bills, doctors, hospitals, and drug companies were able to raise fees and prices without fear of losing business. Medical costs escalated far more rapidly than the rate of inflation.

The Job Corps, which was designed to help poor people get better-paying jobs by providing them with vocational training, was an almost total failure. The cost of the training was high; relatively few trainees completed the courses; and of those that did, few found jobs where they could make use of their new skills. The program had no measurable effect on the national unemployment rate. On balance, the achievements of the Great Society were modest at best, and far below what President Johnson had promised.

Society in Flux

Despite Johnson's extravagant style, his success in getting Kennedy's stalled proposals through Congress, and his landslide defeat of Goldwater, he may well have had some doubts about his Great Society program from the start. The tone of his inaugural address in January 1965 was uncharacteristically restrained. The nation was "prosperous, great, and mighty," he said, but "we have no promise from God that our greatness will endure." He was obviously thinking of the enormous changes that were occurring in the country. He spoke of "this fragile existence," and he warned the people that they lived "in a world where change and growth seem to tower beyond the control, and even the judgment of men."

The population was expanding rapidly. During the depressed thirties it had increased by 9 million; in the fifties it rose by more than 28 million, and the trend was continuing. Population experts observed startling shifts within this expanding mass. The westward movement had by no means ended with the closing of the frontier in the 1890s. One indication of this was the admission of Hawaii and Alaska to the Union in 1959. More significant was the growth of the "sun belt"—Florida and the states of the Southwest. California added more than 5 million to its numbers between 1950 and 1960, and in 1963 it passed New York to become the most populous state in the Union. Nevada and Arizona were expanding at an even more rapid rate.

The climate of the Southwest was particularly attractive to older people, especially after the perfection of mass-produced room air conditioners, and the population growth reflected the prosperity that enabled pensioners and other retired persons to settle there. At the same time the area attracted millions of young workers, for it became the center of the aircraft and electronics industries and the government's atomic energy and space programs. These industries displayed the best side of modern capitalism: high wages, comfortable working conditions, complex and efficient machinery, and the marriage of scientific technology and commercial utility.

The same industries employed increasing numbers of women because much of the work demanded dexterity rather than brute strength. Yet being gainfully employed did not seem to discourage women from marrying and having children: in 1940 about 15 percent of American women in their early 30s were unmarried, in 1965 only 5 percent.

Advances in transportation and communication added to geographical mobility. In the postwar decades the automobile appeared to enter its golden age. In the booming 1920s, when the car became an instrument of mass transportation, about 31 million autos were produced by American factories. During the 1950s, 58 million rolled off the assembly lines; during the 1960s, 77 million.

Gasoline use rose sharply. The more mobile population drove further in more reliable and more comfortable vehicles over smoother and less congested highways. And the new cars were heavier and more powerful than their predecessors. Gasoline consumption first touched 15 billion gallons in 1931; it soared to 35 billion gallons in 1950 and to 92 billion in 1970. A new business, the motel industry (the word, typically American, was a combination of *motor* and *hotel*), developed to service the millions of tourists and businessmen who burned all this fuel on their travels.

The development of the Interstate Highway System, begun under Eisenhower in 1956, was a major cause of increased mobility. The new roads did far more than facilitate long-distance travel; they accelerated the shift of population to the suburbs and the consequent decline of inner-city districts.

Despite the speeds that cars maintained on them, the new highways were much safer than the

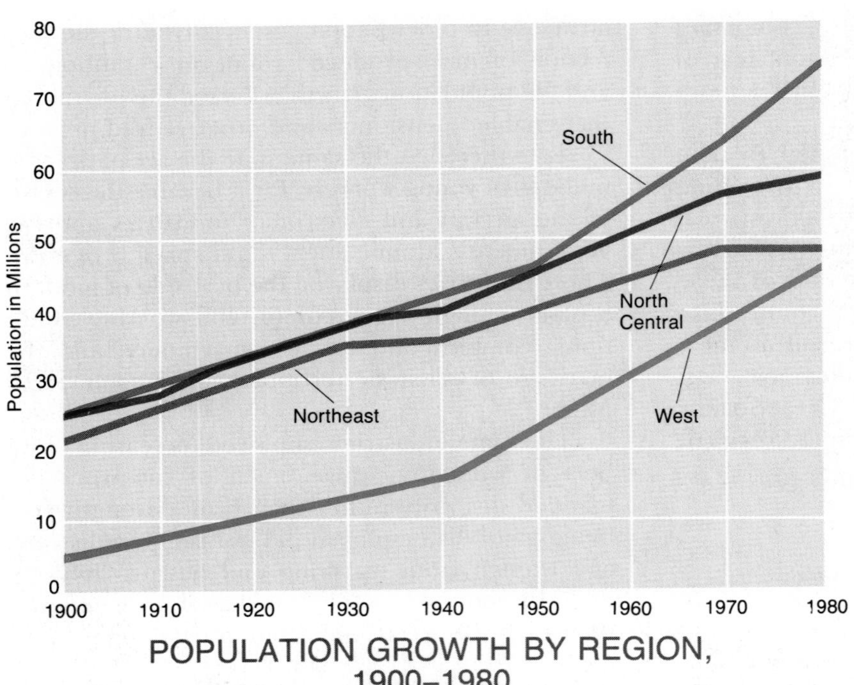

The total population of the United States in 1980 was 226.5 million. During the decade 1971–1980, the West was the fastest growing region, the Northeast the slowest. The South had been the largest region since the 1950s, but it also grew 20 percent during the 1970s owing to migration to the Sunbelt. The North Central region increased only 4 percent in this same period.

old roads. The traffic death rate per mile driven fell steadily, almost entirely because of the interstates. On the other hand, the environmental impact of the system was frequently severe. Elevated roads cut ugly swaths through cities, and the cars they carried released tons of noxious exhaust fumes into urban air. Hillsides were gashed, marshes filled in, forests felled—all in the name of speed and efficiency.

Although commercial air travel had existed in the thirties and had profited from wartime technical advances in military aircraft, it truly came of age when the first jetliner—the Boeing 707, built in Seattle, Washington—went into service in 1958. Almost immediately jets came to dominate long-distance travel, while railroad passenger service and transatlantic liners declined in importance.

Another important postwar change was the advent of television as a means of mass communication. Throughout the 1950s the public bought sets at a rate of 6 or 7 million annually; by 1961 there were 55 million in operation, receiving the transmissions of 530 stations. During the sixties the National Aeronautics and Space Agency (NASA) began launching satellites capable of transmitting television pictures to earth, and the American Telephone and Telegraph Company orbited private commercial satellites that could relay television programs from one continent to another.

Television combined the immediacy of radio with the visual impact of films, and it displayed most of the strengths and weaknesses of both in exaggerated form. It swiftly became indispensable to the political system, both for its coverage of public events and as a vehicle for political advertising. Its handling of the events following President Kennedy's assassination, of national conventions and inaugurations, and of other news developments made history come alive for tens of millions. It brought sports events before the viewer vividly, attracting enormous audiences and producing so much money in advertising revenue that the economics of professional sports was revolutionized. Team franchises were bought and sold for millions, and star players commanded salaries in the hundreds of thousands.

Some excellent drama was presented, especially on the National Educational Television network, along with many filmed documentaries. *Sesame Street,* a children's program presented on the edu-

A graphic example of one effect of modern highway construction: Interstate 80 slashes its way through an older neighborhood in Paterson, New Jersey.

cational network, won international recognition for its entertainment value and for its success in motivating underprivileged children. Commercial television indirectly improved the level of radio broadcasting by siphoning off much of the mass audience; more radio time was devoted to serious discussion programs and to classical music, especially after the introduction of frequency modulation (FM) transmissions.

The entertainment offered by most television stations was generally abominable; Newton Minow of the FCC called it a "vast wasteland." The lion's share of television time was devoted to uninspired and vulgar serials, routine variety shows, giveaway and quiz programs designed to reveal and revel in the ignorance of the average citizen, and reruns of old movies cut to fit rigid time periods and repeatedly interrupted at climactic points by "commercials." Most sets had poor accoustic qualities, which made them inferior instruments for listening to music. Serious discussion programs were too often relegated to inconvenient times, and there were not enough of them. Yet children found television fascinating, remaining transfixed before the screen when—their elders said—they should have been out of doors or curled up with a book.

Another defect of television's virtues was its capacity for influencing the opinions and feelings of viewers. The insistent and strident claims of advertisers punctuated every program with monotonous regularity. Politicians discovered that no other device or method approached television as a means of reaching large numbers of voters with an illusion of intimacy. Since television time was expensive, only candidates who possessed or had access to huge sums could afford to use the medium—a dangerous state of affairs in a democracy. In time Congress clamped a lid on campaign expenditures, but

Astronaut Edwin Aldrin on the moon, July 1969. Reflected in his helmet visor are flight commander Neil Armstrong, who took this picture, and part of their spacecraft. Television enabled some 600 million people to see the historic event.

this action did not necessarily reduce the amounts spent on television, with its capacity to reach so many people.*

"A Nation of Sheep"

Another postwar change was the marked broadening of the middle class. In 1947 only 5.7 million American families had what might be considered middle-class incomes—enough to provide something for leisure, entertainment, and cultural activities as well as for life's necessities. By the early 1960s more than 12 million families, about a third of the population, had such incomes. As they prospered, middle-class Americans became more culturally homogeneous and broader-gauged in their interests.

The percentage of immigrants in the population declined steadily; by the mid-sixties over 95 percent of all Americans were native-born. This trend contributed to social and cultural uniformity. So did the rising incomes of industrial workers and the changing character of their labor. By 1962 about 90 percent of all industrial workers enjoyed such "fringe benefits" as paid vacations and medical insurance at least partially financed by their employers, and nearly 70 percent participated in pension plans. The growth of pension funds made the union officials who managed them powers in the financial world. The merger in 1955 of the two great labor federations, the AFL and the CIO, added to the prestige of all union labor as well as to the power of the new organization.

As blue-collar workers invaded the middle class

* The government now provides substantial public funds to major candidates in presidential elections.

by the tens of thousands, they moved to suburbs previously reserved for junior executives, shopkeepers, and the like. They shed their work clothes for business suits. They took up golf. In sum, they adopted values and attitudes commensurate with their new status—which helps explain the growing conservatism of labor unions. During the Great Depression, when they were underdogs of sorts, the unions fought for social justice. In the 1960s many union workers seemed more interested in preserving their gains against the ravages of inflation and taxation then they were in social reform.

Sociologists and other commentators on contemporary affairs found in the expansion of the middle class another explanation of the tendency of the country to glorify the conformist. They attributed to this expansion the blurring of party lines in politics, the national obsession with "moderation" and "consensus," the complacency of so many Americans, their tendency, for example, to be at once more interested in churchgoing and less concerned with the philosophic aspects of religion than their forebears were. In *The Lonely Crowd* (1950), David Riesman drew a distinction between old-fashioned "inner-directed" people and new "other-directed" conformists who were group-centered, materialistic, and generally accommodating rather than tough and uncompromising. William Whyte's best-selling *Organization Man* (1956) and Sloan Wilson's novel *The Man in the Grey Flannel Suit* (1955) dealt with the same phenomenon. One prominent divine complained of "the drive toward a shallow and implicitly compulsory common creed," a "religion-in-general, superficial and syncretistic, destructive of the profounder elements of faith." Yet no one could deny that the new middle class had more creature comforts (automobiles, household appliances, even swimming pools).

More debatable was the impact of the expansion of the middle class on national standards of taste. For a time after World War II the nation seemed on the verge of a literary outburst comparable to that which followed World War I. A number of excellent novels based on the military experiences of young writers appeared, the most notable being Norman Mailer's *The Naked and the Dead* (1948) and James Jones's *From Here to Eternity* (1951). Unfortunately, a new renaissance did not develop. The most talented younger writers rejected materialist values but preferred to bewail their fate rather than rebel against it. Jack Kerouac, founder of the "beat" (for beatific) school, reveled in the chaotic description of violence, perversion, and madness. At the other extreme, J. D. Salinger, perhaps the most popular writer of the 1950s and the particular favorite of college students—*The Catcher in the Rye* (1951) sold nearly 2 million copies in hardcover and paperback editions—was an impeccable stylist, witty, contemptuous of all pretense; but he too wrote about people entirely wrapped up in themselves.

In *Catch-22* (1955), the book that replaced *The Catcher in the Rye* in the hearts of college students, Joseph Heller produced a war novel at once farcical and an indignant denunciation of the stupidity and waste of warfare. In *The Victim* (1947), *The Adventures of Augie March* (1953), *Herzog* (1964), and many other novels, Saul Bellow described characters possessed of their full share of eccentricities and weaknesses without losing sight of the positive side of modern life. Bellow won many literary awards, including a Nobel prize.

All these novelists and a number of others whose books were of lesser quality were widely read. Year after year sales of books increased, despite much talk about how televison and other diversions were undermining the public's interest in reading. Sales of paperbacks, first introduced in the United States in 1939 by Pocket Books, reached enormous proportions: by 1965 about 25,000 titles were in print and sales were approaching 1 million copies *a day*.

Cheapness and portability only partly accounted for the popularity of paperbacks. Readers could purchase them in drugstores, bus terminals, and supermarkets as well as in bookstores. Teachers, delighted to find out-of-print volumes easily available, assigned hundreds of them in their classes. And there was a psychological factor at work: the paperback became fashionable. People who rarely bought hardcover books purchased weighty volumes of literary criticism, translations of the works of obscure foreign novelists, specialized historical monographs, and difficult philosophical treatises now that they were available in paper covers.

The expansion of the book market, like so many other changes, was not an unalloyed benefit even for writers. It remained difficult for unknown authors to earn a decent living. Publishers tended to concentrate their interest and their money on authors already popular and on books aimed at a mass audience. Even among successful writers of unquestioned ability, the temptations involved in large advances and in book club contracts and movie rights diverted many from making the best use of their talents.

The Painter's Eye

American painters were affected by the same forces that influenced writers. In the past the greatest American artists had been shaped by European influences. This situation changed dramatically after World War II with the emergence of abstract expressionism, or action painting. This "New York school" was led by Jackson Pollock (1912–1956), who composed huge abstract designs by laying his canvas on the floor of his studio and squeezing paint on it directly from tube or pot in a wild tangle of color. The abstract expressionists were utterly subjective in their approach to art. "The source of my painting is the Unconscious," Pollock explained. "I am not much aware of what is taking place; it is only after that I see what I have done." Pollock tried to produce not the representation of a landscape but, as the critic Harold Rosenberg put it, "an inner landscape that is part of himself."

Untutored observers found the abstract expressionists crude, chaotic, devoid of interest. The swirling, dripping chaos of the followers of Pollock, the vaguely defined planes of color favored by Mark Rothko and his disciples, and the sharp spatial confrontations composed by the painters Franz Kline, Robert Motherwell, and Adolph Gottlieb required too much verbal explanation to communicate their meaning to the average observer. On the other hand, viewed in its social context, abstract expressionism reflected, like so much of modern literature, the estrangement of the artist from the world of the atomic bomb and the computer, a revolt against contemporary mass culture with its unthinking acceptance of novelty for its own sake.

The experimental spirit released by the abstract expressionists led to op art, which employed the physical impact of pure complementary colors to produce dynamic optical effects. Even within the

Jackson Pollock's "drip" paintings rejected all traditional techniques and representational subjects, resulting in a purely abstract expression. The title of this large 1950 canvas—it's about 17 by 9 feet—is Autumn Rhythm.

Along with Andy Warhol, Roy Lichtenstein is recognized as a master of pop art.

rigid limitations of severely formal designs composed of concentric circles, stripes, squares, and rectangles, such paintings appeared to be constantly in motion, almost alive.

"Op" was devoid of social connotations; another variant, pop art, playfully yet often with acid incisiveness satirized many aspects of American culture: its vapidity, its crudeness, its violence. The painters Jasper Johns, Roy Lichtenstein, and Andy Warhol created portraits of mundane objects such as flags, comic strips, soup cans, and packing cases. Op and pop art reflected the mechanized aspects of life; the painters made use of technology in their work—for example, they enhanced the shock of vibrating complementary colors by using fluorescent paints. Some artists imitated newspaper-photograph techniques by fashioning their images of sharply defined dots of color. Others borrowed from contemporary commercial art, employing spray guns, stencils, and masking tape to produce flat, "hard-edge" effects. The line between "op" and "pop" was frequently crossed, as in Robert Indiana's *Love,* which was reproduced and imitated on posters, Christmas cards, book jackets, buttons, rings, and a postage stamp.

Color and shape as ends in themselves, stark and often on a heroic scale, typified the new styles. Color-field painters covered vast planes with flat, sometimes subtly shaded hues. Frank Stella, one of the most universally admired of the younger artists, composed complicated bands and curves of color on enormous, eccentrically shaped canvases. To an unprecedented degree, the artist's hand—the combination of patience and skill that had characterized traditional art—was removed from painting.

The pace of change in artistic fashion was dizzying—far more rapid than changes in literature. Aware that their generation was leading European artists instead of following them gave both artists and art lovers a sense of participating in events of historic importance.

As with literature, the effects of such success were not all healthy. Successful artists became national personalities, a few of them enormously rich. For these, each new work was exposed to the glare of publicity, sometimes with unfortunate results. Too much attention, like too much money, could be distracting, even corrupting, especially for young artists who needed time and obscurity to develop their talents. "Schools" rose and fell in rapid order, it seemed, at the whim of one or another influential critic or dealer. Being different was more highly valued than aesthetic quality or technical skill. No matter how outlandish, "the newest thing" attracted respectful attention. The idea of the avant-garde as a revolt of creative minds against the philistinism of the middle class no longer had meaning, despite the fact that the existence of an expanding middle class made the commercial success of modern art possible.

Two Dilemmas

The many changes of the era help to explain why President Johnson expressed so much uncertainty in his inaugural address. Looking at American society more broadly, two dilemmas seem to have confronted people in the 1960s. One dilemma was that progress was often self-defeating. Reforms and innovations instituted with the best of motives often made things worse rather than better. Instances of this dilemma, large and small, are so numerous as to defy summary. DDT, a powerful chemical developed to kill insects that were spreading disease and destroying valuable food crops, proved to have lethal effects on birds and fish—and perhaps indirectly on human beings. Goods manufactured to make life fuller and happier (automobiles, detergents, electric power) produced waste products that disfigured the land and polluted air and water. Cities built in order to bring culture and comfort to millions became pestholes of crime, poverty, and depravity.

Change occurred so fast that experience (the recollection of how things had been) tended to become less useful and sometimes even counterproductive as a guide for dealing with current problems. Foreign policies designed to prevent wars, devised on the basis of knowledge of the causes of past wars, led, because the circumstances were different, to new wars. Parents who sought to transmit to their children the accumulated wisdom of their years found their advice rejected, often with good reason, because that "wisdom" had little application to the problems their children had to face.

The second dilemma was that modern industrial society placed an enormous premium on social cooperation, at the same time undermining the individual citizen's sense of being essential to the proper functioning of society. The economy was as complicated as a fine watch; a breakdown in any one sector had ramifications that spread swiftly to other sectors. Yet specialization had progressed so far that individual workers had little sense of the importance of their personal contributions and thus felt little responsibility for the smooth functioning of the whole. Effective democratic government required that all voters be knowledgeable and concerned, but few could feel that their individual voices had any effect on elections or public policies. The exhaust fumes of millions of automobiles poisoned the air, but it was difficult to expect the single motorist to inconvenience himself by leaving his car in the garage when his restraint would have no measurable effect on total pollution. "One person just can't feel that she's doing anything," a frustrated teenager wrote. "I can use soap instead of detergent . . . but what good do I feel I'm doing when there are people next door having a party with plastic spoons and paper plates?"

People tried to deal with this dilemma by joining groups; then the groups became so large that members felt as incapable of influencing them as they did of influencing the larger society. The groups were so numerous and had so many conflicting objectives that instead of making citizens more socially minded they often made them more self-centered. The organization—union, club, party, pressure group—was a potent force in society. Yet few organizations were really concerned with the common interest, though logic required that the common interest be regarded if individuals or groups were to achieve their special interests.

These dilemmas produced a paradox. The United States was the most powerful nation in the world, its people the best educated, the richest, and probably the most energetic. American society was technologically advanced and dynamic; American traditional values were idealistic, humane, democratic. Yet the nation seemed incapable of mobilizing its resources intelligently to confront the most obvious challenges, its citizens unable to achieve much personal happiness or identification with their fellows, the society helpless in trying to live up to its most universally accepted ideals.

In part the paradox was a product of the strengths of the society and the individuals who made it up. The populace as a whole was more sophisticated. People were more aware of their immediate interests, less willing to suspend judgment and follow leaders or to look on others as better qualified to decide what they should do. They belonged to the "me generation"; they knew that they lived *in* a society and that their lives were profoundly affected *by* that society, but they had trouble feeling that they were part *of* a society.

President Johnson recognized the problem. He hoped to solve it by establishing a "consensus" and building his Great Society. No real consensus emerged; American society remained fragmented, its members divided against themselves and often within themselves. Awareness of the complexities and contradictions of life and human institutions was a mark of increasing maturity but also a source of uncertainty and insecurity.

The Costs of Prosperity

The vexing character of modern conditions could be seen in every aspect of life. The economy, after decades of hectic expansion, accelerated still more rapidly. The gross national product approached a trillion dollars, but inflation was becoming increasingly serious. Workers were under constant pressure to demand raises—which only served to drive prices still higher. Socially the effect was devastating; it became impossible to expect workers to see inflation as a social problem and to restrain their personal demands. Putting their individual interests before those of the whole, they were prepared to disrupt the economy whatever the social cost. Even public employees traditionally committed to a no-strike policy because they worked for the entire community—teachers, garbage collectors, fire fighters, the police—succumbed to this selfish, if understandable, way of looking at life.

Economic expansion resulted in large measure from technological advances, and these too proved to be mixed blessings. As we have seen, World War II needs stimulated the development of plastics like nylon, of synthetic rubber, and of radar, television, and other electronic devices. After the war these products came into their own. Plastics invaded field after field—automobile parts, building materials, adhesives, packaging materials.

In 1951 scientists began to manufacture electricity from nuclear fuels; in 1954 the first atomic-powered ship, the submarine *Nautilus,* was launched. Although the peaceful use of atomic energy remained small compared to other sources of power, its implications were immense. Equally significant was the invention of the electronic computer, which revolutionized the collection and storage of records, solved mathematical problems beyond the scope of the most brilliant human minds, and speeded the work of bank tellers, librarians, billing clerks, statisticians—and income tax collectors.

Computers lay at the heart of industrial automation, for they could control the integration and adjustment of the most complex machines. In automobile factories they made it possible to produce entire engine blocks automatically. In steel mills molten metal could be poured into molds, cooled, rolled, and cut into slabs without the intervention of a human hand, the computers locating defects and adjusting the machinery to correct them far more accurately than the most skilled steelworker, and in a matter of seconds. Taken in conjunction with a new oxygen smelting process six or eight times faster than the open-hearth method, computer-controlled continuous casting promised to have an impact on steelmaking as great as that of the Bessemer process in the 1870s.

The material benefits of technology commonly had what the microbiologist René Dubos described as "disastrous secondary effects, many of which are probably unpredictable." The consumption of petroleum necessary to produce power soared and began to outstrip supplies, threatening shortages that would disrupt the entire economy. The burning of this fuel released unmeasurable tons of smoke and other polluting gases into the atmosphere, endangering the health of millions. "Life is enriched by one million automobiles," Dubos noted, "but can be made into a nightmare by one hundred million."

The vast outpouring of flimsy plastic products and the increased use of paper, metal foil, and other

As environmental issues became more prominent, shots like this view of raw sewage being dumped into the Niagara River appeared more often in the popular press. This photo was taken by Alfred Eisenstaedt for Life *in 1968.*

"disposable" packaging materials seemed about to bury the country beneath mountains of trash. The commercial use of nuclear energy also caused problems. Scientists insisted that the danger from radiation was insignificant, but the possibility of accidents could not be eliminated entirely, and the safe disposal of radioactive wastes became increasingly difficult.

Even an apparently ideal form of scientific advance, the use of commercial fertilizers to boost food output, had unfortunate side effects: phosphates washed from farmlands into streams sometimes upset the ecological balance and turned the streams into malodorous death traps for aquatic life. Above all, technology increased the capacity of the earth to support people. As population increased, production and consumption increased, exhausting supplies of raw materials and speeding the pollution of air and water resources. And where would the process end? Viewed from a world perspective, it was obvious that the population explosion must be checked or it would check itself by pestilence, war, starvation, or some combination of these scourges. Yet how to check it?

New Racial Turmoil

President Johnson and most of those who supported his policies expected that the 1964 Civil Rights Act, the Economic Opportunity Act, Medicare and Medicaid, and the other elements in the war on poverty would produce an era of racial peace and genuine social harmony—the Great Society that everyone wanted. The change that occurred in the thinking of the black radical Malcolm X seemed a straw in the wind. In 1964 Malcolm left the Muslims and founded his own Organization of Afro-American Unity. While continuing to stress black self-help and the militant defense of black rights, he now saw the fight for racial equality as part of a larger struggle for all human rights. "What we do . . . helps all people everywhere who are fighting against oppression," he said. Yet as in so many other aspects of modern life, progress itself created new difficulties. Early in 1965 Black Muslim fanatics, furious at his defection, assassinated Malcolm X while he was making a speech in favor of racial harmony.

The assassination was an act of vengeance, not

of social protest. More significant was the fact that official white recognition of past injustices was making blacks more insistent that all discrimination be ended. The very process of righting past wrongs gave them the strength to fight more vigorously. Black militancy, building steadily during the war and the postwar years, had long been ignored by the white majority; in the mid-sixties it burst forth so powerfully that the most smug and obtuse white citizens had to accept its existence.

The Student Nonviolent Coordinating Committee, which had been born out of the struggle for racial integration, had become by 1964 a radical organization openly scornful of integration and any form of interracial cooperation. Even Martin Luther King, Jr., the herald of nonviolent resistance, became more demanding. A few weeks after Malcolm's death, King led a march from Selma, Alabama, to Montgomery as part of a campaign to force Alabama authorities to allow blacks to register to vote. His marchers were brutally assaulted by state policemen who wielded clubs and tossed canisters of tear gas. Liberal opinion was shocked as never before. Thousands of people descended on Selma to demonstrate their support for the black cause.

The slogan of the radicals was "Black Power," an expression that was given national currency by Stokely Carmichael, chairman of SNCC. Carmichael, a West Indian by birth, had grown up in Harlem. In the early 1960s he had worked ceaselessly for black rights in the South, and as a result he had spent considerable time in southern jails. By 1964, although still willing to work with black moderates such as King, he was adamantly opposed to cooperating with white civil rights activists of any stripe. "The time for white involvement in the fight for equality has ended," Carmichael announced in 1966. "If we are to proceed toward true liberation, we must set ourselves off from white people." Since whites "cannot relate to the black experience," the movement "should be black-staffed, black-controlled, and black financed."

"Integration is a subterfuge for the maintenance of white supremacy," Carmichael said on another occasion. Blacks should have their own schools, their own businesses, their own political parties, their own (that is, African) culture.

Black Power caught on swiftly among militants. This troubled white liberals because people like Carmichael refused "to discriminate between degrees of inequity" among whites. Liberals feared that Black Power would antagonize white conservatives. They argued that since blacks made up only about 11 percent of the population, any attempt to obtain racial justice through the use of naked power was sure to fail.

Meanwhile, black anger erupted in a series of destructive urban riots. The most important occurred in Watts, a ghetto of Los Angeles, in August 1965. A trivial incident—police officers halted a motorist who seemed to be drunk and attempted to give him a sobriety test—brought thousands into the streets. The neighborhood almost literally exploded: for six days Watts was swept by fire, looting, and bloody fighting between local residents and 15,000 National Guardsmen, called up to assist the police. Order was restored only after 34 persons had been killed, more than 850 wounded, 3,100 arrested. Property damage in Watts came to nearly $200 million.

The following summer saw similar outbursts in New York, Chicago, and other cities. In 1967 further riots broke out. In Newark, New Jersey, 25 were killed in a July outburst that lasted four days. In Detroit a few days later, what may have been the worst race riot since the Civil War erupted. The death toll in Detroit came to 43 and looting and arson assumed monstrous proportions. Then, in April 1968, the revered Martin Luther King was murdered in Memphis, Tennessee, by a white man, James Earl Ray.* Blacks in more than a hundred cities swiftly unleashed their anger in paroxysms of burning and looting. White opinion was shocked and profoundly depressed. The death of King appeared to destroy the hope that his doctrine of pacific appeal to reason and right could solve the racial problem.

Public fear and puzzlement led to many investigations of the causes of the riots, the most important being that of the commission headed by Governor Otto Kerner of Illinois, which President Johnson appointed following the murder of King. The conclusions of most of the studies were complex but fairly clear. Race riots had a long history

* Ray fled to England but was apprehended, extradited, convicted, and sentenced to 99 years in prison.

in the United States, but the outbursts of the 1960s were different. Earlier troubles usually began with attacks by whites that led to black counterattacks. Riots of the Watts type were begun by blacks. Although much white-owned property was destroyed, the fighting was mostly between blacks and law enforcement officers trying to control them. White citizens tended to avoid the centers of trouble, and blacks seldom ranged outside their own neighborhoods.

The rioters were expressing frustration and despair; their resentment was directed more at the social system than at individuals. As the Kerner commission put it, the basic cause was an attitude of mind, the "white racism" that deprived blacks of access to good jobs, crowded them into slums, and, for the young in particular, eroded all hope of escape from such misery. Ghettos bred crime and depravity—as slums always have—and the complacent refusal of whites adequately to invest money and energy in helping ghetto residents, or even to acknowledge that the black poor deserved help, made the modern slum unbearable. While the ghettos expanded, middle-class whites tended more and more to "flee" to the suburbs or to call on the police "to maintain law and order," a euphemism for cracking down hard on deviant black behavior no matter how obvious the connection between that behavior and the slum environment.

The victims of racism employed violence not so much to force change as to obtain psychic release; it was a way of getting rid of what they could not stomach, a kind of vomiting. Thus the concentration of the riots in the ghettos themselves, the smashing, Samsonlike, of the source of degradation even when this meant self-destruction. When fires broke out in black districts, the fire fighters who tried to extinguish them were often showered with bottles and bricks and sometimes shot at, while above the roar of the flames and the hiss of steam rose the apocalyptic chant "*Burn, baby, burn!*"

The most frightening aspect of the riots was their tendency to polarize society on racial lines. Advocates of Black Power became more determined to separate themselves from white influence; they exasperated white supporters of school desegregation by demanding schools of their own. Extremists formed the Black Panther party and collected weapons to resist the police. "Shoot, don't loot," the radical H. Rap Brown advised all who would listen. The Panthers demanded public compensation for injustices done to blacks in the past, pointing out that following World War II, West Germany had made payments to Jews to make up for Hitler's persecutions. In 1968 they nominated Eldridge Cleaver, a convict on parole, for president. Although Cleaver was an articulate and intelligent man whose autobiographical *Soul on Ice,* written in prison, had attracted much praise, his nomination for the presidency widened the racial breach.

Middle-class city residents often resented what seemed the "favoritism" of the federal government and state and local administrations, which sought through "affirmative action" to provide blacks with new economic opportunities and social benefits. Efforts to desegregate ghetto schools by "busing" children out of their local neighborhoods was a particularly bitter cause of conflict.

These developments caused a powerful "white backlash." Persons already subjected to the pressures caused by inflation, specialization, and rapid change that were undermining social solidarity, and worried by the sharp rise in urban crime rates and welfare costs, found black radicalism infuriating. In the face of the greatest national effort in history to aid them, blacks (they said) were displaying not merely ingratitude but contempt.

The Unmeltable Ethnics

The struggles of blacks for equality went hand in hand with those of Mexican-Americans, principally in the Southwest. After World War I, thousands of Mexicans flocked into the region. They could do so legally because the restrictive immigration legislation of the 1920s did not apply to Western Hemisphere nations. When the Great Depression struck, Mexican-Americans were the first to suffer—about half a million were either deported or "persuaded" to return to Mexico during the 1930s. During World War II and again between 1948 and 1965 federal legislation encouraged the importation of braceros (temporary farm workers), and many other Mexicans entered the country illegally. The latter were known as *mojados,* or "wetbacks," because they often slipped across the border by swimming the Rio Grande. In general, Mexican-Americans were badly housed, underpaid, and subject to all sorts of discrimination.

César Chávez holds an informal meeting with a group involved in the grape pickers' union activities in Delano, California, in 1968. The women in the foreground wear kerchiefs printed with the union symbol.

Spanish-speaking residents of the Southwest were for a time largely apolitical; they tended to accept their fate with resignation, to mind their own business, not to "make trouble." But in the early 1960s a new spirit of resistance arose. Leaders of the new movement called themselves Chicanos. The Chicanos demanded better schools for their children and easier access to higher education. They urged their fellows to take pride in their traditions and culture, to demand their rights, to organize themselves politically. As with the blacks, the dominant middle-class majority adjusted itself to Chicano demands grudgingly and very slowly.

One Chicano nationalist group, Alianza ("the alliance"), led by Reies López Tijerina, tried to secede from New Mexico, an act that brought it into confrontation with the army and ended with Tijerina in prison. Another, the Crusade for Justice (headed by Rodolfo "Corky" Gonzales, a professional boxer, poet, and politician), focused on achieving social reforms and setting up political action groups. Its slogan, *Venceremos,* was Spanish for Martin Luther King's pledge: We shall overcome.

The Chicano leader with the widest influence was César Chávez, who concentrated on what superficially was a more limited goal—organizing migrant farm workers into unions. Chávez, who was born in 1927, grew up in migrant camps in California; he had no schooling beyond the seventh grade. After serving in the navy during World War II he went to work for the Community Service Organization, a group seeking to raise the political consciousness of the poor and to develop self-help programs for them. Chávez became general director of the CSO but resigned in 1962 because he felt it was not devoting enough attention to the plight of migrant workers. He then founded the National Farm Workers' Association, later known as the United Farm Workers' Organizing Committee.

In 1965 the grape pickers in his union in Delano, California, struck for higher wages and union recognition. Chávez, seeing in the strike an opportunity to attack the very structure of the migrant labor system, turned it into a countrywide crusade. Avoiding violence, he enlisted the support of church leaders; he organized sit-ins, a march on the state capital, and then a national consumer boycott of grapes. He demonstrated convincingly that migrant workers could be unionized and that the militant demands of minorities for equal treatment did not necessarily lead to separatism and class or racial antagonism.

Nevertheless, racial controversies continued. Militant Indians (they preferred to be called Native Americans) used the term "Red Power" as the blacks spoke of Black Power. The National Indian Youth Council and later the American Indian Movement (AIM) demanded the return of lands taken illegally from their ancestors. AIM leaders sought total separation from the United States; they envisaged setting up states within states such as the Cherokees had established in Georgia in Jacksonian days. In 1973 some of the radicals occupied the town of Wounded Knee, South Dakota (site of one of the most disgraceful massacres of Indians in the 19th century), and held it at gunpoint for weeks.

Militant ethnic pride characterized the behavior of many white Americans too. Italian-Americans, Polish-Americans, and descendants of other "new immigrant" groups eagerly studied their histories in order to preserve their cultures and where necessary revive dying traditions. The American "melting pot," some historians now argued, had not amalgamated the immigrant strains as completely as had been thought. Ethnic diversity became for some an end to be desired, despite the possibility that differences might as easily inspire conflict as harmonious adjustment.

For white "ethnics," the concern for origins was in part nostalgic and romantic. As the number of, say, Greek-Americans who had ever seen Greece declined, the appeal of Greek culture and the sense that some Greek-Americans had of belonging to a distinct cultural group increased. For blacks, whose particular origins were obscured by the catastrophe of slavery, awareness of their distinctiveness was more important. Racial pride was a reflection of the new black militancy and the achievements that blacks had made in the postwar period. There was a black on the Supreme Court (Thurgood Marshall, tactician of the fight for school desegregation). President Johnson had named the first black to a Cabinet post (Robert Weaver, secretary of housing and urban development). The first black since reconstruction (Edward W. Brooke of Massachusetts) was elected to the United States Senate in 1966. A number of large cities, including Atlanta, Georgia, elected black mayors.

The color line was broken in major league baseball in 1947, and soon all professional sports were open to black athletes. Where the reign of black heavyweight boxing champion Jack Johnson (1908–1915) had inspired an open search for a "white hope" to depose him, and where the next black champion, Joe Louis (1937–1949), was accepted by whites because he "knew his place" and was "well behaved," it was possible for champion Muhammad Ali to be a hero to both white and black boxing fans despite his often bizarre behavior, his militant advocacy of racial equality, and his adoption of the Muslim religion.

Their achievements and advances aside, black Americans had found real self-awareness. The attitude of mind that ran from the lonely Denmark Versey to Frederick Douglass and to W. E. B. Du Bois had become the black consensus.

Women's Liberation

Concern for improving the treatment of minorities encouraged American women—as it frequently had in earlier times—to speak out more forcefully for their own rights. During the immediate postwar period the women's movement had been relatively quiescent. However, pressures were mounting because social and economic conditions were changing. When the war ended, many women who had taken jobs because of the labor shortage did not meekly return to the home. Some worked to help pay for their veteran-husbands' war-interrupted educations, others to counterbalance the onslaughts of inflation, still others (some married, some not) simply because they enjoyed the money and the independence that jobs made possible. Between 1940 and 1960 the proportion of women workers doubled, and thereafter it increased still more rapidly. The rise was particularly swift among married women, and the difficulties faced by anyone trying to work while having to perform household duties both increased the resentment of these workers and encouraged their husbands to accept changes in male and female family responsibilities.

Married or single, more numerous or not, women workers faced job discrimination of many kinds. In nearly every occupation they were paid less than men who did the same work. Many interesting jobs that they were capable of holding were either closed to them entirely or doled out on the basis of some illogical and often unwritten quota system. In challenging occupations where they could find employment they were rarely given a chance to rise to positions of leadership. Many women objected to this state of affairs even in the 1950s; in the 1960s their protest erupted into an organized and vociferous demand for change.

One of the earliest leaders of the new women's movement was Betty Friedan, whose book *The Feminine Mystique* (1963) sold over a million copies. Friedan argued that advertisers, popular magazines, and other opinion-shaping forces were undermining the capacity of women to use their intelligence and their talents creatively. They were stifling women's potential by a pervasive and not very subtle form of brainwashing designed to convince women of the virtues of domesticity. "The only way for a woman . . . to know herself as a person is by creative work of her own," she wrote.

Betty Friedan, author of The Feminine Mystique, *spearheaded women's rights demonstrations like the National Women's Strike in August 1970. The strike called on women to boycott four consumer products whose advertising the protesters considered insulting to women.*

Friedan had assumed that if able women acted with determination, employers would recognize their abilities and stop discriminating against them. This did not happen. In 1966 she and other feminists founded the National Organization for Women (NOW). Copying the tactics of black activists, NOW called for equal employment opportunities and equal pay as civil rights. "An active, self-respecting partnership with men" was the objective.

Soon the women's movement became more militant. As black radicals had moved from racial integration to Black Power, so radical women shifted from talk of a partnership with men to war between the sexes. In 1967 NOW came out for an equal rights amendment to the Constitution, for changes in the divorce laws, and for the repeal of laws against abortion. Some radical feminists advocated raising children in communal centers and doing away with marriage as a legal institution. "The family unit is a decadent, energy-absorbing, destructive, wasteful institution," one prominent feminist declared.

Militants attacked all aspects of the standard image of the female sex. Avoiding the error of the Progressive Era reformers who had fought for the vote by stressing differences between the sexes (the supposed "purity" and high moral character of women), they insisted on total equality. Clichés such as "the fair sex" and "the weaker sex" made them see red. They insisted that the separation of "Help Wanted—Male" and "Help Wanted—Female" classified ads in newspapers violated the Civil Rights Act of 1964. They took courses in self-defense in order to be able to protect themselves from muggers, rapists, and casual mashers. They denounced the use of masculine words like *chairman* (favoring *chairperson*) and of such terms as *mankind* and *men* to designate people in general.* They substituted *Ms.* for both *Miss* and *Mrs.* on the ground that the language drew no such distinction between unmarried and married men.

Many women rejected the position even of moderate feminists like Betty Friedan, but few escaped being affected by the women's movement. The presence of women in new roles—as television commentators, airline pilots, police officers—did not prove that a large-scale shift in employment patterns had taken place. Yet even the most unregenerate male seemed to recognize that the balance of power and influence between the sexes had been altered. The Civil Rights Act of 1964 had outlawed job discrimination based on sex, and government agencies and the courts were steadily increasing the pressure on employers to conform to its terms.

Rethinking Public Education

Young people were in the forefront in both the fight for the rights of blacks and the women's liberation movement. In a time of uncertainty and discontent, full of conflict and dilemma, youth was affected more strongly than the older generations, and it reacted more forcefully. No institution escaped its criticisms, not even the vaunted educational system, which, youth discovered, poorly suited its needs. This was still another paradox of modern life, for American public education was probably the best (it was certainly the most comprehensive) in the world.

After World War I, under the impact of Freudian psychology, the emphasis in elementary education shifted from using the schools as instruments of social change, as John Dewey had recommended, to using them to promote the emotional development of the students. "Child-centered" educators played down academic achievement in favor of "adjustment." It probably stimulated the students' imaginations and may possibly have improved their psychological well-being, but observers soon noted that the system produced poor work habits and fuzzy thinking and fostered plain ignorance. Although "educationists" insisted that they were not abandoning traditional academic subjects, they surely deemphasized them. "We've built a sort of halo around reading, writing, and arithmetic," one school principal charged.

The demands of society for rigorous intellectual achievement made this distortion of progressive education increasingly less satisfactory. Following World War II, critics began a concerted assault on the system. The leader of the attack was James B. Conant, former president of Harvard. His book *The American High School Today* (1959) sold nearly half a million copies, and his later studies of teacher education and the special problems of urban schools also attracted wide attention. Conant flayed the schools for their failure to teach English grammar and composition effectively, for neglecting foreign languages, and for ignoring the needs of both the brightest and the slowest of their students. He insisted that teachers' colleges should place subject matter above educational methodology in their curricula.

The success of the Russians in launching their first *Sputnik* in 1957 increased the influence of critics like Conant. To match this achievement, the United States needed thousands of engineers and scientists, and the schools were not turning out enough graduates prepared to study science and engineering at the college level. Suddenly the schools were under enormous pressure, for with more and more young people desiring to go to college, the colleges were raising their admission standards. The "traditionalists" thus gained the initiative, academic subjects a revived prestige. The National Defense Education Act of 1958 supplied a powerful stimulus by allocating funds for upgrading work in the sciences, foreign languages, and other subjects and for expanding guidance services and experimenting with television and other new teaching devices.

Concern for improving the training of the children of disadvantaged minority groups (Mexican-Americans, Puerto Ricans, Indians, blacks) pulled the system in a different direction. Many of these children lived in horrible slums, often in broken homes. They lacked the incentives and training that middle-class children received in the family. Many did poorly in school, in part because they were

* The difficulty here was that this form of discrimination was built into the structure of the language. Even the word *woman* derives from the Anglo-Saxon *wif-mann,* "wife of a man." Efforts to avoid the use of masculine words in general references led to such awkward expressions as *his/her* and *(s)he.*

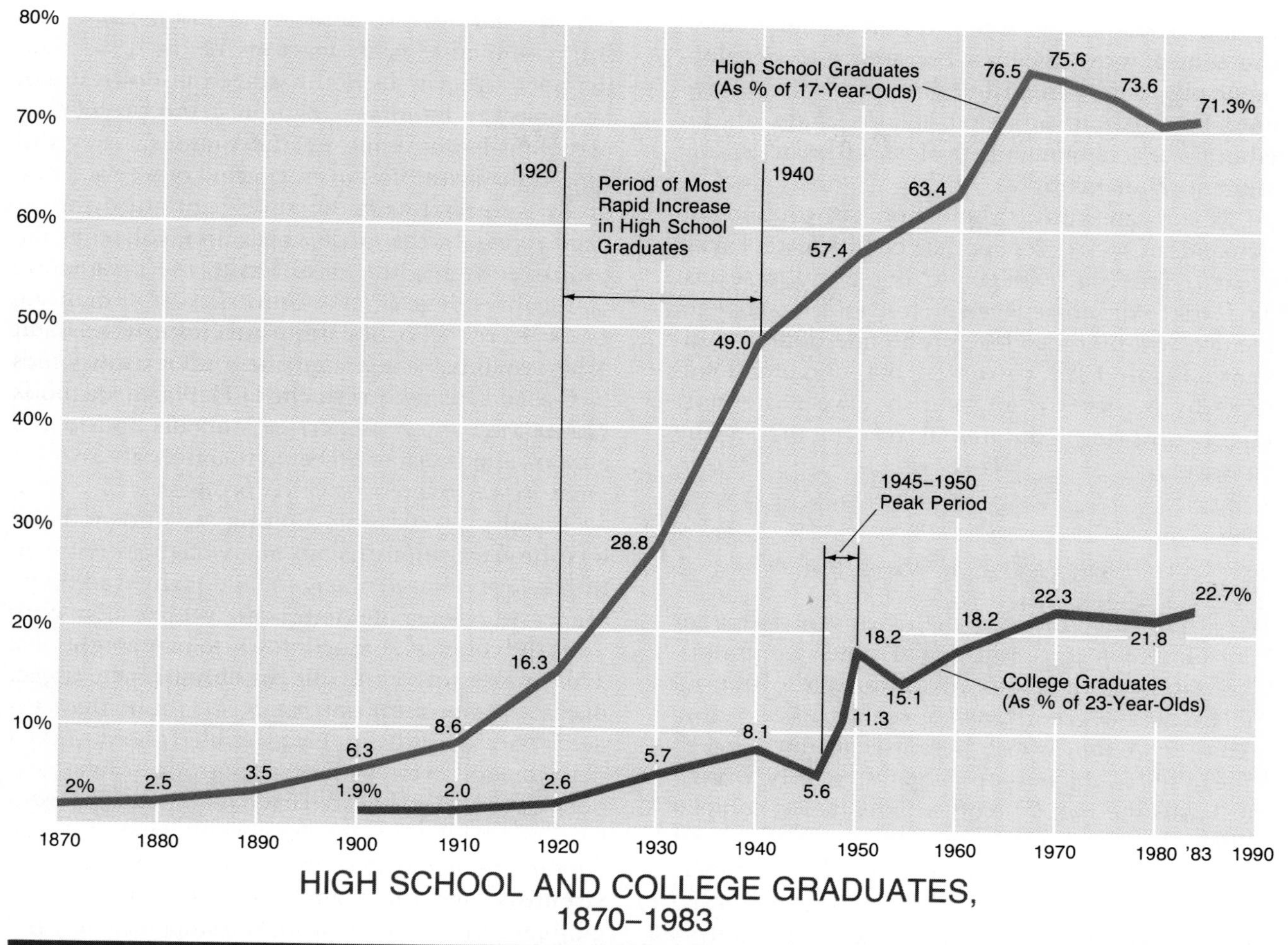

Lyndon Johnson's Elementary and Secondary Education Act, passed in 1965, was a landmark in the century-long expansion of high school education and directly influenced college education in the United States. The most rapid increase in high school graduates occurred between 1920 and 1940, but the number of graduates as a percentage of all people age 17 was greatest in 1967. The peak period for college graduates, 1945 to 1950, reflects the GI Bill after World War II.

poorly motivated, in part because the system was poorly adapted to their needs. But catering to the needs of such children threatened to undermine the standards being set for other children. In the cities, where blacks and other minorities were becoming steadily more numerous, many schools failed to serve adequately either the disadvantaged or those fairly well off. Added to the strains imposed by racial conflicts, the effect was to create the most serious crisis American public education had ever faced.

The post-*Sputnik* stress on academic achievement profoundly affected higher education too. "Prestige" institutions such as Harvard, Yale, Columbia, Stanford, Swarthmore, and a dozen other colleges, able to pick and choose among floods of applicants, became training centers for the intellectual elite. The federal and state governments, together with private philanthropic institutions such as the Carnegie Corporation and the Ford Foundation, poured millions of dollars into dormitory and classroom construction, teacher education, and scholarship funds. At the graduate level the federal government's research and development program, administered by the National Science Foundation, provided billions of dollars for laboratories, equipment, professors' salaries, and student scholarships.

At the same time, population growth and the demands of society for specialized intellectual skills caused American colleges to burst at the seams. To bridge the gap between high school and college, the two-year junior college proliferated. Almost unknown before 1920, there were 600-odd junior colleges by the late sixties, and they were the most rapidly growing educational institutions in the country.

Students in Revolt

For a time after the war, the expansion of higher education took place with remarkable smoothness. Thousands of veterans took advantage of the GI Bill to earn degrees, and thousands more young men and women whose parents had not gone to college seized the new opportunity eagerly. During the 1950s the mood among students was complacency.

In the 1960s the mood changed. The members of this college generation had grown up during the postwar prosperity and had been trained by teachers who were, by and large, New Deal liberals. Modern industrial society with its "soulless" corporations, its bloodless computers, and its equally unfeeling human bureaucracies made them feel insignificant and powerless, despite the material and social advantages it brought them. The "advantages" also made them feel guilty when they thought about the millions of Americans who did not have them. The existence of poverty in a country as rich as the United States seemed intolerable, race prejudice both stupid and evil. The response of their elders to McCarthyism appeared contemptible—craven cowardice of the worst sort—and dangerous. In the age of the atom, rabid anticommunism might end in nuclear war.

If these students had little tolerance for injustice, they seemed to have none at all for personal frustration. Their dissatisfaction often found expression in public protests, riots, and other troubles. The first great outburst convulsed the University of California at Berkeley in the fall of 1964. Angry students, many veterans of the 1964 fight for black rights in the South, staged sit-down strikes in university buildings to protest the prohibition of political canvassing on the campus. They disrupted the institution over a period of weeks. Hundreds were arrested; the state legislature threatened reprisals; the faculty became involved in the controversy; and the crisis led to the resignation of the president of the University of California, Clark Kerr. The situation was exacerbated by American involvement in the war in Vietnam, which increased steadily during the late 1960s (see pages 899–902). Large numbers of students considered all wars immoral and objected to university involvement in war-related research projects.

Equally significant in altering the student mood was the frustration that so many of them felt with the colleges. Rapid change made many traditional aspects of college life outmoded, yet like all institutions the colleges adapted slowly to new conditions. The "now" generation lost patience with the glacial pace of campus adjustment. Regulations that students had formerly merely grumbled about evoked determined, even violent opposition. Dissidents denounced rules that restricted their personal lives, such as prohibitions on the use of alcohol and the banning of members of the opposite sex from dormitories. They complained that required courses inhibited their intellectual development. They demanded a share in the government of their institutions, long the private preserve of administrators and professors.

Beyond their specific dissatisfactions, radical students developed an almost total refusal to endure anything they considered wrong. The knotty social problems that made their elders gravitate toward moderation led these students to become intransigent absolutists. The line between right and wrong became for radicals as sharply defined as the edge of a ruler. Racial prejudice was evil: it must be eradicated. War in a nuclear age was insane: armies must be disbanded. Poverty amid plenty was an abomination: end poverty *now.* To the counsel that evil can be eliminated only gradually, that misguided persons must be persuaded to mend their ways, that compromise was the path to true progress, they responded with scorn. Extremists among them, observing the weaknesses of American civilization, adopted a nihilistic posi-

Student sit-ins kept professors and staff from gaining access to their offices on many campuses. A typical incident was photographed at a "liberated building" on the Columbia University campus in April 1968.

tion—the only way to deal with a "rotten" society was to destroy it; reform was impossible, constructive compromise corrupting.

Other young people were so "turned off" by the modern world that they tried to retreat from it, finding refuge in communes, drugs, and mystical religions. Unwilling to confront the two dilemmas described above, they developed a "counterculture" so directly opposite to the way of life of their parents' generation as to suggest to critics that they were still dominated by the culture they rejected. Being part of the counterculture of the "hippie" world meant not caring about money, or material goods, or power over other people. Love was more important than wealth or power, feelings more significant than thought, natural things superior to anything artificial.

Charles Reich, a professor at Yale, praised this view of the world in *The Greening of America* (1970). Reich gave a course on "Individualism in America." One semester he had over 500 students, not one of whom failed. According to the *Yale Course Guide*, published by students, Professor Reich "thinks kids are neat and what can be bad about someone telling you how the system and the older generation have warped and destroyed things for us?"

Critics found the radical students infantile, old-fashioned, and authoritarian: infantile because they could not tolerate frustration or delay, old-fashioned because their absolutist ideas had been exploded by several generations of philosophers and scientists, authoritarian because they rejected majority rule and would not tolerate views in disagreement with their own. And critics pointed out that the hippies' rejection of material values put them unwittingly in conflict with poor people and disadvantaged minorities.

The radicals were seldom numerous in any college, but they were organized in groups such as the Students for a Democratic Society (SDS) and were totally committed. On campus after campus in the late sixties they roused large numbers of their less extreme fellows to take part in sit-ins and other disruptive tactics. Frequently professors and administrators played into their hands, being so offended by their methods and manners that they refused to recognize the legitimacy of some of their demands.

At Columbia in 1968, SDS and black students occupied university buildings and refused to leave unless a series of "non-negotiable" demands (concerning such matters as the university's involvement in secret military research and its relations with minority groups living in the Columbia neighborhood) were met. When, after long delays, President Grayson Kirk called in the police to clear the buildings, a riot broke out in which dozens of students, some of them innocent bystanders, were clubbed and beaten. General student revulsion at the use of the police led to the resignation of Kirk and to the enactment of many university reforms.

The turmoil seemed endless. Extremist groups were torn by factionalism but—it was the bane of modern society—the ability of small groups to disrupt did not diminish.

One heartening aspect of the situation was the increased number of black students attending college. Almost without exception the colleges tried to increase black enrollments even when it meant allocating large percentages of their scholarship funds and lowering academic entrance requirements to compensate for the poor preparation many of these students had received in the schools.

Black college students tended to keep to themselves, and they demanded more control over all aspects of their education than did the typical white. They wanted Black Studies programs taught and administered by blacks. Achievement of these goals was difficult because of the shortage of black teachers and because professors—including most black professors—considered student control of appointments and curricula unwise and in violation of the principles of academic freedom. Nevertheless the general academic response to black demands was accommodating; if "confrontations" occurred frequently, they were usually resolved by negotiation. Unlike white radical students, blacks tended to confine their demands to matters directly related to local conditions. Although generalization is difficult, probably the majority of academics drew a distinction between black radicals, whose actions they found understandable even when they could not in conscience approve of them, and white radicals, most of whom they thought self-indulgent or emotionally disturbed.

The Sexual Revolution

Young people made the most striking contribution to the revolution that took place in the late 1960s in public attitudes toward sexual relationships. Here change came with startling swiftness. Almost overnight (it seemed in retrospect) conventional ideas about premarital sex, contraception and abortion, homosexuality, pornography, and a host of related matters were openly challenged. Probably the behavior of the majority of Americans did not alter radically. But the majority's beliefs and practices were no longer automatically acknowledged to be the only valid ones. It became possible for individuals to espouse different values and to behave differently with at least relative impunity. Actions that in one decade would have led to social ostracism or even to imprisonment were in the next decade accepted almost as a matter of course.

The causes of this revolution were complex and interrelated; one change led to others. More efficient methods of birth control and antibiotics that cured venereal disease removed the two principal practical arguments against sex outside marriage; with these barriers down, many people found their moral attitudes changing. Almost concurrently, the studies of Alfred C. Kinsey, *Sexual Behavior in the Human Male* (1948) and *Sexual Behavior in the Human Female* (1953), which were based on thousands of confidential interviews with persons from nearly every walk of life, revealed that where sex was concerned, large numbers of Americans did not practice what they preached. Premarital sex, marital infidelity, homosexuality, and various forms of perversion were, Kinsey's figures showed, far more common than most persons had suspected, among women as well as among men.

Once it became possible to look at sex in primarily physical and emotional terms and to accept the idea that one's own urges might not be as uncommon as one had been led to believe, it became much more difficult to object to any sexual activity practiced in private by consenting adults. Homosexuals, for example, began openly to admit their feelings and to demand that the heterosexual society cease to harass and discriminate against them.

Sexual freedom also contributed to the revival of the women's rights movement of the 1960s. For one thing, freedom involved a more drastic revolution for women than for men. Effective methods of contraception obviously affected women more directly than men, and the new attitudes heightened women's consciousness of the way the old sexual standards and patterns of family living had restricted their entire existence. In fact the two revolutions interacted with each other in innumerable ways, some clear, others obscure. Concern for job equality fed the demand for day-care centers for children. But an advocate for legalized abortion could be motivated by the belief that women should be as free not to have children as to have them, or by concern for sexual rights as such. And was a militant who denounced "male chauvinist pigs" a feminist or a lesbian?

That the sexual revolution in its many aspects served useful functions was beyond dispute. Reducing irrational fears and inhibitions was liberating for many persons of both sexes, and it tended to help young people form permanent associations on the basis of deeper feelings than their sexual drives. Women surely profited from the new freedom, just as a greater sharing of family duties by husbands and fathers opened men's lives to many new satisfactions. The sexual revolution undoubtedly contributed to the steep decline of the birthrate that set in at the end of the 1960s.

Like other changes, the revolution produced new problems, and some of its results were at best ambiguous. Equality could mean the loss of special advantages for women as well as the shuffling off of restrictions. An equal rights amendment to the Constitution, critics claimed, would sweep away valuable laws protecting working women. For young people, sexual freedom could be very unsettling; sometimes it generated social pressures that propelled them into relationships they were not yet prepared to handle, with grave psychological results. Equally perplexing was the rise in the number of illegitimate births. Easy *cures* did not eliminate venereal disease; on the contrary, the relaxation of sexual taboos produced what public health officials called a veritable epidemic of gonorrhea, a frightening increase in the incidence of syphilis, and the emergence of a deadly new disease, acquired immune deficiency syndrome (AIDS).

Exercising the right to advocate and practice previously forbidden activities involved subjecting people who found those activities offensive—still a large proportion of the population—to embarrassment and even to acute emotional distress. To some people pornography seemed ethically wrong, and to most feminists it seemed degrading to women. Abortion raised difficult legal and moral questions. The rights of women to control their own bodies and of society to protect itself from having to care for unwanted children were arguments in favor of abortion. But what of the unborn child? A vigorous right-to-life movement sprang up, its supporters calling for the overturn of the Supreme Court decision (*Roe* v. *Wade*) that made abortion legal. Such questions exacerbated already serious social conflicts. Clearly, however, the sexual revolution was not about to end, the direction of change not to be reversed.

SUPPLEMENTARY READING

Titles marked with an asterisk have been published in paperback.

J. F. Heath, **Decade of Disillusionment: The Kennedy-Johnson Years** (1980), and A. J. Matusow, **The Unraveling of America*** (1984), are good surveys, while W. M. O'Neill, **Coming Apart: An Informal History of the 1960s*** (1971), and Godfrey Hodgson, **America in Our Time** (1976), deal more broadly with the decade. On Kennedy, consult H. S. Parmet, **Jack: The Struggles of John F. Kennedy** (1980) and **JKF: The Presidency of John F. Kennedy** (1983), together a fair-minded account. A. M. Schlesinger, Jr., **A Thousand Days*** (1965), and Theodore Sorensen, **Kennedy*** (1965), are rich in eyewitness detail but extremely pro-Kennedy.

On Johnson, see Rowland Evans and Robert Novak, **Lyndon B. Johnson*** (1966), Tom Wicker, **JFK and LBJ*** (1968), E. F. Goldman, **The Tragedy of Lyndon Johnson*** (1969), and Doris Kearns, **Lyndon Johnson and the American Dream*** (1976). The political developments are covered in the Matusow volume and in Congressional Quarterly Service, **Congress and the Nation** (1965, 1969), and J. L. Sundquist, **Politics and Policy** (1968). Economic policies are discussed in S. E. Harris, **Economics of the Kennedy Years*** (1964), the election of 1964 in T. H. White, **The Making of the President*** (1965). Peter Wyden, **Bay of Pigs** (1979), and Elie Abel, **The Missile Crisis** (1966), describe the most important foreign policy crises of the era. On the changes of the period, see J. K. Galbraith, **The Affluent Society*** (1958) and **The New Industrial State*** (1967), dealing with the economy, and also Paul Goodman, **Growing Up Absurd*** (1960), Kenneth Kenniston, **The Uncommitted*** (1965), and C. A. Reich, **The Greening of America*** (1970).

Population trends are described in C. and I. B. Taeuber, **The Changing Population of the United States** (1958), the movement to the suburbs in R. C. Wood, **Suburbia*** (1959). For television, see G. A. Steiner, **The People Look at Television** (1963). Daniel Hoffman (ed.), **Harvard Guide to Contemporary American Writing** (1979), contains convenient discussions of postwar literature. Morris Dickstein, **Gates of Eden: American Culture in the Sixties** (1977), is part history, part literary criticism, part memoir. Modern art is discussed in J. I. Bauer, **Revolution and Tradition in Modern American Art** (1951), Samuel Hunter, **Modern American Painting and Sculpture*** (1959), and Barbara Rose, **American Art Since 1900*** (1967).

For the causes and character of the poverty and urban problems that led Johnson to devise his Great Society program, see Michael Harrington, **The Other America*** (1962), J. C. Donovan, **The Politics of Poverty*** (1967), Oscar Lewis, **La Vida: A Puerto Rican Family in the Culture of Poverty*** (1966), Mitchell Gordon, **Sick Cities: Psychology and Pathology of American Urban Life*** (1963), R. C. Weaver, **The Urban Complex*** (1964), and Jane Jacobs, **The Death and Life of Great American Cities*** (1962).

Students of contemporary race relations should begin with a number of highly personal books by blacks. James Baldwin, **The Fire Next Time*** (1963), first called the new black anger to white attention, but see also M. L. King, Jr., **Stride Toward Freedom*** (1958), Malcolm X, **Autobiography*** (1966), Stokely Carmichael and C. V. Hamilton, **Black Power: The Politics of Liberation in America*** (1967), and Eldridge Cleaver, **Soul on Ice*** (1967). Other important books on race relations include C. E. Silberman, **Crisis in Black and White*** (1964), K. B. Clark, **Youth in the Ghetto** (1964), L. E. Lomax, **The Negro Revolt*** (1963), S. B. Oates, **Let the Trumpet Sound** (1982), a life of Martin Luther King Jr., Clayborne Carson, **In Struggle: SNCC and the Black Awakening of the 1960s** (1981), and August Meier and Elliott Rudwick, **CORE: A Study in the Civil Rights Movement*** (1973). The **Report*** of the National Advisory (Kerner) Commission on Civil Disorders (1968) is full of interesting material. M. S. Meier and Feliciano Rivera, **The Chicanos*** (1972), provides a sympathetic discussion of the problems and aspirations of Mexican-Americans, but see also Joan London and Henry Anderson, **So Shall Ye Reap: The Story of César Chávez & the Farm Workers' Movement** (1970), A. F. Corwin, **Immigrants—and Immigrants** (1978), and J. R. Garcia, **Operation Wetback** (1980). The revived interest in ethnicity is discussed in Michael Novak, **The Rise of the Unmeltable Ethnics** (1972), and Thomas Sowell, **Ethnic America** (1981).

The literature on the women's movement is voluminous and difficult to evaluate. In addition to W. H. Chafe, **The American Woman*** (1972) and **Women and Equality*** (1977), see Betty Friedan, **The Feminine Mystique*** (1963), Jo Freeman, **The Politics of Women's Liberation** (1975), S. M. Rothman, **Woman's Proper Place** (1978), and C. N. Degler, **At Odds*** (1981).

Educational trends are discussed in Richard Hofstadter and C. D. Hardy, **The Development and Scope of Higher Education in the United States** (1952), Jacques

Barzun, The House of Intellect* (1959), R. N. Sanford (ed.), **The American College** (1962), R. O. Bower (ed.), **The New Professors** (1960), Martin Mayer, **The Schools*** (1961), A. E. Bestor, **The Restoration of Learning** (1955), J. B. Conant, **The American High School Today*** (1959) and **Slums and Suburbs*** (1964), and Robert Coles, **Children of Crisis*** (1967). On militancy among college students, see Kenneth Kenniston, **Young Radicals** (1968), S. M. Lipset and P. G. Altbach (eds.), **Students in Revolt** (1969), Roger Kahn, **The Battle of Morningside Heights** (1970), and Kirkpatrick Sale, **SDS** (1973). See also Irwin Unger, **The Movement: A History of the American New Left** (1974), and Theodore Roszak, **The Making of a Counter-Culture** (1969).

PORTFOLIO NINE

U.S. Culture Overseas

As one of the world's two "superpowers," the United States influences events in every corner of the globe. The impact of American wealth and power (and also of American ideas and values) is observable almost daily in the headlines of newspapers both in the United States and in other countries. Who is elected president, what party controls Congress, how prices are moving on the New York Stock Exchange, and similar events hold the attention of political and business leaders in Europe, Asia, and Latin America almost as closely as they do the attention of their counterparts in the United States. But the influence of the United States on other lands takes many less weighty forms, forms that in both obvious and subtle ways profoundly affect the lives and thoughts of ordinary people everywhere. This portfolio provides some examples of this type of influence.

Japan: A movie theater in Tokyo advertises *The Day After,* an American film about the aftermath of an atomic war. The vivid mushroom cloud image lends an ironic touch to the placid Japanese street scene.

Mickey Mouse's kingdom is worldwide. Below is the main entrance to the Tokyo Disneyland. For another of Mickey's outposts, see the photo on page 894 of this portfolio.

A recent fad of Japanese teenagers involved dressing up in 1950s American garb and dancing elaborately choreographed routines to rock music. Above, an older woman in traditional *tabis* and *zoris* looks doubtfully at the goings-on of the younger generation.

Peking: Coca-Cola and other American soft drinks have even invaded the communist world. At the Imperial Palace in China's capital, cases of Coke are stacked awaiting refrigeration.

Singapore: Blue jeans, first made by Levi Strauss during the California gold rush (see Portfolio Six), became stylish in the 1950s and 1960s, when they were worn by movie stars like Marlon Brando (*The Wild One*). This Singapore shop sells blue denim chic.

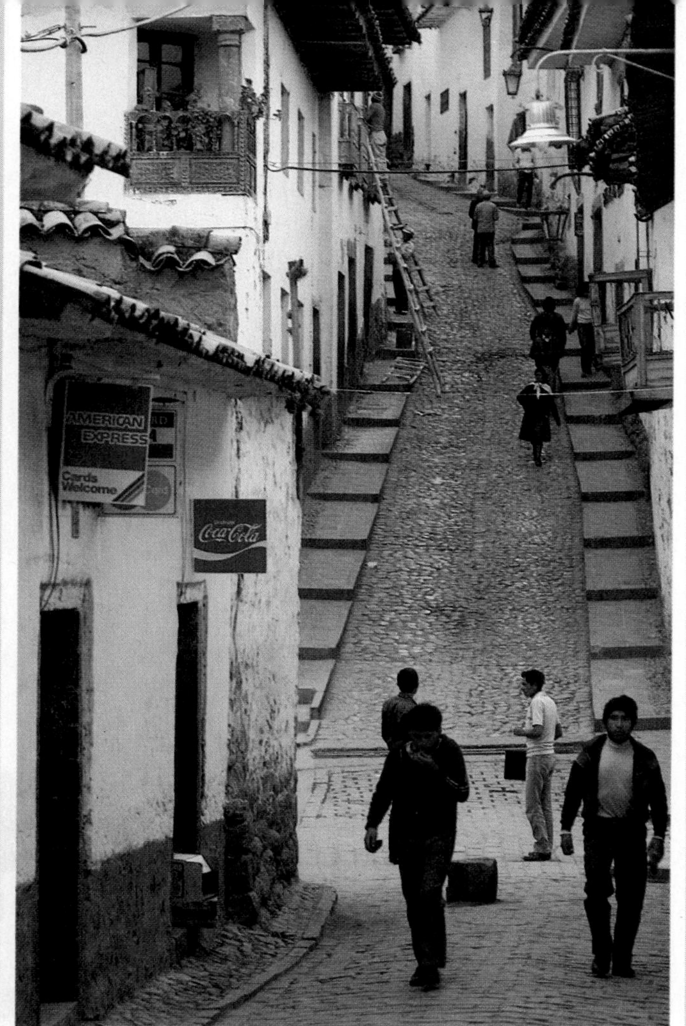

Peru: Calle Loreto in the picturesque mountain town of Cuzco is far removed from Main Street, U.S.A., but American Express, VISA, MasterCard, and Coke are doing business there as in other foreign countries.

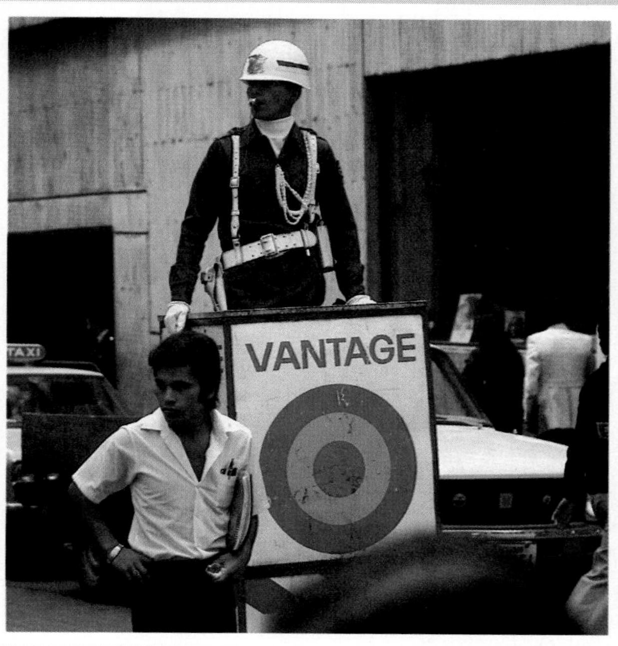

Ecuador: The traffic cop's platform in a Quito street serves as a billboard advertising the American cigarette Vantage.

Brazil: A Rio de Janeiro filling station carries Esso (Exxon in the U.S.) gasoline and alcohol fuel—popular in Brazil—as well as the ubiquitous Coca-Cola.

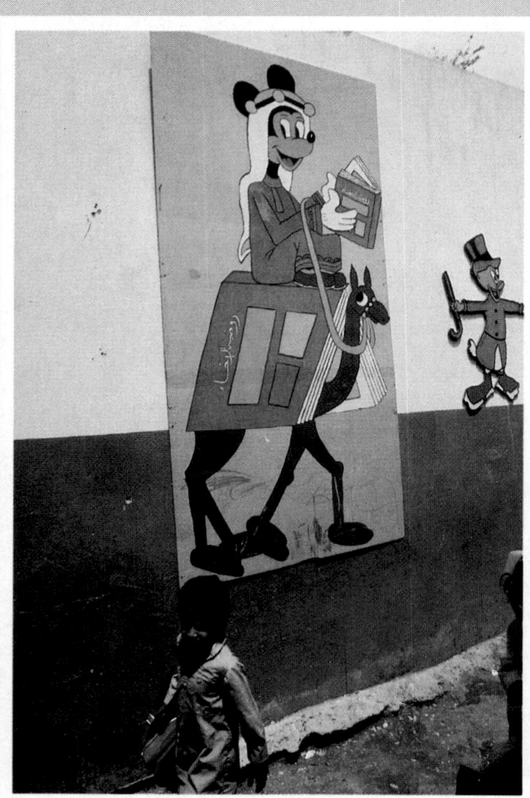

Saudi Arabia: Some Saudi Arabian children enjoy a few of the comforts and conveniences that many American children have. The babies may wear Pampers (upper left); their clothes may be laundered in GE automatic washing machines (upper right); and Mickey Mouse (left), in a burnoose riding a camel, is there on a poster encouraging them to read.

Kuwait: An oil-rich country on the Saudi Arabian peninsula, Kuwait has a formidable appetite for American goods and services. A parking lot (note the minaret in the background) is full of American-made cars, which became a status symbol in Arab countries during the 1970s. An American-style supermarket offers Kuwaiti customers a wide assortment of food and other items.

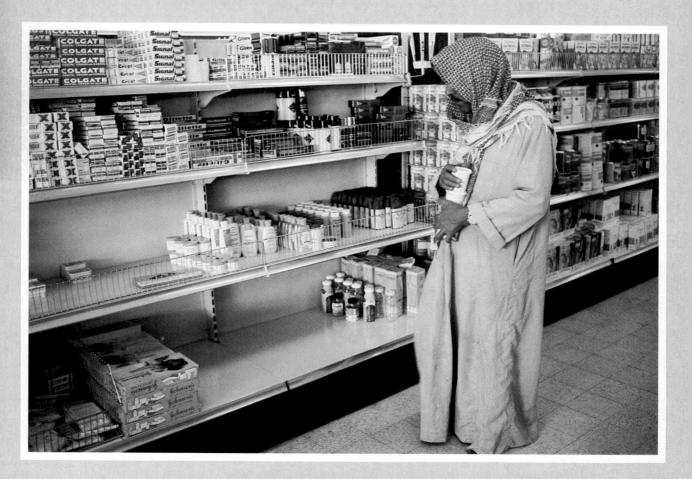

Zambia: In this African country, a store on the American model sells Western-style cooking equipment.

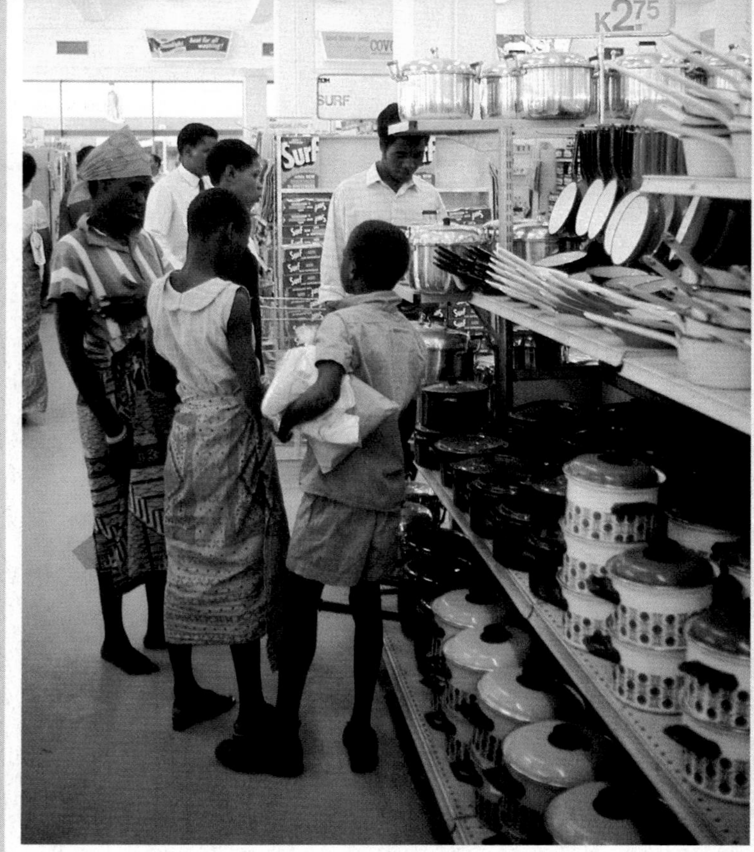

Russia: Blue jeans and rock music are a part of Russian life these days. In June 1986, a rock concert was given as a benefit for the victims of the Chernobyl nuclear power plant disaster. The tradition of benefit rock concerts began in 1971 with the Bangladesh refugee benefit concert in New York involving American, British, and Indian performers.

Senegal: One American firm with worldwide markets is IBM. In the Ministry of Finance in Dakar, a computer technician works with a sophisticated IBM data processing system.

30
Vietnam and Watergate

The obstruction of justice thing is a [expletive deleted] hard thing to prove in court. PRESIDENT RICHARD M. NIXON, *April 16, 1973*

In the fall of 1967 President Lyndon Johnson seemed to have every intention of running for a second full term. Whether he would be reelected was not clear, but that any Democrat could prevent this shrewd and powerful politican from being nominated seemed out of the question. Nevertheless, within a few months opposition to him had become so bitter that he withdrew as a candidate for renomination. The cause of this opposition was his handling of a conflict on the other side of the world—the war in Vietnam.

The War in Vietnam

When Vietnam was divided following the defeat of the French in 1954, a handful of American military "advisers" were sent there to train a South Vietnamese army. As time passed, more American aid and "advice" were dispatched in a futile effort to establish a stable government. Procommunist forces, now called Vietcong, soon controlled large sections of the country, some almost within sight of the capital city of Saigon.

Gradually the Vietcong, drawing supplies from North Vietnam and indirectly from China and the Soviet Union, increased in strength. In response more American money and more military advisers were sent to bolster Ngo Dinh Diem's regime. By the end of 1961 there were 3,200 American military men in the country; by the time Kennedy was assassinated in November 1963, the American military presence had risen to more than 16,000. However, no combat troops were involved and only 120 Americans had been killed.

The Diem government, despite the assistance, could not suppress the Vietcong rebels, and it steadily alienated more South Vietnamese interests. Shortly before Kennedy was assassinated, a group of South Vietnamese generals overthrew Diem and killed him. (American officials encouraged the coup without realizing that the generals planned to execute Diem.)

In August 1964, after announcing that North Vietnamese gunboats had fired on American destroyers in the Gulf of Tonkin, President Johnson demanded, and in an air of crisis obtained, an authorization from Congress to "repel any armed attack against the forces of the United States and to prevent further aggression."

With this blank check, and buttressed by his sweeping defeat of Goldwater in the 1964 presidential election, Johnson sent *combat* troops to South Vietnam and directed air attacks against targets in both South and North Vietnam. At first the American ground troops were supposed to be merely teachers and advisers of the South Vietnamese troops. Then they were said to be there to defend air bases, with the understanding that they would return fire if they were attacked. Next came word that the troops were being used to assist South Vietnamese units when they came under enemy fire. In fact the Americans were soon attacking the enemy directly, mounting "search and destroy missions" aimed at clearing the foe from villages and entire sections of the country.

Johnson's "escalation" of the American commitment occurred piecemeal and apparently without plan. At the end of 1965, 184,000 Americans were in the field; a year later, 385,000; after another year, 485,000. By the middle of 1968 the number exceeded 538,000. As the scope of the action broadened, the number of American casualties rose. Each increase in the number of troops was met by corresponding increases from the other side. Russia and China sent no combat troops but stepped up their aid, and thousands of North Vietnamese regulars filtered across the 17th parallel to join the Vietcong insurgents. The United States was engaged in a full-scale war, one that Congress never declared. Johnson based his actions on the controversial Gulf of Tonkin resolution.

From the beginning the war divided the American people sharply. Defenders of the president's policy, who were called hawks, emphasized the nation's moral responsibility to resist aggression and what President Eisenhower had called the "domino" theory. The domino theory was based on an analogy with the western powers' failure to resist Hitler before 1939. It predicted that if the communists were allowed to "take over" Vietnam, they would soon take its neighbors, then *their* neighbors, and so on until all Asia had been conquered. The United States was not an aggressor in Vietnam, the hawks insisted, and they stressed Johnson's oft-expressed willingness to negotiate a general withdrawal of "foreign" forces from the country, which the communists repeatedly rejected.

American opponents of the war, called doves, argued that the struggle between the South Viet-

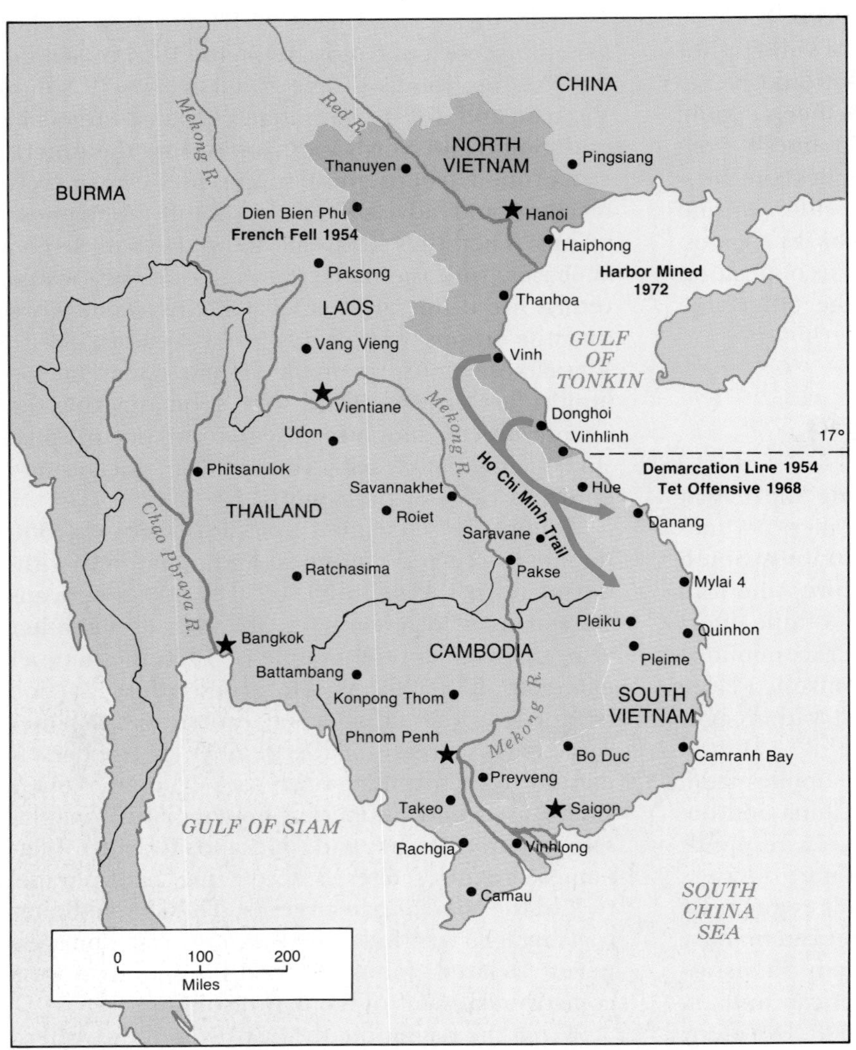

SOUTHEAST ASIA, 1954–1975

namese government and the Vietcong was a civil war in which Americans should not meddle. They stressed the repressive, undemocratic character of the Diem regime and of those that followed as proof that the war was not a contest between democracy and communism. They objected to the massive aerial bombings (more explosives were dropped on Vietnam between 1964 and 1968 than on Germany and Japan combined in World War II), to the use of napalm and other chemical weapons such as the defoliants that were sprayed on forests and crops and which wreaked havoc among noncombatants, and to the killing of civilians by American troops. Senator J. William Fulbright, chairman of the Foreign Relations Committee, had introduced the Gulf of Tonkin Resolution in 1964. By 1967 he was calling the war "unnecessary and immoral" and describing American participation in it as a "false and dangerous dream of an imperial destiny."

The doves discounted the domino theory, pointing both to the growing communist split into Chinese and Russian camps and to the traditional hostility of all Vietnamese to the Chinese, which they claimed made Chinese expansion into Southeast Asia unlikely. And they deplored the heavy loss of American life—over 40,000 dead by 1970. The cost of the war, which came to exceed $20 billion a year, was still another reason the doves opposed it. In large part because so many people objected to the war, Johnson refused to ask Congress to raise taxes to pay for it. The deficit forced the government to borrow huge sums, which caused interest rates to soar, adding to the upward pressure on prices.

Although Johnson's financial policies were shortsighted if not outrightly irresponsible, and although his statements about the war were often lacking in candor, he and his advisers believed they were defending freedom and democracy. What became increasingly clear as time passed and the costs mounted was that military victory was impossible. Yet American leaders were extraordinarily slow to grasp this fact. Repeatedly they advised the president that one more escalation (so many more soldiers, so many more air raids) would break the enemy's will to resist. The smug arrogance bred by America's brief postwar monopoly of nuclear weapons persisted in some quarters long after the monopoly had been lost. As late as 1965 McGeorge Bundy, President Johnson's special assistant for national security affairs, apparently told an interviewer (he later claimed to have been misunderstood) that "the United States was the locomotive at the head of mankind, and the rest of the world the caboose." And like the proverbial donkey plodding after the carrot on the stick, Johnson repeatedly followed the advice of hawks like Bundy.

For a long time, as opinion polls demonstrated, a majority of the American people believed he was correct. Patriotism and pride, along with the costly "lessons" of 1931–1939 and a stubborn refusal to

Graphic proof of the effectiveness of defoliation: at top, an unsprayed mangrove forest; at bottom, a mangrove forest that had been sprayed with herbicides in 1965 as it looked in 1970.

admit that a mistake had been made, held them to this course.

The Election of 1968

Gradually the doves increased in number. Students, for idealistic reasons and because they resented being drafted to fight in Vietnam; businessmen, alarmed by the effects of the war on the economy; and others for different reasons became increasingly dissatisfied with the president's policy.

As late as the fall of 1967, opposition to the war, in Congress and elsewhere, remained disorganized. It was especially vehement on college campuses, some students objecting because they thought the United States had no business intervening in the Vietnam conflict, others because they feared being drafted, still others because so many students were obtaining educational deferments while young men who were unable to attend college were being conscripted. Then, in November 1967, Senator Eugene McCarthy of Minnesota, low-keyed, rather introspective, never a leading figure in the upper house, announced that he was a candidate for the 1968 Democratic presidential nomination. Opposition to the war was his issue.

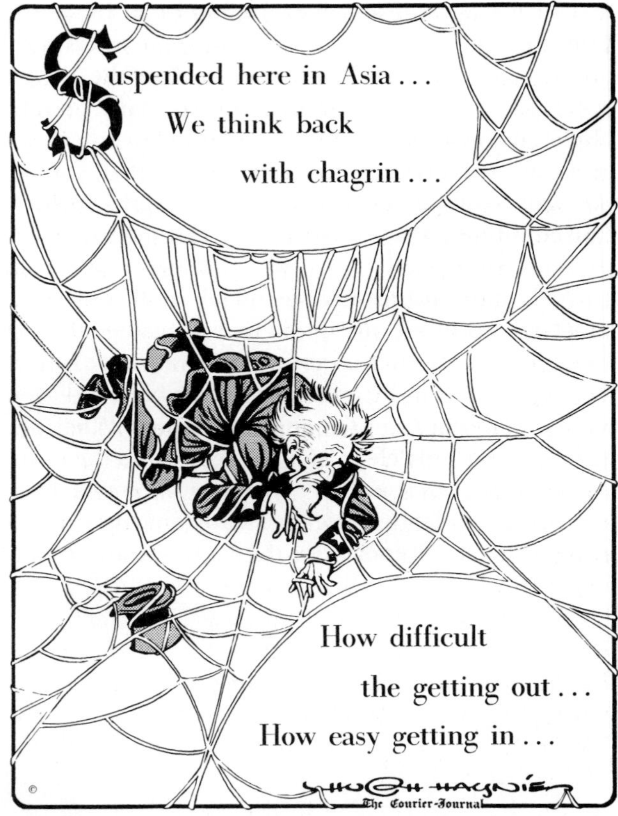

Hugh Haynie of the Louisville Courier-Journal *drew this pointed 1968 cartoon comment about U.S. involvement in Vietnam.*

Preventing Johnson from getting the Democratic nomination in 1968 seemed on the surface impossible. Aside from the difficulty of defeating a "reigning" president, there were the domestic achievements of Johnson's Great Society program: the health insurance program for retired people, greatly expanded federal funding of education and public housing, to say nothing of the Civil Rights Act of 1965, which provided for federal registration of black voters in districts where they had been systematically kept from the polls. McCarthy took his chances of being nominated so lightly that he did not trouble to set up a real organization. He entered the campaign only to "alleviate . . . this sense of political helplessness." Someone, he decided, must step forward to put the Vietnam question before the voters.

Suddenly, early in 1968, on the heels of the latest announcement by the American military that the communists were about to crack, North Vietnam and Vietcong forces launched a general offensive to correspond with their Lunar New Year (Tet). Striking 39 of the 44 provincial capitals, many other towns and cities, and every American base, they caused chaos throughout South Vietnam. They held Hue, the old capital of the country, for weeks. To root them out of Saigon the Americans had to level large sections of the city. Elsewhere the destruction was total, an irony highlighted by the remark of an American officer after the recapture of the village of Ben Tre: "It became necessary to destroy the town to save it."

The Tet offensive was essentially a series of raids; the communists did not expect to hold the cities indefinitely, and they did not. Their losses were enormous. Nevertheless the psychological impact in South Vietnam and in the United States made Tet a clear victory for the North. American pollsters reported an enormous shift of public opinion against further escalation of the fighting. When General William C. Westmoreland described

Tet as a communist defeat and when it came out that the administration was considering sending an additional 206,000 troops to South Vietnam, McCarthy, who was campaigning in New Hampshire, suddenly became a formidable figure. Thousands of students and other volunteers flocked to the state to ring doorbells in his behalf. On election day he polled 42 percent of the Democratic vote.

The political situation was monumentally confused. Many New Hampshire voters had supported McCarthy because they believed that Johnson was not prosecuting the war vigorously enough and saw voting for another person as a way to rebuke him. Before the primary, former attorney general Robert F. Kennedy, brother of the slain president, had refused either to seek the Democratic nomination or to support McCarthy, though he disliked Johnson intensely and was opposed to his policy in Vietnam. McCarthy's strong showing caused Kennedy to reverse himself. He entered the race. Had he done so earlier, McCarthy might have withdrawn in his favor, for Kennedy had powerful political and popular support. After New Hampshire, McCarthy understandably decided to remain in the contest.

Confronting this confusion, President Johnson withdrew from the race. Vice-President Hubert H. Humphrey then announced his candidacy, though not until it was too late for him to enter the primaries. Kennedy carried the primaries in Indiana and Nebraska. McCarthy won in Wisconsin and Oregon. In the climactic contest in California, Kennedy won by a small margin. However, immediately after his victory speech in a Los Angeles hotel, he was assassinated by Sirhan Sirhan, a young Arab nationalist who had been incensed by Kennedy's support of Israel. In effect, Kennedy's death assured the nomination of Humphrey; most professional politicians distrusted McCarthy, who was rather diffident and aloof for a politician.

The contest for the Republican nomination was far less dramatic, though its outcome, the nomination of Richard M. Nixon, would have been hard to predict a few years earlier. After his defeat in the California gubernatorial election of 1962, Nixon moved to New York City and joined a prominent law firm. He remained active in Republican affairs, making countless speeches and attending political meetings throughout the country. In 1967 Governor George Romney of Michigan seemed the likely Republican nominee, but he failed to develop extensive support. While Governor Nelson Rockefeller of New York was widely mentioned, conservative Republicans would not forgive his refusal to help Goldwater in 1964, and he decided not to enter the race. Nixon (who had campaigned hard for Goldwater in 1964) announced his candidacy in February 1968. After Romney withdrew in the midst of the New Hampshire contest, he swept the primaries and won an easy first-ballot victory at the Republican convention.

Nixon then astounded the country and dismayed liberals by choosing Governor Spiro T. Agnew of Maryland as his running mate. Aside from the fact that he had little national reputation ("Spiro who?" jokesters asked), Agnew had taken a tough, almost brutal stand on such matters as racial disturbances, urban crime, and other social problems. Nixon chose him primarily to attract southern votes.

Placating the South seemed necessary because Governor George C. Wallace of Alabama was making a determined bid to win enough electoral votes for his American Independent party to prevent any candidate's obtaining a majority. Wallace was flagrantly antiblack and anti-intellectual. (College professors were among his favorite targets. In attacking them he used such worn images as "ivory-tower folks with pointed heads" and—more inventive—people without "sense enough to park a bicycle straight.") He seemed sure to attract substantial southern and conservative support. He denounced federal "meddling," the "coddling" of criminals, and the forced desegregation of schools. He ridiculed intellectuals, planners, and any form of professional ability or mental distinction. Nixon's choice of Agnew appeared to be an effort to appeal to the groups that Wallace attracted.

This Republican strategy disturbed liberals and heightened the tension surrounding the Democratic convention, which met in Chicago in late August. Humphrey delegates controlled the convention. The vice-president had a solid liberal record on domestic issues, but he had supported Johnson's Vietnam policy with equal solidity. Those who could not stomach the Nixon-Agnew ticket and who opposed the war faced a difficult choice. Several thousand activists representing a dozen groups, and advocating tactics ranging from orderly demonstrations to civil disobedience to indiscriminate violence, descended on Chicago to put pressure on the delegates to repudiate the Johnson Vietnam policy.

In the tense atmosphere that resulted, the party hierarchy overreacted. Mayor Richard J. Daley, whose ability to "influence" election results had often been demonstrated, most recently in the Kennedy-Nixon campaign (see page 854), ringed the convention with barricades and policemen to protect it from disruption. This was a reasonable precaution in itself. Inside the building the delegates nominated Humphrey and adopted a war plank satisfactory to Johnson. Outside, however, provoked by the abusive language and violent behavior of radical demonstrators, an army of policemen tore into the protesters, in Norman Mailer's graphic phrase "like a chain saw cutting into wood," brutally beating dozens while millions watched on television in fascinated horror.

At first the mayhem at Chicago seemed to benefit Nixon by strengthening the convictions of many voters that the tougher treatment of criminals and dissenters that he and Agnew were calling for was necessary. Those who were critical of the Chicago police tended to blame Humphrey, whom Mayor Daley supported. Nixon campaigned at a deliberate, dignified pace. He made relatively few public appearances, relying instead on carefully arranged television interviews and taped commercials prepared by an advertising agency. He stressed firm enforcement of the law and his desire "to bring us together." As to Vietnam, he would "end the war and win the peace," by just what means he did not say. Agnew, in his blunt, coarse way, assaulted Humphrey, the Democrats, and left-wing dissident groups. (Critics who remembered Nixon's own political style in the era of Joseph McCarthy called Agnew "Nixon's Nixon.")

The Democratic campaign was badly organized. Humphrey was subjected to merciless heckling from antiwar audiences. He seemed far behind in the early stages. Shortly before election day, President Johnson helped him greatly by suspending air attacks on North Vietnam, and in the long run the Republican strategy helped too. Black voters and the urban poor had no practical choice but to vote Democratic. Gradually Humphrey gained ground, and on election day the popular vote was close: Nixon slightly less than 31.8 million, Humphrey nearly 31.3 million. Nixon's electoral college margin, however, was substantial—301 to 191. The remaining 46 electoral votes went to Wallace, whose 9.9 million votes came to 13.5 percent of the total. Despite Nixon's triumph, the Democrats retained control of both houses of Congress.

Nixon as President

When he took office in January 1969, Richard Nixon projected an image of calm and deliberate statesmanship; he introduced no startling changes, proposed no important new legislation. The major economic problem facing him, inflation, was primarily a result of the heavy military expenditures and "easy money" policies of the Johnson administration. Nixon cut federal spending and balanced the 1969 budget, while the Federal Reserve Board forced up interest rates in order to slow the expansion of the money supply. The object was to reduce the rate of economic growth without causing heavy unemployment or precipitating a recession (the word *depression* had apparently passed out of the vocabulary of economists). Even its supporters admitted that this policy would check inflation only slowly, and when prices continued to rise, there was mounting uneasiness. Labor unions demanded large wage increases. The problem was complicated by mounting deficits in the United States' balance of trade with foreign nations, the product of an overvaluation of the dollar that encouraged Americans to buy foreign goods.

In 1970 Congress passed a law giving the president power to regulate prices and wages. Nixon had opposed this legislation, but in the summer of 1971 he decided to use it. First he announced a 90-day price and wage freeze (Phase I) and placed a 10 percent surcharge on imports. Then he set up a Pay Board and a Price Commission with authority to limit wage and price increases when the freeze ended (Phase II). These controls did not check inflation completely—and they angered union leaders, who felt that labor was being shortchanged—but they did slow the upward spiral. A 7.9 percent devaluation of the dollar in December 1971 helped the economy by making American products more competitive in foreign markets.

In handling other domestic issues, the president was less firm, sometimes even confused. He advocated a bold plan for shifting the burden of welfare

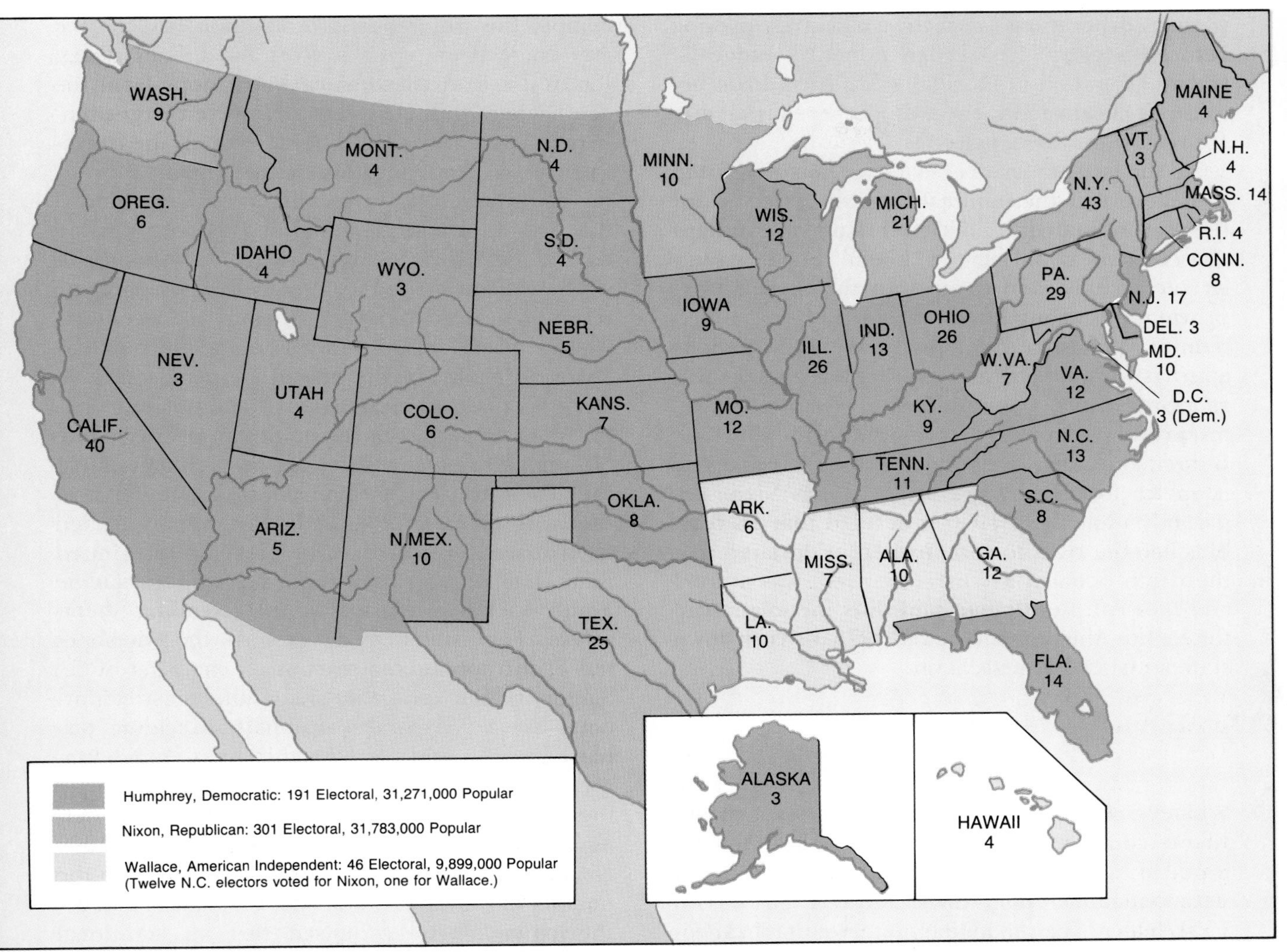

THE ELECTION OF 1968

payments in all the states, and he came out for a "minimum income" for poor families, which alarmed his conservative supporters. These measures got nowhere in Congress. On the other hand, Nixon and his attorney general, John N. Mitchell, were so openly resistant to further federal efforts to force school desegregation on reluctant local districts as to dismay southern moderates and northern liberals. And in his eagerness to add what he called "strict constructionists" to the Supreme Court, which he believed had swung too far to the left in such areas as race relations and the rights of persons accused of committing crimes, Nixon allowed himself to be drawn into two foolish confrontations with the Senate.

When Chief Justice Earl Warren retired from the Court in June 1969, Nixon named a respected conservative, Warren E. Burger, the new chief justice. This caused no difficulties. But Nixon blundered when he sought to fill the seat of Justice Abe Fortas, who had resigned under fire after it came out that he had accepted fees from questionable sources while on the bench. Nixon first selected Judge Clement F. Haynesworth, Jr., of South Carolina, whom the Senate rejected because of his having failed to disqualify himself when cases involving corporations in which he had invested came before his court. His second nominee, Judge G. Harrold Carswell of Florida, was turned down because of his alleged racist attitudes and his mediocre record on the bench.

In the face of a mass of evidence, Nixon refused to believe that the nominations were rejected for the reasons stated; he declared that "no southern conservative" could run the "liberal" Senate gauntlet successfully, and to prevent the Senate from proving him wrong he nominated Harry A. Blackmun of Minnesota. Blackmun won the unanimous approval of the Senate. Since Nixon's analysis was as incorrect as his political tactics were ineffective, his prestige suffered accordingly. And while the Burger court was less liberal than the Warren court, it was far from being as conservative as Nixon apparently wanted. In 1970 it decided that 18-year-olds had the right to vote; in 1972 it declared that the death penalty, as currently used, was a cruel and unusual punishment and thus in violation of the Eighth Amendment; and in 1973 it struck down state antiabortion legislation.

"Vietnamizing" the War

Whatever his difficulties on the domestic front, Nixon considered the solution of the Vietnam problem his chief task. When the war in Southeast Asia first burst upon American consciousness in 1954, he had favored military intervention in keeping with the containment policy. As controversy over American policy developed, he had supported most of the actions of presidents Kennedy and Johnson. During the 1968 campaign he played down the Vietnam issue. Though he insisted he would end the war on "honorable" terms if elected, he suggested nothing very different from what Johnson was doing.

In office, Nixon proposed a phased withdrawal of all non–South Vietnamese troops, to be followed by an internationally supervised election in South Vietnam. The North Vietnamese rejected this scheme and insisted that the United States withdraw it forces unconditionally. Their intransigence left the president in a difficult position. Probably the majority of Americans considered his proposal eminently fair. With equal certainty a majority was unwilling to increase the scale of the fighting to compel the communists to accept it, and as the war dragged on, costs in lives and money rising, the desire to extricate American troops from the conflict became more intense. However, large numbers of Americans would not face up to the consequences of gratifying this desire: ending the war on the communists' terms. Nixon could not compel the foe to negotiate meaningfully, yet every passing day added to the strength of antiwar sentiment, which, as it expressed itself in ever more emphatic terms, in turn led to deeper divisions in the country.

The president responded to the dilemma by trying to build up the South Vietnamese armed forces so that American troops could pull out without the communists overrunning South Vietnam. He shipped so many planes to the Vietnamese that they came to have the fourth largest air force in the world. The trouble with this strategy (called Vietnamization) was that for 15 years the United States had been trying without success to make the South Vietnamese capable of defending themselves. For complicated reasons—the incompetence, corruption, and reactionary character of the Saigon regime probably being the most important—South Vietnamese troops had seldom displayed much enthusiasm for the kind of tough jungle fighting at which the North Vietnamese and the Vietcong excelled. Nevertheless, efforts at Vietnamization were stepped up; and in June 1969 Nixon announced that he would soon reduce the number of American soldiers in Vietnam by 25,000. In September he promised that an additional 35,000 men would be withdrawn by mid-December.

These steps did not quiet American protesters. On October 15 a nationwide antiwar demonstration, Vietnam Moratorium Day, organized by students, produced an unprecedented outpouring all over the country. This massive display produced one of Vice-President Agnew's most notorious blasts of adjectival invective: he said that the moratorium was an example of "national masochism" led by "an effete corps of impudent snobs who characterize themselves as intellectuals." A few days later he called on the country to "separate" radical students from society "with no more regret than we should feel over discarding rotten apples from a barrel," which at least had a quality of terseness that most of Agnew's pronouncements lacked.

A second Moratorium Day brought a crowd estimated at 250,000 to Washington to march past the White House. The president was unmoved. He could not be influenced by protests, he insisted, and during one of the Washington demonstrations he passed the time watching a football game on television. On November 3, he defended his policy in a televised speech. He stressed the sincerity of his peace efforts, the unreasonableness of the communists, the responsibility of the United States to protect the South Vietnamese people from communist reprisals and to honor its international commitments. He announced that he planned to remove all American ground forces from Vietnam. The next day, reporting a flood of telegrams and calls supporting his position, he declared that a "silent majority" of the American people approved his course.

For a season, events appeared to vindicate Nixon's position. A gradual reduction of military activity in Vietnam had reduced American casualties to what those who did not find the war morally unbearable considered "tolerable" levels. Troop withdrawals continued in an orderly fashion. A new lottery system for drafting men for military duty eliminated some of the inequities in the selective service law.

But the war continued. Early in 1970 reports that in 1968 an American unit had massacred civilians, including dozens of women and children, in a Vietnamese hamlet known as Mylai 4, revived the controversy over the purposes of the war and its corrosive effects on those who were fighting it. The American people, it seemed, were being torn apart by the war: one from another according to each one's interpretation of events, many within themselves as they tried to balance the war's horrors against their pride, their detestation of communism, and their unwillingness to turn their backs on their elected leader.

Nixon's most implacable enemy could find no reason to think he wished the war to go on. Its human, economic, and social costs could only vex his days and threaten his future reputation. When he reduced the level of the fighting, the communists merely waited for further reductions. When he raised it, many of his own people denounced him. If he pulled out of Vietnam entirely, other Americans would be outraged.

Perhaps his error lay in his unwillingness to admit his own uncertainty, something the greatest presidents—one thinks immediately of Lincoln and Franklin Roosevelt—were never afraid to do. Facing a dilemma, he tried to convince the world that he was firmly in control of events, with the result that at times he seemed more like a high school valedictorian declaiming sententiously about the meaning of life than the mature statesman he so desperately wished to be. Thus he heightened the tensions he sought to relax—in America, in Vietnam, and elsewhere.

Late in April 1970 Nixon announced that Vietnamization was proceeding more rapidly than he had hoped, that communist power was weakening, that within a year another 150,000 American soldiers would be extracted from Vietnam. A week later he announced that military intelligence had indicated that the enemy was consolidating its "sanctuaries" in neutral Cambodia and that he was therefore dispatching thousands of American troops to destroy these bases.* He was escalating (dread word) the war. He even resumed the bombing of targets in North Vietnam. "You've got to electrify people with bold decisions," he told the Joint Chiefs of Staff. "Let's go blow the hell out of them."

To foes of the war, Nixon's decision seemed so appallingly unwise that some of them began to fear that he had become mentally unbalanced. The contradictions between his confident statements about Vietnamization and his alarmist description of powerful enemy forces poised like a dagger 30-odd miles from Saigon did not seem the product of a reasoning mind. His failure to consult congressional leaders or many of his personal advisers before drastically altering his policy, the critics claimed, was unconstitutional and irresponsible. His insensitive response to the avalanche of criticism that descended on him from the universities, from Congress, and from other quarters further disturbed observers.

Students took the lead in opposing the invasion of Cambodia. Young people had been prominent in the opposition to the war from early in the conflict. Some objected to war in principle. Many more believed that this particular war was wrong because it was being fought against a small country on the other side of the globe where America's vital inter-

* American planes had been bombing Cambodia for some time, but this fact was not known to the public (or to Congress) until 1973.

An Ohio National Guard skirmish line of gas-masked troops advances up a hill on the campus of Kent State University, May 4, 1970. A moment later the guardsmen turned and fired upon student antiwar demonstrators, killing four.

ests did not seem to be threatened. As the war dragged on and casualties mounted, student opposition to the draft became intense. For some the reason was obvious—they did not want to be drafted. Others (including many of the above) objected because the universal military service required was anything but universal. Thousands of students avoided the draft simply by remaining in college; poor and disadvantaged young men did most of the fighting.

Nixon's shocking announcement triggered many campus demonstrations. One college where feeling ran high was Kent State University in Ohio. For several days students there clashed with local police; they broke windows and caused other damage to property. When the governor of Ohio called out the National Guard, angry students showered the soldiers with stones. During a noontime protest on May 4 the guardsmen, who were poorly trained in crowd control, suddenly opened fire. Four students were killed, two of them women who were merely passing by on their way to class.

While the nation reeled from this shock, two black students at Jackson State University were killed by Mississippi state policemen. A wave of student strikes followed, closing down hundreds of colleges, including many that had seen no previous unrest. Moderate students by the tens of thousands had joined with the radicals.

The almost universal condemnation of the invasion and of the way it had been planned and announced to the country shook Nixon hard. He backtracked, pulling American ground troops out of Cambodia quickly. But he did not change his Vietnam policy, and in fact Cambodia apparently stiffened his determination. As American ground troops were withdrawn, he stepped up air attacks. The balance of forces remained in uneasy equilibrium through 1971. But late in March 1972 the North Vietnamese again mounted a series of assaults throughout South Vietnam. The president responded with heavier bombing, and he ordered the approaches to Haiphong and other northern ports sown with mines to cut off the communists' supplies.

Détente

But in the midst of these aggressive actions, Nixon and his principal foreign policy adviser, Henry Kissinger, devised a bold and ingenious diplomatic offensive. First Nixon sent Kissinger secretly to

China and the Soviet Union to prepare the way for summit meetings with the communist leaders. Both the Chinese and the Russians agreed to the meetings, so in February 1972, Nixon and Kissinger flew to Peking to consult with Mao Tse-tung, Premier Chou En-lai, and other Chinese officials. The United States agreed to support the admission of China to the United Nations and to develop economic and cultural exchanges with the Chinese. Although these results appeared small, Nixon's visit, ending more than 20 years of adamantine American refusal to accept Mao's revolution, marked a dramatic reversal; as such it was hailed in the United States and elsewhere in the world.

In May, Nixon and Kissinger flew to Moscow. This trip also produced striking results. The mere fact that it took place while war still raged in Vietnam was remarkable. More important, however, the meeting resulted in a Strategic Arms Limitation Treaty (SALT). The two powers agreed to stop making nuclear ballistic missiles and to reduce the number of antiballistic missiles in their arsenals to 200.

Nixon and Kissinger called the new policy *détente,* a French term meaning the relaxation of tensions between governments. They sought not so much harmony as agreement as to the rules governing their rivalry with the Chinese and especially with the Soviets. SALT did not end the production of atomic weapons, but such was the worldwide fear of a nuclear holocaust that any check on American and Russian arms production was encouraging. That both China and the Soviet Union had been willing to work for improved relations with the United States *before* America withdrew from Vietnam was also significant. This fact, plus the failure of their offensive to overwhelm South Vietnam, led the North Vietnamese to make diplomatic concessions in the interest of getting the United States out of the war. Kissinger began negotiating seriously with their representatives in Paris in the summer of 1972. By October the draft of a settlement

President and Mrs. Nixon talking with Mao Tse-tung and Chou En-lai through an interpreter during the Nixon trip to Peking in February 1972.

calling for a cease-fire in place, the return of American prisoners of war, and the withdrawal of United States forces from Vietnam had been hammered out. Shortly before the presidential election Kissinger announced that peace was "at hand."

Nixon in Triumph

A few days later President Nixon was reelected, defeating the Democratic candidate, Senator George McGovern of South Dakota, in a landslide—521 electoral votes to 17. McGovern carried only Massachusetts and the District of Columbia.

McGovern's campaign had been hampered by divisions within the Democratic party and by the discovery, shortly after the nominating convention, that the vice-presidential candidate, Senator Thomas Eagleton of Missouri, had in the past undergone electric shock treatments following serious psychological difficulties. After some hesitation, which left many voters with the impression that he was indecisive, McGovern forced Eagleton to withdraw. Sargent Shriver, former head of the Peace Corps, took Eagleton's place on the ticket. The affair hurt McGovern badly. Nevertheless, Nixon understandably interpreted his convincing triumph as an indication that the people approved of everything for which he stood.

Suddenly Nixon loomed as one of the most powerful and successful presidents in American history. His bold attack on inflation, his tough-minded handling of the foreign trade question, even his harsh Vietnamese policy suggested decisiveness and self-confidence, qualities he had often seemed to lack. His willingness, despite his long history as a militant "cold warrior," to negotiate with the communist nations in order to arrive at a détente that would lessen world tensions indicated a new flexibility and reasonableness. His landslide victory appeared to demonstrate that a large majority of the people approved his way of tackling the major problems of the times.

His first reaction was to try to extract more favorable terms from the Vietnamese communists. Announcing that they were not bargaining in good faith over the remaining details of the peace treaty, he resumed the bombing of North Vietnam in December 1972, this time sending the mighty B-52s directly over Hanoi and other cities. The destructiveness of the attacks was great, but their effective-

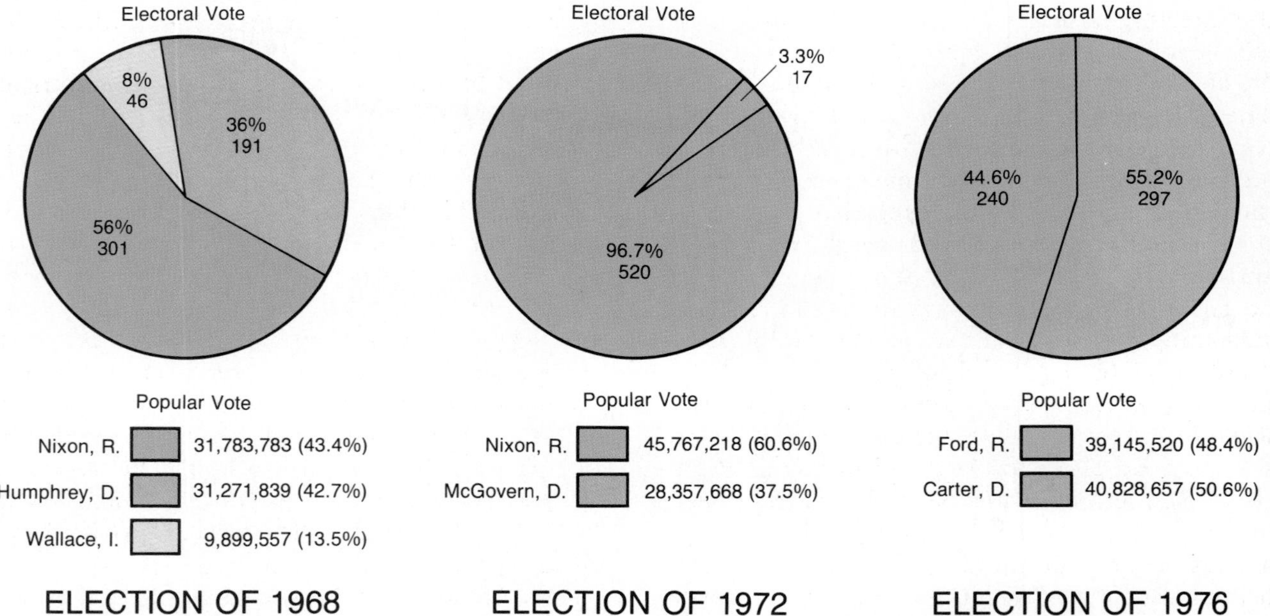

REPUBLICAN ADVANCE CHECKED

ness as a means of forcing concessions from the North Vietnamese was at best debatable, and they led for the first time to the loss of large numbers of the big strategic bombers.

Nevertheless, both sides had much to gain from ending the war. In January 1973 a settlement was finally reached. The North Vietnamese retained control of large sections of the South, and they agreed to release American prisoners of war within 60 days. When this was accomplished, the last American troops were pulled out of Vietnam. Nearly 46,000 Americans had died in the long war, and over 300,000 more had been wounded. The cost had reached a staggering $109 billion.

Whatever the price, the war was over for the United States, and Nixon took the credit for having ended it. He immediately turned to domestic issues, determined, he made clear, to change the direction in which the nation had been moving for decades. He sought on the one hand to strengthen the power of the presidency vis-à-vis Congress and on the other to decentralize administration by encouraging state and local management of government programs. He announced that he intended to reduce the interference of the federal government in the affairs of individuals. People should be more self-reliant, he said, and he denounced what he called "permissiveness." Overconcern for the interests of blacks and other minorities must end. Criminals should be punished "without pity." No person or group should be coddled by the state. These aims brought Nixon into conflict with liberal congressmen of both parties, with the leaders of minority groups, and with people concerned about the increasing power of the executive.

The conflict came to a head over the president's anti-inflation policy. After his second inauguration he ended Phase II price and wage controls and substituted Phase III, which depended on voluntary "restraints" (except in the areas of food, health care, and construction). This approach did not work. Prices soared; it was the most rapid inflation since the Korean War. In an effort to check the rise, Nixon set a rigid limit on federal expenditures; to keep within the limit, he cut back or abolished a large number of social welfare programs, and he reduced federal grants in support of science and education. He even impounded (refused to spend) funds already appropriated by Congress for purposes of which he disapproved.

Impoundment created a furor on Capitol Hill, and when Congress, despite the fact that the Democrats had a majority in both houses, failed to override presidential vetoes of bills challenging his policy, it appeared that Nixon was in total command. The White House staff, headed by H. R. Haldeman ("the Prussian") and John Ehrlichman, dominated the Washington bureaucracy like princes of the blood or oriental viziers and dealt with legislators as though they were dealing with lackeys or eunuchs. When asked to account for their actions they took refuge behind the shield of executive privilege: the doctrine, never before applied so broadly, that discussions and communications within the executive branch were confidential and therefore immune from congressional scrutiny. Critics began to grumble about a new "imperial presidency." No one seemed capable of checking Nixon at any point.

Watergate

On March 19, 1973, James McCord, a former FBI agent accused of burglary, wrote a letter to the judge presiding at his trial. His act precipitated a series of disclosures that disrupted and then destroyed the Nixon administration.

McCord had been employed during the 1972 presidential campaign as a security officer of the Committee to Re-elect the President (CREEP). At about 1 A.M. on June 17, 1972, he and four other men had broken into Democratic headquarters at the Watergate, an apartment house and office building complex in Washington. The burglars had been caught rifling files and installing electronic eavesdropping devices. Two other Republican campaign officials were soon implicated. Their arrest aroused suspicions that the Republican party was behind the break-in. Nixon denied this. "I can say categorically," he announced on June 22, "that no one on the White House staff, no one in this Administration presently employed, was involved in this very bizarre incident." Most people evidently took the president at his word, and the affair did not materially affect the election. When brought to trial early in 1973, most of the defendants pleaded guilty.

McCord, who did not, was convicted by the jury. Before Judge John J. Sirica imposed sentences on the culprits, however, McCord wrote his letter. High Republican officials had known about the burglary in advance and had persuaded most of the defendants to keep their connection secret, McCord claimed. Perjury had been committed during the trial.

The truth of McCord's charges swiftly became apparent. The head of CREEP, Jeb Stuart Magruder, and President Nixon's lawyer, John W. Dean III, admitted their involvement. Dean claimed in testimony before a special Senate Watergate investigation committee headed by Sam Ervin, Jr., of North Carolina, that Nixon had participated in efforts to cover up the affair. Among the disclosures that emerged over the following months were these:

That the acting director of the FBI, L. Patrick Gray, had destroyed documents related to the case.

That large sums of money had been paid the burglars at the instigation of the White House to insure their silence.

That agents of the Nixon administration had burglarized the office of a psychiatrist, seeking evidence against one of his patients, Daniel Ellsberg, who had been charged with leaking classified documents relating to the Vietnam War. (This disclosure led to the immediate dismissal of the charges against Ellsberg by the presiding judge.)

That the Central Intelligence Agency had (perhaps unwittingly) supplied equipment used in this burglary.

That CREEP officials had attempted to disrupt the campaigns of leading Democratic candidates during the 1972 primaries in a number of illegal ways.

That a number of corporations had made large contributions to the Nixon reelection campaign in violation of federal law.

That E. Howard Hunt, one of the Watergate criminals, had earlier forged State Department documents in an effort to make it appear that President Kennedy had been implicated in the assassination of President Ngo Dinh Diem of South Vietnam.

That the Nixon administration had placed wiretaps on the telephones of some of its own officials as well as on those of newspapermen critical of its policies without first obtaining authorization from the courts.

These revelations led to the discharge of John Dean and to the resignations of most of Nixon's closest advisers, including Haldeman, Ehrlichman, and Attorney General Richard Kleindienst. They also raised the question of the president's personal connection with the scandals. This he steadfastly denied. He insisted that he would investigate the Watergate affair thoroughly and see that the guilty were punished. He refused, however, to allow investigators to examine White House documents, again on grounds of executive privilege, which he continued to assert in very broad terms.

In the face of Nixon's denials, John Dean, testifying under oath before the Ervin committee, stated flatly and in circumstantial detail that the president had been closely involved in the Watergate coverup. (Before testifying, Dean consulted with the conservative Senator Barry Goldwater, a Nixon supporter. When he explained what he was going to say, Goldwater replied: "Hell, I'm not surprised. That goddam Nixon has been lying all of his life.") Dean had been a persuasive witness, but—unlike Goldwater—many people were reluctant to believe that a president could lie so cold-bloodedly to the entire country. Therefore, when it came out during later hearings of the Ervin committee that the president had systematically made secret tape recordings of White House conversations and telephone calls, the disclosure caused a sensation. It seemed obvious that these tapes would settle the question of Nixon's involvement once and for all. Again he refused to allow access to the evidence.

One result of the scandals and of Nixon's attitude was a precipitous decline in his standing in public opinion polls. Calls for his resignation, even for impeachment, began to be heard. Yielding to pressure, he agreed to the appointment of an "independent" special prosecutor to investigate the Watergate affair, and he promised the appointee, Professor Archibald Cox of the Harvard Law School, full cooperation.

Cox swiftly aroused the president's ire by seeking access to White House records, including the tapes, and by digging into a number of other questions, such as the relationship between the administration and the International Telephone and Telegraph Company, which, it was charged, had offered to pay $400,000 toward the expenses of the 1972 Republican convention in return for favorable treatment of an antitrust case. When Nixon refused to turn over the tapes, Cox obtained a subpoena from Judge Sirica ordering him to do so. The administration appealed and lost in the appellate court. Then, while the case was headed for the

Supreme Court, Nixon ordered the new attorney general, Elliot Richardson, to dismiss Cox. Both Richardson, who had promised the Senate during his confirmation hearings that the special prosecutor would have a free hand, and his chief assistant, William Ruckelshaus, resigned rather than do so. The solicitor general, third-ranking officer of the Justice Department, carried out Nixon's order.

These events, which occurred on Saturday, October 20, were promptly dubbed the Saturday Night Massacre. They caused an outburst of public indignation. Congress was bombarded by thousands of letters and telegrams demanding the president's impeachment. The House Judiciary Committee, headed by Peter W. Rodino, Jr., of New Jersey, began an investigation to see if enough evidence for impeachment existed.

Once again Nixon backed down. He agreed to turn over the tapes to Judge Sirica with the understanding that while relevant materials would be presented to the grand jury investigating the Watergate affair, nothing would be revealed to the public. He then named a new special prosecutor, Leon Jaworski, and promised him access to whatever White House documents he needed. However, it soon came out that some of the tapes were missing and that an important section of another had been deliberately erased.

Gary Trudeau and his politically biting cartoon strip Doonesbury *enlivened the Vietnam and Watergate years.* Doonesbury *became the first cartoon strip to win a Pulitzer Prize. (Ron Ziegler was President Nixon's press secretary.)*

More Troubles

The nation had never before experienced such a series of morale-shattering crises. While the seemingly unending complications of Watergate were unfolding during 1973, a number of unrelated disasters struck. First, pushed by a shortage of grains resulting from massive Russian purchases authorized by the administration as part of its détente with the Soviet Union, food prices shot up—wheat from $1.45 a bushel to over $5. Nixon imposed another price freeze, which led to shortages, and when the freeze was lifted, prices resumed their steep ascent. Then Vice-President Agnew (defender of law and order, foe of permissiveness) was accused of income tax fraud and of having accepted bribes while county executive of Baltimore and governor of Maryland. After vehemently denying all the charges for two months, Agnew (to escape a jail term) admitted in October that he had been guilty of tax evasion and resigned as vice-president. (He was fined $10,000 and placed on three years' probation, and the Justice Department published a 40,000-word description of his wrongdoings.)

Under the new Twenty-fifth Amendment, President Nixon nominated Gerald R. Ford of Michigan as vice-president, and he was confirmed by Congress. Ford, a graduate of the University of Michigan and the Yale Law School, had served continuously in Congress since 1949, as minority leader since 1964. His positions on public issues were close to Nixon's; he was an internationalist in foreign affairs and both conservative and a convinced Republican partisan on domestic issues.

Not long after the Agnew fiasco, Nixon, responding to charges that he had paid almost no income taxes during his presidency, published his 1969–1972 returns. They showed that he had paid only about $1,600 in two years during which his income had exceeded half a million dollars. Although Nixon claimed that his returns were perfectly legal—he had taken huge deductions for the gift of some of his vice-presidential papers to the National Archives—the legality and the propriety of his deductions were questionable. Combined with charges that millions of dollars of public funds had been spent on improvements for his private residences in California and Florida, the tax issue further eroded his reputation, so much so that he felt obliged, during a televised press conference, to assure the audience: "I am not a crook."

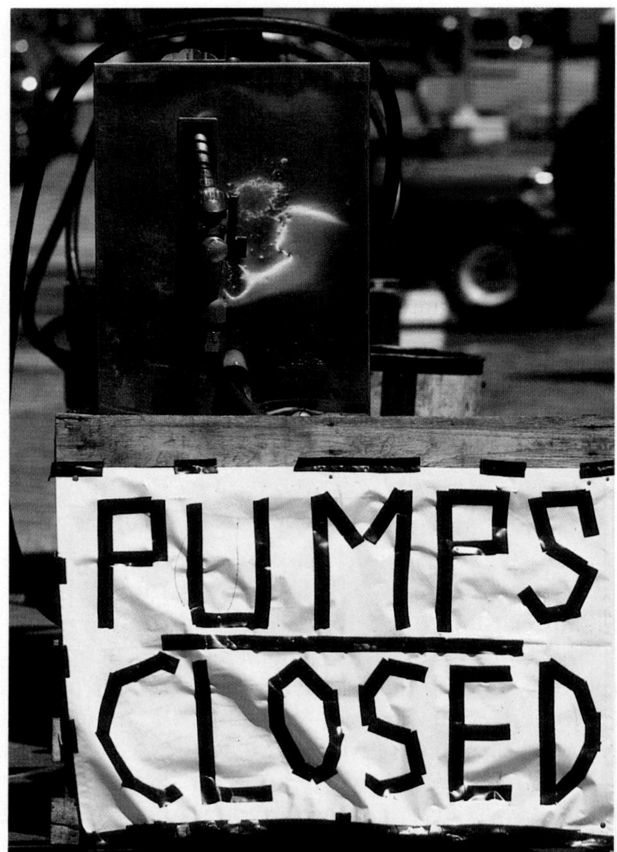

Gas stations all over the country began running out of gas in 1973; the shortage worsened through the winter and into 1974.

The Oil Crisis

Still another disaster followed as a result of the new war that broke out in October 1973 between Israel and the Arab states. The fighting, while bloody, was brief and inconclusive; a truce was soon arranged under the auspices of the United States and the Soviet Union. But in an effort to force western nations to compel Israel to withdraw from lands held since the "six-day" war of 1967, the Arabs cut off oil shipments to the United States, Japan, and most of western Europe. A worldwide energy crisis ensued.

The immediate shortage resulting from the Arab oil boycott was ended by the patient diplomacy of Henry Kissinger, whom Nixon had made secretary of state at the beginning of his second administration. After weeks of negotiating in the spring of 1974, first with Egypt and Israel, then with Syria and Israel, he obtained a tentative agreement which involved the withdrawal of Israel from some of the territory it had occupied in the 1967 war. The Arab nations then lifted the boycott.

A revolution had taken place. From the middle of the 19th century until after World War II the United States had produced far more oil than it could use. However, the phenomenal expansion of oil consumption that occurred after the war soon absorbed the surplus. By the late 1960s American car owners were driving more than a trillion miles a year. Petroleum was being used to manufacture nylon and other synthetic fibers as well as paints, insecticides, fertilizers, and many plastic products. Oil and natural gas became the principal fuels for home heating. Natural gas in particular was used increasingly in factories and electric utility plants, because it was less polluting than coal and most other fuels. The Clean Air Act of 1965 speeded the process of conversion from coal to gas by countless industrial consumers. Because of these developments, at the outbreak of the 1973 Arab-Israeli war the United States was importing one-third of its oil.

In 1960 the principal oil exporters—Venezuela, Saudi Arabia, Kuwait, Iraq, and Iran—had formed a cartel, the Organization of Petroleum Exporting Countries (OPEC). For many years OPEC had been unable to control the world price of oil, which, on the eve of the 1973 war, was about $3 a barrel. The success of the Arab oil boycott served to unite the members of OPEC, and when the boycott was lifted they boldly announced that the price was going up to $11.65 a barrel.

The announcement caused consternation throughout the industrial world. Soaring prices for oil meant soaring prices for everything made from petroleum or with petroleum-powered machinery. In the United States gasoline prices doubled overnight and the trend of all prices rose at a rate of over 10 percent a year. This "double-digit" inflation, which afflicted nearly all the countries of the world, added considerably to President Nixon's woes.

The Judgment: Expletive Deleted

Meanwhile, special prosecutor Jaworski continued his investigation of the Watergate scandals, and the House Judiciary Committee pursued its study of the impeachment question. In March 1974 a grand jury indicted Haldeman, Ehrlichman, former attorney general John Mitchell, who had been head of CREEP at the time of the break-in, and four other White House aides for conspiring to block the Watergate investigation. The jurors also named Nixon an "unindicted co-conspirator," Jaworski having informed them that their power to indict a president was constitutionally questionable. Judge Sirica thereupon turned over the jury's evidence against Nixon to the Judiciary Committee. Then both the Internal Revenue Service and a joint congressional committee, having separately audited the president's income tax returns, announced that most of his deductions had been unjustified. The IRS assessed him nearly half a million dollars in taxes and interest, which he agreed to pay.

In an effort to check the mounting criticism, Nixon late in April released edited transcripts of the tapes he had turned over to the court the previous November. If he had expected the material to convince the public that he had been ignorant of the attempt to cover up the administration's connection with Watergate, he was sadly mistaken. In addition to much incriminating evidence, the transcripts provided a fascinating and to most persons shocking view of how he conducted himself in private. His repeated use of foul language, so out of keeping with his public image, offended millions. The phrase "expletive deleted," inserted in place of words considered too vulgar for publication in family newspapers, became overnight a catchword. Nixon appeared to be ignorant of the simplest legal principles. In conversations he seemed confused and indecisive and lacking in any concern for the public interest. The publication of the transcripts led even some of his strongest supporters to demand that he resign. And once the Judiciary Committee obtained the actual tapes, it became clear that the White House transcripts were in crucial respects inaccurate. Much material prejudicial to the president's case had been suppressed.

Yet impeaching a president seemed so drastic a step that many people felt more direct proof of Nixon's involvement in the cover-up was necessary. Nixon insisted that all the relevant information was contained in these tapes; he adamantly refused to turn over others to the special prosecutor or the Judiciary Committee.

With the defendants in the Watergate case demanding access to tapes that they claimed would prove their innocence, Jaworski was compelled either to obtain them or to risk having the charges dismissed on the ground that the government was withholding evidence. He therefore subpoenaed 64 additional tapes. Nixon, through his lawyer James St. Clair, refused to obey the subpoena. Swiftly the case of *United States* v. *Richard M. Nixon* went to the Supreme Court.

In the summer of 1974—after so many months of alarms and crises—the Watergate drama reached its climax. The Judiciary Committee, following months of study of the evidence behind closed doors, decided to conduct its deliberations in open session. While millions watched on television, 38 members of the House of Representatives debated the charges. The discussions revealed both the thoroughness of the investigation and the soul-searching efforts of the representatives to render an impartial judgment. Three articles of impeachment were adopted. They charged the president with obstructing justice, misusing the powers of his office, and failing to obey the committee's subpoenas. Except in the case of the last article, many of the Republicans on the committee joined with the Democrats in voting aye, a clear indication that the full House would vote to impeach.

DEPRESSION, PROSPERITY, AND INFLATION, 1921–1985

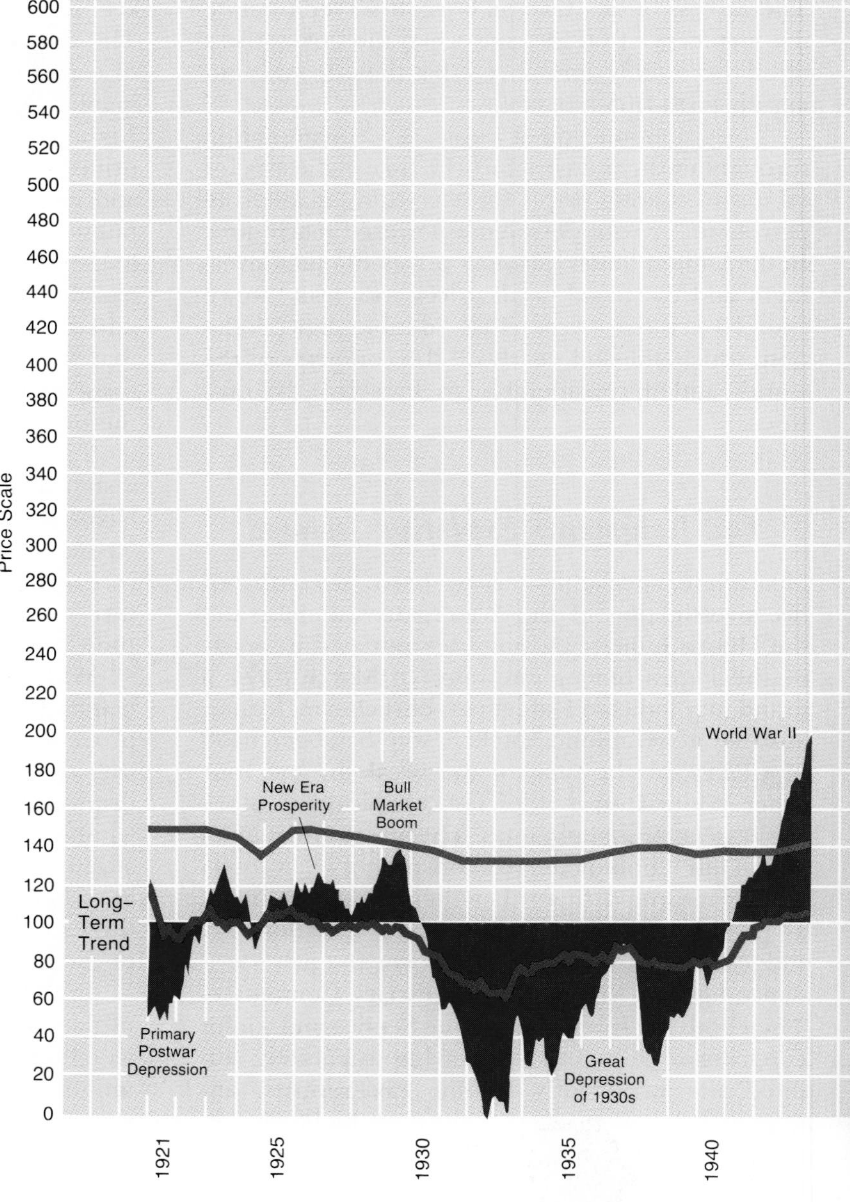

Here is the third of three price graphs. The price scale on the left axis applies to the blue line; it shows wholesale prices as they have varied around the long-term trend line of 100. Prices were much below normal during the Great Depression of the 1930s and were held down by price controls during World War II, but since then they have sky-rocketed, especially during OPEC oil cartel petroleum price hikes in the 1970s. On the right axis scale is the price of a gallon of gas; the green curve reflects OPEC's inflationary influence.

On the eve of the debates, the Supreme Court had ruled unanimously that the president must turn over the 64 subpoenaed tapes to the special prosecutor. Executive privilege had its place, the Court stated, but no person, not even a president, could "withhold evidence that is demonstrably relevant in a criminal trial." For reasons that soon became obvious, Nixon seriously considered defying the Court. Only when convinced that to do so would make his impeachment and conviction certain—and would compel his lawyer, St. Clair, to withdraw from the case—did he agree to comply.

He would not, however, resign. Even if the House impeached him, he was counting on his ability to hold the support of at least 34 senators (one-third plus one of the full Senate) to escape conviction. But events were passing beyond his control. The 64 subpoenaed tapes had to be transcribed

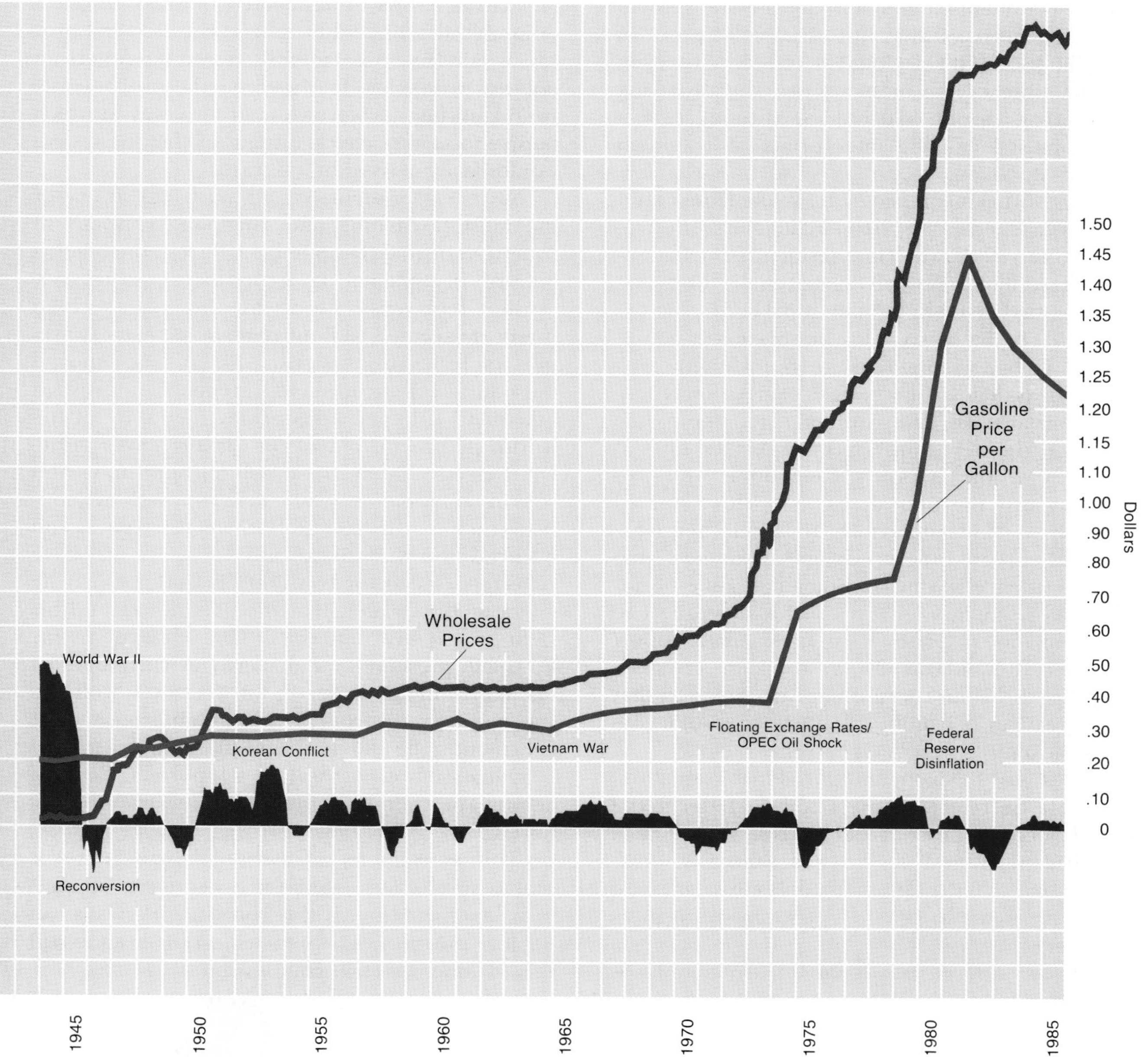

and analyzed; following the Supreme Court decision, Judge Sirica pointedly ordered St. Clair to prepare this material promptly.

Incredibly, up to this time St. Clair had not listened to the tapes; Nixon had assured him that they contained no relevant evidence and had refused to allow him to judge the correctness of this statement for himself. Now St. Clair *had* to listen, and when he did, Nixon's fate was sealed. Three recorded conversations between the president and H. R. Haldeman on June 23, 1972 (less than a week after the break-in and only one day after Nixon had assured the nation that no one in the White House had been involved in the affair), proved conclusively that Nixon had tried to obstruct justice by engaging the CIA in an effort to persuade the FBI not to follow up leads in the case on the spurious ground that national security was involved.

The president's defenders had insisted not so much that he was innocent as that solid proof of his guilt had not been demonstrated. Where, in the metaphor of the moment, was the "smoking gun"? That weapon had now been found, and it bore unmistakably the fingerprints of President Richard M. Nixon.

Exactly what happened in the White House after St. Clair listened to the Nixon-Haldeman conversations is not yet known. The president's chief advisers pressed him to release the material at once and admit he had erred in holding it back. This he did on August 5; that in so doing he specifically admitted that he had withheld information from his lawyer suggests that St. Clair, whose professional reputation was at stake, had played a major role. When they read the new transcripts, all the Republican members of the Judiciary Committee who had voted against the impeachment articles reversed themselves. Understandably, they felt betrayed; they had accepted the president's assurances that all the evidence was in, and they had gone on record before millions of eyes in his defense. The last remnants of Nixon's congressional support crumbled. Republican leaders told him categorically that the House would impeach him and that no more than a handful of senators would vote to acquit him.

On August 8 Nixon announced his resignation. "Dear Mr. Secretary," his terse official letter to the secretary of state ran, "I hereby resign the Office of President of the United States. Sincerely, Richard Nixon." The resignation took effect at noon on August 9, when Gerald Ford was sworn in as president.

The meaning of "Watergate" became immediately the subject of much speculation. Whether Nixon's crude efforts to dominate Congress, to crush or inhibit dissent, and to subvert the electoral process would have permanently altered the American political system had they succeeded is probably beyond knowing. However, the orderly way in which these efforts were checked suggests that the system would have survived in any case.

Nixon's own drama is and must remain one of the most fascinating and enigmatic episodes in American history. Despite his fall from the heights because of personal flaws, his was not a tragedy in the Greek sense. Even when he finally yielded power he seemed without remorse or even awareness of his transgressions. Although he enjoyed the pomp and circumstance attendant on his high office and trumpeted his achievements to all the world, he was devoid of the classic hero's pride. Did he really intend to smash all opposition and rule like a tyrant, or was he driven by lack of confidence in himself? His stubborn aggressiveness and his overblown view of executive privilege may have reflected a need for constant reassurance that he *was* a mighty leader, that the nation accepted his right to exercise authority. One element in his downfall, preserved for posterity in videotapes of his television appearances, was that even while he was assuring the country of his innocence most vehemently, he did not look like a victim of the machinations of overzealous supporters. Perhaps at some profound level he did not want to be believed.

This explanation of Richard Nixon, however tentative, is at least comforting—it makes him appear less menacing. If it is correct, Americans can deplore the injuries he inflicted on society and still feel for him a certain compassion.

SUPPLEMENTARY READING

Titles marked with an asterisk have been published in paperback

On the election of 1968, T. H. White's **The Making of the President, 1968*** (1969) is lively and entertaining, while Joe McGinniss, **The Selling of the President, 1968*** (1969), is a fascinating account of the Republican advertising and television campaign. There is as yet no adequate biography of Nixon, but his own **RN: The Memoirs of Richard Nixon** (1978) offers some insights into his character and view of political life, and Garry Wills, **Nixon Agonistes*** (1970), is a thoughtful though unfriendly analysis. See also William Safire, **Before the Fall** (1975), and Rowland Evans, Jr., and R. D. Novak, **Nixon in the White House*** (1971). White's **The Making of the President, 1972*** (1973) and **Breach of Faith: the Fall of Richard Nixon** (1975) are less satisfactory than his earlier volumes.

The literature on the war in Vietnam is already enormous. Stanley Karnow, **Vietnam: A History** (1983), is a straightforward narrative account, but see also Guenter Lewy, **America in Vietnam*** (1980), Frances FitzGerald, **Fire in the Lake*** (1972), and David Halberstam, **The Best and the Brightest*** (1972), which contains a mass of detail on the evolution of American policy, based on extensive interviews. William Shawcross, **Side-Show: Kissinger, Nixon, and the Destruction of Cambodia*** (1979), is extremely critical, and Norman Mailer, **The Armies of the Night*** (1968), is a vivid account of an antiwar demonstration in Washington.

R. S. Litwak, **Détente and the Nixon Doctrine** (1984), is a useful study of U.S.-Russian relations in the Nixon era, and Henry Kissinger's memoirs, **White House Years** (1979) and **Years of Upheaval** (1982), are important though, like most such works, self-serving.

A convenient summary of the almost infinite complexities of the Watergate affair is New York Times (ed.), **The End of a Presidency*** (1974), but see also Carl Bernstein and Robert Woodward, **All the President's Men*** (1974) and **Final Days*** (1976), J. W. Dean, **Blind Ambition*** (1976), and Leon Jaworski, **The Right and the Power*** (1976).

31
Our Times

"Shucks, I don't think [Jerry Ford] can chew gum and walk at the same time. . . . He's a nice fellow, but he spent too much time playing football without a helmet." LYNDON B. JOHNSON

"Call me Jimmy." PRESIDENT JAMES EARL CARTER, *1977*

"[Reagan] has contributed a spirit of good will and grace to the Presidency and American life generally." SENATOR EDWARD M. KENNEDY, *1986*

The country greeted the accession of Gerald Ford to the presidency with a collective sigh of relief. Most observers considered Ford unimaginative, certainly not brilliant. But he was hardworking and—most important under the circumstances—his record was untouched by scandal. Although he was an almost automaton-like Republican partisan, nearly all the Democrats in Congress liked him. He was Nixon's opposite as a person, being gregarious and open, and he stated repeatedly that he took a dim view of Nixon's high-handed way of dealing with Congress. The president and Congress must work together in the nation's interest, he insisted. Being a most ordinary person, earnest but limited, Ford appeared unlikely to venture beyond conventional limits or to act rashly. This was what nearly everyone wanted of the president in the wake of Nixon.

Ford as President

Ford obviously desired to live up to public expectations, yet he was soon embroiled in controversy and subject to considerable criticism, not all of it partisan. At the outset he roused widespread resentment by pardoning Nixon for whatever crimes he had committed in office, even any, if such existed, that had not yet come to light. Not many Americans wanted to see the ex-president lodged in jail; nevertheless, pardoning him seemed both illogical and incomprehensible when he had admitted no guilt and had not yet been officially charged with any crime. (Nixon's instant acceptance of the pardon while claiming to have done no wrong was also illogical, but it was not incomprehensible.)

Ugly rumors of a deal worked out before Nixon resigned were soon circulating, for the pardon seemed grossly unfair. Why should Nixon go scot-free when his chief underlings, Mitchell, Haldeman, and Erlichman, were being brought to trial for their part in the Watergate scandal? (All three were eventually convicted and jailed.)

Ford displayed inconsistency and apparent incompetence in managing the economy. He announced that inflation was the major problem and asked patriotic citizens to signify their willingness to fight it by wearing WIN buttons (Whip Inflation Now). Almost immediately the economy entered a precipitous slump. Production fell and the unemployment rate rose above 9 percent. The president was forced to ask for tax cuts and other measures aimed at stimulating business activity. While pressing for these measures, he continued to fulminate against spending money on social programs designed to help the urban poor.

That Ford would never act rashly proved to be an incorrect assumption. In the spring of 1975 North Vietnamese forces increased their attacks in South Vietnam. Dispirited, short of guns and ammunition, and incompetently led, the South Vietnamese armies fell back, then fled headlong, then dissolved. As the communists advanced, tens of thousands of South Vietnamese asked for asylum in the United States, and about 140,000 were successfully evacuated. Thousands more were callously abandoned, though their earlier collaboration with the Americans made their situation in a communist-controlled Vietnam precarious. Ford had always taken a hawkish position on the Vietnam War. As the military situation deteriorated, he urged Congress to pour more arms into the South to stem the North Vietnamese advance. The legislators flatly refused to do so, and late in April Saigon fell. The long Vietnam War was finally over.

Two weeks earlier local communists of a particularly radical persuasion had overturned the pro-American regime in Cambodia. On May 12 Cambodian naval forces seized the American merchant ship *Mayaguez* in the Gulf of Siam. President Ford, apparently frustrated by his inability to prevent the communists from taking over South Vietnam and Cambodia, reacted to the seizure without fully investigating the situation or allowing the new regime time to respond to his perfectly proper demand that the *Mayaguez* and its crew be freed. He ordered marine units to attack Tang Island, where the captured vessel had been taken. The assault succeeded in that the Cambodians released the *Mayaguez* and its crew of 39, but 38 marines died in the operation. Since the Cambodians had released the ship before the marines struck, Ford's reflexive response was probably unnecessary, though it was popular with a majority of Americans.

After some hesitation Ford decided to seek the Republican presidential nomination in 1976. He was opposed by ex-governor Ronald Reagan of California, a movie actor turned politician who was the darling of the Republican right wing. Reagan's campaign was well organized and well financed.

He was an excellent speaker, where Ford proved somewhat bumbling on the stump. The contest was close, both candidates winning important primaries and gathering substantial blocs of delegates in nonprimary states. At the convention in August, Ford obtained a slim majority. That he did not win easily, possessed as he was of the advantage of incumbency, made his chances of election in November appear slim.

In the meantime the Democrats had chosen James Earl Carter, a former governor of Georgia, as their candidate. Carter's rise from almost total obscurity was even more spectacular than that of George McGovern in the 1972 campaign and was made possible by the same forces: television, the democratization of the delegate-selection process, and the absence of a dominant leader among the Democrats.

Carter had been a naval officer and a substantial peanut farmer and warehouse owner before entering politics. He was elected governor of Georgia in 1970. While governor he won something of a reputation as a southern public official who treated black citizens fairly. (He hung a portrait of Martin Luther King, Jr., in his office.) Carter's political style was informal—he preferred to be called Jimmy. During the campaign for delegates he turned his inexperience in national politics to advantage, emphasizing his lack of familiarity with the Washington establishment rather than apologizing for it, and trying to make a virtue of being an "outsider." He repeatedly called attention to his integrity and deep religious faith. "I'll never lie to you," he promised voters, a pledge that no candidate would have bothered to give before Nixon's disgrace. Carter entered nearly all the Democratic primaries and campaigned hard in nonprimary states. Running against many different candidates, he won few decisive victories. Nevertheless, he accumulated delegates steadily and went to the convention in New York City in July with a solid majority.

When the final contest began, Carter had a large lead. Most of it soon evaporated. Reagan supporters among the Republicans swung behind Ford, and the prestige of the presidency was another asset. Both candidates were vague with respect to issues. Ford made much of the need to control inflation, Carter of the distressingly high unemployment that the nation was enduring. Three televised debates between the candidates attracted huge audiences without enlightening the public or generating a trend toward either candidate.

As election day approached, pollsters predicted an extremely close contest, and they were right: Carter won, 297 electoral votes to 241, having carried most of the South, including Texas, and a few large industrial states. A key element in his victory was the fact that he got an overwhelming majority of the black vote (partly on his record in Georgia, partly because Ford had been unsympathetic toward the demands of the urban poor). He also ran well in districts dominated by labor union members and throughout the South. The public's wish to punish the party of Richard Nixon was probably a further reason for his victory.

The Carter Presidency

Carter shone brightly in comparison with Nixon, and he seemed more forward-looking and imaginative than Ford. He tried to give a tone of democratic simplicity and moral fervor to his administration. After delivering his inaugural address, he walked with his wife and small daughter Amy in the parade from the Capitol to the White House instead of riding in a limousine. He enrolled Amy, a fourth grader, in a largely black Washington public school. For his first talk on television he wore a sweater instead of a coat and tie, an advertisement for both his informality and the need to conserve energy by turning down thermostats. Soon after taking office he held a "call-in"; for two hours he answered questions phoned in by people from all over the country. From time to time thereafter he organized "town meetings" in small cities at which he fielded questions and chatted with ordinary citizens.

In foreign affairs Carter announced that he intended to deal with all nations in a fair and humane way. He would put defense of "basic human rights" before all other concerns. At home he would fight inflation by reducing government spending and balancing the budget, and he would stimulate the economy by cutting taxes and creating jobs for the unemployed. He advanced an admirable if complicated plan for conserving energy and reducing the dependence of the United States on OPEC oil.

In the front row, from the left: Israeli Prime Minister Begin, President Carter, President Sadat of Egypt, and Moshe Dayan of Israel. The four were on a break from their negotiations at Camp David, so Carter gave them a tour of the battlefield at Gettysburg.

Carter achieved several notable diplomatic successes. He negotiated treaties with Panama that provided for the gradual transfer of the isthmian canal to that nation and guaranteed its neutrality (see footnote, page 649). Critics denounced this "retreat," but in 1978, after long debate, the Senate ratified the treaties. The president also carried forward the Nixon-Ford policy of restoring relations with Communist China by ending official American recognition of Taiwan. In January 1979 the first exchange of ambassadors with the People's Republic of China took place. Six months later another Strategic Arms Limitation Treaty (SALT II) was signed with the Soviet Union.

Carter's most striking diplomatic achievement was the so-called Camp David Agreement with Israel and Egypt. Avoiding war in the Middle East was crucial because war in that part of the world was likely to result in the cutting off of oil supplies from the Arab nations. In September 1978 the president of Egypt, Anwar Sadat, and Prime Minister Menachem Begin of Israel came to the United States at Carter's invitation to negotiate a peace treaty ending the state of war that had existed between their two countries for many years. For two weeks they conferred at Camp David, the presidential retreat outside the capital. Carter was in constant attendance, and his patient work as a mediator had much to do with their successful negotiations. In the treaty Israel promised to withdraw from territory captured from Egypt during the "six-day" war of 1967. Egypt in turn recognized Israel as a nation, the first Arab country to do so.

Carter's handling of domestic problems did not go nearly so well. He made many excellent appointments, but put so many Georgians in important posts that his administration took on a most parochial character. Six of seven top White House aides came from his home state, as did his attorney general, the director of the Office of Management and Budget, the ambassador to the United Nations, and many lesser officials. Most of these people, like their boss, had little or no experience in national affairs. The administration developed a reputation for submitting complicated proposals to Congress with great fanfare and then failing to follow them up.

Sometimes Carter seemed to forget about supposedly vital measures that he had claimed required urgent action. In fact his memory was fine; the trouble was that he became too involved in the details of too many issues. Whatever matter he was considering at the moment seemed to absorb him totally—other urgent matters were allowed to drift. When he was working with Sadat and Begin at Camp David, he paid almost no attention to anything else for nearly two weeks.

This tendency frequently caused him to shift policies sharply when he returned to matters he had put aside. One journalist counted seven distinct changes of approach in Carter's economic policy in three years. While running for office he had emphasized the need to restrain inflation, but early in 1977 he came out for a $50 income tax rebate for individuals that would almost surely have caused prices to rise. When that idea ran into stiff congressional resistance, Carter turned to something else. And so it went.

His energy policy was equally inconsistent. He proposed raising the tax on gasoline and imposing a new tax on "gas guzzlers," cars that got relatively few miles per gallon. But he did not press for these measures, and he waffled on the important question of deregulating the price of American crude oil until late in his term.

In the face of so much frustration it was perhaps only human that Carter tended to blame others for his troubles. In a heralded television speech he described a national "malaise" that, he said, had sapped the people's energies and undermined civic pride. Although there was some truth in this observation, the effect was to make the president seem both ineffective and petulant.

A Time of Troubles

National self-confidence was indeed at a low ebb. The crises of the Cold War had subsided and the hot war in Vietnam was over, but the United States had lost a considerable portion of its international prestige. To a degree this was unavoidable. The very success of American policies after World War II had something to do with the decline of American influence in the world. The Marshall Plan, for example, enabled the nations of western Europe to rebuild their economies; thereafter they were less dependent on outside aid, and in the course of pursuing their own interests they sometimes adopted policies that did not seem to be in the best interests of the United States. Under American occupation, Japan rebuilt its shattered economy. By the 1960s and 1970s it had become one of the world's leading manufacturing nations.

Similarly, to the extent that American aid to underdeveloped countries had improved their economies, they were more likely to act independently and not necessarily in ways that benefited the United States. On the other hand, when American aid was ineffective or used to bolster unpopular local regimes, American prestige also suffered. And the failure of the United States to achieve its objectives in the Vietnam War had a debilitating effect on its influence abroad long after the war ended.

At home the decay of the inner sections of the great cities was a continuing cause of concern. The older cities seemed almost beyond repair. Carter visited the South Bronx section of New York City in 1977. He was shocked to see block after block of rubble and rows of empty, fire-blackened buildings. He pledged that the federal government would clean up and rebuild this wasteland, but when his term ended that part of the South Bronx and similar parts of many cities remained barren ruins.

Crime rates were high in the inner cities, public transportation dilapidated and expensive, other city services undermanned and inefficient, the schools crowded, students' performances poor. Blacks, Hispanics, and other minorities made up a large percentage of the population in decaying urban areas. That they had to live in such surroundings made a mockery of the commitment made by the civil rights legislation of the 1960s and Lyndon Johnson's Great Society program to treat all people equally and improve the lives of the poor.

The most disturbing problem that vexed the nation in the Carter years was soaring inflation. Prices had been rising for an unprecedentedly long period and in recent years at an unprecedentedly rapid pace (see graph, page 916). In 1971 an inflation rate of 5 percent had so alarmed President Nixon that he had imposed a price freeze. In 1979 a 5 percent rate would have seemed almost deflationary—the actual rate was nearly 13 percent.

Double-digit inflation had a devastating effect on the poor, the retired, and others who were living on fixed incomes. However, the squeeze that price increases put on these unfortunates was only part of the damage done. Inflation discouraged people from making long-term investments, and as time passed and the rate of inflation increased, it caused many to stop saving entirely. People began to *anticipate* inflation. They bought goods they did not really need, and without much regard for cost, on the assumption that whatever today's price, tomorrow's would be much higher. This behavior increased demand and thereby pushed prices up still more. Put differently, when the interest paid by savings banks was lower than the inflation rate, it seemed foolish to save money.

At another level, a kind of "flight from money" began. Well-to-do individuals transferred their assets from cash to durable goods such as land and houses, gold, works of art, jewelry, rare postage stamps, and other "collectibles." Interest rates rose rapidly as lenders demanded higher returns to compensate for expected future inflation.

Congress raised the minimum wage to help low-paid workers cope with inflation. It pegged social security payments to the cost of living index in an effort to protect retirees. Thereafter, when prices rose social security payments went up automatically. The poor and the pensioners got some immediate relief, but the laws made balancing the federal budget more difficult and the increased spending power of the recipients caused further upward pressure on prices. Inflation seemed to be feeding upon itself, and the price spiral seemed unstoppable.

The federal government made matters worse in several ways. People's wages and salaries rose in response to inflation, but their taxes went up more rapidly because higher dollar incomes put them in higher tax brackets. This "bracket creep" caused resentment and frustration among middle-class families. There were "taxpayer revolts" as many people turned against long-accepted but expensive government programs for aiding the poor. Inflation also increased the government's need for money. Year after year it spent more than it received in taxes. By thus unbalancing the budget it pumped billions of dollars into the economy, and by borrowing to meet the deficits and pushing up interest rates, it increased the costs of all businesses that had to borrow.

In 1978 President Carter proposed voluntary wage and price guidelines in another effort to apply the brakes. Unions and manufacturers responded fairly well, but the guidelines did not apply to the prices that were going up most rapidly. These were oil, houses, and food. Finally Carter named a conservative banker, Paul A. Volcker, as chairman of the Federal Reserve Board. Volcker belonged to the monetarist school of economics, which taught that the way to check inflation was to limit the growth of the money supply. Under his direction the Board adopted a tight-money policy, which caused already high interest rates to soar.

High interest rates hurt all borrowers, but they were especially damaging to the automobile and housing industries. American car manufacturers had been experiencing hard times because of the competition of Japanese and European automobiles, which gave better gasoline mileage and were seemingly better built than most American vehicles. High interest charges depressed sales still more by raising monthly payments on car purchases beyond the means of many prospective buyers. Automobile workers were among the highest paid in American industry, but tens of thousands of them were out of work. One of the "Big Three" manufacturers, Chrysler, teetered on the edge of bankruptcy, saved only by government-guaranteed loans. Soaring mortgage rates had a similar effect on the sale of homes. The housing slump meant unemployment for thousands of carpenters, bricklayers, and other construction workers and bankruptcy for many builders.

The Iranian Crisis

It was unfair to blame Carter for all the nation's troubles and particularly for the inflation. Blame him people did, however, and by the autumn of 1979 his standing in public opinion polls was extremely low—barely one respondent in four approved his handling of his office. Blameless or not, he had failed to provide the fresh point of view and the firm leadership that he had promised in the 1976 campaign. His chances of being elected to a second term seemed dim.

At this point a dramatic upheaval in the Middle East revived his prospects. On November 4, 1979, about 400 armed Moslem militants broke into the American Embassy compound in Teheran, Iran, and took everyone within the walls captive.

Iran was a leading producer of petroleum and an enthusiastic member of OPEC. However, unlike the leaders of the Arab states, the shah of Iran, Mohammed Riza Pahlevi, had been a close ally of the United States. Over the years the shah had bought billions of dollars worth of American arms. Iran possessed the most powerful military force in the region; it seemed, as President Carter said in 1977, "an island of stability" in the troubled Middle East.

The appearance of stability was deceptive because the shah was extremely unpopular. He suppressed liberal opponents brutally. At the same time, his attempts to introduce western ideas and methods in Iran caused economic disruption and angered conservatives. Moslem religious leaders were particularly offended by such "radical" policies as the shah's tentative efforts to improve the position of women in Iranian society. Because his American-supplied army and his American-trained secret policy kept the shah in power, his opponents hated the United States almost as much as they hated their autocratic ruler.

Throughout 1977 riots and demonstrations convulsed Iran. When the shah's soldiers fired on protesters, the bloodshed caused more unrest. Early in 1978 the whole seemed to rise against him, and the shah was forced to flee the country. A revolutionary government headed by a revered religious leader, the Ayatollah Ruhollah Khomeini, who had recently returned to Iran in triumph after a long exile in France, assumed power.

The Iranian crisis produced striking visual images that appeared worldwide in the press and on TV. These militants burned the American flag a few days after they seized the embassy.

Khomeini denounced the United States, the "Great Satan" whose support of the shah, he claimed, had caused the Iranian people untold suffering. When President Carter allowed the shah, who had been living in Mexico, to come to the United States for medical treatment, the Iranian revolutionaries were convinced that an attempt would be made to restore him to his throne. The seizure of the Teheran embassy resulted.

The militants announced that the captive Americans would be held as hostages until the United States returned the shah to Iran for trial as a traitor. They also demanded that the shah's vast wealth be confiscated and surrendered to the Iranian government. Of course President Carter rejected these demands. (He had no choice in the matter; deporting the shah, who had entered the United States legally, and confiscating his property were not possible under American law.) Instead he froze Iranian assets in the United States and banned trade with Iran until the hostages were freed.

Carter wanted to rescue the hostages, but there seemed to be no way to do so. Even going to war would surely result in their execution—and the deaths of others as well. He gave some consideration to blockading Iranian ports in order to force their release, but that could have no immediate effect and it might alarm the Arab states and lead to another cutoff of Middle Eastern oil. And there was always the danger of Soviet intervention.

The American public and most foreign observers approved of the president's restraint. If he made any mistake, it was a consequence of his habit of focusing so intently on one matter at a time. This exaggerated the importance of the hostage issue. Some critics believed that Carter was playing into the hands of the Iranians by calling attention to the fact that they could hold the mighty United States at bay.

A stalemate developed. The Iranians released the women and black captives, but the others, more than 50 in number, were subjected to countless indignities and in some cases were physically abused. Months passed. Even after the shah, who was terminally ill with cancer, left the United States for Panama, the Iranians remained adamant.

The crisis produced a remarkable emotional response in the United States. For the first time since the Vietnam War the entire country agreed on something. One result of this was a revival of Carter's political fortunes. Before the attack on the Teheran embassy, Senator Edward M. Kennedy of Massachusetts, youngest brother of John F. Kennedy, had decided to run against Carter in the Democratic presidential primaries. He seemed a likely winner until the seizure of the hostages, but that event caused the public to rally round the president. Carter took clever political advantage of the national concern. He refused to campaign in the primaries, insisting (without good reason) that the crisis made his constant presence in Washington essential.

Meanwhile the Nixon-Kissinger policy of détente, which Carter continued, suffered a number of setbacks. The impact of Soviet grain purchases on prices while Nixon was still president caused considerable grumbling. Then Carter's emphasis on human rights focused attention on the Soviet government's restrictions on the freedom of its citizens to criticize the regime. The harsh treatment of dissidents and the government's refusal to allow Soviet Jews to leave the country further eroded American support for détente. So did Russian backing of a Marxist regime in the former Portuguese colony of Angola in southern Africa.

Then, in December 1979, the Soviet Union sent troops into Afghanistan in order to overthrow a government of which it disapproved. Since Afghanistan bordered Iran, some analysts believed that the invasion was a prelude to Soviet intervention in that troubled country.

Carter denounced the invasion and warned the Russians that he would use force if necessary to keep them out of Iran and the other lands bordering the Persian Gulf. He stopped shipments of American grain and technologically advanced products, such as computers, to the Soviet Union, and he withdrew the Strategic Arms Limitation Treaty (SALT II), which he had sent to the Senate for ratification. He refused to allow American athletes to compete in the Olympic games, which were held in the summer of 1980 in Moscow, and he began a new arms buildup. Most people seemed to approve of Carter's handling of the Afghan situation; his ratings in opinion polls rose.

Nevertheless the hostages languished in Iran. In April 1980 Carter finally ordered a team of marine commandos flown into Iran by helicopter in a desperate attempt to rescue them. The raid was a fiasco. Several helicopters broke down. While the others were gathered at a desert rendezvous south of Teheran, Carter called off the attempt. In the confusion of a night departure there was a crash and eight commandos were killed. The Iranians

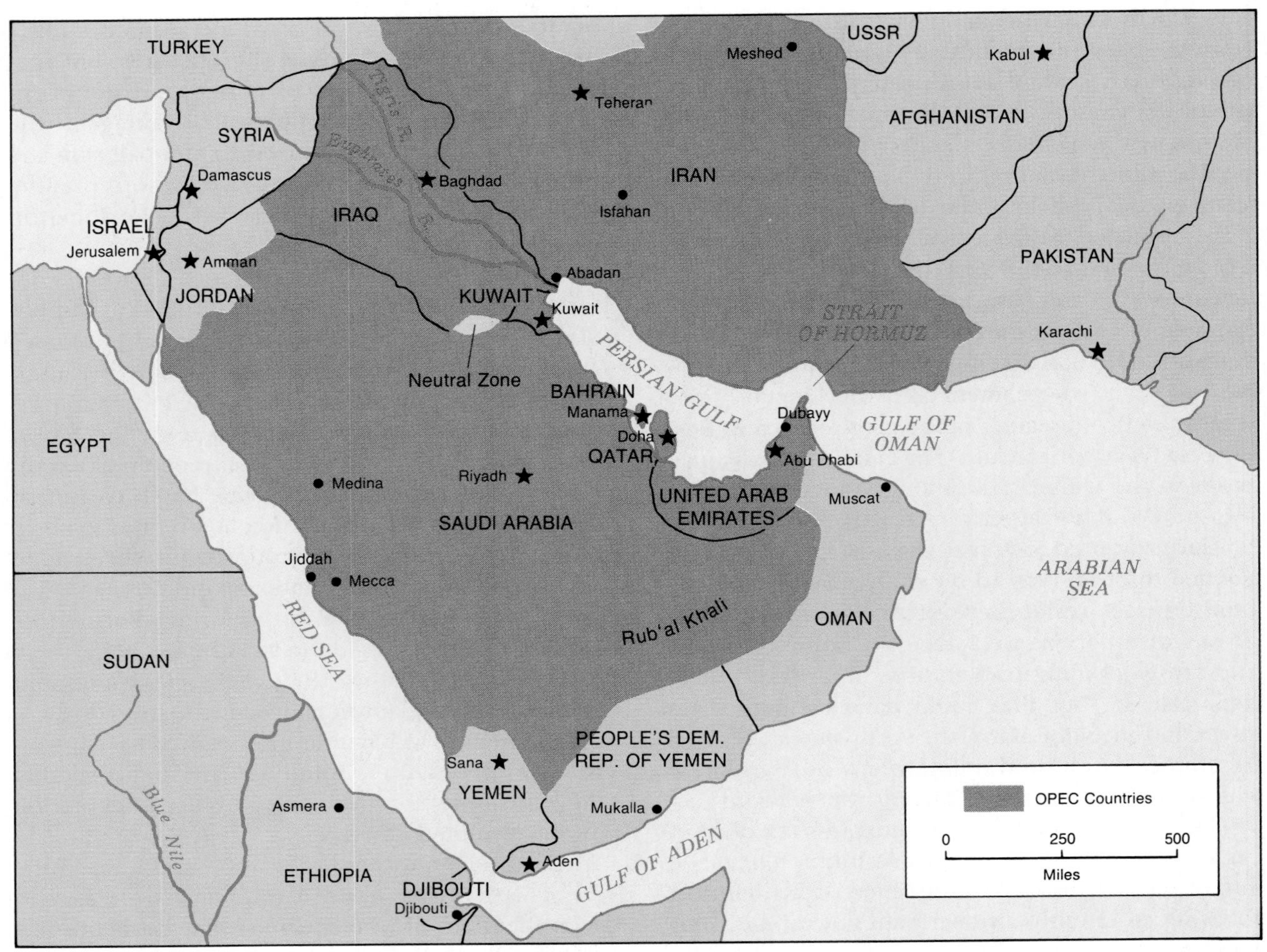

THE MIDDLE EAST

made political capital of the incident, gleefully displaying on television the wrecked aircraft and captured American equipment. Unlike Carter's earlier actions, the raid was widely criticized. (Even before it began Secretary of State Cyrus Vance had quietly resigned on the ground that it was almost sure to result in many casualties and that if it succeeded the Iranians would only seize other Americans in the country.) And so, the stalemate continued. In July 1980 the shah, who had moved from Panama to Egypt, died. It made no difference to the Iranians.

The Election of 1980

Despite the failure of the raid, Carter beat Kennedy decisively in the most important primaries without stirring from the White House. He had more than enough delegates at the Democratic convention to win nomination on the first ballot. His Republican opponent in the campaign that followed was Ronald Reagan, the former movie actor and governor of California who had almost defeated Gerald Ford for the nomination in 1976. At 69, Reagan was the oldest person ever nominated for president by a major party. However, his age was not a serious handicap in the campaign; he was physically trim and vigorous and seemed no older than most other prominent politicians.

Reagan had grown up a New Deal Democrat, but during and immediately after World War II he became disillusioned with liberalism. He denounced government inefficiency and high taxation. As president of the Screen Actors' Guild he attacked the influence of communists in the movie industry. After his movie career ended (he always insisted that he had *not* been typed as "the nice guy who didn't get the girl"), Reagan did publicity for General Electric for a number of years. In 1960 he left GE to work for various conservative causes. He campaigned for Barry Goldwater during the 1964 presidential contest. Two years later, at the urging of a group of California conservatives, he ran for governor of that state and was elected. He was a controversial governor, in part because, despite his professed conservatism and his emphasis on economy, government spending in California increased dramatically during his term. Despite, or perhaps because of this shift, he was easily reelected in 1970.

The 1980 presidential campaign ranks among the most curious in American history. One of Reagan's opponents at the Republican convention, Congressman John Anderson of Illinois, refused to accept defeat and ran for president as an independent. He did so, he announced, because he thought both Carter and Reagan had little genuine popular support.

Indeed, many citizens appeared unable to decide whom to vote for. Of those who expressed a preference, many did so without enthusiasm. Anderson's problem was that he too inspired relatively little enthusiasm among voters. "None of the above" seemed the true desire of many citizens as they contemplated the list of candidates.

Both Carter and Reagan spent much time explaining why the other was unsuited to be president. Carter defended his record, though without much conviction. Reagan promised to install a "New Federalism": he would transfer some functions of the federal government to the states, on the theory that local governments reflected both the will and the wisdom of the citizenry better than the remote, bureaucracy-ridden government in Washington. He denounced criminals, drug addicts, and all varieties of immorality, and spoke in support of patriotism, religion, family life, and other "old-fashioned" virtues. These were positions subscribed to by all successful politicians, but Reagan advanced them with a sincerity that won him the enthusiastic backing of fundamentalist religious sects and other conservative groups. He also promised to reduce spending and cut taxes, insisting at the same time that the budget could be balanced and inflation sharply reduced.

Reagan's tendency to depend on popular magazine articles, half-remembered conversations, and other informal sources for his economic "facts" reflected a mental imprecision that alarmed his critics, but his sunny disposition and his "laid-back" style compared favorably with Carter's personality. The president seemed tight-lipped and tense even when flashing his habitual toothy smile. A television debate between Carter and Reagan pointed up their personal differences but apparently had little effect on public opinion.

Because so many people said they were undecided, the contest seemed close—"too close to call," most experts said on election eve. It did not turn out that way. The voting was light, but those who cast ballots gave Reagan over 43 million votes to Carter's 35 million and Anderson's 5.6 million. Reagan won a big electoral college majority, 489 to 49. Even more unexpected were the results of the congressional elections. The Republicans gained control of the Senate and cut deeply into the Democratic majority in the House of Representatives. Clearly the country had turned in a conservative direction.

Carter devoted his last weeks in office to the continuing hostage crisis. War had broken out between Iran and Iraq in September. The additional strain on an Iranian economy already shattered by revolution raised hopes that Ayatollah Khomeini would release the captive Americans. Iran needed both the assets Carter had frozen and spare parts for its American-made planes and tanks. With Algeria acting as intermediary, American and Iranian diplomats worked out an agreement. Reagan avoided involvement in the negotiations, but to put pressure on the Iranians he announced that he opposed paying "ransom" for "people who have been kidnapped by barbarians." Perhaps fearing that the new president might take some drastic action, Iran at last agreed to release the hostages in return for its assets in the United States. After 444 days in captivity, the 52 hostages were set free on January 20, the day Reagan was inaugurated.

Reagan as President

Despite his amiable, unaggressive style, Reagan acted rapidly and with determination once in office. He hoped to change the direction in which the country was moving. He would replace inflation with price stability, an active, expanding federal government with more dependence on the states and still more dependence on individual initiative. The marketplace, not bureaucratic regulations, should govern most economic decisions. At the same time, Reagan called for greatly increased military expenditures. He believed that the Soviet Union had taken advantage of the relaxation of international tension associated with détente to gain military superiority over the United States.

Cutting taxes was his first priority. He asked Congress to lower income taxes by 30 percent over three years and he demanded steep reductions in federal spending, focused chiefly on social services such as student loans, and welfare payments and food stamps that went to poor people. He promised that despite these cuts he would maintain a "safety net" under the poor to protect them from real deprivation, and he insisted that in the long run they and everyone else would benefit from his program.

Reagan's tax policy was based on what was known as "supply-side economics." He claimed that since the tax cut would leave people with more money, they would invest in productive ways rather than spend the excess on consumer goods, and that the new investment would result in increased production, more jobs, prosperity, and therefore more income for the government despite the lower tax rates. There was a superficial similarity between this argument and the reasoning behind the successful tax cut proposed by President Kennedy in 1963 and engineered by President Johnson in 1964. However, the danger of inflation was much greater in 1981. Many congressmen hesitated, but the mandate of Reagan's big election victory was hard to resist and the income tax was reduced by 25 percent, only slightly less than the president had asked for.

In August 1981 Reagan displayed his determination in convincing fashion when the nation's air traffic controllers went on strike despite the fact that they were forbidden by law to do so. Reagan ordered them to return to work. Most of the controllers, feeling that their demands were just and that the airlines could not operate without them, refused to obey this order. Reagan therefore discharged all 11,400 of them and began a crash program to train replacements. Even after the strike collapsed, the president refused to rehire the strikers. The air controllers' union was destroyed.

An event unrelated to economic policy added greatly to the president's popularity. On March 30, while leaving a Washington hotel, he was shot in the chest by one John W. Hinckley, Jr.* Although he was seriously wounded, Reagan reacted coolly and with his usual self-deprecating style. When he was wheeled into the operating room for emergency surgery, he told the team of doctors before going under the anesthetic that he hoped they were all Republicans. Later he complained of his bad luck—he had been wearing a brand new suit and now it was ruined. It was hard to oppose such bravery and good humor. That he made a swift and total recovery despite his age further increased the admiration of the country.

Helped by the votes of conservative Democrats, Reagan won congressional approval of a Budget Reconciliation Act that reduced government expenditures on domestic programs by $39 billion. In August 1981 Congress also gave him most of the tax cuts he had asked for. The law lowered individual income taxes by 25 percent over three years. Since the percentage was the same for everyone, high-income taxpayers received a disproportionately large share of the savings. Business taxes were liberalized, and capital gains, gift, and inheritance levies were reduced. To further encourage investment, the law authorized anyone with earned income to invest up to $2,000 a year in an individual retirement account (IRA). This money, and the interest or dividends it earned, would not be taxed until the individual retired.

Reagan kept his campaign promise to eliminate many government regulations affecting businesses. Long and complicated antitrust suits against International Business Machines and American Telephone and Telegraph, two of the largest corporations in the country, were dropped.

"Reaganomics," as administration policy was called, was certainly not a new theory. Carter had also advocated tax cuts, reduced federal spending, and the tight money policy adopted by chairman Paul Volcker of the Federal Reserve Board, whom he had appointed. During his term the airlines were freed from control by the Civil Aeronautics Board. But Reagan's supply-side economics was old-fashioned to the point of being antique. It differed little

* Two security officers and Reagan's press secretary were also wounded by Hinckley.

from the policy conservative economists had favored in the Great Depression, which critics had derided as the "trickle-down" theory. As the economist James Tobin said in 1981, "old doctrines and policies, new forty years ago," were to be replaced by "new doctrines and policies, old forty years ago."

Tobin and most other economists did not think that Reaganomics would work. By December 1982 the economy was in a full-scale recession. More than 10 percent of the work force was unemployed. The combination of lower tax rates and a slumping economy was further unbalancing the budget. In 1983 the federal deficit topped $195 billion, up from $59 billion only three years earlier. Month after month the Treasury was forced to borrow billions; its needs kept interest rates high.

Only the fact that inflation was slowing brightened the gloomy picture. Several causes contributed to this much-desired result. High unemployment and the economic slowdown gradually reduced consumer demand for goods and services. People began to worry about the future, and that weakened the inflationary psychology that had led them to spend in anticipation of further price increases. Most significant were the declining prices of gasoline and other petroleum products. Conservation and increased production by non-OPEC countries such as Mexico, Norway, and Great Britain gradually turned chronic shortages into an oil glut. The oil "shocks" of 1973 and 1979 had caused other prices to soar; the glut caused them to fall, though much less abruptly. All in all, the rate of inflation fell from more than 12 percent to less than 4 percent by 1984. When inflation moderated, the Federal Reserve Board relaxed its tight money policy. Interest rates then declined somewhat, making it easier to finance the purchase of homes and automobiles. The new lower tax rates left people with more spendable income for all kinds of purchases. Business began to pick up. Unemployment, while still high, fell below 8 percent in 1984.

But the recovery did not lead to much new business investment. People seemed to be spending their additional income on consumer goods. Together with the federal deficits caused by the large increase in military expenditures, this spending also prevented interest rates from going down as far as economists had hoped they would when inflation slackened.

Many of Reagan's advisers urged him to reduce the military budget and seek some kind of tax increase in order to bring the government's income more nearly in line with its outlays. However, the president insisted that the military buildup was necessary because of the threat to world peace posed by the Soviet Union. He called Russia an "evil empire" and pursued a hard-line anticommunist foreign policy nearly everywhere. With the reluctant support of the governments of the western democracies, where many citizens feared Soviet retaliation against their countries, he installed new nuclear cruise missiles in Europe. Claiming that in Central America the communists were supplying arms to the left-wing Sandinista government of Nicaragua and encouraging communist rebels in El Salvador, he sought to undermine the Nicaraguan regime and bolster the conservative government of El Salvador. He also used American troops to overthrow a Cuban-backed regime on the tiny Caribbean island of Grenada.

In 1982 the continuing turmoil in the Middle East plunged the Reagan administration into a new crisis. Israel had invaded Lebanon to destroy PLO units that were staging raids on northern Israeli settlements from bases there. Israeli troops easily overran much of the country, but in the process the Lebanese government disintegrated and fighting broke out among Lebanese Christians and various Moslem sects. In an effort to end the bloodshed, Reagan agreed to send American troops to serve as part of an international peacekeeping force. Essentially their role was to act as a buffer between the occupying Israelis and the contending Lebanese units in and around Beirut. Before long, however, Israel pulled its troops back to southern Lebanon. Then the peacekeeping units came under fire from the different Lebanese factions. Soon the Americans were reduced to maintaining control of the Beirut airport, where they were under almost constant shelling.

At this point it would probably have been wise to withdraw, but Reagan believed that American prestige was at stake. Tragedy resulted in October 1983 when a fanatical Moslem crashed a truck loaded with explosives into a building at the airport housing American marines. The building collapsed, killing 239 marines. Early the next year, prestige or no, Reagan removed the entire American peacekeeping force from Lebanon.

Four More Years

Being a sitting president with an extraordinarily high standing in public opinion polls, Reagan was nominated for a second term at the 1984 Republican convention without opposition. The Democrats' choice was not so easily made. The leading candidate was Walter Mondale of Minnesota, who had been vice-president under Carter. He was opposed in the primaries by half a dozen others, the most prominent being Senator John Glenn of Ohio, the former astronaut, and the Reverend Jesse Jackson, a civil rights activist. Mondale seemed the likely winner until he was defeated in the New Hampshire primary by Senator Gary Hart of Colorado, who before then had seemed to have little chance. Hart aimed his campaign chiefly at younger voters; he claimed to offer "new ideas," and he accused Mondale of catering to "special interest groups" such as organized labor.

Hart also won in other New England states, but the Mondale forces rallied in the South and Middle West. One by one, the less successful candidates dropped out, until only Mondale, Hart, and Jackson were left. Jackson had little chance of winning, but being an excellent speaker as well as the first black to make a serious run for the presidential nomination of a major party, he roused the enthusiasm of millions of blacks. Tens of thousands of them responded to his appeal that they register and vote in the coming election.

The contest was fairly close between Mondale and Hart, but by the time of the Democratic convention, Mondale had a majority of the delegates. He was nominated on the first ballot. He then electrified the country by choosing Representative Geraldine Ferraro of New York as his running mate.

Ferraro had a liberal voting record in Congress, and she was known to be an effective professional politician. Although Mondale undoubtedly chose her because she was a woman—Democrats expected that she would win the votes of many Republican women and that her selection would counter the claims of Mondale's critics that he was unimaginative and overly cautious—she seemed well-qualified for the office. On the stump she drew large crowds and proved to be an excellent campaigner.

Reagan began the campaign with several important advantages. He was especially popular among religious fundamentalists and other social conservatives. President Nixon had spoken of a "silent majority." By 1980 the kind of people he was referring to were no longer silent, if ever they had been. The Reverend Jerry Falwell's Moral Majority sought to organize them, and by 1984 the Moral Majority had become a powerful political force. Falwell was against drugs, the "coddling" of criminals,

Walter Mondale and Geraldine Ferraro held a press conference in Minnesota shortly after the Democratic nominating convention in July of 1984.

homosexuality, communism, and abortion. While not openly antiblack, Falwell's organization disapproved of forced busing and other government policies designed to help blacks and other minorities. Of course, like all law-abiding people, Walter Mondale was also against many of the things that Falwell and his followers denounced, but Reagan was against them all. In addition, Reagan was in favor of government aid to private schools run by church groups, something dear to the hearts of Moral Majority types despite the constitutional principle of separation of church and state.

But the Moral Majority, despite its name, was far from being an actual majority. Reagan's support was much more broadly based. Like Reagan, a very large proportion of the population did not trust the Soviet Union and therefore approved of the president's insistence on increasing the military budget. Voters were concerned about unemployment and the persistence of poverty in the nation, and they certainly wished that interest rates and the federal budget deficit would come down. These were all problems that Reagan had been unable to solve, but with inflation slackening and tax rates reduced they seemed less pressing. The president's personality was another important plus—voters continued to admire his informal yet firm style, and his stress on patriotism and other "old-fashioned" virtues. He was a confirmed optimist, telling the voters over and over that things were getting better and that four more years of Republican leadership would make them better still.

The tendency of voters to support a sitting president when the economy was on the rise was still another advantage. As the campaign progressed, the economy continued to improve and unemployment fell to a bit over 7 percent. Business investment finally picked up and inflation remained low. Interest rates, while high, were moving down slowly but steadily, in part because foreigners were buying U.S. securities in large amounts.

Despite Reagan's many advantages, the Democrats did not lack arguments to use against his reelection. Many Americans believed that Reagan's insistence on reducing spending on social services was heartless. These critics pointed out that in 1983, 35 million people, more than 15 percent of the population, were officially classified as poor, up from 11.4 percent in 1978. They also noted that despite the economic recovery, millions of workers were still unemployed, that the big federal deficits were keeping interest rates high, and that high interest rates at a time of relatively low inflation proved that administration policies were of special benefit to the rich. Other opponents charged that the president's harsh criticisms of the Russians had only escalated international tensions. They predicted that increasing the already enormous stocks of nuclear weapons and designing still more lethal ones would make an atomic war more likely, rather than serving as a deterrent.

From the start Mondale emphasized the difficulties that he saw ahead for the nation. All the president's economic policies, he said, favored the well-to-do and hurt the poor, women, and minorities. Mondale also tried to focus attention on the huge increase in the federal deficit that Reagan's policies had produced, and he accused the president of misleading the public by saying that he would not raise taxes if reelected.

These were conventional campaign tactics. But Mondale, in a daring move, announced in his acceptance speech at the Democratic convention that he *would* raise taxes if elected. This promise, most unusual for a person running for office, was another attempt to counter his reputation for political caution.

Most polls showed Reagan far in the lead when the campaign began, and this remained true throughout the contest. Reagan's advanced age (73) was a legitimate issue, but when asked by a reporter during a television debate with Mondale whether he thought "the age question" important, he responded with a quip: he would not make an issue of his opponent's youth and inexperience. Optimism and opportunity were his catchwords. Mondale, he said, "sees America wringing her hands. We see America using her hands. He sees America divided by envy. . . . We see an America inspired and uniting for opportunity."

This tactic proved effective. Nothing Mondale or Ferraro did or said affected the president's popularity. Bad news, even his own mistakes, had so little effect on his standing that people began to call him "the Teflon president." On election day he got nearly 60 percent of the popular vote and lost only in Minnesota, Mondale's home state, and in the District of Columbia. His Electoral College margin was overwhelming, 523 to 13.

The Democratic coalition of industrial workers,

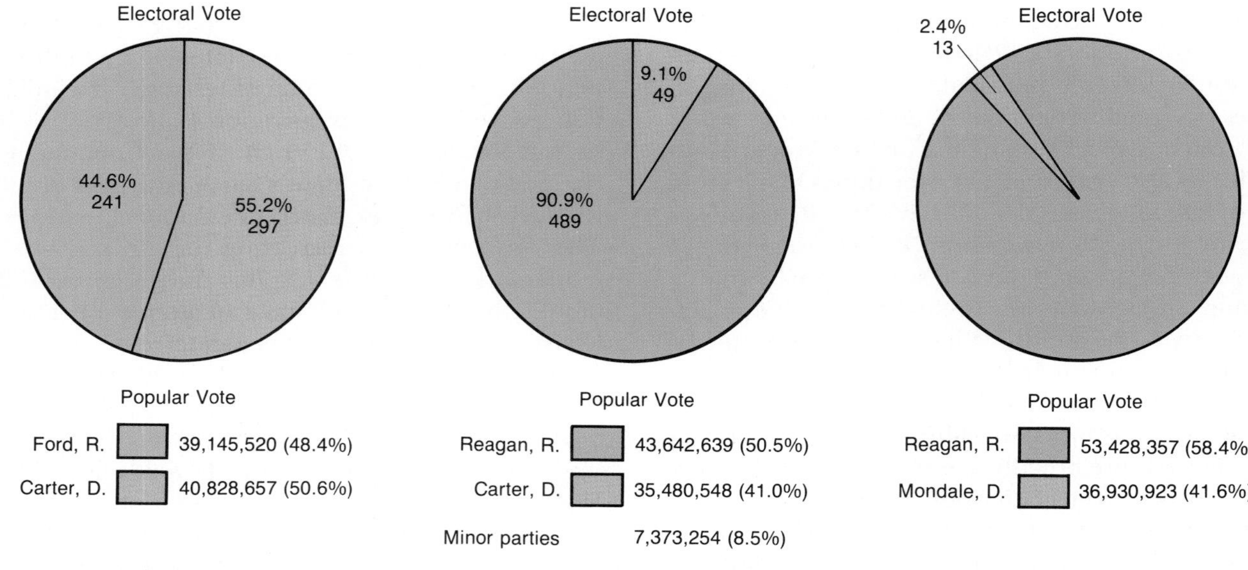

THE REAGAN REVOLUTION?

farmers, and the underprivileged that Franklin Roosevelt had put together half a century earlier had fallen apart. Of its elements, only the blacks, who voted overwhelmingly for Mondale, remained loyal, and their unity may have had something to do with the shift of so many white Democrats to Reagan. Nor had the Democratic strategy of nominating a woman for vice-president proved effective; far more women voted for Reagan than for the Mondale-Ferraro ticket.

Reagan's triumph, like the two landslide victories of Dwight Eisenhower in the 1950s, was primarily a personal one. The Republicans made only minor gains in the House of Representatives and actually lost two seats in the Senate. Some political experts speculated that Reagan would soon become a lame-duck president. Could he turn his popularity with voters into the congressional votes needed to enact the laws he desired?

The Reagan Revolution

Reagan's agenda for his second term closely resembled that of his first. In foreign affairs, he ran into continuing congressional resistance to his requests for military support for his anticommunist crusade in Central America. In particular, the legislators hesitated to supply war materiel to the "Contras" who were fighting the Sandinista government of Nicaragua. Reagan called the Contras "freedom fighters," but many of them were at least as undemocratic as the people they were seeking to overthrow. In addition, memories of Vietnam caused many people to fear getting involved in Central American conflicts. Nevertheless, Reagan insisted that the safety of the nation depended on supplying the Contras with military aid. Combining this appeal with some presidential arm twisting and the judicious dispensing of patronage, he finally got Congress to appropriate $100 million for the anti-Sandinista rebels.

Reagan's anti-Soviet policies, and particularly his belligerent rhetoric, attracted no better than lukewarm support among all but the most fervent American anticommunists. This was particularly true after Mikhail S. Gorbachev became the Russian premier in March 1985. Gorbachev seemed at least on the surface more moderate and flexible than his predecessors. (He was certainly more concerned about public opinion in the western democracies.) The Soviets announced that they would continue to honor the unratified SALT II (see page 927), whereas Reagan, arguing that the Russians had not respected the limits laid down in the pact, seemed bent on pushing ahead with the expansion and modernization of America's nuclear arsenal. He sought funds for the National Aeronautics and Space Administration (NASA) to develop an elaborate computer-controlled strategic defense initiative, popularly known as Star Wars, that would supposedly be capable of destroying enemy missiles in outer space where they could do no damage.

After NASA's spectacular Apollo program, which sent six expeditions to the moon between 1969 and 1972, the space agency's prestige was beyond measurement. Its Skylab orbiting space station program (1973–1974) was equally successful. Next, shortly after the beginning of Reagan's first term, the manned space shuttle *Columbia,* launched by rocket power, was able, after orbiting for several days, to return to earth intact, gliding on its stubby, swept-back wings to an appointed landing strip. *Columbia* and other shuttles were soon transporting satellites into space for the government and private companies, and its astronauts were conducting military and scientific experiments of great importance.

Congress, however, boggled at the enormous estimated cost of Star Wars, which some feared would mount into the trillions of dollars. Costs aside, the idea of relying for national defense on the complex technology involved in controlling machines in outer space suffered a further setback in February 1986, when the space shuttle *Challenger* exploded shortly after takeoff, killing its seven-member crew.

The president was more successful in winning support for his get-tough-with-terrorists policy. After the destruction of the Marine barracks in Lebanon by a terrorist in 1982, Reagan had wisely refrained from retaliating. Exactly which group was responsible and—more important—where that group was located could not be determined. Nevertheless, Reagan had sharply criticized President Carter for not using force during the Iranian hostage crisis, a fact that the Democrats did not fail to call to his attention. He was prepared to act decisively against terrorists when circumstances made such action possible.

Such an opportunity presented itself in October 1985 when four Arab terrorists seized control of the Italian cruise ship *Achille Lauro* in the eastern Mediterranean. They threatened to blow up the ship unless 50 Palestinians in Israeli jails were freed. However, after killing an elderly Jewish-American tourist and tossing his body into the sea, the terrorists surrendered to Egyptian authorities on condition that they be provided with safe passage to Libya on an Egyptian airliner. They chose Libya because the president of that nation, Muammar al-Qaddafi, was a bitter enemy of Israel and the United States and an open supporter of terrorist activities.

The American tourist the terrorists had murdered was an invalid confined to a wheelchair. Reagan, like most people horrified by this wanton cruelty, and as president prepared to retaliate, ordered American warplanes to intercept the airliner. Navy F-14 jets then forced the Egyptian pilot to land in Italy, where the terrorists were taken into custody.

Next President Reagan challenged Qaddafi more directly. The Libyan leader claimed that the territorial waters of his country extended 200 miles offshore. This limit would put the entire Gulf of Sidra (see map) within his domain. No naval power recognized the 200-mile limit. Nevertheless, Qaddafi drew an imaginary "line of death" on the north edge of the Gulf and swore that he would destroy any unfriendly ship that crossed it. Reagan responded by ordering ships from the Sixth Fleet into the Gulf, and when Qaddafi, as expected, sent gunboats to challenge them, navy planes destroyed the gunboats and bombed Libyan shore installations.

Qaddafi then ordered Libyan secret agents in West Germany to bomb a club frequented by American servicemen. One soldier and one civilian were killed in the attack and many people were injured. Reagan retaliated by launching a massive air strike against Libyan bases from airfields in Great Britain. The European reaction to this bold action was one of great alarm, but in America the public responded enthusiastically. The president's popularity rating, already remarkable, reached an all-time high.

Reagan's domestic policies also remained those of his first term. His basic objectives—to reduce the scope of federal activity, particularly in the social welfare area; to simplify the tax system and lower income tax rates; and to increase the strength of the armed forces—did not change. Though debate continued about particular measures, even among Democrats, efforts to reverse the trends the president had put in motion practically disappeared. Despite the steep tax cuts of the first term

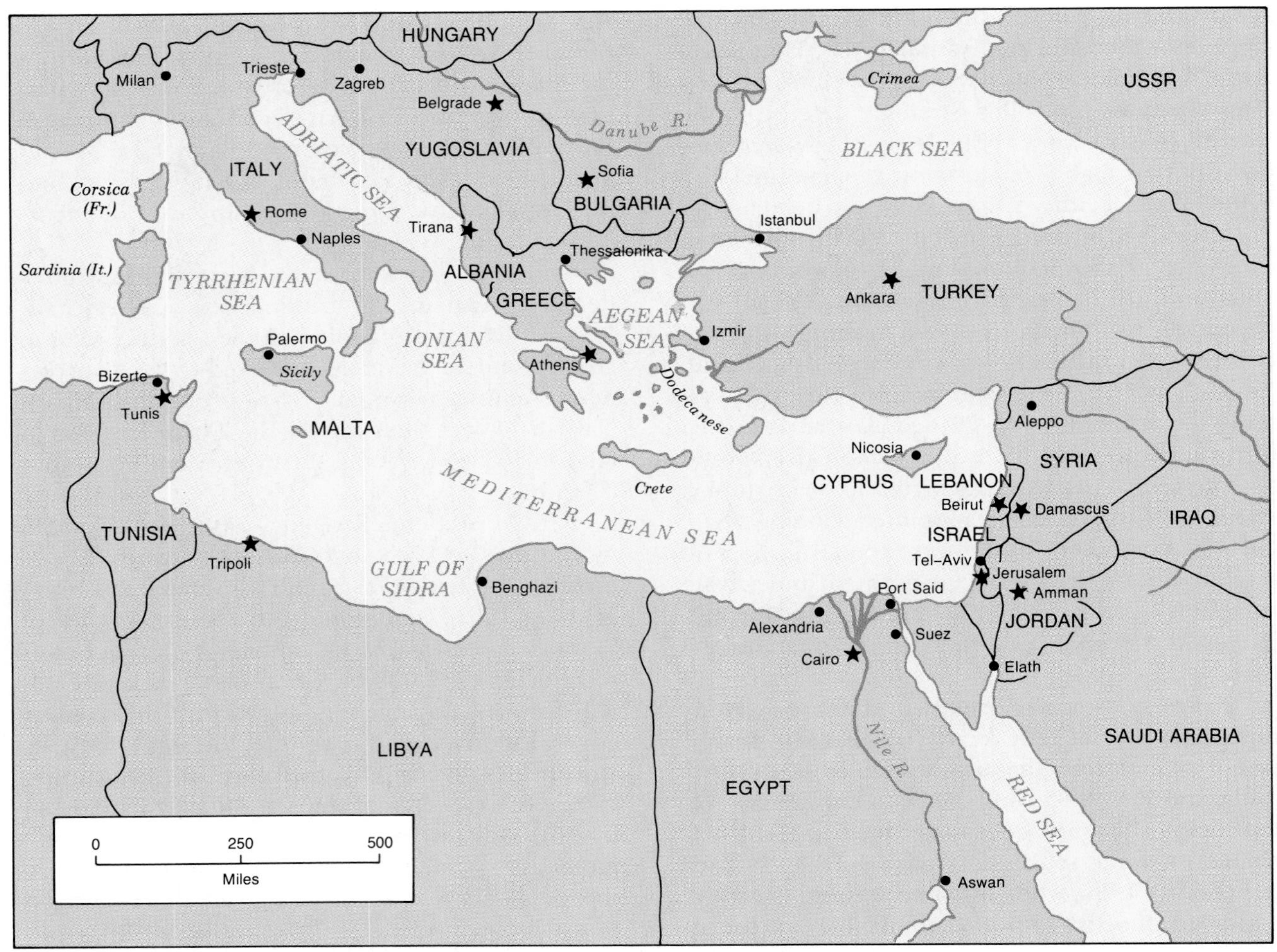

THE EASTERN MEDITERRANEAN

and the fact that the top tax on personal incomes had already been reduced from 70 percent to 50 percent, nearly all the leaders of both parties agreed to a further lowering of tax rates. The Income Tax Act of 1986 lowered the top levy on personal incomes from 50 percent to 28 percent and the tax on corporate profits from 46 percent to 34 percent. "When I think of coming here with the tax rate at 70 percent and ending my first term under 30 percent, it's amazing," one delighted Republican senator told reporters.

To make up for these cuts, the new law did away with most of the tax shelters and special credits that large numbers of corporations and well-to-do individuals had used to reduce their tax bills. (In practice, the new corporate rate was expected to bring in much more money than had actually been collected under the old one.) The law also relieved 6 million low-income people from paying any federal income tax at all. In general, the objective was fairness—defined as a system that required people with similar incomes to pay at least roughly equal taxes. But in the course of achieving this goal, the law undermined the principle of progressive taxation—the practice, dating back to the first income tax enacted after the adoption of the Sixteenth Amendment in 1913, of requiring high-income people to pay a larger *percentage* of their

One of the politer epithets used by Qaddafi's critics was "Maddog." In Dan Wasserman's cartoon, an apprehensive-looking Europe does not seem a bit pleased about Reagan's action.

income than those with smaller incomes. The new law, set to take effect over two years, had only two rates: 15 percent on taxable incomes below $17,850 for individuals and $29,750 for families, and 28 percent on incomes above those limits. A family with a taxable income of $30,000 would pay at the same rate as one with $300,000—or, for that matter, one with $300 million, should any such exist.

The idea that the government should use the tax system to shape social policy or to influence how individuals invest their money received a sharp setback. This was thoroughly in keeping with Reagan's political philosophy, and with that of many Democrats as well. Senator William Bradley of New Jersey, a leader in the liberal wing of the Democratic Party and an early advocate of tax simplification, put it clearly: "No longer will people invest for tax purposes," he said in support of the measure. "They will invest in things that have real value in the marketplace."

Reagan advanced another of his objectives more gradually, but with effects that seemed likely to be long lasting. This was his appointment of conservatives whenever openings occurred in the federal judiciary. The trend was highlighted in 1986 when Chief Justice Warren C. Burger resigned his post. To replace him the president named Associate Justice William H. Rehnquist, probably the most conservative member of the Supreme Court, and he filled the vacancy with Antonin Scalia, a judge reported to be even more conservative than Rehnquist. It was estimated that by the end of his term, Reagan would have appointed well over half of all the members of the federal bench.

Whither America?

But if the "Reagan Revolution" seemed to have triumphed by the middle of the president's second term, many powerful forces were at work that neither he nor any individual or political party could effectively control. The falling price of petroleum, for example, had eased inflationary pressures and helped fuel recovery from the recession. This was a major reason for the president's popularity. Yet cheaper oil dealt a devastating blow to the economies of Texas and other oil-producing states in the Southwest, a region where support of Reagan's policies was particularly strong. Falling oil prices also forced the OPEC countries and other oil-producing lands to cut back on their imports of manufactured goods, which hurt all the industrial nations. Mexico was particularly hard hit, since it depended on money earned by exporting petroleum for a very large percentage of its foreign purchases. The situation was so serious that Mexico was not able even to pay the interest on its debts

A common unfortunate side effect of farm bankruptcy is the auction of the farm's physical assets. Here heavy-duty equipment is being auctioned at an Illinois farm.

to foreign banks without further loans, loans which the banks were increasingly hesitant to make. Indeed, many American banks suffered heavy losses when domestic and foreign oil-related loans went sour.

A similar situation developed in the nation's agricultural heartland. In the 1970s, a time of rising agricultural prices, large numbers of farmers borrowed heavily to expand output. With the price of land and farm products rising steadily because of double-digit inflation, it seemed safe to do so. Between 1975 and 1983 farm mortgage debts soared from less than $50 billion to more than $112 billion, and by 1985 the total debt of American farmers had reached $215 billion. In 1985 about half the farmers in the country were in debt and interest payments on their debts came to $21 billion.

But by that time inflation had slowed to a crawl because of the tight money policy, and because of other factors world agricultural prices were falling steeply. In the 1981–1982 crop year, American farmers exported nearly 2 billion bushels of wheat, for which they received about $8 billion. Four years later, exports fell below a billion bushels, worth between $3 and $4 billion. The net income of the average Illinois farmer in 1981 was $17,676. In 1983 the average Illinois farmer *lost* $5,786. For thousands of farmers in Illinois and other hard-hit states, and for many of the rural banks that had lent these farmers money, the slump meant bankruptcy.

More generally, the huge annual deficits of the federal government continued in good times; the deficit was $179 billion in 1985 and experts predicted that, should the economy fall into recession, it would soar to new heights. The nation continued to import far more goods than it sold abroad. By the mid-1980s imports were exceeding exports by more than $100 billion annually, and in 1986 the United States became a net borrower, owing foreigners more than they owed Americans for the first time since World War I.

These trends were alarming, but reversing them meant adopting policies that might do more harm than good. Reducing the deficit would mean higher taxes or cuts in federal spending, both unpopular ideas. Reducing imports meant doing without desirable products, injuring the economies of friendly nations, and imposing protective tariffs that would raise the cost of goods and that might trigger a disastrous trade war. Exporting more called for improving the quality or reducing the price of American products, and for persuading foreign nations to modify trade restrictions, all difficult tasks.

The makeup of the American people, always

The most recent wave of immigrants has changed the face of America's cities just as earlier ethnic groups did. Street scenes from Union City, New Jersey, and Berkeley, California, reveal strong Hispanic—in this case Cuban—and Vietnamese influences.

in a state of flux, was changing at a rate approaching that of the first decade of the century, when the "new" immigration was at its peak. After the Immigration Act of 1965 had put an end to the national origins concept, a drastic change occurred. In the 1970s, more than 4 million immigrants entered the country, and the vast majority of these newcomers were Asians and Latin Americans. This trend continued; of the 570,000 who came in 1985, more than half were from Korea, the Philippine Islands, Vietnam, and other Asian nations, and another 40 percent were from Latin America, most of these from Mexico. In addition, hundreds of thousands more people entered the country illegally each year, most crossing the long, sparsely settled border of northern Mexico.

As in earlier times, the newcomers met with a mixed reaction. Most were hardworking and willing to take menial jobs that "native" Americans scorned. Some were refugees fleeing from repressive regimes in Vietnam, Cuba, Haiti, and Central America, and these were received sympathetically in most cases. But others became public charges; still others, lawbreakers. Most tended, like their predecessors, to crowd together in ethnic neighborhoods where their unusual customs often roused the suspicion of older inhabitants. Spanish could be heard more often than English in sections of Los Angeles and San Antonio, and also in Miami, where tens of thousands of Cubans had settled, and in New York, where the majority of Hispanics had come from Puerto Rico and other Caribbean lands. By 1980 there were about 6.5 million Hispanic Americans in the southwestern states, a large percentage, of course, native-born citizens.

Although demands that immigration be restricted surfaced, no overwhelming pressure to check the flow could be perceived. Perhaps because so many citizens were themselves the children of immigrants, there was more tolerance and a better understanding of the contributions the newcomers were making than during earlier periods when large numbers were entering the country. The celebration of the one hundredth anniversary of the Statue of Liberty in 1986 caused the nation to reflect on the courage and high hopes of the millions who had come to America over the years. With government officials, well-do-do manufacturers, film stars, and sports figures not commonly known to be the children of immigrants coming forward to offer moving testimony about their parents' experiences—their hard work, their sacrifices, their gratitude for the chance to live in America, the land of freedom and opportunity—talk of closing the gates again subsided.

Reagan's conservative supporters tended to be ambivalent about the new immigrants. They admired the way so many Asian newcomers worked hard and lived frugally in order to accumulate enough capital to start their own shops and small businesses. But they worried about the cost of educating immigrant children, and about the demands of immigrant groups that the public schools provide instruction in their native tongues as well as English.

That so many people were entering the country illegally Reaganites found appalling. The administration tried to check the flow of illegal immigrants from Mexico into the southwestern states. The depressed condition of the Mexican economy, made worse by the steep decline in the price of oil, caused the number of people attempting to slip across the border to increase still further. Even Americans most sympathetic to these desperate "undocumented aliens" agreed that control was desirable. But the long border was difficult to police; many "illegals" were stopped and sent back, but the flow continued.

Reagan, his conservative supporters, and indeed people of all types and persuasions, were deeply disturbed by other trends that neither the government nor any organized force seemed capable of checking. The traditional family, consisting of a husband and wife and their children, the man a "breadwinner," the woman a "housewife," seemed in danger of ceasing to be typical. (With more than half the married women in the nation holding down jobs, such families could not possibly be typical in the statistical sense.) An ever-larger percentage of American families were headed by single parents, in most of these cases by women. In every year of the Reagan administration, more than 1.1 million marriages ended in divorce. Moreover, the tendency of couples to live together without getting married continued, helping to explain why the number of illegitimate births rose steadily. So did the number of abortions. In 1974, the first year after the Supreme Court decided that women had a constitutional right to have unwanted pregnancies terminated, 763,000 Americans had legal abortions. In 1981, the number rose to 1.3 million.

The Reagan administration devoted much talk and considerable hard effort to reducing the amount of crime in the country. Yet little progress was made, despite the fact that the number of persons confined in state and federal prisons reached 464,000 in 1985, an all-time high. A campaign to wipe out the traffic in marijuana, heroin, cocaine, and other illegal drugs resulted in many arrests, but drugs remained widely available. Indeed, some became so available that they fell in price, thus encouraging their use by more people. Cocaine, once considered an expensive and relatively harmless substance, became, in a cheap and potent form called "crack," a problem of epidemic proportion, used by people of every age and from every walk of life.

Certain other trends that the Reagan administration either encouraged or at least did not oppose were producing massive social and economic changes, the ultimate effects of which were difficult to predict. Labor union membership had begun to decline long before 1981, but by 1985 it was down to about 19 percent of the workforce. Reagan's tough stand against the air traffic controllers probably encouraged employers to resist unions more stubbornly, but a far more important cause of the decline was the continuing shift of the economy from unionized manufacturing industries such as steel and chemicals to industries such as electronics that employed white-collar workers who were traditionally difficult to organize. The increased use of computers and automatic machinery meant fewer workers in many fields, another reason for the decline.

A related trend was the merger movement, which saw often unrelated companies swallowing up one another in unprecedented fashion. By using borrowed funds, corporations could even buy businesses far larger than themselves, though the result left the new organization burdened with heavy debts. The deregulation movement begun under President Carter and Reagan's abandonment of strict enforcement of the antitrust laws certainly encouraged this trend, but it was a worldwide phenomenon and one which was producing an economy that transcended national boundaries. Huge multinational corporations could shift their operations across national boundaries, thus avoiding tariffs and other restrictions. By producing goods in countries in Asia and Latin America where labor costs were low and trade unions weak or nonexistent, they were making larger profits (and incidentally strengthening the economies of these lands). But they were also contributing to the decline of unions and quite possibly adding to the number of unemployed in the United States and other "advanced" industrial nations.

The Imponderable Future

If historians can locate suitable records and other sources about a past event, they are able to explain, or at least make plausible guesses about, what it was and why it happened at that time, no matter how remote. Historians are also probably better than most other people at explaining how things got to be the way they are at any present moment. This is because events have causes and results, and these are things that historians are trained to study and understand. But historians are no better than anyone else at predicting the future. Results, quite obviously, come after the events that cause them; it takes time for them to unfold, which means that "at present," even the most hardworking and intelligent historians do not know anything important about what the future will bring.

Another way of putting this is to point out that in the modern world just about everything that happens is in some way related to everything else that is going on. There are far too many things happening (all producing results of some kind) for anyone to sort out which of them is going to have what effect on events that will happen tomorrow, let alone next year or in the 21st century. "Then" (whether tomorrow or next year or the 21st century) historians will be able to study those particular events that interest them and puzzle out their chief causes—but not "now."

Yet "now" is where we happen to be, and thus this book, so full of events and their causes and results, must end inconclusively. No one knows what will happen next. But of course not knowing what will happen next is one of the main reasons life is so interesting.

SUPPLEMENTARY READING

Authoritative works on recent history are hard to find. On Gerald Ford, see Clark Mollenhoff, **The Man Who Pardoned Nixon** (1976), Richard Reeves, **A Ford, Not a Lincoln** (1975), and Ford's autobiography, **A Time to Heal** (1979). Betty Ford's frank **The Times of My Life** (1978) is a cut above most such memoirs.

For the Carter years, see Betty Glad, **Jimmy Carter in Search of the Great White House** (1980), which is critical of Carter's style and actions. Zbigniew Brzezinski, **Power and Principle** (1983), discusses the foreign policy of the administration, while Michael Ledeen and William Lewis, **Debacle** (1981), covers the Iranian hostage crisis.

Books dealing with Reagan and his administration include Hedrick Smith, **Reagan, the Man, the President** (1980), Robert Dallek, **Ronald Reagan: the Politics of Symbolism** (1984), and Rowland Evans and Robert Novak, **The Reagan Revolution** (1981). On Reagan foreign policy, see J. J. Kirkpatrick, **Dictatorships and Double Standards** (1982), and Strobe Talbott, **The Russians and Reagan** (1984). Contrasting views of recent conservative trends are provided by Alan Crawford, **Thunder on the Right** (1980), and Richard Viguerie, **The New Right: We're Ready to Lead** (1981). See also John Kater, **Christians on the Right: The Moral Majority in Perspective** (1982).

TIME LINE 7 ▪ America and the World in Our Century, 1890–1986

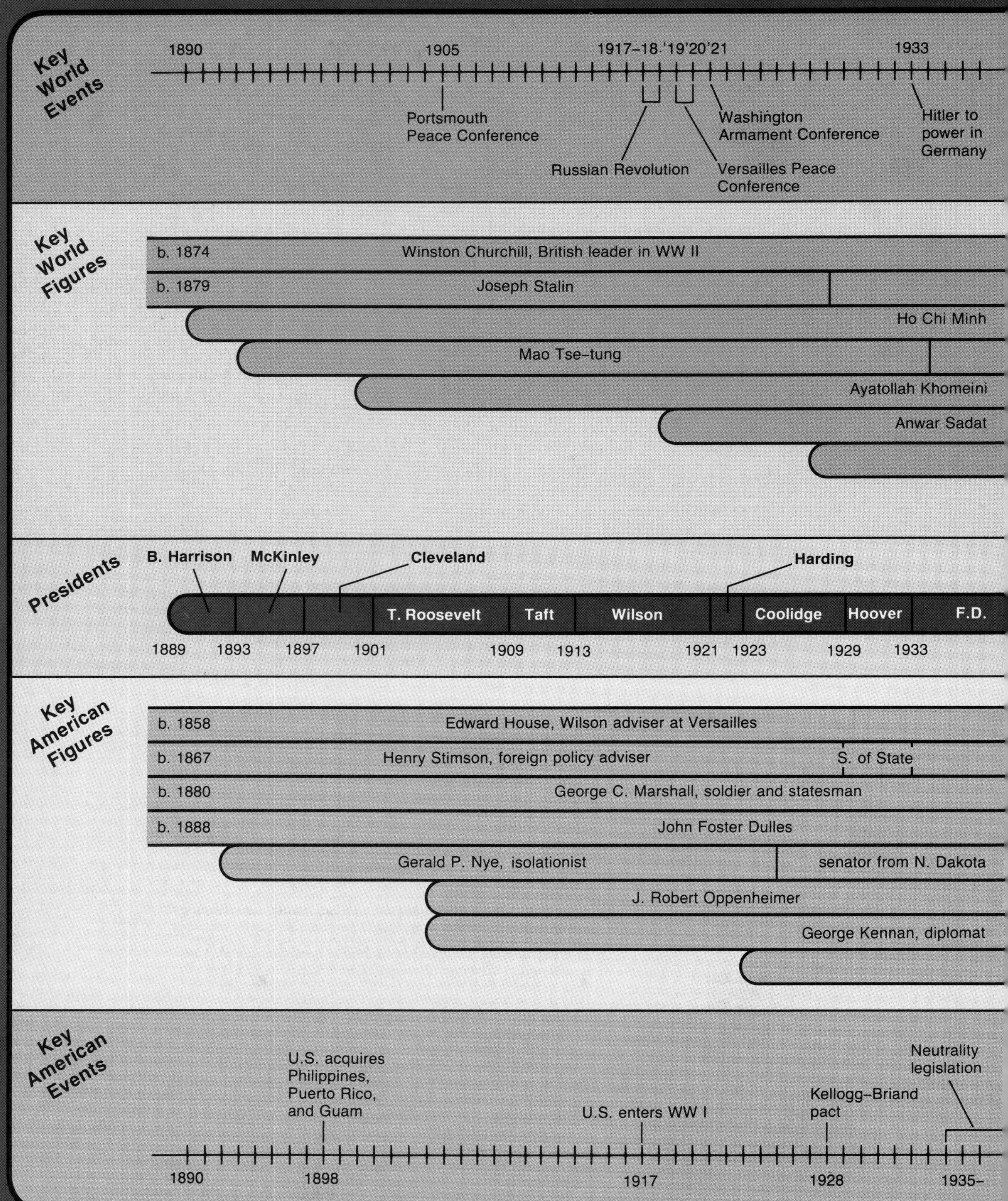

Key World Events
1890
1905
1917–18.'19'20'21
1933
Portsmouth Peace Conference
Russian Revolution
Washington Armament Conference
Versailles Peace Conference
Hitler to power in Germany
Key World Figures
b. 1874
Winston Churchill, British leader in WW II
b. 1879
Joseph Stalin
Ho Chi Minh
Mao Tse–tung
Ayatollah Khomeini
Anwar Sadat
Presidents
B. Harrison
McKinley
Cleveland
Harding
T. Roosevelt
Taft
Wilson
Coolidge
Hoover
F.D.
1889
1893
1897
1901
1909
1913
1921
1923
1929
1933
Key American Figures
b. 1858
Edward House, Wilson adviser at Versailles
b. 1867
Henry Stimson, foreign policy adviser
S. of State
b. 1880
George C. Marshall, soldier and statesman
b. 1888
John Foster Dulles
Gerald P. Nye, isolationist
senator from N. Dakota
J. Robert Oppenheimer
George Kennan, diplomat
Key American Events
U.S. acquires Philippines, Puerto Rico, and Guam
U.S. enters WW I
Kellogg–Briand pact
Neutrality legislation
1890
1898
1917
1928
1935–

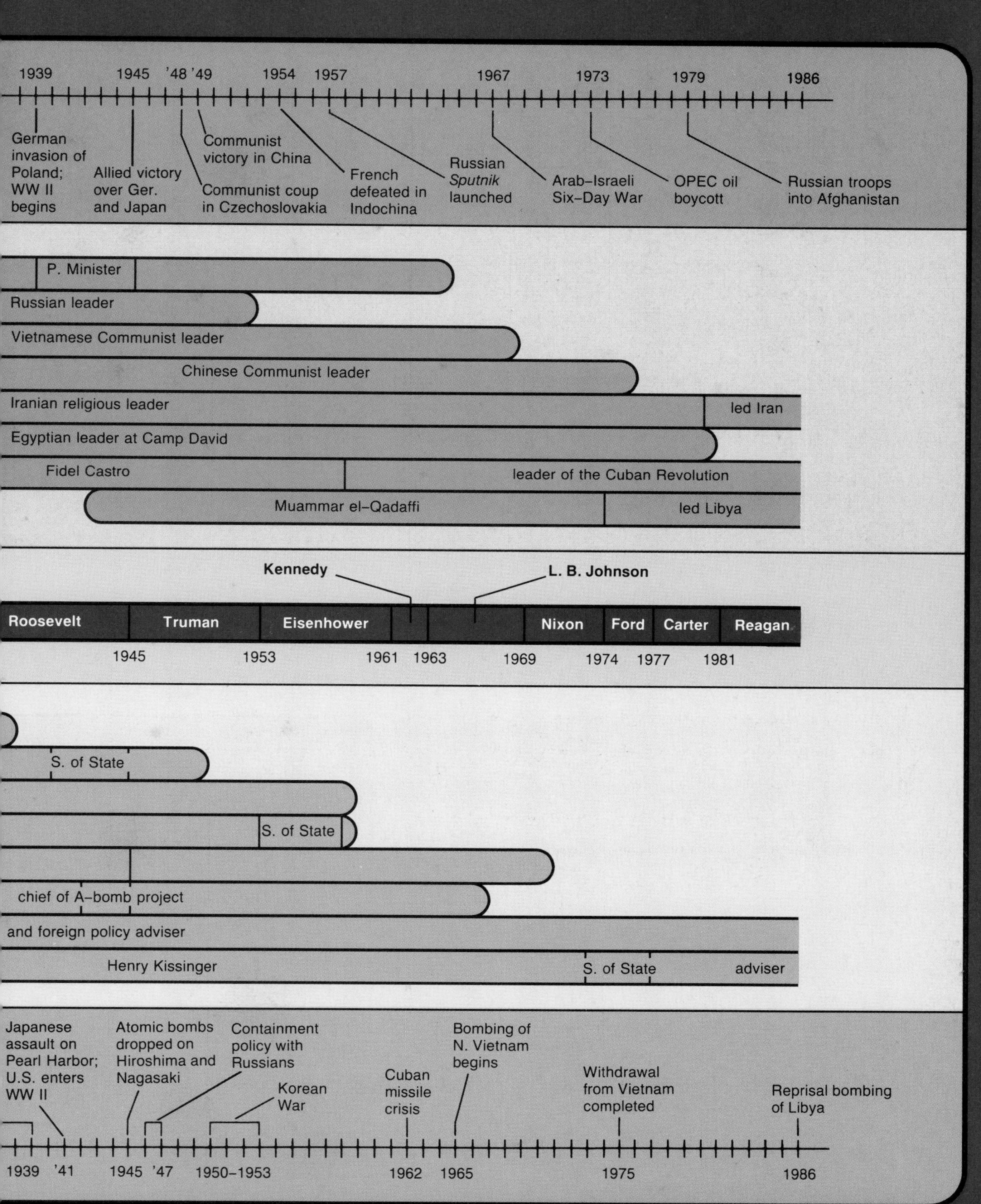

1939
1945
'48
'49
1954
1957
1967
1973
1979
1986
German invasion of Poland; WW II begins
Allied victory over Ger. and Japan
Communist victory in China
Communist coup in Czechoslovakia
French defeated in Indochina
Russian *Sputnik* launched
Arab–Israeli Six-Day War
OPEC oil boycott
Russian troops into Afghanistan
P. Minister
Russian leader
Vietnamese Communist leader
Chinese Communist leader
Iranian religious leader
led Iran
Egyptian leader at Camp David
Fidel Castro
leader of the Cuban Revolution
Muammar el-Qadaffi
led Libya
Kennedy
L. B. Johnson
Roosevelt
Truman
Eisenhower
Nixon
Ford
Carter
Reagan
1945
1953
1961
1963
1969
1974
1977
1981
S. of State
S. of State
chief of A-bomb project
and foreign policy adviser
Henry Kissinger
S. of State
adviser
Japanese assault on Pearl Harbor; U.S. enters WW II
Atomic bombs dropped on Hiroshima and Nagasaki
Containment policy with Russians
Korean War
Cuban missile crisis
Bombing of N. Vietnam begins
Withdrawal from Vietnam completed
Reprisal bombing of Libya
1939
'41
1945
'47
1950–1953
1962
1965
1975
1986

The Declaration of Independence

When in the Course of human events, it becomes necessary for one people to dissolve the political bands which have connected them with another, and to assume among the Powers of the earth, the separate and equal station to which the Laws of Nature and of Nature's God entitle them, a decent respect to the opinions of mankind requires that they should declare the causes which impel them to the separation.

We hold these truths to be self-evident, that all men are created equal, that they are endowed by their Creator with certain unalienable Rights, that among these are Life, Liberty and the pursuit of Happiness. That to secure these rights, Governments are instituted among Men, deriving their just powers from the consent of the governed, That whenever any Form of Government becomes destructive of these ends, it is the Right of the People to alter or to abolish it, and to institute new Government, laying its foundation on such principles and organizing its powers in such form, as to them shall seem most likely to effect their Safety and Happiness. Prudence, indeed, will dictate that Governments long established should not be changed for light and transient causes; and accordingly all experience hath shown, that mankind are more disposed to suffer, while evils are sufferable, than to right themselves by abolishing the forms to which they are accustomed. But when a long train of abuses and usurpations, pursuing invariably the same Object evinces a design to reduce them under absolute Despotism, it is their right, it is their duty, to throw off such Government, and to provide new Guards for their future security.—Such has been the patient sufferance of these Colonies; and such is now the necessity which constrains them to alter their former Systems of Government. The history of the present King of Great Britain is a history of repeated injuries and usurpations, all having in direct object the establishment of an absolute Tyranny over these States. To prove this, let Facts be submitted to a candid world.

He has refused his Assent to Laws, the most wholesome and necessary for the public good.

He has forbidden his Governors to pass Laws of immediate and pressing importance, unless suspended in their operation till his Assent should be obtained; and when so suspended, he has utterly neglected to attend to them.

He has refused to pass other Laws for the accommodation of large districts of people, unless those people would relinquish the right of Representation in the Legislature, a right inestimable to them and formidable to tyrants only.

He has called together legislative bodies at places unusual, uncomfortable, and distant from the depository of their Public Records, for the sole purpose of fatiguing them into compliance with his measures.

He has dissolved Representative Houses repeatedly, for opposing with manly firmness his invasions on the rights of the people.

He has refused for a long time, after such dissolutions, to cause others to be elected; whereby the Legislative Powers, incapable of Annihilation, have returned to the People at large for their exercise; the State remaining in the mean time exposed to all the dangers of invasion from without, and convulsions within.

He has endeavoured to prevent the population of these States; for that purpose obstructing the Laws of Naturalization of Foreigners; refusing to pass others to encourage their migration hither, and raising the conditions of new Appropriations of Lands.

He has obstructed the Administration of Justice, by refusing his Assent to Laws for establishing Judiciary Powers.

He has made Judges dependent on his Will alone, for the tenure of their offices, and the amount and payment of their salaries.

He has erected a multitude of New Offices, and sent hither swarms of Officers to harass our People, and eat out their substance.

He has kept among us, in times of peace, Standing Armies without the Consent of our legislature.

He has affected to render the Military independent of and superior to the Civil Power.

He has combined with others to subject us to a jurisdiction foreign to our constitution, and unacknowledged by our laws; giving his Assent to their acts of pretended legislation:

For quartering large bodies of armed troops among us:

For protecting them, by a mock Trial, from Punishment for any Murders which they should commit on the Inhabitants of these States:

For cutting off our Trade with all parts of the world:

For imposing taxes on us without our Consent:

For depriving us in many cases, of the benefits of Trial by Jury:

For transporting us beyond Seas to be tried for pretended offences:

For abolishing the free System of English Laws in a neighbouring Province, establishing therein an Arbitrary government, and enlarging its Boundaries so as to render it at once an example and fit instrument for introducing the same absolute rule into these Colonies:

For taking away our Charters, abolishing our most valuable Laws, and altering fundamentally the Forms of our Governments:

For suspending our own Legislature, and declaring themselves invested with Power to legislate for us in all cases whatsoever.

He has abdicated Government here, by declaring us out of his Protection and waging War against us.

He has plundered our seas, ravaged our Coasts, burnt our towns, and destroyed the lives of our people.

He is at this time transporting large armies of foreign mercenaries to compleat the works of death, desolation and tyranny, already begun with circumstances of Cruelty & perfidy scarcely paralleled in the most barbarous ages, and totally unworthy the Head of a civilized nation.

He has constrained our fellow Citizens taken Captive on the high Seas to bear Arms against their Country, to become the executioners of their friends and Brethren, or to fall themselves by their Hands.

He has excited domestic insurrections amongst us, and has endeavoured to bring on the inhabitants of our frontiers, the merciless Indian Savages, whose known rule of warfare, is an undistinguished destruction of all ages, sexes and conditions.

In every stage of these Oppressions We have Petitioned for Redress in the most humble terms: Our repeated Petitions have been answered only by repeated injury. A Prince, whose character is thus marked by every act which may define a Tyrant, is unfit to be the ruler of a free People.

Nor have We been wanting in attention to our British brethren. We have warned them from time to time of attempts by their legislature to extend an unwarrantable jurisdiction over us. We have reminded them of the circumstances of our emigration and settlement here. We have appealed to their native justice and magnanimity, and we have conjured them by the ties of our common kindred to disavow these usurpations, which, would inevitably interrupt our connections and correspondence. They too have been deaf to the voice of justice and of consanguinity. We must, therefore, acquiesce in the necessity, which denounces our Separation, and hold them, as we hold the rest of mankind, Enemies in War, in Peace Friends.

We, therefore, the Representatives of the united States of America, in General Congress, Assembled, appealing to the Supreme Judge of the world for the rectitude of our intentions, do, in the Name, and by Authority of the good People of these Colonies, solemnly publish and declare, That these United Colonies are, and of Right ought to be Free and Independent States; that they are Absolved from all Allegiance to the British Crown, and that all political connection between them and the State of Great Britain, is and ought to be totally dissolved; and that as Free and Independent States, they have full Power to levy War, conclude Peace, contract Alliances, establish Commerce, and to do all other Acts and Things which Independent States may of right do. And for the support of this Declaration, with a firm reliance on the Protection of Divine Providence, we mutually pledge to each other our Lives, our Fortunes and our sacred Honor.

John Hancock,

Josiah Bartlett, Wm Whipple, Saml Adams, John Adams, Robt Treat Paine, Elbridge Gerry, Steph. Hopkins, William Ellery, Roger Sherman, Samel Huntington, Wm Williams, Oliver Wolcott, Matthew Thornton, Wm Floyd, Phil Livingston, Frans Lewis, Lewis Morris, Richd Stockton, Jno Witherspoon, Fras Hopkinson, John Hart, Abra Clark, Robt Morris, Benjamin Rush, Benja Franklin, John Morton, Geo Clymer, Jas Smith, Geo. Taylor, James Wilson, Geo. Ross, Caesar Rodney, Geo Read, Thos M:Kean, Samuel Chase, Wm Paca, Thos Stone, Charles Carroll of Carrollton, George Wythe, Richard Henry Lee, Th. Jefferson, Benja Harrison, Thos Nelson, Jr., Francis Lightfoot Lee, Carter Braxton, Wm Hooper, Joseph Hewes, John Penn, Edward Rutledge, Thos Heyward, Junr., Thomas Lynch, Junor., Arthur Middleton, Button Gwinnett, Lyman Hall, Geo Walton.

The Constitution of the United States

We the people of the United States, in Order to form a more perfect Union, establish Justice, insure domestic Tranquility, provide for the common defence, promote the general Welfare, and secure the Blessings of Liberty to ourselves and our Posterity, do ordain and establish this CONSTITUTION for the United States of America.

ARTICLE I

Section 1. All legislative Powers herein granted shall be vested in a Congress of the United States, which shall consist of a Senate and House of Representatives.

Section 2. The House of Representatives shall be composed of Members chosen every second Year by the People of the several States, and the Electors in each State shall have the Qualifications requisite for Electors of the most numerous Branch of the State Legislature.

No Person shall be a Representative who shall not have attained to the Age of twenty-five Years, and been seven Years a Citizen of the United States, and who shall not, when elected, be an Inhabitant of that State in which he shall be chosen.

Representatives and direct Taxes shall be apportioned among the several States which may be included within this Union, according to their respective Numbers, which shall be determined by adding to the whole Number of free Persons, including those bound to Service for a Term of Years, and excluding Indians not taxed, three fifths of all other Persons. The actual Enumeration shall be made within three Years after the first Meeting of the Congress of the United States, and within every subsequent Term of ten Years, in such Manner as they shall by Law direct. The Number of Representatives shall not exceed one for every thirty Thousand, but each State shall have at Least one Representative; and until such enumeration shall be made, the State of New Hampshire shall be entitled to chuse three, Massachusetts eight, Rhode-Island and Providence Plantations one, Connecticut five, New-York six, New Jersey four, Pennsylvania eight, Delaware one, Maryland six, Virginia ten, North Carolina five, South Carolina five, and Georgia three.

When vacancies happen in the Representation from any State, the Executive Authority thereof shall issue Writs of Election to fill such Vacancies.

The House of Representatives shall chuse their Speaker and other Officers; and shall have the sole Power of Impeachment.

Section 3. The Senate of the United States shall be composed of two Senators from each State, chosen by the Legislature thereof, for six Years; and each Senator shall have one Vote.

Immediately after they shall be assembled in Consequence of the first Election, they shall be divided as equally as may be into three Classes. The Seats of the Senators of the first Class shall be vacated at the Expiration of the second Year, of the second Class at the Expiration of the fourth Year, and of the third Class at the Expiration of the sixth Year, so that one-third may be chosen every second Year; and if Vacancies happen by Resignation, or otherwise, during the Recess of the Legislature of any State, the Executive thereof may make temporary Appointments until the next Meeting of the Legislature, which shall then fill such Vacancies.

No Person shall be a Senator who shall not have attained to the Age of thirty Years, and been nine Years a Citizen of the United States, and who shall not, when elected, be an Inhabitant of that State in which he shall be chosen.

The Vice President of the United States shall be President of the Senate, but shall have no vote, unless they be equally divided.

The Senate shall chuse their other Officers, and also a President pro tempore, in the absence of the Vice President, or when he shall exercise the Office of the President of the United States.

The Senate shall have the sole Power to try all Impeachments. When sitting for that purpose, they shall be on Oath or Affirmation. When the President of the United States is tried, the Chief Justice shall preside: And no person shall be convicted without the Concurrence of two thirds of the Members present.

Judgment in Cases of Impeachment shall not extend further than to removal from Office, and disqualification to hold and enjoy any Office of honor, Trust, or Profit under the United States: but the Party convicted shall nevertheless be liable and subject to Indictment, Trial, Judgment, and Punishment, according to Law.

Section 4. The Times, Places and Manner of holding

Elections for Senators and Representatives, shall be prescribed in each state by the Legislature thereof; but the Congress may at any time by Law make or alter such Regulations, except as to the Places of Chusing Senators.

The Congress shall assemble at least once in every Year, and such Meeting shall be on the first Monday in December, unless they shall by Law appoint a different Day.

Section 5. Each House shall be the Judge of the Elections, Returns and Qualifications of its own Members, and a Majority of each shall constitute a Quorum to do Business; but a smaller number may adjourn from day to day, and may be authorized to compel the Attendance of absent Members, in such Manner, and under such Penalties, as each House may provide.

Each House may determine the Rules of its Proceedings, punish its Members for disorderly Behavior, and, with the Concurrence of two thirds, expel a Member.

Each House shall keep a Journal of its Proceedings, and from time to time publish the same, excepting such Parts as may in their Judgment require Secrecy; and the Yeas and Nays of the Members of either House on any question shall, at the Desire of one fifth of those Present, be entered on the Journal.

Neither House, during the Session of Congress, shall, without the Consent of the other, adjourn for more than three days, nor to any other Place than that in which the two Houses shall be sitting.

Section 6. The Senators and Representatives shall receive a Compensation for their Services, to be ascertained by Law, and paid out of the Treasury of the United States. They shall in all Cases, except Treason, Felony, and Breach of the Peace, be privileged from arrest during their Attendance at the Session of their respective Houses, and in going to and returning from the same; and for any Speech or Debate in either House, they shall not be questioned in any other Place.

No Senator or Representative shall, during the Time for which he was elected, be appointed to any civil Office under the Authority of the United States, which shall have been created, or the Emoluments whereof shall have been increased, during such time; and no Person holding any Office under the United States shall be a Member of either House during his continuance in Office.

Section 7. All Bills for raising Revenue shall originate in the House of Representatives; but the Senate may propose or concur with Amendments as on other bills.

Every Bill which shall have passed the House of Representatives and the Senate, shall, before it become a Law, be presented to the President of the United States; If he approve he shall sign it, but if not he shall return it, with his Objections, to that House in which it shall have originated, who shall enter the Objections at large on their Journal, and proceed to reconsider it. If after such Reconsideration two thirds of that House shall agree to pass the bill, it shall be sent, together with the objections, to the other House, by which it shall likewise be reconsidered, and if approved by two thirds of that House, it shall become a Law. But in all such Cases the Votes of both Houses shall be determined by Yeas and Nays, and the Names of the Persons voting for and against the Bill shall be entered on the Journal of each House respectively. If any Bill shall not be returned by the President within ten Days (Sundays excepted) after it shall have been presented to him, the Same shall be a Law, in like Manner as if he had signed it, unless the Congress by their Adjournment prevent its Return, in which Case it shall not be a Law.

Every Order, Resolution, or Vote to which the Concurrence of the Senate and House of Representatives may be necessary (except on a question of Adjournment) shall be presented to the President of the United States; and before the Same shall take Effect, shall be approved by him, or being disapproved by him, shall be repassed by two thirds of the Senate and House of Representatives, according to the Rules and Limitations prescribed in the Case of a Bill.

Section 8. The Congress shall have Power To lay and collect Taxes, Duties, Imposts and Excises, to pay the Debts and provide for the common Defence and general Welfare of the United States; but all Duties, Imposts and Excises shall be uniform throughout the United States;

To borrow money on the credit of the United States;

To regulate Commerce with foreign Nations, and among the several States, and with the Indian Tribes;

To establish an uniform Rule of Naturalization, and uniform Laws on the subject of Bankruptcies throughout the United States;

To coin Money, regulate the Value thereof, and of foreign Coin, and fix the Standard of Weights and Measures;

To provide for the Punishment of counterfeiting the Securities and current Coin of the United States;

To establish Post Offices and post Roads;

To promote the Progress of Science and useful Arts, by securing for limited Times to Authors and Inventors the exclusive Right to their respective Writings and Discoveries;

To constitute Tribunals inferior to the Supreme Court;

To define and punish Piracies and Felonies committed on the high Seas, and Offences against the Law of Nations;

To declare War, grant Letters of Marque and Reprisal, and make Rules concerning Captures on Land and Water;

To raise and support Armies, but no Appropriation

of Money to that Use shall be for a longer Term than two Years;

To provide and maintain a Navy;

To make Rules for the Government and Regulation of the land and naval forces;

To provide for calling forth the Militia to execute the Laws of the Union, suppress Insurrections and repel Invasions;

To provide for organizing, arming, and disciplining the Militia, and for governing such Part of them as may be employed in the Service of the United States, reserving to the States respectively, the Appointment of the Officers, and the Authority of training the Militia according to the discipline prescribed by Congress;

To exercise exclusive Legislation in all Cases whatsoever, over such District (not exceeding ten Miles square) as may, by Cession of particular States, and the acceptance of Congress, become the Seat of Government of the United States, and to exercise like Authority over all Places purchased by the Consent of the Legislature of the State in which the Same shall be, for the Erection of Forts, Magazines, Arsenals, dock-Yards, and other needful Buildings;—And

To make all Laws which shall be necessary and proper for carrying into Execution the foregoing Powers, and all other Powers vested by this Constitution in the government of the United States, or in any Department or Officer thereof.

Section 9. The Migration or Importation of such Persons as any of the States now existing shall think proper to admit, shall not be prohibited by the Congress prior to the Year one thousand eight hundred and eight, but a tax or duty may be imposed on such Importation, not exceeding ten dollars for each Person.

The privilege of the Writ of Habeas Corpus shall not be suspended, unless when in Cases of Rebellion or Invasion the public Safety may require it.

No Bill of Attainder or ex post facto Law shall be passed.

No capitation, or other direct, Tax shall be laid unless in Proportion to the Census or Enumeration herein before directed to be taken.

No Tax or Duty shall be laid on Articles exported from any State.

No Preference shall be given by any Regulation of Revenue to the Ports of one State over those of another: nor shall Vessels bound to, or from, one State, be obliged to enter, clear, or pay Duties in another.

No Money shall be drawn from the Treasury, but in Consequence of Appropriations made by Law; and a regular Statement and Account of the Receipts and Expenditures of all public Money shall be published from time to time.

No Title of Nobility shall be granted by the United States: And no Person holding any Office of Profit or Trust under them, shall, without the Consent of the Congress, accept of any present, Emolument, Office, or Title, of any kind whatever, from any King, Prince, or foreign State.

Section 10. No State shall enter into any Treaty, Alliance, or Confederation; grant Letters of Marque and Reprisal; coin Money; emit Bills of Credit; make any Thing but gold and silver Coin a Tender in Payment of Debts; pass any Bill of Attainder, ex post facto Law, or Law impairing the Obligation of Contracts, or grant any Title of Nobility.

No State shall, without the Consent of the Congress, lay any Imposts or Duties on Imports or Exports, except what may be absolutely necessary for executing its inspection Laws: and the net Produce of all Duties and Imposts, laid by any State on Imports or Exports, shall be for the Use of the Treasury of the United States; and all such Laws shall be subject to the Revision and Control of the Congress.

No State shall, without the Consent of Congress, lay any duty of Tonnage, keep Troops, or Ships of War in time of Peace, enter into any Agreement or Compact with another State, or with a foreign Power, or engage in War, unless actually invaded, or in such imminent Danger as will not admit of delay.

ARTICLE II

Section 1. The executive Power shall be vested in a President of the United States of America. He shall hold his Office during the Term of four years, and, together with the Vice President, chosen for the same Term, be elected, as follows:

Each State shall appoint, in such Manner as the Legislature thereof may direct, a Number of Electors, equal to the whole Number of Senators and Representatives to which the State may be entitled in the Congress; but no Senator or Representative, or Person holding an Office of Trust or Profit under the United States, shall be appointed an Elector.

The Electors shall meet in their respective States, and vote by Ballot for two persons, of whom one at least shall not be an Inhabitant of the same State with themselves. And they shall make a List of all the Persons voted for, and of the Number of Votes for each; which List they shall sign and certify, and transmit sealed to the Seat of the Government of the United States, directed to the President of the Senate. The President of the Senate shall, in the Presence of the Senate and House of Representatives, open all the Certificates, and the Votes shall then be counted. The Person having the greatest Number of Votes shall be the President, if such Number be a Majority of the whole Number of Electors appointed;

and if there be more than one who have such Majority, and have an equal Number of Votes, then the House of Representatives shall immediately chuse by Ballot one of them for President; and if no Person have a Majority, then from the five highest on the List the said House shall in like Manner chuse the President. But in chusing the President, the votes shall be taken by States, the Representation from each State having one Vote; a quorum for this Purpose shall consist of a Member or Members from two-thirds of the States, and a Majority of all the States shall be necessary to a Choice. In every Case, after the Choice of the President, the Person having the greatest Number of Votes of the Electors shall be the Vice President. But if there should remain two or more who have equal votes, the Senate shall chuse from them by Ballot the Vice President.

The Congress may determine the time of chusing the Electors, and the Day on which they shall give their Votes; which Day shall be the same throughout the United States.

No person except a natural-born Citizen, or a Citizen of the United States, at the time of the Adoption of this Constitution, shall be eligible to the Office of President; neither shall any Person be eligible to that Office who shall not have attained to the Age of thirty-five years, and been fourteen Years a Resident within the United States.

In Case of the Removal of the President from Office, or of his Death, Resignation, or Inability to discharge the Powers and Duties of the said Office, the same shall devolve on the Vice President, and the Congress may by Law provide for the Case of Removal, Death, Resignation, or Inability, both of the President and Vice President, declaring what Officer shall then act as President, and such Officer shall act accordingly, until the disability be removed, or a President shall be elected.

The President shall, at stated Times, receive for his Services a Compensation, which shall neither be increased nor diminished during the Period for which he shall have been elected, and he shall not receive within that Period any other Emolument from the United States, or any of them.

Before he enter on the execution of his Office, he shall take the following Oath or Affirmation:—"I do solemnly swear (or affirm) that I will faithfully execute the Office of President of the United States, and will, to the best of my Ability, preserve, protect, and defend the Constitution of the United States."

Section 2. The President shall be Commander in Chief of the Army and Navy of the United States, and of the Militia of the several States, when called into the actual Service of the United States; he may require the Opinion, in writing, of the principal Officer in each of the executive Departments, upon any subject relating to the Duties of their respective Offices, and he shall have Power to Grant Reprieves and Pardons for Offences against the United States, except in Cases of Impeachment.

He shall have Power, by and with the Advice and Consent of the Senate, to make Treaties, provided two thirds of the Senators present concur; and he shall nominate, and by and with the Advice and Consent of the Senate, shall appoint Ambassadors, other public Ministers and Consuls, Judges of the supreme Court, and all other Officers of the United States, whose Appointments are not herein otherwise provided for, and which shall be established by Law: but the Congress may by Law vest the Appointment of such inferior Officers, as they think proper, in the President alone, in the Courts of Law, or in the Heads of Departments.

The President shall have Power to fill up all Vacancies that may happen during the Recess of the Senate, by granting Commissions which shall expire at the End of their next Session.

Section 3. He shall from time to time give to the Congress Information of the State of the Union, and recommend to their Consideration such Measures as he shall judge necessary and expedient; he may, on extraordinary occasions, convene both Houses, or either of them, and in Case of Disagreement between them, with respect to the Time of Adjournment, he may adjourn them to such Time as he shall think proper; he shall receive Ambassadors and other public Ministers; he shall take Care that the Laws be faithfully executed, and shall Commission all the Officers of the United States.

Section 4. The President, Vice President and all civil Officers of the United States, shall be removed from Office on Impeachment for, and Conviction of, Treason, Bribery, or other high Crimes and Misdemeanors.

ARTICLE III

Section 1. The judicial Power of the United States, shall be vested in one supreme Court, and in such inferior Courts as the Congress may from time to time ordain and establish. The Judges, both of the supreme and inferior Courts, shall hold their Offices during good Behaviour, and shall, at stated Times, receive for their Services, a Compensation, which shall not be diminished during their Continuance in Office.

Section 2. The judicial Power shall extend to all Cases, in Law and Equity, arising under this Constitution, the Laws of the United States, and treaties made, or which shall be made, under their Authority;—to all Cases affecting ambassadors, other public ministers and consuls;—to all cases of admiralty and maritime Jurisdiction;—to Controversies to which the United States shall be a Party;—to Controversies between two or more

States;—between a State and Citizens of another State;—between Citizens of different States,—between Citizens of the same State claiming Lands under Grants of different States, and between a State, or the Citizens thereof, and foreign States, Citizens or Subjects.

In all Cases affecting Ambassadors, other public Ministers and Consuls, and those in which a State shall be Party, the supreme Court shall have original Jurisdiction. In all the other Cases before mentioned, the supreme Court shall have appellate Jurisdiction, both as to Law and Fact, with such Exceptions, and under such Regulations as the Congress shall make.

The trial of all Crimes, except in Cases of Impeachment, shall be by Jury; and such Trial shall be held in the State where the said Crimes shall have been committed; but when not committed within any State, the Trial shall be at such Place or Places as the Congress may by Law have directed.

Section 3. Treason against the United States, shall consist only in levying War against them, or in adhering to their Enemies, giving them Aid and Comfort. No Person shall be convicted of Treason unless on the testimony of two Witnesses to the same overt Act, or on Confession in open Court.

The Congress shall have power to declare the Punishment of Treason, but no Attainder of Treason shall work Corruption of Blood, or Forfeiture except during the Life of the Person attained.

ARTICLE IV

Section 1. Full Faith and Credit shall be given in each State to the public Acts, Records, and judicial Proceedings of every other State. And the Congress may by general Laws prescribe the Manner in which such Acts, Records and Proceedings shall be proved, and the Effect thereof.

Section 2. The Citizens of each State shall be entitled to all Privileges and Immunities of Citizens in the several States.

A Person charged in any State with Treason, Felony, or other Crime, who shall flee from Justice, and be found in another State, shall on demand of the executive Authority of the State from which he fled, be delivered up, to be removed to the State having Jurisdiction of the crime.

No Person held to Service or Labour in one State, under the Laws thereof, escaping into another, shall, in Consequence of any Law or Regulation therein, be discharged from such Service or Labour, but shall be delivered up on Claim of the Party to whom such Service or Labour may be due.

Section 3. New States may be admitted by the Congress into this Union; but no new State shall be formed or erected within the Jurisdiction of any other State; nor any State be formed by the Junction of two or more States, or parts of States, without the Consent of the Legislatures of the States concerned as well as of the Congress.

The Congress shall have Power to dispose of and make all needful Rules and Regulations respecting the Territory or other Property belonging to the United States; and nothing in this Constitution shall be so construed as to Prejudice any Claims of the United States, or of any particular State.

Section 4. The United States shall guarantee to every State in this Union a Republican Form of Government, and shall protect each of them against Invasion; and on Application of the Legislature, or the Executive (when the Legislature cannot be convened) against domestic Violence.

ARTICLE V

The Congress, whenever two-thirds of both Houses shall deem it necessary, shall propose Amendments to this Constitution, or, on the Application of the Legislatures of two-thirds of the several States, shall call a Convention for proposing Amendments, which, in either Case, shall be valid to all Intents and Purposes, as part of this Constitution, when ratified by the Legislatures of three-fourths of the several States, or by Conventions in three-fourths thereof, as the one or the other Mode of Ratification may be proposed by the Congress; Provided that no Amendment which may be made prior to the Year One thousand eight hundred and eight shall in any Manner affect the first and fourth Clauses in the Ninth Section of the first Article; and that no State, without its Consent, shall be deprived of its equal Suffrage in the Senate.

ARTICLE VI

All Debts contracted and Engagements entered into, before the Adoption of this Constitution, shall be as valid against the United States under this Constitution, as under the Confederation.

This Constitution, and the Laws of the United States which shall be made in Pursuance thereof; and all Treaties made, or which shall be made, under the Authority of the United States, shall be the supreme Law of the Land; and the Judges in every State shall be bound thereby, any Thing in the Constitution or Laws of any State to the Contrary notwithstanding.

The Senators and Representatives before mentioned, and the Members of the several State Legislatures, and all executive and judicial Officers, both of the United States and of the several States, shall be bound by Oath or Affirmation to support this Constitution; but no religious Test shall ever be required as a qualification to any Office or public Trust under the United States.

ARTICLE VII

The Ratification of the Conventions of nine States shall be sufficient for the Establishment of this Constitution between the States so ratifying the same.

Done in Convention by the Unanimous Consent of the States present the Seventeenth Day of September in the Year of our Lord one thousand seven hundred and Eighty seven, and of the Independence of the United States of America the Twelfth. In Witness whereof We have hereunto subscribed our Names.

Go. Washington, *President and deputy from Virginia; Attest* William Jackson, *Secretary; Delaware:* Geo. Read,* Gunning Bedford, Jr., John Dickinson, Richard Bassett, Jaco. Broom; *Maryland:* James McHenry, Daniel of St. Thomas' Jenifer, Danl. Carroll; *Virginia:* John Blair, James Madison, Jr.; *North Carolina:* Wm. Blount, Richd. Dobbs Spaight, Hu Williamson; *South Carolina:* J. Rutledge, Charles Cotesworth Pinckney, Charles Pinckney, Pierce Butler; *Georgia:* William Few, Abr. Baldwin; *New Hampshire:* John Langdon, Nicholas Gilman; *Massachusetts:* Nathaniel Gorham, Rufus King; *Connecticut:* Wm. Saml. Johnson, Roger Sherman;* *New York:* Alexander Hamilton; *New Jersey:* Wil. Livingston, David Brearley, Wm. Paterson, Jona. Dayton; *Pennsylvania:* B. Franklin,* Thomas Mifflin, Robt. Morris,* Geo. Clymer,* Thos. FitzSimons, Jared Ingersoll, James Wilson, Gouv. Morris.

Articles in Addition to, and Amendment of, the Constitution of the United States of America, Proposed by Congress, and Ratified by the Legislatures of the Several States, Pursuant to the Fifth Article of the Original Constitution.

AMENDMENT I [1791]

Congress shall make no law respecting an establishment of religion, or prohibiting the free exercise thereof; or abridging the freedom of speech, or of the press; or the right of the people peaceably to assemble, and to petition the Government for a redress of grievances.

AMENDMENT II [1791]

A well regulated Militia, being necessary to the security of a free State, the right of the people to keep and bear Arms shall not be infringed.

* Also signed the Declaration of Independence

AMENDMENT III [1791]

No Soldier shall, in time of peace, be quartered in any house, without the consent of the Owner, nor in time of war, but in a manner to be prescribed by law.

AMENDMENT IV [1791]

The right of the people to be secure in their persons, houses, papers, and effects, against unreasonable searches and seizures, shall not be violated, and no Warrants shall issue, but upon probable cause, supported by Oath or affirmation, and particularly describing the place to be searched, and the persons or things to be seized.

AMENDMENT V [1791]

No person shall be held to answer for a capital or otherwise infamous crime, unless on a presentment or indictment of a Grand Jury, except in cases arising in the land or naval forces, or in the Militia, when in actual service in time of War or public danger; nor shall any person be subject for the same offence to be twice put in jeopardy of life or limb; nor shall be compelled in any criminal case to be a witness against himself, nor be deprived of life, liberty, or property, without due process of law; nor shall private property be taken for public use, without just compensation.

AMENDMENT VI [1791]

In all criminal prosecutions, the accused shall enjoy the right to a speedy and public trial, by an impartial jury of the State and district wherein the crime shall have been committed, which district shall have been previously ascertained by law, and to be informed of the nature and cause of the accusation; to be confronted with the winesses against him; to have compulsory process for obtaining witnesses in his favor, and to have the Assistance of Counsel for his defence.

AMENDMENT VII [1791]

In suits at common law, where the value in controversy shall exceed twenty dollars, the right of trial by jury shall be preserved, and no fact tried by a jury, shall be otherwise reexamined in any Court of the United States, than according to the rules of the common law.

AMENDMENT VIII [1791]

Excessive bail shall not be required, nor excessive fines imposed, nor cruel and unusual punishments inflicted.

AMENDMENT IX [1791]

The enumeration in the Constitution, of certain rights, shall not be construed to deny or disparage others retained by the people.

AMENDMENT X [1791]

The powers not delegated to the United States by the Constitution, nor prohibited by it to the States, are reserved to the States respectively, or to the people.

AMENDMENT XI [1798]

The Judicial power of the United States shall not be construed to extend to any suit in law or equity, commenced or prosecuted against one of the United States by Citizens of another State, or by Citizens or Subjects of any Foreign State.

AMENDMENT XII [1804]

The Electors shall meet in their respective States and vote by ballot for President and Vice-President, one of whom, at least, shall not be an inhabitant of the same State with themselves; they shall name in their ballots the person voted for as President, and in distinct ballots the person voted for as Vice-President, and they shall make distinct lists of all persons voted for as President, and of all persons voted for as Vice-President, and of the number of votes for each, which lists they shall sign and certify, and transmit sealed to the seat of the government of the United States, directed to the President of the Senate;—The President of the Senate shall, in the presence of the Senate and House of Representatives, open all the certificates and the votes shall then be counted;—The person having the greatest number of votes for President, shall be the President, if such number be a majority of the whole number of Electors appointed; and if no person have such majority, then from the persons having the highest numbers not exceeding three on the list of those voted for as President, the House of Representatives shall choose immediately, by ballot, the President. But in choosing the President, the votes shall be taken by states, the representation from each state having one vote; a quorum for this purpose shall consist of a member or members from two-thirds of the states, and a majority of all the states shall be necessary to a choice. And if the House of Representatives shall not choose a President whenever the right of choice shall devolve upon them, before the fourth day of March next following, then the Vice-President shall act as President, as in the case of the death or other constitutional disability of the President.—The person having the greatest number of votes as Vice-President, shall be the Vice-President, if such number be a majority of the whole number of Electors appointed, and if no person have a majority, then from the two highest numbers on the list, the Senate shall choose the Vice-President; a quorum for the purpose shall consist of two-thirds of the whole number of Senators, and a majority of the whole number shall be necessary to a choice. But no person constitutionally ineligible to the office of President shall be eligible to that of Vice-President of the United States.

AMENDMENT XIII [1865]

Section 1. Neither slavery nor involuntary servitude, except as a punishment for crime whereof the party shall have been duly convicted, shall exist within the United States, or any place subject to their jurisdiction.

Section 2. Congress shall have power to enforce this article by appropriate legislation.

AMENDMENT XIV [1868]

Section 1. All persons born or naturalized in the United States, and subject to the jurisdiction thereof, are citizens of the United States and of the State wherein they reside. No State shall make or enforce any law which shall abridge the privileges or immunities of citizens of the United States; nor shall any State deprive any person of life, liberty, or property, without due process of law; nor deny to any person within its jurisdiction the equal protection of the laws.

Section 2. Representatives shall be apportioned among the several States according to their respective numbers, counting the whole number of persons in each State, excluding Indians not taxed. But when the right to vote at any election for the choice of electors for President and Vice-President of the United States, Representatives in Congress, the Executive and Judicial officers of a State, or the members of the Legislature thereof, is denied to any of the male inhabitants of such State, being twenty-one years of age, and citizens of the United States, or in any way abridged, except for participation in rebellion, or other crime, the basis of representation therein shall be reduced in the proportion which the number of such male citizens shall bear to the whole number of male citizens twenty-one years of age in such State.

Section 3. No person shall be a Senator or Representative in Congress, or elector of President and Vice-President, or hold any office, civil or military, under the United States, or under any State, who, having previously taken an oath, as a member of Congress, or as an officer of the United States, or as a member of any State legislature, or as an executive or judicial officer of any State, to support the Constitution of the United States, shall have engaged in insurrection or rebellion against the same, or given aid or comfort to the enemies thereof. But Congress may by a vote of two-thirds of each House, remove such disability.

Section 4. The validity of the public debt of the United States, authorized by law, including debts incurred for payment of pensions and bounties for services in suppressing insurrection or rebellion, shall not be questioned. But neither the United States nor any State shall assume or pay any debt or obligation incurred in aid of insurrection or rebellion against the United States, or any claim for the loss or emancipation of any slave; but all such debts, obligations, and claims shall be held illegal and void.

Section 5. The Congress shall have the power to enforce, by appropriate legislation, the provisions of this article.

AMENDMENT XV [1870]

Section 1. The right of citizens of the United States to vote shall not be denied or abridged by the United States or by any State on account of race, color, or previous condition of servitude—

Section 2. The Congress shall have power to enforce this article by appropriate legislation.

AMENDMENT XVI [1913]

The Congress shall have power to lay and collect taxes on incomes, from whatever source derived, without apportionment among the several States, and without regard to any census or enumeration.

AMENDMENT XVII [1913]

The Senate of the United States shall be composed of two Senators from each State, elected by the people thereof, for six years; and each Senator shall have one vote. The electors in each State shall have the qualifications requisite for electors of the most numerous branch of the State legislatures.

When vacancies happen in the representation of any State in the Senate, the executive authority of such State shall issue writs of election to fill such vacancies: *Provided,* That the legislature of any State may empower the executive thereof to make temporary appointments until the people fill the vacancies by election as the legislature may direct.

This amendment shall not be so construed as to affect the election or term of any Senator chosen before it becomes valid as part of the Constitution.

AMENDMENT XVIII [1919]

Section 1. After one year from the ratification of this article the manufacture, sale, or transportation of intoxicating liquors within, the importation thereof into, or the exportation thereof from the United States and all territory subject to the jurisdiction thereof for beverage purposes is hereby prohibited.

Section 2. The Congress and the several States shall have concurrent power to enforce this article by appropriate legislation.

Section 3. This article shall be inoperative unless it shall have been ratified as an amendment to the Constitution by the legislatures of the several States, as provided in the Constitution, within seven years from the date of the submission hereof to the States by the Congress.

AMENDMENT XIX [1920]

The right of citizens of the United States to vote shall not be denied or abridged by the United States or by any State on account of sex.

Congress shall have power to enforce this article by appropriate legislation.

AMENDMENT XX [1933]

Section 1. The terms of the President and Vice-President shall end at noon on the 20th day of January, and the terms of Senators and Representatives at noon on the 3d day of January, of the years in which such terms would have ended if this article had not been ratified; and the terms of their successors shall then begin.

Section 2. The Congress shall assemble at least once in every year, and such meeting shall begin at noon on the 3d day of January, unless they shall by law appoint a different day.

Section 3. If, at the time fixed for the beginning of the term of the President, the President elect shall have died, the Vice-President elect shall become President. If a President shall not have been chosen before the time fixed for the beginning of his term, or if the President elect shall have failed to qualify, then the Vice-President elect shall act as President until a President shall have qualified; and the Congress may by law provide for the case wherein neither a President elect nor a Vice-President elect shall have qualified, declaring who shall then act as President, or the manner in which one who is to act shall be selected, and such person shall act accordingly until a President or Vice-President shall have qualified.

Section 4. The Congress may by law provide for the case of the death of any of the persons from whom the House of Representatives may choose a President whenever the right of choice shall have devolved upon them, and for the case of the death of any of the persons from whom the Senate may choose a Vice-President whenever the right of choice shall have devolved upon them.

Section 5. Sections 1 and 2 shall take effect on the 15th day of October following the ratification of this article.

Section 6. This article shall be inoperative unless it shall have been ratified as an amendment to the Constitution by the legislatures of three-fourths of the several States within seven years from the date of its submission.

AMENDMENT XXI [1933]

Section 1. The eighteenth article of amendment to the Constitution of the United States is hereby repealed.

Section 2. The transportation or importation into any State, Territory, or possession of the United States for delivery or use therein of intoxicating liquors, in violation of the laws thereof, is hereby prohibited.

Section 3. This article shall be inoperative unless it shall have been ratified as an amendment to the Constitution by conventions in the several States, as provided in the Constitution, within seven years from the date of the submission hereof to the States by the Congress.

AMENDMENT XXII [1951]

No person shall be elected to the office of the President more than twice, and no person who has held the office of President, or acted as President, for more than two years of a term to which some other person was elected President shall be elected to the office of the President more than once.

But this Article shall not apply to any person holding the office of President when this Article was proposed by the Congress, and shall not prevent any person who may be holding the office of President, or acting as President, during the term within which this Article becomes operative from holding the office of President or acting as President during the remainder of such term.

AMENDMENT XXIII [1961]

Section 1. The District constituting the seat of Government of the United States shall appoint in such manner as the Congress may direct:

A number of electors of President and Vice President equal to the whole number of Senators and Representatives in Congress to which the District would be entitled if it were a State, but in no event more than the least populous State; they shall be in addition to those appointed by the States, but they shall be considered, for the purposes of the election of President and Vice President, to be electors appointed by a State; and they shall meet in the District and perform such duties as provided by the twelfth article of amendment.

Section 2. The Congress shall have power to enforce this article by appropriate legislation.

AMENDMENT XXIV [1964]

Section 1. The right of citizens of the United States to vote in any primary or other election for President or Vice President, for electors for President or Vice President, or for Senator or Representative in Congress, shall not be denied or abridged by the United States or any State by reason of failure to pay any poll tax or other tax.

Section 2. The Congress shall have the power to enforce this article by appropriate legislation.

AMENDMENT XXV [1967]

Section 1. In case of the removal of the President from office or his death or resignation, the Vice President shall become President.

Section 2. Whenever there is a vacancy in the office of the Vice President, the President shall nominate a Vice President who shall take the office upon confirmation by a majority vote of both houses of Congress.

Section 3. Whenever the President transmits to the President pro tempore of the Senate and the Speaker of the House of Representatives his written declaration that he is unable to discharge the powers and duties of his office, and until he transmits to them a written declaration to the contrary, such powers and duties shall be discharged by the Vice President as Acting President.

Section 4. Whenever the Vice President and a majority of either the principal officers of the executive departments, or of such other body as Congress may by law provide, transmit to the President pro tempore of the Senate and the Speaker of the House of Representatives their written declaration that the President is unable to discharge the powers and duties of his office, the Vice President shall immediately assume the powers and duties of the office as Acting President.

Thereafter, when the President transmits to the President pro tempore of the Senate and the Speaker of the House of Representatives his written declaration that no inability exists, he shall resume the powers and duties of his office unless the Vice President and a majority of either the principal officers of the executive departments, or of such other body as Congress may by law provide, transmit within four days to the President pro tempore of the Senate and the Speaker of the House of Representatives their written declaration that the President is unable to discharge the powers and duties of his office. Thereupon Congress shall decide the issue, assembling within 48 hours for that purpose if not in session. If the Congress, within 21 days after receipt of the latter written declaration, or, if Congress is not in session, within 21 days after Congress is required to assemble, determines by two-thirds vote of both houses that the President is unable to discharge the powers and duties of his office, the Vice President shall continue to discharge the same as Acting President; otherwise, the President shall resume the powers and duties of his office.

AMENDMENT XXVI [1971]

Section 1. The right of citizens of the United States, who are 18 years of age or older, to vote shall not be denied or abridged by the United States or any state on account of age.

Section 2. The Congress shall have the power to enforce this article by appropriate legislation.

Presidential Elections, 1789–1984

Year	Candidates	Party	Popular Vote*	Electoral Vote**
1789	**George Washington**			69
	John Adams			34
	Others			35
1792	**George Washington**			132
	John Adams			77
	George Clinton			50
	Others			5
1796	**John Adams**	Federalist		71
	Thomas Jefferson	Democratic Republican		68
	Thomas Pinckney	Federalist		59
	Aaron Burr	Democratic Republican		30
	Others			48
1800	**Thomas Jefferson**	Democratic Republican		73
	Aaron Burr	Democratic Republican		73
	John Adams	Federalist		65
	Charles C. Pinckney	Federalist		64
1804	**Thomas Jefferson**	Democratic Republican		162
	Charles C. Pinckney	Federalist		14
1808	**James Madison**	Democratic Republican		122
	Charles C. Pinckney	Federalist		47
	George Clinton	Independent Republican		6
1812	**James Madison**	Democratic Republican		128
	DeWitt Clinton	Federalist		89
1816	**James Monroe**	Democratic Republican		183
	Rufus King	Federalist		34
1820	**James Monroe**	Democratic Republican		231
	John Quincy Adams	Independent Republican		1
1824	**John Quincy Adams**	Democratic Republican	108,704 (30.5%)	84
	Andrew Jackson	Democratic Republican	153,544 (43.1%)	99
	Henry Clay	Democratic Republican	47,136 (13.2%)	37
	William H. Crawford	Democratic Republican	46,618 (13.1%)	41
1828	**Andrew Jackson**	Democratic	647,231 (56.0%)	178
	John Quincy Adams	National Republican	509,097 (44.0%)	83

* Because only the leading candidates are listed, popular vote percentages do not always total 100.
** The elections of 1800 and 1824, in which no candidate received an electoral vote majority, were decided in the House of Representatives.

Year	*Candidates*	*Party*	*Popular Vote**	*Electoral Vote***
1832	**Andrew Jackson**	Democratic	687,502 (55.0%)	219
	Henry Clay	National Republican	530,189 (42.4%)	49
	William Wirt	Anti-Masonic	33,108 (2.6%)	7
	John Floyd	National Republican		11
1836	**Martin Van Buren**	Democratic	761,549 (50.9%)	170
	William H. Harrison	Whig	549,567 (36.7%)	73
	Hugh L. White	Whig	145,396 (9.7%)	26
	Daniel Webster	Whig	41,287 (2.7%)	14
1840	**William H. Harrison**	Whig	1,275,017 (53.1%)	234
	(**John Tyler,** 1841)			
	Martin Van Buren	Democratic	1,128,702 (46.9%)	60
1844	**James K. Polk**	Democratic	1,337,243 (49.6%)	170
	Henry Clay	Whig	1,299,068 (48.1%)	105
	James G. Birney	Liberty	62,300 (2.3%)	
1848	**Zachary Taylor**	Whig	1,360,101 (47.4%)	163
	(**Millard Fillmore,** 1850)			
	Lewis Cass	Democratic	1,220,544 (42.5%)	127
	Martin Van Buren	Free Soil	291,263 (10.1%)	
1852	**Franklin Pierce**	Democratic	1,601,474 (50.9%)	254
	Winfield Scott	Whig	1,386,578 (44.1%)	42
1856	**James Buchanan**	Democratic	1,838,169 (45.4%)	174
	John C. Frémont	Republican	1,335,264 (33.0%)	114
	Millard Fillmore	American	874,534 (21.6%)	8
1860	**Abraham Lincoln**	Republican	1,865,593 (39.8%)	180
	Stephen A. Douglas	Democratic	1,382,713 (29.5%)	12
	John C. Breckinridge	Democratic	848,356 (18.1%)	72
	John Bell	Constitutional Union	592,906 (12.6%)	39
1864	**Abraham Lincoln**	Republican	2,206,938 (55.0%)	212
	(**Andrew Johnson,** 1865)			
	George B. McClellan	Democratic	1,803,787 (45.0%)	21
1868	**Ulysses S. Grant**	Republican	3,013,421 (52.7%)	214
	Horatio Seymour	Democratic	2,706,829 (47.3%)	80
1872	**Ulysses S. Grant**	Republican	3,596,745 (55.6%)	286
	Horace Greeley	Democratic	2,843,446 (43.9%)	66
1876	**Rutherford B. Hayes**	Republican	4,036,572 (48.0%)	185
	Samuel J. Tilden	Democratic	4,284,020 (51.0%)	184
1880	**James A. Garfield**	Republican	4,449,053 (48.3%)	214
	(**Chester A. Arthur,** 1881)			
	Winfield S. Hancock	Democratic	4,442,035 (48.2%)	155
	James B. Weaver	Greenback Labor	308,578 (3.4%)	
1884	**Grover Cleveland**	Democratic	4,874,986 (48.5%)	219
	James G. Blaine	Republican	4,851,981 (48.2%)	182
	Benjamin F. Butler	Greenback Labor	175,370 (1.8%)	

Year	Candidates	Party	Popular Vote*	Electoral Vote**
1888	**Benjamin Harrison**	Republican	5,444,337 (47.8%)	233
	Grover Cleveland	Democratic	5,540,050 (48.6%)	168
1892	**Grover Cleveland**	Democratic	5,554,414 (46.0%)	277
	Benjamin Harrison	Republican	5,190,802 (43.0%)	145
	James B. Weaver	People's	1,027,329 (8.5%)	22
1896	**William McKinley**	Republican	7,035,638 (50.8%)	271
	William Jennings Bryan	Democratic; Populist	6,467,946 (46.7%)	176
1900	**William McKinley** (**Theodore Roosevelt,** 1901)	Republican	7,219,530 (51.7%)	292
	William Jennings Bryan	Democratic; Populist	6,356,734 (45.5%)	155
1904	**Theodore Roosevelt**	Republican	7,628,834 (56.4%)	336
	Alton B. Parker	Democratic	5,084,401 (37.6%)	140
	Eugene V. Debs	Socialist	402,460 (3.0%)	
1908	**William H. Taft**	Republican	7,679,006 (51.6%)	321
	William Jennings Bryan	Democratic	6,409,106 (43.1%)	162
	Eugene V. Debs	Socialist	420,820 (2.8%)	
1912	**Woodrow Wilson**	Democratic	6,286,820 (41.8%)	435
	Theodore Roosevelt	Progressive	4,126,020 (27.4%)	88
	William H. Taft	Republican	3,483,922 (23.2%)	8
	Eugene V. Debs	Socialist	897,011 (6.0%)	
1916	**Woodrow Wilson**	Democratic	9,129,606 (49.3%)	277
	Charles E. Hughes	Republican	8,538,221 (46.1%)	254
1920	**Warren G. Harding** (**Calvin Coolidge,** 1923)	Republican	16,152,200 (61.0%)	404
	James M. Cox	Democratic	9,147,353 (34.6%)	127
	Eugene V. Debs	Socialist	919,799 (3.5%)	
1924	**Calvin Coolidge**	Republican	15,725,016 (54.1%)	382
	John W. Davis	Democratic	8,385,586 (28.8%)	136
	Robert M. La Follette	Progressive	4,822,856 (16.6%)	13
1928	**Herbert C. Hoover**	Republican	21,392,190 (58.2%)	444
	Alfred E. Smith	Democratic	15,016,443 (40.8%)	87
1932	**Franklin D. Roosevelt**	Democratic	22,809,638 (57.3%)	472
	Herbert C. Hoover	Republican	15,758,901 (39.6%)	59
	Norman Thomas	Socialist	881,951 (2.2%)	
1936	**Franklin D. Roosevelt**	Democratic	27,751,612 (60.7%)	523
	Alfred M. Landon	Republican	16,681,913 (36.4%)	8
	William Lemke	Union	891,858 (1.9%)	
1940	**Franklin D. Roosevelt**	Democratic	27,243,466 (54.7%)	449
	Wendell L. Willkie	Republican	22,304,755 (44.8%)	82
1944	**Franklin D. Roosevelt** (**Harry S Truman,** 1945)	Democratic	25,602,505 (52.8%)	432
	Thomas E. Dewey	Republican	22,006,278 (44.5%)	99

Year	Candidates	Party	Popular Vote*	Electoral Vote**
1948	**Harry S Truman**	Democratic	24,105,812 (49.5%)	303
	Thomas E. Dewey	Republican	21,970,065 (45.1%)	189
	J. Strom Thurmond	States' Rights	1,169,063 (2.4%)	39
	Henry A. Wallace	Progressive	1,157,172 (2.4%)	
1952	**Dwight D. Eisenhower**	Republican	33,936,234 (55.2%)	442
	Adlai E. Stevenson	Democratic	27,314,992 (44.5%)	89
1956	**Dwight D. Eisenhower**	Republican	35,590,472 (57.4%)	457
	Adlai E. Stevenson	Democratic	26,022,752 (42.0%)	73
1960	**John F. Kennedy**	Democratic	34,227,096 (49.9%)	303
	(**Lyndon B. Johnson,** 1963)			
	Richard M. Nixon	Republican	34,108,546 (49.6%)	219
1964	**Lyndon B. Johnson**	Democratic	43,126,233 (61.1%)	486
	Barry M. Goldwater	Republican	27,174,989 (38.5%)	52
1968	**Richard M. Nixon**	Republican	31,783,783 (43.4%)	301
	Hubert H. Humphrey	Democratic	31,271,839 (42.7%)	191
	George C. Wallace	Amer. Independent	9,899,557 (13.5%)	46
1972	**Richard M. Nixon**	Republican	45,767,218 (60.6%)	520
	(**Gerald R. Ford,** 1974)			
	George S. McGovern	Democratic	28,357,668 (37.5%)	17
1976	**Jimmy Carter**	Democratic	40,828,657 (50.6%)	297
	Gerald R. Ford	Republican	39,145,520 (48.4%)	240
1980	**Ronald Reagan**	Republican	43,899,248 (51%)	489
	Jimmy Carter	Democratic	36,481,435 (41%)	49
	John B. Anderson	Independent	5,719,437 (6%)	
1984	**Ronald Reagan**	Republican	54,455,075 (59%)	525
	Walter F. Mondale	Democratic	37,577,185 (41%)	13

Vice Presidents and Cabinet Members, by Administration

Washington, 1789–1797

Vice-President	John Adams	1789–1797
Secretary of State	Thomas Jefferson	1789–1793
	Edmund Randolph	1794–1795
	Timothy Pickering	1795–1797
Secretary of War	Henry Knox	1789–1794
	Timothy Pickering	1795–1796
	James McHenry	1796–1797
Secretary of Treasury	Alexander Hamilton	1789–1795
	Oliver Wolcott, Jr.	1795–1797
Postmaster General	Samuel Osgood	1789–1791
	Timothy Pickering	1791–1794
	Joseph Habersham	1795–1797
Attorney General	Edmund Randolph	1789–1793
	William Bradford	1794–1795
	Charles Lee	1795–1797

John Adams, 1797–1801

Vice-President	Thomas Jefferson	1797–1801
Secretary of State	Timothy Pickering	1797–1800
	John Marshall	1800–1801
Secretary of War	James McHenry	1797–1800
	Samuel Dexter	1800–1801
Secretary of Treasury	Oliver Wolcott, Jr.	1797–1800
	Samuel Dexter	1800–1801
Postmaster General	Joseph Habersham	1797–1801
Attorney General	Charles Lee	1797–1801
Secretary of Navy	Benjamin Stoddert	1798–1801

Jefferson, 1801–1809

Vice-President	Aaron Burr	1801–1805
	George Clinton	1805–1809
Secretary of State	James Madison	1801–1809
Secretary of War	Henry Dearborn	1801–1809
Secretary of Treasury	Samuel Dexter	1801
	Albert Gallatin	1801–1809
Postmaster General	Joseph Habersham	1801
	Gideon Granger	1801–1809
Attorney General	Levi Lincoln	1801–1805
	Robert Smith	1805
	John C. Breckinridge	1805–1806
	Caesar A. Rodney	1807–1809
Secretary of Navy	Robert Smith	1801–1809

Madison, 1809–1817

Vice-President	George Clinton	1809–1813
	Elbridge Gerry	1813–1817
Secretary of State	Robert Smith	1809–1811
	James Monroe	1811–1817
Secretary of War	William Eustis	1809–1812
	John Armstrong	1813–1814
	James Monroe	1814–1815
	William H. Crawford	1815–1817
Secretary of Treasury	Albert Gallatin	1809–1813
	George W. Campbell	1814
	Alexander J. Dallas	1814–1816
	William H. Crawford	1816–1817
Postmaster General	Gideon Granger	1809–1814
	Return J. Meigs, Jr.	1814–1817
Attorney General	Caesar A. Rodney	1809–1811
	William Pinkney	1811–1814
	Richard Rush	1814–1817
Secretary of Navy	Paul Hamilton	1809–1813
	William Jones	1813–1814
	Benjamin W. Crowninshield	1814–1817

Monroe, 1817–1825

Vice-President	Daniel D. Tompkins	1817–1825
Secretary of State	John Quincy Adams	1817–1825
Secretary of War	George Graham	1817
	John C. Calhoun	1817–1825
Secretary of Treasury	William H. Crawford	1817–1825

Monroe, 1817–1825 (continued)

Postmaster General	Return J. Meigs, Jr.	1817–1823
	John McLean	1823–1825
Attorney General	Richard Rush	1817
	William Wirt	1817–1825
Secretary of Navy	Benjamin W. Crowninshield	1817–1818
	Smith Thompson	1818–1823
	Samuel L. Southard	1823–1825

John Quincy Adams, 1825–1829

Vice-President	John C. Calhoun	1825–1829
Secretary of State	Henry Clay	1825–1829
Secretary of War	James Barbour	1825–1828
	Peter B. Porter	1828–1829
Secretary of Treasury	Richard Rush	1825–1829
Postmaster General	John McLean	1825–1829
Attorney General	William Wirt	1825–1829
Secretary of Navy	Samuel L. Southard	1825–1829

Jackson, 1829–1837

Vice-President	John C. Calhoun	1829–1833
	Martin Van Buren	1833–1837
Secretary of State	Martin Van Buren	1829–1831
	Edward Livingston	1831–1833
	Louis McLane	1833–1834
	John Forsyth	1834–1837
Secretary of War	John H. Eaton	1829–1831
	Lewis Cass	1831–1837
	Benjamin Butler	1837
Secretary of Treasury	Samuel D. Ingham	1829–1831
	Louis McLane	1831–1833
	William J. Duane	1833
	Roger B. Taney	1833–1834
	Levi Woodbury	1834–1837
Postmaster General	William T. Barry	1829–1835
	Amos Kendall	1835–1837
Attorney General	John M. Berrien	1829–1831
	Roger B. Taney	1831–1833
	Benjamin F. Butler	1833–1837
Secretary of Navy	John Branch	1829–1831
	Levi Woodbury	1831–1834
	Mahlon Dickerson	1834–1837

Van Buren, 1837–1841

Vice-President	Richard M. Johnson	1837–1841
Secretary of State	John Forsyth	1837–1841
Secretary of War	Joel R. Poinsett	1837–1841
Secretary of Treasury	Levi Woodbury	1837–1841
Postmaster General	Amos Kendall	1837–1840
	John M. Niles	1840–1841
Attorney General	Benjamin F. Butler	1837–1838
	Felix Grundy	1838–1840
	Henry D. Gilpin	1840–1841
Secretary of Navy	Mahlon Dickerson	1837–1838
	James K. Paulding	1838–1841

William Harrison, 1841

Vice-President	John Tyler	1841
Secretary of State	Daniel Webster	1841
Secretary of War	John Bell	1841
Secretary of Treasury	Thomas Ewing	1841
Postmaster General	Francis Granger	1841
Attorney General	John J. Crittenden	1841
Secretary of Navy	George E. Badger	1841

Tyler, 1841–1845

Vice-President	None	
Secretary of State	Daniel Webster	1841–1843
	Hugh S. Legaré	1843
	Abel P. Upshur	1843–1844
	John C. Calhoun	1844–1845
Secretary of War	John Bell	1841
	John C. Spencer	1841–1843
	John M. Porter	1843–1844
	William Wilkins	1844–1845
Secretary of Treasury	Thomas Ewing	1841
	Walter Forward	1841–1843
	John C. Spencer	1843–1844
	George M. Bibb	1844–1845
Postmaster General	Francis Granger	1841
	Charles A. Wickliffe	1841
Attorney General	John J. Crittenden	1841
	Hugh S. Legaré	1841–1843
	John Nelson	1843–1845

Secretary of Navy	George Badger	1841
	Abel P. Upshur	1841
	David Henshaw	1843–1844
	Thomas W. Gilmer	1844
	John Y. Mason	1844–1845

Polk, 1845–1849

Vice-President	George M. Dallas	1845–1849
Secretary of State	James Buchanan	1845–1849
Secretary of War	William L. Marcy	1845–1849
Secretary of Treasury	Robert J. Walker	1845–1849
Postmaster General	Cave Johnson	1845–1849
Attorney General	John Y. Mason	1845–1846
	Nathan Clifford	1846–1848
	Isaac Toucey	1848–1849
Secretary of Navy	George Bancroft	1845–1846
	John Y. Mason	1846–1849

Taylor, 1849–1850

Vice-President	Millard Fillmore	1849–1850
Secretary of State	John M. Clayton	1849–1850
Secretary of War	George W. Crawford	1849–1850
Secretary of Treasury	William M. Meredith	1849–1850
Postmaster General	Jacob Collamer	1849–1850
Attorney General	Reverdy Johnson	1849–1850
Secretary of Navy	William Preston	1849–1850
Secretary of Interior	Thomas Ewing	1849–1850

Fillmore, 1850–1853

Vice-President	None	
Secretary of State	Daniel Webster	1850–1852
	Edward Everett	1852–1853
Secretary of War	Charles M. Conrad	1850–1853
Secretary of Treasury	Thomas Corwin	1850–1853
Postmaster General	Nathan K. Hall	1850–1852
	Sam D. Hubbard	1852–1853
Attorney General	John J. Crittenden	1850–1853
Secretary of Navy	William A. Graham	1850–1852
	John P. Kennedy	1852–1853
Secretary of Interior	Thomas M. T. McKennan	1850
	Alexander H. H. Stuart	1850–1853

Pierce, 1853–1857

Vice-President	William R. King	1853–1857
Secretary of State	William L. Marcy	1853–1857
Secretary of War	Jefferson Davis	1853–1857
Secretary of Treasury	James Guthrie	1853–1857
Postmaster General	James Campbell	1853–1857
Attorney General	Caleb Cushing	1853–1857
Secretary of Navy	James C. Dobbins	1853–1857
Secretary of Interior	Robert McClelland	1853–1857

Buchanan, 1857–1861

Vice-President	John C. Breckinridge	1857–1861
Secretary of State	Lewis Cass	1857–1860
	Jeremiah S. Black	1860–1861
Secretary of War	John B. Floyd	1857–1861
	Joseph Holt	1861
Secretary of Treasury	Howell Cobb	1857–1860
	Philip F. Thomas	1860–1861
	John A. Dix	1861
Postmaster General	Aaron V. Brown	1857–1859
	Joseph Holt	1859–1861
	Horatio King	1861
Attorney General	Jeremiah S. Black	1857–1860
	Edwin M. Stanton	1860–1861
Secretary of Navy	Isaac Toucey	1857–1861
Secretary of Interior	Jacob Thompson	1857–1861

Lincoln, 1861–1865

Vice-President	Hannibal Hamlin	1861–1865
	Andrew Johnson	1865
Secretary of State	William H. Seward	1861–1865

Lincoln, 1861–1865 (continued)

Secretary of War	Simon Cameron	1861–1862
	Edwin M. Stanton	1862–1865
Secretary of Treasury	Samuel P. Chase	1861–1864
	William P. Fessenden	1864–1865
	Hugh McCulloch	1865
Postmaster General	Horatio King	1861
	Montgomery Blair	1861–1864
	William Dennison	1864–1865
Attorney General	Edward Bates	1861–1864
	James Speed	1864–1865
Secretary of Navy	Gideon Welles	1861–1865
Secretary of Interior	Caleb B. Smith	1861–1863
	John P. Usher	1863–1865

Andrew Johnson, 1865–1869

Vice-President	None	
Secretary of State	William H. Seward	1865–1869
Secretary of War	Edwin M. Stanton	1865–1867
	Ulysses S. Grant	1867–1868
	John M. Schofield	1868–1869
Secretary of Treasury	Hugh McCulloch	1865–1869
Postmaster General	William Dennison	1865–1866
	Alexander W. Randall	1866–1869
Attorney General	James Speed	1865–1866
	Henry Stanbery	1866–1868
	William M. Evarts	1868–1869
Secretary of Navy	Gideon Welles	1865–1869
Secretary of Interior	John P. Usher	1865
	James Harlan	1865–1866
	Orville H. Browning	1866–1869

Grant, 1869–1877

Vice-President	Schuyler Colfax	1869–1873
	Henry Wilson	1873–1877
Secretary of State	Elihu B. Washburne	1869
	Hamilton Fish	1869–1877
Secretary of War	John A. Rawlins	1869
	William T. Sherman	1869
	William W. Belknap	1869–1876
	Alphonso Taft	1876
	James D. Cameron	1876–1877
Secretary of Treasury	George S. Boutwell	1869–1873
	William A. Richardson	1873–1874
	Benjamin H. Bristow	1874–1876
	Lot M. Morrill	1876–1877
Postmaster General	John A. J. Creswell	1869–1874
	James W. Marshall	1874
	Marshall Jewell	1874–1876
	James N. Tyner	1876–1877
Attorney General	Ebenezer R. Hoar	1869–1870
	Amos T. Ackerman	1870–1871
	G. H. Williams	1871–1875
	Edwards Pierrepont	1875–1876
	Alphonso Taft	1876–1877
Secretary of Navy	Adolph E. Borie	1869
	George Robeson	1869–1877
Secretary of Interior	Jacob D. Cox	1869–1870
	Columbus Delano	1870–1875
	Zachariah Chandler	1875–1877

Hayes, 1877–1881

Vice-President	William A. Wheeler	1877–1881
Secretary of State	William B. Evarts	1877–1881
Secretary of War	George W. McCrary	1877–1879
	Alexander Ramsey	1879–1881
Secretary of Treasury	John Sherman	1877–1881
Postmaster General	David M. Key	1877–1880
	Horace Maynard	1880–1881
Attorney General	Charles Devens	1877–1881
Secretary of Navy	Richard W. Thompson	1877–1880
	Nathan Goff, Jr.	1881
Secretary of Interior	Carl Schurz	1877–1881

Garfield, 1881

Vice-President	Chester A. Arthur	1881
Secretary of State	James G. Blaine	1881
Secretary of War	Robert T. Lincoln	1881
Secretary of Treasury	William Windom	1881
Postmaster General	Thomas L. James	1881
Attorney General	Wayne MacVeagh	1881
Secretary of Navy	William H. Hunt	1881
Secretary of Interior	Samuel J. Kirkwood	1881

Arthur, 1881–1885

Vice-President	None	
Secretary of State	Frederick T. Frelinghuysen	1881–1885
Secretary of War	Robert T. Lincoln	1881–1885
Secretary of Treasury	Charles J. Folger Walter Q. Gresham Hugh McCulloch	1881–1884 1884 1884–1885
Postmaster General	Timothy O. Howe Walter Q. Gresham Frank Hatton	1881–1883 1883–1884 1884–1885
Attorney General	Benjamin H. Brewster	1881–1885
Secretary of Navy	William H. Hunt William E. Chandler	1881–1882 1882–1885
Secretary of Interior	Samuel J. Kirkwood Henry M. Teller	1881–1882 1882–1885

Cleveland, 1885–1889

Vice-President	Thomas A. Hendricks	1885–1889
Secretary of State	Thomas F. Bayard	1885–1889
Secretary of War	William C. Endicott	1885–1889
Secretary of Treasury	Daniel Manning Charles S. Fairchild	1885–1887 1887–1889
Postmaster General	William F. Vilas Don M. Dickinson	1885–1888 1888–1889
Attorney General	Augustus H. Garland	1885–1889
Secretary of Navy	William C. Whitney	1885–1889
Secretary of Interior	Lucius Q. C. Lamar William F. Vilas	1885–1888 1888–1889
Secretary of Agriculture	Norman J. Colman	1889

Benjamin Harrison, 1889–1893

Vice-President	Levi P. Morton	1889–1893
Secretary of State	James G. Blaine John W. Foster	1889–1892 1892–1893
Secretary of War	Redfield Proctor Stephen B. Elkins	1889–1891 1891–1893
Secretary of Treasury	William Windom Charles Foster	1889–1891 1891–1893
Postmaster General	John Wanamaker	1889–1893
Attorney General	William H. H. Miller	1889–1891
Secretary of Navy	Benjamin F. Tracy	1889–1893
Secretary of Interior	John W. Noble	1889–1893
Secretary of Agriculture	Jeremiah M. Rusk	1889–1893

Cleveland, 1893–1897

Vice-President	Adlai E. Stevenson	1893–1897
Secretary of State	Walter Q. Gresham Richard Olney	1893–1895 1895–1897
Secretary of War	Daniel S. Lamont	1893–1897
Secretary of Treasury	John G. Carlisle	1893–1897
Postmaster General	Wilson S. Bissell William L. Wilson	1893–1895 1895–1897
Attorney General	Richard Olney Judson Harmon	1893–1895 1895–1897
Secretary of Navy	Hilary A. Herbert	1893–1897
Secretary of Interior	Hoke Smith David R. Francis	1893–1896 1896–1897
Secretary of Agriculture	Julius Sterling Morton	1893–1897

McKinley, 1897–1901

Vice-President	Garret Hobart Theodore Roosevelt	1897–1901 1901
Secretary of State	John Sherman William R. Day John M. Hay	1897–1898 1898 1898–1901
Secretary of War	Russell A. Alger Elihu Root	1897–1899 1899–1901
Secretary of Treasury	Lyman J. Gage	1897–1901
Postmaster General	James A. Gary Charles E. Smith	1897–1898 1898–1901
Attorney General	Joseph McKenna John W. Griggs Philander C. Knox	1897–1898 1898–1901 1901
Secretary of Navy	John D. Long	1897–1901
Secretary of Interior	Cornelius N. Bliss Ethan A. Hitchcock	1897–1899 1899–1901
Secretary of Agriculture	James Wilson	1897–1901

Theodore Roosevelt, 1901–1909

Vice-President	Charles Warren Fairbanks	1905–1909
Secretary of State	John M. Hay	1901–1905
	Elihu Root	1905–1909
	Robert Bacon	1909
Secretary of War	Elihu Root	1901–1904
	William Howard Taft	1904–1908
	Luke E. Wright	1908–1909
Secretary of Treasury	Lyman J. Gage	1901–1902
	Leslie M. Shaw	1902–1907
	George B. Cortelyou	1907–1909
Postmaster General	Charles Emory Smith	1901–1902
	Henry C. Payne	1902–1904
	Robert J. Wynne	1904–1905
	George B. Cortelyou	1905–1907
	George von L. Meyer	1907–1909
Attorney General	Philander C. Knox	1901–1904
	William H. Moody	1904–1906
	Charles J. Bonaparte	1906–1909
Secretary of Navy	John D. Long	1901–1902
	William H. Moody	1902–1904
	Paul Morton	1904–1905
	Charles J. Bonaparte	1905–1906
	Victor H. Metcalf	1906–1908
	Truman H. Newberry	1908–1909
Secretary of Interior	Ethan A. Hitchcock	1901–1907
	James R. Garfield	1907–1909
Secretary of Agriculture	James Wilson	1901–1909
Secretary of Labor and Commerce	George B. Cortelyou	1903–1904
	Victor H. Metcalf	1904–1906
	Oscar S. Straus	1906–1909

Taft, 1909–1913

Vice-President	James S. Sherman	1909–1913
Secretary of State	Philander C. Knox	1909–1913
Secretary of War	Jacob M. Dickinson	1909–1911
	Henry L. Stimson	1911–1913
Secretary of Treasury	Franklin MacVeagh	1909–1913
Postmaster General	Frank H. Hitchcock	1909–1913
Attorney General	George W. Wickersham	1909–1913
Secretary of Navy	George von L. Meyer	1909–1913
Secretary of Interior	Richard A. Ballinger	1909–1911
	Walter Lowrie Fisher	1911–1913
Secretary of Agriculture	James Wilson	1909–1913
Secretary of Labor and Commerce	Oscar S. Straus	1909
	Charles Nagel	1909–1913

Wilson, 1913–1921

Vice-President	Thomas R. Marshall	1913–1921
Secretary of State	William Jennings Bryan	1913–1915
	Robert Lansing	1915–1920
	Bainbridge Colby	1920–1921
Secretary of War	Lindley M. Garrison	1913–1916
	Newton D. Baker	1916–1921
Secretary of Treasury	William Gilbert McAdoo	1913–1918
	Carter Glass	1918–1920
	David F. Houston	1920–1921
Postmaster General	Albert Sidney Burleson	1913–1921
Attorney General	James Clark McReynolds	1913–1914
	Thomas Watt Gregory	1914–1919
	A. Mitchell Palmer	1919–1921
Secretary of Navy	Josephus Daniels	1913–1921
Secretary of Interior	Franklin Knight Lane	1913–1920
	John Barton Payne	1920–1921
Secretary of Agriculture	David F. Houston	1913–1920
	Edwin T. Meredith	1920–1921
Secretary of Commerce	William C. Redfield	1913–1919
Secretary of Labor	William Bauchop Wilson	1913–1921

Harding, 1921–1923

Vice-President	Calvin Coolidge	1921–1923
Secretary of State	Charles Evans Hughes	1921–1923
Secretary of War	John W. Weeks	1921–1923
Secretary of Treasury	Andrew W. Mellon	1921–1923
Postmaster General	Will H. Hays	1921–1922
	Hubert Work	1922–1923
	Harry S. New	1923
Attorney General	Harry M. Daugherty	1921–1923
Secretary of Navy	Edwin Denby	1921–1923
Secretary of Interior	Albert B. Fall	1921–1923
	Hubert Work	1923
Secretary of Agriculture	Henry C. Wallace	1921–1923
Secretary of Commerce	Herbert C. Hoover	1921–1923
Secretary of Labor	James J. Davis	1921–1923

Coolidge, 1923–1929

Vice-President	Charles G. Dawes	1925–1929
Secretary of State	Charles Evans Hughes	1923–1925
	Frank B. Kellogg	1925–1929
Secretary of War	John W. Weeks	1923–1925
	Dwight F. Davis	1925–1929
Secretary of Treasury	Andrew W. Mellon	1923–1929
Postmaster General	Harry S. New	1923–1929
Attorney General	Harry M. Daugherty	1923–1924
	Harlan Fiske Stone	1924–1925
	John G. Sargent	1925–1929
Secretary of Navy	Edwin Derby	1923–1924
	Curtis D. Wilbur	1924–1929
Secretary of Interior	Hubert Work	1923–1928
	Roy O. West	1928–1929
Secretary of Agriculture	Henry C. Wallace	1923–1924
	Howard M. Gore	1924–1925
	William M. Jardine	1925–1929
Secretary of Commerce	Herbert C. Hoover	1923–1928
	William F. Whiting	1928–1929
Secretary of Labor	James J. Davis	1923–1929

Hoover, 1929–1933

Vice-President	Charles Curtis	1929–1933
Secretary of State	Henry L. Stimson	1929–1933
Secretary of War	James W. Good	1929
	Patrick J. Hurley	1929–1933
Secretary of Treasury	Andrew W. Mellon	1929–1932
	Ogden L. Mills	1932–1933
Postmaster General	Walter F. Brown	1929–1933
Attorney General	William D. Mitchell	1929–1933
Secretary of Navy	Charles F. Adams	1929–1933
Secretary of Interior	Ray L. Wilbur	1929–1933
Secretary of Agriculture	Arthur M. Hyde	1929–1933
Secretary of Commerce	Robert P. Lamont	1929–1932
	Roy D. Chapin	1932–1933
Secretary of Labor	James J. Davis	1929–1930
	William N. Doak	1930–1933

Franklin D. Roosevelt, 1933–1945

Vice-President	John Nance Garner	1933–1941
	Henry A. Wallace	1941–1945
	Harry S Truman	1945
Secretary of State	Cordell Hull	1933–1944
	Edward R. Stettinius, Jr.	1944–1945
Secretary of War	George H. Dern	1933–1936
	Henry A. Woodring	1936–1940
	Henry L. Stimson	1940–1945
Secretary of Treasury	William H. Woodin	1933–1934
	Henry Morgenthau, Jr.	1934–1945
Postmaster General	James A. Farley	1933–1940
	Frank C. Walker	1940–1945
Attorney General	Homer S. Cummings	1933–1939
	Frank Murphy	1939–1940
	Robert H. Jackson	1940–1941
	Francis Biddle	1941–1945
Secretary of Navy	Claude A. Swanson	1933–1940
	Charles Edison	1940
	Frank Knox	1940–1944
	James V. Forrestal	1944–1945
Secretary of Interior	Harold L. Ickes	1933–1945
Secretary of Agriculture	Henry A. Wallace	1933–1940
	Claude R. Wickard	1940–1945
Secretary of Commerce	Daniel C. Roper	1933–1939
	Harry L. Hopkins	1939–1940
	Jesse H. Jones	1940–1945
	Henry A. Wallace	1945
Secretary of Labor	Frances Perkins	1933–1945

Truman, 1945–1953

Vice-President	Alben W. Barkley	1949–1953
Secretary of State	Edward R. Stettinius, Jr.	1945
	James F. Byrnes	1945–1947
	George C. Marshall	1947–1949
	Dean G. Acheson	1949–1953
Secretary of War	Robert P. Patterson	1945–1947
	Kenneth C. Royall	1947
Secretary of Treasury	Fred M. Vinson	1945–1946
	John W. Snyder	1946–1953
Postmaster General	Frank C. Walker	1945
	Robert E. Hannegan	1945–1947
	Jesse M. Donaldson	1947–1953
Attorney General	Tom C. Clark	1945–1949
	J. Howard McGrath	1949–1952
	James P. McGranery	1952–1953
Secretary of Navy	James V. Forrestal	1945–1947
Secretary of Interior	Harold L. Ickes	1945–1946
	Julius A. Krug	1946–1949
	Oscar L. Chapman	1949–1953

Truman, 1945–1953 (continued)

Secretary of Agriculture	Clinton P. Anderson	1945–1948
	Charles F. Brannan	1948–1953
Secretary of Commerce	Henry A. Wallace	1945–1946
	W. Averell Harriman	1946–1948
	Charles W. Sawyer	1948–1953
Secretary of Labor	Lewis B. Schwellenbach	1945–1948
	Maurice J. Tobin	1948–1953
Secretary of Defense	James V. Forrestal	1947–1949
	Louis A. Johnson	1949–1950
	George C. Marshall	1950–1951
	Robert A. Lovett	1951–1953

Eisenhower, 1953–1961

Vice-President	Richard M. Nixon	1953–1961
Secretary of State	John Foster Dulles	1953–1959
	Christian A. Herter	1959–1961
Secretary of Treasury	George M. Humphrey	1953–1957
	Robert B. Anderson	1957–1961
Postmaster General	Arthur E. Summerfield	1953–1961
Attorney General	Herbert Brownell, Jr.	1953–1958
	William P. Rogers	1958–1961
Secretary of Interior	Douglas McKay	1953–1956
	Fred A. Seaton	1956–1961
Secretary of Agriculture	Ezra Taft Benson	1953–1961
Secretary of Commerce	Sinclair Weeks	1953–1958
	Lewis L. Strauss	1958–1959
	Frederick H. Mueller	1959–1961
Secretary of Labor	Martin P. Durkin	1953
	James P. Mitchell	1953–1961
Secretary of Defense	Charles E. Wilson	1953–1957
	Neil H. McElroy	1957–1959
	Thomas S. Gates, Jr.	1959–1961
Secretary of Health, Education, and Welfare	Oveta Culp Hobby	1953–1955
	Marion B. Folsom	1955–1958
	Arthur S. Flemming	1958–1961

Kennedy, 1961–1963

Vice-President	Lyndon B. Johnson	1961–1963
Secretary of State	Dean Rusk	1961–1963
Secretary of Treasury	C. Douglas Dillon	1961–1963
Postmaster General	J. Edward Day	1961–1963
	John A. Gronouski	1963
Attorney General	Robert F. Kennedy	1961–1963
Secretary of Interior	Stewart L. Udall	1961–1963
Secretary of Agriculture	Orville L. Freeman	1961–1963
Secretary of Commerce	Luther H. Hodges	1961–1963
Secretary of Labor	Arthur J. Goldberg	1961–1962
	W. Willard Wirtz	1962–1963
Secretary of Defense	Robert S. McNamara	1961–1963
Secretary of Health, Education, and Welfare	Abraham A. Ribicoff	1961–1962
	Anthony J. Celebrezze	1962–1963

Lyndon Johnson, 1963–1969

Vice-President	Hubert H. Humphrey	1965–1969
Secretary of State	Dean Rusk	1963–1969
Secretary of Treasury	C. Douglas Dillon	1963–1965
	Henry H. Fowler	1965–1969
Postmaster General	John A. Gronouski	1963–1965
	Lawrence F. O'Brien	1965–1968
	Marvin Watson	1968–1969
Attorney General	Robert F. Kennedy	1963–1964
	Nicholas Katzenbach	1965–1966
	Ramsey Clark	1967–1969
Secretary of Interior	Stewart L. Udall	1963–1969
Secretary of Agriculture	Orville L. Freeman	1963–1969
Secretary of Commerce	Luther H. Hodges	1963–1964
	John T. Connor	1964–1967
	Alexander B. Trowbridge	1967–1968
	Cyrus R. Smith	1968–1969
Secretary of Labor	W. Willard Wirtz	1963–1969
Secretary of Defense	Robert F. McNamara	1963–1968
	Clark Clifford	1968–1969
Secretary of Health, Education, and Welfare	Anthony J. Celebrezze	1963–1965
	John W. Gardner	1965–1968
	Wilbur J. Cohen	1968–1969
Secretary of Housing and Urban Development	Robert C. Weaver	1966–1969
	Robert C. Wood	1969
Secretary of Transportation	Alan S. Boyd	1967–1969

Nixon, 1969–1974

Vice-President	Spiro T. Agnew	1969–1973
	Gerald R. Ford	1973–1974
Secretary of State	William P. Rogers	1969–1973
	Henry A. Kissinger	1973–1974
Secretary of Treasury	David M. Kennedy	1969–1970
	John B. Connally	1971–1972
	George P. Shultz	1972–1974
	William E. Simon	1974
Postmaster General	Winton M. Blount	1969–1971
Attorney General	John N. Mitchell	1969–1972
	Richard G. Kleindienst	1972–1973
	Elliot L. Richardson	1973
	William B. Saxbe	1973–1974
Secretary of Interior	Walter J. Hickel	1969–1970
	Rogers Morton	1971–1974
Secretary of Agriculture	Clifford M. Hardin	1969–1971
	Earl L. Butz	1971–1974
Secretary of Commerce	Maurice H. Stans	1969–1972
	Peter G. Peterson	1972–1973
	Frederick B. Dent	1973–1974
Secretary of Labor	George P. Shultz	1969–1970
	James D. Hodgson	1970–1973
	Peter J. Brennan	1973–1974
Secretary of Defense	Melvin R. Laird	1969–1973
	Elliot L. Richardson	1973
	James R. Schlesinger	1973–1974
Secretary of Health, Education, and Welfare	Robert H. Finch	1969–1970
	Elliot L. Richardson	1970–1973
	Casper W. Weinberger	1973–1974
Secretary of Housing and Urban Development	George W. Romney	1969–1973
	James T. Lynn	1973–1974
Secretary of Transportation	John A. Volpe	1969–1973
	Claude S. Brinegar	1973–1974

Ford, 1974–1977

Vice-President	Nelson A. Rockefeller	1974–1977
Secretary of State	Henry A. Kissinger	1974–1977
Secretary of Treasury	William E. Simon	1974–1977
Attorney General	William B. Saxbe	1974–1975
	Edward H. Levi	1975–1977
Secretary of Interior	Rogers C. B. Morton	1974–1975
	Stanley K. Hathaway	1975
	Thomas S. Kleppe	1975–1977
Secretary of Agriculture	Earl L. Butz	1974–1976
	John A. Knebel	1976–1977
Secretary of Commerce	Frederick B. Dent	1974–1975
	Rogers C. B. Morton	1975–1976
	Elliot L. Richardson	1976–1977
Secretary of Labor	Peter J. Brennan	1974–1975
	John T. Dunlop	1975–1976
	W. J. Usery, Jr.	1976–1977
Secretary of Defense	James R. Schlesinger	1974–1975
	Donald H. Rumsfeld	1975–1977
Secretary of Health, Education, and Welfare	Casper W. Weinberger	1974–1975
	F. David Mathews	1975–1977
Secretary of Housing and Urban Development	James T. Lynn	1974–1975
	Carla Anderson Hills	1975–1977
Secretary of Transportation	Claude S. Brinegar	1974–1975
	William T. Coleman, Jr.	1974–1977

Carter, 1977–1981

Vice-President	Walter F. Mondale	1977–1981
Secretary of State	Cyrus R. Vance	1977–1980
	Edmund S. Muskie	1980–1981
Secretary of Treasury	W. Michael Blumenthal	1977–1979
	G. William Miller	1979–1981
Attorney General	Griffin B. Bell	1977–1979
	Benjamin R. Civiletti	1979–1981
Secretary of Interior	Cecil D. Andrus	1977–1981
Secretary of Agriculture	Robert Bergland	1977–1981
Secretary of Commerce	Juanita M. Kreps	1977–1979
	Philip M. Klutznick	1979–1981
Secretary of Labor	F. Ray Marshall	1977–1981
Secretary of Defense	Harold Brown	1977–1981
Secretary of Health, Education, and Welfare	Joseph A. Califano, Jr.	1977–1979
	Patricia Roberts Harris	1979
Secretary of Health and Human Services	Patricia Roberts Harris	1979–1981
Secretary of Housing and Urban Development	Patricia Roberts Harris	1977–1979
	Moon Landrieu	1979–1981
Secretary of Transportation	Brock Adams	1977–1979
	Neil E. Goldschmidt	1979–1981
Secretary of Energy	James R. Schlesinger, Jr.	1977–1979
	Charles W. Duncan, Jr.	1979–1981
Secretary of Education	Shirley M. Hufstedler	1979–1981

Reagan, 1981–		
Vice-President	George Bush	1981–
Secretary of State	Alexander M. Haig, Jr.	1981–1982
	George P. Schultz	1982–
Secretary of Treasury	Donald T. Regan	1981–1985
	James A. Baker, III	1985–
Attorney General	William French Smith	1981–1985
	Edwin A. Meese, III	1985–
Secretary of Interior	James C. Watt	1981–1983
	William P. Clarke, Jr.	1983–1985
	Donald P. Hodel	1985–
Secretary of Agriculture	John R. Block	1981–1986
	Richard Lyng	1986–
Secretary of Commerce	Malcolm Baldridge	1981–
Secretary of Labor	Raymond J. Donovan	1981–1985
	William E. Brock	1985–
Secretary of Defense	Caspar W. Weinberger	1981–
Secretary of Health and Human Services	Richard S. Schweiker	1981–1983
	Margaret M. Heckler	1983–1985
	Otis R. Bowen	1986–
Secretary of Housing and Urban Development	Samuel R. Pierce, Jr.	1981–
Secretary of Transportation	Andrew L. Lewis, Jr.	1981–1983
	Elizabeth Hanford Dole	1983–
Secretary of Energy	James B. Edwards	1981–1982
	Donald P. Hodel	1982–1985
	John S. Herrington	1985–
Secretary of Education	Terrel H. Bell	1981–1985
	William J. Bennett	1985–

Justices of the Supreme Court

Chief Justices in italics.

	Term of Service	Years of Service
John Jay	1789–1795	5
John Rutledge	1789–1791	1
William Cushing	1789–1810	20
James Wilson	1789–1798	8
John Blair	1789–1796	6
Robert H. Harrison	1789–1790	—
James Iredell	1790–1799	9
Thomas Johnson	1791–1793	1
William Paterson	1793–1806	13
*John Rutledge**	1795	—
Samuel Chase	1796–1811	15
Oliver Ellsworth	1796–1800	4
Bushrod Washington	1798–1829	31
Alfred Moore	1799–1804	4
John Marshall	1801–1835	34
William Johnson	1804–1834	30
H. Brockholst Livingston	1806–1823	16
Thomas Todd	1807–1826	18
Joseph Story	1811–1845	33
Gabriel Duval	1811–1835	24
Smith Thompson	1823–1843	20
Robert Trimble	1826–1828	2
John McLean	1829–1861	32
Henry Baldwin	1830–1844	14
James M. Wayne	1835–1867	32
Roger B. Taney	1836–1864	28
Philip P. Barbour	1836–1841	4
John Catron	1837–1865	28
John McKinley	1837–1852	15
Peter V. Daniel	1841–1860	19
Samuel Nelson	1845–1872	27
Levi Woodbury	1845–1851	5
Robert C. Grier	1846–1870	23
Benjamin R. Curtis	1851–1857	6
John A. Campbell	1853–1861	8
Nathan Clifford	1858–1881	23
Noah H. Swayne	1862–1881	18
Samuel F. Miller	1862–1890	28
David Davis	1862–1877	14
Stephen J. Field	1863–1897	34
Salmon P. Chase	1864–1873	8
William Strong	1870–1880	10
Joseph P. Bradley	1870–1892	22

* Never confirmed as Chief Justice.

	Term of Service	Years of Service
Ward Hunt	1873–1882	9
Morrison R. Waite	1874–1888	14
John M. Harlan	1877–1911	34
William B. Woods	1880–1887	7
Stanley Matthews	1881–1889	7
Horace Gray	1882–1902	20
Samuel Blatchford	1882–1893	11
Lucius Q. C. Lamar	1888–1893	5
Melville W. Fuller	1888–1910	21
David J. Brewer	1890–1910	20
Henry B. Brown	1890–1906	16
George Shiras, Jr.	1892–1903	10
Howell E. Jackson	1893–1895	2
Edward D. White	1894–1910	16
Rufus W. Peckham	1895–1909	14
Joseph McKenna	1898–1925	26
Oliver W. Holmes, Jr.	1902–1932	30
William R. Day	1903–1922	19
William H. Moody	1906–1910	3
Horace H. Lurton	1910–1914	4
Charles E. Hughes	1910–1916	5
Willis Van Devanter	1911–1937	26
Joseph R. Lamar	1911–1916	5
Edward D. White	1910–1921	11
Mahlon Pitney	1912–1922	10
James C. McReynolds	1914–1941	26
Louis D. Brandeis	1916–1939	22
John H. Clarke	1916–1922	6
William H. Taft	1921–1930	8
George Sutherland	1922–1938	15
Pierce Butler	1922–1939	16
Edward T. Sanford	1923–1930	7
Harlan F. Stone	1925–1941	16
Charles E. Hughes	1930–1941	11
Owen J. Roberts	1930–1945	15
Benjamin N. Cardozo	1932–1938	6
Hugo L. Black	1937–1971	34
Stanley F. Reed	1938–1957	19
Felix Frankfurter	1939–1962	23
William O. Douglas	1939–1975	36
Frank Murphy	1940–1949	9
Harlan F. Stone	1941–1946	5
James F. Byrnes	1941–1942	1
Robert H. Jackson	1941–1954	13
Wiley B. Rutledge	1943–1949	6

	Term of Service	*Years of Service*
Harold H. Burton	1945–1958	13
Fred M. Vinson	1946–1953	7
Tom C. Clark	1949–1967	18
Sherman Minton	1949–1956	7
Earl Warren	1953–1969	16
John Marshall Harlan	1955–1971	16
William J. Brennan, Jr.	1956–	—
Charles E. Whittaker	1957–1962	5
Potter Stewart	1958–1981	23
Byron R. White	1962–	—
Arthur J. Goldberg	1962–1965	3
Abe Fortas	1965–1969	4
Thurgood Marshall	1967–	—
Warren E. Burger	1969–1986	18
Harry A. Blackmun	1970–	—
Lewis F. Powell, Jr.	1971–	—
*William H. Rehnquist***	1971–	—
John P. Stevens III	1975–	—
Sandra Day O'Connor	1981–	—
Antonin Scalia	1986–	—

** Chief Justice from 1986 on.

Territorial Expansion

Louisiana Purchase	1803
Florida	1819
Texas	1845
Oregon	1846
Mexican Cession	1848
Gadsden Purchase	1853
Alaska	1867
Hawaii	1898
Philippines	1898–1946
Puerto Rico	1899
Guam	1899
American Samoa	1900
Canal Zone	1904
U.S. Virgin Islands	1917
Pacific Islands Trust Territory	1947

Population, 1790–1980

1790	3,929,214
1800	5,308,483
1810	7,239,881
1820	9,638,453
1830	12,866,020
1840	17,069,453
1850	23,191,876
1860	31,443,321
1870	39,818,449
1880	50,155,783
1890	62,947,714
1900	75,994,575
1910	91,972,266
1920	105,710,620
1930	122,775,046
1940	131,669,275
1950	151,325,798
1960	179,323,175
1970	204,765,770
1980	226,504,825

Picture Credits

Chapter-Opening Illustrations

Chapter 1 Detail of map, Theodor de Bry, *America* (Frankfurt, 1590): New York Public Library; Astor, Lenox and Tilden Foundations.
Chapter 2 Ralph Earl, *Angus Nickelson Family:* Museum of Fine Arts, Springfield, Mass.
Chapter 3 Cockpit Hill factory, Derby: ceramic teapot, "Stamp Act Repeal'd," ca. 1766: Essex Institute, Salem, Mass.
Chapter 4 John Trumbull, *Death of General Mercer at the Battle of Princeton,* 1787–1794: Yale University Art Gallery.
Chapter 5 Anonymous tapestry, "Washington's Triumphal Entry into New York," 1783: Abby Aldrich Rockefeller Folk Art Center, Williamsburg, Va.
Chapter 6 Sevres porcelain urns, "Thomas Jefferson" and "John Adams," ca. 1826–1827: Private collection; photo by Ronald L. C. Kienhuis.
Chapter 7 Michel Felice Corne, *Battle of the USS* Constitution *and HMS* Guerriere," 1812: New Haven Colony Historical Society, gift of Mrs. Philip S. Galpin, 1886.
Chapter 8 John Caspar Wild, *Cincinnati,* 1835: Cincinnati Historical Society.
Chapter 9 Robert Cruickeshank, *All Creation Going to the White House,* 1829: White House Historical Association.
Chapter 10 J. Hill, *Broadway, New-York,* 1835: New York Public Library, Stokes Collection.
Chapter 11 William Sidney Mount, *The* Herald *in the Country,* 1853: The Museums at Stony Brook; gift of Mr. and Mrs. Ward Melville.
Chapter 12 Emanuel Gottlieb Leutze, *Westward the Course of the Empire Takes Its Way,* 1861: National Museum of American Art, Smithsonian Institution; bequest of Sara Carr Upton.
Chapter 13 Eastman Johnson, *A Ride for Liberty—The Fugitive Slaves,* ca. 1862: The Brooklyn Museum; gift of Miss Gwendolyn O. L. Conkling.
Chapter 14 Advertisement for *Uncle Tom's Cabin,* 1852: The Granger Collection.
Chapter 15 Lincoln visiting Gen. McClellan and officers at Antietam: Brown Brothers.
Chapter 16 Currier & Ives, "The First Colored Senators and Representatives in the 41st and 42nd Congress of the United States," 1872: The Granger Collection.
Chapter 17 T. L. Dawes, "Mining on the Comstock," 1872: Bancroft Library, University of California.
Chapter 18 Cartoon of John D. Rockefeller, *Puck,* March 6, 1901: New-York Historical Society.
Chapter 19 "The Anarchist Riot in Chicago," from *Harper's Weekly:* New York Public Library: Astor, Lenox and Tilden Foundations.
Chapter 20 John Ross Key, *Administration, Mining, and Electrical Buildings from Wooded Island, World's Columbian Exposition,* 1894: Chicago Historical Society.
Chapter 21 Compton & Dry, "1888 Democratic National Convention, St. Louis" (detail): Missouri Historical Society.
Chapter 22 Joseph Keppler, Jr., "The Eagle of American Imperialism," 1904: The Granger Collection.
Chapter 23 President Theodore Roosevelt: Brown Brothers.
Chapter 24 George Luks, *Blue Devils of Fifth Avenue,* 1917: The Phillips Collection.
Chapter 25 Capt. Lindbergh, the Atlantic hero, flies to Croydon: The Bettmann Archive.
Chapter 26 Boardman Robinson, *Going West,* 1933: National Museum of American Art, Smithsonian Institution; gift of Mr. and Mrs. Alexander Lowenthal and Family.
Chapter 27 The National Memorial Cemetery of the Pacific in Punchbowl Crater, Honolulu: © Joe Solem/Camera Hawaii, Inc.
Chapter 28 Atomic bomb test, Yucca Flat, Nevada: Loomis Dean, *Life* magazine, © 1955 Time, Inc.
Chapter 29 Peace parade, Washington, D.C.: Art Resource.
Chapter 30 Nixon, Haldeman, Kissinger, and Ehrlichman: Arthur Schatz, © Time, Inc.
Chapter 31 Ronald Reagan boarding Air Force One: J. L. Atlan/Sygma.

Portfolios (listed by page number)

Portfolio One: **32** Gold face of Asantehene Kofi Karikari: The Wallace Collection, London. Ashanti goldweights (climbing tree, carpentry): Collection of Mr. and Mrs. Chaim Gross; photo by Ronald L. C. Kienhuis. Ashanti goldweight (pounding yams): Trustees of the British Museum. **33** Yam festival, from T. E. Bowdich, *A Mission . . . to Ashantee,* 1819: New York Public Library; Astor, Lenox and Tilden Foundations. "Commerce des Esclaves," from F. Froger, *Relation d'un Voyage . . . aux Cotes d'Afrique . . . , 1698:* Library Company of Philadelphia. *Slave Deck of the* Albanoz: National Maritime Museum, Greenwich, England. **34** Shield decorated with feathers: Württembergisches Landesmuseum. Obsidian-turquoise skull mask: Museum of Mankind, British Museum. Moctezuma's law court, in *Codex Mendoza:* Bodleian Library. **35** Political map of Tenochtitlán, in *Lienzo de Tlaxcala:* Tozzer Library, Harvard University. Aztec picture writing, in *Codex Porfirio Diaz:* Tozzer Library, Harvard University. **36** Tribute roll in Spanish, in *Codex Mendoza:* Bodleian Library. Mexicans laboring, in *Codice Osuna:* Tozzer Library, Harvard University. **37** Photograph of Walpi pueblo: Museum of the American Indian, Heye Foundation. Hopi man spinning cotton: Museum of the American Indian, Heye Foundation. Hopi man weaving a woman's black dress: Photo Archives, Denver Museum of Natural History. **38** Kwa (Eagle Kachina), early 20th century: photo by Susan Middleton, courtesy California Academy of Sciences, San Francisco. *Kiva* mural: Museum of Northern Arizona. **39** Leroy Kewanyama, *Man with Rabbit, Woman Running to Put It in a Sack:* Museum of the American Indian, Heye Foundation. Delegates to meet with Brigham Young: Museum of the American Indian, Heye Foundation.

Portfolio Two: **80** Van Bergen farm, Hudson Valley: New York State Historical Association, Cooperstown. **81** John White, "Pomeiooc": Trustees of the British Museum. **82** Greenway: South Carolina Historical Society. Thomas Coram, *View of Mulberry (House and Street)*: Carolina Art Association/Gibbes Art Gallery. New England salt-box house: Richard Candee. **83** Quaker marriage contract with Richard Penn's stamp: Historical Society of Pennsylvania. Anon., *Baby in Red High Chair:* Abby Aldrich Rockefeller Folk Art Center, Williamsburg. **84** Anon., *The Cheney Family:* National Gallery of Art, Smithsonian Institution; gift of Edgar William and Bernice Chrysler Garbish. **85** Payne Limner, *Alexander Spotswood Payne and His Brother, John Robert Dandridge Payne, and Their Nurse,* 1790–1800: Virginia Museum of Fine Arts; gift of Miss Dorothy Payne. **86** Ephrata Cloister: Sister's House (Saron) and Meeting House (Saal): Ephrata Cloister, Pennsylvania Historical and Museum Commission. Bruton Parish Church: Colonial Williamsburg. **87** Rocky Hill Meeting House, Amesbury, Mass., 1795: Society for the Preservation of New England Antiquities, Boston, Mass. Mary Nash stone, Hatfield, Mass., 1725: Daniel and Jessie Lie Farber. William Dickson stone, Cambridge, Mass., 1692: Daniel and Jessie Lie Farber.

Portfolio Three: **194** Portrait by Gilbert Stuart, 1805: National Portrait Gallery/Thomas Jefferson Memorial Foundation. **195** Bust by Jean-Antoine Houdon: New-York Historical Society. Photo of Monticello exterior: © 1982 Langdon Clay. **196** Thomas Jefferson's elevation study of Monticello: Massachusetts Historical Society/University of Virginia Library. Sketch for gravestone and epitaph: Library of Congress. **197** Thomas Jefferson's study of grounds plans for Monticello: Massachusetts Historical Society/University of Virginia Library. **198** Monticello drawing room with harpsichord and music stand: © 1982 Langdon Clay. **199** View from bed with telescope and surveying equipment: © 1982 Langdon Clay. Monticello entry hall with buffalo head and bones: © 1982 Langdon Clay. **200** Close-up of polygraph and revolving chair: © 1982 Langdon Clay. **201** Daguerreotype of Isaac Jefferson by John Plumbe, ca. 1845: University of Virginia Library. Slave-owning document: Massachusetts Historical Society/ University of Virginia Library.

Portfolio Four: **316** Lewis & Clark watercolor map: American Philosophical Society. **317** Karl Bodmer, *Buffalo and Elk on the Upper Missouri:* Enron Art Foundation/Joslyn Art Museum, Omaha, Nebr. Alfred Jacob Miller, *Throwing the Lasso,* 1836: Yale University Library. **318** Karl Bodmer, facsimile of Indian painting, "Mató-Tópe, Mandan Chief": Enron Art Foundation/ Joslyn Art Museum, Omaha, Nebr. **319** Samuel Seymour, *Kiowa Encampment,* 1820: Yale University Library, Western Americana. Alfred Jacob Miller, *Fort Laramie,* 1836–1837: Yale University Library, Western Americana. **320** Karl Bodmer, *Settler's Farm in Indiana,* 1836: Enron Art Foundation/Joslyn Art Museum, Omaha, Nebr. William T. Ranney, *Advice on the Prairie,* 1853: M/M J. Maxwell Moran, Paoli, Pa. **321** H. Warre, sketch of Oregon City, 1845: American Antiquarian Society. **322** William Rich Hutton, San Francisco in 1847: Henry E. Huntington Library and Art Gallery. S. F. Marryat, *San Francisco and the Bay,* 1851: New-York Historical Society. **323** Gold Rush advertisement, "Ocean Express": The Granger Collection.

Portfolio Five: **480** "Freedom to the Slave," 1863: Library Company of Philadelphia. **481** Edwin White, *Thoughts of Liberia,* ca. 1830–1840: New-York Historical Society. George Fuller, "Cotton Press and Gin, February 2, 1858": Private Collection. Five generations of a South Carolina slave family; photo by T. H. O'Sullivan, 1862: Library of Congress. **482** "Meeting in the African Church, Cincinnati, Ohio," *Frank Leslie's Illustrated Newspaper,* April 30, 1853: Library of Congress. Thomas Rice playing "Jump Jim Crow" on the Bowery, 1833: Museum of the City of New York. **483** Edwin Taylor, *American Slave Market,* 1852: Chicago Historical Society. Bill of sale for Ned: The Old Slave Mart Museum, Charleston, S.C. **484** Currier & Ives, "The Gallant Charge of the 54th Mass. (Colored) Regiment . . . July 18, 1863": Museum of the City of New York. **486** Winslow Homer, *A Visit from the Old Mistress,* 1876: National Museum of American Art, Smithsonian Institution. **487** Sharecropper cabin with slaughtered hogs: Library of Congress. W. L. Sheppard, "Workers Stripping Tobacco in Danville, Virginia," *Harper's Weekly,* January 29, 1887: Virginia State Library.

Portfolio Six: **564** Charles W. Witham, "Grand View of Baxter Street": Theatre and Music Collection, Museum of the City of New York. **565** Alfred Stieglitz, "The Steerage": The Museum of Modern Art, New York; gift of Alfred Stieglitz. Edward Moran, *Unveiling of the Statue of Liberty,"* 1886: Museum of the City of New York. **566** Lewis Hine, Italian mother and child, Ellis Island: New York Public Library. Ellis Island—stethoscope examination: Brown Brothers. **567** Orchard Street looking south from Hester Street, 1898: The Byron Collection, Museum of the City of New York. Lewis Hine, communal faucet in tenement: International Museum of Photography at George Eastman House. Mulberry Bend, ca. 1890; photo by Langill & Darling: Museum of the City of New York. **568** Lewis Hine, labor agency on lower West Side, New York City, 1910: New York Public Library. Immigrant family sewing garments in tenement: Culver Pictures. **569** Poster advertising land in the West, 1870s: The Granger Collection. Nels Wickstrom and family, Wisconsin, 1893: State Historical Society of Wisconsin. **570** Levi Strauss ad, 1870s: Levi Strauss & Co. **571** Jacob Riis: The Granger Collection. Mother Frances Xavier Cabrini: UPI/Bettmann Newsphotos. Nikola Tesla: The Bettmann Archive. Felix Frankfurter: UPI/Bettmann Newsphotos. Sidney Hillman: The Granger Collection. Irving Berlin: The Bettmann Archive.

Portfolio Seven: **684** "Look! The Boss Has a Woman to Write His Letters": National Archives and Record Service. **685** Visiting nurse on Henry Street rooftop: Visiting Nurse Service of New York. Lewis Hine, *Carolina Cotton Mill,* 1908: George Eastman House. Black domestic servant: Valentine Museum, Richmond, Virginia. **686** Triangle Shirtwaist Co. fire: Brown Borthers. Women's Trade Union League demonstration: Brown Brothers. **687** Rose Schneiderman, president of New York Women's Trade Union League: Brown Brothers. Labor organizing poster: Courtesy ILGWU archives, photo by Jack Deutsch. **688** YWCA war effort poster: The Granger Collection. Cooking class, Vassar College, ca. 1918: Brown Brothers. **689** Women polishing cars, Northern Pacific Railroad: Brown Brothers. Woman streetcar conductors, 1918: Brown Brothers. Women welding bombs, munitions factory, ca. 1917: The Granger Collection. **690** Woman schoolteacher, 1920s: The Bettmann Archive, Inc. Secretary metering mail, Eastman Kodak: National Archives and Record Service. Women and men in corn-husking plant: Brown Brothers. **691** Reginald Marsh, *Subway, 14th St.,* 1930: Private collection, New York; photo by Ronald L. C. Kienhuis.

Portfolio Eight: **750** Edward Hopper, *Early Sunday Morning,* 1930: Whitney Museum of American Art. John Marin, *Sun Spots,*

1920: The Metropolitan Museum of Art; Alfred Stieglitz Collection. **751** Georgia O'Keeffe, *Cow Skull: Red, White, and Blue,* 1931: The Metropolitan Museum of Art; Alfred Stieglitz Collection. Thomas Hart Benton, *Romance,* 1931/32: Archer M. Huntington Art Gallery, The University of Texas at Austin; lent by James and Mari Michener. **752** Reginald Marsh, *Twenty Cent Movie,* 1936: Whitney Museum of American Art. Louis Bouché, *Ten Cents a Ride,* 1942: The Metropolitan Museum of Art; George A. Hearn Fund. Ben Shahn, *Willis Avenue Bridge,* 1940: Collection, The Museum of Modern Art, New York; gift of Lincoln Kirstein. **753** John Steuart Curry, *Comedy,* 1937: King's Highway Elementary School, Westport, Conn. **754** Arshile Gorky, *Agony,* 1947: Collection, The Museum of Modern Art, New York; A. Conger Goodyear Fund. Mark Rothko, *Number 10,* 1950: Collection, The Museum of Modern Art, New York; gift of Philip Johnson. Franz Kline, *New York, N.Y.,* 1953: Albright-Knox Art Gallery, Buffalo, N.Y.; gift of Seymour H. Knox. **755** Robert Motherwell, *Elegy to the Spanish Republic 108,* 1965/67: Collection, The Museum of Modern Art, New York; Charles Mergentine Fund. Willem de Kooning, *Woman and Bicycle,* 1952/53: Whitney Museum of American Art. **756** Jasper Johns, *Target With Four Faces,* 1955: Collection, The Museum of Modern Art, New York; gift of Mr. and Mrs. Robert C. Scull. Josef Albers, *Homage to the Square: Apparition,* 1959: Solomon R. Guggenheim Museum. **757** Andrew Wyeth, *Albert's Son,* 1959: National Gallery, Oslo, Norway; photo by J. Lathion.

Portfolio Nine: **890** Japanese movie marquee—*The Day After:* Jim Anderson/Woodfin Camp. **891** Harajuku Park, Tokyo—teens in 1950s clothes: Chuck Fishman/Woodfin Camp (above); Paul Chesley/Woodfin Camp (below). Tokyo Disneyland: James H. Simon/Picture Cube. **892** Peking—Imperial Palace Hotel, Coca-Cola bottles: Marc Bernheim/Woodfin Camp. Singapore—"UIS Jeans Centre": Jim Anderson/Woodfin Camp. **893** Peru—street in Cuzco, Amex sign: John Curtis/Taurus Photos. Ecuador—Quito, traffic cop with Vantage ad: Allan Price/Taurus Photos. Brazil—filling station in Rio de Janeiro: Charles Marden Fitch/Taurus Photos. **894** Saudi Arabia—Bedouins carrying Pampers box: Robert Azzi/Woodfin Camp. Saudi Arabia—GE washers in store: Bill Strode/Woodfin Camp. Saudi Arabia—Mickey Mouse on a camel: Robert Azzi/Woodfin Camp. **895** Kuwait—American cars in parking lot: Robert Azzi/Woodfin Camp. Kuwait—supermarket shelves: Robert Azzi/Woodfin Camp. **896** Zambia—supermarket shelves: M & E Bernheim/Woodfin Camp. Russia—benefit concert for Chernobyl, 1986: Frederique Hibon/Sygma. **897** Senegal—IBM computer: M & E Bernheim/Woodfin Camp.

Text (listed by page number)

Chapter 1: **4** Theodor de Bry, engraving of Columbus departing from Palos, 1590: New York Public Library, Rare Book Collection. **10** Great Temple and Plaza of Tenochtitlán (16th century), reconstructed by Ignacio Marquina: Courtesy Department Library Services, American Museum of Natural History. **12** John White, Indians "sitting at meat": Courtesy of the Trustees of the British Museum. **15** Sir Francis Drake: Virginia Historical Society. **17** Engraving from Captain John Smith's *Generall Historie of Virginia,* 1624: Library of Congress. **21** "The Anabaptist/The Brownist/The Familist/ The Papist," 1641: New York Public Library, Picture Collection. **23** New England primer: American Antiquarian Society. **27** Carington Bowles, "An East Perspective View of the City of Philadelphia . . . ," 1731–36: New York Public Library, Stokes Collection. **29** William Penn, letter from England, 1682: Library of Congress. **30** "t' Fort nieuw Amsterdam op de Manhattans," ca. 1626–28 (pub. 1651): Museum of the City of New York.

Chapter 2: **43** Christopher von Graffenried, drawing of Indians with captives, 1711: Burgerbibliothek, Bern, Switzerland. **45** Indenture agreement, April 29, 1718: Historical Society of Pennsylvania. **47** Announcement of sale of slaves, Charleston, S.C., May 6, 1763: Library of Congress. **50** Indigo processing: Charleston (S.C.) Library Society. **51** Aquatint, idealized view of slave life, from J. Ferrario, *Les Costumes des Peuples . . . ,* Milan, 1827: Library Company of Philadelphia. **54** Patrick Henry arguing against clergy's claim for higher wages: Virginia Historical Society. **57** *The Mason Children: David, Joanna, and Abigail,* attributed to the Freake-Gibbs Painter, 1670: The Fine Arts Museums of San Francisco; gift of Mr. and Mrs. John D. Rockefeller 3rd. **62** T. H. Matteson, *Examination of a Witch,* 1855: Essex Institute, Salem, Mass.; photo by Mark Sexton. **65** David Martin, portrait of Benjamin Franklin, 1767: The White House Historical Association; photo by National Geographic Society. **72** Advertisement, "A Large Spaneil . . . ," New York *Weekly Journal,* November 26, 1733: New-York Historical Society. **73** Phyllis Wheatley, "An Elegiac Poem, on the Death of . . . George Whitefield," Boston, 1770: Library Company of Philadelphia. **76** William Bartram, watercolor drawings, "A seed vessell . . . A large land snale" and "The Alegator of St. Johns": Natural History Museum, London. **77** David Rittenhouse, orrery, 1950s restoration: Princeton University Observatory.

Chapter 3: **90** Portrait of Gov. John Winthrop: American Antiquarian Society. **95** Engraving of sugar refining, from P. Pomet, *A Compleat History of Drugs . . . ,* London, 1712: Library Company of Philadelphia. **96** F. Bartoli, portrait of Cornplanter (Ki-oh-twog-ky), 1796: New-York Historical Society. **100** Thomas Davies, watercolor of seizure of Louisbourg, 1758: Royal Artillery Museum, London. **106** J. W. Barber, wood engraving of New Hampshire stamp master in effigy, from *Interesting Events in the History of the U.S.,* 1829: Metropolitan Museum of Art; bequest of Charles Allen Munn. **108** "The Repeal, or the Funeral of Miss Ame-stamp," London, 1766: Library Company of Philadelphia. **110** John Singleton Copley, portrait of Samuel Adams, ca. 1771: Museum of Fine Arts, Boston. **111** Paul Revere, engraving of Boston Massacre: American Antiquarian Society. **112** Broadside, "Whereas it has been reported . . . ," Boston, December 2, 1773: Massachusetts Historical Society. **113** Cartoon, "The Bostonians in Distress": Colonial Williamsburg Foundation. **114** Cartoon, "The Alternative of Williams Burg": Colonial Williamsburg Foundation.

Chapter 4: **120** Amos Doolittle after Ralph Earle, "Engagement at the North Bridge in Concord," Plate III: Chicago Historical Society. **122** John Trumbull, detail from *Declaration of Independence,* 1786: Yale University Art Gallery. **132** De Grasse blockading Yorktown: Anne S. K. Brown Military Collection, Brown University Library. **133** "The Times, Anno 1783," 1783: Library Company of Philadelphia. **135** Requisition issued by George Washington, December 20, 1777: Historical Society of Pennsylvania. **137** Proclamation by Royal Governor Lord Dunmore, November 25, 1775: Virginia State Library. **140** Thirteen-star flag: Smithsonian Institution, National Museum of American History, Division of Armed Forces History. **143** Charles Willson Peale, portrait of George Washington, 1776: Brooklyn Museum.

Chapter 5: **148** Whitehall Plantation on the Mississippi, after Christophe Colomb: Historic New Orleans Collection. **150** Benjamin Henry Latrobe, *View of Part of the Ruins of*

Norfolk, watercolor, 1796: Maryland Historical Society. **153** Charles Willson Peale, miniature of James Madison, 1783: Albert E. Leeds Collection. **157** Convention room, Independence Hall (restored): Independence National Historic Park, Philadelphia. **159** "The Federal Edifice," from *The Massachusetts Centinel,* August 2, 1788: New-York Historical Society. **161** Amos Doolittle after Lacour, "Federal Hall, the Seat of Congress," 1789: New York Public Library, Stokes Collection. **163** James Sharples, portrait of Alexander Hamilton, ca. 1796: National Portrait Gallery.

Chapter 6: **174** "The Times: A Political Portrait—Triumph Government, Perish All Its Enemies," ca. 1790: New-York Historical Society. **177** Recruiting poster, 1798: Historical Society of Pennsylvania. **179** John Trumbull, portrait of John Adams, 1793: National Portrait Gallery. **181** Cartoon, "The Providential Detection": Library Company of Philadelphia. **182** Map of Washington, D.C., 1790: Library of Congress. **183** Charles Saint-Mémin, portrait of Thomas Jefferson: Worcester Art Museum. **185** Stephen Decatur's raid on Tripoli, Italian engraving, 1805: The Granger Collection. **188** Burr-Hamilton duel, reproduced from 19th-century lantern slide: New-York Historical Society. **191** Lewis and Clark diary drawings of fish and duck: American Philosophical Society.

Chapter 7: **204** Gilbert Stuart, portrait of John Randolph, 1805: National Gallery of Art, Washington; Andrew W. Mellon Collection. **205** Charles Saint-Mémin, portrait of Aaron Burr, 1805: New-York Historical Society. **208** Alexander Anderson, embargo cartoon, 1807: New-York Historical Society. **210** Benjamin Henry Latrobe, "A Conversation at Sea," 1797: Maryland Historical Society. **212** Portrait of "The Open Door," younger brother of Tecumseh, in McKennery and Hall, *History of the Indian Tribes,* 1836: Library Company of Philadelphia. **214** Ambroise Louis Garneray, *Battle of Lake Erie:* Chicago Historical Society. **218** "A Scene on the Frontier as Practiced by the Humane British and Their Worthy Allies," ca. 1813–18: Library Company of Philadelphia. **220** Hyacinthe Laclotte, "Battle of New Orleans": Historic New Orleans Collection.

Chapter 8: **232** Asher B. Durand, portrait of John Quincy Adams, 1835: New-York Historical Society. **233** Francis Alexander, "Black Dan" portrait of Daniel Webster, 1835: Hood Museum of Art, Dartmouth College. **235** Attributed to Charles Bird King, portrait of John C. Calhoun, ca. 1818–25: National Portrait Gallery, transfer from the National Gallery of Art; gift of Andrew W. Mellon. **236** Portrait of Henry Clay, after John Neagle, 1824: Chicago Historical Society. **240** David Claypoole Johnston, "A Foot-Race,": Library Company of Philadelphia. **242** Anonymous, "Pawtucket Bridge and Falls": Rhode Island Historical Society. **247** Frontispiece from *American Slave Trade,* 1822; engraving by Alexander Lawson after sketch by Alexander Rider: Library of Congress. **252** Robert Fulton, self-portrait and portrait of his wife, after Elizabeth Emmett: New-York Historical Society. **253** "Front View of St. Louis," from Eugene Charles Dupré's *Atlas,* St. Louis, 1838: Library Company of Philadelphia. **258** Chester Harding, portrait of John Marshall, 1828: Boston Atheneum.

Chapter 9: **265** Laban S. Beecher, figurehead of Andrew Jackson, 1834: Museum of the City of New York. **268** "Office Hunters for the Year 1834": Library Company of Philadelphia. **270** G. P. A. Healey, "Webster's Reply to Hayne," 1829: Boston Art Commission. **273** Henry L.ewis, slaughter of Black Hawk's braves, from *Das Illustrierte Mississippithal,* 1854: New York Public Library, Rare Book Division. **274** Charles Lesueur, "James Jamy, Choctaw, April 17, 1830": Musée d'Histoire Naturelle, Le Havre, France. **276** Henry Inman, miniature of Nicholas Biddle: private collection. **278** "Set To Between Old Hickory and Bully Nick," 1834–35: Library Company of Philadelphia. **283** Daguerreotype of Martin Van Buren, 1848: National Archives and Record Service. **285** Mass rally election of 1840, Cincinnati: Cincinnati Historical Society.

Chapter 10: **292** Léon Noël, lithograph of Alexis de Tocqueville: Yale University Library, Beinecke Rare Book and Manuscript Collection. **293** Henry Sargent, *The Dinner Party,* ca. 1825: Museum of Fine Arts, Boston; gift of Mrs. Horatio Lamb. **296** "Lure of American Wages," ca. 1855: Museum of the City of New York. **296** Barfoot for Darton, "Progress of Cotton," Plate No. 6: Yale University Art Gallery, Mabel Brady Garvan Collection. **299** *Lowell Offering,* December 1845: The Bettman Archive. **301** Joseph H. Davis, *The Tilton Family,* 1837: Abby Aldrich Rockefeller Center for American Folk Art. **302** Daguerreotype of Amos Bronson Alcott: The Granger Collection. **303** Engraving of Charles Grandison Finney: The Granger Collection. **304** Shaker bedroom: Hancock Shaker Village, Hancock, Mass. **306** C. C. A. Christensen, "The Nauvoo Temple": Brigham Young University. **307** Daguerreotype of Dorothea Linde Dix: The Granger Collection. **310** Daguerreotype of William Lloyd Garrison by Southworth and Hawes: The Metropolitan Museum of Art; gift of I. N. Phelps Stokes, Edward S. Hawes, Alice Mary Hawes, Marion Augusta Hawes, 1937. **311** Portrait of Frederick Douglass by Ritchie: New-York Historical Society. **312** Daguerreotype of Elizabeth Cady Stanton and her daughter Harriot, 1856. Library of Congress.

Chapter 11: **326** Charles Willson Peale, *The Peale Family,* ca. 1790–1810: New-York Historical Society. **328** William Furness, portrait of Ralph Waldo Emerson: The Pennsylvania Academy of the Fine Arts; gift of Horace Howard Furness. **329** Photograph of Walden Pond: Thoreau Lyceum, Concord, Mass. **330** Samuel S. Osgood, portrait of Edgar Allan Poe, ca. 1845: New-York Historical Society. **332** Daguerreotype of Walt Whitman: National Archives and Record Service. **334** Photograph of Otis House by architect Charles Bulfinch: Society for the Preservation of New England Antiquities. **335** "Iron Warehouse of John B. Wickersham, no. 312 Broadway, New York," 1854: Library of Congress. **336** William Sidney Mount, *Eel Spearing at Setauket,* 1845: New York State Historical Association, Cooperstown. **337** Hiram Powers, *The Greek Slave,* 1847: The Newark Museum; gift of Franklin Murphy Jr., 1926. Photograph © The Newark Museum. **338** Anon., "Girls' Evening School," ca. 1840: Museum of Fine Arts, Boston; M. and M. Karolik Collection. **340** Anon., "A Lecture by James Pollard Espy, Meteorologist, at Clinton Hall . . . ," ca. 1841: Museum of the City of New York. **343** Photograph of Maria Mitchell: Vassar College Library, Special Collections.

Chapter 12: **348** Daguerreotype of John Tyler, ca. 1850: Chicago Historical Society. **349** T. Gentilz, *Fall of the Alamo, March 6, 1836,* 1885: Library of Congress. **350** "The Great Prize-Fight," 1844: New-York Historical Society. **354** J. Goldsborough Bruff, "Seeing the Elephant No. 1" and "Seeing the Elephant No. 5," ca. 1850: Yale University, Beinecke Library. **356** "Volunteers for Texas," 1846: Library of Congress. **357** Currier & Ives, "The Battle of Resaca de la Palma, May 9, 1846": Museum of the City of New York. **360** Daguerreotype of Gen. John E. Wool and staff, Saltillo, Mexico, 1846: Yale University, Beinecke Library. **363** Southworth & Hawes, daguerreotype of Henry Clay, ca. 1845–50: The Metropolitan Museum of Art; gift of I. N. Phelps Stokes, Edward S. Hawes, Alice Mary Hawes, Marion Augusta Hawes, 1937. Southworth & Hawes, daguerreotype of Daniel Webster, 1851: The Metropolitan Museum of Art;

gift of I. N. Phelps Stokes, Edward S. Hawes, Alice Mary Hawes, Marion Augusta Hawes, 1937. **368** "Conquering Prejudice," ca. 1850: Worcester Art Museum, Worcester, Mass.
Chapter 13: **372** "Sale of Estates, Pictures and Slaves in the Rotunda, New Orleans," in J. S. Buckingham, *Slave States of America* (London, 1842): New-York Historical Society. **374** Franz Hölzlhuber, "Rice Fields in the State of Arkansas," 1856–60, and "Sugar Harvest in Louisiana and Texas," 1856–1860: Glenbow Foundation, Calgary, Alberta. **375** "Insurrection in Virginia!" in *The Liberator,* September 1831: American Antiquarian Society, Worcester, Mass. **376** "Deck of the Bark *Wildfire,*" in *Harper's Weekly,* June 2, 1860: Library of Congress. **380** Frontispiece, Carstensen and Gildemeister, *New York Crystal Palace* (New York, 1854): New-York Historical Society. **382** "Boom and Bust in the Early Republic, 1790–1860": Adapted from *American Business Activity from 1790 to Today,* 57th Edition, January 1986, AmeriTrust, Cleveland, Ohio. **383** Samuel Waugh, "The Battery, the Bay and Harbor of New York," ca. 1855: Museum of the City of New York. **384** "Five Points District, New York," 1827: New-York Historical Society. **387** Hill & Bennett, "New York from Brooklyn Heights," 1837: New-York Historical Society. **388** E. L. Henry, "The Camden and Amboy Railroad, with the Engine 'Planet' in 1834," 1905: Kennedy Galleries, New York. **392** "Michigan Avenue from the Lake," ca. 1860–65: Library of Congress. **393** Steamer *Princess* at mail line packet landing for Vicksburg, Natchez, and New Orleans, ca. 1850–60: Courtesy the Historic New Orleans Collection.
Chapter 14: **398** Broadside, "Caution! Colored People of Boston," April 21, 1851: Library of Congress. Anon., wood engraving of Rev. Josiah Henson: New-York Historical Society. **400** Gesson Ogata, "First Landing at Kurihama, July 14, 1853": United States Naval Academy Museum. **401** Daguerreotype of Stephen A. Douglas, ca. 1860: Library of Congress. **403** Albert J. Fountain, Jr., *The Signing of the Gadsden Purchase,* 1929: Courtesy of Mary Veitch Alexander, Gadsden Museum, Mesilla, N.M. **406** Daguerreotype, "Free-State Battery," 1856: Kansas State Historical Society, Topeka. **407** "Southern Chivalry—Argument versus Clubs," 1856: Library Company of Philadelphia. **408** G. P. A. Healey, portrait of James Buchanan, 1859: Smithsonian Institution, National Portrait Gallery. **412** Alexander Hesler, daguerreotype of Abraham Lincoln, June 3, 1860: Chicago Historical Society. Daguerreotype of Lincoln, April 10, 1865: Library of Congress. **415** Thomas Hovenden, *The Last Moments of John Brown,* 1884: The Metropolitan Museum of Art; gift of Mr. and Mrs. Carle Stoeckel, 1897. **419** "The True Issue," 1860: Library of Congress.
Chapter 15: **424** "Are We to Have War?" New York *Herald,* April 8, 1861: New-York Historical Society. **427** John Robertson, portrait of Jefferson Davis, 1863: Museum of the Confederacy, Richmond, Va. **429** Anon., "Panic on the Road between Bull Run and Centerville," 1861: Museum of Fine Arts, Boston. **432** "Confederate raider *Nashville* being towed into port": Mariners' Museum, Newport News, Va. **433** 5th Corps ammunition train crossing a pontoon bridge: Library of Congress. **436** Julian Vannerson, photo of Robert E. Lee, 1863: Library of Congress. **438** Matthew Brady, "Havoc effect of a 32-lb shell": National Archives and Record Service. **440** Adalbert Johann Volck, "Lincoln Writing the Emancipation Proclamation": Museum of Fine Arts, Boston; M. and M. Karolik Collection. David Gilmore Blythe, "Abraham Lincoln Writing the Emancipation Proclamation," 1863: Museum of Art, Carnegie Institute; gift of Mr. and Mrs. John F. Walton. **441** Recruiting poster, 12th Mass. Battery: Library of Congress. **442** "U.S. Colored Infantry at Fort Lincoln": National Archives and Record Service. **444** Matthew Brady, photo of Ulysses S. Grant, 1863: Library of Congress. **450** Richard N. Brooke, *Furling the Flag:* West Point Museums Collection, U.S. Military Academy. **451** Ruins of Tredegar Iron Works, Richmond, April 1865: National Archives and Record Service.
Chapter 16: **458** Matthew Brady, daguerreotype of Andrew Johnson: Library of Congress. **459** Matthew Brady, daguerreotype of Thaddeus Stevens: Library of Congress. Matthew Brady, daguerreotype of Benjamin Wade: Library of Congress. **465** Schneider & Fuchs, "The Fifteenth Amendment and Its Results," 1870: The Granger Collection. **467** "The Dual Legislature of the State of South Carolina," *Frank Leslie's Illustrated Newspaper,* December 23, 1876: The Granger Collection. **469** "Primary School for Freedmen, in Charge of Mrs. Green," *Harper's Weekly,* June 23, 1866: New-York Historical Society. **470** The Shores Family, Custer Co., Nebraska, 1887: Nebraska State Historical Society. **473** Carpetbaggers being hanged, Tuscaloosa *Independent Monitor,* September 1, 1868: Alabama Dept. of Archives and History, Montgomery. **475** "I Feed You All!" 1875: New-York Historical Society.
Chapter 17: **490** Kills Two, "An Indian Horse Dance": Yale University Library, Coe Collection. **492** General Sherman and aides in council with Indian chiefs, Fort Laramie, 1868: Culver Pictures. **494** Advertisement for buffalo robes, Hart, Taylor & Co., Boston, October 1, 1876: New-York Historical Society. **495** Geronimo and Natiche with their sons, preparing to surrender to Gen. Crook: National Archives and Record Service. **498** Anon. portrait of Booker T. Washington: National Park Service, Tuskegee Institute National Historic Site; photo by John Scott. **500** "The California Pioneers," ca. 1850: The Granger Collection. **503** 30-horse combines, wheat harvest, Stockton, California, 1907: Library of Congress. **504** J. K. Hillers, railroad bridge near Santa Fe, New Mexico: National Archives and Record Service. **506** Old map of Atlantic & Pacific Railroad: National Archives and Record Service. **507** Andrew J. Russell, meeting of the rails at Promontory, Utah, May 10, 1869: The Granger Collection. **511** S. D. Butcher, masked Nebraska ranchers cutting fence, 1885: Nebraska State Historical Society, S. D. Butcher Collection.
Chapter 18: **516** Herman Decker, *Lonsdale Wharf, Providence, Rhode Island,* 1878: Museum of Art, Rhode Island School of Design; Mary B. Jackson Fund. **519** Poster for Northern Pacific Railroad land grants: Chicago Historical Society. **520** Strip mining, Mesabi Range, 1899: Minnesota Historical Society. **521** Oil Creek Railroad, Pennsylvania, ca. 1860–70: Drake Well Museum, Titusville, Pa. **523** Thomas Edison with wax-cylinder phonograph, 1888: Edison National Historic Site, National Park Service, U.S. Dept. of the Interior. Women in factory: Brown Brothers. **526** Edward Steichen, photo of J. P. Morgan, 1906: Museum of Modern Art; gift of A. Conger Goodyear. **527** Theobald Chartran, portrait of Andrew Carnegie, 1895: Museum of Art, Carnegie Institute, Pittsburgh; gift of Mr. Henry Clay Frick. **528** Photo of John D. Rockefeller: Brown Brothers. **530** Woolworth's, New York City, ca. 1911: Brown Brothers. **532** "The Age of Giant Enterprise, 1861–1920": Adapted from *American Business Activity from 1790 to Today,* 57th Edition, January 1986, AmeriTrust, Cleveland, Ohio. **535** "The Modern Laocoön," New York *Daily Graphic,* April 25, 1874: Library of Congress.
Chapter 19: **541** Knights of Labor meeting: New York Public Library, Picture Collection. **543** Bilingual handbill for mass meeting at Haymarket, Chicago, 1886: Chicago Historical Society. **545** National Guard firing on Pullman strikers, 1894: The Granger Collection. **546** Eugene Debs addressing a So-

cialist Party gathering: National Archives and Record Service **549** Frank Beard, cartoon about unrestricted immigration, 1885: The Granger Collection. **551** Jacob Riis, "Bandit's Roost, Lower East Side," New York *Sun,* 1887: Museum of the City of New York. **553** Thomas Nast, "Let Us Prey," *Harper's Weekly,* September 23, 1887: Library of Congress. **554** Trolleys on lower Broadway, New York, ca. 1890: Brown Brothers. **559** Alice Kellog Tyler, portrait of Jane Addams, 1896: Chicago Historical Society.

Chapter 20: **574** Frances Benjamin Johnston, students working on construction, ca. 1900–1905: Library of Congress, courtesy of National Park Service, Tuskegee Institute National Historical Site; photo by John Scott. **577** John Singer Sargent, portrait of Joseph Pulitzer, 1905: Courtesy of Joseph Pulitzer, Jr. Caricature of William Randolph Hearst as "The Yellow Kid": Sacramento *Bee,* 1898. **580** Smith College students setting out on geology field trip, ca. 1880–1890: Smith College Archives. **586** Frederick Waddy, caricature of Mark Twain, 1872: The Granger Collection. **589** Cartoon of authors: *Life,* 1897. **590** Thomas Eakins, Marey wheel photo of an unidentified model, 1884: Philadelphia Museum of Art; gift of Charles Bregler. **591** Thomas Eakins, *The Swimming Hole,* 1883: Permanent Collection, The Fort Worth Art Museum; photo by David Wharton. **592** Mary Cassatt, *Mother and Child:* Metropolitan Museum of Art, George A. Hearn Fund, 1909. **594** Henry and William James, ca. 1900: The Bettmann Archive.

Chapter 21: **600** Joseph Keppler, "None but Millionaires Need Apply," *Puck,* March 12, 1890: New-York Historical Society. **601** Louis Dalrymple, "Getting Troublesome Again," 1896: The Granger Collection. **605** Currier & Ives, "Farmer Garfield Cutting a Swath to the White House," 1880: The Granger Collection. **608** Bernhard Gillan, "Phryne Before the Chicago Tribunal," *Puck,* 1884: Culver Pictures. **609** Anders Zorn, portrait of Grover Cleveland: National Portrait Gallery, Smithsonian Institution. **613** Guthrie, Oklahoma, May 1889: University of Oklahoma Library, Western History Collections. **615** Mary Elizabeth Lease: Culver Pictures. **617** W. A. Rogers, "Mutiny!—Can the Captain Regain Control of the Ship?" *Harper's Weekly,* April 14, 1894, p. 345: New York Public Library; Astor, Lenox and Tilden Foundations. **619** William Jennings Bryan: The Granger Collection. **621** William McKinley campaigning on his front porch, 1896: The Granger Collection.

Chapter 22: **633** "Well, I Hardly Know Which to Take First!" Boston *Globe,* May 28, 1898: Library of Congress. **635** Louis Dalrymple, "Some Time in the Future," 1895: The Granger Collection. **636** "Prophescopic-Scoopagraph!" Sacramento *Bee,* May 16, 1898. **638** William Glackens, *Transports Anchored in the Bay, June 10th:* Library of Congress. William Glackens, *Night After San Juan:* Wadsworth Atheneum, Hartford; gift of Henry Schnakenberg. **641** Filipino guerrillas captured at Pasay and Paranaque, 1899: Library of Congress. **643** "His Foresight," *Puck,* 1901: Culver Pictures. **647** Cooperating forces preparing to enter the Forbidden City, Peking, 1900: National Archives and Record Service. **649** Panama Canal cartoon, New York *Times,* 1914: Copyright © 1914 by The New York Times Company. Reprinted by permission.

Chapter 23: **654** William Balfour-Ker, *From the Depths,* in John Ames Mitchell, *The Silent War,* 1906: New York Public Library; Astor, Lenox and Tilden Foundations. **655** "The Smile That Won't Come Off," New York *Telegram,* May 5, 1906: Bell & Howell, Inc. **657** William Glackens, *The Green Car,* 1910: The Metropolitan Museum of Art, New York: Arthur H. Hearn Fund. **658** Marcel Duchamp, *Nude Descending a Staircase, No. 2,* 1912: Philadelphia Museum of Art; Louise and Walter Arensberg Collection. **659** Robert La Follette, Cumberland, Wisconsin, 1897: State Historical Society of Wisconsin. **663** Suffrage Parade, New York, May 6, 1911: Culver Pictures. **667** Theodore Roosevelt in lions' den: Culver Pictures. **669** Coal miners' strike, Shenandoah, Pa., 1902: Brown Brothers. **671** "Best" tonic advertisement, ca. 1890–1900: The Granger Collection. **672** William Howard Taft playing golf: Culver Pictures. **674** E. W. Kemble, Bull Moose cartoon, *Harper's,* ca. 1910: Culver Pictures. **678** John T. McCutcheon, "A Near-Futurist Painting," Chicago *Tribune,* April 3, 1913: Library of Congress. **681** Winold Reiss, portrait of W. E. B. DuBois, ca. 1925: National Portrait Gallery, Smithsonian Institution.

Chapter 24: **695** American camp at Colonia Dublan, Mexico: Companies G and H in trenches, ca. 1916: National Archives and Record Service. **698** Warning notice to transatlantic passengers by German embassy, New York *Times,* 1915: Brown Brothers. **700** Wilson 1916 campaign van: UPI/Bettmann Newsphotos. **701** *"U-Boote Heraus!"* poster, ca. 1914: The Granger Collection. **704** Rival Horse Meat & Sausages, Inc., 1917: National Archives and Record Service. **706** "You: Buy a Liberty Bond Lest I Perish!", 1917: New-York Historical Society. **707** Removing statue of Germania, April 1, 1918: Minnesota Historical Society. **710** Yankee doughboys in a trench, Argonne Forest, September 1918: National Archives and Record Service. American major in the basket of an observation balloon, Argonne Forest, June 1918: National Archives and Record Service. **713** "Big Four," Hotel Crillon, Paris, December 1918: The Granger Collection. **715** "Overweighted," *Punch,* March 26, 1919: Punch Publications, Ltd.

Chapter 25: **721** William Gropper cartoon: *The Liberator,* February 1920. **723** John Steuart Curry, *Baptism in Kansas,* 1928: Whitney Museum of American Art, purchase. acq. no. 31.159. **726** Ben Shahn, *Prohibition Alley:* Museum of the City of New York. **727** Ku Klux Klan initiation ceremony, ca. 1920–25: Kansas State Historical Society. **729** Sacco and Vanzetti arriving at court, April 1927: Brown Brothers. **731** F. Scott Fitzgerald: Brown Brothers. Ernest Hemingway: John F. Kennedy Library. **734** Charlie Chaplin in *One A.M.:* Museum of Modern Art/Film Stills Archive, New York. **735** Jacob Lawrence, *The Migration of the Negro* (Panel 1), 1940–1941: The Phillips Collection. **738** Warren G. Harding: Library of Congress. **740** *Life* cover, March 6, 1924: Culver Pictures. **743** Henry Ford: Courtesy of Ford Motor Company. **745** Charles Lindbergh, May 20, 1927: The Granger Collection.

Chapter 26: **760** James Rosenberg, "Oct. 29 *Dies Irae*": Philadelphia Museum of Art; purchased: Lola Downin Peck Fund. **762** Bread line: National Archives and Record Service. **764** John Steinbeck: Magnum Photos: Erich Hartmann. William Faulkner: Black Star: Bern Keating. **766** Franklin D. Roosevelt and admirers, Warm Springs, Ga., 1933: UPI/Bettmann Newsphotos. **772** Frances Perkins visiting steel plant: Brown Brothers. **774** Ben Shahn, *Years of Dust,* 1937: Museum of Modern Art, New York; gift of the designer. **776** Huey Long: The Bettmann Archive. Father Charles Coughlin on radio, Detroit: UPI/Bettmann Newsphotos. **778** Cartoon, Uncle Sam and federal agencies: © 1935, 1963 Condé-Nast Publications, Inc. *Vanity Fair,* July 1935. New York Public Library; Astor, Lenox and Tilden Foundations. **781** "No Boost for the Administration Make-Up Department," New York *Tribune,* 1937: Culver Pictures. **782** Sit-down strikers: Wide World Photos. **785** Arthur Rothstein, photo of evicted sharecroppers, Missouri, 1939: Library of Congress. **787** H. Hospers, Jicarilla older person's home, ca. 1935–40: Photo Archives, Denver Museum of Natural History.

Chapter 27: **794** Members of the Women's International League for Peace and Freedom, ca. 1918: Library of Congress.

798 "They Shall Pay!" Los Angeles *Times* cartoon reprinted in *The Outlook,* January 1923: Library of Congress. **799** Jim Berryman, "His Recovery Means a Lot to Me!" ca. 1934: Library of Congress. **800** Daniel R. Fitzpatrick, "Fellow diplomats—," 1938: The Granger Collection. **801** Peace rally, Germany, ca. 1920: American Friends Service Committee. Billboard, "Never Again! Save Sons and Dollars," 1930s: American Friends Service Committee. **803** German poster, 1938: The Granger Collection. **804** P. Barlow, "Here's the way I look at it. . . . , *The New Yorker,* July 6, 1940: © 1940, 1968, *The New Yorker, Inc.* **807** Devastation at Pearl Harbor: UPI/Bettmann Newsphotos. **808** Justin Murray, "Birds of Our Time: Plate 1, Franklin D. Roosevelt (*Unitus Andguidus*)," 1945: Library of Congress. **811** Margaret Bourke-White, "Women in Steel": *Life* Magazine, © 1943 *Time* Inc. **813** Dorothea Lange, Mochida family, Hayward, California, May 8, 1942: National Archives and Record Service. **816** Bill Mauldin, Willie and Joe cartoon: NewsAmerica Syndicate for Mauldin and Wil-Jo Associates. U.S. Infantry, Battle of the Bulge, Belgium: National Archives and Record Service. **820** Ruins of Hiroshima's Museum of Science and Industry: UPI/Bettmann Newsphotos.

Chapter 28: **824** "An Unexpected Guest," cartoon with wartime bedfellows Uncle Sam and John Bull: Culver Pictures. **825** Oscar Berger caricature of Molotov's cocktail party, New York *Times,* 1945: Copyright © 1980 by The New York Times Company. Reprinted by permission. **827** Churchill, Roosevelt, and Stalin at Yalta, February 1945: The Granger Collection. **829** Ferman Martin, Truman vs. Taft-Hartley labor bill, Houston *Chronicle,* February 1949: Culver Pictures. **834** Berlin airlift: UPI/Bettmann Newsphotos. **835** Truman with Chicago *Daily Tribune* headline, November 1948: UPI/Bettmann Newsphotos. **838** David Douglas Duncan, 1st Marine Division, November 1950: © David Douglas Duncan, *Life.* **840** Joseph McCarthy, March 1950: UPI/Bettmann Newsphotos. **843** Stephens portrait of Eisenhower: National Portrait Gallery, Smithsonian Institution. **845** John Foster Dulles, 1956: UPI/Bettmann Newsphotos. **846** Herblock, "Don't Be Afraid—I Can Always Pull You Back," 1956: From *Herblock's Special for Today* (Simon & Schuster, 1958); by permission of Herbert Block. **848** Russian freighter in Suez Canal, January 12, 1957: UPI/Bettmann Newsphotos. **852** Little Rock Central High School, September 4, 1957: UPI/Bettmann Newsphotos.

Chapter 29: **858** John F. Kennedy: Magnum Photos: Cornell Capa. **859** Martin Luther King, Jr., praying with fellow demonstrators, Selma, Ala., February 1, 1965: UPI/Bettman Newsphotos. **860** Malcolm X, May 10, 1963: UPI/Bettmann Newsphotos. Macpherson, "Bully!" cartoon, nursemaid Khruschev and baby Castro, Toronto *Star,* April 1963: Reprinted with permission, The Toronto Star Syndicate. **863** Lyndon B. Johnson, July 6, 1966: UPI/Bettmann Newsphotos. **869** Interstate 80 under construction, Paterson, N.J.: Monkmeyer Press Photo Service: Hugh Rogers. **870** Edwin Aldrin walking on the moon, July 1969: UPI/Bettmann Newsphotos. **872** Jackson Pollock *Autumn Rhythm,* 1950: Metropolitan Museum of Art, Gerald A. Hearn Fund. **873** Roy Lichtenstein, *Masterpiece,* 1962: Photo courtesy Leo Castelli Gallery, New York. **876** Alfred Eisenstadt, sewage in Niagara River, 1968: *Life* Magazine, © Time Inc. **879** César Chávez, Delano, Calif., 1968: Arthur Schatz, © Time Inc. **881** Betty Friedan, August 25, 1970: UPI/Bettmann Newsphotos. **885** Student sit-in demonstration, Columbia University, April 1968: UPI/Bettmann Newsphotos.

Chapter 30: **901** Before and after defoliation in Vietnam: Wide World. **902** Hugh Haynie, "How difficult the getting out . . ." Louisville *Courier-Journal,* 1968: Courtesy the *Courier-Journal,* Louisville. **908** Troops charging just before Kent State shootings, May 1970: UPI/Bettmann Newsphotos. **909** Nixon and Mao Tse-tung in Peking, February 1972: Woodfin Camp & Associates. **913** Gary Trudeau, Watergate cartoon: Copyright 1973 by G. P. Trudeau. Reprinted with permission of Universal Press Syndicate. All rights reserved. **914** Gasoline shortage, 1973–74: © Sepp Seitz 1983/Woodfin Camp & Associates. **916** "Depression, Prosperity, and Inflation, 1921–1985": Adapted from *American Business Activity from 1790 to Today,* 57th Edition, January 1986, AmeriTrust, Cleveland, Ohio.

Chapter 31: **923** Begin, Carter, Sadat, and Dayan at Gettysburg: © Jim Moore/Gamma Liaison. **926** Iranians burning U.S. flag, October 11, 1979: Alain Mingam/Gamma Liaison. **932** Mondale and Ferraro, Minnesota, July 1984: Tannenbaum/Sygma. **937** Dan Wasserman, "Get Ready—," Boston *Globe:* Dan Wasserman, © 1986 Los Angeles Times Syndicate. **938** Farm auction, Illinois, 1984: Jeff Lowenthal/Woodfin Camp. **939** Cubans neighborhood, Union City, N.J.: Chuck Fishman/Woodfin Camp. Vietnamese billiard hall, Calif., 1985: P. F. Bentley/Photoreporters.

Index

Note: Italicized page numbers refer to maps and graphs.

THE UNITED STATES IN THE WORLD

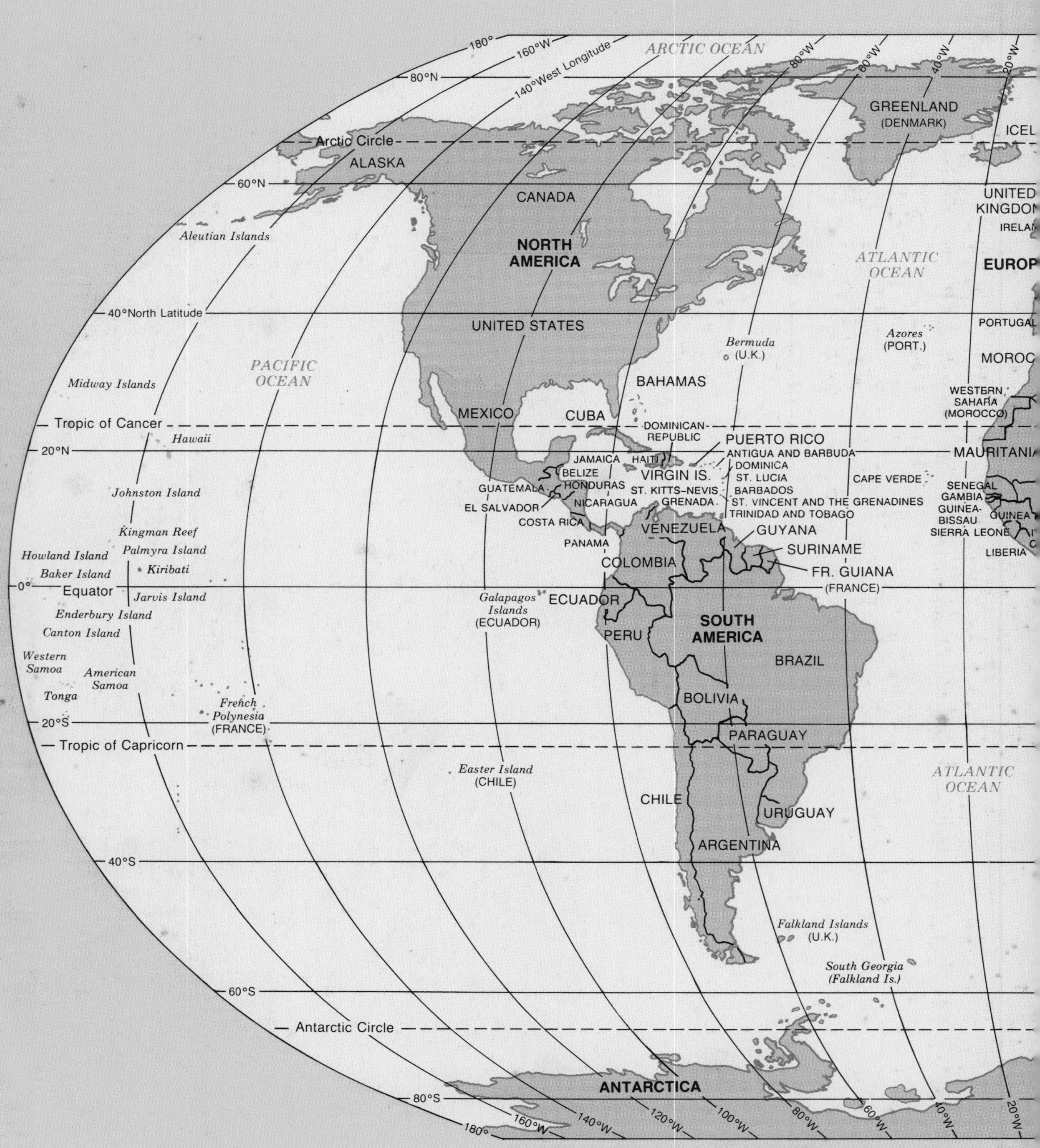

ARCTIC OCEAN
180°
160°W
140°West Longitude
80°W
60°W
40°W
20°W
80°N
60°N
40°North Latitude
20°N
0°
Equator
20°S
40°S
60°S
80°S
Arctic Circle
Tropic of Cancer
Tropic of Capricorn
Antarctic Circle
GREENLAND
(DENMARK)
ICEL
ALASKA
CANADA
UNITED
KINGDOM
IRELA
Aleutian Islands
NORTH
AMERICA
ATLANTIC
OCEAN
EUROP
UNITED STATES
PORTUGAL
Bermuda
(U.K.)
Azores
(PORT.)
MOROC
PACIFIC
OCEAN
Midway Islands
BAHAMAS
WESTERN
SAHARA
(MOROCCO)
MEXICO
CUBA
DOMINICAN
REPUBLIC
PUERTO RICO
Hawaii
ANTIGUA AND BARBUDA
MAURITANIA
JAMAICA
HAITI
DOMINICA
BELIZE
VIRGIN IS.
ST. LUCIA
CAPE VERDE
HONDURAS
GUATEMALA
ST. KITTS-NEVIS
BARBADOS
SENEGAL
GAMBIA
Johnston Island
EL SALVADOR
NICARAGUA
GRENADA
ST. VINCENT AND THE GRENADINES
GUINEA-
BISSAU
GUINEA
TRINIDAD AND TOBAGO
COSTA RICA
VENEZUELA
GUYANA
SIERRA LEONE
Kingman Reef
PANAMA
SURINAME
LIBERIA
Howland Island
Palmyra Island
COLOMBIA
FR. GUIANA
(FRANCE)
Baker Island
Kiribati
Jarvis Island
Galapagos
Islands
(ECUADOR)
ECUADOR
Enderbury Island
SOUTH
AMERICA
Canton Island
PERU
BRAZIL
Western
Samoa
American
Samoa
Tonga
BOLIVIA
French
Polynesia
(FRANCE)
PARAGUAY
Easter Island
(CHILE)
ATLANTIC
OCEAN
CHILE
URUGUAY
ARGENTINA
Falkland Islands
(U.K.)
South Georgia
(Falkland Is.)
ANTARCTICA
160°W
140°W
120°W
100°W
80°W
60°W
40°W
20°W